Panic Disorder With Agoraphobia
Agoraphobia Without History of Panic Disorder
Specific Phobia
Social Phobia
Obsessive-Compulsive Disorder
Posttraumatic Stress Disorder
Acute Stress Disorder
Generalized Anxiety Disorder
Anxiety Due to General Medical Condition
Substance-Induced Anxiety Disorder

Somatoform Disorders

Somatization Disorder
Undifferentiated Somatoform Disorder
Conversion Disorder
Pain Disorder
Hypochondriasis
Body Dysmorphic Disorder

Factitious Disorders

Dissociative Disorders

Dissociative Amnesia
Dissociative Fugue
Dissociative Identity Disorder
Depersonalization Disorder

Sexual and Gender Identity Disorders

Sexual Dysfunctions Sexual Desire Disorders; Arousal Disorders; Orgasmic Disorders; Sexual Pain Disorders; Sexual Dysfunction Due to a General Medical Condition

Paraphilias Exhibitionism, Fetishism, Frotteurism, Pedophilia, Sexual Masochism, Sexual Sadism, Transvestic Fetishism, Voyeurism

Gender Identity Disorders

Eating Disorders

Eating Disorders Anorexia Nervosa; Bulimia Nervosa

Sleep Disorders

Primary Sleep Disorders Dyssomnias; Parasomnias;

Sleep Disorders Related to Another Mental Disorder
Other Sleep Disorders

Impulse-Control Disorders not Elsewhere Classified

Intermittent Explosive Disorder; Kleptomania; Pyromania; Pathological Gambling; Trichotillomania

Adjustment Disorders

Other Conditions That May Be a Focus of Clinical Attention

Psychological Factors Affecting Medical Conditions
Medication-Induced Movement Disorders
Other Medication-Induced Disorder
Relational Problems
Problems Related to Abuse or Neglect
Additional Conditions That May Be a Focus of Clinical Attention

Axis II

Personality Disorders

Paranoid Personality Disorder
Schizoid Personality Disorder
Schizotypal Personality Disorder
Antisocial Personality Disorder
Borderline Personality Disorder
Histrionic Personality Disorder
Narcissistic Personality Disorder
Avoidant Personality Disorder
Dependent Personality Disorder
Obsessive-Compulsive Personality Disorder

Mental Retardation (Specified as to Severity)

Mild Mental Retardation
Moderate Mental Retardation
Severe Mental Retardation
Profound Mental Retardation
Mental Retardation, Severity Unspecified

ABNORMAL PSYCHOLOGY

THE PROBLEM OF MALADAPTIVE BEHAVIOR

EIGHTH EDITION

Irwin G. Sarason
University of Washington

Barbara R. Sarason
University of Washington

PRENTICE HALL
Upper Saddle River, New Jersey 07458

Library of Congress Cataloging-in-Publication Data

Sarason, Irwin G.
   Abnormal psychology : the problem of maladaptive behavior / Irwin
  G. Sarason, Barbara R. Sarason. — 8th ed.
     p.   cm.
   Includes bibliographical references and index.
   ISBN 0-13-356411-8
   1. Psychology, Pathological.   I. Sarason, Barbara R.   II. Title.
RC454.S28   1995
616.89—dc20   95-20168
                                        CIP

Acquisitions editor: Heidi Freund
Project manager: Maureen Richardson
Development editor: Barbara Muller
Marketing manager: Lauren Ward
Copy editor: Winnifred Davis
Creative director: Leslie Osher
Interior design: Circa '86
Cover art: *Faces* by Linda Frichtel
Cover design: Carole Anson
Photo editor: Lorinda Morris-Nantz
Photo researchers: Eloise Marion and Joelle Burrows

© 1996 by Prentice-Hall, Inc.
Simon & Schuster/A Viacom Company
Upper Saddle River, NJ 07458

Printed in the United States of America

10 9 8 7 6 5 4 3 2 1

ISBN 0-13-356411-8

Prentice-Hall International (UK) Limited, *London*
Prentice-Hall of Australia Pty. Limited, *Sydney*
Prentice-Hall Canada, Inc., *Toronto*
Prentice-Hall Hispanoamericana, S.A., *Mexico*
Prentice-Hall of India Private Limited, *New Delhi*
Prentice-Hall of Japan, Inc., *Tokyo*
Simon & Schuster Asia Pte. Ltd., *Singapore*
Editora Prentice-Hall do Brasil, Ltda., *Rio de Janeiro*

To three individuals whose ability to adapt we admire
(in order of their appearance) Sue, Jane, and Don

BRIEF CONTENTS

CONTENTS

CHAPTER 4   CLASSIFICATION AND ASSESSMENT

CHAPTER 5   STRESS, COPING, AND MALADAPTIVE BEHAVIOR

CHAPTER 6   PSYCHOLOGICAL FACTORS AND PHYSICAL SYMPTOMS

CHAPTER 10   MOOD DISORDERS

CHAPTER 11   SCHIZOPHRENIC DISORDER: CHARACTERISTICS AND PROBABLE CAUSES

CHAPTER 12   SCHIZOPHRENIC DISORDER: PSYCHOLOGICAL RESEARCH, TREATMENT, AND OUTCOME

CHAPTER 13   COGNITIVE IMPAIRMENT DISORDERS

CHAPTER 17   THERAPIES AND THEIR OUTCOMES

CHAPTER 18   SOCIETY'S RESPONSE TO MALADAPTIVE BEHAVIOR

PREFACE

A few months ago, a friend said to us, "Writing a new edition must be like having children. You practice with the first one and after that it's a snap." We smiled, mentally noted the friend's naïveté, and wondered what our friend would say if she had actually raised children. However, we realized there was a tiny core of truth to what she had said: Experience helps in writing a textbook—but no more than it helps in parenting a child. Almost all parents know that the second and third children are a little easier than the first born. But if that's all that is said about parenthood, a lot has been left out! Each child presents unique challenges and rewards, and later children are definitely not simply new, easier-to-deal-with replicas of the first one.

INTERACTIONAL PERSPECTIVE

This eighth edition of *Abnormal Psychology*, although easier than the first edition, has presented numerous challenges and rewards. We were challenged to review and rethink our concepts of maladaptive behavior and how we might best communicate key themes to readers. We continue to believe that failures of adaptation are best understood with an interactional perspective that incorporates both personal (for example, temperament, heredity, motivations) and situational (for example, traumatic experiences, having a psychologically troubled parent or spouse) variables. As we reaffirmed our belief in the general value of the interactional perspective, we considered how to make this view more useful in discussions of specific types of maladaptive behavior. We realized that every individual's life—whether heroic, tragic, or (seemingly) ordinary—can be characterized in terms of two factors, vulnerability and resilience, each of which involves both personal and situational variables. Personal characteristics and experiences engendered by the social environment produce a unique combination of vulnerability and resilience that influences how well an individual functions under particular circumstances. In a sense, each person has a unique vulnerability-resilience signature that is an important outcome determinant beyond the contributions of particular life events.

In the case of seriously disordered behavior, the vulnerability factors usually far outweigh the individual's resilience, his or her ability to bounce back when confronted with difficulties and reverses. Yet, even seriously disturbed individuals may have significant assets. A young adult suffering from schizophrenia might have high intelligence, some occupational skills, and an understanding job supervisor. A mentally retarded child might be temperamentally calm, relate well to others, and have parents who are emotionally supportive as well as skilled in helping their child be self-sufficient and enjoy life. The vulnerability-resilience balance and its effect on a variety of disorders is a theme of the eighth edition. In accounting for clinical phenomena, this balance provides a conceptual complement to the interactional perspective.

How might this conceptual tool of vulnerability and resilience be employed to make the topic of abnormal psychology come alive for the reader? We have taken two approaches. First, as appropriate, we analyze pertinent clinical factors and show how therapeutic interventions can be understood as efforts to enhance personal resiliency. Second, we discuss normal individuals who, despite adversity and vulnerability and because of their resilience, have triumphed over life's challenges and stresses. For example, in Chapter 1 we describe Jamel Oeser-Sweat, a teenager who became a finalist in the nationwide Westinghouse Science Talent Search despite a home situation that exposed him to such vulnerability factors as poverty, a psychologically troubled mother, and an absent father. In Chapter 5, which deals with the role of stress in mental disorder, we tell the story of 68-year-old Harvey Weinstein who was kidnapped and experienced for many days the horrors of confinement, hunger, and probable death, but used creative adaptive techniques including thoughts of reunion with his loved ones to deal with these stresses. He continued to show this positive outlook and fighting spirit until he was rescued by the police.

PEDAGOGY. . . DESIGNED TO ENGAGE

Jamel Oeser-Sweat and Harvey Weinstein illustrate another facet of our approach to this edition, the importance of pedagogy. We have tried to present each topic in a way that interests and involves readers, helps them understand the point being made, and encourages them to know more. A pedagogical tool new to this edition is the use of four series of boxed features.

The *Resilience and Vulnerability* series explores the roles of vulnerability and resilience in maladaptive behavior.

The *Case Study* series presents clinical material that brings to life key ideas related to particular clinical disorders.

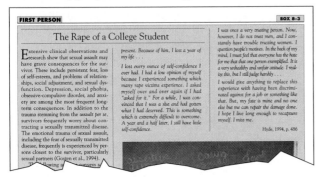

The *First Person* series presents accounts of mental illness told by people who have experienced it.

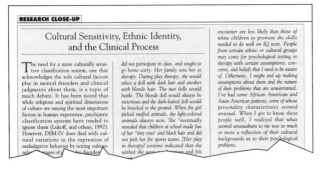

The *Research Close-Up* series reviews in depth, particular techniques, methods, and findings.

We believe these boxes will expand understanding by demonstrating the relevance of research to the clinical enterprise. For example, Chapter 1 contains a Research Close-Up box that introduces the clinical trial as a method of evaluating particular interventions, such as psychotherapy. Ten years ago, clinical trials had relevance principally for the field of medicine. The only clinical trials pertinent to the field of abnormal psychology were those related to evaluating the clinical effectiveness of drugs, such as tranquilizers and anti-psychotic medications. Today, important clinical trials are being conducted to evaluate the effectiveness of various forms of psychotherapy, and there are now hard data showing the effectiveness of psychological therapies. We give several examples of clinical trials throughout the book.

To strengthen the pedagogical thrust of the eighth edition, we increased the number of summary tables. These tables, which were extremely popular in the previous edition, bring together the essential points pertinent to a given disorder, treatment, or idea. For example, Chapter 5 contains a table summarizing the effects of bereavement, and Chapter 13 has a table integrating evidence on the prevalence of dementia. We have also made structural changes for pedagogical purposes. For example, we moved the chapter on anxiety disorders to follow the chapter on psychological aspects of physical conditions. The presentations of illustrations, graphic material, tables, and artwork have been completely redone to increase their interest and learning value. As in the past, we have given special attention to writing style, striving for simplicity of language while recognizing the multidimensional character of many phenomena.

NEW TO THE EIGHTH EDITION

We have updated every chapter to reflect recent research, advances in theory, and new developments in areas of clinical practice (for example, the effects of managed-care programs). We describe the content of DSM-IV, its contributions, and the controversy over its approach. We were excited by the number of theoretical advances, research discoveries, and practical gains in the field since the previous edition—not only useful and important increments to previous knowledge, but entire topics that emerged from relative obscurity to move to the forefront. These topics came into prominence in a very short period of time and are now changing the way we understand and treat abnormal behavior. Among the topics discussed in this edition that have made a recent quantum jump into the limelight are the following: recovered memories and the false memory syndrome;

amnestic disorders; dissociation viewed as a continuum; the relationship between marital satisfaction and sexual dysfunction; evidence of the interactional effects and intertwined roles of biological and situational factors; the increasing need to select particular combinations of treatment components rather than employing only one therapeutic approach; use of dialectical behavior therapy for borderline disorder; and the clinical and theoretical importance of cultural diversity and ethnic identity.

This last topic has become particularly important in the study of maladaptive behavior and its treatment. Many clinicians have long recognized that cultural diversity and ethnic identity need to be taken into account. Now there is a convincing empirical basis demonstrating the role of these factors, and as a result, their importance is more widely acknowledged and acted upon.

The eighth edition also contains many changes that reflect the field's recent revision of domains and conceptual frameworks. For example, Chapter 3 includes expanded coverage of cognitive and social learning theoretical approaches, including Aaron Beck's theoretical, as well as his therapeutic, advances. Chapter 3 also presents a framework that integrates several of the leading theories of abnormal behavior. The concept of coping discussed in Chapter 5 emphasizes the useful distinction between adaptive and maladaptive coping. In several chapters new epidemiological and survey research data are presented. Also expanded in this edition is coverage of rapidly developing topics such as sleep disorders, pain disorders, the effects of emotions on immune-system functioning, brain imaging, and autistic disorders. Although we reviewed several thousand articles, we used only about 500 of them and deleted a comparable amount of material. In doing so, we are not only providing students with the most current knowledge of clinical and research findings and newly important topics, but also focusing their attention with conceptual clarity and organization.

The final challenge in revising has been to follow the maxim of good gardeners: Prune judiciously, remove weak growth, and retain the strong limbs. Good architects have a similar maxim when revamping an existing structure: make the new addition seem an integral part of the whole. We were intent on producing a healthy plant open to air and light or a compact and functional building that is not a hurriedly-built structure with additions and patches here and there. We believe we have been good gardeners and/or builders in producing a text reflecting current consensus, which retains the strengths of earlier editions and looks to the future but is unencumbered by material that is no longer current.

TEACHING AND LEARNING PACKAGE

For the Instructor

The Instructor's Resource Manual with Handouts and Transparency Masters
Ronald G. Evans, Washburne University, has expanded the Instructor's Manual section to include lecture questions and suggestions, chapter overviews, learning objectives, lecture and discussion topics, class activities and video suggestions. The Instructor's Manual also contains 100 handouts and transparency masters that introduce key concepts found in the text. These have been prepared by Alan Swinkels, St. Edwards University.

The Test Item File Written by Katherine Kitamann, University of Virginia, this manual contains over 1800 revised test questions, including multiple choice and short answer essay. All questions reviewed by Joseph Palladino, University of Southern Indiana, a text-construction specialist.

Prentice Hall Test Manager For both the PC and the Macintosh. This feature allows users to select or edit existing items, inset additional questions, and provides a wide range of printing and scrambling options.

Prentice Hall Color Transparencies for Abnormal and Cinical Psychology Series II Add visual impact to the study of abnormal and clinical psychology with these color illustrations. Designed for large classroom settings, the set includes many illustrations in addition to the ones found in the text, offering a wealth of additional resources to enhance lectures and reinforce student learning.

ABC News/PH Video Library for Abnormal Psychology

■ **ABC News/PH Video Library, Abnormal Psychology** Segments from award-winning ABC News programs, including *20/20*, *Primetime Live*, and *Nightlight* cover issues such as drugs and alcoholism, psychotherapy, autism, crime motivation, and depression, plus many more.

■ **ABC News/PH Video Library, Abnormal and Clinical Psychology Series II** Segments from award-winning ABC News programs, including *20/20*, *Primetime Live*, and *Nightline* cover issues such as suicide, eating disorders, Alzheimer's disease, and schizophrenia, plus many more.

■ **Patients as Educators: Video Cases in Abnormal Psychology by James. H. Scully, Jr., M.D., and Alan M. Dahms, Ph.D., Colorado State University** This exclusive video contains a series of 10 patient interviews illustrating a range of disorders. Each interview is preceeded by a brief history of the patient and a synopsis of some major symptoms of the disorder, and ends with a summary and a brief analysis.

FOR THE STUDENT

The Study Guide Created by Christina Harnett, College of Notre Dame of Maryland, the Guide is greatly expanded and more closely coordinated with the Test Item File. It contains chapter outlines, learning objectives, chapter overviews, key terms and concepts, practice multiple-choice, true/false, critical thinking, and short-answer essay questions.

New York Times Abnormal Psychology Supplement *The New York Times* and Prentice Hall are sponsoring Themes of The Times, a program designed to enhance access to current information of relevance in/ the classroom. Through this program, the core subject matter provided in the text is supplemented by a collection of time-sensitive articles from one of the world's  most distinguished newspapers, *The New York Times*. These articles demonstrate the vital, ongoing connection between what is learned in the classroom and what is happening in the world around us.

To enjoy the wealth of information of *The New York Times* daily, a reduced subscription rate is available. For information, call toll-free: 1-800-631-1222.

Prentice Hall and The New York Times are poud to co-sponsor Themes of the Times. We hope it will make the reading of both textbooks and newspapers a more dynamic, involving process.

Asking the Right Questions in Abnormal Psychology This book by Stuart M. Keeley, Bowling Green State University, presents a basic critical-thinking methodology, then asks students to apply this method to a variety of classic research studies in psychopathology.

Prentice Hall CD-ROM for Abnormal and Clinical Psychology An exciting new interactive multimedia tool for your students, Contact your local Prentice Hall Representative for a detailed description of the package's features and capabilities.

ACKNOWLEDGMENTS

We are grateful to many people who have helped in the creation of this eighth edition. We particularly want to recognize the contributions of Prentice Hall Psychology Editor, Heidi Freund, who has been exceptionally supportive and has revealed the most stellar of troubleshooting qualities. Without Heidi's efforts, our job would have been more difficult. Our Development Editor, Barbara Muller, read the entire manuscript and provided many valuable suggestions. We also thank many others at Prentice Hall, including Maureen Richardson, Project Manager, Leslie Osher, Creative Director, Carole Anson, Senior Designer and Tricia Kenny, Manufacturing Buyer. We have also benefited by the thoughtful in-depth chapter reviews by

Karen Smith, Ph.D.
University of Georgia

Lois E. Layne
Western Kentucky University

Anthony F. Fazio
University of Wisconsin Milwaukee

Carolin Keutzer, Ph.D.
University of Oregon

Stephanie Stein
Central Washington University

Eric J. Cooley
Western Oregon State College

Mark J. Krejci
Concordia College

Salvatore J. Cantanzaro
Illinois State University

Philip J. Kinney, Ph.D.
LehighUniversity

Lawrence Simkins, Ph.D.
University of Missouri-Kansas City

These helped us greatly.

On the home front, we owe a great deal to the indefatigable Betty Johnson, whose typing skills and patience endured through the innumerable rewrites we generated in producing this new edition. We also thank Kim Kauffman for helping to sort the many boxes of materials we had accumulated in preparation for writing the eighth edition, as well as Phil Ullrich and Ty Lostutter who contributed their help in checking references and typing the indexes.

Irwin and Barbara Sarason are deeply interested in the multiple causes of maladaptive behavior and how it can be effectively treated. They are perhaps best known for their work on the role of social support as a modifier of stress and a promoter of mental health and adaptive coping. The questions of individual vulnerability and resilience and how adaptation can be encouraged have been of particular interest to them. A current focus of their research is how relationships with family and friends can be protective and aid individuals in coping with daily stresses and strains as well as helping to promote overall psychological adjustment. The topic of social support in general, and as a function of specific relationships, has implications for understanding individual development, abnormal behavior, health status, and the factors within the psychotherapeutic relationship that contribute to positive clinical outcomes. The Sarasons believe that a major ingredient of psychotherapy is the therapist's communication of acceptance and positive evaluation of the patient. Beyond the psychotherapeutic relationship, their work suggests that even vulnerable people who feel that they are accepted and valued by others are more likely to cope well with stress and are less likely to develop maladaptive symptoms. In addition, their work focuses attention on prevention and ways in which communities can become more supportive places to live.

The effects of ethnic and cultural differences on expectations of oneself and others have been an important recent research focus for the Sarasons. They see the need for mental health professionals to develop increased understanding and respect for cultural differences. The stresses of the immigrant experience, the impact of being a member of a minority in our society, and the intergenerational conflicts associated with such status may enhance vulnerability but also allow a focus on individual resilience and moderator effects.

Irwin Sarason received his B.A. degree from Rutgers University and Barbara Sarason received her B.A. degree from Depauw University. They first met while graduate students at the University of Iowa. Each has a Ph.D. degree with a specialization in clinical psychology from Indiana University. After completing their clinical internships in West Haven, Connecticut, they moved to Seattle. Irwin Sarason is currently professor and Barbara Sarason is research professor in the Psychology Department at the University of Washington.

The Sarasons have published over 300 articles and many books on such topics as anxiety, stress and coping, personality research, social support, and techniques for facilitating behavioral change. They have each lectured extensively in the United States, Japan, and throughout Europe.

CHAPTER ONE

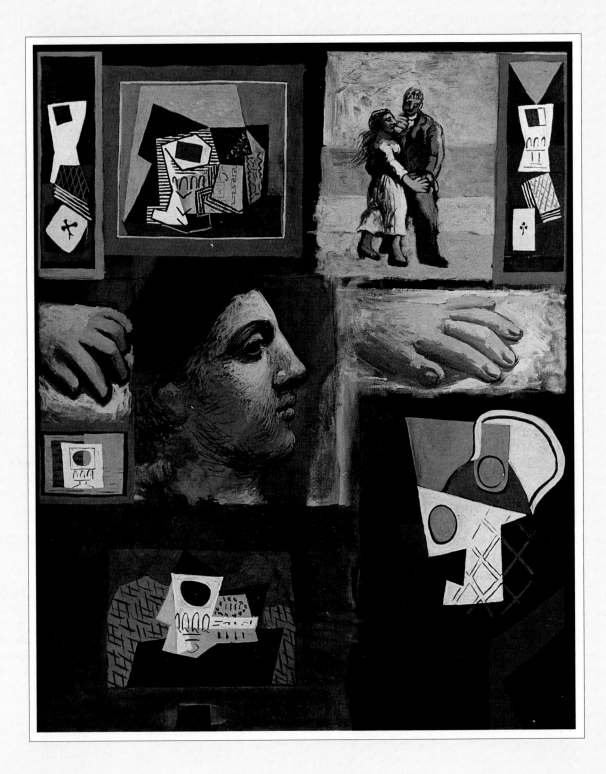

Pablo Picassc, *Etudes*, 1920.

Musee Picasso, Paris/Art Resource, New York. © 1995

Artists Rights Society (ARS), New York/SPADEM, Paris

ABNORMAL PSYCHOLOGY

Bob Cates had felt tense, anxious, and worried a lot of the time during his entire stay at the large university he attended. There seemed to be so much to do. However, in his senior year, despite the fact that he was usually an energetic person, even small things seemed to require a major effort. He felt particularly overwhelmed at pressure points like taking exams, writing papers, and having to say things in class.

> It is worse to be sick in soul than in body, for those afflicted in body only suffer, but those afflicted in soul both suffer and do ill.
>
> PLUTARCH, MORALIA: Affections of soul and body, sec. 501 E. About 95 A.D.

For reasons that were not clear, Bob became increasingly depressed and began to feel that he couldn't go on much longer. His classes, and life in general, seemed less and less worth the effort they required. He couldn't concentrate on his school work and spent several hours each day sitting in his dormitory room—sometimes, just staring into space.

Bob Cates' friends noticed the changes in his behavior and mood and were concerned. As a result of their encouragement, Bob went to the University Counseling Service and had a series of sessions with a counselor. The questions that passed through the counselor's mind included the following:

What is Bob experiencing at the present time—what is he feeling and thinking about?

How serious is the problem that he is experiencing and to what degree is he aware of its seriousness?

What are the causes of Bob's problem—is the problem due to something that has arisen in his current situation or is it a continuation of a long-term, perhaps lifelong, pattern?

What can be done to help Bob overcome his unhappy state?

What is going on in a particular person's life that results in unhappiness and disordered behavior? What can be done to alleviate the problem? These questions are the focus of abnormal psychology. In the case of Bob Cates, the problem was part of a long-term pattern, but it was also related to things going on in his current life situation. His parents had always emphasized the importance of hard work and achievement. His excellent high school record showed to what degree he had learned to strive for success. What seemed to have happened at the university (many of the facts were far from clear) was that for the first time he began to question the values on which his need to achieve was based. As his counseling proceeded, he came to see that in many subtle ways his parents had shaped him to be a "producer." During his junior year, when he was beginning to think about what to do after completing his education, Bob began to feel that he could never achieve as much as his parents wanted him to. This thought had a nagging, depressing effect on him. The future seemed hopeless, and he felt helpless to do anything about it. After several counseling sessions Bob admitted that he had had suicidal thoughts, although he had never seriously considered taking his own life.

What Is Abnormal Behavior?

How abnormal is Bob Cates? While there is no basis for concluding that Bob is "crazy," he definitely has had serious difficulties in adjusting to college. Just how much pressure his parents actually placed on him is not answered by the available information. The fact that he spent hours just sitting in his room, together with his suicidal thoughts, suggests that he was experiencing adjustment difficulties that were much greater than those that are typical for college students.

In this book we will see cases of abnormal behavior both more and less serious than that of Bob Cates. Box 1-1 conveys the wide range of experiences that people have in response to either identifiable stimuli or unknown processes within themselves. The likelihood of a return to normal functioning and a relatively distress-free life is greater when the cause of the problem can be identified than when it is a mystery.

Because our goal is not simply the description of abnormal behavior, we will review theoretical frameworks within which instances of human failure, inadequacy, and unhappiness have been conceptualized. At the same time we will also review basic research pertinent to theories of abnormal behavior. This review of existing theory and research will give us a general framework within which to interpret the wide variety of human problems that find expression in abnormal behaviors. This framework emphasizes the roles played by stress, personal vulnerabilities, and resiliency. How we cope depends on the amount of stress we undergo, together with our limitations and our ability to bounce back under pressure.

Mental disorders, like anything unusual, may make us uncomfortable and even a little frightened. A mentally ill person should not be seen as evil, however, merely as different. **Abnormal psychology** is the area within psychology that is focused on maladaptive behavior—its causes, consequences, and treatment. Abnormal psychology deals with how it feels to be different, the meanings that get attached to being different, and how society deals with people whom it considers to be different. The spectrum of differentness is wide, ranging from reality-defying delusions and severe debilitation to worries and behavioral quirks that we would be better off not having but that do not interfere significantly with our daily lives.

An example of this milder end of the spectrum is a man who was an eminently successful district attorney, was elected governor of New York on three occasions, and was almost elected president of the United States in 1948. This man, Thomas E. Dewey, reached the pinnacle of success, displaying such qualities as rectitude, efficiency, precision, and a nearly limitless capacity for hard work. Yet it was just this combination of traits that made Dewey seem too good to be true. For example, he was never late or absent in his first twelve years of schooling. He lacked a sense of humor and seemed to enjoy life only when he was achieving some goal. He also had personal rigidities that restricted the spontaneity so important in public figures. For example, he had a phobia about germs. When he toured prisons, he would not touch a doorknob without first wiping it off with a folded handkerchief concealed in his palm. He also drank three quarts of water a day because of its presumed healthful effects. Dewey achieved much, but had he been less rigid he might have achieved even more; perhaps more important, he might have been a happier person (R. N. Smith, 1982).

Governor Dewey's differentness was quite mild in comparison to problems like those experienced by Joan Houghton. Houghton's break with reality required intensive treatment during a 5-week period of hospitalization. After her recovery she wrote an account of her experiences.

My mother and I sat next to each other in the waiting room while my father investigated admission procedures. A young man was seated near us. Perspiration dripped across his brow and down his cheeks. In silence I took a tissue from my purse, moved close to him and gently wiped the moisture from his face. I reassured him that everything would be fine.

Then my father rejoined us. We went together to a small room where I met Kay, the psychiatric social worker assigned

The Experience of Distress

Most people who have emotional problems refer to the distress they are experiencing. Distress can arise because of recognizable causes or it can be the result of processes that are very difficult to comprehend. Nancy Raine described her thoughts and feelings after having been raped in a way that can only evoke our understanding and sympathy.

I know how to mark my birthday, my wedding anniversary, even the anniversary of my brother's death. But the day I was raped? How should I observe the passing of another year? . . . I can never again be that woman who locked her door and felt safe. My husband, my mother, my friends still suffer their own brand of helplessness when they try to imagine the content of my memory. My father, who spent his life in law enforcement, leaves the room if the subject of rape in general, or my rape in particular, creeps into the conversation. Why remind them? And dare they remind me, when they secretly hope I might be "over it" at last?

On this anniversary, more or less safe

in the cradle of the day's routine, I began to think back. To the first anniversary, when I realized that I had to stop talking about what happened to me because the people who loved me could not bear to hear it. The second, when I pretended to myself I was "over it." The third, when I realized I wasn't. The fourth, when I was in treatment for posttraumatic stress syndrome. The fifth, when I was convinced my treatment wasn't helping and secretly wondered if I had the guts to kill myself. The sixth, during a lunch date, when I told a woman I barely knew that our meeting was occurring on the anniversary of my rape. I spoke matter-of-factly, afraid she might gather up her black briefcase and suddenly remember a dentist's appointment.

(Raine, 1994, p. 34)

Billy Henderson, who is currently living in the community but had been in mental hospitals on three occasions, responded to the question, "Tell me about yourself," in a way that can only leave us puzzled and worried about his ability to function.

My hands feel paralyzed and I feel under unbearable stress. I'm going to do something.

I believe in free elections of the Protection and Advocacy for Military Intelligence Officers (PAMIO). The Secretary of the Department of Insubordinate Criminals (DIC) is confused about the Genetic Research Committee (GRC) and needs to be brief and redirected. In addition, the oatbran fiasco needs to be analyzed and publicized. I feel strongly about these issues as well as some even more basic ones, including:

- *Mental institutions function by "denying the self" in their victims.*
- *Love should be withdrawn from evil so that it takes its deserved fall.*
- *People suffer as public martyrs for the existence of loves that threaten power (power is the ability to mistreat people with impunity).*
- *A new support group is needed for people who have in common things that were but aren't (for example, victims of electric shock "therapy").*

---

to my case, and a psychiatrist (whose name I don't recall). We talked a few minutes. I was presented with a piece of paper and instructed to sign my name. Obediently, I wrote "Saint Joan" on the paper, not realizing that I was voluntarily admitting myself to a state mental hospital. . . . At the time of my hospitalization I had both a sense of death and a rebirth about me. My first psychotic episode appeared as a private mental exorcism, ending with the honor of sainthood and the gifts of hope and faith.

(Houghton, 1982, pp. 548–549)

The Stigma of Abnormal Behavior

Although Joan Houghton's recovery enabled her to obtain and hold a job at the National Institute of Mental Health and to write sensitively about her experience, she faced many barriers that made the recovery process more difficult than it had to be. Her ordeal continued after discharge from the hospital.

The crisis of mental illness appeared as a nuclear explosion in my life. All that I had known and enjoyed previously was suddenly transformed, like some strange reverse process of nature, from a butterfly's beauty into a pupa's cocoon. There

was a binding, confining quality to my life, in part chosen, in part imposed. Repeated rejections, the awkwardness of others around me, and my own discomfort and self-consciousness propelled me into solitary confinement.

My recovery from mental illness and its aftermath involved a struggle—against my own body, which seemed to be without energy and stamina, and against a society that seemed reluctant to embrace me. It seemed that my greatest needs—to be wanted, needed, valued—were the very needs which others could not fulfill. At times, it felt as though I were trying to swim against a tidal wave.

(Houghton, 1980, p. 8)

The following incident illustrates what swimming against that tidal wave was like.

One Sunday I went to church alone after being absent for several weeks. The minister (who knew of my history, faith, and strong belief in God) began his sermon with reference to the devil. He said, "If you ever want to be convinced of the existence of the devil, you should visit a mental institution." To illustrate his point, he described people who had lost control of their bodily functions, who screamed out obscenities. I left church after the sermon, drove home vowing never to re-

turn to that church as long as that minister preached from the pulpit. At home, however, I began to replace my anger with doubt. Maybe I misunderstood.

At my invitation the minister visited our home to discuss his philosophy about mental illness and the mentally ill. His visit was our last encounter. Not only did he see evil in mental illness but he conveyed an unforgiving attitude to those who have the misfortune of residing in mental hospitals.

(Houghton, 1980, p. 10)

As Houghton's account makes clear, people who are noticeably deviant may experience prejudice and discrimination. The stigma associated with mental illness may express itself directly, as when people outrightly reject individuals who behave in abnormal ways, or indirectly, as when former mental patients anticipate rejection even though they have not been rebuffed by anyone. In the course of socialization we all develop ideas about how mental patients are viewed and treated. If we are not mental patients ourselves, these beliefs may be relatively unimportant to us, applicable only to people on the margins of our lives. For those who do become patients, however, the beliefs become personally relevant. If they think that people devalue and discriminate against mental patients, they feel threatened. They may keep their personal worries and preoccupations a secret, or they may remove themselves from any social situation where they might be rejected. The resulting social withdrawal, uncertainty, and tentativeness affect their job performance, their relationship with others, and their opinion of themselves.

Although mental health professionals often conclude that severe mental illness stems from organic or brain-based disorders, the general public does not share this view. For example, one survey found that 71 percent of respondents thought severe mental illness was due to emotional weakness, 65 percent thought bad parenting was to blame, 35 percent cited sinful behavior, and 45 percent believed that the mentally ill bring on their illness and could will it away if they wished (Judd, 1990).[1] Further, while psychologists believe much mental illness can be cured or most maladaptive behavior greatly reduced, a full 43 percent of survey respondents thought mental illnesses are incurable. Only 10 percent believed that severe mental disorders had a biological basis and involved the brain. A challenge to the field of abnormal psychology is to correct such misperceptions that distort the nature of abnormal behavior and may contribute to such stigmatization.

[1]The percentage of responses across the categories adds to more than 100, because the respondents had the option of choosing more than one possible cause.

Adaptive and Maladaptive Behavior

The bulk of the behaviors studied by abnormal psychology are related to human failures and inadequacies. These failures in living are due mainly to failures in adaptation. **Adaptation** involves the balance between what people do and want to do, on the one hand, and what the environment (the community) requires, on the other.

Adaptation is a dynamic process. Each of us responds to our environment and to the changes that occur within it. How well we adapt depends on two factors: our personal characteristics (skills, attitudes, physical condition) and the nature of the situations that confront us (for example, family conflict or natural disaster). These two factors jointly determine whether we survive, are content, and prosper, or whether we fall by the wayside. Because nothing—not ourselves, not the environment—stays the same for very long, adaptation must take place all the time. The extremely rapid rate of change in the modern world puts a particular strain on our ability to adapt. Moreover, successful adaptation to one set of conditions is not a guarantee of successful adaptation to others.

Adaptation and Adjustment Scientists sometimes draw a distinction between *adaptation* and *adjustment*. **Adaptation** can refer to survival of the species, whereas **adjustment** refers to individual mastery of the environment and the sense of being at peace with oneself. In many instances this distinction is valid and useful. In certain cases, however, it oversimplifies the human situation. Unlike those of animals, the adaptive successes and failures of human beings cannot be measured simply in terms of the survival and reproduction of the species. For most people in the modern world, concerns about quality of life and level of contentment far overshadow the need to satisfy biological requirements. Human beings have developed subtle language forms, a refined level of thinking, superior problem-solving skills, intricate social relationships, and complex communication processes, all of which affect behavior and its interpretation. The notion that a failure to adapt may affect survival of the species has some credibility—individuals' feelings of failure may damage their social relationships, and the human gene pool might be significantly affected by the failure of such people to marry and have children. On the other hand, many individuals with certain types of inadequacies, who would probably be unable to hold their own in a subsistence economy, can survive and reproduce in the modern world because of social institutions such as welfare programs, Social Security, and health insurance.

Biological factors aside, how we live and how we feel about the way we live are important factors in human adaptation. For the authors of this book, adaptation refs to people's ability or inability to modify their behavior in response to changing environmental requirements. This book, therefore, focuses primarily on people's personal and social adaptations.

Maladaptive Versus Deviant Behavior All maladaptive behavior is deviant behavior. However, deviant or unusual behavior is not necessarily maladaptive. This can be seen in the case of Albert Einstein. At the age of 12, Einstein decided to devote his life to solving the "riddle of the huge world." Early in his career, while working as a patent office examiner, he wrote five papers that eventually changed our view of the universe. Although public recognition of the importance of Einstein's theory was many years away, his ability to think about the properties of matter in a completely new way began almost at once to influence the thought of physicists. While other kinds of deviant behaviors, such as wearing very bright ties, refusing to travel by airplane, drinking 10 cups of coffee a day, and needing to read in bed for two hours before falling asleep, are not as productive as Einstein's behavior and may seem odd or annoying, people who act in these ways do not need major rehabilitative efforts to live happy, productive lives. The person who wrote this letter to "Dear Abby" may be quiet and shy, but she does not seem to be abnormal.

Thank you for printing the letter from the teen-age girl who was struggling with shyness.

I, too, am a very shy and quiet person. I've been this way all my life. I can't tell you how many people have said, "You sure are quiet." I can't imagine anyone going up to a person and saying, "You sure have a big mouth!"

I would like to reassure everyone that I know I am quiet, but I am a very well-adjusted, happy person who enjoys being quiet. I am quiet because I have nothing to say, and I don't want to fill the quietness with empty chatter. I would find it quite exhausting to make small talk, or worse yet, try to be the life of the party.

In the past, I have tried to talk more and be more outgoing so people would like me better, but it did not become me. . . . It was not natural.

It has taken me years to like myself just the way I am. I have many friends who like me just the way I am, so to the others who are disturbed by my quietness and shy personality, please leave me alone. Please don't try to make me feel that there is something wrong with me because I am different from you who feel compelled to talk all the time.

Abby, if you print this—and I hope you do—you will be doing an enormous favor to all the shy, quiet people who read your column. There are more of us than you could possibly imagine.

(*Seattle Times*, July 18, 1993, p. L3)

Describing behavior as **maladaptive** implies that a problem exists; it also suggests that vulnerability in the individual, inability to cope, or exceptional stress in the environment has led to problems in living. Students of maladaptive behavior are especially interested in behavior that is not merely different or deviant but that also represents a source of concern to the individual, to his or her family and friends, or to society. This means, for example, that students of maladaptive behavior direct more of their attention toward those with very low IQs than toward those with high IQs, or toward those who are not happy rather than toward those who are extremely content.

There are many causes of maladaptations. In some instances—for example, in certain forms of brain damage—an organic cause is uncovered. In other cases, undesirable present or past social relationships—for example, an incestuous relationship—may be implicated. In still other cases, a combination of these factors along with a stressful event, such as the death of a loved one or the birth of a child, plays a decisive role.

Maladaptations range from chronic fears that are troubling but not disabling to severe distortion of reality, and inability to function independently. A person may simply be unhappy about his or her maladaptive behavior, or the community may be worried about what might happen if the person is not removed from society. Throughout this book many different kinds of maladaptive behavior will be described, along with the social reactions they evoke.

Vulnerability, Resiliency, and Coping

When we talk about how well people adapt, it is important to consider the conditions under which the adaptations are made. The same person may handle a frightening or difficult situation well at one time and maladaptively at others. Some people may behave adaptively in the same situation that others handle poorly. This diversity suggests that it is insufficient to argue that maladaptive behavior occurs simply because of the nature of the situation or stress associated with a particular event.

Stress, our reaction to a situation that poses demands, constraints, or opportunities, is usually not wanted. People are likely to experience psychological stress when they have to deal with an unexpected or unusual change, such as a natural disaster. They are likely to experience even greater stress than usual when the change occurs at the same time as a severe life crisis (such as the death of a loved one) or at the beginning of a critical developmental period (such as adolescence). As Table 1-1 shows, the average number of stressful life events (such as family disturbances, serious illness of a parent, brother, or sister) is greater for clinical cases than for comparable control persons.

TABLE 1–1
Negative Life Events and Personal Maladjustment

Clinical Group		Average Number of Negative Life Events
Conduct disorders	Cases	1.18
	Controls	.36
Mild mood disorders	Cases	1.13
	Controls	.36
Severe mood disorders	Cases	.84
	Controls	.22
Somatic symptoms disorders	Cases	1.04
	Controls	.19

Source: Based on Goodyer, Kolvin, and Gatzanis, (1985). Reprinted with permission from the *British Journal of Psychiatry.*

Despite these general differences between cases and controls, increasing attention is being given to the fact that some people—even those with clinically diagnosed disorders—are not sidetracked by stress. They seem to roll with the punches and function well in the face of adversity. We might think of *risk* and *protective factors* as characterizing each person's life. The risk factors contribute to vulnerability and the protective factors to resiliency.

Vulnerability refers to how likely we are to respond maladaptively to certain situations. An individual can be an effective coper in one situation but not in another. Vulnerability may be increased through heredity, such as having a schizophrenic parent, by certain personality characteristics such as a tendency to worry or feel anxious, by the lack of certain skills such as the ability to make decisions calmly, or by a buildup of unexpected negative experiences. Some people are more vulnerable in all situations because they deal less effectively with what happens to them in daily life. Others are more vulnerable simply because of a combination of recent stressful events. Certainly people are more vulnerable in particular kinds of situations that remind them of former problems or difficulties. For example, upon seeing a child swept away in a river, a person who had seen one of her younger brothers killed in an accident when she was 5 might freeze, while someone who had not had such an experience might be able to act in time to save the child.

Certain life conditions in and of themselves increase people's vulnerability and increase their risk of maladaptive behavior. People who share these conditions become a part of a high-risk group that is more likely than the rest of the population to experience the negative effects of stress. Population groups that may be at high risk for certain conditions include children and adolescents, the aged and the disabled, and disadvantaged minority groups.

Protective factors may compensate for high-risk elements in someone's life and contribute to **resiliency,** the ability to function effectively in the face of adversity and to "bounce back" following significant stress. There are people who, despite their exposure to multiple risk factors, do not show the dire consequences one might expect under the circumstances. Sometimes, the competence associated with resiliency coexists with emotional disturbance, undesirable living conditions, and personally threatening experiences. For example, there is evidence that a significant number of abused children do not succumb to a sense of hopelessness as their inevitable fate (Zimrin, 1986). These children do not exhibit manifest psychiatric symptoms and are not suicidal or self-destructive. Their resiliency enables them to maintain a positive outlook on life and turn away from despair, passivity, and defeatism. While there usually are negative consequences to their abusive experiences, these children seem to have a certain toughness and positive outlook on life (see Box 1-2).

Resilient people are often described as being good copers. **Coping** refers to how people deal with difficulties and attempt to overcome them. **Coping skills** are the techniques available to an individual in making such attempts. A number of general skills are useful in handling stressful situations. These include thinking constructively, dealing with problems as they arise, behaving flexibly, and providing feedback to oneself about which tactics work in a given situation and which ones do not. How useful any particular skill will be depends upon the nature of the situation and the individual's vulnerabilities and assets. Having an effective repertory of coping skills strengthens a person's sense of self-control and self-direction. By gaining greater control over our behavior, we may be able to alter environmental conditions that influence us.

Clinical interventions are ways of helping people deal with their vulnerabilities and improve their re-

The Resilient Budding Scientist

Seventeen-year-old Jamel Oeser-Sweat is a member of a fatherless family who lives in an apartment in a New York City housing project. Jamel's mother had been a foster child, has a chronic psychological disorder, and has been hospitalized for this condition (necessitating Jamel being placed in a group home). When Jamel comes home at the end of the day, he passes drug dealers who ask "What do you want?" and young ladies who make eyes at him. At his housing project he sometimes has to stand on his toes in the elevator to avoid the urine puddles. His family only recently acquired a telephone.

What makes Jamel remarkable is his resiliency. In 1994, he was named one of 40 finalists in the nationwide Westinghouse Science Talent Search scholarship competition. The project that led to this recognition was an experiment he conducted at Mount Sinai Medical Center on bacteria showing that certain materials could cause skin lesions and other diseases if not decontaminated regularly. In 1993, he received a top award in the New York City Science Expo and an invitation to have dinner with the mayor.

Because life in the projects held little for Jamel Oeser-Sweat, he plunged himself into a range of activities, finding people along the way who cared for him and advised him. Although his grades were not exceptionally high, one teacher noticed how quickly Jamel was able to synthesize difficult information and arranged for him to participate in a special Mount Sinai program. On his own, Jamel decided to tutor children in a Harlem elementary school (see Figure 1-1).

There is a certain sadness to Jamel (he has been told he rarely smiles). But he is highly intelligent, has a strong desire to help others, and is able to establish rewarding supportive relationships—for example, with the teacher who noticed his exceptional ability to process information. In the face of overwhelmingly negative life experiences, he is a case study, not of pathology, but of resiliency.

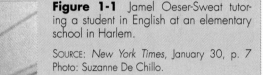

Figure 1-1 Jamel Oeser-Sweat tutoring a student in English at an elementary school in Harlem.

SOURCE: *New York Times,* January 30, p. 7 Photo: Suzanne De Chillo.

siliency. The intervention selected for someone who is experiencing a short-term crisis, such as the serious illness of a loved one, might be a tranquilizing drug. In this case, the tranquilizer reduces vulnerability to intense anxiety experienced over a specific period of time. In other cases, insight into the person's desires, motivations, and conflicts is needed in order to help the individual cope more effectively with stress and become less vulnerable to the crises that are the inevitable ingredients of every human life. Sometimes the person needs to learn new skills or behaviors that are effective in dealing with difficult situations. For some people, the way they think about a situation needs to be changed. If a low test grade makes you think, "I'm dumb; it's no use trying to finish this course," later academic performance might be very different than it would be if you thought, "I didn't study very effectively; I'd better organize my work better and check with the professor before the next test to ask about the points that aren't clear." Clinicians thus will vary their approaches depending on their assessment of the factors in a given case and the psychological perspective or viewpoints they favor.

One of the guiding principles of this book is that each person has a particular set of vulnerability and resiliency factors that influence how well he or she adapts to life's circumstances. In addition, people differ in how supportive their environment is in helping them adjust to adversity. Seven-year-old Denton may adapt well when he has a sympathetic teacher, when his parents are getting along well, and when he is healthy. However, if he has a teacher whom he hates, if his parents bicker half the night and are on the edge of divorce, and if he is constipated, he may become much more upset about not being a starting player on his soccer team than he might otherwise. Or if Mrs. Block has just lost an important client for her firm and comes home to find someone has smashed into her car as it sat parked in the driveway, and then her 12-year-old son tells her he has just left his violin on the school bus, she may not respond as constructively as she might under other circumstances.

The concepts of vulnerability and resiliency have implications not only for treatment and prevention but also for improving our understanding of the determinants of maladaptive behavior. Research on these topics is gathering momentum and helping us better understand their source (Schuldberg, 1993). For example, after reviewing the pertinent literature, Garmezy (1993) concluded that three dimensions of resiliency seem especially important: (1) *temperamental factors*, such as activity level and responsiveness to others; (2) *family factors*, such as warmth, cohesion, and caring; and (3) *external support*, such as neighbors, parents of friends, and clergymen who are supportive and actively want to help. In illustrating this last factor, Garmezy (1993, pp. 134–135) relates the following anecdote:

> In the foyer of a walk-up apartment building in Harlem there was a large frame on the wall within the entrance way. The photographs of children who lived in the apartment building were pasted on the frame with a written request that if anyone saw any of these children endangered on the street to bring them back to the apartment house. My thoughts focus on those who conceived the idea, put up the sign, and joined in providing photographs of their children. Can there be a better example of adult competence and concern for the safety of children? Is this effort not a dramatic reflection of what we mean when we seek to describe "protective" factors on behalf of the well-being of children under stress?

In this book we will present a number of different perspectives on why maladaptive behavior occurs and how adaptive behavior can be substituted for it. Running through our discussion of abnormal psychology will be a consideration of the effects of vulnerability and resiliency on the outcome of any particular situation. The more we understand what causes an individual to feel stressed, and the more we can identify the factors that produce vulnerability, the clearer the sources of the maladaptive behavior will be and the more likely we will be to come up with effective treatment procedures. This search for understanding is what the study of abnormal psychology is all about.

The Epidemiology of Maladaptive Behavior

While the primary task of a clinician is to diagnose and treat illness in individual patients, the epidemiologist investigates the occurrence of illness in populations and identifies factors (for example, heredity and family history) that influence their occurrence. Psychologists use findings from **epidemiological research** to help them understand patterns and possible relationships between maladaptive behaviors of certain populations or groups and a variety of environmental and behavioral factors. Information for epidemiological research may come from analyses of various types of data, such as hospital and clinic records, the geographical distribution of mental disorders, and the types of community facilities available for the treatment of the mentally disturbed. For example, a study of institutional records has shown that the northeastern and Pacific Coast regions of the United States have had consistently higher rates of schizophrenia over an 83-year period than have other regions of the country (Torrey & Bowler, 1990). Research is needed to identify the reasons for these geographical differences.

Another example of the role of epidemiological research emerges from the finding that a number of basic personal factors, such as age and sex, have been shown to be correlated with types of disorders and use of clinical facilities (National Institute of Mental Health, 1990). Table 1–2 shows the rates per 100,000 population for different age groups admitted to outpatient facilities for the treatment of mental and behavioral problems. It is noteworthy that children and youth are admitted at a higher rate relative to their number in the

TABLE 1–2 Admission to Outpatient Mental Health Services[a]	
Age Group	**Rate**
Under 18	872.3
18–24	1098.9
25–44	1276.2
45–64	567.4
65 and over	229.6
All ages	888.6
[a]Rates per 100,000 civilian population Source: Based on National Institute of Mental Health (1990), p. 164.	

population than are both the elderly and those aged 45 to 64. In contrast, the admission rates for the elderly are low relative to their number in the population.

Epidemiologists are interested in identifying the environmental causes of particular conditions, especially those causes associated with a community's way of life. The Broad Street pump incident is one of the most famous examples of epidemiological inquiry and its use in furthering public health. In 1848, during a severe cholera epidemic in London, a study of the disease's distribution within the city was carried out. The investigation showed that the outbreak had a geographical center, a water pump in Broad Street. It was further found that two groups of people within that area—inmates of an institution and employees of a brewery—did not develop the illness in anything like epidemic proportions. Each of these groups had its own well, and brewery workers drank beer rather than water at work. On the basis of this information, the Broad Street pump was dismantled and the epidemic was brought under control. This example is especially interesting because it shows how epidemiological detective work can contribute to human well-being even when the cause of a condition is unknown—in 1848 the microorganisms that cause cholera had not yet been identified.

Prevalence, Incidence, and Risk Factors

Epidemiologists conduct surveys to estimate the extent of a health problem. Although their primary focus is on the occurrence of various types of abnormality, epidemiologists also gather information about the frequency of behavior in the normal population. This information often provides a valuable context for interpreting statistics about conditions that are clearly pathological. For example, one survey of approximately 45,000 Americans found that one-third have poor mental and physical health at least one day a month. Indicators of poor mental health status included stress, depression, and emotional problems. The elderly (75 years and older) reported fewer poor mental health days (1.9) than those between the ages of 18 and 24 (3.4). American Indians and Alaska natives had the highest number of "not good" days (3.8), while Asians and Pacific Islanders had the lowest number (2.3 days). Women had 3.3 poor mental health days compared with men (2.2 days). People who were separated or divorced reported more poor days (5.4 and 3.9, respectively) than the never married and married (3.0 and 2.4). Table 1-3 summarizes findings related to self-reports of subpar mental health.

Another recent survey has shown that close to one in two Americans—48 percent—has experienced a mental disorder at some point in their lives, and 30 percent suffer from one in any given year (Kessler et al., 1994).

TABLE 1–3
Self-Reported Bad Days (Recent Mental Health)

Question	Response	Percent
(Number of days when mental health was not good during the 30 days preceding the survey)	0 days	68.5
	1–2 days	9.9
	3–7 days	10.6
	8 or more days	10.9

Source: Centers for Disease Control and Prevention

These odds that someone will suffer from a mental disorder over a lifetime are much higher than have been found in previous years. Weight needs to be given to this study because it was a comprehensive survey using face-to-face interviews with more than 8,000 people between the ages of 15 and 54 in 34 states. The survey found that the most common disorder was major depression, with 10 percent of Americans experiencing the problem in a given year and 17 percent having had major depression at some point in life. The second most common disorder was alcohol dependence, with 7 percent having the problem during a given year and 14 percent at some point in life. The most severe psychiatric disorders were concentrated among a small number of people who tend to suffer from several disorders at once.

Epidemiological research has identified a number of factors that must be attended to in order to ensure the accuracy of survey results. These include representative sampling of the population, clearly worded questions asked, and careful training of interviewers. Table 1-4 gives the definitions of a number of concepts used in epidemiological research.

Two types of information are obtained in epidemiological surveys. **Prevalence** data describe the frequency of occurrence of a given condition among a certain population at a particular point in time. For example, if, on a given date, 100 cases of depression were counted in a

TABLE 1–4
Epidemiological Concepts

Incidence. The rate of new cases during a defined period of time (for example, one year).
Prevalence. The rate of both new and old (existing) cases for a defined period of time (for example, 6-month prevalence).
Lifetime prevalence. The proportion of people in the general population who ever had a particular disorder.
Risk factor. A specific characteristic or condition whose presence is associated with an increased likelihood that a specific disorder is present, or will develop at a later time.

community of 1,000 people, the prevalence rate would be 10 percent. A recent study has concluded that one in five Americans has an active behavioral disorder, and the best estimate is a 32 percent lifetime prevalence for a disorder of some type (Robins & Regier, 1991). **Incidence** data relate to the number of *new* cases of a specific condition that arise during a particular period of time. For example, if 10 people who had not been depressed at the time of the prevalence study became depressed during the next year, the incidence rate would be 1 percent.

In addition to prevalence and incidence, another important epidemiological concept is **risk factor.** This concept is based on the finding of a statistically significant association between a disorder and a factor (for example, lung cancer and smoking; cardiovascular disease and high cholesterol level). For example, the following are risk factors that have been identified for violent behavior (Reid & Balis, 1987):

- History of aggressive, destructive behavior
- History of repeated traffic violations (reckless driving, etc.)
- History of abuse and neglect in childhood
- Childhood history of severe hyperactivity and restlessness
- Habitual alcohol use and dependence
- Suicidal attempts and gestures
- Hypersexuality
- Low frustration tolerance
- Low self-esteem and failure to achieve
- Inability to examine one's own behavior
- Impulsivity
- Self-centeredness

When risk factors are identified, they may be useful in suggesting prevention efforts. For example, children who have been abused or neglected might be given the opportunity to have positive experiences with caring adults as a step toward preventing long-term frustration and anger. Risk factors can serve as early warning signs of the need for intervention regarding particular conditions.

The value of identifying risk factors is reflected in a study of the relationship between diagnosis of abnormal behavior and the likelihood of committing violent acts. Only a small minority of all people who commit violent acts are psychotic, and they are responsible for relatively little violent crime. However, there is a statistical connection between psychosis (particularly schizophrenia) and violence and between drug and alcohol-related disorders and violence (J. C. Beck, 1994; Torrey, 1994). The research shows that psychotic delusions and hallucinations may provide the individual with a rationale for violence because of the need to counterattack. If

substance abuse through some combination of education and treatment were reduced and if more effective long-term treatment of patients with psychotic disorders were provided, violence in these groups might be substantially reduced.

Epidemiological research on a large representative sample of residents in several cities has shown that persons diagnosed with anxiety disorders have low rates of violence while those diagnosed with schizophrenia have slightly elevated rates (Swanson et al. 1990). Young males of lower socioeconomic status are found to be at substantially higher risk levels. The other important finding of the Swanson study concerns the relationship between the number of diagnostic categories used in describing individuals and the risk of violent behavior. As Figure 1-2 shows, the rate of reported violent behavior increases sharply with the number of diagnostic categories assigned by clinical workers. A greater number of diagnostic categories might be taken as an indicator of the complexity of a case and the gross amount and variety of psychopathology present. Thus, the more symptoms and problems someone has, the more likely that violent behavior will be among them. We should bear in mind the limitations of this epidemiological survey, however. The reports of violent behavior came from the survey respondents themselves. The study's conclusions need to be confirmed by independent assessments of the occurrence of violent behavior.

In addition to establishing connections between various factors, epidemiological surveys have proven valuable in correcting some false assumptions (Robins &

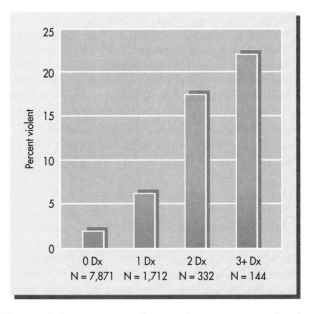

Figure 1-2 Percentage of respondents reporting violent behavior by the number of diagnoses (Dx).

Source: Swanson, Holzer, Ganju, & Jono. (1990). *Hospital and Community Psychiatry*, p. 767.

Regier, 1991). It had been thought that minority groups must have high rates of antisocial personality and substance abuse disorders because they have high rates of arrest and incarceration. However, recent evidence suggests that the high arrest and incarceration rates among minority groups cannot be explained simply by diagnoses of antisocial personality and substance abuse disorders. Until recently it had been generally assumed that women are particularly liable to develop psychological problems. However, recent surveys have shown that psychological disorders in men are as common or slightly more common than in women. Women are more likely to have depressive and anxiety disorders while men are more apt to have substance abuse and antisocial personality disorders (Robins & Regier, 1991).

Mental illness has an effect not only on diagnosed individuals, but also on their family members. An estimated 30 to 40 million people experience some direct consequences because of their close ties with mentally ill individuals (Research on Mental Illness and Addictive Disorders, 1985). In this book, we will focus not only on the effect of maladaptive behavior on the person whose problems are described but also on the impact of the problem on family members—parents, husbands, wives, and children. Table 1-5 lists several factors that are significantly related to the presence of mental illness. It seems clear that interpersonal, economic, and educational factors play important roles in the frequency of abnormal behaviors. There is also evidence that people who have good coping skills and supportive friends and relatives are less likely to suffer psychological distress than those who do not (Horwitz, 1984).

TABLE 1–5
Factors Associated with Rates of Diagnosed Mental Disorder

1. *Age.* Younger people have higher rates than older people.
2. *Marital Status.* Separated, divorced, and single people have higher rates than the married and widowed.
3. *Education.* Less educated people have higher rates than people who have more education.
4. *Personal Income.* The lower the income, the higher the rates.
5. *Employment Status.* Unemployed people have higher rates than employed people.
6. *Contact with Friends.* Lack of social contacts is associated with relatively high rates.
7. *Satisfaction with Relationships with Friends and Relatives.* The greater the satisfaction, the lower the rates.
8. *Marital Happiness.* The greater the degree of marital happiness, the lower the rates.

Source: Based on Leaf, P.J., Weissman, M.M., Myers, J.K., Tischler, G.L., and Holzer, C.E. (1984).

Seeking Help for Abnormal Behavior

People seek help for a variety of reasons and from a variety of clinical facilities.

Reasons for Clinical Contacts

Some people seek professional help because they are dissatisfied with themselves and certain aspects of their lives; others do so because of concerns expressed by family members, friends, or co-workers; still others are forced to see clinicians because they have gotten into trouble in the community.

Personal Unhappiness In the following case, personal unhappiness seems to have been the factor that led this person to seek help.

> Jack Farmer was a 40-year-old executive in a large multinational corporation. From all outward appearances, any differences he might have had from other people were positive. Whatever weaknesses he had were minor. For example, his athletic ability was probably below average. The opinion of his company and community was that Jack Farmer was a very well-functioning individual. While he and his wife and two children got along reasonably well, Jack had some concerns that had shaped his family role, particularly as his children approached high school age. These concerns had to do with the burdens of family responsibility, especially the need he felt to ensure his family's happiness should anything happen to him. He occasionally commented to his wife that television commercials about the need to have plenty of life insurance seem to have been written specifically with him in mind. However, Jack was concerned about more than money. He felt that he should be a closer friend to his children and less distant from his wife than he often was. He was also very concerned about the issue of nuclear waste and the pollution of the natural environment. His concerns often led to his feeling blue and hopeless about the future.
>
> One Sunday Jack read a newspaper article about a local mental health center that had opened recently. The article pointed out that the center's services were not restricted to severely disturbed individuals, that perfectly normal people who have hit a rough spot in their lives might find it valuable to talk with an expert about their personal problems. After several weeks of internal debate ("Could I be a little crazy?," "I'd be ashamed if my friends ever found out that I went to a shrink"), Jack decided to go to the mental health center.

By conventional standards, Jack Farmer's case is not serious. He sought help because of personal dissatisfactions and concerns. Wrestling further with his personal tensions seemed worse to him than his fear of being stigmatized if he sought professional help.

The Concerns of Others Sometimes it is difficult even for professionals to decide what the dividing line should be between maladaptive and merely unusual behavior. In the following case, there was no agreement about whether the woman concerned was psychotic (out of touch with reality) and needed institutionalization, or whether her behavior was simply unusual and presented no hazard to her or her family.

Mary Waverly was in her late twenties. A university graduate, she had run a successful boutique in a large western city until shortly before the birth of her daughter, Alice, who is now 2 years old. During the year before Alice was born, Mary's mother had been treated for cancer. She died when Alice was fourteen months old. During Alice's first year and a half, the baby had surgery several times to correct a birth defect.

Recently, Mary's husband attempted to have her committed to a psychiatric hospital. He said he was concerned about their daughter's welfare. Mary had become preoccupied with rather unusual religious ideas. Although she came from a very religious family, until recently, when she joined a cult group, her behavior had not seemed out of the ordinary. Since joining the group she refused to have sexual relations with her husband because he was not a "believer." Although she seemed to take good care of her child, she made all decisions only after listening to the "voice of the Lord."

When Mary Waverly was examined, her judgment did not seem impaired, her intelligence was found to be above average, and her religious thoughts, although they took up a great deal of her time, did not seem to differ from those of other enthusiastic converts to cult groups. A pediatrician examined her daughter and reported that she was well cared for. A question was raised about what Mary Waverly might do if she thought God told her to harm her child or someone else. Neither of the clinicians who examined her was willing to give a definite answer to this question.

Mary Waverly didn't think she had a mental disorder and didn't think she needed treatment. One of the clinicians agreed. He believed that her behavior was unusual but that she was not mentally ill. Another clinician thought she was a paranoid schizophrenic who should be hospitalized for drug therapy. What should be done when professionals disagree? In this case, after hearing the conflicting views, Mr. Waverly decided not to press for hospitalization.

Legal and Community Problems Mild personal maladaptations like Jack Farmer's affect the lives of the individual and possibly a small number of other people. Mary Waverly's behavior was a matter of concern to her husband because he was worried that she might harm their daughter. In the case of Charles Clay, a legal problem arose over something he had done.

Charles Clay, aged 45, owned what had been a successful 24-hour-a-day grocery store. Now, however, he was having increasing difficulty containing his anger toward his customers. Until five years ago he had been a cheerful, friendly merchant. Then his wife died, and his personality seemed to change. Increasingly he worried that people were trying to shoplift his merchandise. (There was a problem with a few high school students who frequented his store right after school.) As time went on, he began to confront customers with his suspicions and even to demand that some of them submit to being searched.

Not surprisingly, Charles' business began to decline. When this happened, he got very angry and even more suspicious. The culminating event occurred when a woman entered the store, walked around for a few minutes, and then bought a newspaper. When he tried to search her (at the same time yelling, "Don't tell me you were just looking around!"), she ran from the store and summoned the police. The ensuing police investigation led him to seek advice from his lawyer, who had been a friend since high school. Although Charles insisted that "there is nothing the matter with me," his anger and suspiciousness bothered his lawyer. Using tact and persuasion, the lawyer got him to agree to visit a psychiatrist. Unfortunately, the visit did not work out well. He was reluctant to talk about his concerns with the psychiatrist and was angered by what he viewed as the psychiatrist's inquisitiveness. He refused to return for a second visit. Nevertheless, the lawyer was able to get Charles out of trouble with the police. Unfortunately, several months later he was arrested and convicted of physically attacking another customer.

Many people saw Charles Clay as having problems that he refused to recognize. In spite of the social consensus about the maladaptive quality of his behavior, he gave himself a clean bill of health. In part because of his failure to perceive his own behavior accurately, he eventually got into trouble with the law. His first contact with the police did not result in formal charges; the community's agents recognized his psychological difficulties, and the focus of their attention was on helping a citizen with his personal problems. The second contact, however, resulted in punishment for a crime. Society had decided that he was not going to help himself and moved to protect itself.

Gross failure to see oneself accurately, as illustrated by the case of Charles Clay, is characteristic of several of the most serious forms of maladaptive behavior. In such cases, it is a highly positive development if the person begins to suspect that his or her behavior is contributing to difficulties in getting along with others.

Sources of Help

People whose behavior is maladaptive can receive help in various types of facilities staffed by several types of mental health specialists.

Types of Treatment Facilities Despite the decrease in recent years in number of beds in state mental hospitals, these institutions continue to play an important role in caring for the most disturbed and troublesome patients in the U.S. mental health system. State hospitals serve as 24-hour emergency backups, the institutions of last resort and ultimate responsibility. Nevertheless, most experts agree about the desirability of treating people in the community as early as possible so as to avoid institutionalization.

Community-based treatment has become a more realistic possibility for some disturbed individuals because of an increase in the availability of community facilities, changes in state laws regarding involuntary hospitalization and the detaining of disturbed individuals in mental hospitals, and the discovery that a variety of drugs effectively control much of the violent and bizarre behavior associated with mental patients. The number of community treatment and care facilities has increased over threefold since 1955, and the trend toward treating people in the community is now firmly established. Figure 1-3 shows some of the mental health services that are available today.

Since the 1960s there has been a movement to **deinstitutionalize,** or return to the community, mental patients whose problems can be expected to continue for long periods. Under the banner of community-based care, many of them now live in group homes, boarding houses, residential hotels (often in undesirable neighborhoods), and subsidized apartments. This change, based partly on concern for the civil rights of the individual, is also a result of scientific advances like the use of antipsychotic drugs. These make it possible for many people to function adaptively enough so that they don't need to be institutionalized, although many of these individuals still behave in marginal, ineffective fashion. The development of community support programs in conjunction with established therapeutic programs for chronically mentally ill individuals offers promise of better lives for many people. At the present time, however, a compre-

(a)

(b)

(c)

Figure 1-3 A variety of community mental health services provide for the many different mental health needs that exist in any community. (a) Group homes provide for living arrangements with opportunities for independent living, self-care, and contact with others. (b) Community clinics and outpatient facilities enable patients to receive treatment while still residing in the community. (c) Not all mental health services are provided by professionals. This parent volunteer is discussing drug problems with a teen group.

hensive range of residential, therapeutic, and social services is not available in many communities. As a result, many people who might be able to function in a protected environment or with some types of psychological support or supervision of antipsychotic medication end up as part of the homeless population, often in large urban areas. Chapter 17 will look at this problem in more detail.

Types of Mental Health Specialists Most of the behavior patterns with which this book deals are of special interest to four groups of mental health specialists: clinical and counseling psychologists, psychiatrists, psychiatric social workers, and psychiatric nurses. A **clinical psychologist** holds a graduate degree, usually a Ph.D. or Psy.D. and specializes in abnormal behavior. Clinical psychologists are trained to diagnose and treat personality problems that are not medical or organic in nature. They also plan and conduct research investigations. **Counseling psychologists** may hold a Ph.D. or an Ed.D. degree and work with clients experiencing current life stress. A **psychiatrist** is a physician (an M.D.) with postgraduate training and experience in treating emotional disorders. Psychiatrists have legal responsibilities in commitment proceedings and in the supervision of mental hospitals. Somatic therapies, such as drugs and electroconvulsive therapy, are administered by psychiatrists.

A **psychiatric social worker,** holder of a graduate degree in social work, is most often concerned with the link between a person who displays problematic behavior and his or her home environment. Psychiatric social workers are trained in mental health care and how to work with families and help them utilize social agencies or other community resources to get practical help with such things as finances. A **psychiatric nurse** has special training in the care of mentally ill patients. Psychiatric nurses play a variety of roles. They are skilled in working closely with patients and understanding their needs so that all contacts the patient has with others during a hospitalization have as much of the therapeutic focus as possible. Within hospital settings, psychiatric nurses often supervise ward personnel and train them in the approach they should take with each patient.

The activities of these mental health workers, especially of psychiatrists, clinical psychologists, and social workers often overlap. For example, all three are trained to conduct psychotherapy and counseling. Table 1-6 shows the numbers of men and women among these mental health specialists.

The following account by a clinical psychologist accurately reflects the diversity of activities in which most clinicians engage.

I wish the time passed more slowly because there is just so much to do. From talking to my clinician friends I know I'm not alone in feeling that way. Part of the problem is that most of us don't just do one thing. Sure, some do mainly therapy and others are primarily diagnosticians. But most of us do many things.

Take me, for example. I work in a big-city general hospital that has two wards for psychiatric cases and a large outpatient clinic. Many of these patients are not in very good contact with reality. In some cases police officers picked them up because they were wandering aimlessly around town in the middle of winter, in the dead of night. In other cases, they are people who have had some recent situational stress and are just not able to come to terms with it.

In still other cases, physicians who have patients on other wards in the hospital ask us for help. Yesterday, for example, a surgeon referred a case to me because the patient, who is supposed to undergo abdominal surgery tomorrow, has been in such a psychological panic that the doctor felt something had to be done—and he didn't know what to do. So far, I've talked with the patient twice. Really, all I did was listen and let her ventilate her feelings. You'd be amazed how much just listening in a sympathetic and supportive manner does to help a person who is going through a stressful situation. When I told the surgeon that this patient was very worried about getting too strong a dose of anesthetic and dying he was amazed. He said the patient had never mentioned that worry to him.

About 20 percent of my time is spent dealing with problems nonpsychiatric physicians need help with.

TABLE 1–6 Number of Clinically Trained Mental Health Personnel			
Professional Group	**Total Number**	**Number of Men**	**Number of Women**
Psychology	56,530	35,275	21,255
Psychiatry	30,642	25,348	5,294
Social work	81,737	23,050	58,687
Psychiatric nursing	10,567	444	10,123
Source: Based on *Mental Health, United States.* (1990).			

Perhaps 30 percent is spent doing therapy either on the wards or in the outpatient clinic. Another 20 percent involves administering psychological tests to patients with particular problems. The rest of the time I do research. That's what usually gets squeezed out when a number of pressing clinical problems arise. That's when I most need a time-stretcher. But all the pressure is nothing compared to how much I like what I'm doing. I wouldn't trade with anybody.

The work of professionals in the mental health field is especially challenging because it requires the ability to think on one's feet correctly and quickly size up a problem ("Is this person depressed enough to be thinking about suicide?"), and devise appropriate and sometimes unusual treatment plans for clients. This means that while clinicians strive for complete objectivity in their work and try to use proven techniques, they often must devise on-the-spot tactics to deal with the particular problem confronting them.

Two points should be noted regarding the clinical workers we have described. One is that various professionals play important roles in helping people who are behaving maladaptively improve their level of functioning. For example, counseling psychologists evaluate the interests and aptitudes of hospitalized patients and help prepare them vocationally for a return to the community. The other point is that the various professional groups concerned with diagnosis and treatment of maladaptive behavior often have different theoretical perspectives. For example, psychologists tend to emphasize the link between patients' psychological state and their social ties (for example, their relationships with family and friends), while psychiatrists often take a much more biological approach to treatment, for example, by prescribing medications (Wyatt & Livson, 1994).

Research in Abnormal Psychology

Scientific investigation, or the use of the scientific method, has greatly increased our understanding of abnormal behavior, how to treat it, and how to prevent it. As a consequence, observation and fact have replaced beliefs and hope in the effort to help people suffering from behavior disorders.

Some scientists have contributed to clinical progress either by accident or as an offshoot of some other interest. For example, some advances in developing tranquilizing drugs came from the observation that drugs that were being used for other purposes also decreased anxiety. However, most of the scientific information on which contemporary abnormal psychology is based comes from in-depth studies of deviant people. Although researchers may differ on their interpretation of data, they agree that careful observation is essential for scientific progress.

Observing Behavior

Certain sciences, such as astronomy and anatomy, are basically descriptive in nature. Scientists in those two disciplines concentrate on using careful observations to describe heavenly or earthly bodies. Psychologists also do research that is descriptive in nature. By describing various behaviors and the specific circumstances under which they seem to occur, researchers can obtain important information about potential cause-and-effect relationships. Observation and description are often the first steps in the scientific process; eventually they lead to the formulation of hypotheses that can be tested experimentally and applied in clinical situations. As can be seen in the following description, observation plays an important role in psychological treatment:

> I noticed that Mr. R. never looked directly at me. He answered my questions but always looked the other way. He seemed terribly shy and afraid. I was tempted to ask him what he was afraid of, but decided not to because he might take my comment as a criticism.

Some clinicians might have decided to ask Mr. R. about his apparent fearfulness. However, all would agree on the importance of carefully observing and noting his anxious behavior.

The scientific process always begins with some kind of noteworthy observation. Researchers often stumble onto important discoveries quite by accident. When this happens, a good researcher heeds B. F. Skinner's advice: "When you run into something interesting, drop everything and study it" (Skinner, 1959).

One problem in psychological research is that people cannot be completely disinterested observers of themselves. Personal values, goals, and interests, together with cultural norms, influence our judgments about the success or failure of human adaptation. Maladaptation is neither a universal nor a timeless concept. Behavior that may be quite adaptive in one society may be a failure in another.

With this in mind, how do scientists study human behavior objectively? They record responses, describe events and the conditions surrounding them, and then draw inferences about causes. In order to overcome the effects of personal bias, several observers make reports on each of the individuals or events under study. Reliability increases when these observers have a common frame of reference, agree on which particular aspects of behavior to emphasize (and which not to emphasize), and when they do not have to draw too many inferences from their observations. Observational methods are used in specially created laboratory conditions as well as in naturally occurring situations.

Observation is more than simply using one's eyes in a seemingly straightforward way. Certain questions must be asked first: What types of responses should be selected for observation? How capable is the observer of making reliable and unbiased observations? Will the observer's presence influence the behavior that he or she wants to study? Is it preferable to observe behavior within naturally occurring settings or under controlled laboratory conditions? Should observations be limited to motor responses (walking, running), verbal responses (phone conversations, requests for help), or expressive behavior (smiling, crying)? How long a period of time is needed for reliable observation? Is time sampling needed—that is, should observations be gathered during several different time intervals? Even mental patients who hallucinate frequently do not engage in this kind of behavior all the time; time sampling can provide data on the conditions under which certain types of responses are most likely to occur.

Reliable observations can provide useful records of both the incidence of behavior in a given environment and the events that elicit and maintain it. An example of how observational research can correct commonsense but incorrect assumptions is found in a study of the frequency of interactions between patients and staff on a mental hospital ward (Eldred et al., 1964). One might assume that the staff members' goal of helping their patients would lead them to spend most of their time interacting with the patients. However, as Figure 1-4 shows, the rate at which staff members interacted with other staff members was approximately double the rate at which they interacted with the patients. The low rate of interaction among the patients themselves also seems surprising, but it is typical of the social isolation found on the wards of many mental hospitals.

Although they are subjective and therefore are susceptible to personal bias, **self-observations** can be useful in clinical research. For example, a patient who had been admitted to a mental hospital because of depression was asked to keep track of her mood (level of sadness) and activity (number of social exchanges with hospital staff or other patients). Figure 1-5 shows a progressively less depressed mood and increased social activity during her first 15 days of hospitalization. In this case, there was good agreement between the patient's self-observations and the observations made by the hospital staff. This concordance will not always be the case. As we all know, the people with whom we come into contact in our daily lives may not see us as we see ourselves (see Figure 1-6).

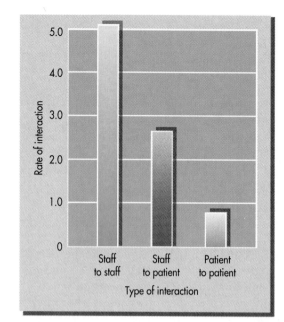

Figure 1-4 Rates of interaction for different patient and staff relationships.

Source: Adapted from Eldred, Bell, Longabaugh, & Sherman. (1964), p. 4.

Self-observations are useful in keeping records of the responses to clinical treatment. In the case of the patient whose self-observations are recorded in Figure 1-5 the treatment was complex, consisting of a benign hospital environment, daily individual and group psychotherapy, and medication. It would be interesting to compare the self-observation records of groups of comparable patients whose treatment consisted of only one of these elements—the hospital environment, psychotherapy, or medication alone—as well as all the possible combinations of these treatments.

Types of Observational Data The value of observations is greatest when what is to be observed is defined explicitly. Four types of data are of special interest in observational research:

1. The stimuli that elicit particular types of responses—for example, the influence of family members' behavior (such as criticism or hostility) on a person who is prone to become depressed.
2. The subjective response to the stimuli—for example, the person's feelings when he or she is criticized.
3. The behavioral response to the stimuli—for example, the person's level of social activity after receiving criticism.
4. The consequences of the behavior—for example, how does the hospital environment respond when the person behaves in a depressed manner?

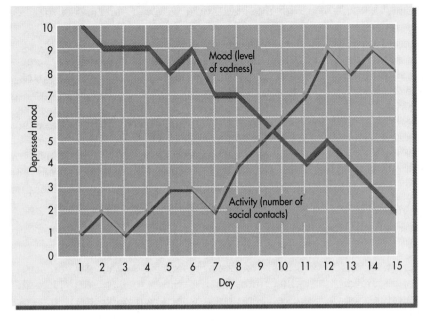

Figure 1-5 The mood and activity changes in a patient treated for depression. The patient's mood ratings are based on her self-observations.

and understand what was observed. Typically, the path of scientific understanding involves these steps:

1. Initial, often informal, observations
2. Tentative hypotheses to explain the meaning of the observations
3. Further observations (if possible, under controlled conditions), to test the hypotheses
4. Theory building

Scientists like to proceed from observation to theory because they want to figure out why or how a particular phenomenon occurs. Behaving just as lay people would, they use reason, logic, and sometimes simple guesswork to arrive at an initial and tentative explanation. However, whereas casual observers may be satisfied with such a tentative answer, scientists recognize it as only tentative and go on to test their understanding by "if . . . then . . ." hypotheses that can be evaluated (for example, "if patients are concerned about rejection by the therapist,

Types of Observational Methods The types of observations made and the observational methods employed depend on a number of factors, including the hypothesis being investigated and the situations in which the observations must be made. Observations might be made by means of hidden videotaping equipment, by visible observers who do not interact with the people they are studying, or by participant observers who become actively involved in the behavior they are observing. Each of these methods has advantages and disadvantages. For example, secret videotaping allows us to observe behavior without the knowledge of the individual who is being observed, but this technique is often questionable for ethical reasons. Participant and nonparticipant observations have been used by anthropologists and sociologists as well as by psychologists. However, any observer may affect people's behavior simply by being present. Participant observers may damage their objectivity by becoming overinvolved with the people they are studying. Nonparticipant observers may come to superficial conclusions because they are not involved enough. Each of these techniques can be valuable, and each has both supporters and critics.

The Role of Theory

While bird watchers, museumgoers, and children in the back seat of a car may observe—often very precisely—what is going on around them, scientists seek to make observations that not only describe what is going on but also explain it. Scientific study involves a continuous interplay between observations and attempts to explain

"You are fair, compassionate, and intelligent, but you are perceived as biased, callous, and dumb."

Figure 1-6 Drawing by Mankoff; copyright 1985 *The New Yorker Magazine, Inc.*

then they will be uncomfortable in therapy," or "if children are frustrated, then they are likely to behave aggressively"). They then proceed to collect the observations needed either to support or refute the hypothesis. If the hypothesis is supported by their observations, they return to their original "Why?" question and attempt to formulate increasingly broad concepts and principles that go beyond initial observations. This is the way that theories are developed.

Good theories have a number of functions. First, they are able to incorporate many existing facts, observations, and relationships within a single, broad explanatory framework. Second, additional hypotheses may be derived from the theory and tested, and may lead to new observations. In this way theories provide a foundation on which to build knowledge. If new observations do not support the theory, it may be modified or discarded. However, it will still have served a valuable function by leading to the discovery of new knowledge and to the development of an even better and more inclusive theory.

In order for a theory to be useful, it must be capable of being tested and refuted. It should be able to specify the types of relationships that are not possible as well as those that are. If it seems able to account for everything and anything, even seemingly contradictory facts, it is not a good scientific theory. The essence of the scientific method is systematic observation and the use of objective procedures to identify cause-and-effect relationships.

The Research Journey

The path of research from observation to theory is a little like going on an automobile trip. There is a lot more to the journey than knowing where one is and where one wants to go. What route should be followed? Will there be detours? Would bad weather make a difference? How should one prepare for the trip? Following are some of the important steps in the scientist's research journey:

1. *Specifying the topic as clearly as possible*. Suppose you are intrigued by psychotherapy. Why are you drawn to that topic? Is it because you think verbal interchanges are crucial to achieving therapeutic change? Or are you more interested in the interpersonal relationship between client and therapist?
2. *Reviewing the relevant literature*. Some library work can save a researcher a lot of time and frustration. Studying the pertinent books and journals can answer many questions: How have other people dealt

with this idea? What were the outcomes of their research?
3. *Defining the variables*. A variable is any aspect of a person, group, or setting that is measured for the purposes of the study in question. **Independent variables** are conditions manipulated by the researcher in order to investigate their effects on particular outcomes (for example, behavioral changes) that are called **dependent variables.**
4. *Developing a specific hypothesis*. A **hypothesis** is a statement to be proved, an idea that has been formulated so that it may be evaluated using scientific methods. A hypothesis is a kind of educated guess that states a predicted relationship between events or variables. It is typically stated in the form "If A exists, then B will occur."
5. *Selecting a research strategy*. What plan of action will permit the hypothesis to be tested? Does the researcher plan to see each subject on one occasion (for example, at the beginning or end of psychotherapy), or will several observations be necessary in order to test the hypothesis? Should an experiment be conducted? Conducting an experiment means systematically varying one or more conditions for some groups but not for others. Is experimental research possible in a particular clinical setting?
6. *Conducting the study*. The research should be carried out objectively enough to permit others to replicate it. Therefore, all the steps in the research process must be specified. For example, how was the sample of subjects selected? Were the subjects chosen on the basis of age, sex, or intelligence? If so, the selection variables must be specified.
7. *Analyzing the results*. How did the group or groups perform? What is the likelihood that the results are simply due to chance? An analysis of research results usually includes making a distribution of the scores obtained by subjects; calculating relevant **descriptive statistics,** the numerical measures (scores) that enable a researcher to describe certain aspects of subjects' performance (for example, the mean or average); and calculating **inferential statistics,** the statistics that are used for judgments about the probability that the results are due to chance.
8. *Reporting research findings*. Writing up a piece of research not only permits communication of ideas and findings to others but also forces researchers to think through all that they have done and the meaning that might be attached to it. Going public serves an important communication function. The scientific journey would be much less valuable if research results were not written up and published.

Types of Research

Researchers use a variety of methods to better understand maladaptive behavior. We will focus on clinical observations here because of the valuable insights they provide about individual cases. Clinical studies also suggest profitable directions for projects involving various samples of subjects and methods. The following sections will discuss the most common types of clinical observations.

Case Studies Case studies involve detailed observations of a single patient's behavior. The clinician tries to organize many observations conceptually. In most case studies, explanations of the events occur after the fact, and there is little, if any, opportunity to rule out other possible explanations by controlling for them. Even the most intensive study of an individual case cannot assure us that we have isolated the true causes of the behavior. Nevertheless, such studies can provide important leads for more controlled research. Clinicians recognize that each case is different because of the particular circumstances surrounding the case, and cases may become more complicated because of client's verbal reports. Troubled people more often than not leave out important information in telling their stories to clinicians. They frequently fail to remember significant experiences and the feelings and thoughts related to them. Each case study thus is unique, although with experience clinicians become sensitive to commonalities that aid them in understanding and helping people.

Correlational Studies In correlational studies, researchers investigate relationships between uncontrolled events. These studies show us that two things are associated (see Figure 1-7), but they do not explain which factor causes what. For example, a correlational study may identify a significant relationship between socioeconomic or marital status and severity of psychopathology. Although we do not know which is the contributing factor, a potentially important association has been singled out.

Both case studies and correlational studies provide bases for hypotheses. In evaluating a hypothesis it is important to decide on the observations that are relevant to it and the conditions under which those observations should be made. The conditions might be the same for all subjects or different for designated groups. In assessment studies, the conditions are the same, the aim being to gather information under standard conditions for purposes of description and prediction. In experimental studies, the conditions are varied so as to test hypotheses about the effects of the conditions.

"WHICH IS IT— DO PEOPLE HATE US BECAUSE WE DRESS THIS WAY, OR DO WE DRESS THIS WAY BECAUSE PEOPLE HATE US?"

(a)

FRANK AND ERNEST   by Bob Thaves

I DON'T CARE WHAT YOU SAY ABOUT HIM — — WE DIDN'T HAVE THIS KIND OF WEATHER WHEN RICHARD NIXON WAS PRESIDENT!

(b)

Figure 1-7 It is dangerous to infer causality from correlational data. (a) the witches are trying to infer causality on the basis of an association they have observed; (b) the man's data are recollections of past events, which can be notoriously unreliable. The recollections could be correlated with his current mood.

SOURCE: (a) By permission of Sidney Harris and *Saturday Review World;* copyright 1987 by Sidney Harris. (b) "Frank and Ernest" drawing by B. Thaves. Reprinted by permission of NEA, Inc.

Assessment Studies The purpose of **assessment studies** is to provide an objective account of behavior at any given time. Assessment methods range from recording how often certain responses occur in natural situations to noting the types of behavior displayed in specially created settings such as interviews. Assessment is not simply a measuring device; it is a general approach to observing and interpreting behavior. As such, it extends beyond traditional procedures such as interviews and tests in much the same way that the concept of intelligence and the judgments based on it extend beyond the tests used to measure it.

Assessment data can be used in a number of ways. They might be employed to predict future behavior, to identify correlates of present behavior, or to measure the likelihood of a positive reaction to therapeutic procedures. For example, a study of junior high school students might indicate the type of person who is most likely to engage in antisocial behavior in the future; a comparison of the assessed characteristics of depressed individuals might point out those who are most likely to commit suicide; and a comparison of the personality traits of people who respond positively to psychotherapy and those who respond negatively might help in screening candidates for therapy. Assessment research ranges from in-depth studies of one or a few people to surveys of large populations.

When people are assessed, several kinds of data are usually gathered, including age, sex, personal history, and number of previous hospitalizations. This information can be intercorrelated and the degree of relationship among the various items determined. Assessment studies, which often involve large samples of subjects and sophisticated assessment techniques, are limited by their correlational nature; despite this limitation, they have much to contribute to the study of abnormal behavior. This is particularly true when, for practical or ethical reasons, it is not possible to manipulate conditions experimentally. Suppose, for example, that we wanted to study the possibility that having been abused as a child increases the likelihood that one will abuse one's own children. It would be highly unethical as well as impractical to subject an experimental group of children to severe abuse and then wait 20 years to see whether or not they beat their own children. However, information obtained through assessment about such a correlation could be of great value in understanding the causes of abuse, and could perhaps be used in selecting high-risk parents for programs designed to prevent abuse.

As an alternative, we might find ways to measure the amount of abuse parents received when they were children as well as the extent to which they now abuse their own children. For each of a large group of parents, we could obtain a score for each of the two abuse variables—each parent's reports of being abused as a child and some measure of his or her abusiveness as a parent—and then determine what kind of relationship, if any, exists between the two sets of measures. If being abusive and having been abused are correlated, that would provide a potentially useful clue to how child abuse could be prevented. For instance, perhaps parental counseling and training for people who were abused as children would be of preventive value.

If we find a positive correlation, we might be tempted to conclude from the data that child abuse is caused by parents having been abused as children. This is certainly a possibility, but it is important to remember that *correlation* is not the same as *cause*. There are other possible explanations for the positive correlation. It may be, for example, that guilt about abusing their own child causes parents to exaggerate the extent to which they were abused as children. Another possibility is that some other variable that was not measured in the study (such as some form of psychological disturbance) actually caused the parent to be the target of abuse as a child and causes him or her to become a child abuser as an adult. We simply cannot be certain which of these and other possible causal relationships may account for the positive correlation between recalled childhood experiences and present adult behavior.

Longitudinal Studies One way to deal with limitations inherent in assessment studies is the **longitudinal study,** whose goal is to observe and record the behavior of people over long periods—perhaps 20 or 30 years. This type of study is costly, time-consuming, and often frustrating to the investigator, who may not live to see the study completed. There are other problems as well. The nature of the group under study may change greatly as people move or die. The methods chosen at the beginning of the study may become outdated. The importance of new variables that were ignored in the study may become recognized by the scientific community. For these reasons, few longitudinal studies are done. Nevertheless, because they deal so directly with the developmental process, the value of such studies is widely recognized.

Figure 1-8 illustrates the predictive value of longitudinal studies. Researchers were able to identify a group of men who at ages 8 to 10 had been socially withdrawn and inhibited (Caspi & Elder, 1988). Because they had been studied over a period of more than 20 years, it was possible to relate social withdrawal in childhood to these men's experiences at three adult life transitions: getting married, becoming a father, and beginning a work career. As Figure 1-8 shows, men with a childhood history of social withdrawal marry at a significantly older age than men with no such behavioral history—the difference between the groups is 3 years. Not surprisingly, delayed age at marriage corresponds with delayed parenthood. Finally, withdrawn behavior in childhood seems to hinder men's transition into an occupational career. Men with a childhood history of withdrawn behavior assumed a work career 3 years after the majority of their peers were already established in an occupation.

The delays in life transitions revealed by this study can generate conflicting obligations and options that may enhance stress and the risk of maladaptation. Evidence about the connection between withdrawn behav-

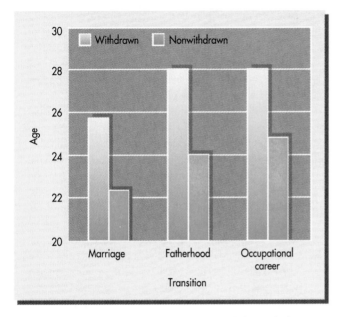

Figure 1-8 Timing of life transitions by withdrawn behavior in childhood.

SOURCE: Based on Caspi & Elder. (1988)

ior in childhood and disorganization later in life could be of value in developing programs to improve the social adjustment of withdrawn children.

Follow-up Studies One type of research that avoids some of the logistical problems of longitudinal studies, but still has longitudinal features, is the **follow-up study.** In such studies, people are given an initial assessment and then are contacted again months or years later to see whether there have been any changes in their behavior during that time. Follow-up studies are used to assess the effects of different therapeutic approaches as well as to observe the development of particular condi-

tions. For example, a follow-up study might be carried out to determine how well people who have been discharged from a mental hospital have adjusted to life in the community. Figure 1-9 summarizes the results of a study that explored the relationship between the amount of television viewing at 8 years of age and the seriousness of criminal acts at age 30. The figure shows that the seriousness of crimes was proportional to TV-viewing frequency at age 8 for both males and females. While this relationship may not be causal, the fact that child TV viewing was predictive of crime seriousness in adulthood suggests the need to investigate the TV-viewing experiences of children. What are the characteristics of children who do a lot of TV viewing? What sorts of programs do they watch?

Cross-Sectional Studies The **cross-sectional study** is a useful way to assess the views or status of one or more groups of people at any given point in time. Cross-sectional studies are the most common assessment method used by social scientists. Because no follow-up is required, these studies are less time-consuming and expensive than longitudinal studies. A public opinion poll is an example of a cross-sectional study that is carried out in the field. The epidemiological surveys described earlier in the chapter were cross-sectional studies.

Experimental Studies Experimental research involves the observation and assessment of behavior, but with an important additional ingredient. In **experimental studies,** or **experiments,** variables can be manipulated. This degree of control is impossible in many real-life situations. Because experimenters can control the variables in the laboratory, they can more easily isolate and record the causes of the behavior they observe. For certain purposes, research with animals is valuable because it per-

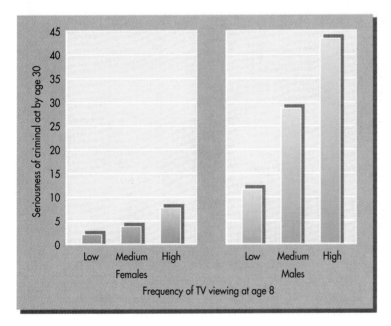

Figure 1-9 Seriousness of criminal acts by age 30 as a function of frequency of television viewing at age 8.

SOURCE: Eron. (1987). p. 440. Copyright 1987 by the American Psychological Association. Reprinted by permission of the author.

mits the manipulation of experimental variables and the control of unwanted factors to an extent usually not possible with people.

The variables that are manipulated by researchers in experiments are **independent variables; dependent variables** are any observed changes in behavior due to the manipulation. Psychological experiments are designed to discover relationships between environmental conditions and behavior. Figure 1-10 illustrates a conventional experimental design. For example, an experiment might be done to discover the relationship between the temperature in a room and people's performance on a test. In this experiment the independent variable would be the temperature. The experimenter would use a different tem-perature for each experimental room. The dependent variable would be the test scores. If the average test scores for the individuals in the rooms were significantly different, the experimenter would conclude that this result was related to the different temperatures in the rooms in which the groups of individuals worked. Asking people how they felt under both conditions would be simpler, but the results would not be nearly as accurate or objective.

Types of Experiments There are two general types of experiments. The first type is the **hypothesis-testing experiment,** in which the researcher makes a prediction based on a theory and then conducts an experiment to see whether the prediction is correct. In the following excerpt, a psychologist outlines her plan for such a study.

I'm interested in determining whether, if children have an early close, secure relationship with an adult, what psychologists call attachment, they will have fewer problems getting along with other children when they enter school. My hypothesis is that if children are securely attached when they are very young, their social skills will be better and they will be less likely to be described as having behavior problems.

I have some records of nursery school children's behavior in a situation designed to measure attachment. In that research setup, a young child and his or her mother sit together in an attractive room with some playthings. Then a "stranger" (a research worker) comes into the room and sits down. After a while the mother leaves; she comes back a short time later. The way the child behaves, both while the mother is gone and when she returns, is a measure of attachment. If the child does not cling to the mother when the stranger enters, and if the child continues to play with the toys, is not distressed when she leaves, and greets her warmly but does not cling to her when she returns, the child is said to be securely attached.

Now those children are in the first grade, and I want to determine whether those who were securely attached in nursery school behave differently from the other children in either stressful or nonstressful situations. For one-half of each of the attachment groups, I am observing the children in a frustrating situation where they are given an impossible task to solve. For the other half of each group, I will give the children another task that is not difficult but takes a fairly long time to do. My hypothesis is that children who are securely attached will work longer at the impossible task than the other attachment group. For the other task, I expect no difference between the two groups. I base these predictions on the

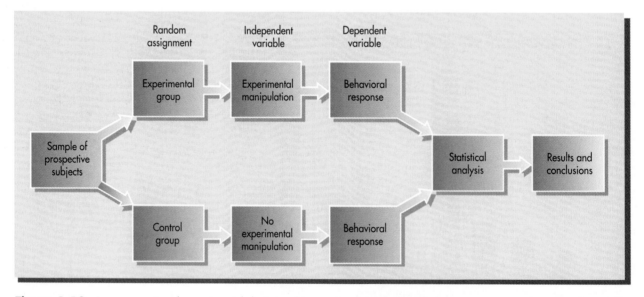

Figure 1-10 In a conventional experimental design, subjects are randomly assigned to an experimental or control group for manipulation of the independent variable. Their dependent variable behaviors are then measured; differences between the two groups of subjects are assessed through statistical analysis to determine the effects of the independent variable.

idea that children who are securely attached in their early years develop feelings of competence and tolerance of frustration superior to those of children who did not have a positive attachment experience.

The second type of experiment, the **behavior-change experiment,** is concerned primarily with the development of therapeutic techniques. It is also designed to test hypotheses, but in this case the goal is to make an immediate contribution to the development of practical rehabilitative techniques. For example, a behavior-change experiment might test the hypothesis that supervised work experiences are significantly more effective than group psychotherapy in changing the attitudes and behavior of convicted criminals. The researcher who wrote the following account is studying schizophrenia. However, the researcher's goal is a very practical one: improving the social skills of those with schizophrenia.

I'm trying to devise procedures that will help patients with schizophrenia return to the community more quickly and be more effective when they make their return. My approach is to start with one obvious deficiency of the patients: inadequate social skills. They just don't do a very good job of relating to other people. What I've been doing is finding out, by asking them questions and observing them, what social skills the patients lack; for example, they have a lot of trouble introducing themselves to strangers and making small talk. I'm modeling—that is, demonstrating—for them various ways of being effective in social situations. I also have a control group that doesn't get the social skills training, as well as a group that participates in discussions about how to handle social situations but gets no modeling. If I'm on the right track, follow-ups should show that the modeling group is better able to adjust back into the community than the control group and maybe also better than the discussion group.

An increasingly important type of behavior change experiment is the clinical trial. A **clinical trial** is a planned experiment designed to determine the effectiveness of a treatment by comparing the outcomes in a group of patients given the test treatment with those in a comparable group of patients receiving a control treatment. Thus, both groups are treated and followed over the same period of time. There might also be an untreated control group. Clinical trials are costly because they usually require a large number of subjects who are studied at several clinical centers over a considerable period of time. Box 1-3 gives an in-depth look at the clinical trial.

Experiments With Animals For obvious reasons, certain types of experimentation cannot be carried out using human subjects. For example, it would be impossi-

ble—and unethical, even if it were possible—to try to observe and control the course of a person's life. However, the telescoped life span of nonhuman primates like monkeys makes it possible to study the long-term consequences of early experiences. Under controlled conditions these experiences can be observed either as they unfold or after experimental manipulations. Animal studies permit levels of control and ways of carrying out experimental manipulations that are not possible with humans. As a consequence, animal experimentation plays an important role in the study of abnormal behavior.

Animal studies can be used to investigate both biological and social factors in behavior. One example of research with a biological focus is the investigation of the effects of drugs. Researchers have fed monkeys large doses of drugs that are believed to cause depression and have noted their effects on the animals' behavior. Such experiments have shown that depression-inducing drugs lead to decreases in the general activity and exploratory behavior of monkeys.

A group of drugs called amphetamines, which function as stimulants, produce psychotic symptoms in people. Once the effects of amphetamines on animals are shown to be similar, animals that had been injected with amphetamines can then be given antipsychotic drugs to determine whether they are able to counteract the amphetamine's psychosis-inducing action. Research has shown that rats and humans exhibit some similar symptoms when treated with amphetamines, and we now know that certain antipsychotic drugs are effective in reversing the effects of amphetamines on rats.

Another example of animal studies with a biological focus can be seen in the work of Harry Harlow and his co-workers. They were interested in the effects of early experience on the later development of monkeys. Infant monkeys show a number of innate behaviors, such as clinging and sucking. When the infants are separated from their mothers and reared with other young monkeys, their clinging behavior lasts much longer than it does for mother-reared monkeys (see Figure 1-11a). Young monkeys also begin to show innate fear behavior when they are about 2 months old. When they are reared with other monkeys, the fear behaviors do not disappear but last into adulthood (Suomi and Harlow, 1978).

When infant monkeys are not only separated from their mothers but reared in isolation for 6 months, they show several disturbed behaviors. They suck themselves, constantly rock back and forth, and are very timid. When their isolation ends, they behave very aggressively toward other monkeys. The research showed, however, that monkeys that are reared in isolation for 6 months can later develop normally if they are "treated"

The Clinical Trial

Because of the lack of effective treatments, for a long time the study of abnormal behavior was primarily descriptive. Now the situation is different. Today a major goal of clinical researchers is evaluation of the effectiveness of *specific* forms of therapy for *specific* types of patients. Potentially practical treatments for a number of conditions are now available and require careful evaluation. This type of evaluation requires methodological rigor and the ability of researchers to draw conclusions about the target intervention that are applicable, not just to a particular clinician, clinic, or hospital, but to entire regions and populations.

Clinical trials are studies of patients that systematically test the safety and effectiveness of new therapies and compare the results with standard treatment. Whether the condition in question is cancer, or heart attack, or depression, clinical trials are the only sure way to determine whether one approach is better—or worse—than another. Clinical trials offer the potential benefits of promising new treatments to the trial participants and to all patients who will come after them.

The most scientifically sound method of determining the therapies that are effective and those that are not is the randomized controlled clinical trial. Eligible participants are given either the experimental treatment, in addition to standard therapy, or a placebo, an intervention or medication that resembles the one being studied but has no specific benefit. Participants cannot choose which group or condition of the study they will be in and, in the best trials, neither the patients nor the evaluating doctors know which treatment is being given to whom until the study is complete. The use of placebos is particularly important in trials of experimental drugs because about one-third of patients improve just because they are being studied.

An example of a clinical trial is the ongoing National Institute of Mental Health Treatment of Depression Collaborative Research Program, a comparison of brief psychotherapy interventions and medications for the treatment of nonhospitalized depressed people (Elkin, 1994). This clinical trial involves four treatment approaches including combinations of psychotherapy and antidepressant drugs, as well as a placebo. The project was designed to determine the effectiveness of psychotherapy and drugs singly and in combination. In order to increase the generalizability of the results, the project was carried out at three clinical centers in the United States. The treatments at these centers were provided by experienced therapists who had been carefully selected to take part in the program and received further training in their respective treatment approaches. The patients were followed for 18 months after the end of treatment. This experiment showed that, in comparison with the control condition, both the psychotherapy and medication groups improved. However, the control group also showed some improvement, thus demonstrating the need for appropriate groups with which treatment interventions can be compared. Chapter 10 will review treatment approaches and research on depression.

Clinical trials are costly because they require seven major steps, summarized in Table 1–7. The research design of each clinical trial must be planned, the procedures in the treatment(s) specified, patients recruited into the study, the treatment(s) given, one or more posttrial follow-ups carried out to assess long-term effects, data analyzed, and a report of results written (usually in the form of journal articles or a book). The complexity of a clinical trial is demonstrated by the need for research subjects to complete all phases of the treatment and participate in the follow-up (for example, by filling out questionnaires at specified intervals). Each trial must make a concerted effort to maintain patient interest and participation by assuring that each clinical center in which the trial is carried out is easily accessible (public transportation and parking must be available), has pleasant physical surroundings, and treats patients with courtesy and dignity.

In a sense, complex clinical trials in abnormal psychology are indications of the field's success. There would be no need for clinical trials if there were no interventions that seemed likely to help people overcome their difficulties.

TABLE 1–7
Steps in Clinical Trials

1. Research design
2. Specification of all intervention procedures
3. Patient recruitment
4. Implementation of the intervention(s)
5. Long-term follow-up of treatment effects
6. Data analysis
7. Report writing

---

by therapist monkeys. The most successful therapist monkeys were 3-month-olds who still showed a great deal of clinging behavior. They clung to the isolates affectionately (see Figure 1-11b). The isolates soon responded, and within 6 months their behavior was hard to distinguish from that of their therapists (Suomi & Harlow, 1972).

Young monkeys separated from their mothers often show symptoms similar to depression in humans. Depression in young monkeys may be preceded by a protest phase characterized by immediate frantic activity that appears to reflect attempts to communicate with and locate the missing mother. The depression is often followed by a detachment phase in which the young monkey shows an emotional detachment or aloofness from its mother upon reunion. This phase has been observed in human children when in the presence of mothers from whom they have been separated (Rosenblum & Paully, 1987).

Experiments With Humans A study by Abrams and

(a)

(b)

Figure 1-11 (a) All monkeys go through a clinging stage, but monkeys reared without their mothers show a greatly prolonged period of clinging. (b) A young monkey, still in the clinging stage, can be an effective therapist for an older monkey reared in isolation.

Wilson (1979) illustrates the power of the experiment in identifying a factor that is relevant to a particular type of behavior. The researchers were interested in the relationship between alcohol and social anxiety in women. The subjects were paid female undergraduates selected from volunteers who reported only moderate drinking. Two independent variables, alcohol dose and expectancy, were manipulated by randomly assigning subjects to one of four groups: expect alcohol and receive alcohol, expect alcohol and receive placebo, expect placebo and receive alcohol, or expect placebo and receive placebo. (A **placebo** is an inactive substance whose effect on a person's behavior depends on his or her expectations.) The experimental manipulation was **double-blind;** that is, neither the subject nor the experimenter knew what the subject was drinking. Unlike the cartoon in Figure 1-12, records are kept of which subjects are assigned to each group, but those who evaluate the subjects' behavior or progress and the subjects themselves do not know the assignment. All of the subjects were told that both alcohol and nonalcohol groups would be tested in the study and that they had been randomly assigned to either the alcohol-only group or the nonalcohol-only group. Under the guise of prepar-ing for a breathalyzer test, the subjects gargled with a mouthwash that reduced their sensitivity to taste. The drinks were mixed from labeled bottles in full view of the subject, and the glasses in the "receive placebo" group were surreptitiously smeared with vodka. Finally, the breathalyzer was altered to give false feedback.

After the drink manipulation and breathalyzer test, the subjects were placed in a controlled social interaction with a male confederate. The dependent variables included physiological measures of anxiety (heart rate and skin conductance) taken before, during, and after the interaction; self-report measures of anxiety taken before and after the interaction; and observer ratings of the anxiety shown by each subject during the interaction.

The experiment showed that women who believed that they had consumed alcohol, whether or not their drinks actually contained it, showed significantly increased levels of physiological arousal compared with those who believed that they had drunk only tonic water. Accord-ing to ratings made by observers, subjects who believed that they had consumed alcohol showed greater discomfort in the social interaction (see Figure 1-13). This experiment highlights the decisive role that subjects' expectations can play in their behavior and in their ability to cope.

"IT WAS MORE OF A 'TRIPLE-BLIND' TEST. THE PATIENTS DIDN'T KNOW WHICH ONES WERE GETTING THE REAL DRUG, THE DOCTORS DIDN'T KNOW, AND, I'M AFRAID, NOBODY KNEW."

Figure 1-12   Copyright 1993 by Sidney Harris.

Research Design, Statistical Analyses, and Inferences

Planning is a key feature of scientific research. Researchers must identify their goals and figure out how to reach them. Is the goal to describe some phenomenon (such as the social behavior of depressed individuals),

establish a correlation between events (such as the association between viewing violent television programs and committing crimes), or demonstrating a cause-and-effect relationship between independent and dependent variables (such as the effects of psychotherapy and medication on depressed mood)? Some types of behavior can be studied only in their natural settings where little or no control is possible; others can be studied under controlled laboratory conditions. Where they are appropriate, controlled experiments have the advantage of exposing subjects to conditions that permit a good test of the researcher's hypothesis. A well-controlled experiment has high **internal validity** because the results can be attributed to manipulation of the independent variable rather than to some extraneous or confounding variable. The independent variable could be a condition far removed from the subject's life. However, if the condition mirrors what happens in the "real world," the experiment also has **external validity.** Scientific observation results in data that are usually numerical in nature. Statistical procedures allow the researcher to summarize and bring order to data, as well as to measure relationships among variables.

Descriptive Statistics Descriptive statistics are used to summarize observations. The summaries might be of patients' responses to psychological tests, the ages at which various types of patients develop their conditions, and clinicians' ratings of patients' progress. **Measures of central tendency** provide descriptive numerical summaries of a group's behavior. The three most commonly used measures of central tendency are the **mean** or arithmetic average; the **median,** the point that cuts the distribution of scores in half, so that half of the rank-or-

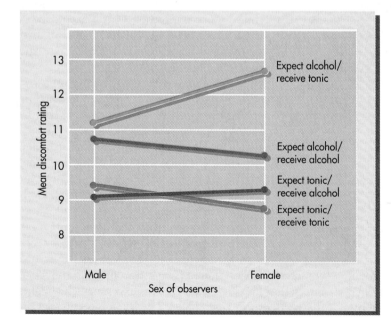

Figure 1-13   Mean discomfort ratings by drink content, expectancy, and sex made by observers who rated videotapes of subjects' social interactions.

SOURCE: From Abrams, D. B., and Wilson, G. T. (1979). Effects of alcohol on social anxiety in women, *Journal of Abnormal Psychology, 88,* 161–173. Copyright 1979 by the American Psychological Association. Reprinted by permission of the authors.

dered scores fall above it and half below it, and the **mode,** the score that the largest number of subjects obtained. Because of its desirable mathematical properties, the mean is typically favored in statistical analyses.

Measures of central tendency, such as the mean, provide information about the average score in a distribution. However, knowing the average score in a distribution does not provide all of the information required to describe a group of scores. In addition, **measures of variability** are required. The simplest idea of variability is the **range,** which is merely the difference between the highest and lowest scores. The most commonly used measure of variability is the **standard deviation,** whichtakes into account all of the scores in the distribution rather than only the highest and lowest.

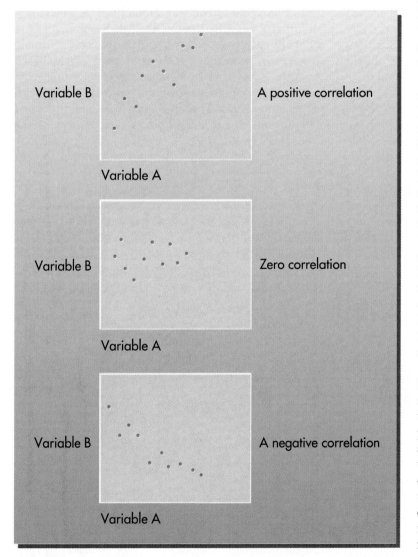

Figure 1-14 Correlation coefficients can be computed between pairs of variables, A and B, in which we might be interested—for example, in intelligence and performance in school; socioeconomic level and anxiety; and self-rated stress and social skills.

The standard deviation reflects the size of the deviation of the scores in the distribution from the group mean.

Inferential Statistics Whereas descriptive statistics help us characterize a group of subjects, it is often important to make comparisons among two or more groups (for example, the mean IQs of students at two high schools). **Inferential statistics** help us determine whether any observed differences between groups should be attributed to chance or to some systematic factor (the socioeconomic status of students at the schools, for example). Statistical tests, such as the *t-test*, evaluate the **null hypothesis,** the theory that the groups really do not differ. If the null hypothesis is rejected, it is unlikely that the observed differences could have arisen by chance. Statistical tests yield what is known as a *level of significance*, which is determined by comparing the results of the statistical tests with a set of probability tables.

Correlation Coefficients Quite commonly, clinicians or researchers are interested not so much in how groups might differ, but in how variables that represent characteristics of some particular sample or population are related to each other. The **correlation coefficient** provides this information. Correlation coefficients can range from − 1.00 to + 1.00. A coefficient of + 1.00 means that there is a perfect positive association between two variables. A correlation of − 1.00 signifies a perfect negative, or inverse, relationship, and a correlation of .00 means that there is no relationship between the variables. Figure 1-14 illustrates three kinds of correlation results.

Interpreting Results of Research There are many types of statistical tests, some of which are complex. For example, some procedures involve evaluating the relationships among combinations of three or more variables. But regardless of the procedures employed, interpretation of the results obtained is required in light of the research design and methods employed. The experiment is a powerful scientific tool, but it is not infallible. Certain factors can seriously undermine the validity of research results. Four of the most serious issues that researchers must consider in conducting studies and interpreting results are confounding of variables, reactivity, demand characteristics, and expectancy effects. How we interpret the results of research depends not only on the outcomes of the statistical tests employed but also on how well the research was conducted; that is, how successful the researcher has been in eliminating these biasing factors.

Confounding occurs when uncontrolled variables affect the dependent variable in a way that is mistakenly attributed to the independent variable. For example, some depressed individuals might be given psychotherapy while others serve as control group. Comparing the two groups might show a statistically significant difference in depressed mood, with the group that received psychotherapy showing less depression after psychotherapy than the control group. This result would suggest that psychotherapy is a useful treatment for depression. But what if the experimental and control groups differed in age, sex, or initial level of depression? These possibly confounding variables would lead us to be very cautious about any statistically significant results we might obtain.

Reactivity refers to changes in behavior that occur when subjects know they are being observed or studied. If subjects in a laboratory experiment react to being observed by behaving differently from the way they would outside the laboratory, we might easily draw false conclusions from the experimental results.

Demand characteristics are features of research situations that give subjects information about how they are expected to behave. Subjects may pick up these clues about the nature of a study and how they are "supposed" to behave. Some patients in psychoanalysis might report more dreams than patients in other forms of psychotherapy because their analysts may communicate that reporting and analyzing dreams is what they want their patients to do. Because demand characteristics can be a threat to valid results, researchers often feel a need to hide the true intent of their experiments.

Expectancy effects can be a source of bias in experiments if they lead to systematic errors in observations. In a study involving tranquilizers, some experimenters might rate patients who have been taking tranquilizing drugs as being less anxious because in past research such drugs were found to reduce anxiety. In this case, scientists should be blind with regard to the drug being taken. Researchers' expectancies about what will happen in a given situation might actually influence the observations they make.

An additional factor that influences the results of research is **sampling.** A researcher virtually can never study every member of the larger group to which experimental results are expected to apply. We are almost always restricted to a segment, or sample, of that larger group, which is called the population. If valid conclusions are to be drawn, the sample must reflect the important characteristics of that larger population. Public opinion pollsters thus use samples that possess the important characteristics (age, gender, political party, geographical location, and so on) in the same proportion as contained in the general population. The responses of such a representative sample are therefore likely to mirror those of the larger population. Clearly, interpretation of research investigations depends on the nature of the samples studied—if the sample does not adequately reflect the general public, results will have a limited application.

Ethical Aspects of Research

Although the cartoon in Figure 1-15 is humorous, it deals with a very serious and important issue in the conduct of research: the need to protect the rights and dignity of the subjects who are studied. Regardless of the scholarly merits of doing research, investigators should never place people in either physical or psychological jeopardy. Subjects should be informed regarding what the experiment is about and any hazards associated with participation in it. They also must be clearly told that they are free to withdraw from the experiment at any time. If deception must be used, the subjects must be completely debriefed after the experiment, and the en-

Figure 1-15 Research subjects should not be subjected to experiences that are harmful or intimidating.

tire procedure explained to them. Special measures must be taken to protect confidentiality.

As a result of the increasing emphasis on the protection and welfare of both human and animal subjects used in psychological research, psychologists now must restrict their experimentation with certain groups of people who are not in a position to give their consent, such as children, the mentally retarded, and seriously disturbed mental patients. When such people, or others who are not able to give consent, are involved, consent must be obtained from their parents or guardians. Strict guidelines are also being developed for research in prisons. No prisoner can be forced to participate in research or penalized for refusal to do so, and in the case of rehabilitative programs, prisoners must be permitted to share in decisions concerning program goals. Researchers must adhere to the ethics of research or risk serious legal and professional consequences.

WHAT IS ABNORMAL BEHAVIOR?

Abnormal psychology deals with how it feels to be different, how others interpret these differences, and how society deals with those it considers different. An understanding of the roles of **stress, personal vulnerabilities,** and **resiliency** is important in interpreting abnormal behavior.

The Stigma of Abnormal Behavior Beliefs and assumptions about mental illness affect the way people respond to someone who shows abnormal behavior. Those who behave in unusual ways or have been diagnosed as having a mental illness may be rejected by others, either directly or indirectly. Many false beliefs exist about the causes and the outcome of mental illness.

Adaptive and Maladaptive Behavior Adaptation, as the term is used in this book, refers to people's ability or inability to modify their behavior in response to changes in their environment. Deviant or unusual behavior is often *not* maladaptive. **Maladaptive** behavior refers to behavior that causes problems in living. Maladaptive behavior ranges from relatively minor but troubling fears to severe distortion of reality and inability to function independently.

VULNERABILITY, RESILIENCY, AND COPING

Stress refers to people's reactions to situations that pose demands, constraints, or opportunities. **Vulnerability** refers to the likelihood of maladaptive response. Vulnerability is affected by heredity, personality factors, lack of certain skills, a history of negative life events, and certain environmental conditions. **Resiliency** is the ability to function effectively in the face of adversity and to recover from the effects of stress. Resilient people are often good copers. **Coping skills** are the techniques—such as constructive thinking and flexibility—that people use to deal with stress. A person's level of coping varies from time to time because of differences in vulnerability and resiliency in various types of situations.

REASONS FOR CLINICAL CONTACTS

Personal Unhappiness Although to an outsider a person may be functioning well, feelings of anxiety, depression, or a feeling of failure to reach one's potential may motivate an individual to seek therapeutic help.

The Concerns of Others Even if people do not view their own behavior as maladaptive or abnormal, others who know them well may see either present or potential problems and urge them to seek professional contact.

Legal and Community Problems If a person's maladaptive behavior is seen as a threat to others, legal or community agencies often become involved.

THE EPIDEMIOLOGY OF MALADAPTIVE BEHAVIOR

Epidemiologists look for clues about the causes of disorders by investigating environmental, personal, and behavioral characteristics that are associated with different rates of various disorders.

Prevalence, Incidence, and Risk Factors Prevalence data describe the frequency of occurrence of a condition at a given point in time. **Incidence** data are the number of *new* cases occurring during a given period. **Risk factors** are personal or situational characteristics that have been found to have a significant association with a disorder.

SOURCES OF HELP

Types of Treatment Facilities Facilities for the treatment of mental disorders range from inpatient treatment at state hospitals and in psychiatric wards of general hospitals to outpatient-based treatment in the community. These outpatient facilities include hospital emergency rooms, mental health clinics, and the services of mental health workers. The movement for **deinstitutionalization** returned many people to the community without providing sufficient community facilities to care for them adequately.

Types of Mental Health Specialists Mental health specialists include **clinical psychologists, counseling psychologists, psychiatrists, psychiatric social workers,** and **psychiatric nurses.** Each of these professional specialties requires different training. Although the responsibilities ordinarily given to each group differ, they often carry out similar therapeutic activities.

RESEARCH IN ABNORMAL PSYCHOLOGY

Observing Behavior Observation is the beginning stage in the scientific process. It is important to recognize that observations are susceptible to cultural and personal bias. To make observation useful it is necessary to determine such things as the types of responses to be observed, how the observer's presence will affect the behavior, and the period of time necessary for reliable observation. In addition to observation by others, **self-observation** by the client can provide useful research data. The data obtained from observation can include the stimuli that elicit particular responses, the subjective and behavioral responses to particular stimuli, and the environmental consequences of certain behaviors.

The Role of Theory Theories in abnormal psychology often begin with informal observations in clinical settings. Researchers then make hypotheses based on their observations and test these through further observations, preferably under controlled conditions. As these studies show whether or not each hypothesis is supported by research findings, a theory can be built. Theories are used to relate many facts into a single framework and also to provide new questions for researchers to test in a systematic manner. For this reason it is very important that theories are constructed to be testable and refutable.

The Research Journey The vital steps in scientific research are: specifying the topic, reviewing the literature, defining the variables to be measured, developing the hypothesis, selecting a research strategy, conducting the study, analyzing the data, and reporting the research findings. Both **independent variables,** or those that are manipulated by the researcher, and **dependent variables,** or outcomes, must be specified.

Types of Research **Case studies** provide descriptions of single individuals who are usually studied through many observations. **Correlational studies** provide information about how much variables are related or associated, but like case studies they do not show cause and effect. **Assessment studies** describe behavior at any given time. They can be used for prediction of future behavior or to identify correlates of present behavior, but, like case and correlational studies, they cannot be used to show causality. **Experimental studies** can be used to infer causality. Two major types of experimental studies are the **hypothesis-testing experiment** and the **behavior-change experiment.**

Research Design, Statistical Analysis, and Inferences Researchers need to identify their goals and plan their studies so as to attain them. Statistical procedures enable a researcher to summarize data and measure relationships among variables. The results are calculated in terms of both **descriptive statistics,** or numerical measures, and **inferential statistics,** which are used to provide information about whether the results might be due to chance. Included among descriptive statistics are **measures of central tendency,** which include the **mean, median,** and **mode.** The **range** of scores is a simple measure of variability. The most commonly used variability measure is the **standard deviation.** Inferential statistics are used to evaluate the **null hypothesis** (to determine whether the groups in an experimental study differ). These statistics can be used to determine the **level of significance** or the probability that the results occurred by chance. When the results of an experiment are interpreted, several factors that can negatively affect the validity of the results must be kept in mind. The factors include **confounding of variables, reactivity** of subject behavior, **demand characteristics** of the experiment, and **expectancy effects.**

ETHICAL ASPECTS OF RESEARCH

Researchers must not treat people without their informed consent, and must never treat them in a way that might possibly cause them either physical or psychological harm. Potential subjects must be informed about the nature of the experiment and any risks it might involve, and their written consent must be obtained. They must be given a chance to withdraw and, if any deception is used, they must be debriefed afterwards by having the procedures explained. All data from research must be kept confidential so that no one except the researchers will know the subjects' responses.

CHAPTER TWO

Rembrandt Harmensz van Rijn, *Self Portrait*, 1629.
Giraudon/Art Resource, New York

THE HISTORICAL BACKGROUND OF ABNORMAL PSYCHOLOGY

To really understand people, we need to know what has happened in their lives. To really understand current ideas and practices concerning abnormal psychology, we need to learn about its origins and history.

Those who cannot remember the past are condemned to repeat it.

GEORGE SANTAYANA,
The Life of Reason,
1905–1908

Historical Views of Abnormal Behavior

Someone might observe that modern techniques are surely much more effective, enlightened, and sophisticated than those used in earlier times, and ask: Why not concentrate on them instead of getting bogged down in accounts of the past? The trouble with this approach is that it misses important links between the past and the present. Much of what seems modern is an outgrowth of the past, not a rejection of it. In abnormal psychology, as in other fields of study, there are fewer completely new ideas than one might think. A review of the history of abnormal psychology provides a context within which the best of the modern discipline can be understood.

People have always been concerned about their physical well-being, their social relationships, and their place in the universe. They have posed many questions about these issues and have evolved theories about them. Some of those theories seem almost universal. They can be observed in many parts of the world and in many periods of human history. Perhaps the greatest benefit of studying the history of abnormal psychology is the discovery that certain theories of maladaptive behavior have occurred over and over again.

One ancient theory that is still encountered today holds that abnormal behavior can be explained by the operation of supernatural and magical forces such as evil spirits or the devil. In societies that believe in this theory, therapy generally involves **exorcism,** that is, removing the evil that resides in the individual through counter-magic and prayer. Although this view is most prevalent in nonliterate cultures, it is still found in industrialized societies and often exists side by side with more modern approaches. For example, many people who use folk healers also seek assistance from health care professionals. Professionals can improve the effectiveness of the help they provide by understanding what folk healers do and why their patients seek them out.

In many societies the **shaman** or medicine man, a magician who is believed to have contact with supernatural forces, is the medium through which spirits communicate with human beings (see Figure 2–1). Through the shaman, an afflicted person can learn which spirits are responsible for his or her problem and what needs to be done to appease them. To accomplish this, the shaman conducts a seance in which he displays intense excitement and often mimics the abnormal behavior he seeks to cure. Through mystical utterances, violent movements, and by acting out his dreams, the shaman reveals messages from spirits. Often the liberation of an evil spirit from the patient's body is expressed through what appears, through sleight of hand, to be the actual expulsion of an object, such as a stone, from the patient's ear or mouth. These rituals are based on specific theories about supernatural forces or evil powers as the cause of abnormal behavior and as the basis of therapeutic change.

It is tempting to view seemingly primitive beliefs about mental illness as part of the dead past. Yet the fact is that even in a relatively advanced and enlightened society like the United States there is a wide range of views about the causes of personal problems. The following case, reported in 1977, concerned a 33-year-old man from a rural area near Little Rock, Arkansas:

Figure 2-1 A shaman anoints a man with holy water to protect him from evil spirits as the latter embarks on a pilgrimage.

The patient had been having seizures recently and had become increasingly irritable and withdrawn from his family. He was hospitalized, and when he could no longer be detained safely on the neurology service, he was transferred to the psychiatric ward, where he became increasingly more agitated, confused, and almost delirious. He became very fearful whenever people approached him, and he began to hallucinate. He finally slowed down after being given 1000 mg of chlorpromazine (a tranquilizer), but the necessity for bed restraint remained. All neurological findings, including a brain scan, proved normal. After two weeks of hospitalization the patient suffered a cardiac arrest. All efforts to revive him failed. An autopsy provided no reason for the death. After he died, the patient's wife told staff members that her husband had been seeing a "two-headed," an older woman considered by the community to be a witch who cast spells and healed people. The widow stated that her husband had angered the two-headed and that she had caused his death.

—Golden, 1977, p. 1425

Reports of "two-headeds" in Africa and other places describe them as people with voodoo powers who are able to cause sickness, insanity, and death. The power of such beings apparently is related to the victim's belief in them. The effect of the shaman's behavior both in curing disorders and causing them illustrates the interrelationship of people's beliefs and emotional reactions and their physical and psychological health.

Shamans are currently active in many countries. In Taiwan there are professional shamans, while in China the shamans are part-time practitioners of an illegal activity. Approximately 70 percent of rural Chinese with mental illnesses consult shamans (Shengxian & Phillips, 1990). Many of the families of these people are not even aware of the existence of mental hospitals. Since they often perceive disturbed behavior as the outcome of intervention by the spirit world, they seek out shamans for assistance.

A recurring theme in the history of abnormal behavior is the belief that individuals behave strangely because their bodies are not working right. Such people are thought to have something wrong with them, an organic defect that affects a specific organ rather than the whole body. The source of the presumed defect varies according to the nature of the abnormality, the society's cultural beliefs, and—particularly in the modern era—scientific knowledge.

The finding of ancient skulls with holes in them that were not caused by battle wounds has led some anthropologists to conjecture that abnormal behavior was sometimes treated by means of a procedure called **trephination.** In this technique a sharp tool such as a stone was used to make a hole in the skull about 2 centimeters in diameter (see Figure 2–2). Evidence that

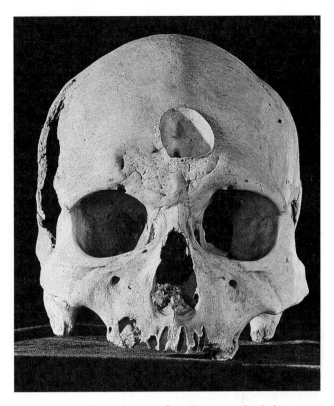

Figure 2-2 The technique of trephining involved chipping a hole in the person's skull. The healing that took place on this skull shows that some individuals actually survived the operation.

trephination was performed as early as 3000 to 2000 B.C. has been uncovered in eastern Mediterranean and North African countries. Studies of trephined skulls suggest that the operation often was not fatal, a remarkable achievement given the difficulty of the procedure. Trephination may have been done to permit demonic spirits to escape. However, because of the absence of written records and the fact that our only data are the trephined skulls themselves, we need to be cautious in speculating about their significance (see Figure 2–3).

Another general approach to the causes of abnormal behavior reflects what might be called the psychological perspective. According to this point of view, behavioral disturbances are caused by inadequacies in the way an individual thinks, feels, or perceives the world. According to the psychological perspective, people are at least potentially capable of examining their own thinking and modifying their behavior in light of that examination. Many modern psychotherapists see their task as helping people learn to think more rationally about themselves and their social relationships.

All three of these perspectives—mystical, organic, and psychological—have recurred throughout the history of Western civilization, beginning with the Greeks.

Figure 2-3 A mural depicting the ancient Incas of Peru performing trephination.

The Ancient Western World

The philosophers of ancient Greece were the earliest to write about the psychological and organic approaches to deviance. At the height of their civilization, the Greeks emphasized the rational analysis of the natural world. The concepts of motivation and intelligence were among those that they invented in their efforts to explain the behavior they observed in everyday life. Although we tend to see the modern era as the period in which human beings have sought to extend the boundaries of human understanding through the application of reason, the foundations for this period were laid by the writings of the ancient Greek philosophers. The main difference between us and the Greeks of antiquity is that we have access to all the knowledge that has accumulated in the past 2,000 years, as well as the tools of the scientific method.

Even in ancient Greece, knowledge evolved over a period of several centuries. At the time that Homer created the *Iliad* and the *Odyssey* (about 800 B.C.), disturbed or psychotic behavior was interpreted as a form of punishment for offenses against the gods. ("Those whom the gods would destroy, they first make mad.") In the battle scenes in the *Illiad*, Homer typically described his heroes as suddenly possessed by feelings of power that are engendered in them by the gods. States of insanity were believed to be created in the same way. Therapy took place in a group of temples dedicated to Asclepius, the god of healing. Each temple was a maze-like structure in which mental patients walked and slept and ultimately reached the center. In the process it was believed that Asclepius attended to their dreams and healed them.

In the centuries after Homer, the idea that a person's life is in the hands of the gods gradually declined, at least among educated citizens. The Greek philosophers became increasingly curious about aspects of the individual that might explain normal as well as abnormal behavior. Extreme mental deviations and disorders came to be viewed as natural phenomena for which rational treatments might be developed.

The ancient Egyptians, as well as the Mesopotamians and Hebrews, believed the seat of the mind to be in the heart. When the Pharaohs were embalmed, the heart was venerated, but the brain was removed and thrown away. For the Greeks, however, the brain was the seat of the mind. (Shakespeare referred to the lingering heart–mind controversy in Act III of *The Merchant of Venice* when he wrote: "Tell me where is fancie bred in the heart or in the head.") Despite his lack of anatomical knowledge, the Greek physician Hippocrates (460–377 B.C.) looked to the brain in his efforts to explain why people behave as they do. He described the brain as the interpreter of consciousness and the body's most important organ.

Hippocrates described epileptic seizures and concluded that they were caused by a diseased brain. He also wrote about depression, states of delirium, psychosis, irrational fears (what we now call phobias), and hysteria (organic symptoms in the absence of an organic disturbance). He and his followers became known for their ability to recognize and treat mental illness. Their thera-

Figure 2-4 Hippocrates, an older contemporary of Plato, was born in 460 B.C. He attended the medical school on the island of Cos and traveled to many cities both to practice and to teach. Over the centuries his influence grew. His writings include material that today would be called textbooks, articles, case histories, and speeches.

peutic techniques consisted of rest, bathing, and dieting. There is even a record of Hippocrates appearing as an expert witness at the trial of an insane person. Today physicians continue to pay their debt to Hippocrates by taking the Hippocratic oath when they graduate from medical school (see Figure 2–4).

Three other Greek philosophers—Socrates (470–399 B.C.), Plato (427–347 B.C.), and Aristotle (384–322 B.C.)—also deserve mention for their contributions to abnormal psychology. Socrates was interested in self-exploration and considered reasoning to be the cornerstone of the good life and personal happiness. He believed in using inquiry to further knowledge; his goal was to teach by asking questions instead of giving answers. Today this procedure—called the Socratic method—is a valuable teaching tool as well as a component of the scientific method.

Socrates' most famous student, Plato, developed the **organismic point of view.** He saw behavior as a product of the totality of psychological processes. Like many modern writers, Plato believed that disturbed behavior grew out of conflicts between emotion and reason. In contrast to those who saw abnormal behavior as having a physical cause, he stressed the power of ideas, going so far as to say that the mind is the only true reality of human existence. According to Plato, the ideal individual is, above all, guided by reason. In his *Laws*, he expressed the belief that people who have lost their reason should be separated from society: "No lunatic shall be allowed to be at large in the community; the relatives of such persons shall keep them in safe custody at home by such methods as they contrive, on penalty of fine." Plato's belief is similar to that which has been held by many societies in the past. However, as time went on separation of the mentally ill from others in the community became the responsibility of the government rather than of the family. The large institutions created to care for the mentally ill are described later in this chapter. Since the middle of the 1960s, an emphasis on the civil rights of those who are mentally ill has resulted in the closure of many of these institutions and the return of many patients to the community and, for those that have them, to the care of family members.

Aristotle, a pupil of Plato and the teacher of Alexander the Great, wrote extensively on the nature of reasoning and consciousness and also sought to analyze human emotions. He described and speculated about a number of emotional and motivational states, including anger, fear, envy, courage, hatred, and pity. He believed that anger occurred when a person was subjected to what he or she experienced as injustice and wrongdoing; he saw fear as the awareness of danger with an expectation of loss, defeat, or rejection. Like most of the Greek philosophers, Aristotle placed the highest value on reason and application. He also believed that the various forces in the body need to be in balance for reason to prevail.

Galen (A.D. 130–200), the greatest Roman physician, consolidated and augmented the Greek theories of mind and body. Galen extended ancient theories about the role of the four humors in personal character and temperament. The four **humors** (fluids of the body) were blood, black bile, yellow bile, and phlegm. Each of the humors was believed to be associated with a certain temperamental quality, and imbalances among the humors were believed to cause various disorders. For Galen, psychological characteristics were expressions of bodily processes and as such were influenced by the particular blend or balance of the four humors. Galen's the-

Figure 2-5 These medieval woodcuts reflect the view that temperamental qualities result from excesses of the four humors. From left to right: The man with plenty of blood who has a changeable temperament; the hot-tempered man with an excess of yellow bile; the sluggish man with too much phlegm; and the man with too much black bile who is melancholic.

ories were popular through the medieval period (see Figure 2–5).

The rational approach of the ancient philosophers laid the groundwork for modern science. It led to attempts to classify abnormal behavior according to some consistent scheme. It temporarily replaced magic and religious explanations of abnormal behavior with a quest, through observation and reason, for natural causes. Except for a break during the Middle Ages, that quest has continued until the present time.

The Middle Ages

A host of changes accompanied the decline of ancient Greek culture and the rise and fall of the Roman Empire. Perhaps the two most obvious causes of these changes were the invasions of Western Europe by barbarian tribes and the growth of the Christian religion. The invaders, whose ideas were primitive compared to those of the Greeks and Romans, caused great social unrest, while the Christian religion served to comfort people in troubled times. The church also acted as a unifying force when the civil government of Rome finally fell.

The unrest of the Middle Ages was intensified by nearly constant warfare as well as by the Black Death and other epidemics that came without warning and wiped out hundreds of thousands of people. During this period fear and terror spread like brush fires, causing many outbreaks of group hysteria. The nature of these outbreaks varied. Some groups of people behaved like packs of wolves, and others danced in the streets, making spiderlike movements.

During the early Middle Ages the importance of the Christian spirit of charity, particularly toward stigmatized groups such as the severely mentally disturbed, cannot be overestimated. For example, in Gheel, Belgium, the church established a special institution for the care of retarded and psychotic children. As they improved, these children were often placed with local sympathetic families (see Figure 2–6). Also during this period, music and dance were thought to cure insanity by restoring the chemical balance within the body (see Figure 2–7).

One figure in the early Christian era, the theologian and philosopher Saint Augustine (A.D. 354–430), stands out because he helped lay the groundwork for modern psychodynamic theories of abnormal behavior. Writing extensively about feelings, mental anguish, and human conflict, he was perhaps the earliest forerunner of today's psychoanalysts. It was not so much the topics he dealt with as the way he approached them that most resembles the psychoanalytic method of today. Saint Augustine used introspection, or examination of his own thoughts, feelings, and motives, to discuss mental processes like the conflict between pleasure and discipline. He worked almost ruthlessly toward a complete, if painful, self-analysis, and in his *Confessions* he revealed his innermost thoughts, temptations, and fears.

Figure 2-6 One place where moral therapy has survived is Gheel, Belgium. Founded after the miracle cure of five "lunatics" at the shrine of Saint Dymphna in the thirteenth century, the colony has continued its work to the present. Over 2,000 patients like this man live in private homes under few restrictions; there they work with their host families at everyday tasks until they have recovered.

By demonstrating that introspection and exploration of the individual's emotional life could be valuable sources of psychological knowledge, Saint Augustine made an important contribution to modern abnormal psychology. Unfortunately, these efforts were not followed up during the late Middle Ages. As the church's

control and influence increased, so did its role in governmental affairs, and it was religious dogma, not civil law, that became the supreme voice of authority. The church came to control the practice of medicine, defining its goals and prescribing treatments for various conditions. To the degree that this control reflected a feeling of charity toward people suffering hardships of various kinds, the church played a positive role. To the extent that it was intolerant, authoritarian, and repressive, however, its role was decidedly negative.

The legacy of rationality that the Middle Ages had inherited from the Greek philosophers was quickly abandoned in the late medieval period. Demonology and superstition gained renewed importance in the explanation of abnormal behavior. Church authorities felt the need for a definitive document on the apprehension and conviction of witches and sorcerers, whom they saw as the primary agents of evil. That need was met in 1484 with the publication of *Malleus Maleficarum* (*The Witches' Hammer*) by Fathers Henry Kramer and James Sprenger, a highly influential work that became a basic reference for investigators of diabolical phenomena.

In the late Middle Ages, although many people continued to take a benign, naturalistic view of mental illness, antiintellectualism and belief in magic and witchcraft increased. Many people believed strongly in exorcism, the casting out of evil spirits from the body of an afflicted person (see Figure 2–8). Nevertheless, it is difficult to draw firm conclusions about the mental status of the witches who were put on trial during the Middle Ages, since the available evidence is sparse and scattered. However, research has shown that many of the "witches" who were put on trial in New England during the sixteenth and seventeenth centuries were persecuted social outcasts rather than people suffering from mental disorders (Demos, 1982; Schoenman, 1984; Spanos, 1978).

History does not move in a simple, uncomplicated way. The *Malleus Maleficarum* described a case of a young man who could not restrain himself from protruding his tongue or shouting obscenities whenever he tried to pray. It attributed this problem to demonic possession. However, Paracelsus (1493–1541) vigorously attacked such notions. Like the Greeks before him, he pictured maladaptations as caused by natural phenomena, although, as a believer in astrology, he felt that such phenomena lay within the stars and planets, not within the individual. In the six-

Figure 2-7 In this medieval engraving, the insane are shown being led through a dance, in an effort to improve their mental condition.

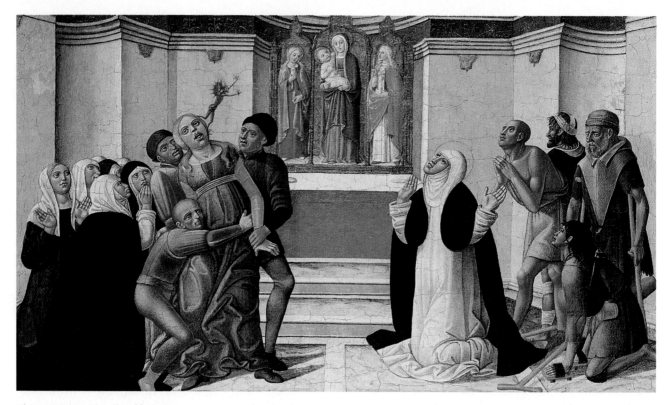

Figure 2-8 This late fifteenth-century painting by Girolamo Di Benvenuto, *Saint Catherine Exorcising a Possessed Woman,* shows Saint Catherine of Siena casting the devil out of a possessed woman. The devil is seen fleeing from the woman's head.

teenth century another rational thinker, Juan Huarte (1530–1589), wrote one of the first treatises on psychology, *Probe of the Mind.* In it he distinguished between theology and psychology and argued forcefully for a rational explanation of the psychological development of children.

In addition to thoughtful individuals like Paracelsus and Huarte, there were some relatively enlightened governments and some serious efforts to care for mentally troubled individuals. In England, for example, the Crown had the right and duty to protect the mentally impaired, who were divided into two categories: natural fools and persons *non compos mentis.* A **natural fool** was a mentally retarded person whose intellectual capacities had never progressed beyond those of a child. **Persons *non compos mentis*** (Latin for "not of sound mind") did not show mental disability at birth. Their deviant behavior was not continuous, and they might show long periods of recovery. (For reasons that are not clear, by the fifteenth century the term "lunatic" had replaced the phrase *"non compos mentis"* and "idiot" had replaced "natural fool.")

There is also evidence that hearings to judge a person's mental status and legal competency were held as early as the thirteenth century (Neugebauer, 1979). Such examinations were designed to assess a person's orientation, memory, and intellect. The following description of Emma de Beston, which dates from 1383, is typical of the reports that were based on such examinations.

> *The said Emma, being caused to appear before them, was asked whence she came and said that she did not know. Being asked in what town she was, she said that she was at Ely. Being asked how many days there were in the week, she said seven but could not name them. Being asked how many husbands she had had in her time she said three, giving the name of one only and not knowing the names of the others. Being asked whether she had ever had issue by them, she said that she had had a husband with a son, but did not know his name. Being asked how many shillings were in forty pence, she said she did not know. Being asked whether she would rather have twenty silver groats than forty pence, she said they were of the same value. They examined her in all other ways which they thought best and found that she was not of sound mind, having neither sense nor memory nor sufficient intelligence to manage herself, her lands or her goods. As appeared by inspection she had the face and countenance of an idiot.*
>
> —O'Donoghue, 1914, pp. 127–128

The Renaissance

The Renaissance was a period of increased humanism, curiosity about nature, and interest in scholarship. Yet persecution continued of the people society did not like.

Figure 2–9 is an example of the less than compassionate view of insanity that was commonplace. Many medical authorities devoted much time to investigating skin blemishes, which were believed to indicate points of contact with Satan. The idea of magical cures embodied in shamanism was evident in the popular therapy of removing stones from the head (see Figure 2–10).

Although the influence of *Malleus Maleficarum* continued to be felt for centuries, gradually the idea that irrational behavior could be explained rationally gained renewed attention. It followed that detailed descriptions of the behavior in question were needed. Johann Weyer (1515–1576), a sixteenth-century physician, was one of the major contributors to this development. In an age of unbridled superstition, Weyer emphasized psychological conflict and disturbed interpersonal relationships as causes of mental disorder. His enlightened humanism undoubtedly saved countless mentally ill people from death at the stake. Weyer had the courage to insist that witches were mentally disturbed individuals rather than creatures of Satan. He vigorously asserted the need to treat such people medically rather than theologically.

On the basis of careful psychological examination of mental patients, Weyer described a wide range of abnormal behavior, including the disorders known today as paranoia, epilepsy, psychosis, depression, and persistent nightmares. In *The Deception of Demons* he specifically attacked the preposterous claims of the *Malleus Maleficarum*. He argued that clinical treatment must be oriented toward meeting the needs of disturbed people rather than merely following rules of clerical institutions. He spent much time talking with and observing his patients because he felt that he could not treat psychopathology without firsthand knowledge of it. The knowledge led him to the conclusion that inner experiences (such as psychological conflict) and disturbed relationships with others were significant causes of mental

Figure 2-10 This early sixteenth-century painting by the Dutch painter Hieronymous Bosch shows an operation for removing stones from the head. An old phrase used even today to describe a mentally unbalanced person is "He has stones (or rocks) in his head." In the sixteenth and seventeenth centuries, quacks took advantage of this superstition and pretended to cure insanity by making a superficial incision in the patient's scalp and "extracting" small stones that were supplied by a confederate standing behind the patient.

Figure 2-9 This sixteenth-century woodcut shows a method for curing insanity. An insane man's head is held in an oven while demons and troublesome thoughts exit through the top of the oven.

illness. Weyer's writings represent a major step toward the separation of abnormal psychology from theology.

The Age of Reason and the Enlightenment

The seventeenth century, known as the Age of Reason, and the eighteenth century, known as the Enlightenment, have been so labeled because during these two centuries reason and the scientific method came to replace faith and dogma as ways of understanding the natural world. During these two centuries major advances were made in such diverse fields as astronomy, biology, and chemistry. Scientists and philosophers alike emphasized the need to support assertions with observations of natural phenomena.

Although human emotions and motivations are

less accessible to direct observation than the moon, the human circulatory system, or molecular structures, a number of philosophers and scientists focused on the subjective experiences of human beings. Baruch Spinoza (1632–1677) anticipated modern approaches to psychology and physiology with his argument that mind and body are inseparable. Much current writing in psychology is reminiscent of Spinoza's writings, in which he discussed psychological causation and the roles of emotions, ideas, and desires in human life. Spinoza even referred to unconscious mechanisms that influence behavior. His main contribution to abnormal psychology was his argument that psychological processes, though they are not directly observable, are equal in importance to the material processes of the natural world. The English physician William Harvey (1578–1657), best known for his work on the human circulatory system, also wrote about the relationships between the psychological and physiological sides of life.

Among the perceptive observers of the human experience in every age have been playwrights, novelists, and poets. During the Age of Reason, a number of authors probed especially deeply into the problems of human motivation and emotions. The clearest examples can be found in many plays of William Shakespeare (1564–1616), particularly *Hamlet*. Hamlet wants to take revenge on his uncle but consistently hesitates to act. Psychoanalysts have interpreted this hesitation as a reflection of Hamlet's neurotic conflicts concerning his mother, who had married the uncle after the death of Hamlet's father. Another literary work that dealt with human emotions was *The Anatomy of Melancholy*, by Robert Burton (1577–1640) (see Figure 2–11). In this book Burton focused on the emotional core of depression and called attention to an observation that clinical workers have often made: depressed people tend to be very angry not only with themselves but with all others as well. Burton, a professor of divinity at Oxford, based his description and analysis of depression on his own experience.

These literary developments mirror the longstanding conflict between psychological and physical explanations of abnormal behavior. However, during the seventeenth and eighteenth centuries both groups—those who analyzed subjective experience and those who sought to identify physical defects—finally rejected the idea that demons and supernatural forces were the causes of abnormal behavior. As a consequence, by the end of the eighteenth century superstition had been almost totally replaced by a commitment to rationality, scientific observation, and humane treatment of the mentally ill.

In England the movement toward humane treatment gained impetus as a result of the psychotic breakdown suffered by King George III in 1765. This event precipi-

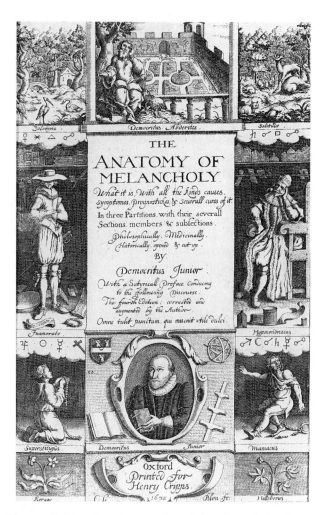

Figure 2-11 The title page from Robert Burton's book, written under the name of Democritus Junior. At the top center is a picture of Democritus the Elder in his garden, while a portrait of the author is at the bottom. The three larger pictures on each side illustrate some of the causes of melancholy. Jealousy, love, and superstition are on the left; solitude, hypochondriasis, and mania are on the right. At the bottom are two herbs, borage and hellebore, that were thought to help cure melancholia.

tated a constitutional crisis and made many people aware that even prominent individuals were not immune to mental derangement. Madhouses had existed in England for many years, but only in 1774 did Britain pass its first parliamentary act licensing such institutions and regulating the admission of patients to them.

From the late seventeenth to the nineteenth century interest rose in **physiognomy**, the art of judging character, personality, and feelings from the form of the body, particularly the face (see Figure 2–12). In the early nineteenth century another new approach to abnormal psychology emerged. Franz Joseph Gall (1758–1828), a physician, studied the brains of different kinds of people (young, old, deranged) and gathered evidence suggesting that brain size and mental development are related.

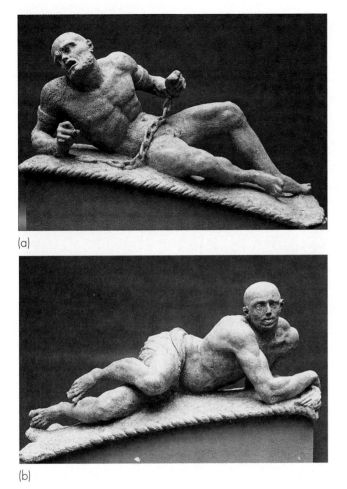

(a)

(b)

Figure 2-12 These statues, originally above the gates of the Bethlehem Hospital in London, are generally taken as representations of Raving Madness (*a*) and Melancholy Madness (*b*). They exemplify the then growing interest in physiognomy, or gauging emotions from the appearance of the body and face. (See page 45 for more on Bethlehem Hospital.)

ducing of vomiting, special diets, exercise programs, and physiotherapy. Like most of his contemporaries, Cullen used severe restraints and straitjackets to control violently disturbed individuals.

An even more famous example of the quest for organic explanations of abnormal behavior is the career of a Viennese physician, Franz Anton Mesmer (1734–1815). In 1774 Mesmer heard of the work of some English physicians who were treating certain diseases with magnets. He then treated a patient by making her swallow a preparation containing iron and attaching three magnets to her body, one on her stomach and two on her legs. Following her dramatic recovery, Mesmer speculated about the mechanisms that had brought about the cure. We would all agree with his first conclusion: the favorable result could not reasonably be explained by the action of the magnets alone. But Mesmer, a flamboyant and ambitious man, went on to assert that the magnets had simply reinforced or strengthened

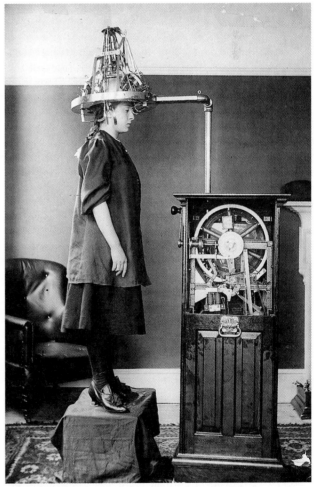

Figure 2-13 The Lavery electric phrenometer, invented in 1907, was designed to measure bumps on the head. Such bumps were thought to indicate the location of different psychological faculties.

On the basis of this evidence he formulated the theory of **phrenology,** according to which discrete psychological "faculties" were located in specific areas of the brain. Gall believed that bumps and indentations on the surface of the skull were accurate reflections of the underlying brain parts. Figure 2–13 shows a device that was used to measure these irregularities. Interest in this now-discredited theory lasted a long time: the journal of the Ohio State Phrenological Society was published until 1938, and the British Phrenological Society was in existence until 1967.

Two additional examples that illustrate the growing interest in physical approaches to mental illness are the ideas of Cullen and Mesmer. The Scottish physician William Cullen (1712–1790) believed that neurotic behavior was caused by physical defects of the nervous system. Cullen's therapeutic efforts seem naive, but they were a logical outgrowth of his organic orientation. He treated his patients with cold dousings, bloodletting, in-

Figure 2-14 *Mesmer treated his patients using a* baquet, *a round tub in which he placed bottles of magnetized water. This eighteenth-century engraving shows patients using rods and ropes connected to the tub to touch the afflicted areas on their bodies.*

the primary cause of the cure: his personal or animal magnetism.

While Mesmer's idea of animal magnetism seems ridiculous today, it fit reasonably well with some of the scientific beliefs of his time. In the eighteenth century it was widely believed that the planets influenced both physiological and psychological aspects of behavior. Mesmer contended that all human beings were endowed with a special magnetic fluid, a kind of sixth sense that, when liberated, could cure and prevent all illnesses (see Figure 2–14). Furthermore, he was convinced that he possessed an unusual abundance of the fluid. Mesmer believed that a gesture with his hands was enough to make his patients feel the transmission of his magnetic force.

Mesmer's patients entered a thickly carpeted, dimly lit room amid soft music and perfumed air. They held hands, forming a circle around the *baquet*, a tub filled with magnetized water. Mesmer entered, dressed in an elegant cloak and carrying a sword. These dramatics were deliberately created to accomplish the emotional crisis needed for the cure.

Many testimonials claimed that Mesmer's treatment had been helpful. However, the mechanism of his therapy had more to do with the power of suggestion than with human magnetic fluids. His animal magnetism was a forerunner not of an organic cure, but rather of a complex psychological means of influencing attitudes and behavior. Mesmer thus was an important figure in the history of hypnosis, a clinical technique that, while far removed from Mesmer's *baquet*, still relies on suggestion as a means of influencing the patient's state of awareness.

The Reform Movement

The growth of a scientific attitude toward mental disorders—an attitude that began in the eighteenth century—contributed to an increase in compassion for people who suffered from them. This new compassion became the basis for the reform movement of the nineteenth century. Philippe Pinel (1745–1826), a leader in the reform of French mental hospitals, had expressed great sympathy for the plight of the deranged. He firmly believed that they required humane care and treatment. Although this orientation is widely accepted by both professional workers and the public today, Pinel's ideas were far from commonplace in his time. Pinel had to fight against the view that institutions for the insane were needed more to protect society than to help the deranged (Weiner, 1992).

An interesting aspect of the growth of Pinel's humanism was the influence of Jean-Baptiste Pussin, a former patient at a hospital where Pinel worked. After being discharged Pussin was given a job at the Hospice de Bicêtre, the major asylum for male patients, where he eventually became superintendent of the ward for incurable mental patients. Research has shown that it was Pussin, not Pinel, who removed the chains from patients at the Bicêtre (Weiner, 1979). Pussin forbade cruelty toward patients and routinely dismissed attendants who mistreated them. Pinel learned much from Pussin, and when he was appointed head of the Salpêtrière, the women's asylum, he insisted that Pussin come with him.

Other reformers in Europe and America also had to fight many battles to achieve their goals. An example of the less-than-human methods that they opposed were the "ships of fools," or ships whose captains were paid to take the mentally ill away from the offended community. The community usually didn't seem to care that the lives of the passengers often ended at the bottom of the sea thousands of miles from home.

An important step toward humane treatment of the mentally ill occurred on May 25, 1815, when the British House of Commons ordered a "Parliamentary Inquiry into the Madhouses of England." One of these, the Hospital of St. Mary of Bethlehem in London, had become known for the noise and chaos prevailing within it. The activities in this "madhouse" were of such great interest to the public that visitors often came to observe the antics of the patients. Tickets were even sold to this popular tourist attraction (see Figure 2-15), from which the word *bedlam* is derived. A full-scale investigation was initiated after incidents of physical abuse at Bethlehem Hospital were revealed by a citizen's committee, which rallied public support for enlightened legislation on behalf of the mentally ill.

One of the leaders of the citizen's reform committee was William Hone, a political satirist. Hone described the formation of the committee as follows.

Figure 2-15 This drawing by William Hogarth, for his series "Rake's Progress" shows two women visitors who have purchased admission tickets to view the antics of the patients. Although it is hard for us to believe today, tickets for such viewings were sold at Bethlehem Hospital in London until the late eighteenth century and people enjoyed the novelty of these sights much as though they were attending a circus.

> I was at a Coffee Shop in Fleet Street sitting next to Alderman Waithman, when the illustrator George Cruikshank came in. We talked, as we often did, on the subject of madhouses, of the abuses and cruelty to the patients—
>
> I then proposed forming a committee to investigate the Lunatic Asylums.
>
> Thus self-authorized, we knocked at the door of one Asylum after another. George Cruikshank drew the pictures and I took notes.

Cruikshank's graphic portrayals of the inhuman conditions endured by the mentally ill were a major factor in bringing about reform (see Figure 2–16).

By the middle of the nineteenth century, the growing acceptance of humanitarian ideas had led to a broad recognition of the need to reform social institutions. Vigorous movements were begun to establish protective and benign asylums for the mentally ill. These movements were given impetus by Pinel's *Treatise on Insanity*, written at the beginning of the nineteenth century, in which he called for the application of scientific principles in place of guesswork in arriving at treatments for

Figure 2-16 The illustrator George Cruikshank's dramatic pictures of the mistreatment of mental patients helped bring about reform legislation. This engraving shows a son visiting his mother during her confinement in Bethlehem Hospital.

disturbed behavior. Classifying his patients according to observable characteristics, such as melancholy and delirium, Pinel sought to devise specific treatments for them. For example, here is how he described the optimal treatment of melancholia and depression:

> Patience, firmness, humane feeling in the manner of directing them, continuous watchfulness in the wards to prevent outbursts of anger and exasperations, pleasant occupations varied according to differences in taste, various types of physical exercise, spacious quarters among trees, all the enjoyments and tranquillity of country living, and from time to time soft and melodious music, all the easier to obtain since there is almost always in these establishments some distinguished musician whose talents languish for want of exercise and cultivation.
>
> Pinel, 1809, pp. 258–260

Figure 2-17 As a result of the reform movement, mental hospitals made special efforts to provide patients with cheerful surroundings and enjoyable entertainment. For example, the Middlesex County Lunatic Asylum in England held elaborate parties for its patients on New Years Day.

The sometimes huge asylums for the insane that were built in the nineteenth century came into existence because it was felt that the only way to treat mentally disturbed people was to isolate them from the damaging influences of family, friends, and community. Accompanying this view was the belief in **moral treatment.** This approach mirrored Pinel's treatment plan for depression. It sought to control and rehabilitate the patient through a fixed schedule that encouraged regular habits; kind treatment with a minimum of restraint; a daily visit from the hospital superintendent, who assumed the role of persuader and inspirational leader; calm, pleasant surroundings; accommodations that separated patients with different degrees of disturbance; proper diet; some medication; and organized physical and mental activities (see Figure 2–17).

The programs of hospitals that employed moral-treatment approaches seemed to be most effective when the patients and staff shared common religious, ethnic, and cultural values; when caseloads were held to a relatively small size; when the hospital superintendent was charismatic and inspirational; and when adequate funds to run the hospitals were available (Morrissey & Goldman, 1986).

An important feature of the European reform movement was the creation of institutions for the treatment of psychologically troubled children. At the beginning of the nineteenth century, childhood was marked by a high infant mortality rate and an early entry into the adult work world, for example, in the coal mines, cotton mills, and other factories. Up to the 1850s children were placed into exactly the same institutions as adults. They were locked up in prisons—in 1816, 3,000 prisoners in various London jails were under 20, almost half under 17 years of age. Many were placed in workhouses.

The inadequate or nonexistent facilities for children came about in part due to the then-standard definition of insanity as the loss of reason. Childhood, it was believed, was the time before reason was acquired. By the middle of the nineteenth century, however, textbooks dealing with psychological abnormalities included sections on children, using such terms as "the insanity of early life." Eventually, special institutions were developed not only for the care and treatment of disturbed children but also for those who were mentally retarded (Scull, 1993).

The Reform Movement in America The eighteenth century was not a good time to be insane in the fledgling British Colonies; often the mentally ill simply languished in jail. In early colonial days the mentally ill generally were ignored until they required some action because they were thought to be a nuisance or a menace to the community. In this way, the insane became identified with criminals and paupers. In some communities, a group of these people would be loaded into a stagecoach in the middle of the night and dumped in the town square of some distant locale. The Philadelphia Almshouse, erected in 1732, illustrates the type of public institution in which the mentally ill were placed. The almshouse served the poor, the infirm, and the psychologically disturbed. In 1750, Benjamin Franklin wrote that the Almshouse "was by no means fitted" to treat the mentally ill and that they needed treatment in a separate hospital.

The second half of the seventeenth century saw the gradual growth of a reform movement. For example, Virginia's royal governor, Francis Fauquier, persuaded the House of Burgesses to build a hospital for "ideots and lu-

(a)

(b)

(c)

Figure 2-18 (a) The Colonial Williamsburg restoration in Virginia features a reconstruction of the Public Hospital for Persons of Insane and Disordered Minds, America's first public institution exclusively for the mentally ill. (b) In the eighteenth century the inmates inhabited bare, depressing cells. (c) By the midnineteenth century, comfortable housing had become an important part of treatment.

naticks"; the hospital opened on October 12, 1773 (see Figure 2–18). Benjamin Rush (1745–1813), a signer of the Declaration of Independence, is often credited with the founding of American psychiatry. He believed that "madness" was caused by engorgement of the blood vessels of the brain. Although the treatment methods that he advocated (bleeding, purging, and water cures) today seem more like punishment than therapy, his work took place in a hospital rather than in a custodial institution, and his methods were intended to reduce pressure on the brain's blood vessels and thus reduce mental illness. The Pennsylvania Hospital, where Rush introduced his new treatment methods, was the first hospital in America to admit mentally ill patients. His *Medical Inquiries and Observations upon the Diseases of the Mind*, published in 1812, was the first American textbook on psychiatry and was used as a basic reference for over 50 years. Figure 2–19 shows a reproduction of a "tranquilizer" chair designed by Rush. It was intended to calm patients by restraining them and depriving them of the use of their senses.

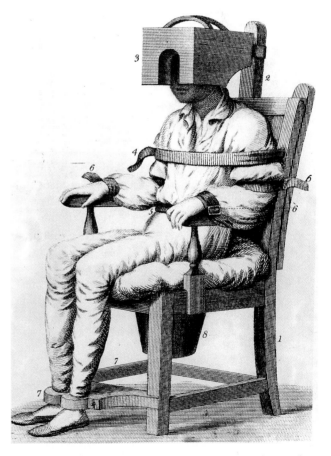

Figure 2-19 This engraving shows the tranquilizing chair developed by Benjamin Rush. Although it may appear more humane than some of the methods used earlier, today such restraints would be viewed as non-therapeutic.

Figure 2-20 Dorothea Dix sought to replace prescientific "therapies" for violent patients with more humane treatment approaches.

The lack of humane treatment and decent facilities for the insane in America appalled Dorothea Dix (1802–1887), a Boston schoolteacher who devoted much of her life to reforming institutions for the indigent. (See Figures 2–20 and 2–21.) By 1847 she had vis-

ited 18 penitentiaries, 300 county jails and houses of correction, and 500 almshouses where the mentally ill were kept. Through her personal efforts 32 mental hospitals were constructed. Illustrative of the humane treatment movement is the art therapy program developed in the 1880s at the Institute of Pennsylvania Hospital (see Figure 2-22).

In 1908, an American businessman named Clifford Beers recorded his experiences as a mental patient in his book *A Mind that Found Itself* (see Box 2-1). After his recovery Beers became determined to make changes in the conditions of mental hospitals, and his book helped him gather support for a citizens' reform group, the National Committee for Mental Hygiene (now called the National Association for Mental Health), which was founded in 1909. The group promoted social programs aimed at preventing mental illness as well as ensuring humane treatment of the mentally ill.

Despite the progress toward more humane treatment of mental patients in the nineteenth century, the mentally ill continued to be persecuted well into the twentieth century. An example is provided by Albert Deutsch, who published a shocking exposé of the mistreatment of patients at the Philadelphia State Hospital for Mental Diseases during the 1940s:

> The male "incontinent ward" was like a scene out of Dante's Inferno. Three hundred nude men stood, squatted and sprawled in this bare room. . . . Winter or Summer, these creatures never were given any clothing at all. . . . Many patients . . . had to eat their meals with their hands. There weren't nearly enough spoons or other tableware to go around. . . . Four hundred patients were herded into one barn-like dayroom intended for only 80. There were only a few benches; most of the men had to stand all day or sit on the splintery floor. There was no supervised recreation, no occupational therapy. . . . Only two attendants were on this

Figure 2-21 The crib was one of the prescientific "therapies" for violent patients that Dorothea Dix sought to abolish.

Figure 2-22 1880s' art therapy workshop of the Institute of Pennsylvania Hospital.

ward; at least 10 were needed. The hogs in a near-by pigpen were far better fed, in far greater comfort, than these human beings.

—Deutsch, 1948, pp. 49–50

Today conditions such as Deutsch described are unlikely to exist and many institutions provide a high standard of care. However, while the quality of care in many mental hospitals has improved over time, the deinstitutionalization movement begun over 25 years ago has resulted in a lower standard of care for many people affected by mental illness and an increase in the suffering for some. For instance, the situation of homeless mentally ill persons in many ways parallels the less humane treatment of the mentally ill in earlier periods of history. Deinstitutionalization and some of its consequences are discussed further in both chapters 1 and 18.

Our review of the history of abnormal psychology has emphasized two themes: (1) the changing beliefs about what abnormal behavior is and what it should be about, and (2) the need for humane approaches to the mentally disturbed. An increasingly important theme of the twentieth century is recognition of research as a path to rational understanding and treatment. In the next section we explore important first steps toward a science of abnormal psychology.

Psychological and Organic Views of Abnormal Behavior

The causes of abnormal behavior have yet to be determined fully, and debates on this issue recur continually. Is abnormal behavior caused by disturbances in bodily functioning or by subjective experiences, thoughts, and

motivations? We will see in chapter 3 that a dichotomy between organic and psychological causation is becoming less and less tenable. However, in the past such a dichotomy has often dominated the study of abnormal behavior.

The Psychological Approach

Eighteenth-century theories emphasized **rational thinking** as the way to achieve personal and social adjustment. During the first half of the nineteenth century, however, the important role of **irrational thought** in both normal and abnormal behavior attracted much more attention. This shift in emphasis took place as part of the so-called Romantic reaction against the view of philosophers and scientists who gave little weight to the role of emotions, motivations, and internal conflicts in human behavior. Many clinical workers and researchers began to view internal conflicts as a major cause of personal unhappiness and failure to adapt socially. This focus on emotion and irrational feelings laid the groundwork for Sigmund Freud's early twentieth century writings about mental processes and their relationship to disturbed behavior (see chapter 3).

The reaction against pure rationalism directed more attention to the inner life of the person than to any other aspect of human existence. The German psychiatrist Johann Christian Heinroth (1773–1843) theorized that mental illness resulted from internal conflicts between unacceptable impulses and the guilt generated by those impulses, and that the individual is often unaware of these conflicts. What distinguished theories like Heinroth's from those of his predecessors was their attempts to provide an account of the whole person, the inner life, and the mental stresses and strains that underlie observable behavior. This was in contrast to the rationalist view that the scientific study of abnormal behavior primarily required meticulous observation and description of disordered behaviors, along with classification of those behaviors.

Heinroth's ideas are strikingly similar to Freud's notion that impulses clash with conscience and result in anxiety, unhappiness, and socially inappropriate behavior. Freud, like Heinroth, recognized that this clash might take place at an unconscious level and that awareness of these conflicts was a means of understanding and resolving them, and hence a way of correcting maladaptive behavior. Despite these similarities, Freud seems to have been only slightly acquainted with Heinroth and the other participants in the Romantic reaction. One reason for this was that by the midnineteenth century, long before Freud's work began, the pendulum

A Protest That Had an Effect

Clifford Beers's book, *A Mind that Found Itself*, is the story of his treatment in mental hospitals during a period of psychosis and a protest against the often cruel treatment of patients in institutions for the mentally ill. Its description of what Beers endured gripped the imagination of readers and helped gain popular support for the American mental health movement (see Figure 2–23). After his recovery Beers carried on a lifelong crusade that helped revolutionize the care of the mentally ill. In the following excerpt Beers describes his agony when he was restrained in a camisole or straitjacket, a canvas device that was used to restrict movement of unruly patients. In this case Beers believed that the attending physician had laced the jacket unnecessarily tight because of his anger at Beers's behavior.

No incidents of my life have ever impressed themselves more indelibly on my memory than those of my first night in a straitjacket. Within one hour of the time I was placed in it I was suffering pain as intense as any I ever endured, and before the night had passed it had become almost unbearable. My right hand was so held that the tip of one of my fingers was all but cut by the nail of another, and soon knifelike pains began to shoot through my right arm as far as the shoulder. After four or five hours the excess of pain rendered me partially insensible to it. But for fifteen consecutive hours I remained in that instrument of torture; and not until the twelfth hour, about breakfast time the next morning did the attendant so much as loosen a cord.

During the first seven or eight hours, excruciating pains racked not only my

arms, but half of my body. Though I cried and moaned, in fact, screamed so loudly that the attendants must have heard me, little attention was paid to me. . . . I even begged the attendants to loosen the jacket enough to ease me a little. This they refused to do, and they even seemed to enjoy being in a position to add their considerable mite to my torture.

After fifteen interminable hours the straitjacket was removed. Whereas just prior to its putting on I had been in a vigorous enough condition to offer stout resistance when wantonly assaulted, now, on coming out of it, I was helpless. When my arms were released from their constricted position, the pain was intense. Every joint had been racked. I had no control over the fingers of either hand, and could not have dressed myself had I been promised my freedom for doing so.

For more than the following week I suffered as already described, though of course with gradually decreasing intensity as my racked body became accustomed to the unnatural positions it was forced to take. The first experience occurred on the night of October 18th, 1902. I was subjected to the same unfair, unnecessary, and unscientific ordeal for twenty-one consecutive nights and parts of the corresponding twenty-one days. On more than one occasion, indeed, the attendant placed me in the straitjacket during the day for refusing to obey some trivial command. This, too, without an explicit order from the doctor in charge, though perhaps he acted under a general order.

During most of the time I was held also in seclusion in a padded cell. A padded

Figure 2-23 Clifford Beers became an effective advocate for humane treatment of mental disorders after his own experiences in a mental institution.

cell is a vile hole. The side walls are padded as high as a man can reach, as is also the inside of the door. One of the worst features of such cells is the lack of ventilation, which deficiency of course aggravates their general unsanitary condition. The cell which I was forced to occupy was practically without heat, and as winter was coming on, I suffered intensely from the cold.

—Beers, 1981 [1908], pp. 107, 110–111

---

had begun to swing in a quite different direction—toward the search for biological causes of abnormal behavior.

The Organic Approach

Just as Heinroth was the champion of the psychological approach to abnormal behavior, another German psychiatrist, Wilhelm Griesinger (1817–1868), led the search for bodily causes. He argued that most mental disorders were caused by the direct or indirect influence of disturbances in brain function. While he was a staunch advocate of humane treatment and was himself a sensitive observer of human conflict, Griesinger firmly believed that the organic, rather than the psychological, origins of human maladaptation and unhappiness were predominant. His slogan was "mental diseases are brain diseases."

Behind this perspective was the assumption that the material (brain cells) almost invariably causes the mental manifestation (personal unhappiness). The major implication of this viewpoint was that it was necessary to find out more about how the body (particularly the nervous system) works. One way of doing so was to dissect the brains of mentally disturbed individuals after their deaths. Researchers reasoned that the unusual behaviors exhibited by those individuals had been caused by structural abnormalities in the brain. Through direct examination of the brains of such people, they hoped to discover relationships between the brain and behavior. From this point of view, introspection as a path to understanding psychological disturbance held little appeal. Nor was there much interest in how thoughts direct observable behavior.

Emil Kraepelin (1856–1926), who was influenced by Griesinger, also believed that abnormal behavior was caused by organic disturbances. Kraepelin's major contribution was his attempt to construct a classification system that would encompass most of the disorders that required treatment and hospitalization. He distinguished between two especially serious and debilitating conditions, dementia praecox and manic-depressive psychosis, and believed that they were specific diseases with specific organic causes.

The Approaches Converge

Toward the end of the nineteenth century, important developments took place on both the physical and psychological fronts. The French neurologist Jean Martin Charcot (1825–1893) continued to believe that organic disturbances were of crucial importance, but he used a psychological approach in studying and treating his patients. The patients in whom Charcot was most interested were **hysterics,** people who suffered from physical complaints for which no organic causes could be found. Hysterics complained of loss of sensation in the skin,

pains in various parts of the body, blindness and other visual impairments, tics, muscular contractions that resembled epileptic seizures, difficulty in walking, or paralysis. In addition to this wide variety of inexplicable symptoms, Charcot observed some psychological consistencies in hysterical patients, notably what he called *la belle indifference*: although a person who had become paralyzed could be expected to be depressed about it, Charcot's patients seemed unconcerned about their condition. Charcot also noticed that hysterical patients had their own incorrect theories of bodily functioning and that their physical symptoms were compatible with those theories. He diagnosed many of these cases as "traumatic paralysis."

Despite his orientation toward organic causes, Charcot became impressed with his psychological observations and came to the conclusion that mental states were indeed related to hysterical symptoms. He therefore developed a technique for hypnotizing hysterical patients. While they were in a hypnotic trance, he suggested to them that their symptoms (for example, paralysis of a part of the body) would disappear. In many cases the symptoms indeed vanished completely. Charcot also was able to induce hysterical symptoms in normal individuals by giving them appropriate suggestions while they were under hypnosis. Hypnosis is still used today in the treatment of some disorders, but the approach is much more complex than Charcot's reliance on mere suggestion as a way to remove symptoms.

Throughout France and Europe Charcot gained great prestige; he was referred to as the "Napoleon of neuroses." He became known as a charismatic clinician and teacher (see Figure 2–24). The following account describes some of his miraculous cures:

Figure 2-24 This portrait of Charcot shows him demonstrating the typical behavior of a hysteric, using a female patient as an example. Notice her fainting posture. Such dramatic behavior is typical of a hysterical episode.

Many patients were brought to Charcot from all over the world, paralytics on stretchers or wearing complicated apparatuses. Charcot ordered the removal of those appliances and told the patients to walk. There was, for instance, a young lady who had been paralyzed for years. Charcot bade her stand up and walk, which she did under the astonished eyes of her parents and of the Mother Superior of the convent in which she had been staying. Another young lady was brought to Charcot with a paralysis of both legs. Charcot found no organic lesion: the consultation was not yet over when the patient stood up and walked back to the door where the cabman, who was waiting for her, took off his hat in amazement and crossed himself.

—Ellenberger, 1970, p. 95

One of Charcot's students, Pierre Janet (1859–1947), extended his work and concluded that hysteria was due to a splitting off from conscious experience of certain ideas that continued to influence behavior. He observed that under hypnosis many patients recalled upsetting events that seemed to be related to the onset of their symptoms. He found that in some cases, when patients expressed the strong feelings they had experienced at the time the original events took place, their symptoms weakened temporarily or disappeared.

Besides strengthening the view that psychological causes played a role in a significant number of behavioral disorders, Charcot and Janet helped broaden the scope of behavior that was studied by abnormal psychology. Their patients, though they were troubled people who needed help, were not thought of as insane or crazy.

One of the many clinical workers who came to France especially to study with Charcot was Sigmund Freud (1856–1939). Freud had received his medical training as a neurologist and initially believed that the ultimate causes of abnormal behavior were biological. Like Charcot, however, he chose to explore aspects of mental life that seemed to be related to psychological discomfort and maladaptive behavior. Also like Charcot, Freud became increasingly interested in noncatastrophic conditions such as hysteria and phobias. Chapter 3 discusses Freud's theories in some depth, as well as other currently influential psychological, social, and organic theories dealing with the understanding and treatment of abnormal behavior.

The Stage Is Set

The history of abnormal psychology is the story of how communities have responded to people who were different and did not fit in. The ups and downs, the advances and retreats, leave us with a feeling of cautious optimism about the power of the intellect to comprehend and de-

vise ways of helping individuals who are unable to adapt to community norms.

Ideas about abnormality are almost never brand new. As we have seen, they have a history that in some cases is very long. Moreover, they are often complex. Attitudes toward deviant individuals have always reflected the social dynamics that prevailed at the time. An example of the link between what is going on in a society (its values, prejudices, and the like) and how it conceives of mental illness has been provided by studies of the role of women in the nineteenth century. Theories that asserted that there were sex-based differences in the tendency to engage in abnormal behavior were an outgrowth of cultural stereotypes and the social status quo. Not only were women regarded as subordinate to men, they were also believed to be more prone to nervous and emotional disorders. Biological factors were assumed to play a role in these differences. Some of Sigmund Freud's writings reflect this sexist assessment; for example, early in his career he assumed that the strong sexual repression he observed in women was the cause of what he viewed as their intellectual inferiority (Ellenberger, 1970).

Because we are so close to our own times, we tend to lose sight of many of the basic assumptions and beliefs that direct the thinking of our contemporaries about a wide variety of topics. If we look back at earlier periods, these assumptions and beliefs are easier to see, and they often seem strange. For example, during the 1880s and 1890s, Freud's developing theories had to compete with ideas that seem naive today. One such idea was the notion that masturbation is a sign of serious personality disorder. People who masturbated were described as moral degenerates, as deceitful, selfish, and full of cunning. Excessive masturbation was believed to result in "masturbational insanity." Another popular idea was that there was a connection between blushing and psychological functioning: excessive blushing indicated inner moral failings, whereas inability to blush reflected psychological weakness (Skultans, 1979).

Policies regarding the treatment of abnormal behavior have been influenced by the public's concerns and priorities. For example, the American public puts a premium on speed and often seems to feel that a quick solution is best. Thus in the 1960s and 1970s public opinion favored a drastic reduction in the number of residents in mental hospitals. Because an effective system of halfway houses and other support services had not been established, masses of hurriedly discharged mental patients had to make their own way into unprepared and largely hostile communities. Few were able to make the transition successfully.

This book is devoted to modern theory, research, and practice concerning abnormal behavior. Everyone has read dozens of newspaper and magazine articles describing breakthroughs that will soon eliminate certain types of mental disorders. Too often the solutions do not materialize, because the breakthrough has been interpreted too simplistically. As the scientific method has uncovered information on a variety of fronts, the need to recognize the complexity of most forms of maladaptation has become clearer.

HISTORICAL VIEWS OF ABNORMAL BEHAVIOR

It is important to know about the history of abnormal psychology because certain perspectives about deviance—mystical, organic, and psychological—have continued to recur throughout history. Some early mystical beliefs concerning the role of supernatural or magical forces in the origin of abnormal behavior are still found in many cultures. From this point of view, therapy often involves **exorcism,** or the removal of the evil through countermagic or prayer. This practice is often performed by a **shaman,** or folk healer. Another perspective links abnormal behavior with organic defect. Early evidence of this view is found in skulls from prehistoric times that show evidence of **trephination,** chipping holes in the skull. The psychological perspective suggests that abnormal behavior is related to disturbances in the way a person thinks or perceives the world and that these disturbances are potentially modifiable.

The Ancient Western World In ancient Greece disturbed behavior was originally interpreted as punishment for offenses against the gods. Later, several Greek philosophers, beginning with Socrates, held a more psychological view and considered reasoning to be basic to adaptive behavior. Plato developed the **organismic point of view,** which explained behavior as an overall expression of a person's psychological process. He thought of disturbed behavior as arising from internal conflicts between reason and emotion. Galen, a Roman physician, taught that psychological characteristics were expressions of bodily process influenced by a balance of the **four humors.**

The Middle Ages During the Middle Ages, contrasting views of mental illness existed. Saint Augustine helped lay the groundwork for modern psychodynamic theory through his use of introspection to discuss mental processes. During the late Middle Ages, the church played both important positive and negative roles in the treatment of the mentally ill. The *Malleus Maleficarum* was an influential book that focused on the apprehension and conviction of witches and sorcerers. It played an important role in the persecution of the mentally ill who were often perceived as agents of diabolical forces. During this same period, rational thinkers Paracelsus and Juan Huarte attacked superstitious beliefs. Some governments, such as that in England, took responsibility for the protection of those who were mentally ill. There, two categories of persons, called **natural fools** and **persons** *non compos mentis,* were considered to need this protection.

The Renaissance During the late fifteenth and the sixteenth centuries, despite an increase in learning, witches were still persecuted and the influence of *Malleus Maleficarum* was still strong. However, Weyer, in an influential book, *The Deception of Demons,* argued for clinical treatment for the mentally ill rather than religious persecution. Weyer emphasized disturbed interpersonal relationships and psychological conflict as causes of mental disorder.

The Age of Reason and the Enlightenment In the seventeenth and eighteenth centuries, scientific knowledge increased greatly. Philosophers such as Spinoza wrote about the roles of emotions, ideas, and desires in life and made reference to unconscious mechanisms that influence behavior. Scientists such as Harvey wrote about the relationship between the physiological and psychological aspects of life. Literature also dealt with emotion and motivation. Many of Shakespeare's plays focus on the effects of emotion on behavior. Burton, in his book the *Anatomy of Melancholy,* described and analyzed depression from a psychological viewpoint. New ideas appeared, such as **physiognomy,** the art of judging personality from physical appearance, and **phrenology,** the view that mental faculties could be "read" from feeling the bumps on a person's head. Mesmer developed the idea of animal magnetism, which led to the use of **hypnotism** as a treatment for mental disorder.

The Reform Movement The movement toward more humane treatment of the mentally ill began with the development of **moral treatment** by Pinel in France. In England, Hone and Cruikshank spearheaded a governmental review of conditions in London's St. Mary of Bethlehem hospital, the institution whose terrible conditions for patients was the origin of the word "bedlam." In the nineteenth century, special institutions were developed to care for and treat children who were mentally ill or retarded. The reform movement in the United States was led first by Rush, later by Dix, and then by Beers, who used his experiences as a patient to improve conditions in mental hospitals.

PSYCHOLOGICAL AND ORGANIC VIEWS OF ABNORMAL BEHAVIOR

Because much is yet to be learned about the causes of abnormal behavior, the debate over the role of psychological factors and bodily functioning is ongoing.

The Psychological Approach The emphasis on **irrational thought** arose in the early nineteenth century as a reaction to the focus on **rational thinking** that characterized the Age of Reason. Heinroth described mental illness as the result of internal conflicts between unacceptable impulses and the guilt those impulses caused. About 100 years later, Freud had similar ideas despite the prevailing beliefs in his day about the biological basis for abnormal behavior.

The Organic Approach Griesinger argued that mental disorders are the result of disturbances in brain function. Later,

Kraepelin used this view to construct a classification system for serious disorders. He distinguished between *dementia praecox* and *manic-depressive psychosis*, disorders that he believed had specific organic causes.

THE APPROACHES CONVERGE

Charcot was especially interested in **hysteria.** Although he believed in organic causes, he concluded that mental states were related to hysterical symptoms. He used hypnosis and suggestion to cure hysterical patients. Janet found that patients' symptoms were decreased by their expression of strong feelings that had been experienced earlier during an upsetting event. Work with Charcot helped Freud form his theoretical perspective.

THE STAGE IS SET

Attitudes about abnormal behavior and ideas about appropriate treatment reflect the social values and prejudices of the time. It is important to keep this historical perspective in mind as emphasis shifts between biological and psychological explanations and treatments for abnormal behavior.

CHAPTER THREE

Jasper Johns, Target with Four Faces, 1955. Assemblage; encaustic and collage on canvas with
objects, 26 X 26", surmounted by 4 tinted plaster faces in wood box with hinged front.
Box closed, 3 3/4 X 26 X 3 1/2"; overall dimensions with box opened, 33 5/8 X 26 X 3".
The Museum of Modern Art, New York. Gift of Mr. and Mrs. Robert C. Schull.
Photograph © 1995 The Mueum of Modern Art, New York.

THEORETICAL PERSPECTIVES ON MALADAPTIVE BEHAVIOR

Fred Price, age 38, has been experiencing occasional pain in his chest for two months. He is a high school vice-principal in a large city, a high-pressure job requiring many daily contacts with teachers and students. The teachers often have complaints and the students almost always are having problems or causing them. Fred's task is to handle the problems effectively and quickly. He has put off seeing a doctor, attributing the chest pain to indigestion associated with stress at work. In fact, Alka Seltzer seemed to help somewhat. Recently he and his wife have been arguing a lot, often about money: braces for one child's teeth, tuition and living expenses for his oldest child who wants to go to college away from home, and nursing home expenses for his wife's mother. Last night, during an especially fierce argument with his wife, he had another bout of chest pains that took several hours to subside even after he took Alka Seltzer. Afterwards Fred began thinking about the fact that his father had his first heart attack at the age of 47. Like Fred, his father had had a demanding job that took a lot out of him, leaving him exhausted at night. In the morning Fred called his doctor for an appointment.

It would be difficult to summarize Fred Price's problems in a neat, straightforward manner. Is he a man who is about to have a heart attack? If so, is it because he has "bad" genes that make him prone to have one? Or, might his somatic problems simply be expressions of a high anxiety level engendered by a stressful job? Are his physical resources or stress-coping skills inadequate to handle the demands of being a vice-principal of an inner-city high school? What role do family pressures and marital discord play in his symptoms? Like most of us, Fred Price is a complex person. His thoughts, behavior, and physical status probably have multiple determinants. From the information provided, it is not possible to determine the likely cause or causes of his symptoms and apparent unhappiness.

Clinicians and researchers have developed theories they hope will be helpful in identifying the causes of behavioral maladaptation and physical illness. These theories guide clinicians as they inquire into the determinants of maladaptation.

The Role of Theory in Abnormal Psychology

Everyone wants to know why things happen. Scientific theories are created to organize what we know and explain what it means. Theories are never complete, because there are different ways of looking at what we do know and because there are always some pieces missing from our knowledge. Even an incomplete theory is useful, however, if it provides a perspective for examining the information we have. A good theory will also help us decide what new information we need.

Clinical workers and researchers operate on the basis of formal theories, but they also use informal theories or hunches based on past experience. A psychiatrist, clinical psychologist, or social worker who is assigned a case will use a particular theoretical perspective to analyze the available information. We all use theoretical perspectives in our lives, which serve as lenses that reflect and shape our conceptions of human nature. Thus according to one theoretical perspective a bad cold may be thought of as a viral infection; according to another it may be simply "God's will"; and according to your mother it may be "your own fault for getting your feet wet."

The diversity of theories in abnormal psychology is wide. We will review six theoretical perspectives that are particularly influential today: (1) the **biological perspective,** which emphasizes the role of bodily processes; (2) the **psychodynamic perspective,** which emphasizes the role of anxiety and inner conflict; (3) the **behavioral perspective,** which examines how the environment influences behavior; (4) the **cognitive perspective,** which looks to defective thinking and problem solving as causes of abnormal behavior; (5) the **humanistic–existential perspective,** which emphasizes our uniqueness as individuals and our freedom to make our own decisions; and (6) the **community–cultural perspective,** which is concerned with the roles of social relationships and the impact of socioeconomic conditions on maladaptive behavior.

Which of these theoretical perspectives is right? In Jewish lore there is a story about a couple who came to their rabbi for marriage counseling. The rabbi interviewed each partner separately about the problems in their relationship and then met with them together. They asked him who was right and who was wrong. The rabbi told the puzzled couple, "You are both right." The rabbi's observation also applies to these theoretical perspectives. Each one deals with pieces of reality, but the pieces are often quite different. Some theories are more pertinent to an understanding of the causes of stress, others to the ways in which we cope, and still others to the nature of human vulnerabilities. Consequently, there is no reason why we should commit ourselves to a particular theoretical position and feel called upon to explain all abnormal behavior in terms of its concepts. With a topic as complex as abnormal behavior, it is a good idea to remember that even a respected theory may be too simple an explanation.

It is also important to note that theories are not static. In the previous chapter we saw that through the centuries explanations of deviance have undergone wide swings. New facts exerted an influence on existing theories, but so did people's beliefs, which may or may not have scientific validity. Besides accommodating new facts or changes in public attitudes, a new theory may be developed as a reaction to weaknesses in a currently popular theory. Although all of the basic theoretical viewpoints discussed in this chapter are important and are actively used and researched today, it is worthwhile to keep in mind that each was a reaction to the situation prevailing at the time it was initially proposed.

The Orientation of This Book

We believe that the six theoretical perspectives described in this chapter merit attention because each deals with a significant piece of the puzzle of maladaptive behavior. What should the various theories be telling us? As we stated in chapter 1, we think of maladaptive behavior in terms of personal vulnerabilities and resiliency. What is it we bring to situations that pushes us in the direction of functioning effectively or ineffectively? Although the words vulnerability and resiliency may not occupy prominent places in all of the theories we will review, the theories do in fact deal with issues related to these characteristics. For example, each of us has biological assets and liabilities, as well as assets and liabilities in the way we think, perceive ourselves and others, and cope with various types of stress.

Because each of us is probably both vulnerable and resilient in particular ways, a profile of assets and liabilities is needed for each person. In addition to this profile, methods are needed for reducing vulnerabilities and increasing resiliency. The six theoretical perspectives we will review approach this need in several ways. For example, biological theories focus attention on somatic interventions, such as tranquilizing or antipsychotic drugs; psychoanalysis seeks to help people cope more effectively with disturbing thoughts and emotions; behavioral theories are concerned with modifying specific types of undesirable behavior; and cognitive theories have led to therapeutic techniques for changing unrealistic ideas.

Because each of us is a complex product of biology and experience, ultimately we will need ways of integrating the variables, mechanisms, and treatments inherent in each theoretical position. The field of abnormal psychology is not yet at this point. But the need for theoretical integration becomes more evident with each passing year of research and clinical experience. Clues to integration are becoming discernible. In addition to understanding each of these six traditional theoretical perspectives, we need to think about ways in which they might be combined or integrated so as to provide a well-rounded picture of the individual. In a sense, this chapter is about the building blocks for the integrative theories that we hope will emerge by the next century.

The Biological Perspective

In our review of the history of abnormal psychology in chapter 2, we saw that the idea that bodily disturbances cause disordered behavior has been around for a long time. It is not surprising that the biological perspective gained renewed popularity in the eighteenth and nineteenth centuries, when great leaps forward in anatomy, physiology, and genetics made it seem reasonable that a biological cause might eventually be found for every disorder, be it physical or behavioral. Major impetus for the biological point of view came from findings about the relationship between bodily infections and defects, on the one hand, and disordered behavior, on the other.

Recent information about the role of biological factors supports the argument that such factors are important to some, but certainly not all, mental conditions. Modern advances in several areas of biology and medicine have continued to motivate researchers. For example, equipment and techniques like the positron emission tomography (PET) scan and the computerized

tomography (CT) scan, which make it possible to see how the brain works without the use of surgical or other invasive procedures, are beginning to permit previously unthought-of studies of the relationships between behavior and the brain. And research on heredity and genetics has shown that certain chromosomal defects are responsible for metabolic disorders, such as phenylketonuria, that in turn may lead to specific forms of mental retardation. The list of behavioral problems in which biological processes play at least some role is lengthening, as is the list of biologically based therapies.

Most people distinguish between the body and the mind, although the meanings attached to these words vary widely. **Body** refers to organs, muscles, bones, and brain; **mind** usually refers to attitudes, feelings, and thoughts. Although we generally speak as if the worlds of body and mind were totally separate, the separation between body and mind is actually an intellectual invention rather than a reality. Cognitive and bodily processes are closely intertwined, though how much weight one assigns to each process in accounting for maladaptive behavior depends on one's view. And new evidence may alter prevailing views from time to time.

At its most extreme, the biological viewpoint assumes that all maladaptive behavior is due to a disordered body structure or function. Such a disorder can be explained by an inherited defect that may cause permanent damage, by a defect acquired through injury or infection before or after birth, or by a more or less temporary physiological malfunction caused by some condition that is present at a particular time, such as a high fever caused by a temporary infection. A less extreme view, which still emphasizes the importance of biological functioning, recognizes that maladaptive behavior is a joint product of three types of disordered processes: in the body (for example, a hormonal deficiency), in psychological functioning (for example, a tendency toward shyness), and in the social environment (for example, a high unemployment rate in the community). This interactional view is discussed later in the chapter.

Biological Influences in Abnormal Behavior

A number of biological factors influence the behavior of organisms. How we behave and think depends not only on the action of each by itself but also on the interrelationships among them. Genetic factors, the brain and nervous system, and the endocrine glands all play important roles in psychological processes and in abnormal behavior.

Genetic Factors The field of genetics has expanded dramatically in recent years. Evidence that genetic abnormalities account for a significant number of medical problems has led researchers to seek hereditary roots for maladaptive behavior as well. Available evidence suggests that genetic factors may contribute to such diverse disorders as schizophrenia, depression, criminality, and mental retardation. The idea that people can inherit certain behavioral tendencies arouses skepticism among some people who feel it conflicts with egalitarian ideals and conjures up a specter of "biological determinism." Yet research, particularly within the past two decades, has shown that few dimensions of behavior seem to be immune to the effects of genetic factors.

A major factor in some genetic abnormalities is irregularities in the structure or number of an individual's chromosomes. **Chromosomes** are threadlike bodies that are present in pairs in all body cells. Humans have 46 chromosomes in each cell. **Chromosomal anomalies** are likely to produce abnormalities in the brain. For instance, persons with Down syndrome, a type of mental retardation, have three # 21 chromosomes instead of two.

Arranged linearly along the chromosomes are the **genes,** each of which occupies its own characteristic position or **locus.** In contrast to the 46 chromosomes that are contained in a cell, an estimated 100,000 genes function as the elements of human heredity. More than 4,000 diseases are known to result from failure or abnormality of a gene, but in most cases the actual genes have not been identified or assigned to any particular chromosome. While maps of chromosomes, called **karyotypes,** have assisted geneticists in identifying chromosomal anomalies for some time, mapping the human **genome**—the complete set of a person's genes—that is currently under way is likely to have a revolutionary effect on biology. It is no exaggeration to say that current maps of human chromosomes compare in accuracy to the navigational charts that guided the explorers to the New World. Mapping the human genome could yield maps comparable to today's most detailed geological surveys (see Figure 3–1).

Scientists do know that faulty genes, or genes that are defective in some way, can exist in the absence of obvious chromosomal deviations and may cause metabolic or biochemical abnormalities. Particular genes influence behavior through a long series of steps. Their influence may be modified by events that happen before and after birth, as well as by the actions of other genes. The basis for gene action is a complex substance, **deoxyribonucleic acid** (DNA), that is found in the chromosomes. The discovery of DNA as the means by which genetic information is transferred led to the discovery of how genes work.

Sometimes a specific gene is present that has been identified as causing a certain characteristic or disease, yet the person may show no sign of the problem or perhaps only mild symptoms. The term **penetrance** has been used to refer to the percentage of cases in which, if

Figure 3-1 The development of radioactive markers now enables scientists to examine films of genetic material.

a specific gene is present, a particular trait, characteristic, or disease will actually manifest itself in the fully developed organism. For example, the molecules of DNA you receive from your parents may carry the blueprint for a strong, sturdy body. But this will not automatically make you an athlete. Your nutrition, the amount of exercise and training you get, and your motivation, as well as any illnesses or injuries you experience before or after your birth, will all influence how your genetic predisposition toward physical strength is expressed.

Behavior Genetics A young but rapidly developing field is **population genetics,** the study of the distribution of genes throughout groups of people who mate with each other. Such information is used in predicting the incidence of certain genetically carried disorders. For example, Tay-Sachs disease is a form of retardation that is caused by genes carried by some Jews whose ancestors came from a particular area of Europe.

Behavior geneticists study the effects of genetic inheritance on behavior. Behavioral genetic research with humans usually takes one of two forms: analysis of family histories or twin studies. Genealogical studies begin with an individual who manifests a particular trait. His or her relatives are then assessed to see whether they have the same trait. When such an analysis is carried out over at least two generations, some inferences about family genetics can be drawn. Twin studies are a more direct way of studying the effects of heredity on behavior. **Monozygotic** (identical) twins have been compared with **dizygotic** (fraternal) twins

Figure 3-2 These identical twins were reunited at age 31 for the first time since they were adopted by two different families shortly after birth. They found that despite different upbringing they were very similar in many of their habits, interests, and even in their choice of occupation, fire fighting.

with respect to a variety of behaviors. Because monozygotic twins develop from the same fertilized egg, they have identical genes and hence identical heredities. Dizygotic twins, on the other hand, are the products of two entirely different eggs. If monozygotic twins exhibit a particular behavior disorder more often than dizygotic twins do, the identical heredity of the monozygotic pair may be the important factor.

The degree of **concordance** in twin studies refers to the relationship between twins or other family members

with respect to a given characteristic or trait. If both twins show the trait, the pair is described as concordant (see Figure 3–2). If they do not, the pair is described as discordant. For example, studies have shown that the concordance rate for schizophrenia is high for monozygotic twins and drops precipitously for dizygotic twins of the same sex. The drop is even greater for dizygotic twins of opposite sexes. However, the fact that the concordance rate is not 100 percent for monozygotic twins suggests that environmental influences play a role. Figure 3–3 presents concordance rates for monozygotic and dizygotic twins for several types of maladaptive behavior. Although there is a very strong suggestion of a genetic component in these disorders, we must not forget that experience can lessen or emphasize the effects of any hereditary tendency.

The latter point is illustrated by a study of a set of identical triplets, all of whom suffered from serious chronic disorders (McGuffin et al., 1982). Two of the brothers had periods of auditory hallucinations and other clear schizophrenic symptoms. Between these periods they functioned at a low level and were unable to work. The third brother also had psychotic periods (although not as clearly schizophrenic), but he was able to function at a relatively high level and could hold a job between his psychotic episodes. His IQ was higher than that of his brothers, and his relationship with his father was much less stormy than theirs. This case demonstrates that even

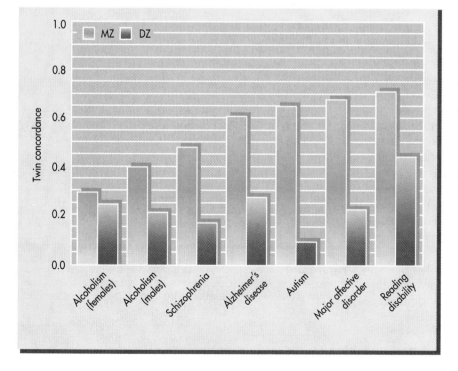

Figure 3-3 Identical twin (monozygotic, MZ) and fraternal twin (dizygotic, DZ) concordances for behavioral disorders. Genetic influence is substantial for schizophrenia, Alzheimer's disease, autism, major affective disorder, and reading disability. The concordance for diagnosed alcoholism is much more modest, particularly for females. Interestingly, autism—characterized by severe impairment in social relationships, communication, and activity—was assumed until the 1970s to be primarily environmental in origin.

when people have identical heredities, their levels of functioning may vary in important ways.

The extent to which genes affect behavior has been a subject of debate for at least the last two centuries. In the nineteenth century, fierce battles were fought in what has come to be known as the nature–nurture controversy. Heredity (nature) and environment (nurture) were seen as separate and distinct forces that worked in an either/or fashion. Either nature determined a certain behavior, or nurture did; you couldn't have it both ways. Today, however, most psychologists hold the view that the interplay of many forces—in particular the interaction between the information carried by genes and the experience provided by the environment—determines behavioral patterns.

Research has shifted from simply demonstrating the existence of genetic influence to exploring its details and interactions with other factors. The focus of attention is now on "nature *and* nurture" rather than "nature *versus* nurture." For example, studies of the developing visual systems of mammals have shown that the visual cortex is, to a large extent, ready to be used at birth. Yet if animals are deprived of early visual experience, dramatic changes in the structure of their visual cortex will occur. There is a critical period early in visual development in which both innate neural wiring and visual experience must interact in order to ensure proper development of the visual system. Similarly, the genes that predispose one toward schizophrenia may not be expressed except under special environmental circumstances; for instance, conditions of great stress. Throughout life, experience continues to modulate the fine pattern of cortical connections, allowing us to acquire new skills and knowledge. The operations of the brain result from a balance between inputs from heredity and environment—nature and nurture—and this balance should also be reflected in research into the biological basis of behavior.

As the case above and others suggest, close and constant as it may seem, even the family environment affects children differently. Children growing up in the same household have different experiences. They may be at different ages when the family's income and social status rise and fall. They are treated differently by parents and their brothers and sisters. Birth order, age spacing, and sex differences are important. Furthermore, children have different experiences outside the family, with schoolmates, teachers, and friends. Random events of all kinds may also have effects that are compounded over time and make children in the same family different in unpredictable ways. Current work by behavioral geneticists suggests that differences in personality among family members are accounted for by a com-

bination of genetic differences among the children and the effects of the **non-shared environment** (the unique relationships and life experiences of each child).

The Nervous System and the Brain The nervous system is the body's master control center. It consists of increasingly complex structures that appear as one moves up the evolutionary scale. The three-pound grapefruit-size brain that you carry around inside your skull is the most complex structure in the known universe. It can even wonder about itself.

The Nervous System The nervous system has two major divisions: the **central nervous system,** which includes all the nerve cells (neurons) of the brain and spinal cord, and the **peripheral nervous system,** which includes all the neurons connecting the central nervous system with the glands, muscles, and sensory receptors (see Figure 3–4). The peripheral nervous system also has two divisions: the **somatic system,** which transmits information from sense organs to the muscles responsible for voluntary movement, and the **autonomic sys-**

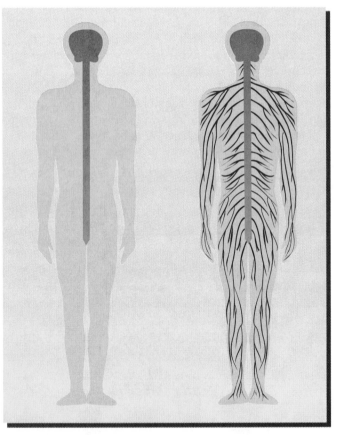

Figure 3-4 The central nervous system and the peripheral nervous system. The central nervous system (CNS) (left) consists of the brain, brain stem, and spinal cord; the peripheral nervous system (PNS) (right) includes all nerve fibers extending to and from the rest of the body. The CNS acts on the world through the PNS (a brain without a mouth cannot speak); it also learns about the world through the PNS (a brain without eyes cannot see).

tem, which directs the activity of the glands and internal organs.

The fundamental unit of the entire nervous system is the **neuron,** or nerve cell, which has a long extension called the **axon** and several shorter extensions called **dendrites.** The function of nerve cells is to transmit electrical impulses to other nerve cells and to structures outside the nervous system (such as muscles and glands). A typical nerve cell receives a messenger chemical, or **neurotransmitter,** from other nerve cells through specific receptor sites on its dendrites. It changes the chemical signal to an electrical one and sends it through the axon. When the electrical signal reaches the tip of the axon, the nerve cell releases molecules of neurotransmitters that pass through a tiny region called the **synapse** and are taken up by specific receptors on the dendrites of adjacent nerve cells. This process can be repeated many times to transmit signals throughout the nervous system (see Figure 3–5).

The Brain The brain is easily the most complex part of the nervous system (see Figure 3–6). Its two cerebral hemispheres are highly developed centers for processing sensory information. The **cerebral cortex,** the convoluted layer of gray matter that covers each hemisphere, controls our distinctively human behavior. The cortex has areas that monitor hearing, vision, body sensations, and other processes. Disturbances in specific parts of the brain (caused, for example, by tumors) will result in specific behavioral deficits (for example, loss of speech). Electrical stimulation of certain areas of the cerebral cortex also produces specific motor responses or sensory effects.

The brain and its neurons are active continuously. This activity occurs spontaneously as well as in response to external stimulation. The activity of nerve cells generates electrical energy, and the voltage differences between cells or regions can be amplified and measured as brain potentials. A record of these brain potentials, called an **electroencephalogram** (EEG), shows a pattern of brain waves. Researchers have found that most behavioral states have distinct brain wave patterns. For example, the patterns designated as beta waves dominate during wakefulness, whereas theta and delta waves characterize deep sleep. Researchers have also been able to correlate brain wave patterns with psychological functions such as dreaming and attention, and with abnormalities caused by tumors or by the unusual electrical activity found in epilepsy (see Figure 3–7).

The Brain and Behavior Abundant evidence exists that various behavioral deficits result from defects in the central nervous system, but many questions remain unanswered. Frequently, neither the particular type of deficit nor the available information about possible organic damage is sufficiently clear-cut to permit a high

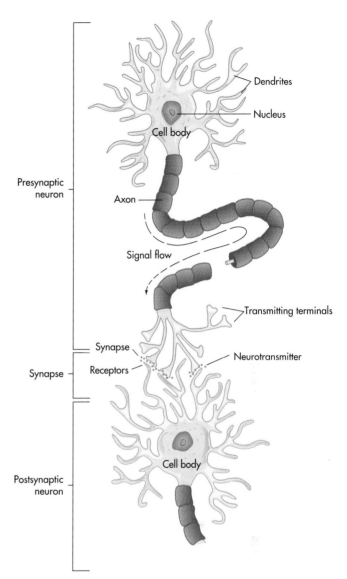

Figure 3-5 The relationship between a pair of typical neurons. A neuron consists of a cell body and two types of extensions—dendrites and an axon. Specific receptors or dendrites receive neurotransmitter molecules from the axons of adjacent neurons. This transfer sets up an electrical impulse in the receiving neuron by the nerve terminal at the tip of its axon. The arrival of the impulse at the nerve terminal causes the release of neurotransmitter molecules (shown by dots), which diffuse across a small gap (the synapse) to receptors on the dendrites of the next neuron. The process can be repeated many times to send signals throughout the brain and the rest of the nervous system.

degree of certainty about the causes of behavior. A person who experiences memory losses and thought disturbances may have fallen on his or her head, but the actual effects of the fall on brain tissue may not be obvious.

An important part of current brain research concerns recently identified systems within the brain. For example,

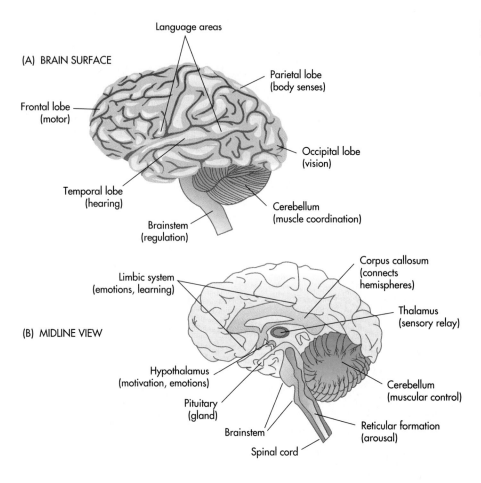

Figure 3-6 The human brain. (a) The surface of the left hemisphere with major areas and their functions labeled. (b) A midline view of the right hemisphere with major areas and structures and their functions labeled.

(A) BRAIN SURFACE

Language areas

Parietal lobe
(body senses)

Frontal lobe
(motor)

Occipital lobe
(vision)

Temporal lobe
(hearing)

Cerebellum
(muscle coordination)

Brainstem
(regulation)

(B) MIDLINE VIEW

Limbic system
(emotions, learning)

Corpus callosum
(connects
hemispheres)

Thalamus
(sensory relay)

Hypothalamus
(motivation, emotions)

Pituitary
(gland)

Cerebellum
(muscular control)

Brainstem

Reticular formation
(arousal)

Spinal cord

work on the basic psychology and biology of motivation has resulted in the discovery of the brain reward system in higher animals. The brain reward system involves the hypothalamus and structures of the limbic system. The **limbic system** is part of the primitive, lower part of the cortex and is associated with emotional and motivational functions; the **hypothalamus,** located above the roof of the mouth, plays a role in motivation and emotions but also has connections with many other areas of the brain. Activation of the brain reward system by electrical stimulation produces an intense feeling of pleasure that is much more powerful than ordinary reinforcers, such as food and sex. In experimental work with rats it has been found that if an electrode is implanted so that an animal can deliver a weak shock to its own brain reward system by pressing a lever, it will do so at a very fast rate. If the animal is starved and then given a choice between food and electrical self-stimulation, it will self-stimulate until it starves to death.

Early researchers who studied the brain reward system had no idea that their work might be related to addiction to substances like opium, but unexpected recent evidence is rapidly changing the situation. Researchers have discovered that there are chemical receptors on neurons in certain regions of the brain that respond to opiates. In fact, the greatest concentration of these opiate receptors is in the brain reward system. Moreover, the brain produces substances called **endorphins** that activate these receptors; they are even more powerful analgesics (pain relievers) than opium and, when administered directly, are addictive.

The endorphins work like keys in a lock. They fit only into sites, or receptors, that are specifically designed to accept them. Because the endorphins are similar to opium and related chemicals, knowledge of how they work may lead to a better understanding of drug addiction and its treatment. There are, of course, equally important environmental, psychosocial, and personality factors that influence the actual addictive behaviors. If scientists can create nonaddictive chemicals that function like the opiates, they may be able to ease pain of all kinds, including the pain connected with stopping a heroin habit. Before this can happen, however, much more information about the brain reward system and endorphins is needed.

Frontiers of Brain Research New discoveries are changing old concepts of how the brain develops and works. Two of the most surprising discoveries indicate

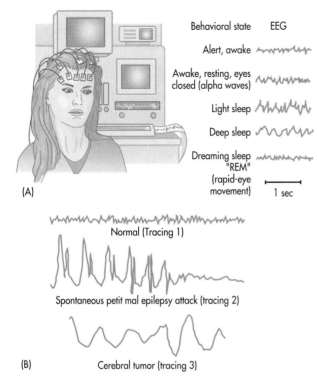

Behavioral state   EEG

Alert, awake ~~~~~~~~

Awake, resting, eyes
closed (alpha waves) ~~~~~~~~

Light sleep ~~~~~~~~

Deep sleep ~~~~~~~~

Dreaming sleep
"REM"
(rapid-eye
movement) ~~~~~~~~
                        1 sec

(A)

Normal (Tracing 1)

Spontaneous petit mal epilepsy attack (tracing 2)

Cerebral tumor (tracing 3)

(B)

Figure 3-7 An EEG and three EEG tracings. (a) An electroencephalogram (EEG) uses scalp electrodes to measure the activity of specific types of neurons. Particular EEG patterns are associated with certain behavioral states, as depicted here. (b) EEG tracings from patients who have different disorders are often visually distinguishable from one another and from those of normal subjects. Tracing 1 shows a normal EEG. Tracing 2 shows the onset of wave and spike discharges that are characteristic of petit mal epilepsy, a disorder in which sudden transitory disturbances of brain function may cause brief periods of loss of consciousness. Tracing 3 demonstrates the slow wave activity that is often associated with a cerebral tumor.

(1) that the brain uses the outside world to shape itself, and (2) that it goes through critical periods in which brain cells require specific types of stimulation to develop such powers as vision, language, smell, muscle control, and reasoning. A related discovery is that the brain has the ability to change rapidly as it physically reshapes itself into a kind of biological map of the outside world. Researchers now believe that genes, the chemical blueprints of life, establish the framework of the brain, but the external environment provides the customized finishing touches. The new discoveries are overturning the old concept of a static brain—a self-contained unit that slowly begins the process of learning from a preset, unchangeable set of rules, like a tape recorder that stores whatever words it happens to hear. Now, thanks to advances in molecular biology and genetics, new imaging techniques, and a better understanding of the role of environmental influences, it is clear that the brain adapts to many types of experiences.

The brain learns and remembers throughout life by using the same processes it uses to shape itself in the first place: constantly changing its network of trillions of connections between cells as a result of stimuli from its environment. Although we cannot say for sure exactly what the implications of further advances in our understanding of how the brain works will be for abnormal psychology, it is safe to guess that it will be considerable and, perhaps, surprising.

The Endocrines Your body contains a marvelous system of glands and nerves that quickly organizes your heart, lungs, liver, kidneys, blood vessels, and bowels, causing them to work at top efficiency in an emergency. And when the threat ends, that same glandular system calms everything down.

Several glands, including the pituitary, thyroid, adrenal, and gonadel (sex) glands, as well as the part of the pancreas that produces insulin, make up the endocrine system (see Figure 3-8). These glands are ductless: the endocrines, unlike the salivary glands or

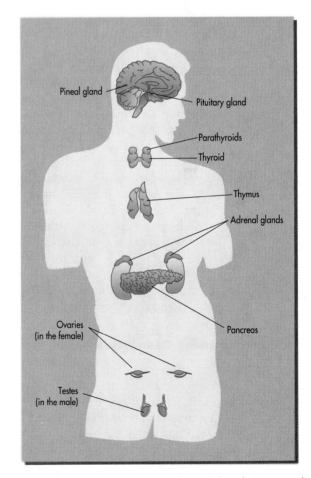

Pineal gland
Pituitary gland
Parathyroids
Thyroid
Thymus
Adrenal glands
Ovaries
(in the female)
Pancreas
Testes
(in the male)

Figure 3-8 The endocrine glands and their location in the body.

tear glands, have no ducts for delivery of the substances they produce. Instead, they discharge those substances directly into the bloodstream, which carries them to all parts of the body. Hormones secreted by the endocrine glands act as chemical messengers (the word "hormone" is derived from a Greek word meaning "messenger"). They correlate our reactions to external events and coordinate bodily growth and development.

Hormones are very potent, so it takes very little of them to exert an influence over their specific target cells. Cells that respond to hormones are genetically endowed with special surface molecules, or "receptors," that detect even very low hormone concentrations. Once these cells receive a hormone, they initiate a series of adjustments within the cell that are dictated by the hormone. Hormones will usually increase the cell's activity temporarily.

In the study of abnormal psychology there is particular interest in the role played by the endocrine glands in dealing with stress. The word **stressor** is often used to refer to a condition that makes it harder to achieve or maintain biological and psychological adaptation. Examples of stressors to which the endocrine glands respond are biological factors such as disease germs and psychological experiences such as receiving an insult or engaging in combat. The hormones secreted by the glands help us mobilize our physical resources to deal with stressors by fighting or escaping.

The stress response involves the pituitary gland and the part of the adrenal gland called the **adrenal cortex.** In times of stress the brain is activated and sends messages to one of its structures, the hypothalamus, which is close to the pituitary gland. The hypothalamus releases a substance called **corticotrophin-releasing factor** (CRF), which goes to the pituitary to form and release another chemical, **adrenocorticotrophic hormone** (ACTH). ACTH is released into the bloodstream and can go directly to the adrenal cortex, where it causes the adrenal cortex to form and release **adrenal corticosteroids,** which affect the brain's and the body's response to mental and physical stress. Some researchers have used the level of these steroids as an indicator of the degree of stress experienced by the individual.

The Neurosciences Revolution

Exciting as developments in the fields of genetics, neurology, and endocrinology have been, equally impressive are recent advances in our understanding of their interrelationships. A new interdisciplinary field has emerged, called **neuroscience.** Researchers in the neurosciences aim to understand the relationship between the structure and function of the brain and human thoughts, feelings, and behavior. The neuroscience disciplines include:

- *neuroanatomy*—the study of brain structure;
- *neuropathology*—the study of disease processes caused by disorders of brain structure;
- *neurochemistry*—the study of the chemical processes that control brain function;
- *neuropharmacology*—the study of the effects of drugs on the brain;
- *neuropsychology*—the study of the relationship between various psychological or mental functions and brain structure;
- *neuroendocrinology*—the study of the relationship between glandular function and brain function.

Considering the brain from all these perspectives, the brain has three major aspects. First, it is a complex *physical and chemical system* in which numerous enzymes, receptors, and other active molecules operate under subtle gene regulatory mechanisms. Neuroscientists seek to clarify how the brain functions as a molecular–cellular machine. This may pave the way for describing the basis for a number of problems, for example, what happens within the brain as people age. Second, the brain is a highly complex and flexible *information system* comprising billions of cells with capabilities for surpassing modern computers by far. Finally, the human brain, the pinnacle of evolution, developed its functional capacity to such an extent that it eventually became the *center of complex processes* tied to thought, emotion, and behavior. With recent progress in cognitive neuroscience, it is possible to foresee a time when we may be able to understand who we are.

The neurosciences seek to protect the brain when it is healthy and to heal it when it is ill. As more and more neuroscience research has been undertaken, it has become increasingly clear that a multitude of factors may cause mental illness. At present, we can only partially understand these causes. We do know, however, that several forms of mental illness are due to different types of brain abnormalities, including the loss of nerve cells and excesses or deficits in chemical transmissions between neurons. We can also attribute some maladaptive behaviors to defects in the wiring or circuitry pattern within the nervous system, to deficiencies in the command centers of the brain, or to the way messages move through the nervous system. The tendency to develop such abnormalities may run in families and therefore be partially hereditary. A broad range of environmental factors (for example, infections, nutrition, head injuries, or even the shocks and stresses of everyday life) may also play important roles in causing some mental illnesses.

The value of the neurosciences' multidisciplinary approach can be illustrated with the disorder of Parkinson's disease. Parkinson's disease was described by James Parkinson in 1817. It has been called the "shaking palsy" because its victims suffer from a tendency to shake, most noticeably in their hands, as well as a tendency to become stiff and rigid, sometimes to such a degree that they are nearly paralyzed. A significant percentage of people with Parkinson's disease, particularly the elderly, develop lapses of memory, disorientation, and poor judgment. As techniques to study brain structures were developed, it was found that victims of this disease had a loss of nerve cells in a particular and quite small part of their brains called the **substantia nigra.** Neurochemists have shown that certain neurochemical abnormalities contributed to this loss. Spurred on by this clue, neuropharmacologists have found that giving Parkinson's patients the substance L-dopa could correct this neurochemical deficiency. The use of L-dopa has revolutionized the treatment of Parkinson's disease. Patients who receive it often have a marked decrease in their symptoms, particularly rigidity. Many patients who were nearly incapacitated are now able to live normal lives.

The case of Parkinson's disease illustrates how the neuroscience disciplines interrelate closely, with discoveries in one branch often put to use by researchers or clinicians in another branch. Neuroscientists have shown that behavior, perception, and cognition are results of integrated actions of networks of nerve cells. Understanding the complex activities of the nervous system requires identifying the relevant anatomical connections and chemical factors. Sensitive techniques now permit study of the discrete molecular events that take place at the synapses, the junctions between nerve cells where clinically useful treatments are known to exert their actions. Great strides have been made in identifying transmitter substances and the process of neural transmission pertinent to a number of types of maladaptive behavior. Box 3-1 presents an example of how the neurosciences have deepened our understanding of an aspect of behavior most of us take for granted, sleep. Sleep is a complex process that is influenced by neurophysiological processes, personal preoccupations, and recent experiences.

Brain Imaging In the 1970s, advances in applied physics and computer science laid the basis for the later development of instruments that permit the study of both brain anatomy and brain function in living individuals. The development of neuroimaging has provided a window through which the brain can be viewed. **Computed tomography** (CT), in which images are collected on X-ray film was the first neuroimaging technique applied to the study of abnormal behavior. It requires processing by a computer of 51,200 pieces of data to generate visually and physically mean-

ingful images. More recent imaging technology has produced several, even more sophisticated, types of equipment. **Magnetic resonance imaging** (MRI) now provides the capacity to examine brain anatomy visually and to measure it quantitatively with a resolution of approximately one millimeter in a routine, rapid, and efficient manner.

The MRI image is derived from signals generated by changes in the levels of electromagnetic radiation from tissues under observation. MRI can make out details one tenth the size that can be detected with CT and it discriminates much better between different types of brain tissue. **Magnetic resonance spectroscopy** (MRS) extends the capacity of magnetic resonance to permit the study of tissue chemistry and metabolic function. **Single photon emission computed tomography** (SPECT) is an imaging technique that provides direct measurement of cerebral blood flow and several specific physiological and neurochemical features of the brain. SPECT is being used to study brain function while subjects perform various kinds of cognitive tasks. Thus, it is now possible to compare the SPECTs of anxious, depressed, or schizophrenic individuals. Although more precise and flexible than SPECT, **positron emission tomography** (PET) is much more costly and complex (Figure 3-9). Consequently, SPECT can be more widely available and more suitable for general use than PET. Use of PET scans has provided greater understanding of the role of neurotransmitters in brain function and mental disorders. Prior to their development, researchers had been hampered by the lack of techniques for directly assessing the way these substances function in the living human brain.

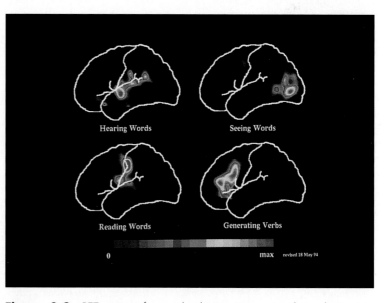

Figure 3-9 PET scans of normal subjects give researchers clues as to what areas of the brain are involved in everyday activities and how the metabolism in the brain is affected.

What Goes on When We Sleep—and When We Can't? What Can We Do About Sleep Difficulties?

Whether it is the sole problem or part of a more complex clinical picture, a sleep disorder can increase vulnerability to other difficulties (for example, doing poorly in school). While they may not reach clinical proportions, many people have occasional sleep problems. For this reason, we all need to maximize our resilience when these problems arise.

Sleep disturbances affect about one third of the U.S. population. Patients with sleep problems are concerned not only about the immediate distress and discomfort caused by inability to sleep, but also about the effects of their sleep deficit on family life, employment status, and general social adjustment. Sleep disorders accompany a number of forms of maladaptive behavior (including depression, which is discussed in chapter 10).

Aids to a Satisfying Sleep

The fact that these types of biological processes have been identified as significant contributors to whether and how deeply we sleep does not mean that an individual is powerless to change a faulty sleep pattern. Attention to the following behavioral and environmental factors can help us be more resilient and maximize the benefits of sleep.

1. Sleep as much as needed to feel refreshed during the following day. Restricting the time in bed seems to solidify sleep, but excessively long times in bed seem related to fragmented and shallow sleep.
2. Get up at the same time each day, seven days a week. (A regular waking time in the morning leads to regular times of sleep onset.)
3. A steady daily amount of exercise probably deepens sleep.
4. Insulate your bedroom against sounds (carpeting, insulated curtains, closing the door).
5. Excessively warm rooms may disturb sleep; keep the room temperature moderate.
6. Hunger may disturb sleep. A light snack at bedtime may help sleep.
7. Try to avoid excessive liquids in the evening, in order to minimize the need for nighttime trips to the bathroom.
8. Avoid caffeinated beverages in the evening.
9. Avoid alcohol in the evening. Although alcohol helps tense people fall asleep more easily, the ensuing sleep is then broken up.
10. People who feel angry and frustrated because they cannot sleep should not try harder and harder to fall asleep but should turn on the light, leave the bedroom, and keep occupied by an unstimulating activity like reading a boring book. Return to bed only when sleepy. Get up at your regular time the next day, no matter how little you slept.
11. The chronic use of tobacco disturbs sleep.
12. If you find yourself waking up and looking at the clock, put the clock under the bed or cover it up.

Sleep Disorders

The field of sleep disorders is a relatively new one, having existed only for about 25 years. The field has developed rapidly because of increased recognition of the scope of problems related to many people's difficulties in sleeping and advances in knowledge about the sleep process. Sleep disorders include a wide variety of conditions that include:

1. **Primary sleep disorders,** abnormalities in the sleep-wake cycle for which identifiable causes are not available. There are two types of primary sleep disorder: **dyssomnias,** which involve abnormalities in the amount, quality, or timing of sleep and **parasomnias,** which are characterized by abnormal behavioral or physiological events occurring in association with sleep, specific sleep stages, or sleep-wake transitions. **Primary insomnia,** in which the individual complains of difficulty in initiating or maintaining sleep, is an example of a dyssomnia.

Nightmares that occur repeatedly and lead to awakening is an example of a parasomnia.
2. **Sleep disorder related to another mental disorder** marked by prominent complaints of sleep disturbance that result from a diagnosable mental disorder (often involving a high level of anxiety or depression). Insomnia might be categorized as a primary sleep disorder if it occurs in the absence of a diagnosable mental disorder or as a sleep disorder related to another mental disorder if there are diagnosable features, such as anxiety or depression.
3. **Sleep disorder due to a general medical condition** in which there is a prominent complaint of sleep disturbance that results from the direct physiological effects of a general medical condition on the sleep-wake system. Some forms of both insomnia and excessive sleeping (**hypersomnia**) could be due to a diagnosable medical condition.
4. **Substance-induced sleep disorder** in which prominent complaints of sleep disturbance result from the use of a substance, such as a drug or medication. Drug (e.g., alcohol, cocaine) abuse could be a cause of some sleep disorders.

Because no structural pathology has been identified for most sleep disorders, their diagnoses are usually based on clinical features (symptoms) and abnormal physiology. An issue that arises in diagnosing sleep disorders is the question: When does the symptom become a disorder in its own right? The boundary between a sleep disorder and an annoying sleep disturbance that falls within the normal range is often unclear (Figure 3-10).

In the following case, the patient would be diagnosed as having **narcolepsy,** a primary sleep disorder marked by irresistible attacks of sleep.

Sidney is a 16-year-old high school student who recently developed a problem with excessive daytime sleepiness. Periodically during the day she suddenly falls asleep for several seconds to a minute. Often this occurs in the middle of a class. Sometimes she awakes to find the teacher standing over her calling her name and some of the other students laughing.

Several of the teachers have

BOX 3-1

Figure 3-10 This multiple exposure shows the tossing and turning as well as attempts at distracting himself by reading of a man who is unable to fall asleep. Insomnia produces not only unpleasant hours of trying to sleep, but also creates a state of perpetual tiredness and frustration concerning inability to fall asleep or stay asleep.

spoken to Sidney and her parents about sleeping in class. She explains that she can't control the sleeping but her teachers are reluctant to believe her. The sleep episodes have made it difficult for Sidney to keep up with her studies because she misses important information during class. Several of her friends are sympathetic and help by loaning her class notes. One friend says, "I can always tell when you're asleep. Your mouth drops open or your head falls on your chest."

Sleep terror disorder is another primary sleep disorder that is characterized by the repeated occurrence of sleep terrors—abrupt awakenings from sleep usually beginning with a panicky scream or cry.

Jeremy is a 25-year-old man who has been working long hours to finish an important project in his company. He often comes home late, feeling exhausted, eats a small dinner with his wife, and goes to bed.

In the last few weeks he has had several strange and disturbing experiences during the night. They usually occur one to two hours after he goes to sleep. His wife describes the episodes as

follows, "Jeremy suddenly sits bolt upright in the bed, screams, and looks panicky." The first time it happened, his wife was so startled that she woke up and jumped out of bed. She continued with her description, "I looked at Jeremy. His eyes were wide open, he was sweating and breathing fast. When I sat next to him I could feel his heart racing. I tried to find out what was wrong but he wouldn't respond." A minute or two later Jeremy awoke and looked at his wife. When she asked him what was wrong he replied, "I feel terrified but I don't know why." She held him for a few minutes until he fell asleep again. In the morning Jeremy did not remember anything about the episode. The succeeding episodes were similar but his wife became accustomed to them and was less startled.

Polysomnography

Polysomnography is the monitoring of multiple bodily parameters during sleep.

Today, valuable information about what goes on when we sleep is coming from neuroscience research conducted in sleep laboratories (see Figure 3-11), in which a number of biological processes

are monitored while subjects sleep. Through such sleep studies, researchers in the neurosciences have significantly contributed to an understanding of the complex processes involved in sleep. Some of their findings include the following.

1. Stages of sleep can be marked by specific types of events, such as EEG patterns and eye blinking.
2. Sleep occurs in cycles. The distribution of wakefulness across an eight-hour nocturnal period has been described for each successive hour (the first hour has more wakefulness than any of the remaining seven hours).
3. Most bodily processes slow down at sleep onset and may be further reduced later in sleeping.
4. At least three groups of neurotransmitters play roles in sleep.
5. The secretion of certain hypothalamic–pituitary hormones are closely related to sleep-wake cycles.

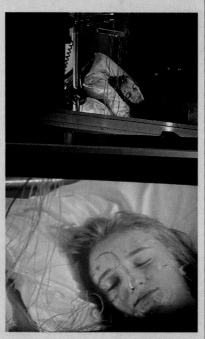

Figure 3-11 In the sleep laboratory an infrared video system is used to unobtrusively monitor subjects as they sleep throughout the night. Electrodes connected to this woman's face and head allow scientists in the sleep laboratory to monitor and record the electrical activity from her heart and brain as well as the muscle activity from her face and neck as she sleeps.

The various imaging techniques are now being used in the search for clues to evaluate and measure the functions and dysfunctions of the brain. As yet, these techniques have not identified large consistent differences, say, between people who have schizophrenia and those who are depressed. Research will have to deal with a number of methodological issues that, if not attended to, could lead to negative results in such comparisons. For example, there is so much variability in the size of brain structures that the size distributions of structures from the groups compared often overlap substantially. Imaging studies that have included patients with Alzheimer's disease have found significant differences between this group and control subjects. PET scan studies of people with obsessive-compulsive and affective disorders also may reveal distinctive brain features. There is some evidence of imaging differences between people who as children had been diagnosed as having an attention-deficit disorder and other groups. Although many different imaging techniques may be useful for studying disease processes and may be applicable to assessing and understanding brain function in individual patients, none of the imaging techniques has as yet yielded a clear and definitive diagnostic laboratory test (Buchsbaum, 1993).

Psychoneuroimmunology Psychoneuroimmunology is a new field of study that links psychological, neural, and immunological processes. The case below illustrates how these processes may interact in an individual.

Larry Jackson, a 50-year-old high school teacher, was divorced five years ago, and had had a series of infections and fevers, swollen lymph nodes, and a nagging cough ever since his high-school-age daughter had died four years previously. Recently he had experienced severe respiratory difficulties, as a result of which he had been hospitalized. The three months prior to the hospitalization had been particularly stressful because of disagreements with the school principal, who seemed always to be annoyed with him. While he was in the hospital, treatment with antibiotics resulted in some symptomatic improvement, but he continued to feel weak and the lymph node swelling persisted. A lymph node biopsy showed the existence of some cancerous cells. His physician was not sure how Jackson's physical symptoms were related or caused, but the doctor concluded, after several conversations with his patient, that Jackson had not yet gotten over his daughter's death. Jackson seemed to work very hard at denying his grief over the daughter's death. He never expressed the feelings that the doctor felt would be normal under the circumstances.

Many physicians have noted associations between significant losses, like a daughter's death, and subsequent illness. The association often seems greatest when the person experiencing the loss is unable to express strong emotions, for example, the grief that normally accompanies personal tragedies. Cases like Jackson's have led researchers to the hypothesis that the stress evoked by major losses and separations disrupts the body's immune system and thereby contributes to a host of physical illnesses.

The immune system has two major tasks: recognition of foreign materials (called **antigens**), and inactivation and/or removal of these materials. The immune system influences a person's susceptibility to the course of a disease. It consists of several distinct groups of cells called **lymphocytes.** Recent research has provided a preliminary understanding of how stress and emotional factors lead to hormonal changes that can sometimes decrease the efficiency of the immune system and thus increase susceptibility to disease. This is exactly what has been found in studies of immune system changes of persons taking academic exams (Kiecolt-Glaser and Glaser, 1992).

The first demonstration of a relationship between bereavement and alterations in the functioning of the immune system was a study of 26 surviving spouses of patients who either had been fatally injured or had died after a prolonged illness (Bartrop et al., 1977). Although the effects were not large, the evidence suggested diminished immune system functioning among the survivors. Subsequent research has shown that bereavement caused by the death of a spouse is associated with a suppression of immunity and that the absence of a supportive social network also contributes to suppression of the immune system (Stein et al., 1987). Furthermore, certain psychological states, such as loneliness, depression, and feelings of helplessness, have a negative impact on the immune system. In this connection it is noteworthy that Jackson's divorce had occurred a year before his daughter's death. The divorce had greatly restricted his social network. He had fewer contacts with other people and lacked social relationships that made it easy for him to express his grief, loneliness, and anger at the terrible things that had happened to him.

Psychoneuroimmunologists study three bodily systems simultaneously—the nervous, endocrine, and immune systems—that can communicate with one another through complex chemical signals. It is possible that some people who exhibit severe emotional and behavioral abnormalities show psychoneuroimmunological abnormalities as well. This possibility is being investigated, particularly in people suffering from either of two severe psychological conditions, schizophrenia and depression.

Integration of Biological and Psychological Systems

For many years chemicals have been known to influence behavior—for example, to reduce pain and induce sleep. Chemicals are used extensively in treating maladaptive behavior. Several kinds of psychoactive drugs (antipsychotic, antianxiety, and antidepressant drugs) are often highly effective in reducing particular types of maladaptive behavior. The introduction of antipsychotic drugs resulted in a sharp decline in the number of patients in mental hospitals. Prior to the introduction of the antipsychotic drugs, there had been a steady increase in the number of hospitalized mental patients. The use of those drugs has greatly reduced and even eliminated hospital stays for many individuals.

The biological perspective has proven fruitful because of the therapies, such as drugs, that it has produced, and also because of the questions it has raised. If the abnormal behavior of schizophrenics can be muted or eliminated by certain chemical compounds, can schizophrenia be regarded merely as a sign of a specific chemical disorder in the nervous system? Unfortunately, this sort of question can almost never be answered in a true-or-false fashion. For example, there are also instances in which purely psychological treatment of schizophrenic disorder has led to marked reductions in bizarre behavior.

To what degree can maladaptive behavior be viewed as a disease? The boundaries between health and disease are far from clear, partly because of the roles played by psychological, social, and cultural factors as well as biological ones. Given the multiple factors that affect people, an extreme organic perspective is likely to be overly simplified. More likely to stand the test of time is a model that views maladaptive behavior as a product of these interacting factors. Although it does not provide a final answer, the biological perspective has enhanced our understanding of one of these sets of factors.

From the standpoint of abnormal psychology, it is important to relate biological processes to maladaptive behavior. Theories about these relationships range from those that reject the importance of the relationship for most disorders, to those that see value in exploring them but do not draw many firm conclusions, to those that argue that mental illnesses are diseases in the same sense as cancer or high blood pressure. However, there is growing evidence that cancer and high blood pressure are not pure illustrations of physically caused conditions. Most diseases are probably caused by multiple determinants, including physical, environmental, psychological, and hereditary factors. Disentangling these various kinds of causes from one another can be a difficult scientific problem.

It is clear that the multiple causes of mental illness, like those of cancer and high blood pressure, are only partially understood. The biological perspective implies that many types of abnormal behavior are due largely to factors beyond people's control—primarily to the type of brain and body people are born with and the environment in which they are nourished. While this point of view may seem extremely deterministic, it is not totally so. Most theorists recognize that, to varying degrees, biological systems have plasticity. For example, the brain has built into it the ability to adapt and change in response to injury or changes in the environment. The limits that biological processes place on behavior and the degree to which those processes can be influenced represent topics of current research and theory.

The Psychodynamic Perspective

The **psychodynamic perspective** is based on the idea that thoughts and emotions are important causes of behavior. Psychodynamic approaches to behavior assume that, to varying degrees, observable behavior (overt responses) is a function of intrapsychic processes (covert events). Not all psychodynamic theorists emphasize the same inner events and the same sources of environmental stimulation, but they do agree that personality is shaped by a combination of inner and outer events, with emphasis on the inner ones. Sigmund Freud, the originator of the psychodynamic perspective, believed that eventually all behavior could be explained by bodily changes; however, because so little was known in his time about the relationships between the body and the personality, he actually gave biological factors little emphasis. Nevertheless, impressed by Charles Darwin's theory concerning the importance of emotions, Freud directed his attention to their influences over thought. Freud believed that to understand behavior it is necessary to analyze the thoughts preceding and associated with it, and that to understand those thoughts, a person's deepest emotions and feelings must be explored.

Because thoughts and feelings are not directly observable, psychodynamic theorists must infer them. They relate their inferences about inner processes to important features of overt behavior. The following account by a psychotherapist illustrates how this process is done:

By the fourth session I realized that he had never mentioned his father. It seemed as if there wasn't and never had been a father. I asked myself: How could it be that this man who is so unhappy and has so many problems fails to even mention his father? I guessed that he was either so ashamed of his father that he couldn't talk about him or he harbored so much anger toward him that consciously or unconsciously he couldn't deal with it. I decided to wait and see what would happen rather than push the client in the direction of talking about something that was very sensitive for him.

During the ninth session he told me about a dream he had had the night before. A large dark man sat at a table and a small child watched from a corner as the man ate great quantities of food and ordered a small, frightened woman to bring him more and more. After he ate each helping he would raise a gun and shoot down a few people who were standing in a row against the wall.

The client reported how frightened he had felt during the dream. As we discussed his associations to the dream, it became clear to me that the man in the dream represented his father. After several more sessions he told me he felt very angry with me because I constantly told him what to do and verbally cut him down. After pointing out that in reality I had said almost nothing, I asked him if I seemed like the man in the dream. Finally the dike burst. For the rest of the session and the next one all of his seething hatred toward his father came out. He blurted out that when he was a child he had seen his father strike his mother several times. When he saw this happen, he had wanted to kill his father.

This example shows the complex information-processing task confronting therapists. This therapist not only attended carefully to what the patient said and how he behaved but also drew pertinent inferences (for example, that the patient's failure to mention his father might be significant) and made important decisions (for example, to wait and see what happens rather than ask questions about his father).

Apart from the contribution that psychodynamic theories have made to our understanding of human behavior, they seem especially influential because they are the systems out of which all types of psychotherapy developed. While clinical psychoanalysis as originated by Freud is infrequently used today, its basic elements and the theory of mental events underlying it have greatly influenced the development of the entire field of psychotherapy.

Freud and Psychoanalysis

Sigmund Freud, a Viennese neurologist, is clearly one of the most influential writers of this century, admired for his wit, intellect, and willingness to revise and improve his theories as his clinical experience grew. Freud began his practice at a time when there were few effective forms of treatment in most fields of medicine. Effective treatment generally depends on an understanding of the causes of a disorder, and at that time, although accurate diagnoses could sometimes be made, little was

known about the causes of disease, whether physical or mental. A disorder that was particularly common during the late 1800s was hysteria, the presence of physical problems in the absence of any physical causes. Like other well-trained neurologists of his time, Freud originally used hypnosis to help his hysterical patients lose their symptoms. Then a friend, Joseph Breuer, told Freud that while under hypnosis one of his patients had recalled and understood the emotional experience that had led to the development of her symptoms, and that her symptoms had then disappeared. For a time Freud and Breuer used this method of recapturing memories with some success. However, because some patients were not easy to hypnotize and sometimes the positive effects did not last long, Freud began to develop his method of psychoanalysis, in which the patient recaptures forgotten memories without the use of hypnosis. Freud's psychoanalytical method made him enormously influential among European clinicians. By the time that he visited the United States in 1909, his reputation had already spread across the Atlantic (see Figure 3-12).

Freud's Theories of Personality Freud's theories of personality may seem complicated because they incorporate many interlocking factors, but two basic assumptions underlie them all: psychic determinism and the conscious-unconscious dimension.

Figure 3-12 Freud's visit to the United States in 1909 was important in extending his influence in North America. He is shown here at Clark University in Worcester, Massachusetts with some of the pioneers of psychoanalysis and psychology. From left to right in the front row are Freud, G. Stanley Hall, and Carl Jung. Standing behind them are A. A. Brill, Ernest Jones, and Sandor Ferenczi.

The principle of **psychic determinism** states that all behavior, whether overt (a muscle movement) or covert (a thought), is caused or determined by prior mental events. The outside world and the private psychic life of the individual combine to determine all aspects of behavior. As a clinical practitioner, Freud sought to modify unwanted behavior by identifying and eliminating its psychic determinants.

Freud assumed that mental events such as thoughts and fantasies vary in the ease with which they come to the individual's awareness. For example, aspects of mental life that are currently in awareness are **conscious.** Mental contents that are not currently at the level of awareness but can reach that level fairly easily are **preconscious.** Mental contents that can be brought to awareness only with great difficulty are **unconscious.** Freud was interested mainly in how these unconscious mental contents could influence overt behavior (see Figure 3-13).

Freud was especially intrigued by thoughts and fantasies that seem to go underground but then reappear at the conscious level. He asserted that the level of intrapsychic conflict was a major factor in determining our awareness of particular mental events. According to Freud, the classic example of intrapsychic conflict results when a young boy desires to take his father's place in relation to his mother but at the same time feels love and affection for his father. Freud believed that the greater the degree of intrapsychic conflict, the greater the likelihood that the mental events connected with it would remain unconscious. The more massive the

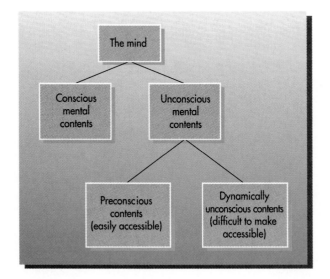

Figure 3-13 Freud's model of the mind. Freud viewed the mind as having conscious and unconscious portions. Material in the unconscious portion varies in the ease with which it can be brought to consciousness. The more intense the emotions linked with unconscious thoughts, the greater the difficulty in bringing them to the level of awareness.

unconscious conflict, the greater the person's vulnerability to stress. Freud believed that behavior disorders that occur after childhood are caused by a combination of early traumatic experiences and later experiences that trigger the emotions and unresolved conflicts associated with the early events.

Freud contended that hidden emotions or drives are involved in human conflict. He referred to these drives as **libido** and believed that they were a form of psychic energy analogous to the individual's supply of physical energy. Just as some people are more athletic, some have stronger libidos. Freud also believed that the psychic energy or drive level of the individual sets up an inner state of tension that must somehow be reduced. In general, libido can be seen as desire for pleasure, particularly sexual gratification.

One novel feature of Freud's theory was his emphasis on sexuality. This emphasis was no doubt related to the often prudish, repressive atmosphere of Vienna at that time. The concept of sexuality within psychoanalytic theory is very broad and, rather than referring only to sexual intimacy, can be equated with the individual's total quest for pleasure and gratification. Freud also saw the process of development as being expressed in sexual terms.

Stages of Psychosexual Development Freud's theory of personality development placed tremendous emphasis on the effects of experiences that occur during the first five years of life. During this period children pass through a number of stages during which their libido is focused on a series of pleasure-giving or erogenous zones in the body. Those zones are the mouth, the anus, and the genitals, resulting in the **oral, anal,** and **phallic psychosexual stages.** In the phallic period, which occurs at about age 3, the child's pleasure in touching his or her genitals is accompanied by fantasies related to the sexual and aggressive impulses the child feels towards his or her parents. The child then enters a more or less sexually inactive latency period, which lasts until adolescence, when the sexual impulses are once again activated. If all has gone well to this point, the individual reaches the **genital stage,** in which pleasure comes from a mature heterosexual relationship. In well-socialized adults the self-centered sexuality of earlier psychosexual stages blossoms into mature love and the individual becomes capable of genuine caring and adult sexual satisfaction.

What happens to children during these psychosexual stages helps mold their adult personalities. If they are unsuccessful in resolving the psychosexual conflicts that accompany a given stage or are severely deprived or overindulged, they may become fixated at one stage or another. **Fixation** is an arrest in personal development caused by the unresolved difficulties experienced at a given stage. Moreover, even if people resolve their conflics successfully, severe difficulties later in life may cause them to **regress,** or adopt some of the feelings or behavior of earlier, more satisfying stages.

Freud's ideas about psychosexual development are undoubtedly the most controversial aspect of his theory. Although many theorists agree that childhood experiences are very important in personality development, many of them reject Freud's assertions about childhood sexuality.

The Psychic Apparatus For Freud, the mental world of the individual is divided into three structures: the **id,** the **ego,** and the **superego.** A basic distinction is made between the ego and the id. The id is a completely unorganized reservoir of psychic energy. The ego, on the other hand, is a problem-solving agent. Whereas the id is concerned simply with maximizing pleasure, the ego's efforts are directed toward maximizing pleasure within the constraints of reality. The id says, "I want it now." The ego says, "Okay, but first we have to do our homework" or "No, that's illegal." The ego performs the valuable functions of avoiding danger or coping with it when avoidance is not possible. There are three major sources of danger for the individual: the environment,

his or her id impulses, and guilt. Guilt comes from the third structure of the psychic apparatus, the superego, which represents the person's moral code and reflects social values as expressed by parents, schools, and so on. The superego uses guilt to keep the id in line. The superego might say, "Work is more important than pleasure" or "You know that's wrong" (see Figure 3-14).

In early infancy the id is in control of all phases of behavior. Freud described the thought processes of the infant as **primary process thinking,** or thinking that is characterized by inability to discriminate between the real and the unreal, between the "me" and the "nonme," as well as by inability to inhibit impulses. Primary process thinking reflects uninhibited adherence to the **pleasure principle**—the immediate satisfaction of needs and desires without regard for the requirements of reality. The desire for immediate gratification that characterizes primary process thinking is dominant in childhood. Thus, most children, when given a piece of candy, eat it immediately, whereas an adult might wait until after lunch. A child who can't get immediate gratification often shifts its goal in order to achieve gratification in some other way. Thus, a baby that is crying for

Figure 3-14 The id, ego, and superego can give very different messages. See if you can identify which one is the source of each message in this cartoon. The answers are at the bottom.

SOURCE: Drawing by R. Chast; © 1983 *The New Yorker Magazine, Inc.*

its bottle may gratify itself at least temporarily by sucking vigorously on its thumb.

Secondary process thinking is characteristic of older children and adults and is dependent on the development of the ego. The adult has learned to wait for gratification. Saving money for a goal—a new stereo system, a nest egg for old age—rather than going out for an expensive dinner on payday would be an example. The adult is also less likely than the child to substitute another object for gratification. An adult will generally keep working for the originally desired object even if setbacks occur.

Primary process thinking is still found in adults. It can be seen in humor, in dreams, in the parent who feels better after coming home and yelling at the children because her boss criticized her on the job, and in the person who eats a pint of ice cream out of the container while standing right in front of the refrigerator. However, maladaptation is considered to exist only when the primary process plays an overriding role in the adult's behavior.

Anxiety Freud defined **anxiety** as a response to perceived danger or stress. He distinguished between two kinds of anxiety-provoking situations. In one, of which birth might be the best example, anxiety is caused by stimulation that exceeds the organism's capacity to handle it. In the other, Freud assumed that psychic energy (libido) accumulates if inhibitions and taboos keep it from being expressed. This accumulated energy may build up to the point where it may overwhelm the controls of the ego. When this happens, a panic or traumatic state results. Psychoanalysts believe that these traumatic states are likely to occur in infants and children who do not know how to cope with much of their environment.

Anxiety often arises in anticipation of danger rather than after a dangerous situation has actually occurred. Anxiety, like physical pain, thus serves a protective function by signaling the approach of danger and warning us to prepare our defenses. Anxiety can also indicate inability to cope with danger. The meaning of anxiety is a central problem of psychoanalysis.

Defense Mechanisms Freud believed that the ego was not helpless in the face of the demands of the id, the outside world, and the superego. Anxiety alerts the individual to danger, such as the presence of an intense unconscious conflict or unacceptable wish. If this anxiety cannot be managed by direct action, so that the wish can be gratified, the ego initiates unconscious defenses in order to ward off awareness of the conflict. A variety of defensive responses to perceived danger are possible. Since everyone experiences danger, the use of these responses, called **defense mechanisms,** clearly is not a special characteristic of maladaptive behavior. Defense mechanisms are used, either singly or in combination, by all people at one time or another. The level of adaptive behavior depends on the repertory of defenses available to the individual (Vaillant, 1994).

The most important and basic of the defense mechanisms is **repression.** Freud called it the cornerstone on which psychoanalysis rests. Repression, like other defenses, is directed at both external dangers, such as fear-arousing events, and internal dangers, such as wishes, impulses, and emotions that cry out for gratification but arouse guilt. Repression reduces anxiety by keeping anxiety-laden thoughts and impulses out of the person's consciousness. In Figure 3-15, each of the drivers seems to be repressing the thought expressed in the caption.

Repression is often described as motivated forgetting. It is necessary to distinguish between two kinds of forgetting: forgetting neutral mental content such as an unimportant telephone number is not the same as forgetting a traumatic childhood experience. Psychoanalysts are not nearly as interested in neutral material as they are in personally significant events. For instance, a recent college graduate may forget to go for a job interview if she is afraid that she will fail and not be hired, or a man may forget to attend the wedding of his brother to a woman that he himself was attracted to. In each case, the forgetting is real. The person is not making an excuse but actually is unaware of the engagement at the time. The effort required to achieve such repression sometimes makes other behavior less effective. The person is, in a sense, preoccupied with the effort to maintain the repression. Sometimes repressed thoughts and wishes leak out and are expressed indirectly. Table 3-1 lists some other defense mechanisms.

Clinical Psychoanalysis Psychoanalysis is both a theoretical perspective and a clinical technique. As a clinical technique, it takes time. One of its conditions usually is that both patient and analyst make a commitment to the process for an indefinite period. Freud believed that much unhappiness and ineffectiveness are caused by forgotten conflicts that occurred long ago. Many a psychoanalyst has commented that a lifetime of difficulty cannot be straightened out in a few months.

Today most psychoanalysts are physicians who receive special training in the field of psychiatry and even more specialized analytic training. Some people without medical training, including psychologists, are also qualified to do psychoanalysis. All psychoanalysts believe that the roots of maladaptive behavior may be found in early childhood experiences and in infantile thoughts and feelings that persist into later life. They believe that insight into what went on in childhood enables the individual to adopt more mature and effective ways of living a happier, more productive adult life.

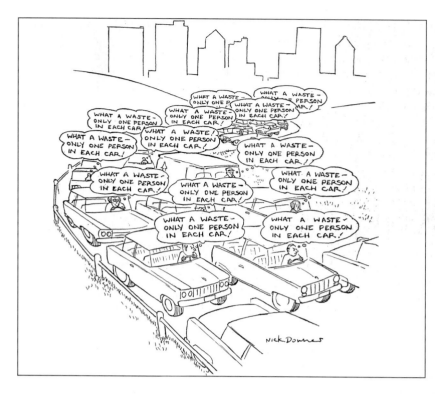

Figure 3-15 These drivers may be repressing the thought, "What a waste—I'm the only person in this car."

Shortly after sitting down in a good restaurant for his first date with a charming girl, a young man noticed he was beginning to get a stomachache. To his dismay it continued to increase, threatening to destroy his pleasure in the dinner or even force him to leave. He wondered what could have caused it. Then he remembered a relationship discovered during his analysis: repressed or suppressed anger at his mother or other females tended to be correlated with stomachaches, especially if it was produced by feelings of rejection. At the moment he had not been aware of any anger or rejection. The minute he recalled his correlation, he understood the problem.

When he had asked this girl for a date for that Saturday she had said: "Oh, it's too bad, I've already accepted an invitation to go dancing. But wait, I'm being picked up somewhat late; we could have a leisurely dinner together." He felt trapped and exploited. Refusing her suggestion would be gauche, but a leisurely dinner spoiled his chances for another date and the best part of this precious evening in New York.

But once he focused his thought on this problem, it occurred to him that she might have made the suggestion because she really wanted to see him. He tested this by asking for a date for the next time he could come to New York. She accepted with pleasure; his stomachache disappeared. In this case, the relationship between specific emotions and a stomachache had already been learned. Its becoming clearly conscious led to an awareness of the emotions and their source that had been crowded out of consciousness by responses to the social situation. This new awareness then led on to solution of the problem (Miller, 1992, pp. 12–13).

Many of Freud's ideas emerged from his studies of the dreams, fantasies, and memories of his patients. He developed the technique of **free association,** which calls for patients to express their thoughts and feelings as freely as possible during analysis. With censorship (defense) reduced in this way, Freud hoped to gain a clearer picture of the conflicts underlying maladaptive behavior. As his work proceeded, it occurred to him that dreams might provide evidence about the workings of unconscious impulses. Clinical psychoanalysis places great weight on the interpretation of dreams and other types of fantasy and their relationship to thought and behavior (see Figure 3-16).

Psychotherapists agree that not all cases of maladaptive behavior are suitable for psychoanalysis. There are several situations in which psychoanalysis might not be recommended. For example, a person might not have adequate financial resources to pay for the many sessions needed, or might lack the necessary intellectual resources, particularly the verbal skill to engage in the required level of communication. Freud believed that the most severe mental disorders, psychoses, could not be treated successfully with psychoanalysis.

TABLE 3–1
Some Defense Mechanisms Used in Addition to Repression

Freud mentioned a number of defense mechanisms, but he devoted most of his attention to repression as an all-inclusive defense. His daughter, Anna Freud, defined most of the concepts we refer to today as defense mechanisms.

Displacement

A shift of feelings and attitudes from one object to another, more acceptable substitute.

Examples:

A man is critized by his boss and then feels angry. He comes home and yells at his wife (yelling at the boss might be too dangerous).

A young woman feels sexually attracted to her older brother. She finds a person in her office who has the same dry sense of humor and curly hair as her brother and quickly becomes very attracted to him.

Intellectualization

Dealing with problems as interesting events that can be explained rationally and that have no anxiety or emotional content attached to them.

Examples:

A woman whose husband has just died discussed the inadequacy of America's mourning rituals, rather than her anger at her husband for leaving her.

A man who has just seen a bank robbery in which five people near him were gunned down talks about how interesting it was to observe the variety of ways that the people present reacted to the murders.

Reaction Formation

Expressing an unacceptable impulse by transforming it into its opposite.

Examples:

A person who is attracted by the excitement and brutality of war becomes an overly zealous pacifist.

A mother who feels angry and rejecting toward her child checks many times to see if the child is all right during the night and worries excessively about her safety on the way to and from school.

Denial

Refusal to acknowledge the anxiety-arousing aspects of the environment. The denial may be related only to the emotions connected to an idea or event or it may involve failure to acknowledge the event itself. Denial is often seen in adults who are under very severe stress often related to loss or failure.

Examples:

A husband, when told that his wife has incurable cancer, remains convinced that she will recover.

A student who has to take a final exam on material she doesn't understand, tells herself the exam is really not important and goes to a movie instead of studying the material with which she is having trouble.

Identification with the Aggressor

Adopting the traits or mannerisms of a feared person.

Examples:

A child who is afraid of his father takes on certain of his characteristics.

A member of the American Nazi Party who is the son of a concentration camp survivor.

Projection

Characteristics or impulses that arouse anxiety are externalized by attributing them to others. Psychotics are particularly likely to use projection.

Examples:

Nazis in Germany who started World War II insisted that they did so because of aggressive threats from other countries.

A man who has a strong desire to have extramarital affairs but feels guilty about it constantly accuses his wife of being unfaithful to him even though he has no evidence.

Regression

Going back to earlier ways of behaving that were characteristic of a previous development level. Typical of people who go to pieces under stress.

Examples:

A wife goes home to her mother every time she and her husband have a quarrel.

A student consoles himself, whenever things get rough, with several hot fudge sundaes, repeating behavior learned when his mother gave him ice cream to make him feel better after a scraped elbow or a disappointment.

Sublimation

A socially useful course of action developed when more direct forms of gratification are blocked.

Examples:

A teenager with strong aggressive feelings expresses them without danger by becoming a football player.

Someone with strong erotic feelings expresses them in a socially approved way by becoming a painter of nudes.

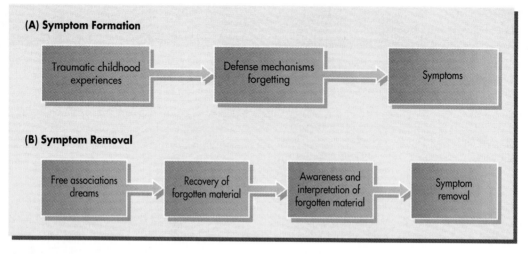

Figure 3-16 Processes hypothesized by Freud to be involved in symptom formation and removal. Symptoms (abnormal behavior, worries, unhappiness) result from emotion-laden traumatic childhood experiences that, while defended against and forgotten, continue to exert unconscious influences that distort behavior, thought, and emotions. In the accepting, benign atmosphere of the psychoanalytic session, clues to the forgotten material come to the fore and are interpreted. Realization of the infantile quality of the forgotten material permits the individual to give up the symptoms.

Contemporary Approaches to Psychoanalysis

Several psychoanalysts have disagreed with aspects of psychoanalytic theory as created by Freud. Among the early revisionists, Carl Jung (1875–1961) and Alfred Adler (1870–1937), both were originally members of Freud's inner circle of supporters. Both men had much more optimistic conceptions of human nature than Freud did. Jung did not think that all behavior is determined by earlier events. His emphasis on the need to emphasize spiritual qualities as well as rational ideas and his interest in Eastern religious thought have made him popular with many people today. Adler believed that people could be changed for the better through the creation of social conditions designed to develop realistic and adaptive lifestyles. For example, children have to be helped to overcome the inferiority that they naturally feel in comparison to adults. Consequently, Adler attached great importance to training parents in effective childrearing techniques, and to the early education of children. He was a strong believer in the need to prevent psychological disorders rather than simply treat them after they occur.

Erik Erikson (1902–1994) is a central figure in contemporary psychoanalytic theory. His theory is a psychosocial one that emphasizes the "mutual fit between the individual and environment—that is, of the individual's capacity to relate to an ever-changing life space of people and institutions, on the one hand, and, on the other, the readiness of these people and institutions to make him part of an ongoing cultural concern" (Erikson, 1975, p. 102). Erikson stressed the role Freud

assigned to the ego, but he gave it additional qualities such as the needs for trust and hope, industry, intimacy and love, and integrity. He thought of the ego as a strong creative force that can deal effectively with problems.

Of special interest to psychologists is Erikson's idea of stages of development. Unlike Freud, who believed that development was essentially completed early in life, Erikson saw development as a lifelong process. Erikson's view reflects his interest in the interpersonal and cultural needs of the developing individual. He described a life cycle of stages, each of which presents the individual with tasks to be achieved. Whereas Freud centered development around psycho*sexual* stages of the infant and child, Erikson directed attention to psycho*social* stages throughout the life cycle. Failure to resolve the conflicts of a particular stage makes coping at succeeding stages more difficult. Erikson's stages range from the acquisition of a sense of trust in others—developed particularly in relation to the mother during the first year of life—to a satisfaction with oneself and one's accomplishments and a sense of order and meaning in life developed in later years. In between these stages, and at particular periods of life, individuals who successfully meet life cycle challenges develop a sense of autonomy and self-control, initiative and purpose, industriousness, a fulfilling self-concept and sense of identity, the ability to form satisfying intimate ties with others, and the ability to lose themselves in work and significant interpersonal relationships.

Object relations theorists offer another approach to psychoanalytic theory. While working within a psychoanalytic framework, these practitioners emphasize the view that the mind is made up of internal representations of significant others, who are referred to as objects. Object-relations proponents focus attention on the emotional bonds between one person and another. Melanie Klein (1882–1960), a controversial British pioneer in the psychoanalysis of children, gave great emphasis to complex, presumably "pre-wired" object fantasies that she believed occurred in very young infants. Other object-relations theorists, including those who differ with Klein, give central importance to the concept of **splitting,** the capacity of an infant to divide a single object (for example, mother) into separate good and bad mothers depending on the infant's experience of gratification or frustration. They believe that splitting is common in several types of maladaptive behavior in which an individual has developed a poor capacity for loving and reacting appropriately to others.

Self-psychology is a relatively recent theory put forth by Heinz Kohut (1913–1981), an Austrian psychoanalyst who spent much of his professional life in the United States. Kohut held that a person's self-concept is the central organizer of psychological development. His approach to personal development focuses on the maturation of the sense of self from its infantile state of fragility and fragmentation into the cohesive and stable structure of adulthood. The sexual and aggressive drives so emphasized by Freud are not the forces of psychological development for Kohut. That role is played instead by the self. Kohut believed that psychological disorder results when there are major deficits in the structure of the self. Undesirable early experiences—for example, inadequate mothering and attention—can interfere with development of the self. Therapists who adhere to self-psychology see their task as helping to repair the damage done by previous unloving relationships and environments. They seek to facilitate in the patient a healthy sense of self, a satisfactory and reasonably stable level of self-esteem, and the ability to take pride in accomplishments. These practitioners also aim to instill an awareness of and responsiveness to the needs of others while patients learn to respond to their own needs.

Contemporary theorists have helped broaden the perspectives of psychoanalysis, particularly through their emphasis on the role of distorted interpersonal relationships in maladaptive behavior. They have insisted that disordered behavior and thought must be viewed as outgrowths of the individual's efforts to cope with personal crises in a world peopled by others. In presenting their views, these theorists have deemphasized the role of biology in personality and instead have looked to the social environment for explanations of maladaptive behavior.

Evaluating Psychoanalytic Theory

Psychoanalytic theory contains many ideas about the nature of perception and thought, human development, psychopathology, and treatment. However, its formulations are difficult to study scientifically because the events they hypothesize are not directly observable. Because psychoanalytic theory contains many general and somewhat unclearly defined concepts, it is hard to evaluate objectively. It seems to be better at explaining what has already happened than at predicting future events.

Since psychoanalytic concepts are difficult to prove experimentally, some researchers have tended to reject them out of hand. Others recognize that certain psychoanalytic concepts are vaguely stated and in fact untestable, but nevertheless feel that scientific investigations should be conducted whenever possible.

Is psychoanalysis a theoretical framework within which human behavior can be studied scientifically, or is it a therapeutic method? These two possibilities are not inconsistent, as Freud pointed out on several occasions. A full evaluation of psychoanalysis will be possible only when its effectiveness as a therapy for maladaptive behavior has been objectively assessed and its links with the scientific method have been strengthened.

The problematical proliferation of accusations of sexual and other types of abuse from people, many guided by their therapists, who suddenly remember what they years or decades ago allegedly repressed has hurt the reputation of some psychodynamic therapists. Although Freud almost certainly would have regarded most of these charges with skepticism, his theory of repression and the unconscious has been used to assert the authenticity of some hard-to-believe "memories." Without doubting that childhood sexual abuse is widespread and underreported, some clinicians and researchers have asked the question: Can memories of repeated incest and other bizarre incidents be so repressed that the victim is totally unaware of them until they emerge during therapy? The "recovery" of false memories may be more the product of some overzealous therapists than theories of psychotherapy.

The Behavioral Perspective

Give me a dozen healthy infants, well-formed, and my own specified world to bring them up in and I'll guarantee to take any one at random and train him to become any type of specialist I might select, doctor, lawyer, artist, merchant-chief, and yes, even beggarman and thief, regardless of his talents, penchants, tendencies, abilities, vocations, and race of his ancestors.

—Watson, 1925, p. 82

For John B. Watson (1878–1958), an American psychologist who was the founder of behaviorism, development was a thoroughly mechanical affair. The complete personality—by which Watson meant the whole system of overt behavior—was built up out of the conditioning process. Although many contemporary learning theorists are not as confident as Watson about the simplicity of the processes of behavior acquisition and behavior change, the behavioristic approach continues to exert a powerful influence.

Just as dissatisfaction with a narrow biological orientation was one factor in the development of the psychodynamic perspective, the **behavioral perspective** developed in part because psychologists found many of Freud's ideas about the mind vague, complicated, and untestable. These theorists thought that the same behaviors examined by Freud could be explained in a simpler fashion and in a way that would make it possible to study them experimentally. The behavioral perspective asserts that human beings behave according to the dictates of their environment.

Both the psychoanalytic and behavioral approaches are deterministic, but each finds the source of behavior in a different place. (**Determinism** means that every event or act is caused by what has happened before, not by the overt decisions of the individual.) Psychologists using the behavioral perspective focus on learning. They view behavior as a product of stimulus–response (S–R) relationships, not of intrapsychic events. They do not delve into the past or try to get people to figure out why they are the way they are. To change behavior, they concentrate on altering the relevant aspects of the environment, particularly sources of reinforcement.

A **reinforcer** is an event whose occurrence increases the probability that a certain stimulus will evoke a certain response. Reinforcers reward the individual for doing the right thing or not doing the wrong thing. If the reward is desirable enough, the individual is likely to keep on performing properly as long as the response is reinforced. The response can be either an approach response (asking for another glass of milk) or an escape or avoidance response (running from a pursuer or refusing to go out at night). A **positive reinforcer** increases the probability that the proper response will be made by giving the individual something pleasant. A **negative reinforcer,** on the other hand, increases the probability that the proper response will be made by taking away something unpleasant as soon as that desired response occurs.

Punishment, another way of changing behavior, is an unpleasant consequence for a wrong response. For example, a wife may positively reinforce her husband for not drinking by having sex with him only when he is sober; she may negatively reinforce his drinking by stopping her nagging when he stops drinking; and she may punish him for drunkenness by locking him out of the house. Table 3-2 illustrates the differences between reinforcement and punishment and contrasts them with **extinction,** still another way of changing behavior.

Positive and negative reinforcers and punishment have been applied to a variety of situations. Smiles, gold stars, and hugs are often highly effective in stimulating productive behavior in schoolchildren, and frowns or scolding may be used to discourage undesirable behavior. However, punishment, a negative consequence of behavior that is intended to discourage its repetition, is not very effective when used alone. It may cut down on undesired behavior, but it does not necessarily stimulate productive activity, since the person does not learn an acceptable substitute behavior.

The use of reinforcement in research on maladaptive behavior has followed two general paradigms: classical conditioning and operant conditioning.

Classical Conditioning

In **classical conditioning,** the response that an organism automatically makes to a certain stimulus is transferred to a new stimulus through an association between the two stimuli. The most famous classical conditioning experiment was the Russian physiologist Ivan Pavlov's (1849–1936) investigation of salivation in dogs. Pavlov placed a hungry dog in a harness and turned on a light at certain intervals. The dog did not salivate in response to the light, which was the **conditioned stimulus** (CS). After a few such trials, meat powder was delivered immediately after the CS had been turned on. Since the dog was hungry, it salivated—an **unconditioned response** (UR)—upon presentation of the **unconditioned stimulus** (US), the meat powder. After a number of trials in which turning on the light was followed by delivery of meat powder, Pavlov found that the dog salivated when the light was turned on even if food did not follow. A **conditioned response** (CR) to the light had been established. Pavlov also carried out experiments with sounds, such as the ringing of bells, as the conditioned stimulus.

In some classical conditioning situations, the US is painful. Unpleasant US's are used when the goal is to strengthen **avoidance** or **escape responses.** For instance, an electric fence gives pets or cattle a mild but uncomfortable shock when they touch it. The sight of the fence alone then becomes enough to cause them to stay within a certain limited area. Conditioned responses that are not reinforced periodically through the presence of the US become weaker and ultimately disappear from the organism's repertoire of responses. This disappearance of a previously learned response is called **extinction.**

Students of maladaptive behavior have been intrigued by the process of classical conditioning because it seems to explain fear, anxiety, and other types

TABLE 3–2
Some Mechanisms of Behavior Change

	Definition	Examples
Positive Reinforcement	Encouraging any behavior by using a desired reinforcer as a reward.	Giving a child candy when he brings in a homework assignment. Saying "good girl" when a baby swallows a spoonful of cereal.
Negative Reinforcement	Encouraging any behavior by removing an aversive stimulus when the behavior occurs.	Ceasing to scold a child when he hangs up his coat after throwing it on the floor. Giving in to a roommate or spouse to bring an unpleasant argument to an end.
Punishment	Aversive stimulus given as a result of an undesired behavior in an attempt to suppress that behavior in the future.	Slapping a child for swearing at you. Sending a child to her room because she broke her brother's toy.
Extinction	Supressing behavior by removing the reinforcers for it.	Ignoring a child when he has a temper tantrum. Removing all rock records from the record collection of your roommate, who likes only rock music and plays the stereo too often for your comfort.

of emotional reactions. Some of these reactions may come about because of accidental classical conditioning. A child who has been bitten by a dog may fear all dogs and, through generalization, other types of animals as well. Classical conditioning is also the basis for some therapies. An example is **systematic desensitization,** a therapeutic procedure whose goal is to extinguish a conditioned response. This procedure might be used to help a woman who has been afraid of cars ever since she was injured in a serious auto crash. At first she was merely uncomfortable in a car, but finally she became so fearful that she could not even look at a picture of a car. A diagram of the classical conditioning situation would look like this:

Unconditioned stimulus	→	Unconditioned response
Car crash and injury		*Fear*
Conditioned stimulus	→	Conditioned response
Car		*Fear*

Through a series of steps that break down the bond between the conditioned stimulus and the conditioned response and substitute another conditioned response, the woman's fear could be removed. First she would be taught to relax, then to imagine she was looking at an automobile ad in a magazine. Her relaxed state would counteract the anxiety response. Once she could do this successfully, she might be asked to look at a real ad, then to look at a real car, to touch a car, to imagine herself in a car, and so on. At each step she would relax first and then experience the conditioned stimulus. In this way a new conditioning bond would be built up between a car and a relaxed state.

Operant Conditioning

In **operant conditioning,** the organism must make a particular response before the reinforcement occurs. The organism "operates" on its environment and produces an effect. The American psychologist B. F. Skinner (1904–1990) is famous for demonstrating the effectiveness of operant conditioning. Skinner devised an experimental "Skinner box," in which a rat will press a bar repeatedly if this activity is reinforced by pellets of food falling into a dish (see Figure 3-17). Whereas classical conditioning makes use of natural as well as contrived responses, operant conditioning deals with responses that occur relatively infrequently prior to being reinforced.

A diagram of operant conditioning looks like this:

Response

↓

Reinforcement

↓

Increased probability
of repetition of response

For example, in teaching a child to talk, parents reward the child with smiles and hugs whenever she says a desired word. These parental behaviors are positive reinforcements; they increase the chance that the child will repeat the word.

We hear over and over again how complex human behavior is. We point to our lofty thoughts, fine feelings, and obscure motives. But those who use the behavioral perspective see human behavior as complex for other reasons. Even the simplest act can be seen as a chain of responses, each of which needs to be learned. Few of us get things right the first time. Children are particularly likely to become discouraged and give up if reinforcement is withheld until they do something perfectly. Thus, **shaping**—obtaining the desired response by reinforcing successfully better approximations of it—is one of the basic processes in operant conditioning.

Considerable thought and planning are needed to decide what sorts of reinforcers are best for achieving particular behavior-shaping goals. In some situations an effective reinforcer may be rejected for purely practical reasons. A teacher who wanted to control disruptive behavior in the classroom probably could not use candy as a reinforcer, because it might have an undesirable effect on the pupils' appetites. In addition to deciding which reinforcers would be most effective and practical, it is necessary to decide on a **schedule** for reinforcing particular types of responses. The following case, which involves shaping verbal behavior in a 13-year-old boy with a suspected hearing problem, illustrates these elements.

Figure 3-17 B. F. Skinner, one of the most influential psychologists of the twentieth century, is shown here demonstrating the famous Skinner box used in many of his operant-conditioning experiments. Because we tend to see figures such as Skinner as being somewhat larger than life, the following account by his daughter on one of the last days of his life is both touching and enlightening: *I set up a cot in his study and brought in my guitar. For an hour I played for him—all of the classical pieces I could play reasonably well. It pleased him. He hadn't heard me play in some time and commented on the "richness" of the sound. . . . Later, in his bed, a Japanese-designed sleeping cubicle in the far corner of his study, we talked. I sat on the edge, holding his hand, as so many times, dewy-eyed, he had held mine when putting me to bed as a child. Only this time there were tears in both of our eyes.*

(Vargas, 1990, p. 410)

Benjie, who wore a hearing aid, had never been observed to make verbal responses (except for occasional grunts). He did not smile, cry, or interact meaningfully with others in any way. A reinforcement program was instituted in which candy was used as both a positive and a negative reinforcer. In addition to negative reinforcement (removal of a previously earned piece of candy), mild punishment (a slap on the hand) was used. This was how the operant treatment of Benjie began:

a. *The experimenter sat across from Benjie and said, "Do you hear me, Benjie? If you do, nod your head." The experimenter nodded his head in the hope that Benjie would imitate him and gave Benjie some candy. Initially, Benjie made no head-nodding response.*

b. *Next, the basic procedure remained the same; however, candy was made contingent on the head-nodding response. Soon, Benjie was making 100 percent imitative head-nodding responses.*

c. *In the next procedure, the experimenter stood behind Benjie when giving the verbal cue. Benjie responded by nodding his head. This was the first indication to the experimenters that Benjie did, in fact, have the ability to hear verbalizations given at a normal conversational volume. From that point on Benjie did not wear his hearing aid in the laboratory or at home.*

This reinforcement procedure was not effective in inducing Benjie to make sounds. Because he seemed unresponsive to rewards, the experimenters decided to try a food deprivation schedule as a means of modifying Benjie's behavior. At breakfast, as soon as he made a sound he received a bite of food. This procedure proved to be effective. When he was hungry, he would make sounds at the command, "Benjie, tell me something." Eventually he came to respond to the command even when he was not hungry. After several months Benjie responded with a vocal sound every time a verbal command was directed toward him.

—Knowles and Prutsman, 1968, p. 2

Although the ethical guidelines for working with subjects would generally prohibit the use of food deprivation as a way of motivating behavior, this kind of approach may be used in very special situations such as this one. Here the acquisition of a new behavior is important for treatment, and less intrusive ways of promoting the needed change are not effective. Another example of this controversial approach to behavior change is the use of mild electric shock or other painful stimulus to treat disturbed and retarded children who are self-mutilating; that is, they constantly inflict injury on themselves by knocking their heads against the wall, pulling out their own hair, and so on. The use of this technique has been debated by both professionals and the courts, but because of the lack of any effective alternative it is often considered to cause less damage to the patient than the self-inflicted behavior.

Social Learning Theory

Social learning theorists emphasize the idea that a number of factors combine to shape social behavior and mediate the influence of learning experiences. Although social learning theorists generally agree that covert events serve as mediators between external stimuli and overt behavior, the extent of the role of such events is not clear.

Modeling has received considerable attention from social learning theorists. They believe that reinforcement is not always necessary for learning to occur. **Modeling** can be used to change behavior because people are able to learn by watching how other people do things. Opportunities for observational learning arise when another person—a model—performs some response or group of responses. One of the first learning theorists to point this out was Albert Bandura (b. 1925). He emphasized that the observer does not need to have had practice in making the observed response and does not necessarily have to be reinforced in order to learn it. Exposure to models whose behavior and skills we admire plays an important role in our personal development and contributes to our self-esteem (see Figure 3-18). Models may have desirable or undesirable effects on those who observe their behavior.

Clinical studies support the conclusion that observational learning plays a part in the acquisition of maladaptive behavior. Anxiety in patients can often be traced to modeling experiences. A severe phobia, for example, may represent an exaggeration of a major or

Figure 3-18 While modeling behavior can occur at all ages, it is seen most clearly in children.

minor fear observed in a parent. Watching television is basically a symbolic modeling experience, especially for children. Noticeable and sometimes dramatic changes in behavior can result from modeling experiences. Terms like **vicarious learning, social facilitation, copying,** and **identification** are terms used to characterize this process.

Modeling exposes the observer to the specific responses displayed by the model. Even more important, it provides the observer with food for thought. A child who observes continual arguing between parents forms a concept of what marriage is like. Poor people who observe the parade of commercials on television come to believe that most other people are free from financial worries. Modeling, then, not only illustrates possible overt behavior but also contributes to the formation of concepts, attitudes, and needs. **Role playing,** or practicing behavior shown by a model, is another important learning technique.

The way in which modeling and role playing can strengthen adaptive behavior is illustrated by the case of John R., an unemployed 18-year-old who had been placed in a juvenile correction facility for stealing a car. Therapists noted that his problem was not simply a failure to adhere to social norms but a weak behavioral repertoire.

A particularly serious deficiency was his fear about and inadequacy in job interview situations. He had never had an opportunity to observe the effective behavior of others in situations that required putting one's best foot forward. In the institution he was given the opportunity to observe job interview behavior as modeled by persons (noninmates) who were effective in this area. On several occasions John observed simulated job interviews and then practiced being interviewed himself. After leaving the institution, he found that the modeling experience had helped him. He reported that while waiting for an actual job interview he had remembered and thought about the behavior he had observed. He then mentally rehearsed how he might handle himself when confronted by the personnel manager. He was hired, he felt, because of the new skill and security he brought to the previously traumatic job interview situation. His increased skill and security seemed to result from his having a better idea of what to expect in a job interview.

A strength of social learning theory is its recognition of two developmental aspects of behavior. One is the individual's history of experiences, including various types of events and associated conditioning and modeling. The other aspect, less well understood, but no less important, is how the individual analyzes and interprets past experiences. Much of what is learned, especially after the early years of childhood, occurs implicitly, that is, without being a direct consequence of external environmental

effects. **Implicit learning** takes place when an individual arranges memories of experiences (such as his father's need to read the newspaper right after dinner) into new patterns of thought (such as the role of the reading as a barrier to family interaction). As the child develops an extensive symbolic repertory of words and images, he is no longer dependent on actual environmental experience to learn. Instead, children can manipulate their growing storehouses of symbols and images, imagine new attainments, and thus develop new strategies for dealing with the environment. Similarly, by reorganizing their internal symbolic world, adults supplement the external world with novel thoughts that in turn provide new opportunities for learning and self-administered reinforcements. The emphasis that social learning theorists have placed on the role of the individual as an information processor has increased over time so that most researchers in this field now speak of their view as *cognitive* social learning theory.

While the behavioral perspective focuses attention on the role of the external environment in shaping and governing our actions, cognitive social learning theorists believe that the environment often exerts its influence on behavior indirectly through the individual's thought processes. Our behavior is affected by our memories of the past and anticipations of the future as well as by impactful stimulus configurations.

The Cognitive Perspective

People are disturbed not by things, but by the views which they take of them.

—Epictetus, first century A.D.

If the Greek philosopher Epictetus were alive today, he would likely be a cognitive psychologist. The word "cognitive" comes from the Latin word *cognitare*, meaning "to have known." Cognitive psychology addresses human beings as information processors and problem solvers. The cognitive view seeks to account for behavior by studying the ways in which the person attends to, interprets, and uses available information.

Like the psychodynamic perspective, the **cognitive perspective** is concerned with internal processes. Rather than stressing urges, needs, and motivations, however, it emphasizes how people acquire and interpret information and use it in solving problems. Unlike psychoanalysis, it places great emphasis on mental processes that we are aware of or can rather easily be made aware of, as opposed to hidden motivations, feelings, and conflicts. Its approach has been contrasted with the learning perspective's emphasis on the external environment as a prime cause of behavior. Typically, the cognitive perspective pays more attention to our present thoughts and problem-solving strategies than to our personal histories. However, histories of cognitions also receive some attention (Sarason, 1979). The relationships among emotions, motivations, and cognitive processes and thus the overlap between the cognitive perspective and other approaches is becoming more evident.

In its view of the individual as information processor, the cognitive perspective holds that people are continually collecting, storing, modifying, interpreting, and understanding both internally generated information and environmental stimuli. Humans are seen as active, selective seekers, creators, and users of information, and behavior is viewed as both a product and an initiator of mental acts and environmental changes. The mental life of the individual is conceived of as consisting of **schemata** (plural of *schema*) that contain information in particular domains such as parents, work, and pets. Through their influence on cognitive processes, schemata enable people to identify stimuli quickly, cluster them into manageable units, fill in missing information, and select a strategy for obtaining further information, solving a problem, or reaching a goal (Weary & Edwards, 1994).

From a clinical standpoint, self-schemata are especially important. They organize and guide not only our social experiences but any experiences that are personally relevant. Personally relevant experiences are often laden with emotions and are likely to reflect an individual's prior learning history. Self-schemata are capable of distorting a person's perceptions of reality. Schemata that concern our self-evaluations influence not only how we feel about ourselves but also how we relate to others. For example, **self-efficacy** refers to the strength of our convictions about our personal effectiveness. People may imagine potential difficulties as more formidable than they are in reality if they perceive themselves as ineffective in important types of situations. Inappropriate or maladaptive behavior in those situations may confirm the individual's self-perception as inadequate, helpless, or cowardly. This confirmation may cause the person to avoid problematic situations or reduce his or her task-relevant efforts. A vicious cycle is thereby created and perpetuated.

The cognitive perspective on personality has led to a variety of theories. Among the best known of these are those of Dollard and Miller, Kelly, Bandura, and Beck.

Maladaptive Behavior and Cognition

Many psychological disorders involve serious cognitive disturbances. These disturbances may not be just symptoms but actual causes of the disorders. Several cognitive theorists have suggested some of the causal pathways.

John Dollard and Neal Miller John Dollard (1900–1980) and Neal Miller (b. 1909) tried to relate human learning to psychodynamic processes as well as to external events. Although thinking, feeling, perceiving, and other covert processes cannot be observed, they can be inferred. They are usually called **hypothetical constructs** (because there is no way to prove that they really exist) or **intervening variables** (because they are presumed to intervene between environmental stimuli and behavior).

Dollard and Miller (1950) thought they saw parallels between learning theory and Freudian theory in the area of personality development. For example, the reinforcement principle and Freud's pleasure principle have the same general function: people are more likely to do what makes them feel good. Dollard and Miller also made use of cognitive concepts by describing maladaptive behavior as a joint product of unfortunate life experiences and maladaptive thinking. They viewed gaining insight into the roots of one's behavior as acquiring self-awareness responses. Despite their preference for describing behavior in terms of habits and learning, they emphasized the individual's cognitive resolution of conflicts.

George Kelly The product of George Kelly's (1905–1966) extensive study of the nature of personal experience was his psychology of **personal constructs.** Kelly (1955) concluded that people's personal constructs reflect how they interpret or develop ideas about themselves, the world, and future events. Personal constructs are the way in which each person builds his or her own reality by sorting people and events into categories. Kelly believed that each person is constantly engaged in problem solving and that personal constructs are an important means of organizing information about interpersonal relationships.

There are wide differences between the personal constructs of different individuals. People may perceive the same event in entirely different ways. For example, suppose two lovers break up. One observer may describe the event as simple incompatibility, while another may believe that one person "jilted" the other. Another might say that the breakup was due to "parental meddling"; still another might see it as a "blessing in disguise."

Kelly was not a supporter of the concepts of hidden psychodynamics and the unconscious. He often referred to what he whimsically termed "Kelly's first principle": "If you don't know what is wrong with clients, ask them; they may tell you." Although he recognized that we might not be aware of all of our personal constructs at any given time, he tended to reject Freud's belief that the greater part of mental life is hidden from view. He also tended to reject the emphasis placed by psychoanalysis on what happened to a person in the past. For Kelly, the important thing was the distinctive set of personal constructs that guide a person's life at the present time.

Kelly stressed the role of personal constructs as causes of emotional reactions. We feel anxious when we don't know how to handle a situation, when we become aware that our system of constructs does not encompass a problem that has arisen. Thus, Kelly believed that cognitions precede emotions. He saw psychotherapy as a way of demonstrating to clients that their constructs are hypotheses rather than facts. Once clients realized this, he encouraged them to test their constructs so that the maladaptive ones could be replaced with more useful ones.

Albert Bandura In addition to his emphasis on social learning theory, Albert Bandura has more recently emphasized the symbolic and cognitive aspects of learning as opposed to the stimulus–response aspects (see Figure 3-19). According to Bandura (1981, 1986), we can solve problems symbolically without having to resort to trial-and-error behavior because we can foresee the consequences of our behavior and act accordingly. For example, we buy fire insurance because we think about what might happen if our house burned down. Similarly, in preparing for our first winter camping trip, we assemble protective gear because we can anticipate the effects of a blizzard. The ability to anticipate consequences operates in more routine behaviors as well as in special instances like these.

Figure 3-19 Albert Bandura's work on modeling, as well as his more recent work on self-regulation, has been important not only theoretically but also in the development of new therapeutic approaches.

Bandura (1978) is interested in studying self-regulation, or learning by internal reinforcement, as opposed to modifying behavior by external reinforcement alone. Many cognitive psychologists are developing techniques by which people who lack behavioral self-control can be helped to acquire it. The following examples illustrate techniques for strengthening self-control that make use of cognitive mechanisms.

1. A student studies every night even though no test has been announced.
2. A heavy smoker teaches herself nonsmoking behavior.

In the first case, the student may motivate himself by means of cognitive representation of future consequences. That is, he may think about how bad he would feel if he scored poorly on the next test or how stressful it would be to try to learn all the information the night before the test. Another motivation may be his own goal-setting behavior. He wants to receive a high grade for the course. Whenever he feels like turning on the television set or stopping for a snack, he visualizes how he will feel if he attains his goal. When people evaluate their own behavior in this way, they tend to persist until they achieve their goals.

In the second example, each time the former smoker has the impulse to smoke, she may imagine an X-ray of lungs afflicted by cancer, or she may see herself coughing and unable to breathe. Such self-generated cognitive mechanisms would provide negative reinforcement for her thoughts about smoking.

Aaron Beck The key concept in Beck's theory is the **schema** as an enduring cognitive structure that represents an individual's organized knowledge in a particular domain (Figure 3-20). A schema directs attention to new information and guides the retrieval of stored information, the integration of information, and related inferences and interpretations. Schemata exert important influences over (1) affect and feelings and (2) behavioral responses. For Beck, maladaptive behavior results from dysfunctions of the cognitive system, for example, highly idiosyncratic schemata that are not consistent with reality. Dysfunctional schemata concerning the self (for example, "I am a selfish person") often develop early in life in response to certain situations and are reactivated later in life. This can result in distortions, such as catastrophizing about the consequences of being less than perfect (Beck & Emery, 1985; Beck et al. 1979).

The content of these idiosyncratic schemata influence the type of maladaptive behavior a person displays. For example, a depressed person might attend unduly to failure, rejection, and their consequences. Beck's cogni-

Figure 3-20 Aaron Beck has applied his cognitive theory to the understanding and treatment of several types of maladaptive behavior, including depression, anxiety, and personality disorders.

tive therapy is intended to help patients restructure their thinking and gather evidence to refute the validity of the illogical beliefs that are maintaining their abnormal behaviors. This restructuring often involves revising negative interpretations of events, viewing the future less pessimistically, and thinking more positively about oneself. For Beck, psychological difficulties are due to automatic thoughts, faulty assumptions about the motivations and reactions of others, and negative self-statements. These are examples of the cognitive distortions with which Beck's theory and therapy deal:

- "My life is wasted unless I am a success."
- "It is awful to be disapproved of by people important to you."
- "A person should do well at everything she or he undertakes."

Cognitive Therapies

The idea that maladaptive thoughts are the cause of maladaptive behavior and that people must be taught new ways of thinking has been used as a basic approach by many therapists. Several forms of therapy are based on the cognitive perspective.

Rational-emotive therapy, developed by Albert Ellis, is based on the belief that behavior depends more on individual belief systems and ways of interpreting situations than on objective conditions. Ellis contends that all effective psychotherapists, whether or not they realize it, function as teachers for their clients. They help their clients to review, reperceive, and rethink their lives; to question their irrational beliefs; and to modify their unrealistic and illogical thoughts, emotions, and behaviors. Ellis regards both intense emotions and maladaptive behavior as the modifiable consequences of thoughts. He admits that faulty beliefs are probably formed in childhood. However, he feels that finding out how people got to be the way they are is less important than helping them respond more constructively to their present situation.

In rational-emotive therapy the clinician explains and demonstrates productive thinking, persuades the client to think and behave in more effective ways, and discusses homework assignments. Through such assignments the client might practice ways of behaving more assertively with co-workers or family members without alienating them (Ellis, 1962, 1970; Smith, 1982).

George Kelly used a variety of tactics to help his clients explore and modify their personal constructs. Most often he used a traditional interview format in which he and his client talked about specific personal constructs and the roles they led the client to play in social relationships. In addition, he used **fixed-role therapy,** in which clients experimented with (by acting out) new roles that might result from particular revisions in their personal-construct systems. Kelly believed that people have difficulty simply trying out new ways of behaving; hence he was very supportive of these experimental efforts (Niemeyer & Niemeyer, 1985).

Aaron Beck (1976) also thinks that the job of the therapist is to help clients restructure their thinking and replace maladaptive thoughts with thoughts that are more helpful in coping with stressful situations. Beck's work was originally focused on the cognitions of depressed individuals, but recently his approach has been extended to the problems of anxiety and personality disorders (Beck & Emery, 1985; Beck et al., 1990). Beck thinks that people's emotions and behavior are based largely on the way they view the world. In his view, many people exaggerate their difficulties and minimize the possibility that anything can be done about them. Applying this idea in therapy, it becomes important to identify those beliefs (for example, "People don't like me") that shape personal interpretations of events and facilitate or inhibit action. Beck believes that people generally have broad goals that are very important to them but that may not be completely in their awareness. The therapist's job is to help translate the client's stated aspirations and inhibitions into these underlying goals. Beck's cognitive therapeutic approach is illustrated in chapter 10.

The cognitive perspective seeks to understand how dysfunctional and irrational thought patterns create emotional problems. Clinicians who take the cognitive perspective analyze distress and maladaptive behavior in terms of what we tell ourselves about situations rather than the external situations themselves.

The Humanistic–Existential Perspective

The humanistic-existential perspective presents a sharp contrast to the theoretical approaches described so far. Its roots are found in a number of philosophical and religious systems that have stressed the dignity, inherent goodness, and freedom of human nature. The growth of this perspective within psychology was partly a product of this tradition and partly a reaction to the less flattering conceptions of human nature that are characteristic of psychoanalysis and radical behaviorism.

One of the central assumptions of the humanistic view is that in every person there is an active force toward **self-actualization,** a striving to be "all that you can be." When the human personality unfolds in a benign environment that gives these creative forces free rein, the positive inner nature of the human being emerges. Human misery and pathology, on the other hand, are fostered by environments that frustrate the individual's natural tendencies toward self-actualization.

Closely related to the humanistic movement is the existential perspective, which became popular in Europe after World War II, as psychologists and philosophers sought to understand how the horrors of the war could have occurred and how certain people were able to rise above them and find meaning in life. While the humanistic theories focus on the process of self-actualization, existential theorists emphasize self-determination, choice, and the responsibility of the individual to rise above environmental forces. "We are our choices," maintains the existentialist. "Our existence and its meaning are squarely in our own hands, for we alone can decide what our attitudes and behaviors will be."

Humanistic-existential theorists believe that scientific psychology is missing the mark when it dwells only on observable behavior and neglects the person's inner life. They believe that inner experiences and the search for the meaning of existence are the core of the individual and hence should be the focus of psychology. They therefore regard introspection as a valid and, indeed, indispensable source of psychological information.

Rogers' Conception of the Self

Carl Rogers (1902–1987), one of the leaders of humanistic psychology (see Figure 3-21) used the self-image as the centerpiece of his perspective on personality (1951, 1959, 1980). Rogers related the ability to achieve self-understanding and self-actualization to the individual's self-regard and perception of acceptance by others. An adult who felt wanted and highly valued as a child is

Figure 3-21 Carl Rogers.

likely to have a positive self-image, to be thought well of by others, and to have the capacity for self-actualization. Optimal adjustment results in what Rogers calls the fully functioning person and is characterized by a low level of anxiety. Anxiety is due to uneasiness or tension resulting from inconsistencies between people's self-perceptions and their ideas of what they would like to be.

Although the ways in which they conceptualized behavior contrast sharply, both Rogers and Freud developed their theoretical positions on the basis of similar observational data: the behavior of clients and therapists in psychotherapy. However, Rogers rejected the psychoanalytic notion that people are irrational and unsocial by nature. He asserted, on the contrary, that each person is basically rational, socialized, and constructive.

For Rogers, psychotherapy is a situation in which anxious, troubled people with low self-regard and distorted perceptions of themselves and the world seek help. Rogers thinks that healthy people are those who move away from roles created by the expectations of others, that is, they do not pretend to be something they are not. Instead, they learn to trust themselves and reject the false selves that others have created for them. Neurotic and psychotic people, on the other hand, have self-concepts that do not match their experiences. They are afraid to accept their own experiences as valid, so they distort them, either to protect themselves or to win approval from others. A therapist can help them give up these false selves.

The task for Rogerian therapists is neither to provide interpretations nor to give advice. Rather, the therapist must accept clients as having worth and dignity in their own right despite their problems. This acceptance means that the therapist must understand the client's feelings, no matter how positive or negative they are or how much they contradict the therapist's own attitudes.

Rogers believed that "there is no such thing as scientific knowledge; there are only individual perceptions of what appears to each person to be such knowledge" (1959). This statement expresses the humanistic-existentialist view that inner experience and a search for individual meaning should be the focus of psychology.

The Existential Point of View

Existentialists believe that people are free to choose among alternative courses of action. If this is true, why are so many people unhappy and dissatisfied? Why does maladaptive behavior exist? For one thing, not everyone chooses wisely. A person can choose to act either authentically or inauthentically. To act **authentically** means to freely establish one's own goals. To act **inauthentically** means to let other people dictate those goals. For each person there are also certain givens that place definite limits on what he or she may become. These may be characteristics that are present at birth, such as learning ability, physical appearance, or the presence of a disabling disease, or they may be environmental, including the influence of parents and later of school and peers. These expand or contract the individual's chances for fulfillment based on the qualities present at birth. The primary task of the therapist, according to this view, is to help empty, lonely people expand their experiences and fulfill their own uniqueness, that is, to help them make constructive choices.

The humanistic-existential perspective is more a philosophical position than a formal scientific theory. However, it does address crucial aspects of human existence. Humanistic-existential writers believe that scientific psychology misses the mark if it dwells on observable behavior and neglects the individual's inner life, particularly motivations and personality styles.

The Community–Cultural Perspective

Many people see mental illness as a personal health problem or as a character defect. In contrast, from the **community-cultural perspective,** maladaptive behavior results from inability to cope effectively with stress. It is not viewed as a disease or problem that exists only within the individual; instead, it is seen as at least partly a failure of the individual's social support system. This system includes the person's spouse, parents, siblings, relatives, friends, teachers, employer, religious adviser, and others, as well as community organizations and government agencies. Cultural factors might play a role in the failure of someone's support network to be helpful, not because the network members desire to play a negative role, but rather because the values, beliefs, and habits prevalent in a particular culture may apply to certain situations. Cultural variations can play a role either in the maladaptive behavior for which clinical help is sought or in the therapy situation, for example, when the therapist is unfamiliar with the cultural realities of the client's life.

Community psychologists, proponents of the community perspective, do not deny the role of life history or genetic makeup in causing maladaptive behavior, but these are not seen as necessarily sufficient to produce such behavior. For example, a person vulnerable to schizophrenia may develop hallucinations for many reasons: biochemical factors, traumatic early experiences, or unusual social relationships are all possibilities. However, the presence of an especially strong stressor or the breakdown of the person's social support system may be equally important in producing the schizophrenic behavior.

The community approach attempts to reduce maladaptive behavior through preventive measures, by intervening in people's lives before catastrophes occur. Such measures include a variety of special programs: discussion or mutual support programs for recently separated, divorced, or widowed people; preschool enrichment programs for children from low-income, single-parent homes; combined school programs and child care facilities for teenage single parents; day-care centers for elderly people who may not be able to live self-sufficiently. Implicit in community psychology is the belief that the effects of social disorganization (such as slums, bad schools, and high unemployment rates) are a major cause of many personal problems. For this reason, mental health professionals with a community orientation tend to become involved in efforts to change society by lobbying for legislation and becoming actively involved in community affairs.

Community psychologists study the social environment and factors related to it, such as socioeconomic status. When the living places of people who are identified as psychologically and socially impaired are plotted on a map, it can be shown that the frequency of such problems is much higher in certain areas than in others. **Social-causation theories** argue that the poor schools, crime, inadequate housing, and prejudice often found in low-income, deteriorating neighborhoods may increase the stress experienced by already vulnerable people. The **social-selection theory,** on the other hand, argues that lower socioeconomic groups show a greater incidence of maladaptive behavior because people who do not function well tend to experience downward social mobility. Recent research suggests that, while social causation is implicated in depression, antisocial behavior, and substance abuse, social selection is implicated in schizophrenia (Dohrenwend et al., 1992).

Those who believe in the community-cultural perspective are more likely to support the social-causation theory. They point out that, while social selection may be a factor, the theory does not rule out the stress-producing situations—related to cultural disparities or encountered by low-income people—that may aggravate existing disorders. Such people may have not only less power to control their environment but also fewer resources for dealing with stress. For a variety of reasons, including the difficulty of carrying out controlled research in community settings, one cannot completely rule out either the social-selection or the social-causation theory. One or the other might apply to certain types of disorders. In either case, psychologists with a community-cultural perspective see a need to develop special programs aimed at reducing cultural disparities and counteracting undesirable aspects of urban life such as poverty and overcrowding. Such programs would improve the lives of the general population as well as those of people with specific psychological problems.

Social Roles and Labeling

All individuals belong to cultural and social groups. These groups shape people's behavior by providing the distinctive reinforcements, punishments, and models that are part of life in a particular cultural setting. The members of a cultural or social group share a set of meanings or symbols, experience a feeling of unity, and participate in a network of mutual obligations. The group or groups to which a person belongs influence nearly every aspect of his or her life.

Social roles are particular functions that a person plays as a member of a social group. Some theorists have maintained that we always attempt to project an image and that, in fact, we have no true self. This position is presented by Erving Goffman (1959), who argues that in all of our encounters with other people we adopt particular roles. Each role is accompanied by a script that includes different actions and signals. In effect, we vary our behaviors continuously as the situation requires. This viewpoint implies that there is no such thing as a fixed personality.

Less extreme than this position, and more widely accepted, is the composite position: There is a basic personality that is overlaid with situational role playing. Research has shown that a number of factors influence the roles people play in social relationships. These factors are often important because they serve to label an individual in a particular way. **Labeling** occurs whenever people are categorized on some basis, whether that basis is relevant and fair or not. Labels can be destructive because they draw attention to one aspect of the person while ignoring other aspects that make him or her unique. (Would you like to be labeled as a slob simply because you don't like to put your shoes away at night?) Some labels, such as "good student" and "loyal friend," are desirable, but many others carry negative social con-

notations. For example, the role of mental patient is widely viewed as socially unacceptable, and the label of mentally ill often causes permanent damage. The damage takes many forms, including discrimination by others and feelings of self-doubt and inadequacy.

Contributions of the Community–Cultural Perspective

What we know at present suggests that cultural, social, and economic factors play roles in emotional expression and maladaptive behavior. For example, children's levels of distress and depression increase sharply when they live in an environment in which adults express high levels of anger and behave aggressively. There is some evidence that this responsiveness to family discord is greater for boys than it is for girls (Cummings & Davies, 1994).

The community-cultural perspective has been influential in producing new approaches to maladaptive behavior and in reaching segments of the population whose psychological needs hitherto have been ignored. It has been effective both in changing the perspective of academic thinking and in altering social policy. As important, it has raised questions for future research whose answers will contribute to our understanding of both the cultural and social causes of maladaptive behavior and ways the social environment can enhance the lives of children and adults. Included among these questions are: How does stress in personal lives and in the community influence whether maladaptive behavior occurs? Can the community provide social support that either prevents maladaptive behavior or limits its undesirable effects? How can communities best meet the needs of special groups such as chronically mentally ill people, recent immigrants, and the homeless?

An Integrative Approach

We have reviewed six widely varying perspectives on the causes and treatment of maladaptive behavior. You may be wondering how these perspectives relate to the rest of the book. Which one is emphasized most? We think you should know our biases and how our views will affect what you learn in this book.

We have attempted to use the most valuable contributions of each viewpoint in our discussions of abnormal behavior. Abnormal behavior can result from any or all of a large number of factors. One perspective may contribute more than another under one set of conditions; under a different set, another viewpoint may be more useful. Our approach, which is shared by many other psychologists, is interactional. That is, what we think about and how we behave usually depends on *interactions* among several factors. These factors combine in giving direction to our lives. For example, the state of our health, concerns about parental expectations, self-doubts, our past experiences and present values, and our cultural background interact in influencing our approach to an upcoming final exam. We might feel perfectly healthy, have had rewarding experiences with taking exams in the past, and not feel strong cultural pressures to attain a certain level of performance on exams; but if we feel a lot of pressure from our parents to get perfect grades, have troubling self-doubts, and feel a responsibility to society to be very successful, anticipating and taking the exam might be an unpleasant experience. It would be even more unpleasant if, in addition, we had a bad cold.

The factors emphasized by the six theoretical perspectives can be thought of as contributing to our vulnerability and resiliency. We might be vulnerable to poor performance because of our worries and those of our parents regarding the consequences of not being successful. At the same time, being intelligent, resourceful, and hard-working helps us be resilient under academic stress. The way a situation influences behavior depends on our particular mix of vulnerability and resiliency and the conditions we are confronting. These conditions together with personal characteristics can be thought of as interacting or combining to produce a special product, the individual's behavior. Why maladaptive behavior occurs in some people and not in others can be understood in this way.

In addition to influencing final behavior, personal and environmental factors also can influence each other. For example, someone who is aggressive and always gets into fights is likely to alienate other people and thereby reduce social support. At the same time, someone who experiences a succession of stressful life events may become discouraged and feel pessimistic about a positive outcome.

This interactional approach not only provides a general framework for thinking about maladaptive behavior but also allows for specification of the factors that are especially pertinent to particular disorders. For example, while in the past schizophrenia may have been thought of as being caused by demonic possession, we now know that certain personal and environmental factors, as well as specific biological conditions, play roles in the incidence of this serious disorder. Researchers today are investigating the possible relevance to schizophrenia of a large variety of these factors, including the following personal variables (Gottesman, 1991):

1. A reduced capacity for information processing in situations requiring attention to complex stimuli
2. Hyperactivity of the autonomic nervous system to aversive stimuli in the environment
3. Poor social and coping skills

There is also evidence that these environmental factors contribute to the incidence of schizophrenia and its recurrence:

1. Stressful life events
2. A nonsupportive social network

Research has shown that it is particular combinations of these personal vulnerabilities and environmental handicaps, not their individual existence, that pose special risks for people with tendencies toward various types of maladaptive behavior.

Another example of the application of the interactional approach can be seen in the study of depression. For instance, there is evidence that many people do not become depressed for either purely mental or purely environmental reasons. A full understanding of depression requires information about both the person's internal state and the state of his or her social and community ties. Depression can be viewed as despair over a severe loss or disappointment from which, for a longer or shorter time, there seems to be no escape. Recovery from this crisis depends on whether the situation changes and/or how the person's cognitions about the situation change.

Each of us has expectations and goals that color our thoughts. A stamp collector probably has different thoughts when going to the post office than a noncollector does. Our thoughts serve as **mediators:** they provide links between informational inputs and behavioral outputs, just as an intermediary in the business world links a manufacturer and a retailer. Several theories of abnormal behavior deal with the mediating process, though there are differences of opinion about which ones are most important. The various theoretical perspectives reflect these differences by focusing on such different mediators as chemical processes in the body, drives and emotions, thinking styles, values and needs, or the social milieu.

Each of us confronts diverse situations each day. They provide us with information (pleasant, unpleasant, frightening, reassuring) and often call forth certain reactions. The information available to us influences our way of looking at things. At the same time, our personal characteristics—our skills and vulnerabilities—help determine how we handle the situations to which we must respond. As psychologists and authors, we are interested in what makes an individual vulnerable to particular situations, what kind of stressors cause maladaptive behavior to appear, and how people can be helped to deal better with stressors and to compensate for their vulnerabilities.

THE ROLE OF THEORY IN ABNORMAL PSYCHOLOGY

Theories play an important role in guiding research on the causes of behavioral maladaptations and physical illness. The six currently influential theoretical perspectives are: (1) the biological perspective, (2) the psychodynamic perspective, (3) the behavioral perspective, (4) the cognitive perspective, (5) the humanistic–existential perspective, and (6) the community–cultural perspective. Each of these theories has something to contribute to the understanding of maladaptive behavior, personal vulnerabilities, and one's resiliency in coping with challenging situations.

THE BIOLOGICAL PERSPECTIVE

The **biological perspective** concerns the role bodily disturbances play in disordered behavior. The bodily disturbance may be due to a genetic defect, an injury or infection before or after birth, or to a more or less temporary physiological malfunction caused by some condition present at a particular time.

Biological Determinants of Abnormal Behavior Genes, the elements of human heredity, are transmitted from parent to child in the form of **DNA.** DNA is found in the **chromosomes,** present in pairs in all body cells. **Behavior genetics** emphasizes the interaction of heredity and environment. Research in behavior genetics is carried out either through the study of family histories or through studies of twins. The two major divisions of the nervous system are the **central nervous system** (CNS), the nerve cells in the brain and spinal cord, and the **peripheral nervous system,** the neurons connecting the CNS with the glands, muscles, and sensory receptors.

The Neurosciences Revolution Neuroscience is a new interdisciplinary field aimed at understanding the relationship between thinking, feeling, and behavior and the structure and function of the brain. The use of new techniques to study molecular-level events at the synapse as well as scanning techniques that make possible the study of the living brain are contributing to the understanding of relationships between the brain and behavior. **Psychoneuroimmunology** is an area of research focused on the effects of psychological and neural events on immunological processes.

Integration of Biological and Psychological Systems One major contribution of the biological perspective is drug therapy. A variety of drugs are used in treating maladaptive behavior. However, it is important to recognize the multiple determinants of abnormal behavior that include interactions among the physical environment, psychological factors, and biological functioning.

THE PSYCHODYNAMIC PERSPECTIVE

The **psychodynamic perspective** is based on the idea that thoughts and emotions are important causes of behavior.

Freud and Psychoanalysis Freud developed **psychoanalysis,** a method in which the patient recaptures forgotten memories without the use of hypnosis. The two most basic assumptions of Freud's theories of personality are **psychic determinism** and the **conscious-unconscious dimension.** The latter includes three levels of consciousness: the **conscious, preconscious,** and **unconscious.** Freud's theory placed great emphasis on the first five years of life. During this period he thought that the **libido,** or basic human drives, was focused on a series of specific erogenous zones or sources of pleasure. His theory divided the mental world into three structures—the **id,** the **ego,** and the **superego.** Freud also placed great emphasis on the concept of **anxiety** and on the use of **defense mechanisms** to ward off anxiety. He believed the most important of the defense mechanisms was **repression.**

Contemporary Approaches to Psychoanalysis Psychoanalytic theory has been modified by many later theorists. Erikson developed a **psychosocial** theory. He described a series of stages of development over the entire life cycle. **Object-relations** theory was developed by psychoanalysts such as Klein. Kohut developed a theory of **self-psychology.**

Evaluating Psychoanalytic Theory Psychoanalysis is both a theoretical framework and a therapeutic method. Its full evaluation will be possible only when its therapeutic effectiveness can be objectively assessed and its concepts explored using scientific methods, such as the experiment.

THE BEHAVIORAL PERSPECTIVE

The behavioral perspective focuses on behavior as a response to stimuli in the environment. Behaviors that receive **reinforcement** or reward have an increased probability of occurring again. **Negative reinforcement** occurs when something unpleasant is taken away after the behavior occurs. **Punishment** provides a negative consequence for the behavior.

Classical Conditioning In **classical conditioning,** the response that occurs automatically to one stimulus is transferred to a new stimulus by pairing the two stimuli.

Operant Conditioning In **operant conditioning** the response precedes the reinforcement.

Social Learning Theory Social learning theorists do not believe that direct reinforcement is always necessary for learning. They stress the use of **modeling,** or observational learning, as the way a great deal of behavior, especially social behavior, is learned. **Role playing,** or practice of the modeled behavior, is also an important learning technique.

THE COGNITIVE PERSPECTIVE

The **cognitive perspective** focuses on how people acquire and interpret information and use it in problem-solving. Each person develops **schemata** that contain information about different domains in a person's life and assist in information processing and strategy development. In the study of maladaptive behavior, **self-schemata** are particularly important.

Maladaptive Behavior and Cognition Dollard and Miller combined elements of the psychodynamic, learning, and cognitive perspectives. They saw maladaptive behavior as a result of both unfortunate life experiences and maladaptive thinking. According to Kelly, each person builds a view of the world by sorting people and events into categories. He called these categories **personal constructs,** and thought the role of psychotherapy was to help people replace maladaptive personal constructs with more adaptive ones. Bandura is especially interested in **self-regulation** through the use of internal rather than external reinforcement. For Beck, maladaptive behavior results from dysfunctional cognitions, highly idiosyncratic schemata that are not consistent with reality.

Cognitive Therapies Rational-emotive therapy, developed by Ellis, is based on the idea that behavior is more a function of belief systems than of actual conditions. The therapist's role is to explain, demonstrate, and assist the client in practicing more productive ways of thinking. **Fixed-role therapy,** developed by Kelly, focuses on assisting clients to act out new roles that may help them revise their personal-construct systems. Beck focuses on helping clients replace maladaptive thoughts with more effective coping techniques. His work intially focused on depression but now also includes problems with anxiety as the major symptom.

THE HUMANISTIC–EXISTENTIAL PERSPECTIVE

The **humanistic** perspective assumes that in every person there is an active force toward **self-actualization.**

Rogers' Conception of the Self Rogers emphasized the importance of the **self-image.** He believed a primary role of the therapist was the total acceptance of the client as a person of worth.

The Existential Point of View Existentialists focus on the need to help people to establish their own goals and then to make constructive choices to reach these.

THE COMMUNITY–CULTURAL PERSPECTIVE

The **community–cultural perspective** directs attention to the roles played by community-wide factors (for example, poverty) and cultural diversity in maladaptive behavior. **Community psychologists** focus on the failure of social support systems as the cause of maladaptations. They emphasize preventive intervention—such as special programs in schools—and programs for specific groups that are at high risk because they need help in solving problems of living.

Social Roles and Labeling Social roles are defined by the person's group and the functions of the person in that group. Each role has a script that determines how the person is expected to act in different situations. **Labeling** is the result of categorizing people on some basis, such as the social group to which they belong, without attention to their individual characteristics.

CONTRIBUTIONS OF THE COMMUNITY–CULTURAL PERSPECTIVE

Social, economic, and cultural factors play roles in emotional expression and maladaptive behavior. Community psychology has been influential in reaching people whose needs have been ignored by the other perspectives that focus more on treating the individual instead of changing the environment. How best to provide support in the community setting is still a question that needs extensive research.

AN INTEGRATIVE APPROACH

All of the perspectives make contributions to identifying personal vulnerabilities and factors in resiliency that relate to maladaptive behavior, its prevention, and its treatment. In an interactional approach an important issue is how these factors combine with stressful life experiences to produce the various types of maladaptive behavior.

CHAPTER FOUR

Dick Jemison, *Earthnote 1*, 1994.
Courtesy of Riva Yares Gallery, Santa Fe, N.M. And Scottsdale, Az.

CLASSIFICATION AND ASSESSMENT

Robert Frank, a 37-year-old married man, has come to a community mental health center because some of his thoughts have been bothering him.

For as long as he can recall, he has been introverted and somewhat fearful of people. He has wanted social contact but, because of his fearfulness, has usually been unsuccessful in forming relationships. At the time he has come to the center, he has been keeping certain disturbing thoughts to himself. In the past he had discussed these thoughts with his wife and with clinicians at a mental hospital. He thinks he is being spied upon by some unknown group, which he believes to be a government intelligence agency. He also feels that his television set is providing him with special messages and that an attempt is being made to control his will and thoughts. He has a job in a large corporation. In the judgment of his supervisor, he has performed well in the past but recently his work has deteriorated somewhat.

Frank has been hospitalized twice, after which he seemed to make a good adjustment back into the community. Six months ago his mother's death upset him greatly. During the past few months he has increasingly restricted his social activities to members of his family and, even with them, has been somewhat withdrawn. He has come to the community mental health center because the thoughts are becoming more persistent. His discomfort level is increasing, and he realizes that he is becoming more incoherent; he wants to avoid another hospitalization if at all possible.

The clinical worker who talked with Frank wanted to assess the seriousness of his problem and evaluate vulnerability and resiliency factors in his life. The fact that he has been hospitalized twice reflects his vulnerability to becoming preoccupied with paranoid thoughts. But he also seems to be resilient in important ways: He has a job that until recently he performed well and has had good recoveries from his two hospitalizations. The clinician hoped to use all the information at her disposal in order to recommend the most practical and effective therapeutic program. She went through a series of steps gathering and interpreting information about Frank.

To increase the accuracy of their interpretations, clinicians often make use of the experiences of other professionals in evaluating behavior. Classification systems are particularly valuable because they represent attempts to organize what a great many clinical workers know about the various types of problems they deal with. The classification of personal problems is based on assessments of what clients say and how they behave. Both current life conditions and past experiences are taken into account. Classification is not simply an intellectual exercise, however. It has far-reaching effects on the lives of people who exhibit maladaptive behavior as well as on the activities of clinical workers.

Classification: Categories of Maladaptive Behavior

The need to classify various types of personalities and personal problems has long been recognized. Since the time of Hippocrates, classification systems have continually been revised to incorporate new knowledge and changing viewpoints. Nevertheless, the classification of abnormal behavior is still in an early stage of evolution, partly because of the arbitrary nature of the process of attaching labels to people. For example, there is no precise point at which an excessive drinker becomes a full-blown alcoholic, or when the tension you feel when you are alone in a strange room becomes the intense dread known as claustrophobia.

A classification statement, or **diagnosis,** places a disorder within a system of conventional groupings based on important similarities in symptoms. Most classification systems in psychology are organized in hierarchical fashion, just as they are in the natural sciences. Thus, in the system that is used to classify animal life, human beings are members of the species *Homo sapiens*, genus *Homo*, which is a subdivision of the family Hominidae, of the order Primates, of the class Mammalia, of the phylum Chordata, of the kingdom Animalia. Similarly, manic episode is a subdivision of bipolar disorder, which in turn is one of the major disorders in the family of mood disorders.

While classification is generally regarded as a scientific and clinical tool, we should remember that all people continually use some form of classification in their daily lives. The people we meet, the day's weather, and other everyday experiences are all put into groups on the basis of similarities to past experiences or of other ways of classifying events. Classification is a way of trying to understand and to learn from experience. Without a classification system, everything that happens to us would be unique. We could not prepare for the future in any way (see Figure 4-1).

Advantages and Disadvantages of Classification

General use of a widely recognized classification system is very important. If every clinical worker created his or her own system, communication problems would be enormous. For example, it would be difficult to make use of research data on effective treatment. In addition, classification systems are useful for statistical purposes. Government and other planning agencies need records of how often various types of maladaptation occur. Without such records, it would be impossible to say whether the incidence of certain forms of maladaptation was increasing or decreasing. Moreover, to the extent that the categories used in established classification systems are distinctive and can be rated reliably, they contribute to the planning of treatment programs and facilities.

Still, the usefulness of classification for understanding the causes of some disorders and treating them remains controversial, as shown by the following comments by an experienced clinician.

> You would think that after working with troubled people for 20 years I'd know what their major problems are and what I should be diagnosing. Yet I'm not really sure what diagnosis is, what it should be, or how it can do more than just name and pigeonhole. I classify cases because it helps me keep records and communicate with other clinicians. At the same time, my major job is to treat people, to decide what I can do that will help them figure out what they should do to make their lives happier and more worthwhile. People are different more than they are similar. Two people may come in with a similar symptom, such as delusions of grandeur, but the mechanisms that produce the symptom may be different. I wish diagnosis helped me better understand the basis for the conditions I diagnose.

The idea of classifying maladaptive behaviors has been criticized on several counts. Most important to many people is the fact that a diagnosis puts a label on a person. Labeling might make it difficult for a former

Figure 4-1 In this cartoon, Linus is discovering how to classify an event ("I'll slug you right back") so he can better prepare for the future.

patient to get a job, gain admission to a professional program, obtain custody of a child, and the like. Another argument is that many diagnoses are not useful because the diagnostic categories are imperfect and the same label may be assigned to behaviors that appear similar but have different causes and require different treatment.

Yet, on balance, the case for classification is a strong one. It is easy to defend the idea that each patient is unique, yet nothing can be done to help an individual without referring to general principles. What is known about an individual case, however detailed, can be utilized only if the case is viewed within the context of existing knowledge. At the same time, general principles will have validity only if they are based on observation of individuals.

There are two major sources of unreliability in diagnoses. One concerns clinical judgment: Differences in therapists' clinical training and theoretical orientation may lead to different diagnoses. The other major source of unreliability is that diagnostic labels are attached to people, and no two people (or their problems) are alike. The same person might also describe his or her problem differently on two separate occasions depending on how he or she was feeling at the time or what events relating to the problem had occurred recently. Diagnosticians may change their original assessment of a case, or two people with similar problems might describe their conditions differently and therefore be classified differently.

Ambiguities and inconsistencies also arise because most clinics and hospitals are burdened with more cases than they can handle. Leisurely and protracted study aimed at accurate classification is often impossible. Another factor in classification difficulty is the range of problems treated by a particular clinical facility. The staff of a facility that treats a narrow range of disorders may tend to describe and interpret its cases differently than would the staff of a more broadly based institution. Diagnostic methods will achieve a firmer scientific basis as assessment becomes more standardized and less susceptible to distortion by such factors. Table 4-1 lists some of the important features of a good classification system. Currently, for most types of maladaptive behavior, the characteristics listed in Table 4-1 remain goals—they are not yet achievements.

TABLE 4–1
Characteristics of a Good Clinical Classification System

1. Provides information about the cause or causes of a condition.
2. Provides a common language for communication among clinicians and researchers.
3. Enables clinicians to give patients and their families a short- and long-term outlook.
4. Indicates possible treatment.
5. Suggests paths to prevention.

Vulnerability, Resiliency, and Coping

The authors' interactional approach to abnormal psychology has definite implications for the process of classification. This approach argues that abnormal behavior must be understood in the context of several factors: the recent stressful events in a person's life, such as a bereavement or loss of a job; the person's general vulnerabilities, such as a tendency toward low self-esteem possibly engendered by early childhood experiences or a highly reactive nervous system; and what the individual has going for him or her, such as coping skills, intellectual ability, and family and friends who are willing and able to help. An especially important asset in coping with stress is resiliency, the ability to think clearly and function well despite adverse circumstances.

Classifying abnormal behavior should be a matter of creating a complete portrait of a person rather than simply marking a point on a graph. In classifying a person who is experiencing a problem, we want to know not only what the problem is—for example, Frank's belief that he is being spied on—but also the context of the problem. In Frank's case, the context includes (1) recent experiences that may have aroused stress and led to the worsening of his condition, (2) his vulnerabilities or weaknesses, and (3) his assets or strengths. The fact that Frank has experienced long periods of good adjustment (for example, being able to hold a job) is encouraging and should not be ignored. Optimally, the way we classify people should tell us something about their future prospects and likely responses to therapeutic efforts.

The Multiaxial Approach

Over the years, classification or diagnosis has meant many things; the simple assignment of a name or label as well as a statement providing information about several aspects of a particular case. (The root of "diagnostic" means "thorough knowledge.") Official classifications of mental disorders first came into use in the United States in 1840, with the adoption of a one-item classification scheme. In the census that year, "idiocy" was the single label used to categorize mental illness. By the 1880 census, there were eight categories for mental disorders.

Today, practitioners make use of a **multiaxial classification system** designed to summarize the diverse information relevant to an individual case rather than to provide a single label. Instead of merely assigning a case to a category (such as schizophrenia), clinicians using a multiaxial system can describe an individual in terms of a set of clinically important factors, or *axes*. The American Psychiatric Association's multiaxial classification system is currently so widely accepted that it is easy to lose sight of the fact that the multiaxial feature is a relatively new development in the classification of mental disorders. The first multiaxial system was presented as recently as 1980, in the *Diagnostic and Statistical Manual of Mental Disorders* (referred to as DSM-III). A revision of DSM-III, referred to as DSM-III-R, was published in 1987. Like its predecessors, DSM-IV is a multiaxial system with five axes.

A multiaxial system is primarily concerned with the description of clinical problems. Its categories take note of the etiology, or cause, of the disorder when it can be identified (although some critics of DSM maintain that this system does not pay sufficient attention to etiology), as well as the subjective experiences of clients (for example, how worried or angry they seem to be) and their assets and liabilities. DSM-IV provides information about the context in which abnormal behavior occurs as well as a description of the behavior.

DSM-IV

The axes of DSM-IV provide information about the biological, psychological, and social aspects of a person's condition.

- *Axis I* reports most of the disorders or conditions in the classification system. Personality disorders and mental retardation are reported on Axis II. When necessary to accurately describe a given individual, more than one disorder can be listed on Axis I. In such a case, the principal diagnosis is listed first.
- *Axis II* deals with personality disorders and mental retardation, both of which begin in childhood or adolescence and usually persist into adult life. An example would be the personality disorder in which there is an unwarranted tendency to interpret the actions of other people as threatening. Axis II may also be used for noting maladaptive personality features and defense mechanisms that do not meet all the criteria for a personality disorder.
- *Axis III* describes general medical conditions that seem relevant to a case (for example, the client's history of heart attacks).

- *Axis IV* describes psychosocial and environmental problems (for example, housing problems, a negative life event, or family stress). In some cases, these problems may stem from adjustment difficulties created by the disorder.
- *Axis V* is a global assessment of the individual's psychological, social, and occupational functioning. The clinician makes a **global assessment of functioning (GAF)** rating on a scale from 1 to 100. *Low* ratings indicate that individuals pose dangers to themselves or others. *High* ratings indicate good or superior functioning (for example, being involved in a variety of activities and showing effectiveness in interpersonal relationships).

The case of Robert Frank presented at the beginning of the chapter might be classified as follows:

Axis I: Paranoid schizophrenia
Axis II: Avoidant personality disorder
Axis III: No apparent medical conditions
Axis IV: Several severe problems
Axis V: GAF = 55 (moderate to severe symptoms)

An innovation of the DSM-IV system is that it provides criteria for coding the relatively subjective factors of Axes IV and V. Axis IV provides guidelines for rating the overall severity of recent events (death of a child, retirement) and long-lasting circumstances (unemployment or serious chronic illness). Guidelines for Axis V pertain to level of functioning (violence to self or others, conflict with co-workers). The behavior of two severely disturbed people would probably be interpreted differently and even treated differently if one had a history of good relationships with others and an excellent work record while the other had a history of social inadequacy and inability to hold a job.

The more complete the available information about a given case, the more reliable the classification and ratings will be. Often, particularly in acute or emergency cases, a classification is made even though there are major informational gaps. In such cases, the classification is considered to be tentative and may be revised as more information is acquired.

The Major Diagnostic Categories

Beginning with DSM-III in 1980, a special effort has been made to be as specific as possible in describing major diagnostic categories and in listing the symptoms and factors relevant to particular disorders. These include the typical features of the disorder, the age at which it usually develops, its likely progression or outcome, the amount of social and occupational impairment involved, possible complications (for example,

suicide attempts by depressed individuals), aspects of a person's life that increase the risk of a severe disorder, sex differences, and relevant family patterns. Table 4-2 lists indicators such as these, which the clinician observes in making classifications.

Axis I Categories As stated earlier, Axis I includes all the clinical disorders except personality disorders and mental retardation.

- **Disorders Usually First Diagnosed in Infancy, Childhood, or Adolescence** (excluding mental retardation, which is diagnosed on Axis II). These include disruptive behavior, gender identity disorders, and learning disorders.
- **Delirium, Dementia, and Amnestic and Other Cognitive Disorders.** Impairments in cognition—for example, memory deficit, language disturbance, failure to recognize or identify objects—that appear to be caused by one or more substances and/or general medical conditions.
- **Mental Disorders Due to a General Medical Condition.** Mental disorder in association with a general medical condition that is judged to be its cause.
- **Substance-Related Disorders.** Conditions marked by adverse social, behavioral, psychological, and physio-

---

TABLE 4–2
Clinical Observations and Symptoms Used in DSM-IV Classification

While a given symptom may be part of several different clinical pictures (for example, headaches may be present in cases marked by high anxiety, hypochondriasis, or somatic complaints), this list suggests the kinds of data clinicians attend to and that go into a psychiatric diagnosis. The presence of *groups* of symptoms characteristic of a particular disorder increases the likelihood of accurate classification.

Anxiety
Behavior
Cognitive functioning (attention, memory)
Eating disturbance
Energy level
Mood
Motor activity
Occupational and social impairment
Perceptual disturbance
Personal appearance
Personality traits
Physical symptoms
Sleep disturbance
Speaking manner
Thought content

logical effects caused by seeking or using one or more substances (for example, alcohol, cocaine, and amphetamines).

- **Schizophrenia and Other Psychotic Disorders.** Significant distortion in the perception of reality, impaired capacity to reason, speak, and behave rationally or spontaneously; impaired capacity to respond with appropriate affect and motivation (e.g., delusions, hallucinations, incoherence, and social isolation).
- **Mood Disorders.** Abnormal mood characterized by depression, mania, or both symptoms in alternating fashion. Depression is indicated by sadness, gloominess, and dejection; mania is indicated by excitement, irritability, and expansiveness.
- **Anxiety Disorders.** High levels of anxiety, tension, and worry over extended periods of time that may be accompanied by avoidance of feared situations, ritual acts, or repetitive thoughts.
- **Somatoform Disorders.** Physical symptoms for which no medical causes can be found; persistent worry about having a physical illness; exaggerated concern about minor or imagined physical defects in an otherwise normal-appearing person.
- **Factitious Disorders.** Physical or behavioral symptoms that are voluntarily produced by the individual, apparently in order to play the role of patient and often involving chronic blatant lying.
- **Dissociative Disorders.** Temporary (often sudden) disruptions in the normal functions of consciousness (e.g., loss of memory, consciousness, or identity).
- **Sexual and Gender Identity Disorders.** Difficulty in the expression of normal sexuality (e.g., confusion about gender identity, decreased sexual desire or arousal, sexual acts and fantasies involving the production of suffering or humiliation for either sexual partner, and sexual activity with children or nonconsenting adults).
- **Eating Disorders.** Significant disturbances in eating (e.g., anorexia, binge eating).
- **Sleep Disorders.** Disturbances in the process of sleep (e.g., difficulty in going to sleep or staying asleep, excessive daytime sleepiness, disturbances of the sleep-wake cycle).
- **Impulse Control Disorders Not Elsewhere Classified.** Repeated expression of impulsive acts that lead to physical or financial damage to the individual or another person, and often result in a sense of relief or release of tension (e.g., assaultive acts, stealing objects that are not needed, setting fires, and recurrent maladaptive gambling).
- **Adjustment Disorders.** Persistent emotional or behavioral reactions in response to an identifiable stressor (such as a negative life event). The reactions may be dominated by depressed mood, anxiety, and withdrawal.
- **Other Conditions That May Be a Focus of Clinical Attention.** Presence of one or more psychological or behavioral factors that adversely affect a general medical condition; medication-induced movement disorders; family relationship problems; problems related to abuse or neglect; extended bereavement reactions.

Axis II Categories Personality disorders and mental retardation. These conditions begin in childhood or adolescence and continue into adult life without much change. Axes I and II are separated so that when individuals are evaluated, these continuing characteristics, which may affect personality or cognitive, social, or motor functioning, will be taken into consideration. Axis II may also be used to indicate prominent maladaptive personality features that do not meet the threshold for a personality disorder. Axis II may not distinguish clearly enough between personality styles or traits that are commonly seen in the general population but appear to cause few problems for the individual and the rigid, clearly maladaptive personality styles that lead to personal unhappiness or ineffectiveness. Imperfect as it may be, however, this attempt to include personality factors in psychiatric classification is a step forward.

- **Personality Disorders.** Pervasive and enduring patterns of maladaptive behavior and thought that begin by early adulthood, often interfere with normal interpersonal relationships, and reduce personal effectiveness. Subjective distress may or may not be present. Personality disorders specified in DSM-IV include:

  paranoid personality disorder
  schizoid personality disorder
  schizotypal personality disorder
  antisocial personality disorder
  borderline personality disorder
  histrionic personality disorder
  narcissistic personality disorder
  avoidant personality disorder
  dependent personality disorder
  obsessive-compulsive personality disorder
  personality disorder not otherwise specified.

- **Mental Retardation.** Disorders marked by delays in development in many areas. These disorders are predominantly characterized by pervasive impaired intellectual functioning as well as specific learning problems. Intelligence levels range from mild (IQ ranging from 50 to 70) to profound (IQ below 20 or 25).

Evaluation of the DSM Multiaxial Approach

DSM-III, DSM-III-R, and DSM-IV differ from earlier classification manuals in their emphasis on describing clinical problems rather than interpreting them and listing specific criteria for each diagnostic category. This change came about as a result of widespread concern that psychiatric diagnoses are often unreliable because they are based on guesses about the underlying causes of problems. A review of earlier diagnostic systems will illustrate the path clinicians have taken in classifying abnormal behavior.

DSM-I, published in 1952, and DSM-II, published in 1968, were significantly smaller volumes than DSM-III, DSM-III-R, and DSM-IV. Recent DSM's are so much larger due to the greater scope of maladaptations covered, the greater use of examples of particular classifications, and their intent as a reliable and unambiguous description of disorders. The language of both DSM-I and DSM-II was heavily influenced by psychoanalytic theory, and the manuals focused on internal nonobservable processes. As a result, clinicians' diagnoses often varied greatly. In contrast, the recent DSMs have used much more precise language. Another reason for the superiority of the most recent DSMs is that extensive field trials were carried out in their development. These trials, involving thousands of patients and hundreds of clinicians, made it possible to check for ease of usage and reliability and to correct deficiencies before publication.

Although they represent advances in clinical classification, no one believes that the most recent DSMs are the final word on the subject of diagnosis. Among their limitations are continued reliance on impressionistic clinical judgments (for example, in estimating the severity of a disorder). DSM-IV might best be viewed as a set of guidelines for characterizing clinical problems. It is concerned primarily with the description of these problems.

The time intervals between the several versions of DSM have become progressively shorter. This acceleration is due to rapid advances in knowledge about the various types of maladaptive behavior that must be taken into account in diagnosis and to efforts to improve the reliability of the diagnostic system. Whereas the first multiaxial DSM (DSM-III) represented a major innovation in the concept of classification, DSM-IV reflects the need to fine-tune the diagnostic system. Another important reason for producing DSM-IV such a short time after DSM-III-R was the desirability of an internationally standardized system. Extensive research throughout the world on mental disorders requires that worldwide diagnostic systems be as similar as possible if researchers in all countries are to be able to take advantage of new information. The World Health Organization's International Classification of Diseases (ICD) includes maladaptive behavior as one section and is widely used through much of the world. Over the years, those who developed the ICD and DSM systems have been cooperating and sharing information in an effort to make the systems more similar. Work on DSM-IV was accelerated so that the two systems would have updated versions of increased similarity available at about the same time.

DSM-III and its successors have sought to be quite specific about the criteria for using each diagnostic category. It appears that these manuals have successfully achieved that objective. By emphasizing descriptions of behavior rather than theoretical ideas about its cause, the DSM approach has reduced the amount of inference needed to make a particular diagnosis, and has increased reliability. Not only have recent manuals increased the dimensions for describing particular disorders, they have greatly increased coverage of the range of disorders. This increase is especially evident in the extensive coverage of childhood disorders.

Although much more research is needed in order to make a definitive evaluation of the DSM multiaxial approach, practitioners agree that it has been successful in facilitating communication among clinicians and contributing to more reliable classification. For example, prior to DSM-III clinicians often complained about the difficulty, using available classification criteria, of distinguishing between certain affective disorders and schizophrenia. Furthermore, as a consequence of too-vague criteria, diagnoses of schizophrenia were made more often than this disorder actually occurs in the population. Evidence since introduction of DSM-III suggests that this overrepresentation of schizophrenia diagnoses has been much reduced (Adamson, 1989).

It is possible that the comprehensiveness of the multiaxial approach is a mixed blessing. Clinicians show a high level of agreement in classifying patients on broad general diagnostic categories, such as depression and juvenile delinquency, and less consistency in classifying finer subdivisions within these general categories (Rutter & Shaffer, 1980). Much research will be required in order to determine the breadth and specificity needed to maximize the value of current multiaxial approaches.

Critics have argued that recent DSMs have paid too much attention to how a person appears at a particular point in time (for example, upon admission to a clinic or hospital) and not enough to his or her prior history and developmental crises. The DSM system has also been criticized for providing little information about the causes of abnormal behavior. Several writers argue that since the publication of DSM-III, etiology has not been given sufficient attention in classification, and that both description of and inferences about the processes involved in maladaptive behavior are needed (Vaillant, 1984).

Despite these criticisms, most practitioners recognize the unique value of the multiaxial approach. By including axes that pertain to severity of stress and previous level of adjustment, as well as to long-lasting personality patterns, DSM-IV reflects the need for integrating what is known about people's vulnerabilities, assets, and stressful life events with what is observed in their behavior. Efforts are continuing to improve the existing axes in the light both of the research findings and of the needs of practicing clinicians.

Despite the shortcomings in the axis system, there nevertheless seems little doubt that DSM-IV is an improvement over previous diagnostic systems. Many of its limitations grow out of limitations in our understanding of what mental health and mental disorder are. Any classification system can be no better than available knowledge and attitudes about what is being classified. As we will see later in this chapter, experts who have devoted their entire careers to studying a specific topic such as schizophrenia have strong differences of opinion about what types of behavior should be examined. The greatest contributions of DSM-III, DSM-III-R, and DSM-IV may turn out to be the new knowledge that results from the arguments they have stimulated.

Research on Classification

Research on the classification of abnormal behavior has focused on the role of clinical judgment in classification and on the effects of the labeling process. Information is also needed on how complex a classification system should be. How many categories should it have? Which variables must be assessed in making a diagnosis? Which variables should be optional? In what way should an individual's life story be taken into account in assessing his or her present behavior? The psychoanalytic perspective might lead to the conclusion that information about early childhood is essential to assessment, whereas a behavioristic viewpoint might emphasize a detailed description of present-day behavior. A diagnosis is not simply a label that is attached to a client by a clinician; it is a complex product of present knowledge and opinion about maladaptive behavior. As such, diagnosis is not an immutable process. Rather, it changes with advances in knowledge and alterations in what society defines as a problem.

Earlier we mentioned the importance of achieving agreement among clinicians in classifying cases. Until about 20 years ago, diagnosis was handicapped by the low reliability of diagnostic agreement. **Reliability** is concerned with whether a classification decision is reproducible, either by the same clinician at a different time or by different clinicians. In order to have high reliability the defining characteristics of a class or the criteria that must be met in order to establish class membership must be clearly defined. For example, it must be clearly specified which specific symptoms all patients in this class would have in common and which symptoms would cause their exclusion from the class. Reliability can be assessed with several specific statistical tools. Often, reliability is simply assessed by the

degree of agreement when the same patient is diagnosed by several different clinicians. However, simply using the percentage of agreement overlooks the possibility that some clinical agreement might occur by chance. A clinician who sees schizophrenia in a high percentage of his or her cases will show a fair amount of chance agreement with other clinicians in using the label of schizophrenia. A reliability index, the **kappa statistic,** corrects the amount of observed agreement for the amount of chance agreement. This correction is based on information about the overall frequency with which clinicians use particular classifications. By correcting for chance agreement, use of the kappa statistic provides a truer estimate of diagnostic reliability and has become the standard method for indexing agreement in studies relating to classification.

Validity is concerned with the appropriateness of the classification system—whether or not the classification groups together people whose symptoms arise from the same causes and respond to similar treatments. An ideal demonstration of the validity of a diagnosis requires similar causes and mechanisms underlying the symptoms of all those with the same diagnosis. A more usual way to view validity is the predictability of clinical course and outcome and the most effective treatment approach. The highly specific descriptions of most DSM categories have greatly increased the reliability of the diagnoses made using the system, but the validity of many of DSM classifications has yet to be fully established. One of the reasons for this is that not enough is known about the causes of many disorders. It is likely for instance, that some DSM-IV categories may contain disorders with very different causes despite the similar symptoms that are the basis for the classification. Another problem is that the DSM system allows a diagnosis if the person has only a certain number of symptoms from a much larger list. This means that two people who have the same diagnosis may have just a few symptoms in common. Determining more about the similarity of causation within the same diagnostic group is currently a major focus of research.

Clinical Judgment A variety of data go into classification statements. In arriving at a diagnosis, the clinician goes through a series of problem-solving and decision-making steps. The more complete and standardized the data and the more explicit the intervening cognitive steps, the greater the reliability of the diagnosis. This holds true whether we are talking (1) about a clinician making a diagnosis on two different occasions using the same data or (2) about two clinicians making independent diagnoses on the basis of the same information.

Studies of clinical judgment have been carried out in order to determine just how the clinician's role affects the reliability of classification. When diagnostic criteria are described clearly and intensive training is given in their use, and when the clinicians using them employ comparable methods, the reliability of diagnoses increases significantly. Additional factors also affect clinical judgments. One such factor is that certain disorders are more easily classified than others (for example, the reliability of diagnoses for organic brain disorders is higher than that of diagnoses for schizophrenia). Irrelevant or tangential information, such as labels, may throw a clinician off course. In addition, the attitudes and characteristics of diagnosticians often influence the judgments they make. A study using the 10th revision of the International Classification of Diseases (ICD-10) showed that explicit diagnostic criteria similar to those provided by DSM-IV contributed to agreement among clinicians in patient classification (Sartorius et al., 1993). However, there was less agreement regarding personality disorders than most other conditions because the participating clinicians found the categories of these disorders somewhat difficult to use.

Research on clinical judgment suggests that even though they may not carry out formal research projects, clinicians use a research process in making their diagnoses. Like more research-oriented scientists, clinicians make observations, integrate them, and draw conclusions on the basis of the evidence they have gathered.

Evidence gathered in formal research on clinical judgment has helped identify factors that contribute to disagreement and error in day-to-day clinical research. Among them are the following:

1. *Client factors.* The client is not a constant. In fact, he or she may contribute to differences in clinical opinion by behaving in different ways at different times. If one clinician assesses an individual who is in the midst of an alcoholic delirium, while another clinician's assessment is carried out several days after the delirium has lifted, differences in classification would not be surprising.
2. *Method factors.* Clinicians who use different assessment techniques might describe people who are actually similar as being different.
3. *Criteria factors.* Clinicians who have different standards for classifying cases might differ in their diagnoses.
4. *Clinician factors.* Clinicians differ in how they assess data. Personality differences among clinicians, as well as differences in training and theoretical orientation, influence the clinician's information processing.

Clinicians differ in how they process information and in how much they can keep track of. Computers may prove to be valuable aids to clinical assessment because they are capable of scanning and retaining larger amounts of information than a human diagnostician can. Whether or not clinicians are aided by computers, the process by which they form judgments and make decisions is an important part of research on classification and the clinical process. One variable, whose role in clinical encounters is increasingly being recognized, the clinician's cultural sensitivity, is discussed in Box 4-1.

Classification is a necessary first step toward introducing order into discussions of the nature, causes, and treatment of maladaptive behavior. It is essential to determine and to increase the reliability and validity of the labels attached by clinicians to patterns of maladaptive behavior and to people.

Assessment: The Basis of Classification

While efforts are made to improve classification systems, clinical workers must employ currently available methods in their work. The major methods used to assess behavior in clinical settings include interviews, psychological tests, and behavioral assessment. Assessment methods of other aspects of individual's behavior have also been developed and are discussed later in the chapter.

Structured interviews are used primarily in two settings in which information obtained in a standard way is particularly important. One of these settings is in large institutions where a client will be assigned to treatment only after initial information is collected and a group of health professionals have discussed a diagnosis and agreed on an initial treatment plan. In this type of setting it is especially important that information on all clients be obtained in a uniform manner so that the conference concerning the treatment plan is minimally affected by the particular person who gathered the data and also so that all needed information is likely to be obtained. The other major setting for structured interviews is one in which research is being carried out. Again the ability to obtain client data that can be meaningfully compared with data on many other individuals is of crucial importance. In contrast to these situations, clinicians who will carry out the treatment program themselves often develop individual approaches to gathering data. They may find that a standardized interview makes it more difficult to begin forming a relationship with the client. In addition, they may fit their interview approach to their own personalities and to information they have personally found important in treating other clients.

Although there is agreement about the need to develop valid ways of characterizing individuals, clinicians disagree on how this can best be accomplished. Because no single assessment tool is considered foolproof, assessment is commonly approached in more than

Cultural Sensitivity, Ethnic Identity, and the Clinical Process

The need for a more culturally sensitive classification system, one that acknowledges the role cultural factors play in mental disorders and clinical judgments about them, is a topic of much debate. It has been noted that while religious and spiritual dimensions of culture are among the most important factors in human experience, psychiatric classification systems have tended to ignore them (Lukoff, and others, 1992). However, DSM-IV does deal with cultural variations in the expression of maladaptive behavior by noting culture-related features of particular disorders.

Ethnic identity is a significant cultural variable that influences a person's self-concept and sense of belonging with other members of an ethnic group, based on shared characteristics. It can influence a person's willingness to seek help concerning a mental health problem and the way in which the problem is described to a professional worker. As the following case demonstrates, ethnic identity can also play a role in the nature of the problem. The case involves a 7-year-old, fourth-generation Japanese American who negatively evaluates physical characteristics of her ethnic group.

The girl frequently did not want to go to school and was withdrawn at home and at school. When she was at school, she avoided playing with the other children,

did not participate in class, and sought to go home early. Her family sent her to therapy. During play therapy, she would select a doll with dark hair and another with blonde hair. The two dolls would battle. The blonde doll would always be victorious and the dark-haired doll would be knocked to the ground. When the girl picked stuffed animals, the light-colored animals always won. She "eventually revealed that children at school made fun of her "tiny eyes' and black hair and did not pick her for sports teams. [Her play in therapy] sessions indicated that she wished she were not Japanese and felt anger toward her parents, blaming them for the differences in her eyes. [She reasoned that] if her parents were not Japanese, she would not be experiencing the ostracism she now faced." (Nagata, 1989, p. 103)

This case shows the need for clinicians to be sensitive to cultural differences and to see the world the way the patient does. The following comments by a psychologist who works in a culturally diverse urban setting exemplify clinicians' growing recognition of the role of ethnic identity in clinical interactions:

People with different ethnic backgrounds often pose special challenges for me. They may have had unusual or harmful experiences. For example, the environments that African American children

encounter are less likely than those of white children to promote the skills needed to do well on IQ tests. People from certain ethnic or cultural groups may come for psychological testing or therapy with certain assumptions, concerns, and beliefs that I need to be aware of. Otherwise, I might end up making assumptions about them and the nature of their problems that are unwarranted. I've had some African American and Asian American patients, some of whose personality characteristics seemed unusual. When I got to know these people well, I realized that what seemed unusualness to me was as much or more a reflection of their cultural backgrounds as to their psychological problems.

The following comments by a psychiatrist working for the first time in a rural Appalachian setting reinforce the need for clinicians to question assumptions that they might make about regional differences:

Religious and folk beliefs—which some call superstitions—of Appalachian people are fascinating but do not seem to be as strong a guiding force as I had originally assumed. I have come to appreciate how much rural people take care of their own. Many mentally disturbed patients have help from family and people in the community to make sure they take their medications, eat properly, and are living comfortably. Working with the people of Appalachia offers many rewards: a rich and diverse culture; a refreshing, interconnected life; and patients who, to me,

one way in order to yield a more complete and accurate description of the individual.

Psychological tests differ from interviews in that they restrict the client's freedom of expression. Just as it is easier to quantify and compare scores on a multiple choice test than on an essay test, the responses obtained on psychological tests can be more readily quantified and compared than the more open-ended and unstructured responses obtained in interviews. A tester's observation of how individuals approach particular test items often provides valuable insights into significant aspects of their everyday lives (Table 4-3). To achieve a well-rounded picture of the individual, most clinicians interpret assessment results in light of behavioral observations made in less restricted situations.

The Interview

The interview continues to be the most widely used assessment tool. Clinical interviews are of two types: assessment and therapeutic. The purpose of the **assessment** or **diagnostic interview** is to gather information and assess behavior. On the basis of the client's verbal and nonverbal behavior during the interview, the interviewer tries to understand why the client is seeking help and what, from a therapeutic standpoint might be done. The **therapeutic interview** (or therapy session) occurs after a preliminary assessment has been made. Its aim is to modify maladaptive behavior and attitudes.

Interviews usually involve two individuals, the inter-

Box 4-1

Therapists need to take into account the ethnic identities and viewpoints of their patients.

are surprisingly hopeful, optimistic, and flexible.

There has not been enough research on the roles played by ethnic and cultural differences in diagnosis and treatment of abnormal behavior. In some respects, members of minority groups may view and react to the world just like all other people; in other respects, they may see it differently (for example, as a result of exposure to racism). In recent years, personality and maladaptive behavior research has increased concerning these similarities and differences and the impact of feeling different from most people in one's community (Jackson, 1991; Uba, 1994). Research on cross-cultural comparisons of emotional disturbance and its expression is also increasing. For example, it has been

shown that depression often has very different meanings and forms of expression in different societies. Most cases of depression worldwide are experienced and expressed in bodily terms of aching backs, headaches, fatigue, and a wide assortment of other somatic symptoms that lead patients to regard this condition as a physical problem. Only in contemporary Western societies is depression seen principally as an intrapsychic experience ("I feel blue") and, even in these societies, many cases of depression are still lived and coped with as physical conditions (Jenkins, and others, 1991).

Comparisons of Asian American groups with other groups in the population has yielded valuable information. The preponderance of research has indicated that many Asian Americans tend to somaticize their mental health prob-

lems (Uba, 1994). That is, it seems that they manifest their worries, guilt feelings, and strong negative emotions (such as depression) as physical complaints. The tendency to somaticize mental health problems may be a reflection of Asian American cultural values that emphasize avoiding shame and maintaining the honor of the family. Somatic problems do not carry the stigma or negative social consequences that psychological problems do. Perhaps Asian Americans present their problems as somatic rather than emotional problems because they are more comfortable talking about physical problems than psychological ones. Clinicians need to take account of the meanings people in various groups attach to expressing emotion-laden thoughts and having certain kinds of difficulties.

---

viewer and the client, although other people, such as family members, are sometimes included. Family members may also be interviewed separately. Treatment decisions are often based largely on the data gathered in an assessment interview, which may begin as a telephone call and then be followed up in a face-to-face setting. Table 4-4 lists four important components of the clinical interview.

Content of the Interview Assessment interviewers seek to identify problems and determine the nature and extent of maladaptive behavior. Typically, interviewers begin by trying to find out how the client describes, understands, and interprets his or her problem. In some cases, the complaint is nonspecific, such as "I feel tense

and worried all the time." In other cases, it may seem deceptively clear, as in "My child is hyperactive—I can't control him." Then the interviewer may inquire into the history of the problem. In the course of obtaining this information, the interviewer may get a better understanding of the stressing agents present in the client's life as the problem was developing.

Initial interviews often are relatively unstructured. Depending on the problem and how it is described, the interviewer may have to move back and forth among a number of topics. However, an attempt is made to answer the following questions:

1. *Who is the client?* That is, what is his or her name, age, ethnic and cultural background, marital status,

What do testers notice? In addition to the test responses themselves, testers are attentive to how clients approach tasks, how they react emotionally, and how they relate to the tester. These are some of the behavioral observations the tester may note and use in writing a case report.

1. How persistent is the client? Keeps trying? Gives up easily?
2. Is the client able to concentrate on the task at hand?
3. What is the client's attitude toward the test? Casual or serious? Competitive?
4. What is the client's problem-solving style? Methodical? Reasoned? Impulsive? Fragmented?
5. What emotions does the client exhibit? Is he or she anxious about being tested? Angry? Depressed?
6. How does the client react to failure or possible failure? Gets upset at failures? Expects to fail?
7. How does the client react to the tester? As an authority figure? As an adversary?
8. How verbally expressive is the client? Articulate? Monosyllabic?

and occupation? What led to his or her decision to obtain professional help?

2. *How does the client think and feel about life at this time?* What are the client's preoccupations and feelings?
3. *What is the history of the problem and the client's developmental background?* Depending on the particular problem, an inquiry might be made into the physical and emotional climate of the home during the client's infancy and childhood, as well as the client's sleep patterns, physical and motor development, and sexual and social development.
4. *What is the client's present psychological state?* What is noteworthy about the client's speech, thought, judgment, cooperativeness, and social skills?
5. *How vulnerable and how resilient is the client?* What are the client's assets and liabilities?

During an assessment interview, many aspects of behavior must be observed and noted. These include the client's general appearance and grooming, voice and speech patterns, the kinds of thoughts described, as well as facial expression, posture, and style of movement.

People with serious problems state facts, opinions, attitudes, and, in some cases, distortions and lies. They behave in a variety of ways: they may sigh, gesture, avert their eyes, tap their feet, smile, or grimace at the interviewer. As a consequence of this flood of responses, the interviewer usually can extract and use only a small per-

centage of the data presented during the interview. On the other hand, some clients hesitate to discuss their problems openly and provide very little information. Answers to questions such as, "How does your wife get on your nerves?" can differ widely in honesty, clarity, and feeling. Unanticipated reactions by the client and indications that he or she is not in contact with reality must be noted. In the following case, a woman is talking about a physician she had wished to consult.

> *Patient: I wanted to see him desperately, and called once and then again. I got him the third time. But did he come? No, he didn't. But he should have, shouldn't he?*
> *Interviewer: I don't know. Can you tell me more about . . .*
> *Patient: You're interested in part of my story, aren't you?*
> *Interviewer: Yes.*
> *Patient: Would you like me to write it down for you?*
>
> *The interviewer gives the patient paper and pencil and the patient proceeds to write the following: "alpha, beta, gamma, delta, epsilon, epsilon, bactrim, bacterium, back." The patient concluded by writing her signature.*

There is no apparent connection between the failure to make contact with the physician, the Greek alphabet, and the antibiotic bactrim. During the interview, the interviewer noted several indicators of incoherence and delusions as the patient talked about her life.

Interviewers need to observe the relationship between their clients' verbal and nonverbal behaviors. Often what interviewers hear contradicts what they see. The client's verbal manner may be calm and dispassion-

While these components are found in virtually all types of clinical interviews, they are especially pertinent to the diagnostic interview.

1. *Rapport.* Rapport relates to how the interviewer and client relate to each other. To achieve rapport, the interviewer seeks to put the client at ease and show interest in the problem being discussed.
2. *Technique.* Depending on the client and the problem, the interviewer selects techniques to build rapport and to obtain information. Techniques range from open-ended questions to a tactful challenge of something the client has said.
3. *Mental status.* To determine the mental level at which the client is functioning, the interviewer will evaluate his or her answers to questions. Are they clear or fuzzy, pleasant or angry, reality-oriented or full of strange and bizarre ideas?
4. *Diagnosis.* The interviewer is continually revising his or her formulation of the client's problems and personality. This process includes a diagnosis.

ate even though tension is evident from nonverbal signs such as sweating and handwringing. In some cases, gestures, movements, and facial expressions yield clues to the sources of a client's anxiety. Experienced clinicians are adept at observing nuances of behavior that clients are unaware of or believe they are suppressing successfully, as can be seen in the following interview:

> *During the interview she held her small son on her lap. The child began to play with his genitals. The mother, without looking directly at the child, moved his hand away and held it securely for a while. Later in the interview the mother was asked what she ordinarily did when the child played with himself. She replied that he never did this—he was a very "good" boy. She was evidently entirely unconscious of what had transpired in the very presence of the interviewer.*
>
> —Maccoby and Maccoby, 1954, p. 484

Another interviewer recorded the frequency of a client's "blouse-clutching" behavior during an assessment interview (see Figure 4-2), and noted a particularly high frequency of this behavior during one portion of the interview (Mahl, 1968). The client had at that time been describing how, at the age of 8, she and her twin sister had been told that they had "killed their mother" during their birth.

The Role of the Interviewer Every type of assessment involves taking a behavior sample for the purpose of predicting future behavior. Much of the behavior that is sampled in an interview is self-description. To facilitate the planning of treatment, the interviewer must establish valid relationships between the responses made during the interview and the client's behavior in current or future life situations. If the interview behavior is not representative of the client's characteristic response ten-

dencies, inappropriate treatment decisions may be made. The interviewer attempts to construct a situation that, within a short period, provides reflections of complex lifelong patterns.

In most applied settings assessment interviewers make mental and written notes, subjectively interpreting the behavior sample as it unfolds. A truly objective evaluation of an interview, however, cannot focus on the client alone. Because each interview involves a developing and distinctive relationship between the interviewer and the client, their characteristics jointly influence what takes place during the interview. Research supports clinical impressions that interviewers are a major factor in the interview. Are they accurate observers of the client's behavior? Do they unduly influence the behavior of the person being interviewed? These questions arise frequently in discussions of interviewing. Interviewers don't always note or interpret correctly much of what goes on in an interview. In both assessment and therapeutic interviews, the interviewer's behavior may influence the data obtained, as well as how those data are analyzed. The following are some interviewer characteristics that might influence the course of an interview and its content:

- age
- gender
- ethnicity
- professional background
- interviewing style
- personality pattern
- attitudes and values
- expectations

As the following case suggests, the unique characteristics and styles that both the client and interviewer bring to the clinical situation make it difficult to perfectly standardize clinical interviews.

> *The interviewer knew nothing about Robert Hatton except that he was 19 years old, had just begun his studies at a large university, and had a skin condition of apparently recent origin. The skin condition included redness, breaking out in large welts, and itchiness. Hatton had come to the Student Health Service for the skin condition, but the ointment prescribed gave only minor, temporary relief. Because the physician who treated him suspected that the problem might be a result—at least in part—of psychological factors, she recommended that he talk with a clinical psychologist who was a consultant on the staff of the Student Health Service in order to investigate whether any psychological factors were playing a role in his symptoms.*
>
> *The first thing Hatton mentioned to the psychologist was the skin condition, how annoying and disruptive it was*

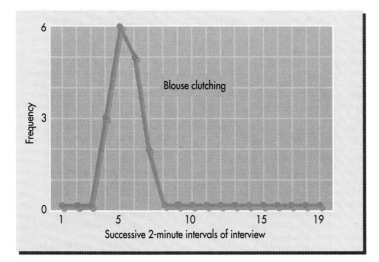

Figure 4-2 Frequency of one nonverbal response (blouse clutching) during an interview.

because of the incessant itching, and his puzzlement at being referred to a psychologist. During the initial interview he sweated a lot, occasionally had to catch his breath, and tapped his foot continually. Noting the stigma Hatton seemed to feel about talking with what he called "a mental specialist," the psychologist made the following internal analysis of the situation: "If Robert's skin condition does have a psychological component, he has to learn that it is okay to talk to me. My main job right now is to listen and not to ask a lot of questions that make Robert think he's crazy."

The psychologist did ask some questions ("Have you had skin problems in the past? Under what circumstances?" "How do you like it at the university?"), but mainly she listened patiently, avoiding making quick judgments about what the client had to say, and carefully observed what the client said and did, as well as what topics seemed to be upsetting to him. While avoiding aloofness, the psychologist maintained a detached but friendly attitude. When Hatton expressed concern about his ability to succeed at the university, the clinician did not say, "You're obviously intelligent enough to be very successful at this university," even though Hatton's vocabulary and manner of expressing himself were obviously outstanding. (She mused to herself, "What good would it do if I told Robert what all his friends and relatives tell him? What he is saying is that he's scared and really is worried about flunking out. I've got to let him know I realize what he is going through. The flip reassurance of other people hasn't done him one bit of good.")

The interview was uncomfortable for both Hatton and the psychologist. Hatton was tense, and there were long pauses during which he seemed unable to think of anything to say. Each of these pauses posed a conflict for the interviewer. ("If the pause is too long and too uncomfortable, he might decide not to come to see me again. On the other hand, what clients say after pauses is often very significant. I've got to steer along just the right path with Robert.") The interviewer noted whenever the client was experiencing too much anxiety or felt that he needed a show of interest and support.

The clinical psychologist had seen many cases in which physical problems (such as skin conditions) were related to the stress of university life. But she did not want to pigeonhole Hatton. Her main goal in the initial interview was to establish a relationship of mutual trust with him. She liked him, wanted to help him, and thought she could. But the first task was to accept him as a likable, unique person and hope that he would want to come back. Apparently her approach worked, because Hatton came back four times, as a result of which much information was brought out and the clinical picture became clearer. What emerged was a person of exceptional potential for whom the university created an intense stress because of the need he felt to be worthy of all the sacrifices his family was making for him. While he wanted to reward his parents for their help, he was also deeply angered at the way in which they blithely assumed he would make Phi Beta Kappa if he avoided being lazy.

On the basis of the series of interviews, the psychologist pieced together a picture of an intense stress reaction because of all the pressures to which Hatton felt he was being subjected. The psychologist did not know for sure what had caused the skin condition, but she felt that it might have been an accompaniment of the anxious thoughts connected with going to the university. Her recommendation to Hatton and to the referring physician was that psychotherapy might be helpful. Because the student health service did not provide psychotherapy sessions, the psychologist recommended to Hatton that he see a psychotherapist who might help him decide on his own goals in life, rather than uncritically accept his parents' goals for him. After a series of 20 therapy sessions, Hatton was much less anxious, his skin condition was gone, and he felt more accepting of both himself and his parents.

The clinical psychologist who talked with Hatton was not following a standard interview format, nor did she feel under pressure to uncover a lot of factual material. Rather, she quickly saw the need to establish an accepting working relationship with someone who came to the interview with hesitancy and reservations. Such a relationship-building orientation is valuable in most clinical interviews.

One important interviewing skill is the ability to size up a situation quickly and to devise an appropriate clinical strategy in light of the assessment. In the following case, the interviewer quickly picked up on the patient's denial of having a problem and turned the focus to how others might have perceived the problem. The 25-year-old patient was a man diagnosed as experiencing a manic episode, a condition marked by a euphoric, hyperactive state and impaired judgment.

Patient:	By the way, before we start, I just wanted to tell you that everything I say, there's no bullshit. It's the truth.
Interviewer:	Why don't we begin by your telling me exactly what it was that got you into the hospital?
Patient:	I was transferred from City Hospital.
Interviewer:	O.K., what got you into that hospital?
Patient:	I was pretending to be an undercover cop.
Interviewer:	You were pretending to be an undercover cop? How come?
Patient:	How come? I had just seen the movie Serpico. And I knew I could do a better job.
Interviewer:	Was it recently that you saw the film?
Patient:	About two months ago.
Interviewer:	This had been going on for some time then?

Patient:	Yeah.
Interviewer:	So, how long has it been since you were last feeling well?
Patient:	Last feeling well? Right now!
Interviewer:	You've been feeling well, then?
Patient:	Oh, yeah. I've been feeling well for the past . . . I've been feeling well for a long time.
Interviewer:	However, going into the hospital means that other people are not certain that you're well.
Patient:	Of course! That's what I've been dealing with.
Interviewer:	Well, then, let's rephrase the question. How long has it been since others have felt that there was something the matter with you?
Patient:	That began about three months ago. I was telling my sister that I could take any amount of cyanide or mescaline, or any other drug, and that it wouldn't have any effect on me at all. She didn't believe me.

The Structured Interview We noted earlier that standardized procedures increase the reliability of classifications of abnormal behavior. This makes a lot of sense, since standardization guarantees that clinicians will at least ask the same questions of each person they interview. An argument against standardized interviews is that they do not give the clinician the flexibility needed to form a productive relationship with a client. However, there is no reason for a clinical worker not to use a standardized format in one interview and a more flexible one in another.

Structured, or standardized, interviews use a standard series of questions to determine whether specific symptoms are present. Standardization is achieved by providing the interviewer with a glossary of symptom definitions, a series of questions pertinent to symptoms, a set of topics requiring information, and cut-off points that indicate when to stop probing on a particular topic. The clinician also is given instructions for rating, in numerical terms, the presence and severity of symptoms. Most structured interviews permit the interviewer to depart from the standardized form under specified circumstances. The interviewer also has the option of pursuing lines of inquiry (including a return to a former line of questioning or a jump to a completely different section) that are suggested by the client's responses.

The Diagnostic Interview Schedule The **Diagnostic Interview Schedule** (DIS) illustrates the potential of the structured interview (Malgady and others, 1992; Robins and others, 1981). The DIS is designed to permit diagnosis of selected disorders, such as panic disorder. A person who has a panic disorder has recurrent anxiety attacks that often occur unpredictably, though certain situations, such as riding on a bus, may become associated with a panic attack. Panic attacks are noted for their frequency, severity, and symptoms that include sweating, trembling, faintness, and heart palpitations. The section of the DIS that pertains to panic disorder provides the following questions and offers procedures for interpreting the answers and deriving the appropriate classification.

- Did a panic attack occur?
- How many attacks have occurred?
- What are the symptoms?
- Are the attacks repetitive rather than isolated?
- Are the attacks characteristic of the person's life rather than confined to a brief, atypical period?
- At what age did the attacks begin?
- Are the attacks explainable as symptoms of another disorder?
- Is the person tense, nervous, or high-strung between attacks?

The DIS has continued to evolve and now includes procedures, probes, and criteria appropriate for use with specific clusters of symptoms. New clusters are added periodically. Questions are asked not only about symptoms but also about recent and past experiences associated with their onset. For example, in the case of bulimia, whose main symptom is binge eating, questions are asked about the types of food eaten, the respondent's mood during and after the binge, the environment in which the eating is done, how the binges are terminated, associated weight gain, and efforts to prevent weight gain. The onset and most recent occurrence of the disorder are determined from the dates of the first and most recent binges.

The DIS can be employed by professional and nonprofessional interviewers who have been trained in its use. Table 4-5 lists examples of some of the types of interview questions used. Training (a week-long course), supervision, quality control in the use of the interview, and periodic retraining sessions are recommended with the use of the DIS. Programs for computer scoring of interview data are available. Studies are being carried out to determine the feasibility of using computers either to directly administer the DIS or to aid the interviewer in administering it.

Research has shown that both professional and nonprofessional DIS users tend to agree with each other and with the impressions gained by clinicians in non-DIS psychiatric interviews (Helzer et al., 1985). While the goal of an instrument like the DIS is to assess the occurrence of specific symptoms, determining whether that

TABLE 4–5
Examples of Questions Used in Structured Interviews

TABLE 4–5
Examples of Questions Used in Structured Interviews

How old were you the first time you were bothered by these particular fears?

Has there ever been a period of two weeks or more when you felt worthless, sinful, or guilty?

Have you ever gotten into physical fights while drinking?

For how many weeks, months, or years did you continue to have no interest in an activity that had meant a lot to you before?

Has there ever been a period of two weeks or more when you had a lot more trouble concentrating than is normal for you?

Has there ever been a period of two weeks or more when you wanted to die?

goal has been achieved is not a simple matter as there is no objective and absolute standard against which to measure results. Nevertheless, clear specification of diagnostic definitions is a major achievement because it makes possible uniform diagnostic methods for diverse populations and places.

Instruments like the DIS, based on specific clinical criteria, have the potential to make comparability across studies a reality. However, much more research will be needed to determine whether this potential can be fully realized. Research on the DIS and similar instruments is proceeding at an accelerating pace. One of the findings of that research is that lay interviewers (that is, nonprofessionals) are able to use the DIS in a reliable fashion and that their judgments tend to agree with those of professionals (Helzer et al., 1987).

Structured diagnostic interviews vary in the degree to which the interview is structured. The **Structured Clinical Interview** for DSM (SCID) is less structured than the DIS and encourages the interviewer to ask follow-up questions based on clinical judgment. Its reliability in making diagnoses appears to be satisfactory (Spitzer et al., 1992; Williams et al., 1992).

Intelligence Tests

Intelligence tests were the first widely recognized psychological assessment tool. During the latter part of the nineteenth century, intelligence was equated with fast reflexes and sensitivity to the environment. Efforts to assess intelligence therefore relied heavily on sensory and other discrimination tasks. The English scientist Francis Galton sought to evaluate intelligence by measuring such things as reaction time, ability to discriminate between weights, sensitivity to pain, and ability to differentiate tones.

As the study of intelligence has evolved, it has come to be thought of as having two components: general intelligence, demonstrated by a global capacity to solve problems, and specific abilities, such as spatial perception. In examining intelligence, psychologists have focused on two main areas. One area is theoretical and is broken down into three general categories: what intelligence is, where it comes from, and how it works. The second area is practical—the goal of constructing tests to measure characteristics that can be used to predict future achievements. The tests that psychologists construct are related to their theories of intelligence. For example, theories about the relationship between brain damage and perceptual and motor skills have resulted in efforts to measure deficits in these skills (see Figure 4-3).

The Binet Tests In the late nineteenth and early twentieth centuries, the French psychologist Alfred Binet developed a series of tests that differed noticeably from those that had previously been used to measure intelligence. Binet viewed intelligence as something that grows with age; older children are, on average, more intelligent than younger ones. He sought to measure reasoning, ability to understand and follow directions, and the exercise of judgment or good sense. The child's score on the original Binet test was expressed as a mental level corresponding to the age of normal children whose performance reached the same level.

Later the term "mental age" was substituted for "mental level" and an intelligence quotient (IQ) was computed by dividing the person's test score, or mental age (MA), by his or her chronological age (CA) and multiplying the result by 100. In equation form,

$$IQ = \frac{MA}{CA} \times 100$$

The current test, called the Stanford-Binet scales, has undergone periodic revisions. Stanford-Binet scores are now derived from norms based on how much the individual's score deviates from the mean score for a particular age.

In its first three editions the Binet test yielded one overall score. Use of the Binet-type tests declined beginning in the 1960s, partly because the tasks on the Binet scales did not lend themselves to separate, reliable, quantitative analyses. Perhaps the most important reason for the relative decline in the use of the Binet scales was that they were designed primarily for work with children. As a result of these criticisms, the fourth edition yields several different scores, and many of the items have been rewritten to apply to adults as well as children (Thorndike and others, 1986). The new edition resembles the widely used Wechsler tests, discussed below, more than did the earlier editions.

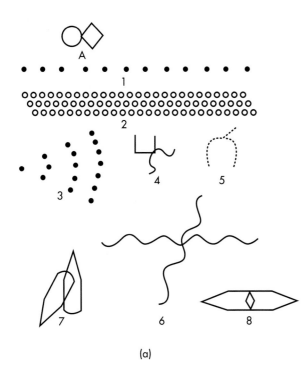

Figure 4-3a Perceptual performance in a case of organic brain damage. The Bender Visual-Motor Gestalt Test (1938) is a deceptively simple task in which the subject is asked to copy geometric forms like these.

SOURCE: From Bender Visual-Motor Gestalt Test, published by American Orthopsychiatric Association, 1938.

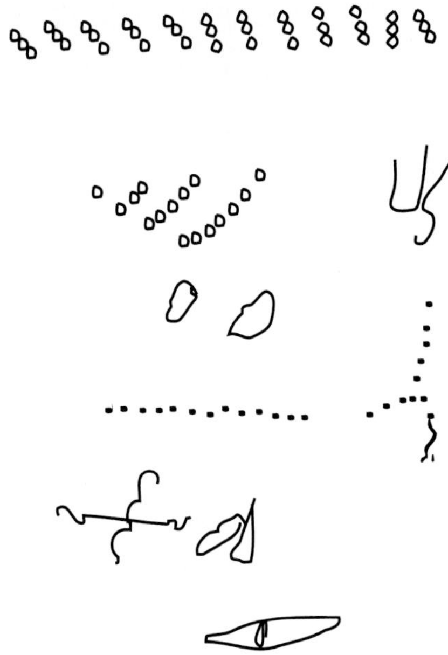

Figure 4-3b The Bender-Gestalt protocol of a patient suffering from organic brain damage.

SOURCE: From Lacks (1984), p. 34. Copyright 1984 by John Wiley & Sons. Reprinted by permission.

The Wechsler Tests David Wechsler (1955, 1958) regarded the Binet tests as deficient because they produced only a single score. He believed that intelligence is an aggregate of abilities and should be measured as such. The current version of the Wechsler test for those 16 years and older, **Wechsler Adult Intelligence Scale-Revised** (WAIS-R), published in 1981, consists of eleven subtests, of which six are verbal and five nonverbal. An important advantage of a test like the WAIS is that in addition to yielding an aggregate score, each of its subtests can be scored separately.

Three IQs are obtained on the Wechsler scales. **Verbal IQ** reflects level of attainment on subtests dealing with general information, comprehension, ability to think in abstract terms, and arithmetic. **Performance IQ** reflects level of attainment on tasks requiring solution of puzzles, substitution of symbols for digits, and reproduction of designs. Finally, the **Full Scale IQ** represents the total score on the test. The WAIS-R is the most popular test for assessing adult intelligence. It is used in clinical, educational, and vocational evaluations of individuals aged 16 and up (Kaufman, 1990).

The success of Wechsler's Adult Intelligence Scales led to the development of the **Wechsler Intelligence Scale for Children** (WISC). The WISC was developed as a downward extension of the adult level WAIS (see Figure 4-4). It uses the same categories of subtests and many of the same items as the WAIS with some easier items added. Like the WAIS, it also provides a Verbal IQ, a Performance IQ, and a Full Scale IQ.

For use with even younger children, the **Wechsler Preschool and Primary Scale of Intelligence** (WPPSI) was developed. This test's revision in 1989 (WPPSI-R) improved the instrument's content, broadened its scope, and updated norms. Just as most subtests on the WISC are downward extensions and adaptations of the WAIS, the majority of the subtests on the WPPSI are downward extensions of the WISC subtests. The additional subtests cover the same general skills as subtests on the WAIS and WISC, but the material is presented differently because of the age of the children to be tested. For example, instead of being asked to use blocks to reproduce a series of designs, the child is asked to copy simple designs using a colored pencil. Like the WAIS and the WISC, the WPPSI provides verbal, performance, and full scale scores that then can be converted into IQ scores.

Figure 4-4 The child is completing one of the puzzle like tasks that make up the object assembly subtest of the WISC.

Kaufman Assessment Battery for Children The **Kaufman Assessment Battery for Children** (K-ABC) has come into frequent use because of concern about the effects of a child's cultural experiences on test results. The K-ABC is designed to incorporate ideas from cognitive psychology and neuropsychology into the assessment of intelligence (Kaufman & Kaufman, 1983). The K-ABC consists of 16 subtests, some for older and some for younger children. The tests fall into several categories: sequential processing, such as remembering a series of digits or hand movements; simultaneous processing, such as arranging a series of related pictures in the correct order; and tests that measure school experience more directly, such as naming pictures of well-known places and objects (see Figure 4-5). Many of the tests do not require a verbal response, and those that do require a few words at most. In most cases, the child can respond by pointing or in other nonverbal ways. The test has been described as a way to learn more about the child's approach to problem-solving and learning tasks. The test's emphasis on short-term memory has been questioned by some critics, but the test authors argue that what is being measured is not memory as such but the sequential and simultaneous processing abilities that are defined as intelligence by cognitive psychologists.

Although the K-ABC tests have been described as being particularly fair to minority children, scores on these tests show the same black–white differences that are seen on other intelligence tests. However, the K-ABC tests do demonstrate that if parental education is taken into account, there is little racial or ethnic difference on many nonverbal reasoning tasks. The similarities in performance are due primarily to the tests' emphasis on short-term memory.

Personality Assessment

Research on personality has stimulated the development of a variety of tests, rating scales, and questionnaires aimed at measuring personality differences. These devices can be useful shortcuts to understanding behavior. Think how long it takes you to get to know a person; in many situations psychologists do not have that kind of time. Personality tests and other assessment methods are used in clinical settings in making diagnoses, estimating the client's strengths and weaknesses, deciding whether treatment is required, and planning the treatment to be used. For example, special assessment aids have been developed to diagnose the types of personality disorders classified on DSM-IV's Axis II. Table 4-6 gives examples of items used to classify particular personality disorders.

Personality Inventories The success of intelligence tests in predicting future achievement led researchers to try to develop similar ways to measure personality. But personality isn't something that can be measured by a total score that is high, medium, or low. The testlike measures used in personality assessment are meant to indicate the types of characteristics that combine to make up an individual's personality.

Rather than testing general knowledge or specific skills, **personality inventories** ask people questions about themselves. These questions may take a variety of forms. When taking such a test, you might have to decide whether each of a series of statements is accurate as a self-description, or you might be asked to respond to a series of true–false questions about yourself and the world. Several inventories require the respondent to rate a set of statements on a scale based on how well they reflect his or her characteristics. Modern personality inventories yield several scores, each of which is intended to represent a distinct aspect of the personality.

Since its introduction in 1943, the **Minnesota Multiphasic Personality Inventory** (MMPI) has been one of the most widely used psychological tests. A revision, entitled MMPI-2, was published in 1989; it consists of 567 items. In developing MMPI-2, the wording of many of the original MMPI items was updated and a number of items were dropped, changed, or added. The standardization of MMPI-2 was superior to that of the original MMPI because of the new normative sample's

(a)

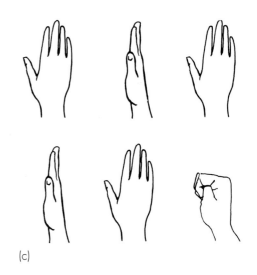

(c)

(b)

(d)

Figure 4-5 Some of the tasks from the Kaufman-ABC. In the Face Recognition subtest, the child is shown a picture of a face, such as (a) for 5 seconds and is then asked to select that same individual from a group picture such as (b). In the Hand Movements subtest the examiner tells the child, "Watch my hand," and after making the series of hand movements, says, "Now, you try it." Two series of movements appropriate for children who are aged two and one-half are illustrated (c). In the Gestalt Closure subtest, the child is shown a series of partially completed drawings such as (d). The task is to name the object pictured, in this case a bird.

greater size, geographic representativeness, and racial balance. Although there is still much work to be done in analyzing the MMPI-2, it appears to be a successful revision and should be used as widely as the original MMPI (Graham, 1993).

The MMPI-2 includes 10 scales related to different groups of clinical disorders (the scales are usually referred to by the abbreviations in parentheses): hypochondriasis (Hs), depression (D), hysteria (Hy), psychopathic deviate (Pd), masculinity-femininity (Mf), paranoia (Pa), psychasthenia (Pt), schizophrenia (Sc), hypomania (Ma), and social introversion (Si). In addition to these standard clinical scales, there are numerous special scales—for example, the 16-item Anger scale reflects irritability, impatience, grouchiness, and hot-

headedness. People who sometimes feel like swearing or smashing things may get high scores on this scale (Butcher, 1990). Scores on MMPI-2 scales can be compared with those of the normal standardization group and samples of reliably diagnosed clinical cases.

Besides the clinical scales, the MMPI-2 also includes several validity or control scales. These were designed to assess test-taking attitudes and response biases that might distort the picture presented by the clinical scale scores alone. High scores on these scales may indicate invalid clinical scale profiles. The validity scales consider the tendency of people to create a favorable impression, and consist of items dealing with minor flaws and weaknesses to which most people are willing to admit. People with high L (or Lie) scores appear

TABLE 4–6
Assessing Axis II Personality Disorders: Sample of Items

Axis II Classification	Sample Item
Paranoid personality disorder	"Certain people will take unfair advantage of me if they get the slightest chance."
Antisocial personality disorder	"Before I was 15 years old, people were already giving me a hard time for breaking the rules at home or school."
Avoidant personality disorder	"When people look at me, I am afraid that they will criticize or make fun of me for being strange or weird."
Obsessive-compulsive personality disorder	"I often get so involved in making each detail of a project absolutely perfect that I never finish."
Schizoid personality disorder	"Other people's feelings just don't move me one way or the other."

Source: Based on Klein et al., 1993

impossibly good and virtuous. The F scale (or validity score) was designed to detect deviant or atypical ways of responding to test items. High scores on this scale indicate those people who describe themselves as having a number of rare and improbable characteristics. While the F scale was included to reflect people's carelessness and confusion in taking the MMPI, it has also come to be seen as a good indicator of psychopathology.

The K scale (or defensiveness score) is more subtle than the L and F scales and covers several different content areas in which a person can deny problems (for example, suspiciousness, worry). Its construction was based on the observation that some open and frank people may obtain high scores on the clinical scales while others who are very defensive may obtain low scores. The K scale was devised to reduce these biasing factors. People who get high K scores are defensive; they tend to answer "False" to items like "I feel bad when others criticize me." K corrections are made on a number of clinical scales in order to compare the scores of people who differ in these tendencies.

In addition to the L, F, and K scales that were part of the original MMPI, MMPI-2 has three new validity scales. The Fb scale is intended to reflect a subject's tendency to answer later items in the test booklet differently than those that occur earlier. The VRIN scale provides an indication of subjects' tendencies to respond inconsistently to MMPI-2 items. Inconsistencies can result when subjects do not read the content of the items and respond instead in a random or near-random way. The TRIN scale was developed to identify subjects who respond indiscriminately by giving either mainly true responses (acquiescence) or mainly false responses (nonacquiescence) without taking into account the meaning of the item statement.

Table 4-7 describes the MMPI-2's clinical and validity scales. The principal application of the MMPI-2 is in deciding how to classify a given case. In general, the greater the number and magnitude of deviant scores on the MMPI-2, the more likely it is that the individual is severely disturbed. In making diagnostic decisions, the MMPI-2 user must be adept at interpreting not only the scores on the individual scales but also the pattern of those scores in a particular person's profile. For example, the assessor cannot assume that a high score on the schizophrenia scale indicates the presence of schizophrenia. Other psychotic groups may show high elevation on this scale, and persons with schizophrenic disorder often score higher on other scales than on the Sc scale.

Rating Scales There are many other personality assessment techniques. The **rating scale** is one of the most venerable and versatile of these. Rating scales present respondents with a question that focuses on a concept, person, or situation and asks them to select from a number of choices. The rating scale is similar in some respects to a multiple-choice test, but its options represent degrees of a particular characteristic.

An example of a rating scale item is "To what degree are you shy?" People might be asked to place this item on a scale ranging from "Not at all" to "Extremely." They can do this graphically by placing a check mark at an appropriate point on a continuum. Rating scales can be used to rate other people's behavior as well as one's own. For instance, a teacher might use rating scales to rate his or her students. In this case the item above might read "To what degree is this student shy?" An example of this use of rating scales in clinical work is the assessment of children's ability to pay attention to what is going on around them and to exercise self-control. The degree to which children possess these abilities is an indicator of their personal development. Many clinical problems in children are related to the inability to delay responding until the desired time, to plan activities, and to engage in socially appropriate behavior. Kendall and Wilcox (1978) devised a convenient series of rating scales to assess children's self-control. Their measure, the **Behavior Rating Scale for Children,** has

TABLE 4–7
The MMPI-2: Clinical and Validity Scales

The name, abbreviation, and number of each scale is given. (Clinical workers typically refer to the clinical scales by number rather than by name or abbreviation.) Interpretations are given for high scores on the scales.

Name and Abbreviation	Scale Number	Interpretation of High Scores
Clinical Scales		
Hypochondriasis (Hs)	1	Bodily preoccupation; pessimistic
Depression (D)	2	Depressed; lacks self-confidence
Hysteria (Hy)	3	Psychologically motivated physical symptoms; lacks insight
Psychopathic deviate (Pd)	4	Antisocial tendencies: impulsive
Masculinity–femininity (Mf)	5	Sex-role conflict
Paranoia (Pa)	6	Suspiciousness; resentful
Psychasthenia (Pt)	7	Anxiety; insecure
Schizophrenia (Sc)	8	Bizarre thinking; withdrawn
Hypomania (Ma)	9	Excessive psychomotor activity; unrealistic goals
Social introversion (Si)	0	Social anxiety; shy
Validity Scales		
L scale	—	Need to present unrealistically favorable impression
F scale	—	Severe psychological disturbance
K scale	—	Defensiveness; inhibited
Fb scale	—	Inattention to some items
VRIN scale	—	Inconsistent responses
TRIN scale	—	Acquiescence or nonacquiescence biases

proven reliable and can be used in a variety of settings and by untrained observers such as parents.

The Behavior Rating Scale for Children presents the rater with 33 questions, each of which is responded to on a 7-point rating scale (1 = always, 7 = never). The following are some representative items from the scale.

- Does the child sit still?
- Does the child disrupt games?
- Does the child think before he or she acts?
- Does the child grab for the belongings of others?
- Is the child easily distracted from his or her work or chores?

Another type of rating scale, the **visual analogue scale** (VAS) has been used in clinical and research settings to measure a variety of subjective phenomena, such as pain, anxiety, and craving for substances such as cigarettes. One or several VASs might be used in a given study. A VAS provides a convenient, easy, and rapidly administered measurement strategy (Wewers & Lowe, 1990). However, the applicability of these scales is limited by subjects' ability to conceptualize and understand the method itself, that is, to translate a personal perception of an abstract concept to a linear unit. Figure 4-6 shows examples of different types of visual analogue scales that measure pain and anxiety.

Rating scales, like self-report questionnaires, are not immune to inaccuracy. One possible biasing factor, the **halo effect,** results when an individual rates a person more favorably than is realistic on a specific characteristic because the rater has a generally favorable reaction to the person. Other methodological problems include the tendency to want to say only nice things about oneself or someone else, and the tendency to overuse the midrange of the scales. Research has shown that many of these problems can be reduced through careful wording of items, instructions to the rater, use of minimally ambiguous concepts and scales, and in some cases, actual training in making ratings.

Projective Techniques One group of assessment specialists believes that the more freedom people have in picking their responses, the more meaningful the description and classification that can be obtained. Because personality inventories do not permit much freedom of choice, some clinical psychologists prefer to use **projective techniques,** in which a person is shown ambiguous stimuli and asked what he or she thinks they are about. Some clinicians believe that projective techniques are very sensitive to unconscious dimensions of

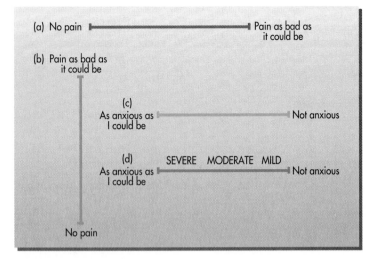

personality. Defense mechanisms, latent impulses, and anxieties have all been inferred from data gathered in projective situations.

The **Rorschach inkblots,** developed by the Swiss psychiatrist Hermann Rorschach (1884–1922), consist of ten cards, half colored and half black and white (see Figure 4-7). The test is administered by showing the cards, one at a time, and asking the person to describe what he or she sees in them. There are no right or wrong answers. After the person has responded to the inkblots in a free-association manner, the examiner asks questions about particular responses ("What gave you that impression?" "What made it seem like a _____?"). Besides recording what is said in response to the inkblots, the examiner also notes the person's mannerisms, gestures, and attitudes. Figure 4-8 offers a lighter view of the Rorschach test and its origins.

Rorschach developed the inkblot test as part of an experimental effort to relate perception to personality.

He believed that people's responses to inkblots could serve as clues to their basic personality traits. There are some striking examples of ability of the Rorschach to assess important aspects of personality. For example, Sirhan Sirhan, a 24-year-old Palestinian immigrant, assassinated presidential aspirant Robert F. Kennedy on June 5, 1968. Sirhan fostered his identity as an Arab and hated Zionists whom he equated with Nazis. His hatred of Zionists generalized to all Jews. Sirhan gave the following response to the inkblot shown in Figure 4-7b (Meloy, 1992):

> I don't know, it's a desert plant. Grows very tall—not a cactus. I don't know the name. The colors shock me—no—I don't know—I feel very jittery—I can't hold still,—it stirs me. I read this magazine article on the 20th anniversary of the State of Israel. It was in color—that color—I hate the Jews. There was jubilation—I felt that they were saying in the article, we beat the Arabs—it burns the shit out of me, there was happiness and jubilation.

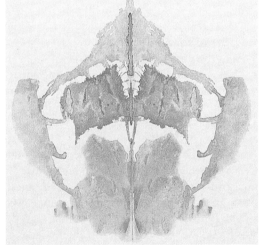

Figure 4-7b This Rorschach inkblot, produced a variety of responses, including: 1. "Looks like a long tunnel or channel in the center." 2. "On its side, I see a crabby old man frowning, with a long nose. I don't like him." 3. "There is a head of a camel in the middle there—no body, just the head."

Figure 4-7a As the client responds to the Rorschach card, the clinician records both verbal responses and behavior.

Because of a large number of negative findings in research studies using the Rorschach, many users of projective techniques became dubious about the validity of the Rorschach inkblots as perceptual indicators of personality. However, the test can still be used in analyzing people's social behavior and the content of their responses. Attempts to elicit assistance from the examiner and the use of stereotyped verbal responses are examples of observable types of behavior in the Rorschach situation. Also, there have been a number of attempts to develop a Rorschach scoring system that is more psychometrically sound. Among these is an ambitious effort to provide a uniform system for interpreting the Rorschach that has been developed by Exner (1994). Research so far completed suggests that the use of this system permits comparability among findings of different researchers.

Like the Rorschach test, the **Thematic Apperception Test** (TAT) employs ambiguous stimuli to which people can respond in a free manner. The TAT uses pictures that show people engaging in a variety of activities; hence, it is less ambiguous than the Rorschach inkblots. The total test consists of 30 picture cards and one blank card, although in most test situations not all of the cards are used. The cards are presented one at a time, and the client is asked to make up a story describing the scene in each picture, the events that led up to that scene, and the events that will grow from it. The client is also asked to describe the thoughts and feelings of the people in the story. As the client looks at the card and tells the story, the clinician not only records the story itself but notes behavior such as pauses, facial expressions, and changes in tone of voice.

Figure 4-9 Cards from the Thematic Apperception Test are more structured than the Rorschach stimuli yet they also produce many different responses. This card produced the two very different stories in the text.

Henry A. Murray (1893–1988), the author of the TAT (Murray, 1936), described the picture in Figure 4-9 (Card 12-F) as a portrait of a young woman, with a weird old woman grimacing in the background. Following is a story about that picture that was told by a 37-year-old woman who was diagnosed with a paranoid schizophrenia and was also depressed. How might her story be interpreted? Note the perceptual distortion that changed the usual mother-daughter relationship into a father-son relationship. (The examiner's questions are indicated in parentheses).

It's an old man standing behind a young man thinking, or knows what this young man should do, what he has ahead of him. He is very tired [old man] and the young man has a lot more—I can't explain it. The young man hasn't had the experience and gone through as much as the old man. That's all I think of now. (Relationship?) There is no relationship. I said father and son though didn't I? (Related?) No. (Happening?) They're both concentrating on life. (Explain?) Well, the old man, as I said, is concentrating on what the young man has ahead of him. (?) Whatever he chooses. (What did old man go through?) He looked like he had gone through suffering. (Explain?) Suffering from living. (?) Working hard. (Else?) No. (?) Well, I thought of other

Figure 4-8 Drawing by R. Chast; © 1989 *The New Yorker Magazine*, Inc.

things. The trouble he'd had. (?) Family troubles. (Story!) They lived way out in a lonely place, worked and existed. Nothing much to do, and they became very tired, and that's all.

—Schafer, 1948, pp. 188–189

Here is the response to the same card that was given by a 27-year-old married woman who would probably be diagnosed as having an anxiety disorder. How does it compare with the first response?

[Shakes head, swallows.] The old woman must be either the mother or the grandmother of the young woman. The young woman has a strong face. She has lots of character. The old woman has a sly expression on her face or around her mouth. If it wasn't for that expression on her face, I might try to interpret it. I can't imagine why she looks that way. The old woman looks like she worked hard all her life. (?) I don't know, just can't imagine. If this old lady had a different expression on her face, say, one of worry. . . . (?) Then I'd say she must be cherishing a lot of ambitions for the girl. Maybe she would be hoping that the girl would do things she always wanted to do. Maybe her ambitions would be realized in this woman.

—Schafer, 1948, p. 258

These two stories to the same picture differ in several ways, in addition to the unusual perceptual distortion of the 37-year-old woman. While her story reveals little concerning the relationship between the two people in the picture, the 27-year-old woman is very much involved in their feelings, motives, and personalities. The 27-year-old woman seems much more absorbed in the story-telling task than is the 37-year-old woman.

Clinical interpretation of a TAT story usually begins with an effort to determine the character with whom the person seems to have identified. Attention is paid to such variables as the person's behavior in the testing situation, characteristics of his or her utterances, the way the stories are told, the stories' emotional tone, and the conscious and unconscious needs that are revealed by the story content.

Whereas Rorschach viewed his test as an experimental perceptual task, Murray conceived of the TAT as a probe of the unconscious. Most contemporary users of projective techniques such as these consider them to be methods of tapping unconscious processes, an emphasis that is derived largely from the influence of psychoanalytic theory. Some psychotherapists use TAT responses as clues to hidden problem areas that require in-depth exploration.

In addition to the Rorschach and the TAT, many types of tasks are used as projective stimuli. In a **word-association test,** for example, a list of words is presented one at a time, and the client is asked to respond with the first word or idea that comes to mind. Clinicians are most interested in how long it takes a person to respond and how unusual the associations are. The **sentence-completion technique** is a logical extension of word associations. Here the subject is presented with a series of incomplete sentences and asked to complete them. Sentence-completion methods are typically analyzed in terms of the attitudes, conflicts, and motives reflected in them. The following are typical sentence stems:

- I worry about _____.
- My mother _____.
- What makes me mad is _____.
- My greatest regret is _____.

Other widely used projective methods include asking people to draw pictures of themselves and others, to finger paint, or to tell stories. These approaches have been used as means of increasing knowledge about fantasy, its determinants, and its behavioral correlates. At times their clinical application has been based more on theoretical usefulness than on objectively demonstrated validity. Researchers who are concerned with the evaluation of clinical tools continue to study these techniques.

Behavioral Assessment

Behavioral assessment has grown out of the behavioral-therapy movement. It is often used to identify response deficits, which are then treated through the use of behavioral methods such as reinforcement schedules and modeling. Clinicians often use behavioral observations to get information that cannot be obtained by other means. Examples of such observations include the frequency of a particular type of response, such as physical attacks on others on the school playground, or observations by teachers of certain behaviors of a school child such as frequent interruptions in the classroom. In either case, observational data must meet the same standards of reliability as data obtained by more formal measures.

Consider the case of a 10-year-old boy who, according to his teacher, is doing poorly in his schoolwork and, according to his parents, is difficult to manage at home and doesn't get along with other children. A measure of the boy's general intelligence, which might help to explain his poor schoolwork; personality tests, which might reveal trends related to his inadequate social relationships; an interview with him to provide insights into his view of the problem; and an interview with his parents, since the boy's poor behavior in school may be symptomatic of problems at home—all could be supplemented by behavioral assessments to add valuable information. Appropriate types of behavioral observations might include observations of his activities and response patterns in school; observations of his behavior in a specially created situation, such as a playroom with many interesting toys and games; and observations of his behavior at home—while he is interacting with one or both of his parents as well as while he is playing alone or with friends.

Making all of these assessments would be a major undertaking and not practical under most circumstances. Because of the variety of data that are potentially available, the assessor must decide which types of information are most feasible and desirable under a given set of circumstances. In most cases, the clinician is interested in both subjective and objective information. Subjective information includes clients' thoughts, their emotions, and their worries and preoccupations. Interviews, personality inventories, and projective techniques provide indications of subjective experience, although considerable clinical judgment is needed to infer what is going on within the client from the way he or she responds to a test. In contrast, objective information includes the person's observable behavior and usually does not require the assessor to draw complex inferences about such topics as attitudes toward parents, unconscious wishes, and deep-seated conflicts. Behavioral assessment is directed toward this latter type of observation (see Figure 4-10).

The following are some of the questions likely to be covered in behavioral assessments. Notice the absence of references to unconscious motivations or intrapsychic tensions.

1. What is the problem as described by the clinician?
2. Who are the people involved in the problem (for example, parents, spouse)?
3. Under what circumstances is the problem most in evidence?
4. What reinforcers contribute to maintenance of the problematic behavior?
5. What is the developmental history of the problem?
6. What are the assets and liabilities of the client's behavioral repetoire?
7. How modifiable are aspects of the client's situation that bear on the problem, and how can modification be made?

Baseline, or **operant, observations** are a type of behavioral observation that is becoming increasingly popular. These observations are recordings of response frequencies in particular situations before any treatment intervention has been made. They can be used in several ways. Observations might be made simply to describe a person's response repertory at a given time. For example, the number of aggressive responses made by children of different ages might be recorded. Such observations also provide a baseline for judging the effectiveness of behavior modification techniques. A similar set of observations, made after behavior modification procedures have been used, could be compared with the baseline measurement as a way of determining how well the therapy worked. For example, here are some questions that behavioral observations of schoolchildren can

Figure 4-10a This child's aggressive behavior in a playroom situation is being rated by observers through a one-way mirror. Behavioral observations made in a controlled environment are helpful to clinicians because they make comparisons among children more meaningful.

Figure 4-10b Children's behavior can also be observed in a natural setting. Aggressive behavior on a playground can be rated by observers. Because the situation is less standardized and other children are involved, these naturalistic ratings may be less easily compared. At the same time, the observed behavior may give important information about the child's everyday behaviors.

answer concerning the effectiveness of a special program to train teachers in the handling of children with particular types of behavioral problems:

1. Is the student engaged in an activity other than schoolwork?
2. Is the student looking around and not engaged in any other activity?
3. Is the student interacting with one or more other students?
4. Is the student interacting with the classroom teacher?

Cognitive Assessment

Just as it is important to know what a person does and how his or her behavior affects other people, it is also necessary to assess the thoughts that may lie behind the behavior. **Cognitive assessment** provides information about thoughts that precede, accompany, and follow maladaptive behavior. It also provides information about the effects of procedures whose goal is to modify both how someone thinks about a problem and how he or she behaves.

Cognitive assessment can be carried out in a variety of ways. For example, questionnaires can sample people's thoughts after an upsetting event. Electronic beepers have been used to signal subjects to record their thoughts at certain times of the day. There are also questionnaires to assess the directions people give themselves while working on a task and their theories about why things happen as they do.

Cognitions play an important role when a person is trying to concentrate on an intellectual task (see Figure 4-11). Anyone who has taken exams knows that worrying about one's ability, the possibility of failure, and what other students might be doing interferes with effective performance. But while thoughts that reflect worry have undesirable effects, thoughts that are directed toward the task at hand are helpful. The Cognitive Interference Questionnaire (Sarason & Stoops, 1978) was developed to assess the degree to which people working on important tasks have thoughts that interfere with their concentration. Subjects respond to the questionnaire by indicating how often thoughts like the following ones enter their minds while they are working on an assigned task.

- I thought about how others have done on this task.
- I thought about things completely unrelated to this task.
- I thought about how poorly I was doing.
- I thought about something that made me angry.
- I thought about something that happened earlier in the day.

The assessment of thoughts and ideas is a relatively new development. It has received impetus from the growing

Figure 4-11 People have different kinds of thoughts while taking an exam. Worries or thoughts that are unrelated to the exam interfere with good performance.

evidence that thought processes and the content of thoughts are related to emotions and behavior (Booth-Butterfield, 1991). Cognitive assessment provides information about adaptive and maladaptive aspects of people's thoughts and the role thoughts play in the processes of planning, making decisions, and interpreting reality.

Relational Assessment

Maladaptive behavior always occurs in some environmental context. One person might hallucinate only when other people are not present. Another person might become angry, and even violent, only when in the presence of certain other individuals. Because of the importance of an individual's social context, this book emphasizes an interactional approach to abnormal psychology that directs attention to the interrelationships among personal and situational variables. Our relationships with other people are important types of contextual variables; clinicians thus recognize the importance of making **relational assessments,** or evaluating key relationships, such as those within a family. Families are complex units of people who, while they may be alike in some ways, are unique individuals each with a particular set of needs, behavioral styles, emotions, and beliefs about themselves and the world in which they live (see Figure 4-12).

Clinicians try to develop ways of characterizing a person's social relationships, both with the outside environment and with other individuals. Are the person's relationships assets or liabilities? In chapter 5 we will discuss measures of social support that assess how supportive a person perceives the environment to be. In addition to this global sense of support, information is needed about specific features of a person's key close relationships. Each person can be viewed as one component of the numerous two-or-more-person interactions that fill daily activity. How does the person function in these interactions? What are his or her relational or interpersonal skills?

The family is one of the most powerful interactional systems affecting all people. To conceptualize patients without considering the dynamics of their family is to see half a picture at best. To plan treatment without considering the needs and opinions of the patient's family might represent an invitation to treatment failure. Moreover, whether clinicians admit it or not, the patient's family is often psychologically present, representing a powerful determining force in the patient's behavior. For this reason, interviewers need to make some type of assessment that gathers information about both individual family members and the family as a system. The following topics about the family might be brought up in a clinical interview.

- What were holidays like at your house?
- Who makes the decisions in your family?
- What kinds of things did your brothers and sisters like to do?

Figure 4-12 Drawing by R. Chast; © 1987 *The New Yorker Magazine,* Inc.

- Tell me a little about what kinds of things your parents used to argue about?

Because of the important role the family plays in shaping personality and the development of maladaptive behavior, researchers are beginning to develop ways of objectively measuring close relationships, such as those within a family. For example, Pierce (Pierce et al., 1991) has developed the *Quality of Relationships Inventory* to assess various aspects of close relationships with specific people (for example, with family members, romantic partners, or friends). This inventory obtains quantified responses from subjects to such questions as:

- To what extent could you turn to your mother for advice about problems?
- How much does your father like you?
- How much does your mother want you to change?
- How critical of you is your brother?
- How often does your sister make you angry?

Another relational assessment tool, the *Family Environment Scale* (Moos, 1974), asks subjects to describe the overall social climate within their families by responding to items like these:

- There are a lot of spontaneous discussions in our family.
- In our family each person has different ideas about what is right and wrong.
- In our family, we are strongly encouraged to be independent.

Clinicians can use the results of these assessments to understand more about the client's social network. If several family or network members complete these measures, the clinician has a better idea of how representative the client's views are of the quality of the relationships and the general atmosphere in the immediate social environment. If the client is being treated in a family setting, with other family members present at therapy sessions, the measures give the clinician valuable clues about family relationships.

Bodily Assessment

Insights into clients' feelings and motivations are provided by their expressive behavior and how their bodies function. Sophisticated devices have been developed to measure such physiological changes as pupil dilation, blood pressure, and electrical skin responses under specific conditions.

Figure 4-13a The portable blood pressure monitor allows a person's blood pressure to be recorded automatically at predetermined times without interfering with his or her normal daily activities. Here we see a physician instructing a patient in the use of a monitor. While engaging in normal daily activities, the monitor can be placed on the man's belt or in his coat pocket.

Technological advances are making it possible to monitor an individual's physiological state on a continuous basis. Sweat, heart rate, blood volume, the amounts of different substances in the bloodstream, and blood pressure can all be recorded and correlated with the presence or absence of certain psychological conditions such as stress. This approach seems promising.

An example of the use of automated assessment can be seen in the measurement of blood pressure. It is now possible to measure blood pressure while a person is engaged in everyday activities. Such measurement is a considerable medical advance, since resting blood pressure readings may not give a full picture of changes in pressure or provide an accurate 24-hour average. Ambulatory monitors can show changes in a patient's blood pressure throughout the day and during sleep (see Figure 4-13a). Such data are useful in diagnosing cases of high blood pressure in which cognitive and behavioral factors play important roles. These data may also be important in the selection and evaluation of treatment programs.

Figure 4-13b shows the pattern of blood pressure changes for a 45-year-old woman during a typical day. The patient had been diagnosed as having chronically elevated blood pressure, but as the figure shows, the readings actually covered a wide range. Other studies of patients who had been diagnosed as having high blood

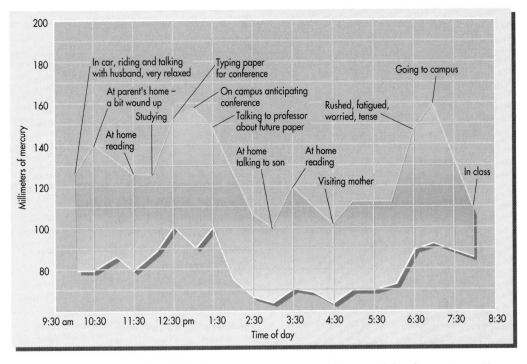

Figure 4-13b An ambulatory blood pressure monitor was used to record the changes in a 45-year-old woman's blood pressure during a one-day period. The chart is annotated with descriptions of the subject's daily activities. The top line charts the systolic blood pressure and the bottom line the diastolic blood pressure. Systolic pressure represents the higher point in the blood pressure cycle as the heart contracts and sends the blood through the circulatory system. Diastolic pressure represents the low point in the pressure cycle, which occurs as the heart fills with blood.

SOURCE: Werdegar et al., 1967, p. 103.

pressure have shown that blood pressure readings taken in the doctor's office may be significantly higher than readings taken during normal activity, even though the office readings are usually taken after a period of rest.

Another measure of emotional response is the **polygraph,** or lie detector. It records physiological reactions (heart rate, blood pressure, respiration rate, and galvanic skin response). Its use has been criticized because it violates the right of privacy and the right to avoid self-incrimination. Even more important, questions have been raised about its reliability and validity. Criminal cases suggest that the accuracy of the polygraph in judging guilt can be made with 75 to 97 percent accuracy, but the rate of false-positives (people who are innocent but whose polygraph records suggest guilt) is too high to use the polygraph as the sole basis of determining guilt or innocence (Council on Scientific Affairs, 1986).

Research may suggest novel applications of the polygraph in the field of mental health. For example, it may be possible to use the polygraph to determine what situations or topics caused a particular emotional reaction on the part of a client. This knowledge might provide some clues about areas that should be explored during therapy. In one study (Abrams, 1973), the polygraph was used in much the same way that a word-association test would be used. Stimulus words—some neutral, some thought to be especially relevant—were read to each of 20 psychiatric patients while they were attached to a polygraph. Figure 4-14 shows a typical set of polygraph tracings from this study. Respiration is at the top, galvanic skin response in the center, and a combination of heart rate and blood pressure at the bottom. (The **galvanic skin response** [GSR] is an increase in the electri-

cal conductivity of the skin that occurs when sweat glands increase their activity.) Stimulus word 23, *window,* was included as a neutral control word. However, instead of the expected lack of response, the patient showed a definite reaction to it. On the other hand, while there is a response to *sex,* it does not compare with the GSR to *window.* The patient later disclosed that he had considered committing suicide by jumping out a window. Word 26, the therapist's name, resulted in a large GSR, a slight rise in blood pressure, and suppression of breathing. In contrast, the patient reacted relatively little to neutral word 27, *pen.*

Biofeedback, described in chapter 6, is being used increasingly in the treatment of certain bodily complaints. The patient receives continuous reports of a particular index of bodily functions, such as blood pressure, and is helped to find ways of bringing the index within normal limits. Thus, the opportunity to monitor one's own behavior and bodily functioning can have a therapeutic effect.

Techniques of bodily assessment are becoming more and more sophisticated and play increasingly important roles in diagnosis. At several points in this book we will describe a variety of **brain imaging techniques** such as those mentioned in chapter 3 that enable clinicians to study in great detail the brain anatomy of patients, to observe shifts in metabolic activity as the brain responds to cognitive and perceptual tasks, and to measure quantitatively the neurochemical activity of neurotransmitter circuits in the brain. These brain imaging techniques may make it possible to identify the anatomical, metabolic, and neurochemical bases of mental illnesses.

Assessment techniques help in defining the nature and scope of clinical problems, selecting appropriate

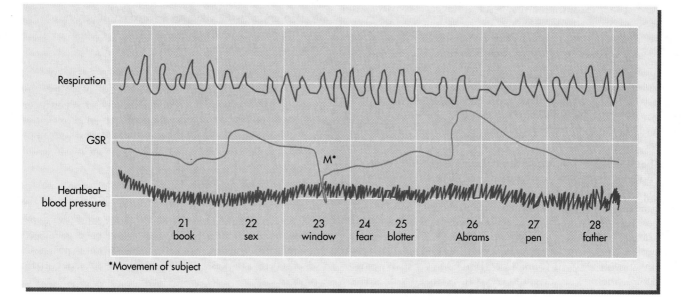

Figure 4-14 Polygraph tracing for one psychiatric patient. Stimulus words are numbered.
SOURCE: Abrams, 1973, p. 95.

treatments, and evaluating the results from treatment. The use of multiple techniques (for example, interview, projective techniques, and bodily assessment) may provide a particularly firm basis for valid clinical judgments.

As theories of maladaptive behavior become more comprehensive and more firmly based on scientific findings, approaches to classification can be expected to change. Assessment and classification methods help clinicians describe disordered behavior and plan therapeutic interventions to change it. What is assessed and how people are classified and treated depend on what we know about the factors involved in abnormal behavior.

CHAPTER SUMMARY

CLASSIFICATION

Classification is necessary in all branches of knowledge. In the area of personality and abnormal behavior, classification is based on assessment of what clients say and how they behave; it also takes account of events they have experienced in the present as well as their past histories. In abnormal psychology the classification of a person is referred to as a **diagnosis.** The diagnosis places the person's disorder within an existing system or grouping of disorders.

Advantages and Disadvantages of Classification An ideal classification system for abnormal behavior would group together behaviors with similar causes. However, in the field of abnormal psychology not enough is known about the causes of many disorders to do this. Therefore, the classification is a descriptive one in which different types of disorders are described in detail. On the one hand, even a descriptive classification system is valuable—for communication concerning treatment, in research, and for statistical purposes. On the other hand, classification may result in labeling that creates stigmatization. If the groupings in the system are incorrect because of incomplete knowledge, they make it harder for researchers to see true relationships between disorders.

Vulnerability, Resiliency, and Coping In classifying individuals, it is important to characterize their problems within the context of their stresses as well as of their vulnerabilities, resiliency, and coping abilities.

The Multiaxial Approach A multiaxial diagnostic system is designed, not to provide a simple label, but to summarize information about several aspects of the person's history and behavior. Since 1980, the diagnostic system used for most purposes in the United States, the **Diagnostic and Statistical Manual of Mental Disorders** (DSM), has used a multiaxial system. This system began with DSM-III in 1980 and has continued with DSM-III-R and DSM-IV. DSM-IV has five axes: Axis I, the primary diagnosis; Axis II, personality disorders and mental retardation; Axis III, relevant physical conditions; Axis IV, recent stresses; and Axis V, a global assessment of psychosocial functioning, currently and in the past year.

The Major Diagnostic Categories Axis I includes groupings for developmental disorders, serious cognitive disorders, substance-related disorders, sleep disorders, schizophrenia and other psychotic disorders, mood disorders, anxiety disorders, somatoform disorders, dissociative disorders, sexual disorders, factitious disorders, impulse control disorders not classified elsewhere, eating disorders, adjustment disorders, and psychological factors that affect a physical condition. Axis II includes personality disorders and mental retardation.

Evaluation of DSM-IV The DSM-IV approach is to use highly specific, descriptive diagnostic criteria for each category. This approach increases the reliability of diagnoses among clinicians. DSM-IV is more comprehensive and includes many more disorders and subdivisions of different disorders than previous editions. But more research is needed to know whether these additional classifications are justified. Overall, the changes in DSM-III, DSM-III-R, and DSM-IV have added clarity to the diagnostic process.

Research on Classification Unreliability in diagnosis or classification made by the clinician is based on the characteristics of the diagnostic system and a variety of other factors. These include client factors—the way the client is behaving at a particular time; method factors such as the different assessment techniques used by clinicians; criteria factors that are a function of baselines the clinician develops as a result of the type of patients seen; and factors related to the clinician's own personality and theoretical orientation. Research on classification must take into account all of these factors and how they interact with the characteristics of the diagnostic system.

ASSESSMENT: THE BASIS OF CLASSIFICATION

Because no single assessment tool is perfect, a variety of different ways of characterizing individuals have been developed. The major methods include interviews, psychological tests, and behavioral assessment as well as more specialized approaches.

The Interview The **interview** can be used for both diagnosis and therapy. Initial interviews are often relatively unstructured, but during the intake interview the clinician tries to determine why the client came for help, the current state of the client's mood and view of life, the history of the problem, and how the client is currently functioning. Interviewers typically note both verbal and nonverbal behavior of the client. Personal characteristics of the interviewer as well as the client determine how the interview will proceed. It is important for the clinician to be culturally sensitive, for example, with regard to the client's ethnic identity. The clinician needs to have the ability to size up the situation quickly and adopt the appropriate clinical strategies to assess the problem clearly. In some circumstances, a structured interview format such as the **Diagnostic Interview Schedule** is useful to increase comparability across interviews and help to ensure that the same types of information are gathered about each client.

Intelligence Tests The first standardized **intelligence tests** were developed by Alfred Binet. These yielded an **intelligence quotient** (IQ) score based on dividing the child's **mental age** by his or her actual or chronological age and multiplying by 100. Although this method is no longer used, the term *IQ* has remained in use. Currently, the scores on the Binet test as well as other intelligence tests are determined by deviation from a predetermined norm based on test results of a large and representative sample of people. At present, the **Wechsler tests** are the most frequently used intelligence tests. These tests report three different IQ scores: a **Verbal IQ,** a **Performance IQ,** and a **Full Scale IQ,** which represents the total score on the test. There is a series of Wechsler tests, each suitable for a different age group. These include the **Weschler Adult Intelligence Scale (WAIS-R),** the **Wechsler Intelligence Scale for Children (WISC),** and the **Wechsler Preschool and Primary Scale of Intelligence (WPPSI).** Currently, the **Kauffman Assessment Battery for Children (K-ABC),** a test based on ideas from cognitive psychology and neuropsychology and designed to reduce cultural bias in intelligence testing, is used extensively for testing children.

Personality Assessment Personality assessment encompasses many different approaches. These include personality inventories, rating scales, and projective tests. **Personality inventories** ask people questions about themselves. Because personality is not conceptualized as a single construct, most personality tests yield several scores. The **Minnesota Multiphasic Personality Inventory** (MMPI) is a widely used personality inventory. **Rating scales** present a series of items and allow the respondent to select from a number of choices, often concerning the degree to which the item is descriptive of him or her. A variation of the rating scale is the **visual analogue scale.** This approach is often used to measure the degree of some sensation experienced by the client. **Projective techniques** use ambiguous stimuli to which the client is asked to respond. These are most often used by clinicians with a psychodynamic orientation. Two well-known projective techniques are the **Rorschach inkblots** and the **Thematic Apperception Test** (TAT).

Behavioral Assessment Behavioral assessment focuses on observations of the frequency of particular types or categories of response. It is often used to identify response deficits. **Baseline or operant** observations are used to describe a person's response repertory at a particular time. Behavioral observations may be made either in a controlled setting or in the person's natural environment.

Cognitive Assessment Cognitive Assessment provides information about thoughts that precede, accompany, and follow maladaptive behavior. Questionnaires and beepers are often used in cognitive assessment. Cognitive assessment has been used most extensively in studying the factors that affect concentration on important tasks.

Relational Assessment Because people's behavior is affected by their interpersonal relationships, it is important to assess both general and specific social relationships. One important area of relationships for many people is family relationships. Relationships can be assessed either as general categories such as family or at the level of specific relationships such as mother, brother, or best friend.

Bodily Assessment A person's inner state can be assessed by measuring bodily functions such as blood pressure, heartbeat, respiration, and galvanic skin response. Biofeedback techniques have been developed that allow a person to monitor and to learn to control his or her own bodily responses.

CHAPTER FIVE

Rimma Gerlovina and Valerily Gerlovin, *Maze*, 1990.
Steinbaum Krauss Gallery, New York.

STRESS, COPING, AND MALADAPTIVE BEHAVIOR

One morning, while brushing her teeth, Sheila Mason noticed a small lump on her gum. It didn't hurt, but she was sure that it had not been there before. She wondered whether it might be related to an upset stomach or a cold, but there had been no recent changes in her diet and she felt fine. She was worried about the lump, but at the same time she didn't want to bring a trivial symptom to the attention of her physician or dentist. After three days the lump was still there. It was no bigger than it had been when she had first noticed it, and it still didn't hurt. Sheila concluded that it was not her responsibility to decide whether or not the lump was a trivial symptom. That was the professional's job. Having decided to get an expert to look at the lump, Sheila was left with only one question: Should she call her physician or her dentist?

Grace Dolby, married and the mother of two children, felt a small but noticeable lump in her right breast. Her first reaction was one of alarm bordering on panic, but then she told herself it was really nothing. She must have been mistaken. Then she simply tried to stop thinking about the lump. She put it out of her mind whenever her thoughts strayed to the topic. She also said nothing to anyone else about it for over two months and made a tremendous effort to wish it away. Grace was usually outgoing and cheerful, but during those months her husband, Jack, noticed that she had become moody, tense, and depressed. At times she also seemed distant and preoccupied. Toward the end of the two-month period, Grace's moodiness and distance from others (including her children) increased. Her sleep became fitful, and she had frequent headaches (even though previously she had almost never had them). If her husband insisted that she tell him what the matter was, her reply was always, "Nothing's the matter. I'm perfectly normal." Finally, one evening during lovemaking Jack felt the lump in her breast, and despite Grace's protests that it was "nothing" he insisted that she see the family physician.

Just about the only thing that Sheila Mason and Grace Dolby have in common is that they discovered lumps that worried them. The two women dealt with their worries in quite different ways. After some doubt about whether she should undergo a clinical examination, Sheila made a rational decision to seek help. She realized that there was a chance the lump could be serious but that she could not evaluate the possibility herself and that the longer she waited, the worse it would be.

In contrast, Grace Dolby seemed unable to act realistically and decisively. She first attempted to cope with the discovery of the lump in her breast by unsuccessfully trying to deny that it was really there. She then tried to tell herself that it "wasn't anything." The stress aroused by her discovery could only temporarily be reduced by denial and secrecy. She was still unable to deal with the reality of the lump.

Such a situation would be stressful for anyone. Most people who find themselves in such a situation go to a doctor immediately. Grace Dolby's response is considered maladaptive mainly because it did not work; the lump (or reality) did not go away. In fact, Grace's behavior simply increased the amount of stress she experienced. A clinician working with Grace would want to understand the personal needs, motivations, and dispositions that combined with the situation (discovery of the lump) to produce her decision to be secretive and not to act. What made Grace Dolby so much more vulnerable to stress than Sheila Mason?

In this chapter we describe ways in which people react to stress. We emphasize examples of maladaptive behavior in response to two types of situations: those that arise suddenly (an earthquake, a sudden illness, becoming a crime victim), and those that develop more gradually or represent life transitions such as marriage (see Figure 5-1). We examine the concept of stress, explore the different ways in which people handle it, and review three clinical conditions (adjustment disorders, posttraumatic disorders, and dissociative disorders) in which stress plays an identifiable role. Even though the behavioral reactions observed in the three conditions seem quite different, stress plays a crucial role in each, and its removal is often followed by improvement.

Because this is the first chapter in which we study particular disorders in some depth, it is worthwhile to anticipate an observation that has been made many times by both experienced clinicians and students: The various disorders are not conveniently arranged so that they have mutually exclusive features. Although stress is the main topic of this chapter, we will also refer to stress as we discuss other forms of maladaptation. What is distinctive about the disorders discussed here is that the sources of stress are often more evident than they usually are in other forms of abnormal behavior.

Figure 5-1 Everyone has times when they must deal with stress. Stress may build up gradually as the consequence of an ongoing unsatisfactory work or life situation or as the result of an upcoming life transition such as college graduation, marriage, or becoming a parent. Stress may also result from sudden catastrophes, for example, unexpected illness and serious and traumatic life events caused by outside forces. Here we see a postal worker who is reacting to a suddenly occurring stressful event, a shoot-out that occurred in a post office in Dearborn, Michigan, in 1993. For unknown reasons, but possibly as a result of accumulated job stress, an average of about 500 violent acts involving postal workers take place in the United States each year. While this postal worker is dealing with a completely unanticipated stress, the person responsible for the shoot-out was probably reacting to a stressful life situation that developed over a long period of time.

Stress and Coping

In Chapter 1 we said that the term *stress* refers to situations that pose demands, constraints, or opportunities. However, a stress-arousing situation for one person might be a neutral event for another. Whether a certain situation is stressful for us or not depends on how we appraise a life event and how we rate our ability to deal with it.

People differ not only in the life events they experience but also in their vulnerability to them. A person's **vulnerability** to stress is influenced by his or her temperament, coping skills, and the available social support. Vulnerability increases the likelihood of a maladaptive response to stress. For example, unloved children are more vulnerable and generally at greater risk of developing behavior disorders than those who are loved

(Werner & Smith, 1992). While vulnerability implies a heightened risk of a negative outcome, personal resiliency may reduce such a likelihood. Factors contributing to **resiliency** include having a positive self-concept, being alert and independent, enjoying new experiences, and being able to form meaningful and rewarding relationships with other people (Werner, 1993).

Temperament can be an asset or liability depending on the life situation the individual confronts. Temperament comprises those aspects of a person's behavior (particularly those having to do with feelings and emotions) that show some significant degree of consistency over time and from one life situation to another. Activity level, mood, and distractibility illustrate temperamental attributes that can influence how effectively we handle situations. For example, an abundance of energy in a highly active person can be an asset when it is used in the pursuit of specific, planned goals, but a liability in situations where hasty judgments, commitments, and responses should be avoided. Adjustment problems may occur when temperamental factors prevent people from meeting their own or others' expectations. For example, children with a tendency to withdraw from new stimuli may experience excessive stress if their parents or teachers demand rapid adjustment to new conditions (such as entering nursery school). Researchers are attempting to identify the origins of temperament (for example, heredity, biological make-up, parental attitudes, and sociocultural factors) (Chess, 1990).

Coping Skills

Coping skills—characteristic ways of dealing with difficulties—influence how we identify and try to solve problems. People who cope successfully do not only know how to do things. They also know how to approach situations for which they do not have a readily available response.

The coping skills that people bring with them to life experiences (their expectations, fears, skills, hopes) influence how much stress they feel and how well they cope with it. Experience and success in coping with similar situations, well-founded self-confidence, and the ability to remain composed and "think on one's feet" instead of falling to pieces when faced with a problem, all contribute to realistic appraisals of and responses to situations. These characteristics are products of personality development, which, in turn, is influenced by social relationships.

A task-oriented, matter-of-fact response to a tough situation is usually more effective than becoming anxious, angry, or defensive. Failure to be task-oriented can happen for a variety of reasons. A person may simply lack the coping resources needed to take a matter-of-

fact approach. In that case, the situation is beyond his or her capabilities. It could also be that certain elements of the situation may prevent an individual from taking a constructive approach to it. For example, a man might have the coping resources needed to be assertive with other men but not with women. His vulnerability with regard to women might keep him from complaining about being shortchanged by a waitress, whereas he would be quick to complain if he were shortchanged by a waiter.

In trying to identify the basis for a particular behavioral coping response, it is necessary to analyze carefully what is going on in the situation, together with the person's assets and liabilities (coping resources and vulnerabilities). In addition, attention must be paid to how the person sizes up the situation and his or her coping resources. Grace Dolby, the subject of the second case at the beginning of the chapter, had in the past experienced many physical symptoms that required action—such as high temperature and skin rash. The lump in her breast, however, was different because of its life-threatening implications. Her mother had died when Grace was 4 years old, and Grace was concerned about depriving her children of the maternal love and attention that she had missed as a result of her mother's early death. Perhaps her intense concern about abandoning her children made Grace particularly vulnerable to her symptom and resulted in her denial of its significance.

Like Grace, many people with bodily symptoms cope with them by denying them. They may intentionally ignore them and try to keep thoughts of them out of awareness or they may misinterpret them. A common response to the chest pain of a heart attack is denial of its significance. It has been estimated that 80 to 90 percent of people who experience such pain attribute it to other causes, usually indigestion (Hackett & Cassem, 1975). Once the possibility that it might be a heart attack strikes them, they think, "It couldn't be happening to me." This thought alone seems to be enough to keep them from seeking medical help. Even some physicians, who should know better, have gone jogging when they experienced chest pains in order to "prove it's nothing." Clearly, there is a common tendency to deny the true significance of pain despite its severity, intensity, or duration (Breznitz, 1988).

This denial holds true for psychological pain as well. Many people deny the reality of an unhappy or unsatisfying marriage rather than seek counseling or even a divorce. People who have lost their jobs may blame their employers instead of recognizing their own inadequacies as employees. They may put off looking for work because they "deserve a rest," denying even to themselves that they are afraid of being fired again. As Table 5-1 shows, denial can play a reality-distorting role at various stages of a stressful experience.

TABLE 5-1
Types of Denial of Stress

Type of Denial	Example
1. Denial of provided information	"No one ever told me about it."
2. Denial of information about a threat	"No one ever told me there was anything to worry about."
3. Denial of personal relevance	"It doesn't apply to me."
4. Denial of urgency	"No need to hurry."
5. Denial of vulnerability	"No matter what happens, it can't happen to me."
6. Denial of emotion	"I'm not scared."
7. Denial of the emotion's relevance	"I'm scared, but there is no reason to feel that way."

Heightened stress levels have detectable, although perhaps not immediately noticeable, psychological consequences. For example, a significantly higher percentage of depressed and suicidal people than of people with other disorders have had undesirable recent experiences. The undesirable events that contribute most to depression include the departure or loss of significant people in one's life during the previous year (see chapter 10).

The psychological disorders discussed in this chapter begin with a specific event that has definable characteristics and has special meaning for the person involved. This event is then appraised or processed, and as a result of the appraisal, the person's emotions or thoughts (fears, plans) are aroused and coping strategies are considered. The end product is some response that reflects the level of stress as well as the person's resources and vulnerabilities. Box 5-1 contrasts coping patterns of two people each of whom lived through a terrible experience.

The Coping Process In coping, people use their personal resources to master a problem, overcome or sidestep an obstacle, answer a question, or resolve a dilemma. Different coping strategies are effective in different types of situations. People who generally cope successfully have a varied array of personal resources, which include the ability to:

1. Seek pertinent information.
2. Share concerns and find consolation when needed.
3. Redefine a situation so as to make it more solvable.

4. Consider alternatives and examine consequences.
5. Use humor to defuse a situation.

A growing body of research is devoted to the question of how people can be helped to cope more effectively with stress (Hodgkinson & Stewart, 1991; Lazarus, 1991). One finding of this research is that what you don't know *can* hurt you. People who know what to expect beforehand are better able to cope with stress than people who do not know what lies ahead. Many surgical patients, for example, suffer unnecessarily because they have not been warned that they will have considerable pain after the operation. It has been shown that patients are less anxious and recover faster when the surgery and recovery process are explained to them before the operation takes place.

In one study (Anderson, 1987), 60 men undergoing coronary bypass grafts were divided into three groups. One group received the hospital's standard preparation: a brochure on the procedures and a short visit from a nurse to answer questions. The other groups watched a videotape that followed a patient through the operation and recovery. In addition, one of these groups received advance instructions in the physical therapy exercises—such as deep breathing to expand their lung capacity—that they would be doing to help recovery.

While 75 percent of those with the standard preparation suffered after the surgery from acute hypertension—a condition that can endanger coronary bypass patients in the first 12 hours after surgery—less than 45 percent of those who saw the tape had the problem. The patients who viewed the tape also had less anxiety as they waited in the hospital before the surgery and reported less stress and seemed more relaxed to nurses in the week after the surgery. The group that received extra instruction in the physical therapy went into surgery feeling even less anxious than the other groups.

Learning the specific skills needed in stressful situations helps individuals cope more effectively. Many people enter dangerous situations without proper training. For example, many hiking and mountain climbing accidents are a result of poor training and preparation. Besides learning specific skills, individuals can be trained for stressful situations by being put through a series of experiences that are graded from relatively low to relatively high in stress. In addition, observing a model who copes with stress in an effective way can help people about to enter a strange or dangerous situation.

Sometimes people fail to cope with stress because a high level of arousal interferes with their ability to concentrate on adaptive thoughts. Because such people do not observe their own thoughts, feelings, and behaviors in challenging situations, they fail to engage in constructive problem solving. Learning general skills for coping with stress involves learning how to think con-

Adaptive and Maladaptive Coping

Harvey Weinstein, 68 years old and in the clothing apparel business, was kidnapped in a matter of 20 seconds after he had finished breakfast and emerged from a New York diner near his office. A man held a knife to his throat and pushed him into a car. He was taken to a scraggly urban woodland near a highway and city parkland. For 12 days, Mr. Weinstein was forced to remain hunched in a 4-foot-wide pit as his family and police detectives frantically sought his freedom and conducted fruitless nightmarish negotiations over ransoms demanded by his captors. Mr. Weinstein never knew where he was or what precisely he was trapped in. When the police located him, Mr. Weinstein had lost over 15 pounds and was, not surprisingly, a bit shaky. (His captors had lowered water and some fruit into his pit during the ordeal.) As soon as he was found by the police, while still in the pit, he asked for a cellular phone and called his family. The police quoted him as saying, "Sorry I'm putting you through what I'm putting you through. I'm in a hole." When he was helped out of the pit, he said, "I'm going to hug and kiss all my beautiful people."

Mrs. A, a woman in her early 40s, came to a psychiatrist's office to talk about a traumatic experience she had had almost two years previously. She came to the office appearing angry and suspicious, although her behavior was polite and socially correct. She chose the chair farthest from the psychiatrist and closest to the door. Nearly two

years before, she had been shot and critically wounded in an incident with an acquaintance in her own home. After a long hospitalization and convalescence her physical recovery is complete, but her life has totally changed. She has moved to another area. She stays in her house. In a market, she scans the surroundings, expecting to be shot. Seeing a man with a hat like that of her assailant is enough to produce a marked physiological arousal response. She avoids contact with family and former friends. She has not been able to return to work. Her sleep is poor. She dreams of the shooting and its aftermath. After such dreams, fear can leave her feeling weak for days.

All of us would agree that these two people had extremely traumatic experiences.

Why did Mr. Weinstein get over his quickly (a few days after regaining his freedom, Mr. Weinstein said, "I feel great!"), while Mrs. A continues to relive her awful experience? Among Mr. Weinstein's outstanding characteristics is his resiliency, reflected in his ability to be task-oriented when faced with challenges, and his good, warm relationships with other people. While he was trapped in the pit, Mr. Weinstein thought of his foxhole experience as a Marine decades earlier. As an 18-year-old Marine corporal in World War II, he had seen some fierce fighting. Sitting in the armored cave of an amphibious tank, he had survived shellfire and smoke. He told detectives, "I survived this kind of thing once. I knew I could survive it again. I closed my eyes and I was back there. That's what got me through this. I kept thinking, 'I am a Marine. I can survive this.'"

Harvey Weinstein, who was kidnapped and spent five days in an underground pit, embraces his sons Mark and Dan as he talks with reporters about his ordeal. His thoughts about his family helped him endure the capitivity.

structively, solve problems, behave flexibly, and provide feedback to oneself about the tactics that work and those that do not (see Table 5-2).

The following examples of useful statements that people can make to themselves to prepare for and deal with stressful situations have been used in training programs directed toward strengthening cognitive skills. In such training, the statements are modeled for each participant, who is then given an opportunity to rehearse them while imagining being in stressful situations (Freeman and others, 1989).

PREPARING FOR A STRESSFUL SITUATION
- "I should work out a plan for dealing with this problem."
- "I'm not going to worry about what happens; I'll just prepare myself in the best way I can."

CONFRONTING A STRESSFUL SITUATION
- "I'm just going to take one step at a time. I can do it."
- "I want to be sure to stick to what's really important."

COPING WITH FEELINGS OF BEING OVERWHELMED
- "Sure I'm scared—but that's normal."
- "I know I'm afraid, but I've got to do things that will help me cope."

TABLE 5–2
Aids to Behavioral Coping

1. *Be task-oriented.* Focus only on the task confronting you. It is not productive to spend time with thoughts or feelings that are unrelated to accomplishing the task. Being task-oriented means that you are concentrating completely on the job at hand. Negative or disruptive thoughts and emotions are the enemies of task orientation.
2. *Be yourself.* Don't role play. You will be more effective acting naturally than trying to fit a role. Place your confidence in *yourself,* not in the role.
3. *Self-monitor.* Pay attention to the way you are thinking and feeling in a given situation. It is important to learn about what causes stress for you and about your personal reactions to stress. Effective self-monitoring is your early warning system. It can alert you to the necessity of using the other coping skills to prevent a blowup.
4. *Be realistic about what you can achieve.* Know your own limits as well as your strengths.
5. *Use your sense of humor.* At times, laughter is the best medicine—don't lose your sense of humor.
6. *Have a constructive outlook.* Try to look for the positives in the people around you. Don't be too quick to conclude that people are behaving the way they are just to upset you. Put yourself in the other person's shoes—from that point of view his or her behavior may make perfect sense.
7. *Use supportive relationships.* Compare notes, blow off steam, and get support from your friends. Don't draw into yourself when you are feeling stressed. Remember that we all "get by with a little help from our friends."
8. *Be patient with yourself.* Don't punish yourself for not achieving perfection. Your mistakes should become learning experiences, not times for heavy self-criticism. Keep your expectations of yourself at a reasonable level.

REINFORCING SELF-STATEMENTS
- "I controlled my tension—and I did it."
- "I must be pretty good to be able to handle a crisis like that one."

As the above statements show, people who cope effectively with stressful situations have learned to direct their thoughts along productive lines and to avoid being distracted by fear and worry. Actors, quarterbacks, and other people who are often in the limelight soon learn that attention to the task at hand is more constructive than self-preoccupied thoughts ("There are 100,000 people out there waiting for me to fumble that ball"). They also learn to anticipate problems that might complicate a stressful situation and to think about the way to deal with them. (The person in Figure 5-2 is admirably resourceful in this regard.) Actors come to accept that they will occasionally get their lines mixed up and that deemphasizing their mistakes and moving on to the next line reduces the impact of their errors. On the other hand, the thoughts of some people who are prone to stress disorders are saturated with self-blame and catastrophizing ("The worst will surely happen").

Social Support

Our social network includes people on whom we can rely, people who let us know that they care about, value, and love us. Someone who believes that he or she belongs to a social network experiences **social support.** Evidence is increasing that maladaptive ways of thinking and behaving occur disproportionately among people with few social supports. The amount and adequacy of social support available to a person play a part in both vulnerability and coping (Sarason et al., 1990). Vulnerability to physical and psychological breakdown increases as social support decreases. That is, social support serves as a buffer against the upsets of living in a complex world. Not only is social support very helpful during a period of stress (it is nice to know that there are people pulling for us in a tough situation), but it is also helpful in times of relative calm. It gives us the security and self-confidence to try out new approaches and gain additional coping skills. With an expanded repertory of coping skills, we are in a better position to handle demands, frustrations, and challenges when they do arise.

Figure 5-2

The Wall Street Journal, 1994, p A15. Reprinted by permission of Cartoon Features Syndicate, Inc.

Research aimed at measuring social support is under way. The Social Support Questionnaire (SSQ) provides information about how much social support people think they have and how satisfied they are with it (Sarason et al., 1983). This information is then scored on separate Availability and Satisfaction scales. Table 5-3 lists some of the items on the SSQ. One interesting finding of research using the SSQ is that there is only a moderate correlation between the Availability and Satisfaction scores. There appears to be no minimum number of social supports that ensures satisfaction for everyone. For some people, a small number of close friends and relatives is satisfying, whereas others seem to need ties to many different people.

Research with the SSQ has also revealed relationships between social support and physical health. In general, people who have had many recent undesirable experiences are more likely to get sick than those who have been more fortunate. However, people who have high levels of social support are less vulnerable to illness even when they have experienced a recent misfortune (Sarason et al., 1985).

Maladaptive ways of thinking and behaving are more common among people who have few social supports, particularly within their families. Strong family ties seem to encourage self-reliance. Self-reliance and reliance on others are not only compatible but comple-mentary. Social support facilitates coping with crisis and adapting to change.

Why do some people have many rewarding ties that help them smooth out the rough spots in their lives, while others are lonely and socially isolated? Are the number and quality of social ties simply a matter of luck? There is evidence that people with high and low levels of social support as assessed by the SSQ differ in the social skills needed to attract the interest of others (Sarason et al., 1985). When engaging in a conversation with a stranger, people who are high in social support feel more competent, comfortable, and assured than people who report having few social supports. In addition, people who are low in social support tend to be perceived by others as being less interesting, dependable, friendly, and considerate than people who are high in social support. They are also less wanted as friends and co-workers and report feeling more lonely. There appears to be a strong link between social skills and social support. People with low levels of support may not believe that other people could be interested in them. This belief would tend to increase their vulnerability to stress, especially in situations that called for interactions with other people. Training in social skills might not only increase their interpersonal effectiveness but also help reduce their perception of social isolation.

As we have seen, the coping process involves a num-

TABLE 5–3
The Social Support Questionnaire

The *Social Support Questionnaire* (SSQ) consists of 27 items, four of which are presented here. After answering each item, the test taker is asked to indicate his or her level of satisfaction with the support available by marking a 6-point rating scale that ranges from "very satisfied" to "very unsatisfied." The SSQ yields scores relating to *Availability* of and *Satisfaction* with social support.

Who do you know who you can trust with information that could get you in trouble? (This item is completed as an example).

_____ No one	A) R.N. (brother)	D) T.N. (father)	G)
	B) L.M. (friend)	E) L.M. (employer)	H)
	C) R.S. (friend)	F)	I)

Whose lives do you feel that you are an important part of?

_____ No one	A)	D)	G)
	B)	E)	H)
	C)	F)	I)

Whom can you really count on to distract you from your worries when you feel under stress?

_____ No one	A)	D)	G)
	B)	E)	H)
	C)	F)	I)

Who helps you feel that you truly have something positive to contribute to others?

_____ No one	A)	D)	G)
	B)	E)	H)
	C)	F)	I)

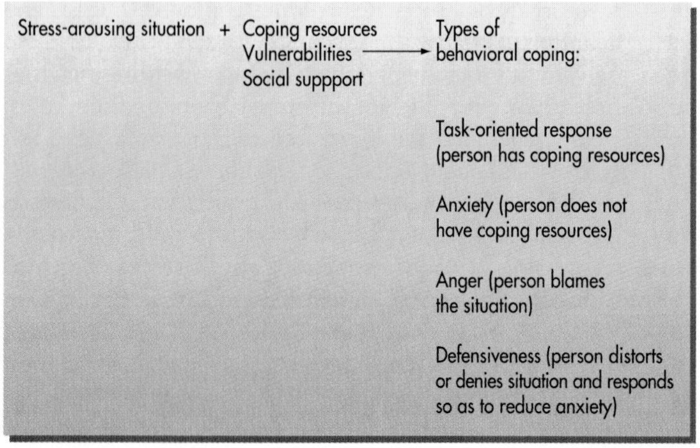

```
Stress-arousing situation + Coping resources        Types of
                            Vulnerabilities  ——————> behavioral coping:
                            Social suppport

                                                     Task-oriented response
                                                     (person has coping resources)

                                                     Anxiety (person does not
                                                     have coping resources)

                                                     Anger (person blames
                                                     the situation)

                                                     Defensiveness (person distorts
                                                     or denies situation and responds
                                                     so as to reduce anxiety)
```

Figure 5-3 The stress-coping process. How a person actually copes with a stress-arousing situation depends on the person's skills or coping resources, vulnerabilities, and the presence of a supportive social network.

ber of interacting factors. Figure 5-3 summarizes the role of three especially important factors in this process: individuals' coping resources, their vulnerabilities, and their perceptions of available social support.

Stressful Situations and Life Transitions

The interacting factors in Figure 5-3 come into play in a variety of stress-arousing contexts that require the individual to make some type of adjustment. Since stress has undesirable effects on behavior, thought, and bodily functioning, it is important to build up a person's resources for behavioral coping. The experience of stress involves uncomfortable psychological feelings. Physical aspects—blood pressure, hormone levels, and brain waves—are also affected by stress. Very high levels of stress can result in trembling, stuttering, and a decline in the effectiveness with which tasks are carried out.

There is often little consistency in people's reactions to stress. That is, one person might react to stress primarily in a bodily way, another might develop psychological symptoms, and yet another might show a profound deterioration in performance. Responses to stress involve bodily, psychological, and behavioral systems, but the correlation among these systems is often low. Table 5-4 lists ways in which the three systems may react to stress.

There seems to be some truth to the commonly held belief that everyone has a breaking point. The more stress people experience, the more likely they are to break down either physically or psychologically. Dealing with several stressful situations at the same time obviously places great demands on a per-

son's resources, but stress can also have cumulative effects.

Research has shown that people who have experienced multiple stressors in the recent past are especially susceptible to depression, anxiety, and overreactivity of physiological systems (Noshpitz & Coddington, 1990). There is growing reason to believe that mental or physical breakdowns could be predicted if there were a way to quantify how stressful certain life experiences are. For this reason, researchers have sought ways of assessing those experiences. Because recent experiences often exert a more powerful influence and are more easily recalled than those that occurred many years before, efforts have been made to quantify stressful life changes for specific time periods, such as the past year. Questionnaires have been constructed to assess not only whether certain events have occurred in the recent past, but also how the individual perceived the event and felt its impact (Cohen, 1988; Sarason et al., 1978). These questionnaires deal with events such as being fired from a job, getting a new job, breaking up with a boyfriend or girlfriend, and experiencing financial difficulties. While the

TABLE 5-4
Some Psychological, Bodily, and Behavioral Reactions to Stress

Psychological Responses

Feeling upset
Inability to concentrate
Irritability
Loss of self-confidence
Worry
Difficulty in making decisions
Racing thoughts
Absent-mindedness

Bodily Responses

Rapid pulse
Pounding heart
Increased perspiration
Tensing of arm and leg muscles
Shortness of breath
Gritting of teeth

Behavioral Responses

Deterioration in performance effectiveness
Smoking and use of alcohol or other "recreational" drugs
Accident proneness
Nervous mannerisms (foot tapping, nail biting)
Increased or decreased eating
Increased or decreased sleeping

occurrence of any one particular event might not put a person at a greater risk for an adverse outcome (such as getting sick), the occurrence of several different kinds of events close together in a brief period of time would create significant added risk.

Stress-Arousing Situations

Two broad types of stress-arousing conditions that require adjustment are situations that arise in life, often unexpectedly, and developmental transitions. The death of a close friend illustrates the need for a situational adjustment; going to college is an example of a transitional adjustment. Such stress-arousing conditions have varying characteristics. Following are some of the ways in which challenging situations and circumstances vary.

1. *Duration.* Stressful situations differ in duration. A job interview lasts for a short time, whereas a marital quarrel might last for hours or days.
2. *Severity.* Situations vary in the severity of the circumstances confronting the individual. In general, a minor injury is easier to cope with than a major injury.
3. *Predictability.* In some cases predictability is high (we know what is going to happen), whereas in others predictability is low. The amount of stress caused by a request to give an oral presentation in class would depend on whether the request was made on the spot or was a previously given assignment.
4. *Degree of loss of control.* One of the most upsetting aspects of a situation is the feeling that one is unable to exert any influence on the circumstances. For example, earthquake victims can do nothing to prevent or control the quake's initial impact and aftershocks.
5. *The individual's level of self-confidence.* Lack of self-confidence often results in reduced personal effectiveness, even though the person may really know how to handle the situation. For example, a recently divorced woman may feel ill at ease in social situations that she was able to handle very well during her marriage.
6. *Suddenness of onset.* Suddenness of onset influences how prepared we are to cope with a particular situation. An accident is usually completely unexpected, whereas the crises of adolescence build up gradually.

Accidents, natural disasters, and military combat are examples of situations that typically evoke high levels of stress and may result in emotions so intense they interfere with normal functioning. Their psychological impact comes from actual physical injury or threat of injury and from the possibility of loss of life.

Extreme stressors set in motion a cycle of reactions aimed at restoring an equilibrium between the person's self-concept and the new realities of his or her life. Pre-existing personality characteristics may interfere with an adaptive response after a disaster. People who see themselves as incompetent, who tend to respond defensively to challenges (for example, by using denial or projection), who have conflicts involving themes similar to some aspect of the disaster, or who believe that their past thoughts might somehow have influenced what happened—such people are likely to have long-lasting maladaptive reactions to traumatic situations. These prolonged reactions usually include feeling dazed and having intrusive thoughts and images about the traumatic event. Such thoughts and images may interfere with the ability to sleep.

Personal Crises Stressors can be widespread events that affect many people, such as an airplane crash, or they can be a highly personal crisis. The death of a loved one, the loss of a job, and the need to care for a parent who has an incurable illness are all examples of personal crises. Rape is another type of personal crisis whose frequency of occurrence and seriousness are now receiving increased attention (Koss, 1993). Rape affects men as well as women, married as well as single persons. Date rape is a particularly serious problem among adolescent- and college-age persons (see Box 5-2).

The fears that persist after the experience of rape tend to restrict and control the victim's life (Ruch et al., 1991). The most prevalent fears are of being alone, of strangers, of going out, and of darkness. Women who have been victims of sudden and violent assaults by strangers are especially likely to remain fearful and depressed for a long time, and they are also more likely to avoid dating for a long period.

From the behavioral perspective, a rape is part of a real life, classical-conditioning situation in which the threat of death or physical damage elicits a strong autonomic arousal—fear. Any stimulus that is present during the rape—darkness, a man with a particular appearance, being alone—becomes associated with the fear response. These cues then become conditioned stimuli that independently evoke fear and anxiety. Because some of these stimuli are often encountered by the victim in her daily life, she may begin to use avoidance behavior to escape them. This decreases the likelihood that the conditioned fear response will dissipate over time. Behavior therapy offers a way of overcoming these problems. By using both cognitive and behavioral techniques, victims can learn to overcome their avoidance behavior and thus extinguish their anxiety.

Since an estimated 10 to 20 percent of rape victims have continuing problems of sexual dysfunction several years after the rape, they may also be helped by sex ther-

Date Rape

College women are a high-risk group for sexual assault. Nationally, the age group with the highest rape victimization rate is the 16–19 year olds with the age 20–24 group having the second highest rate (Ward et al., 1991). About 16 percent of women college students in two different surveys reported that they had been raped by someone they knew or were dating (Sherman, 1985). In another survey of a representative sample of university students, 6 percent of the women replied "yes" to the question, "Have you ever been raped?" However, when the definition was broadened somewhat, percentages went up substantially; 21 percent of the women said that they had had sexual intercourse with a man when they didn't really want to because they had felt pressured by his continual arguments (Koss & Oros, 1982). Eleven percent of the college men in the surveys said they had forced a woman to have intercourse. A typical story was something like what happened to a 20-year-old college student in Pittsburgh.

She met him two years ago at a fraternity party on a neighboring campus. His dashing good looks, she recalls now, coupled with his shy grin and friendly manner made him appear "sweet, but not macho." They talked and danced for hours, and later that evening, he took her in his arms and they kissed.

When he asked if she would like to get something to eat, she agreed. But instead of heading toward a nearby restaurant, he swerved onto a side street, pulled over to the curb and stopped the car. Then he raped her.

—Sherman, 1985, p. 17

Sexual activity that goes farther than one of the participants would like is not new among college students, nor are the forces behind it. But the term "date rape" is recent, and this label itself may have given such activity a new identity, defining nonconsensual sex between dates or acquaintances as a form of male assault rather than a form of female fault.

Research with both high school and college students shows that a sizable minority of students do not believe that date rape is definitely unacceptable behavior (Mahoney, 1983). Men who have been charged with rape by women they have known or dated are often befuddled by the current situation. Many of them have been conditioned to believe that initial refusals are an essential part of a "mating game" ritual, one that dictates that women must resist somewhat to make themselves more attractive to men.

Several studies have examined the attitudes of college students toward date rape. In one such study, based on questionnaire responses of college students, those students who were more accepting of date rape were less sure that forcible date rape is really rape, were more traditional in their attitudes toward women, were more self-permissive about pre-marital sex with friends or acquaintances, and had less knowledge about sex than other students (Fischer, 1986). A measure of acceptance of force in sexual intercourse was found to be correlated with how often college men admitted using force to have intercourse, how much force was used, and with a lower degree of social responsibility and social conscience (Rapaport & Burkart, 1984). Research also has shown that alcohol and drugs play important roles in date or acquaintance rape. Approximately 75 percent of the men and 55 percent of the women involved in date rape had been drinking or taking drugs prior to the incident (Abbey, 1991; Ward, 1991). The role of alcohol was especially important in combination with participation in party-related activities.

Because research findings show that students' perceptions of what is sexually appropriate have an important influence on their behavior, many schools have begun to educate students about the role that attitudes play in sexual intimacy and about the relationship of behaviors that impair judgment, such as heavy drinking, to the occurrence of date rape. This type of educational program not only heightens student awareness of the problem, but also provides information about how to cope in situations that might be likely to result in unwanted sexual intercourse (see Figure 5-4).

Figure 5-4 These students are watching a video used in school-sponsored programs designed to combat date rape by increasing awareness about the rights of individuals and factors that increase vulnerability and to illustrate coping strategies.

apy that takes into account anger and resentment toward men, guilt and self-blame, and attitudes toward their partners that may be a residue of the rape. Victims of uncontrollable events, such as rape, blame themselves for what has happened beyond what an objective assessment suggests is realistic. Such self-blame is illustrated in this account of a rape victim's experience.

The young woman who was raped after the fraternity party berated herself initially for not picking out some flaw in her assailant's character. She recalls wondering whether her blouse was too low-cut, or whether she had said or done anything to provoke the assault. "It took me a long time," she says ruefully, "to realize that it wasn't my fault."

—Sherman, 1985, p. 19

Rape victims need to know what to do and where to go after the rape in order to obtain medical, mental health, social, and legal services. They also need immediate and follow-up medical care for physical trauma, collection of medicolegal evidence, prevention of venereal disease, and protection against unwanted pregnancy. Rape victims need to be listened to and helped to talk about their experience, as well as to be given basic information and assistance in making decisions about further steps to be taken. An important source of help for rape victims is rape-relief centers where information and psychological support are available (see Figure 5-5).

Bereavement and Grief While we now know that rape is much more prevalent than had previously been thought to be the case, the near universality of experiencing the death of a loved one has been obvious for a long time. More than 2 million people can be expected to die in a single year in the United States alone. Of these, more than 16,000 are children between the ages of 1 and 14, and as many as 38,000 are young people between the ages of 15 and 24. More than 40,000 babies die before reaching the age of 1 year. For each of these deaths, there are left behind bereaved persons at an increased risk of harm to their mental and physical health (Stroebe et al., 1993).

Bereavement refers to the loss of someone significant through that person's death. The normal course of recovery from bereavement often extends to a year or more, and such a pattern of recovery is not considered to be an adjustment disorder. It is only when a person's response differs from this normal pattern, and coping difficulties and emotional distress continue without gradual improvement, that the diagnosis of adjustment disorder would be given. Table 5-5 lists behavioral and physiological changes frequently observed in the period following the loss of a loved one.

Grief is the emotional or affective response to the loss. The symptoms of grief are part of a normal recovery process and not a sign of pathology. Nevertheless, grief

Figure 5-5 Rape relief centers provide information about medical and legal services for rape victims as well as immediate supportive interactions. Such centers attempt to reduce the feelings of social stigma experienced by many rape victims.

takes more prolonged, pervasive, and complicated forms than many people realize. These forms vary greatly; there is no uniform and orderly succession of stages through which all bereaved people must pass. However, certain phases are observed often enough to be recognized as, if not typical, at least common after the death of a husband, wife, or child. The first reactions are often shock, numbness, bewilderment, and a sense of disbe-

TABLE 5–5
Behavioral and Physiological Aspects of Bereavement in Adults

Behavioral Changes	Physiological Changes
Crying	Muscular weakness
Agitation, restlessness	Sighing
Preoccupation with image	Sleep disturbance
of the deceased	Immunological changes
Social withdrawal	Endocrine changes
Decreased concentration	Cardiovascular changes
and attention	Decreased body weight
Depressed mood	
Anxiety	

Source: Based on Hofer, 1984.

lief—even denial of the reality for a time. This reaction is common even when the death was anticipated. After a few days numbness turns to intense suffering. Grieving people feel empty. They are repeatedly reminded of the person who has died. Waves of crying sweep over them with each reminder; they may have dreams and even hallucinations in which the dead person is still alive (Clayton, 1990).

After this comes a period of despair, as the grieving person slowly accepts the loss. The dominant feelings are sadness and inability to feel pleasure. Tense, restless anxiety may alternate with lethargy and fatigue. Physical symptoms are common—weakness, sleep disturbances, loss of appetite, headaches, back pain, indigestion, shortness of breath, heart palpitations, and even occasional dizziness and nausea.

Grieving persons may alternate between avoiding reminders of the deceased and cultivating memories (see Figure 5-6). Some desperately seek company, and others

Figure 5-6 Bob Ojeda, a Cleveland Indians' pitcher, was injured in a boating accident that caused the deaths of two of his teammates. Ojeda recovered from his physical injuries, but the psychological impact of his teammates' deaths persisted. For a while after the accident he wanted to run away from the world, and from himself. He went to Stockholm for two days—just got on a plane and left without telling anyone. He shut out his wife, Ellen, because he tried to suppress the event, hoping it might just go away. It was terrible for her, too, since she wanted to help and didn't understand his reaction. When he first returned to the Indians, he felt estranged, as if he was a reminder to them of the accident—a ghost, a burden—and he seemed to distance himself.

withdraw. Sadness is mixed with anger—at doctors who failed, at friends and relatives thought to be unappreciative, even at the dead person for abandoning the living. The motives of people who try to help are sometimes suspect, and grieving persons may alienate their friends by irritability and quarrelsomeness. Most painful of all is self-reproach for having treated the deceased badly or having done too little to prevent the death. For example, there is evidence that a spouse's recovery from grief is quicker and more complete when the marriage was happy (Stroebe et al., 1993). When the grieving process becomes abnormal, the bereaved person may suffer persistent anxiety or depression produced by morbid or unresolved grief. In such a case psychotherapy may be helpful.

Research on grief and the failure of some bereaved people to resume a normal life in a reasonable period of time is needed because bereavement is so common and because popular ideas about how people do or should respond to loss may not be correct. One focus of this research concerns high-risk factors for poor outcome of bereavement. Table 5-6 summarizes evidence on this topic (Sanders, 1993). Studies are also being conducted on the role of counseling and psychotherapy in overcoming intense grief reactions. Enabling bereaved persons to explore their loss and express their feelings about it and encouraging them to focus on the present and future can be helpful.

Life Transitions

Whereas disasters and many personal crises are imposed on people from outside, other crises grow out of the individual's own path of personal development. Some of the transitions in the life cycle that can cause stress are the following.

1. Birth and attainment of coordination between mother and infant

TABLE 5–6 **Factors that heighten risk for poor outcome of bereavement**
■ Sudden unexpected deaths, including suicide, murder, and stigmatized deaths (for example, death due to AIDS)
■ Ambivalence toward and dependency on the deceased
■ Death of a parent
■ Perceived lack of social support
■ Concurrent crises (for example, illness in other family members)
■ Reduced material resources
■ Gender of a surviving spouse (widowers are often at higher risk than widows)

2. Initial steps toward independence and transition to an out-of-home facility (school, day-care center)
3. The biological and social changes that mark puberty and adolescence
4. Major educational transitions, such as going to college
5. Entry into the world of work
6. Marriage
7. Bearing and rearing children
8. Moving to a new place of residence
9. Children's milestones
10. Retirement

The period of adolescence illustrates the role stress plays in a life transition.

Adolescence The role of cultural factors in adolescence cannot be overestimated. As a reasonably distinct period of life, adolescence might be described as a by-product of the Industrial Revolution. Prior to that event there had been no need to provide a special niche for people who were biologically no longer children but to whom society did not find it convenient to assign adult roles. Since the Industrial Revolution, the age at which individuals are admitted to adult occupational roles has repeatedly been raised, with the result that the period of adolescence has been lengthened. The stress experienced by adolescents has been increased by the lack of agreement about when adolescence ends as well as by the greater number of life choices young people have to make.

Adolescence can be divided into early, middle, and late periods. The dominant theme of early adolescence, approximately ages 12 to 14, is the individual's response to changes in sex hormone levels and a general growth spurt. For girls, the onset of puberty comes at an increasingly early age—the average age at first menstruation has declined from 16.5 years in 1860 to 12.5 years today. The comparable events of puberty for boys lag approximately two years behind those for girls.

By the end of this early period, the young teenager has acquired a body that is quite different from the one he or she had as a child. Changes in body image have a significant effect on an adolescent's self-concept. How well an adolescent likes his or her body often depends on how other people respond to it. For example, late-maturing boys generally show more personal and social maladjustment at all stages of adolescence than those who mature early. They tend to be characterized by negative self-concepts, prolonged dependency, and feelings of rejection by important peer groups. The picture is different for girls. Early-maturing girls often lack poise and are submissive in their social relationships. Late-maturing girls, on the other hand, seem more outgoing and self-assured.

The extent to which the unpredictable moodiness, depression, anger, and emotionality often seen in early adolescence are related to changes in sex hormone levels is unclear. It has been shown, however, that adolescence does not necessarily have to be a stormy and stressful time. Parental interest, reasonable guidelines, and support, particularly from the same-sex parent, play important roles in helping the younger teenager make the necessary developmental transitions.

During midadolescence (roughly 15 to 17 years of age), the teenager receives increasing responsibility and more privileges (for example, holding down a part-time job; driving a car). There are also increases in stress created by the fact that the adolescent is in many ways a marginal character: too old to be treated as a child, too young to have the rights of an adult. Perhaps the most noteworthy developmental occurrence in midadolescence is the gradual shift from a here-and-now perspective to a point of view that is oriented toward the future. In addition, the individual becomes less self-absorbed and grows increasingly concerned with values and ideals.

In late adolescence, teenagers begin to relinquish their parents as primary attachment figures. Living with the family, which is seen as protection by some adolescents and as restraint by others, can now come to an end. Some individuals move directly into the adult roles of marriage and full-time work, whereas others enter a more or less extended adolescence through college or job-training experience. Major tasks of this period include development of a personal identity, renegotiation of the relationship to the family, and the development of stable and enduring ties to others. Late adolescence can be difficult for a variety of reasons, including high unemployment rates among teenagers and young adults as well as high crime rates and the problems posed by alcoholism and drug abuse.

During this period adolescents often feel isolated and in limbo. Various factors contribute to this adolescent loneliness. The adolescent experiences new desires and expectations that may not be readily satisfied but that disrupt existing personal relationships. A predisposition to loneliness may originate in such personality characteristics as shyness and low self-esteem and may be intensified by cultural factors such as the existing social network.

We have noted that everyone has a breaking point and that breakdowns can occur either as a result of sudden personal crises or gradually developing life transitions. In either case, an effective repertoire of coping skills and the availability of supportive friends and family keep the individual from feeling overwhelmed by stressors.

Clinical Reactions to Stress

Stress plays a role in most of the conditions that make up abnormal psychology. Stress disorders that require clinical attention are pathological because they go beyond expected, normal emotional and cognitive reactions to severe personal challenges. Table 5-7 lists some of the normal and abnormal responses to stress. As the table makes clear, many normal responses become abnormal reactions when symptoms persist and are excessive. Successful coping often involves the individual's somehow coming to terms with overwhelming feelings such as sadness or anger. For example, one researcher (Bohmfalk, 1991) documented the case of a physician who, while delivering terrible news to families of patients with dismal or hopeless prognoses, would develop an irrational urge to laugh. The doctor had to learn to face the overwhelming distress he felt in delivering such news. The physician described how conveying bad news to a particular patient's family helped him to face his own distress and free himself of his urge to laugh.

The patient and her family were perfectly typical. The girl was neither beautiful nor brilliant, her family neither overbearing nor solicitous. Their deep concern for her fate was overblown by neither guilt nor persecution. Her severe injuries were ordinary, her operation went smoothly, and there was no problem over several days with any aspect of her care. She just wasn't going to survive. This time, however, after bracing myself for the ultimate family conference and hoping I would be able to suppress an involuntary smile or chuckle, something wonderfully different happened. As

the parents, grandparents, and siblings accepted my report and began to cry quietly, tears began flowing down my face. I had no guilt, I had nothing for which to apologize; I hadn't even come to know this family very well. But there I was, crying right along with them. I didn't want to cry, it just happened. I didn't feel stupid or self-conscious. I simply felt really sad.

. . . Since those initial belated tears, I never had to fight an inappropriate smile. Misery is no longer a laughing matter.

—Bohmfalk, 1991, p. 1245

This section will review three conditions, which, though dealt with by DSM-IV in different ways, are all linked to stress arousal, strong emotional reactions—that may be denied, and clinical symptoms. In *adjustment disorders*, a recent increase in life stress precedes what is usually a temporary maladaptive reaction. *Posttraumatic disorders* are often more complicated because of the possibility of delayed and recurring reactions to stress. *Dissociative disorders* are among the most dramatic and puzzling forms of abnormal behavior and are usually preceded by an upsurge of stress that the individual cannot handle.

Adjustment disorders are considered to be more straightforward than the other two conditions. This lack of ambiguity may be due to the fact that in an adjustment disorder specific stressful experiences can be identified as having occurred recently in the patient's life, and prospects of recovery are relatively good. While specific stressors can also be identified in a posttraumatic disorder, they are often more dramatic and overwhelming than those seen in adjustment disorders, their effects last over a longer period of time, and recovery prospects are less positive. One source of controversy about posttraumatic disorders is the question of the reliability of information about the patient's personality prior to the traumatic event. Clinicians must evaluate how much of the posttraumatic disorder is attributable to the event and how much to the patient's vulnerabilities before the event. Varying interpretations of dissociative disorders depend upon the weight given to a number of factors, including the stressors that immediately precede clinical flare-ups, stressors that may have occurred early in the person's life, and biological causes. A major challenge in the real world of maladaptive behavior is the multiplicity of factors involved in most cases.

TABLE 5–7
Normal and Abnormal Responses to Stress

Normal Responses	Abnormal Responses
Feeling strong emotions subsequent to the event (for example, fear, sadness, rage)	Being overwhelmed by intense emotions; experiencing panic or exhaustion
Resistance to thinking about the event; denial	Extreme resistance to thinking about the event (for example, through use of drugs); massive denial
Having unwanted, intrusive thoughts about the event	Having disturbing, persistent images and thoughts that interfere with usual functioning
Temporary physical symptoms (headaches, stomach distress)	Strong, persistent bodily reactions (for example, continuing headaches, chronic stomach pains)
Resuming one's normal pattern of life	Long-term problems in ability to love and work

Adjustment Disorder

A person with an **adjustment disorder** is someone who has not adapted as well as the average person to one or more stressors that have occurred in the previous three months. The stressors might involve a developmental transition (such as marriage, divorce, having a child, or menopause), or they might be situational (such as changing schools, getting a new supervisor at work, or having been socially rejected), or they might be multiple stressors that have recently accumulated. (DMS-IV deals with bereavement reactions as a special condition and does not categorize them—despite several similarities—as adjustment disorders.) Most of the time a person's maladaptive reactions to these stressors tend to disappear when the stressful circumstances dissipate or when the person learns how to live with new conditions. In the following case, the stressful transition to marriage resulted in an adjustment disorder.

Mark Catton, aged 23, had recently married. He and his wife had known each other for two years at college and were deeply in love. Their getting married seemed a perfectly logical consequence of their affection for each other. The first several weeks after the wedding were wonderful for the couple. They looked forward to their evenings together and often took short trips on the weekend.

One evening at dinner Dorothy talked about a new salesman at her office. She described him as intelligent, handsome, and charming. When Dorothy used the word "charming," something seemed to click inside Mark. He wondered why she had chosen that particular word to describe the new salesman, as well as why she talked so much about someone she had known for only a day. During the next few weeks Dorothy made several additional references to the salesman. Her liking for him was more obvious with each reference. Each time it came up, Mark became increasingly suspicious and depressed. When Dorothy worked until late in the evening twice in one week, his suspiciousness and depression increased. When he confronted her with his suspicion that she was dating the salesman, Dorothy displayed shock and outrage.

During the next few weeks Mark became increasingly depressed. His depression was interrupted only by occasional outbursts of venom directed toward Dorothy. Their sex life soon ceased to exist, and their evenings were filled with silence. The problem reached clinical proportions when Mark began to stay in bed all day. It took great effort for Dorothy to get him to see a psychotherapist, although by this time even Mark knew that something was very wrong.

During his sessions with the psychotherapist Mark came to see how unrealistic his expectations about marriage were. He also was able for the first time to bring all of his thoughts and feelings out into the open. One recollection about his parents seemed particularly important. He remembered that

when he was about 6 or 7 his parents had quarreled a great deal, apparently over his father's suspicion about his mother's activities at home while he was at work. His father had accused his mother of infidelity and had been very nasty. Mark couldn't remember exactly how the situation had been resolved. Although he had not thought about the incident for years, it became very meaningful to him, and discussing it in psychotherapy seemed to help him.

Mark Catton's case is interesting because it shows so clearly the interaction between past and present experiences. His own marital problems, created by his irrational suspicions about his wife's activities, seemed to be linked to things his wife had told him about the salesman and to his unrecognized dread that what his father had feared was actually being inflicted on him. One additional point about this case is that Mark had no history of suspiciousness and depression. Both reaction patterns had apparently been ignited simply by getting married. His psychological functioning deteriorated primarily because of the expectations and concerns he had brought to the marital situation, not because of a traumatic development within the marriage. His psychotherapy experience (which consisted of 11 sessions) enabled Mark to resume a normal, gratifying marital relationship.

Depression, anxiety, disturbances in conduct (truancy, fighting, reckless driving), disrupted sleep patterns, deterioration in performance at work or school, and social withdrawal are typical behaviors of individuals who have adjustment disorders. Table 5-8 lists information pertinent to making a DSM-IV diagnosis of adjustment disorder. The severity of the disorder is not directly proportional to the severity of the stressor, because personality characteristics as well as cultural or group norms contribute to how well an individual copes with a given set of circumstances. However, one characteristic of adjustment disorders is that the behavior displayed is in excess of what would normally be expected under the circumstances. A return to pre-stressor functioning within 6 months can be expected and the chances of complete recovery when the stress level comes down are good. An adjustment disorder usually

---

TABLE 5–8
Information Needed in Making an Adjustment Disorder Diagnosis

- Time of onset and duration of the stressor (symptoms must develop within 3 months after onset).
- Duration of symptoms (usually less than 6 months).
- Depressed mood, and/or
- Anxiety, and/or
- Inappropriate or antisocial conduct

does not involve extremely bizarre behavior and is not part of a lifelong pattern of maladaptation.

Posttraumatic Stress Disorder

Whereas the stressors in adjustment disorder are within the range of common experience, **posttraumatic stress disorders** (PTSD) involve more extreme experiences (such as disasters) whose effects may extend over a long period. The traumas range from those that are directly experienced (for example, being threatened with death) to those that are witnessed (for example, a family member being threatened with death). The onset of the clinical condition in posttraumatic disorders varies from soon after the trauma to a long time afterward. In DSM-IV, these disorders are considered to be acute if the condition begins within 3 months of the trauma and delayed if symptoms emerge more than 6 months after the event. The chances of complete recovery are better in the acute form than in the delayed form. Although preexisting psychological difficulties may intensify posttraumatic disorders, many people who develop these disorders do not have a history of psychiatric problems.

A frequent characteristic of posttraumatic disorders is a tendency to reexperience the event. Painful and intrusive recollections and recurrent dreams or nightmares are common. The reexperiencing of a traumatic event may have an aura of unreality about it. When this happens, the person feels emotionally anesthetized amid an unstoppable flood of thoughts about the event.

In addition to reexperiencing the stressor, people who are suffering from posttraumatic disorders may show excessive autonomic arousal, hyperalertness, difficulty in concentrating on or completing tasks, and difficulty falling asleep. A symptom that often occurs in children who have experienced trauma is an exaggerated startle response. These symptoms may increase when the individual is exposed to cues related to the traumatic event (for example, when a victim of an automobile accident sees a car crash in a movie). Preoccupation with the traumatic event may also lead to decreased interest in social relationships, intimacy, and sexuality. Painful guilt feelings are common, as are depression, restlessness, and irritability. In some cases, there may be outbreaks of impulsive behavior, usually of a nonviolent nature (for example, unexplained absences from work), and abuse of alcohol or drugs.

In the following case, there was a short interval between the stressor and the onset of the posttraumatic condition. This case illustrates how denial can be used to blunt the strong feelings aroused by a stressful event.

Harry is a 40-year-old truck dispatcher. He had worked his way up in a small trucking firm. One night he himself took a

run because he was shorthanded. The load was steel pipes carried in an old truck. This improper vehicle had armor between the load bed and the driver's side of the forward compartment but did not fully protect the passenger's side.

Late at night Harry passed an attractive and solitary girl hitchhiking on a lonely stretch of highway. Making an impulsive decision to violate the company rule against passengers of any sort, he picked her up.

A short time later, a car veered across the divider line and entered his lane, threatening a head-on collision. He pulled over the shoulder of the road into an initially clear area, but crashed abruptly into a pile of gravel. The pipes shifted, penetrated the cab of the truck on the passenger's side and impaled the girl. Harry crashed into the steering wheel and windshield and was briefly unconscious. He regained consciousness and was met with the grisly sight of his dead companion.

The highway patrol found no identification on the girl, the other car had driven on, and Harry was taken by ambulance to a hospital emergency room. No fractures were found, his lacerations were sutured, and he remained overnight for observation. His wife, who sat with him, found him anxious and dazed that night, talking episodically of the events in a fragmentary and incoherent way so that the story was not clear.

The next day he was released. Against his wife's wishes, he returned to work. From then on, for several days, he continued his regular work as if nothing had happened. There was an immediate session with his superiors and with legal advisors. The result was that he was reprimanded for breaking the rule about passengers but also reassured that, otherwise, the accident was not his fault and he would not be held responsible. As it happened, the no-passenger rule was frequently breached by other drivers. This fact was well known throughout the group.

For several days after the accident Harry thought about it occasionally, but he was surprised at how little emotion he felt. However, despite his good performance at work, Harry's wife reported that he thrashed around in his sleep, ground his teeth, and seemed tenser and more irritable than usual. A month after the accident he had a nightmare in which mangled bodies appeared. He awoke in a state of anxiety. During the following days he had recurring, upsetting images of the girl's body. He developed a phobia about driving to and from work, increased his consumption of alcohol, had outbursts of temper at minor frustrations, and began feeling intense guilt about the accident.

In psychotherapy an effort was made to understand the significance of the accident for Harry. Initially Harry resisted describing to the therapist the circumstances surrounding the accident. After this resistance subsided, his strong feelings— the guilt, fears, and anger—emerged and were discussed. Because of complex and defensive motives, Harry could not accept and integrate his traumatic perceptions of the accident. They were stored, but not forgotten. He came to understand that two themes had been most upsetting to him: guilt over his relief at the fact that the girl had been the victim instead of him, as well as guilt over his sexual fantasies about her; and anxiety over the realization that he had come so close to being the victim. Bringing these themes into focus enabled Harry to be more open about himself and to take a problem-solving rather than a defensive stance toward his situation. Psychotherapy enabled him to look at himself in a more realistic way, to feel comfortable doing so within the supportive-therapy situation, and to achieve an improved adaptation.

—Adapted from Horowitz, 1974, p. 769–771

What happens in posttraumatic stress? In coping with trauma, an individual uses a huge amount of psychological energy to fend off thoughts about it. Although the event has ended, it is relived daily, and there is an irrational fear that it will happen again. It is this fear that causes hypervigilance and agitation. Intrusive thoughts, images, and dreams may become so preoccupying that the person cannot engage in normal work or relationships.

In some cases of maladaptive reactions to trauma there may be an alternation of intrusive thinking and denial. In the intrusive state, the individual cannot stop having frightening thoughts related to the traumatic event. In the denial state, the individual ignores the implications of threats and losses, forgets important problems, and may show a withdrawal of interest in life. Table 5-9 lists symptoms of the intrusive and denial phases of posttraumatic disorders.

Posttraumatic stress disorder, in which the reaction continues over a considerable period of time, is now an established psychiatric diagnosis, but it is still a controversial one. DSM-IV distinguishes PTSD from **acute stress disorder,** a diagnosis limited to conditions in which the symptoms occur within 1 month of the extreme stressor. Because PTSD requires more than 1 month of symptoms, the diagnosis is not used during this initial one-month period. Epidemiological evidence suggests that the prevalence of PTSD typically ranges from 1 to 14 percent depending on the population sampled and how PTSD symptoms were assessed. Recent findings suggest that PTSD is more prevalent than has been thought to be the case (Solomon, et al., 1992). About 20 percent of wounded Vietnam veterans showed symptoms of PTSD (Helzer and others, 1987). A study of people who had been present at a mass-murder spree in a cafeteria found that 20 percent of the men and 36 percent of the women later met the criteria for PTSD (North, et al., 1994) (see Figure 5-7).

There is some evidence that preexisting emotional and behavioral difficulties constitute vulnerabilities and increase the likelihood of PTSD. In one study, 72 percent of individuals with PTSD diagnoses had pre-stress histories of psychological disorders (Smith et al., 1990). Prominent among the pre-stress diagnoses of adult PTSD patients were depression and alcohol abuse. A recent study has provided information concerning certain conditions conducive to development of PTSD. The study dealt with the aftermath of the 1991 fires in the Oakland, California, hills (Koopman, et al., 1994). The major finding was that those who react with an apparently unwarranted calm may be particularly prone to posttraumatic distress problems such as severe anxiety, sleep disruptions, or flashbacks, which may not surface until months or even years later. There was also evidence that they may also be inclined to put themselves in danger during a disaster because they ignore the reality of the peril. The heightened risk occurs particularly in those whose steadiness during a catastrophe is a result of symptoms of dissociation that include lack of emotional reaction, a feeling that the events are unreal, or disorientation. Thus, those who tend to shut out reality in stressful situation are at heightened risk for a later severe posttraumatic disorder.

Certain symptoms may be related to the type of trauma experienced, such as whether or not the individual played a role in causing the traumatic event (for example, by driving a car recklessly or speeding). Victims of crimes involving violence and humiliation (for example, rape) often feel both intensely fearful and ashamed. Rape victims often show this type of reaction. Their anger at being victimized and the lack of control they feel concerning the event results frequently in long-term effects like those discussed earlier in the chapter. The severity, duration, and proximity of an individual's exposure to the traumatic event are the most important factors affecting the likelihood of developing this disorder.

TABLE 5–9
Symptoms of Intrusive Thinking and Denial in Posttraumatic Stress Disorders (Symptoms May Alternate)

Symptoms of Intrusive Thinking

Sleep and dream disturbances
Awareness of ideas and feelings related to the traumatic event
Preoccupation with the event
Compulsive repetitions of actions related to the event

Symptoms of Denial

Selective inattention
Amnesia (complete or partial)
Use of fantasy to counteract real conditions
Withdrawal

Source: Adapted from Horowitz, 1986. Copyright © 1986 by the American Psychological Association. Reprinted by permission of the author.

Figure 5-7 Few of Sarajevo's 60,000 children escaped the devastating effects of the war between Serbs and Muslims for control of the Bosnian capitol. At least 6,000 of these children have died in the civil war and many others have experienced extreme stress. Figure 5-7a shows psychiatrist Arshad Husain conducting an actual group therapy session with Bosnian children. Because of the scarcity of trained mental health personnel, he is also using the session to train the teachers shown in the foreground to enable them to work therapeutically with children in their classes. Figures 5-7b and 5-7c, drawings by Bosnian children affected by post-traumatic stress disorder, graphically portray the horrors of their experience.

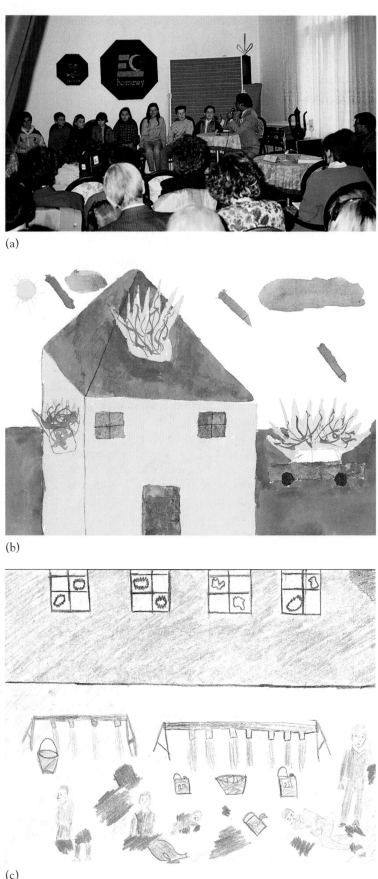

(a)

(b)

(c)

Psychotherapy can often be helpful in reducing these effects because it helps victims not only to view the experience in a more objective way but also to express the strong emotions they may have felt forced to suppress in conversations with friends and relatives. Behavioral therapies designed to reduce anxiety by means of repeated or extended, real or imaginary, exposure to objectively harmless yet feared stimuli have been used successfully in some cases of PTSD. Psychodynamic and cognitive therapy approaches have also been found to be helpful. Drug treatments, such as antidepressants and tranquilizers, appear to be less effective than psychological therapies (Solomon et al., 1992).

Dissociative Disorders

Dissociative disorders are disturbances or alterations in the functions of identity, memory, and consciousness. The disturbance may come about suddenly or gradually and may last only a brief period or be long-lasting and chronic. The person's identity may be temporarily forgotten or a new identity assumed or there may be a feeling that one's sense of reality is lost. The maladaptive behaviors that arise from dissociative disorders provide a striking contrast to those that arise from post-traumatic stress disorders and adjustment disorders. Stress plays a major role in all three, yet the reactions involved appear to be poles apart. Once again we see that similar situations can elicit drastically different responses in people with different dispositions and vulnerabilities.

People with dissociative disorders seem to use a variety of dramatic maneuvers to escape from the anxieties and conflicts aroused by stress. Their behavior involves sudden, temporary alterations of consciousness that serve to blot out painful experiences. In contrast, in posttraumatic stress disorders, individuals cannot get the distressing experiences that they have undergone out of their minds; those with adjustment disorders show milder disturbances and decreased ability to cope, but their behavior clears up when they learn to adapt to a stressor when the stressor is removed.

Many dissociative disorders appear to begin and end abruptly and are precipitated by stressful experiences. Although these disorders usually occur after childhood, in most cases there is a history of serious family turmoil. Separation from parents in early childhood and abuse by parents have frequently been reported (Putnam, 1991).

The dissociation often involves feelings of unreality, estrangement, and depersonalization, and sometimes a loss or shift of self-identity. Less dramatic, but somewhat similar, examples of dissociation are commonly observed in normal adults and children. When the first impact of bad news or a catastrophe hits us, we may feel as if everything is suddenly strange, unnatural, and different (estrangement), or as if we are unreal and cannot actually be witnessing or feeling what is going on (depersonalization). These are not classified as dissociative disorders but are useful to help in understanding what the much more severe dissociative disorder is like.

The Dissociation Continuum Before turning to the dramatic behavioral patterns seen in the dissociative disorders, we need to note a growing interest on the part of researchers in the possibility that dissociative processes fall along a continuum ranging from normal to pathological. Examples of pathological processes are the bizarre behavior seen in multiple personality and fugue states, both of which we will describe.

As a process, dissociation can be viewed as a severing of the connections between ideas and emotion. This happens to all of us when we divide our attention between two or more simultaneous tasks. From this perspective, dissociation might be regarded as an attribute that facilitates dividing one's attention. It might also play a role in fantasy, imagination, and acting. A good actor is able to become immersed in various types of roles. Could it be that dissociation becomes pathological only when a significant trauma occurs and the individual loses control of dissociative processes? Might a person high in dissociative ability who suffers a trauma use dissociation as a defense that normally might be adaptive? Researchers have only recently begun to study these questions. A first step in this effort is the assessment of individual differences in dissociation. Table 5-10 contains examples of items currently being used in making this assessment. By studying how these items relate

to various types of behavior, it may be possible to determine the degree to which the tendency to dissociate is a basic personality trait. A dissociation trait might have multiple components that influence the extent to which people can compartmentalize their experiences, identity, memory, perception, and motor function.

Dissociation should not be considered inherently pathological and it might not lead to significant distress, impairment, or help-seeking behavior. Furthermore, cross-cultural studies have found that dissociative states are a common and accepted expression of cultural activity or religious experience in many societies (Spiegel, 1994).

DSM-IV classifies four conditions as dissociative disorders:

1. Dissociative amnesia
2. Dissociative fugue
3. Dissociative identity disorder
4. Depersonalization

All of these disorders involve large memory gaps and drastic changes in social roles.

Dissociative Amnesia Amnesia involves extensive, but selective, memory loss in the absence of indications of organic change (for example, head injuries). The memory losses characteristic of amnesia are too extensive to be explained by ordinary forgetfulness. Some people cannot remember anything about their past. Others can no longer recall specific events, people, places, or objects while their memory for other, simultaneously experienced events remains intact.

Amnesia is usually precipitated by a physical accident or an emotionally traumatic event such as an intensely painful disappointment. Cases of amnesia demonstrate, as Ernest Hilgard (1986) has noted, that the unity of consciousness is illusory. Our conscious representation of our actions is incomplete; our attention is usually

---

TABLE 5–10
Examples of Questionnaire Items Intended to Place Individuals on the Dissociation Continuum

I like to fantasize about doing interesting and exciting things.
Sometimes the things around me do not seem quite real.
Sometimes while driving a car, I suddenly realize that I don't remember what has happened during all or part of the trip.
I have such a vivid imagination that I really could "become" someone else for a few minutes.
Sometimes I feel as if there is someone inside me directing my actions.

divided among two or more streams of thought or courses of action. Unconscious systems of ideas may come to be split off from the major personality and exist as subordinate personalities, capable of becoming represented in consciousness under certain conditions. The following account illustrates the power of such unconscious forces.

A young man who was dressed in work clothes came to the emergency room of a hospital in the city in which he lived with the complaint that he did not know who he was. He seemed dazed, was not intoxicated, and carried no identification. After being kept in the hospital a few days, he woke up one morning in great distress, demanding to know why he was being kept in the hospital and announcing that he had to leave immediately to attend to urgent business.

With the recovery of his memory, the facts related to his amnesia emerged. The day his amnesia began, he had been the driver in an automobile accident that resulted in the death of a pedestrian. Police officers on the scene were convinced that the driver had not been in the wrong: The accident had been the pedestrian's fault. The police told the driver to fill out a routine form and to plan to appear at the coroner's inquest. The man filled out the form at the home of a friend and accidentally left his wallet there. Later after mailing the form, he became dazed and amnesic. He was led to the hospital by a stranger. This amnesia was probably related to the stress of the fatal accident, fear of the inquest, and worry that he might actually have been responsible for the accident.

—Based on Cameron, 1963, pp. 355–356

While amnesia is probably the most common dissociative disorder, there are no accurate statistics on the incidence of any of the dissociative disorders. Dissociative amnesias are seen more often in adolescents and young adults than in children and older people, and occur more often among females than males.

There are several types of dissociative amnesia:

Localized amnesia, in which the individual fails to recall events that occurred during a particular period of time (for example, the first few hours after a profoundly disturbing event).
Selective amnesia, in which the person can recall some, but not all, of the events during a particular period of time.
Generalized amnesia, which involves a recall failure that encompasses the person's entire life. This type occurs rarely.
Continuous amnesia, the inability to recall events subsequent to a specific time, up to and including the present.
Systematized amnesia, the loss of memory for certain categories of information, such as memories relating to a particular person.

Dissociative fugue. **Dissociative fugue** has as its essential feature unexpected travel away from home and customary workplace, the assumption of a new identity, and the inability to recall the previous identity. The travel and behavior seen in a person experiencing a fugue are more purposeful than any wandering that may take place in dissociative amnesia. Such a person sets up a new life in some distant place as a seemingly different person. The fugue state, or amnesic flight, usually ends when he or she abruptly "wakes up," mystified and distressed at being in a strange place under strange circumstances (see Figure 5-8).

Fugues, like amnesia, are often precipitated by intolerable stresses, such as marital quarrels, personal rejection, military conflict, and natural disasters. Fugues are usually of brief duration, with complete recovery and lit-

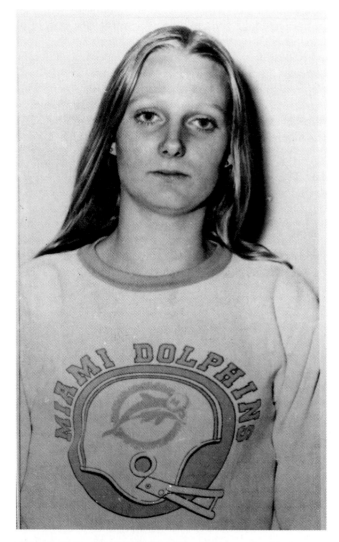

Figure 5-8 Police distributed this photograph of a woman found wandering on a New Jersey highway in the hope that someone would recognize her. When she was found she was unable to remember her name, where she lived, or how she came to be walking along the highway.

tle likelihood of recurrence. After "waking up," the person frequently has no recollection of the events that took place during the fugue. The following case illustrates a fugue state with massive amnesia.

Samuel O., a graduate student, impoverished and far from home, was invited to dinner at the home of an instructor whom he had known when they were socioeconomic equals in another town. He accepted the invitation because he was lonely and hungry, but he regretted it almost at once because his clothes were shabby. He thought, in retrospect, that the instructor had seemed condescending. That evening he left his rooming house in plenty of time for the dinner, but he failed to show up at the instructor's home. Two days later he was picked up by the police in a neighboring state. He could vaguely remember riding a freight train, talking with strangers, and sharing their food, but he had no idea who he was, where he had come from, or where he was going.

Later on, the young man was able to remember the events leading up to the fugue and something of what went on during it. When he started out for the instructor's house, he was still experiencing strong conflict about going there. He was ashamed of his appearance, resentful over the condescension, and afraid to express what he felt and call the dinner off. On his way, he was held up at a grade crossing by a slowly moving freight train. He had a sudden impulse to board the train and get away. When he acted on this impulse, he apparently became amnesic.

—Based on Easton, 1959, pp. 505–513

People experiencing a fugue generally appear to be without psychopathology and do not attract attention. Most fugues do not involve the formation of a new identity. However, the person might assume a new name or take up a new residence.

Dissociative Identity Disorder. **Dissociative identity disorder,** often referred to as *multiple personality,* is the most dramatic of the dissociative disorders. In this disorder, an individual assumes alternate personalities, like Dr. Jekyll and Mr. Hyde. Each personality has its own set of memories and typical behaviors. Frequently none of the personalities has any awareness of the others. In other cases, there is a one-way amnesia in which personality A is aware of the experiences of personality B while B remains unaware of A.

While multiple personality is a rare disorder, it is of increasing interest because of the marked increase in the number of cases currently being described in the clinical literature and the linkage that has been made in many of these cases between multiple personality and traumatic childhood experiences. The improved diagnostic criteria for the disorder that first appeared in DSM-III are thought to have contributed to the increased number of reported cases (Kluft, 1991). Many more female than male dissociative identity

disorders have been reported, the ratio being about 4 to 1 (Kluft, 1988).

Clinically, the personalities' behavioral differences and disparate self-concepts seem striking and puzzling. They may experience themselves as being of different genders, ages, and sexual orientations. They may have separate wardrobes, possessions, interests, and interpersonal styles. Their values, beliefs, and problems may diverge. They may even have different handwritings, handedness, speech patterns, and accents.

In the following case, a 38-year-old woman named Margaret B. was admitted to a hospital with paralysis of her legs following a minor car accident that had occurred 6 months earlier.

She reported that until three years before her admission to the hospital she had enjoyed smoking, drinking, visiting nightclubs, and otherwise indulging in parties and social activities. At that point, however, she and her husband, who was an alcoholic, were converted to a small, evangelical religious sect. Her husband achieved control of his drinking, she gave up her prior social indulgences, and the two of them became completely immersed in the activities of the church.

[The] history revealed that she often "heard a voice telling her to say things and do things." It was, she said, "a terrible voice" that sometimes threatened to "take over completely." When it was finally suggested to the patient that she let the voice "take over," she closed her eyes, clenched her fists, and grimaced for a few moments during which she was out of contact with those around her. Suddenly she opened her eyes and one was in the presence of another person. Her name, she said, was "Harriet." Whereas Margaret had been paralyzed, and complained of fatigue, headache and backache, Harriet felt well, and she at once proceeded to walk unaided around the interviewing room. She spoke scornfully of Margaret's religiousness, her invalidism and her puritanical life, professing that she herself liked to drink and "go partying" but that Margaret was always going to church and reading the Bible. "But," she said impishly and proudly, "I make her miserable—I make her say and do things she doesn't want to." At length, at the interviewer's suggestion, Harriet reluctantly agreed to "bring Margaret back," and after more grimacing and fist clenching, Margaret reappeared, paralyzed, complaining of her headache and backache, and completely amnesic for the brief period of Harriet's release from her prison.

—Nemiah, 1988, 247–248

The clash between Margaret's religiousness, on the one hand, and her inclinations to indulge in pleasure, on the other, is a frequent theme in cases of multiple personality. It is noteworthy that as a child Margaret had had a playmate, Harriet, to whom she had been very devoted. When they were both 6 years old Harriet had died of an acute infectious disease. Margaret had been deeply upset at her friend's death and wished that she had died in Harriet's place. Perhaps internalizing the image of her dead friend had in some way protected Margaret from prolonged despair and sorrow at her loss. As Margaret grew older, that internalization became the depository for all of her unacceptable impulses and feelings.

Many clinicians think of dissociative identity disorder as a psychological adaptation to traumatic experiences in early childhood. These experiences are severe and dramatic; examples include being dangled out of a window or being the victim of sexual sadism. In addition to having experienced harsh trauma in childhood, people with dissociative identity disorder seem prone to go into spontaneous hypnotic trances. Such a temporary defense may become stabilized into this disorder when the child faces repeated, overwhelming trauma.

Some researchers question whether dissociative identity disorder represents anything more than an extreme form of the normal ability to present a variety of distinctive "selves." An important reason for such disagreements about dissociative identity disorder is that cases of this disorder are rare, making it difficult to do good research and to compare cases seen at different times under different circumstances. Despite methodological difficulties, studies of dissociative identity disorder are proceeding on a number of fronts.

One provocative lead in dissociative identity disorder research relates to the possible role of brain abnormalities. Some studies have found that people with multiple personalities have an elevated risk for epileptic seizures (Benson et al., 1986). It is possible that there is a connection between seizures and the switch between personalities. However, while some cases of epilepsy may involve a neurological condition that is associated with dissociative identity disorder, the strength and basis of the association are not yet established. Future work is needed to explore the possibility of a biological basis to the capacity to dissociate, the ways in which stress early in life and later on interact with biological factors, and the development of effective therapies. Clinicians believe that establishing a secure, trusting relationship with the therapist is essential for therapeutic progress (Kluft, 1988). When such a relationship is achieved, it becomes possible to deal with conflicts among the personalities and help the patient move toward cooperation among them and, optimally, integration of the personalities (Spanos, 1994).

In most cases of dissociative identity disorder, the emergence of new personalities begins in early childhood, frequently in response to severe physical and sexual abuse. The emerging personalities appear to be a means of protecting themselves and they often create another self to handle the stressor (Putnam, 1991). Over time, the protective functions served by the new personality remain separate in the form of an alternate person-

ality. In the majority of cases of dissociative identity disorder, the individual tries to hide the alternate personalities. This tendency to "hide" alternate personalities may be contributing to a large number of erroneous diagnoses in such cases.

Depersonalization While **depersonalization** is usually included among the dissociative disorders, some clinicians question its inclusion because it does not entail memory disturbances. In depersonalization there is a change in self-perception, and the person's sense of reality is temporarily lost or changed. Someone who is experiencing a state of depersonalization might say, "I feel as though I'm in a dream" or "I feel that I'm doing this mechanically." Frequently the individual has a feeling of not being in complete control of his or her actions, including speech. The onset of depersonalization is usually rapid and causes social or occupational impairment. The state of estrangement from oneself gradually disappears.

The following case illustrates several features of depersonalization:

> A 24-year-old graduate student sought treatment because he felt he was losing his mind. He had begun to doubt his own reality. He felt he was living in a dream in which he saw himself from without, and did not feel connected to his body or his thoughts. When he saw himself through his own eyes, he perceived his body parts as distorted—his hands and feet seemed quite large. As he walked across campus, he often felt the people he saw might be robots; he began to ruminate about his dizzy spells—did this mean that he had a brain tumor?
>
> . . . He often noted that he spent so much time thinking about his situation that he lost contact with all feelings except a pervasive discomfort about his own predicament. . . .
>
> . . . [H]e was preoccupied with his perception that his feet had grown too large for his shoes, and fretted over whether to break up with his girlfriend because he doubted the reality of his feelings for her, and had begun to perceive her in a distorted manner.
>
> —Kluft, 1988, p. 580

As is true with most clinical cases, explanations for several aspects of this case are by no means obvious. Why does the student often see people as robots? What might account for the distortions in his bodily perceptions? Nevertheless, the case provides several examples of depersonalization. These include the doubts about his own reality, feeling as though he is living in a dream, and losing contact with his feelings.

People with depersonalization disorders may have either a persistent sense of depersonalization or suffer recurrent episodes. In either case, they perceive themselves as having lost their usual sense of reality, or as having had it changed. They feel as if they are in a dream and fear losing their sanity. A number of cases have been reported in which depersonalization seemed to be a response to extreme stress (Kluft, 1988).

Interpreting Dissociative Disorders Dissociation seems to represent a process whereby certain mental functions that are ordinarily integrated with other functions presumably operate in a more compartmentalized or automatic way, usually outside the sphere of conscious awareness or memory recall. It might be described as a condition in which information—incoming, stored, or outgoing—is actively deflected from its usual or expected associations. This phenomenon results in alteration of the person's thoughts, feelings, or actions so that information is not associated or integrated with other information as it normally or logically would be.

The dissociative disorders are difficult to explain for several reasons. Often it is unclear whether a given case involves dissociation or is some sort of psychotic manifestation. Also, it is often difficult to obtain the information needed to draw reasonable conclusions. In the dissociative identity disorder case of Margaret, for example, one wonders about the stressors that led to Harriet's emergence. How important were the loss of the 6-year-old playmate and the recent changes in Margaret's adult life? To what extent did Margaret forget or distort events that occurred when she was a child? While the source of stress is easy to identify in adjustment and posttraumatic disorders, in the dissociative disorders the source might not be obvious at all. Dissociative disorders may be related to combinations of vulnerability factors (for example, certain aspects of biological makeup) and stresses that occurred many years before maladaptation reached clinical proportions. Because human beings are able to distort their memories, considerable probing is often needed to determine the true nature of the stress.

Dissociative disorders are often discussed in psychodynamic (dissociation as a defense mechanism) and cognitive (dissociation as a memory failure) terms. These disorders help the individual escape from reality and seem to facilitate the expression of a variety of pent-up emotions. They have been interpreted as attempts to escape from excessive tension, anxiety, and stimulation by separating some parts of the personality from the rest. When there are no indications of a recent experience that might have functioned as a stressor, these perspectives raise questions about earlier stressors that might still have symbolic meaning for the individual. (Margaret's loss of Harriet illustrates this possibility.) In treating dissociative disorders, many clinicians seek to uncover the dissociated memories and to help the individual face them and deal with them more directly. Psychoanalysis, behavior therapy, hypnosis, and videotaped interviews combined with sedative drugs have all been useful for this purpose.

Reactions to stress can lead to clinical problems. Adjustment disorders involve behavioral deterioration following a stressful experience. However, as the stress level lowers, the individual usually returns to normal. Posttraumatic stress disorders are set in motion by unusual stressful experiences and may persist long after the traumatic event has ended. Though dissociative disorders also often follow stressful experiences, these disorders occur in people who have psychological vulnerabilities including a tendency to sever the connection between ideas and emotions and a strong need to escape from unpleasant realities.

Treating Stress-Related Problems

People often overcome their maladaptive reactions to stress in the course of time, but help from an expert may speed up the process. The clinician has two broad functions: (1) to provide social support for troubled people, and (2) to strengthen their coping skills. Several procedures are used in treating stress-related problems.

Supportive Therapy

It is hard to recover from a stress-related disorder if one is or feels socially isolated. Because most stress reactions involve feelings of inadequacy and isolation, many people can be helped by sympathetic listening and encouragement. Though they use different terms, both psychodynamically and humanistically oriented clinicians emphasize the client-therapist relationship as a means of facilitating adaptive coping. Freudians describe their efforts in this regard as strengthening the client's ego. When the ego is able to manipulate reality more effectively, it can handle the id's incessant demands with less stress. The Rogerian therapist's acceptance of clients as they are, coupled with recognition of their strengths and deemphasis of their failings, helps clients feel more positive about themselves and creates a supportive climate. Clients who receive supportive therapy often comment with relief that the therapist did not criticize them either directly or indirectly for their handling of difficult situations. Within a supportive environment clients can relax enough to engage in problem solving and the careful consideration of alternatives that had previously seemed impossible.

Being supportive may not be easy for the therapist. Working with dissociative disorders can be arduous and demanding. Many therapists, sensitive to their patients' isolation, find it difficult to be both accessible and able to set reasonable and nonpunitive limits. In dissociative identity disorders, it is particularly difficult to follow the threads of the separate personalities.

Drugs and Sedatives

A variety of antianxiety and antidepressive drugs are available to help people who have experienced trauma. While they are not a cure, such drugs can be of value in overcoming panic states and other maladaptive reactions to intense short-term stress. Tranquilizers are often used along with such psychological approaches as supportive therapy.

Relaxation Training

It is possible for people to learn ways of helping themselves deal with stress. It is well known that people can learn to regulate voluntarily certain effects of the autonomic nervous system. Such regulation, in turn, can affect their emotional state. For example, anxiety can be caused by the sensation of tension that is experienced when muscle fibers are shortened or contracted, as they are during stress. Conversely, tension cannot be present when muscle fibers are lengthened or relaxed. Relaxation training involves the following steps:

1. Focusing attention on a series of specific muscle groups
2. Tensing each group
3. Maintaining tension for five to seven seconds
4. Telling oneself to relax and immediately releasing tension
5. Focusing attention on each muscle group as it relaxes

Relaxation training is used not only as a technique in its own right but also as a basis for other therapies. It is applicable to a wide variety of stress-related problems and can be readily taught both individually and in groups.

Systematic Desensitization

This procedure consists of combining relaxation training and a hierarchy of anxiety-producing stimuli to gradually eliminate the fear of a specific situation. The person learns to maintain the relaxed state while imagining anxiety-associated stimuli from the various stages of the hierarchy. The result is often a significant reduction in his or her fears.

Cognitive Modification

Behavioral problems can arise in part because an individual persists in a particular maladaptive line of thought. If someone can be guided to think about a situation in a different, more productive way, adaptive coping may become possible. Cognitive modification involves learning new internal dialogues and new ways of thinking about situations and about oneself. In this sense, cognitive modification is a step toward productive problem solving.

Social Intervention

Some therapists prefer to treat troubled individuals alone, whereas other therapists feel that they can be more helpful if they treat people within their social contexts. Family therapy, in which all members of the family go into treatment together, is based on the latter idea. In some instances the clinical worker might even decide to make one or more home visits to observe the family's interactions in more natural surroundings.

CHAPTER SUMMARY

STRESS AND COPING

How people cope with stress depends on their vulnerability and resiliency. **Vulnerability** increases the likelihood of a maladaptive response to stress, **resiliency** decreases it. Having a positive self-concept, enjoying new experiences, and having good interpersonal relationships contribute to resiliency.

Coping skills refer to a person's ability to deal with different types of situations. People who are effective copers usually have a variety of techniques available and are able to choose those most appropriate for the situation. These effective copers also learn to direct their thoughts toward problem solving and are able to avoid distraction caused by fear and worry.

Social Support Social support, the feeling of being cared about, valued, and loved by others, can help make people less vulnerable to stress. This belief that social support is available also encourages people to develop new ways to cope during periods that are not highly stressful. Researchers have shown a relationship between the availability of social support and both psychological and physical health.

STRESSFUL SITUATIONS AND LIFE TRANSITIONS

Stress can have undesirable effects on behavior, thought, and bodily functioning. Because different people react to stressors in different ways, the correlation between particular stressors and their effects on the different bodily symptoms is often low. It is particularly hard for people to deal with several stressors that occur at nearly the same time. However, the cumulative effects of stressors over a long period of time can also have a negative effect on a person's mental and physical health. Questionnaires are often used to assess what events a person has experienced in the recent past as well as how he or she perceived the events and reacted to them.

Stress-Arousing Situations Stress can arise either from specific situations or from developmental transitions. Stressful events vary in several ways: duration, severity, predictability, degree of loss of control, self-confidence of the person, and suddenness of onset. Accidents, natural disasters, and military combat all can bring about high levels of stress and may result in a posttraumatic stress disorder. Stress may also be the result of a personal crisis such as being raped or bereaved.

Life Transitions Life transitions, such as going to college, getting a job, having a baby, and moving, may also be stressful. Adolescence is a time of particular stress because of physical changes, role changes, and changes in parent-child relationships.

CLINICAL REACTIONS TO STRESS

Among the disorders that seem most related to stress are adjustment disorders, posttraumatic disorders, and dissociative disorders.

Adjustment Disorder An **adjustment disorder** is a reaction to recent stress and usually disappears when the stress level decreases. Common symptoms of adjustment disorder are depression, anxiety, disruptive or reckless behavior, sleep problems, deterioration in performance, and social withdrawal.

Posttraumatic Disorders Posttraumatic stress disorder (PTSD) may occur after an extreme stress such as a natural disaster, a serious accident, or participation in battle or other war-related situations. PTSD symptoms vary widely, but may include recurrent dreams, flashbacks, impaired concentration, and emotional numbing. Those who experience PTSD after a stressful experience are likely to have had pre-stress histories of psychological disorder.

Dissociative Disorders Sudden temporary alterations of consciousness that blot out painful experiences are characteristic of **dissociative disorders.** Four conditions are included in this group: Dissociative amnesia, dissociative fugue, dissociative identity disorder, and depersonalization. **Dissociative amnesia** involves extensive, but selective, memory loss that has no known organic cause. This disorder is often associated with overwhelming stress. In **dissociative fugue,** the person loses identity, leaves home, and sets up a new life in a distant place. The fugue usually ends suddenly when the person suddenly "wakes up" with no memory of events that occurred during the fugue. **Dissociative identity disorder** often seems to be associated with traumatic experiences in childhood. In this disorder the person assumes alternate personalities that may or may not be aware of each other. **Depersonalization** involves a dreamlike state in which the person has a sense of being separated both from self and from reality. This state may be persistent or recurrent. In this disorder it is often difficult to identify the source of the stress.

TREATING STRESS-RELATED PROBLEMS

A variety of approaches are used either alone or in combination to treat stress-related disorders.

Supportive Therapy In **supportive therapy** the therapist provides acceptance and a noncritical attitude in order to give the client an opportunity to relax enough to engage in problem solving.

Drugs and Sedatives Drugs and sedatives act on the nervous system to allow the person to feel a temporary decrease in stress. This treatment is often combined with a psychological therapeutic approach.

Relaxation Training Relaxation training is a structured approach to tension reduction that also helps to decrease feelings of stress enough that the person can focus on working out problems.

Systematic Desensitization Systematic desensitization is a process designed to eliminate fear in specific types of situations by pairing relaxation techniques with imagining the presence of the anxiety-associated stimuli.

Cognitive Modification Cognitive modification is the process of learning to think about or construe anxiety-producing situations in a different way.

Social Intervention Social intervention involves treating not just the individual with the problem, but also involving family members in the treatment process.

CHAPTER SIX

Jaune Quick-to-See Smith, *Osage Orange*, 1985.
Steinbaum Krase Gallery, New York.

PSYCHOLOGICAL FACTORS AND PHYSICAL SYMPTOMS

People get upset when they hear that someone they know has been diagnosed with cancer. A number of people I told began to cry. People said they would pray for me. All this might sound like an outpouring of love and support, but it was also scary. For a while I reacted to any expression from others with anger, feeling that everyone thought I was dying. At times I worried that my understanding of my illness was incorrect, reasoning that others must know something that I don't about my prognosis or that I was denying the seriousness of my condition. I spent a lot of time reassuring others, trying to feel that they weren't viewing me as a person with "one foot in the grave."

These reactions make social support a more complex issue than it might at first appear. . . . While having people around me to help and support me was invaluable, it also was a burden, taking energy I needed for other things. There is, however, one exception to this ambivalence. I quickly discovered the comfort of being with other people who were diagnosed with cancer.

. . . [O]ne day some colleagues asked about my chemotherapy. After telling them about the regimen one listener invited me to agree with her that it was wonderful that such potentially lifesaving drugs were available. I couldn't respond. You see, I hate my chemotherapy drugs. I loathe ordering them from the pharmacy, smelling them, feeling them in my hand, and taking them. But to express this to her would involve a lot of explaining, assuring her that I don't intend to stop my treatments, stating that, of course, I am glad we have these drugs, etc. I don't have to do that with another cancer patient. When a woman also being treated for breast cancer fairly spit out the name of one of her drugs I understood what she was feeling. When I complained that I was tired of being bald, a colleague with cancer didn't tell me I looked great, urge me to hang in there, or get teary. He simply said "I know." Similarly, when he and I joke about our experiences we are being funny, not poignant, touching, or brave. It's good to be able to gripe and joke unselfconsciously.

—Shore, 1989, p. 25

The previous chapter showed that the combination of stress and vulnerability can lead to maladaptive psychological outcomes. Under certain conditions, it can also lead either to physical symptoms or to bodily complaints without discernible malfunction. A physical symptom is not necessarily a result of stress. For example, peptic ulcers are often regarded as psychologically caused even though the scientific basis for such an assertion has not been established (Weiner, 1991). However, there is evidence that (1) acute and chronic stressors play a role in certain types of physical conditions, (2) vulnerability and resiliency influence bodily functioning and recovery from illness, and (3) for some people, bodily complaints seem to be a way of coping with stress. As Elsie Shore's account of her experience with cancer conveys, psychological stress frequently accompanies serious illness regardless of its cause. Social support can be most helpful in such situations.

While well-intentioned people can add to stress when their supportive efforts do not meet the needs of the ill person, informal, warm, accepting relationships, such as the one described, can have a significant influence over bodily function. For example, there is evidence that the quality of close relationships (that is, the degree to which warmth and positive thoughts characterize them) can influence the functioning of the immune system (Kennedy et al., 1990). Rewarding interpersonal relationships and social support contribute to resiliency when individuals confront threats to health and well-being. An example of this is Supreme Court Justice Sandra Day O'Connor, who several years ago had breast cancer that necessitated a mastectomy. Her husband accompanied her to doctors' appointments to provide support and to ensure she didn't miss any important information. While the availability of caring others contributed to her resiliency and speedy recovery, recognition of her responsibilities to loved ones also played a positive role: "You'd better shape up and make a go of this because you're causing a lot of distress for other people." (*Seattle Times*, November 4, 1994, p. A4).

Evidence suggesting that psychological and social factors may play important roles in health and fitness—an idea that has intrigued clinical workers and patients alike for a long time—is increasing. In this chapter we will review existing information about the relationships among personality, environment, and illness, and examine how psychological and social variables operate in health and illness. We will then emphasize several groups of conditions marked by actual tissue damage or impairment and that appear to be linked to certain personality and environmental factors. These conditions are often referred to as **psychophysiological** or **psychosomatic disorders.**

After reviewing these disorders, we will discuss another group of conditions, those that involve physical complaints with no detectable tissue damage or impairment. These conditions have been referred to as **somatoform disorders** because they suggest somatic impairment when there is no evidence that any exists. A third group of conditions that will be dealt with are **factitious disorders.** People with factitious conditions, as the name implies, have physical or psychological complaints that appear to be simulated and under their voluntary control. In other words, they seem to be faking.

Many of the disorders covered in this chapter are thought to result from frequent, intense, and prolonged physiological arousal. Whereas some people respond to stress primarily with bizarre thoughts and behavior, others respond primarily with physical symptoms ranging from cancer to migraine headaches. But while it is known that there are wide differences in individual patterns of physiological, cognitive, and behavioral reactions to stress, the mechanisms behind those patterns remain unclear. Whatever the mechanisms turn out to be, it is now certain that they involve interactions among personal variables (for example, attitudes and physiological patterns) and situational variables (such as past and recent life experiences and social supports): Illness clearly results from multiple factors.

Psychological, Social, and Bodily Interactions

Awareness that one's state of mind can influence one's body has a long history (see chapter 2). In the eighteenth century Mesmer claimed that he could modify the course of physical symptoms by using his personal "magnetism." In the nineteenth century Charcot pioneered the use of hypnosis in the treatment of bodily complaints, and early in this century Freud applied psychoanalytic concepts to physical symptoms. Freud believed that somatic symptoms had symbolic significance; they represented compromises among forbidden impulses, intrapsychic conflicts, and the need to defend oneself from anxiety. In the 1930s and 1940s a number of clinicians attempted to integrate Freudian ideas into a growing body of knowledge concerning the bodily aspects of emotional experiences. During this period the **psychosomatic hypothesis** became popular. According to this theory, bodily symptoms can be caused by a blocking of emotional expression.

Recent research work has focused on how bodily reactions change when people are exposed to various emotion-arousing stimuli. For example, emotional tension has been shown to influence the autonomic nervous system and the endocrine glands. One of the endocrine glands, the adrenal medulla, releases its hormones when the situation calls for "fight or flight." As a result, the rates of breathing, heartbeat, and muscle tension increase. These and other bodily changes caused by emotional responses to stress prepare the organism to meet challenges (Selye, 1976). For example, pituitary and adrenal hormones are influenced by events that occur in the course of conflicts between husbands and wives. Marital researchers typically ask couples to discuss a topic on which they are known to disagree. The researchers then note differences in behavior during these discussions. Recent studies have shown that conflict and hostility in such discussions are closely linked to changes in the levels of several hormones and blood pressure (Malarkey et al., 1994). The changes are especially great for people prone to anger in a variety of situations. The health consequences remain to be determined of these exaggerated bodily responses to conflict (see Figure 6-1).

The Biopsychosocial Model

Today most researchers look at physical symptoms from an interactional viewpoint: Bodily defects may cause psychological problems, and psychological problems may in turn cause bodily defects. When psychological factors are involved in illness, their role is usually indirect. For example, personality characteristics by themselves may not cause an illness like asthma, but in combination with hypersensitive lungs and certain situational stresses, they may play an important role.

In the last two decades, emphasis has been placed on the interaction between psychological states and social and biological variables. According to the **biopsychoso-cial model,** a person can be regarded as a system with interacting biological, psychological, and social subsystems (Engel, 1977). Sources of vulnerability and resiliency exist throughout this system. The model can be illustrated by some of the complex activities involved in brain function. The brain processes both physical and nonphysical inputs (environmental events, ideas); it generates thoughts and behavior; and it regulates bodily functions. At any given moment the brain's circuitry permits simultaneous "programming" of data pertaining to the biological, psychological, and social spheres. The challenge facing researchers is to identify the factors and conditions that play roles in this complex type of information processing.

Biopsychosocial problems often arise when people's lives are disrupted by environmental changes, challenges, and constraints. The word **homeostasis** refers to the mechanism by which an organism mobilizes itself to restore a dynamic equilibrium in the face of these disruptions. At present most researchers and clinicians believe that, for any given individual, a host of variables—physical, psychological, and social—contribute to the phenomenon that we call "getting sick." The idea that illness is due simply to the influence of external agents seems outmoded. While it is true that there are individual differences in the vulnerability of bodily organs to disease, these differences must be considered in light of personality characteristics, environmental factors, and the general condition of the body. The biopsychosocial point of view is not limited to the causes of illness. It is also relevant to prevention and treatment, major fields of concern to the specialty areas of behavioral medicine and health psychology (see Box 6-1).

Stress and Illness

There is growing evidence that stress plays an important role in illness and health. We have observed that stress leads to diverse bodily reactions. The heart, lungs, and digestive, endocrine, and nervous systems, among others, work overtime when people experience stress. When these systems are consistently overloaded throughout long periods of a person's life, the likelihood increases that some sort of physical weakness or disturbance will occur. It makes good medical sense, therefore, to study the personal characteristics and aspects of life that go along with strong and persistent stress reactions or that might predispose a person to psychological or physical breakdown. Stress is created when individuals face difficult situations and have to ask themselves, "How am I going to handle this

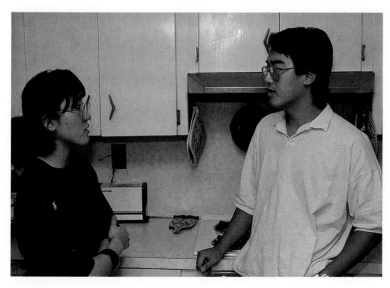

Figure 6-1 A married couple being physiologically monitored while engaged in discussion about a family conflict. Monitored data are obtained through unobtrusive sensors. Although the couple is aware that their bodily reactions are being monitored, there are no noticeable physical indications that this is happening. Comparisons can be made between their physiological responses under neutral, ordinary conditions and when they are discussing topics that are conflict-laden.

Behavioral Medicine and Health Psychology

The biopsychosocial model's emphasis on interrelating factors has contributed to the development of two new fields, behavioral medicine and health psychology. These fields are based on the idea that combinations of biological, psychological, and social factors influence an individual's health, vulnerability to disease, and reactions to disease. Studies in these fields strongly indicate that virtually every ill that can befall the body—from the common cold to cancer and heart disease—can be influenced, positively or negatively, by a person's mental state, lifestyle, and social relationships. By unveiling the mechanisms behind these effects, research may point to new ways of preventing and treating disease.

Behavioral medicine is concerned with ways of improving diagnosis, treatment, and rehabilitation by using psychological techniques that help people adopt healthier ways of living. An important goal of behavioral medicine is the improvement of service delivery by providers of health care. Researchers in behavioral medicine are particularly concerned with direct patient evaluation and treatment.

The related field of **health psychology** is directed toward the prevention of disease. Health psychologists seek to reduce health risks by changing people's thinking and living habits. Researchers in health psychology tend to be concerned with broader topics, including the acquisition and modification of behavior that influences health or is guided by concerns about health. Since as much as 50 percent of mortality from the leading causes of death can be traced to such behaviors as inactivity, poor nutrition, and smoking, health psychologists seek to strengthen those behaviors that contribute to good health.

Both behavioral medicine and health psychology are concerned with reducing the stressfulness of illness and, wherever possible, preventing such stress. Preven-

tion often involves helping people to make healthful lifestyle changes. Examples of targets of prevention efforts are smoking, a form of voluntary behavior clearly harmful to health and a major cause of cancer; alcohol abuse, which contributes to cirrhosis of the liver; injuries from accidents and violence; and overeating and underexercising which contribute to obesity, high blood pressure, and diabetes. The great need for effective health promotion techniques is suggested by the facts presented in Table 6-1.

Behavioral medicine and health psychology are interdisciplinary fields that integrate the behavioral and biomedical sciences. Common to both of these fields is a philosophy that emphasizes individual responsibility as a means of maximizing health. According to this view, health is a personal achievement, and people's behavior influences whether they attain it or not. Physical, mental, social, and economic factors all influence health and recovery from illness. The doctor-patient relationship, the relationship of gender to longevity, and a biopsychosocial approach to the common cold are areas in which these factors play roles.

The doctor-patient relationship The character of the relationship between doctor and patient influences patients' perceptions of their problems and clinical outcomes as well. A good relationship contributes to the patient's morale and perception of the doctor as truly interested in his or her welfare. This patient's perception of his doctor contributed to strong negative emotions:

I guess in becoming a great surgeon you forgot those early courses in doctor-patient relations: that patients tend to panic and imagine the worst; that they need reassurance. You said outright that I had two malignant tumors that must be removed at once. That meant cancer.

TABLE 6–1
Facts About Health in the United States

About one-fourth of the adult population is 20 percent or more above desirable body weight.

About one-half of adults experience at least a moderate amount of stress in a 2-week period.

Forty percent of the population say they exercise or play sports, but only 28 percent are very physically active.

About 30 percent of persons 18 years of age and over smoke cigarettes.

Fifty percent of young mothers, 18 to 24 years of age, with less than 12 years of education have smoked in the year preceding the birth of their last child.

The word scared the hell out of me. I broke out in a sweat. But you didn't seem to notice. You frowned your usual frown and said that radiation or chemotherapy were not options. You gave no explanation and I was too clobbered to ask.

In contrast, it is highly likely that this doctor plays a positive and important role in his patients' lives:

I have practiced medicine long enough to sense intuitively that even when a person with significant medical problems has a presenting complaint, more than half the time the complaint is related to stress. On a daily basis, therefore, I assess the disease process and adjust the medical management as needed, but my joy comes from listening carefully, helping people to identify their stressors, providing my best advice when I think it is appropriate, but always offering my caring and understanding—especially when I see that the problem, as presented, is

one?" or "Can I do it?" (Figure 6-2). These are some of the skills whose absence increases stress and the risk of illness:

1. Ability to adapt to changes in environmental demands

2. Ability to handle strong feelings and emotions, and to express them realistically

3. Ability to interpret demands, constraints, and opportunities correctly

4. Ability to form rewarding, lasting interpersonal ties, particularly love relationships

BOX 6-1

insoluble. I am both rewarded and fascinated to observe that people feel better just by recognizing that I care.

Gender and Longevity Gender is a significant factor in longevity. While women live longer than men, the cause of this difference is unclear. Probably both genetic and lifestyle factors play roles. Sex differences in longevity are smaller in nonindustrial than in industrial societies. To a large extent this distinction reflects smaller sex differences in mortality for coronary heart disease in nonindustrial societies. In industrial societies like the United States, higher male mortality rates seem to be related to society's expectations that men be more aggressive, adventurous, ambitious, and hard-driving than women. If these expectations were changed, would male mortality rates become lower as a result? As more and more women hold jobs and support families, will their mortality rates go up? We do not have definite answers to these questions. Research that compares mortality among men who differ in their need to adopt traditional male roles and among women who differ in their conceptions of female roles may clarify this issue.

Stress and Colds Both observation and experiments suggest that stress increases susceptibility to colds and other respiratory infections. In a one-year study of a hundred subjects, throat cultures were taken every three weeks for bacteria, and blood was drawn every four months for antibodies to cold viruses. Events that caused stress, as indicated by diaries, were four times more likely to precede than to follow new infections. People who developed a cold or bacterial infection had often been feeling more angry and tense than usual, and these feelings were not early signs of illness, since they appeared an average of four days before the physical symptoms. The effect persisted even with controls for sex, family history of respiratory infections, family size, and allergies (Cohen & Williamson, 1991).

A recent experiment provides even more persuasive evidence for a connection between stress and colds. Four hundred and twenty subjects (154 men and 266 women) were exposed to one of five cold viruses after answering questionnaires on psychological stress, personality, health practices, and behavior. The following three measures of stress were used: occurrence of certain events (job loss, death in the family, moving, divorce, and so on) in the previous year; feeling frightened, upset, nervous, sad, angry, or irritated; and feeling unable to cope with current demands (Cohen et al., 1991).

Before exposure and a month afterward, the researchers asked about cold symptoms and tested for antibodies to the cold viruses. They found that the more stress a person was under, the greater the chance of infection (as indicated by the presence of antibodies). Among the 25 percent of subjects under greatest stress, 90 percent became infected; among the 25 percent under least stress, 74 percent became infected. But once they became infected, people under stress were no more likely to develop cold symptoms. In other words, stress increased the danger of infection itself, not the resulting discomfort (which is produced by the immune system's defenses against the virus).

Listening with empathy and understanding to the patient's spoken and unspoken concerns is an important factor in reducing the stress of hospitalization and in aiding recovery.

The proportion of women compared to men in this group of senior citizens preparing for a lesson at a Texas tennis court provides evidence of the longer life expentancy of women.

Only some of the people who are biologically predisposed to a particular condition actually fall ill. Others who are equally biologically vulnerable are able to cope effectively and thus reduce the negative effects of stress on health. The chance of onset of illness may vary with a number of factors, including age, the particular form of the illness, and what is going on in the person's life. These interacting factors provide a clue to why it is practically impossible to make statements like, "John Jones got pneumonia because he had been working overtime for two months" or "Mary Smith developed ulcers because she is such a nervous person." Many peo-

Figure 6-2 Being well-prepared for challenges reduces the risk of illness due to stress. For example, research on police officers assigned to dangerous tactical and negotiation units who have received intensive training and supervision do not show an unusually high number of psychological or physical stress-related symptoms.

SOURCE: Messer, 1994.

ple develop pneumonia without working overtime, and most people can work overtime without becoming sick. Similarly, many people who develop ulcers do not appear to be especially nervous, and most nervous people do not develop ulcers.

As noted earlier, stress causes a variety of physical changes. Among other things, it stimulates hormonal secretions (particularly those of the pituitary and adrenal glands), activates the autonomic system, brings about biochemical changes, and alters the brain's electrical level. Although all people have these reactions to stress, the strength and pattern of the reactions depend not only on the nature of the stressful stimulus but also on the individual's biological characteristics, personality, and life experiences. Recent and past life experiences play important roles in influencing our appraisal of situations and the coping mechanisms we use to deal with stress.

Psychophysiological Disorders

The body is made up of many millions of cells that, grouped together, form organs whose functions overlap to produce the body's systems. In this section, we review a number of bodily systems that have been approached from a biopsychosocial point of view and that are believed to be related to psychological processes.

Several groups of such physical disorders in which personality and social factors may play a part have been studied over the years. There is no evidence that these conditions are directly attributable to the mental state of the individual or that a person suffering from one of these disorders has a completely different personality from a person suffering from another disorder or none at all. What is becoming increasingly clear, however, is that people—not just cells or organs—have diseases and that diseases must be studied in the context of people's physical, psychological, social, and cultural environments.

The term **psychophysiological disorder** has traditionally been applied to physical conditions in which psychologically meaningful events are closely related to bodily symptoms. Psychophysiological disorders might be thought of as end products of biopsychosocial processes. A large number of physical problems have been studied from a psychophysiological standpoint. These include disorders of the cardiovascular, respiratory, gastrointestinal, musculoskeletal, and genitourinary systems, as well as of the skin. Both clinical data and informal observations suggest the importance of psychological factors in many of these disorders. Consider the following case.

A 38-year-old mother of four children had a five-year history of attacks of hives, a skin condition characterized by itching, burning, and stinging. During these attacks, areas of her face, trunk, waist, thighs, and arms would swell. There would be swelling even on her tongue and inside her respiratory passages. The attacks initially occurred about once a month, but at the time that she sought help, their frequency was closer to once every four or five days. Each attack was accompanied by depression and nausea.

An examination in an allergy clinic yielded negative results. After a psychiatrist placed the patient on tranquilizing drugs, the incidence of hives declined markedly. Further study indicated that her attacks usually occurred when she was experiencing intense stress. For example, when she was having marital difficulties and was forced to face the possibility that her husband might leave her, she had an especially severe series of attacks. At one point she felt so overwhelmed by situational stresses that she was hospitalized. During this period she was protected from family tensions, and her hives disappeared completely. After leaving the hospital the patient entered psychotherapy on a twice-a-week basis. In these sessions she was able to express her frustrations at leading a very restricted life because of her small children's demands and her husband's inability to see why she might need time away from home. Another point that emerged in therapy was the patient's inability to express to her husband how much she needed to have him acknowledge her value as a person, not just as the mother of his children. After several months of therapy, she felt able to tell her husband about her unfulfilled psychological needs as well as her resentment and frustra-

tion. At the time that therapy ended, she had been completely free from hives for four months.

In this case, it seems clear that this particular woman's skin condition was linked to events and conditions in her personal life. A major hurdle for the researcher is figuring out how to proceed from relationships that may be at work in a given case to generalizations that could apply to whole groups of people.

Headaches

Headaches may be the most commonly reported painful bodily signal. Although the majority of headaches are not associated with significant organic disease, they nonetheless can be debilitating. Every year an estimated 80 percent of Americans suffer from at least one headache, and 10 to 20 percent go to a physician with headaches as their primary complaint. Headaches also are a major reason given for absenteeism from work or avoidance of other undesired social or personal activities.

The pain of a headache has three components.

1. Physiological changes (usually either muscular contractions or blood vessel dilation)
2. The subjective experience of pain (aching, distress, fatigue, and so on)
3. Behavior motivated by the pain (for example, pill

taking, withdrawal from family and social activities, absence from work).

Not all headaches are alike and there are wide differences in people's sensitivity to the physiological changes that signal the beginning of a headache (see Table 6-2).

Muscle-contraction or **tension headaches,** distinguished by changes in skeletal muscles, are probably the most common form of head pain. The person reports an aching, dull, pressing feeling; the scalp may feel tender if pressed with the hand; and there are persistent sensations of band-like pain or tightness in the head. The exact cause of muscle-contraction headaches has not yet been pinpointed. Research suggests that tension headache sufferers are emotionally hyperreactive to pain and to stress (Lehrer & Murphy, 1991).

Migraine headaches are localized on one side or on the front of the head. They are severe, tend to recur, and are often accompanied by a variety of somatic symptoms. The throbbing, pulsating pain characteristic of migraines may last for several hours. Nausea and vomiting are common. In some cases, the dilated cranial artery is visible and tender.

Unlike muscle-contraction headaches, migraines are usually preceded by a sensory, motor, or mood disturbance, called an *aura.* There may be ringing in the ears; tingling, numbness, or weakness of a limb; extreme sensitivity to light; visual blurring; distorted depth perception; nausea; or unaccountable emotional changes.

TABLE 6–2
Differentiating Features of Common Types of Headaches

	Muscle-contraction headache	Migraine	Cluster headache
Sex	No difference	More frequent in women	More frequent in men
Quality of pain	Pressure, tightness, band-like	Throbbing	Piercing, burning, excruciating
Time of onset	Often afternoon or evening	Often early mornings and weekends	Soon after onset of sleep, and daytime
Mode of onset	Gradual	Abrupt or gradual	Abrupt
Duration	Hours, days, or weeks	Hours, 1 to 2 days	20 minutes to 2 hours
Precipitating or aggravating factors	Emotional stress or not apparent	Emotional stress, menstruation, alcohol, certain foods, change in weather	Alcohol, lying down, REM sleep
Associated symptoms or signs	No specific symptoms except tenderness of scalp or neck muscles	Nausea, vomiting, irritability, tender scalp	Tearing of eyes, nasal stuffiness and discharge
Personality traits	Competitive, conscientious	Perfectionistic, neat, efficient	Specific traits not identified
Age of onset	Adolescence; early adulthood	Puberty to menopause	20 to 50 years of age

Many migraine suffers have a family history of such headaches, but whether this is due to heredity or to common living experiences is unclear. Migraine attacks may begin with stressful life changes such as puberty, going to college, or starting a job. Migraines occur more often in women. A significant percentage of migraine sufferers are prone to experience feelings of depression and anxiety, although the basis for this relationship is unclear (Breslau & Davis, 1993).

To someone unfamiliar with migraines the agony of them may be hard to appreciate. An account by the prominent novelist Joan Didion (Figure 6-3) describes what the experience is like.

> *Three, four, sometimes five times a month, I spend the day in bed with a migraine headache, insensible to the world around me. Almost every day of every month, between these attacks, I feel the sudden irrational irritation and the flush of blood into the cerebral arteries which tell me that migraine is on its way, and I take certain drugs to avert its arrival. If I did not take the drugs, I would be able to function perhaps one day in four. . . .*
>
> *Once an attack is under way, no drug touches it. When I am in a migraine aura (for some people the aura lasts fifteen minutes, for others several hours), I will drive through red lights, lose the house keys, spill whatever I am holding, lose the ability to focus my eyes or frame coherent sentences, and generally give the appearance of being on drugs, or drunk. The actual headache, when it comes, brings with it chills, sweating, nausea, a debility that seems to stretch the very limits of endurance. That no one dies of migraine seems, to someone deep into an attack, an ambiguous blessing.*
>
> —Didion, 1979, pp. 168–172

In the past, it was believed that migraine is caused by narrowing followed by dilation of blood vessels. This idea is now being replaced by the idea that a wave of cerebral electrical activity may cause the aura, or warning sensation, and headaches develop when the wave reaches pain-sensitive blood vessels. What triggers this wave? Stress, hunger, hormone fluctuations, foods, alcohol, too much sleep, caffeine withdrawal, or noise are chief suspects. It has recently been found that serotonin, a nerve cell messenger, becomes depleted in the brain during a migraine attack. Some disturbance in serotonin function seems to be a central component, if not the primary culprit, in producing the pain and other symptoms of migraines. Drug companies are now working on the development of compounds that can correct a dysfunction in the brain chemistry of migraine sufferers.

Migraine headaches often respond positively to drugs that constrict the arteries in the scalp. Psychotherapists have observed significant improvement in some people who suffer from chronic headaches, but little or no improvement in people who have migraines only occasionally. There have been reports of the successful use of behavior therapy and biofeedback in some cases of migraine.

Cluster headaches are often confined to one side of the head with pain that is excruciating, the pain hitting a peak in three to five minutes and disappearing within an hour. Patients often are pain-free for long periods of time but then experience a series of headaches over several weeks, sometimes several in one day. The headaches often occur at night and wake people from sound sleep. Patients often pace and sometimes bang their heads against the wall in an attempt to quell the pain. Cluster headaches are more common in men.

Biofeedback Pain has to do with bodily signals that are so amplified they hurt us. Some other types of bodily signals are not so readily perceived and require amplification. **Biofeedback** has been used in behavioral medicine to treat such problems as hypertension, highly volatile blood pressure, and epilepsy (see Figure 6-4). This technique provides a way of extending self-control procedures to deal with a variety of physiological behaviors that were formerly thought to be involuntary responses, such as heart rate, blood pressure, and brain waves. Such behaviors were thought to be beyond conscious control until researchers became aware of indi-

Figure 6-3 Joan Didion, a prominent novelist, suffers from frequent migraine headaches. Her description of them conveys a clear picture of what the experience is like.

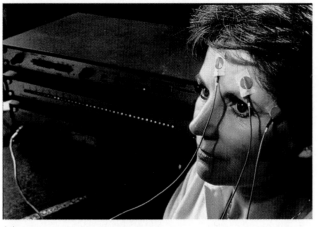

(a)

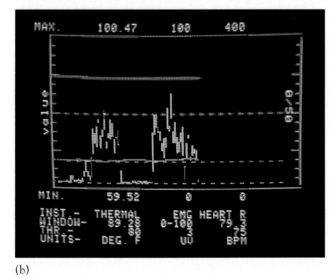

(b)

Figure 6-4 Biofeedback training can help clients control a variety of physiological responses. Photo (a) shows a client with the biofeedback apparatus. Photo (b) shows the video monitor that visually presents the responses as they occur.

viduals who apparently are able to control them. One such person, a Yoga practitioner named Swami Rama, was studied intensively at the Menninger Foundation (Green, 1972). Laboratory tests showed that, among other things, Rama was able to speed up and slow down his heart rate at will, to stop his heart from pumping blood for 17 seconds, to cause two areas of his palm a few inches apart to change temperature in opposite directions until their temperature differed by 10 °F (the "hot" side of his palm became rosy whereas the "cold" side became ashen), and to produce widely differing brain wave patterns at will.

Rama was not unique, although the extent of his control is startling. Humans and animals can learn to control their heart rate, blood pressure, brain waves, and other behaviors. For humans, no external reinforcement of the behavior seems to be necessary. All that is required

is that the individual be given information in the form of feedback from the response system in question. Just as we could never learn to shoot a basketball accurately if we did not receive visual feedback and feedback from our muscles, we cannot learn to control our heart rate or brain waves unless we receive some kind of feedback on physiological changes as they occur. The feedback then serves as a reinforcer for the desired change.

Ordinarily we do not get feedback on such responses as blood pressure and brain waves, but through biofeedback—which precisely measures physiological events and converts the electronic signals into visual or auditory feedback—we can be made aware of our own physiological responses. This process has been used to train people to control the physiological responses of the brain, muscles, and cardiovascular and glandular systems, and has been applied to a variety of clinical problems, including cardiac disorders, high blood pressure, headaches, anxiety, and neuromuscular disorders such as cerebral palsy. Clients come in for regular biofeedback sessions until they learn to recognize and control their bodily signals reliably without the help of the biofeedback apparatus.

Although there is no longer any question that people can learn to control a wide range of bodily functions, there are questions about the overall effectiveness of biofeedback compared to relaxation training for migraine headaches or assertiveness training for tension headaches. There is evidence that skills learned through biofeedback training are lost rather quickly when training stops. As researchers continue to identify the limitations of biofeedback, it becomes more apparent that these techniques are not the cure-all that overenthusiastic proponents initially believed they would be. But it is equally clear that biofeedback can be successfully applied to certain problems. An important goal of current research is to determine how and when biofeedback techniques can be used most effectively to enhance control over physiological and psychological responses.

Cardiovascular Disorders

Every affection of the mind that is attended with either pain or pleasure, hope or fear, is the cause of an agitation whose influence extends to the heart.

—William Harvey, 1628

Written more than 350 years ago, Harvey's allusion to an intimate association between neural factors and the heart received some attention in anecdote and fable, yet was not subjected to systematic scientific inquiry until the second half of the twentieth century.

The heart is a highly specialized muscle that pumps blood to the body. The blood flows through the body in an unending loop of blood vessels called the *circulatory system.* Each day the human heart beats approximately 100,000 times, delivering the equivalent of 4,300 gallons of blood to all parts of the body. The arteries provide food and oxygen to the cells, while the veins remove carbon dioxide and waste products. The term **cardiovascular disorders** refers to pathological conditions that are related to the functioning of the heart and blood vessels. There is growing evidence that psychological and social factors play a role in two major cardiovascular disorders: coronary heart disease and hypertension. These conditions have caused over half of all deaths in the United States for more than 40 years.

Coronary Heart Disease The leading cause of death and disability in the United States is **coronary heart disease** (CHD), accounting for 40 percent of all deaths. A million new cases are identified annually. CHD is produced by lesions of the coronary arteries, the arteries that circulate blood within the heart itself. In CHD one or more of the three coronary arteries are partially or totally obstructed by deposits, called **plaques,** that thicken the arterial wall. When the coronary arteries become rigid and narrow as a result of these plaque deposits, the supply of blood to various portions of the heart muscle is temporarily or permanently cut off.

CHD takes a variety of forms. In **angina pectoris,** people suffer from periodic chest pains caused by an insufficient supply of oxygen-rich blood to the heart. The insufficient blood supply is related to plaque buildup (referred to as **atherosclerosis**) in the arteries. A **myocardial infarction,** also caused by an insufficient blood supply to the heart, is more serious than angina pectoris because it involves a more complete curtailment of the heart's blood supply. When people speak of a heart attack, they are usually referring to a myocardial infarction.

A significant factor in heart attacks is stress. From the Stone Age to the present day, human beings have responded to environmental challenges and threats by releasing larger amounts of adrenal and other stress hormones, followed by increases in heart rate and respiration and dilation of the vessels that transport blood to the muscles. Although these responses are adaptive or even life-saving when the threat is a wolf pack, you would do better without them if you are stuck in a traffic jam. In fact, not only are these primitive physiological responses of little help in dealing with most modern-day problems, but they may actually be related to the development of disease.

Stress seems to contribute to coronary disease through the body's general reactions to aversive stimulation. Under arousing conditions, hormonal substances called **catecholamines** are secreted. Two of the catecholamines, **epinephrine** and **norepinephrine,** accelerate the rate of arterial damage and ultimately can lead to heart attacks. Identifying which people are most likely to have heart attacks under high levels of stress and learning what steps lead from psychological stress to cardiac damage, are both topics of current research.

Personal Factors and CHD Factors known to increase the risk of CHD include age (older people are at greater risk), cigarette smoking, high blood pressure, high cholesterol level, and diabetes. A recent study found that men who complain of high anxiety are up to six times more likely than calmer men to suffer sudden cardiac death (Kawachi et al., 1994). Answering affirmatively to questions such as, "Do strange people or places make you afraid?" and "Do you often become suddenly scared for no good reason?" seemed to reflect a strong vulnerability factor.

Some studies have also implicated such factors as obesity, heredity, and lack of physical exercise. These factors may not be causes of CHD; they may simply be correlated with it. Even the most predictive of the risk factors still fails to identify more than half of the new cases of CHD. How these factors are related to the incidence of heart attack in a given individual is not yet known precisely.

There are important differences between men and women. While most middle-aged heart attack victims are men, heart attacks that occur in later life are a principal cause of death for both men and women. Heart disease is the leading cause of death in women after the age of 66; in men it is the leading killer beginning at age 39. Women often have chest pains for a long time before a heart attack; in men, such pains more often mean a heart attack has already begun. Researchers are currently examining the reasons for these differences. There may be important biological differences between the sexes in the functioning and development of the heart and cardiovascular system.

Death due to CHD has decreased more than 35 percent in the last 40 years, and recently this decrease has accelerated. Factors that may be contributing to the decline in mortality are improved medical services, the development of coronary care units in hospitals, advances in surgical and medical treatment of CHD, and improved control of blood pressure. Life-style changes such as less smoking, better eating habits, and increased physical fitness also seem to play an important preventive role.

Personal Life Styles and CHD Personal lifestyle patterns may play a significant role in CHD. Studies of twins living in the same community can play a valuable role in answering this question. A study conducted in Sweden (Liljefors & Rahe, 1970) provided a unique set of data about the relationship between CHD, personality, and life style. The sample consisted of 32 pairs of identical male twins, 42 to 67 years of age, who were discordant for CHD—that is, only one member of each pair had a heart condition. Virtually all the twins had been raised together at least until their early teens.

The twins' characteristic behavior patterns in four areas—devotion to work, lack of leisure, home problems, and life dissatisfactions—were assessed through interviews. The overall results are reflected in a comparison of one of the pairs of twins. Although the twins were at the same hereditary risk, the twin with CHD had a high pressure job during parts of the year and because he was self-employed may have experienced more stress throughout the year because of concerns about the success of his business. He reported continuing to feel a lack of sufficient time for his tasks and perhaps for this reason had fewer periods of relaxation than his twin. In addition, he seemed dissatisfied with his achievements and his ability to carry out his business dealings effectively while his twin was relatively satisfied with his progress. Since the twins examined were discordant for CHD, the researchers concluded that life style as well as heredity is an important factor in the disease. A more recent study (Kringlen, 1981) has provided further support for this hypothesis.

Based on their clinical observations as cardiologists, Meyer Friedman and Ray Rosenman (1974) developed their ideas about the existence of a heart-attack prone personality pattern. They thought that people who are habitually hurried, competitive, and hostile would tend to be heart-attack prone. They labelled these people **Type A personalities.** People who lived less pressured and hard-driving lives they called **Type B personalities.**

Specially designed interviews and questionnaires have been used to assess Type A tendencies. One study showed that during eight and a half years of follow-up, Type A men had more than twice as much heart disease as Type B men (Rosenman and others, 1975). This difference could not be explained simply in terms of traditional risk factors, such as cigarette smoking, because those factors had been equalized for the two groups.

One type of investigation that may help chart the relationship between personality and CHD and also clarify the way that known risk factors combine to bring about physical illness is the longitudinal or prospective study. Most clinical problems have been studied retrospectively, that is, after the fact. After someone gets sick, the doctor inquires about past illnesses and experiences that might explain the current problem. More powerful—but also more time-consuming and costly—is

the prospective, or before-the-fact, investigation. Such a study gathers information over a relatively long period. Because prospective studies are longitudinal, they can provide a picture of how a person's thinking, behavior, and bodily reactions unfold over time. Depending on the data gathered, this approach permits the researcher to identify interactions between particular personality variables and important life events and the effects of those interactions on the person's health.

The Framingham study is an example of a prospective investigation (Haynes et al., 1980). A group of 5,127 adult residents of Framingham, Massachusetts, have volunteered to participate in a study on coronary heart disease for the rest of their lives. They have been monitored for the incidence of illness, hospitalization, and death since 1948. Every two years each participant is given a physical examination that includes blood tests, electrocardiograms, X rays, and blood pressure readings. Several physical risk factors have been identified by the Framingham study, including elevated blood pressure, cholesterol level, and cigarette smoking. The study has confirmed that weight gains result in elevated blood pressure and thus indirectly increased the risk of coronary heart disease.

A subgroup of 1,674 Framingham participants between the ages of 45 and 77 was assessed for Type A tendencies and then followed up over an 8-year period (Haynes et al., 1980). Women between the ages of 45 and 64 who developed CHD scored significantly higher on the Type A measure and exhibited more suppressed hostility (not showing or discussing anger), tension, and anxiety than women who remained free of CHD. Type A women developed twice as much CHD as Type B women. Although working women tended to have higher Type A scores than housewives, being a housewife did not protect Type A women from higher rates of CHD. Figure 6-5 shows that working women under 65 years of age were almost twice as likely to develop CHD if they exhibited Type A rather than Type B behavior. Among housewives in the under-65 age group, CHD incidence among Type As was almost three times greater than among Type Bs. Figure 6-6 shows the association of Type A behavior with CHD incidence among white- and blue-collar men in the 45 to 64 and 65 to 74 age groups. The association was statistically significant only among men holding white-collar jobs. The results of the Framingham study suggest that the Type A behavior pattern operates independently of the usual coronary risk factors (such as blood pressure, age, and weight).

Despite many positive results concerning this relationship there have also been some contradictory findings. For example, one study found that Type A men who had had heart attacks were *less* likely than Type Bs to have recurrences (Ragland & Brand, 1988). This

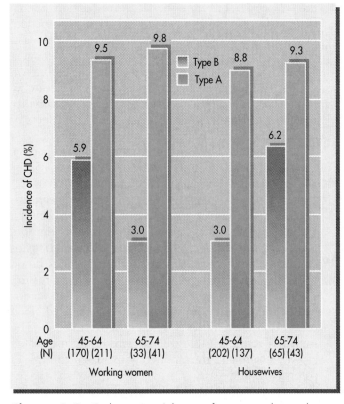

Figure 6-5 Eight-year incidence of coronary heart disease among Framingham working women and housewives with Type A and Type B behavior patterns.

Source: Findings from the Framingham study; adapted from Haynes, Feinleib, & Kannel, 1980.

unexpected result, as well as other findings not consistent with the Type A formulation, might have been due to methodological aspects of the particular investigations or to some factor that has not yet been identified (Dimsdale, 1988). In any case, there is good reason to believe that the original Type A–CHD relationship proposed by Friedman and Rosenman needs some revision.

Because the Type A pattern has many elements, researchers are exploring facets of the pattern that might be of special importance. Work on two topics currently being investigated—hostility and physiological reactivity—may help clarify relationships among personality, behavior, and CHD.

According to one hypothesis, hostility may be the most active Type A ingredient, and there is evidence that people who are hostile, angry, cynical, and suspicious of others have an especially high risk of fatal coronary disease (Barefoot et al., 1987). The results found for women in the Framingham study who were classified as Type A were consistent with this hypothesis. They showed that suppressed hostility was an important predictor of CHD for this group. It may be that the impatience, ambition, and work drive seen in so many Type A people is not nearly as important from a cardiovascular standpoint as their hostility (expressed or suppressed)

and cynical view of other people's motivations. Table 6-3 presents sample questionnaire items designed to measure such cynical hostility. In one study, husbands and wives rated each other's hostility level. As Figure 6-7 shows, the higher the spouse-rated hostility, the greater the likelihood of CHD (Kneip et al., 1993).

Because hostility has a number of aspects, it will be necessary to isolate its components and relate these to clinically significant events, such as whether people have heart attacks. Three components that merit study are (1) distrust of others (expecting someone to cheat or take advantage of you), (2) feeling very angry when you find someone cheating (the person in the 10-item supermarket express line who has 12 items) and (3) showing anger (telling the person with 12 items that he or she is a cheater). If cynical attitudes and hostile emotions cause biological responses that lead to coronary disease, clinicians may be able to devise ways of changing disease-producing thoughts and feelings. Further research on hostility and CHD is needed to assess this relationship and possible responses to it (Barefoot et al., 1991).

Another possible reformulation of the Type A pattern is suggested by evidence that Type As are more physiologically reactive than other people. This excitability might be the most active ingredient in the Type A personality (Manuck et al., 1989). It has been hypothesized that perhaps there are two groups of people, hot and cold reactors, with the cold reactors showing normal cardiovascular responses (blood pressure, heart rate) to stress, and hot reactors displaying abnormally intense cardiovascular responses (Eliot & Buell, 1983). Hot and cold reactors might not differ in terms of their overt behavior, but the hot reactors might experience steep blood pressure surges under

TABLE 6–3
Questionnaire Items Used to Assess Cynical Hostility

Subjects are asked to circle the word "Never," "Sometimes," "Often," or "Always" as it best describes their behavior in these situations. It is believed that people who circle "Often" or "Always" in answer to these items are in a high-risk heart disease group.

1. When anybody slows down or stops what I want to do, I think they are selfish, mean, and inconsiderate.
2. When anybody does something that seems incompetent, messy, selfish, or inconsiderate to me, I quickly feel angry or enraged. At the same time, my heart races, my breath comes quickly, and my palms sweat.
3. When I have such thoughts or feelings (No. 2), I let fly with words, gestures, a raised voice, and frowns.

Source: MacDougall et al., 1981

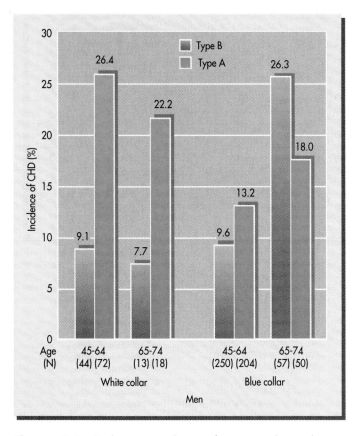

Figure 6-6 Eight-year incidence of coronary heart disease among white-collar and blue-collar Type A and Type B men in the Framingham study.

SOURCE: Adapted from Haynes, Feinleib, & Kannel, 1980.

stress. If this proves to be the case, measurements of the Type A pattern by means of questionnaires and interviews may not be as direct a predictor of cardiac disorders as measurements of actual cardiovascular responses under stressful conditions.

Stressful Events and CHD

Researchers have found that particular stressful episodes—meeting a deadline, for example, or getting fired—affect the cardiovas-cular system temporarily (such as by raising blood pressure). Also, some sudden, personally meaningful events seem to set off major cardiovascular reactions. For example, separations from and losses of loved ones often bring about the need for sudden life-style changes and may culminate in a heart attack, as shown in the following case.

Harry Allen's wife had suffered from lung cancer for many months. Her death came slowly and painfully. For Allen, aged 54, the loss and grief were overwhelming. Every-

one knew that the cancer was incurable and that death was approaching. Yet it came as a terrible shock to Allen. Four months before his wife's death, Harry had had a thorough physical examination that included an electrocardiogram. The electrocardiogram as well as the other studies relevant to heart function were completely negative. Yet two days after his wife's death Allen collapsed and died of a massive heart attack.

The role of social losses and social isolation in recovery from heart attacks has been explored in a large number of studies. In one investigation, 2,320 male survivors of myocardial infarctions were assessed to identify factors that were predictive of how long they would live after having had a heart attack (Ruberman et al., 1984). One important factor was education, with the better-educated subjects living longer. Life stress and social isolation, both alone and in combination, also emerged as significant predictors of mortality. Life stress was defined by subjects' reports concerning such problems as job difficulties, divorces and separations, accidents, and criminal victimization. Social isolation was defined in terms of contacts with friends and relatives and membership in social, church, and fraternal organizations.

In Figure 6-8, graphs *a* and *b* show that when the effects of life stress and social isolation were evaluated separately, each of these factors was significantly associated with increased probability of mortality. The risk of death for men who were high in life stress was double the risk for men who were low in life stress. A similar relationship was found when men who were high and low in social isolation were compared. The combined effect of these two factors is shown in graph *c* of Figure 6-8. For men who were high in both life stress and social isolation, the risk of dying was four times greater than for men who were

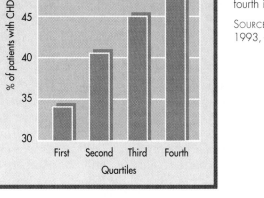

Figure 6-7 Percentage of patients with coronary heart disease as a function of spouses' ratings of partner's hostile outlook. The first quartile includes the lowest ratings of hostility; the fourth includes the highest.

SOURCE: Based on Kneip et al., 1993, p. 305.

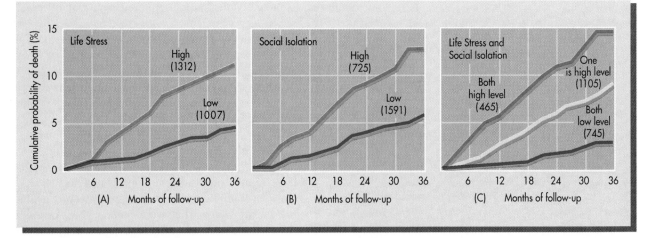

Figure 6-8 Cumulative probability of death under conditions of stress, social isolation or both as a function of number of months that subjects were followed up after myocardial infarction.

SOURCE: Adapted from Ruberman, Weinblatt, Goldberg, and Chaudhary, 1984, p. 555. Reprinted by permission of *The New England Journal of Medicine*, 9 (1984), p. 555.

low in both life stress and social isolation. The middle line in graph c presents the risk of dying for men who were high in either life stress or social isolation.

As Figure 6-8 makes clear, it is valuable to have evidence concerning the relationship between sudden personal cataclysms, such as the death of a loved one or loss of a job, and coronary heart disease; equally significant is information about the effects of less intense, but persistent, aspects of a person's life style. Deficits in social support have been found to be associated with CHD but the basis for the associations remains to be specified (Shumaker & Czajkowski, 1994).

Community Life Style and CHD Life style refers to a way of life that reflects the values and attitudes of an individual or group. Our jobs, interests, and social relationships show the effects of our life styles, but the type of community in which we live may also play a role. A recent study has provided evidence that there may be an important relationship between the general pace of life in a community and the incidence of cardiovascular disorders (Levine et al., 1989). Thirty-six small, medium, and large metropolitan areas across the United States were compared using four indicators of pace of life:

1. How fast people walked
2. How fast people talked
3. The speed with which bank tellers worked
4. The proportion of individuals wearing watches (presumed to be an indicator of concern with time.)

The researchers found that pace of life was strongly related to death rates from coronary heart disease both across cities and across regions of the country. A faster pace played a role in higher rates of CHD, while communities with slower paces of life had lower rates of CHD.

Cultural Factors and CHD Studies that compare different cultures and the process of social change also provide evidence concerning the role of life-style factors in disease. In general, low rates of CHD tend to be found in parts of the world where tradition and family ties are strong. Cross-cultural data have provided a broader perspective on the relationship between psychosocial experience and physical breakdown. Japan, for example, has one of the lowest rates of heart disease in the world, while the United States has one of the highest. The rate of death from CHD for Japanese men between the ages of 35 and 64 is 64 per 100,000 population; the comparable figure for American men is 400 per 100,000.

Can CHD-prone Life Styles Be Changed? Researchers are exploring the possibility of reducing the susceptibility to CHD using psychological training (Haaga, 1987). A variety of cognitive and behavioral techniques have been tried with Type As, including self-control training, learning to think about situations in less intense ways, and being attentive to the problems created by personal beliefs that emphasize urgency and the need to gain immediate control over events. There is some basis for believing that learning to think and act differently exerts a positive influence on the health of Type As. For example, one study found that Type A men who had already had a heart attack were less likely to have another attack if they had participated in a cognitive-behavior counseling program after the first heart attack (Thoresen et al., 1982). In regard to the connection between hostility and CHD, perhaps angry people can become more aware of their hostile tendencies and modify them, or perhaps they can learn to be more trusting of and have more empathy with other people.

Another group of researchers has tried to help healthy successful Army colonels engage in fewer Type A behaviors (Gill et al., 1985). The colonels participated in a series of counseling sessions that dealt with ways of modifying beliefs and attributions that underlie Type A behavior. They were also given advice on how to avoid potentially stressful situations, and engaged in role plays in which they practiced less highly pressured ways of coping with situations. The findings support the conclusion that the Type A attributes of anger, irritation, and impatience are not necessary aspects of the drive, ambition, creativity, and hard work needed by military leaders. The study showed that the colonels became less prone to Type A behaviors and that their ability to function as leaders was in no way impaired, but actually might have been improved.

There are wide regional and cultural differences in a large country like the United States. For example, according to a survey done some years ago, the town of Roseto, Pennsylvania, had a remarkably low death rate, especially from heart attacks. These low rates might seem surprising, since both the men and women of Roseto tended to be overweight and their diets, smoking, and exercise patterns were similar to those in other communities. What seemed to contribute most to the relatively low death rate was the way in which the people lived. Almost all Roseto's residents were of Italian descent and the town's neighborhoods were very cohesive. Family relationships were extremely close, supportive, and traditional. Men were likely to be the uncontested heads of their families. Personal and family problems tended to be worked out with the help of relatives, friends, and the local priest.

Although Roseto had these stable features, like all American communities, it had begun undergoing constant change. Young men and women were marrying non-Italians from other towns. The birth rate was declining, church attendance was down, and people were moving outside the old areas into more distant suburban neighborhoods. By the mid-1970s after many of these changes had occurred, a striking increase in the rate of heart attacks and sudden death was noticed, particularly among men under 55 (Egolf et al., 1992; Wolf & Bruhn, 1993). Apparently this social change was weakening Roseto's sources of social and emotional security, with important consequences for the health and longevity of its inhabitants.

Hypertension Hypertension is what most people describe as high blood pressure. A blood pressure level that is over 140 when the heart contracts (systolic pressure) and does not fall below 90 when the heart relaxes (diastolic pressure) is usually considered high. High blood pressure indicates that there is resistance to the flow of blood through the cardiovascular system. This condition places pressure on the arteries and forces the heart to work harder to overcome the resistance. Among younger adults (aged 25 to 44), men have higher blood pressures than women. Among older adults (aged 65 to 74), this pattern is reversed. Blood pressure readings of African-American adults typically exceed those of white adults. The basis for higher rates of hypertension among African Americans has not yet been identified.

High blood pressure is a major contributor to cardiovascular disorders and is one of the conditions that creates increased risk of heart attacks. Usually it is a silent or symptomless risk because the hypertensive individual might show no observable signs of a medical problem for many years. Hypertension may well be the most common, major, chronic disease in the United States today.

Clinical observations indicating that many hypertensives show wide variability in blood pressure readings and seem emotionally on edge much of the time have led to speculation about the causes and treatment of this disorder. Chronic anger and anger suppression have been identified as particularly important factors (Chesney & Rosenman, 1985). While everybody is exposed to anger-provoking situations, according to one theory, hypertensives experience chronic anger because of their inability to express it or assert themselves in a socially desirable manner. Psychotherapists believe that within the warm acceptance of the psychotherapeutic setting, angry, anxious people can gain insight into and mastery over their tendency to experience strong emotional reactions. However, firm empirical support for this approach is not yet available.

Some support is emerging for a behavioral approach to hypertension that directs attention to the specific types of situations associated with elevated blood pressure. Lack of competence in dealing with situations that call for assertiveness may be a specific behavioral deficit of many hypertensives. Assertiveness, defined as the ability to stand up for one's rights, express feelings, and avoid mistreatment by others, is a vital interpersonal skill and an indicator of social competence. People who are low in assertiveness tend to be mistreated, fail to express their feelings, and are frequently unable to have their needs met. Researchers have been able to show that hypertensives respond positively to behavioral training that involves the modeling and role-playing of appropriate assertiveness. As the social competence of these individuals increases, in many cases their blood pressure declines (Manuck et al., 1985); thus, strengthening the social skills of hypertensives may prove to be of clinical value.

Another line of research concerns the relationship between relaxation and blood pressure. Some reduction in blood pressure can be achieved by teaching relaxation skills to hypertensives. Herbert Benson (1977) has developed relaxation exercises that involve four elements: a repetitive mental device, a passive attitude, decreased muscle tension, and a quiet environment. His approach uses instructions like the following:

Sit quietly in a comfortable position. Close your eyes. Deeply relax all your muscles, beginning at your feet and progressing up to your face. Keep them deeply relaxed.

Breathe through your nose. Become aware of your breathing. As you breathe out, say the word "one" silently to yourself. Continue for 20 minutes. You may open your eyes to check the time, but do not use an alarm. When you have finished, sit quietly for several minutes, at first with closed eyes and later with opened eyes.

Do not worry about whether you are successful in achieving a deep level of relaxation. Maintain a passive attitude and permit relaxation to occur at its own pace. Expect distracting thoughts. When these distracting thoughts occur, ignore them and continue repeating "one."

Practice the technique once or twice daily, but not within two hours after a meal, since the digestive processes seem to interfere with elicitation of anticipated changes.

—Benson, 1977, p. 153

The simple method outlined by Benson often leads to lower blood pressure, as well as to other bodily changes that accompany relaxation. Figure 6-9 shows the types of results that have encouraged clinicians to use relaxation techniques with hypertensives. As the figure makes clear, relaxation led to lower systolic blood pressure during the day and also while the subjects were asleep. There were similar results obtained for diastolic pressure.

There is also evidence that the combined use of relaxation and biofeedback has particularly good long-term effects on blood pressure (Jacob et al., 1987). These benefits must be considered along with certain drawbacks, including cost, side effects, and difficulty in getting some patients to take antihypertensive medications. These medications have been shown to be effective in reducing blood pressure.

One study relating job stress to blood pressure elevation focused attention on the environment's role in hypertension (Schnall et al., 1990). In a study of 215 male workers (ranging from garbage collectors to stockbrokers) who were between the ages of 30 and 60, difficult work environments were found to cause sustained round-the-clock effects on hypertension. The most problematic work environments were relatively low-level jobs in which high psychological demands were combined with little control over the work process and little use of skills. Inability to exert an influence on the work situation increased the likelihood of high blood pres-

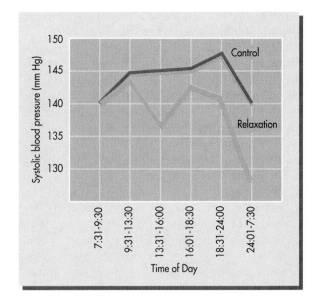

Figure 6-9 Systolic blood pressures for hypertensives who were given relaxation training and for an untreated control group. Blood pressure readings were taken during six time periods beginning with 7:31 to 9:30 A.M.

SOURCE: Adapted from Agras, Taylor, Kraemer, Allen, & Schneider, *Archives of General Psychiatry, 37,* p. 861. © 1980 American Medical Association.

sure. If a high-stress job included latitude to control the situation there was no increase in blood pressure. Twenty-one percent of all subjects suffered job strain. These men faced as much as three times greater risk of having high blood pressure than did those without job strain. The men between the ages 30 to 40 who had high-stress jobs showed a thickening of the heart's left ventricle, or chamber, a condition that often precedes coronary disease and heart attacks. These men had all worked on the job for at least 3 years, none was more than 20 percent overweight, and none had suffered heart disease before the study began. The finding of a significant relationship between high job stress and increased heart mass held regardless of the subject's alcohol intake, and whether or not the subject was a smoker.

For some people with hypertension, stress is the main cause, and relaxation and biofeedback may solve the problem entirely. For others, stress is not a factor at all, and medication may be the best approach to the problem. Hypertension has many possible causes, and the relaxation response should only be expected to help in cases when stress is at least a significant component.

Cancer

A growing number of research efforts are investigating whether psychological variables are related in some way to the occurrence and growth of cancer and to recovery from the disease.

Animal studies suggest that certain early life experiences (for example, daily handling by laboratory caretaking personnel or separation of young rats from their mothers) result in decreased or increased cancer susceptibility respectively. Another critical factor is the animal's ability to develop an adaptive coping response. Exposure to acute *escapable* stress does not influence tumor growth appreciably; however, the identical amount of *uncontrollable* stress markedly exacerbates tumor growth (O'Leary, 1990). Both animal studies and clinical observations of humans have revealed that uncontrollable stress is related to cancer growth (Sklar & Anisman, 1981). Stimulated by such findings, research is now being carried out on the roles of stress and personality in human cancers. One of these studies has shown that medical students whose psychological profiles indicated a relatively restricted capacity for close interpersonal relationships were especially prone to develop cancers 20 to 25 years later (Shaffer et al., 1987).

One hypothesis that has been suggested is that people who have difficulty handling strong feelings are more prone to develop cancers than people who can appropriately ventilate their emotions. Some researchers have focused attention particularly on feelings of depression. In one study, the MMPI (see chapter 4) was administered to over 2,000 middle-aged employed men. Two decades later only the MMPI Depression score was associated with increased risk of death (Persky et al., 1987; Shekelle et al., 1981). Whether psychological depression can be described as a direct or indirect cause of increased risk of death from cancer was not answered by this study. To answer that question we will need more information about the biology of psychological depression and its relationship to the growth of cancer cells.

While the role played by psychological factors in the development of cancer remains to be clarified, there is no question about the stressful impact of receiving a cancer diagnosis and having to live with the illness.

I knew from the outset that I had some form of cancer because the doctor didn't equivocate. "If it's ovarian, we can cure you," were his words, as I recall them. "If it's anything else, we can't." I took the news calmly, agreeing that immediate hospitalization was the most prudent course of action. The tears, the terror, didn't hit until hours later, sometime deep in that first, sleepless hospital night. And it was months before the real subtlety of his statement hit me. "We can cure you" doesn't necessarily mean "We will cure you."

Beyond the anxiety engendered by the illness itself, cancer exposes patients to physical and emotional stress from painful and sometimes emotionally difficult treatments and their side effects. Counseling and psychotherapy may lighten the load. For example, one clinical study suggested that group psychotherapy may be useful in helping cancer patients cope with their disease (Spiegel et al., 1989). The lives of women with breast cancer were lengthened by a year and a half when they participated in group psychotherapy; these women also reported significant reductions in their anxiety and pain. This study is particularly impressive because the 86 subjects had been randomly assigned to therapy and control groups, and all patients in both groups received standard medical treatment, including surgery and radiation or chemotherapy.

While further research will be needed to specify the most beneficial elements of group psychotherapy, the social support it provides is probably among them. Having supportive social ties contributes to resiliency and helps people cope with traumatic experiences of various types (see Figure 6-10). Cancer tends to stigmatize its victims and this often leads to social isolation and strong negative emotions.

The evidence implicating psychological factors in cancer is still tentative; similar emotional states have been associated with a variety of physical disorders. One of the greatest needs in cancer research is for longitudinal studies that begin before people develop cancer symptoms. Obviously, such studies are difficult to conduct because no one can tell in advance that a person will develop a malignancy. The ideal study would be one in which a large representative sample of apparently healthy people is assessed psychologically and then followed up to determine those individuals who develop cancer and whether its incidence can be predicted by psychological data collected before the cancer was identified.

We saw in chapter 3 that the immune system, the body's surveillance system, plays a role in regulating susceptibility to cancers, infections, allergies, and other diseases. There is evidence that psychological, behavioral, and environmental factors influence the functioning of the immune system in humans. Immunological consequences of stressors have been observed in such diverse situations as space flight, sleep deprivation, school examinations, bereavement, and depressive states. Not only exposure to multiple or chronic life stressors, but also loneliness, strong negative emotions, low levels of social support, and intense work pressures seem to lower the effectiveness of a person's immune system (Coe, 1993; Herbert & Cohen, 1993a; Herbert & Cohen, 1993b; Vollhardt, 1991). For example, many college students show decreased immune system functioning during exam periods (Jemmott & Locke, 1984; McClelland et al., 1985). This fact may help explain why they have so many illnesses during this time. Another example of this relation is a Canadian study of accountants that was conducted during the eight weeks preceding the deadline for filing income taxes and six months thereafter

Figure 6-10 Bald but beautiful. The classmates of 11-year-old Ian O'Gorman (center), a cancer patient, shaved their heads so that Ian would not feel out of place. Ian's teacher was so inspired that he, too, shaved his head.

Source: *Seattle Times,* March 10, 1994, p. A3.

(Dorian & Garfinkel, 1987). The accountants not only experienced high levels of psychological distress, but they also showed a decline in immune system function at the peak tax-filing periods. How this increasing evidence of stress–immune system relationships relates to cancer will require careful study, as will the possibility that therapeutic stress reduction can enhance immune functioning (Glaser & Kiecolt-Glaser, 1994).

Researchers who study possible behavioral factors in cancer must take into account some important facts and issues. Cancer is not a single disease but a group of different diseases sharing a common pattern of destructive, uncontrolled cellular growth. Psychosocial factors could theoretically affect at least two different stages of cancer: the initiation of a new cancer and the progression of an established cancer. Research to this point suggests that the main behavioral contributions to cancer initiation include smoking and poor nutrition. And although current research—such as some of the studies discussed in this section—point to a link between psychosocial factors and cancer outcome, the role of morale, mood, and attitude remains less well established and is controversial.

Asthma

Although the cause is unknown, **asthma** appears to be an allergic condition that results in reversible obstruction of the bronchial passages. People who have asthma chronically wheeze, cough, and have difficulty breath-

ing. To the patient, asthma means labored breathing, a feeling of constriction in the chest, gasping, and apprehension. About 30 out of 1,000 people in the United States have asthma.

Asthma patients often report that intense emotional states accompany acute attacks of labored breathing. This is not surprising: One can quickly measure one's emotional state by how easy it is to breathe. It has long been recognized that psychological variables contribute to asthma attacks. According to one theory, asthmatics share a common personality type and similar unconscious conflicts. However, there is little evidence to indicate that asthmatics are psychologically any more deviant than the general population. Another theory holds that characteristic personality features are the result, rather than the cause, of the restricted activities of severe asthmatics (Vachon, 1989).

Although the search for the cause and cure of asthma continues, a number of psychological and situational factors that seem to maintain or worsen asthma attacks have been studied successfully. The value of objective study of clinical cases is suggested by an experiment conducted with asthmatic children in Denver (Purcell et al., 1969). Parents of asthmatic children have been described as overcontrolling people who create an emotionally tense home environment. Clinical evidence has indicated that removing the children from the home and placing them in an institutional setting often reduces their asthmatic symptoms. Purcell and his colleagues wished to discover the effects of separating asthmatic children from their families while keeping their home environment relatively constant.

The experimental design involved an initial qualification period during which asthmatic symptoms were assessed, a preseparation period, a separation period, and reunion. During the two-week separation period the child's family lived in a nearby motel or hotel and had no contact with the asthmatic child, who remained within the family home, playing and attending school as usual. A substitute parent cared for the child at home during the separation period. Wheezing declined precipitously during the separation and increased again during reunion (see Figure 6-11). A Norwegian study recently yielded results that corroborated the Denver study (Askildsen et al., 1993).

Family relationships rather than physical aspects of the home environment thus appear to be conducive to asthmatic symptoms, although the psychological mechanism involved is unclear. One possibility is that the breathing obstruction that is characteristic of asthma may be produced by stress-induced activity of the auto-

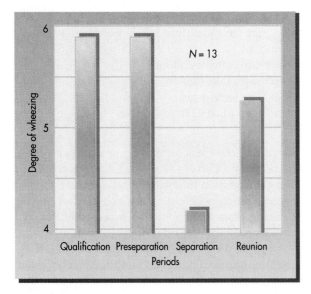

Figure 6-11 Mean daily scores for clinical evidence of wheezing during each period in the Denver asthma study.

Source: Reprinted by permission of Elsevier Science Publishing Co., Inc.; from K. Purcell, K. Brady, H. Schall, J. Muser, L. Molk, N. Gordon, and J. Means. The affect of asthma in children of experimental separation from the family, *Psychosomatic Medicine, 31*, pp. 144–164. Copyright © 1969 by the American Psychosomatic Society, Inc.

nomic nervous system, which stimulates mucus secretion, increased blood flow, and constriction of the bronchial tubes. Situational variables and personal vulnerability appear to combine in producing symptoms of asthma. Asthma has a strong genetic component and psychological factors alone are not sufficient to cause the disease. But in some people who have inherited a tendency for hyperreactive airways, stress and emotional factors may precipitate asthma attacks or make them more severe.

Although study of the roles of social and personality factors in health and illness is a relatively recent development, there is already considerable evidence that, along with other factors, they can be very important. Our anxieties and preoccupations, as well as our rewarding social ties, probably interact with biological variables (for example, heredity) and environmental occurrences (for example, stressful life events) in influencing how we cope while healthy and how well we recover from illness.

Somatoform Disorders

Many of the bodily complaints that physicians are asked to treat suggest physical pathology, but no actual impairment can be found. Although failure to diagnose a case medically might be due to a doctor's lack of

knowledge or to a faulty laboratory test, in a large group of cases psychological rather than physiological factors are responsible for the symptoms. These cases, which do not seem to be produced consciously, are characterized as **somatoform disorders.** This category includes several conditions in which bodily complaints play an important role (Kirmayer et al., 1994). Table 6-4 summarizes the major types of somatoform disorder described in DSM-IV.

Somatization Disorders

Somatization disorders are marked by multiple somatic complaints that are recurrent or chronic. This condition is often referred to as *Briquet's syndrome* because a physician by that name described it in detail in 1859. The most common complaints are headaches, fatigue, heart palpitations, fainting spells, nausea, vomiting, abdominal pains, bowel troubles, allergies, and menstrual and sexual problems. With this wide assortment of complaints, it is not surprising that somatizing patients are constantly going to the doctor, changing doctors, and undergoing probably unneeded surgery. Figure 6-12 compares the frequency of major surgical procedures for patients who were classified as somatizers and for normal controls.

Individuals with this disorder have a several-year history, beginning before age 30, of seeking treatment for or becoming impaired by multiple physical complaints that do not appear to be intentionally feigned. DSM-IV's criteria for this disorder include at least four pain symptoms in different bodily sites, two gastrointestinal

---

TABLE 6–4
Somatoform Disorders Described in DSM-IV

Somatization disorder. Multiple somatic complaints that may extend over a period of years; characterized by a combination of pain, gastrointestinal, sexual, and pseudoneurological symptoms.

Conversion disorder. Unexplained symptoms or deficits affecting voluntary motor or sensory function that suggest a medical condition; psychological factors are judged to be associated with the symptoms or deficits.

Hypochondriasis. Preoccupation with the idea that one has or might get a serious disease and misinterpretation of bodily symptoms or bodily functions.

Body dysmorphic disorder. Preoccupation with an imagined or exaggerated defect in physical appearance.

Pain disorder. Pain is the predominant feature of the clinical picture and psychological factors are judged to have an important role in its onset, severity, exacerbation, or maintenance.

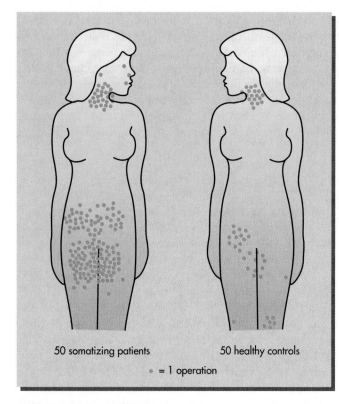

Figure 6-12 The complaints of somatizing patients often lead to unnecessary surgery. These two figures compare the number and location of major surgical procedures in 50 somatizing patients and 50 control subjects. Three times as much body tissue was removed from the somatizing patients as from the controls.

SOURCE: Based on Cohen et al., 1953.

symptoms without pain, one sexual symptom without pain, and one symptom or deficit suggesting a neurological symptom.

Patients with somatization disorders believe that they are sick, provide long and detailed histories in support of their belief, and take large quantities of medicines. Almost always, the chronic multiple complaints of somatizers are accompanied by a characteristic personality pattern and by difficulties in social relationships. They share many of the features of histrionic personality disorders, including a self-centered attitude and exaggerated expressions of emotion. Anxiety and depression are common features, as is manipulativeness, which may take the form of suicide threats and attempts. Somatizers impress people as being immature and overly excitable. Somatization disorder differs from hypochondriasis in that hypochondriacs focus on the *fear* of having a specific disease or diseases while the person with a somatization disorder tends to be preoccupied with the *symptoms*.

The complaints in somatization disorders are usually presented in a dramatic, vague, or exaggerated way. Somatizers tend to use vivid images in describing events and their reactions to them. For example:

- I wake up in the morning stiff as a board.
- My heart feels as if iron bands were being tightened around it.
- I throw up every half hour.
- I can't even take liquids.
- I feel as weak as a cat.
- I really can't take it much longer.

Somatizing disorders seem to occur mainly in women; approximately 1 percent of women have the condition. It is not uncommon for a family to have more than one somatizer. Since people who are classified as having a somatizing disorder tend to be suggestible, the high prevalence of the disorder in certain families may reflect the influence of a somatizing parent (usually the mother) rather than heredity. The vagueness of somatization complaints makes it difficult to do good research on the disorder (for example, the researcher is frequently left to wonder about possible organic causes of the symptoms).

Conversion Disorders

People with **conversion disorders** report that they have lost part or all of some basic bodily function. The disturbance does not seem to be under voluntary control and cannot be explained in terms of the principles of medical science. Paralysis, blindness, deafness, and difficulty in walking are among the symptoms reported by these patients. The onset of symptoms in conversion disorders often follows a stressful experience and may be quite sudden. Psychodynamic theorists believe that the symptoms represent an underlying psychological conflict.

Conversion symptoms seem to be naive inventions developed without regard for the actual facts of anatomy. In the case of **glove anesthesia,** for example, the individual may be unable to feel anything in one hand, although the arm has normal sensation. This is anatomically impossible because the sensory nerve supply to this part of the body is organized so that glove anesthesia could not be a result of a neurological disorder.

Although conversion symptoms often seem to appear for no obvious reason, they can frequently be traced to specific precipitating events. Complicating the task of diagnosing conversion disorders is the fact that at times they cannot easily be distinguished from somatically rooted symptoms. One clue that helps make the distinction is a characteristic feature of conversion disorders that has been termed *la belle indifférence* (the beautiful indifference): Whereas the individual may experience intense anxiety in other areas of life, his or her lack of concern about what seems to be an incapacitating physical disturbance is remarkable and not typically associated with similar symptoms associated with true somatic disorders.

Clinical conversion cases usually involve a single disturbance during any one period. Different bodily sites might be affected in subsequent episodes. The symptoms often allow the person to escape from frustrating or challenging situations through physical incapacity. When the pressures of these experiences wane, the physical symptoms weaken. Secondary gain may also occur when the person derives something from a physical symptom (such as attention, affection, or a pension) that he or she might not get otherwise. Because histrionic tendencies and excitability are characteristic of people who have these bodily reactions, their symptoms often tend to be highly dramatic as well as incapacitating.

Hypochondriasis

Hypochondriasis is diagnosed if a person has a persistent (6 months or longer) belief that she or he has a serious illness, despite medical reassurance, a lack of physical findings, and failure to develop the disease. Such persons often show poor insight in that they do not recognize that their concern is excessive.

Hypochondriacs have an obsessive preoccupation and concern with the condition of their bodily organs and continually worry about their health. Because they fear developing a disease they carefully track all potential symptoms by keeping themselves attuned to even the most minute changes in bodily functioning. They tend to misunderstand the nature of the significance of physiological activity and to exaggerate symptoms when they occur. Here is a physician's account of one of his hypochondriacal patients:

Harold Yocum kept the most extensive diary of any patient I have ever seen. Harold was a dapper little guy, standing perhaps five feet four. A local retail clerk, he was always impeccably dressed: sharp creases on his suit trousers (always a suit), carefully knotted ties, handkerchief in the breast pocket just so, highly polished wing tips, carefully clipped nails, and sharply parted hair with the long sweep over the bald spot. Harold was single and I could never get much social history from him—perhaps he didn't have much social history. He had some college education and had worked as a clerk for many years, but he never chatted about personal activities, friends, or hobbies. Efforts to engage him in such conversation made him uncomfortable, so after a few visits, I stopped trying. Indeed, after a few visits there was no opportunity to try. We had to review the diary. . . . He began to include more and more in his diary—time and dose of medication, general feelings, minor aches and pains, food-stuffs consumed, coffee and cola intake. He even developed his own stress scale and described evacuations in great detail—time, quantity, color.

Soon the volume of material was too much for his spiral-bound notebook and he began to bring in laboriously typed reports.

—Burnside, 1987, p. 1802

Body Dysmorphic Disorders

Individuals with this disorder have a preoccupation with an imagined defect or morbidly excessive concern about a minor unwanted feature of their physical appearance.

Denny is a 21-year-old man who is concerned about his appearance. One day when he was age 13, Denny was looking in the mirror while combing his hair and noticed that his nose was slightly crooked. He examined it closely from several angles and became convinced that it was abnormal. At breakfast he asked his mother to look at his nose. "It looks fine to me," she said. Denny was not reassured. At school he asked his best friend Steve, "Does my nose look alright to you?" "You mean aside from the big zit," Steve laughed. Denny frowned, "I mean, does it look crooked to you." Steve looked at Denny with a slight smile and said, "It's a nose. What do you want from it? Let's go to lunch."

Despite reassurances from friends and family, Denny continued to be concerned about his nose. He became so self-conscious about his nose that he often held his hand up to cover it when he spoke with people. By the time he was age 18, Denny began to investigate the possibility of plastic surgery to straighten his nose. When he was age 21, he made an appointment with a plastic surgeon for an evaluation.

(Fauman, 1994, p. 245)

People with body dysmorphic disorder commonly have imagined or slight flaws of the face or head such as hair thinning, acne, wrinkles, scars, or excessive facial hair. Other common preoccupations include the shape, size, or some other aspect of the nose, eyes, mouth, teeth, or head. Most individuals with this disorder experience marked distress over their supposed deformity, often describing their preoccupations as "intensely painful" and "devastating." Feelings of self-consciousness about their "defect" may lead to avoidance of work or public situations.

Pain Disorders

Severe prolonged pain either without organic symptoms or greatly in excess of what might be expected to accompany organic symptoms is classified as a pain disorder. There is often a temporal relationship between the occurrence of an actual, threatened, or fantasized interpersonal loss and complaints of pain (Mikail et al., 1994). The complaints may be used to evoke social responses, such as attention, from others. Examples of impairment resulting from the pain include inability to work or attend school, frequent use of the health-care system, the pain becoming a major focus of the individual's life, substantial use of medications, and interpersonal problems such as marital discord and disruption of the family's normal lifestyle. Important factors that appear to influence recovery from pain disorder are the individual's participation in regularly scheduled activities (e.g., work) despite the pain and resistance to allowing the pain to become the determining factor in his or her life. Pain disorder can be acute or chronic and difficult to diagnose because, while in some cases either psychological or physical factors seem to predominate, often the picture observed by the clinician is mixed.

Pain Saying "It hurts" is the result of an appraisal process that often leads to going to the doctor. Pain is influenced by biological, psychological, and social factors. The condition of our bodily systems obviously plays an important role in how we interpret signals coming from within our body. But our psychological state is also involved and, for this reason, pain is one of the more mysterious and elusive aspects of illness and its treatment. Social factors influence the perception of pain as well. When one member of a family reports pain, the other members may respond with attention and expressions of concern. This response may serve as a stimulus for more reports of pain.

The word pain is derived from the Greek *poine*, meaning "punishment." By the middle of this century, it became clear that pain was a complex, multiply-determined experience. One barrier to the treatment of pain is the difficulty people have describing it objectively. If you have a lump you can point to it, or if a bone is broken, it can be seen in an x-ray. Pain does not have these objective references. Yet, almost everyone must cope with periods of acute or chronic pain. Table 6-5 lists some self-management strategies that are useful in coping with pain.

A number of recent approaches to pain have focused on pain behaviors (for example, complaining about pain) and the conditions that strengthen or weaken them. In some cases pain is related to a physical disorder that can be identified—for example, pain related to a deterioration of the discs that separate and cushion the bones in the spinal column. Even in situations where the source of the pain can be identified in bodily changes, some people experience incapacitating pain while others with what seems to be very similar changes do not. Psychological approaches have focused on these behaviors and the conditions that strengthen or weaken them. Another class of pain behaviors has no such clear antecedents. Despite careful medical investigations, no organic changes can be found. The following case shows how operant conditioning procedures are clinically effective in bringing about behavioral changes related to pain when no physical cause can be identified.

The patient was a 19-year-old man who had been admitted to a hospital with complaints of pain in the lower back, hips, and both legs, and great difficulty in walking, sitting, and standing. An exhaustive medical study determined that his symptoms were unrelated to physical causes, and the case was diagnosed as a psychological disorder.

The operant therapy consisted of visits by a young assistant to the patient's room three times daily. During these visits the assistant spent approximately ten minutes talking to the patient about topics unrelated to his disorder. During an initial three-day period she encouraged him to walk but provided him with no reinforcement for doing so. During the next three-day sequence she instructed the patient to walk and reinforced him when this happened. Reinforcement consisted of comments such as "Good," "That's great," and "You're doing fine," accompanied by attention, friendliness, and smiling. Reinforcements were not given during

---

TABLE 6–5
Self-Management Strategies for Coping With Pain

Relaxation and biofeedback. Muscle relaxation decreases or prevents muscle spasms, reduces and controls muscle tension and helps control other physiological mechanisms (such as changes in brain chemicals) involved in nervous system arousal and pain production. Relaxation and biofeedback, described earlier in the chapter, can help reduce common forms of chronic pain.

Cognitive restructuring. Cognitive restructuring entails revising the way you think about your pain problem by rewriting your internal "script." Pain sufferers have found it useful to record in diaries when their pain is particularly severe; what the situation was at the time of the pain; what they thought about and felt before, during, and after the pain episode; and what they tried to do to decrease the pain. In doing this, they have sometimes been able (1) to identify thoughts and cues that trigger tension and anxiety that make the pain worse, and (2) to restructure or revise those of their thoughts that heighten stress and pain.

Distraction. Conjuring up pleasant, pain-free visions and thinking about topics not related to pain can help distract pain sufferers from becoming overly preoccupied with how much it hurts. Focusing on the environment and specific tasks (for example, how to study for an upcoming exam) instead of paying attention to your body can also help.

Exercise. There is some evidence that physical workouts can ease pain by facilitating the release of neurotransmitters that serve as natural painkillers in the body. Exercise regimens for people with chronic pain usually entail working each day toward a specific goal—one that is difficult but still attainable.

the following three-day period, but they were reinstituted during the final three days of the experimental therapeutic program.

—Hersen and others, 1972, pp. 720–721

This pattern of intervention is called an **A-B-A-B research design.** Such a design is useful in assessing the reasons for clinical change in a particular case because it can be carried out with only one subject who also serves as his or her own control in the period when no reinforcement is given. The A-B-A-B approach is used most often to determine whether operant-conditioning procedures are effective in bringing about behavioral changes. It consists of obtaining a baseline measure of the target behavior (A), instituting reinforcement-contingency procedures (B), removing the contingency so that the conditions that were present during the baseline period are reinstated (A), and reintroducing the phase-B contingency (B). This *repeated-measures design* is a very powerful method for isolating the conditions that control behavior.

Figure 6-13 summarizes the results of the program described in the above case. During the instruction period there was no increase in walking, but the addition of reinforcement resulted in increased walking. When reinforcing contingencies are discontinued, there is usually a gradual decrease in the target behavior. In this case, contrary to what might be expected however, improvement continued during the second period in which no reinforcement was given. Uncontrolled and unscheduled reinforcement by other patients may have contributed to this continued improvement. The greatest improvement occurred during the final phase of the program when reinforcement by the assistant had resumed.

Somatoform disorders involve physical symptoms that cannot be explained by current knowledge of how the body works. Collaborative research carried out by medical and behavioral scientists can help us obtain a clearer picture of how the mind and the body interact and why certain people report symptoms in the absence of any apparent physical basis. The pattern of inter-relationships is not well understood and probably quite complex.

Factitious Disorders and Malingering

Although somatoform disorders and problems that have traditionally been described as psychophysiological (for example, asthma and peptic ulcers) are different in a number of respects, they have in common the fact that the person with the disorder assumes the role of a patient—someone who receives attention and care. Another group of conditions that are characterized by

the same feature is **factitious disorders.** But in these conditions, physical and psychological symptoms are voluntarily self-induced by the patient. They may involve a total fabrication or an exaggeration of a preexisting condition.

In a factitious disorder the only apparent goal is the *desire* to assume the role of patient. The person often has a history of uncontrollable lying, demands for attention from professional people, and dramatic accounts of vague pains. Classifying a set of symptoms as factitious may be quite difficult. The dramatic way in which the patient presents his or her problems usually arouses suspicion; however, many individuals with this disorder have managed to gather quite a bit of medical information and, as a consequence, may be good enough actors to make their symptoms seem credible (Feldman & Ford, 1993).

Factitious disorders typically begin during early adulthood and are often stimulated by hospitalization for a genuine physical problem. Because of their dramatically presented but vague symptoms, individuals with factitious disorders undergo frequent hospitalizations during

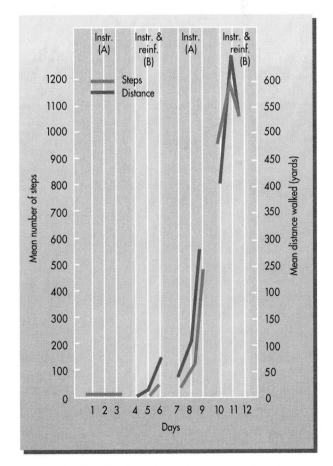

Figure 6-13 The chart shows changes in walking behavior during the four conditions of the repeated-measures design. Mean number of steps and of distance are shown as a function of instructions and reinforcements.

which unnecessary surgery may be performed. While somatization disorders are more common in women, factitious disorders are more prevalent among men. Although the symptoms of somaticizers and those with factitious disorders are the same, the somaticizers believe they are really ill but those with factitious disorder are merely seeking attention by manufacturing symptoms.

The term **Munchausen syndrome** refers to an extreme type of factitious disorder marked by repeated, knowing simulation of disease for the sole purpose of obtaining medical attention. A patient with this syndrome may travel great distances to appear at hospitals with dramatic and plausible, yet false, histories that convince physicians and staff members that he or she is suffering from an acute illness. The syndrome is named after Baron von Munchausen, an eighteenth-century German cavalry officer who became legendary for concocting elaborate lies. Patients with this syndrome tell incredible tales about their medical histories. They also fake symptoms; for example, they may pretend to be in pain, put blood in a urine sample, or manipulate a thermometer to create an impression of fever. Sometimes they go even further, inflicting real injury on themselves by burning or cutting themselves, taking dangerous drugs, or injecting foreign material into their veins. Often they persuade doctors to perform unnecessary surgery. They may spend most of their lives moving from one hospital to another, trying to be admitted. Once in a hospital, they refuse to comply with its rules and make constant demands for attention. The following case illustrates a typical example of Munchausen syndrome.

A woman staggered into the emergency room of a New York City hospital bleeding from the mouth, clutching her stomach, and wailing with pain. It was some entrance. Even in that setting, forever serving bleeders and clutchers and wailers, there was something about her, some terrible star quality that held stage center. Her pain was larger than life.

She told a harrowing story: A man had seduced her, then tied her up, beaten her, forced her to surrender money and jewelry on threat of death. She had severe pain in her lower left side and an unbearable headache.

She was admitted, and exhaustively tested. Nothing could be found; no reason for the bleeding or the pain; the specialists were left scratching their heads.

Then, one day, a hospital aide came upon these items in her bedside table: a needle, syringe, and a blood thinner

called heparin. Eureka. Inject yourself with enough blood thinner and you, too, can take stage center in an emergency room.

Confronted, she denied all charges. The stuff was not hers; someone was trying to frame her; if nobody believed her, she would check out of this place and find doctors who really cared. And off she went. Later, it was learned that she had recently been in two other hospitals: the same story, same symptoms, and same sequence of events.

—Lear, 1988, p. 21

A particularly disturbing variant of Munchausen syndrome is one in which a mother produces symptoms of disease in her child and then presents the child for treatment. The mother's concern may be convincing because she herself feels a need to be cared for; it is as though she regards the child's body as an extension of her own. The child goes along with the mother because the relationship is so close and intense and the activity so exciting.

Having a factitious disorder is not the same thing as **malingering.** People with factitious disorders simply crave attention and want to be taken care of. Malingerers, on the other hand, seek medical care and hospitalization in order to achieve some specific goal such as compensation, a disability pension, or evasion of the police. Whereas multiple complaints and hospitalizations seem almost a continuous pattern in factitious disorders, malingering often ends abruptly when the patient gets what he or she wants. In contrast, people with factitious disorders seem incapable of stopping their lying and manufacturing of symptoms. However, both of these conditions are self-induced, and both increase in response to high levels of stress.

Distinguishing factitious disorder or malingering from other conditions can be difficult. The judgment that a particular symptom is under voluntary control occasionally is made by excluding all other possible causes. Distinguishing between a factitious disorder and malingering also poses problems. When the clinician is not fully aware of the particular purpose for which the malingerer manufacturers his or her symptoms, the chances of misdiagnosis increase. An act of malingering might, under certain circumstances, be considered adaptive (for example, when a prisoner of war fakes an illness), but factitious disorders are almost always seen in people with severe, lifelong personality disturbances.

CHAPTER SUMMARY

PSYCHOLOGICAL, SOCIAL, AND BODILY INTERACTIONS

The **psychosomatic hypothesis** which became popular some 50 or 60 years ago, linked a person's development of certain bodily symptoms with the lack of emotional expression. Contemporary research has focused on bodily reactions to various emotion-arousing stimuli or stressors.

The Biopsychosocial Model The biopsychosocial model considers the interaction of the person's biological, psychological, and social subsystems. In this view, psychological factors usually play indirect roles in illness in that they combine with biological vulnerabilities of the person. The product of their interaction determines the effect of different levels of stress on the individual. This view emphasizes the concept of **homeostasis,** in which a living organism attempts to restore its dynamic equilibrium when it is exposed to stressors. **Behavioral medicine** and **health psychology** are concerned with reducing the stressfulness of illness and, wherever possible, preventing it.

Stress and Illness Stress occurs when a person feels unable to control important aspects of life. Skills whose presence decrease stress and risk of illness include ability to adapt to environmental change, to handle strong emotions, to interpret the situation correctly, and to form positive close relationships. There is growing evidence that stress can play a role in illness. Stress occurs when a person feels unable to control important aspects of life. Skills whose presence decreases stress and risk of illness include the ability to adapt to environmental change, to handle strong emotions, to interpret a situation correctly, and to form close positive relationships.

PSYCHOPHYSIOLOGICAL DISORDERS

Headaches Headache pain, which may have a variety of causes, is often treated with **biofeedback,** a technique that helps the clients use self-control procedures to gain more control over body functions such as muscle tension and other reactions to stress.

Cardiovascular Disorders Cardiovascular disorders are pathological conditions related to the functioning of the heart and blood vessels. In coronary heart disease, deposits—called **plaques**—thicken the walls of the coronary arteries and decrease the supply of blood available to produce a condition called **atherosclerosis.** This buildup can result in **angina pectoris** (chest pain) or in a **myocardial infarction** (what is usually called a heart attack). **Stress** is thought to contribute to the risk of coronary heart disease because in stressful situations the body secrets more of hormonal substances called **catecholamines.** Two of these, **epinephrine** and **norepinephrine** accelerate the rate of arterial damage. Many personal lifestyle factors can increase stress as can separation from or loss of a loved one. Living in a fast-paced society also increases risk of heart disease, presumably because it increases stress. When stress and social isolation are both present in a person's life, the risk of dying from heart disease is much higher than for people who are low in stress experiences and high in social support. People who have **Type A** personalities are very demanding of themselves and others and tend to operate under high pressure. Their higher risk for coronary heart disease may be due primarily to the hostility that permeates their lives. **Hypertension,** or high blood pressure, is also a risk factor for heart disease. Behavioral methods, including assertiveness training, relaxation training, and biofeedback, are helpful in lowering blood pressure in some cases.

Cancer Uncontrollable stress may be related to cancer growth. Some research indicates that both depression and inability to express strong feelings may be associated with greater risk of cancer. Although evidence linking psychological forces and cancer is still tentative, group psychotherapy has been shown to be associated with longer life expectancy for women with breast cancer. There is some evidence that stress–immune system relationships are related to cancer and that stress reduction can enhance immune functioning.

Asthma is an allergic condition that causes bronchial obstruction and seems to have a psychological component, as well as a genetic one.

SOMATOFORM DISORDERS

Somatoform disorders are bodily complaints for which no actual physical impairment can be found. Somatization, conversion, body dysmorphic, and pain disorders, as well as hypochondriasis, are included under this classification.

Somatization Disorders Patients with **somatization disorders** (also called *Briquet's syndrome*) have multiple and recurrent or chronic bodily complaints. These complaints are likely to be presented in a dramatic and exaggerated way.

Conversion Disorders The symptoms of **conversion disorders** are the reported loss of part or all of some basic body function, for instance the paralysis of some portion of the body or a sensory function such as ability to see. This loss does not seem under voluntary control although the symptoms do not fit with the facts of anatomical structures. One symptom of conversion disorder is *belle indifference,* the lack of concern about what seem to be incapacitating physical symptoms.

Hypochondriasis People affected with **hypochondriasis** show unrealistic fears of illness and are excessively preoccupied about their health.

Body Dysmorphic Disorders People with **body dysmorphic disorders** are preoccupied with imagined or exaggerated bodily defects. They experience great distress over their supposed deformity.

Pain Disorders **Pain disorders** involve reports of extreme and incapacitating pain without any identifiable organic symptoms or that is greatly in excess of what would be expected based on the organic symptoms found. These disorders can be acute or chronic and difficult to diagnose.

FACTITIOUS DISORDERS AND MALINGERING

Factitious disorders have symptoms that are voluntarily induced by the patient, presumably in an effort to receive attention and care. **Munchausen syndrome** is an extreme form of this disorder in which the person deliberately simulates the symptoms of disease by faking symptoms and even manipulating the results of medical tests. **Malingering** differs from factitious disorders because the person reports the symptoms to achieve some specific goal, such as an insurance settlement.

CHAPTER SEVEN

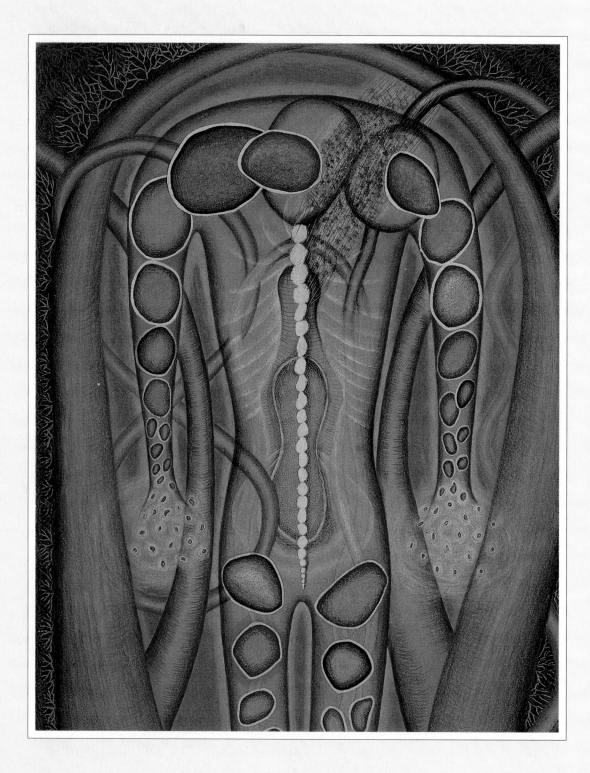

Marcy Hermansader, *Transparent Being Series #1-86*, 1986.
Photo courtesy Janet Fleisher Gallery, Philadelphia

ANXIETY DISORDERS

CASE A: SUSAN

I wish I could tell you exactly what's the matter. Sometimes I feel like something terrible has just happened when actually nothing has happened at all. Other times I'm expecting the sky to fall down any minute. Most of the time I can't point my finger at something specific. Still, I feel tense and jumpy. The fact is that I am tense and jumpy, almost all the time. Sometimes my heart beats so fast, I'm sure it's a heart attack.

Little things can set it off. The other day I thought a supermarket clerk had overcharged me a few cents on an item. She showed me that I was wrong, but that didn't end it. I worried the rest of the day. I kept going over the incident in my mind, feeling terribly embarrassed at having raised the possibility that the clerk had committed an error. The tension was so great, I wasn't sure I'd be able to go to work in the afternoon. That sort of thing is painful to live with.

CASE B: PAUL

It happened without any warning, a sudden wave of terror. My heart was pounding like mad, I couldn't catch my breath, and the ground underfoot seemed unstable. I was sure it was a heart attack. It was the worst experience of my life.

CASE C: SHARON

I can't tell you why I'm afraid of rats. They fill me with terror. Even if I just see the word *rat*, my heart starts pounding. I worry about rats in restaurants I go to, in my kitchen cupboard, and anywhere I hear a noise that sounds like a small animal scratching or running.

CASE D: MIKE

Before I come home from work I spend half my time wondering whether a burglar has broken into the apartment. As soon as I get home I check every room, under the bed, and in the closets. Before going to sleep I probably check the lock on the front door 50 times. I feel better after each check, but then my concern wells up and I have to go check again.

The problems described in these four cases are different, but they have one feature in common: the experience of strong anxiety. In Susan's case, which illustrates a *generalized anxiety disorder*, the anxiety is chronic and is felt in a variety of situations. Paul is describing a *panic attack*, in which the anxiety is sudden and overwhelming. People who experience one or more panic attacks worry a great deal about whether and where another attack may take place. Sharon has a *phobic disorder*, in which anxiety is aroused by a specific type of situation, animal, or object. Mike's case is an example of an *obsessive-compulsive disorder*, in which thinking certain thoughts and neglecting to do certain things (like checking the lock on the front door) arouse intense anxiety and concern.

Everyone has worries and fears, even the rich and famous (see Figure 7-1). Freud argued that anxiety can be adaptive if the discomfort that goes with it motivates people to learn new ways of approaching life's challenges. But whether it is adaptive or maladaptive, the discomfort can be intense. The anxious person who is waiting for the worst to happen is often unable to enjoy a personal life, or to gain gratification from work. Anxious people may thus prevent themselves from experiencing positive outcomes in life.

Figure 7-1 Even successful people known for their toughness and daring may have powerful fears that dictate their behavior. Tony Dorsett, one of football's greats, makes no secret of his fear of sleeping in the dark.

"I've always been a person afraid of the dark. I was taught that when you have complete darkness, that's when spirits walk. In our house when I was growing up, all the doors were always cracked a little bit at night so you could get light into the room. You come in my house now and you're gonna see light everywhere. Even now when I sleep, I leave the bathroom light on and leave the door cracked. And I'm not ashamed to tell you."

The term **anxiety** is usually defined as a diffuse, vague, very unpleasant feeling of fear and apprehension. The anxious person worries a lot, particularly about unknown dangers. In addition, the anxious individual shows combinations of the following symptoms: rapid heart rate, shortness of breath, diarrhea, loss of appetite, fainting, dizziness, sweating, sleeplessness, frequent urination, and tremors. All of these physical symptoms accompany fear as well as anxiety. Fear differs from anxiety because people who have fears can easily state what they are afraid of. People who feel anxious, on the other hand, are not aware of the reasons for their fear. Thus, even though fear and anxiety involve similar reactions, the cause of worry is readily apparent in the former case but is not at all clear in the latter.

This chapter focuses on the serious maladaptive aspects of anxiety, but it is useful to remember that anxiety has many causes and that all people experience it at some time in their lives. It is normal for people to experience anxiety when faced with stressful, threatening situations, but it is abnormal to feel strong, chronic anxiety in the absence of a visible cause.

The characteristics of anxiety include feelings of uncertainty, helplessness, and physiological arousal. A person who experiences anxiety complains of feeling nervous, tense, jumpy, and irritable. Often he or she has difficulty falling asleep at night. An anxious person becomes fatigued easily and has "butterflies in the stomach," as well as headaches, muscle tension, and difficulty in concentrating. There is growing evidence that people suffering from anxiety disorders are overly sensitive to threat cues. Such individuals may exhibit a heightened sensitivity, vigilance, or readiness to attend to potential threats. Table 7-1 lists common symptoms of anxiety and self-descriptions given by people with high levels of anxiety. The experience of intense anxiety may occur after an event has taken place, in anticipation of a future event, or when a person decides to resist a preoccupying idea, change an undesirable aspect of behavior, or approach a fear-arousing stimulus.

In chapter 5 we discussed one kind of anxiety disorder, the posttraumatic stress disorder, which occurs after an intensely traumatic event such as a serious accident or natural disaster. In this chapter we discuss four types of disorders in which the causes of anxiety usually are not so clear. A generalized anxiety disorder is marked by chronic anxiety over a long period (at least several months). A panic disorder consists of recurrent, sudden anxiety attacks in which the individual experiences intense terror and dread. In phobic disorders, the anxiety has an identifiable cause—for example, being near dogs or having to speak to a group. When the stimulus is not present, the phobic person's tension level is relatively low. In obsessive-compulsive disorder, anxiety results from efforts to prevent undesirable outcomes.

TABLE 7–1
Common Anxiety Symptoms and Self-Descriptions Indicative of High Anxiety

Symptoms

1. Nervousness, jitteriness
2. Tension
3. Feeling tired
4. Dizziness
5. Frequency of urination
6. Heart palpitations
7. Feeling faint
8. Breathlessness
9. Sweating
10. Trembling
11. Worry and apprehension
12. Sleeplessness
13. Difficulty in concentrating
14. Vigilance

Self-Descriptions

1. I am often bothered by the thumping of my heart.
2. Little annoyances get on my nerves and irritate me.
3. I often suddenly become scared for no good reason.
4. I worry continuously and that gets me down.
5. I frequently get spells of complete exhaustion and fatigue.
6. It is always hard for me to make up my mind.
7. I always seem to be dreading something.
8. I feel nervous and high-strung all the time.
9. I often feel I can't overcome my difficulties.
10. I feel constantly under strain.

The individual is plagued with a recurrent need to ward off disaster by thinking about certain ideas and/or performing certain acts.

Many clinicians used to describe people who were suffering from anxiety disorders as neurotic. In DSM-II, an early version of the classification system that was strongly influenced by the psychodynamic perspective, the word "neurosis" was used to describe disorders marked by anxiety, personal dissatisfaction, and inappropriate (but not psychotic) behavior. These disorders were grouped together because it was thought that they all arose from somewhat similar, unconscious, mental processes and motivations. Though this view may some day be substantiated, today such a view is not widely held.

Most current schemes for classifying maladaptive behavior involve identifying its source and using the obvious presence of marked anxiety as the criterion for including maladaptive behavior in the group of **anxiety disorders.** This chapter is restricted to a discussion of disorders in which the individual is abnormally anxious, either generally or under certain circumstances, but still

has adequate contact with reality and is rarely incapacitated enough to require institutionalization. The role of anxiety in several other disorders is described in later chapters. We will look first at specific characteristics of the various anxiety disorders and examine some similarities and differences among them. In the latter part of the chapter we will discuss particular therapeutic approaches to these disorders.

Although the anxiety disorders include a wide range of maladaptive behavior, the various conditions can usually be categorized in one of two groups: (1) the frequent experience of anxiety, worry, and apprehension more intense and longer lasting than the anxiety experienced by the average person in everyday life; and (2) the frequent development of avoidance, ritual acts, or repetitive thoughts as a means of protecting the individual from experiencing the anxiety.

Generalized Anxiety Disorder

Generalized anxiety disorder might best be described as consisting of prolonged, vague, unexplained, but intense fears that do not seem to be attached to any particular object. They resemble normal fears, but there is no actual danger, and in most cases danger is not even imagined to be present. In one recent study, a group of patients with various types of anxiety disorders were asked, "Do you worry excessively about minor things?" Ninety-one percent of those diagnosed as having generalized anxiety disorder answered yes to this question, a much higher percentage than for any of the other anxiety disorder groups (Sanderson & Barlow, 1990). Although a diagnosis cannot be made definitively on the basis of a cartoon, Ziggy in Figure 7-2 may have an anxiety disorder, most likely generalized anxiety disorder.

In generalized anxiety disorder, anxiety persists for six months or longer and is not attributable to recent life experiences. The symptoms of generalized anxiety disorder usually include motor tension, hyperactivity of the autonomic nervous system, dread of the future, and hypervigilance. These symptoms may be experienced individually or in combination.

1. *Motor tension.* Individuals with this symptom are unable to relax, keyed up, and visibly shaky and tense. Strained facial expressions are common, as are furrowed brows and deep sighs. Such individuals are easily startled.
2. *Autonomic reactivity.* In individuals with this symptom, the sympathetic and parasympathetic nervous systems seem to be working overtime. There is some combination of sweating, dizziness, pounding or racing heart, hot or cold spells, cold and clammy hands,

Figure 7-2 *Ziggy*, by Tom Wilson.

SOURCE: Copyright © 1994, Ziggy and Friends, Inc. Dist. by Universal Press Syndicate.

upset stomach, lightheadedness, frequent urination or defecation, lump in the throat, and high pulse and respiration rates.

3. *Apprehensive feelings about the future.* People with generalized anxiety disorders worry about what the future holds for them, for people close to them, or for their valued possessions.

4. *Hypervigilance.* People who suffer from generalized anxiety adopt a sentrylike stance in their approach to life. They constantly scan the environment for dangers (not necessarily of a physical nature), although often they cannot specify what the dangers might be. This excessive vigilance is related to their hyper-aroused state. Because they are always alert to potential threats, they are easily distracted from tasks on which they are working. Their hypervigilance also contributes to difficulty in falling asleep.

Generalized anxiety is a common disorder and more common among women than men. One study conducted in three cities found that between 4.1 and 6.6 percent of the population had experienced a generalized anxiety disorder during their lives (Robins & Regier, 1991). Another recent study found that over 5 percent of people between the ages of 15 and 45 have had the symptoms of generalized anxiety disorder at least once during their lifetime. Being older than 24 years of age, separated, widowed, divorced, unemployed, or a homemaker tended to be associated with having the symptoms (Wittchen et al., 1994).

A study of patients diagnosed as having a generalized anxiety disorder found that seven symptoms were especially characteristic of the group studied (Marten et al.

1993). These symptoms are summarized in Table 7-2. While the cause of the anxiety is usually hard to identify, environmental events and recent experiences may play a role. One study found that in a large number of cases of generalized anxiety disorder, the sufferers had experienced important negative and unexpected events in the months before the anxiety reached clinical proportions (Blazer et al., 1987).

Panic Disorder

Pan, the Greek god of woods and fields, was blamed for the inexplicable dread sometimes felt by travelers in lonely places. His name has been given to a disorder identified by sudden, overwhelming, apparently senseless terror. **Panic disorders** may attack with no warning (see Figure 7-3). The indicators of panic disorder are

---

TABLE 7–2
Most Characteristic Symptoms of Generalized Anxiety Disorder Patients (N = 204)

1. Irritability
2. Restlessness
3. Muscle tension
4. Difficulty concentrating
5. Sleep difficulties
6. Feeling keyed up
7. Feeling fatigued

Source: Based on Marten et al., 1993

Figure 7-3 John Madden, a 6 foot 4 inch, 240-pound former football player and head coach of the Oakland Raiders professional football team, is now a well-known TV sports personality. While he was flying across the country, Madden experienced a severe panic attack, left the plane at a stop halfway across the United States, and has never flown again. He is shown here in the luxury bus—donated for his use by Greyhound—that now serves as his home as he travels across the country.

similar to those of generalized anxiety disorder except that they are greatly magnified and usually have a sudden onset. However, there are differences between generalized anxiety disorder and panic disorder in their risk factors, rates of occurrence, and family relationships (Weissman, 1990).

People with panic disorder may not be anxious all the time. Instead, they have unanticipated anxiety attacks that recur after periods (perhaps several days) of normal functioning. Severe palpitations, extreme shortness of breath, chest pains or discomfort, trembling, sweating, dizziness, and a feeling of helplessness mark the panic attacks. The victims fear that they will die, go crazy, or do something uncontrolled, and they report a variety of unusual psychosensory symptoms (see Table 7-3). In addition to recurrent unexpected panic attacks, panic disorder patients also display persistent concern about having additional attacks and what the attacks might imply.

Panic attacks range in length from a few seconds to many hours and even days. They also differ in severity and in the degree of incapacitation involved. In the following case, frequent panic attacks had a definitely incapacitating effect.

A 30-year-old housewife comes to a psychiatric clinic complaining that she is afraid she will no longer be able to care for her three young children. In the past few months she has suffered repeated episodes of dizziness and shortness of breath, with chest pains, heart palpitations, headaches, and uncontrollable trembling. During these episodes the world seems strange and unreal, and she has a sense of impending doom. Once she went to a hospital, irresistibly convinced that she was having a heart attack. Her doctor told her that

she was physically healthy and suggested that she relax, work less hard, and develop more interests outside her family, but the attacks became more intense and frequent, and finally he referred her to the clinic.

Although she used to be gregarious and outgoing, she is now afraid to leave home except in the company of her husband or her mother. She avoids supermarkets and department stores, and says that any crowded place makes her uneasy. When she has to be in an unfamiliar building, she tries to stay near the door and checks for windows and exits. She will no longer drive a car, ride a train, or board a boat. Bridges terrify her. She says that she trembled with fear even on the way to the clinic. Last summer the family did not take their usual vacation, because she did not think she could tolerate being so far from home. Now she wants her mother to stay with her when the children are at home, because she is afraid that if one of the children had an accident she would be unable to help.

—*The Harvard Mental Health Letter*, March 1990, p. 1

TABLE 7–3
Common Features of Panic Attacks

Shortness of breath or the feeling of being smothered
Dizziness, unsteadiness, or faintness
Trembling, shaking, or sweating
Heart palpitations or a racing heart rate
Choking, nausea, or stomach pain
Numbness or tingling; flushing or chills
Chest pain or discomfort
A sense of "strangeness," of being detached from oneself or one's surroundings
Fear of going crazy, losing control, or dying

The term **panic attack** denotes an abrupt surge of intense anxiety rising to a peak that either is cued by the presence, or thoughts, of particular stimuli or occurs without obvious cues and is spontaneous and unpredictable. In the former case (which is more common), persons experiencing panic often have phobic fears that the stimuli evoke. People who have panic attacks when such evoking stimuli are not present typically do not have phobias as well. Panic disorder affects women more than men, and younger age groups more than the elderly (Robins & Regier, 1991). A recent study found that about 15 percent of the 8,098 individuals surveyed reported the occurrence of a panic attack over their lifetimes, and 3 percent reported a panic attack in the preceding month (Eaton et al., 1994).

Compared to other anxiety disorders, panic attacks appear to be particularly distressing experiences. Generalized anxiety and panic disorders both run in families, although the family incidence rate is much higher for panic disorder. There is no evidence that any specific type of childhood experience predisposes people to these states. Problems often arise in classifying these disorders, because many cases are complicated. (Barlow et al., 1994). Several types of maladaptive behavior may occur simultaneously. Obsessions, compulsions, and phobias might all be observed in a given individual. Severe panic states are sometimes followed by periods of psychotic disorganization in which there is a reduced capacity to test reality.

Box 7-1 presents a case of both anxiety and panic disorder along with an interpretation of its major features. A person who has had a panic attack develops anticipatory anxiety: He or she becomes worried and tense, and is afraid that the panic will recur. In some cases, this type of anticipatory anxiety seems to be a quite realistic fear. Recent research has revealed that persons who experience panic attacks perceive themselves as having impairments in their physical health and emotional well-being, and in occupational and financial functioning. They are heavy users of health-care facilities and emergency departments, and they are much more prone than the general population to think about committing suicide. Twenty percent of patients with panic disorder report that they have attempted suicide (Klerman et al., 1991). In addition to studying suicidal cognitions of people who experience panic attacks, research has revealed certain cognitive processes that occur during these attacks. Ottaviani and Beck (1987) asked persons who had had panic attacks about the types of thoughts they remembered having during the attacks. Subjects reported thoughts of humiliation, losing control, helplessness, and failure.

There is reason to believe that panic and anticipatory anxiety have different sources. Imipramine, a drug used in the treatment of depression, has been shown to prevent the recurrence of panic attacks (Marks, 1987). However, it seems to have no effect on the anticipatory anxiety that panic attacks almost always arouse. That is, subjects treated with imipramine may feel anxious in anticipation of a panic attack but not experience one.

In the past, relatively few attempts had been made to identify and compare the two types of anxiety disorders: (1) generalized anxiety and (2) panic disorders. Now their similarities and differences are being examined and investigated more intensively. For example, one group of researchers has compared the patterns of symptoms, family characteristics, type of onset, and clinical course in generalized anxiety disorder and panic disorder (Anderson et al., 1984). Their findings support the assumption that these conditions are distinct from one another. Table 7-4 compares these disorders with regard to several bodily symptoms. Subjects with generalized anxiety disorder have fewer bodily symptoms than do those with panic disorder. Their histories also show an earlier, more gradual onset. A generalized anxiety disorder has a more chronic course and is more likely to have a favorable outcome. Members of families in which a person suffers from a panic disorder tend to have a relatively high percentage of panic episodes. The comparable percentage for family members of those with a generalized anxiety disorder is much lower.

Panic and generalized anxiety disorders differ most clearly in the diffuseness of the anxiety seen in the latter and its focused intensity in the former. But research has shown that they differ in a number of other ways as well. Table 7-5 lists some of these differences. In addition to investigating the characteristics of panic disorders, researchers are also conducting experiments designed to better understand how the attacks come about. It has been discovered that sodium lactate, when administered intravenously to patients with panic disorder, will often provoke a panic attack, while this does not happen to the general population. A number of research teams are

TABLE 7–4
Percentages of Patients with Panic Disorder and Generalized Anxiety Disorder Reporting Particular Symptoms

Symptom	Panic Disorder	Generalized Anxiety Disorder
Sweating, flushing	58.3	22.2
Heart palpitations	89.5	61.1
Chest pain	68.8	11.1
Faintness, lightheadedness	52.1	11.1
Blurred vision	31.2	0
Feeling of muscular weakness	47.9	11.1

Source: Based on Anderson, Noyes, and Crowe, 1984.

An Anxious, Precise, Demanding Man Seeks Help

An Evaluation of Mr. E.'s Condition

Mr. E., 40 years old and recently married, sought clinical help because he was nervous and worried about his health. These lifelong concerns became worse during his courtship and honeymoon.

Mr. E. has trouble falling asleep if the room is too dark or too light, if he has eaten too much or too little, if the sheets are cold or wrinkled, if he forgets his nose spray, or if there is any noise. He fears nightmares, nocturnal asthma attacks, or dying in his sleep. He often awakes in a panicky sweat with nightmares, typically of being chased or suffocated. He worries that his lost sleep is shortening his life and ruining his work efficiency.

Mr. E. had always been anxious and worried. He expects the worst, dreads each time the phone rings lest it be bad news, and suspects that he has a serious illness. He experiences frequent palpitations, shortness of breath, dizziness, and numb fingers and has had numerous physical exams and electrocardiograms. The negative findings do not reassure him, as Mr. E. is convinced that his doctors are withholding information, and he is determined to have additional checkups until his condition is diagnosed. He also has gastrointestinal flutters, frequent diarrhea or constipation, and occasional nausea and vomiting. His father died of heart disease and his mother of cancer, and he feels confident that he already has, or soon will have, one or both conditions.

Mr. E. is also extremely anxious about his work. He is a stockbroker responsible for large financial transactions and cannot ever relax his concentration, even on vacations. He has also felt considerable performance anxiety about his recently more active sex life and has suffered from consistent premature ejaculation. There are many specific situations that make him intolerably nervous—waiting in line, sitting in the middle of a row at a movie, riding public transportation, wearing a pair of pants a second time without having them cleaned, having dirty dollar bills, and so forth—but he is able to avoid most of them without great inconvenience. Mr. E. has panic attacks at least every few weeks. They tend to occur whenever something new is expected of him, when he is forced to do one of the things he fears, when he must give a talk, and, at times, for no apparent reason.

Mr. E. is a very precise and demanding man who is difficult to live or work with (or to treat). He is controlling, self-absorbed, maddeningly fastidious, and meticulous. He did not marry previously because he had very demanding expectations of a woman, and his worries and habits are intolerable to many women. His wife has begun to complain to him, and he is afraid she may leave unless he is able to change quickly.

—Frances, A.J. and Klein, D.F., Anxious, precise, demanding man seeks help soon after marriage. Hospital and Community Psychiatry 33, 89–90, 1982. Copyright © 1982, the American Psychiatric Association. Reprinted by permission.

Because this is a real-life case, it is more complicated than a textbook outline of a disorder. Mr. E. might be described in terms of either generalized anxiety disorder or panic disorder. However, because of the definite recurring panic attacks, panic disorder seems the more likely primary diagnosis. Mr. E.'s concerns about being precise and meticulous also raise the possibility of an obsessive-compulsive personality disorder. Despite Mr. E.'s protestations to the contrary, he suffers from no apparent physical disorder. A reasonable rating of Mr. E.'s psychosocial stress (his recent marriage) would seem to be moderately severe. Mr. E. might be described as having a fair level of adaptive functioning in the past year. Despite his superior work performance, his social and leisure-time difficulties now suggest a decreased level of functioning.

Thus, Mr. E. might be described as having a panic disorder, features of an obsessive-compulsive personality disorder, no apparent physical disorders, moderately severe stress in the recent past, and moderate but increasing difficulty in functioning.

It is important to remember that experienced clinicians might disagree about this description either because of gaps in what is known about Mr. E. or because of emphasis on different known facts. With additional information, the classification might change. A clinician treating Mr. E. would want to better understand his sexual problems, his conviction that he has cancer or heart disease, and his somatic complaints, for which no bodily cause has been found.

---

seeking to identify the mechanisms by which sodium lactate causes panic attacks. Imipramine significantly decreases the frequency of sodium-lactate-provoked panic attacks.

Phobias

Phobos was the Greek god of fear. His likeness was painted on masks and shields to frighten enemies in battle. The word *phobia*, derived from his name, came to

TABLE 7-5

Characteristics of Panic Disorder in Comparison with Generalized Anxiety Disorder

1. Clinical onset is later.
2. The role of heredity seems to be greater.
3. The ratio of women to men is greater.
4. Alcoholism is more common.
5. While depression is common in both, it is unusually more so in panic disorder.

mean fear, panic, dread, or fright. Unlike people who have generalized anxiety disorders, people who have **phobic disorders** know exactly what they are afraid of. Except for their fears of specific objects, people, or situations, phobic individuals usually do not engage in gross distortions of reality. Nothing physical seems to be wrong with them. However, their fears are out of proportion with reality, seem inexplicable, and are beyond their voluntary control.

One question that inevitably arises in discussions of anxiety is why people spend so much time brooding about vague menaces when there are so many real dangers to worry about. Perhaps the degree of fear we feel about a potentially harmful event is linked not primarily to the degree of threat (in terms of the probability that it will actually happen to us) or even to the amount of injury that we imagine we might sustain if the worst did happen, but to the disturbing quality of the event or situation itself. For example, even though there are three times as many traffic fatalities as there are murders, our thoughts are rarely preoccupied by the danger of an automobile accident. Fear of violent crime, on the other hand, touches many of us. Crucial to the experience of fear is whether people feel that they will be able to respond meaningfully to a situation—that is, whether they will be able to cope.

One of the most interesting aspects of phobias is that the stimuli that evoke them are not random. The most common fear-arousing stimuli tend to be animals, objects, or events that presented real dangers in earlier stages of human evolution (McNally, 1987). Although extreme fear of dogs, snakes, and spiders seems maladaptive today, such fear may have been highly adaptive in earlier times. More "modern" phobias are rare. For example, electric-outlet or pajama phobias occur infrequently, even though these objects are often associated with trauma.

Some researchers believe that human beings are instinctively predisposed or prepared to like or dislike and fear or not fear certain stimuli—snakes, for example (Seligman, 1971). Presumably fears for which we are prepared are products of millions of years of evolution. While this theory seems consistent with some evidence—for example, the many fears of childhood that do not appear to be products of conditioning—many questions remain unanswered (Davey, 1992). Why do people develop fears of objects that have no evolutionary significance? Why are therapeutic interventions effective in treating phobias that might be regarded as being linked to instincts?

Phobics do not need the actual presence of the feared object or situation to experience intense tension and discomfort. The following account by a psychiatrist with an airplane phobia shows that simply imagining a phobia-related event can elicit strong psychological and bodily reactions.

I was pampering my neurosis by taking the train to a meeting in Philadelphia. It was a nasty day out, the fog so thick you could see only a few feet ahead of your face, and the train, which had been late in leaving New York, was making up time by hurtling at a great rate across the flat land of New Jersey. As I sat there comfortably enjoying the ride, I happened to glance at the headlines of a late edition, which one of the passengers who had boarded in New York was reading. "TRAINS CRASH IN FOG," ran the banner headlines, "10 DEAD, MANY INJURED." I reflected on our speed, the dense fog outside, and had a mild, transitory moment of concern that the fog might claim us victim, too, and then relaxed as I picked up the novel I had been reading. Some minutes later the thought suddenly entered my mind that had I not "chickened out" about flying, I might at that moment be overhead in a plane. At the mere image of sitting up there strapped in by a seat belt, my hands began to sweat, my heart to beat perceptibly faster, and I felt a kind of nervous uneasiness in my gut. The sensation lasted until I forced myself back to my book and forgot about the imagery.

I must say I found this experience a vivid lesson in the nature of phobias. Here I had reacted with hardly a flicker of concern to an admittedly small, but real danger of accident, as evidenced by the fog-caused train crash an hour or two earlier; at the same time I had responded to a purely imaginary situation with an unpleasant start of nervousness, experienced both as somatic symptoms and as an inner sense of indescribable dread so characteristic of anxiety. The unreasonableness of the latter was highlighted for me by its contrast with the absence of concern about the speeding train, which if I had worried about it, would have been an apprehension founded on real, external circumstances.

—Nemiah and Uhde, 1989, p. 973

The onset of many phobias is so gradual that it is difficult to tell whether there were any specific precipitating factors. In other cases, the apparent time of onset, although not necessarily the cause, can be pinpointed.

I was riding in my husband's car and I suddenly became terrified. I felt as if I would die. I made him turn around and take me home. I ran into the house and suddenly felt safe. I could not understand what had happened. I had never been afraid of cars. The next day it happened again, and it kept getting worse. Finally, just being on the street and seeing a car would bring on a terrible feeling. Now I just stay at home.

—De Nike and Tiber, 1968, p. 346

Phobias may begin with a generalized anxiety attack, but the anxiety then becomes crystallized around a particular object or situation (for example, elevators, snakes, or darkness). As long as the feared object or situation can be avoided, the anxiety does not reach disturbing proportions. Some objects of phobias—such as cats, cars, and stairs—are considered aspects of everyday life by most of us. Other objects and situations—snakes, death, and heights—are disliked to some extent by most people. However, phobias involve levels of fear that, in addition to being overly intense, interfere with normal living patterns. One study of phobic patients showed that their fears fell into five categories related to (1) separations, (2) animals, (3) bodily mutilation, (4) social situations, and (5) nature (Torgersen, 1979). Table 7-6 gives examples of phobic content that fall into these categories.

Phobias tend to grow progressively broader. For example, one woman had a subway phobia that began with an inability to ride an express train between two fairly distant locations. Gradually the phobia developed until she would have to get off the train at each local stop, wait until her anxiety diminished, get on the next train, get off again at the next stop, and so on, until her destination was reached.

Phobic individuals usually develop ways of reducing their fears. The subway rider was able to get from one place to another. However, the cumbersome procedures people with phobias' devise do not eliminate their fear; indeed, the fear seems always to be one step ahead of them. In one sense, phobic individuals who cannot cross the thresholds of certain rooms or cannot work may be as incapacitated as people with severe psychotic symptoms. In another sense, they are more fortunate than people who exhibit free-floating anxiety, since at least their fears are directed toward a specific object, and they can reduce their anxiety by simply avoiding that object.

Phobias, like other forms of maladaptive behavior, do not occur in isolation. They are usually intertwined with a host of other problems. In consequence, it is difficult to estimate their frequency accurately. One survey of randomly selected residents of a medium-sized Canadian city found that 61 percent of the respondents reported

being much or somewhat more fearful than other people in at least one of several types of situations (Stein et al., 1994). While fears reaching clinical proportions occur much less frequently, phobias are relatively common, being even more prevalent than generalized anxiety disorders (Robins & Regier, 1991).

Rates of phobic disorder are about twice as high for females as males. In both sexes, blacks have higher rates than whites or Hispanics. Phobias typically have their onset in childhood or young adulthood and there is a sharp decline in new cases with age. The mean duration for phobias varies from 24 to 31 years—in other words, the duration tends to be chronic (Boyd et al., 1990). Phobias do not require hospitalization. Professional treatment, when it is given, is usually carried out on an outpatient basis.

Traditionally, phobias have been named by means of Greek or Latin prefixes that stand for the object of the fear, as shown in the following examples:

- Acrophobia: fear of heights
- Agoraphobia: fear of open places and unfamiliar settings
- Aquaphobia: fear of water
- Claustrophobia: fear of closed places
- Xenophobia: fear of strangers

Recently, however, such names have been avoided. People's knowledge of Greek and Latin is not what it once was, and in any case, a staggering number of labels would be needed to take account of the great variety of phobias that have been observed. Today, therefore, phobias are grouped into three general categories: specific phobias, social phobias, and agoraphobia.

Specific Phobias

Specific phobias are a miscellaneous category of marked, persistent, irrational fears. Some examples of specific phobias are intense fear of particular types of animals (for example, snakes, dogs, or rats), claustrophobia, and acrophobia (see Figure 7-4). Specific phobia is the most common type of phobia, with about 11 percent of the population meeting the criteria for specific phobia during their lifetime. (The comparable figures for agoraphobia and social phobia are 5.6 percent and 2.7 percent, respectively.) Unreasonable fears of heights and bugs or other small animals are the most common fears, with over 18 percent of a large surveyed population responding positively to questions about these fears (Robins & Regier, 1991). Two other symptoms—unreasonable fears of water and public transport—were reported by over 10 percent of the sample surveyed.

If you have a specific phobia, it might have begun when you actually did face a risk that realistically provoked anxiety. Perhaps, for example, you found yourself

TABLE 7–6 Examples for Five Categories of Phobias	
Separation fears	Social fears
Crowds	Eating with strangers
Traveling alone	Being watched writing
Being alone at home	Being watched working
Animal fears	Nature fears
Mice	Mountains
Rats	The ocean
Insects	Cliffs, heights
Mutilation fears	
Open wounds	
Surgical operations	
Blood	

Source: From Torgersen, 1979.

in deep water before you learned to swim. Extreme fear was appropriate in such a situation. But if you continue to avoid even the shallow end of a pool, your anxiety is excessive and may be of phobic proportions (see Figure 7-5). For the person with a specific phobia, the degree of distress varies with the prevalence of the avoided situation. For example, a hospital employee who fears blood may be in a constant state of fear because the probability of encountering blood in a hospital setting is high. When the probability of the feared stimulus is low, people with specific phobias are usually free of symptoms. The person who is phobic about drowning is usually not affected by that phobia except in the presence of water or when a beach party is being planned.

Children eventually overcome many of their fears. And while it is not unusual for adults with specific phobias to overcome their fear as a result of a positive experience involving contact with the fear-arousing stimulus, specific phobias tend to be chronic. A variety of therapeutic approaches have been used in treating specific phobias. Procedures that promote association between the fear-arousing stimulus and nonanxiety responses, and at the same time provide information countering mistaken beliefs about the stimulus (for example, that all dogs are ferocious), often have positive effects.

Mary, aged 29, had fainted at the sight of blood or injury ever since she was 4 years old. She and her therapist agreed on specific targets for treatment: watching blood samples being taken from someone else and from herself, coping with her children when they needed first aid for minor injuries, and getting her own varicose veins treated. In her first session, Mary was able to watch a blood sample being taken from her therapist's finger and then having her own finger pricked and a blood sample taken. In the next session, she was asked to imagine situations involving injury and to watch films depicting injuries to others. Between sessions, at home, Mary dealt successfully with some small emergencies with her children and she had her varicose veins injected. At follow-up 8 months later, she reported that she was free of her problem. She was able to enroll in a first-aid class and went freely to movies depicting blood and injury.

—Adapted from Marks, 1978, pp. 135–136

This case illustrates two important points. One is that exposure to fear-arousing stimuli contributes to overcoming specific phobias. The other is that high motivation on the part of client increases the likelihood of success.

Figure 7-4 This painting by George Tooker, titled *Cornice*, captures the fear of heights that acrophobic people feel even when they are in situations much less threatening than the precarious perch shown in the painting—for instance, when they are climbing ladders or standing near the railings of observation platforms.

Source: Columbus Museum of Art, Ohio: Museum Purchase: Howald Fund II.

Figure 7-5 A specific phobia often can be traced to an intense, realistic childhood fear. For example, a child who was never taught to swim and remembers vividly desperate attempts to stay afloat might as an adult continue to be terrified by even shallow water.

Social Phobias

Social phobias are less common than specific phobias—they occur at only about 25 percent the rate of specific phobias—but they can attack with no less force (Robins & Regier, 1991). Social phobias are characterized by fear and embarrassment in dealings with others (see Figure 7-6). Often the individual's greatest fear is that signs of anxiety such as intense blushing, tremors of the hand, and a quavering voice will be detected by people with whom he or she comes into contact. Fear of public speaking and of eating in public are frequent complaints of socially phobic individuals. These problems often begin in late childhood or early adolescence, and may crystallize into a phobia in late adolescence.

> *I sometimes don't get to class because I think the teacher might call on me. My fear doesn't have anything to do with being unprepared if he asks me a question, because I'm almost always well prepared. My grades on exams are always near the top of the class. What I keep thinking about is that the teacher and all the students will see how red my face gets whenever I have to say something in a group.*

Most phobias about interpersonal relationships involve one or more of the following fears: fear of asserting oneself, fear of criticism, fear of making a mistake, and fear of public speaking. People who are afflicted in these ways have much in common. They go through life feeling generally inadequate and have many social and interpersonal difficulties. They attempt to compensate by immersing themselves in school and then in their work, never being really sure of their skills and talents. They dismiss their successes, if any, by saying, "My work isn't really good enough" or "I was just lucky—being in the right place at the right time." They may feel like impostors, fearing that they will be discovered and that the rug will be pulled out from under them.

Two types of social phobia are particularly stubborn, the fears of blushing and eating. Some people are terrified that they will blush in the company of others and are convinced that they will be highly visible and the center of painful attention. If questioned, these people cannot say what is so dreadful about blushing, but it is often evident that shame is an important component of their anxiety. In some cases, a change of color may not be at all evident to the observer, even though the individual insists that he or she feels bright red. The force of their fear, unfounded as it may be, often leads people to restrict their social lives severely. Fear of eating often involves a dread of eating in the company of others. Even this fear may be very specific. For instance, Emma, age 26, became very anxious when she had to eat or drink in the company of anyone she knew. However, she was able to eat or drink in public places without undue distress as long as the other people present were strangers. Table 7-7 gives some guidelines concerning interpersonal behavior that have been found to be helpful in building the resilience of people with social phobias (Marks, 1987).

Figure 7-6 Social phobic individuals avoid situations requiring interpersonal contact. If they cannot stay away from contact with other people, they often experience physical symptoms such as nausea, trembling, and profuse perspiration as well as disabling feelings of anxiety.

TABLE 7–7
Interpersonal Self-Help Techniques for the Person with a Social Phobia

1. Respond to anxiety symptoms by approach rather than withdrawal.
2. Greet people properly, with eye contact.
3. Listen carefully to people and make a mental list of possible topics of conversation.
4. Show that you want to speak; initiate conversation (asking questions is easier, as it switches attention to the person expected to reply).
5. Speak up without mumbling.
6. Tolerate some silences.
7. Wait for cues from others in deciding where to sit, when to pick up a drink, and what to talk about.
8. Learn to tolerate criticism by introducing controversy deliberately at an appropriate point.

Table 7-8 provides some hints that might be useful for a friend or spouse of a phobic person to help the fearful person.

Agoraphobia

One ordinary day, while tending to some chore, taking a walk, driving to work—in other words, just going about his usual business—Leo Green was suddenly struck by a wave of awful terror. His heart started pounding, he trembled, he perspired profusely, and he had difficulty catching his breath. He became convinced that something terrible was happening to him—maybe he was going crazy, maybe he was having a heart attack, maybe he was about to die. He desperately sought safety, reassurance from his family, and some type of treatment program. His doctor could find nothing wrong with him, so he went about his business, until a panic attack struck him again. As the attacks became more frequent, he spent more and more time thinking about them. He worried, watched for danger, and waited with fear for the next one to hit.

He began to avoid situations where he had experienced an attack, then others where he might find it particularly difficult to cope with one by escaping and getting help. He started by making minor adjustments in his habits—going to a supermarket at midnight, for example, rather than on the way home from work when the store tended to be crowded. Gradually, Leo Green got to the point where he couldn't venture outside his immediate neighborhood, couldn't leave the house without his spouse, or sometimes couldn't leave at all. What started out as an inconvenience turned into a nightmare. Like a creature in a horror movie, fear expanded until it covered the entire screen of his life.

This scenario describes a common path in the development of **agoraphobia,** the fear of entering unfamiliar situations. To the outside observer, a person with agoraphobia may look no different from one with a social phobia. Both may stay home from a party. But their reasons for doing so are different. While the socially phobic individual is afraid of the scrutiny of other people, many investigators believe that the agoraphobic individual is afraid of his or her own internal cues. The agoraphobic person dreads the awful anxiety of a panic attack, and is afraid of losing control in a crowd. Minor physical sensations may be interpreted as the prelude to some catastrophic threat to life. In severe cases, the individual may have an irrational fear of leaving the familiar setting of the home; in the most extreme cases, the victim is unable even to walk down the street or go shopping.

Like most other phobias, agoraphobia is more common among women than among men. It often begins in the late teens, although it is also observed in older people. And like other phobias, it waxes and wanes, and it is not uncommon for the object of the fear to change.

TABLE 7–8
Hints for Helping a Phobic Person

1. Never make the assumption that you know what is best; do not force your beliefs.
2. Always provide a way out if he or she is having difficulties (for example, leave the party).
3. Be aware of excuses to avoid the feared situation ("I'm not feeling well today"). Provide encouragement, but do not make a big issue if your suggestion is met with resistance.
4. Don't assume that because something was accomplished successfully one time that the next time will also be easy.
5. Never play tricks by doing something that is different from what you initially agreed upon.
6. If things are going well, suggest trying something a little more difficult.
7. Approach feared situations in gradual steps, never making the decision to go on to the next step yourself.
8. Encourage him or her to practice responses to the feared situation (a party, a dog).
9. While practicing or in the feared situation, don't constantly ask about the person's feelings.
10. If the phobic person practices alone and reports successes to you, share in his or her excitement.

Some cases of agoraphobia are preceded by panic attacks marked by intense anxiety. In many cases of agoraphobia, the phobic symptoms are a complication of panic disorder. People who experience the intense fears that are characteristic of agoraphobia strive to organize their lives in such a way as to minimize exposure to the fear-arousing stimuli.

Recent research suggests that agoraphobic individuals can be divided into two groups, those with and those without panic attacks (Eaton et al., 1994). About 50 percent of people who experience panic attacks go on to develop agoraphobia unless they are treated early with certain drugs. One theory regarding the panic attack–agoraphobia linkage is that an individual is born with a biological vulnerability to panic attacks. Psychosocial factors, such as a pile-up of stressful life events and upsetting situations, can trigger a panic attack in a vulnerable individual. According to this theory, many patients, unaware of the biological roots of panic attacks, conclude that the situations in which the attacks take place must be the culprit. They become increasingly preoccupied with avoiding such situations and constrict their life styles—often at considerable economic and social expense—in the hope of eluding the attack. One patient confided that she had accumulated hundreds of dollars in fines by parking her car illegally in front of her office rather than face the anxiety associated with walking across the parking lot.

Panic attacks can be treated with certain drugs that are effective in treating depression (for example, the tricyclic antidepressants and monoamine oxidase inhibitors). To a significant extent, agoraphobia is a complication of panic attacks that are not treated and therefore are allowed to recur. Antidepressants are effective in suppressing panic but not in reducing anticipatory anxiety and agoraphobia. Behavioral techniques, including graduated exposure to the situation the individual is afraid of, are effective in treating agoraphobia. Some highly motivated agoraphobics are able to carry out this exposure themselves, without the frequent aid of a therapist. The following case illustrates the successful use of this approach.

Ms. A., a 40-year-old woman, had been virtually house-bound for 5 years because of classic agoraphobia. In a 1½-hour session, she, her husband, and I delineated her avoidance profile (those places she avoided regularly because they evoked panic) and worked out an exposure-homework program in which she would slowly habituate to one situation after another. I explained how she should keep a diary of her exposure-homework exercises and asked her to mail them to me. This she did regularly. She diligently carried out her exposure program and within weeks was mobile for the first time in years. She kept up her progress for 4 years without seeing me again, but then she had some family difficulties, which depressed her, and quickly relapsed. She saw me once more for an hour and was encouraged to revive her original exposure-homework program. On doing this she recovered her gains, which continued through follow-up for 9 years, when I last heard from her—a gratifying result for 2½ hours of time from a clinician.

—Marks, 1987, pp. 1163–1164

Agoraphobic individuals are often clinging and dependent. Studies of the histories of severely impaired agoraphobic persons have shown that 50 percent of the patients exhibited separation anxiety in childhood, well before the onset of the agoraphobia (Gittelman & Klein, 1984). The association between childhood separation anxiety and agoraphobia is much stronger in women than in men. Perhaps, in some sense, agoraphobia is a delayed outbreak of childhood separation anxiety. Because separation anxiety is almost always measured by means of retrospective self-reports, there is a need for longitudinal studies that allow for the observation of subjects' behavior in addition to self-reports.

Obsessive-Compulsive Disorder

A man who suffered from fears of contamination from AIDS felt a drop in his eye as he looked up while passing under a building. He became obsessed that the drop was actually from someone spitting out of a window who had

AIDS. He felt compelled to go to every office on the 16 floors of that side of the building and ask if anyone had spit out the window.

This man, diagnosed as having **obsessive-compulsive disorder,** shows the driven quality of the thoughts and rituals seen in people with this condition. While the specific features of the condition vary from case to case, they have in common recurrent obsessions or compulsions that are severe enough to be time consuming (that is, they take more than one hour a day) or cause marked distress or significant impairment. **Obsessive** people are unable to get an idea out of their minds (for example, they are preoccupied by sexual, aggressive, or religious thoughts); **compulsive** people feel compelled to perform a particular act or series of acts over and over again (repetitive hand washing or stepping on cracks in the sidewalk, for example).

Obsessions usually involve doubt, hesitation, fear of contamination, or fear of one's own aggression. The most common forms of compulsive behavior are counting, ordering, checking, touching, and washing. A few victims of obsessive-compulsive disorder have purely mental rituals; for example, to ward off the obsessional thought or impulse they might recite a series of magic words or numbers. About 25 percent of people with an obsessive-compulsive disorder have intrusive thoughts but do not act on them. The rest are both obsessive and compulsive; compulsive behavior without obsessional thoughts is rare (Skodol, 1989).

Compulsive rituals may become elaborate patterns of behavior that include many activities. For example, a man requires that his furniture never be left an inch out of place, and feels a need to dress and undress, brush his teeth, and use the toilet in a precise, unvarying order, all the time doubting whether he has performed this sequence of actions correctly, and often repeating it to make sure. Some theorists believe that compulsive behavior serves to divert attention from obsessive thoughts. In any case, compulsive rituals become a protection against anxiety, and so long as they are practiced correctly, the individual feels safe.

Therapists say there are enormous differences between healthy people with compulsive streaks and those suffering from obsessive-compulsive disorder. Truly obsessive-compulsive people often have family histories of psychiatric difficulties, suggesting a genetic component to the disorder. They are wracked by self-doubt and often are unable to make even simple decisions.

By contrast, healthy people with a few compulsive tendencies tend to work efficiently and organize their daily activities to avoid confusion. They also take pride in their ability to control their emotions—an impossibility for those with obsessive-compulsive disorder. Although obsessive-compulsive people are wracked by guilt over their strange behavior's effects on their families, they continue because they believe their compulsive acts keep themselves and their families safe. Box 7-2 contains three first-person accounts: the first dealing with the development of a compulsion, the second with the experience of obsessive thoughts in a particular situation, and the third with a relapse after encouraging improvement.

The exact incidence of obsessive-compulsive disorder is hard to determine. The victims tend to be secretive about their preoccupations and frequently are able to work effectively in spite of them; consequently, their "problems" are probably underestimated. Obsessive-compulsive disorder is more common among upper-income, somewhat more intelligent individuals. It tends to begin in late adolescence and early adulthood, and males and females are equally likely to suffer from it. A relatively high proportion of obsessive-compulsive individuals—some surveys report up to 50 percent—remain unmarried.

Recent studies have found the lifetime prevalence of obsessive-compulsive disorder in the United States and Canada to be approximately 2.3–2.6 per 100 people with the age of onset occurring in the twenties (Robins & Regier, 1991; Weissman et al., 1994). While this figure is lower than for phobias and generalized anxiety, it is higher than for panic disorder and several other diagnostic groupings. As public awareness of the prevalence of obsessive-compulsive disorder increases, the social stigma associated with it may decrease and encourage those who suffer from it to seek professional help.

The most common features of obsessive-compulsive disorder are the following:

1. The obsession or compulsion intrudes insistently and persistently into the individual's awareness.
2. A feeling of anxious dread occurs if the thought or act is prevented for some reason.
3. The obsession or compulsion is experienced as foreign to oneself; it is unacceptable and uncontrollable.
4. The individual recognizes the absurdity and irrationality of the obsession or compulsion.
5. The individual feels a need to resist it.

The language used by those with an obsessive-compulsive disorder conveys their exaggerated attention to details, their air of detachment, and the difficulty they have in making a decision:

I seem to be stuck with them—the thoughts, I mean. They seem so unimportant and silly. Why can't I think about things I really want to think about? But I can't stop thinking about trivia like did I lock the garage door when I went to work this morning. I've never not locked it and my wife's home anyway. I get depressed when I realize how much time I waste on nothing.

I feel under such pressure, but I can't make a decision. I write out on 3-by-5 cards all the pros and cons, then I study them, consider all the complications that perhaps might bear on the decision, and then I do it again—but I never seem to be able to make up my mind.

Obsessional thoughts often seem distasteful and shameful. Their content generally involves harming others, causing accidents to occur, swearing, or having abhorrent sexual or religious ideas. The person with these thoughts is often very fearful that he or she might act on them and as a result spends a great deal of time avoiding these situations or checking that everything is all right.

Susan, a quiet 30-year-old college graduate who has held the same responsible job for 8 years, worries that she might put razor blades in other people's food. She refuses to drive a car because she fears she would deliberately smash it into another vehicle.

When she makes coffee at work, she worries that she might have slipped poison into it. She checks her clothing when she leaves work to make sure she hasn't tucked a razor blade into a pocket. She is afraid to hold babies or be around small children. She worries that she might suddenly commit some violent act, such as hurling them to the floor.

She won't shop by herself, afraid that she might slip something into the products on the store shelves. Even when accompanied by her boyfriend, she finds herself needing reassurance. "I was OK, wasn't I?" she asks.

Susan has never put sharp objects in food, hurt a baby, or poisoned coffee.

Depending on the situation and the nature of the obsession, the obsessive individual may feel some pride in his or her unwillingness to make a premature decision, or may feel self-contempt when indecisiveness prevents action and allows others to win acclaim. The founder of evolutionary theory, Charles Darwin, is an example of an obsessive person. Only when Darwin faced the possibility of prior publication by a colleague was he able to overcome his obsessive indecisiveness and put *On the Origin of Species* into the hands of a publisher.

The variety of obsessive-compulsive rituals and thoughts is practically unlimited, but investigators have identified four broad types of preoccupations: (1) checking, (2) cleaning, (3) slowness, and (4) doubting and conscientiousness. The following statements illustrate each type.

Checking
■ I frequently have to check things (gas or water taps, doors) several times.
Cleaning
■ I avoid using public telephones because of possible contamination.

Slowness
- I am often late because I can't seem to get through everything on time.

Doubting and Conscientiousness
- Even when I do something very carefully, I often feel that it is not quite right.

When the compulsive rituals or obsessive thoughts begin to interfere with important routines of daily life, they become significant problems that require professional attention. Their bases frequently are not well understood, but because all of us have had some persistent preoccupations with particular acts and thoughts, their interfering effects can easily be appreciated. Obsessive-compulsive preoccupations—checking details, keeping things clean, and being deliberate—often increase during periods of stress. They can have undesirable effects when speedy decisions or actions are required.

Attempts to find out what obsessive-compulsive individuals are afraid of usually fail. Many clinicians believe that fear of loss of control and the need for structure are at the core of the obsessions and compulsions. Whether the disorder reflects the impact of environmental factors or heredity, its incidence is greater among members of some families than among the general population.

A common feature of psychotic behavior is irrational thought, but an obsessive-compulsive person is not considered to be psychotic since he or she is usually aware of the irrationality. In some cases, however, the border between obsessive-compulsive disorder and true psychosis is imprecise.

People who suffer from obsessive-compulsive disorder are very cautious. Like victims of phobias and other anxiety disorders, they unreasonably anticipate catastrophe and loss of control. In general, victims of phobias fear what might happen to them, whereas victims of obsessive-compulsive disorders fear what they might do. There are mixed cases; for example, fear of knives might be associated with the obsessional thought that one will hurt someone if one picks up a knife, and fear of elevators might be brought on by a recurrent impulse to push someone down the shaft. An obsessional thought about shouting obscenities during a sermon might lead the victim to avoid attending church, just as a phobia about the sound of church bells would. Normally, the object of a phobia can be avoided while an obsession cannot be, but again there are mixed cases; a dirt phobia may be as intrusive as an obsession, because dirt is everywhere.

Obsessive thoughts and compulsive rituals shade into phobias to the extent that anxiety accompanies the thoughts or rituals and there is avoidance of situations that evoke them. For example, someone who has a washing ritual will try to avoid dirt, much as a person with a dog phobia avoids dogs. Clinical workers often observe that both obsessive-compulsive and phobic individuals have an unusually high incidence of interpersonal problems. The two disorders differ in that the obsessive-compulsive person's fear is directed not at the situation itself but, rather, at the consequences of becoming involved with it—for example, having to wash afterwards. Another difference is that obsessive-compulsive persons develop a more elaborate set of beliefs concerning their preoccupying thoughts and rituals than phobics do about their fears. Cognitions seem to play a larger role in obsession-compulsion than in phobia. This point is illustrated by the case of a 40-year-old man with a checking compulsion.

The other night my wife and I went to the movies. It was torture even though the movie was great. For about an hour before going I couldn't stop thinking about this need I have to check the doorknob in order to make sure it's locked. I had to get out of the car four times to check the doorknob. When I do that sort of thing, my wife tries to be understanding, but I know she is thinking, "How come once isn't enough?" On the way to the theater I kept worrying about whether the door was locked. I would bet I had similar thoughts a hundred times while at the theater. You can't enjoy yourself under those circumstances, can you?

Interpreting and Treating Anxiety Disorders

Whether it is general or specific to certain situations, anxiety is a major component of the disorders dealt with in this chapter. Anxiety and the things that people do to keep it at manageable levels have been looked at from several theoretical perspectives. Many theories have been offered to explain anxiety disorders. We will discuss the ones that are currently most influential in clinical practice and research.

The Psychodynamic Perspective

Psychodynamic theorists and many other clinicians believe that the major determinants of anxiety disorders are intrapsychic events and unconscious motivations. They believe that anxiety is an alarm reaction that appears whenever a person is threatened. How an individual adapts to the anxiety alarm depends on its intensity, the cue that evokes it, and the person's characteristic response to alarms. It is normal to experience some overt anxiety; the amount of anxiety and the nature of the threat determine whether an instance of anxiety is normal or pathological.

A distinguishing characteristic of clinical anxiety is that an alarm is frequently sounded in the absence of a consciously recognized source of danger. A danger exists, but its basis is vague or totally hidden from view. A tourist may understandably experience overwhelming

Obsessive-Compulsive Disorder

The Development of Compulsions

I'm 18 now, and I've had OCD [obsessive-compulsive disorder] since I was 8 or 9. That's when my special "routines" for getting dressed in the morning started. I'd often miss the school bus, and my mother would have to drive me to school.

Before I could take my morning shower, I had to be sure everything was just right. The folds in the shower curtain had to hang a certain way. The sink, tub, and faucets had to be perfectly clean. I had to remove everyone else's towels from the racks and put them in the hall. Before I even stepped into the shower, I had spent more than half an hour cleaning and organizing the bathroom.

When I turned the shower on, I had a rule that only the cold water could run while I washed my hair. I also had a ritual for washing my hair—I used 30 circular motions, and if I touched either of my ears, I had to start over.

I had more routines for getting dressed. My clothes had to be organized a certain way and put on in a certain order. If any piece of clothing touched the floor, I'd have to take everything off and start again. Eventually my morning routines

took so long that I had to set my alarm for 5 a.m. Even then, I'd be late some days.

At school I had rules about touching things and washing my hands. It was not unusual for me to go into the bathroom 20 times a day to wash my hands. I was afraid my friends would find out about my secrets—so I began to avoid them.

My parents knew something was wrong, but they thought I was just going through an "awkward stage." I knew all my weird routines didn't make sense, but I felt that something horrible would happen if I didn't give in to them.

The compulsive person feels compelled or driven to act a certain way (see Figure 7-7a).

Obsessive Thoughts While Driving

I'm driving down the highway doing 55 MPH. I'm on my way to take a final exam. My seat belt is buckled and I'm vigilantly following all the rules of the road. No one is on the highway—not a living soul.

Out of nowhere an Obsessive-Compulsive Disorder attack strikes. It's almost

Figure 7-7a While frequent washing of one's hands is obviously desirable, a constant focus on the need for hand washing is maladaptive.

magical the way it distorts my perception of reality. While in reality no one is on the road, I'm intruded with the heinous thought that I might have hit someone . . . a human being! God knows where such a fantasy comes from.

I think about this for a second and then say to myself, "That's ridiculous. I didn't hit anybody." Nonetheless, a gnawing anxiety is born. An anxiety I will ultimately not be able to put away until an enormous emotional price has been paid.

I try to make reality chase away this fantasy. I reason, "Well, if I hit someone while driving, I would have felt it." This brief trip into reality helps the pain dissipate . . . but only for a second. Why?

anxiety while walking through a jungle. However, some individuals experience the same kind of anxiety in their own living rooms, for no apparent reason. According to the psychodynamic view, such people's defenses are inadequate to control or contain their anxiety. Figure 7-8 indicates, humorously, that it is possible to develop a defensive posture that effectively masks inner turmoil.

Psychodynamic theorists frequently mention the following as causes of anxiety that reaches clinical proportions: perception of oneself as helpless in coping with environmental pressures, separation or anticipation of abandonment, privation and loss of emotional supports as a result of sudden environmental changes, unacceptable or dangerous impulses that are close to breaking into consciousness, and threats or anticipation of disapproval and withdrawal of love.

The psychodynamic view of phobias stems from two fundamental concepts: (1) psychological conflict and (2) unconscious mental processes. From this standpoint the phobic situation or object has symbolic significance; it can be regarded as a stand-in for something else that

one is frightened of, something that is completely beyond one's awareness. It represents an unresolved psychological conflict, a holdover from childhood. For example, a child who reaches school age at the same time that her brother is born might be very angry at her mother for sending her to school. She might feel that her mother is getting rid of her in order to be alone with the new baby all day. On the way to school each day the little girl passes a house where a vicious German shepherd is chained up. The dog becomes associated with her fantasy about her mother's real reason for sending her to school. The girl manages to get through her childhood all right, but in her twenties she develops a phobia about dogs after her mother has expressed strong disapproval of her future husband.

Obsessive ideas and complusive rituals may direct attention away from significant, distressing, unconscious thoughts. Psychoanalysts believe that these thoughts often involve aggression and rage that may have first been aroused in the battle for autonomy between the growing child and the mother. When the mother is

BOX 7-2

Because the gnawing anxiety that I really did commit the illusionary accident is growing larger—so is the pain. . . .

I start ruminating, "Maybe I did hit someone and didn't realize it . . . Oh my God! I might have killed somebody! I have to go back and check." Checking is the only way to calm the anxiety. It brings me closer to truth somehow. I can't live with the thought that I actually may have killed someone—I have to check it out.

Now I'm sweating . . . literally. I pray this outrageous act of negligence never happened. My fantasies run wild. I desperately hope the jury will be merciful.

—Rapoport, 1989, pp. 21–22

Obsessions are persistent and unwanted thoughts, ideas, or images that the person does not intentionally produce (see Figure 7-7b).

Relapse

I felt I was making real progress. Recently there had only been a glimmer of my obsessions breaking through.

I'd begun to think that perhaps they were behind me, that my life was on the brink of returning to normal.

And then, whammo. There I was spiraling downward into the dark heart of my old obsessions about cancer.

At first I felt only the deep anxiety that always accompanies this obsession, but it was quickly joined by a deep anger and frustration—I couldn't believe this was happening again. Was I never going to be free of this terrible obsessiveness?

But once beyond the initial shock, I began to notice a couple of things about this latest attack. First, my anxiety was not quite as bad as when my obsessions were at their peak a few years ago, and that, in itself, was a small comfort. Second, I found I had a little perspective on them this time that I was able to use as a foundation for recovery.

For example, in looking back at the weeks preceding the attack, I realized they had been filled with stress—the Christmas season. Now, I like Christmas, but as befitting my personality, I go at it each year with a gung-ho attitude. This year, I shopped till I dropped. When I wasn't shopping, I was obsessing about "perfect" gift ideas. I baked too many cookies, made too many ornaments, and spent too much time fussing about an annual Christmas Day dinner with my neighbors. By the time the holidays were over, I was in an ideal mental state for a return of my symptoms.

I tried to reduce my stress by lowering my expectations for my household duties for awhile. I also made a greater effort to get out by myself more—I am an at-home parent of two young chil-

Figure 7-7b For someone who has obsessive thoughts about the possibility of injuring another person while driving, a noneventful ride down an empty highway can become a highly upsetting experience.

dren, and if you've ever had that responsibility, I don't need to tell you what it can do to your stress level. Finally, I reviewed some of the behavioral techniques that I hadn't had to employ for some time, and found that they were still just as effective.

The result is that I'm improving—not quite back to the level I was at before the attack, but definitely better.

especially demanding and has unreasonably high expectations about when the child should meet certain developmental challenges (such as toilet training), the child may be forced to bottle up his or her anger. This unacceptable anger expresses itself deviously later in life.

Freud emphasized the roles of several defense mechanisms in the development of obsessive-compulsive disorders. These include isolation, undoing, and reaction formation. Through **isolation,** emotions are separated from a thought or act, which then becomes obsessive or compulsive. However, the emotion is not completely barred from consciousness and constantly threatens to break through the controls that have been imposed upon it. **Undoing** is illustrated by an individual who thinks obsessively, "My father will die" whenever he

Figure 7-8 From a psychodynamic standpoint, inconsistencies between Snoopy's overt and covert behavior would be explained in terms of intrapsychic conflicts and attempts to resolve them.

SOURCE: PEANUTS reprinted by permission of UFS, Inc.

turns off a light. This thought compels him to turn around, touch the switch, and say, "I take back that thought." The compulsive act could be said to "undo" what he feared might result from the initial obsessive thought, which might be rooted in an underlying aggressive impulse toward the father. **Reaction formation** is illustrated by a mother who compulsively checks her children's rooms dozens of times while they are asleep; she is overly solicitous about her children because of her underlying resentment toward them.

Psychotherapy, the main clinical tool of the psychodynamically oriented clinician, is intended to help people expose and deal with the psychodynamic roots of their maladaptive behaviors. Most psychotherapists believe that such behaviors occur when a person becomes preoccupied with relieving or eliminating anxiety. They feel that by gaining insight into the unconscious roots of anxiety, the person can direct his or her activity toward altering or abandoning unwanted behavior. Chapter 17 reviews some of the major aspects of research on psychotherapy and other therapeutic approaches.

The Behavioral Perspective

Instead of speaking of symptoms caused by underlying events, behavioral psychologists focus on acquired responses and response tendencies. They believe that the general principles of learning can be applied to the understanding of all behavior, including anxiety disorders. According to behavioral theorists, anxiety that reaches clinical proportions is a learned or acquired response, a symptom that has been created by environmental conditions, often within the home.

B. F. Skinner, a leading behaviorist (see chapter 3), objected to any references to mental events (thoughts or feelings) as explanations of behavior; he preferred to rely almost exclusively on observable stimulus and response (S and R) variables. Other theorists emphasize S and R variables but have gone one step beyond Skinner in dealing with internal events as well. Dollard and Miller (1950) were among the earliest theorists to broaden the psychology of learning to include mental events. They went so far as to agree with psychodynamic theorists that there is a personal history behind the development of neurotic disorders (now called anxiety disorders) and that psychotherapy (the "talking therapy") is the optimum means of modifying it.

If neurotic behavior is learned, it should be unlearned by some combination of the same principles by which it was taught. We believe this to be the case. Psychotherapy establishes a set of conditions by which neurotic habits may be unlearned and nonneurotic habits learned. Therefore, we

view the therapist as a kind of teacher and the patient as a learner. In the same way and by the same principles that bad tennis habits can be corrected by a good coach, so bad mental and emotional habits can be corrected by a psychotherapist. There is this difference, however. Whereas only a few people want to play tennis, all the world wants a clear, free, efficient mind.

—Dollard and Miller, 1950, pp. 7–8

Learning concepts such as conditioning, reinforcement, and extinction have increasingly been applied to the study of anxiety disorders. Several new, clinically useful techniques, collectively referred to as **behavior therapy** are the most valuable outcomes of these applications. Research in behavior therapy has been directed at discovering the variables that help defuse highly emotional responses.

Exposure Therapies A common element in most behavior therapies is exposing the client to stimuli that evoke discomfort until he or she becomes used to them. Much research has been carried out in which clients are exposed to feared stimuli and are prevented from making an avoidance or escape response. The client is strongly urged to continue to attend to the anxiety-eliciting stimuli despite the stressful effects that usually accompany this effort.

Exposure therapy has been used in treating both phobic and obsessive-compulsive disorders. A critical element of the treatment is motivating the client to maintain contact with the actual noxious stimuli or with their imagined presence until he or she becomes used to them. This might mean, for example, exposing a compulsive hand washer to dirt until the hand washing no longer occurs, or encouraging such a person to think about dirt, perhaps imagined first as household dust and later as particularly noxious dirt such as vomit or feces. The therapist's task is to identify all components of the stimulus that evoke an avoidance or escape response and to continue the exposure until the evoked response no longer occurs.

Three types of therapy based on the exposure principle are systematic desensitization, implosive therapy, and in vivo exposure. In **systematic desensitization** a series of fear-arousing stimuli, carefully graded from mild to strongly fearful, are used. Only when a client is comfortable with one level of fear-producing stimuli is the next, slightly stronger stimulus introduced. **Implosive therapy** refers to therapist-controlled exposure to the imagined re-creation of a complex, high-intensity, fear-arousing situation. **In vivo exposure** means that the individual experiences the actual feared situation rather than imagining it under the therapist's direction. In vivo exposure may be conducted gradually, beginning with low levels of stimulus intensity, or rapidly, by exposing the client immediately to high-intensity and prolonged stimulation. This rapid, intense exposure is called **flooding.**

Systematic desensitization, which is used primarily in the treatment of strong fears, is based on conditioning principles. The client is taught to relax and then is presented with a series of stimuli that are graded from low to high according to their capacity to evoke anxiety. The treatment of a death phobia illustrates how systematic desensitization is used. The patient's fears are arranged in a hierarchy, with the items in the hierarchy ranging, in descending order, from human corpses to funeral processions, black clothes, and floral wreaths. The therapy begins with items that are low in the hierarchy, such as seeing a wreath. The therapist tries to teach the client to remain relaxed while imagining or actually seeing a wreath. When the client can maintain a relaxed state consistently, the therapy proceeds with stimuli that are higher in the hierarchy.

A therapist does not try to produce cures overnight with conditioning procedures. Usually, the process of reducing the level of an emotional response to a stimulus that should be neutral is a gradual one. Clinical applications of systematic desensitization have shown that clients who are treated in this way become less upset by previously feared situations and better able to manage their anxiety. It is possible that the most effective part of systematic desensitization is the client's exposure to gradually increasing levels of fear-arousing stimuli under nonthreatening conditions. Individuals who can mentally rehearse being exposed to the upsetting, fear-arousing situations show particularly high levels of improvement.

Implosive therapy is based on the belief that many conditions, including anxiety disorders, are outgrowths of painful prior experiences. For the patient to unlearn them, the original situation must be re-created so that it can be experienced without pain. Therapists who use implosion ask their clients to imagine scenes related to particular personal conflicts and to re-create the anxiety felt in those scenes. The therapist strives to heighten the realism of the re-creation and to help the patient extinguish the anxiety that was created by the original aversive conditions. In addition, the client is helped to adopt more mature forms of behavior. Implosive therapy uses the methods and ideas of both behavioral and psychodynamic theories. Although it is not uniformly effective in reducing anxiety, research to date suggests that it, like desensitization, can reduce many intense fears (Gelder et al., 1989).

The term *in vivo* exposure means that the exposure is carried out in a real-life setting, not simply in the imaginations of the client and the therapist as they sit in the therapist's office. The difference between in vivo exposure and flooding might be compared to the difference between wading into a swimming pool and jumping in at the deep end. An example of flooding might be an agoraphobic client who experienced intense anxiety anywhere outside her home who might be asked to go to a crowded shopping center with the therapist and remain there until her desire to escape disappeared. Researchers have reported that when using this procedure, someone with a specific fear can lose it in only three sessions (Marks, 1987). Exposure, in combination with cognitive therapy, has also been found to be therapeutic for persons with panic disorder (Barlow et al., 1989; McNally, 1990).

In the treatment of most anxiety disorders, exposure has produced consistently good results, with improvements lasting for up to several years. The longer the exposure to the critical stimulus, the better the results. How well exposure treatment works depends on the client's motivation and on specific factors in his or her life. For example, when compulsive rituals are triggered by home cues (which is true in many cases), treatment needs to be conducted in the home setting. Failure to improve can usually be traced to failure to comply with treatment instructions, particularly by not seeking exposure to fear-arousing stimuli. In one study, compulsive people received exposure therapy in their homes (Emmelkamp et al., 1980). The clients' task was to avoid responding compulsively when the evoking stimuli were present. Figure 7-9 shows changes in the clients' ratings of their levels of anxiety when exposed to the evoking stimuli. If the client refrained from compulsive behavior in the presence of the stimuli, the level of anxiety decreased immediately after exposure. The decrease

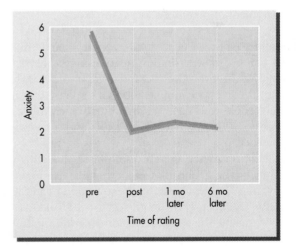

Figure 7-9 Changes in rated anxiety before exposure in vivo (pre), immediately afterwards (post), and at 1- and 6-month follow-up points.

SOURCE: From Emmelkamp, van der Helm, van Zanten, and Plochg, 1980. Reprinted with permission from *Behavior Research and Therapy.* Copyright © 1980, Pergaman Journals, Ltd.

was maintained 1 and 6 months later, in the presence of the formerly compulsion-evoking stimuli.

An important task for future research is to find out *why* exposure is effective. When a client "gets used to" an upsetting stimulus, what is going on? One possible explanation is that as clients find that they can handle a little exposure to upsetting stimuli and note that their anxiety levels subside, they quickly gain confidence in themselves and develop the courage to persist in their efforts to overcome their problems.

The most effective behavioral technique for treating compulsive rituals is a combination of exposure and response prevention. The therapist asks the patient to disclose all obsessions and compulsive patterns, and then prohibits them. A compulsive washer, for example, is allowed to become dirty, or is even made dirty, and then is ordered not to wash. A typical treatment might allow one 10-minute shower every fifth day. Exposure reduces hypersensitivity to dirt as well as its associated anxiety; response prevention eventually eliminates the compulsive ritual. Exposure usually has to be done outside the psychotherapist's office, and trained helpers may be needed—wives, husbands, friends, or nurse-therapists. Exposure in fantasy is less effective, but sometimes it is the only possible way—for example, a patient with a fear of causing a traffic fatality cannot actually run over someone.

Exposure therapy and other behavioral approaches are not highly effective with people who are "pure obsessives," that is, who do not engage in rituals or avoidant behavior. Because depression is a factor in many such cases, antidepressant drugs are often used in the treatment of obsessions.

Modeling Another behavioral approach, **modeling,** is often combined with exposure to anxiety-provoking stimuli. While exposure therapies emphasize removing some of the overwhelming emotional response that may inhibit people who have an anxiety disorder, modeling emphasizes *acquiring* behavioral skills and a feeling of competence.

In addition to acting as a disinhibitor, modeling can function in the acquisition of new skills and response capabilities. For example, a therapist might model a response and then provide corrective feedback as the client performs the same behavior. In addition to the information provided by the modeled behavior, the client receives guidance on his or her own performance. Modeling works especially well with complex behaviors, such as those involved in certain social situations. A therapist can guide the client toward mastery over frightening situations and maladaptive behavior. Modeling and guidance help the client attain a sense of mastery or self-efficacy.

The Cognitive Perspective

The methods developed by behavioral therapists, although they are based on learning principles, have important implications for our understanding of cognitive processes, that is, private or internal processes such as imagery and how we think about ourselves and the world. Therapies such as systematic desensitization, exposure, and modeling affect not only clients' behavior but also how they think about themselves. Furthermore, cognitive activity is often a specific step in behavioral therapy; for example, in systematic desensitization the client is asked to visualize, think about, or imagine certain fear-arousing situations. Cognitive rehearsal in combination with in vivo exposure has been used successfully with phobic and obsessive-compulsive individuals. Available evidence suggests that this procedure is highly effective in ultimately reducing anxiety, regardless of whether the client feels relaxed or anxious during exposure.

Modeling can also have an important cognitive element. Someone who overcomes intense fears as a result of a behavioral-therapy program such as participant modeling acquires more self-confidence and may begin to think about new ways of behaving in situations that were not covered in the modeling program. The way people think about things often changes when they acquire new response capabilities. These cognitive changes can then lead to important behavioral advances. The term **cognitive behavior therapy** refers to clinical procedures based on principles of learning, such as extinction and reinforcement, that emphasize cognitive behavior.

Cognitive Factors in Maladaptive Behavior In addition to the increased interest in cognitive aspects of behavior therapy, there has been a rapid increase in the influence of the cognitive perspective on efforts to understand the anxiety disorders. This perspective emphasizes the ways in which certain thoughts and styles of thinking have undesirable effects on behavior. Thoughts that preoccupy people interfere with attention to the task at hand. Worries, daydreams, and ideas that have nothing to do with the immediate task are distracting and reduce behavioral effectiveness.

According to cognitive theorists, thinking disturbances that occur only in certain places or in relation to specific problems are often sources of anxiety. These thoughts may include unrealistic appraisals of situations and consistent overestimation of their dangerous aspects; for example, the *degree* and *likelihood* of harm may both be exaggerated. Thus, a person's train of thought and mental set can be viewed as vulnerability factors that interact with the characteristics of certain situations. From this point of view, precipitating events (the situation) elicit or magnify an underlying attitude or fear (the vulnerability factor) and give rise to hypervigilance. As this attitude strengthens, danger-related thoughts become more easily activated by less specific, less avoidable situations ("If you look for it, you're sure to find it"). As a result, the anxious individual continually scans internal and external stimuli for danger signals.

An example of this sort of disturbance may be seen in an obsessive person who experiences intense anxiety when having to cross the street and may actually be unable to attempt a crossing. Most people would use the following train of thought.

1. Streets are safe for crossing at green lights or when free of traffic.
2. This street has a green light or is free of traffic.
3. Therefore, this street can be crossed.

The obsessive person's thinking, on the other hand, might go as follows.

1. Streets are safe for crossing at green lights or when free of traffic.
2. This street has a green light or is free of traffic, but if the light suddenly changes or a car appears unexpectedly. . . .
3. Then this street is not safe for me to cross.

Studies of obsessive thinkers have revealed unreasonable beliefs and assumptions. Such people believe that they should be perfectly competent, must avoid criticism or disapproval, and will be severely punished for their mistakes and imperfections. In addition, at some level they seem to believe that thinking certain thoughts or performing certain rituals will help them avoid the disastrous outcomes they imagine are just around the corner. Obsessive-compulsive individuals make arbitrary rules that they must follow (for example, stepping on every seventh crack in the sidewalk). Phobic people also make up rules for themselves that are not reality-based (for example, "Elevators get stuck. If I use one it will get stuck and I might suffocate; therefore, I won't go in an elevator."). Unfortunately, "protective" rituals and rules become very intrusive and can interfere with normal activity.

Cognitive Therapy Cognitive therapists employ a number of techniques. One of these is **cognitive restructuring.** Developed out of the rational-emotive therapy of Albert Ellis (see chapter 3), cognitive restructuring calls the client's attention to the unrealistic thoughts that serve as cues for his or her maladaptive behavior. The therapist helps clients review their irrational beliefs and expectations and develop more rational ways of looking at their lives. For example, many people with anxiety disorders are perfectionists who expect too much of themselves and others and become overly emotional when their unattainable goals are not realized. During therapy sessions emphasis is placed on how the irrational things that people say to themselves can affect their emotions and behavior. The baseball pitcher in Figure 7-10 is being advised to do some cognitive restructuring in order to improve his chances of preventing this skilled batter from getting a hit.

By means of cognitive restructuring, people develop more realistic appraisals of themselves and others. For example, when taking an exam a person might think: "This test is hard. Everyone else seems to think it's going to be simple. They all must know a lot more than I do." Such thoughts are likely to lead to a high degree of anxiety. A cognitive therapist would help this client concentrate on a more adaptive type of thought such as: "I studied hard. I'll just try to answer one question at a time. If I don't know the answer, I'll go on to the next one. No reason for panic. Even people who do well don't know the answer to every question."

Thought stopping is another cognitive technique. It works on the assumption that a sudden distracting stimulus, such as an unpleasant noise, will serve to terminate obsessional thoughts. The client is asked to get the thought firmly in mind; then the therapist loudly says "Stop!" This sequence—obsessional thought followed by "Stop!"—is repeated several times with the client, rather than the therapist, yelling "Stop!" Finally, the client simply mentally says "Stop!" If it is successful, this procedure provides the client with a specific self-control

FORGET ABOUT HIS SIX-MILLION-DOLLAR CONTRACT—
THINK OF HIM AS A GUY WITH TAX PROBLEMS.

Figure 7-10 The catcher is trying to help the pitcher overcome concern about pitching to a superhitter by encouraging the pitcher to think about the batter in a different way.

SOURCE: From *The Wall Street Journal*—permission, Cartoon Features Syndicate.

technique for removing an obsessional thought when it occurs.

A third cognitive technique is **cognitive rehearsal,** through which the client can mentally rehearse adaptive approaches to problematic situations. Cognitive rehearsal is particularly useful for problems that cannot be conveniently simulated in a clinical setting. For example, behavioral rehearsal of social skills by socially phobic individuals requires the presence of a large group of people. However, someone who suffers from a social phobia can imagine being in a group and can mentally rehearse behaviors and internal statements designed to improve his or her interpersonal relationships.

Aaron Beck has developed one of the most influential types of cognitive therapy (Beck & Emery, 1985). He believes that the core psychological problem in anxiety disorders is a vulnerability that grows out of the individual's tendency to devalue his or her problem-solving ability as well as to exaggerate the degree of threat in a problematic situation. Such an individual perceives anxiety-provoking threats to social relationships, freedom, and self-identity.

Beck's cognitive therapy typically consists of five to twenty sessions. A minimal amount of time is spent acquiring background information, searching for the original causes of anxiety, or engaging in unfocused conversation with the patient. Most of the therapy is task-oriented, devoted to solving problems brought up by the patient. The therapist encourages the patient to talk openly about his or her fears and concerns, and conveys empathy for the patient's anxiety. The Socratic method (see chapter 2) is used to help the patient become aware of what his or her thoughts are, examine them for cognitive distortions, and substitute more realistic thoughts. Three steps are involved in cognitive therapy: (1) conceptualizing the patient's problem, (2) choosing strategies and tactics to deal with the problem, and (3) assessing the effectiveness of those strategies and tactics.

In a sense, Beck is arguing that each of us has an inner voice. When that voice interferes with our ability to function adequately, the unproductive thoughts that result must be replaced by productive ones. This is done by correcting thinking errors and having the patient work on pertinent homework assignments. Using these techniques, the patient can develop not only improved ways of thinking but also more effective, less anxiety-producing ways of dealing with difficult situations.

The following exchange occurred in a therapy session in which Beck's approach was applied to a case of panic disorder. Because catastrophic misinterpretation of physiological sensations is a central component of panic disorder, the therapist sought a precise description of the patient's typical attack and helped the patient, an 18-year-old female, become more aware of her misinterpretations.

P (Patient):	*I've felt a couple of times like I was going to have a heart attack.*
T (Therapist):	*Tell me about that.*
P:	*It's just like, it starts to beat so hard, and so fast, that, I mean, it hurts, and you just think, you're just like sitting there going (breathes rapidly to demonstrate how she hyperventilates).*
T:	*What was the effect, do you think, of that particular image or idea on the symptoms themselves?*
P:	*Oh, well, they get worse, as soon as you think . . . (pause).*
T:	*So you have a bodily sensation here at this point in the spiral of anxiety (pointing to diagram). The next step, thoughts that the sensation is a sign of catastrophe, that you're going to have a heart attack. What do you think happens to your thoughts when your heart rate does in fact go up? Because you said it would increase when you had this fear . . .*
P:	*Uh-huh.*
T:	*What would you think then?*
P:	*I just get really scared, and I have to get out of the situation that I'm in. I mean, I have to.*
T:	*O.K. So you see what's happening there. You perceive a danger, which would lead to more anxiety; the anxiety would make the symptoms worse, would make the heart rate even faster; and you interpret that, then, as "I really am giong to have a heart attack." Right?*
P:	*Yeah, but only fleetingly, you know, and then I go "I'm not going to have a heart attack, but I've got to get out of here!"*
T:	*O.K.*
P:	*But, I mean, fleetingly, I've also thought all kinds of, you know, I'm sure . . .*

—Alford and others, 1990, pp. 231–232

Upon identification of her physiological sensations and negative automatic thoughts associated with the sensations, the patient was able to rapidly obtain some distance from her fearful thoughts. At a 5-month follow-up, she reported having no panic attacks after the cognitive therapy ended.

Combining Cognitive and Behavioral Approaches

Some of the most promising efforts to apply psychological techniques to clinical problems involve combining approaches suggested by a variety of theoretical perspectives. Research on the treatment of anxiety disorders illustrates these attempts. In England, Gillian Butler (1988) of Oxford University developed an anxiety-management training program with the following components:

1. Information about the nature of anxiety and what might be expected from treatment;
2. A cognitive component to help with self-identification and response to specific anxiety-provoking thoughts;
3. Use of distractions and relaxation to cope with situations in which anxiety is anticipated;
4. Exposure training for overcoming avoidance behavior;
5. A component designed to instill self-confidence by identifying the person's strong points, by engaging in rewarding and pleasurable activities, and by paying attention to aspects of life in which the person is functioning relatively well.

The treatment program is described in an easy to understand self-help booklet that the client follows. Clients play an active role in setting goals, planning homework assignments, and monitoring their progress. The program has been used in a series of clinical studies with social phobia and generalized anxiety disorder patients. In one study of generalized anxiety disorder, clients were randomly assigned to either the treatment or control conditions. The program, which typically extended over fewer than nine sessions, resulted in significant reductions of anxiety. The therapeutic improvement was maintained at a 6-month follow-up. The significance of these results is reflected in the finding that at posttreatment the anxiety ratings of half of the clients had fallen below the cutoff point that distinguishes a normal from a clinical population. There was some evidence that people with panic disorders also responded favorably to this type of treatment.

The Biological Perspective

Over the years several different types of anxiety reactions have been found to be caused by an individual's biological state. Some of these discoveries have led to the development of medical treatment methods. Although no direct organic cause has been found for most types of anxiety disorders, the findings of physical causation in other conditions suggest the possibility that there are some links between anxieties and biophysical functioning. People whose nervous systems are particularly sensitive to stimulation seem more likely to experience severe anxiety.

Genetic and Environmental Factors Inbreeding experiments with animals have shown that heredity has a strong influence on such characteristics as timidity, fearfulness, and aggressiveness. Evidence also shows that anxiety disorders tend to run in families (Andreasen & Black, 1991).

One study found children of people treated for anxiety disorder were more anxious and fearful, had more school difficulties, worried more about family members and themselves, and had more somatic complaints than did the children of normal parents (Turner et al., 1987). These children also spent more time engaged in solitary activities and were seven times more likely to meet the criteria for an anxiety disorder than children whose families had no history of anxiety disorder. Another study of nearly 4,000 pairs of adult twins attempted to evaluate the separate effects of genetic and environmental factors in anxiety and depression (Kendler, 1986). There was strong evidence of a genetic factor and a statistically significant, but weaker, effect for a family environment factor.

Drug Therapies During the 1950s new medications used in the treatment of severe psychotic disorders were found to have dramatic positive effects. Subsequently, much biological research has also been directed toward developing medications that might be effective for less severe—and often more common—disorders. A number of drugs are now available for treating specific anxiety disorders. Research on their effects and how these are produced is ongoing.

Benzodiazepines Tranquilizing drugs are the most commonly used somatic therapy in the treatment of anxiety. Although placebo reactions may account for some of their effectiveness, psychiatrists and other physicians who prescribe tranquilizers have found them valuable in reducing states of great tension. The literature on the behavioral effects of tranquilizers or antianxiety drugs suggests that these agents reduce the intensity of responses to stimuli that signal punishment and frustration.

In 1960 a group of drugs called **benzodiazepines** were introduced. They are marketed under trade names like Librium and Valium and are used for the treatment of anxiety, tension, behavioral excitement, and insomnia. Figure 7-11 shows the anxiety lowering effect of one dose of a member of this group, diazepam (Valium), on the anxiety experienced when people who were phobic about cats and roaches were exposed to these animals. Similar results were obtained when measuring how close the person would come to the fear-arousing stimulus. It seems clear that a dose of diazepam made phobics better able to tolerate the animals they were afraid of. Although benzodiazepines have been proven effective in reducing anxiety, they have some troubling side effects. These include drowsiness, lethargy, motor impairment, and reduced ability to concentrate. The drugs also produce physiological and psychological dependence.

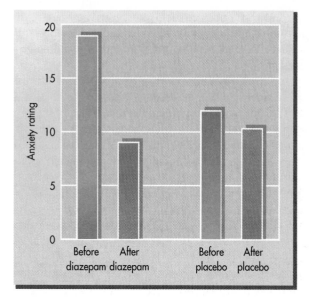

Figure 7-11 Subjective anxiety ratings when confronted with phobic stimuli. "After" measures were made two hours after the subject took either a pill containing diazepam (Valium) or a placebo.

Source: Adapted from Whitehead, Blackwell, and Robinson, 1978, p. 63.

Excessive use may lead to undesirable behavior, including disorientation, confusion, rage, and other symptoms that resemble drunkenness. When taken with alcohol, slowing of physical movements and lack of alertness may intensify dangerously.

Recently, one benzodiazepine derivative, alprazolam, was approved by the United States Food and Drug Administration for the treatment of panic disorders. Alprazolam is fast acting and has fewer unpleasant side effects than other drugs used in the treatment of panic disorders. Its side effects include drowsiness and withdrawal symptoms if a patient stops taking it after long-term use.

Antidepressants Some drugs developed as antidepressants have proven to be effective in treating panic and obsessive-compulsive disorders. One group of antidepressants, the tricyclic drugs (imipramine, clomipramine), appears to have therapeutic effects on many people with these disorders. The tricyclics may be effective in up to two-thirds of those suffering with obsessive-compulsive disorder, by reducing the obsessions and feelings of anxiety and increasing the likelihood of a positive response to behavior therapy designed to eliminate ritualistic responding. Possible side effects of the tricyclic drugs include dry mouth, drowsiness, blurred vision, and seizures.

The successful use of drugs to treat anxiety disorders not only has been of practical value and a stimulus for developing biological theories of anxiety, but also has raised some important questions. For example, why might drugs developed for the treatment of depression be helpful in cases of anxiety? Evidence that antidepressant drugs are useful in treating anxiety disorders suggests that the relationship between anxiety and depression needs careful examination. One study found that all patients in a sample of people diagnosed as depressed also showed anxiety symptoms (Barlow et al., 1986). Significant overlaps of symptoms in different disorders may partially explain some of the seemingly surprising effects that drugs have been found to have on certain groups of patients. These symptom overlaps are referred to as **comorbidity,** the co-occurence of symptoms and conditions in different disorders. Box 7-3 deals with this topic, which is now being widely discussed among clinicians and researchers.

Combining Psychological and Biological Treatments The various theoretical perspectives and the treatment approaches derived from them have often been discussed in competitive terms: Which is the most valid and effective? Of course, it would not be surprising if certain techniques were indeed superior to others in treating particular types of disorders. Research comparing the various treatment approaches to maladaptive behavior is valuable theoretically as well as clinically. Issues involved in such comparisons will be discussed in chapter 17.

The anxiety disorders illustrate the value of research on the possibility that *combinations* of treatment approaches might be optimal for certain kinds of clinical problems. For example, one recent study showed that the combination of alprazolam and cognitive-behavioral treatment was especially effective for panic disorder patients (Spiegel et al., 1994). While the alprazolam was effective in reducing the number of panic attacks, a cognitive-behavioral program that included cognitive restructuring, exposure, and relaxation training was effective in preventing relapses after discontinuation of the alprazolam. Other studies have also shown treatment combinations to be helpful in treating patients with anxiety disorders (Acierno et al., 1993; Clark et al., 1994).

Comorbidity

Patients with anxiety disorders often have features of multiple mental disorders, especially the disturbances of mood found in depression. Although such co-occurrences of thoughts, behaviors, and symptoms appear in a number of other disorders as well, surprisingly little attention has been paid to this phenomenon. Table 7-9 shows the wide range of comorbidity, the co-occurrence of clinical symptoms, among various types of maladaptive behavior. The table indicates, for example, that 77.2 percent of cases of schizophrenia and paranoid disorders in the population studied had only that diagnosis, while 22.8 percent of these cases had multiple diagnoses (that is, diagnoses in addition to the primary one). Comorbidity estimates vary from study to study for several reasons, including the methods employed in making diagnoses and characteristics of the sample surveyed. For example, while 29.8 percent of the cases of anxiety disorder in Table 7-9 involved multiple diagnoses, other studies using different populations and diagnostic methods have found greater comorbidity for anxiety and depressive disorders (Hecht et al., 1989). One study found that, while the risk of suicide in people with panic disorder is high, the risk is even higher in panic disorder cases that involved comorbidity with other disorders (Johnson et al., 1990).

Studies of comorbidity have led clinicians to attend to the fact that more than one disorder can be diagnosed in the same individual. In addition, an individual who meets the full diagnostic criteria for only one disorder may still have an increased frequency of symptoms from other categories—but to an extent that is insufficient to diagnose another disorder. Depending on the disorder, patients diagnosed as having a particular disorder may have relatively greater or lesser risk of having other disorders or other symptoms.

Comorbidity can occur within a given diagnostic category as well as between different ones. For example, there is evidence that the presence of one type of anxiety disorder increases the likelihood of the presence of another. We know persons diagnosed as having social phobias often receive a secondary diagnosis of panic disorder (de Ruiter et al., 1989). Knowing that comorbidity may be high in certain types of cases is valuable to clinicians because it alerts them to the need to probe carefully regarding the possibility of co-occurrences.

Evidence of high comorbidity within a diagnostic category also leads to consideration of the possible need to revise classification criteria. For example, noting that generalized anxiety disorder has been associated with extremely high rates of comorbidity with other types of anxiety disorder, some researchers have suggested that generalized anxiety disorder might be conceptualized as a trait conducive to vulnerability to other types of anxiety disorders rather than as a discrete disorder in its own right (Brown, et al., 1994).

Epidemiological studies of anxiety and mood disorders have revealed several intriguing findings. One is that the risk of depression in individuals with chronic anxiety disorders is greater than the risk of anxiety in individuals with depressive disorders (Maser & Cloninger, 1990). Another is that depressive disorders are more likely to remain free of comorbid anxiety while anxiety disorders are more often complicated by depression after long-term follow-up. There are many issues raised by the comorbidity of mental disorders. One pertains to the role of heredity. Is there a common genetic cause or predisposition for both depression and anxiety or are different environmental exposures responsible for comorbidity? At present we do not have an answer to this question. The association between anxiety and depression could be due to one of the disorders causing or leading to the other. Another possible explanation is that the two disorders have some common genetic cause. Because of increasing attention being given to the topic of comorbidity, research on which of these possibilities is most likely is accelerating (Lilienfeld, et al., 1990).

TABLE 7–9
Percentages of Single and Multiple Diagnoses for Various Diagnostic Categories

Diagnostic Categories	(%) Single Diagnoses	(%) Multiple Diagnoses
Anxiety disorders	70.2	29.8
Affective disorders (depression)	57.4	42.6
Dissociative disorders	50.0	50.0
Adjustment disorders	69.0	31.0
Alcohol-use disorders	13.5	86.5
Psychosexual disorders	13.8	86.2
Schizophrenic and paranoid disorders	77.2	22.8
Mental retardation	14.7	85.3
Organic brain disorders	67.0	33.0

Source: Based on Mezzich, Ahn, Fabrega, & Pilkonis, 1990

GENERALIZED ANXIETY DISORDER

Anxiety is a vague, diffuse feeling that includes both worried thoughts and a combination of physical symptoms. Anxiety differs from ordinary fear in that fear is related to an identifiable cause, while the reasons for the anxiety are often not clear to the anxious person. A person with **generalized anxiety disorder** experiences vague, but intense, concerns and fearfulness that persist over a long period, at least a month, and includes four types of symptoms: motor tension, autonomic reactivity, apprehension about the future, and hypervigilance.

PANIC DISORDER

Panic attacks are severe anxiety attacks that occur unexpectedly and involve severe physical symptoms as well as very strong fears that often involve concern over dying, going crazy, or behaving in an uncontrolled way. Persons with panic disorder experience panic attacks unexpectedly and therefore become very anxious as they worry that another attack may occur. Panic disorder is the least prevalent of all the anxiety disorders. Some panic attacks can be prevented by **imipramine,** a drug used to treat depression. Both generalized anxiety disorder and panic disorder seem to run in families.

PHOBIAS

People who have **phobias** have fears related to specific objects, people, or situations. Phobias often develop gradually or begin with a generalized anxiety attack. Phobias are common disorders that affect women about twice as frequently as men. Phobias often begin before adulthood and are likely to become chronic. Phobias can be grouped into three main types: specific phobias, social phobias, and agoraphobia.

Specific phobias are the most commonly occurring type of phobia. This group includes miscellaneous irrational fears such as intense fear of a certain type of animal or of being in an enclosed place. Specific phobias may arise from an earlier frightening or anxiety-producing situation that originally involved the type of person or situation that later became associated with the phobia. Procedures that use the classical conditioning approach of pairing the phobic stimulus with a nonanxiety response are often used successfully to treat specific phobias.

Social Phobias Intense and incapacitating fear and embarrassment when dealing with others characterize **social phobias.** Fears of blushing when in a social situation or of eating

with others present are two social phobias that are especially difficult to treat successfully.

Agoraphobia Agoraphobia is the term used when people develop a fear of entering unfamiliar situations. Many agoraphobics are afraid to leave their homes so their ability to carry on normal life activities is severely limited. There are two major types of agoraphobia, that with and that without panic attacks. In the former group, panic attacks often begin first and lead to agoraphobia. Panic attacks can often be treated with antidepressant drugs. Agoraphobia can be successfully treated with behavioral techniques in which the agoraphobic is exposed to the feared stimulus, under controlled conditions, with the support of a therapist.

OBSESSIVE-COMPULSIVE DISORDER

People affected by an **obsessive-compulsive disorder** are unable to control their preoccupation with specific ideas or are unable to prevent themselves from repeatedly carrying out a particular act or series of acts that affect their ability to carry out normal activities. The inability to stop thinking about a particular idea or topic is called an **obsession.** The topic of these thoughts is often felt by the person involved to be unpleasant and shameful. The need to perform certain behaviors over and over is called a **compulsion.** Many compulsions deal with counting, ordering, checking, touching, and washing. Compulsive rituals may become very elaborate and contain many activities. Like phobia, obsessive-compulsive disorder tends to begin before adulthood and is more common in women than in men.

INTERPRETING AND TREATING ANXIETY DISORDERS

The Psychodynamic Perspective Psychodynamic theorists suggest several possible causes of anxiety disorders. These include perceptions of helplessness and inability to cope with life situations, fear of abandonment or loss of love, sudden loss of emotional support, and unacceptable impulses that—while still unconscious—are threatening to break into awareness. Freud defined several defense mechanisms that may play a role in obsessive-compulsive disorders. The mechanisms include **isolation, undoing,** and **reaction formation.** Psychodynamically oriented therapists typically deal with anxiety disorders by psychotherapy directed at helping clients gain insight into the unconscious roots of their anxiety.

The Behavioral Perspective The behavioral-learning concepts of conditioning, reinforcement, and extinction are all applied in **behavior therapy.** Behavioral therapists commonly use **exposure therapy** in treating phobic and obsessive-compulsive clients. Three types of therapy based on the exposure principle are **systematic desensitization** in which fear-arousing stimuli are presented in a graded series paired with relaxation exercises, **implosive therapy** in which the client imagines a complex and highly arousing fear situation, and **in vivo exposure** in which the person actually is present in the feared situation. **Flooding** refers to the rapid, intense exposure of stimulation in an in vivo exposure situation. **Modeling** is used to help clients acquire adaptive and correct maladaptive responses.

The Cognitive Perspective Many of the behavioral therapies such as systematic desensitization include cognitive rehearsal. **Cognitive-behavior therapy** is based on the learning principles of extinction and reinforcement that include emphasis on cognitive behavior. Cognitive therapy focuses on a number of techniques that are usually combined with various behavioral exercises. These include **cognitive restructuring, thought stopping,** and **cognitive rehearsal.**

The Biological Perspective Strong evidence for a genetic factor in anxiety disorders is shown in studies of both animals and humans. There is also some weaker evidence of an environmental factor. A number of drugs are now used for treating specific anxiety disorders. The **benzodiazepines** or tranquilizing drugs such as Valium are the most frequently prescribed drugs used in the general treatment of anxiety. One benzodiazepine derivative, alprazolam, has recently become popular for treating panic disorders. One group of antidepressant drugs, the **tricyclics,** are used successfully in treating obsessive-compulsive disorder especially in combination with behavior therapy. It is thought that one reason antidepressant drugs are useful in treating anxiety is because of the overlap in symptoms and conditions in the different disorders. This overlap is referred to as **comorbidity.** Combinations of biological and psychological treatment techniques have been found to be often more effective than either approach alone.

CHAPTER EIGHT

Pablo Picasso, *The Kiss*, 1925.

Private collection; Art Resource, New York. © Artists Rights Society, New York/SPADEM, Paris.

SEXUAL VARIATIONS AND DISORDERS

CASE A: LAURA

I told my parents because I wanted to share with them. Now I would tell people NEVER to tell their parents. DO NOT. I suppose it depends on the family. If you have a working relationship or communication with them. No, I'd say keep the relationship you now have. They don't need to know. I remember all the agony I went through in telling them. . . .

CASE B: JAMES

Well, when I first told my mother she said, "Well, it's no news to me. You're the same person." When I told my sister and brothers, they were scared. But I told them that I didn't choose to be gay, but I do choose to be happy. But I made it very clear to them. I told them that if they couldn't accept me for the person I am and always will be, then that was too bad. . . . When my sister first met Steve, she loved him. She said, "You better hang on to him. You've really got yourself a catch!"

—Meyer, 1990, p. 71

These two experiences of announcing to family members that one is homosexual show how varied responses to the "news" can be. The prevalence of homosexuality, how it is expressed, and how family and community respond to it, vary from culture to culture and from time to time. For example, in ancient Greece homosexuality was commonly accepted, and even encouraged. Today, many Americans disapprove of homosexuality and believe that it is a kind of mental illness. Others see it simply as one of several acceptable types of sexual orientation. Both of these views might be considered an improvement over earlier beliefs that regarded this type of sexual orientation as a sin or heresy.

This chapter deals with many variations in sexual behavior, ranging from behavior that is universally regarded as disturbed to behavior that some people simply don't like. Although the focus of this book is primarily on abnormal behavior, it is important to have a broad frame of reference in reviewing highly charged and often controversial topics like sexual variation.

Changing Views of Sexual Behavior

Sexual behavior of all types has never ceased to be a topic of great interest. Over the centuries ideas about sexuality and sexual deviance have undergone drastic changes. During the fourth century B.C. the Greeks regarded sex as a pleasurable part of nature, to be enjoyed with partners of either sex. This open view of sexuality contrasts sharply with the prevailing view during the period between the fall of Rome and the fifteenth century, when church authorities were obsessed with the notion of sex as a sin. During that period many thousands of Europeans were tortured into confessing erotic encounters with the devil, after which they were publicly burned alive. Entire villages in southern Germany and Switzerland were exterminated in this way.

The price that women had to pay to be rescued from this fate was to renounce all sexual or erotic thoughts. By the mid-nineteenth century, the idea of women as morally pure, erotically apathetic, and sexually inert had reached a peak. Women were expected to engage in sexual behavior only as a way of satisfying their husbands and carrying out their obligation to become mothers. Despite these expectations, however, pornography, prostitution, and venereal disease flourished.

From time to time, some brave souls have been willing to question popularly held ideas about the role of sexuality in human behavior. One of these individuals, Sigmund Freud, used material gathered from many patients to illustrate the negative effects of a repressive view of sexuality. Freud traced the sexual deviations of adults to significant events in childhood. Although some aspects of his theories continue to be controversial, Freud stimulated a rethinking of the role of sexual feelings in development. He argued that all people are innately bisexual. Although psychosexual development usually progresses along a heterosexual course, some circumstances, such as inability to resolve the Oedipus complex, might result in adult homosexual behavior. In general, Freud's view of homosexuality was that it is simply a variation of sexual development. In a letter to a mother who had written to him asking for therapy for her son, he wrote:

> Homosexuality is assuredly no advantage, but it is nothing to be ashamed of, no vice, no degradation, it cannot be classified as an illness; we consider it to be a variation of sexual function produced by a certain arrest of sexual development. Many highly respectable individuals of ancient and modern times have been homosexuals, several of the greatest men among them (Plato, Michelangelo, Leonardo de Vinci, etc.). It is a great injustice to persecute homosexuality as a crime, and cruelty too.
>
> —Freud, 1935/1951, p. 786

Havelock Ellis was another important influence on views about sexuality. Ellis wrote books and articles that focused on the range of sexual behavior that occurred in the lives of ordinary people. He recognized that it was common for both men and women to masturbate, and emphasized the psychological rather than physical causes of many sexual problems. It was Ellis who suggested that objective surveys be taken to find out what happens in ordinary sexual relationships. This useful suggestion was not acted upon until fairly recently.

Surveys of Sexual Behavior

While the frequency with which people engage in various sexual practices has for a long time been of great interest and much discussed, it is only recently that concerted scientific efforts have been made to gather pertinent facts. It is virtually impossible (as well as socially unacceptable) to obtain direct measures of the sexual behaviors of members of a community. Consequently, we must rely on individuals' self-reported sexual behavior. As with all surveys of sensitive issues, these self-reports are likely to contain some bias. Intentional misreporting (that is, nonreporting or overreporting), incomplete recall, misunderstanding of survey questions, and selective participation in a survey can reduce the reliability and validity of the data (Seidman & Rieder, 1994).

Alfred Kinsey, a biologist at Indiana University, conducted a series of in-depth interviews with volunteers about their sex lives and published his findings for men in 1948 and for women in 1953. His research was the first major objective survey of sexual practices. However, his data were limited by the fact that his subjects were self-selected people who were probably more sexually interested and interesting than a randomly selected group. While scientists have recognized the need to improve on Kinsey's pioneering studies and obtain information about current sexual practices, the federal government has been squeamish about providing financial support for surveys of sexual behavior.

Fortunately, the National Opinion Research Center at the University of Chicago recently carried out a study of 3,432 randomly selected American men and women between the ages of 18 and 59 (Laumann et al., 1994). The participation was high for a survey—80 percent agreed to discuss the facts of their sexual lives.

The survey found that Americans have sex about once a week, but a third of adult Americans have sex a few times a year or not at all (see Table 8-1). The median number of sexual partners over a lifetime for men is six. For women, the median number is two. More than 80 percent of Americans had only one partner or no partner in the past year and just 3 percent of women and men had five or more partners in the past year. Seventy-five percent of married men and 85 percent of married women say they have remained faithful. The people who have the most sex and are the happiest with their sex lives are monogamous couples.

Depending on how the question is asked, people have a variety of responses on their sexual preferences. Five percent of men report having had a sexual encounter with another man as an adult, while 2.8 percent say they are homosexual or bisexual. Four percent of women report having had a sexual encounter with another woman, while 1.5 percent say they are homosexual or bisexual (see Table 8-2). Geography plays an important role in the formation of homosexual communities. About 9 percent of the men and 3 percent of the women living in the nation's largest cities identify themselves as homosexual or bisexual. These findings help explain why the incidence of homosexuality has been subject to such dispute. Homosexuals are likely to cluster in large cities, but overall, they are a tiny fraction of the population.

In order to inform debates over combating teen pregnancies, Americans need to know why teenage girls have sex for the first time. The reasons have changed over the decades. In previous generations, most women said they had sex for the first time because of affection for their partner, and only a small number said the reason was peer pressure. In contrast, 37 percent of the younger women who participated in the recent survey said the reason they had sex for the first time was peer pressure and only 35 percent said it was out of affection for their partner.

TABLE 8–1
How Often Do People in Different Age Groups Have Sex?
Percentages of various age groups reporting frequencies of sex

Four or more times a week		A few times a month		Not at all	
Men	Women	Men	Women	Men	Women
Age 18–24		Age 18–24		Age 18–24	
12%	12%	24%	32%	15%	11%
Age 25–29		Age 25–29		Age 25–29	
11%	10%	31%	38%	7%	5%
Age 30–34		Age 30–34		Age 30–34	
7%	8%	35%	35%	10%	8%
Age 35–39		Age 35–39		Age 35–39	
5%	3%	40%	38%	7%	11%
Age 40–44		Age 40–44		Age 40–44	
6%	7%	44%	46%	7%	15%
Age 45–49		Age 45–49		Age 45–49	
6%	3%	33%	41%	13%	16%
Age 50–54		Age 50–54		Age 50–54	
5%	2%	45%	40%	8%	19%
Age 55–59		Age 55–59		Age 55–59	
1%	2%	42%	30%	16%	41%
All Ages 18–59		All Ages 18–59		All Ages 18–59	
8%	7%	36%	37%	10%	14%

Source: Laumann et al., 1994

Description	Men	Women
Identified themselves as homosexual or bisexual	2.8	1.4
Had sex with person of same sex at least once since puberty	5.3	3.5
Felt desire for sex with person of same sex	7.7	7.5
Total reporting some same-sex desires or experiences	10.1	8.6

Source: Laumann et al., 1994

The survey also found that men think about sex more than women and are drawn to a wider range of sex practices (see Table 8-3). Compared to earlier surveys, the most recent findings show a widening range of sex practices for both men and women. Studies of college students reflect this trend. There appears to have been an increase in and acceptance of oral-genital sexual behavior among college students. Kinsey had found that oral sex was considered more intimate than intercourse and seldom occurred until intercourse had been experienced. Herold and Way (1983) found just the reverse. In their study, two-thirds of the women who were still virgins had experienced oral sex. This suggests a change in attitudes regarding the level of intimacy represented by oral sex as compared to intercourse.

The passage of time since these earlier surveys has brought with it changes in social customs, especially those related to increased acceptance of sexual relationships of nontraditional types, increased frequency of cohabitation before marriage, and increased rates of divorce and remarriage. In addition, concerns about AIDS and contracting the HIV virus seem to have had an impact on the sexual behaviors of many individuals. For all these reasons there is a need for continuing surveys of sexual practices.

Homosexuality

Homosexual behavior is sexual behavior with a member of one's own sex. **Homosexuals** are individuals who prefer to engage in sexual activity with members of their own sex over an extended period. Female homosexuality is often called **lesbianism.** Many homosexuals engage in sexual activity only with members of the same sex and are not attracted to members of the opposite sex. However, many homosexuals have heterosexual fantasies and can be sexually aroused by members of the opposite sex. A person's belief that he or she is a homosexual does not depend on actual behavior. Someone with no sexual experience at all may think of himself or herself as a homosexual. In recent years the term "gay" has been used by homosexuals to describe their life style because they feel that the term has fewer negative implications than "homosexual." Individuals, both males and females, who wish to publicly acknowledge their homosexual orientation usually use the term "gay."

Attitudes Toward Homosexuality

Homosexuality illustrates the changing character of views about sexual behavior, and the degree to which sexual behavior can become a sociopolitical issue. Society's stigmatizing of homosexuals can be very harmful

TABLE 8–3
The Appeal of Various Sexual Practices: Percentages of Respondents

	Degree of appeal to men ages 18–44				Degree of appeal to women ages 18–44			
	Very	Some-what	Not really	Not at all	Very	Some-what	Not really	Not at all
Vaginal intercourse	83%	12%	1%	4%	78%	18%	1%	3%
Watching partner undress	50	43	3	4	30	51	11	9
Receiving oral sex	50	33	5	12	33	35	11	21
Giving oral sex	37	39	9	15	19	38	15	28
Active anal intercourse	5	9	13	73	—	—	—	—
Passive anal intercourse	3	8	15	75	1	4	9	87
Group sex	14	32	20	33	1	8	14	78
Same-sex partner	4	2	5	89	3	3	9	85
Sex with a stranger	5	29	25	42	1	9	11	80
Forcing someone to do something sexual	0	2	14	84	0	2	7	91
Being forced to do something sexual	0	3	13	84	0	2	6	92

Source: Laumann et al., 1994

and lead to anxiety, self-doubt ("What's wrong with me?"; "I'm not normal"), and a perceived need to be "cured."

> In the bad old days, when homosexuality was considered a mental illness, a friend of mine was trying to go straight. He was seeing a distinguished psychoanalyst who believed (and still believes) that what some call a life style and still others call a crime is a psychiatrically treatable disorder. Through six years of anguished analysis, my friend changed his sexual orientation and married. His wife was wonderful—they had been friends for years—but he died unexpectedly of a heart attack at the age of 42, six months after the wedding. I am not superstitious, and I don't blame anyone, least of all his wife: he was happy with her. But a nagging question remains: Is it possible that my friend's doctor was trying to change something that should have been left alone?
>
> He had been homosexual for years, and had had at least one stable long-term relationship. But he lived in a society that condemned him on religious and medical grounds. He "freely" chose to change through psychoanalysis. But this was a limited sort of freedom, and though he in fact did change—as some have—he did not live to find out how the change would work.
>
> —Konner, 1989, p. 60

Public attitudes have tended to stigmatize homosexual activity to such an extent that many of those engaging in it have suffered social and legal mistreatment far beyond the domain of sexual behavior. During recent years, gay activism has increased markedly, as homosexuals have battled discrimination and social stigmatization (see Figure 8-1). The need for such battles varies from country to country and culture to culture. In a recent public opinion poll, 57 percent of American respondents said that gays cannot be considered good role models for children, and 53 percent said that they believe that homosexual relationships between consenting adults are morally wrong. Twenty-one percent said they would not knowingly buy from a homosexual salesperson (*Time Magazine*, June 27, 1994, p. 57). Contrasting with this negativism and ambivalence is the situation in Denmark, the first country in the world that legalized (in 1989) same-sex marriages—or *registered partnerships*, as they are called. More than 2,000 homosexual couples have wed under the Danish registered partnership law.

> Erik Ladefoged and Kim Norgaard, surrounded by 30 family and friends, finally were able to formally tie the knot in 1989 after living together for more than 20 years. "We were [married] between two heterosexual couples. Before us was a young couple, and after us came an elderly couple," recalls Mr. Norgaard, 47, an airline employee, showing off photographs of the ceremony and a champagne reception that followed.
>
> The couple found to their surprise that the wedding was an emotional experience, symbolic not only as a public declaration of their love, but of their nation's acceptance of them. "I thought it would be a formality. But our friends were singing a traditional Danish wedding song. I was happy all over. It was great to be gay and have the official handshake and smile of the state," notes Mr. Ladefoged, a 49-year-old school teacher. "It's extremely important that society said, "'It's different but it's OK for you, there's a place for you.'"
>
> (*Wall Street Journal*, June 8, 1994, p. 1)

Research evidence may also be playing a role in changing attitudes toward homosexuality. Although not too long ago homosexuality was considered to be a diagnosable disorder, it is not listed as a psychiatric condition in DSM-IV. Both the American Psychiatric Association and the American Psychological Association have voted to remove homosexuality from the list of mental illnesses. Contributing to this diagnostic change has been evidence indicating that lesbians and gay men do not differ in psychological adjustment from heterosexual women and men (Rothblum, 1994). Furthermore, the adjustment of children with lesbian or gay parents does not appear to differ from that of children with heterosexual parents (Patterson, 1992).

Homosexuals, like heterosexuals, may be anxious or depressed and are not

Figure 8-1 Gay Pride activities provide social support for homosexual individuals by visibly demonstrating their numbers. Such activities also provide a way for homosexuals to publicly state their sexual preferences rather than hide them.

always emotionally stable, but homosexuality is clearly not a form of mental illness. However, the psychological impact of the current high AIDS-associated death rate in the gay community as well as the personal loss of friends as a result of AIDS is likely to result in an increased amount of stress experienced by gay individuals. Research has shown that mean levels of psychological distress among gay men at risk for AIDS are significantly higher than in the general population (Chuang et al., 1989; Joseph et al., 1990). As we have stated throughout this book (see expecially chapters 1 and 5), high stress is associated with a higher rate of disorders of various types. Thus homosexual individuals may be at some higher risk for disorder, not because of their homosexuality itself, but because of current stress factors disproportionately affecting those in the gay community.

Origins of Sexual Orientation

The origins and determinants of sexual orientation, both heterosexual and homosexual, pose unanswered questions of genuine scientific interest. Recently researchers have focused attention on the roles of biological factors and learning in the development of sexual preferences. For example, one study suggested that there may be anatomical differences between the brains of homosexual and heterosexual men (LeVay, 1991). The study found that among homosexual men who had died from AIDS-related diseases, a part of the hypothalamus (a brain region that influences sexual behavior) had the anatomical form usually found in women rather than the form typical of heterosexual men. This finding is not direct evidence that brain structure causes homosexuality, but it suggests the need to explore areas of the brain that might relate to sexual preference. One problem in this study is that because the subjects had AIDS, the results might not apply to the overall population.

How much of sexual orientation is determined by genes and/or hormonal levels? One group of researchers has related male homosexuality to a small stretch of DNA on the X-chromosome (Homer et al., 1993). Other researchers have looked at the role of hormonal mechanisms (Bancroft, 1994). While these and other biological approaches to sexual preference are intriguing, it is most likely that sexual orientation grows out of the interplay of multiple determinants in which psychosocial factors as well as biological factors are important. An interactional approach to sexual orientation opens the possibility of multiple pathways to the development of sexual orientation.

Bisexual behavior, in which partners of either sex may be preferred at different times, is a sexual orientation that is beginning to receive scientific attention. **Bisexuals** engage in sexual activity with both men and women. The incidence of bisexuality in Western societies is difficult to estimate. At present, the relevant factors in its development remain to be identified. Sometimes the bisexual individual has a long heterosexual relationship and then a long homosexual relationship. Or the order might be reversed. Sometimes both relationships go on during the same period. One 23-year-old woman described her bisexual experience as follows.

I had been dating a guy I was very friendly with for about a year with a good sexual relationship. Then I suddenly found myself making it with my roommate, who slowly but expertly introduced me to how two women make love. I really enjoyed both kinds of sex and both personal relationships, so I continued them for some while until my graduate school career was over and I moved to a new town.

—Masters, Johnson, and Kolodny, 1988, p. 439

Sexual Dysfunction

Homosexuals may experience psychological distress because of social stigmatization. The distress caused by sexual dysfunction, on the other hand, is usually a very private matter about which other people have no knowledge. Both heterosexuals and homosexuals can experience sexual dysfunction.

A **sexual dysfunction** or **disorder** can be defined as persistent impairment of sexual interest or response that causes interpersonal difficulty or personal distress. Sometimes the dysfunction is independent of, and sometimes it results from, other psychological disorders or physical conditions (Catalan et al., 1990). If the problem is due *entirely* to organic factors, it is not given this diagnosis. A predisposition may be created by upbringing, personality, lack of information, or early sexual trauma. More immediate, precipitating causes include conflict with the partner, infidelity, age, depression, or an accidental failure produced by fatigue, stress, anxiety, or alcohol. The disorder may be sustained by anticipation of failure, the partner's reaction, poor communication, and limited sexual skills. Because of the large number of factors that might be involved in sexual disorders, clinicians must sensitively inquire about many aspects of sexual activity (see Table 8-4).

Sexual dysfunction often can be traced to a personality problem or some difficulty in the partners' relationship. However, as Box 8-1 shows, it should not be assumed that marital and sexual satisfaction always go together. The following are some of the frequent psychological contributors to sexual dysfunction:

1. A restricted ability to express warm and tender emotions.
2. Worries about rejection or criticism.

TABLE 8-4
Information Needed in Diagnosing and Treating Sexual Dysfunction

1. The nature of the dysfunction (e.g., lack of interest in sexual activity, inability to achieve orgasm)
2. When the sexual difficulty first became apparent (how long ago? in what situation?)
3. With what frequency has the difficulty been encountered (with each sexual partner? frequently or occasionally?)
4. The course of the dysfunction (acute or gradual in onset?)
5. What the patient thinks is the cause of the difficulty (e.g., "Maybe I'm just getting older")
6. What have the patient and partner done to correct the dysfunction, and with what results?

Source: Based on Moore, 1989

3. Inhibitions about nakedness or displaying one's body.
4. Difficulty with authority and concerns about being dominated.
5. Feelings of low self-esteem.

Sexuality is a biological function like digestion or respiration, and adequate sexual functioning, like good digestion or normal breathing, requires freedom from agitated feelings or excessive tension and control. A psychophysiological disorder may develop through the mutual reinforcement of fears, excessive expectations, physical responses, and the partner's reaction. For example, a man may become anxious when his female partner is slow to achieve orgasm; his anxiety may make it still more difficult for her, which may increase his anxiety level further and lead to erectile dysfunction.

Types of Sexual Dysfunction

Problems people encounter in sexual activity may occur in any of four stages of the sexual-response cycle. The stages include the following periods.

1. *Appetitive:* the presence of fantasy about sexual activity and a feeling of desire
2. *Excitement:* a period of subjective pleasure and physiological changes, including penile erection in the male and swelling and lubrication of the female genitals
3. *Orgasm:* the peaking of sexual pleasure and the release of sexual tension, as shown by ejaculation in the male and rhythmic muscle contraction in the pelvic area for both males and females
4. *Resolution:* a sense of relaxation and well-being. Men cannot produce an erection or experience orgasm during the resolution period, while women may be able to respond almost immediately to additional stimulation.

Sexual problems can occur during any of these stages. In the appetitive stage, physical conditions such as high blood pressure or diabetes can inhibit sexual desire. Some people simply seem to be at the low end of the normal distribution of sexual desire. These problems usually come to the attention of a clinician only when they become a source of concern to the individual or his or her partner.

Sexual problems can also occur at the excitement stage of the cycle. The male may fail to attain or hold an erection until the completion of intercourse. This problem is called **erectile dysfunction.** In females, a problem at this stage is inability to attain or maintain the swelling-lubrication response until the sex act is completed. This inability is often brought about by **inhibited sexual excitement.** Problems at each stage of sexual response may be a function of the individual and occur no matter who the partner is, or they may be a function of some aspects of a particular relationship and occur only with a specific partner.

Inhibited sexual desire in either men or women was not regarded as a distinct problem or even named as a separate diagnosis until about ten years ago. This diagnosis now encompasses both lack of interest in and active aversion to sex. Low sexual desire is not always easy to define and cannot be judged merely by the frequency of sexual activity, which varies a great deal. (Mohr & Beutler, 1990).

In women, inhibited sexual excitement means insufficient lubrication of the vagina to allow entry of the penis. Inhibited excitement or arousal in men means failure to attain or hold an erection sufficiently to complete coitus (sexual intercourse). It may be either primary (that is, the man has never been able to sustain an erection long enough for coitus) or secondary (the man has been able to complete intercourse successfully in the past). The former is rare, the latter common. About one-eighth of men fail to retain an erection long enough to permit entry into the vagina and ejaculation at least a quarter of the time, and the proportion rises with age. Erectile dysfunction is the main problem of more than half of men who request treatment for sexual disorders (Sadock, 1989).

One technique that is used in evaluating a man's capacity to have an erection is measurement of changes in penis size during sleep, or **nocturnal penile tumescence** (NPT). Erection normally occurs during rapid eye movement (REM) sleep—the period of sleep associated with dreaming and indicated by the rapid darting of the eyeballs beneath the closed lids. Researchers have developed physiological recording instruments to measure NPT (Meisler & Carey, 1990). A fairly reliable test for nocturnal erections is the use of a snap gauge—a device that springs open when the penis enlarges. There are also several techniques for measuring blood flow and

BOX 8-1

The Marital Relationship, Psychological Adjustment, and Sexual Dysfunction

While many people think that marital and sexual satisfaction go together, research on these topics reveals a surprising and more complicated picture. Significant levels of sexual dysfunction are found even in "normal" samples or among patients at general medical clinics. For example, Ellen Frank and her colleagues (1978) recruited couples as the "normal control sample" for a broader investigation, and found that sexual dysfunction (problems of desire, arousal, orgasm and genital pain) was reported by 40 percent of the men and 63 percent of the women, with 50 percent and 77 percent, respectively, reporting sexual "difficulty." Of special note, 83 percent of subjects described themselves as happily married.

Marital researchers have often found a close relationship between one person showing "withdrawal" and the other person expressing "hostile" or "demanding" behaviors, with wife demand/husband withdrawal occurring more frequently than the reverse pattern. These elements can produce a vicious cycle of increasing demands met by further withdrawal. Also, the more partners differ from each other in the amount of intimacy and distance they prefer, the greater their marital distress. As a result, we could expect marital distress in a situation where women did not feel that their husbands were intimate enough with them. We might also expect perceived male withdrawal (also a common response to a sexual problem) to be associated with higher levels of female hostility.

Ellis and Heiman (1992) designed a study to look more closely at these issues. Participants were 36 men seeking treatment for sexual dysfunction and their wives or current female partners (see Figure 8-2). All men reported erectile disorders, with several also reporting low sexual desire (thought to be secondary to the erectile problem) or premature ejaculation. None of the female partners reported a sexual dysfunction. The couples had been married for an average of 21 years (range, 1–44 years) and with an average of two children.

The couples' scores on indexes of marital adjustment were well within normal limits, suggesting that couples' marital functioning overall was intact. Scores on a measure of psychological symptoms were also within the normal range, though husbands scored slightly higher than wives on a few of the subscales (depression, hostility, and somatization, or a concern about physical functioning). Spouse scores were generally similar on the marital and psychological symptom scales, and on a self-reported stress rating (averaging 5 on a 10-point scale).

Ellis and Heiman looked at the variables that were most closely associated with overall marital adjustment. In the more distressed marriages, wives had higher ratings of depression and husbands had higher ratings of loneliness or alienation. Interestingly, wives' marital adjustment was correlated with *both* their own and their husbands' psychological functioning, while husbands' marital ratings were related more to their own psy-

Figure 8-2 The participation in therapy of both partners in cases of sexual dysfunction is important because clinicians need to know, not only about the presenting symptoms, but also the context in which they occur and how the partners view the problem.

chological functioning than to that of their wives.

The available evidence is consistent with two conclusions:

1. Sexual problems can occur in the context of a well-functioning marriage and with psychologically healthy individuals. A sexual problem does *not necessarily* signify a problem with an individual or a relationship.

2. The responses of men and women to a sexual problem within marriage are likely to differ. Within the context of a male sexual problem, women's depression and men's loneliness/alienation may be the most closely related to marital functioning. These psychological responses make sense in the context of a male erectile problem, since both partners may feel rejected. One can suppose that the two patterns—male withdrawal and female depressive symptoms—react with and maintain each other.

---

blood pressure in the penis. If the man experiences NPT, the cause of the erectile problem is likely to be psychological rather than physiological.

Anxiety stemming from personal conflict or from concern over a physical problem is often an important psychological factor in erectile dysfunction. Physical causes include early undiagnosed diabetes, hormonal imbalances, and the use of narcotics and alcohol. In the past, hidden psychopathology or psychodynamic conflicts was believed to be the main psychological cause of this type of sexual dysfunction. More recently, however, recognition has been given to **performance anxiety,** in which a man's preoccupation with sexual adequacy interferes

with his performance. One 34-year-old man's comment is typical.

> *After a while, the problem becomes so predictable that you start to make excuses in advance. It's as though you lose any chance of having sexual pleasure because you become preoccupied with the notion of failure. And that failure hits you right in the gut—you don't feel like much of a man.*
>
> —Masters et al., 1985, p. 502

Figure 8-3 illustrates the many sources of stress that may interact with biological vulnerabilities to result in problems of sexual performance for men.

Both males and females may experience problems in the orgasm phase of the sexual-response cycle. In the male, these take the form of premature ejaculation or delayed or absent ejaculation. In the female, they take the form of a delay or absence of orgasm after a normal excitement phase. **Premature ejaculation,** in which the man is unable to inhibit ejaculation long enough for his female partner to experience orgasm through intercourse, is probably the most common type of male sexual dysfunction. The man's failure to control his orgasm often results in his feeling sexually inadequate. According to one viewpoint, the male experiences anxiety as he reaches high levels of erotic arousal, and the anxiety triggers the involuntary orgasm.

In **retarded ejaculation,** on the other hand, the ejaculatory response is inhibited. Men with this problem respond to sexual stimuli with erotic feelings and a firm erection, but they are unable to ejaculate. In severe cases, the male may prolong intercourse for a long time, engage in fantasy, and drink alcohol, all to no avail. Although physical injuries may be responsible for the problem in some cases, a variety of psychological factors that contribute to the occurrence of retarded ejaculation include ambivalence toward the sexual partner, strongly suppressed anger, and a religious upbringing that engenders sexual guilt.

The chief disorder of the orgasm phase in females is **anorgasmia**—inability to achieve orgasm after normal excitement either through masturbation or coitus. About 5 to 10 percent of women suffer from primary anorgasmia; they have never been able to achieve orgasm. Secondary anorgasmia is the main problem for the vast majority of women who come to clinics for the treatment of sexual disorders. Some women with anorgasmia have few other symptoms; others suffer from

inhibited excitement, tension, irritability, and physical symptoms during sexual activity.

Psychological and situational factors can be an important cause of inhibited female orgasm. Psychological factors include unresolved conflicts over sexual activity and disturbances in the relationship between the partners. In many cases, however, the explanation is simpler: Inadequate stimulation during lovemaking can damage a woman's ability to become sexually responsive. In such cases, the therapist attempts to sensitize both partners to each other's sexual needs, explaining, for example, that a woman is more difficult to arouse than a man. Some women are unable to experience an orgasm without manual stimulation of the clitoris, which has a larger number of sensitive nerve endings than the vagina. This may represent a normal variation in sexual response. Most women do not have an orgasm each time they have intercourse, and about 15 percent of women never have orgasms (Cole, 1985). Anorgasmia can decrease a woman's overall sexual responsiveness as well as lead to depression and a decreased sense of self-esteem. As one 19-year-old college student said,

> There's so much talk about orgasms that I've been wondering what's wrong with me, that I don't have them. I used to enjoy sex a lot, but lately it's a bad scene because I just get reminded of problems.
>
> —Masters et al., 1988, p. 506

Other problems can also occur that often make sexual intercourse difficult. Both men and women may experience **dyspareunia,** a recurrent or persistent genital pain that occurs before, during, or after intercourse (Meana & Binik, 1994). Women also may be affected by **vaginismus.** This disorder makes intercourse difficult or impos-

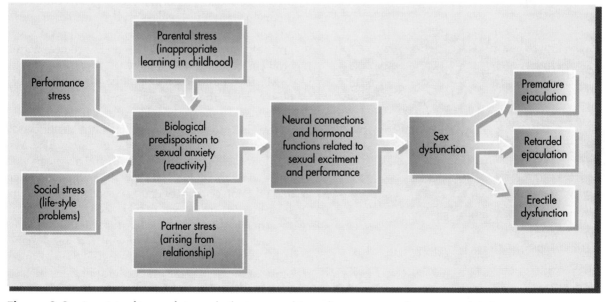

Figure 8-3 A variety of types of stress—both remote and immediate—can contribute to sexual dysfunction in men. SOURCE: Cole, 1985, p. 341. Reprinted with permission of the *British Journal of Psychiatry*.

sible because of involuntary spasms of the outer portion of the vagina.

Treatment of Sexual Dysfunction

Most present day sex therapy represents an integration of sex therapy procedures stemming from psychodynamic approaches, family systems therapy, and cognitive-behavioral techniques (LoPiccolo, 1994). The decision to request help for a sexual disorder is difficult for most people, and the attitude of the person who hears the complaint is important. Whether a sexual problem is ultimately mentioned at all and the vagueness of the problem presented often depend on whether the therapist seems to have some knowledge of the sexual problems and can discuss them without embarrassment. Once the client has indicated that the problem involves sexual activity it is important for the interviewer to get detailed information about the patient's medical history and physical symptoms as well as family background, early sexual development, work history, and use of drugs and alcohol. For some disorders both a physical examination and a psychological evaluation are necessary. Although great advances have been made in the medical treatment of sexual dysfunction, particularly impotence, generally psychological and relationship therapy continue to be the most effective treatment for sexual problems within relationships (Crowe & Jones, 1992). The therapist should have a clear and detailed idea of the patient's physical acts, emotional responses, fantasies during sex, and expectations. For instance, Figure 8-4 suggests that the man's expectations do not mesh with the experience of his sexual partner.

Usually sex therapy is requested by a couple. It is important to know how the partners feel about each other apart from the sexual relationship, how the rela-

"Multiple? Are you kidding? It wasn't even fractional!"

Figure 8-4

SOURCE: *Playboy*, February 1979. Reproduced by special permission of *Playboy* Magazine; Copyright © 1979 by *Playboy*.

tionship has changed (sexually or otherwise), how well they communicate, whether one partner is more interested in sex than the other, and which one is more eager for treatment. The therapist must see each partner separately in case there are subjects they do not want to discuss in each other's presence, such as fantasies, masturbation, infidelity, or feelings about their partner's sexual attractiveness.

In addition to dealing with factors specific to a given case, sex therapists have three general goals for the couple:

1. to engender an atmosphere of mutual communication
2. to decrease the fear of failure
3. to shift attention away from the fear of failure to the experience of sensory pleasure

The Masters and Johnson Approach Over a 10-year period the research team of William Masters, a gynecologist, and Virginia Johnson, a behavioral scientist, studied the sexual responses of 694 men and women under controlled laboratory conditions. Masters and Johnson's studies (1966, 1970) have been largely responsible for giving the laboratory study of human sexual behavior and the treatment of sexual dysfunctions scientific credibility and respectability.

Since the publication of Masters and Johnson's first two books in 1966 and 1970, sex therapy has emerged as a discipline in its own right. While they recognize that many sexually dysfunctional people are dysfunctional in other areas of their personal and social lives, Masters and Johnson believe that short-term treatment directed primarily at sexual problems can help most people who experience such dysfunctions. They have observed that becoming sexually functional has a positive influence on a person's anxiety level as well as on his or her self-esteem. A man who is anxious but has a good sex life is probably happier than a man who has to deal with a sex problem in addition to anxiety.

Masters and Johnson emphasize the treatment of couples, not just the person who seems to have a problem. This does not mean that the partner is seen as the cause of the difficulty, but rather that both members of the relationship are affected by the problem. The Masters and Johnson approach uses a man and a woman working together as therapists. The therapy program is intensive and takes place daily over a two-week period. It emphasizes instruction in the sexual needs of both partners, together with exercises in erotic stimulation. Specific homework assignments are given that are designed to help couples become more aware of their own sexual sensations. The therapy procedure includes basic information about the sexual organs and the physiology of the sexual response for clients who lack this information (most of the people who come for treatment, in fact).

The presentation of this basic information often has important therapeutic benefits in itself.

Emphasis is also placed on communication, nonverbal as well as verbal, between partners. Because couples who seek treatment typically place lovemaking exclusively under the man's control, sexual intercourse may be attempted only when he indicates that he is interested. The belief of many women that they will be rejected if they are sexually assertive continues to be widespread. In many cases of sexual dysfunction, the most effective treatment may not be complex physical or psychotherapeutic tactics, but simply providing information about sexual relationships and encouraging meaningful communication between sex partners.

Sensate focus is probably the best known of Masters and Johnson's sexual-retraining techniques. The rationale behind sensate focus is that sexually dysfunctional couples have lost the ability to think and feel in a sensual way because of the various stresses and pressures they associate with intercourse. They therefore have to be reacquainted with the pleasures of tactile contact. Each partner learns not only that being touched is pleasurable, but that exploring and caressing the partner's body can be exciting and stimulating in itself. The couple is encouraged to engage in sensate focus under conditions that are dissimilar to those associated with the anxieties, frustrations, and resentments of their former lovemaking. Intercourse is prohibited throughout the early stages of treatment because that simple requirement can reduce tension in both sexual and nonsexual areas of the relationship. Masters and Johnson thought this ban on intercourse made sensate focus particularly effective in treating performance anxiety. However, other therapists have suggested that a deemphasis rather than a ban is more helpful to couples (Lipsius, 1987).

The couples technique of therapy is especially appropriate in treating premature ejaculation, since this is often more upsetting to the woman than to the man. If premature ejaculation is the problem, the therapists often introduce a method known as the "squeeze technique" that helps recondition the ejaculatory reflex. The woman is taught to apply a firm, grasping pressure on the penis several times during the beginning stages of intercourse. This technique reduces the urgency of the need to ejaculate.

When the couple's problem is related to an orgasmic dysfunction in the woman, the treatment includes an exploratory discussion to identify attitudes that may be related to the woman's inability to attain orgasm. Then the couple is given a series of graduated homework assignments. If the woman is willing, she begins by exploring her own bodily sensations, stimulating herself by masturbating. As she becomes more comfortable with this technique, her partner begins to participate in the sessions through kissing and tactile stimulation. The importance of the woman's clear and assertive communication of her reactions and desires to her partner is strongly emphasized.

Masters and Johnson have reported very low failure rates of their treatment programs for both heterosexual and homosexual couples. However, their findings have been criticized, primarily because their reports are not completely clear on such topics as who is selected and who is rejected for the program and how success and failure are defined (Cole, 1985). Nevertheless, their techniques are far superior to earlier methods of treating sexual disorders.

The Behavioral and Cognitive Approaches Looked at from a behavioral perspective, the Masters and Johnson technique of sensate focus is reminiscent of systematic desensitization in that it leads to the substitution of a pleasurable response for anxiety. Sex therapists often create a sort of hierarchy in which certain parts of the body initially are designated as "out of bounds" and then are gradually included as progress is made. Although orthodox systematic desensitization can be used to eliminate specific anxieties (such as feeling uncomfortable while looking at a man's genitals), the more global sensate focus appears to be appropriate in dealing with the various diffuse anxieties experienced by sexually dysfunctional individuals.

The methods used by Masters and Johnson have been further refined by many behaviorally oriented therapists. For instance, relaxation, modeling, and a variety of cognitive elements have been introduced into treatment plans. The case presented in Box 8-2 illustrates this combined approach to the treatment of sexual dysfunction.

Researchers are paying increasing attention to both the cognitive and fantasy underpinnings of sexual behavior. Sexual fantasies can occur while daydreaming or during masturbation or sexual intercourse (see Figure 8-5). It is now recognized that being aroused by a given fantasy (for example, linking sex to physical violence or an exotic locale or someone other than one's partner) is not necessarily a sign of maladaptation (Meuwissen & Over, 1991). Fantasies can be a means of self-stimulation that heighten the experience of sex with another person. Among the most common sex fantasies are thinking of an imaginary lover, imagining being overpowered or forced to surrender, pretending to engage in a sex act that is usually regarded as repugnant, and reliving a previous sexual experience. Analyzing the emotional meanings of sexual fantasies and how the fantasies become linked to behavior is a challenge being taken up by researchers. Fantasy can be a useful technique for some individuals with sexual dysfunctions. They may be able to utilize it to heighten their level of arousal during sexual activity.

A Cognitive-Behavioral Approach to Sexual Dysfunction

Treatment in the following case involved both cognitive and behavioral elements. The elements included identifying thoughts and situations that were upsetting to the client, modeling, and rehearsal.

The client was a 24-year-old lawyer who after six months of marriage was upset by his frequent inability to obtain or retain an erection. His history suggested that his mother had been a dominating woman of whom he was fearful and that he was also unwilling to challenge or criticize his wife in any way even though he often felt considerable resentment toward her. He seemed to feel that expressing his feelings was not manly. After several therapeutic sessions directed at his irrational attitudes, he and the therapist composed a carefully worded speech for the client to deliver to his wife.

"Grace, I have something very important and very serious to discuss with you. It concerns you, me, our marriage, and life in general. I want you to please hear me out without interrupting me. . . . I was raised by my mother to bottle up my feelings, especially in relation to women. In thinking over this attitude, I now realize that this is crazy and even dishonest. I feel, for instance, that if I resent the fact that you turn to your father for advice in matters about which I have more knowledge than he, I ought to express my resentment instead of hiding it from you. I feel that when you order me about and treat me like a child, I ought to tell you how I really feel about it instead of acting like an obedient puppy dog. And most important of all, when you go ahead and make plans for me without consulting me, and especially when you yell at me in front of your parents, maybe I should quit acting as if I didn't mind and let you

know how strongly I really react inside. What I am getting at is simply that in spite of my love and affection for you, I would really rather be unmarried than be a henpecked husband like my father."

This little monologue was rehearsed several times during a one-hour session until playbacks on a tape recorder convinced the therapist that the client was ready to confront his wife and that he would do so in a forthright and sincere manner. Rehearsal techniques were used in preparing the patient to cope with tears, interruptions, denials, counterallegations, etc. His assignment was then put into effect. The patient reported that his wife "heard me out without interruption. . . . [She] seemed a little upset, but agreed that I should not withhold or conceal my feelings. I felt incredibly close to her and that night we had very good sex."

—Lazarus, 1971, pp. 156–157

Figure 8-5 This eighteenth-century block print by Harunobu shows a young girl fantasizing about her lover while she masturbates.

SOURCE: Harunobu, *A Fantasy* (late 1760s): Trustees of the British Museum.

The Kaplan Approach Some therapists believe that behavioral methods are useful for many sexual problems, but that other problems require a combination of behavioral approaches with psychodynamically oriented therapy for one or both partners. One of the foremost proponents of this view is Helen Singer Kaplan (1974, 1979). Kaplan, a psychoanalyst, believes that standard sex therapy methods are effective when sexual problems are based on mild and easily diminished anxieties and conflicts. However, there are many individuals whose symptoms are rooted in more profound conflicts. Kaplan thinks that this is especially true in the cases of men and women who lack sexual desire and men who have difficulty maintaining an erection. For these problems, Kaplan and her coworkers have developed a lengthy and individualized treatment program that involves traditional sex therapy and psychodynamically oriented sessions, sometimes with one of the clients and sometimes with both partners. The case of Sam and Susie illustrates Kaplan's approach.

Susie, 28, and Sam, 30, had been married four years and have 3-year-old twin sons. The chief complaint was Susie's lack of desire. The couple had a good relationship, each felt in love with the other, and they were judged to be good parents. During their marriage they had had intercourse only three times. During the last two years they had had no physical contact because any attempt by Sam to hold or kiss Susie resulted in "hysterics," that is, she had an anxiety attack. The couple were referred to Kaplan after nine months of weekly sessions at a sex therapy clinic had not produced improvement.

The ordinary sensate focusing or pleasuring activities threw Susie into an anxiety state. In addition, when there was any improvement Susie would effectively resist or sabotage the treatment by trying to do too much. For example, if the assignment were to lie next to Sam in bed and hold his hand, she might try to have him caress her breast as well. This would then precipitate her anxious feelings. The therapist discussed this behavior with Susie and gave her the job of controlling the progress of desensitizing her anxiety. She was to select only tasks that were within her comfort-zone, that is, those that produced only tolerable anxiety.

Susie also had a more general problem with fun and pleasure. Whenever she allowed herself to experience them, she developed sharp headaches. As the desensitizing of her phobic avoidance of sexual contact progressed, Susie had a series of dreams about "dead relatives buried in the basement that needed to be removed." A central threatening figure was her deceased father. After discussions with the therapist about Oedipal feelings toward her father and the transfer of some of these feelings to her husband, Susie's father disappeared from her dreams.

After further sessions along with her husband that focused on guilt over pleasure, Susie's pleasure anxiety had decreased, her relationship with her husband was more open, and the couple was having satisfying intercourse at least once per week.

—Adapted from Kaplan, 1979, pp. 73–75

The Effectiveness of Sex Therapy

Great variations in the success rate for sex therapy have been reported by researchers (Cole, 1985). Successes reported range from 39 to 98 percent. Part of the problem in assessing effectiveness is that the measurement of success is often poorly defined in the research and few follow-up studies are reported. As a result, long-term changes are unknown. The particular treatment approach used does not seem to affect the success rate. One study compared Masters and Johnson's technique with a modified technique using only one therapist and another technique that combined efforts to improve communication and behavioral methods, such as relaxation training and contracts (Crowe et al., 1981). All three approaches led to improvement lasting at least one year for couples with problems of erectile dysfunction, anorgasmia, and loss of sexual interest. There was no difference in effectiveness among the various therapies.

Findings like these suggest that research is needed to determine which therapeutic elements are actually helpful and which elements are unnecessary. For instance, decreasing anxiety about sexual performance has been a focus of many approaches to sex therapy. However, anxiety is a complex construct that has behavioral, cognitive, and physiological aspects. The heightened physiological response that is part of anxiety has been shown to increase, not decrease, sexual response (Beck & Barlow, 1984). However, the cognitive aspects—for instance, interfering thoughts and problems of focusing attention—have a negative effect on arousal. Such thoughts may increase because of the demand for performance when the partner is clearly aroused. These findings suggest that attempts to decrease the physiological aspects of anxiety may be ineffective or even counterproductive, whereas practice in screening out distracting thoughts might be most helpful.

If sex therapy is unsuccessful, its effects and the feelings it arouses may provide new insight for both the patient and the therapist. Some patients find the exercises mechanical or boring; this reaction may indicate hostility toward the partner, fear of rejection, or even performance anxiety about touching and caressing. Some people feel guilty about their own fantasies or are jealous of their partner's fantasies. The partner may sabotage the therapy by a critical attitude, detachment, or loss of interest. A common source of sexual problems is the relationship between the partners. Sometimes they have greatly differing expectations of the marriage or love affair. They may be chronically angry at each other or engaged in a power struggle. Sometimes both partners are unsure about how close they want to be, but this ambivalence takes a peculiar form in which one demands sexual intimacy and the other retreats. The recommended treatment for such problems is psychotherapy. The type of psychotherapy depends more on the therapist and patient than on the specific sexual disorder.

Gender Identity Disorder

Gender identity, a basic feature of personality, refers to an individual's feeling of being male or female. Children become aware that they are male or female at an early age, and once formed, their gender identity is highly resistant to change. Gender identity is different from sexual preference. Sexual preference refers to whether a person desires a sexual partner of the same or the opposite sex; it does not refer to the person's sexual self-concept.

Gender Identity Problems in Childhood

In **gender identity disorder of childhood,** children who have not yet reached puberty may show considerable distress at being male or female and will express intense desires to be of the opposite sex. For instance, a girl may vehemently state her desire to be a boy or even insist that she is a boy. She may refuse to wear ordinary feminine clothing and insist on wearing the clothing typical of males including boys' underwear and other accessories. She may also deny her gender by such behaviors as refusing to urinate while in a sitting position or by the insistence that she either already has or will grow a penis. Boys show the same types of behavior in reverse. In addition to playing with girls' toys and wanting to dress as a girl, a boy may say that he wants to be a woman when he grows up and that his penis and testes are disgusting or that they will disappear as he grows older.

Problems that may relate to gender identity come to clinical attention when parents become concerned because their child's behavior and social relationships are not like those of other children of the same sex and age. For instance, this mother is worried that her son is and will continue to be sexually abnormal.

My boy is showing feminine tendencies and has ever since he was two years old. It started out real cute. His sister had dress-up clothes at her grandparents', and when he got to be about two years old, he'd dress up in these clothes and hats and high heels, and he was just real cute. We thought it was something he'd pass. Now he will be eleven years old this month, and he does this in secret. I just felt like now was the time to investigate it.

—Green, 1974, p. xxi

If a young child's behavior is typical of that of children of the opposite sex, it does not always mean that the child has a gender identity problem. Often parents are not aware of how much their own behavior contributes to the behavior of their children. The mother quoted earlier may have encouraged her son to dress in women's clothes by telling him how cute he was then, and at no other time. When this is the case, counseling may be helpful. Parents can be trained to reinforce sex-appropriate behavior in the home—for example, by giving the child special attention or a material reinforcer when he or she is behaving appropriately. This approach has been found to be effective in helping children acquire new sex roles (Rekers, 1977).

Despite advances in the study of sexual practices, questions frequently arise as to how maladaptive a certain type of behavior is. Children who act out inappropriate sex roles early in their development may drop this behavior as they get older. The 5-year-old tomboy or sissy may simply be going through a phase. However, children who dress in the clothes of the opposite sex and whose play follows the patterns of the other sex, have an increased likelihood of developing a homosexual orientation in adulthood (Money, 1987). A longitudinal study compared boys with extremely feminine interests and behavior in childhood with boys in a control group (Green, 1987). Eleven years later 75 percent of the previously feminine boys were either bisexual or homosexual in fantasy and/or behavior. All but one of the boys in the control group were heterosexual.

Gender Identity Disorder in Adults

Gender identity disorders in adults can take two forms: **transexualism** and **nontranssexual gender identity disorder.** Transsexuals experience an intense desire and need to change their sexual status, including their anatomical structure. In contrast, although adults with nontranssexual gender-identity disorder feel a discomfort and inappropriateness about their assigned sex and often cross-dress, they are not preoccupied with getting rid of their primary and secondary sexual characteristics and acquiring those of the other sex.

Although the number of cases of transsexualism is very small (according to one estimate, only 1 per 100,000 people for females and 1 per 30,000 for males), the behavior has aroused a great deal of curiosity. Scientific interest in transsexualism derives mainly from the light that such cases may shed on the general nature and development of gender identity. When a child's strong desire to be a member of the opposite sex continues into adulthood, transsexualism may result. The problem begins to surface at puberty, when maturational changes in the body emphasize biological gender. In the follow-up study of feminine boys described in the last section (Green, 1987), one boy seemed to have transsexual feelings. Though clinicians agree on the value of studying the lives of transsexuals, the use of medical techniques to bring about bodily changes that conform to the transsexual's gender identity remains controversial.

Changing a male transsexual into a female involves administering female hormones to reduce hair growth and stimulate development of the breasts, removing the male genitals, and creating an artificial vagina. Changing a female into a sexually functioning male is more difficult because the artificially constructed penis cannot become erect by natural means or feel tactile stimulation. An inflation device is sometimes implanted in the penis to make artificial erection possible. The long-term success of this method, however, is still in doubt.

Many of the candidates who apply to clinics for what is called sexual-reassignment surgery show considerable psychological disturbance. In one group of patients who applied to a university gender identity clinic, 92 percent of the males and 60 percent of the females showed other psychological disturbances in addition to problems with sexual identity (Levine, 1980). For this reason, clinicians stress the need to assess each candidate carefully before deciding whether to carry out the medical steps needed for a sex change. After people who are emotionally stable and likely to adjust well to surgery are selected, most reputable centers still require a number of preliminary steps before the surgery is carried out. This degree of caution is needed because the surgical procedures are irreversible.

After patients have been selected, they usually are required to spend one or two years prior to the surgery living in the community as a member of the opposite sex. During this period hormone injections are used to alter secondary sex characteristics such as breast size or muscle definition. This period serves as psychological preparation for life as a member of the other sex and also provides a realistic experience of what that life may be like. Psychotherapy is also often required during the presurgical period. Sometimes clients have what might be called "magical" hopes regarding the surgery. The psychotherapeutic sessions can give them a chance to look at their underlying feelings and perhaps become more comfortable as hetero- or homosexuals.

What happens to those who undergo the surgery? Several transsexuals have written about their experiences. One is Jan Morris, whose autobiography is entitled *Conundrum* (1974). James Humphrey Morris was a highly regarded English foreign correspondent. At age 17 he had been an officer in one of Britain's crack cavalry regiments. As a correspondent for *The Times* of London, he covered the successful attempt by Hilary and Tenzing to climb Mount Everest. He covered wars and rebellions the world over and also wrote 15 books on history and travel. Then James became Jan. Jan Morris refers to her former self as a woman trapped in a man's body.

At age 3 or 4 James Morris realized that he was a girl who had been born into the wrong body. As an adult he enjoyed the company of women but did not desire to sleep with them. He married at 22, and he and his wife had five children. As middle age neared, he became depressed, had suicidal thoughts, and finally sought a transsexual change. Hormones were used to enlarge his breasts and soften his body to more feminine lines. After surgery to complete the process begun by the hormone pills, Morris divorced his wife. Jan Morris reports that she feels like the person she always wanted to be. (See Figure 8-6a-c). She says the children of her former marriage treat her as an aunt.

Although Jan Morris appears to have had a rewarding transsexual experience, in general the results of sexual reassignment have been disappointing. During the 1980s several prominent medical centers stopped doing transsexual surgery because the benefits were doubtful. In a long-term follow-up in male-to-female transsexuals, only one-third were judged to have a fair or good sexual adjustment (Lindemalm et al., 1986). More than half of the patients were unchanged in social adjustment. Almost one-third considered their sex-reassignment surgery to have been a mistake.

Transsexualism is a prime example of the interactional point of view. Sex is a matter of anatomy and physiology, but gender identity is strongly influenced by psychological, social, and cultural factors. It is likely that there may be a small group of transsexuals for whom sexual-reassignment therapy is an effective treatment. For many more, who are likely to have significant personality problems and other psychopathology, the surgery does not provide an answer to their mental health problems; instead, the problems may worsen. Some individuals become deeply depressed after surgery, while others have transient psychotic episodes.

Nontranssexual gender-identity disorder also produces discomfort about one's assigned sex. However, people with this disorder lack the preoccupation for acquiring the sexual organs and other physical characteristics of the opposite sex that is characteristic of transsexuals. Instead they focus on fantasizing that they are of the opposite sex or actually acting out that role through cross-dressing. This cross-dressing differs from that of transvestites, discussed later. Although transvestites obtain sexual gratification from cross-dressing, they are not dissatisfied with their biological sex. They wish to remain male but become sexually excited by wearing women's clothes.

The Paraphilias

Not everyone is sexually excited by the same stimuli. Some individuals can gain sexual gratification only from particular objects or situations. While many of these sexual behaviors are practiced in private or with consenting adult partners and do not cause harm to other people, paraphilic imagery may be acted out with a nonconsenting partner in a way that does cause harm. DSM-IV describes three general classes of **paraphilia** (which means attraction to the deviant).

1. preference for the use of a nonhuman object for sexual arousal
2. repetitive sexual activity with humans that involves real or simulated suffering or humiliation
3. repetitive sexual activity with nonconsenting partners

(a)

(b)

(c)

Figure 8-6 (a) James Morris in 1960. (b) Jan Morris in 1974. (c) A note written by Morris to the authors.

I always seem to have been fascinated by rubber boots. I cannot say exactly when the fascination first started, but I must have been very young. Their spell is almost hypnotic and should I see someone walking along with rubber boots, I become very excited and may follow the person for a great distance. I quickly get an erection under such circumstances and I might easily ejaculate. I often will take the boots to bed with me, caress them, kiss them, and ejaculate into them.

—Epstein, 1965, pp. 515–516

Fetishism

Fetishism, a psychological state in which a non-living object (fetish) serves as a primary source of sexual arousal and consummation, is an example of a sexual deviation that is not usually addressed by the law. Most fetishists are solitary in their activities, although in some cases they commit crimes to acquire their favorite fetishes (often undergarments, boots, or shoes). Fetishists are almost always male, and the fetish varies widely from the clearly erotic (such as an article of women's underwear, especially underwear that has been worn, stained, and not yet laundered) to objects with little apparent connection with sexuality. Fetishism often begins in adolescence.

Rubber fetishes are particularly popular. Some rubber fetishists derive sexual excitement merely from wearing rubber garments. Others dress in them or want their partner to wear them during sexual activity because the garments are necessary for them to become sexually aroused. One rubber fetishist describes the role played by rubber boots in his sexual behavior.

Fetishism is one of the most puzzling of all forms of sexual behavior. It is chronic, and in some cases the collection of fetishistic objects is the main activity in the individual's life. No one has been able to explain adequately fetishists' sexual attachment to diverse objects. Although theories range from those that stress unconscious motivation to those that hypothesize impaired neural mechanisms such as are found among epileptics, the causes of this unusual type of sexual behavior remain shrouded in mystery (Wise, 1985).

Fetishists do not often seek therapy. In one large London hospital only 60 cases were diagnosed in a 20-year period (Chalkley & Powell, 1983). Of these, about 30 percent were referred by the courts, mainly because of their theft of fetishistic objects. About a third of the patients came for treatment because of anxiety about their fetishistic behavior. About 20 percent came for other reasons; the fetish was identified only after they had begun treatment. Treatment based on learning principles has been applied to fetishism with some success. In aversion therapy, for example, the fetish object is paired, either actually or in fantasy, with an unpleasant stimulus such as electric shock or a sense of overwhelming embarrassment.

Transvestic Fetishism

A transvestite often uses clothing as a sexual stimulant or fetish. Transvestism literally means "cross-dressing." Figure 8-7 shows a male cross-dresser. Transvestic behavior in men ranges from occasional solitary wearing of female clothes to extensive involvement in a transvestic subculture. Some males wear a single item of women's apparel (for example, underwear or hosiery) under their masculine attire, while others dress entirely as females and wear makeup. While cross-dressed, male transvestites often masturbate.

DSM-IV describes **transvestite fetishism** only in het-

Figure 8-7 Many transvestites, also known as crossdressers, are in committed and satisfying relationships with female partners. A married couple, Davida (left) and Corinne, are shown here with Davida in crossdress. Although some male transvestites gain sexual gratification while crossdressed, others, particularly those who have passed adolescence and early manhood, seem to experience aesthetic pleasure and release from the responsibilities of the male role. Photo by Mariette Pathy Allen, New York City. From her book, *Transformations.*

The personal masculine attributes that first attracted you to me are, as you know, an integral part of my personality, just as my transvestism is. It has always been a part of me. . . . We are only make-believe girls, and we know always that we are really men, so don't worry that we are ever dissatisfied with manhood, or want to change forever into a woman. When we are dressed in feminine clothes and attain as close a resemblance as possible to a real girl, we do certainly pretend that we are girls for that short time, but it is a pretense and definitely not a reality.

—Prince, 1967, pp. 80–81

An unusual study some years ago of a nationwide sample of transvestites provided comprehensive descriptions of their behavior and attitudes (Bentler & Prince, 1969, 1970). Compared with a nontransvestite group, the transvestites were more inhibited in their interpersonal relationships, less involved with other individuals, and more independent. In general, they gave evidence of being less able to seek sympathy, love, and help from others and seemed to be happier when they temporarily shed the responsibilities of the male gender role to others. However, in many areas of personality they did not differ significantly from nontransvestites.

erosexual males. Women are not usually considered to be transvestites, probably because our society allows them to dress in most masculine styles. However, cases of female cross-dressing have been described. For example, Billy Tipton was a successful jazz musician who began his career in jazz clubs in the 1930s. Tipton had been married and had adopted three sons. When he died in 1989, the funeral director discovered that he was biologically a woman (see Figure 8-8).

References to cross-dressing can be found throughout history. King Henry III of France, who reigned from 1574 to 1589, cross-dressed publicly and wished to be addressed and treated as a woman. Joan of Arc (1412–1431) wore her hair short and preferred to dress as a man. Most transvestic fetishists are heterosexual men who dress in women's clothes, often starting in adolescence. When not cross-dressed, the transvestite usually exhibits masculine behavior and interests.

Although some clinicians have contended that transvestism and transsexualism are basically similar, there are a number of differences between these two conditions. Transsexuals wish to change their genitals and live as members of the opposite sex. They do not experience sexual arousal when cross-dressing. Transvestites, on the other hand, may become sexually aroused when cross-dressing but continue to identify themselves as members of their biological sex.

A male transvestite gave this explanation for his behavior in a letter to his wife.

Figure 8-8 The Billy Tipton Trio: Tipton (center), Ron Kilde, and Dick O'Neil. "I never suspected a thing," O'Neil said after he found out, on Tipton's death, that Tipton was a woman.

Psychologists have emphasized several perspectives—psychodynamic processes, conditioning, and biological predisposition—in discussing transvestism. Many clinicians believe that transvestism develops in the context of disturbed parent-child relationships. Others see it as a product of aberrant psychosexual development. Behaviorists see it as a conditioned response that is susceptible to aversion therapy in which dressing in women's clothing is paired with an aversive stimulus. Behavioral training aimed at fostering confidence and adequacy in playing a conventional sex role has also been suggested. Some recent therapy is focused on reducing the guilt and anxiety associated with cross dressing.

Covert sensitization seems to be particularly useful in treating transvestism and other paraphilias. In this procedure clients are first asked to imagine as vividly as possible the sexually arousing behavior that they are trying to eradicate, and to follow these thoughts with equally vivid aversion imagery (for example, being discovered and embarrassed). This approach was used for a 31-year-old transvestite, a married police officer who sought help for uncontrollable urges to dress in women's clothing and appear in public. The client had a 16-year history of transvestism that had earlier resulted in his discharge from the Marine Corps. His wife had threatened to divorce him because of his cross-dressing. In treatment, he was asked to form images of deviant sexual scenes as well as aversive images of their undesirable consequences. The following is an example of the material used in the covert sensitization for this case.

You are in your house alone, and you are feeling lonely. You get the urge to put on the clothing, so you enter the bedroom and open the closet. You begin to get aroused as you decide what to wear. As you put on the clothing, you can see the colors and feel the clothing on your hands. You really are turned on as you put on the bra, panties, nylons, wig. You feel like playing with yourself as you apply your makeup, but you can't wait to go out. As you leave the house, you get very excited. You are touching your penis through the panties as you're driving. And then you hear sirens! The police pull you over, and it's your fellow policemen. They start to laugh and call for other police cars. A crowd is gathering, and they know you're a man. The officers throw you around and take you to the station. The women are disgusted, and the chief will take your gun and badge. You are humiliated, and they call you "sick." Your kids are crying as they return from school because others tease them about having a perverted father. Look what you've done to yourself!

—Brownell et al., 1977, pp. 1146–1147

Covert sensitization has been successful in treating transvestic fetishism. Figure 8-9 shows the average percentages of full erection (measured by penis circumference) during a baseline period, during covert sensitization, and upon follow-up. The figure also shows self-reported changes in sexual arousal to transvestite stimuli. Both the physiological and self-report measures revealed a sizable decrease in sexual arousal. In addition, physiological and self-reported arousal in response to heterosexual stimuli increased. The client, who had received prior treatment for his sexual difficulties, was surprised at the effectiveness of the covert sensitization.

For some transvestic fetishists it is not the clothes themselves that are exciting, but rather the ability to fool the public and be taken for a woman. One transvestic fetishist was asked if he would feel happier if social custom allowed people to dress as they wished in public.

"Heavens, no," he smiled. "Merely to be allowed to wear women's clothes in public is nothing. It is the challenge of being so much like a woman that no one knows I'm a man

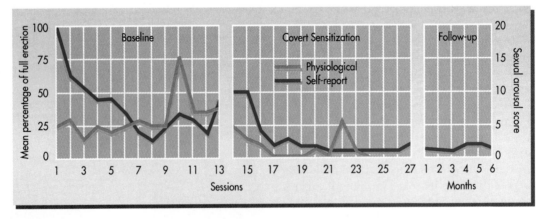

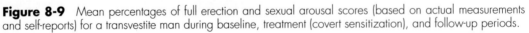

Figure 8-9 Mean percentages of full erection and sexual arousal scores (based on actual measurements and self-reports) for a transvestite man during baseline, treatment (covert sensitization), and follow-up periods.

SOURCE: Adapted from Brownell, Hayes, and Barlow, 1977. Copyright © by the American Psychological Association. Adapted by permission of the authors.

that turns me on. The combination of doing something that I want to, that everyone says is impossible and is forbidden anyway, produces in me an arousal which, because it is in a sexual context, becomes sexual arousal."

—Gosselin and Wilson, 1980, p. 67

Sexual Sadism and Masochism

For some people, inflicting or experiencing pain and indignity is linked to sexual gratification. Many people incorporate mildly painful acts—such as biting, nipping, and spanking—into their sexual practices. When both partners enjoy them, these activities can enhance sexual pleasure. However, sadists and masochists often go beyond mild pain and, moreover, cannot enjoy sex any other way. To the **sadist,** achieving orgasm depends on humiliating others or inflicting pain on them. This is often referred to as "discipline." To the **masochist,** sexual satisfaction depends on "bondage"—suffering, humiliation, pain, and ill treatment at the hands of others. Sadism and masochism occur in both heterosexual and homosexual relationships, but, like other sexual deviations, they are poorly understood. Both sexual masochism and sadism are chronic conditions. When they are severe, serious injury or death may result for the victim. Some clinical workers have conjectured that the roots of sadism and masochism are to be found in childhood; others have mentioned possible biological factors. One area that would seem to merit study is the fantasy life of these individuals—for example, the thoughts associated with their sexual activities.

The sexual masochist experiences arousal through his or her own suffering, preferably by being humiliated and beaten. Masochists have fantasies, often beginning in childhood, in which they are bound, tortured, raped, or otherwise abused in ways that they cannot prevent. These fantasies and acts are far more common in males than in females. Five features are found in most cases of sadomasochism: (1) agreement as to which partner is to be dominant and which one submissive; (2) awareness by both partners that they are role playing; (3) the consent of both participants; (4) a sexual context; and (5) a shared understanding by both participants that their behavior is sadomasochistic (Weinberg et al., 1984).

In sadomasochistic relationships the participants agree on the limits beforehand.

My wife and I do play dominance and submission games, and maybe we have the marks to prove it on occasion. But the one playing top dog watches like a hawk to make sure we stop when the other one doesn't like it any more.

—Gosselin & Wilson, 1980, p. 69

Often a signal is set up so that the submissive partner can stop the session at any time if the agreed-upon

boundaries are exceeded. One sadomasochistic prostitute explained her approach.

When you have a new client, what I used to do was I used to sit down and I would talk to them first and find out exactly what they wanted. Because sometimes you can get into a session with somebody and get very brutal and that's not what they want. There's heavy dominance and there's light dominance and there's play acting, roles, all different kinds. So the best thing to do is to sit down and talk to somebody first, initially.

—Weinberg, 1978, p. 290

When sadomasochism is a person's predominant sexual style, the most common way of reaching other sadomasochistic devotees is the use of ads in sadomasochistic magazines. For example:

Beautiful Dominatrix, 24. A true sophisticate of the bizarre and unusual. I have a well-equipped dungeon in my luxurious home. You will submit to prolonged periods of degradation for my pleasure. Toilet servitude a must. I know what you crave and can fulfill your every need.

A very pretty 30-year-old female has fantasies about receiving hand spankings on bare behind. I've never allowed myself to act out any of the fantasies. Is there anyone out there who'd like to correspond with me about their fantasies or experience with spanking?

—Weinberg & Falk, 1980, pp. 385–386

As these examples show, the ads contain code messages. "Toilet servitude," for instance, refers to handling feces or being defecated on. Sadomasochistic experiences can also be enhanced by hoods, paddles, enema equipment, adult diapers, and other paraphernalia sold in sex shops (see Figure 8-10). Many of these "sex boutiques" can be found in middle-class neighborhoods.

Sadomasochists may be heterosexual, bisexual, or homosexual in their choice of partners. A questionnaire study showed few differences among these groups (Breslow et al., 1986). In general, subjects in all three groups felt that their sadomasochistic interests were natural ones that were present in childhood. People in all three groups used ads to make contact with others with similar interests. Few subjects in any of the groups reported being sexually abused as children, although a sizeable minority felt emotionally abused. In general, the homosexual respondents sometimes tended to take the dominant and sometimes the submissive role in their sadomasochistic activities. Heterosexual and bisexual subjects were about equally divided into "predominantly dominant," "predominantly submissive," or "adopting either" roles. Although more men than women seem to

Figure 8-10 This sex shop mannequin is dressed in the leather, restraints, and chains that are attractive to many sadists and masochists.

be interested in sadomasochism, in one survey using questionnaires placed in a sadomasochistic contact magazine, 40 percent of those who responded were female (Breslow and others, 1985).

Voyeurism

Some sexual variations are not physically harmful but may victimize innocent people. One example is **voyeurism,** the impulse to spy on others, usually strangers. The French word "voyeur" means "watcher." The voyeur is subject to an irresistible, repetitive urge to spy on others through windows or doors, in public toilets, in parks, or on beaches, and particularly enjoys watching other people have sex. Like the exhibitionist (to be described shortly), the voyeur or "peeping Tom" is male and achieves sexual gratification from doing something forbidden. Also like the exhibitionist, the voyeur is usually harmless and will run if he is discovered. In some cases, however, usually after feeling intensely stimulated or provoked, the voyeur will let his presence be known—for example, he may exhibit his

genitals and ask his victim to touch him or even to masturbate him. Cases have been known in which the voyeur tried to force the victim to have sexual intercourse with him, but such cases are exceptional.

Voyeurism begins in early childhood and usually continues over a long period. Fifty percent of those arrested for voyeurism are later rearrested for similar acts. About one-fourth of the men who are arrested for peeping are married. When voyeuristic acts are related to life stress, the impulse to commit them usually decreases when the stress dissipates. While voyeurs show few signs of serious mental disorders, they usually have unsatisfying heterosexual relationships.

Exhibitionism

Exhibitionists, who are always males, repeatedly expose their genitals to unsuspecting strangers in public places as a way of experiencing sexual arousal. The exhibitionist does not want to harm anyone; his act of exposure is done for his own sexual gratification. His arousal is apparently heightened by seeing people react with amazement or shock when he unexpectedly shows his penis. Exhibitionists expose their genitals mainly to women and children. One-third of all people arrested for sex offenses are exhibitionists, and about 20 percent of these are arrested more than once (Hyde, 1994).

Exhibitionism can begin between preadolescence and middle age, but it occurs most frequently during the twenties. An exhibitionist has an irresistible, compulsive need to expose his genitals, and he does so despite the anxiety, depression, and shame he feels as a result. Acts of genital exposure often seem to be triggered by feelings of excitement, fear, restlessness, and sexual arousal. When overcome by these feelings, the exhibitionist is driven to find relief. Both psychodynamic and behavioral therapies (particularly aversion therapy) have been tried with exhibitionists. Although both methods seem to achieve some success, the results are unpredictable (Hyde, 1994).

Pedophilia

Pedophilia is the term used to describe a disorder that includes intense and recurrent sexual urges and sexually arousing fantasies involving some form of sexual activity with a child who has not reached the age of puberty. To be classified as a pedophile the person must either have acted on these urges or be very distressed by them. The sexual attractions of pedophiles are very specific. For instance, the only children who may be seen as arousing may be girls from the ages of 8 to 10. The behavior is usually a chronic one that continues over a long time. However, periods of high stress tend to increase the frequency of pedophilic behavior. In about 90 percent of all cases, the pedophile is someone whom the child knows (Hyde, 1994).

Pedophilic behavior may take a variety of forms, including exposure of the pedophile's sexual body parts to the child; kissing, hugging, and fondling the child in a sexual way; touching sexual parts of the child's body or inducing the child to touch or fondle the pedophile's sexual organs; or attempted or actual intercourse with the child. Most of the victims do not seek the assistance of public services. Clearly, better preventive and therapeutic measures are needed. Youngsters need to be taught to protect themselves and the public needs to be educated about the nature of the problem.

Pedophiles are likely to repeat the behavior after being apprehended. Some, but not all, child sex abusers can be classified as pedophiles. In most cases, a pedophile will have had sexual contacts with children both in and outside of the family and prefers children for sexual targets. Many pedophiles do report being sexually abused as children, although researchers do not have much data on this disorder.

Perspectives on the Paraphilias

Human sexual behavior is varied. It has its underpinnings in a biological substrate for physiological expression and is strongly influenced by the socialization process. When sexual behavior greatly diverges from the norm, and especially when it is harmful to others, researchers attempt to understand it better by defining its characteristics. Defining and classifying these deviant sexual behaviors has been difficult, however, because they are: (1) committed by a small percentage of the population; (2) usually concealed by their participants; and (3) constantly modified by adaptations to social changes. One hallmark of the paraphilias that researchers have been able to identify is that these unusual or bizarre acts are insistently and involuntarily repetitive (Hyde, 1994).

No single theory has so far been able to explain the development of paraphilic behavior. Each of the theoretical perspectives has implications for research in terms of definition of the variant behavior, preferred type of treatment, appropriate treatment goals, and ways of assessing treatment outcome.

The psychodynamic perspective views paraphilic behavior as a reflection of unresolved conflicts during psychosexual development (Freud, 1969). This view leads to long-term treatment that aims to change personality structure and dynamics and also alter overt behavior and sexual fantasies.

The behavioral perspective views sexual variance as something learned by the same rules as more usual sexual behavior—through conditioning, modeling, reinforcement, generalization, and punishment. From this perspective the definition of variant sexual behavior would be based on the individual's personal discomfort with the behavior and any conflict between this behavior and the rules of society. The treatment, which can be as short as one day or much longer, is based on understanding the immediate antecedents and consequences of the behavior and on developing alternate forms of sexual arousal. Treatment effectiveness is based on overt behavior as measured by self-monitoring and psychophysiological measures. Various types of aversion therapy have been tried with individuals with paraphilias, but this approach has generated a great deal of controversy because of the pain and discomfort created. Covert sensitization that involves imagined unpleasant events seems to avoid some of the ethical questions surrounding the use of physical punishment. A broader behavioral view from the social-learning perspective explains the variant behavior as a substitute for more appropriate social and sexual functioning, or inability to form a satisfactory marital relationship. The treatment goal is to assist the client to form satisfactory relationships through teaching interpersonal skills. Outcome measures here are client's self-reports of satisfying sexual and nonsexual relationships with significant others.

The biological perspective deals with heredity, prenatal hormonal environment, and a focus on the biological causes of gender identity. The treatment goals include suppression not only of the variant behaviors but also of sexual responsiveness in general and may involve the use of hormonal treatments or surgery. But until the side effects of hormonal treatments and long-term behavior changes can be assessed accurately, it is difficult to draw any conclusions about the therapeutic effects of this type of treatment for paraphiliacs. The outcome is usually measured in terms of psychophysiological responses as well as of sexual activity.

No one type of treatment seems to be clearly superior for the paraphilias. Much of the research has severe shortcomings and consists of single-subject studies without control subjects. These shortcomings are not surprising, considering the difficulty of doing research in this area. There is tentative evidence across many studies that behavioral treatment may be effective in reducing or eliminating some paraphilic sexual behavior and increasing appropriate sexual behavior instead (Kilmann et al., 1982). Many of the therapeutic efforts reported used a variety of behavioral treatments that included aversion therapy. The programs were most effective when they were tailored for the specific problems of the individual paraphiliac. Conventional counseling or psychotherapy has not been very effective in modifying paraphiliacs' behavior. The reasons for resistance to treatment are unclear.

Sexual Victimization

Some sexual deviations involve a participant who is either unwilling, uninformed, vulnerable, or too young to give legal consent. Among the clearest examples of such deviations are rape and child sexual abuse. When individuals who practice these deviations come into contact with the law, they are usually known as **sex offenders** and are subjected to a variety of treatments as well as to imprisonment. Some cases of rape and child sexual abuse are examples of paraphilias; others are examples of gratification through aggression or, in the case of child sexual abuse, desire for an easily obtainable and easily coerced sexual partner.

Research on sexual victimization has proceeded in two directions, one dealing with the effects on the victim and the other with the characteristics of perpetrators and the settings in which victimizations occur. Together, these two areas of investigation help us view a complete picture of these abhorrent crimes.

Rape

Rape, or having sexual intercourse forcibly and without the partner's consent, is a seriously underreported crime. Only about 15 to 20 percent of all rapes are reported to authorities—probably because of the emotional trauma experienced by the victim. As we saw in chapter 5, the trauma can be severe. Box 8-3 contains a personal account of the rape experience.

The great majority of convicted rapists are sent to civil prisons for fixed sentences, but some states maintain special treatment facilities for sexual offenders, particularly those who are violent. While both male and female rapes occur, females are overwhelmingly the victims of sexual assaults. However, many cases of male rape—by other males—have been reported in prison populations.

Rapes fall into three general categories: power rape, anger rape, and sadistic rape. In **power rape,** the rapist, who usually feels inadequate and awkward in interpersonal relationships, intimidates the victim with threats of physical harm. In **anger rape,** the rapist seems to be seeking revenge on women in general and expresses his rage through physical and verbal abuse. He seems to get little or no sexual satisfaction from the rape. The third and rarest type, **sadistic rape,** combines sexuality and aggression and focuses on the suffering of the victim (Prentky & Knight, 1991).

In chapter 5, we looked at the effects of rape on its victims. Here the focus is on the rapist. What kinds of men commit these crimes? Can sexual aggression be predicted? Past sexual aggression against adults does tend to be predictive of future sexual aggression against adults (Hall, 1990). But while it is useful to have this informa-

tion, it is also important to know how persons who were not previously sexually aggressive in behavior develop this trait. Many variables may play roles in sexual aggression, including past sexual experiences such as victimization and deviant sexual arousal, general level of willingness to commit aggression, impulsivity, lack of respect for society's rules, deficient social skill, and a tendency to lose control under the influence of alcohol. More research is needed on the effects of these variables individually and in combination.

Men between the ages of 20 and 24 form the largest group arrested for rape. The next most-frequent group are 15- to 19-year-old males. Adolescent males aged 12 through 19 account for almost a quarter of the forcible rapes against all ages of victims (Davis & Leitenberg, 1987). As might be expected, rapes committed by adolescents tend to occur on weekends, at night, and in the summer. Burglary is often committed along with these rapes. Peer pressure seems to be a large factor in rape by adolescents, since sexual assaults are frequently committed as part of a group. In one study, 27 percent of rapes committed by offenders under the age of 21 involved multiple offenders. The proportion of adolescent rapists who are complete strangers to the victim varies widely, ranging from 42 to 91 percent (Vinogradov et al., 1988).

Child Sexual Abuse

As was explained in the section on pedophilia, although pedophilics engage in child sexual abuse, not all child sexual abusers are pedophilics. The child abuser may seek sexual gratification from children because they are available, rather than because of the particular attraction to them seen in pedophilia. Unlike pedophilics, these other child abusers are not drawn exclusively to children as sexual objects and often will choose any of a variety of sexual targets available to them.

According to one review of the evidence, each year in the United States 100,000 to 500,000 children suffer abuse in the form of sexual molestation and a larger number are sexually abused, but they do not report this exploitation for fear of retaliation, embarrassment, or unknown consequences (Fuller, 1989). The very acts that may be the most harmful, those carried out by someone, such as a family member, with continued access to the child, are the least likely to be reported. Special materials—such as dolls—have been developed to help clinicians interview young children to determine whether sexual abuse has occurred (see Figure 8-12). Research is needed to determine the usefulness of such materials. For example, the most common criticism of the dolls is that they are overly suggestive to young, sexually naive children (Everson & Boat, 1994). However, in addition to identifying victims, uses of the dolls

The Rape of a College Student

Extensive clinical observations and research show that sexual assault may have grave consequences for the survivor. These include persistent fear, loss of self-esteem, and problems of relationships, social adjustment, and sexual dysfunction. Depression, social phobia, obsessive-compulsive disorder, and anxiety are among the most frequent long-term consequences. In addition to the trauma stemming from the assault *per se*, survivors frequently worry about contracting a sexually transmitted disease. The emotional trauma of sexual assault, including the fear of sexually transmitted disease, frequently is experienced by persons closest to the survivor, particularly sexual partners (Gosten et al., 1994).

The following account conveys some of the immediate effects of rape and ensuing long-term difficulties.

I left the party to go outside to cool off from dancing. I thought I was alone. Apparently, I was followed from the party. My rapist caught me in a very dark place, threw me down, knocked me out, and raped me.

It would have been to my advantage if I had remained unconscious. But, I regained consciousness just as he was climaxing. At that moment I hated everything that my femininity symbolized. He was deriving the utmost physical pleasure at the cost of my dignity and, more importantly, at the cost of my future.

The cuts and bruises healed but the mental torture remained and will always be

present. Because of him, I lost a year of my life . . .

I lost every ounce of self-confidence I ever had. I had a low opinion of myself because I experienced something which many rape victims experience. I asked myself over and over again if I had "asked for it." For a while, I was convinced that I was a slut and had gotten what I had deserved. This is something which is extremely difficult to overcome. A year and a half later, I still have little self-confidence.

I was once a very trusting person. Now, however, I do not trust men, and I constantly have trouble trusting women. I question people's motives. In the back of my mind, I must feel that everyone has the hate for me that that one person exemplified. It is a very unhealthy and unfair attitude. I realize this, but I still judge harshly . . .

I would give anything to replace this experience with having been discriminated against for a job or something like that. But, my fate is mine and no one else but me can repair the damage done. I hope I live long enough to recapture myself. I miss me.

Hyde, 1994, p. 486

Figure 8-11 One way to deal with the trauma of rape is to take part in a Rape Survivor group. Here one group member participates in a confidence building exercise in which she lists on the blackboard the positive qualities that the other women in the group see in her.

---

include assisting to focus the child's attention in a nonthreatening manner on sexual issues and body parts.

Surveys of child sexual abuse have often yielded very different rates because they used varying definitions of sexual abuse. Some defined sexual abuse in terms of physical contact, ranging from touching or fondling to sexual intercourse or oral-genital or anal-genital contact. Other surveys included noncontact abuse, such as exposure of the offender's genitals or requests for sexual involvement. Partly as a result of these different definitions, and partly as a result of different survey techniques, the survey rates of abuse range widely.

Because child abuse often becomes a legal issue, questions have been raised about whether the truthfulness of children's reports of child abuse could be relied upon. A survey of professionals who frequently deal with child abuse found that, in general, they believed that the reports were accurate (Conte et al., 1991). The factors they considered in authenticating the reports included physical indicators of abuse such as sexually transmitted diseases, tears or enlargements of tissue, age-inappropriate sexual knowledge, children's descriptions that were consistent over time or that detailed a progression of sexual activity, and sexualized play or precocious or seductive behavior during the interview. The only factor

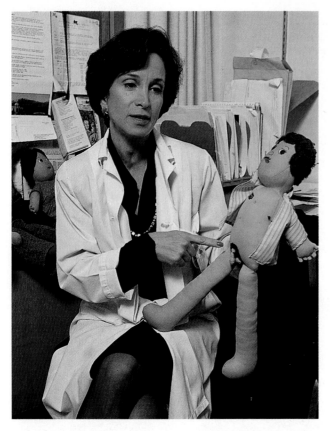

Figure 8-12 Anatomically correct dolls can be used to aid in interviewing child victims of sexual abuse, for court testimony and play therapy. The dolls, available in several racial types, have anal, oral, and genital openings, breasts or penises, and pubic hair. They also have movable tongues and fingers to aid in the description of oral molestation or masturbation.

SOURCE: From Real People Dolls, Hylands Anatomical Dolls, Inc., 4455 Torrance Blvd., Suite 310, Torrance, CA 90503.

that these experts felt might contribute to distortions in the children's reports was their status as subjects in custody battles.

What are the characteristics of families and individuals that may mean a high risk of sexual abuse? Children in step-, foster, and adoptive families seem to be most likely to be victimized (Russell, 1984). Other high-risk groups are children in families where there is marital discord and families in which physical violence and spouse abuse are frequent (Walker, 1984). These groups usually show disruption in family relationships, lack of supervision of children, and focus of attention by the parents on their own concerns rather than on those of the children.

What are the effects of sexual abuse in childhood? In the short term the child may show sexual preoccupation including excessive or public masturbation and an unusual interest in sexual organs and sex play. Another likely result is frequent physical complaints and problems such as rashes, vomiting, and headaches, none of which can be explained by medical examination. Some researchers think that at puberty the problems may intensify. What results carry over into adulthood is unclear. Sexual abuse in childhood may result in problems of depression and low self-esteem as well as in sexual difficulties, either avoidance of sexual contact or, on the other hand, promiscuity or prostitution. Research studies suggest that the kinds of abuse that appear to be the most damaging are those that involve father figures, genital contact, and force (Browne & Finkelhor, 1986).

As reports of sexual abuse of children have increased, ways to protect children are now being carried out. Some information campaigns have concentrated on children's contacts with strangers—for example, "Never get into a car with anyone you don't know," "Never go with someone who says he or she has some candy for you." However, in the majority of reported assaults children are victimized by people they know. To prevent this kind of assault, children need to be taught to recognize signs of trouble and to be assertive enough to report them to a responsible adult. How to accomplish this task represents an important challenge to prevention-oriented researchers.

Incest While definitions of **incest** vary, it is generally recognized as sexual contact between persons who are closely biologically related (for example, father–daughter, mother–son, brother–sister). Most attention has been given to sexual abuse involving a father and daughter. Incest differs from pedophilia in that pedophiles are usually not biologically related to the child they victimize. An important question concerning incest is whether those who commit it also are a danger to children outside the family. One study found that 49 percent of one group of incestuous fathers abused children outside of the family at the same time they were abusing their own children. Of these men, 18 percent were also raping adult women (Abel et al., 1988). Childhood sexual abuse is often associated with poor psychological adjustment and behavior disorders (Cahill et al., 1991; Swett et al., 1990).

CHANGING VIEWS OF SEXUAL BEHAVIOR

A look at history shows that views concerning sexuality have at some times been permissive and at other times restrictive. One area of sexuality in which views have varied both over time and across cultures is sexual preference.

SURVEYS OF SEXUAL BEHAVIOR

Most information concerning sexual practices comes from survey research. Because patterns of sexual practices are known to have changed over time, there is need for frequent surveys that focus on representative samples of the population. The most recent survey found that monogamous couples report having sex most frequently and are the happiest with their lives.

HOMOSEXUALITY

Homosexual behavior refers to sexual behavior with members of one's own sex. Surveys indicate that it is not unusual for people to have at least some experience with homosexual behavior in their lifetimes. **Homosexuality** refers to sexual preference for one's own sex that endures over an extended period. The term **gay** is increasingly used to refer to this behavior because of the feeling that the term has fewer negative associations. Many people who identify themselves as gay adopt this self-label during adolescence.

Attitudes toward Homosexuality Public attitudes have tended to stigmatize homosexual activity to such an extent that many of those engaging in this activity have suffered social and legal mistreatment far beyond the domain of sexual behavior.

Origins of Sexual Orientation It is likely that sexual orientation is the result of multiple determinants in which both psychosocial and biological factors play a role. Bisexual behavior is a sexual orientation in which preferred partners are sometimes of one sex and sometimes of the other.

SEXUAL DYSFUNCTION

A persistent impairment of sexual interest or response is called a **sexual dysfunction.** A sexual dysfunction is often associated with anxiety about performance or cultural inhibitions.

Types of Sexual Dysfunction Sexual problems can occur in any of four stages of the sexual response: appetitive, excitement, orgasm, or resolution. **Erectile dysfunction** refers to the inability of a man to maintain an erection until the completion of intercourse. Problems of erectile dysfunction are often associated with **performance anxiety.** Women may have problems of **inhibited sexual excitement** that result in an inability to maintain a swelling-lubrication response. For women, a problem that often brings them to clinics is **anorgasmia**—the frequent inability to achieve orgasm.

Treatment of Sexual Dysfunction When a person seeks therapy for a sexual dysfunction or disorder, the clinician should get detailed information about medical history, physical symptoms, developmental history, drug and alcohol use, present relationships, and stressors. Sex therapy is often carried out by working with the couple rather than one person. The therapist attempts to decrease fear of failure and to focus on sensory pleasure rather than on the sex act itself. A frequent way of carrying this out is to use **sensate focus,** a sexual retraining technique developed by Masters and Johnson in their pioneering work on sex therapy. Behavioral and cognitive elements are widely used in current treatment of sexual dysfunction. Some therapists use an approach that combines these elements with a more traditional psychodynamic approach. One advocate of such an approach is Kaplan.

The Effectiveness of Sex Therapy More research is needed to interpret the widely differing results reported for sex therapy. Many therapists believe that aspects of the relationship between the members of the couple may be a major force in a negative therapeutic outcome.

GENDER IDENTITY DISORDER

Gender Identity Problems in Childhood Gender indentity refers to a person's sexual self-concept, the feeling of being male or female. In **gender identity disorder of childhood,** children who have not yet reached puberty express extreme distress at their gender and intense desires to be of the opposite sex.

Gender Identity Disorder in Adults Transsexualism refers to the intense desire by adults to change not only their sexual identity but also their anatomical status. Adults who have **nontranssexual gender identity disorder** are uncomfortable with their assigned sex and may frequently **cross-dress,** that is, wear clothes of the opposite sex. However, they are not preoccupied with changing their physical sexual characteristics the way that transsexuals are.

THE PARAPHILIAS

The term **paraphilia** means attraction to the deviant. Three general classes of paraphilias include: preference for use of nonhuman objects for sexual arousal, sexual activity with humans with sexual arousal based on real or simulated suffering or humiliation, and repetitive sexual activity with nonconsenting partners.

Fetishism Fetishism refers to the use of a nonliving object as a primary source of sexual arousal and consummation.

Transvestic Fetishism. **Transvestic fetishism** refers to someone who seeks sexual stimulation through cross-dressing. Transvestic fetishists continue to identify with their biological sex, and when not cross-dressed, show behaviors and interests consistent with their sex. Covert sensitization has been used successfully in treating transvestic fetishists.

Sexual Sadism and Masochism A **sadist** achieves orgasm through humiliating or inflicting pain on others. A **masochist** achieves sexual gratification and orgasm under circumstances of humiliation and ill treatment by others. Sadism and masochism occur in both heterosexual and homosexual relationships.

Voyeurism Voyeurism refers to the achievement of sexual gratification through watching or spying upon others, particularly when they are dressing, undressing, or engaging in sexual activity. The socially forbidden nature of the activity seems to be a major factor in producing the voyeur's sexual excitement.

Exhibitionism Exhibitionists are males who gain sexual arousal from exposing their genitals to strangers in public settings.

Pedophilia A pedophile targets children as the main source of sexual gratification. Pedophilic behavior includes a variety of types: forcing the child to fondle the adult's sexual organs, the sexual fondling and caressing of the child by an adult, and attempted or actual intercourse.

Perspectives on the Paraphilias Each of the perspectives have something to offer in understanding the paraphilias. Because many of the paraphilic behaviors are carried out in private and only occasionally come to public attention, and because they vary so greatly, little research has been carried out on them and their causes are poorly understood. Conventional psychotherapy seems ineffective in treating paraphilias. Biological treatments involving hormones have been used but long-term effects have not yet been evaluated. Behavioral therapy using aversion techniques has been tried but is found objectionable by many people on ethical grounds. Cognitive-behavioral approaches involving covert desensitization may be helpful in some cases.

SEXUAL VICTIMIZATION

Sex offenders are those who come into contact with the law because their sexual deviations involve a participant who is unwilling, uninformed, vulnerable, or too young to give legal consent. Some of these sexual offenses are examples of paraphilias, while others are related to gratification of aggressive impulses or the desire for an easily obtainable sexual partner.

Rape Rape is defined as forcible sexual intercourse with an unconsenting partner. A number of personal characteristics may play a role in the likelihood of carrying out a rape. These include past experiences of sexual victimization, deviant sexual arousal, aggressive or impulsive behaviors, social skills deficits, and a tendency to lose control under the influence of alcohol.

Child Sexual Abuse Because of differences in the definition of child sexual abuse, results of surveys concerning its frequency vary widely. The number of cases reported is also much smaller than those presumed to have occurred, partly because abuse by a family member is often not reported at the time.

Incest Incest refers to sexual contact between persons who are biologically related. An incestuous relationship as a child is often associated with poor psychological adjustment and behavior disorders in adulthood.

CHAPTER NINE

Jim Dine, *The Storage Jars,* 1991.
Enamel, oil and epoxy on bronze, cloth, steel and wood bookshelf: 78 X 47 X 31, five jars: 33″ high.
Photo courtesy PaceWildenstein, New York.

PERSONALITY DISORDERS

John, a 50-year-old retired policeman, sought treatment a few weeks after his dog had been run over and died. Since that time he had felt sad, tired, and had experienced trouble sleeping and concentrating.

John lived alone, and for many years had virtually no conversational contacts with other human beings beyond a "Hello" or "How are you?" He preferred to be by himself, found talk a waste of time, and felt awkward when other people tried to initiate a relationship. He occasionally spent some time in a bar, but always off by himself and not really following the general conversation. He read newspapers avidly, and was well informed in many areas, but took no particular interest in the people around him. He was employed as a security guard, but was known by fellow workers as a "cold fish" and a "loner." They no longer even noticed or teased him, especially since he never seemed to notice or care about their teasing anyway.

John floated through life without relationships except for that with his dog, which he dearly loved. At Christmas he would buy the dog elaborate gifts and, in return, would receive a wrapped bottle of scotch that he bought for himself as a gift from the dog. The loss of his pets had been the only events in his life that had caused him sadness. He experienced the death of his parents without emotion, and felt no regret whatever at being completely out of contact with the rest of his family. He considered himself different from other people, and regarded emotionality in others with bewilderment.

—Adapted from Spitzer et al., 1989, pp. 249–250

Dr. B., a 41-year-old family practitioner, was getting ready to leave his office at 6 P.M. to rush home and have supper before attending his son's final high school basketball game. The hospital called to inform him that one of his obstetric patients had arrived in Labor and Delivery and was currently showing 5 cm of cervical dilation. He knew that one of his partners was covering obstetrics that night, but he felt compelled to run by the hospital to check her before going home. After checking her, he decided to stay through the delivery, necessitating his missing his son's last game. After the delivery, the physician sat in the locker room and wept. He felt terribly guilt-ridden over missing the game, and as he reflected on the evening, he could not understand why he had not simply handed the case over to his partner. He poignantly stated later that he was not even emotionally attached to this particular patient. His own narcissism had gotten the best of him: i.e., he felt that he and he alone had to be the one to deliver the baby, as though his partner could not have performed exactly the same function.

—Gabbard, 1985, p. 2928

What do these two men have in common? How are they different? Do they have problems of clinical proportions?

John sought treatment because he feels terribly distraught. However, most clinicians would be confident that John also has some sort of mental disorder because of the extreme intensity of his reaction to the death of his dog and the time the reaction has lasted. His Axis I diagnosis (see chapter 4) would probably be adjustment disorder with depressed mood because his distress is clearly linked to an identifiable stressor, the dog's death. But this Axis I classification does not completely capture all the major features of John's life. His longstanding pattern of not wanting or enjoying close relationships with other people, including his family, always choosing solitary activities, and only rarely experiencing strong emotions, coupled with an absence of oddities and eccentricities of behavior, speech, or thought, is indicative of schizoid personality disorder, an Axis II classification. Clinicians would maintain that it was the presence of the schizoid personality disorder that made John particularly vulnerable to the stress of his pet's death.

Dr. B. is probably not suffering from a mental disorder of any kind, but he may be somewhat compulsive when it comes to feeling responsible for his patients' welfare. When that compulsivity gets out of hand it can cause him temporary distress as it did in this case. Yet he seems to be functioning well in his medical practice and his personality style is shared by many physicians who often feel an exaggerated sense of responsibility (Gabbard, 1985). This style may show itself in both adaptive and maladaptive ways. In one poll of 100 randomly selected physicians, all of them described themselves as "compulsive personalities" (Krakowski, 1982).

John's and Dr. B.'s cases illustrate what both clinicians and the public would agree on—that everyone has a distinctive set of personal characteristics and that these traits affect behavior. John's life style seems to have contributed to his protracted bereavement, while Dr. B.'s compulsivity probably makes him the dedicated doctor he is (although, along with that dedication, there are occasional temporary personal upsets, such as missing his son's game).

A person's characteristic ways of responding are often referred to as his or her **personality.** Most people's personality styles do not affect their behavior similarly in all situations. Personality styles can be maladaptive if an individual is unable to modify his or her behavior when the environment undergoes significant changes that call for different approaches. If personality characteristics are not flexible enough to allow an individual to respond adaptively to at least an ordinary variety of situations, a disorder may be present.

When personality styles become pathological, they can impair an individual's functioning in important situations and can lead to anxiety, feelings of distress, and unhappiness. The point at which a personality style becomes a personality disorder is unclear. **Personality disorders** are longstanding, maladaptive, and inflexible ways of relating to the environment. Such disorders can usually be noticed in childhood or at least by early adolescence, and may continue through adult life. They severely limit an individual's approach to stress-producing situations because his or her characteristic styles of thinking and behavior allow for only a rigid and narrow range of responses. Studies of personality disorders within the general population estimate their prevalence to be between 10 and 13 percent (Weissman, 1993).

Classifying Personality Disorders

Personality disorders pose problems for people who construct classification systems, as well as for textbook writers and teachers of abnormal psychology. They seem important, and their existence can easily be recognized even by nonprofessional observers, yet little is known about their origins and development. With the exception of the antisocial personality disorder, and until recently the borderline personality disorder, very little research has been done on these problems, probably because they often are not dramatic or severely incapacitating and many people who might have such a disorder never seek help in dealing with their problems.

Although the maladaptive behavior that is typical of personality disorders sometimes causes great distress to the people involved, they find it difficult to change the way they think about and respond to situations. The clinical problems are intensified when, as is usually the case, the person does not regard his or her behavior patterns as maladaptive or undesirable, even if the unpleasant and counterproductive consequences of those behaviors are obvious to others. As we will see in this chapter, this situation is perhaps most evident in cases of antisocial personality.

Personality disorders are diagnosed on DSM-IV's Axis II. Mental retardation is also diagnosed on this axis. Because these two conditions have in common a lifetime or near-lifetime duration and stability, there are not likely to be periods of improvement or change. A diagnosis of personality disorder can be made only when a person's inflexible long-lasting behavior pattern or personality style causes important problems in social situations or on the job, or when it results in a high level of personal distress. Table 9-1 lists three groups of major personality disorders; Figure 9-1 shows their frequency as well as how that frequency is divided between men and women.

Unlike the near permanent disorders diagnosed on Axis II, Axis I disorders, called **symptom disorders,** may

---

TABLE 9–1
Major Personality Disorders and Their Characteristics

Odd or Eccentric Behavior

1. *Paranoid:* Tense; guarded; suspicious; holds grudges
2. *Schizoid:* Socially isolated with restricted emotional expression
3. *Schizotypal:* Peculiarities of thought, appearance, and behavior that are disconcerting to others; emotionally detached and isolated

Dramatic, Emotional, or Erratic Behavior

1. *Antisocial:* Manipulative; exploitive; dishonest; disloyal; lacking in guilt; habitually breaks social rules; childhood history of such behavior; often in trouble with the law
2. *Borderline:* Cannot stand to be alone; intense, unstable moods and personal relationships; chronic anger; drug and alcohol abuse
3. *Histrionic:* Seductive behavior; needs immediate gratification and constant reassurance; rapidly changing moods; shallow emotions
4. *Narcissistic:* Self-absorbed; expects special treatment and adulation; envious of attention to others

Anxious or Fearful Behavior

1. *Avoidant:* Easily hurt and embarrassed; few close friends; sticks to routines to avoid new and possibly stressful experiences
2. *Dependent:* Wants others to make decisions; needs constant advice and reassurance; fears being abandoned
3. *Obsessive-compulsive:* Perfectionistic; overconscientious; indecisive; preoccupied with details; stiff; unable to express affection

---

come or go. Symptom disorders may be triggered by events or environmental factors and may disappear when conditions change, or when a person is taught new behaviors. People with Axis I disorders often see themselves as having personal problems (symptoms) that are troublesome and require treatment. People with Axis II disorders are far more likely to say that their difficulties are attributable to the environment (for example, their family or co-workers) and that they do not need clinical treatment.

Frequently a person has both a personality disorder and a symptom disorder. The relationship between personality disorders and symptom disorders is unclear, but the relationship is obviously a close one. One theory holds that personality disorders may be thought of as vulnerabilities, with each personality disorder associated with vulnerability to only some of the symptom disorders. For example, schizotypal personalities are thought to be susceptible to schizophrenia, dependent personalities to depression, avoidant personalities to social phobias, and borderline and antisocial personalities to drug and alcohol abuse. While this idea of increased vulnerability has some support, it is not a certainty. Another classification scheme might include personality disorders as milder forms of symptom disorders. For example, schizotypal disorder might be a mild form of schizophrenia and borderline disorder might be a form of mood disorder.

In some instances, the classification statements of Axis II are used to provide information that bears on the primary diagnosis of Axis I. In other cases, a personality disorder referred to on Axis II is the individual's major problem. Many combinations are possible. A person may have a diagnosis on both Axes I and II. For example, Henry A. had psychotic symptoms that called for a diagnosis of schizophrenia. Before his present schizophrenic episode, however, Henry A. had shown several characteristics—odd speech, social isolation, suspiciousness, and hypersensitivity to real or imagined criticism—that had significantly impaired his effectiveness in a variety of situations. Because of the different types of behaviors Henry A. showed, he was diagnosed using both Axis I and Axis II. The term "premorbid" means that before the schizophrenic symptoms developed, the personality disorder already existed.

- Axis I: Schizophrenia, paranoid, chronic
- Axis II: Schizotypal personality disorder (premorbid)

In another case, Gerry B. showed similar personality characteristics, but there was no basis for an Axis I diagnosis. Her diagnosis would be as follows.

- Axis I: _____
- Axis II: Schizotypal personality disorder

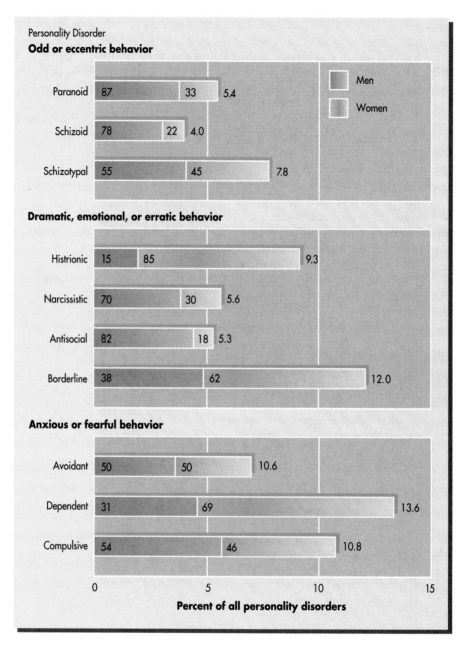

Figure 9-1 Not all personality disorders occur with equal frequency and not all affect men and women equally. Each bar shows what percent of all personality disorders is represented by each disorder. The different colored portions of each bar represent the proportion of men and women given this diagnosis. The total does not add up to 100 percent because some personality disorders do not fit any of these categories.

SOURCE: Data from Millon, 1986.

A third individual, Deborah C., had characteristics of the same personality disorder seen in Henry A. and Gerry B. However, she had additional characteristics that fit another personality disorder. In this case both personality disorders would be diagnosed.

- Axis I: _____
- Axis II: Schizotypal personality disorder; borderline personality disorder

Personality disorders produce relatively unreliable diagnostic classifications. One difficulty in deciding on the appropriateness of an Axis II diagnosis is the unclear boundary between those personality characteristics within normal limits and those representing disordered behavior. Another problem is that some of the Axis II categories overlap a great deal. Rather than being separate disorders, they represent different degrees of the same general behaviors. In fact, about two thirds of the patients who meet the criteria for one personality disorder will also meet the criteria for at least one more (Widiger, 1991). A third problem is that some personality disorders also overlap Axis I categories. For instance, in one study more than half of the individuals who were diagnosed as borderline also had a major affective disorder (Frances & Widiger, 1986). Recent research has shown that when clinicians use standardized interviews (interviews following a structured format) their interrater reliability is higher than for clinicians who conduct relatively freewheeling interviews (Loranger et al., 1994; Zimmerman, 1994).

If disorders are to be classified into separate types, their criteria should be distinct and mutually exclusive, and the number of ambiguous cases should be relatively few. Some DSM categories—for example, schizophrenia, the affective disorders, and the organic disorders—are relatively distinct from each other, although there are some fuzzy areas between them. But as we have seen, this is not true of personality disorders, many of whose diagnostic criteria overlap.

Some of these classification problems come about because so little is known about most personality disorders. Another difficulty stems from the so-called **prototypal approach** used in DSM-IV. Each disorder has a list of possible characteristics, and if more than a specific number are met, the diagnosis of that disorder is given. This means that no single listed characteristic must necessarily be shared by everyone diagnosed with a particular personality disorder. For instance, for a diagnosis of paranoid personality disorder, a person must have any four from a list of seven characteristics. This means that any two people given this classification might have quite different characteristics (Livesley et al., 1994).

Despite the drawbacks and uncertainties associated with the disorders listed in DSM-IV Axis II, the attempt to incorporate personality disorders into the classification process still represents a major advance. Prior to DSM-III, the diagnosis of mental disorders gave primary attention to the more obvious conditions now classified on Axis I. DSM-III's placement of the personality disorders on a separate axis highlights their importance to, coexistence with, and contribution to other disorders. In this way, Axis II represents a pioneering step toward a classification system applicable to the whole person. As research proceeds on this novel approach to diagnosis, it is likely that ways will be found to solve some of the classification problems mentioned above.

In this chapter, we will discuss the personality disorders in terms of the three groupings outlined in Table 9-1: odd or eccentric behaviors; dramatic, emotional or erratic behaviors; and fearful or anxious behaviors. While there are a number of other reasonable categorizations, this grouping provides an approachable structure for understanding these disorders.

Odd or Eccentric Behavior

Disorders in this group are marked by odd, eccentric, isolative, or suspicious behavior. Individuals with a diagnosis falling within this group may read hidden demeaning or threatening meanings into benign remarks, seem detached from social relationships, and have difficulty forming close relationships.

Paranoid Personality Disorder

People with **paranoid personality disorder** have several outstanding characteristics: unwarranted feelings of suspiciousness and mistrust of other people; hypersensitivity; the expectation—without sufficient justification—that they will be exploited or harmed by others; and a tendency to read hidden demeaning or threatening messages into benign remarks or events (for example, suspecting that a neighbor put out trash early to annoy them). It is very difficult for such people to have close relationships with others because they are constantly expecting treachery. The following case provides an account of a typical paranoid personality.

A 36-year-old single white male engineer was referred for psychiatric evaluation, with his grudging cooperation, by his project manager. He described his current work situation as very tense because his co-workers had been "ganging up" on him, giving him the most difficult assignments and sometimes removing the crucial information he needed from the relevant files. He said they did this "because they like to see me sweat." He had changed jobs four times in the past six years because of similar problems at previous jobs. Aside from his frequent contact with a sibling, the patient was socially isolated. He stated, "I've never trusted people. All they want to do is take advantage of you." He was tense, aloof, and obviously very angry at his co-workers. He was hypervigilant and made several comments indicating that he felt that the interviewer might not "see things my way." There was no evidence of psychosis or depression.

—Siever and Kendler, 1986, p. 199

Paranoid individuals rarely seek clinical help. If a situation becomes so difficult that they are forced to seek help (for example, if they are required to work closely with other people), the therapist's hardest task is to penetrate the barrier of suspiciousness. They are also hypersensitive to criticism, making it especially difficult for them to function in subordinate positions. They have a strong fear of losing independence and the power to shape events. Just the feeling of being in a position of lower rank or lesser power might be intolerable (Akhtar, 1990).

People with paranoid personality disorder often seem cold, humorless, devious, and scheming. These characteristics do not promote close, rewarding relationships. Perhaps because people with this kind of personality keep to themselves and rarely become intimate with others, many of their unusual ideas remain unnoticed. Their performance is often impaired because their preoccupation with searching for hidden motives and special meanings limits their ability to consider and understand whole situations. When problems occur, they are often work-related, since work is an area in which interpersonal contacts are difficult to avoid.

Table 9-2 lists the major clinical features in DSM-IV Axis II of paranoid personalities. As we stated earlier, all of the features do not have to be present for this classification to be used—four or more of the characteristics might justify use of the diagnosis.

Schizoid Personality Disorder

Individuals with **schizoid personality disorder** are reserved, socially withdrawn, and seclusive (see Figure 9-2). They prefer solitary work activities and hobbies and lack the capacity for warm, close relationships. Such people rarely express their feelings directly. Not only do they have few relationships with others, but they also seem to have little desire for them. In any case, they often have poor social skills, although their speech and behavior patterns are not unusual or eccentric. They also lack a sense of humor and seem detached from their environment. When, in her book *The White Album*, Joan Didion uses the phrase "only marginally engaged in the dailiness of life," she could be describing the detachment of people with schizoid personality disorders. Perhaps because of this detachment, males with schizoid personality disorder seldom marry. Females are more likely to marry, possibly by accepting a marriage offer rather than seeking it.

John, whose social isolation was described at the beginning of the chapter, would probably be described as having a schizoid personality disorder. Although the

Figure 9-2 Spending time alone, withdrawn from others, is typical of people with schizoid personality disorders. They often appear quite detached from life around them.

man in the following example did not complain of social isolation (and schizoid individuals rarely do), his stable solitary existence was a central part of his personality. He also showed a rigidity in his personal life and was not concerned about others' opinions of him as long as they let him alone.

> A 46-year-old single white male accountant sought professional consultation on the advice of a colleague because of persistent feelings of dissatisfaction and depression following a change in his work situation. Although he retained his position at his firm, where he had worked for 20 years, many of his more important responsibilities had been shifted to a younger colleague. He had always worked well in a rather autonomous position in the firm but now felt that his daily work routine had been disrupted and he no longer had meaningful tasks to accomplish. It turned out that he had always been socially isolated, with social contacts limited to acquaintances at work, and followed a rather prescribed pattern of reading the newspaper and watching television as his evening recreation. He at times saw a married sister and her family on weekends. This limited life style had been tolerable for him for some time and he appeared relatively indifferent to the opinions of co-workers as long as he could count on being assigned his quota of accounts. His redefined position left him with less work to do and an unclear role in the firm. He felt as if "the rug had been pulled out from under me." In the consultation, he was a quiet man who, although cooperative,

TABLE 9–2
Clinical Features of Paranoid Personality Disorder

A person having at least four of these characteristics might be considered to have a paranoid personality disorder.

1. Expects, without sufficient basis, to be exploited or harmed by others.
2. Questions, without justification, the loyalty or trustworthiness of peers and associates.
3. Reads hidden demeaning or threatening meanings into benign remarks or events.
4. Bears grudges or is unforgiving of insults or slights.
5. Is reluctant to confide in others because of unwarranted fear that the information will be used against him or her.
6. Perceives attacks on his or her character or reputation that are not apparent to others and is quick to react with anger or to counterattack.
7. Has recurrent suspicions, without justification, regarding fidelity of spouse or sexual partner.

was difficult to engage affectively. He spoke with little emotion and mumbled at times, exhibiting no sense of attachment to other people in his life, but only to his "way of doing things," which he had great difficulty in changing.

—Siever and Kendler, 1986, p. 192

The emotional responses of schizoid individuals seem rather flat as well as cold. The kinds of frustrations that arouse expressions of anger in most people elicit little observable hostility from these individuals. They often seem vague, self-absorbed, absent-minded, and not very aware of or interested in what is going on around them. Some of these people can support themselves if they find socially isolated jobs. Many of them, however, have problems at work because of the contact with other people that most jobs require. Since schizoid people are not bothered by their lack of personal relationships, they are poor prospects for therapy (Akhtar, 1987).

Table 9-3 lists the clinical features of schizoid personalities described in DSM-IV. As with all the personality disorders, the presence of every feature is not required for use of the classification.

Schizotypal Personality Disorder

People with **schizotypal personality disorder** are characterized by oddities of thinking, perceiving, communicating, and behaving. These deviations are never as extreme as those found in cases of full-blown schizophrenia. Still, clinicians often feel the need to probe for the possibility of major distortions, such as hearing voices and having ideas that do not seem to make sense. Box 9-1 shows how clinicians explore these possibilities.

People with schizotypal personality disorder, like schizoid individuals, are seclusive, emotionally shallow, and socially unskilled. The speech patterns of the two

---

TABLE 9–3
Clinical Features of Schizoid Personality Disorder

A person having at least four of these characteristics might be considered to have a schizoid personality disorder.

1. Neither desires nor enjoys close relationships, including being part of a family.
2. Almost always chooses solitary activities.
3. Few, if any, activities provide pleasure.
4. Indicates little, if any, desire to have sexual experiences with another person.
5. Appears indifferent to the praise or criticism of others.
6. No close friends or confidants (or only one).
7. Shows emotional coldness, detachment, and little variation in emotions.

---

groups are quite different. People with a schizoid personality disorder have no oddities of speech although they may lack social skills. Those with a schizotypal personality disorder, on the other hand, often are not understood because they either use unusual words and phrases or use common words in unusual ways. They also are likely to express ideas unclearly. At times—usually when they are under stress—their thinking deteriorates and they may express ideas that seem delusional. These cognitive and perceptual characteristics are probably the most important ones in distinguishing schizotypal personality disorder from borderline and schizoid personality disorders (Widiger et al., 1987).

The behavior of people with a schizotypal personality disorder may, at times, border on the bizarre. Much of the time they seem suspicious, superstitious, and aloof. The following case illustrates a number of the characteristics of schizotypal personality disorder.

A 41-year-old man was referred to a community mental health center's activities program for help in improving his social skills. He had a lifelong pattern of social isolation, with no real friends, and spent long hours worrying that his angry thoughts about his older brother would cause his brother harm. He had previously worked as a clerk in civil service, but had lost his job because of poor attendance and low productivity.

On interview the patient was distant and somewhat distrustful. He described in elaborate and often irrelevant detail his rather uneventful and routine daily life. He told the interviewer that he had spent an hour and a half in a pet store deciding which of two brands of fish food to buy, and explained their relative merits. For two days he had studied the washing instructions on a new pair of jeans—Did "Wash before wearing" mean that the jeans were to be washed before wearing the first time, or did they need, for some reason, to be washed each time before they were worn? He did not regard concerns such as these as senseless, though he acknowledged that the amount of time spent thinking about them might be excessive. When asked about his finances, he could recite from memory his most recent monthly bank statement, including the amount of every check and the running balance as each check was written. He knew his balance on any particular day, but sometimes got anxious if he considered whether a certain check or deposit had actually cleared.

He asked the interviewer whether, if he joined the program, he would be required to participate in groups. He said that groups made him very nervous, and he was unsure if he could "stand" participating in them.

—Spitzer et al., 1989, p. 154

Noteworthy features of this case include the absence of close friends or confidants, belief that he has magical powers (worrying that his angry thoughts would cause

Probing for Schizotypal Thinking

The following interview was productive because of the interviewer's sensitivity and ability to communicate empathy for the patient's feelings and thoughts.

I (Interviewer):   Where shall we begin?

P (Patient):   I may as well start with them, the character disorders.

I: Tell me about them!

P: I think the people who give you the most trouble—that's who they are.

I: It sounds as if some people bother you a lot.

P: You see, it all depends. I hate the character disorders who are cruel and who hurt you. You can feel their aggressive thoughts, but I quit my job so they can't get at me anymore.

I: It must feel awful to be harassed by those people.

P: I just have to stay away from them.

I: Did they try to harm or persecute you?

P: It's their thoughtlessness that hurts you.

I: Have they ever tried to follow you, observe your house, tap your phone, bug your bedroom, or living room?

P: No, but I'm surprised that you ask. Are you in tune with them?

I: I want to understand how they bother you, how they get to you.

P: The way they look at you, the way they don't talk to you.

I: Have you heard any voices ever?

P: My own thoughts, I think them in words. I imagine how they would sound if I were to speak them out loud. There is the quality of sound in thoughts. Thoughts go beyond

people. They interconnect and survive.

I: Do you have access to those interconnecting thoughts? Are you familiar with ESP?

P: I can sense them, I can sense the hostile thoughts of the character disorders.

I: Tell me about these character disorders! Who are they?

P: Those people who impose on your thoughts—you meet them everywhere. These thoughtless, callous mental morons.

I: Do you think they are like a fraternity? Sticking together and conspiring against you?

P: No, they are not like a conspiracy—more here and there, you know, just like people you meet and don't like. I don't think they are organized. It's more like a mind game.

—Othmer and Othmer, 1994, pp. 414–415

---

his brother harm), constricted affect (reflected in his being "distant" in the interview), odd speech (providing elaborate and often irrelevant details), and social anxiety. Because of this man's eccentricities of thought and speech he would be classified as schizotypal rather than schizoid.

Schizotypal individuals probably have more than the average risk of an episode of schizophrenia later in life. A 15-year follow-up of patients with schizotypal personality disorder suggests that this category represents a borderline group between health and schizophrenia (McGlashan, 1986). Since many cases of schizophrenia are presumed to have a hereditary, biological component, schizotypal individuals probably share this genetic characteristic. There is evidence that schizotypal personality disorder is common among individuals who have a twin or close relative with the disorder (Torgersen et al., 1993).

Table 9-4 lists clinical features of schizotypal personality disorder. Persons with paranoid, schizoid, and schizotypal personality disorders have in common a degree of social detachment and the presence of "odd" or idiosyncratic behavior that can be observed in much more extreme form in schizophrenia. Paranoid personality disorder focuses attention on suspiciousness and mistrust of others; schizoid personality disorder on the

TABLE 9-4
Clinical Features of Schizotypal Personality Disorder

A person having at least five of these characteristics might be considered to have a schizotypal personality disorder.

1. Inappropriate ideas of reference (the belief that the conversation, smiling, or other actions of people have reference to oneself).
2. Excessive social anxiety that does not diminish with familiarity and tends to be associated with paranoid fears rather than negative judgments.
3. Odd beliefs or thinking that one has magical powers (e.g., "others can feel my feelings").
4. Unusual perceptual experiences including bodily illusions.
5. Odd speech and thinking (e.g., very vague, circumstantial, overelaborate).
6. Paranoid ideas or suspiciousness.
7. Odd or eccentric behavior or appearance (e.g., unusual mannerisms, talking to self, odd speech).
8. No close friends or confidants (or perhaps only one) other than relatives, primarily because of lack of desire for contact, pervasive discomfort with others, or eccentricities.
9. Inappropriate or constricted affect (e.g., is cold, aloof).

preference for solitary activities, without there necessarily being distortions in perceptions of reality; and schizotypal personality disorder focuses on eccentricity and cognitive-perceptual distortions. Because of overlaps among these odd and eccentric behaviors and between them and some other Axis II and Axis I classifications, there is no complete agreement about their clinical uniqueness. Agreement is probably least for schizotypal personality disorder because research has shown that it is often closely related to schizophrenia and might simply be a weak form of that disorder (Siever et al., 1991). However, the schizotypal classification does meet the Axis II requirements of enduring patterns of perceiving, relating to, and thinking about the environment and oneself. The criteria for schizotypal personality disorder refer to persistent disturbances in perception and cognition of relations between self and others. These disturbances are not limited to periods of stress; they are present virtually all the time. Research is needed to establish the contribution this Axis II classification can make to the diagnostic process.

Dramatic, Emotional, or Erratic Behavior

The first group of personality disorders, which we have just reviewed, is composed of individuals with withdrawn behavior. The second category contains people who seek attention and whose behavior is often highly noticeable and very unpredictable.

Histrionic Personality Disorder

For people with **histrionic personality disorder,** getting the attention of others is a high priority (see Figure 9-3). Their motto might be "All the world's a stage"; in interpersonal relationships, they often act out a role, such as "the star" or "the victim." These people strike others as vain and immature and tend to speak in a dramatic, exaggerated, and gushing manner.

This classification is used in cases that are marked by exaggerated expression of emotion, stormy interpersonal relationships, a self-centered attitude, and manipulativeness. The manipulativeness might manifest itself in suicidal gestures, threats, or attempts, as well as in other attention-getting behaviors such as dramatic physical complaints. Histrionic patients often come to the attention of therapists because of a drug overdose or other form of suicide attempt.

Histrionic individuals often react too quickly to situations that require some analysis and thought. They don't always focus their attention long enough to perceive the details of a situation, and as a result they tend to respond with emotionally tinged generalities. When people with histrionic personalities are asked to describe

Figure 9-3 Histrionic personalities may be overly concerned with physical attractiveness and making a striking or dramatic impression.

something, they generally respond with impressions rather than facts. For example, a therapist who was taking a case history from a client and had made repeated efforts to get a description of the client's father reported that the patient "seemed . . . hardly to understand the sort of data I was interested in, and the best she could provide was, 'My father? He was wham-bang! That's all—just wham-bang!'" (Shapiro, 1965, p. 111).

Histrionic individuals often operate on hunches and tend to stop at the obvious. Not only are they suggestible and easily influenced by the opinions of others, but they are also easy to distract. Their attention is easily captured and just as easily turned toward something else. Thus, their behavior has a scattered quality. These problems of attention also lead histrionic people to appear incredibly naive about many commonplace things.

Psychoanalyst Anthony Storr (1980) has interpreted histrionic behavior as a pattern that is often adopted by individuals who do not feel able to compete with others on equal terms and believe that no one is paying attention to them. Storr thinks that such people may have been disregarded by their parents as children. Although the child repeatedly tried to get the parents to think of him or her as an individual, those attempts failed. The child then became demanding and resorted to all kinds of dramatic behaviors in order to be noticed. This interpretation may help to explain another characteristic of these histrionic individuals—their frequent complaints of poor health—for example, weakness or headaches. The less attention the parents paid to the child, the more the child had to shout or dramatize to get their attention. Histrionic individuals carry these extreme behaviors into adulthood.

Perhaps because of such childhood experience, histrionic people may also feel unlovable and may react to this feeling by trying to make themselves sexually irresistible. Women in particular may dress and behave seductively yet not really desire intimate sexual activity. Women are more likely than men to be diagnosed as histrionic (Pfohl, 1991). Table 9-5 lists several clinical features frequently observed in cases of histrionic personality disorder. In the following case, the interviewer inquires about a sleep problem for which the patient was seeking clinical consultation.

I: *Tell me about your sleep problems.*

P: *Oh, it's terrible. There are whole nights when I can't sleep at all. I toss and turn, and I get up in the morning without having closed my eyes for even a second.*

I: *This happens only some nights?*

P: *It happens when I have these terrible, terrible fights with my husband. He just tears me to pieces. (Patient rolls her eyes dramatically upward.)*

I: *Does he or anybody else notice what you are going through?*

P: *They don't have the foggiest idea. I can scream and yell and they still don't understand.*

I: *When you have these fights, is your mood affected?*

P: *I get these devastating depressions and I have to cry the whole time.*

—Othmer and Othmer, 1989, p. 402

Even though this patient talks freely, she isn't able to provide needed information. For example, she is unable to describe precisely the circumstances of the fights with her husband. She expresses her suffering in an exaggerated way typical of histrionic personality disorder and she is reluctant to furnish the facts.

Narcissistic Personality Disorder

The word "narcissism" comes from the classical myth about a young man, Narcissus, who fell in love with his reflection in a pond. Because he could never grasp his own image, he despaired and died of his own anguish.

TABLE 9–5
Clinical Features of Histrionic Personality Disorder

A person having at least five of these characteristics might be considered to have a histrionic personality disorder.

1. Rapidly shifting, but basically shallow, expressions of emotions.
2. Overly concerned with physical attractiveness.
3. Inappropriately sexually seductive in appearance or behavior.
4. Uncomfortable when not the center of attention.
5. Excessively impressionistic speech, which lacks detail.
6. Intolerant of, or excessively frustrated by, situations that do not work out exactly as desired.
7. Apparent view of relationships as possessing greater intimacy than is actually the case (e.g., refers to an acquaintance as a "dear, dear friend").
8. Exaggerated expressions of emotion with much self-dramatization.

Several critical factors play roles in **narcissistic personality disorder:** an extreme sense of self-importance and the expectation of special favors, a need for constant attention, fragile self-esteem, and lack of empathy or caring for others (see Figure 9-4). People with a narcissistic personality disorder are often preoccupied with fantasies of unlimited success and brilliance, power, beauty, and ideal love relationships. They may think of their problems as unique and feel that only other equally special people are able to understand them. The case of Robert Graham illustrates many of the characteristics of narcissistic personality disorder.

Graham, a successful 30-year-old actor, contacted a therapist because he was having trouble with a new stage role. In it he had to play a character who was deeply depressed by the death of his wife. As Graham said, he had trouble portraying "a character who was so involved with a woman that his life essentially ended simply because she died."

In his first interview he told the therapist what a good actor he was. "I don't wish to be immodest, but I am uniquely talented." Throughout his life he had been told he was "uniquely cute" and "gifted." He could be charming and entertaining and used these abilities to make other people feel "special" as a way of furthering his career. He seemed to respond to others with a feeling of contempt and remarked that other people were gullible and "easily taken in by experiences."

Graham's relations with women puzzled him. He began dating and had sexual activity early and had romances with a series of women as he grew older. However, in each romance he would gradually lose interest after a short period and usu-

Figure 9-4 Even if they do not have the characteristics that would result in a diagnosis of narcissistic personality disorder, many theatrical performers are very high in narcissism. The characteristics of performers' jobs may increase whatever narcissistic tendencies they already possess. Their success often demands that they focus great attention on their youthful appearance, personal attractiveness, and other aspects of their self-image. Adoration by fans may also increase performers' feelings of self-absorption and of being special people.

ally start an affair with another woman before breaking off with the first. He gave little thought to his former partner after breaking off each relationship. "It is almost as if people are playthings and I need lots and lots of new toys." His account of his life sounded as if he had never grieved or been depressed.

—Adapted from Spitzer et al., 1983, pp. 71–74

Table 9-6 lists characteristics frequently seen in narcissistic personality disorder. As with other personality disorders, all clinical features do not have to be present for the classification to be used. Rather, the characteristics in the table can be viewed as a prototype or composite of narcissistic disorders. The presence of more than half the features in a given case would justify use of the diagnosis.

The category of narcissistic personality disorder was introduced into DSM because mental-health professionals were seeing an increase in cases in which the prob-

TABLE 9–6
Clinical Features of Narcissistic Personality Disorder

A person having at least five of these characteristics might be considered to have a narcissistic personality disorder.
1. Grandiose sense of self-importance, exaggeration of personal achievements and talents, and need for recognition of one's superiority by others.
2. Preoccupations with fantasies of unlimited success, power, and beauty.
3. Sense of one's specialness and uniqueness that can be appreciated only by other special or high-status people or institutions (e.g., employers).
4. Requires excessive admiration and attention.
5. Sense of entitlement, expects especially favorable treatment or automatic compliance with personal expectations.
6. Exploits other people, takes advantage of them.
7. Lacks empathy for other people's needs and feelings.
8. Often envious of others or believes others are envious of him or her (resents privileges or achievements of those regarded less special or deserving).
9. Arrogant, haughty behavior or attitudes.

lem seemed to be excessive self-concern and an inflated sense of one's own importance and uniqueness (see Figure 9-5). In addition, in recent years several psychoanalysts have focused on personal development in the early years of life, the development of the self as a separate entity, and narcissism as an aspect of self-development.

Relatively little research has been done on the classification of narcissistic personality disorder. One study used a structured interview, the Diagnostic Interview for Narcissism (DIN), designed to cover content areas that might be especially relevant to the diagnostic picture in narcissistic personality disorder (Gunderson et al., 1990). After the interviews were completed, the answers were coded into content areas and the results were statistically analyzed to determine the categories of response that best identified people with this disorder.

Borderline Personality Disorder

Borderline personality disorder was officially recognized as a diagnosis in 1980. Since that time the borderline category has been used so widely that 20 percent of psychiatric patients are given this diagnosis and it is estimated to occur in 3 to 5 percent of the general population (Frances & Widiger, 1986). About two thirds of those with borderline personality disorder are female. A heterogeneous group of individuals receive this diagnosis, but they share a number of characteristics, including unstable personal relationships, threats of self-destruc-

Figure 9-5 This sign suggests that Dr. Holgdbrn may have become a specialist in narcissistic personalities from observing his own behavior.

SOURCE: Harley Schwadron.

A person having at least five of these characteristics might be considered to have a borderline personality disorder.

1. Frantic efforts to avoid real or imagined abandonment.
2. Unstable and intense interpersonal relationships.
3. Persistent and markedly disturbed, distorted, or unstable sense of self (e.g., a feeling that one doesn't exist or embodies evil).
4. Impulsiveness in such areas as sex, substance use, crime, and reckless driving.
5. Recurrent suicidal thoughts, gestures, or behavior.
6. Emotional instability with periods of extreme depression, irritability, or anxiety.
7. Chronic feelings of emptiness.
8. Inappropriate intense anger or lack of control of anger (e.g., loss of temper, recurrent physical fights).
9. Transient, stress-related paranoid thoughts or severe dissociative symptoms.

tive behavior, chronic range of cognitive distortions, fears of abandonment, and impulsivity.

Intense clinging dependency and manipulation characterize the interpersonal relationships of those with borderline personality disorder and make interaction with these people very difficult. They seem to wish for a dependent and exclusive relationship with another person. This desire for dependency is clear to outside observers but vehemently denied by the borderline individual. As a part of this vehement denial, such individuals devalue or discredit the strengths and personal signficance of others. This often takes the form of extreme anger when the other person sets limits for the relationships, or when a separation is about to occur. In addition to anger, the borderline individual uses manipulative behavior to control relationships, such as complaining about physical symptoms and making and carrying out self-destructive threats. Table 9-7 lists major clinical features of borderline personality disorder.

Self-destructive behaviors have been called "the behavioral specialty" of those with borderline personality disorder. Table 9-8 shows the frequency of self-destructive acts in one group of borderline individuals. Overdosing with drugs and wrist-slashing are most common. In recent years severe bulimia (an eating disorder discussed in chapter 15) has become a common self-destructive tactic (Gunderson & Zanarini, 1987). Such behaviors are designed to call forth a "saving" response from another significant person. Persons with borderline personality disorder often are a continuing burden for the police and hospitals.

Self-destructiveness is the characteristic of borderline individuals that generates the most discomfort in those who attempt to help them. The therapist's hope of saving an endangered life is alternately encouraged and then dashed by the client's spiteful efforts at self-destruction. Therapists often experience intense feelings of responsibility for borderline clients. The therapist's initial efforts to be supportive when the client threatens suicide can lead to increased responsibility for the client's life and increased involvement outside of the therapy sessions. Unless the controlling nature of the client's responses are interpreted in the therapy sessions, the situation may become unworkable for the therapist. It is necessary to make the client understand that the therapist cannot be manipulated by threats of suicide and that the client must work to understand these self-destructive urges without acting them out. If this effort is not successful, the threats of self-destruction will recur, and the risk to the client will be even greater if the therapist fails to respond on cue. This danger is illustrated by the following example.

A borderline patient periodically rented a motel room and, with a stockpile of pills nearby, would call her therapist's home with an urgent message. He would respond by engaging in long conversations in which he "talked her down." Even as he told her that she could not count on his always being available, he became more wary of going out evenings without detailed instructions about how he could be reached. One night the patient couldn't reach him due to a bad phone connection. She fatally overdosed from what was probably a miscalculated manipulation.

—Gunderson, 1984, p. 93

TABLE 9–8
Total Number of Self-destructive Acts Described by 57 People With Borderline Personality Disorder

Category	Number of Acts	Behavior Pattern
Suicide threats	42	To get attention To cause trouble In rage
Overdose	40	No usual pattern Barbiturates most frequent
Self-mutilation	36	Wrist-slashing most frequent, then body banging, then burning, puncturing, or hair removal
Drug abuse	38	Polydrug abuse most frequent, next amphetamines or alcohol binges, then marijuana
Promiscuity	36	Usually under the influence of drugs or alcohol
Accidents	14	Reckless driving

Source: Adapted from Gunderson, 1984, p. 86.

Their strong need for a relationship leads borderline persons to have chronic and long-lasting fears that the people on whom they are dependent will abandon them. These fears are related to the extreme panic they feel when alone. As a defense against this fear, borderline people are compulsively social. But despite this need for social interaction, many of their behaviors repel people. These include their intense anger and demands, suspiciousness, and their impulsivity. They deal with stress by being sexually promiscuous, getting into fights, and binge eating and purging.

Marked emotional instability with sudden shifts to anxiety, and continued depression or irritability—which may last only a few hours and never more than a few days—are typical of borderline personality disorder, as is illustrated in the following description by a patient.

"I was alone at home a few months ago; I was frightened! I was trying to get in touch with my boyfriend and I couldn't. . . . He was nowhere to be found. All my friends seemed to be busy that night and I had no one to talk to. . . . I just got more and more nervous and more and more agitated. Finally—bang!—I took out a cigarette and lit it and stuck it

into my forearm. I don't know why I did it because I didn't really care for him all that much. I guess I felt I had to do something dramatic."

—Stone, 1980, p. 400

Borderline individuals also show disturbance in their concepts of identity: uncertainties about self-image, gender identity, values, loyalties, and goals. They may have chronic feelings of emptiness or boredom and be unable to tolerate being alone. The following anecdote illustrates the behavior of a borderline individual.

A 27-year-old woman was married and had two small children. She had had a stormy adolescence, having been forced into sexual relations with a brother six years her senior whom she at first idolized and later feared. Their relationship continued until just before she left home for college, when she told her parents of it. In the ensuing emotional turmoil, she made a gesture of suicide (overdose of aspirin) but was not hospitalized. . . . Outwardly flirtatious, although inwardly shy and ill at ease, she felt intensely lonely and went through a period of mild alcohol abuse and brief sexual affairs in an effort to cope with her anxiety and sense of inner emptiness. At age 19, she married a classmate and dropped out of school.

Fairly at ease in the first years of her marriage, she became anxious, bored, and given to fits of sadness and tearfulness after the birth of her second child. Her mood fluctuated widely from hour to hour, day to day, but negative feelings were greatly intensified on the three or four days before her period. Her husband had grown less attentive as the family expanded, in response to which she became increasingly irritable, provocative, and at times abusive (smashing plates, hurling insults). Her husband began to carry on an extramarital relationship, which she eventually discovered. At that point, she became seriously depressed, lost sleep and appetite, began to abuse alcohol and sedatives, and made several gestures of suicide, including one instance of cutting her wrist. On two occasions she hid for several nights in motels without informing anyone where she was. Each time she took her 8-year-old daughter with her, as though to protect her from the "designs" she imagined her husband had on their elder girl. After the wrist-cutting incident, when she had also left a note apologizing for being a "failure" as a wife and mother, she was hospitalized. She understood the unrealistic nature of her suspicions, as she explained to the hospital staff, but could not shake off the morbid doubts she experienced.

—Stone, 1986, p. 210

Distinguishing Borderlines From Other Groups The word "borderline" suggests a marginal level of functioning, something that borders on becoming something else. Originally the term was used to describe a marginal or milder form of schizophrenia. Today, some researchers argue that borderline patients actually represent the boundary between personality disorders and mood disorders. Indeed, about half of those with borderline personality disorder can also be diagnosed as having a mood disorder. Such individuals are also likely to have a family history of mood disorder. However, people with several other types of personality disorders are equally as likely to be depressed. Relatives of those with borderline personality disorder are more likely to share this diagnosis than are family members of those with other personality disorders—that is, the disorder seems to "breed true" (Zanarini et al., 1988). This likelihood supports the view that borderline personality is a disorder in its own right.

Despite the evidence obtained from family studies, some researchers have been unable to distinguish borderline disorder from histrionic personality disorder and antisocial personality disorder (Pope et al., 1983). Figure 9-6 shows the overlapping characteristics between borderline personality disorder and the other personality disorders in the same diagnostic cluster. Overlap may also occur with a personality disorder in another cluster. Sometimes patients who are diagnosed as borderline and those who are diagnosed as schizotypal seem similar. However, the schizotypal and borderline categories have different emphases. The schizotypal category stresses cognitive symptoms: thinking that one has magical

powers, ideas of reference, suspicious thought. The borderline category stresses affective or emotional symptoms: feelings of emotional instability, emptiness, boredom, and inappropriate and intense anger. Schizotypal individuals are socially isolated; in contrast, borderline individuals cannot stand being alone. Despite these problems of overlap with depression and with other personality disorders, research findings provide support for the borderline personality disorder as a true category of pathologies rather than as a combination of several groups (Zalewski & Archer, 1991).

Research Into Causes of Borderline Personality Disorder Probably because of the relatively large number of cases diagnosed as borderline personality disorders and also because borderline individuals are likely to make frequent suicidal gestures, more research on causes and treatment has been carried out with this disorder than with many of the other personality disorders (Weaver & Clum, 1993). Most of the theories about its cause also focus on a disturbed early relationship between a preborderline child and his or her parents. There are a variety of descriptions of what this relationship might be like (Gunderson & Zanarini, 1987). Some focus on the attachment experience in early childhood,

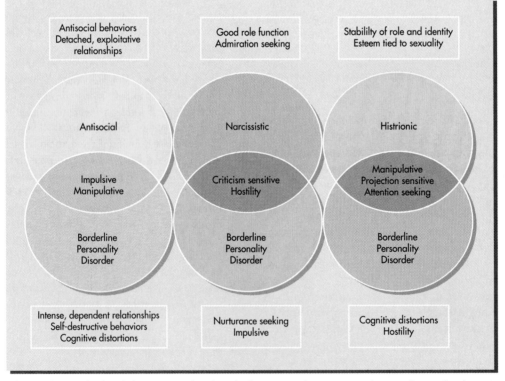

Figure 9-6 The borderline personality disorder has some characteristics that overlap with other personality disorders in the dramatic, emotional, or erratic behavior category. The similar characteristics are shown in the overlapping circle segments. Characteristics that distinguish between the two disorders are shown in the boxes above and below each pair.

SOURCE: Adapted from Gunderson and Zanarini, "Current Overview of the Borderline Diagnosis." *Journal of Clinical Psychiatry*, Supplement 48(8), (1987), p. 7.

while others point to parents who fail to provide adequate attention to the child's own feelings so that he or she never develops an adequate sense of self (Alder & Buie, 1979). Some theorists focus on parental abuse (both sexual and physical) in adolescence, as well as divorce, alcoholism, and other stressors (Linehan, 1987). It is clear from all these examples, however, that such stressors in the family occur often and children do not develop borderline personality disorder. This finding suggests that borderline disorder may be associated with some genetic vulnerability. The disorder probably develops through a combination of neurobiological, early developmental, and later socializing factors. *Splitting* is Kernberg's (1975) theoretical explanation of the extreme changeability that can be seen in the borderline person's relationships to others. He defined **splitting** as the failure to integrate the positive and negative experiences that occur between the individual and other people. Rather than perceiving another individual as a loving person who sometimes accepts and sometimes rejects—for example, a mother who sometimes hugs and sometimes disciplines a young child—the borderline individual shifts back and forth between these contradictory images.

Clinical Treatment of Borderline Personality Disorder A first step in planning treatment for any disorder is to identify its most distinctive features. Recent research has suggested three especially important problems in cases of borderline personality disorder (Hurt & Clarkin, 1990):

1. *Identity disturbances* reflected in borderline individuals' chronic feelings of emptiness or boredom and intolerance of being alone. These people have a strong need for involvement with others and a reliance on external support for self-definition.
2. *Affective disturbances* reflected in their intense, inappropriate anger, instability of emotions, and unstable interpersonal relationships. Borderline individuals often lead stormy, dramatic lives.
3. *Impulse disturbances* reflected in their self-damaging acts and impulsive behaviors.

Various therapeutic approaches deal with these core issues in different ways. Psychodynamically oriented clinicians believe that most borderline individuals can best be treated in intensive face-to-face psychotherapy sessions at least three times a week over a period of several years. In these sessions the therapist plays a more active structuring role than is usual in classical psychoanalysis. At the beginning the emphasis is on present behavior rather than childhood experiences, and rather than allowing the transference relationship to develop fully, the therapist explicitly describes and discusses the client's apparent distortions of reality—for example, the client's perceptions of the therapist.

Although psychoanalysts were among the first clinicians to describe and treat borderline personalities, clinicians of several theoretical perspectives are now developing therapies for these people. Cognitively oriented therapists focus on the borderline individual's limitations in three areas: automatic thoughts, cognitive distortions, and unrealistic underlying assumptions (for example, that people are either all good or all bad) (Linehan, 1989). Cognitive therapy thus concentrates on identifying and changing cognitions so as to permit better reality testing. Behavior therapists direct attention elsewhere, to the borderline person's defective behavioral repertoire. They try to teach patients better social skills and to help them manage their anxiety so as to not become overwhelmed with affective reactions. Biologically oriented clinicians make use of various types of medication in treating borderline individuals. In general, medication alone is mildly effective, with patients perhaps improving from severely to moderately impaired. Combinations of several therapeutic approaches may prove to be particularly effective. For example, medications together with psychotherapy and family support could be useful in dealing with the borderline person's multiple problems. Further research is needed in developing therapeutic approaches that will help these unstable people who lead such chaotic lives (see Box 9-2).

Long-Term Prospects for Borderline Individuals It was originally thought that because of their depressive and sometimes psychoticlike symptoms, borderline individuals would eventually develop a traditional illness such as schizophrenia or a major mood disorder. However, several follow-up studies show that this rarely happens; instead, borderline personality disorder tends to remain roughly the same over time (Plakun et al., 1985; Stone & Stone, 1988).

Follow-ups over 10 years or less show that the unstable relationships, poor work performance, and symptom levels usually continue. Longer-term follow-up studies show that borderline individuals who have received intensive treatment and are from high socioeconomic levels have a fairly good chance of developing full-time employment. Interpersonal relations also improve after a long unstable period during the young adult years (Stone et al., 1987). About a third of these borderline patients eventually marry and establish their own families. However, the range of outcomes is wide and many of those with borderline personality disorder continue to have severe interpersonal and occupational problems. One negative outcome is suicide. Probably 8 to 10 percent of borderline individuals actually kill themselves, although this figure is small compared to the number of

Does Dialectical Behavior Therapy Help?

Given the complexities of borderline personality disorder (BPD), it would not be surprising if a treatment approach incorporating elements of several of the traditional therapies is needed to help people with this condition. Marsha Linehan (1993) has developed a new approach, called **dialectical behavior therapy** (DBT), that builds on a variety of cognitive, behavioral, and psychodynamic concepts. The word *dialectical* describes the contradictions that dominate the borderline person's thinking and the need for him or her to learn that human relationships are not just a matter of love or hate and that there are middle grounds.

Linehan's approach is aimed particularly at the suicidal threats, gestures, and attempts seen in many borderline individuals. This approach uses a combined format of individual and group psychotherapy that is time-limited (usually one year) and makes explicit what the patient's, as well as the therapist's, responsibilities are (e.g., missing four sessions of group or individual therapy in a row results in termination of the treatment). Her therapy is active in that she deals directly, and early, with several key issues in the lives of the borderline individual—for example, coping with anger and impulses to self-destructive behavior. Therapeutic sessions provide patients with opportunities to learn ways of tolerating and expressing distressing emotions. Emphasis in therapy is placed on the patient's acquiring a better understanding of her or his vulnerabilities and

strengths, developing more reasonable expectations regarding other people, and improving stress-coping skills.

Linehan has asked two question that are useful in evaluating any treatment approach: (1) What is the theory behind the therapy? and (2) Does the therapy work? She sketches her therapy in the following way:

> Many borderline patients react to themselves with extreme loathing, bordering on self-hate. All but a few feel enormous shame in general, and shame about their own abuse history, the troubles they have caused, and their present emotional reactivity in particular. Cherishing oneself is the opposite of these emotional reactions. Thus, the therapist must target the self-hate, the self-blame, and the sense of shame. Although work on this target is a lifelong process, substantial progress should be made before therapy ends.

> One thing the therapist must be especially careful to do before therapy ends is to reinforce patient self-respect that is independent of the therapist. That is, the therapist must ultimately pull back and relentlessly reinforce within the therapeutic relationship self-validation, self-care, self-soothing, and problem-solving without reference to the therapist. I hasten to add, however, that this stance does not suggest that patients should learn to be independent of all people. Interpersonal dependence, asking for and accepting nurturing, soothing, and active assistance from others are crucial for most

people's well-being (Linehan, 1993, p. 160).

> My patients often ask me whether they will ever get better, whether they will ever be happy. It is a difficult question to answer. Surely they can get better and happier than they are when they first come to see me. And, yes, I believe that life can be worth living even for a person who has at one time met criteria for BPD. I am less certain, however, whether anyone can ever completely overcome the effects of the extremely abusive environments many of my patients have experienced. . . . The relationship with the therapist may be the best one an individual ever finds—not necessarily because of deficiencies on her part, but because the ability of our society to provide community and companionship is limited, even for many of its best members (Linehan, 1993, p. 461).

Although research on DBT is in its early stages, results to date seem promising. One study followed patients during treatment that lasted one year and comparable patients receiving therapies other than DBT. The DBT patients were less likely to drop out of therapy and less likely to make suicidal threats and gestures (Linehan et al., 1991). A later study did follow-ups a year after completion of treatment and also found a reduction of suicidal threats and gestures (Linehan, et al., 1993). The most recent study found that DBT reduced patients' anger levels and increased their social competence (Linehan et al., 1994).

---

suicide attempts by people with this diagnosis. Another frequent negative outcome is alcohol abuse.

Antisocial Personality Disorder

Antisocial personality disorder is associated with crime, violence, and delinquency occurring after the age of 15. This diagnosis is not given until age 18, however its essential characteristics include a history of continuous and chronic conduct disorder (discussed in chapter 15) in the period before the age of 15. After the age of 15, the individual must have shown a pervasive pattern indicating disregard for the rights of others and violations of those rights. Such behaviors must include at

least three of the types of actions listed in Table 9-9. Convicted murderer Gary Gilmore fits this description well (see Box 9-3).

Although Gary Gilmore's antisocial traits may have led him to commit crimes, it is important to distinguish between criminal or aggressive behavior and antisocial personality disorder.

From the standpoint of abnormal psychology, the defining properties of antisocial personalities are not so much the particular acts they perform (e.g., robbing a bank or shoplifting), as their distinctive deeply ingrained approach to life. They always seem to be participating in a game in which other individuals exist as pieces to be manipulated and utilized, and it is this game

TABLE 9–9
Clinical Features of Antisocial Personality Disorder

A person having at least three of these characteristics might be considered to have an antisocial personality disorder.

1. Failure to conform to social norms (violating laws).
2. Deceitfulness, manipulativeness.
3. Impulsivity, failure to plan ahead.
4. Irritability, aggressiveness.
5. Reckless disregard for the safety of self or others.
6. Consistent irresponsibility.
7. Lack of remorse after having hurt, mistreated, or stolen from another.

playing that leads these people to get into trouble with the law. At their worst, these people can be cruel, sadistic, or violent. They seldom show anxiety and don't feel guilt. Freudians would maintain that the mind of the antisocial personality is totally lacking the "moral police officer" role of the superego. Antisocial personalities do not see themselves as the cause of their problems, but rather see the tough spots they find themselves in as due to flaws in other people. Despite their frequent violation of the rights of others, many individuals with antisocial personality disorder do not have criminal records. A large epidemiological survey of the community found that more than half the people whose histories caused them to be classified as having antisocial personality disorder did not have a significant history of arrests despite continuous and chronic antisocial behavior (Robins & Regier, 1991). Such people were also unlikely to have sought help in a traditional clinical setting except under circumstances when it seemed to them that seeking such help would enable them to avoid legal consequences arising from their actions.

The case of Bert is not as dramatic as that of Gary Gilmore, but is representative of many people who are diagnosed as having an antisocial personality disorder yet who never come in contact with the law or, if they do, are not convicted of a crime. These people treat others callously without any apparent concern. They seem to feel no guilt even at harming those closest to them. The excitement of taking chances and of manipulating others seems to be their prime motivators. They either lack an ability to foresee consequences or they consider the consequences unimportant.

After graduating from high school and having a few dead-end jobs, Bert wanted to go into business for himself. He asked his parents, who had a modest income and some savings for their retirement, to lend him the money he needed to get started. Within 5 months Bert was out of business, his par-

ents' money "lost," as he put it. Several months later, having found a new business opportunity, Bert again pleaded with his parents to borrow the money he needed. They agreed, and again Bert's opportunity fizzled. His parents desperately wanted to help Bert and to believe in him. So great was their need and so successful was Bert in "conning" his parents that they repeatedly helped him engage in activities that were doomed to failure. Bert craved the excitement of going into business for himself, but was unable either to attend to all the details involved in running a business or to plan ahead. He was magnificent in playing the role of the charming young man on the way up. When he failed, he felt no regrets concerning his failure's implications for his parents and others who had helped him.

Research Into Causes of Antisocial Personality Disorder Researchers of antisocial personality have been hampered by the fact that it is so much easier to identify antisocial personalities among individuals who have been convicted of crimes than among the general population. Consequently, the group on which research is based may not be typical of all people with an antisocial personality disorder. One researcher approached this methodological problem in a unique way: She inserted the following ad in a Boston counterculture newspaper.

Wanted: charming, aggressive, carefree people who are impulsively irresponsible but are good at handling people and at looking after number one. Send name, address, phone, and short biography proving how interesting you are to . . .
—Widom, 1978, p. 72

Widom's ad drew 73 responses, of which about two thirds were from males. About one third of the responses seemed to meet the criteria for a diagnosis of antisocial personality disorder. The respondents were interviewed and given a battery of psychological tests. Some of the characteristics of the group are shown in Table 9-10. The researcher concluded that the main difference between her sample and prison samples was that the people who answered her ad had somehow been able to avoid conviction after arrest or detention by the police. In other respects they seemed very similar to prison inmates.

Researchers have looked at many aspects of antisocial individuals—their life histories, psychological and physiological functioning, and personality characteristics—in order to understand why these people behave as they do. The biological perspective has yielded a number of interesting findings. There is increasing evidence that heredity may play a role in both criminality and antisocial behavior (Gottesman & Goldsmith, 1994). A Swedish study revealed that adopted children who were separated at birth from biological parents who met the criteria for antisocial personality disorder showed more

Antisocial Personality Disorder

The case of Gary Gilmore (Figure 9-7) illustrates many characteristics of antisocial personality disorder. While Gilmore experienced short-term distress when things did not go well, the distress usually concerned, "How can I get out of this fix?" rather than any long-term personal anxieties, fears, or worries.

Gilmore was convicted of two murders and sentenced to death. When he was executed in 1977, he was the first person to be put to death in the United States in 11 years. Although he refused to appeal his conviction, several appeals were made on his behalf and his execution was delayed three times. During this period, while newspapers featured stories on his "fight for the right to be executed," he attempted suicide twice.

Gilmore reported that he had begun drinking at the age of 10 and later had used a variety of illegal drugs—amphetamines, cocaine, and LSD. He displayed an antisocial personality pattern very early. In spite of his high intelligence, his school grades were poor, he was often truant, and he was repeatedly accused of stealing from his schoolmates. At age 14 he was sent to a juvenile center for stealing a car; after his release he was sent to jail several times for burglaries; and at age 20 he was sent to the state penitentiary for burglary and robbery.

It seems like things have always gone bad for me. It seems like I've always done dumb things that just caused trouble for me. I remember when I was a boy I would feel like I had to do things like sit on a railroad track until just before the train came and then I would dash off. Or I would put my finger over the end of

a BB gun and pull the trigger to see if a BB was really in it. Sometimes I would stick my finger in water and then put my finger in a light socket to see if it would really shock me.

—Spitzer et al., 1983, p. 68

Gilmore was evaluated to determine whether he was competent to stand trial. His IQ was found to be 129, in the superior range. His general knowledge was surprisingly good for someone with so little education. He was proud of his vocabulary and read both fiction and news magazines avidly. There was no indication of any organic problems. He reported no bizarre or unusual thoughts except when on drugs. Personality tests revealed no thought or mood disturbances. He slept soundly, had a good appetite, and was not depressed or worried. "I almost never get blue. Though I've made a mess of my life, I never stew about the things I have done."

Gilmore showed the characteristic behaviors of an antisocial personality. He disobeyed rules at home and at school, drank, and used illegal drugs at an early age. By 14 he had been arrested for car theft. While he was in prison he was known for his cruel and violent behavior. He seemed to lack sympathy and felt no guilt. He never had a steady job or a long-lasting relationship.

Although Gary Gilmore shared some of his early experiences with professionals who interviewed him, he said very little about his early life in terms of family relationships. This appeared to be an area he was reluctant to discuss or even think about. Seventeen years after Gary

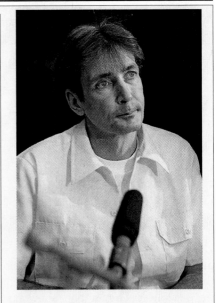

Figure 9-7 Gary Gilmore in 1977.

Gilmore's death, his younger brother, Mikal Gilmore, a professional writer and columnist, wrote a book in which he discussed some of the Gilmore's family life and provided some clues that might help to understand Gary's behavior (Gilmore, 1994). Mikal Gilmore described a family in which violence and child abuse were daily occurrences, a family in which the children lived in fear of the consequences of their misdeeds and experienced both physical punishment and extreme psychological mistreatment at the hands of their father. Mikal makes the point in his book that these events were never discussed in the family and that he, himself, felt he could not be free of their influence until he had confronted them by writing the family story which ended in the violent deaths of his father and both his brothers.

antisocial behavior later in life than control subjects (Bohman et al., 1982).

How antisocial behavior might be inherited is not yet clear. Researchers have connected habitually violent and antisocial tendencies with the neurochemistry of the body. Impulsive physical violence and aggression in humans is related to very low levels of one of the neurotransmitters, serotonin, and one of its metabolites in the spinal fluid (Virkkunen, 1983). Other research has focused on patterns of brain wave activity. For example, some researchers have demonstrated a relationship between one type of electrical brain activity, slow alpha

waves, and later antisocial behavior (Volavka, 1990). In normal individuals, alpha-wave frequency is known to decrease with relaxation and drowsiness and to increase with tension, so the slow alpha waves suggest that some antisocial individuals have a lower than normal arousal level. This may mean that sensory inputs that would be disturbing to most people would not be strong enough to excite antisocial individuals. Such people may crave increased stimulation and may therefore seek out unusual forms of excitement. The brain wave patterns found in people who fit the criteria of antisocial personality disorder have some resemblance to those that

TABLE 9–10 Characteristics of Subjects Interviewed by Widom[a]	
Characteristic	Percentage of Subjects
Arrest Records:	
Detained	17.9
Arrested as an adult	64.3
Convicted as an adult	17.9
Incarceration:	
As a juvenile	10.7
As an adult	32.1
Psychiatric Hospitalization:	
Hospitalized at some time	21.4
Treated as an outpatient only	46.4
Suicide attempts	28.6
Number with both psychiatric and arrest	
records	46.4
Parental separation:	
Broken homes	21.4
Divorce	7.1
Parental psychopathology	7.1
Parental alcoholism	17.8

[a]The subjects averaged 25 years of age (from 19 to 47 years old). All except one were white.

Source: Widom, 1978

occur normally in children and adolescents rather than those of adults. This similarity suggests that at least one subgroup of people with this disorder may have delayed cerebral maturation (Reid, 1986).

Another physiological factor—anxiety—has been studied in antisocial individuals. It had seemed reasonable to assume that people who met the criteria for antisocial personality would also show little anxiety compared to other individuals. But this assumption may be true only in a limited sense. Schalling (1978) found that while antisocial personalities seem to worry less than other people, they nevertheless experience all of the common somatic and muscular indicators of anxiety (high heart rate, shortness of breath, tense muscles). If we divide anxiety into its cognitive part—worry—and its physiological components—the body's responses to fear—antisocial individuals seem to lack the cognitive component of anxiety.

From a cognitive perspective, the study of antisocial behavior focuses on moral development (Kegan, 1986). Just as in the case of psychophysiological factors, the idea of a delay in moral development has been suggested. Between the ages of 7 and 11, normal children can tell when someone else treats them unfairly. If they have been treated unfairly in the past, when an opportu-

nity arises they will "make up" for the past unfairness by striking back when someone else is vulnerable. For example, after being teased for being the shortest player on the peewee basketball team and then growing several inches, instead of feeling empathy for smaller kids the child will think, "Now it's my turn," not, "I'll treat younger kids differently."

A new morality normally begins to develop at about the age of 13. Then children think about the fairness of their own actions rather than concentrating on getting even. Cognitive theorists describe this as the development of the ability to reason in abstract terms and to understand the concept of partnership. From this point of view, those with antisocial personality disorder are developmentally arrested at the 7- to 11-year-old level because they are not concerned about the effects of their behavior on others.

In general, antisocial personality disorder cannot be explained simply by social class, bad associates, membership in a deviant subgroup, residence in a high-crime neighborhood, or brain damage. The disorder does seem to occur frequently in chaotic home environments.

There is evidence that abused and/or neglected children are at greater risk of being diagnosed as having antisocial personality disorder when they are adults (Luntz & Widom, 1994). Childhood victimization may be a significant predictor of antisocial personality disorder symptoms. In all likelihood, an adequate explanation of antisocial personality disorder will require approaches that simultaneously examine environmental, physiological, genetic, and temperamental variables.

Clinical Treatment of Antisocial Personality Disorder The following excerpt from a therapy session with 29-year-old Brett, illustrates some of the important features of antisocial personality disorder. For most of his late adolescence and early adult life, Brett had frequently schemed to cheat "the system" and to take what he wanted without paying for it. He used this approach not so much from lack of money to pay as for the excitement and pleasure that resulted when he was successful. Notice how the cognitively oriented therapist deftly tries to get Brett to think about costs associated with "beating the system."

Therapist: How well has the "beat-the-system" approach actually worked out for you over time?

Brett: It works great . . . until someone catches on or starts to catch on. Then you have to scrap that plan and come up with a new one.

Therapist: How difficult was it, you know, to cover up one scheme and come up with a new one?

Brett: Sometimes it was really easy. There are some real pigeons out there.

Therapist:	Was it always easy?
Brett:	Well, no. Sometimes it was a real bitch. Like beating the phone system. That really ended up in a big hassle. There was really no way to cover it up, and everyone gave me such a hard time.
Therapist:	Was it very easy to come up with an alternative plan?
Brett:	Not for the phones. I never did come up with another plan.
Therapist:	How about at other times? Did beat-the-system plans come to you very easily—I mean, ones that actually worked?
Brett:	Well, I came up with lots of good ones, but it was tough coming up with something that would really pay off.
Therapist:	Did a good plan last a long time, or were new ones frequently required?
Brett:	Seems like I'm always needing a good plan to beat the system.
Therapist:	Do you think it's ever easier to go with the system instead of trying to beat it in some way?
Brett:	Well, after all that I have been through, I would have to say yes, there have been times that going with the system would have been easier in the long run. By the time I'm done paying legal fees, I will have shelled out more than my tuition would ever have cost me. But . . . it's such a challenge to beat the system. It feels exciting when I come up with a new plan and think I can make it work. Going with the system might not even occur to me.

—Beck, Freeman, and Associates, 1990, p. 171

The following excerpt from an interview with a person diagnosed as antisocial personality disorder illustrates the sensitivity with which clinicians must approach aspects of a patient's life that the individual might prefer not to admit to or discuss. In this case, the clinician needs to inquire into the patient's fighting. Does he get into fights because of living in a violent neighborhood or is he frequently the instigator?

Clinician:	Do some of them try to hassle you?
Patient:	Yeah sure, but that's all part of the game.
Clinician:	Have any of them tried to push you around?
Patient:	Yeah, a couple of them but I set them straight.
Clinician:	How do you mean?
Patient:	I kicked their asses.
Clinician:	Well, you look like you're in pretty good shape. I imagine you can take care of yourself pretty

	well. What about in the past, what types of fights have you been in?
Patient:	Oh, I been in a few now and then. People know not to mess with me. I grew up in a tough neighborhood and you had to know how to fight to survive.
Clinician:	When you were fairly young, let's say between the ages of say 15 and 25, how many fights do you think you were in, 20, 30?
Patient:	I'm bad but not that bad . . . oh, let's see, maybe about 15, who knows, it could have been as high as 20.
Clinician:	Did you ever get hurt?
Patient:	Nah, not really, but I did a number on a few of those guys.
Clinician:	Did you ever put anyone in the hospital?
Patient:	Yeah, there was one dude that I cut up pretty good, but he really deserved it, trust me.
Clinician:	Earlier you told me that you drank a fair amount in the past but have completely stopped now, which you deserve a lot of credit for. Back when you were drinking, did you sometimes feel on edge, almost like you needed a good fight, so you went looking for one, perhaps the alcohol making it a little more difficult to control your anger?
Patient:	Sometimes, yeah, sometimes . . . especially if I was pretty strung out, I would be just plain nasty, and I started my fair share of fights. But usually I was just protecting myself or the guy really had it coming to him.
Clinician:	It certainly sounds like you know how to handle yourself in a fight. Did you use to run in a gang or how did you learn how to defend yourself so well?
Patient:	Like I said, where I grew up you had to learn how to fight, and I did hang out with a gang for a couple of years.

—Shea, 1988, pp. 375–376

In this interview, the clinician discovers that while the patient comes from a tough neighborhood, he is a frequent instigator of fights. The clinician enters the potentially loaded topic of fighting by asking, "Do some of them try to hassle you?", referring to the patient's fellow residents at a drug rehabilitation center. Asking the question in this way enables the topic of fighting to be brought up without attributing blame to the patient. Once the patient is talking freely about fights, the clinician focuses on his history of fights and his role in them. Had the clinician prematurely asked, "Do you pick a lot of fights?", he probably would have gotten a defensive answer. The clinician skillfully compliments the patient ("Well, you look like you're in pretty good shape . . . ") and makes it easy for the patient to admit to fighting by associating it with the use of alcohol. This approach not only provides needed diagnostic information, but it also helps build a working relationship with the patient.

People with antisocial personality disorder are not usually helped by traditional methods of psychotherapy. Their lack of empathy and social responsibility are major deterrents to establishing therapeutic rapport and commitment to change. The antisocial patient may at times experience a greater investment in outwitting the therapist than in effecting positive changes. Whenever possible, the therapist tries to raise questions in the patient's mind about beliefs that might result in antisocial behavior and negative outcomes— for example, the idea that wanting something or wanting to avoid something justifies a particular course of action.

A correctional facility or other type of highly structured, well-controlled setting may be the only means of managing some antisocial patients. An effective residential treatment center forces antisocial personalities to stay for months or years in a program with rigid rules so firm that they cannot talk their way out (Reid & Balis, 1987). In such a situation, the participants initially become depressed because they are forced to face their lack of inner feelings and their inability to establish meaningful relationships with others. The major goals of the entire program are to increase the person's ability to feel emotions, to think constructively about the future, to trust other people, and to develop empathy. Such a program emphasizes *milieu therapy*, an approach in which all the staff work together to provide consistent support and long-term stable relationships.

Another type of program has similar goals but can be carried out in the community. A judge may sentence young male first-offenders, or other men who are good prospects for improvement, to the program with prison as the alternative. The offender is required to begin schooling or a job immediately and to return to an unlocked treatment center for the remaining time. Gradually he is given more physical freedom. Throughout the program he is also expected to be responsible for his behavior and that of others in the program. He is also expected to repay his victims for their losses and to pay his living expenses. If he fails in the program, his alternate sentence, prison, immediately takes effect. Many people with antisocial personalities find this type of program very stressful. Often as many as 50 percent drop out and return to prison. For those who do successfully complete the program, however, the re-arrest rate has been significantly lower than the rate for similar people from traditional prison or halfway house settings.

Anxious or Fearful Behavior

Disorders in this group share many characteristics with the personality disorders already described. What sets them apart is that each of these disorders has a prominent component of anxiety or fear.

Avoidant Personality Disorder

Avoidant personality disorder is characterized by low self-esteem, fear of negative evaluation, and a pervasive behavioral, emotional, and cognitive avoidance of social interaction. In therapy, avoidant personalities express a desire for affection, acceptance, and friendship; yet frequently, they have few friends and share little intimacy with anyone. Fear of rejection plays a key role in influencing these people to keep away from personal attachments. They won't enter into a relationship unless the other person provides unusually strong guarantees of uncritical acceptance. Table 9-11 lists clinical features of this disorder.

The seclusiveness of avoidant personalities differs from that of people with schizoid personality disorder because, unlike the latter group, avoidant people do want to enter into relationships. The conflict they feel is over wanting affection and, at the same time, doubting their acceptance by others. They cannot seem to rid themselves of the belief that any overtures of friendship will end in pain and disillusion. They are caught between wanting human contact and dreading it. People with avoidant personality disorder seem timid and withdrawn and perhaps also cold and strange to those

---

TABLE 9–11
Clinical Features of Avoidant Personality Disorder

A person having at least four of these characteristics might be considered to have an avoidant personality disorder.

1. Anticipates and worries about being rejected or criticized in social situations.
2. Has few friends despite the desire for them.
3. Is unwilling to get involved with people unless certain of being liked.
4. Avoids social or occupational activities that involve significant interpersonal contact.
5. Inhibits development of intimate relationships (despite wishing for them) because of fear of seeming foolish, being ridiculed, and feeling shamed.
6. Possesses low self-worth because of self-perceived social ineptness and lack of personally appealing qualities.
7. Unusually reluctant to engage in new situations or activities for fear of embarrassment.

who have superficial contact with them. However, to those who know them well, they appear anxious and extremely sensitive. Some of these feelings come from doubts about their own competence.

One coping mechanism that those with avoidant personality disorder are likely to use is hypervigilance. They continuously assess all their human contacts for signs of deception, humiliation, and negative reactions. As a result, they are able to detect the most minute traces of indifference or annoyance. They make mountains out of molehills. This technique of constantly scanning the environment is a self-defeating one, however, because it increases the likelihood that they will pick up just the kind of negative response they expect. In addition, their nervousness can result in making their companions uncomfortable, which can further damage the quality of their relationships with others.

Another maneuver that avoidant personalities use is to narrow their range of activities in order to cut off upsetting stimuli. Someone with an avoidant personality disorder may patronize only a small number of shops and restaurants so as to avoid encountering unfamiliar people or situations, or may even avoid shopping and other everyday activities because they seem too tiring or uncomfortable. Such people may also exaggerate the potential dangers of certain situations; for example, they may refuse to use buses or trains even though others do not doubt their safety. The lives of people with avoidant personality disorders are controlled by fears of looking foolish or being embarrassed. One unfortunate consequence of this retreat from contact with others and from new experiences is that it gives these individuals more time to be preoccupied with their own thoughts and to relive earlier painful experiences. The retreat also inhibits the development of social skills that might provide increased feelings of self-efficacy in dealing with interpersonal situations. Both these factors lead to a vicious cycle which makes new social contacts harder.

Avoidant personality disorder was added to the official DSM classification system in 1980. As yet little research has been done that gives insight into its causes or the most effective treatment approaches. One question concerning this disorder has to do with its discriminability from social phobia. One study compared individuals with social phobia and those diagnosed as avoidant personality disorder as they performed in a social role-play test and gave a speech (Turner et al., 1986). Although the two groups reported equal levels of anxiety and similar anxious thoughts, those patients diagnosed as avoidant personality showed poorer social skills than those with social phobia. Further research is needed to evaluate overlaps between avoidant personality disorder and other classifications.

Dependent Personality Disorder

People with **dependent personality disorder** have two basic characteristics. First, they passively allow other people to make all the important decisions in their lives because they lack confidence and feel that they are unable to function independently. Second, to ensure that they will not lose this dependent position, such people subordinate their own needs to the needs and demands of others. Dependent personalities fear separation and have an excessive need to be taken care of. As a consequence, they are submissive and clinging (Bornstein, 1992).

Dependent individuals try to make themselves so pleasing that no one could possibly wish to abandon them. They are self-effacing, ever agreeable, and continually ingratiating. If left on their own, they feel empty, extremely anxious, and unable to function. They may feel anxiety even when the dependent relationship is intact because of the pervasive worry that the dominant figure might be lost in some way—for example, through death or divorce. Table 9-12 lists the clinical features of dependent personality disorder.

Dependent individuals feel that they must act meek and obedient in order to hold onto other people. They also behave affectionately and admiringly toward their protectors. In many cases this behavior may actually be an effective coping technique. The dominant partner will then feel useful, strong, and competent and will want to encourage the relationship. Sometimes, how-

---

TABLE 9–12
Clinical Features of Dependent Personality Disorder

A person having at least five of these characteristics might be considered to have a dependent personality disorder.

1. Is unable to make everyday decisions without excessive advice and reassurance from others.
2. Allows or encourages others to make important life decisions (e.g., getting married, where to live, having children).
3. Has difficulty expressing disagreement with others because of fear of their anger or loss of support.
4. Has difficulty independently initiating activities because of lack of confidence in personal judgment or abilities.
5. Goes to excessive lengths to obtain nurturance and support from others.
6. Feels uncomfortable or helpless when alone because of exaggerated fears of inability to care for himself or herself.
7. Indiscriminately seeks another relationship to provide nurturing and support when a close relationship ends.
8. Is frequently preoccupied with fears of being left to care for himself or herself.

ever, things go wrong. The dominant individual may tire of the constant need to demonstrate affection and support and may behave abusively or seek to be rid of the leechlike attachment of the dependent partner. (Hirschfeld et al., 1991.)

The following case is an example of a dependent personality. The subject has allowed his mother to make the important decision as to whether he should marry his girl friend.

> *Matthew is a 34-year-old single man who lives with his mother and works as an accountant. He sought treatment because he was very unhappy after having just broken up with his girl friend. His mother had disapproved of his marriage plans, ostensibly because the woman was of a different religion. Matthew felt trapped and forced to choose between his mother and his girl friend, and since "blood is thicker than water," he had decided not to go against his mother's wishes. Nonetheless, he was angry at himself and at his mother, and believed that she would never let him marry and was possessively hanging on to him. His mother "wore the pants" in the family and was a very domineering woman who was used to getting her way. Matthew was afraid of her and criticized himself for being weak, but also admired his mother and respected her judgment—"Maybe Carol wasn't right for me after all." He alternated between resentment and a "Mother knows best" attitude. He felt that his own judgment was poor.*
>
> —Adapted from Spitzer et al., 1989, pp. 123–124

The causes of dependent personality disorders are unclear. One suggestion is that dependent individuals had overprotective parents who made life so easy for them as children that they never learned coping skills. Other theorists have suggested that dependent children were insecurely attached to their mothers or other caregivers or did not have close and trusting relationships with others during childhood. So far both of these ideas are interesting but untested hypotheses (Hirschfeld et al., 1991).

As with avoidant personalities, assertiveness training may be useful in treating dependent people. It may be difficult to convince these individuals that their coping styles need to be changed; sometimes a consciousness-raising therapy group is used before direct treatment is attempted.

As with other personality disorders we have discussed, more research is needed on this disorder's overlap with other conditions, its causes, and effective treatment strategies. Working with clients who have dependent personality disorders can be rewarding to the therapist when they develop the ability to function independently, but reaching that point can be difficult and frustrating. Many dependent people revel

in the early stages of therapy. Then at some point they come to the realization that therapy isn't a passive experience. They begin to understand that therapy isn't just a matter of someone (the therapist) showing an interest in them. What happens then can be a turning point in therapy—or the therapy can turn into a dead end.

Obsessive-Compulsive Personality Disorder

Obsessive-compulsive personality disorder is similar to obsessive-compulsive anxiety disorder (discussed in chapter 6), but the two disorders are different. People with obsessive-compulsive personality disorder are rigid and restricted in their behavior, but they do not show obsessional thinking that seems to force itself into consciousness, nor do they engage in the kinds of irrational rituals that are performed by people with obsessive-compulsive anxiety disorder. People with the anxiety disorder see their behavior as nonadaptive and distressing, but they cannot stop behaving that way. People with a personality disorder, on the other hand, usually exhibit behavior that is rigid and unadaptive but that they feel is under their control.

Compulsive people have been described as "living machines" (Reich, 1933, 1949). As one patient put it, his life was like "a train that was running efficiently, fast, pulling a substantial load, but on a track laid out for it" (Shapiro, 1965). An obsessive-compulsive personality disorder has several characteristics. One is lack of ability to express many warm and tender emotions. Instead, a person with this disorder seems stiff, formal, and unusually serious. Such an individual is likely to be overly conscientious and inflexible about matters of morality. Extreme perfectionism is also a problem because it focuses on small details, lists, and rulemaking rather than on getting the job done. This rigidity leads to an inability to grasp the "big picture." For instance, in the following example two friends are discussing a house that K is interested in buying. L shows his rigidity in not really listening to what K says but going by his own "rule of house ownership."

> K: *So you think I shouldn't buy it?*
>
> L: *Never buy a house with a bad roof. It will cost you its price again in repairs before you're finished.*
>
> K: *But the builder I hired to look it over did say it was in good condition otherwise.*
>
> L: *The roof is only the beginning. First it's the roof and then comes the plumbing and then the heating and then the plaster.*

K: Still, those things seem to be all right.

L: And, after the plaster, it will be the wiring.

K: But the wiring is . . .

L [interrupts with calm assurance]: It will cost double the price before you're finished.

—Shapiro, 1965, p. 25

This example also illustrates another aspect of compulsive personalities: insistence that their way of doing things be followed, without any awareness of the feelings this creates in other people. K probably really wants to buy the house, and if L's criticisms are, as we suspect, simply evidence of his compulsive personality without any facts attached, K's self-esteem and his positive feelings toward L are not likely to increase as a result of this encounter. People with this disorder focus on rules and neatness and may be disturbed by anything out of place (see Figure 9-8). Excessive concentration on work and productivity is also typical. Even pleasure becomes work.

Figure 9-8   Housekeeping routines or other cleaning or straightening rituals occupy a great deal of time for some obsessive-compulsive people. This person's home library is a source of worry and frustration because of her concern about how to arrange the books. If they are arranged alphabetically by author, then she finds that the different sizes mixed together are visually unpleasing. If she arranges them by size, although they look better, she cannot find a particular book quickly. The result is that she spends a great deal of time both arranging the books and feeling dissatisfied with what she has done.

One such person carefully scheduled his Sundays with certain activities in order to produce "maximum enjoyment." He determinedly set about enjoying himself and became quite upset if anything interfered with his schedule, not merely because he missed the activity, but because his holiday had been spent inefficiently. Another compulsive patient always tried hard, in his social life, to be "spontaneous."

—Shapiro, 1965, p. 32

Finally, obsessive-compulsive personality disorder is characterized by indecisiveness. Individuals with this disorder have great difficulty making decisions because they might be wrong. Their inability to make decisions can be so extreme that they can accomplish relatively little. Their pleasure comes from planning a job, not from doing it.

Despite job problems such as those referred to previously, obsessive-compulsiveness is relatively less likely than other personality disorders to inhibit job performance and is least often confused with misbehavior. Table 9-13 lists the clinical features of this personality disorder.

Someone with an obsessive-compulsive personality disorder usually seeks treatment only when his or her carefully built-up life style is threatened. This may happen when a spouse is exasperated and leaves, when a boss decides to fire the difficult employee, or when there is an accumulation of stressful events that make it impossible to carry on as usual. Psychotherapy is often recommended in such circumstances. Although in the past the therapeutic approach was usually psychodynamic and focused on unconscious processes that might underlie the disorder, in recent years other approaches

---

TABLE 9–13
Clinical Features of Obsessive-Compulsive Personality Disorder

A person having at least four of these characteristics might be considered to have an obsessive-compulsive personality.

1. Perfectionism that interferes with completing tasks.
2. Preoccupation with details, rules, lists, and schedules.
3. Reluctance to delegate tasks or to work with others unless they follow exactly his or her way of doing things.
4. Excessive devotion to work and productivity to the exclusion of leisure activities and friendships.
5. Overconscientiousness and inflexibility about matters of morality or ethics.
6. Perceives money as something to be saved for future catastrophes; is miserly regarding spending for self and others.
7. Inability to discard worn out or worthless objects even when they have no sentimental value.
8. Behavior that is typically rigid and stubborn.

---

have also come to the fore. A cognitive approach directs attention to the content, style, and structure of the individual's thought processes in the belief that it is irrational and dysfunctional thoughts that lead to maladaptive behavior (Beck et al., 1990). For example, automatic thoughts such as "I need to get this assignment done perfectly" may inhibit spontaneity and the expression of feelings. Behavioral approaches that use techniques like exposure therapy (see chapter 7) are also being used, as is group therapy.

Treatment of Personality Disorders

Our knowledge of personality disorders is limited because professionals see a restricted sample of people with these disorders. Unless their difficulties become overwhelming, such individuals tend to be satisfied with their behavior, not intensely unhappy the way an anxious or depressed person might be. As we have seen, people with personality disorders perceive their environment—not their rigid behavior patterns—as the cause of any difficulties they may encounter.

It is important to remember that even individuals who are classified as having a personality disorder may behave appropriately or normally some of the time. However, when coping behaviors are called for, each personality disorder is distinguished by the frequency and intensity with which certain characteristic behaviors appear. For example, someone with a paranoid personality disorder does not always appear to be suspicious, but he or she is much more likely than most people to be inappropriately suspicious. Many people with personality disorders go through life without ever coming into contact with a mental health professional. However, their rigid response styles often lead them to cope ineffectively with their environment. If the environmental stresses become too great, their response styles may become clearly ineffective.

A variety of therapies have been used in treating personality disorders. Although most of these disorders have not been found to be very responsive to drugs in the past, clinicians have recently been using certain psychoactive drugs to treat some people with personality disorders. The drugs currently being assessed include certain antipsychotic drugs; one group of antidepressant drugs, the MAO inhibitors; and lithium. So far the results of drug therapy are not entirely clear. Behavioral techniques such as assertiveness training and systematic desensitization may be helpful for avoidant and dependent patients. Although cognitive therapies seem to be appropriate for deviant cognitive styles, little information on their effectiveness is available. However, dealing with the cognitions that underlie the personality disorders would seem to be a promising approach.

As Box 9-2 showed for borderline personality disorder, there may be considerable merit in developing therapies that combine several treatment approaches. Psychodynamic therapy has been used successfully with personality disorders in which anxious or fearful behaviors play a prominent role (Winston et al., 1994). An intensive milieu therapy that provides clear rules and a stable environment—as well as clear penalties for failure to take personal responsibility for behavior—is being tried as a way to help those with antisocial personality disorder.

Because personality disorders affect interpersonal relationships, they also tend to elicit certain patterns of behaviors from family members or friends. For this reason, any behavior changes that come about through therapy will have an impact on the patterns of these relationships. Group or family therapy thus may be a useful part of the treatment of many individuals with personality disorders. Therapists need to focus the client's attention on the effect of his or her behavior on the behavior of others.

The Outlook for the Personality Disorder Classification

The idea of personality disorders as independent conditions (listed on DSM-IV's Axis II), that might or might not be related to the more traditional disorders (listed on Axis I), is relatively new. Even though clinicians have responded positively to this new system of classifying various personality patterns, many questions and issues remain.

Two questions that inevitably arise are: Are the personality disorders included in DSM-IV the right ones—that is, are they defined in ways that contribute to diagnostic reliability and validity? Are there personality disorders not included in DSM-IV that should be part of the classification system? It has been difficult for professionals to answer these questions because, except for a few of the personality disorders (most notably the borderline classification), research on these conditions has been quite limited. With increased use of Axis II by clinicians and as research evidence accrues, it seems likely that conceptualizations of the personality disorders will change, as well as the diagnostic criteria for their use.

Clinical experience and research may also suggest adding to Axis II some classifications of personality patterns not currently represented. For example, some people show a pervasive sadistic pattern of cruel, demanding, and aggressive behavior to other people; others show a self-defeating or masochistic pattern that leads to disappointment, failure, or mistreatment by others; and still others show a mild, but persistent, depressive mood that is dominated by dejection and cheerlessness. Whether these or other personality patterns should also be included within Axis II is a topic of considerable discussion among clinicians and researchers.

Another important topic concerns how information about the personality disorders can most effectively be presented. Currently, Axis II uses a **categorical model** of classification, in which a disorder is considered to be diagnosed if a certain threshold of criteria is reached or exceeded. As we have seen in the clinical features tables presented throughout this chapter, it is not required that all listed criteria be present in order to use a particular classification. In contrast with this classification model, a **dimensional model** focuses attention on *patterns* of personality characteristics. In a dimensional approach, an individual would be classified not as having a dependent or antisocial personality disorder, but rather as having a personality pattern that reflects the individual's standing on a variety of dimensions. The value of a dimensional approach is that it results in a profile for each person classified. One possibility would be a profile of ratings of the severity of various types of maladaptive personality patterns. While the time for dimensional classification might not yet have come (it involves somewhat novel and complex procedures), with further research to support its value, it might be incorporated into future DSMs.

Understanding and treating personality disorders can be advanced by recognizing their multiple causes. People with these disorders have varied combinations of vulnerability and risk factors on the one hand, and resiliency features on the other. Their traits can best be understood as developing from the interaction of biologically rooted factors, such as temperament, and their many types of life experiences. Social influences can act either as protective factors against personality disorder that buffer the effects of biological and psychological risk, or as risk factors in their own right. Personality disorders are highly complex phenomena and their multidimensional character needs to be borne in mind by researchers and clinicians.

CLASSIFYING PERSONALITY DISORDERS

Personality disorders are longstanding, maladaptive, inflexible ways of relating to the environment. These disorders are diagnosed on Axis II of DSM-IV. Many people with personality disorders also have a diagnosis on Axis I. Personality disorders can be grouped into three categories: odd or eccentric behaviors; dramatic, emotional, or erratic behaviors; and anxious or fearful behaviors.

ODD OR ECCENTRIC BEHAVIOR

Paranoid Personality Disorder People with **paranoid personality disorder** are suspicious and mistrusting of others and hypersensitive; they expect to be taken advantage of, and read hidden meanings into benign remarks or events.

Schizoid Personality Disorder Those diagnosed with **schizoid personality disorder** are withdrawn and seclusive, prefer to work alone, and do not seem interested in warm close relationships with others.

Schizotypal Personality Disorder Schizotypal personality disorder is associated with odd ways of thinking, perceiving, communicating, and behaving—although these deviations are not as extreme as those seen in people diagnosed with a schizophrenic disorder. Some research suggests that this disorder may be related to schizophrenia as a weak form of that disorder.

DRAMATIC, EMOTIONAL, OR ERRATIC BEHAVIOR

Histrionic Personality Disorder People with **histrionic personality disorder** are self-centered, manipulative, and have stormy interpersonal relationships.

Narcissistic Personality Disorder Factors that are important in the diagnosis of **narcissistic personality disorder** are an extreme sense of self-importance, need for constant attention, fragility of self-esteem, and a lack of empathy for others.

Borderline Personality Disorder Those diagnosed as having a **borderline personality disorder** have unstable personal relationships, often threaten and frequently engage in self-destructive behavior, are very impulsive, and tend to have relationships characterized by intense clinging dependency and manipulation of others. Because of the frequency of the borderline diagnosis, more work is done on treatment of this disorder than on the other personality disorders.

Antisocial Personality Disorder Antisocial personality disorder is typified by a chronic and continuous history of behavior that violates the rights of others. This history begins before age 15 and continues into adulthood. In adulthood these individuals continue to have a history of antisocial acts against property and other people, and are likely to be reckless and sexually promiscuous, and to lack remorse for hurting others. Many acts of criminal and antisocial behavior are committed by people who do not fit the classification of antisocial personality disorder. Traditional psychotherapy does not seem effective with individuals with antisocial personality.

ANXIOUS OR FEARFUL BEHAVIOR

Avoidant Personality Disorder People diagnosed as having **avoidant personality disorder** have low self-esteem, worry about negative evaluation by others, and avoid social interactions. Although they desire affection and close relationships, fear of rejection seems to keep these people from seeking such relationships.

Dependent Personality Disorder People with **dependent personality disorder** lack confidence in their ability to function independently. In order to maintain their dependent relationships, they are willing to subordinate their own needs and wishes to those of others.

Obsessive-Compulsive Personality Disorder Obsessive-compulsive personality disorder is characterized by lack of ability to express warm emotions, extreme perfectionism, and a rigid approach to the way things "should" be done.

TREATMENT OF PERSONALITY DISORDERS

Because many people with personality disorders never come to clinicians' attention, researchers have only studied a limited sample of this group. People with personality disorders may not seek clinical help because they see the environment as the source of any problems. They are also likely to behave appropriately much of the time so that their problems do not cause others to refer them for treatment. Therapeutic approaches from each of the perspectives, sometimes in combination, are used for treating these individuals. These include a variety of psychoactive drugs, behavioral techniques such as assertiveness training and systematic desensitization, cognitive therapies, and psychodynamic therapies. Family or group therapies focus on the effects of the behaviors on others.

THE OUTLOOK FOR PERSONALITY DISORDER CLASSIFICATION

Because the current classifications of personality disorders overlap with each other, it is likely that as more research is done the conceptualizations of the disorders may change and new categories may be added. Another possibility is that a dimensional model that focuses on personality patterns might be preferable to the categorical model in current use.

CHAPTER TEN

Sherri Silverman, *Blue Woman in Red,* 1993.
Superstock.

MOOD DISORDERS

It is difficult to put into words how I felt at that time. I guess my major reaction was one of despair—a despair of ever being human again. I honestly felt subhuman, lower than the lowest vermin. Furthermore, I was self-deprecatory and could not understand why anyone would want to associate with me, let alone love me. I became mistrustful and suspicious of others and was certain that they were checking up on me to prove that I was incompetent myself. . . . I had become increasingly concerned about finances. On one hand, I thought that I was receiving extra money that I didn't deserve and, on the other, I was certain that we were going bankrupt. In any case, I was positive that I was going to wind up in jail. When I received my July salary statement it appeared to me that the total was larger than it should be. This frightened me and I told my wife that we should phone the university immediately and arrange to return the extra money before I got into trouble. Gently, my wife told me that she thought the amount of money was correct and there was nothing to worry about. Of course, she was right. . . . I not only pondered my current situation but my whole career as well. I was positive that I was a fraud and a phony and that I didn't deserve my Ph.D. I didn't deserve to have tenure; I didn't deserve to be a Full Professor . . . I didn't deserve the research grants I had been awarded; I couldn't understand how I had written the books and journal articles that I had and how they had been accepted for publication. I must have conned a lot of people.

—Endler, 1990, pp. 41–42

These were the thoughts of a well-known psychologist during a period of severe depression. They illustrate how drastically depression may alter mood, perception, and behavior. A period of mania, on the other hand, leads to quite different thoughts and feelings, as described here:

When I am high I couldn't worry about money if I tried. So I don't. The money will come from somewhere, I am entitled, God will provide. Credit cards are disastrous, personal checks worse. . . . So, I bought twelve snake bite kits, with a sense of urgency and importance. I bought precious stones, elegant and unnecessary furniture, three watches within an hour of one another (in the Rolex rather than Timex class: champagne tastes bubble to the surface, are the surface, in mania), and totally inappropriate siren-like clothes. During one spree I spent several hundred on books having titles or covers that somehow caught my fancy. . . . Once I shoplifted a blouse because I could not wait a minute longer for the woman-with-molasses-feet in front of me in line. I imagine I must have spent far more than $30,000 during my two manic episodes, and God only knows how much more during my frequent hypomanias. I haven't any idea where most of the money went.

—Goodwin & Jamison, 1990, p. 29

Mood Disorders

The two examples given illustrate the wide range of behaviors that may be seen in mood disorders. The three main types of mood disorders are shown in Table 10-1. Depressive disorders and bipolar disorders reflect a disturbance in mood or emotional reaction that is not due to any other physical or mental disorder. These two groups of mood disorders are the focus of this chapter. In addition, approximately one of every ten major depressive episodes is caused by medical illnesses, substance abuse, or medications used to treat another disorder (Clinton, 1993). Mood disorders may occur due to a general medical condition such as cancer, diabetes, or a recent heart attack. Almost one of every four hospitalized medical patients has depressive symptoms (Moldin, 1993). Some of these aspects of depression are discussed in chapter 7. Use of both prescription medications and illegal drugs, as well as exposure to other chemicals, can also produce mood disorder. Some of these effects are discussed in chapter 14.

How Common Are Mood Disorders?

Many researchers have studied the degree to which mood disorders of the two major types shown in Table 10-1, depressive disorders and bipolar disorders, occur in the overall population. One of the best ways to get this information is through an epidemiological study in which a large number of people are surveyed. A team of researchers (Weissman et al., 1990) used a sample of

TABLE 10–1 Types of Mood Disorder	
Depressive Disorders	
Dysthymic disorder	History of depressed mood a majority of the time
Major depressive disorder	One or more major depressive episodes
Bipolar Disorders	
Cyclothymic disorder	Numerous hypomanic episodes and numerous periods of depressive symptoms that do not meet criteria for major depressive episode
Bipolar I disorder	One or more manic episodes and usually one or more major depressive episodes
Bipolar II disorder	At least one hypomanic episode and one or more major depressive episodes but no manic episode or cyclothymia
Other Mood Disorders	
Mood disorder due to a general medical condition Substance-induced mood disorder	

20,000 scientifically selected people from five areas in the United States to carry out the Epidemiological Catchment Area study (ECA). All these people were interviewed and 7.8 percent of them were found to have met the criteria for a mood disorder one or more times in the past. The ECA study found that the reported rate of mood disorder was *generally similar* for whites, Hispanics, and African Americans, although African Americans did report slightly lower rates of mood disorder than the other two groups. Although few racial or ethnic differences were found, there was a dramatic difference in the rate of mood disorder for men and women. Twice as many women as men reported a mood disorder of some type in either the present or the past. This same difference was found for all time periods considered, including a lifetime, one year, or one month. The difference was accounted for by the higher rate of depressive disorders women reported; the rate of bipolar disorder for men and women did not differ significantly.

Depression

The term *depression* covers a variety of negative moods and behavior changes. Some are normal mood fluctuations and others meet the definition of clinical problems. The mood change may be temporary or long lasting. It may range from a relatively minor feeling of melancholy to a deeply negative view of the world and an inability to function effectively. In this section we discuss several aspects of depression—temporarily depressed mood, long-lasting downward or negative mood that may interfere only mildly with effective behavior, and severely depressed mood accompanied by a marked but usually temporary inability to function effectively.

Depressed Mood

The word *depression* is part of our everyday language. How often have you said you felt depressed or blue? These feelings occur in all of us. They may occur in rainy weather, during an annoying cold, or after an argument with a friend. Often an event that is usually expected to be happy ends with such feelings. People may experience the blues after such holidays as Christmas or New Year's Day or after moving to a new home. These feelings of depression based on temporary situations usually fade away quickly. They are quite different from the feelings of being under a black cloud that accompany a depressive episode or major depressive disorder (Hamilton, 1982).

People also use the term depression to describe a sadness that comes from a death in the family. After the death of someone they care deeply about, most survivors experience a depressed mood that is usually called grief. These feelings of depression are entirely normal. As we discussed in chapter 5, common features of grief include physical distress such as sighing, tightness of the throat, an empty feeling in the abdomen, and a feeling of muscular weakness. In addition, there may be preoccupation with the visual image of the dead person, along with guilt and hostile reactions. During the normal process of grieving, the guilt, hostility, feelings of loss, and physical symptoms gradually disappear.

These same symptoms may be the result of any other kind of important loss. For example, the breakup of a dating relationship, or divorce or separation, may also bring about these feelings; they are likely to occur regardless of who wanted to end the relationship. Such feelings often represent a short-term response to stress.

A 24-year-old, single, female nursery-school teacher terminated brief psychotherapy after ten sessions. She had entered treatment two weeks after she discovered that the man she had been involved with for four months was married and wanted to stop seeing her. She reacted with bouts of sadness and crying, felt she was falling apart, took a week's sick leave from her job, and had vague thoughts that the future was so bleak that life might not be worth the effort. She felt that she must be in some essential way "flawed"; otherwise she would not have gotten so involved with someone who had no inten-

tions of maintaining a long-term relationship. She felt that others "would have seen it," that only she was "so stupid" as to have been deceived. There were no other signs of a depressive syndrome, such as loss of interest or appetite or trouble concentrating. She responded to mixed supportive-insight psychotherapy and, toward the end of treatment, began dating a law student whom she met at a local cafe.

—Spitzer et al., 1981, p. 261

Other kinds of stressful life events—losing a job, being turned down for a graduate school program, or losing everything in a fire—may also bring on feelings of depression. These feelings of loss not due to bereavement that are not severe enough to be called mood disorders are classified as an adjustment disorder with depressed mood (adjustment disorders are discussed in chapter 5). In addition, depressed mood is an important symptom in a variety of other disorders including borderline personality disorder, schizophrenia, and physical changes in the brain such as those seen in Alzheimer's disease. In such instances, depression is seen as a response or symptom of a life stress or physical change and is not usually considered to reflect a mood disorder.

Perhaps because the term depression is so much a part of our language and because virtually everyone has experienced "the blues" at one time or another, many people do not regard depression as a problem needing treatment. In a poll of a representative sample of Americans sponsored by the National Mental Health Association, those contacted were divided as to whether depression, defined as a mental disorder that "interferes with one's emotional and physical well-being" was a health problem (46 percent) or a personal weakness (43 percent) (*Psychiatric News*, June 3, 1992, p. 9). About two-thirds of those who believed they had had such a depression reported they had not sought treatment.

Risk Factors

Just as we have said throughout this book the chance that any person may develop a particular disorder is related to that person's biological vulnerabilities, other risk factors in the environment, and the presence or absence of factors that promote resiliency. Risk factors affecting depression include heredity, age, gender, and lack of social support.

Heredity An important risk factor is genetic makeup. Studies of twins and of families clearly suggest a genetic component in both major depression and bipolar disorders. There is a much greater risk of developing a major depression if one's identical twin has had this disorder than if one's parent, brother, or sister has experienced it. The chances of developing the disorder are even less if a person has no close relatives that have ever been given this diagnosis. Figure 10-1 shows how the closeness of

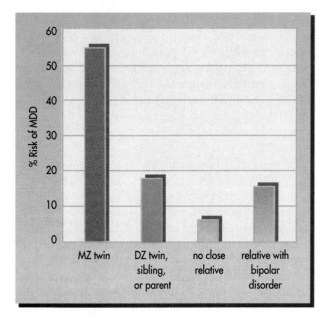

Figure 10-1 Relationship to person with major depressive disorder (MDD). Risk for developing a major depressive disorder based on occurrence of depression or bipolar disorder in family members of varying degrees of genetic closeness.

SOURCE: Data from Gershon et al., (1988). "Mood Disorders: Genetic Aspects." In H. I. Kaplan and B. J. Sadock (eds.) *Textbook of Psychiatry, 5/e.* Williams and Wilkins.

relationship to a person with a major depressive disorder affects a person's risk. Figure 10-1 also indicates that both major depression and bipolar disorders may be associated with the same genetic makeup. Those with relatives with a bipolar diagnosis have almost three times as great a chance of developing a major depression as those who have no family member with either a diagnosis of depression or bipolar disorder.

Family studies have shown that the younger people are when their first major depression occurs, the more likely it is that their relatives will also experience periods of depression. Relatives of people whose first depressive episode had occurred before the age of 20 had an eight-times greater chance of becoming depressed than relatives of normal subjects. Relatives of people who were over 40 when they first had a major depression had little more than the normal risk of depression. This increased risk was found both for relatives of patients who were hospitalized and for relatives of individuals who did not need to be hospitalized (Weissman et al., 1984).

Although major depression has been consistently shown to run in families (Tsuang & Faraone, 1990), much less is known about how heredity affects the clinical features of the disorder such as number and type of symptoms, age at which the first depression occurs, and length of period of severely depressed mood. A sample of 176 pairs of female twins chosen from the Virginia

Twin Registry was used to study these questions (Kendler et al., 1992). Use of such a twin registry provides nonbiased information because—rather than being selected from those who have sought treatment—the names on the register are gathered from a systematic review of all birth certificates over a long period of time. A comparison of the results for monozygotic (MZ) and dizygotic (DZ) twins showed that whether depression was recurrent or not seemed to be affected by genetic factors. However, within the group experiencing recurrent episodes, the actual number of episodes seemed to be related to stressful life experiences not shared by the other twin in the pair rather than to heredity. MZ twins were more likely than DZ twins to be similar in what are called *negative* symptoms of depression (changes in weight, appetite, and sleep). In contrast, treatment-seeking appeared to be related to environmental or family variables rather than to any genetic pattern.

Although genetic factors seem important in many cases of depression, the exact mechanism of inheritance of depression is not clear and may even vary from one family to another. Nongenetic factors, either physical or related to a person's environment or relationships, may be required to produce depression even in people with a genetic vulnerability.

Age Another risk factor for depression is age. The risk for a first episode of any degree of depression is highest in women between the ages of 20 and 29. For men, the similar risk period is between the ages of 40 and 49 (Rorsman et al., 1990). In addition to age, another factor is year of birth or the birth cohort to which a person belongs. Box 10-1 shows that recent cohorts have a higher risk of depression.

Gender One of the greatest risk factors for depression is simply being female. Women are at least twice as likely to experience all types of depressed states than are men. Past researchers have tried to understand this difference in cultural terms. In American culture it has been thought to be more acceptable in general for women than for men to seek help for emotional problems. Women are more likely to consult physicians or mental health experts and to take a psychological view of their problems than they are to see them only in terms of physical symptoms. However, these explanations of more women *seeking treatment* for depression do not explain the higher overall *rate* for depression because the same difference in rate of depressive disorder for women and men has been consistently found in community surveys such as the ECA study described earlier, where people are contacted on a randomized basis and not because they have sought help. One explanation that has been suggested by researchers interested in social support and its effect on health is that while

The Changing Rate of Major Depression

A person's chances of experiencing a major depression are related to the risk factors listed: stressful life events, heredity, age, gender, and the absence of supportive close relationships. But another factor, one harder to understand, seems important as well—a person's birth cohort. This means that the year (or decade) in which people were born has important predictive value for the probability that they will experience depression at any particular age or whether they will experience depression over their lifetime.

Nine independent epidemiological studies as well as three family studies conducted in the 1980s in North America, Puerto Rico, Western Europe, the Middle East, Asia, and the Pacific Rim have all obtained similar results—those born in more recent cohorts have increased risk for major depression compared to those in earlier cohorts (Cross-National Collaborative Group, 1992). This means that there has been an overall increase in major depression over time over all countries. Figure 10-2 shows the results of the large ECA study mentioned at the beginning of this chapter. This figure shows that there is an increase in rate at age 25 that begins with the cohort born between 1935 and 1944. Not only did more people experience a major depression, but those born

in later decades were more likely to experience it at a younger age.

An advantage of comparing results of large epidemiological studies carried out in different places around the world is that differences in findings may provide clues to the help in understanding the study results. For example, because all studies were cross-sectional, the increase in later cohorts might be due to forgetting over time. However, comparison of the results of the different studies suggests memory differences are not an adequate explanation. Studies done in various countries show differences that can be related to stressful events in that area. For example, Figure 10-3 shows the cumulative lifetime cohort rates for Beirut, Lebanon. Those who were 20 years old or younger when the Lebanon wars began in 1975 show the highest cumulative rates. The researchers also found significant short-term fluctuations in rates at different time periods as well as by cohort. In Beirut, for example, there was a dramatic short-term increase from 1950–1960 during a time of political chaos and war. From 1960 to 1970, a period of relative social and economic prosperity and stability, the rate decreased, and increased again during the 1970–1980 period when the Lebanese war again intensified. This period effect is shown in Figure 10-4.

Depression may result from a pileup of life stressors. For example, inhabitants of Beirut, Lebanon, have lived amid destruction and the constant threat of violence for many years. Workers in many countries face the threat of unemployment or as these former workers in Newark, New Jersey, have found, the reality of unemployment lines.

Figure 10-2 Cumulative lifetime rates of major depressive disorder (MDD) in the 5 site Epidemiologic Catchment Area Study.

SOURCE: Cross-National Collaborative Group, 1992, "The changing rate of major depression: Cross-national comparison." *Journal of the American Medical Association,* (1992), Vol. 268, p. 3100.

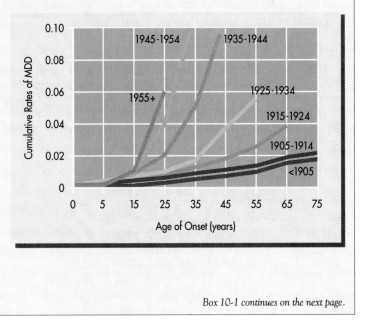

Box 10-1 continues on the next page.

Figure 10-3 Cumulative lifetime rate of major depression (MDD) by birth cohort and age of onset for Beirut, Lebanon, and the surrounding area. Note the elevated risk for the cohort born after 1955.

SOURCE: "The changing rate of major depression: Cross-national comparison." *Journal of the American Medical Association,* (1992), Vol. 268, p. 3100.

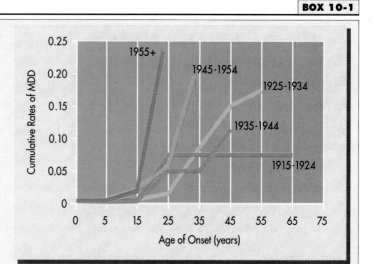

Figure 10-4 Short term overall increase or decrease in major depression is related to political events. The period 1960–1970 was a relatively stable and prosperous period. 1950–1960 and 1970–1980 were periods of war and civil unrest during which depression increased in the population.

SOURCE: "The changing rate of major depression: Cross-national comparison." *Journal of the American Medical Association,* (1992), Vol. 268, p. 3104.

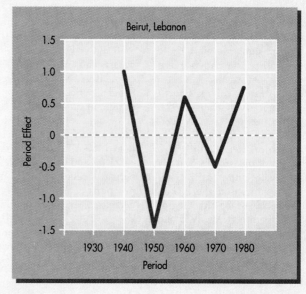

Why is depression increasing worldwide so that younger people are at greater risk? Many explanations have been advanced. Among them are alcohol and drug abuse, changes in marital stability and family structure, changes in employment opportunities, urbanization, and a variety of toxic agents at every site. Although research is being carried out on many of these topics, the comparison of results from large studies in different cultural settings so far makes it possible to say with confidence that there is an increase but that conditions specific to a particular country also play a role.

women in general receive more social support than do men, they are also expected to offer more support (Shumaker & Hill, 1991). Because support-giving often involves them in the problems and stressors experienced by others, women may thus experience more stress than men. This idea is supported by a study that found that much of the difference in rates of depression between men and women from 25 to 45 years of age was explained by the particularly high rate for married women, compared to the rates either for other women or for men (Paykel, 1991). During this age period married women are likely to have an especially high level of stress because of their role in caring for young children in addition to their roles in providing support to their extended families and to their responsibilities in the employment arena.

Social Support Epidemiological studies clearly support an added risk for depression for people who lack close relationships. In addition, social support from relationships has a protective effect once a person is subjected to severe stressors (Henderson, 1992). Recently, more emphasis has been placed on the possible effects of unsupportive behaviors that may also be part of close relationships. Behaviors implying that someone deserves criticism or is unworthy of loyalty are more likely to be related to depression than is the mere absence of support (Harris, 1992). For example, a woman may be protected from depression by the support of her close friend after the woman's son has been arrested for stealing. But if the woman's husband then blames his wife for the son's behavior by saying it was caused by the way she raised him, the support from the friend is no longer effective (Harris, 1992).

Life Events

The teacher described earlier had experienced a stressful event, the breakup of a romance. Although environmental factors such as life events, especially a pile up of stressful events in a short time period, may play a significant role in producing an episode of depression, their effects are generally short in duration. They do not affect a person's long term vulnerability to depression (Kendler and others, 1993). Whether life events produce depression or some other disorder, such as ulcers, for a particular individual may be determined by the person's genetic vulnerability. Life events and genetic vulnerability may also be interrelated. Recent research suggests that neither genes nor family environment is likely to produce life events directly, but both factors may predispose a person to negative life events. This statement indicates that stressful life events are not random but are often associated with a person's vulnerability and life circumstances, not simply with "bad luck" (Kendler, 1993). In addition to individual life events, long-term ongoing life situations such as being caretaker to an invalid spouse or parent or having several young children to care for also put people at risk for depression.

Depressive Disorders

How can we distinguish between the blues or "normal depression" we all feel once in a while and a **depressive disorder** (depression that fits DSM-IV criteria)? Some of the symptoms of depressive disorder include dissatisfaction and anxiety; changes in appetite, sleep, and psychomotor functions; loss of interest and energy; feelings of guilt; thoughts of death; and diminished

concentration. Figure 10-5 shows that many of these symptoms of depression are frequently reported by people who are not classified as having a depressive disor-

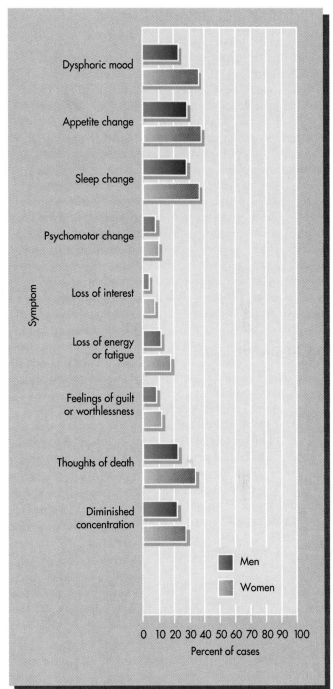

Figure 10-5 Percent of all individuals in the general population surveyed by the Epidemiological Area Catchment Study who reported having experienced each of these symptoms of depression for two weeks or longer.

SOURCE: Reprinted with permission of the Free Press, a Division of Simon & Schuster, Inc. from *Psychiatric Disorders in America* by Lee N. Robins, Ph.D. and Darrel A. Regier, M.D. Copyright © 1991 by Lee N. Robins, Ph.D. and Darrel A. Regier, M.D.

der. For instance, almost 23 percent of men and 36 percent of women in the ECA study reported a period lasting two weeks or more when they felt sad and blue ("dysphoric mood" in the figure). However, only a much smaller proportion of the population (about 3.6 percent of men and 8.7 percent of women) had enough of these symptoms at any one time so that they could be classified as experiencing a depressive episode. If you compare Figure 10-5 with Figure 10-6 you can see that, although these symptoms occur relatively frequently in the general population, they are much more frequent in people who are clinically depressed.

Symptoms of depression like those listed above are also likely to occur in bipolar disorders. For this reason, the term **unipolar disorder** is often used when discussing different types of depressive disorder to distinguish between people who have experienced one or more episodes of depression but no manic or hypomanic episode and those who have a past history that includes at least one episode of mania or hypomania. Individuals who have one or more episodes of mania or hypomania as well as periods of depression are diagnosed as having bipolar disorder. Bipolar disorder is discussed later in the chapter.

Dysthymic Disorder

The milder, less incapacitating form of depressive disorder is **dysthymic disorder.** (The term "dysthymia" comes from the Greek words meaning "defective or diseased mood.") Dysthymic disorder tends to be chronic, often lasting for years, and sometimes is hard to distinguish from a personality disorder. In order to be classified as a dysthymic disorder, the depressed mood or loss of interest or pleasure and other symptoms must be of longstanding duration. Even though this longstanding depressed mood may be interrupted by periods of a few days or a few weeks of normal mood, the depressed feelings are those that dominate over time.

People with dysthymic disorder tend to be depressed most of the day, more days than not, based on their own description or the description of others. They also have at least two of the following problems: difficulties with eating (either poor appetite or overeating), difficulties with sleeping (either insomnia or sleeping too much), constant feelings of tiredness, difficulty concentrating or making decisions, a low opinion of themselves, and feelings of hopelessness. Dysthymic disorder, unlike major depression, shows little variability with age. The rate is stable from age 18 through age 64 and only declines after age 65. The length of a period of dysthymia has been found to extend from between 2 to at least 20 years. The median duration is about 5 years (Keller, 1990).

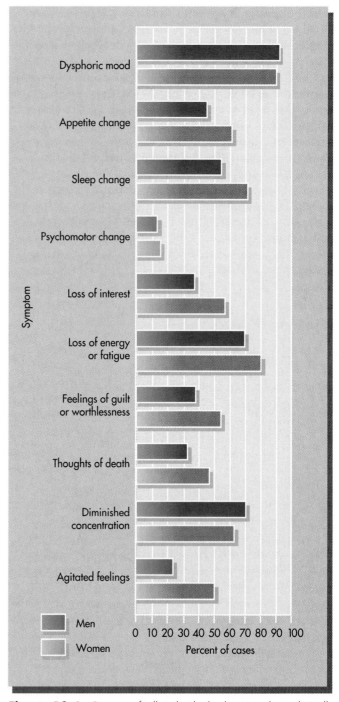

Figure 10-6 Percent of all individuals diagnosed as clinically depressed who report having each of these symptoms of depression.

SOURCE: Reprinted with permission of The Free Press, a Division of Simon & Schuster, Inc. from *Psychiatric Disorders in America* by Lee N. Robins, Ph.D. and Darrel A. Regier, M.D. Copyright © 1991 by Lee N. Robins, Ph.D. and Darrel A. Regier, M.D.

Dysthymic disorder can coexist with any of the other mood disorders, but it is most likely to occur along with a major depressive episode. Periods of intense depression are usually described as time-limited, which means that even without treatment the symptoms tend to lessen over time by some naturally occurring process. In contrast, dysthymic disorder tends to be chronic and persist for long periods, often over years of a person's life. If a person with dysthymic disorder develops symptoms of major depression as well, they are said to have "double depression" because at that time they meet the criteria for both diagnoses. This dual state occurs quite frequently. Almost half of the people studied in the ECA study who had dysthymic disorder also had at least one episode of major depression in their lifetime. Figure 10-7 shows the overlap of the two disorders. If recovery is defined as recovery from both dysthymic disorder and the depressive episode, more than 60 percent of patients had not yet recovered after two years (Keller, 1990).

Dysthymic disorder is likely to begin sometime in the period from childhood to early adulthood. Many researchers believe dysthymic disorder is biologically related to depression and that people with this disorder have a high risk of a major depressive disorder (Howland & Thase, 1991). Individuals diagnosed with dysthymic disorder have some of the same characteristics typically found in those with major depressive disorder. These characteristics include impaired continuity of sleep and abnormal rapid eye movement (REM) sleep periods (Howland & Thase, 1991). This group is also more likely to have relatives who have been diagnosed with a major depressive disorder (Akiskal, 1994).

The following case describes a woman diagnosed with dysthymic disorder whose problems with depression have persisted in spite of extensive psychotherapy. Throughout her adult life she has continued to show dysthymic symptoms. She continually feels inferior and without attraction for others. Even when events should suggest to her that she is attractive or competent, she seems to go out of her way to prove to herself that such is not the case.

The 28-year-old junior executive had obtained a master's degree in business administration and moved to California a year and a half earlier to begin work in a large firm. She told the therapist in her initial interview that she had had extensive psychotherapy previously, but that she was "depressed" about everything: her job, her husband, and her prospects for the future.

Her complaints were of persistent feelings of depressed mood, inferiority, and pessimism, which she claims to have had since she was 16 or 17 years old. Although she did reasonably well in college, she consistently ruminated about those students who were "genuinely intelligent." She dated during college and graduate school, but claimed that she would never go after a guy she thought was "special," always feeling inferior and intimidated. Whenever she saw or met such a man, she acted stiff and aloof, or actually walked away as quickly as possible, only to berate herself afterward and then fantasize about him for many months. She claimed that her therapy had helped, although she still could not remember a time when she didn't feel somewhat depressed.

Just after graduation, she married the man she was going out with at the time primarily because she felt she "needed a husband" for companionship. Shortly after their marriage, the couple started to bicker. She was very critical of his clothes, his job, and his parents; and he, in turn, found her rejecting, controlling, and moody. She began to feel that she had made a mistake in marrying him. Her social life with her husband involves several other couples. The man in these couples is usually a friend of her husband's. She is sure that the women find her uninteresting and unimpressive, and that the people who seem to like her are probably no better off than she.

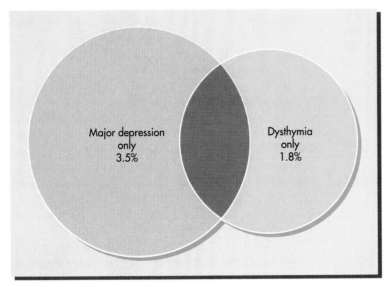

Figure 10-7 Percent of individuals in the ECA study who had overlapping diagnoses—or comorbidity—of major depression and dysthymia over the lifetime compared to the percentages of those in the sample who had only one of these diagnoses.

SOURCE: Reprinted with permission of the Free Press, a Division of Simon & Schuster, Inc. from *Psychiatric Disorders in America*, by Lee N. Robins, Ph.D. and Darrel A. Regier, M.D. Copyright © 1991 by Lee N. Robins, Ph.D. and Darrel A. Regier, M.D.

Major depression
only
3.5%

Dysthymia
only
1.8%

Recently she has also been having difficulties at work. She is assigned the most menial tasks at the firm and is never given an assignment of importance or responsibility. She admits that she frequently does a "slipshod" job of what is given her, never does more than is required, and never demonstrates any assertiveness or initiative to her supervisors. She views her boss as self-centered, unconcerned, and unfair, but nevertheless admires his success.

—Spitzer et al., 1981, pp. 10–11

Major Depressive Disorder

Someone who has major depressive disorder has experienced one or more major depressive episodes without ever experiencing a manic or hypomanic episode.

Major Depressive Episode A major depressive episode is marked by depressed mood or a loss of interest or pleasure in almost all activities and at least four other symptoms from those listed below. These symptoms must last at least two weeks and represent a change from the person's usual functioning. The additional symptoms that may occur in a major depressive episode include: marked weight loss or gain when not dieting, constant sleeping problems, agitated or greatly slowed-down behavior, fatigue, inability to think clearly, feelings of worthlessness, and frequent thoughts about death or suicide. Figure 10-6 showed the incidence of these symptoms among those diagnosed as depressed.

The description of Mrs. B. provides a typical example of a major depressive episode. She was brought to a psychiatrist's office by her concerned husband. When he had called to make an appointment and was told that the first one available was in 10 days, he had responded that he didn't think his wife could wait that long. Mrs. B., the mother of two children, was a 45-year-old legal secretary.

Mrs. B was dressed in wrinkled and slightly soiled clothing. Her hair was carelessly combed and there was a faint body odor about her. Her face was drawn and expressionless. She was helped by her husband into the office where she sat motionless, staring at the floor and occasionally sighing audibly. She said nothing unless asked a simple direct question. Even then her answers were delayed, spoken slowly, and of a droning, monotonous quality. A portion of the interview went as follows:

Dr. R: *What's the trouble that brings you in?*

Mrs. B: *I don't care about anything.*

Dr. R: *What do you mean?*

Mrs. B: *(no response)*

Dr. R: *You look sad.*

Mrs. B: *Yes . . . not sad . . . just nothing.*

Dr. R: *How long have you been like this?*

Mrs. B: *About three weeks . . . getting worse.*

Dr. R: *Has anything like this ever happened to you before?*

Mrs. B: *No.*

Dr. R: *How's your appetite?*

Mrs. B: *No appetite.*

Dr. R: *Have you lost weight these three weeks?*

Mrs. B: *I don't know . . . maybe 10 or 12 lbs.*

Dr. R: *How's your sleeping?*

Mrs. B: *Bad, I wake up every morning about 3 and just lay there.*

Dr. R: *Do you feel bad about anything?*

Mrs. B: *Everything . . . I wish I were dead.*

—Tomb and Christensen, 1987, p. 198

After her interview, Mrs. B.'s husband spoke with the psychiatrist. He said he and his wife had been married 26 years and this behavior was very different from any she had ever shown before. He thought the trouble had begun about a month earlier. At that time she was too tired to take part in her favorite activity, boating.

Gradually she has withdrawn. She doesn't want to see anybody, just wants to rest but I never see her sleeping. I force her to eat. I guess I panicked yesterday when she said she wanted to die.

—Tomb and Christensen, 1987, p. 198

A depressive episode lasts a variable length of time. It may end completely in a few weeks or months or it may merely lessen with some symptoms continuing for a long period. For a few individuals the symptoms may continue to meet the criteria a year later. Although bereavement or loss of a close loved one can result in behavior similar to that classified as a depressive disorder, a bereaved person who experiences these symptoms for two months or less is not considered to have experienced a major depressive episode.

Recurrent Major Depressive Disorder At least half of those people who are diagnosed with a major depressive episode will have at least one more episode in their lifetime. With each additional episode the chances of yet another one increase. A severe life stress may play an important part in the occurrence of the first or even the second episodes of a major depressive disorder. Later episodes seem less likely to be related to a stressful life situation.

Heredity also plays a role. Those who have a close relative with this disorder have up to three times the average risk for also being diagnosed with it. Up to 10 percent of those who initially have a single episode of a major depressive disorder will eventually have a manic episode as well. The initial diagnosis of major depressive disorder will then change to bipolar disorder.

Major Depressive Episode With Psychotic Features

About 15 percent of people with a major depression have some psychotic symptoms, usually delusions (false beliefs about reality). The delusions typically include guilt—"It is my fault that she is ill," punishment—"I am suffering because I am a terrible person," or poverty—"I will go bankrupt and starve in my old age." Sometimes, but more rarely, the delusions do not have depressive themes. Psychotic depression may have some distinct features that differentiate it from other types of major depressive disorder. Some researchers have argued that psychotic depression should be a separate DSM category (Schatzberg & Rothschild, 1992).

Behavior typical of depression with psychotic features is illustrated by the case of a 58-year-old man brought to the emergency room by his wife and son:

> . . . He was working as an architect and doing well until three weeks ago. At that time, he became noticeably more quiet and began to withdraw to his room immediately after dinner. One week ago he refused to go to work, stopped eating, and began to pace the floor at night. He would wring his hands, clench his fists, and cry. He talked of many minor life events as being "major sins" and today began to warn his family that he was really "the devil." "All these years you've mistaken me for your father. I am the devil, Satan himself. No one is more evil and wretched than me. I bring death and

> disease to the world and I will burn in Hell forever." This is the third time in five years he has presented himself in such a state. Each time he has professed the belief that his identity has been mistaken and he is really the devil.

> —Tomb and Christensen, 1987, p. 49

Whether psychotic features are present or not, severe depression is highly visible to others. Not only are those who are severely depressed unable to work or carry on other normal life activities, but they also seem immersed in their own misery. The well-known American artist Jacob Lawrence has captured an artistic view of severe depression in his painting of hospitalized depressed men (see Figure 10-8).

Theoretical Perspectives on Depression

Most researchers think that depression results from an interaction between a person's biological and psychological vulnerabilities and the occurrence of stressful events or difficult ongoing situations in his or her life (Akiskal, 1985). Despite this widely held view that both personal and situational characteristics are important, most of the perspectives discussed in this book try to understand the causes of depression and to find effective treatment approaches while generally looking at only one aspect of this complex interaction. However, these different theoretical approaches to depression have produced different types of studies and different data, which may add to our understanding of the causes and treatment of this complex disorder.

Figure 10-8 In his painting *Depression*, artist Jacob Lawrence has shown the downcast eyes, the drooping head and shoulders, and the shrunken posture of people who are deeply depressed.

Biological Theories

Biological theories assume that the cause of depression lies either in the genes or in some physiological malfunction that may or may not have an inherited base.

Neurotransmitters Whatever the mechanism by which the genetic factor is inherited, its influences are biochemical. Depression is probably the result of a lack of certain chemical neurotransmitters at particular sites in the brain. Neurotransmitter systems, especially the **monoamine neurotransmitters,** have been the most widely studied biological phenomena in depression. The most important monoamines are the **catecholamines** norepinephrine and dopamine and the **indolamine** serotonin. Other neurotransmitters that have been thought to play a role in depression include **gamma aminobutyric acid** (GABA), which seems to inhibit neurotransmitter action and is widely found in the central nervous system, and **acetylcholine,** which is found in both the central and the peripheral nervous systems and can be either an inhibitor or a stimulator of transmission between neurons.

Each of the billions of neurons in the brain interacts with others by electrochemical means. When the neuron is stimulated, it releases neurotransmitters—chemical substances—from **vesicles,** or storage areas, in the presynaptic neuron. The neurotransmitter diffuses across the **synaptic cleft** or space between two neurons (see chapter 3) and interacts with a receptor, which is a highly specialized protein substance, on the outside surface of the postsynaptic neuron. Recent research on antidepressant drugs suggests that serotonin may play a central role in depression. The chemical name for serotonin is *5-hydroxytryptamine*. This chemical is synthesized by the body from the amino acid L-tryptophan in two steps. Figure 10-9 is a greatly simplified diagram that illustrates the activity of a serotonin synapse. The arrival of an electrical impulse or action potential in the presynaptic neuron results in the release of serotonin from vesicles where it has been stored after it has been synthesized from the amino acid tryptophan. The serotonin then moves into the synaptic cleft. Some of it finds its way to specialized receptors in the postsynaptic neuron. The postsynaptic or receiving neuron then alters its electrical and chemical activity. However, serotonin can also be removed from the synapse in two other ways. Reuptake mechanisms in the presynaptic neuron take the serotonin back into the presynaptic neuron where it is reused or chemically returned into an earlier stage of the process by

which it was synthesized in the neuron. Another way serotonin is deactivated is by the enzyme monoamine oxidase (MAO) that normally causes serotonin to change chemically. Both MAO and the reuptake mechanisms decrease the amount of serotonin available at the synapse.

A great deal has been learned about the role of the monoamines, especially serotonin, through studies of the action of different types of antidepressant drugs. Each group of drugs has a different approach to regulating the amount of serotonin in the synapse. The major types of antidepressants and their action are discussed more fully in the therapy section of this chapter. Antidepressants called MAO *inhibitors* work by inhibiting or lessening the ability of MAO to change serotonin into another form—5-hydroxyindole acetic acid (5-HIAA). This MAO inhibitor action leads to a buildup of serotonin in the brain. However, because MAO performs a number of other vital chemical functions in the brain, MAO inhibitors can be very toxic because they affect these other functions as well as altering the amount of serotonin available. In contrast to MAO inhibitors, *tricyclic antidepressants* (so named because of their three-ring chemical structure) work by blocking the reuptake of serotonin back into the presynaptic neuron. This results in a larger supply of serotonin in the synapse. Although tricyclic antidepressants do not have the more dangerous side effects of MAO inhibitors, they cause side effects by blocking the reuptake of norepinephrine and dopamine as well as of serotonin. The increase in

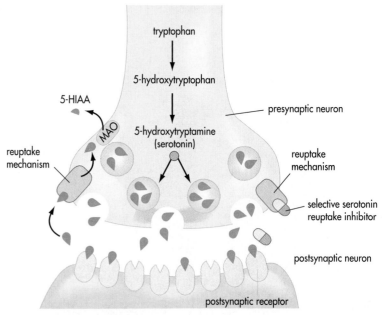

Figure 10-9 Simplified diagram of a serotonin synapse showing release and reuptake of serotonin as well as its binding to postsynaptic receptors.

SOURCE: Jacobs, (1994). "Seratonin, motor activity and depression related disorders." *American Scientist*, 82, p. 459.

these monamines may result in a variety of side effects including dryness of the mouth, constipation, and headaches. A newer group of drugs, called *selective serotonin reuptake inhibitors* limit their action to serotonin and thus cause fewer side effects. Each of these categories of antidepressant drugs is illustrated in Table 10-5 in the section on treatment of depression later in the chapter.

Research using antidepressant drugs showed that their use changed levels of norepinephrine and serotonin rather quickly after the drugs were taken. However, the mood-elevating effects of these changes often could not be observed for several weeks. One possibility is that, initially—when the levels of brain serotonin are increased—a feedback system inhibits the discharge of additional serotonin in order to normalize the situation. This action results in a stable amount of brain serotonin rather than in a net increase (deMontigny et al., 1990). According to this view, after a period of exposure to serotonin in the synapse the receptors become desensitized, resulting in progressively less feedback together with increased serotonin transmission and improvement in symptoms of depression. This desensitization hypothesis seems to account for the time lag between beginning drug therapy and the relief of symptoms, but it still does not completely explain the role of neurotransmitters in depression.

The Search for Markers of Depression Since most scientists agree that not all depressions have similar causes, a great deal of effort has been spent on finding subgroups of depressed patients that have similar characteristics. The study of such subgroups should not only make it easier to understand the causes of depression but, even more important, provide clues to the most effective treatment for a particular individual. A major focus of research in this area is the effort to develop a test that could be used to identify various subgroups just as laboratory tests are used to identify particular strains of bacteria in order to diagnose types of infection.

Hormonal Studies Although much of the biological research on mood disorders is aimed at learning more about biochemical activity, it is also becoming clear that the disorders involve many different organ systems in the body. The close connections of mood disorders with the endocrine system are just beginning to be understood. A high level of cortisol, a hormone produced in the cortex of the brain, has been consistently found in depressed patients. Actions of a variety of neurotransmitters have been thought to be basic steps in this cortisol excess. Research efforts have used neuroendocrine strategies to develop diagnostic tests or markers to define subgroups of patients who respond in specific ways. If these neuroendocrine-based tests could successfully divide patients into meaningful groups, the results

might be potentially useful both in understanding more about the role of hormones in depression and in defining subgroups of depressed patients for whom specific types of treatment or specific antidepressant drugs might be particularly helpful. So far, these efforts have added to general knowledge but have not been useful in a clinical setting.

One example of such a strategy is the **dexamethasone suppression test** (DST) (Carroll, 1985). In this test, patients are given dexamethasone, a steroid that suppresses the production of cortisol. Normally, dexamethasone suppresses the level of cortisol in the blood for about 24 hours. In some depressed patients, however, the suppression does not last that long. The problem with this test is that about 50 percent of people with depression have a normal response to dexamethasone. Thus, if only this test were used to identify depression, 50 percent of the people who are depressed would go undetected. On the other hand, the chances of getting a positive test result when the person is not depressed are less than 10 percent (Rothschild, 1993). Even within the group correctly identified as depressed, the test does not differentiate between depressive disorder and the depressed phase of bipolar disorders. This distinction is important because treatment of the two disorders differs. Another problem is that the dexamethasone-suppressor response has been reported in conditions other than depression—for example, alcoholism, schizophrenia, and eating disorders—as well as in normal individuals who were dieting. It seems unlikely that all these disorders share a common cause. More likely, DST reflects a nonspecific aspect of the severity of the person's disorder (Hirschfeld & Goodwin, 1988). Thus, the DST cannot be viewed as a clear diagnostic sign of depression. Another shortcoming of the DST is that it does not discriminate between people who may be helped by antidepressant drugs and those who would not. Since gaining such information to make appropriate clinical treatment more quickly available is one of the purposes of the search for markers, results of research with the DST have so far been disappointing and its use in clinical settings has decreased.

Scanning Techniques The use of scanning techniques to locate specific receptor sites has already been described. Findings from a variety of scanning techniques—computer tomography (CT), magnetic resonance imaging (MRI), positron emission tomography (PET), and single photon emission computed tomography (SPECT)—from studies of individuals with depression suggest that the disorder is associated with some type of regional brain dysfunction. Dysphoric mood, inability to experience pleasure, helplessness, and feelings of sadness all are shown by these scanning techniques to be associated with changes in blood flow in the cerebrum and/or with differences in metabolism in the frontal-temporal areas of the cortex and other specific brain areas (Cummings, 1993). Improvement as a result of treatment is accompanied by an increased rate of metabolism in the frontal cortex. This indicates that some of the differences observed in PET and SPECT studies are related to the person's current depressed state rather than to consistent characteristics of the individual.

Figure 10-10 shows how PET scans of the brain of a patient with a major depressive disorder indicate changes as the depression decreases as well as the effects of a drug that produces a lessening of depressed behaviors. Figure 10-11 shows a SPECT scan of a vertical interior view of the brain that is similar to the PET findings in showing decreased blood flow in the frontal brain region. An important area of future research using these imaging techniques involves finding whether any of these differences continue after patients have recovered from an episode of depression. Such research is important because we know that the risk of having a depressive episode increases greatly after the first episode has occurred. If the blood flow and metabolism return to normal this suggests that they are a result rather than an initial cause of the depressive episode.

Use of scanning techniques has also created hypotheses about biological causes of depression by documenting changes in brain function or brain anatomy in other disorders in which depression may be a secondary symptom. These disorders include stroke, Huntington's disease, multiple sclerosis, and epilepsy. In each of these disorders, patients who are depressed also show signs of regional brain dysfunction in patterns similar to those found in people whose primary problem is a major depressive disorder. Based on these similarities Cummings (1993) had proposed a model of depression that takes into account both brain blood flow and metabolism as well as the neurotransmitters serotonin, norepinephrine, and dopamine discussed earlier. Figure 10-12 illustrates how the behaviors characteristic of depression may be related directly to the functioning of certain brain structures that are affected by a variety of disorders, some of them genetic in origin. The genetic action may have a direct effect or may affect brain function indirectly by means of changes in neurotransmitter function. The use of scanning techniques can help researchers understand how changes in the living, active brain are related to depression either as a primary disorder or in association with other disorders involving the brain.

Biological Rhythms Differences in biological rhythms may be a way to identify subgroups of depressed

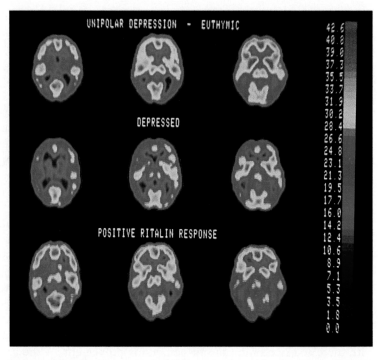

Figure 10-10 Three series of PET scans of unipolar depression illustrate how this technique can be used as an objective measure of the changes in biological activity that accompany certain behavior changes. The center row illustrates the decreased glucose metabolism found in a unipolar depressed patient. (The darker green the area, the less the metabolic activity.) The top row shows how the glucose metabolism increases as a patient naturally recovers from a period of depression. The lower row shows a similar increase in glucose metabolism when an antidepressant improves a patient's behavior.

SOURCE: O. Lingjaerde, (1983), "The biochemistry of depression," in *Acta Psychiatrica Scandinavica Supplementum*, 302, pp. 36–51. Copyright © 1983 Munksgaard International Publishers Ltd., Copenhagen, Denmark [University of California at Los Angeles].

individuals; this approach may also be a way to clarify how biological functioning differs for people who are depressed as compared to those who are not. Regular rhythms in the functioning of human beings and other animals have been recognized for a long time. Of these, the 24-hour or circadian rhythms have been studied most. Seasonal changes may also affect biological rhythms. Seasonal affective disorder (SAD) described in Box 10-2 is a type of depression related to seasonal rather than daily rhythms.

Biological rhythms are controlled or influenced by internal factors, including neurotransmitters, as well as by external factors, such as light. Some circadian rhythms, such as body temperature and sleep activity, are usually synchronized so that their peaks occur at the same time. When these rhythms get out of synchrony, other changes occur. For instance, sleep lasts a long time if a person goes to sleep at the top of the body temperature curve. If, instead, the person goes to sleep near the bottom of the temperature curve, sleep lasts a much shorter time. Depression researchers are interested in

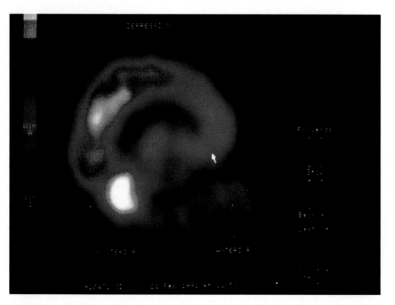

Figure 10-11 A SPECT scan showing the low level of frontal activity in a clinically depressed patient.

Source: From M. S. George, H. A. Ring, D. C. Costa, (1991), *Neuroactivation and Neuroimaging with SPECT*, London: Springer Verlag, as reprinted in *Journal of Clinical Psychiatry, 54,* sup. 11, 1993, p. 9.

how biological rhythms affect sleep because sleep disturbance is frequent in depressed individuals. They tend to have trouble both in going to sleep and in staying asleep. Researchers studying the causes of depression had noted that treatment with antidepressant drugs and also with electroconvulsive therapy (ECT) cause these sleep disturbances to disappear. Table 10-2 lists some of the characteristics of sleep of depressed people.

Sleep has a number of phases that can be measured

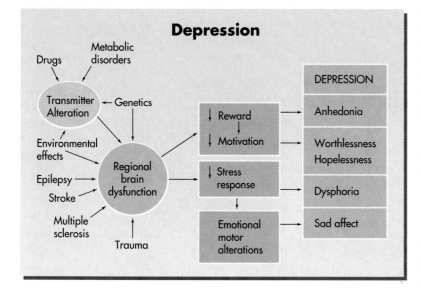

Figure 10-12 A model that associates depression with changes in cerebral blood flow and metabolism.

Source: J. L. Cummings, (1993), "The neuroanatomy of depression," in *Journal of Clinical Psychiatry, 54,* sup. 11, p. 19.

by monitoring the electrical impulses of the brain. The one that is of most interest from the standpoint of depression is REM sleep, during which the eyes rapidly move from side to side and brain wave patterns indicate a peak in brain activity. During REM sleep the serotonin neurons become completely inactive (Jacobs, 1994). In some depressed individuals there is a shortened period between falling asleep and the beginning of the first REM period as well as increased length and intensity of the first REM period of the night (Kupfer et al., 1985). Thus the increased REM period may be related to a decrease in available serotonin. The causal factors in this relationship, however, are unclear.

These connections between REM sleep and serotonin production have led some researchers to study the effect of sleep deprivation on depression. In one study 15 depressed and 15 control subjects experienced a night of total sleep deprivation (Wu et al., 1992). One area of the brain in which the researchers were interested was the limbic system. The limbic system is believed to play a role in emotion and in the production of neurotransmitters. High levels of limbic activity are associated with depression. PET scans were taken the day before and the day after the sleep deprivation. Although not all the depressed patients improved, those who did had PET scans that showed hyperactivity in some limbic areas of the brain before sleep deprivation, but had normal patterns of limbic activity afterward. Depressed individuals who did not improve showed normal limbic patterns both before and afterward. Thus sleep deprivation appeared to affect abnormal limbic function. Research such as this is important in understanding biological factors in depression. The findings of such studies may help to classify depression into various types related to different patterns of regional brain activity. These findings may help clinicians to predict what type of treatment may be most helpful of each subgroup of depressed individuals.

The Psychodynamic View

The psychological study of depression was begun by Sigmund Freud and Karl Abraham, a German physician. Both described depression as a complex reaction to loss (Abraham, 1911/1968; Freud, 1917/1957). Depression, or melancholy, as Freud called it, was grief gone haywire—excessive,

Seasonal Affective Disorder (SAD)

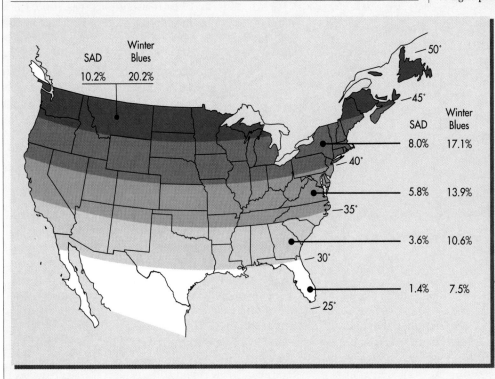

	SAD	Winter Blues
	10.2%	20.2%
	8.0%	17.1%
	5.8%	13.9%
	3.6%	10.6%
	1.4%	7.5%

Figure 10-13 The estimated percentages of seasonal affective disorder and its milder form "winter blues" vary by latitude and the resulting differences in the hours of winter sunlight.

SOURCE: From *The New York Times*, December 29, (1993), p. B7.

Most people live in regions of the world where the number of hours of light per day varies with the season. This is most extreme in the farthest northern and southern parts of the globe where winter daylight is short. In 1984 it was first formally recognized that some people suffered recurrent depression that started in the fall, lasted through the winter, and ended in the spring in a pattern associated with the relative number of hours of seasonal light and darkness (Rosenthal et al., 1984). Symptoms of seasonal affective disorder (SAD) include depressed mood, sluggishness and lethargy, increased appetite and weight gain, and a craving for foods high in carbohydrates. People who live at higher latitudes where the winter darkness is longest are most likely to develop SAD (see Figure 10-13). Women are more at risk than men and younger

Figure 10-14 Bright light from special fixtures can be used to treat seasonal affective disorder.

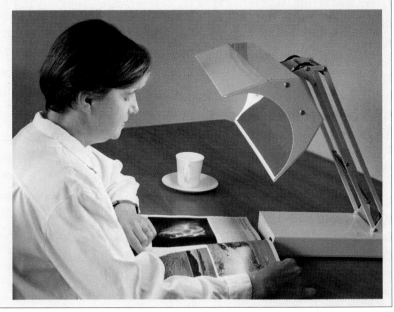

BOX 10-2

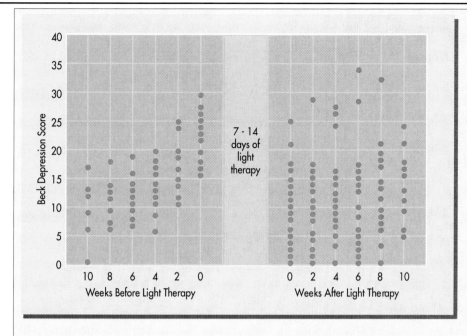

Figure 10-15 Range of Beck Depression inventory (BDI) scores of 31 subjects who were classified as having severe depression (BDI score greater than 15) prior to beginning of 7–14 days of light therapy. Note how depression is increasing before therapy, how it drops for all but a few subjects immediately after therapy, and how it gradually increases for most subjects as the time period after treatment lengthens.

SOURCE: Adapted from Dam et al., 1944, pp. 76, 77.

people are more at risk than older people. Overall, 10 percent of all mood disorders may show a seasonal pattern (Faedda et al., 1993). If people show a pattern of major depressive episode on a seasonal basis for at least two years, DSM-IV adds a phrase, "with seasonal pattern" to their diagnosis. So far it is unclear whether SAD is more closely linked to recurrent major depressive disorder or to bipolar disorder. It may also be linked to eating disorders, especially to the combination of bulimia and anorexia (Brewerton et al., 1994). (See chapter 15 for a discussion of eating disorders.)

SAD can be successfully treated with light therapy (see Figure 10-14). The person being treated usually sits in front of a bright light source for at least two hours a day. Researchers have found that full spectrum bright light is more effective than ultraviolet screened light or colored light (Dam et al., 1994). Dim full-spectrum light exposure seems to have no effect.

Although antidepressants such as MAO inhibitors and psychostimulants related to amphetamines are sometimes used to treat SAD, light therapy is at least as effective and has fewer side effects (Fossey & Shapiro, 1992). Figure

10-15 shows how patients' scores in the Beck Depression Inventory (BDI) changed after light therapy. Similar changes were found using two other self-report measures of depression. Some 7 to 14 days after therapy was stopped the BDI scores again began to increase. This might have been because the length of treatment was not long enough. It might also be that the depression returned because the environmental factor of darkness still was present. Some individuals showed no response improvement from light therapy, suggesting that SAD may have more than one cause.

TABLE 10–2
Major Sleep Disturbances Common to Depression

Generalization	Findings
Shallow sleep	Decreased Stage 3 and 4 (Delta) sleep
	Increased Stage 1 sleep
	Greater sensitivity to noises
Fragmented sleep	Increased awakenings
	Increased stage shifts
	Decreased sleep efficiency
Short sleep	Decreased total sleep time
	Increased time to fall asleep
	Increased early morning wakening
"Intense" REM sleep	Increased REM density (increased eye movement during REM sleep)
REM sleep is advanced toward sleep onset	REM begins sooner after falling asleep
	Increased length and REM density of first REM period
	Increased proportion of REM in first half of night

Source: From S. S. Campbell and J. C. Gillin (1987). Sleep measures in depression: How sensitive? How specific? *Psychiatric Annals, 17,* 647–653.

drawn out, often unrelated to the environment, and seemingly unjustified. Freud described both normal mourning and depression as responses to the loss of someone or something that was loved. However, in contrast to the mourner, the depressed person suffers "an extraordinary diminution of his self-regard, an impoverishment of his ego on a grand scale" (Freud, 1917/1957, p. 246). Freud believed that a depressed person has a strong and punishing conscience or superego. He thought that one reason the conscience becomes so strong is to control the anger and aggressive feelings that otherwise might come forth to hurt others (Freud, 1930).

A different way of conceptualizing depression from a psychodynamic view was suggested by Edward Bibring, an Austrian psychoanalyst (1953). He viewed depression as the emotional expression of the ego's helplessness in maintaining a desired sense of self. He changed the focus from an internal conflict to situations that made a person feel helpless.

Psychoanalytic theorists have suggested that clinical episodes of depression happen because the events that set off the depression revive dimly conscious, threatening views of the self and others that are based on childhood experience. These assumptions appear to be related to a childhood belief that one will never be loved by others, never become worthwhile, and will always lack the ability to control what happens. John Bowlby, a British psychoanalyst, was one of the more prominent theorists who emphasized the importance of loss or separation in childhood to later development. Bowlby thought that separation of a child from its mother or another important figure during early childhood, whether because of illness, travel, or other reasons, created feelings of sadness, anger, and continuing anxiety that might affect the person's emotional relationships in adult life (Bowlby, 1980). Bowlby believed that the childhood experiences that contribute to these feelings are not single events, but develop from long-term patterns of familial interaction. Among these are children's inability to obtain a stable, secure relationship with a parent despite many efforts to be pleasing on the child's part, or children growing up in an atmosphere in which they hear repeatedly about how unlovable or incompetent they are. Some research suggests that a combination of traumatic childhood experiences and acute external stressful events in adulthood is associated with a major depressive episode more than with other forms of depression or bipolar disorder (Alnaes & Torgersen, 1993). The following case illustrates how past experiences may contribute to depression and anxiety in the present.

One depressed woman stated that she became symptomatic when she could no longer keep up with her work and felt herself to be a failure. This explanation was partially true but did not go far enough in describing her actual situation. Later it was revealed that she began to feel anxious and dysphoric when her boss, upon whom she depended for a sense of worth . . . hired another female assistant. This threatened the patient's imagined special status with the boss, and she anticipated that he would favor the new employee, who was erroneously perceived as more able, attractive, and likeable than the patient. Much of this reaction was a recapitulation of the events surrounding the birth of a younger sibling when the patient was five years old. Just as in childhood, she attempted to win back the father's preferential regard by working harder and harder, in order to obtain praise and reassurance.

However, in contrast to her father, the boss did not sufficiently recognize her increased effort, causing her to apply herself even harder so that her work did become too much for her. Therefore, she did become depressed as a result of being overwhelmed by her work; however, the initiative to do more and more was of her own choosing, and the basic reason for it was to become reinstated as the boss/father's favorite.

—Bemporad and Vasile, 1990, pp. 57–58

With the help of the therapist, the client gradually began to understand that her beliefs originated in childhood. As she became aware of these distorted views, other "transference distortions" in her reactions to the therapist appeared. Although she was unaware of doing so, she began to defer toward the therapist as a parental figure. But the therapist, instead of acting out the parental role she expected, helped her to identify and examine the reactions she anticipated. As a result, the client then began to understand how the nature of her past relationships affected her present behavior, that inside this adult was a helpless, needy child who had never felt able to act as she wanted to because of the fear of losing her father's favor. As these old assumptions began to alter, the client was able to be comfortable with the idea that perfection either in one's own eyes or in the eyes of others is not necessary for happiness or love.

A variation of psychodynamic therapy, **interpersonal psychotherapy,** is often used with depressed clients. Interpersonal therapy has some of the same basic concepts as more traditional psychodynamic treatment. Therapists who use this approach believe that depression is best understood in an interpersonal context that emphasizes both people's social effectiveness and the degree to which they experience social support. This therapeutic approach focuses on helping people learn to be more socially effective. For many people who are depressed, effective long-term treatment seems to be associated with improvement in their relationships with their most significant others. Biologically based treatments for depression do not seem to modify these relational problems for many people who are depressed.

The Behavioral Perspective

Behaviorists view depression from a different perspective. When depressed people find themselves in stressful situations, they tend to cope by delaying (seeking more information before taking any action) and attempting to get emotional support from others. Excessive support seeking may be what makes other people feel uncomfortable and guilty and causes them to try to avoid contact with the depressed person. Depressed people may also make many complaints to elicit sympathy and affection. Although those who are on the receiving end of this treatment may respond appropriately at first, after a while they may begin to be annoyed or frustrated. Eventually a vicious cycle develops in which the display of symptoms and frustration of the depressed person's companions increase until the companions begin to say things like, "You could get better if you try," "No one has to act like that," and so forth. These statements merely serve to worsen an already bad situation. Such feelings, whether expressed or not, are probably one reason why people tend to avoid the company of depressed individuals (see Figure 10-16).

Although people who are depressed often seem to take a negative view of their interactions with others, there is considerable evidence that they also make a negative impression on others because of deficits in their social skills (Dykman et al., 1991). A negative spiral results, in which real deficits in performance compound the effects of the negative self-views. Depressed people not only are likely to think others respond to them negatively, but others are more likely to respond negatively because of the depressed people's lack of social skills.

The Cognitive Perspective

Probably the most influential psychological theories of depression today are derived from the cognitive perspective. The cognitive perspective on depression recognizes that not only cognitions but also behavior and biochemistry are important components of depressive disorders. Cognitive therapists believe that when depressive cognitions are changed, behavior and presumably biochemical responses change as well although the mechanisms of such changes have not been identified (Young et al., 1993).

Figure 10-16 This poster, part of a campaign to inform the public about the need to seek treatment for depression, is a response to the fact that symptoms of depression are often not recognized.

According to this view depressed persons consistently interpret events in distorted ways that result in negative views of themselves, their environment, and what may happen in the future. For example, a person who does not receive an expected promotion might think: "I am a worthless person. Everyone thinks poorly of me. If they did not, I would have been selected for the job." A second person in the same situation might think: "R. was chosen for that job I wanted because he had more experience in negotiation. I know I could have done the job, but my qualifications didn't look as impressive on paper." One cause of unjustified negative interpretations may be the presence of **schemas** or ways of coding and interpreting behavior. Although these schemas are thought to have arisen early in life, they continue their influence into adulthood. Table 10-3 contains a summary of the major content areas of early maladaptive schemas. Cognitive therapy techniques are used to counter the effects of schemas and to help the client create new behavioral approaches and alter schemas to make them more adaptive.

Beck's Cognitive-Distortion Model. Aaron Beck's cognitive-distortion model of depression (Beck, 1967, 1976; Beck et al., 1979) has been the most influential of the cognitive approaches to depression. Beck believes that depression can best be described as a **cognitive triad** of negative thoughts about oneself, the situation, and the future. A person who is depressed misinterprets facts in a negative way, focuses on the negative aspects of any situation, and also has pessimistic and hopeless expectations about the future. Table 10-4 illustrates some of these cognitive errors on the part of depressed individuals.

Beck maintains that these cognitions of depressed people are specific to depression and thus differ from the

---

TABLE 10–3
Major Content Areas of Early Maladaptive Schemas

Instability and Disconnection

Abandonment	*Example:* He may find someone better.
Distrust, expectations of being hurt	*Example:* I always get the short end of the stick.
Emotional deprivation	*Example:* No one will listen to me, no one understands me.

Impaired autonomy

Dependence or incompetence	*Example:* I can't take care of things myself.
Vulnerability to harm or illness	*Example:* Feeling that disaster will strike at any time. *I will go broke, I will get mugged if I go out,* etc.
Enmeshment with others	*Example:* My mother won't be happy unless I spend all my free time with her instead of going out with a date.

Undesirability

Defectiveness	*Example:* Feeling that one is *unworthy,* defective, or flawed.
Social undesirability	*Example:* Feeling that one is *outwardly* undesirable to others.
Failure to achieve	*Example:* I am stupid and untalented and will never get a good job.

Restricted self-expression

Subjugation	*Example:* Nobody takes into account what I think when important decisions are made.
Emotional inhibition	*Example:* Difficulty in expressing feelings because doing so may lead to rejection by others.

Restricted gratification

Self-sacrifice	*Example:* Excessive focus on the needs of others at the expense of one's own gratification.
Unrelenting standards	*Example:* A need for perfection in all tasks.
Negativity or pessimism	*Example:* Constant focus on the negative aspects of life and the minimizing of the positive aspects.

Impaired limits

Feelings of entitlement	*Example:* The belief that one should have what one wants without regard to the effect on others.
Insufficient self-control	*Example:* Poor frustration tolerance and self-control that make it difficult to reach personal goals.

TABLE 10–4
Cognitive Errors and the Assumptions From Which They Are Derived

Cognitive Error	Assumption
1. Overgeneralizing	1. If it is true in one case, it applies to any case that is even slightly similar.
2. Selective abstraction	2. The only events that matter are failures, deprivation, etc. Should measure self by errors, weaknesses, etc.
3. Excessive responsibility (assuming personal causality)	3. *I am responsible for all bad things, failures, etc.*
4. Assuming temporal causality (predicting without sufficient evidence)	4. *If it has been true in the past, then it is always going to be true.*
5. Self-references	5. *I am the center of everyone's attention, especially of bad performances or personal attributes.*
6. "Catastrophizing"	6. *Always think of the worst. It is most likely to happen to you.*
7. Dichotomous thinking	7. *Everything is either one extreme or another (black or white; good or bad).*

Source: A. T. Beck (1976), *Cognitive Therapy and the Emotional Disorders.* New York: International Universities Press. Copyright © 1976 by Aaron T. Beck, M. D. Reprinted by permission of the publisher.

thoughts of people with anxiety disorders (Beck et al., 1987). The thoughts of depressed people either focus on negative aspects of the past or reflect a negative outlook on what the future will bring. Those with anxiety as their primary symptom have thoughts that focus on uncertainty and worry about the future. The anxious person worries about what might happen and *whether* he or she will be able to deal with it. In contrast, the depressed person thinks about how he or she has failed in the past, how terrible the future will be and how he or she will be *unable* to deal with it or improve it.

Beck believes that a person who is depressed attributes or blames any misfortune on his or her personal defects. Awareness of these presumed defects becomes so intense that it completely overwhelms any positive self-concepts. Any ambiguous situation is interpreted as evidence of the defect, even if there are more plausible explanations. A good example is provided by Norman Endler's description of his thoughts during his bout of depression (Endler, 1982). Endler went through a period of fear (not at all based on reality) that his family would desert him and he would be unable to cope with everyday living.

I recall a time during the end of August when I took the subway with my wife. She had gone through the turnstile before I did and I was positive that she was going to desert me. She probably had had enough of me and my shenanigans and was fed up with my behavior.

—Endler, 1990, p. 44

After his recovery from this period of depression, Endler recognized the irrationality of such a thought.

Of course nothing could have been further from the truth. Her kindness and devotion, her concern, compassion, and

her love, more than anything else, sustained me during my ordeal. If I had to single out the one person who was most instrumental in my getting better, it would be my wife.

—Endler, 1990, p. 44

Beck also thinks that depressed people tend to emphasize self–other comparisons which further lower their self-esteem. Every encounter with another person becomes the opportunity for a negative self-evaluation. For instance, when talking with others the depressed person thinks: "I'm not a good conversationalist. I'm not as interesting as other people." Beck thinks that the tendency to have these negative cognitions may be related to particular ways of evaluating situations that grow out of childhood experiences. These schemas affect all the elements of the cognitive triad in later life.

Research on the outcome or effects of psychotherapy has raised some questions about whether these negative cognitions cause depression. It is possible that negative thoughts are merely the result of depression, not its causal agent. At present the answer to this question of causality is not clear.

Measuring Cognitions in Depression The work of Beck and others interested in the role of cognitions in depression has led to the development of many ways to measure these cognitions. These measures can be thought of as three general types (Segal & Swallow, 1994). One type, *cognitive product variables*, operates in a person's level of awareness and includes self-critical automatic thoughts and attributions and pessimistic expectations for the future. These can be measured in a direct manner. For example, the Automatic Thoughts Questionnaire (Hollon & Kendall, 1980) asks about the frequency with which each of 30 negative automatic thoughts have "popped" into a person's head in the past week. An example might be "no one understands me." A second type, *cognitive process variables,* cannot be measured so directly. These include the cognitive and social cognitive mechanisms by which people formulate the evaluations and expectations that dominate their awareness. An example of this type of measure is the Rochester Social Comparison Record (Wheeler & Miyake, 1992). Subjects are asked about the circumstances (social interaction, daydream, etc.) of each interpersonal comparison they make, the dimension on which the comparison is made (social skills, intelligence, etc.), the gender and type of relationship with the comparison target, and their mood before and after the interaction. Using this measure, Wheeler and Miyake (1992) were able to show how unfavorable social comparisons were followed by negative affect. The third and least accessible level of cognition is *cognitive schemas* that are thought to operate to store, organize, and direct the processing of personally relevant information. Negative self-schemas are thought to play a central role in depression. One measure used to elicit schemas is the Stroop color–word task (Stroop, 1935). Subjects are asked to name the color of the ink in which a word is printed but to ignore the meaning of the word itself. Slower responses are thought to indicate greater effort to suppress stimulus words that are highly salient—that is, words that are associated with the self-schema. For instance, depressed individuals took longer to name the color in which depressed-content words were printed compared to the color for other words (Gotlib & McCann, 1984).

Attributional Models of Depression One of the cognitive maneuvers Beck discusses is attribution. He predicts that depressed individuals' attributions will be personal—that is, depressed people will blame themselves when anything bad happens. When something good does happen, it will usually be attributed to luck. For instance, one woman was not especially pleased when a short story she had written was accepted for publication; she attributed the acceptance to sheer luck. On the other hand, when one of her articles was rejected, she was distressed because she thought the rejection reflected badly on her. Most nondepressed people do the opposite: They accept responsibility for the good in their lives but tend to blame the situation on others when things do not work out. Figure 10-17 illustrates this difference in attributional thinking. Attributional models of depression do not claim that attribu-

tional style alone is enough to cause depression. These models suggest that attributional style is important only when a person experiences intense or frequent negative events in his or her life (Abramson et al., 1989).

People who are depressed seem to feel helpless to control their environment. They think that, no matter what they do, they will be unable to affect the way things turn out. It is possible that such people learn to be helpless as a result of certain situations they have encountered in the past. Martin Seligman (1974, 1975) first popularized this concept, which is termed **learned helplessness.** Research on the concept of learned helplessness soon showed that some people feel generally helpless and others feel helpless only in certain situations. The explanation of this appeared to lie in the kinds of attributions people make about stressful situations (Abramson et al., 1989). The attribution model fits best in situations that have to do with achievement, such as college performance or vocational success. Other kinds of negative events, such as a death or a friend moving away, may call up different sets of attributions from the same person. Only about one-third of depressed people show this attributional style and those who do show it usually change their attributional style in periods when they are not depressed (Hamilton & Abramson, 1983). This suggests that attributions play a role only for a subgroup of depressed people and raises the question of whether this attributional style is a result or symptom rather than a causal factor in depression.

Some researchers have suggested that there is a subtype of depression, **hopelessness depression,** that links attributional style in a causal chain that leads to the occurrence of depression (Abramson et al., 1989). This chain starts with the perceived occurrence of negative life events or the nonoccurrence of positive life events. It also includes people's characteristic way of viewing

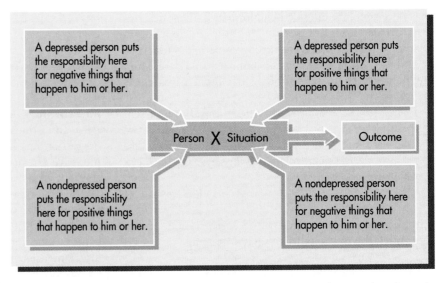

Figure 10-17 A comparison of the attribution process in depressed and nondepressed people.

the causes and consequences of events as well as of evaluating themselves. These personal characteristics work together to determine how a person will respond to the life event. The theory maintains that if the response is one of hopelessness, either about dealing with the event or changing oneself, depression will result.

The hopelessness theory is more similar to the other cognitive theories of depression than is the helplessness theory. It closely resembles Beck's ideas, although with some differences. The hopelessness theory describes a particular subclass of depression, whereas Beck focuses on the role that cognitions play in depression in general. The hopelessness theory also suggests that some people may be invulnerable, or at least much less vulnerable, to depression because of their tendency to attribute negative events not to themselves or ongoing conditions in their environment, but to specific causes or situations that can be expected to come to an end soon.

Cognitive Accuracy in Depression Both Beck's theory and the revised learned helplessness hypothesis stress the inaccuracy of self-perception in depression. But the attributions of depressed people may be more accurate than these theories predict. Experimenters, studying how well people assessed their own social competence, found that depressed patients were quite realistic about their own social skills (Lewinsohn et al., 1980). In contrast, other psychiatric patients and control subjects tended to see themselves as more competent than other people saw them. Even more interesting, the realism of the depressed patients' self-perceptions tended to decrease as therapy progressed. In short, as they became less depressed, the patients became less realistic about their effect on others; they deluded themselves more in the same way the nonpatients do. According to this view the result of cognitive therapy may actually be to encourage a normal lack of realism (Sackeim & Wegner, 1986).

Researchers who study cognitive distortion have focused primarily on negative events. However, attributions concerning positive events may also be important and may play a role in recovery from depression (Needles & Abramson, 1990). As yet the question of the degree of cognitive distortion in depression is far from settled. Many aspects of the cognitive theory of depression have been supported by research including increased negativity of cognitions about the self, increased hopelessness, and the focus on themes of loss. However, evidence that depressive thinking is especially inaccurate or illogical is still weak (Haaga et al., 1991).

The Humanistic-Existential Perspective

Whereas psychodynamic theorists emphasize the loss of a loved object as a central cause of depression, existential theorists focus on the loss of self-esteem. The lost object can be real or symbolic—power, social rank, or money—but the loss itself is not as important as the change in an individual's self-assessment as a result of the loss. Many people base their self-concepts on who they are or what they have: I'm the leader of the factory assembly team; I'm the boss; I'm a member of the exclusive city athletic club; I'm the husband of a famous movie star. Identifications of this kind offer external verification of people's worth in their own minds. The philosopher Kierkegaard expressed this view of the effects of loss very well in the following quotation:

> Despair is never ultimately over the external object but always over ourselves. A girl loses her sweetheart and she despairs. It is not over the sweetheart, but over herself-without-the-sweetheart. And so it is with all cases of loss, whether it be money, power, or social rank. The unbearable loss is not really in itself unbearable. What we cannot bear is being stripped of the external object. We stand denuded and see the intolerable abyss of ourselves.

Humanistic theorists such as Carl Rogers (1951, 1980) emphasize the difference between a person's ideal self and his or her perceptions of the actual state of things as the source of depression and anxiety. They, like Kierkegaard, believe that depression is likely to result when the difference between the ideal and the real selves becomes too great for the individual to tolerate. This discrepancy occurs frequently, especially among people who have high aspirations for achievement and are trying to fill several roles simultaneously. A current example of this problem is the dilemma of many women today. These women may be trying to fill multiple roles—a successful career, a wife who manages the household effectively, and a mother who provides adequate attention for her children. In such a situation it is inevitable that each role is not carried out to its highest potential and therefore the resulting discrepancy between the ideal self and the actual self in each of the multiple roles is often difficult for these women to deal with and is likely to create stress and depressed feelings as well as possible clinical depression in those women who are especially vulnerable.

Depression From a Vulnerability-Resilience Perspective

This chapter has discussed the role in depression of heredity and other biological factors such as neurotransmitter activity, brain structure, and metabolism that may be, but are not necessarily, a result of genetic inheritance. Other personal factors that may play a role in depression include misattributions of the cause of events and the strength of the supportive relationships a person has. Both biological factors and these other personally related factors can contribute to vulnerability or resilience. Together they often determine the outcome when people encounter environmental stressors or what we often call negative life events. (See chapter 5 for a discussion of life events.) Highly personally stressful events, especially those that occur in the context of chronic stress or ongoing difficulties and low levels of support, are especially likely to result in depression (Brown et al., 1987; Patten, 1991).

An example of the vulnerability and resiliency approach can be seen in the life of Abraham Lincoln, an American president who was able to function effectively amid great stress despite a lifetime of periods of great melancholy or what we would now call major depressive episodes. Lincoln was able to overcome a lifetime of periods of deep melancholy to effectively lead the country through one of its most trying periods, the Civil War.

In 1841 he wrote to his law partner in Washington, D.C., "If what I feel were equally distributed to the whole human family, there would not be one cheerful face on the earth. Whether I shall ever be better, I cannot tell. I awfully [sic] forebode I shall not."

Despite his apprehension about the future, Lincoln of course did carry on. However, even during his presidency he experienced periods of depression. The terrible loss of life in the Civil War and the lack of success of the northern forces in the early part of the war affected him greatly. During this period the public and many members of Congress turned against him and doubted his leadership. His visits to the wounded in military hospitals also upset him deeply. He often sat silent, his "soul filled with sadness" (quoted in Grinker, 1979). He felt guilty and full of self-reproach, wanted to die, and had dreams about assassination.

Lincoln's personal life was also filled by negative life events. His marriage to Mary Todd was an unhappy one, his wife was bitterly criticized and villified by Washington society, and two of his children died in childhood (see Figure 10-18). His early life was also difficult: He grew up in extreme poverty, his mother died when he was young, and his father treated him harshly. Despite these adverse conditions, Lincoln showed amazing resiliency and managed to educate himself, become a successful lawyer and politician, be elected to Congress and the presidency and became one of the United States' most revered presidents.

Treatment of Depression

Each of the theoretical perspectives has made a contribution to the treatment of depression. Often two or more perspectives are combined in developing a therapeutic intervention. Although many such combinations

Figure 10-18 One of the tragedies in Lincoln's life was the death in childhood of his son Tod, shown here reading a book with his father.

are possible, the most frequent at present is the use of antidepressant drugs together with cognitive therapy.

Biologically Based Treatment

The two major biologically based treatment approaches are antidepressant medication and electroconvulsive therapy. Of the two, the use of antidepressant drugs is far more common.

Antidepressant Drugs The first effective antidepressants were from two chemical groups, **monoamine oxidase** (MAO) **inhibitors** and **tricyclics** (named from their three-ring chemical structure). More recently a new group of antidepressants with a variety of ring structures has been developed. This group is often referred to as **selective serotonin reuptake inhibitors** (SSRIs) or **second generation antidepressants.** Because of the varied ring structures, non-MAO inhibitor antidepressants are now more properly described as **heterocyclics.**

Table 10-5 lists some of the more widely known drugs in each category. Although these antidepressants may be effective in removing depressive symptoms or at least lessening them, they must be taken under careful medical supervision because they also have a variety of side effects. Because tricyclics also block acetylcholine, a neurotransmitter in the parasympathetic nervous system, their side effects include dry mouth, constipation, dizziness, irregular heartbeat, blurred vision, ringing in the ears, retention of urine, and excessive sweating. In addition, tricyclics may cause tremors and, in older patients, confusion and delirium. They also may affect male sexual functioning by causing difficulties in ejacu-

TABLE 10–5
Examples of Antidepressants Used to Treat Relatively Severe Depressive Symptoms of the Unipolar Type

	Generic Name	Trade Name (example)	General Description
Heterocyclics			
Tricyclic type	amitriptyline	Elavil	Variable effectiveness in moderating symptoms. Slow acting. May take up to three weeks before response is seen. Many side effects.
	desipramine	Norpramin	
	doxepin	Sinequan	
	imipramine	Tofranil	
	nortriptyline	Pamelor	
Selective Serotonin Reuptake Inhibitors	amoxapine	Asendin	Fewer side effects than tricyclics or MAO inhibitors. More specific focus on serotonin receptors. Slow acting as above.
	fluoxetine	Prozac	
	maprotiline	Ludiomil	
	trazodone	Desyrel	
MAO Inhibitors	isocarboxazid	Marplan	MAO inhibitors require restrictions in diet because of serious interactive effects with certain food chemicals. Slow acting as above.
	phenelzine	Nardil	
	tranylcypromine	Parnate	

lation. Many of these side effects decrease after several weeks of drug use. Patients who experience certain side effects may find that shifting to a drug with a different chemical composition will decrease them.

Some of the SSRI antidepressants were developed in order to lessen side effects. They are more specific in their effect on neurotransmitters and thus have fewer unwanted effects. This is important for two reasons. First, some of the side effects may be directly harmful or may be so unpleasant that depressed persons will choose not to use the medication regularly and thus not receive its beneficial effects. Secondly, by giving depressed persons access to drugs that could be toxic in high doses, physicians might also be making it easier for those who feel suicidal to kill themselves with an overdose.

Antidepressants are the drugs most commonly involved in prescription drug overdose, which claims several thousand lives each year. One antidepressant drug, fluoxetine (Prozac) has also been alleged to intensify suicidal desires or other violent behaviors that might continue for several months after the medication had been discontinued. The controversy over the safety of Prozac became strong enough that the Psychopharmacological Drugs Advisory Committee of the Federal Drug Administration (FDA) held a special meeting in 1991 to discuss the matter. The committee concluded that despite some isolated reports, there was no scientific evidence suggesting that Prozac or other antidepressant drugs intensified suicidal desires or other violent behavior. Later research concerning the relative risk of different antidepressants found that, when the total amount of use of each drug was considered, the risk of suicide was much higher for tricyclics than for the newer drugs including Prozac (Kapur et al, 1992).

Prozac has been called a wonder drug (see Figure 10-19) that not only alleviates depression but also has a helpful effect on personality disorders (Teicher et al., 1990, 1993). In the six years after Prozac came on the market more than 10 million people had taken it, making it the second-best-selling drug in the world. Claims for Prozac extend to the desirability of its use for individuals who are not clinically depressed because it makes them "still happier" and "better than well" (Miller, 1994). Such claims have disturbed many mental health professionals. Even representatives of the company that manufactures Prozac have deplored the media's role in making the drug seem to be a personality enhancer. In 1994 the company placed ads in a number of scientific and trade journals stating that Prozac was "intended for use only where a clear medical need exists."

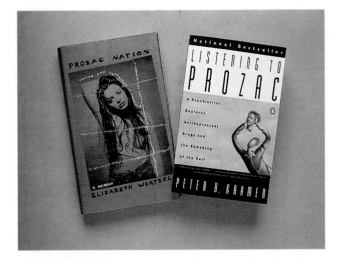

Figure 10-19 The use of Prozac has grown dramatically, not only for depression, but as a "wonder drug" that enhances adjustment. The number of books with the name Prozac in the title reflects public interest in its effects. These two books present somewhat different evaluations of Prozac's use and effectiveness. *Listening to Prozac* takes a positive view of the drug as a self-enhancer as well as an effective antidepressant. In *Prozac Nation*, the author recognizes that Prozac was helpful to her during her bouts of depression but expresses her concern about the frequency with which it and other medications are prescribed as a complete solution to clients' problems.

Which group of drugs and which particular drug within a group will be effective is still usually a matter of trial and error on the part of the physician. Usually, one of the tricyclic or SSRI group of drugs is preferred because the MAO inhibitors have such potentially dangerous side effects. When taken with foods containing a substance called tyramine they may produce a toxic reaction and cause blood pressure to rise to a life-threatening level. Because many common foods, including cheese, chocolate, sour cream, and wine, contain tyramine, the use of MAO inhibitors requires careful dietary monitoring.

Although antidepressant drugs are used widely some researchers have wondered about whether it may be the expectations of the depressed person and the physician that are responsible for the improvements noted in trials that compare the effect of these drugs to that of a placebo. Studies of drug effectiveness are supposed to be double blind, that is, neither the patient nor the therapist knows which individuals are receiving the drug and which the placebo. However, double-blind studies may not achieve this goal because the nonplacebo drugs are recognized by their side effects. In a combined analysis of the results of 22 comparative studies using tricyclic drugs and placebos the difference in outcome between the drug and placebo groups was small. The drugs were more likely to produce improvement than the placebo 58 percent of the time but the difference was barely sig-

nificant statistically (White et al., 1992). Neither the patients nor the therapists were likely to notice more therapeutic effects from the drug therapy compared to the placebo.

Electroconvulsive Therapy One of the problems in treating a severe episode of depression with antidepressant drugs is the time lag between their initial use and the first signs of improvement of the patient's mood. Several weeks may go by before any improvement is seen. If there is concern about suicide, a wait of three weeks or so may seem too great a risk. In such situations, or if drugs are not effective, electroconvulsive therapy may be the treatment used because it produces a more rapid effect. **Electroconvulsive therapy** (ECT) involves passing a current of between 70 and 130 volts through the patient's head. First an anesthetic and a muscle relaxant are administered. (The muscle relaxant is given to prevent injury from the convulsion caused by the electric charge.) The current is then administered through electrodes placed on one or both sides of the head (see Figure 10-20).

ECT is very effective in treating severe depression in which there is a great deal of delusional thinking and when no precipitating event or events can be identified (Rush & Weissenburger, 1994). ECT is also effective for some severe depressions that have not responded to tricyclics or MAO inhibitors. It is not effective for mild depressions (dysthymic disorder and adjustment disorder with depressed mood). Despite its effectiveness the use of ECT has brought forth a good deal of controversy.

Several questions have been raised by those concerned about use of ECT:

■ Does ECT have an effect on brain structure? Does it cause brain damage?

Figure 10-20 A patient is being prepared for an ECT treatment.

- Is there a relationship between abnormalities seen by means of brain scans and the effectiveness or lack of effectiveness of ECT?
- Does ECT provide any insights about brain function and depression?

Early studies had associated ECT with brain damage seen at autopsy in some patients (Friedberg, 1977) but it was not certain whether any damage seen was related to the ECT or had been present before ECT. However, after the development of scanning techniques it became possible not only to examine brain structure in living patients but also to scan both before and after treatment. Results from these repeated scanning procedures suggest that there are no permanent changes in brain structure as a consequence of ECT (Black, 1993). These studies have shown, however, that a relatively high number of the patients referred for treatment already have structural changes in the brain before treatment. Even in these patients ECT does not produce further changes in brain structure (Coffey et al., 1991).

Use of brain-scanning techniques, such as CT and MRI, are beginning to provide information on structural brain abnormalities that may predict poor or good outcome from ECT. Many older adults whose depression is not lessened by medication but who are likely to be helped by ECT have been found, through the use of scanning techniques, to have indications of organic brain changes that may be related to the depressive disorder (Coffey, 1993). Patients who are likely to develop delirium from ECT treatment can also be identified through scanning techniques. The presence of certain brain lesions (e.g., in the basal ganglion area) seemed to be associated with delirium (Figiel et al., 1990).

Scanning techniques, such as PT and SPECT, that focus on function rather than structure are also beginning to be used to study the short- and long-term effects of ECT. Studies using repeated measurements over time are difficult to do because of the radiation to which the scan exposes the patient. The research done so far using PT and SPECT suggests that the decreased metabolic activity, found in the prefrontal area of the brain in many depressed individuals, is increased after a series of ECT treatments (Guze et al., 1991). More patients need to be studied before we can be confident about these results.

In the early years of its use, ECT was estimated to produce improvement in between 80 and 90 percent of patients for whom it was used. After initial enthusiasm with ECT as a treatment for depression its use decreased because of concerns over its safety and generally negative public opinion concerning this method (Persad, 1990). Newer research findings have reduced safety concerns. However, even today, ECT is rarely used unless treatment with antidepressant drugs has been tried

and has been unsuccessful. Under those conditions, about 50 percent of patients show marked improvement after ECT (Sackeim et al., 1990). An increase in use has been predicted by some authorities because ECT reduces time in the hospital and therefore also medical costs.

Sometimes ECT can produce dramatic changes in mood. Norman Endler, the psychologist whose description of his own depression (later diagnosed as a bipolar type) appears at the beginning of this chapter, also described his experience with ECT after both tricyclic and MAO-inhibiting drugs had proved ineffective and the depression was still incapacitating him after 5 months. Endler was faced with a choice between ECT and hospitalization; he reluctantly chose ECT.

Dr. Persad met us on the sixth floor at seven forty-five. He tried to calm me down, and I recall his saying that he had never seen anyone so agitated as I. The prospect of ECT really frightened me.

Beatty [Endler's wife] remained in the waiting area and Dr. Persad and I went into the ECT room. I changed into my pajamas and a nurse took my vital signs [blood pressure, pulse, and temperature]. The nurse and other attendants were friendly and reassuring. I began to feel at ease. The anesthetist arrived and informed me that she was going to give me an injection. I was asked to lie down on a cot and was wheeled into the ECT room proper. It was about eight o'clock. A needle was injected into my arm and I was told to count back from 100. I got about as far as 91. The next thing I knew I was in the recovery room and it was about eight-fifteen. I was slightly groggy and tired but not confused. My memory was not impaired. I certainly knew where I was. Shortly after eight-thirty, I got dressed, went down the hall to fetch Beatty, and she drove me home. At home I had breakfast and then lay down for a few hours. Late in the morning I got dressed. I felt no pain, no confusion, and no agitation. I felt neither less depressed nor more depressed than I had before the ECT. . . . After about the third or fourth treatment I went up to Dr. Persad's office and spoke to him briefly. He asked me if I had noticed any improvement and to what degree. I believed that I had improved 35 to 40 percent. Dr. Persad believed that the improvement was more likely to be 70 to 75 percent.

—Endler 1990, pp. 74–75

After the fifth and sixth treatments had been completed Endler returned to his office. A colleague who had been helping to manage the psychology department in his absence was there.

I asked her to remain. She stated that she would be glad to stay as long as I needed her assistance. By early afternoon Kathy looked at me and said "Norm, you are perfectly fine, you do not need me here." She left and I stayed the rest of the day. As of then I resumed the chairmanship full time. A miracle had happened in two weeks. I had gone from feeling like an emotional cripple to feeling well.

—Endler, 1990, p. 75

Like many people who have a bipolar disorder, Endler experienced another depression about a year after the first. This time, although ECT produced improvement and made it possible for him to work effectively, the depressed mood hung on for several months. Treatment with a combination of antidepressants and lithium led to a quick recovery. In 1989 he wrote that he had been "symptom-free for eight years and am functioning as effectively as I did prior to my depression" without using any medication (Endler, 1989).

Assessment of Biological Treatment Options

Although both ECT and the various drug therapies can be helpful to those with depressive disorders, each option has both positive and negative features. As in the case described above, treatment may help relieve a depression but may not be able to prevent a recurrence. Repeated series of ECT administered if the depression does recur may not be as effective as they were for the first depressive episode. In addition, the long-term effects of repeated series of ECT treatments are not known.

Treatment with antidepressant drugs also presents difficulties. Choosing the best drug is often a trial-and-error affair even for an experienced clinician. This means that effective treatment may be long delayed and the severely depressed person may be at risk for suicide as well as being further demoralized by the concern that treatment may not be helpful. Also, as we have seen, many of the antidepressant drugs have side effects that may range from the merely annoying or uncomfortable, such as dry mouth or constipation, to the life-threatening, such as sudden changes in blood pressure. Just as in the case of ECT, the effects these drugs may have after many years of use are also not known. Some researchers argue that dependence on drugs makes unipolar or bipolar individuals less likely to improve their coping mechanisms and thus increases the chances of their having further affective problems. The attitude of many therapists toward using biological treatment alone is expressed by Silvano Arieti, a well-known psychoanalyst and researcher: "I have never met a patient about whom I could say that his depression came from nowhere and its origin had to be sought exclusively in metabolic disorder" (Arieti & Bemporad, 1978, p. 5).

Behavioral Treatment for Depression

People who are depressed often lack skills necessary to develop satisfying relationships with others. One behav-

ioral approach to this problem is through social skills training. This training has some overlap with interpersonal therapy discussed earlier; however, the two differ greatly because social skills training does not deal with any psychodynamic issues and concentrates solely on appropriate behavior and perhaps also on the cognitions that accompany it. Social skills training normally consists of four parts. First, clients are taught basic verbal and nonverbal skills that focus on small segments of the desired behavior and then, when these are learned, they practice gradually putting the segments together. After rehearsing these larger and larger parts with the therapist, clients are given "homework" assignments in which the goal is to adapt the new skill so it is useful in the everyday environment. Next, clients are trained to be more perceptive about cues other people in the environment give and learn how to change their own behavior according to these environmental changes. Finally clients learn to adopt realistic criteria for performance and are taught how to be self-reinforcing. The following case illustrates the effectiveness of social skills training.

Ms. SJ is a 43-year-old single woman with a master's degree in chemistry. She has worked as a laboratory assistant for a number of years. She came to the clinic complaining of (a) sad mood, (b) low energy, (c) trouble making decisions, (d) feeling worthless, (e) pessimism about her future, and (f) guilt about her unsuccessful past. She was involved in a three-year intimate relationship, which has just ended. This event has rekindled symptoms of depression and a fear that this new episode would be as bad as a previous one ten years earlier.

Standardized role plays revealed difficulties with display of positive and negative assertion, as well as with conversation. She could not give a compliment to another person, particularly a male, and she could not touch a person. . . .

The first focus of clinical treatment was greeting people. Role plays focused on making eye contact with the other person, saying "Hello, I'm Sarah," and smiling. This behavior contrasted sharply with her current style of avoiding eye contact, not smiling, and only speaking if directly spoken to. Many role plays were carried out to train these skills.

As she began to improve in this skill, touching the other person was added. Reverse role plays were first used, and her initial response to a touch on the hand was to become quite scared, to be silent, and to withdraw as fast as possible. Several practices were carried out in conjunction with a homework assignment . . . to observe other people in her clubs and to log each time one person touched another. After one week of observational data, she was astounded at how often people touched. . . .

Conversation role plays were repeated to include touching. After many repetitions, she became comfortable and began to enjoy the contact. Two further existing conversation behaviors were addressed before the first homework: First, she never wore a name tag because she believed that if someone really wanted to know her, they would find out her name. Second, she would always position herself to be out of the way in order not to impede other people. . . . She attended her meetings with instructions (a) to introduce herself and say "Hello, I'm Sarah" to everyone, (b) to wear her name tag, (c) to locate herself in high-traffic areas, and (d) to smile with her greeting and with her departure. . . .

This homework assignment resulted in an astonishing response. People were friendly to her, included her in their conversations, and invited her into some of their activities. . . . This was such a success for her that she wondered why she had not done it before. These behaviors were practiced once more and then monitored. She continued these new behaviors, and they produced invitations to go sailing, to attend a special program in Florida, and to attend a meeting in Massachusetts as well. Her mood brightened considerably. She felt less alone, less like an outsider, and more worthwhile.

—Becker, 1990, pp. 99–100

Therapists who use a social skills training approach usually find it works well with depressed clients (Becker, 1990). If problems do occur, they tend to fall into certain categories: homework follow-through, client crises, and therapist expectations. Clients may refuse to role play or to do the homework assignments. Role play is necessary so that the client gets the practice needed to use new behaviors in the real-life situations called for in the homework assignments. The practice gained from these assignments is in turn critical for success in learning new habits.

Problems may also arise if clients continually bring new crises to therapy. These may take the focus away from the treatment with the result that the clients never learn the skills to solve their own problems. In dealing with a client's life crises, therefore, the therapist must steer a middle ground between focusing exclusively on social skills training and attending to the crisis at hand. Finally, problems in this type of therapeutic approach may occur if an inexperienced therapist tries to move through the training too quickly to get to the primary problem facing the client.

Cognitive Therapy for Depression

Cognitive therapy is often referred to as **cognitive behavioral therapy** because it makes use of both types of theories. The proportion of cognitive and behavioral techniques that are used depends on the client's skills and degree of depression as well as the chosen goals of the therapy. In general, the more severely depressed the client, the more likely the therapist is to use behavioral techniques. In such cases, the first goals would be to

mobilize the client to perform some simple self-help tasks. Later, as the client improves, the therapist may begin to work to help change some dysfunctional thinking by challenging parts of the client's belief system. Although behavioral techniques are used most intensively by cognitive therapists early in therapy, their use continues to some degree throughout the therapeutic treatment.

Cognitive therapists use a well-defined structure for therapy sessions. Each session begins with a discussion of an agenda for the session. After the short list of items are agreed upon, the client and therapist discuss each one. The therapist may begin by asking the client a series of questions to clarify the difficulty. During this questioning, the therapist tries to understand what misinterpretations, unrealistic expectations, or early maladaptive schemas are involved. At the end of the session, the therapist asks the client to provide a summary (often in written form) of the major conclusions from the session. Finally, the therapist usually gives the client a homework assignment designed to assist the client in practicing skills and behaviors worked on during the session. Early in cognitive therapy, the session may be focused on the client's symptoms as well as on behavioral and motivational problems the client brings up for discussion. Once improvement begins in these areas, the therapist shifts the emphasis to the content and pattern that typify the client's thinking.

In the symptom-reduction phase of therapy, one of the aims of the therapist is the eliciting of automatic thoughts. Therapists use several techniques to identify these thoughts including direct questioning, asking the client to use imagery to evoke the thoughts, or causing them to occur by means of a role-play situation. These automatic thoughts are important in understanding the problem. They are the link between outside events and the client's reaction to the event, but they occur so quickly and so frequently that they are often unnoticed by the client. For cognitive therapy to be effective the client must learn to identify these automatic thoughts when they occur. After clients learn to identify these thoughts they are asked to keep a daily record of them. Figure 10-21 illustrates the Daily Record of Dysfunctional Thoughts developed by Beck and his co-workers (Beck et al., 1979). After the client can identify automatic thoughts, then he or she and the therapist approach each thought as a testable hypothesis. This teaches the client that a person's view of reality can be quite different from the reality itself.

Even when clients can identify automatic thoughts and can recognize and correct their cognitive distortions, they are vulnerable to a return of depression if their early maladaptive schemas have not been modified. The therapist tries to link past experiences with present emotions by probing into the client's childhood and what events were linked to the beginning of diffi-

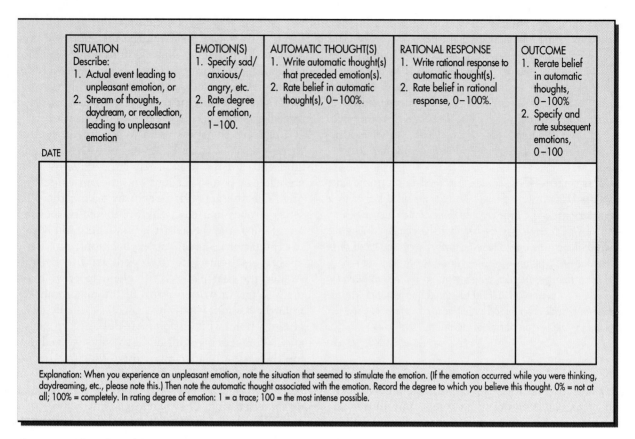

DATE	SITUATION Describe: 1. Actual event leading to unpleasant emotion, or 2. Stream of thoughts, daydream, or recollection, leading to unpleasant emotion	EMOTION(S) 1. Specify sad/ anxious/ angry, etc. 2. Rate degree of emotion, 1–100.	AUTOMATIC THOUGHT(S) 1. Write automatic thought(s) that preceded emotion(s). 2. Rate belief in automatic thought(s), 0–100%.	RATIONAL RESPONSE 1. Write rational response to automatic thought(s). 2. Rate belief in rational response, 0–100%.	OUTCOME 1. Rerate belief in automatic thoughts, 0–100% 2. Specify and rate subsequent emotions, 0–100

Explanation: When you experience an unpleasant emotion, note the situation that seemed to stimulate the emotion. (If the emotion occurred while you were thinking, daydreaming, etc., please note this.) Then note the automatic thought associated with the emotion. Record the degree to which you believe this thought. 0% = not at all; 100% = completely. In rating degree of emotion: 1 = a trace; 100 = the most intense possible.

Figure 10-21 Form for recording a client's Daily Record of Dysfunctional Thoughts.

SOURCE: From Young, Beck, & Weinberger (1993). "Depression." In D. H. Barlow (ed.) *Clinical Handbook of Psychological Disorders,* 3/E, p. 250.

culties with depression. For example, Michelle came to the clinic after she had stopped working and rarely left the house except for shopping (Young et al., 1993). Her depression appeared to have begun when, after visiting her gynecologist, she found she was not pregnant. She reported being happily married until a few months earlier and had been successful as a real estate sales person. She also said she currently felt worthless, unloved, and unappreciated.

After a period of treatment in which she learned to identify and test her dysfunctional thoughts and had successfully completed homework assignments, her depression lessened. The therapist then began the schema-focused phase of the treatment to help prevent a recurrence of the depression.

Michelle's recollection of her early family life was sketchy. She remembered her father as very bright and a good provider who was "hardly ever around." Her mother she recalled as gentle but seemingly passive. While growing up she could not confide in either of them for fear of engendering anger, ridicule, or "worse," especially on the *part of her father. A sister, 2 years her junior, was favored by her parents and "she has remained their darling even up to now."*

Michelle reported no "real" depressive episodes until she started dating and began experiencing feelings of "being terribly lonely and discarded" whenever her relationships suffered. Further questions about her past and her previous experience with psychotherapy revealed several minor episodes of depression, and at least one major depressive episode. Perceived or actual fluctuations in her relationship with Jim, her husband, seemed to have triggered many of her depressive reactions, during their marriage as well as during their courtship. Her previous major depression was triggered by Jim's announcement, after months of dating, that he was breaking up with her.

Young et al., 1993, pp. 269–270

The therapist worked to change Michelle's schemas by examining the evidence for Michelle's feeling that her husband might leave her.

T: Is it possible, based on some of these schemas that we talked about, some of the feelings of being defective or that people will leave you, that you have tended to exaggerate how little Jim is attracted to you?

M: *That would be wonderful if it were true, but I don't think so.*

T: *Well, let's look. What could you point to as evidence that he is attached and committed to you?*

M: *He says he loves me. Often he's happy to see me, to be around me. . . . He compliments me at times when we go out so I know he's attracted to me. He buys me very nice gifts—rings, jewelry, pocketbooks—and he takes me out on weekends. He asks me where I want us to go on vacation. I guess he does think of me.*

T: *Is there any evidence about his leaving you? Has he ever left you or threatened to leave you?*

M: *When we dated he left several times.*

T: *And since you've been married?*

M: *No, not since we've been married. He's never left.*

T: *Did he ever say anything about wanting to leave?*

M: *No.*

Young et al., 1993, pp. 272–273

The therapist also asked Michelle to imagine dialogues with her father in which she expressed anger at him for making her feel abandoned. This helped her see the connection between these feelings and how her schemas were activated both with her husband and in her sessions with the therapist.

Contrasting Psychological Therapies for Depression

It is sometimes difficult to distinguish clearly how the various psychological theories of depression and the therapies derived from them differ. The behavioral approach and Beck's cognitive-distortion theory started out quite differently, but as their related therapies developed, many of the techniques used became more alike. The behavioral approach increasingly emphasized cognitive attributions, and Beck included learning-theory techniques such as behavioral checklists of events and moods and homework assignments.

The same emphasis on feelings of hopelessness and helplessness seen in the cognitive view of depression is also found in the humanistic-existential approach, in which loss of self-esteem and a perceived inability to alter the oppressive demands of society are central ideas. The therapeutic approach of the humanistic-existential group is much less structured than the cognitive or learning therapies but somewhat more direct than psychoanalysis. Unlike psychoanalysis, but instead like learning and cognitive therapies, it is centered on the present rather than on the client's past history. Existential therapy is essentially a talking therapy and does not use the checklists and specific behavioral observations used in learning and cognitive approaches. Psychodynamic therapists stress cognitive distortions, but they tend to focus not only on how these affect present behavior but also on their origins in the client's earlier life. Cognitive theories are also concerned with a person's past experiences as a source of current schema that may produce distorted perceptions or interpretations of others' behavior, but these theories focus less on the past and more on the distortion. For instance, in the information-processing approach, the linking of stressful events and past memories is clarified for the client. It is important to remember that while the psychological theories and their related therapies differ in emphasis, some of their basic ideas are now surprisingly similar.

Effectiveness of Biological and Psychological Therapies for Depression

Most recent comparisons of the usefulness of psychological and biologically-based therapies for depression have focused on comparing the effectiveness of cognitive therapy, pharmacotherapy using tricyclic antidepressants, and a combined cognitive-pharmacotherapy approach. Results of both a large collaborative multicenter study sponsored by the National Institute of Mental Health and a later NIMH-funded study—designed to deal with possible scientifically confounding factors in the original NIMH study—suggested little difference in outcome at the end of treatment by the biological and cognitive therapies (Elkin et al., 1989; Hollon et al., 1992). However, follow-up of patients in the second study over a longer time period suggested that the treatments did seem to produce different effects over time (Hollon et al., 1992). In a follow-up 24 months after the end of the study, patients who had received cognitive therapy were less likely to have had a return of depression than had other groups (see Figure 10-22). Patients who had received short-term pharmacotherapy had the greatest chance of reexperiencing another depressive episode. The number of patients in this study was small and the follow-up over too brief a time to be certain of the meaning of the findings. However, the findings do suggest that risk of a relapse is greatest in the early months after the depressed episode begins, no matter what treatment is used. For this reason treatment should continue for some time after the acute symptoms decrease, but how long such a continuation period should last to be most effective has not been determined.

Although the information from this study cannot give us a final answer, the findings suggest that, at least for some people who are depressed, either antidepressant or a cognitively-based therapy may decrease symptoms

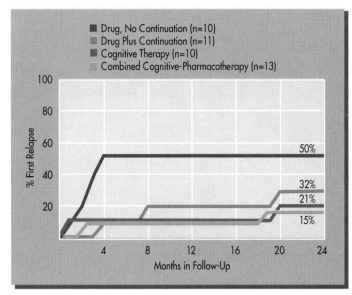

Figure 10-22 A comparison of the percent of those patients, in each of four treatment groups, whose symptoms returned during the follow-up period. Only patients in the Drug Plus Continuation group received any type of treatment during the follow-up period.

SOURCE: Evans et al., "Different relapse following cognitive therapy and pharmacotherapy for depression." *Archives of General Psychiatry*, 49, p. 805.

and shorten a depressive episode. It may be, however, that after discontinuation of therapy the prevention of a new depression episode may be facilitated by prior use of the cognitive approach. Other recent research suggests that another type of psychological therapy, psychodynamic interpersonal therapy, may be as effective as the cognitive approach (Shapiro et al., 1994). In this method, the therapist-client relationship is used as a vehicle for exploring and resolving interpersonal difficulties that may be primary sources of depression.

The Bipolar Disorders

DSM-IV lists four groups of bipolar disorders: cyclothymia, Bipolar I disorder, Bipolar II disorder, and a miscellaneous category for bipolar disorders that don't fit the criteria for any of the other three. Bipolar disorders include both periods of depression as well as periods of manic behavior or its milder variation, hypomanic behavior. Table 10-6 contrasts manic and depressive behavior. The periods of depression that occur in bipolar disorder are not any different from the depression that has already been described in this chapter. The peak incidence of bipolar disorders is during young adulthood, although many people show evidence of the disorder as adolescents.

Bipolar disorders have been traditionally thought to be much less common than depression. The ECA study discussed at the beginning of this chapter found that depressive disorders were four to five times more frequent than bipolar disorder. Some researchers disagree with this finding, however, and believe that the rates of depressive disorder and bipolar disorder are really very similar (Bowden, 1993). The reason depression has been traditionally considered to be more common, according to this view, is that many bipolar individuals are wrongly classified as unipolar because a manic or hypomanic episode has not yet occurred.

Cyclothymic Disorder

Like dysthymic disorder, **cyclothymic disorder** is a chronic state of mood disturbance. In cyclothymic disorder both hypomanic behavior and depressive behavior occur but neither type meets the DSM-IV criteria for a manic episode or a major depressive episode and the behaviors extend over at least a two-year period. Cyclothymic disorder usually begins in adolescence or early adult life. People who are classified as having cyclothymic disorder seem to be a diverse group. Some will later develop bipolar disorder but many may not (Howland & Thase, 1993). Many family history studies have suggested a genetic link between bipolar disorder and cyclothymia (Howland & Thase, 1993). People diagnosed with cyclothymic disorder are more likely to have a close relative with a bipolar disorder than are either normal controls or people diagnosed with unipolar disorder. This difference suggests not only that cyclothymic disorder is more closely associated with bipolar disorder than with unipolar disorder but also that bipolar disorder has genetic causes different from those of unipolar depression.

Bipolar I Disorder

A person with **Bipolar I** disorder will experience episodes of mania and, usually, major depressive episodes as well. A very small number of people may experience one or more periods of mania without ever experiencing depression (Goodwin & Jamison, 1987). As this happens so infrequently these people are nonetheless classified as having a bipolar disorder, because of the expectation that a period of depression will ultimately occur. **Mania** is characterized by a flight of ideas, elevated mood, and increased psychomotor activity. Manic behavior is illustrated by a study of the well-known American poet Robert Lowell (1917–1977) who was affected by bipolar disorder for much of his life. Over a 15-year period his manic episodes followed a repeated pattern. Each time, just as his manic behavior became obvious, Lowell, a married man, started an affair with a young girl.

With his immense charm and erudition, his stature as a famous poet and his quality of infectious enthusiasm, he

TABLE 10–6
Differing Patterns in Manic and Depressive Behavior Found in Bipolar Disorder

	Manic Behavior	Depressive Behavior
Emotional Characteristics	Elated, euphoric	Gloomy, hopeless
	Very sociable	Socially withdrawn
	Impatient at any hindrance	Irritable
Cognitive Characteristics	Racing thoughts, flight of ideas	Slowness of thought processes
	Desire for action	Obsessive worrying
	Impulsive behavior	Inability to make decisions
	Positive self-image	Negative self-image, self-blame
	Delusions of grandeur	Delusions of guilt and disease
	Talkative	
Motor Characteristics	Hyperactive	Decreased motor activity
	Does not become tired	Tired
	Needs less sleep than usual	Difficulty in sleeping
	Increased sex drive	Decreased sex drive
	Fluctuating appetite	Decreased appetite

would court a girl many years his junior. Always successfully. . . . He would then summon his circle of friends to a party to announce the exciting change in his life, and that he was leaving his wife forever. Over the ensuing days his elation would become increasingly frantic until he would be hospitalized and, after 1953 when it first became available, he would be treated with chlorpromazine [an antipsychotic drug]. The elation would be followed by several weeks or months of what he called his "dark, post-manic and pathological self-abasement." The girl would be abandoned and he would return to Hardwick [his wife]. She, for her part, would protest over the intense public humiliation she had been put through, but always took him back. No treatment modality, including attempts at psychotherapy, seems to have altered this pattern until the time he was eventually given lithium.

Powell, 1991, p. 378

Before classifying someone who has experienced a manic episode as having a bipolar disorder, it is important to rule out other causes for the manic behavior. Mania may be caused by certain biochemical factors not related to bipolar disorder. Certain drugs can cause people with no history of affective disorders to experience episodes of mania. Drugs that produce this response include steroids, MAO inhibitors and tricyclic drugs used to treat depression, and L-dopa (used to treat Parkinson's disease). Mania can also result from infections, metabolic disturbances, and the growth of tumors. Mania in these cases is considered a symptom of the change in a person's biochemical state and is not classified as a mood disorder.

Bipolar II Disorder

Bipolar II disorder differs from Bipolar I in that—rather than experiencing one or more florid, dramatic manic episodes such as Robert Lowell's—the manic behavior is present to a lesser degree, called *hypomania* or a *hypomanic episode*. A **hypomanic episode** occurs when there is a distinct period of elevated, expansive, or irritable mood and other manic behaviors, but social or on-the-job functioning is not greatly impaired and the person does not have to be hospitalized. Bipolar II seems to be a separate type of disorder and not a preliminary problem that will later develop into a typical bipolar disorder (Dunner, 1987). People who experience a hypomanic episode may not see it as pathological, although those around them may be concerned about the erratic behavior they see. For the person affected, the feelings of elation and creativity and the driving energy characteristic of the hypomanic state can be positive forces (see Box 10-3).

Is There a Relationship Between Creativity or Leadership and Bipolar Disorder?

A few years ago, a study of British artists and writers revealed that these highly creative people had received treatment for a mood disorder in much higher proportions than would be expected in the general population (Jamison, 1989). Moreover, the incidence for bipolar disorder, relatively rare in the general public, was significantly higher in this creative group. Figure 10-23 summarizes key findings from this study. This scientific study confirms what letters, diaries, and biographical accounts of well-known poets, artists, and composers have related for years: Highly creative people tend to experience extremes of mood, which in turn may fuel the creative process (see Figure 10-23). Such accounts provide fascinating information for those interested in understanding mood disorders.

Leonard Woolf, the husband of Virginia Woolf, a highly creative writer who was affected by bipolar disorder and ultimately killed herself while depressed, described the relationship of her disorder to her creativity this way:

I am quite sure that Virginia's genius was closely connected with what manifested itself as mental instability and insanity. The creative imagination in her novels, her ability to "leave the ground" in conversation, and the voluble delusions of the breakdowns all came from the same place in her mind—she "stumbled after her own voice" and followed "the voices that fly ahead." And that in itself was the crux of her life, the tragedy of her genius.

Woolf, 1964, p. 80

Virginia Woolf seemed to agree. She wrote:

As an experience, madness is terrific. I can assure you, and not to be sniffed at; and in its lava I still find most of the things I write about. It shoots out of one everything shaped, final, not in mere driblets, as sanity does.

Woolf, 1978, p. 180

Certain creative professions seem more prone to bipolar disorder than others. Novelists, playwrights, and composers all appear more likely than average to have a bipolar illness, while poets appear the most likely to be affected. For instance, 36 American poets born since 1900 are represented in *The New Oxford Book of American Verse*, a collection of outstanding poetry. Eight of these, listed in Table 10-7, have well-documented histories of bipolar disorder. This figure may be a low estimate of the total, since the biographical materials for all 36 poets have not yet been researched (Goodwin & Jamison, 1990). Since the rate for bipolar disorder in the general population is less than 1 percent, this group of very talented poets clearly has a significantly higher rate.

Creativity can be shown not only in the arts, but also in political leadership. Some outstanding political leaders of the past, for instance Napoleon Bonaparte, Oliver Cromwell, and Winston Churchill, all experienced periods of both quite severe depression and of high energy, elevated mood, impetuousness, and at times questionable judgment. People who worked with Churchill were impressed by the fertility of his mind and his inexhaustible stream of inventive thought. However, "all those who worked with him also agreed that he needed the most severe restraint put on him, and that many of his ideas, if they

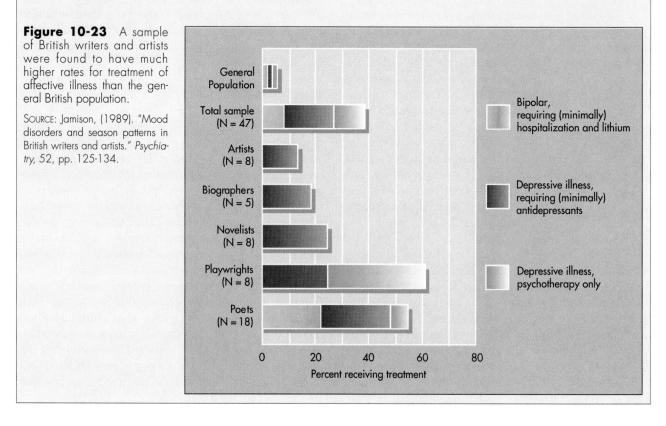

Figure 10-23 A sample of British writers and artists were found to have much higher rates for treatment of affective illness than the general British population.

SOURCE: Jamison, (1989). "Mood disorders and season patterns in British writers and artists." *Psychiatry*, 52, pp. 125-134.

BOX 10-3

Figure 10-24 Although poets seem to be affected by bipolar disorder more frequently than other writers, many well-known novelists, playwrights, and other writers also experienced some form of severe cyclothymia or bipolar illness. Of those pictured here, Virginia Woolf and Ernest Hemingway took their own lives during periods of depression.

(a) Virginia Woolf, English novelist and essayist.

(b) Eugene O'Neill, American playwright.

(c) Ernest Hemingway, American novelist.

had been put into practice, would have been utterly disastrous" (Storr, 1988, pp. 14–15). The other side of his mood swings was documented by his personal physician, who described many conversations with Churchill. In one of them, Churchill ruminated that:

> For two or three years the light faded out of the picture. I did my work. I sat in the House of Commons, but the black depression settled on me. . . . I don't like standing near the edge of a platform when an express train is passing through. I like to stand right back and if possible to get a pillar between me and the train. I don't like to stand by the side of a ship and look down into the water. A second's action would end everything.
>
> Moran, 1966, p. 167

Theodore Roosevelt is an example of a leader who was chronically hypomanic and although he was at times mildly depressed, he did not seem to have the periods of deep depressed mood that characterized the above-mentioned leaders. His life went on at a fast pace. He was overtalkative, often grandiose, restless, and extremely enthusiastic. He was able to get along with very little sleep and worked, wrote, or explored at a frenzied pace. During his lifetime he wrote more than 150,000 letters and a large number of books ranging in topic from naval history to a record of his experiences living in the wilderness.

For all these leaders, even those who were at times incapacitated by depres-

sion, their hypomanic periods produced inspired leadership and a large number of accomplishments. For both these leaders and the creative artists discussed earlier, their bipolar tendencies had a positive effect and enabled them to achieve a great deal. Their enormous accomplishments suggest that sometimes the negative aspects of these serious disorders are so preoccupying to researchers and clinicians that other important aspects of behavior may be overlooked. In spite of findings such as these, it is important to remember that many creative artists and successful leaders have no mood disorder or other type of psychopathology and that many people with mood disorders are not unusually creative or talented in leadership.

TABLE 10–7
Partial Listing of Major 20th Century American Poets, Born Between 1895 and 1935, with Documented Histories of Bipolar Illness

Poet	Pulitzer Prize in Poetry	Treated for Major Depressive Illness	Treated for Mania	Committed Suicide
Hart Crane (1899–1932)		X	X	X
Theodore Roethke (1908–1963)	X	X	X	
Delmore Schwartz (1913–1966)		X	X	
John Berryman (1914–1972)	X	X	X	X
Randall Jarrell (1914–1965)		X	X	X
Robert Lowell (1917–1977)	X	X	X	
Anne Sexton (1928–1974)	X	X	X	X
Sylvia Plath[a] (1932–1963)	X	X		X

[a]Plath, although not treated for mania, was probably bipolar II.

Source: From *Manic-Depressive Illness* by Frederick K. Goodwin and Kay Redfield Jamison. Copyright © 1990 by Oxford University Press, Inc. Reprinted by permission.

The Course of Bipolar Disorder

Bipolar disorder has always been considered to be a condition in which a person experiences multiple episodes of disordered behavior. Not only researchers but also those diagnosed with the disorder have an interest in what to expect in the future. For example, what is the probability of another period of mania or depression? Will the time between these periods increase or decrease? Will repeated periods be more or less severe than when the disorder first occurred? Because there were conflicting answers to these questions the National Institute of Mental Health began a collaborative study of depression that included bipolar disorder. For more than 10 years patients in this study have been systematically followed up (Winokur et al., 1994). An analysis of the data for Bipolar I patients clearly showed the recurrent nature of Bipolar I disorder. Even though the people in the study continued to receive appropriate treatment during the 10-year follow-up, on average they experienced two to three additional manic episodes and two to three depressive episodes during that period. Only 13 percent of the men and 10 percent of the women had no further episodes after their first hospitalization. It had also been thought that the period between episodes of mania and depression might become shorter as time went on, but this was not the case in the study. What was observed, however, was that those who had a family history of mania had more episodes during the 10-year follow-up. Another interesting finding concerned the relationship of bipolar disorder to alcoholism. It had been previously noted that the rate of alcoholism in bipolar patients was very high, about 30 percent (Winokur et al., 1994). The follow-up data showed that if a person was already affected by alcoholism before the first episode of the bipolar disorder, the number of additional episodes he or she experienced during the 10-year period was significantly fewer than the number experienced by people who became alcoholic after they had been diagnosed with bipolar disorder. This suggests that alcoholism may precipitate occurrence of an initial episode of bipolar disorder in a vulnerable person but once alcohol use is controlled the degree of vulnerability decreases.

Causes of Bipolar Disorder

Both genetic inheritance and stress seem to play a role in determining whether a person will develop symptoms of bipolar disorder.

The Role of Heredity Genetic studies of families of people diagnosed with bipolar disorder show that there is a strong tendency for other family members also to have higher than expected risk for a mood disorder of some type including bipolar disorder, unipolar depression, schizoaffective disorder, and possibly cyclothymia (Mitchell et al., 1993). This suggests that these disorders show some genetic characteristics. However, the genetic picture is a complicated one. For example, there is a higher risk for both Bipolar I and Bipolar II disorder for families of individuals with a Bipolar I diagnosis. In contrast, for people with a Bipolar II diagnosis, the risk for bipolar disorder among their family members is increased for Bipolar II but not for Bipolar I (Coryell et al., 1984). Another interesting observation is that, just as has been found with depressive disorder, bipolar disorder seems to show a cohort effect. For those who do not have a family history of affective disorder, the rate of bipolar disorder is higher in individuals born after 1940 (Gershon et al., 1982).

Studies of twins also have been used to help us understand heritability of bipolar disorder. In about half of the cases where one MZ twin had been diagnosed with bipolar disorder, the other twin—whose heredity was, of course, identical—also received that diagnosis (Tsuang & Faraone, 1990). This suggested that heredity plays an important role because the rate for DZ twins or siblings was much lower. Another interesting finding was that even when only one of an MZ-twin pair had been diagnosed with a bipolar disorder, the children of both the diagnosed twin and healthy twin had about an equal risk of developing the disorder (Bertelsen & Gottesman, 1986). This finding, in accord with the vulnerability and resiliency theme of this book, suggests that it is possible not to show disordered behavior despite having the same genetic makeup (as in the MZ-twin parents) but still be just as likely to pass the disorder along to offspring.

Genetic studies of bipolar disorder have also used recombinant DNA technology in an attempt to locate genetic markers. By studying DNA from family members, some of whom have bipolar disorder, researchers have identified genes located on the X Chromosome, Chromosome 6, or Chromosome 11 that occur only in affected family members. Unfortunately other researchers, studying different family groups, have not been able to replicate any of these results. Nevertheless, studies of genetic markers and their placement on specific chromosomes are an important future source of information about heredity of bipolar disorders.

As the general public becomes more aware of the heritability factors in bipolar disorder, clinicians receive more requests for advice concerning the risk of illness for potential offspring. Studies indicate that children of a bipolar parent may have a 13 percent risk of bipolar disorder, a 15 percent risk of unipolar depression, and a 1 percent risk of schizoaffective illness. However, the risk becomes higher when the spouse also has an affective disorder. In that case the risk increases to 50 to 74 percent (Gershon et al., 1982).

Stress and Bipolar Disorder Children of a bipolar parent who also develop a disorder themselves are most likely to live in families in which the bipolar parent has frequent episodes of mania or depression (LaRoche et al., 1985). This increased risk may be a result of a parent's stronger genetic loading that produces more episodes of illness. It may also be a result of stress generated by the parent's behavior. There is now considerable evidence that stress can precipitate manic episodes (Ellicott et al., 1990).

Environmental stressors can sometimes be important in setting off either an initial or an additional manic episode. Two-thirds of manic episodes experienced by patients in one study were preceded by a life-related stress of some kind (Ambelas, 1987). Stressful events can also cause a manic episode in people with a past history of manic episodes or bipolar disorder. For example, when a major hurricane struck Long Island, New York, in 1985, there was a dramatic increase in manic episodes among patients with bipolar disorder who were being treated with lithium (Aronson & Shukla, 1987). All the people who relapsed already had a high level of stress in their lives and most lacked social support from a close, confiding relationship. For each of these people the hurricane resulted in additional stress besides that from the storm itself. For example, two people had to move into their parents' homes where there was a high tension level, another person went into a temporary shelter where she knew no one, and yet another wrecked her boyfriend's new car during the storm and their relationship deteriorated. There is a need for studies of the interaction between genetic vulnerability to bipolar disorder and stressful environmental factors (Mitchell et al., 1993).

A person with a bipolar disorder—because of its episodic nature—usually experiences relapses and also periods of normal or nearly normal functioning. When these changes occur, roles shift within the family (Moltz, 1993). Responsibilities for everyday decision-making need to be redistributed and the hierarchy of authority changes. As one patient's son said, "I have to take myself away from the fact that I'm her son and I have to be the parent. It's hard to do that" (Moltz, 1993, p 416). Another problem is that affect in the family is contagious even under normal circumstances. Living with a depressed person, for example, can cause psychological distress to family members. In one study 40 percent of those living with a person in the midst of a depressed episode were sufficiently distressed themselves to meet the criterion for needing psychological intervention. However, when their family member was not in the midst of such an episode, their own distress faded as well. Mania can also be hard to tolerate.

No other difficulty, not even homicide in the family, has such a high degree of enduring familial chaos nor such a high likelihood that family will be unable to tolerate the patient and give up on him or her.

Lansky, 1988, p. 216

Family members often believe the person with a bipolar or unipolar disorder can control his or her feelings and behavior. This misunderstanding can lead to anger and a sense of failure for all concerned. Family members can also become hypervigilant and interpret any expression of emotion as a signal that another episode of mania or depression is about to begin. Sometimes when a manic episode is in the beginning stages, the person can "pull together" for brief periods and appear self-controlled. This may happen when a family member calls the police or when involuntary hospitalization is imminent and can lead to blame toward family members who are acting appropriately. For example

A woman was forced to call the police to have her husband involuntarily committed after he became violent with her and with their son during a manic episode. Mutual friends blamed her for overreacting, and testified at his commitment hearing that he did not need hospitalization. As a result, he was released without treatment, whereupon he flew to Australia and bombarded his wife and their friends with threatening and harassing phone calls from around the world.

Moltz, 1993, p. 417

Table 10-8 illustrates some of the effects on the family. These effects make it clear that the best treatment approach for bipolar disorder may include not only treating the patient but also educating the family about the disorder and providing them with support. Working with the patient and the family together to improve communication and to deal directly with the issues listed in Table 10-8 can decrease stress for everyone and possibly enhance the resiliency of both patient and family members to episodes of bipolar disorder or other stress-related reactions.

Treatment of Bipolar Disorder

The most common treatment for bipolar disorders today is lithium. Since the first sign of the disorder often is depression, an antidepressant medication may be used. This can have the undesirable effect of bringing on manic behavior rather than simply reducing depressed affect. Unfortunately there is no existing laboratory test that can distinguish between a major depressive episode found in a depressive disorder and the same type of episode as a part of bipolar disorder. For that reason the clinician usually inquires carefully about any relatives

TABLE 10–8
Effects of Bipolar Disorder on Other Family Members

Characteristics of Illness	Effects on Family	Long-Term Consequences
Episodic	More serious consequences	Hypervigilance
	Shifts in roles and authority	Generalization
		Constraints on range of behavior
	Fear of relapse	Taboo on discussion
Affective	Contagion and intensity	Inhibition of growth and development
	Confusion between symptoms and normal moods	
Ambiguous	Problems with responsibility and control	
	Confusion about personality	

Source: Moltz, 1993.

who may have a type of bipolar disorder. If there are such relatives, the chances of a bipolar disorder in the person being treated for a depression are enhanced. As a result, the clinician may choose to use lithium. Lithium is used to treat both the depression and the manic behavior seen in bipolar disorder. Table 10-9 lists some of the lithium-based medications currently used. Lithium may change the chemical balance of the body fluids by replacing calcium, magnesium, potassium, and/or sodium, or it may slow down the release or increase the absorption of norepinephrine. Whatever the process, it seems effective in calming manic behavior and also serves to prevent the depressed phase of the bipolar cycle. Lithium is effective in the treatment of acute mania as well as for depression for some patients with bipolar disorder. It also may have dangerous side effects. The slight difference between an effective and a

toxic lithium dosage is the smallest difference found for any drug routinely prescribed for psychiatric illness (Bowden et al., 1994). As a result of these problems there has been an active search for other effective treatments for bipolar disorder.

Recently another chemical compound, divalproex sodium, has been tried in research studies. In a study of hospitalized acutely manic patients, both divalproex and lithium were more effective than a placebo. Some patients for whom lithium was not previously effective improved when taking divalproex (Bowden, 1993). Before this drug or others are used on a nonresearch basis, a long period of testing is necessary. However, this type of research may result in useful treatment for a group of bipolar patients for whom lithium is not effective.

Even for those who respond to lithium treatment, it may not be effective because many patients find its side effects so negative that they discontinue their medication. A two-year follow-up of patients for whom lithium carbonate was prescribed has raised some doubts about patients' use of this medication except under careful monitoring (Harrow et al., 1990). About one third of those studied had a very poor outcome for which one cause was the tendency of many patients either wholly or temporarily to discontinue their medication against medical advice. There are several possible reasons why this discontinuation occurred. One may be that lithium is abandoned during a low, although not depressed, period in the hope that stopping its use will elevate the person's mood. An even more intriguing reason appears to be unwillingness to give up some of the pleasant cognitive and behavioral changes that come with an elevated mood (Goodwin & Jamison, 1990). These changes include increased sensitivity to the environment, sexual intensity, creativity, and social ease (see Research Close-Up Box 10-3).

In any book on abnormal psychology, the negative or maladaptive aspects of abnormal behavior and the various disorders are likely to be emphasized. It is worth remembering, though, that at least in the case of bipolar disorder, the

TABLE 10–9
Examples of Medications Used to Treat Bipolar Disorder

Generic Name	Trade Names	General Description
lithium carbonate	Carbolith Eskalith Lithonate Lithotabs	Used to treat manic episodes and some severe depressions, especially those that alternate with mania. Effective in reducing or preventing manic episodes but variable with depressions. Many possible side effects if use not closely monitored. High toxic potential.

abnormal mood state may include some positive aspects. Although certainly all those with bipolar disorder are not creative people, and all creative people do not have bipolar disorder, a sizeable proportion of highly creative artists and writers seem to have been affected. For these people, mood changes that preceded or accompanied intense creative episodes have often been indistinguishable from hypomania.

The reaction to taking lithium by creative individuals with bipolar disorder suggests that, for them at least, hypomania and creativity may be closely connected. Such people complain that the continued use of lithium carbonate acts as a "brake" and inhibits creativity so that they are unable to express themselves. They feel that if lithium prevents the high, even if it also might prevent the "low," they would prefer not to take something that would deprive them of a pleasurable and productive state. This effect of lithium on productivity may occur only at the top rung of the creative spectrum (Goodwin & Jamison, 1990).

Suicide

Although suicide is a statistically rare event in the United States, it is the second leading cause of death on college campuses (NCHS, 1990). Suicides among young people 15 to 19 years old increased by 30 percent from 1980 to 1990 (from 8.5 per 100,000 to 11.1 per 100,000) (Silverman, 1993). For 20- to 24-year-olds, although the rate has greatly increased since the 1960s, there was a 7 percent drop during the 1980s. However, the actual numbers (2890 in 1990) remain "much too high" (Otten, 1994). Although college students are often thought to have a higher rate of suicide than nonstudents in their age group, a review of all available studies suggests the rate for college students is about half that for nonstudents of comparable age (Schwartz & Whitaker, 1990). However, another review of the literature suggests that the rate for college students may be anywhere from 5 to 50 per 100,000 (Lipschitz, 1990). Thus, according to this analysis we don't know if the rate is higher, the same, or lower. What is needed are some studies that include data from many schools. When studying a phenomena such as suicide with a low base rate only multiyear, multisite studies can provide a clear answer.

Risk Factors

Because the factors that determine whether a person will attempt suicide are complex, a model that includes both personal vulnerabilities and resilience factors makes sense (see Figure 10-25). Some risk factors such

as psychiatric disorder may be present. Over 90 percent of those who successfully commit suicide have a psychiatric illness at the time of death. Two disorders, mood disorder and alcoholism, are associated with at least three-quarters of all suicides. Other risk factors include personality characteristics such as deficiency in problem solving. This deficiency usually takes the form of a rigid way of looking at problems (Evans et al., 1992). Resiliency may come from protective factors include a socially supportive network and, for women, having young or adolescent children at home (Veiel et al., 1988). Secure financial status and steady employment are also important (Hagnell & Rorsman, 1980). Often, but not always, one or a series of negative life events may be important precipitating factors in a suicide attempt (Heikkinen et al., 1993).

A precipitating factor based on the pain and fear of experiencing another bipolar episode is shown clearly in this excerpt from the suicide letter written by the writer Virginia Woolf to her husband before she drowned herself:

Dearest, I feel certain I am going mad again. I feel we can't go through another of those terrible times. And I shan't recover this time. . . . So I am doing what seems the best thing to do. . . . I don't think two people could have been happier until this terrible disease came. I can't fight any longer.

Bell, 1972, p. 266

Because of this high risk of suicide by those with a mood disorder, it is very important to be able to identify those within the group who are at highest risk so that they can be treated and protected. Table 10-10

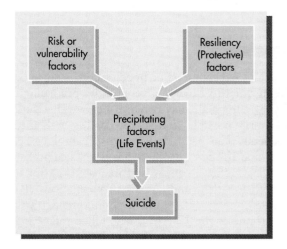

Figure 10-25 Risk and resiliency as well as precipitating life events may play roles in whether a suicide occurs.

TABLE 10–10
Factors Related to Increased Risk of Suicide in Those with Mood Disorders

For treated or untreated individuals

1. History of suicide among family members
2. High level of anxiety
3. Feelings of hopelessness
4. Talk about or threats of suicide
5. Previous suicide attempts

In addition, for those who have had treatment for mood disorder

1. Inadequate treatment
2. Overprescription of tranquilizers
3. Inadequate doses of antidepressant medication (tricyclics)
4. Inconsistent and poor outpatient care and follow-up after hospital discharge

lists a number of predictors that have been found. The majority of people who commit suicide have seen a general physician in the three months before their deaths (Goodwin & Jamison, 1990), suggesting that they were experiencing problems and probably seeking help but perhaps not expressing their concerns clearly. Past studies have shown that physicians tend to underdiagnose depression and often miss histories of suicidal behaviors. Many of the medications used to treat depression and many tranquilizers prescribed for patients experiencing stress and anxiety are highly lethal if taken in large quantities. About half of those who die from an overdose of medication have obtained that lethal dose from a physician in a single prescription.

Hopelessness

Negative expectations or hopelessness is an important theme for those who have suicidal preoccupations. These individuals may come to believe that suicide is their only possible strategy for dealing with insoluble problems. The Beck Hopelessness Scale developed by Beck and his co-researchers has been demonstrated to predict whether a person is at increased risk for suicide in both inpatient and outpatient populations (Beck et al, 1985, 1990). In a study of nonhospitalized patients, all but one of the 17 (94%) who killed themselves had scores above 9 on the Beck Hopelessness Scale. People whose scores were above 9 were 11 times more likely to commit suicide than those with lower scores. Because the individuals in the study had come for therapy for depression the number in the group scoring above 9 was

large (over 1,100 patients). Clearly most of these people (1,038 out of 1,100) did not kill themselves. Yet the Beck Hopelessness Scale identified those with a high suicide potential or risk factor so that clinicians were alerted to the increased risk. It also provided insight into what aspect of depressed thinking might entail the greatest risk. Because Beck and his co-workers have shown that hopelessness can be modified by cognitive therapy, his approach has also promoted more effective treatment (Rush et al., 1982).

Another group of researchers working with the Hopelessness Scale has pointed out the importance of considering hopelessness in the context of other risk factors. In their study of almost 1000 subjects participating in a large research project on the psychobiology of depression, researchers found that for drug and alcohol abusers, a group generally at high risk for suicide, those who were not high in hopelessness were at the highest risk for suicide (Young et al., 1994). Why this is the case is not clear. Perhaps hopelessness may mean something different to drug and alcohol abusers than to nonabusers who are depressed. Or it may mean that those high in hopelessness who are not abusers are low in coping skills, while high-hopeless abusers are at risk because they use denial as a way to deal with problems or they abuse various substances as a way of ridding themselves of hopelessness. Whatever the answer to this puzzling finding, it points out the value of considering the interaction of a number of factors when studying abnormal behavior.

Attitudes Toward Suicide

Different cultures interpret suicide differently. Most Western societies seek to prevent suicide and to interfere with its completion whenever possible. In some other cultures, for example in Japan, long-held traditions considered it an honorable action, perhaps the only acceptable one for a disgraced person.

In a study that investigated the influence of the potential suicide victim's situation on others' attitudes toward acceptability of suicide, college students read one of several fictitious scenarios about a man who decided to kill himself. The different scenarios portrayed the man as suffering from different conditions, including depression of different types, severe physical pain, or terminal bone cancer. This was one scenario:

John, a 45-year-old factory worker, has been suffering for the past 20 years from severe depression. His doctors believe the depression is likely due to a biochemical disorder of the central nervous system. Despite having received a wide variety of therapies (including drug treatments, psychotherapy, and behavior modification), the depression has gotten worse over time. John feels that the doctors have already done all they can, and he has no hope that his symptoms will be reduced. John is currently experiencing a great deal of psychological pain, and is very upset over the fact that his condition is draining the emotional and financial resources of his family and friends. John feels that the quality of his life now is very poor and will only get worse, and he fears that he will be an increasingly large burden to his loved ones. Despite protests from his family and friends, John has decided to kill himself.

Deluty, 1988/89, p. 83

Students answered a series of evaluative questions about the man and his decision. The evaluations were most accepting of the decision when the suicide occurred in response to terminal bone cancer, and least accepting when the cause was described as chronic depression as illustrated above.

Similar results were obtained in a survey of health professionals' views about suicide. Suicide as a response to physical illness was judged as more acceptable than suicide in the face of chronic psychological illness (Hammond & Deluty, 1991). The majority of those who responded to the survey believed that it was possible to make a rational decision to commit suicide. However, although these professionals did not see suicide as morally wrong, they thought it was wrong because of the consequences for the survivors, who often feel extreme guilt and responsibility for not understanding and helping the dead person's distress.

The Impact of Suicide on Others

Suicide is a traumatic event for the surviving family members, co-workers, or classmates. Although any experience of bereavement can cause great sadness, those bereaved by suicide may believe that they will receive less help from potential sources of support, the community will view the death more negatively, and others may experience social discomfort that causes them to avoid the survivor (Calhoun & Allen, 1991).

First Person Box 10-4 illustrates the devastating impact and guilt felt by survivors as well as how important expressions of grief can be. Even in the days immediately after the suicide survivors can be helped by a chance to express their feelings, obtain reassurance, and interpret what happened.

When a member of a group has committed suicide, group discussion and intervention can sometimes be helpful. This type of intervention, called **postvention,** can help survivors deal with their grief and possible feelings of responsibility and guilt as well as serve as a way to prevent others from focusing on the possibility of sui-

---

FIRST PERSON   **BOX 10-4**

Suicide and the Survivors

Suicide has a strong impact on the families of those who killed themselves and on others who knew them. It is more painful for the family than other kinds of death and often harder to accept or acknowledge. Parents may think of the suicide of their adolescent child as an accidental death. They may also experience strong feelings of guilt and shame that may make normal mourning impossible. Young children of a parent who commits suicide are also likely to be seriously disturbed. The surviving parent may claim the suicide was an accident. The child then begins to distrust the parent or doubt the reality of what he or she had observed, or both. Children often feel responsible for a parental suicide or think they should have prevented it. The result of these misperceptions may be a child who is depressed, passive, and self-destructive. Because of the social stigma that surrounds suicide the survivors often avoid talking to others.

In the following paragraphs a wife describes her reactions and those of her 12-year-old son, Richard, to her husband's death.

For me the days that followed [her husband's suicide] were full of pain. The questions pounded at me. Why? Why? But shock numbs; somehow I could cope with memorial-service plans. Like a robot, I did what I had to do. People came and went, and I sat for hours without moving much. I remember not taking my clothes off for two days. I didn't want to move or change anything. Talking was an effort. Eating was an effort.

At the end of a week, after the service was over, the relatives had left, the real loneliness set in, and the guilt. Each night I dreamed that I was soothing Dick, telling him how much I loved him and still love him, feeling in my dreams that if only he knew, then he would be

back and safe. . . . Two months later on the plane as we came home from a Christmas trip to visit Dick's family, Richard said, "I feel like I really miss somebody and I don't even know who." I said, "Don't you think it's Dad?" and the only tears I saw him cry came then. We talk often and he tells me that now he mostly feels mad. "When I start to feel angry or sad," he says, "I try to concentrate really hard on whatever I happen to be doing at the time, like playing ball or riding my bike."

I've found it difficult to be that sensible, to avoid guilt and constant questioning. The notes Dick left said it was his job, that I had nothing to do with what he did. Still, why couldn't I have seen what was happening? Why couldn't I have saved him? He had been the best friend I ever had. I must not have been a good enough friend to him. I wanted to piece it together; I relived every conversation. But there were no answers, and it didn't fit together.

Kenyon, 1979, p. 17

cide as a way of coping with personal difficulties. Such a program is described in the discussion of prevention strategies in chapter 18.

Suicide of a well-known figure often increases calls to crisis centers from people who are concerned about their own suicidal thoughts and can sometimes stimulate a series of suicides by others. When rock-star Kurt Cobain was found dead of an apparent suicide in 1994 a number of his admirers also killed themselves, although most of his fans expressed their sorrow through vigils or other group demonstrations (see Figure 10-26.).

Figure 10-26 Approximately 3,000 people attended a Seattle memorial service for rock star Kurt Cobain. Here Nirvana fans sign a homemade poster during the service.

WHAT ARE MOOD DISORDERS?

A wide range of behaviors are seen in mood disorders. The three main types of **mood disorder** are **depressive disorder, bipolar disorder,** and **other mood disorders** due to general medical conditions or substance-induced.

How Common Are Mood Disorders? Depressive disorder is relatively common. Bipolar disorders are much less common than depressive disorder.

DEPRESSION

Depression can refer to a symptom or a disorder. The symptom of depressed mood does not necessarily mean a person has a mood disorder.

Depressed Mood In everyday language, the word *depression* is usually used to refer to depressed mood in connection with some aspects of the surroundings or with some mild physical symptoms. *Depression* is also used to refer to normal feelings experienced after a significant loss, either a death, a relationship breakup, or failure to attain a significant goal.

Risk Factors Genetic makeup or heredity is an important risk factor for both major depression and bipolar disorder. Age is also a risk factor. Women are particularly at risk during young adulthood, while for men the risk is highest in early middle age. Gender is also related to risk. Twice as many women as men in the general population report a depressive disorder. However, for bipolar disorder the number of men and women who report being affected is approximately equal. Another risk factor is lack of social support, particularly from close relationships. This support may be especially valuable if stressful life events have recently occurred.

Life Events Negative or stressful life events, especially several occurring within a short time, may produce depressive episodes in people who are genetically vulnerable.

DEPRESSIVE DISORDERS

Although some symptoms of depression occur frequently in people who "have the blues" but are not clinically depressed, those who do meet DSM-IV criteria experience more symptoms and symptoms that are more severe. Depressive disorders are sometimes referred to as **unipolar disorders** to differentiate these types of depression from that found in bipolar disorder. There are several categories of depressive disorder.

Dysthymic Disorder A dysthymic disorder is a stable condition in which a depressed mood is dominant over long periods of time even if it is interrupted by short periods of normal mood.

Major Depressive Disorder A major depressive disorder is diagnosed when a person has experienced one or more major depressive episodes but has never experienced either a manic or hypomanic episode. A **major depressive episode** is defined as a period of depressed mood and/or loss of interest or pleasure in most activities, together with some other symptoms, which may include marked change in body weight, constant sleep problems, tiredness, inability to think clearly, agitation or greatly slowed behavior, and thoughts of death. Depressive episodes tend to recur over a person's lifetime. When a person who has experienced one major depressive episode develops the symptoms again at a later time, the diagnosis is changed to **recurrent major depressive disorder.** At least half of those who experience a first episode experience a recurrence. Sometimes someone experiences delusions or other psychotic symptoms during a major depressive episode. The diagnosis then becomes a **major depressive episode with psychotic features.**

THEORETICAL PERSPECTIVES ON DEPRESSION

It is generally thought that depression is the result of an interaction between biological characteristics, psychological vulnerabilities, and stressful events or ongoing stressful life situations. Each of the theoretical perspectives has contributed to the understanding of and the treatments available for depression.

Biological Theories Twin and family studies suggest a genetic component for both major depression and bipolar disorder. The mechanism for the depressed or manic behavior may be the activity of the neurotransmitter systems. The **catecholamines** *norepinephrine* and **dopamine** and the **indolamine serotonin,** have been most widely researched. The study of the effects of various antidepressant drugs including **MAO inhibitors, tricyclics,** and **selective serotonin receptive inhibitors** have led to hypotheses about the role of the neurotransmitters in producing behaviors associated with depression.

Markers of Depression The search for **markers of depression** has been an important research strategy. The markers investigated include hormone activity as measured by the **dexamethasone suppression test,** specific receptor sites in the brain studied by various scanning devices, and the role of biological rhythms, especially in **seasonal affective disorder.**

The Psychodynamic View Freud's view of depression focused on a decrease in self-regard and a punishing conscience that was an attempt to control feelings of anger and aggression. Later psychodynamic theorists believed feelings of helplessness in coping with loss were central to depression. Psychodynamic therapy focuses on helping clients to discover and clarify how past experiences and beliefs can distort interpretations of the present. The client's reactions within the client-therapist relationship are important tools for the therapist in psychodynamic or **interpersonal therapy.**

The Behavioral Perspective Depressed people may engage in excessive support-seeking, which eventually causes distress in those who have contact with them. In both their own estimation and in the view of others, some of those who are depressed may lack important social skills.

The Cognitive Perspective Unjustified negative interpretations of events or interactions are likely to be caused by **schemas** or customary ways of interpreting behavior that are based on experiences earlier in life. Beck's **cognitive distortion model** of depression was the original cognitive view of depression and remains highly influential. The model explains depression as a **cognitive triad** of negative thoughts about oneself, the situation, and the future. Many measures of cognitions have developed as a result of interest in a cognitive theory of depression. Attributional models of depression focus on the **causal attributions** people make, for instance, whether they blame themselves or others. The interest in these attributions originally stemmed from **learned helplessness theory.** A subtype of depression may be **hopelessness depression,** in which the attribution process is important in initiating the depression. Although originally it was believed that depression was associated with negative **cognitive distortions** of reality, some researchers believe that depressed people may distort less than those who are not depressed and that the latter group systematically distort reality in a positive direction.

The Humanistic-Existential Perspective In the humanistic-existential view depression is a loss of self-esteem. These theorists emphasize the difference between the person's ideal self and his or her perception of the actual self. If the difference is too great, depression is likely to result.

Depression From a Vulnerability-Resilience Perspective Biological and personally related factors combine to produce vulnerability or resilience to stressful life events. Although personal qualities play a role, social support is a major factor in lessening the likelihood of stress-related depression.

TREATMENT OF DEPRESSION

Treatment approaches to depression stem from the various theoretical perspectives.

Biologically-Based Treatment Treatments based on biological theories include antidepressant drugs, especially those from the heterocyclic chemical group including **tricyclics** and **selective serotonin receptive inhibitors,** as well as **MAO inhibitors,** and **lithium** compounds. Another biological approach to treatment is **electroconvulsive therapy (ECT).** Biologically-based treatments of depression are often successful in lessening depression. ECT is faster acting than antidepressant medication and also is often used if an effective medication cannot be found.

Behavioral Treatment for Depression An effective behavioral approach to treating depression is **social skills training,** focused both on appropriate behavior and on improved skills in understanding the cues other people give in social interactions.

Cognitive Therapy for Depression Therapy from the cognitive perspective utilizes both cognitive and behavioral elements and is often called **cognitive-behavioral therapy.** Although initially a behavioral approach may be used, as the client improves the therapist works with the client to change his or her dysfunctional thought patterns. One aim of the therapist is to elicit clients' automatic thoughts and eventually to modify their early maladaptive schemas.

Contrasting Psychological Therapies of Depression Although the psychological therapies differ in their approach and emphasis, they have increasingly come to include similar elements.

Efficacy of Biological and Psychological Therapies for Depression Recent large-scale comparisons of the efficacy of different therapeutic approaches to depression have assessed tricyclic antidepressants and a combination of these antidepressants and cognitive therapy. Little difference in short-term outcome was found but long-term follow-up suggested that the cognitive therapy may have helped to prevent later relapse. The studies also suggested that treatment should continue for some time after the major symptoms of depression disappear.

BIPOLAR DISORDERS

Bipolar disorders, sometimes referred to as manic-depressive disorders, include phases of both depression and mania or hypomania. **Mania,** is a state of elevated mood, flight of ideas, and increased psychomotor activity. A **hypomanic episode** refers to a period of manic behavior that is not extreme enough to greatly impair function. DSM-IV lists four bipolar disorders: cyclothymia, Bipolar I disorder, Bipolar II disorder, and a miscellaneous group. **Cyclothymic disorder** includes both hypomanic and depressive behavior that extends over at least a two-year period. **Bipolar I Disorder** includes episodes of mania and usually also major depressive episodes.

Bipolar II Disorder Bipolar II disorder is a variant of bipolar disorder in which there has been no manic episode but at least one hypomanic period as well as a major depressive episode.

The Course of Bipolar Disorder Episodes of bipolar disorder tend to recur. The number of recurrences is greater in those who have a family history that includes bipolar disorder.

Causes of Bipolar Disorder Bipolar disorders show some genetic characteristics. These effects appear complex and differ for Bipolar I and Bipolar II diagnoses. There is considerable evidence that stress can set off episodes of manic behavior in genetically vulnerable individuals.

Treatment of Bipolar Disorder Bipolar disorder is most commonly treated with lithium. However, lithium may be effective only under careful monitoring. Many people, especially those who are in occupations demanding high creativity, are likely to discontinue the medication because they find that the mood changes it causes to be aversive.

SUICIDE

Suicide, although a statistically rare event, is the second leading cause of death on college campuses. Suicide rates of the 15- to 19-year-old group increased by 30 percent from 1980 to 1990, but rates for 20- to 24-year-olds dropped slightly.

Risk Factors Risk factors for suicide include one or more previous suicide attempts and having a psychiatric illness, especially mood disorder or alcoholism. A series of life events may be an important precipitating factor.

Hopelessness Negative expectations or feelings of hopelessness may be important predictors of suicidal behavior for those who do not abuse drugs and alcohol.

Attitudes Toward Suicide Suicide may be culturally approved in some circumstances—in Japan, for example, for a person who has had a serious failure or been dishonored. In the United States attitudes differ depending on the circumstances. Suicide because of a terminal illness may appear more permissible than suicide as a result of psychological distress. Even among those who think suicide morally acceptable, it is viewed negatively because of the consequences for survivors.

The Impact of Suicide on Others Suicide of a family member or other person with whom one has a close relationship can produce guilt feelings and despair. Sometimes—if the suicide is of a person admired but not personally known—strong feelings of sorrow and mourning, even imitative suicidal behavior, can occur.

CHAPTER ELEVEN

Alfredo Castaneda, *To Arrive at the Sea,* 1989.
Mary-Anne Martin/Fine Art, New York.

SCHIZOPHRENIC DISORDER: CHARACTERISTICS AND PROBABLE CAUSES

"All of a sudden things weren't going so well. I began to lose control of my life and, most of all, myself. I couldn't concentrate on my school work, I couldn't sleep, and when I did sleep, I had dreams about dying. I was afraid to go to class, imagined that people were talking about me, and on top of that I heard voices. I called my mother in Pittsburgh and asked for advice. She told me to move off campus into an apartment with my sister.

"After I moved in with my sister, things got worse. I was afraid to go outside and when I looked out of the window, it seemed that everyone outside was yelling 'Kill her, kill her.' My sister forced me to go to school. I would go out of the house until I knew she had gone to work; then I would return home. Things continued to get worse. I imagined that I had a foul body odor and I sometimes took up to six showers a day. . . . Things worsened—I couldn't remember a thing. I had a notebook full of reminders telling me what to do on that particular day. I couldn't remember my school work, and I would study from 6 P.M. until 4 A.M., but never had the courage to go to class on the following day. I tried to tell my sister about it, but she didn't understand. She suggested that I see a psychiatrist, but I was afraid to go out of the house to see him.

"One day I decided that I couldn't take the trauma anymore so I took an overdose of 35 Darvon pills. At the same moment, a voice inside me said, 'What did you do that for? Now you won't go to heaven.' At that instant I realized that I really didn't want to die, I wanted to live, and I was afraid. So I got on the phone and called the psychiatrist whom my sister had recommended."

After more than a year on medication, first in the hospital and then out, J. decided she was well and stopped both medication and therapy. She got a job but quickly lost it. "My friends and family said I was behaving strangely, but I took no notice. I went out dancing practically every night to make up for the time lost while being afraid. . . . "

In the fall she went back to school in Atlanta to finish her senior year. Then she was hospitalized again. "This time things were twice as bad as the first. I no longer heard voices, but the things I saw and dreamed about were far more traumatic. I recall at one point thinking I was Jesus Christ and that I was placed on this earth to bear everyone's sins."

After a month in the hospital J. returned home and received both antipsychotic drugs and psychotherapy as an outpatient. Two years later, still on medication, she was back in college, president of her sorority, "more confident and happy than I have ever been in my life."

—Adapted from O'Neal, 1984, pp. 109–110

This young woman seems to have made a good recovery from several schizophrenic episodes. Before they began, she had been functioning at a high level. She was a good student, an officer in her sorority chapter, president of a campus club, and she had a part-time job and a satisfying relationship with her boyfriend. One predictor of improvement for someone experiencing a schizophrenic disorder is the person's level of adjustment before the symptoms appeared.

Not all people who develop schizophrenia experience such a dramatic recovery, even when they continue to use antipsychotic drugs. The following passage, written by the mother of a son diagnosed with schizophrenic disorder, describes a more common pattern.

When Dan first began to suffer from schizophrenia, our family thought it was just a case of teenage blues. We sent him off to college. By the time he began attacking the refrigerator for reading his mind and threatening family members for using the word "right," we had learned to recognize the disease. We have six children. It was a happy family, and I wish I could say it hasn't changed. Our family isn't destroyed, but it is badly damaged.

We did everything we could to be helpful to Dan. We took him weekly to a psychiatrist, and then tried to see that he took his medicine. Whenever he was released from a hospital, we helped him find a job. We took him around until he found a suitable room in the area, and then once more helped him move his drafting table and other belongings to his new home.

He never took his medicine once he was away from us. Each time he finally began breaking things, and we once more brought the drafting table, suitcases, and sometimes cockroaches back home. Eventually, he would be reaccepted by the hospital, and we sat with heavy hearts while heaving sighs of relief. . . . There has never been a time when we would be surprised to look out the window and see Dan coming up the driveway. This was true especially in the year we were testing adult homes, though we continued calling on Dan, taking him places, and inviting him home for visits. Here is an example of Dan's life during this period:

On August 6, 1981, we drove Dan to Richmond, stopping on the way to buy him a new pair of shoes. Ten days later, . . . we called to find out Dan was in jail. He had eaten a restaurant meal he couldn't pay for and assaulted a policeman.

The manager of the adult home explained Dan's problem to the police, and they released him, but Dan was not happy to be back at the home. . . . He sold his new shoes, pawned his watch, ran up a bill in a friendly Vietnamese cafe, and found new places where he could order a meal only to discover later that he didn't have his billfold. He was constantly asking John to raise his allowance from $20 to $35 a week. Whenever we went to visit him, he would spoil our time together by badgering his father.

[Later, during a period at home,] Dan was getting more and more upset over people "messing with his mind." He finally threatened to kill his younger brother, who moved out to live temporarily with a friend. It wasn't long before Dan was back in the hospital. Though the doctor said there was nothing wrong with him, his lawyer had talked him into volunteering.

While Dan was in the hospital, we once more investigated adult homes, hoping to find one which would please him. By the time he was to be dismissed, we hadn't found anything suitable, and in the end, we presented him with a plan for living at home. He was now 34 years old, and his younger brother, Fred, was away at college, so it would be just the three of us. Here was our proposition:

We welcome you to live at home with us if you take your medicine regularly, eat at meal time, and smoke only in a restricted area. We will give you $30 a week for your expenses, and you will have occasional use of the car after you get your driver's license.

For over a year now, he has been going to the clinic to get his shots. He knows a good thing when he sees it. That $30 never makes it to the end of the week, but if he talks hard enough, he can always get a couple more dollars out of his Dad, who would rather toss him the bills than risk building up his blood pressure.

—Adapted from Piercey, 1985, pp. 155–157

Schizophrenic disorders are a prominent part of the category of mental disorders known as psychotic disorders. A psychotic disorder involves alterations of perception, thoughts, or consciousness; these alterations are called *hallucinations* or *delusions*. Someone who makes incorrect inferences about reality based on these alterations and believes that the inferences are real and actual has a psychotic disorder. A psychotic disorder may also include disorganized speech and behavior. Although psychotic symptoms may be seen in other disorders—for example, substance-induced delirium and major depressive disorder with psychotic features—the psychotic disorders have the psychotic symptoms as their defining or central feature.

Psychotic symptoms often produce the kind of behaviors that were formerly called *madness*, *lunacy*, or *insanity*. Causal factors have been found for some disorders with these symptoms. The causes may be temporary, such as the effect of drugs, reduced availability of oxygen to the brain during high fevers, or extreme vitamin deficiencies, or they may be permanent, for instance, the consequence of infections such as syphilis. However, a specific cause has not been found for many disorders that produce psychotic behavior. Such disorders include, in addition to schizophrenic disorders, some manias, and certain severe depressions.

The Impact of Schizophrenic Disorders

Of all the psychoses, schizophrenic disorders have the most severe impact on people's lives and on the health care system. The ECA Catchment Study described previously found that about 14 in every 1,000 adults (1.4 percent) who live outside of institutions have met the criterion for a diagnosis of a schizophrenic disorder sometime in their lives (Keith et al., 1991). In any given year, about 1 percent of the population is affected by schizophrenia. Despite the relatively small percent of the total United States population affected, the seriousness and incapacitating consequences of schizophrenic disorder means that about 50 percent of those so affected will become severely and permanently disabled, members of the poorest socioeconomic group, and dependent on public assistance funding. Individuals diagnosed with schizophrenic disorder consume about 2.5 percent of total annual health care expenditures, make up 10 percent of the permanently and totally disabled population and constitute as much as 14 percent of the homeless population of some large urban centers (Rupp & Keith, 1993). Worldwide about 20 million people meet the criteria for schizophrenic disorder (Sartorius & de Girolamo, 1991).

In the United States the total treatment cost for schizophrenia is estimated at $16 billion per year. Lost productivity, social welfare costs, and the estimated value of family caregiving added to the treatment cost were estimated to total about $33 billion in 1990 (Rice and Miller, 1992). As an example of the high costs of treating schizophrenia, consider the case of one 32-year-old American woman who became ill when she was 14. In 18 years the direct costs for her care in inpatient settings or in community outpatient settings totaled more than $636,000 in 1983 dollars (Moran et al., 1984). This figure did not include costs for outpatient therapy, health care, emergency room care, and social services, or the costs to her parents, who supported her financially when she was not in a hospital or halfway house.

In addition to the cost in money, the social and psychological costs of schizophrenic disorder are tremendous both to patients and their families and to society. The psychological cost to patients is shown in the very high rates of attempted and completed suicide by those with a schizophrenic diagnosis. About one in every four patients with schizophrenia will try to kill him- or herself, and one in every ten will succeed (Roy, 1986). Those who elect suicide have certain characteristics in common with those in the general population who turn to suicide. They tend to be unmarried and unemployed, live alone, feel hopeless, and have made previous suicide attempts. However, people with a schizophrenic disorder who kill themselves also have certain characteristics unlike those of many suicides. These include youth, a college education, a chronic course of illness with many worsenings and improvements, an awareness of the effects of schizophrenia, fear of further disintegration, and a nondelusional negative view concerning the future (Caldwell & Gottesman, 1990). In addition to financial costs and the emotional costs to families of those with a schizophrenic disorder, it is estimated that family members spend an average of 67 hours per month on behalf of their ill member.

Characteristics of Schizophrenic Disorders

In a person who is experiencing a schizophrenic disorder all the normal mental processes seem to be completely out of kilter. People with schizophrenic disorder hear voices that are not there, speak a language others don't understand, laugh when others see nothing humorous, and seem to lose touch with the real world.

The major characteristics of a schizophrenic disorder include specific patterns of thought content and the form or structure in which thoughts are expressed; changes in perception of the environment and in emotional response; an imperfect differentiation between oneself and the environment; and changes in degree of motivation, in relationships, in level of functioning, and in patterns of body movement. The characteristics of schizophrenic disorder cover a wide range of behaviors, not all of which may occur in any one person. Table 11-1 lists the symptoms that characterize schizophrenic disorder as well as the other principal psychotic disorders. In this chapter we will be concerned primarily with schizophrenia.

Often changes in behavior can be noted before the active psychotic phase of a schizophrenic episode begins. Initially, these are often explained by family members as part of the normal growing-up process and only afterward are seen as the beginning of the disorder. They may include such things as marked social isolation and withdrawal; impairment in functioning in a previous role as a worker, student, or homemaker; impairment in personal hygiene and grooming; inappropriate affect; vague, digressive speech or contentless speech; odd beliefs or thinking that one has magical powers; and/or marked lack of initiative, interests, or energy.

Sometimes it is hard, even for an expert observer, to understand the implications of these early changes. A psychoanalyst wrote this description of his son's behavior in the period before a schizophrenic disorder was diagnosed.

I have often been asked, "When did Gary's illness begin?" If I were his psychiatrist writing up the case history, I would

TABLE 11-1
The Principal Psychotic Disorders

Name	Characteristics
Schizophrenia	Six months or greater duration of disturbance. At least one month of active-phase usually including at least two of the positive symptoms listed in Table 11-2 or one positive and one negative symptom. A decline in social or occupational function must also occur. (Five subtypes include Paranoid, Disorganized, Catatonic, Undifferentiated, and Residual)
Schizophreniform Disorder	Same symptoms as schizophrenia except lasting less than six months. It is not necessary that there be a decline in function for this diagnosis.
Schizoaffective Disorder	The active phase symptoms of schizophrenic disorder occur together with an episode characteristic of a mood disorder. These are preceded or followed by at least two weeks of delusions or hallucinations.
Brief Psychotic Disorder	A psychotic disturbance lasting more than one day but less than one month.
Psychotic Disorder due to General Medical Condition	Psychotic symptoms thought to be physiological results of a general medical condition or illness.
Substance-Induced Psychotic Disorder	Psychotic symptoms thought to be the physiological result of toxin exposure, medication, or drug abuse.
Delusional Disorder	Non-bizarre delusions lasting at least one month without other symptoms that characterize the active phase of schizophrenia.

say, "when he dropped out of Harvard during his sophomore year" or "at the time of his first hospitalization 2 years later." But when the onset of the illness is so insidious, as it was in Gary's case, and as it is in so many of these young people, it is an impossible question to answer. In retrospect, we have reason to believe that his illness started much earlier.

At age 13, while at summer camp, he became depressed for about a month. At age 14 he asked to see a psychiatrist, whom he saw for 4 years. I later learned that Gary was experiencing certain unusual visual imagery in his fantasy life at that time. Otherwise, the psychiatrist thought he was having some not-untypical adolescent conflicts and never, during the course of those 4 years, had any suspicion of any kind of psychosis. During high school Gary quit the tennis team, saying that he wanted to concentrate on his drumming and band work. At the time it seemed reasonable, but in retrospect it was the beginning of a tendency toward isolation. He asked for a single room at Harvard, although he had always been quite gregarious. During his senior year of high school he sent in his application to Amherst College late; not so unusual for many teenagers, but quite unusual for him.

Here we were, sophisticated parents, knowledgeable about emotional troubles, observant and close to our children, yet we could not see that anything terrible was happening to Gary. He could not decide whether to go to Harvard or Haverford. All kids should have such dilemmas, we thought! After all, I went to Harvard and his older brother was already there. Wasn't it understandable that he would be ambivalent about it? He wanted to be his own person. His well-written college essay was preoccupied with issues of moral integrity and concerns about being phony. Weren't these also concerns appropriate for an adolescent?

It was only when his illness was full-blown that we realized that his ambivalence about his college choice was the early manifestation of the profound ambivalence so characteristic of this illness. At its height he might spend many minutes opening and closing the refrigerator door, each action accompanied by a delusional fear and the attempt to avoid it. Only when his illness was diagnosed did we see that the preoccupation with morality and phoniness which he displayed in his essay was the early form of the typical delusions with which he is still struggling. Despite the fact that these symptoms were already beginning to plague him, he was selected as the leading drummer for the Harvard jazz band during his freshman year and was able to maintain a B average. The next year, however, he could no longer do the work and his condition deteriorated.

—Willick, 1994, pp 708–709

Gary subsequently was hospitalized three times, received a variety of antipsychotic medications, and 10 years after leaving Harvard was living in a halfway house.

Positive Symptoms

Two general types of symptoms of schizophrenia, positive and negative, have been identified. **Positive symptoms** reflect a distortion or excess of normal functions. **Negative symptoms,** on the other hand, involve a loss

TABLE 11-2
Positive and Negative Symptoms of Schizophrenic Disorder

Positive Symptoms	Negative Symptoms
Delusions	Flat affect
Hallucinations	Poverty of speech
Disorganized speech	Loss of directedness or motivation
Disorganized and bizarre behavior	Loss of energy
	Loss of feelings of pleasure

or decrease of normal functions. They can be described as behavior deficits. Table 11-2 lists the categories of behavior classified as positive or negative symptoms. At least one positive symptom must be present in the active or acute phase of the disorder for a diagnosis of schizophrenia to be made.

Delusions A delusion is essentially a faulty interpretation of reality that cannot be shaken despite clear evidence to the contrary. Delusions occur in other disorders besides schizophrenia, but in each disorder they have a somewhat different content (See Table 11-3).

Delusions may be expressed in many ways. Some types of delusions occur more often in schizophrenia than in any other type of psychoses. Among these are the belief that everyone can hear the person's thoughts, the belief that others are either inserting thoughts into the person's mind or removing them, or the belief that the person's thoughts, feelings, and impulses are controlled by some external force. All delusions of these types are classified as *bizarre*. If even one bizarre delusion is present, the criterion for two symptoms in DSM-IV is satisfied. Another kind of delusion is *referential*. The person believes that certain gestures or comments, song lyrics, passages in books, etc., are specifically intended for him or her. Additional delusions that are typical of schizophrenia but that occur less often include the belief of being persecuted, grandiose thoughts about being an extremely important person, or ideas with a religious theme. The artist who created the picture in Figure 11-1 expressed some of these types of delusional thinking through his painting. An example of religious themes can be found in the case at the beginning of the chapter, in which the college student described her belief that she was Jesus Christ.

Delusions can result in violent behavior that harms others. In 1994, a stagehand working on the *Today* show was shot and killed after he tried to alert police to an armed man who was trying to enter the NBC studios in midtown Manhattan (see Figure 11-2). The 46-year-old man accused of the shooting told police that the television networks had been spying on him and sending rays through his television set into his brain. He brought an assault rifle to the studio as a result of these delusional thoughts. At other times behavior, although based on delusional thinking, may be highly organized and appears logical. For example, the Army journal *Military Review* recently published an article, entitled "Hell in a Hand Basket: The Threat of Portable Nuclear Arms," that focused on the growing peril of hand-held nuclear weapons that terrorists could easily deliver. C. T. Harrison, the author, was identified in the journal as a commercial pilot with a science degree; a member of the Mensa Society, an organization for those of superior intelligence; and a freelance researcher for several government departments. However, he also was later identified, to the embarrassment of the journal's editors, as someone who was currently institutionalized in a mental health institution (Blumenthal, 1993). He had been confined to the institution nine years earlier with the diagnosis of paranoid schizophrenic disorder after killing his mother and being ruled not guilty by reason of insanity. After they received this information, the journal staff made further inquiries. They discovered that both the FBI and the Secret Service had been investigating Harrison for at least 12 years in connection with death threats against political figures and with a stream of letters in which he iden-

TABLE 11-3
Typical Content of Delusions in Different Types of Psychoses

Disorder	Typical Delusional Content
Schizophrenia	Variety of bizarre content
	Being controlled by others
	Being persecuted by others
	Finding reference to oneself in others' behaviors and in printed materials
Depression (in either unipolar or bipolar disorder)	Unjustified guilt
	Perceived bodily changes (for example, rotting, putrefaction)
Mania	Great self-importance, grandiosity
Delusional Disorder	Loved by celebrity/high status person
	Unfaithful behavior by spouse/lover
	Possession of special (unrecognized) talent

Figure 11-1 The artist who created this picture was, at the time, a hospitalized psychiatric patient who was troubled by a variety of tormenting thoughts. Here he represented his negative view of life and some of the topics that were special areas of conflict for him. Talented as an artist, he made painting his vocation after his recovery.

Figure 11-2 William Tager is escorted by police after being charged with the shooting death of an NBC stagehand outside the *Today* show studio.

tified himself as a member of a fictional terrorist group that claimed responsibility for assassination plots against many world leaders, including the Pope. Yet despite the apparent delusional nature of his thinking, he was able to communicate clearly and logically enough to convince the journal that his paper was worth publishing. In the course of considering the article the editor had spoken with Harrison several times but did not realize he was calling someone who was hospitalized.

Hallucinations Hallucinations account for most of the difficulties a person with schizophrenia experiences in perceiving reality. **Hallucinations** are projections of internal impulses and experiences onto perceptual images in the external world. Although they may occur in other disorders—for example, during the delirium associated with a high fever or as a result of the effects of drugs or other chemicals on the nervous system—only in schizophrenia do hallucinations occur when the person is in a clear, conscious state. Hallucinations can be associated with any of the senses. In the case at the beginning of the chapter, J. had the hallucination of hearing voices threatening to kill her. This kind of *auditory* hallucination is the most common type found in schizophrenia. Many of those with schizophrenic disorder report voices making a running commentary on their behavior or speaking directly to them and issuing orders or accusing them of terrible crimes or actions. Hallucinations may also be related to touch. For instance, the person may feel burning or tingling sensations. Hallucinations associated with smell, while less common, are also typical. Foul odors may be perceived as coming from one's body as a sign of decay and death or of some sexual change. Sometimes hallucinations are somatic, or reflect internal sensations.

> *I began to hallucinate at the age of nine. . . . I would giggle at odd times as I would "see" a troop of elves jump merrily from desk to desk and tweak the teacher's nose. At other times, I would cry out at the sight of my desk biting my dress like a hungry animal. My behavior was annoying, and my explanations were seen as fanciful lies to cover up my disruptive behavior. . . . By late adolescence, I had learned that I could trust no one with the truth.*
>
> —Lovejoy, 1982, p. 605

The frightening quality of hallucinations is illustrated by the experience of a medical student in response to a highly stressful personal situation.

> *One night, after weeks of bunking with anxiety, I was lying in bed, . . . when from the room, barely audible, came a whisper. Calmly, I looked around. Dormitories are noisy. There could be someone walking around outside. I opened my door, peeked side to side at the empty hall, then returned to bed. I rested within my sheets and attempted to relax, when again came a definite whisper. My eyes flashed open and there, almost expected, beside my bed, without certain form, rose a warm shadowy figure, a vibration in the dark that stood nearly motionless, then, after a moment, spoke.*
>
> *"I am here to help you," was the first it said.*
>
> *Terror can freeze. I stood before the specter of my creation (even at the time that thought crossed my mind) frozen by terror. My visitor softly crossed the room and sat lightly on my desk. I could see it had a head and a mouth. Looking close, I saw it grin. I lunged from the room, slamming the door behind me.*
>
> *The hallway was empty. I stared at my door, waiting for the knob to move, just the slightest. But the knob held still. . . .*
>
> *During the next week, my specter returned every night. I dropped out of school and began visiting a psychiatrist. . . .*
>
> *Up till now, I've told only two trustworthy (medical student) friends about my experiences and, curiously, they both*

> *reacted by eagerly asking the same question: "What was it like?" As if it were some psychedelic, amusement-park hallucination, a thrilling fun-for-the-whole-family adventure. One asked, "Was it like having a movie inside your head?"*
>
> *No, it wasn't. It was the fright of close lightning; it was waking up thinking you're blind, with your eyes wide open in the dark. It's lonely seeing what no one else sees. Frightening and lonely. Terror can also isolate. What I have seen and heard I know are not there. But these things I have seen and heard. Even if it's the product of tension, genetics, or unworldly expectations, within the strange casing of my mind, it is real. What is real to the mind is real to the person. Hallucinations can talk, they can walk, they can blind, mute, maim, and they can kill.*
>
> —Name withheld, 1993, pp. 149, 151

Although many hallucinations are frightening, not all hallucinations are accusatory or unpleasant. Sometimes those who experience hallucinations find them so comfortable they are unwilling to give them up because they serve as protections from negative aspects of reality.

Hallucinations have been investigated from several perspectives (Asaad & Shapiro, 1986). From a biological perspective they have been linked to abnormal brain excitability. PET scans have shown greater biochemical activity in the temporal lobe and auditory areas during auditory hallucinations. The neurotransmitter dopamine may also play a role. From the psychodynamic perspective, hallucinations are thought to represent a breakthrough into consciousness of material from the unconscious. Their content is believed to have psychodynamic meaning such as wish fulfillment, aggressive impulses, or a projection of a critical superego or conscience. From a cognitive viewpoint, intelligence level may play an important role in auditory hallucinations because these occur more frequently in people with lower intellectual and development levels. Perhaps auditory hallucinations represent the best way that less intellectually able people can describe stressful experience (Zigler & Levine, 1983).

Disordered Speech Disordered thinking has frequently been considered to be the most important characteristic of schizophrenia. Because disordered thinking is difficult to measure objectively, DSM-IV lays stress on disordered speech instead. **Disordered speech** is often described as a *loosening of associations*, in which the speaker's ideas shift from one topic to another in a way that seems unrelated to everyone else. When the loosening of association is severe the person's speech becomes incomprehensible. An example of loose associations is the answer given by someone with a schizophrenic disorder to the question, "What does this proverb mean, 'Strike while the iron is hot!'?"

It could mean (pause) Hercules! (Could you say more?) I saw the movie Hercules. (Yes . . .) And it means don't iron over your hands and don't strike anybody before you cast the first stone.

—Marengo et al., 1986, p. 498

Researchers have found that individuals with a schizophrenic disorder are likely to ask inappropriate questions and give inappropriate answers (Rutter, 1985). What seems to be missing is the predictability and the repetitions of meaning that are present in normal speech. This may be the reason that interviewers who talk to someone with a schizophrenic disorder may come away confused about the conversation's meaning. Individuals diagnosed with schizophrenic disorder may be highly intelligent, not at all confused, and very painstaking in working out solutions to problems. However, their thought processes do not lead to conclusions based on reality or universal logic.

It is important to remember that not all people with a schizophrenic disorder display peculiar speech. The majority speak coherently most of the time, and peculiar speech is found in other patients about as frequently as it is in those with schizophrenic disorder. (Andreasen & Grove, 1979). To appreciate this point, rate the following examples on a five-point scale from 1, schizophrenic, to 5, normal.

a. *Then, I always liked geography. My last teacher in the subject was Professor August A. He was a man with black eyes. I also like black eyes. There are also blue and gray eyes and other sorts, too. I have heard it said that snakes have green eyes. All people have eyes. There are some, too, who are blind. These blind people are led by a boy. It must be terrible not to be able to see. There are people who can't see, and in addition, can't hear. I know some who hear too much. One can hear too much. There are many sick people in Bürgholzli; they are called patients.*

—Bleuler, 1950, p. 17

b. *Yes, of course, the whole thing wasn't my idea. So, I suppose I'd be perfectly happy if he came back and decided to do it all on his own. If I could make two trips myself, I don't see why he can't.*

—Laffal, 1965, p. 309

c. *Well, I wonder if that part of it can't be—I wonder if that doesn't—let me put it frankly; I wonder if that doesn't have to be continued? Let me put it this way: Let us suppose you get the million bucks, and you get the proper way to handle it. You could hold that side?*

—Gold, 1974, p. 117

When these excerpts were informally rated by several psychologists, item *a* was usually rated as characteristic of schizophrenic speech. It represents the way people

think those with this disorder speak. Item *b* was rated as normal because it is neither bizarre nor obscure. Item *c* was rated moderately characteristic of speech of those with schizophrenic disorder. How do these ratings agree with yours? The results may cause you to readjust your ideas about those with schizophrenic disorder, because *a* and *b* were produced by patients who were diagnosed as having this disorder and *c* is from a conversation by former U.S. President Richard Nixon. According to one study, many of Nixon's colleagues produced similar speech (Gold, 1974). These findings illustrate how, taken out of context in a transcript, even normal speech may sound fractured because thought transitions assumed by those involved are not known to the readers of the transcript.

Hard-to-follow communications may also come from people who have been given diagnoses other than schizophrenic disorder. The following excerpt was produced by a patient who was experiencing a hypomanic episode. (Hypomanic behavior may be seen in bipolar disorder, discussed in chapter 10.)

Women of America, it behooves you one and all to help at this, the most interesting epoch of the World's History, in every way possible, the march of civilization, the march of victory! I will play you Beethoven's Great Symphony with its four fateful opening notes—sol, sol, sol, mi. . . . V.V.V.V. the Day of the Century as dawned.

—Cohen, 1975, p. 1020

Another characteristic of speech in schizophrenic disorder is *poverty of content:* Even though the speaker talks for quite a while, little information is transmitted because what is said is vague, repetitive, stereotyped, and either too abstract or too concrete.

Disorganized Behavior Behavior of those with schizophrenic disorder varies widely and is unpredictable. There may be changes in goal-directed behavior, difficulties in carrying out activities of daily living, and impaired social or interpersonal functioning.

Unpredictability of Behavior. Behavior of those with schizophrenic disorder may be difficult to predict and may seem unrelated to the surroundings. For instance, at times a person may giggle or laugh without explanation. As an example, recall the young woman's account of her childhood giggles when she "saw" elves dancing across her desk. Because her schoolmates could not see the hallucinatory elves, her behavior seemed quite strange and inappropriate. Another inappropriate emotional response that may occur in schizophrenia is sudden, unpredictable, and seemingly inexplicable outbursts of anger. Whether all these inappropriate expressions of emotion are connected to hallucinations and delusions is not known. Some of the angry outbursts may be a result of the ideas of reference mentioned earlier in which behaviors of others or written materials may be falsely interpreted by the person with a schizophrenic disorder as referring to him or her, usually in a derogatory way. At times schizophrenic patients may become wildly aggressive and difficult to control, or they may move about constantly, much like a person experiencing a manic episode, stopping only when exhaustion sets in.

The following comment by a person diagnosed as having a schizophrenic disorder illustrates another type of unpredictable behavior.

I get shaky in the knees and my chest is like a mountain in front of me, and my body actions are different. The arms and legs are apart and away from me and they go on their own. That's when I feel I am the other person and copy their movements, or else stop and stand like a statue. I have to stop to find out whether my hand is in my pocket or not.

—Sass, 1987, p. 16

This description shows both the tendency to excess or seemingly random motor activity called **catatonic excitement** as well as the complete lack of activity called **catatonic rigidity** or posturing. In this case the person may remain motionless in strange postures for many hours, to the point at which circulation is impaired and swelling of body parts such as the feet and ankles occurs.

Changes in goal-directed behavior. Another change that almost always accompanies a schizophrenic disorder is a change in motivation or goal-directed behavior. Such changes are most likely to occur in the early phases of the disorder and again in the period after acute psychosis has passed. Parents often notice the first symptoms of what may become a schizophrenic disorder when their child's school grades begin to fall and the child does nothing but sit around listening to music or watching TV, constantly retreats to his or her bedroom, and avoids contact with others. Problems with goal-directed behavior may become so great that the person has problems with maintaining personal hygiene or eating meals at regular times. Markedly disheveled behavior and unusual dress such as wearing multiple layers of winter coats in summer weather may also occur (see Figure 11-3).

Social or interpersonal functioning. Impairment of interpersonal functioning in schizophrenic disorder may take a number of forms. One behavior that is almost always present in schizophrenia in all its phases is social withdrawal and emotional detachment. The person with schizophrenic disorder may be caught up in personal fantasies and inner experiences to the degree that the outer world is excluded. At some times, too, other problems with social interactions arise because he or she

Figure 11-3 Without appropriate medication, people with schizophrenic disorder may dress in a disheveled fashion and lead disorganized lives.

seems unable to comprehend the most basic social conventions. For example, during at least some phases of the disorder, the schizophrenic person may intrude so much on others' personal space that they become uncomfortable and avoid contact. Such intrusions might involve inserting him- or herself into an ongoing interaction with strangers—for example, joining strangers at a lunch table and interacting in an overly familiar way. Another behavior of this kind involves clinging to others or simply standing only inches away when asking a question. Because those with schizophrenic disorder may have little regard for social convention, some individuals also may display clearly inappropriate sexual behaviors such as public masturbation.

Negative Symptoms

The characteristics discussed so far—hallucinations, delusions, and disorganized speech or behavior are usually called the positive symptoms of schizophrenic disorder. **Negative symptoms** can be described as behavior deficits, and include such behaviors as flattened affect, poverty of speech and of speech content, and lack of directedness. Although they are not found only in people with a diagnosis of schizophrenia, negative symptoms do appear to be more common among schizophrenic patients than among other diagnostic groups (McGlashan & Fenton, 1992). Table 11-4 provides examples of several categories of negative symptoms. The following description characterizes a patient with negative symptoms predominating.

> *He is a single male who has had problems socializing throughout adolescence and does not date. He has a mediocre-to-poor school achievement record and, at best, a sporadic work record. He appears uncoordinated physically and conveys an aura of being different or unusual. Although he may show both positive and negative symptoms in a fluctuating pattern when the disorder just becomes apparent, later a poor level of functioning and a dominance of negative symptoms are seen. The disorder results in a chronic and disabling condition that is likely to require some form of institutionalization or housing in a sheltered environment, such as a group home, for his lifetime.*

Genetic family studies suggest that those diagnosed with schizophrenic disorder who have predominantly negative symptoms are less likely to have relatives diagnosed with either schizophrenic disorder or other disorders in the schizophrenic spectrum than patients who have a predominance of positive symptoms (Baron et al., 1992). This finding has suggested to some researchers that negative symptoms are more likely to be related to nongenetic causes such as pre- or postnatal virus infection, birth complications, and brain damage.

Negative symptoms are often difficult to evaluate because they are more like the end of the continuum of normal behavior than positive symptoms are. Sometimes antipsychotic medications produce as side effects behavior that is very similar to flat affect so that if the symptoms are observed some time after the initial diagnosis they may be a characteristic of medication rather than the disorder itself.

Major Subtypes of Schizophrenia

The subtypes of schizophrenia have their basis in historical views of the disorder (see Box 11-1). Kraepelin described three subtypes of schizophrenia or dementia praecox—*paranoid*, *hebephrenic*, and *catatonic*. When Bleuler broadened the description of the disorder, he added a fourth category, *simple schizophrenia*. These four categories were used for many years. Current DSM-IV categories reflect a modification of these traditional types. They include: *paranoid*, *catatonic*, *disorganized*, and a catchall or *undifferentiated* group. In addition, there is a *residual* category for cases in which the psychotic features are no longer prominent.

The diagnosis most often given to patients with a schizophrenic disorder on their first admission to a mental hospital is schizophrenia of the **paranoid type.** This disorder seems to display itself primarily in cognitive behavior, characterized by delusions and sustained, extreme suspiciousness. Since some aspects of intellectual functioning may be unaffected by the delusional thoughts, under certain circumstances those with the paranoic type of schizophrenic disorder may seem to function relatively well. Figure 11-5 shows the precise and well-organized artistic work of Martin Ramirez who spent most of his life institutionalized at a California state psychiatric hospital. Although he had no previous art training he developed a passion for art after about 20 years in the hospital. His work has been featured in solo and group exhibits.

People with a schizophrenic disorder of the paranoid type misinterpret the world around them. Although they are capable of evaluating the situation correctly, they resist the feedback cues that most people use. Well-defined systems of delusional paranoid thinking can also occur in people who in other respects show well-integrated behavior. Such people are diagnosed as having a delusional disorder rather than schizophrenia of the paranoid type.

It is important to realize that paranoid elements can be observed in a range of disorders as well as in the average person. Everyone engages in paranoid thinking at one time or another. You could probably think of at least one occasion when you have felt that you were being discriminated against or

TABLE 11-4
Examples of Negative Symptom Behavior

Flat Affect	Poverty of Speech	Lack of Directedness
1. Avoidance of eye contact	1. Long lapses before replying to questions	1. Slowed movements
2. Immobile, expressionless face	2. Restriction of quantity of speech	2. Reduction of voluntary movements
3. Lack of emotion when discussing emotional material	3. Failure to answer	3. Inability to initiate
4. Apathetic and uninterested	4. Slowed speech	4. Little interest in social participation
5. Monotonous voice	5. Blocking	
6. Low voice, difficult to hear		

Changing Views of Schizophrenia and their Implications for Classification, Research, and Treatment

Despite the fact that many of the historic views concerning schizophrenia are no longer accepted, many early ideas, such as the subgroups or types of the disorder, and the characteristics of symptoms essential for the diagnosis of schizophrenic disorder still have an influence seen both in the DSM-IV and in the way researchers go about defining questions for their studies. Schizophrenic disorders were not clearly defined until the nineteenth century, although brief descriptions of what today would probably be called schizophrenic disorders are found in writings as early as the Hindu *Ayur Veda* (1400 B.C.) (Kendell, 1983). Despite this early recognition of such a type of disordered behavior, for many centuries descriptions of schizophrenia were much less common and detailed than descriptions of psychotic behavior characterized by mania. This was probably because manic symptoms are more attention-getting and less complex than the varied symptoms shown in schizophrenia.

Dementia Praecox

One of the first writers to classify schizophrenia as a distinct disorder was Emil Kraepelin (1856–1926), a German physician, who called it **dementia praecox.** Kraepelin was the author of the most influential psychiatric textbook of his period. He emphasized that classification depended on the cause of the illness, not just the symptoms observed at a particular time. Kraepelin used the term "dementia praecox" (premature madness) because the onset of the disorder occurred early in life, typically in adolescence. He believed the cause of dementia praecox was irreversible organic deterioration, which would eventually be found to have a specific organic cause and pathology. Although he considered recovery from dementia praecox to be impossible, 16 of the 127 cases he studied seemed to have ended in complete recovery (Kraepelin, 1909, vol. 2, p. 865).

Kraepelin's entire focus was on the symptoms of the underlying deterioration. Consequently he paid no attention to the psychological aspects of schizophrenia and ignored the person's life history, personality, and experiences with the illness. When he did mention psychological features, Kraepelin considered them temporary expedients, expecting that findings from microscopes and test tubes would make it possible to investigate the disease objectively.

The Schizophrenias

One of the first people to emphasize the psychological aspects of the disorder was Eugen Bleuler (1857–1939), a Swiss physician, who was influenced by Freud's work on the neuroses. According to Bleuler, whatever the underlying process might be, many of the symptoms had a psychological cause. Bleuler spoke of "the schizophrenias" instead of using the term *dementia praecox* and broadened the concept of the disorder as well as changing its name. He believed that the symptoms might represent a group of disorders with different causes and outcomes, not a single cause and outcome as Kraepelin had thought. Bleuler noted that although some people with schizophrenic disorders deteriorate, others remain unchanged and some improve. Bleuler also emphasized the role of the environment in schizophrenic disorder. In his view, some individuals might have the potential for developing these disorders, but because particular types of environmental situations did not occur, the disorder remained latent and these people never showed visible signs of schizophrenia. This idea is still current in the concept of vulnerability, discussed later in this chapter and in chapter 12.

Bleuler spoke of this group of disorders as characterized by loss of integration of thinking, emotion, and motivation rather than by gradual deterioration. He summed up the primary characteristics of schizophrenic behavior as the "four A's": alterations in affect, alterations in association, ambivalence, and autism. Associated with these changes, in Bleuler's view, were the secondary symptoms of hallucinations and delusions.

From the 1930s until the 1960s, several important figures in American psychiatry, such as Adolf Meyer and Harry Stack Sullivan, emphasized a broad concept of schizophrenia and psychosis in general, and a concern with the psychodynamics of the behavior and emphasis on interpersonal relationships as causal factors. As a result, emphasis on differential diagnosis—discriminating, for example, between affective disorders and schizophrenia—was thought to be of little importance and the proportion of people who were called schizophrenic increased sharply. When such a large number of people with different symptoms and different outcomes of illness were given the same diagnosis, the chances of effective treatment greatly decreased. As a result of this problem, work began to be focused on narrowing the definition of schizophrenic disorders.

First-Rank Symptoms

Kurt Schneider (1887–1967) was one of the leaders in the effort to make the definition of schizophrenia more concise and easier to reach agreement over. Schneider did not deny that Kraepelin's idea of bodily changes was correct, but he believed that since these changes had not been identified, it was important to divide people into types on the basis of their psychological symptoms. Moreover, Schneider felt that Bleuler's characterization system of the four A's seemed too vague to be interpreted reliably.

Schneider dealt with these problems by describing a series of first- and second-rank symptoms. If first-rank symptoms were present and no organic cause was evident, a diagnosis of schizophrenia was justified. **First-rank symptoms** were all related to hallucinations and delusional thinking; they are now described as the positive symptoms. The hallucinations are likely to be auditory, such as voices keeping up a running commentary on the person's current behavior. The delusions include the belief that thoughts are no longer confined only to the person's mind but are simultaneously broadcast for all to hear. For example, a 21-year-old student said:

Box 11-1 continues on the next page.

As I think, my thoughts leave my head on a type of mental ticker-tape. Everyone around has only to pass the tape through their mind and they know my thoughts.

—Mellor, 1970, p. 17

First-rank symptoms also include experiences of external control, such as having thoughts inserted into one's head or arbitrarily taken away. Patients might report feeling hypnotized or having become robotlike, under the control of others. A female patient reported this type of feeling:

I cry, tears roll down my cheeks and I look unhappy, but inside I have a cold anger because they are using me in this way, and it is not me who is unhappy, but they are projecting unhappiness into my brain. They project upon me laughter, for no reason, and you have no idea how terrible it is to laugh and look happy and know it is not you, but their emotions.

—Mellor, 1970, p. 17

Second-rank symptoms included other symptoms usually associated with schizophrenia that in Schneider's view, could also be found in other psychotic disorders, although he believed that a diagnosis of schizophrenia could be made without first-rank symptoms. His classification system attempted to identify behavioral symptoms of abnormal inner experiences of the individual that would be readily noticed by an examiner, could be easily agreed upon by several observers, and could occur only in schizophrenia.

Schneider was only partially successful in meeting his goals. The first-rank symptoms are easily noticed and are easy for examiners to agree on. However, although they occur frequently in schizophrenia, they are not unique to it. At least one-fourth of patients with bipolar affective disorders also show some of these symptoms (Hoenig, 1984). In addition, the presence or absence of these symptoms does not seem to be related to later functioning and improvement (Silverstein & Harrow, 1981).

Viewing the changing ideas concerning schizophrenic disorder across time makes it clear that each of them has implications for classification, treatment, and research. In chapter 2 we discussed some of the historical views of mental illness and the implications of each for dealing with those persons who were affected by the disorders. Kraepelin's view implied that researchers should be most interested in examining the brain tissue of deceased patients to understand more about how brain anatomy might be related to symptoms. This view did not encourage treatment, since it was thought to be useless, but was the beginning of the formal classification process of mental disorders because it distinguished dementia praecox from disorders involving depression and perhaps mania. Bleuler's view had quite different impli-cations, including treatment approaches that focused on decreasing environmental stress. We can still see the influence of his views as well as those of Meyer and Sullivan in the emphasis on vulnerability and the stress on both environmental factors and aspects of interpersonal relationships that is current today. These views have stimulated research, particularly on family relationships, such as the work on expressed emotion discussed in Chapter 12. Schneider's emphasis on improving symptom description and developing a reliable classification system was a forerunner of the extensive work on classification systems that is continuing today. Adoption of a standard system, such as the DSM-IV, is not only useful in clinical communication but is essential in enabling researchers to compare their findings in meaningful ways. The increase in standardization of classification has been an important stimulus to current research. This historical view suggests that research as we see it today is tied closely to the continuing influence of theories of the past as well as to the knowledge and strategies created by those theorists and the researchers who followed them. As in other areas of research in the field of abnormal psychology the emphasis shifts back and forth between biological and social/psychological processes. The interactional view and the vulnerability and resilience approach that are the focus of this book combine these emphases.

(a)

(b)

(c)

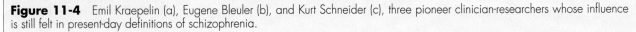

Figure 11-4 Emil Kraepelin (a), Eugene Bleuler (b), and Kurt Schneider (c), three pioneer clinician-researchers whose influence is still felt in present-day definitions of schizophrenia.

Figure 11-5 A graphite and chalk drawing by Martin Ramirez.

SOURCE: From "Schizophrenia and the Heart of Creation," by Christian L. Shriqoi, in *Psychiatric News*, May 6, 1994, p. 12.

talked about or were suspicious of someone else's motives without adequate proof that such things had actually occurred. We can consider paranoid thinking to be a kind of cognitive style that can be expressed as a continuum extending from everyday types of fleeting thoughts to severe delusional thinking that affects all of a person's life (see Table 11-5). Illness, drugs, damage to the brain, some effects of aging, and the experience of severe stress can also produce paranoid thinking even when no disorder is present.

Delusional thoughts in the paranoid spectrum usually fall into one of several categories: the feeling of being persecuted by others; unwarranted jealousy and suspicion of sexual unfaithfulness by one's lover or mate; the feeling that another person has fallen in love with one when there is no evidence for this; and delusions of illness when none exists.

The **catatonic type** of schizophrenic disorder is characterized by psychomotor disturbance that may range from immobility or stupor to excessive motor activity that seems purposeless and unconnected to what is going on in the environment. A person with this type of schizophrenic disorder may refuse to speak and may remain stiffly immobile or may be extremely agitated. *Waxy flexibility* is an extreme form of immobility in which the person's arm or leg remains passively in the position in which it is placed. The individual may show other peculiarities of voluntary movement found in this type of schizophrenic disorder that may include grimacing or the repetitive imitation of others' movements, mannerisms, or speech. A person with agitated catatonic behavior shows extreme psychomotor excitement, talking and shouting almost continuously. Patients who experience prolonged catatonic excitement may be very destructive and violent toward others. As with manic excitement, there is a danger of personal injury or collapse due to exhaustion.

A person diagnosed as having the **disorganized type** of schizophrenia shows incoherence in expression, grossly disorganized behavior, and either flat or extremely inappropriate emotional reactions. Such people behave actively but aimlessly. They may show a childish disregard for social conventions and may resist wearing clothes, or urinate or defecate at inappropriate times. Giggling, silly mannerisms, and inexplicable gestures are common. Usually the long-term outlook for recovery is poor. People with disorganized schizophrenia are likely to have shown symptoms early and to have been poorly adapted even before that time.

In assigning a subtype to the diagnosis, DSM-IV uses the following rules. Paranoid type is assigned if delusions or hallucinations are prominent unless the person also meets the criteria for the catatonic or disorganized type. If they meet either of those other criteria then that diagnosis takes priority. This means that the catatonic subtype diagnosis is used if catatonic symptoms are present even if behaviors characteristic of another type are also seen. Disorganized type is assigned if there is no catatonic behavior but either disorganized behavior or speech or inappropriate or flat affect are characteristic. If a person shows symptoms characteristic of the active phase of schizophrenic disorder but does not meet the criteria for any of these three types, a diagnosis of schizophrenic disorder of the **undifferentiated type** is given.

If someone has previously met the diagnostic criteria for schizophrenic disorder, and no longer has prominent positive symptoms but still continues to have negative symptoms or some very mild residual positive symptoms such as eccentric behavior or odd beliefs, he or she is classified as having schizophrenic disorder of the **residual type.** Behavior of the residual type may represent any of the following situations: a transition between an active psychotic episode and a complete remission, an interlude between psychotic episodes, or a long-term state that may last over many years.

TABLE 11-5
The Range of Disordered Perceptions of Reality with Paranoid Elements

Mild		Moderate		Severe
Average Person	**Paranoid Personality**	**Paranoid Personality Disorder**	**Delusional Disorder (Persecutory or jealous type)**	**Paranoid Schizophrenia**
Occasional suspicious thoughts	A suspicious cognitive style	A suspicious cognitive style so strong that it impairs effective behavior; there are no delusions; reality testing is intact	A stable and chronic delusional system with a specific focus; reality testing good in all other areas	Multiple delusions that are likely to be fragmented, accompanied by marked loosening of associations, obvious hallucinations, and other evidence of disorganization; reality markedly distorted

What Causes Schizophrenic Disorder?

The cause of schizophrenic disorders is not known, although it seems likely that symptoms of schizophrenic disorder are produced by the interaction of vulnerability factors with some kind of environmental stress. Thus, schizophrenic disorder is a good example of the interaction of stressors, vulnerability, and the protective factors that promote resiliency even in biologically vulnerable people. Environmental stress may come from disturbed family relationships, but it might also come from many other sources. Thus in studying schizophrenic disorders it is important to utilize many perspectives, to look at genetic factors, other biological variables, and environmental conditions that may be related to whether or not symptoms of the disorder appear. Box 11-2 describes quadruplets with schizophrenic disorder whose cases were investigated from many perspectives.

Genetic Factors

The importance of genetic factors in the development of schizophrenic disorders has emerged from the results of many family, twin, and adoption studies conducted over at least 75 years. These studies have shown that the risk of development of a schizophrenic disorder is correlated with the closeness of genetic relationship, or genetic overlap with the *index case*, as the person under study is often called. Genetic overlap or the percentage of genes that the relative has in common with the index case

ranges from 100 percent for identical twins to 12.5 percent for great-grandchildren, first cousins, and great nieces and nephews.

Figure 11-10 shows the average risk for developing schizophrenia when family members with different degrees of relationship have been diagnosed with the disorder. The lifetime risk of developing schizophrenia correlates quite well with the proportion of genes shared with an affected family member (Gottesman, 1991). In other words, the more genes that two people have in common, the higher the risk. However, the fact that even for identical twins, who have identical genes, the risk is a little less than 50 percent, suggests other factors at work besides genetics. Another important, well-established research finding that suggests that study of genetic inheritance is not enough to understand schizophrenic disorder is the fact that 89 percent of all people diagnosed with schizophrenic disorder have no known relative with that disorder (Cromwell, 1993).

Although, as Figure 11-10 illustrates, genetic transmission seems to be a factor in schizophrenic disorder, up to the present, no specific mode of genetic transmission has been identified. This means that no chromosome, gene, or DNA segmental locus has been associated with schizophrenic disorder and with that association then replicated or found in later research (Kendler & Diehl, 1993). Before discussing the genetic hypothesis further, we will briefly discuss the common models used in genetic theory and research.

In studies of heredity, predictions based on theoreti-

Investigating Schizophrenic Disorder from a Variety of Perspectives

Investigation of schizophrenic behavior from several perspectives can help in understanding both the disorder and its symptoms. The case of the Genain sisters illustrates how investigations of heredity, brain anatomy and activity, psychophysiological measures, and family interactions can complement one another.

The sisters, who were identical quadruplets, shared the same heredity (see Figures 11-6 and 11-7). Because the odds for identical quadruplets are one in 16 million births, they became celebrities in their home town soon after their birth in 1930. During their childhood, they performed song and dance routines and were so popular that they had a police escort on one early local tour. As they grew older, however, it became clear that they were not developing in a normal way. One sister dropped out of high school. The other three graduated but had trouble holding jobs. During their twenties, all four sisters developed schizophrenic disorders.

Because of the uniqueness of this case (four individuals with identical heredity who all showed schizophrenic behavior could be expected to occur only once in tens of billions of births), a local physi-

cian alerted scientists at the National Institute of Mental Health. The sisters came to Washington, D.C., and were hospitalized there for intensive study in the mid-1950s. During the three years that they spent at NIMH, they were examined from a number of perspectives. To protect their privacy, the sisters were given pseudonyms, corresponding to NIMH's initials—Nora, Iris, Myra, and Hester—and the family was given the name Genain, from the Greek words meaning "dire birth."

Several of the quadruplets' family members had histories of psychological problems. Not only was their father's behavior often bizarre, but his brother, his mother, and his paternal uncle had each had a nervous breakdown.

Even though they had the same genetic risk, the sisters' schizophrenia could have been at least partly the result of environmental factors. For example, as is usual in multiple births, they were all small at birth. All of them spent time in incubators and did not go home from the hospital until they were six weeks old. They grew up in the glare of publicity and constantly heard comments about their similarity. Their father restricted their interactions with other people by refusing to allow them to play with other children or, later, to take part in school activities or to date.

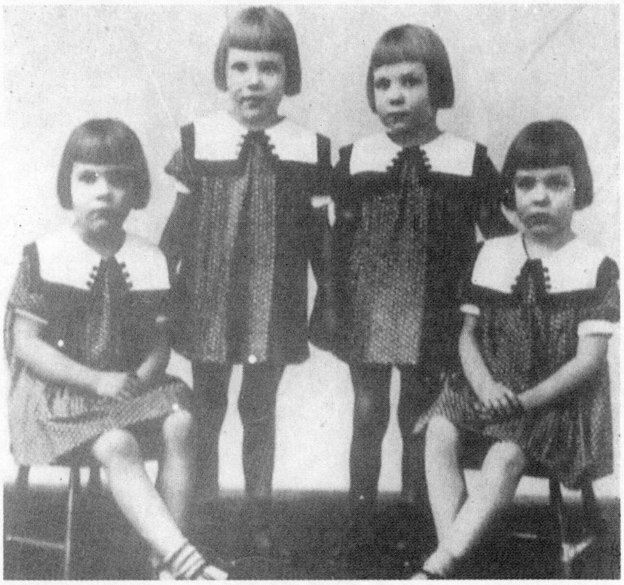

The girls' father also objected to their stay at NIMH and often threatened to take them out of the hospital. Although he was cooperative and cordial at times, he also had considerable hostility toward people. His wife reported that he had tried to choke her several times and said that

she had considered leaving him. At times, he accused his wife of having sexual relationships with his daughters' psychiatrists. During the quadruplets' third year at the hospital, he died.

This report, which reflects the psychodynamic perspective, describes the family relationships in detail:

Mrs. Genain's unfulfilled needs for maternal nurturing found expression in her closeness to Nora. It was the symbiotic tie of mother and infant, one in which the mother does not see the infant as a separate individual but as part of herself. . . . The closeness between them supported a report that Nora was not only her father's "favorite," but her mother's also. . . . Nora was always the first of the babies to be burped after feeding. . . . Nora was also the daughter Mrs. Genain took home for trial visits from the hospital, although Iris' adjustment was also appropriate for home visits.

The central role for Myra was the "independent positive." Mrs. Genain identified Myra with her own independent strivings and actions. . . . Myra was the daughter upon whom Mrs. Genain was prone to lean in times of stress, who often strove for the favored position (which in this family was the protected one) with her mother. . . . She tried to live out the role her mother assigned to her of becoming independent, and the dependent-independent conflict became acute for her when she tried to move out on her own.

The central theme of the role Mrs. Genain assigned to Iris was the "repressed" one. She identified in Iris her own feeling that she must put up with anything. . . . In areas that concerned Iris as an individual, e.g., her abilities and appearance, Mrs. Genain was neither concerned nor interested.

The central theme assigned to Hester was the "negative" one. . . . Hester personified that which Mrs. Genain regarded as undesirable—hostility and sexuality, for example. The perception of these feelings in Hester appeared to have blocked her mother's perception of other human qualities in her. She was the last to be regarded as sick (she had been "bad") and she was not hospitalized before coming to the Clinical Center.

Box 11-2 continues on the next page.

Figure 11-6 The Genain sisters as young children.

Figure 11-7 The Genain sisters as adults.

Later Mrs. Genain did not even consider a time when Hester might come home for home visits from the hospital.

—*Adapted from Rosenthal, 1963, pp. 463–465*

The Genains were invited back to NIMH for a follow-up in 1981. During that period Myra had lived the most normal life. She went to business college and later worked as a secretary. She was the only one of the four sisters to marry and have children. Nora was next best in adjustment. She had worked at least seven years, partly in government training programs. Hester and Iris had each spent more than 15 years in hospitals and had received more antipsychotic drug treatment than either Myra or Nora.

Researchers wondered if scanning techniques, developed after the early

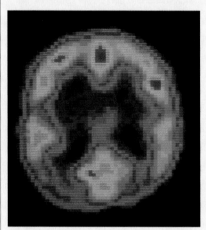

(normal)

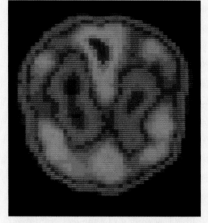

(Nora)

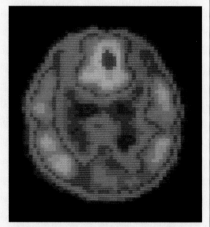

(Myra)

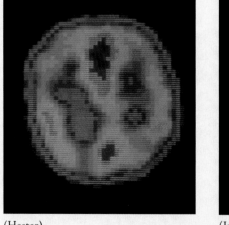

(Hester)

(Iris)

Figure 11-8 The PET scans of the Genain sisters differ from the normal PET scan. Energy use is highest in the frontal lobes of the normal scan. In contrast, the visual areas of the sisters' scans are most active, possibly as a result of hallucinations.

BOX 11-2 continued

study of the sisters, could shed light on the differences in their behavior. The sisters' CT scans appeared normal, but other types of scans showed abnormal patterns. Their PET scans, made when the women were resting, showed activity in the visual areas (see Figure 11-8). Scientists wondered if this was an indication of hallucinations. The PET scans of Myra and Nora, the two sisters who had made the best adjustment, were closer to the normal PET scans than those of the two sisters whose behavior was less adaptive. The Genains also showed much less

alpha brain wave activity than is normal. Since alpha waves appear when people relax or let their minds go blank, the low frequency of alpha waves may also suggest hallucinations.

The sisters were also given Computer Electroencephalographic Tomography scans (CET). CET scans show the electrical activity in the brain, in contrast to PET scans, which show chemical activity (see Figure 11-9). Since CET scans are much cheaper and safer for the subject than PET scans, they can be repeated at frequent intervals. All four Genain sis-

ters showed low levels of alpha waves on the CET scans compared to a control subject. The correspondence between PET and CET scan patterns both in this case and in general research findings seems fairly close (Buchsbaum & Haier, 1987). These findings, when matched with the sisters' behavioral histories and with the earlier test data, may prove a help in relating specific behaviors with environmental factors and biological functioning.

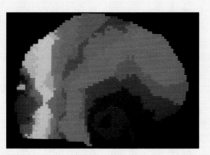
(normal)

(Nora)

(Myra)

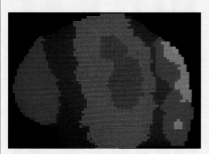
(Hester)

(Iris)

Figure 11-9 CET scans of the Genain quadruplets show low levels of alpha rhythm compared to the normal scan. All these scans were made while the subjects were resting with their eyes shut.

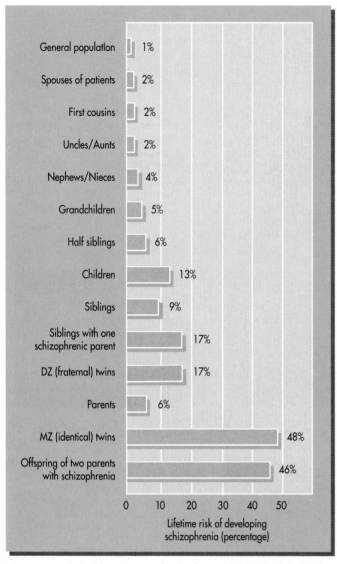

General population — 1%
Spouses of patients — 2%
First cousins — 2%
Uncles/Aunts — 2%
Nephews/Nieces — 4%
Grandchildren — 5%
Half siblings — 6%
Children — 13%
Siblings — 9%
Siblings with one schizophrenic parent — 17%
DZ (fraternal) twins — 17%
Parents — 6%
MZ (identical) twins — 48%
Offspring of two parents with schizophrenia — 46%

0   10   20   30   40   50

Lifetime risk of developing schizophrenia (percentage)

Figure 11-10 The degree of risk of developing a schizophrenic disorder correlates highly with the degree of genetic relationship with someone who has that disorder. These higher risks contrast with the general population risk of 1 percent or—in some studies—as high as 1.4 percent. The column on the left shows the degree of relationship and the length of the bar indicates the lifetime percentage of risk of developing schizophrenia.

SOURCE: From *Schizophrenic Genesis: The Origins of Madness*, by Irving I. Gottesman. Reprinted with permission of W. H. Freeman and Company.

cal models are compared with the observed frequency of occurrence of various characteristics. If the model is a good one, the agreement between prediction and observation should be close. The two major types of models show the transmission of inherited traits by one gene and by more than one gene.

Monogenic models are based on the idea that the genetic transmission that occurs at one locus (the place occupied by a gene pair on a particular chromosome) is all that is necessary to produce a particular characteristic. At any one locus, one gene of the pair may be domi-

nant over the other. That means that the characteristic carried by that dominant gene—say, brown eyes—will be **expressed**; that is, the person will have brown eyes. A recessive trait—for example, blue eyes—will not be expressed unless both members of the gene pair carry the characteristic for blue eyes. This is sometimes referred to as the *Mendelian pattern of heredity.*

In investigating the genetics of schizophrenia, researchers originally looked for distributions based on a monogenic model, but they did not find them. The number of cases of schizophrenia in relatives of schizophrenics is always less than would be expected by monogenic models. One way of explaining this is to use the concept of *penetrance. Penetrance* refers to the degree of probability that if a person has one or two copies of a predisposing gene he or she will show the symptoms to the disorder. According to this idea, a predicted number of individuals will carry the potential for schizophrenia—they will have the right genetic makeup—but not all of them will become schizophrenic because they are not exposed to significant environmental stress.

Polygenic models assume that a number of genes found at specific locations must interact to produce a trait. Many characteristics, including height, weight, and skin color, are thought to be influenced by more than one gene. Some models suggest that a limited number of genes and locations are involved. Other polygenic models, called **multifactorial polygenic models,** do not specify the number of gene loci involved in schizophrenia. Instead, the models assume that there are many loci and that they are interchangeable. Genes at all of these loci may have small additive effects on a person's vulnerability to schizophrenia. According to this view, many people have some predisposition to develop schizophrenia. If their predisposition is over a certain threshold, they will develop a schizophrenic disorder; if their liability is below that threshold, they will not (McGue & Gottesman, 1989). Genetic theorists studying schizophrenic disorder tend to favor multifactorial polygenic models of heredity over other models.

Recent advances in molecular biology have made it possible to study variations in DNA sequence to identify gene locations related to particular disorders. This new technology has been used to understand genetic contributions to various illnesses such as Huntington's disease and muscular dystrophy. A few studies have identified gene locations associated with schizophrenia using several generations of family groups in which there was more than one member with a diagnosis of schizophrenia. So far the findings differ. Some studies have identified some abnormality in chromosome 11 (Holland & Gosden, 1990; Smith et al., 1989; St. Clair et al., 1990). These results have not been supported in another study of family groups (Gill et al., 1993). There are many possible reasons for this disagreement in findings. The varying results from one study to another may be because schizophrenic disorders are not all based on the same genetic transmission. Another possible reason for the disagreement is that the techniques for reading the results from this technology are not yet highly reliable, so that two readings from a blood sample of the same person may not always yield exactly the same result. However, despite the complexity, the techniques of molecular genetic research hold promise for new insights into the genetic aspects of schizophrenia.

Schizophrenic Spectrum Disorders

When the families of individuals diagnosed as having schizophrenic disorder are studied, they seem to include more than the expected number of relatives who are somewhat unusual in their behavior. These relatives dress eccentrically, behave in unusual ways, and seem somewhat limited emotionally or somewhat asocial. A greater than anticipated number of relatives of schizophrenics may also show peculiarities in thinking—believing one has magical powers, for instance. Many researchers believe that there may be some genetic relationship between these behaviors and the schizophrenic disorders. They maintain that the whole spectrum of disordered behaviors should be investigated together and usually discuss all of these under the label of **schizophrenic spectrum disorders.** The relatively greater frequency of these spectrum disorders in the families of those individuals with schizophrenic disorder compared to the frequency in families of nonpatient controls has been observed in a variety of cultures (Varma & Sharma, 1993).

Schizophrenic spectrum disorders include not only unusual emotional responses and cognitive behaviors but also certain personality disorders. For instance, *schizotypal personality disorder* and *paranoid personality disorder* occur more frequently in the families of people who have schizophrenic disorders (Kendler & Diehl, 1993). Other disorders that have sometimes been linked to the schizophrenic spectrum are *schizoaffective disorder* (a category that includes individuals who show significant depression or manic symptoms along with the

development of thought disorder) and other types of psychotic disorders (Kendler et al., 1985). Of all these spectrum disorders schizotypal personality disorder seems to be closest genetically to schizophrenic disorder (Condray & Steinhauer, 1992). The study of the relationships among these disordered behaviors may provide clues to the genetic causes of schizophrenic behavior. The schizophrenic spectrum does not appear to include all types of behavior disorders. For instance, relatives of those with schizophrenic disorder do not seem to be at increased risk for most forms of mood disorders, anxiety disorders, or alcoholism (Kane, 1993).

The idea of spectrum disorder fits in well with the polygenic model discussed in the preceding section. Such a polygenic model can be expanded to include two different levels of liability. Figure 11-11 illustrates such a

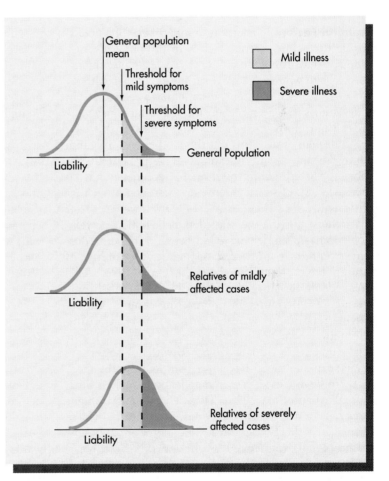

Figure 11-11 These distributions show the liability of mild and severe disorders within the schizophrenic spectrum for the general population and for relatives of those with mild and severe disorders. If the liability is greater than the threshold, the disorder can be noted. Relatives of those who are severely affected have a greater risk for both mild and severe diagnoses than the relatives of those who are mildly affected.

SOURCE: Adapted from *Journal of Psychiatric Research, 21,* M. Baron and N. Risch, "The spectrum concept of schizophrenia: Evidence for a continuum," Copyright © 1987. Reprinted with permission.

model. People to the *right* of the *right-hand* threshold (for severe symptoms) would develop a severe form of schizophrenia while those to the *left* of the *left-hand* threshold (for mild symptoms) would not be schizophrenic. Those *between* the two thresholds would develop a mild form of the disorder. Using a complex statistical technique called *path analysis,* this model seems to predict outcome fairly well for several large sets of data (McGue et al., 1985; Faraone & Tsuang, 1985).

Other Biological Factors

In addition to genetic factors, other biological factors may increase vulnerability to the development of a schizophrenic disorder. These factors include aspects of the prenatal environment as well as anatomical and biochemical characteristics of unknown origin.

Prenatal Factors In addition to inheritance of a predisposition to schizophrenia, factors in the physical environment may also have an effect. For example, infants born in late winter and early spring to families without any history of schizophrenic disorder have been found in some studies to have a higher risk of developing the disorder than children born at other times of the year (O'Callaghan et al., 1991). If the mother had influenza while pregnant, some researchers have presented data showing that the child born of that pregnancy has an increased risk of schizophrenic disorder, at least if that child is female (Takei et al., 1994). However, other researchers studying the same data believe that no relationship has been demonstrated between influenza during pregnancy and the later development of schizophrenic disorder in the child (Crow, 1994). This disagreement is a good example of the problems researchers encounter in interpreting complex sets of correlational data. Whether or not this relationship exists awaits further investigation. In some—but not all—studies, individuals diagnosed with schizophrenic disorder in adulthood have also been found to be more likely to have had obstetric complications at their birth (O'Callaghan et al., 1992). These complications might have been a causal factor themselves or they may have been the result of other developmental or environmental problems experienced by the fetus. Nevertheless, birth complications suggest possible damage to the brain or nervous system.

Another effect of the prenatal environment is sometimes seen in monozygotic (MZ) twins. The genetically identical fetuses may receive differing amounts of blood supply while in the uterus. This may result in one twin weighing considerably more than the other at birth. If one of the twins later develops a schizophrenic disorder, the twin who weighed less at birth is likely to be the one who receives that diagnosis (Torrey et al., 1994). Pre-sumably brain development was negatively affected by this difference in prenatal blood supply.

Brain Structure One finding that has emerged from the use of scanning techniques is that some individuals with schizophrenic disorder have significantly larger **cerebral ventricles** (cavities that contain cerebrospinal fluid) than the ventricles found in the brains of those people without this diagnosis. However, some enlargement of ventricles seems to occur naturally; in general, people's ventricles become larger with age. Enlarged ventricles are also found in other conditions such as alcoholism, traumatic head injuries, and severe mood disorders involving psychosis (Raz & Raz, 1990). Another difficulty in understanding the meaning of enlarged ventricles is that these and other significant brain effects occur in only about one-third of people with schizophrenic disorder who are examined by radiologists.

The results of a study of 15 sets of MZ twins in which only one of each pair had been diagnosed with schizophrenic disorder were of particular interest in understanding the role of enlarged ventricles, because the anatomy of the brains of each pair would be expected to be highly similar (Suddath et al., 1990). The twins with the schizophrenic disorder not only had enlarged lateral and third ventricles compared to their nonschizophrenic twins, but they also were found to have a reduction in the size of their temporal lobes, anterior hippocampus, and left temporal lobe gray matter. Since these areas of the brain are involved in thinking, concentration, memory, and perception, these differences may be associated with some of the characteristic symptoms of schizophrenia. In 14 of these 15 pairs, the twin with the schizophrenic disorder had reduced brain volume when compared to his or her healthy twin.

Figure 11-12 shows scans of one pair of MZ twins that illustrate the differences found in ventricle size in this study. An arrow points to the ventricular area in the brain scan of each twin. One possible explanation of this difference in MZ twins is that the twin with the enlarged ventricles might have experienced some injury before birth. Another interesting finding in this study was that the enlargement in many cases would not have been considered by a specialist to be of abnormal size. It was only in comparison with the healthy twin that the difference in size was apparent. This observation suggests that even subtle changes in ventricle size may be important in the development of schizophrenia. Ventricular enlargement is also associated with other disorders.

Biochemical Brain Abnormalities

There are strong arguments for the assumption that biochemical factors play a role in schizophrenic disorder. An impetus to the search for biochemical clues has been

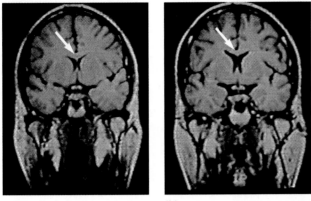

(a)　　　　　　　　(b)

Figure 11-12 When an identical (MZ) twin develops schizophrenia and the other twin does not, one difference found between them is likely to be enlarged ventricles in the affected twin, especially an enlarged third ventricle. The arrows on the MRI scans point out the difference in ventricle size in an unaffected twin (a) and her twin sister (b) who has a diagnosis of schizophrenic disorder.

provided by the effectiveness of some antipsychotic drugs, which are known to produce certain biochemical changes. Recent developments in technology and the discovery of new neurochemical systems in the body have enabled researchers to take a more sophisticated approach to biological differences than was possible in the past. Investigators are now able to look for abnormalities in biochemical *functioning,* using a variety of scanning techniques. For example, research using PET scans shows that people who have a long-standing, chronic schizophrenic disorder tend to have a lower level of metabolism in the frontal and temporal lobes of their brains and a somewhat higher flow at the base of the skull than control subjects (see Figure 11-13).

The Dopamine Hypothesis Just as neurotransmitters are currently thought to be important in at least some types of mood disorders (see chapter 10), biologically oriented research on schizophrenia also stresses the importance of neurotransmitter functioning. In schizophrenia, current research focuses on dopamine. The **dopamine hypothesis,** simply stated, says that an excess of dopamine at certain synapses in the brain is associated with schizophrenic disorder.

The idea that dopamine is involved in schizophrenia comes from two sources. One is the finding that large doses of amphetamines are capable of producing behavior in individuals with no history of psychological difficulties that is very similar to that typical of paranoid schizophrenia. Even more important, low doses of amphetamines worsen the symptoms of some individuals with schizophrenic disorder. Biochemically, amphetamines increase the amounts of both the catecholamines—dopamine and norepinephrine—that are present at the synapse.

The second reason to suspect that dopamine is involved comes from knowledge of the effects of the antipsychotic drugs used to treat schizophrenia. The effectiveness of anti-psychotic drugs in reducing psychotic symptoms is directly related to their success at binding to (that is, blocking) postsynaptic dopamine receptors. Antipsychotic drugs that work by blocking brain receptors for dopamine are able to control positive symptoms in about 80 percent of patients.

Although the dopamine hypothesis is supported by these and other data, it is too simple to explain all the findings. For instance, even when antipsychotic drugs are effective in altering the amount of available dopamine at the synapse, they typically require about six weeks to produce a maximum level of behavioral improvement. What appears to happen is that initially the blockage of the dopamine receptor results in feedback that increases the activity of the dopamine transmitters in the midbrain. However, after some time the neurons are firing so quickly that their effectiveness is actually decreased.

In spite of agreement by many researchers that the dopamine system is overactive in schizophrenic disorder, no one is certain about the mechanisms involved. Because dopamine receptors can now be identified by PET scans, this may provide a useful way of investigating the dopamine hypothesis. For some time two subtypes of dopamine receptors called D_1, and D_2 have been identified. Their presence appears to be concentrated in the basal ganglia, a part of the nervous system that controls movement. Since the distinguishing characteristics of schizophrenic disorder are largely cognitive and emotional rather than movement related, this location was puzzling to researchers. Recently, three additional dopamine receptors, D_3, D_4, and D_5, have been identified. Knowledge of these new receptors may help explain the role of dopamine in schizophrenic disorder (Solokoff et al., 1990; Sunahara et al., 1993). D_3 and D_4 are concentrated in the part of the brain where the symptoms of schizophrenic disorder are thought to originate. Geneticists have also identified distinct neuronal dopamine receptor genes for these receptors. Although individually none of these receptors may be exclusively involved in the dopamine levels in the brain associated with schizophrenic disorder, acting in combination they may help to account for both the positive and negative symptoms. At present at least one family study does not show a difference in D_3 markers in families of patients with schizophrenic disorder and control families. Thus, earlier researchers' optimism that D_3 may have a predisposing role has not been supported (Sabaté et al., 1994). However, as more knowledge of receptor systems grows, more information about how dopamine receptors are involved may be available.

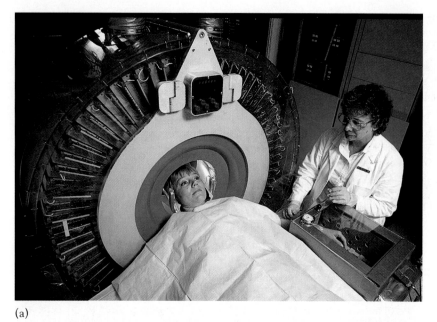

(a)

Figure 11-13 PET scan photos show brain metabolism, the chemical activity currently going on in a living brain. Photo (a) shows how a patient is prepared for a PET scan, photo (b) shows a PET scan of the brain of a normal individual and photo (c) shows a PET scan of a person with a schizophrenic disorder who is not currently receiving antipsychotic medication. Colors toward the red-yellow end of the spectrum indicate a higher rate of metabolic activity and those at the blue-green end a lower rate. Notice the relatively higher frontal metabolism in the normal person and the higher posterior metabolism in the patient.

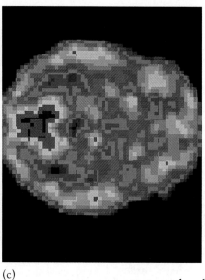

(b)   (c)

Methods of Studying Genetic Transmission and Environmental Factors

A number of methods have been used to study the role of genetics in schizophrenic disorder. These include family, twin, adoption, and cross-fostering studies. Not only do these studies focus on identifying patterns of genetic inheritance, but they also make it possible to determine the role played by environmental factors. Family studies by their nature confound genetic transmission and environment. Twin and adoption studies provide a somewhat less confounded picture. Although twin and adoption studies, in particular, have also been used to learn about hereditary

patterns in other disorders, the serious consequences of schizophrenic disorder have stimulated many large studies, often with long-term follow-up. Therefore, we will describe all of these research tactics here.

Family Studies

A common first step in studying the genetics of any disorder is to determine whether relatives of an affected person are more likely to have that same disorder than are members of the general population. Systematic family studies were started early in this century and have continued ever since. A common way to conduct a family study is to construct a comprehensive diagram of a family tree going back several generations. Then all those people in this family tree who showed symptoms of any disorder are identified. In this way it is possible to see whether a disorder seems to occur in any particular pattern throughout the generations. This pattern can then be matched with predictions based on theoretical models. A family tree to study the occurrence of Fragile X disorder, a condition discussed later in this text, is shown in chapter 16.

In addition to determining specific patterns of heredity for different disorders, family studies provide information about the relationships between schizophrenia and other disorders that may appear in families. If several particular disorders typically occur together in families, this suggests that those disorders may be genetically similar. Such similarity is called the spectrum concept discussed earlier in this chapter.

One factor that may affect the risk for schizophrenia or other disorders is **assortative mating.** This term refers to the tendency for people to mate with those who are similar to them more frequently than would be the case if their choices were random. Assortative mating occurs for physical traits, psychological traits, and behavior disorders. For instance, assortative mating is seen in families of patients with a schizophrenic disorder. The spouses of individuals with schizophrenic disorder are more likely than members of the general public to be diagnosed with the same disorder. As a result their children may get "double doses" of genes associated with schizophrenic disorder.

Although families with both a mother and father with schizophrenic disorder are rare, at least five studies of the adult offspring of such parents have been carried out (Gottesman, 1991). The results of all these studies are similar. In each, about one-third of the children of these parents had developed a schizophrenic disorder. Because some of the children studied were not yet old enough to have passed through the entire period of risk for developing schizophrenia, the estimated lifetime maximum risk for the group as a whole was 46 percent. This risk is much higher than the 17 percent lifetime risk of developing schizophrenic disorder for children with only one parent affected by schizophrenia. The researchers in these studies also found that even the children of these marriages who did not develop schizophrenia had a considerably higher risk of having some other psychiatric diagnosis than does the average child. However, the studies also were in agreement about another, and perhaps quite surprising, finding. About one-quarter of the children in these families showed neither schizophrenic disorder nor other types of disordered behavior. This finding is startling considering not only their genetic inheritance, but also the likelihood these children had experienced a good deal of stress from living in a family with two schizophrenic parents. Box 11-3 presents accounts of the stress experienced by two daughters who grew up with schizophrenic mothers. Although the daughters describe some positive aspects of these relationships, their accounts make clear the difficulties faced by a child growing up in such a household. The finding that a considerable number of children who are not only genetically at risk but also have lived in a difficult and stressful environment do not develop schizophrenic disorder has stimulated research interest in personal resiliency factors and environmental factors such as social support that may promote such good outcomes.

Twin Studies

While family studies can give an overall picture of hereditary risks in schizophrenia and the possible genetic relationships among disorders, twin studies provide a way to focus on the environmental factors that contribute to schizophrenic disorders while keeping hereditary factors constant. This is possible because MZ twins are produced from the same fertilized egg and therefore begin life with identical genetic makeup. Dizygotic (DZ) twins are produced from two fertilized eggs; they have the same genetic relationship as any other siblings. In some rare cases chromosome alterations or gene mutation may occur in only one MZ twin after the original cell division. For example, at least 5 pairs of MZ twins have been reported in which only one twin was affected by Down syndrome (Rogers et al., 1982). This disorder, discussed in chapter 16, results from a trisomy or extra copy of chromosome 21.

About a dozen major twin studies have been carried out. All show that MZ twins have a much greater chance of being concordant for schizophrenia than DZ twins do. However, as we saw earlier in Figure 11-10, the concordance rate for schizophrenia in MZ twins is only about 50 percent. This finding makes it clear that heredity alone is not enough to produce a schizophrenic disorder, at least in most people. One way to learn more about the nongenetic biological factors and environmental factors that may increase vulnerability to schizophrenia is through the study of MZ twins, one of whom is affected by the disorder and one of whom is not. A six-year study of 27 MZ twin pairs who differed or were **discordant** for schizophrenia has been carried out by the National Institute of Mental Health (Torrey et al., 1994). These discordant pairs were compared with 13 twin pairs where both twins had been diagnosed with schizophrenic disorder and 8 normal pairs who served as a control group. Clearly these twins represent a distinctly unique group, so that the findings may not generalize well. Yet the study represents an opportunity to learn more about risk factors, vulnerability, and resilience. One question that interested the researchers was when the affected twin was first observed to become "different." This determination was made from all available information about the twins' developmental histories. Of the 27 twin pairs discordant for schizophrenia, 7 were already seen as different by age 5. No other pairs were seen to become different until age 13 or later (see Figure 11-14).

Adoption Studies

Another way of studying the effects of heredity on the development of schizophrenia is through adoption studies. Adoption studies can give researchers a clearer

Growing Up with a Mother Who Has a Schizophrenic Disorder

These two accounts written by daughters who spent their early lives with mothers who had a schizophrenic disorder show some of the stresses they experienced. They also show how, despite the mothers' illness, there were positive aspects to the mother-daughter relationship.

In the first excerpt, the mother and daughter shared some warmth and positive moments over their mutual love of music and dance.

My mother is a paranoid schizophrenic. In the past I was afraid to admit it, but now that I've put it down on paper, I'll be able to say it again and again: Mother, schizophrenic, Mother, paranoid, shame, guilt, Mother, crazy, different, Mother, schizophrenia.

I have been teaching inpatient children on the children's ward of Bellevue Psychiatric Hospital in New York City for 13 years, and yet I'm still wary of revealing the nature of my mother's illness. When I tell my friends about my mother, even psychiatrist friends, I regret my openness and worry that they will find me peculiar. . . .

On the outside our house resembled those of our neighbors, but on the inside it was so different *that there was no basis of comparison. Our house was a disaster. Everything was a mess. Nothing matched, furniture was broken, dishes were cracked, and there were coffee rings and cigarette burns clear across our grand piano. I was ashamed of our house. It was impossible to bring friends home. I never knew what my mother might be doing or how she would look.*

She was totally unpredictable. At best she was working on a sculpture or practicing the piano, chain smoking and sipping stale coffee, with a dress too ragged to give to charity hanging from her emaciated body. At worst she was screaming at my father, still wearing her nightgown at six o'clock in the evening, a wild look on her face. I was never popular as a youngster, and I blamed my lack of popularity on my mother. . . .

Mother was quite interested in music and ballet, and she took me to every ballet and concert in Kansas City. She always looked terrible when she went out, and more than once she arrived at the theater in her bedroom slippers. I was embarrassed to be seen with her, and before we left home, I would try to convince her to dress properly. She never listened and sometimes became angry, but chic or not, I accompanied her.

I loved music and dance as much as she did. I even gave up Saturday afternoons to stay home with her and listen to the Metropolitan Opera broadcasts, and I loved her most and felt closest to her sitting in front of a gas fire, feeling her bony arm around my shoulders as we listened to the music together. . . .

When I was in high school, Mother and I shared a room with twin beds. When Mother was lying down, she would start to moan as if she were talking in her sleep. "I can't stand that girl. She's evil; she's a bitch. She's just like her father." I was terrorized, but I dared not move. I felt I had to pretend to be asleep, because I didn't want her to know I was listening. . . .

I used to lie in bed, wishing I were dead, believing that I was the worthless girl she was describing. . . . My oldest brother was the target of the same kinds of insults, and we comforted each other. . . .

—Adapted from Lanquetot, 1984, pp. 467–471

In this second account, after a long period of estrangement, the daughter was finally able to understand that her mother cared about her despite the problems that the symptoms of schizophrenia placed in the way.

The period of time during which my mother began to withdraw and isolate herself from others—from my father, from

understanding of the role environment and heredity may play in schizophrenia. There are three basic kinds of adoption studies in research on schizophrenia: those that compare adopted children whose biological parents were diagnosed as having a schizophrenic disorder with adopted children whose parents did not have this disorder; those that examine the incidence of schizophrenic disorder in the biological and adoptive families of adopted children who later develop this disorder; and those that study the relatively rare individuals whose adoptive parents, but not biological parents, develop schizophrenic disorder.

One of the first large adoption studies ever conducted was reported by a group of Danish and American researchers working in Denmark (Cannon and Mednick, 1993; Rosenthal et al., 1968, 1975). Because Denmark and a few other countries have excellent national medical and psychiatric registers as well as adoption registers, marriage registers, and so on, many of the large studies tracing heredity of disorders have been carried out in those countries. First the researchers searched the government adoption register of the Copenhagen area to find the names of parents who had given up their children to nonfamily members for adoption. Then they searched the official psychiatric register to see if they could find the names of any of those parents. The records of those who were found were rated, and those parents who clearly fit a strict definition of schizophrenic disorder were selected. The children who had been given up for adoption by these parents became the index cases. The control group consisted of adopted children whose parents had no psychiatric history. Three of the 39 index cases and none of the 47 controls were given a definite diagnosis of schizophrenic disorder. This high rate (8 percent) in the index group compared to 0 percent in the control group points to a hereditary factor.

In another kind of adoption study, Kety and his col-

BOX 11-3

myself, and from my younger sister—I remember only feeling a sort of desperate denial of anything being wrong or out of the ordinary. Unfortunately, my father . . . was in the Navy and he went overseas a lot. It was during these absences that I would come home from the second or third grade to find my mother sitting alone in our living room, the blinds pulled down, the TV and radio off. On the table next to her chair would be a stack of three to five pieces of burnt, butterless toast and she would stare off into space as she crunched her way through the afternoon. She might greet me then as I came in or she might not. I hurried by, trying not to look at her too closely. . . .

I was aware of her paranoia, and I was aware it was not based on facts. She barricaded the back door with an ironing board after locking it at night. She accused the next door neighbor of stealing our clothes off the clothesline and taking our mail out of the mailbox.

Soon no one visited anymore, not the landlord and his wife, who were our personal friends, not the relatives who lived nearby—no one. It was just we two little girls with our mother who was slipping further and further away from us and, more importantly, from reality. . . .

Later on, this woman's mother was periodically hospitalized.

When my mother would return [from the hospital], her memory fogged from the electric shock treatments or coming out of a daze from drugs, . . . things would be mellow for awhile, and then she would wonder where all her jewelry was?! I would patiently remind her of how she threw it over the fence in the backyard, right before she checked into the hospital the last time. She would look confused first, then suspicious, and finally the paranoia would begin to unravel her life again. Some months later, after hurling all the contents of the refrigerator into the dining room or some other sort of frenzied behavior that our fragile family unit just could not handle, she would be taken back to the hospital. Sometimes my father would have to call the police to escort her away!

Finally, when this woman was 13, her parents were divorced and her mother lived elsewhere.

Life went on for all of us. My mother finally stopped spending time in mental hospitals shortly after I graduated from high school. She seemed to stabilize and find her niche somehow. She also remarried. Later she separated from her new husband, tried living with relatives, tried living alone, reunited with her husband, tried employment, even tried suicide—in short, she began living her life and grow-

ing, in her own way, as we all do. She gets an injection once a month now that keeps her from hearing "the voices." She considers this a miracle, and so do I!

For over 10 years, the woman's mother called her about once a month.

[She] endured many shallow and resentful conversations on my part. She never complained; she endured patiently. She never judged me, although I was judging her so harshly at that time, for not really being there for me as I was growing up. She always blessed me, was proud of me, and loved me.

Only after her own experience in psychotherapy was this daughter able to understand and accept her mother.

[Now] I have been gifted with the rediscovery of my love for my mother. Words cannot effectively describe the feeling of setting aside the broken heart I have been carrying around within me and nursing for some 30 years now. I love my mother just as she is, and that is exactly the way she has always loved me.

—Adapted from Crosby, 1989, pp. 507–509

leagues (1978) took advantage of the Danish government's comprehensive records to locate people in the Copenhagen area who had been adopted and had later developed schizophrenic disorder. They then compared the frequencies of schizophrenic disorder or other disturbances in the adoptees' biological and adoptive relatives. They found that about twice as many blood relatives as adoptive relatives of individuals with schizophrenic disorder had been diagnosed as definitely or possibly having this same disorder. Both rates were higher than those for relatives of a control group of adoptees who had not been diagnosed with schizophrenic disorder. In a later study the same research group studied adoptees in the rest of Denmark and obtained similar results (Kety et al., 1994). Again, adoptees who developed a schizophrenic disorder were twice as likely to have biological relatives who were diagnosed with schizophrenic disorder.

The 1978 study also contained an important subsam-

ple: half-brothers and half-sisters of the adopted individual who had the same father. Half-siblings share 25 percent of their genes, rather than 50 percent as full siblings do. However, half-siblings with a common father do not share the environment in the uterus before birth, nor do they share the same early mothering experience. Both the paternal half-brothers and half-sisters were found to have a greater risk of schizophrenia and schizophrenic spectrum disorders than the control group. This finding gave increased weight to the importance of genetic factors in schizophrenia compared to prenatal factors.

A third kind of adoption study is called a **cross-fostering study.** Such a study asks whether children whose biological parents have not been diagnosed with a schizophrenic disorder but who are reared by an adoptive parent with such a disorder are more likely to develop a schizophrenic disorder than either of two other groups: children with a biological parent with schizophrenia and

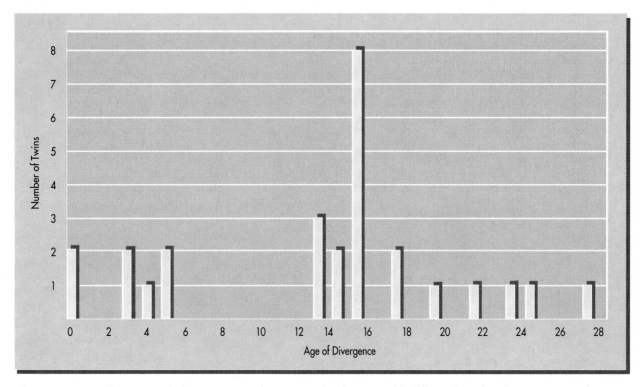

Figure 11-14 The age at which one twin was first perceived to be noticeably different from the other in a group of 27 twin pairs discordant for schizophrenic disorder.

SOURCE: From Torrey et al., 1994, p. 87.

children with no such heredity who are reared by normal individuals. Wender and colleagues (1974) found that it made no difference in the incidence of diagnosis of schizophrenic disorder in children whether they were reared by psychologically healthy adoptive parents or by adoptive parents at least one of whom developed a schizophrenic disorder. In both types of homes, almost twice as many children with schizophrenic heredity as children without such heredity developed schizophrenic disorder. This study suggests that rearing by an adoptive parent diagnosed with schizophrenic disorder does not increase a nonvulnerable person's chances of developing schizophrenia. However, the stress of growing up in an adoptive home that includes a parent with a schizophrenic disorder may increase the risk of developing symptoms of a schizophrenic disorder for genetically vulnerable children—those whose biological parents also had this disorder.

Vulnerability, Resiliency, and Stress

A major theme in this book has to do with vulnerability and resiliency that cause people either to develop some type of disorder or to stay well. The prevailing view of the development of symptoms of schizophrenic disorder fits well with these ideas.

As has been clearly demonstrated in this chapter, genetic factors or other biological vulnerabilities are thought to be important in the development of schizophrenic disorder, but not sufficient in themselves. This interplay of genetic and environmental factors in the production of symptoms of schizophrenic disorder is referred to as the **diathesis-stress theory.** The word *diathesis* means predisposition; the theory means that only people who have some genetic vulnerability will develop schizophrenia, and only if they are exposed to so much stress that they are unable to cope will they experience a range of schizophrenic symptoms. Although the diathesis-stress model can be applied to all behavior, in the area of schizophrenia it has been particularly clearly defined by Joseph Zubin (Zubin et al., 1983; Zubin & Spring, 1977). Zubin's hypothesis assumes that schizophrenia is not a permanent disorder but rather a permanent *vulnerability* to a disorder (see Figure 11-15). According to this theory, each person has a level of vulnerability to schizophrenia determined by both genetic inheritance and prenatal and postnatal physical factors. This level, which may range from no risk to high risk, interacts with stressful events or conditions in a person's life. If the combination exceeds a certain critical level or wellness/illness threshold, schizophrenic behavior will occur. This concept of vulnerability offers one way of understanding why, if one

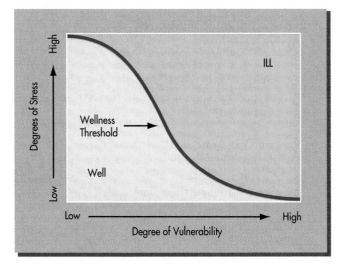

Figure 11-15 The diathesis-stress model of schizophrenia illustrates how vulnerable individuals are likely to become ill when experiencing even a small amount of stress while those with little vulnerability remain well even under a high level of stress.

SOURCE: Adapted from Zubin and Spring, 1977.

identical twin has a schizophrenic disorder, the other twin's chances of also having the disorder are not 100 percent.

An adoption study carried out in Finland supports this point of view (Tienari et al., 1990; 1994). Adopted children whose biological mothers were diagnosed with schizophrenic disorder were paired with adopted children whose biological parents did not have this diagnosis. In order to carry out this study the researchers collected information about the nearly 20,000 women who had been treated in psychiatric hospitals in Finland at some time during a 10-year period. From this group they found 171 women who had been diagnosed with schizophrenic disorder and who had a child who was adopted by a nonrelative Finnish family before the child was 4 years old. We can appreciate the complexity of the tasks required to complete an adoption study by considering the following. First, in this study a large number of cases had to be investigated to determine which of the women in the original sample were diagnosed as schizophrenic, had had a baby, and had given up the baby for adoption. Fewer than 1 in 100 of the original cases qualified. All that effort had to be expended before the study could even get under way.

Some of the other tasks the researchers faced were:

1. Selecting two adopted children as matched controls for each index case;
2. Checking the psychiatric histories of the control children's parents;
3. Administering structured interviews to all the biological mothers, thus providing a diagnosis with which to compare the diagnosis in the hospital records;
4. Interviewing the biological father of each index group member to evaluate whether he had a psychiatric disorder that would add to risk for the child.

In addition, the research team performed an evaluation of the child-rearing environment of each adoptive family for each index and control child, which included the following steps:

1. Interview with the entire family;
2. Joint interview with both adoptive parents;
3. Psychological testing of adoptive parents together and then also with their adoptive child;
4. Comprehensive test battery for each child and each adoptive parent, separately;
5. Follow-up assessments five to seven years after the initial assessment.

Because some of the adopted children have yet to reach or complete the age span of greatest risk for schizophrenia, data from this Finnish study will not be complete for a long time. Thus far in the study the people in the control group are much healthier than those in the index group. Fifteen percent of those in the control group have a severe psychological disorder from the schizophrenia spectrum compared to 30 percent of the index group. One and one-half percent of the control group have developed a psychotic disorder compared to more than 7 percent of the index group. Most interesting of all is the relationship between frequency of psychological problems and the adoptive family environment of the index cases.

The study's findings about the index children, shown in Figure 11-16, support the idea that healthy family environment has a protective effect for children who may be at risk for schizophrenia. In the group of index children reared in psychologically healthy families, none had become psychotic and only 4 percent had a severe psychological disorder. For the index children brought up in severely disturbed families, 11 percent were psychotic and 41 percent had a severe psychological disorder. Compared to the control children in each corresponding family type, the index children were less likely to be psychologically healthy and also were more likely to have a psychosis. These findings, although preliminary until the children have all passed the age of maximum risk, support the view that genetically transmitted vulnerability may be necessary for, or at least increase the likelihood of, occurrence of a schizophrenic disorder, but that disturbed family environment may play an important role in the expression of that vulnerability as a schizophrenic disorder.

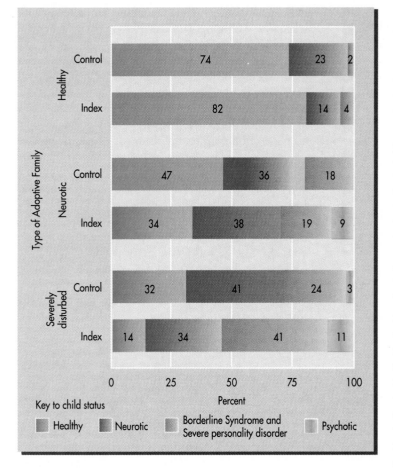

Figure 11-16 Even though adopted children whose biological mothers had a schizophrenic disorder (the index group) are more at risk than adopted children with normal biological mothers (the control group), the atmosphere in the families into which the children are adopted is important in their psychological outcome.

SOURCE: Adapted from Tienari et al., 1990, p. 327.

Community Factors and Stress

More than 50 studies conducted in Canada, Denmark, Finland, Great Britain, Norway, Sweden, and Taiwan, as well as in the United States, have found that people of lower socioeconomic status (SES) are diagnosed with schizophrenic disorder more frequently than people of middle or upper SES. However, researchers have not been able to discover why social class is related to schizophrenia. Two theories—social selection and the social-causation or increased-stress theory—have been posed to explain this relationship. The **social-selection theory** assumes that people who cannot make it in society gradually become lower in SES because of their poor coping skills.

Whereas the social-selection theory points to flaws in the individual as the cause of schizophrenia, an alternative explanation for the greater incidence of schizophrenia in the lower SES group points to flaws in the society itself. The **increased-stress theory** focuses on the amount of stress experienced by people in different

socioeconomic classes. Living in areas with high crime rates, run-down housing, and inadequate schools may be more difficult and stressful than living in more affluent communities. At the same time, lower-SES people have little money or power to cope with the stresses they encounter.

Over many years the results of studies have supported one or the other of these theories. Recent evidence from a study of almost 50,000 Swedish men from whom data were originally obtained when they were called to serve their military obligation supports the increased-stress theory (Lewis et al., 1992). The study found that the incidence of schizophrenic disorder was 1.65 times higher for men brought up in cities than for those who grew up in rural areas. The large number of men in the study made it possible to control for factors that might have differed between urban and rural settings such as drug use, family finances, parental divorce, and family history of psychiatric disorder. The study also did not support the idea of urban drift. The researchers found that the increase in rate varied with the size of the city. Small towns showed a lower rate than large towns and large towns a lower rate than cities. The difference in rate related to degree of urbanization was much greater for schizophrenic disorder than for other diagnoses. These findings support the idea that environmental factors found in cities are associated with an increased risk for schizophrenic disorder. One possible explanation is the higher level of stressful life events that have been found to be more common in cities. Other causes such as greater exposure to viruses or childhood head injuries or a variety of social causes are also possible, but increased stress seems a more likely explanation.

High-risk Studies and the Search for Markers

One way of examining the risk factors in schizophrenia is to study children beginning in infancy or early childhood and compare the records of those who later develop a schizophrenic disorder with those who do not. This type of research has several advantages.

1. The subjects can be studied before those who develop disorders have experienced hospitalization and drugs.
2. None of the researchers, relatives, teachers, or subjects know who will develop a schizophrenic disorder. Potential sources of bias in their observations and reports are thus removed.

3. The information obtained is relatively current when it is gathered. Questions about teenage dating patterns and frequency, for example, are answered more accurately by adolescents than they would be by a 30-year-old schizophrenic patient and his or her 55-year-old mother.
4. The data can be obtained uniformly, not by relying on records from various agencies and individuals working in different ways.

This type of study avoids many problems that arise in dealing with an individual who has been diagnosed with a schizophrenic disorder. For example, it is not necessary to rely on the patients' and their families' sometimes faulty and selective memories of past events. This is especially important because once a diagnosis of schizophrenic disorder has been made, everyone in the family may see past events in a different light. Studying the person and his or her family after schizophrenia has developed tells more about the consequences of having a schizophrenic disorder than about its causes. The diagnosis of schizophrenia means that the person is likely to have already suffered educational, economic, and social failures and may also have experienced hospitalization and extensive drug therapy. These factors alone may explain many of the differences that researchers find between schizophrenic and control groups.

In spite of these advantages, there is one important problem with studies that test people before they become ill and later compare the records for those who develop schizophrenia with those who do not. Since no more than 1.4 percent of all people ever develop a schizophrenic disorder, many thousands of people would have to be tested in order to be sure that the group diagnosed as having schizophrenic disorder would be large enough. One way to cope with this problem is to do a **high-risk** study. This means that the researcher selects for study a group that is thought to have a higher potential or risk of schizophrenia than the population in general. One such group consists of children who have at least one parent with schizophrenic disorder.

Most high-risk studies of children of parents who have been diagnosed with schizophrenic disorder focus on understanding the differences among children who do and do not develop problems despite the fact that all may have a potential genetic vulnerability. The Finnish study described earlier represents a sophisticated high-risk study in which the interaction between environment and heredity could be studied because the subjects were all adopted.

Much research on high-risk subjects has focused on identifying markers for schizophrenia by determining the distinctive early characteristics of children who ultimately become schizophrenic. So far the search for markers suggests several conclusions (Erlenmeyer-Kimling & Cornblatt, 1993; Erlenmeyer-Kimling et al., 1994).

1. Impaired attention is a potentially promising early biobehavioral marker for genetic risk of schizophrenic disorder. The type of impairment seen is similar to that seen in patients diagnosed with schizophrenic disorder.
2. By age 7, more than one-quarter of the high-risk children show attention dysfunctions in comparison to a much lower proportion for those in the control group and among children at hereditary risk for affective disorder, as well.
3. In the high-risk—but not the low-risk—subjects, attentional dysfunction is related to disturbances in adjustment in adolescence and adulthood, including increase in social isolation.

Figure 11-17 presents one theoretical view of how attentional disorder present in early life may affect later behavior and symptoms in people at genetic risk for schizophrenic disorder.

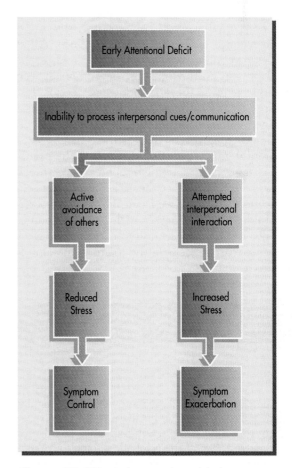

Figure 11-17 A theoretical model showing two alternative social outcomes based on the attentional deficits of those vulnerable to schizophrenic disorder.

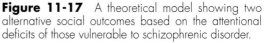

Source: Based on Cornblatt and Keilp, 1994, p. 41.

Another possible marker of risk for schizophrenic spectrum disorder are high levels of parental communication deviance. Such communication deviance has been found to be associated with vulnerability among at-risk children (Miklowitz and Stackman, 1992). This aspect of parental behavior may be a good marker for at-risk children. **Communication deviance** refers to the inability of the parent or parents to maintain a shared focus of attention during interactions with another person. Cross-sectional studies have shown that high communication deviance is associated with schizophrenia in the children of such parents. However, some of the research on communication deviance has raised questions about causality. The parents' communication problems may be a response to unclear communications from the children.

One way to understand the causes and effects of communication problems is through long-term prospective studies. In a high-risk study carried out at the University of California at Los Angeles, the participating families each contained a mild- to moderately-disturbed teenage member (Goldstein, 1985). All of the families had contacted the university-based psychology clinic for help. At the time they were originally seen, the parents were given the Thematic Apperception Test (see chapter 4), which was scored for communication deviance. Fifteen years later the children were rediagnosed and grouped according to the original assessment of parental communication deviance. The number of cases of schizophrenia and schizophrenic spectrum disorders was clearly related to the earlier assessments of communication deviance (see Figure 11-18). Fifty percent of the children in the families with high communication deviance had a diagnosis in the schizophrenic spectrum, compared to 26 percent in the intermediate- and 9 percent in the low-deviance families.

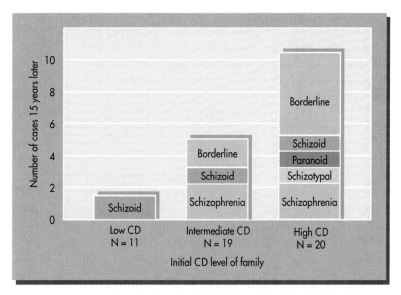

Figure 11-18 When families were divided into three levels of communication deviance (CD), the number of children who were later diagnosed as having a schizophrenic spectrum disorder was clearly different for each type of family.

SOURCE: Adapted from Goldstein, 1985, p. 12. Copyright © 1985 Munksgaard International Publishers, Ltd., Copenhagen, Denmark.

Although high-risk studies are making an important contribution to knowledge about schizophrenia, they have an important drawback. Since only about 11 percent of all people who develop a schizophrenic disorder have one or more parents with the disorder, it may be that the data from these studies apply only to a specific subtype of schizophrenia (Gottesman, 1991). As is true of other research carried out on a specific population—such as college students, members of the armed forces, or relatives of hospital patients—it is not clear what general statements can be made from findings based on a particular group. However, because they focus attention on vulnerabilities, the results of high-risk studies may play an important role in the design of prevention programs.

CHAPTER SUMMARY

THE IMPACT OF SCHIZOPHRENIC DISORDERS

The central or defining characteristic of a **psychotic disorder** is a group of symptoms that involve alterations in perception, thought, or consciousness. Schizophrenic disorders are an important subgroup of the psychotic disorders as well as the group that has the most severe impact both on people's lives and on the mental health system.

CHARACTERISTICS OF SCHIZOPHRENIC DISORDERS

Two general types of symptoms of schizophrenic disorder have

been described—positive symptoms and negative symptoms. Positive symptoms reflect a distortion or excess of normal functions while negative symptoms involve a loss or decrease in normal functioning.

Positive Symptoms Positive symptoms include delusions, hallucinations, disorganized speech, and disorganized behavior. A **delusion** is a faulty interpretation of reality that cannot be shaken by contrary evidence. Although delusions can occur in other disorders, certain types of delusions occur more often in schizophrenic disorder. **Hallucinations,** projections of internal impulses and experiences onto perceptions in the external world, account for most of the difficulties in perception experienced by a person with schizophrenia. Hallucinations can be associated with any of the senses, but are most commonly visual or auditory. **Disordered speech** is often described as a loosening of associations. This means that others have difficulty in following the speaker's train of thought because the connection between ideas is not clear to the listeners. **Disorganized behavior** is also characteristic of those diagnosed with schizophrenic disorder. This behavior is often unpredictable with a tendency to excess or random motor activity. Two extreme types of behaviors seen in this disorder are **catatonic rigidity** or the adopting of unusual postures for long periods and **catatonic excitement** in which a high level of purposeless motor activity occurs that does not seem to be stimulated by external events. A decrease in motivational level and impairment in social or interpersonal functioning are also characteristic of schizophrenic disorder.

Negative Symptoms Negative symptoms include such behaviors as flattened affect, poverty of speech and speech content, and lack of directedness, including decreased interest in social participation.

MAJOR SUBTYPES OF SCHIZOPHRENIA

The subtypes of schizophrenic disorder are based on historical views of the disorder. The **paranoid type** is characterized by extreme suspiciousness and delusions concerning another's motivation. The **catatonic type** involves psychomotor disturbance ranging from immobility to excessive motor activity. The **disorganized type** includes incoherent expression, disorganized behavior, and inappropriate emotional reactions. If none of these three types fit the individual's behavior, the category **undifferentiated type** is used.

WHAT CAUSES SCHIZOPHRENIC DISORDER?

Genetic and other biological factors create vulnerability to schizophrenia. Environmental factors that produce stress or provide support also play a role in determining whether vulnerable individuals develop symptoms of schizophrenic disorder.

Genetic Factors Although genetic transmission seems to be a factor in schizophrenic disorder, at present no specified gene or combination of genes that lead to genetic vulnerability has been identified.

Schizophrenic Spectrum Disorders Some other disorders appear to be genetically linked to schizophrenic disorder. These include schizotypal personality disorder and paranoid personality disorder as well as other types of psychotic disorders.

Other Biological Factors Some aspects of prenatal environment have been associated with schizophrenic disorder. Brain structure, especially enlarged **cerebral ventricles,** and biochemical brain abnormalities, especially related to **dopamine** transmission, may also play a role in vulnerability.

METHODS OF STUDYING GENETIC AND ENVIRONMENTAL FACTORS

Family, twin, adoption, and cross fostering studies are all used to study the roles of genetics and environment in schizophrenic disorder.

Family Studies The lifetime risk of developing schizophrenia correlates well with the proportion of genes shared with an affected family member. In family studies a family tree is constructed to give information about hereditary factors for a disorder. The risk for schizophrenia and other disorders is affected by **assortative mating,** the tendency for people to mate with others similar to themselves. **Genetic specificity** refers to findings that show that different disorders are caused by different genes. The **spectrum concept** refers to the situation in which several genetically related disorders typically occur in the same family.

Twin Studies Twin studies can help to disentangle heredity and environmental factors. Because monozygotic (MZ) twins have identical heredity, and dizygotic twins (DZ) share as many genes as a sibling pair, difference in rates of disorders in MZ and DZ twins suggest the relative contribution of heredity and environment.

Adoption Studies Adoption studies can also help provide information about heredity and environmental factors. The most common pattern for an adoption study is to use medical records to determine whether adopted children who had a biological parent with a schizophrenic disorder were more likely to develop a schizophrenic spectrum disorder than children without this genetic history.

VULNERABILITY, RESILIENCY, AND STRESS

The **diathesis-stress theory** of schizophrenia emphasizes the interaction of biological vulnerability and environmental stress in the development of schizophrenic disorder. Data from adoption studies support this theory.

Community Factors and Stress The lower a person's socioeconomic status the greater the risk of a diagnosis of schizophrenic disorder. This finding has been explained in two ways. The **social-selection theory** assumes that people who have poor coping skills drift toward lower socioeconomic status. The **increased-stress theory** suggests that lower socioeconomic status is associated with greater stress in terms of poorer living conditions and increased crime coupled with fewer coping resources. Recent work supports the increased-stress theory.

High-risk Studies and the Search for Markers Longitudinal studies are useful in examining causal factors in schizophrenic disorder for many reasons. In disorders that occur in a relatively small percent of the population, longitudinal studies usually focus on subjects who are at high risk for the disorder because of the economic cost of including a large number of subjects who are extremely unlikely to develop the disorder. Research with high risk subjects has emphasized the identification of **markers** because an early indicator of especially high vulnerability would be helpful in providing early treatment. To be useful a marker should have several characteristics. Especially important among them are measurement of a stable personal trait, the occurrence or observability of the trait before a disorder develops, and the availability of a reliable and relatively noninvasive manner of assessment. Impaired **attention** in childhood may be a potentially useful marker in high risk subjects. Family **communication deviance** may be a marker for schizophrenic spectrum disorder.

CHAPTER TWELVE

Karel Appel, *Untitled*, 1966.
Jane Kahn Gallery, New York.

SCHIZOPHRENIC DISORDER: PSYCHOLOGICAL RESEARCH, TREATMENT, AND OUTCOME

In 1950 John Nash received his Ph.D. in mathematics from Princeton University (see Figure 12-1). In July of 1958 Nash was singled out by *Fortune* magazine as America's brilliant young star of the "new mathematics." In 1994, the Nobel Prize Committee announced that John Nash was to be one of two individuals who would share that year's Nobel Prize for economics. However, there is more to the story. For much of the time between those two announcements, John Nash's personal and professional life was destroyed by paranoid schizophrenia.

Nash was first labeled a genius as an undergraduate. In graduate school at Princeton he was seen as a loner, odd but brilliant. As a young professor at Massachusetts Institute of Technology he invented a completely new method for approaching what had been thought to be an unsolvable mathematical problem. At age 30 he was hospitalized in a psychiatric hospital. In the months prior to his hospitalization Nash seemed to become another person. His lectures no longer made sense. He experienced fearful delusions. After this hospitalization he fled to Europe and traveled widely there, always convinced that he was being spied on and pursued. He returned to the United States and for the next two decades was repeatedly committed to psychiatric hospitals where many treatments were tried and failed. For most of this period he divided his time between these hospitals and his former wife's home in Princeton, New Jersey. Although they had been divorced after his illness began, she financially and emotionally supported him throughout his long period of illness. She believed strongly that he should stay within the Princeton University mathematics community even if he was not functioning well. During those years he spent time in the university library or walking on campus. He was silent and vacant in appearance but former colleagues were receptive and compassionate. Even though most of them believed his illness would never end they helped him get access to computers and invited him to seminars.

A few years ago he experienced what those colleagues saw as a "miraculous remission" not related to medication or treatment, but perhaps as his wife said "It's just a question of living a quiet life." He became able to do mathematics again and was able to go to Stockholm to receive the prize.

–Adapted from Nasar, 1994, pp. F1, 8

Figure 12-1 John Nash, joint winner of the 1994 Nobel prize in economics.

SOURCE: From *The New York Times*, Dec. 3, 1994 p. 1.

Why Nash developed the disorder or why the symptoms faded is not clear. Perhaps in view of what is known about stress and vulnerability in schizophrenic disorder his wife's analysis was on target. The success of some of the family-focused interventions discussed later in this chapter suggests that the support and acceptance of others, together with few demands or stressors, may be important in preventing relapse and improving functioning.

Attention, Cognition, and the Schizophrenic Process

Since the time of Kraepelin and Bleuler (see Box 11-1) who were instrumental in identifying and defining the disorder, scientists have sought to understand more about the schizophrenic process. The functional significance and neurobiological basis of information processing and attentional dysfunctions have been seen as important research topics in this effort. In 1921 Kraepelin commented on a "certain unsteadiness of attention" in patients he identified by the diagnosis *dementia praecox* (the forerunner of the present category of *schizophrenic disorder*). Bleuler (1911/1950) also noted that "acute attention is lacking" in schizophrenic patients. Especially since 1961 when McGhie and Chapman described the disorders of attention and perception that patients report in the early states of their schizophrenic disorder, many psychological researchers have focused

on understanding the schizophrenic process by quantifying information processing and attentional deficits seen in the disorder. Their studies have operated on the assumption that patients with schizophrenic disorder have important deficiencies in their information processing abilities and that these deficiencies are shown most clearly when the total task involves efficient and rapid information processing and high processing loads, as well as distraction or other stressors. Some of these deficiencies may be *trait-linked*, that is, they may be stable personal characteristics even when a disorder is not apparent. Studies of high-risk children and family members of patients diagnosed with schizophrenic disorder, for example, are based on that assumption. Some of the deficits may also be *state-linked*, that is, they may be associated with an active psychotic process that is not unique to schizophrenic disorder but that may also be seen during manic episodes and psychosis arising from the effects of drugs. A model linking attention and information processing to these state and trait variables is shown in Figure 12-2.

Although both information processing and attention are widely used terms, they are sometimes difficult to define quantitatively for study of either nonpatient or "normal" groups or for those diagnosed with, or at risk for, schizophrenic disorder or other disorders in the schizophrenic spectrum. Some of the measures that researchers have used in information processing and attention in the study of schizophrenic disorder include skin conductance, brain electrical activity, behavior during the Continuous Performance Task, and smooth-pursuit eye movement. The techniques have been used with patients and their family members and have been investigated in relation to measures obtained through various brain imaging techniques. Changes in the information processing and attention of patients as a result of receiving antipsychotic drugs have also been explored.

Overall, the research efforts have provided some experimental confirmations of the relationships shown in Figure 12-2 when applied to schizophrenic disorders. Differences in attention and information processing based on these measures have been related to presence or absence of negative symptoms (Braff, 1989), prognosis and therapy outcome (Zahn & Carpenter, 1978), and trait-linked familial inheritance patterns (Clementz et al., 1992). Some examples of psychological studies of attention and information processing are discussed in the following sections.

Attention Tasks

Researchers have tried to understand what factors contribute to the problems of attention seen in many of

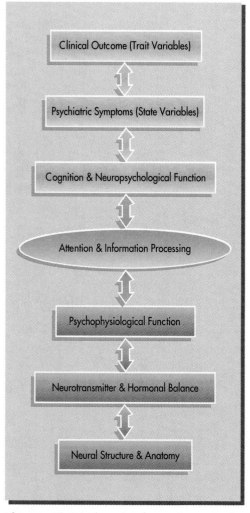

Figure 12-2 The role of attention and information-processing deficits in the symptoms and outcome of schizophrenic disorder.

SOURCE: Adapted from Braff (1993), p. 234.

increased when a distractor tone was added to the task. Under the distractor condition the patient group's response time was much slower than that of the control group. A measure of electrical activity in various parts of the brain was used in this study as a way to link differences in cognitive processing and attention to the difference in reaction time. The brain electrical activity patterns showed that the patients attended much more to the distracting tones than did the control group. This finding supported the hypothesis that the difference in group performance under the distracting condition was at least partly a result of an inability of the patients to focus their attention on one set of stimuli and to ignore other stimuli not relevant to the task. This difficulty may thus divert too much of their information processing resources from the assigned task.

Although this experiment did provide some important information about the reason for poor performance on attentional tasks by patients with schizophrenic disorder, a study of this kind cannot answer the question of whether this distractibility might be a marker for schizophrenia or whether it is merely a symptom of the disorder when it becomes acute. Another study investigated this question by comparing performance on a distraction task by several different groups. The groups included those who had been diagnosed with schizophrenic disorder, those who had not been diagnosed with this disorder but who had a relative with a diagnosis of schizophrenia, and a number of normal controls (Spring et al., 1989). Subjects listened over a headphone to strings of words that included both distractor and target words. The study showed that when distractors were words unassociated with the target words, only the overall performance accuracy of hospitalized patients with schizophrenic disorder was disrupted and the performance of the other groups was not (see Figure 12-3a). This result suggested that disruptions of selective attention might be a sign of an acute schizophrenic episode rather than a marker of risk. However, when specific types of errors were examined, certain kinds of errors were more frequent in all the at-risk groups than in the normal controls (see Figure 12-3b).) This second result suggested that certain types of attentional errors may be markers of vulnerability to schizophrenia, but that only during an acute psychotic episode do these deficits become more general in affecting performance.

Three measures of attention look especially promising as biological markers of risk for schizophrenia in children of schizophrenic mothers (Erlenmeyer-Kimling, 1987). These include the Continuous Performance Task, measures of eye-tracking dysfunction, and the Stroop task.

those with schizophrenic disorder. Attentional problems are of interest, not only in understanding the deficits experienced in schizophrenia, but also in the search for markers of high-risk individuals and development of therapeutic interventions. One possibility is that people who have a schizophrenic disorder are only able to devote part of their information processing resources to the task at hand. The remainder of their attention is abnormally focused on task-irrelevant stimuli. This idea has been supported in some research studies. For instance, in one study patients and controls were asked to push a button as soon as a target tone was heard, and their reaction time was measured (Grillon et al., 1990). Although in general the patients' time was somewhat slower than that of controls, the difference in speed between the groups was greatly

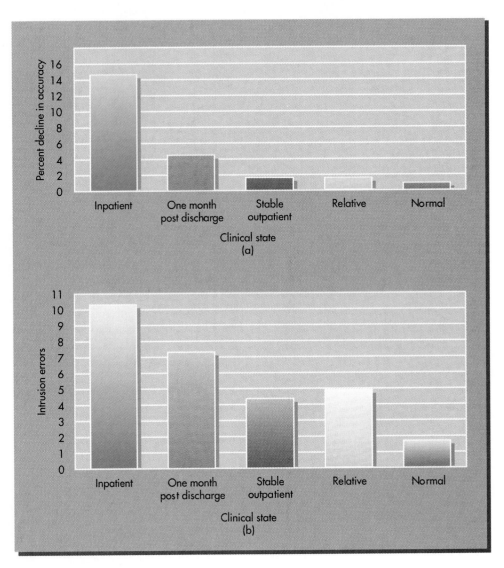

Figure 12-3 Performance of patients hospitalized with schizophrenic disorder on an attentional task compared with the performance of recently discharged and stable out-patients with the same diagnosis, patients' relatives, and a control group.

Source: B. Spring, M. Lemon, L. Weinstein, and A. Haskell (1989), "Distractibility in schizophrenia: State and trait aspects," in *British Journal of Psychiatry, 155*, 63–68. By permission of the Royal College of Psychiatrists.

Continuous Performance Task The **Continuous Performance Task** (CPT) (Rosvold et al., 1956) measures sustained visual attention for periods of up to 20 minutes. The subject is exposed to a series of different stimuli after he or she has been instructed to respond to one particular type of stimulus by pressing a key. Individuals with schizophrenic disorder make more errors both by pressing the key when other types of stimuli, not the assigned one, appear and also by failing to press the key when the correct stimulus appears. This poor performance may be related to a dysfunction in the reticular system in the brain stem (Mirsky & Bakay Pragay, 1984). It may also measure a vulnerability specific to schizophrenic disorder or schizophrenic spectrum disorder. Children of mothers with schizophrenic disorder scored more poorly on the CPT than either children of mothers with other disorders or other children in their classrooms (Nuechterlein, 1983). In another study those children who scored poorly on measures of attention including the CPT and also had a parent diagnosed with schizophrenic disorder were more likely than others in the group to develop schizophrenic disorder in adulthood (Cornblatt et al., 1989).

Eye Tracking Smooth-pursuit eye movements, which, strictly speaking, are not voluntary and cannot be faked, occur only when a person tracks a slowly moving target such as a pendulum. Many research studies show that patients with schizophrenic disorder as well as their close relatives are likely to have abnormalities in eye-tracking performance and other measures related to eye movements (Iacono & Clementz, 1993). Figure 12-4 illustrates the difference between the typical tracking pattern of someone with a schizophrenic disorder and that of a normal control. About 85 percent of the

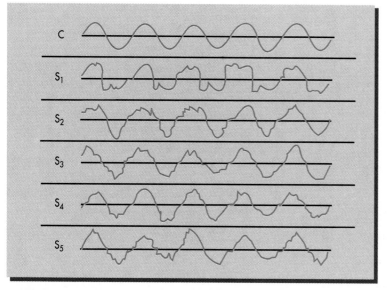

Figure 12-4 Samples of visual-tracking performance by a control subject (C) and five patients with schizophrenia (S1–S5). (The target moved back and forth across a 20-degree arc every 2.5 seconds.)

SOURCE: Iacono and Koenig (1983), p. 39.

patients with schizophrenic disorder who were tested showed abnormal patterns of these smooth-pursuit movements (Siever & Coursey, 1985). About 50 percent of close relatives of those with schizophrenic disorder also show this deviant pattern. In contrast, only 13 percent of relatives of other types of patients show abnormal tracking patterns. Two separate research groups have shown that eye tracking and other eye-movement abnormalities follow a Mendelian pattern of inheritance in studies involving families of patients with schizophrenic disorder (Holzman et al., 1988; Grove et al., 1992). This suggests that it may be possible to find a genetic link associated with abnormal smooth-pursuit eye movements. However, despite the differences in percent of relatives affected for those with schizophrenic disorder or some other DSM-IV disorder, this genetic link may not be specific to schizophrenic disorder or schizophrenic spectrum disorder. Deviant tracking patterns are also found in bipolar disorders, brain lesions, brain damage, and some forms of drug intoxication. Poor trackers, even among people who have not received any psychiatric diagnosis, are likely to show interpersonal difficulties and neurological impairment. Why these relationships exist is not known at present, but even if causal processes are unclear, eye tracking patterns may be useful as markers for early identification of those at risk for a wide group of disorders.

Stroop Task Performance The Stroop task (Stroop, 1935) taps a fundamental aspect of selective attention, the ability to respond to one set of stimuli when another set, with more compelling characteristics, is also available. In the original Stroop task subjects are asked to read the names of color words written in black ink, to give color names from color patches, and to name colors from color words each written in ink of a different color than the color named (color naming interference). Normal subjects are slower to respond, for example, to the red color patch than to the word "red" printed in black ink or red ink. Both responses are faster than when the word *green* is printed in red ink and the subject is asked to name the ink color. Normal subjects are said to show the Stroop effect because they have a harder time ignoring words and attending selectively to colors than in doing the reverse. Because a selective-attention deficit is hypothesized in schizophrenic disorder, subjects with this disorder should show even larger Stroop effects. Figure 12-5 shows that such a difference is found when patients with schizophrenic disorder are compared to a patient-control group.

Information Processing Tasks

Research on information processing and language performance suggests that patients with schizophrenic disorder make poor use of the context of a written selection in, for example, guessing the words deleted from a transcript of speech or arranging sentences in the correct order after they have been randomly rearranged. One reason for this may be that the schizophrenic disorder somehow interferes with the ability to keep the previous context in mind during the presentation of another stimuli and thus the behavior of the patients with schizophrenic disorder is greatly influenced by stimuli in their immediate temporal or spatial environment. This idea was tested in a study in which a word with two meanings, one weak and the other strong, was presented either before or after the context word on a computer screen (Cohen & Servan-Schreiber, 1991). For instance, the word "pen" has a strong linguistic meaning as a writing instrument and also a weaker one as a type of enclosure. In this study the subject saw the word PEN, for example, followed by one of three conditions: (a) a correct weak meaning, context last; (b) a weak correct meaning, context first;

(c) a strong correct meaning, context first. The successive screens presented looked like this:

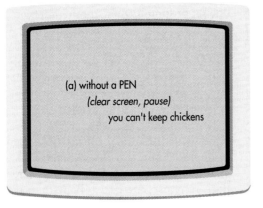

—or—

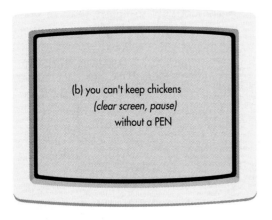

—or—

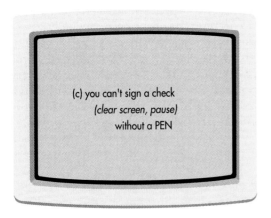

After screen (a), (b), or (c) the subject was presented with the screen in the next column:

The results showed that if the context came first the patients made significantly more dominant-meaning

responses (errors) than the controls when the weak meaning was correct (see Figure 12-6). If the context came last when the weak meaning was correct the patient group and the control group did not differ in the number of dominant meaning responses (errors). This result suggests that if the word was shown last, the patient subjects remembered only the word and not the context that had been presented. Thus they were more likely to give the dominant response just as they would have if the word had been presented to them free of any context. This finding suggested that the impairment observed in language tasks of those with schizophrenic disorder may be similar to the impairments observed in attentional tasks, that is, a difficulty in maintaining and utilizing an internal representation of the context in order to control action.

Thought Disorder

Although disordered cognition is often associated with schizophrenic disorder it can occur in other disorders such as mania and to some degree even in normal, healthy individuals. In one study, tape recordings of responses on the Rorschach personality test were compared for a number of groups, including those with schizophrenic disorder, patients experiencing mania, and normal controls (Solovay et al., 1987). The responses were all rated on a thought disorder index. The group diagnosed with schizophrenic disorder had the highest overall number of thought-disordered responses, although all groups showed some examples of disordered thought of each type measured (see Figure 12-7).

Researchers have wondered whether an above-average degree of thought disorder is simply a symptom of acute psychosis or whether it might also be a marker of vulnerability to schizophrenia. They have found that some degree of disordered thought may show up long

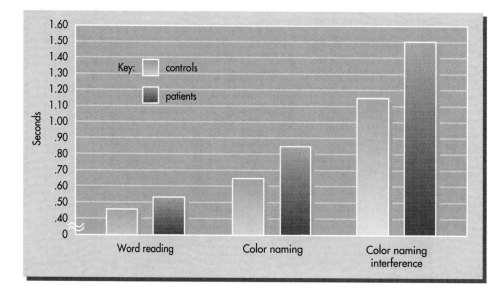

Figure 12-5 Response time in seconds for controls and patients with schizophrenic disorder on three aspects of the Stroop Task.

SOURCE: Adapted from Wysocki and Sweet (1985).

before other signs of a schizophrenic disorder appear and that it may be a permanent characteristic of at least some people who are vulnerable to schizophrenia (Erlenmeyer-Kimling et al., 1993).

A measure of thought disorder can also be useful in assessing the effects of antipsychotic medication. For example, in one study the responses of patients with schizophrenic disorder were evaluated on a thought-disorder index before the patients began drug treatment. The results showed that thought disorder as measured by

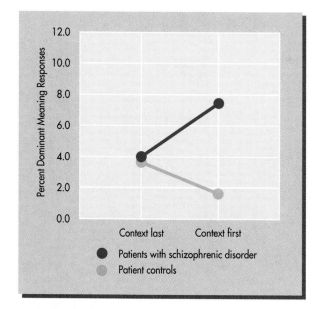

Figure 12-6 Median rates of dominant meaning responses if weak meaning was correct when the context appeared after or before the stimulus word.

SOURCE: From Cohen and Servan-Schreiber (1992), "Context, cortex and dopamine," *Psychological Review*, 99, p. 48.

the index dropped dramatically after the treatment began (see Figure 12-8). The maximum effect was reached in about three weeks, and then a relatively stable level was maintained. These results suggest that the drug therapy was effective in maintaining better cognitive performance. However, the level of disordered thinking shown, even after treatment with antipsychotic drugs, by the patients with schizophrenic disorder remained consistently higher than that of nonschizophrenic individuals.

The cycle set up by the combination of cognitive dysfunction resulting from attentional problems or disordered cognitions and the resulting decrease in coping skills often leads a person to experience high levels of social stress. This may come about because of difficulties in understanding what is expected or because of an inability to deal effectively with problems. Both situations may lead an individual to experience more negative life events, which in turn leads to more stress. Figure 12-9 illustrates how problems in basic cognitive functions such as attention and encoding or information processing may play a role not only in disturbing more complex functions, but also in a lessened ability to deal with life stressors.

Therapeutic Approaches

Because schizophrenic disorder is likely to arise from different sources in different patients, a wide variety of therapies have been developed. Probably the most usual treatment for schizophrenia today is antipsychotic medication. Despite the wide use of these drugs, at least 40 percent of individuals diagnosed as having schizophrenic disorder who also receive medication and use it

Figure 12-7 The frequency of thought-disordered responses of schizophrenic and manic patients was compared with that of control subjects. The figure shows how each group differed from the overall mean (0) in each of several aspects of their performance. (The data were transformed for statistical purposes and the results are reported in terms of z scores).

SOURCE: *Archives of General Psychiatry* (1987), *44*, 13–20. Copyright © 1987, American Medical Association.

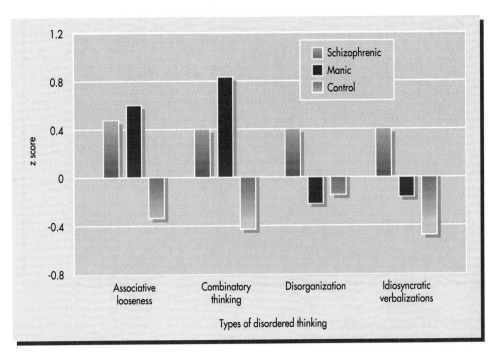

appropriately are likely to experience a relapse within one year of hospital discharge (Johnstone & Geddes, 1994). This makes it clear that additional forms of treatment are needed to supplement the biological drug-based approach. Many of these alternative or additional treatment approaches are focused on decreasing stress because increased stress seems to produce symptoms of psychosis in those genetically vulnerable to schizophrenic disorder. This stress-vulnerability relationship was illustrated in Figure 11-15. Optimal treatment of the disorder usually is considered to combine antipsychotic drugs and a variety of psychosocial approaches including a number of types of social-skills training and family interventions. In addition to these socially focused approaches, a few programs to help individuals adapt to or overcome attentional and information processing problems have been tried out but are yet largely unproven (Green, 1993). In general, individual psy-

Figure 12-8 Mean Thought Disorder Index of patients with schizophrenic disorder at several time points during their hospital stay. Effects of antipsychotic medications appeared quickly and the index reached a stable level but that level continued to be higher than the level for normal individuals ("wo" = end of drug-free "wash-out" period to remove effects of previous medication).

SOURCE: Holzman (1978), p. 367.

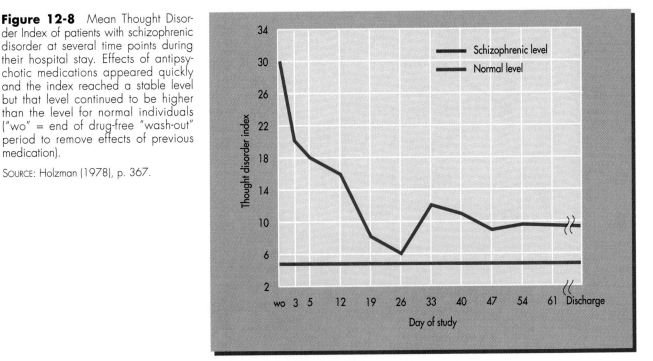

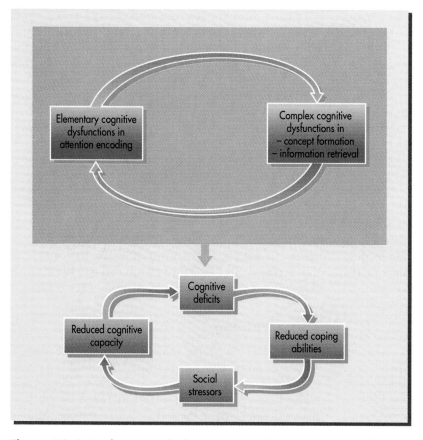

Figure 12-9 Dysfunctions in both elementary and complex cognitive functions may increase stress and diminish coping.

SOURCE: Adapted from Brenner et al. (1992).

chotherapy and psychodynamic or insight-based therapies are no longer used (Mueser & Berenbaum, 1990). One reason for psychotherapy's lack of success may be that psychodynamically oriented therapy provides too much stimulation for patients, especially chronic patients. Psychotherapy may make it harder for patients with a schizophrenic disorder to maintain cognitive control by further diminishing their fragile concept of self versus the environment. Rather than insight, these people need help in focusing their attention on practical skills such as learning more appropriate techniques of social interaction and skills related to everyday living and self-management.

Antipsychotic Drugs

The introduction of antipsychotic drugs in the 1950s revolutionized the hospital treatment of psychosis because the drugs decreased the unusual and hard-to-control behaviors of many patients. The number of patients who had to be hospitalized for long periods was correspondingly reduced, although the number of hospitalizations per patient increased because an in-and-out pattern of hospital stays developed.

Antipsychotic medications available today are often effective in suppressing ongoing psychotic behaviors although they may not prevent a new episode or relapse. However, only about half of all patients with schizophrenic disorder are helped by these drugs (Awad, 1989). Even for those who benefit, antipsychotic medication does not affect negative symptoms of apathy and withdrawal and may not improve higher level problem solving (Goldberg et al, 1993). Despite these limitations, a review of studies conducted over several decades has shown that—on average—early treatment with antipsychotic drugs not only shortens the current psychotic episode for many patients but also improves their long-term outcome (Wyatt, 1991). This suggests that prolonged or repeated psychotic episodes are not only bad in themselves but they may worsen the underlying disorder as well. Those who improve as a result of drug therapy are likely to be advised to remain on a drug program after discharge from the hospital in the hope that continuing medication may dampen symptoms and reduce the chance of relapse. Despite such advice, about half these discharged patients discontinue using the drugs as prescribed on discharge (Weiner et al., 1989). Why do so many individuals refuse to take, or just stop taking, their medication? Some patients appear to lack insight that their symptoms are part of a serious disorder and fail to understand the relationship between treatment and improved functioning (Ghaemi & Pope, 1994). A decrease in symptoms does not usually produce increased insight in this group. Many others seem to be responding to negative side effects of the antipsychotic drugs. For example, callers to a British mental health helpline, although lucid and articulate concerning their medication, indicated their feeling that the medication numbed their senses, caused their motivation to disappear, and made their lives seem meaningless.

"When I take my medication, I feel as though I am walking with lead in my shoes," one young man told me on the telephone. Another told the volunteer who took his call, "I feel emptied out, devoid of ideas." Another young man sent us a poem in which he compares the effect of the drugs with drowning—"I was always under the water gasping for air and sunshine," he writes.

—Wallace, 1994, p. 35

Development of newer antipsychotic drugs having fewer side effects may change this situation for some patients (Meltzer, 1993).

Although almost every person diagnosed with schizophrenic disorder receives antipsychotic drugs at some time, there are no good predictors of which type of drug will be most effective during a psychotic episode (Kane, 1994). Clinicians, therefore, usually must implement what is essentially a trial-and-error approach to find the most beneficial drug for a particular patient. Because it is necessary to try a new drug for several weeks to determine if it will be helpful, this method is problematic. Another serious drawback for the use of most antipsychotic drugs is the potentially irreversible damage to the nervous system that occasionally occurs as a result of their use. This damage usually appears in the form of **tardive dyskinesia,** or involuntary movements of the mouth, lips, tongue, legs, or body. At present there is no way to identify people who are at special risk for this drug side effect. Once tardive dykinesia has developed, its symptoms do not usually become worse with continued antipsychotic medication, but generally—even with medication change—the symptoms do not improve once they appear (Gardos et al., 1994). Because antipsychotic drugs are sometimes given inappropriately or used for too long a time, the risk of these side effects is unnecessarily high for some patients. Some years ago, in 1985, the American Psychiatric Association issued a warning about the need for "cautious use" of antipsychotic drugs. That concern still is present although both researchers and clinicians are increasingly likely to emphasize the need to determine the lowest effective dose for each patient and the drugs with the least side effects.

One of the new generation of antipsychotic drugs, **clozapine** (Clozaril) has the benefit of not being linked to tardive dyskinesia. In addition, clozapine has been found to produce some improvement in two-thirds of patients who had not responded to more traditional antipsychotic drugs (Breier et al., 1993). Clozapine was developed in 1972, but its use was delayed because it was found to cause bone marrow failure and death in some patients (Terkelsen & Grosser, 1990). Now that this risk has been recognized, it can be reduced if physicians who prescribe clozapine carefully monitor their patients. Although the apparent effectiveness of clozapine, and the reduced risk if weekly blood samples are checked, suggests its widespread use, the high cost of treatment has created controversy concerning the use of this drug (Jeffries, 1993).

One problem in carrying out treatment that relies on antipsychotic drugs is the question of patient competence to agree to or refuse the medication. Although the law is clear that no patient should receive medication without his or her informed consent, the cognitive impairment and loss of insight that are primary effects of schizophrenic disorder make the question of competence a difficult one. Often the question of competence comes up only when medication is refused (Jeffries, 1993). Then the question arises, when should a person have the right to refuse treatment? Research studies show that for many people the disorder may, at least temporarily, remit and eventually may not be evident as these individuals grow older. However, because of the informed consent–competence issue, the families of patients who refuse medication as well as clinicians who believe medication necessary for the welfare of the patients are often forced to wait until the psychosis worsens, and the individuals become dangerous to themselves or others, before hospitalization and medication can be required. Then when the patient again improves with medication, competence must be reassessed. If, as a result of this reassessment, the patient is diagnosed as legally competent, he or she may again refuse medication and another cycle of worsening of symptoms and active psychosis may begin.

Skills Training

Many individuals with schizophrenic disorder lack a variety of skills. This is particularly true for those whose disorder appears to be chronic. For these individuals, even if positive symptoms are controlled by antipsychotic drugs, many of these skill deficits remain (Mueser et al., 1991). Such skill deficits can be seen in a number of areas—social interactions, self-care and self-management skills related to independent living, and cognitive skills that appear to be linked with some of the attentional problems discussed earlier.

Social Skills Social skills training, based on social learning theory, seems to decrease symptoms and increase social adjustment but does not appear to prevent another psychotic episode (Bellack & Mueser, 1993). However, this training is often an effective way to improve quality of life after hospital discharge and to decrease the chances of rehospitalization.

Social skills training for those with chronic schizophrenic disorder consists of a highly structured program focused on teaching new, more adaptive interpersonal behavior. For these chronic patients, many of whom have functioned poorly in social interactions for many years, the training may initially focus on very basic components of social skills, such as voice volume and pitch, eye contact, and turn-taking. Even basic skills are broken down into simpler components. As an example, Table 12-1 shows how the behavioral skills for carrying on an ordinary conversation might be divided for training purposes. Such a careful breakdown of specific skills might seem unnecessary to most people. However, it is very important for helping patients who may not have functioned adequately prior to their illness, especially those with predominantly negative symptoms. In the initial stages of treatment an analysis of behaviors

The teaching of these skills can be useful in therapy with patients with mood or personality disorders as well as those with schizophrenic disorders. However, for many patients with schizophrenia the training must initially focus on more basic, lower level skills than for the other diagnostic groups.

Initiating conversations
    Initiating a brief conversation with an acquaintance
    Initiating a brief conversation with a stranger
    Social telephone calls
Maintaining conversations
    Asking questions
    Providing information
    Social reinforcement
    Social perception
Ending conversations
    Timing
    How to break off
    Good-byes
    Judging when the partner wants to leave

Source: Morrison and Wixted, 1989, p. 243.

within each task must be made by the therapist and then taught in small steps to the recovering patients. Later, or with people whose basic skills remain adequate, the therapy may be directed toward more complex behaviors. Other skills, such as assertiveness or on-the-job skills can be treated in the same way.

Self-Care Skills In addition to poor social skills, chronic patients are likely to have inadequate self-care skills. They are often poorly groomed, fail to wash regularly, have poor table manners, and are unable to use public transportation, manage their money, or prepare meals. Behavioral-training methods can also focus on the improvement of these skills. Successful transition for patients from the hospital to the community is predicted better by these skills than by the characteristics of behavior at or during hospitalization (Presly et al., 1982). One series of modules that focus on a variety of social and self-care skills needed for independent living was developed by the UCLA Clinical Research Center. These include patient management of medication and modules of symptoms of relapse, conversational skills and self-grooming skills, and skills related to recreational activities. Table 12-2 illustrates the skills areas

TABLE 12-2
The Skill Areas and Goals from Two of the UCLA Modules for Training Social and Independent Living Skills

Skill Areas	Goals
Skill Areas for Medication Management	
1. Obtaining information about antipsychotic medication.	To gain an understanding of how these drugs work, why maintenance drug therapy is used, and what benefits result from taking medication.
2. Knowing correct self-administration and evaluation of medication.	To learn appropriate procedures in taking medication, and how to evaluate responses to medication daily.
3. Identifying side effects of medication.	To learn the side effects that sometimes result from taking medication and what can be done to alleviate these problems.
4. Negotiating medication issues with health-care providers.	To practice ways of getting assistance when problems occur with medication; for example, how to call the hospital or doctor and how to report symptoms and progress.
5. Using long-acting injectable medication.	To desensitize fears of injections and learn benefits of biweekly or monthly injectable medication.
Skills Areas for Symptom Management	
1. Identifying warning signs of relapse.	To learn how to identify personal warning signs and monitor them with assistance from others.
2. Managing warning signs.	To learn to use specific techniques for managing warning signs and develop an *emergency plan*.
3. Coping with persistent symptoms.	To learn how to recognize persistent symptoms and use techniques for coping with them.
4. Avoiding alcohol and street drugs.	To learn about the adverse effects of alcohol and illicit drugs, and how to avoid them.

Source: Liberman & Corrigan, 1993, p. 242.

for medication and symptom management. Both sets of skills are important in helping prevent a relapse into psychotic behavior or—if such a relapse occurs—to help the individual recognize the relapse signs and seek help.

Cognitive Social Skills Some of the specific cognitive deficits frequent among patients with schizophrenic disorder and appropriate remedial strategies are illustrated in Table 12-3. Many of these deficits have been studied by psychological researchers using measures such as those described in the first part of this chapter. These deficits can be categorized not only in research terms but also at a more applied level, for example, as receiving, processing, and sending skills. Examples of situations broken down in this way are shown in Table 12-4.

Cognitive behavior therapy has been used experimentally to deal with some of these deficits in processing skills—for example, to decrease or make less upsetting chronic auditory hallucinations. These efforts focus on the idea that these hallucinations, arising from inside the patient, are misattributed by him or her to an external source (Bentall et al., 1994). For instance, using this cognitive approach some patients became aware that it was not the voices that were so distressing but their own thoughts about the voices. When they were able to recognize situations that caused the voices to become worse they sometimes were also able to understand that the voices reflected feelings they were unable to express. This allowed them to begin addressing some of these problems with the therapist.

Aaron Beck, one of the originators and foremost proponents of cognitive therapy, believes that although at this time application of the cognitive therapy techniques to treatment of schizophrenia has not been adequately demonstrated, the cognitive approach to stress reduction is consistent with the diathesis-stress model and thus may help vulnerable individuals prevent or reduce their delusional beliefs (Alford & Beck, 1994).

Behavioral techniques have also been used to modify some of the disordered cognitions that affect social problem solving in schizophrenia (Brenner, 1989; Roder et al., 1990). In one program, training was given to increase attention span and discrimination of social cues (Brenner et al., 1989). Patients were shown slides illustrating facial expressions to help them distinguish between expressions of different emotions. The researchers also worked with patients in a group setting to help them recognize cues given by other group members. After 18 months the trained group showed lower symptomatology and better attention, comprehension, and adjustment than the group that received no training (Benton & Schroeder, 1990). Despite these encouraging research findings it is currently unclear whether such training can generalize to new environments and thus be useful in patients' daily lives.

TABLE 12-3
Remedial Strategies for Some Cognitive Deficits of Schizophrenia

Cognitive Deficit	Remedial Strategy
1. Hyperaroused by over-stimulating milieu.	Diminish external distractors, ambient noise, likely interruptions.
2. Difficulty sustaining attention over time.	Keep training tasks brief and focused. Use frequent prompts to regain attentional focus. Use incentive program and self-management to improve prearranged attention goals.
3. Distracted by irrelevant cues.	Keep training site uncluttered of stimuli not germane to modular skill areas.
4. Misinterpret learning points.	Post charts that explain skill areas.
5. Difficulty with speeded tasks.	Proceed slowly through training steps.
6. Easily overloaded by complex tasks.	Conduct task analysis and break tasks down into simpler substeps.
7. Influenced by immediate stimuli in the environment.	Avoid accidental pairing of extraneous variables by providing immediate feedback and reinforcement. After overlearning has occurred, gradually fade feedback and reinforcers.
8. Distracted by hallucinations and poor associations.	Adopt thought-stopping techniques. Self-monitor disordered thought and hallucinations and avoid stressors that may exacerbate them.

Source: Liberman & Corrigan, 1993, p. 246.

Family Interventions

Family interventions have been among the most successful approaches to preventing relapse and promoting better functioning of individuals with a schizophrenic disorder. Psychoeducational programs focus on both the patient and the family. Family members are viewed as an important resource in the social rehabilitation and management of individuals who are released from the hospital after the acute symptoms of an episode of schizophrenic disorder have subsided. Research on family interventions was spurred by the move that occurred in the 1960s to deinstitutionalize patients. Instead of being retained in essentially custodial care in large hospitals many long-time patients were discharged. Many of these individuals returned to their families and, as time went on, it was recognized that negative affect

TABLE 12-4
Examples of Receiving, Processing, and Sending Skills

Receiving Skills	Processing Skills	Sending Skills
I see the man walking towards me with a knife in his hand.	The man approaching me with the knife may try to rob me.	
I hear the police car siren in the distance.	My alternatives to being robbed include: yelling for help, flagging a police car, running.	I yelled for help and waved my arms to stop the police car.
I see a girl sitting alone in the dance hall.	The girl staring at me in the corner may want me to ask her to dance.	
I hear the music in the dance hall.	My alternatives at the dance are: ask the girl to dance, ask someone else to dance, go to the refreshment table instead.	I asked the girl to dance by approaching her, making eye contact, and saying in a pleasant voice, "I'd like to have the next dance with you."

Source: Liberman & Corrigan, 1993, p. 241.

and attitudes expressed about the patient by family members were related to relapse and increased symptoms. In contrast, if the family's attitude toward the patient was positive, the family could serve as an effective source of support and continuity. In addition, it was clear that family members bore a heavy burden when they cared for an ill relative, particularly one with a chronic disorder such as schizophrenia. Interventions designed to provide family members with increased understanding of the disorder and social support were needed.

Expressed Emotion Many of the first studies that promoted family interventions were focused on expressed emotion. **Expressed emotion** (EE) is a measure of the attitudes expressed by family members when talking about the person whose behavior is disturbed (Leff & Vaughn, 1985). Table 12-5 lists the categories of expressed emotion that are measured.

Researchers found that patients hospitalized for schizophrenic disorder who were subsequently discharged and who returned to families high in negative EE were not likely to stay out of the hospital as long as patients whose families were less critical. This was true whether or not the patient was also taking antipsychotic drugs (Leff & Vaughn, 1981; Vaughn & Leff, 1976) (see Figure 12-10). Studies carried out in England and Los Angeles produced similar results (Vaughn et al., 1984).

Negative EE includes criticism, hostility, and emotional overinvolvement (exaggerated emotional response to the illness or extreme protectiveness). Relatives who were rated high in negative EE made such remarks as the following.

I always say, "why don't you pick up a book, do a crossword or something like that to keep your mind off it." That's even too much trouble.

I've tried to jolly him out of it and pestered him into doing things. Maybe I've overdone it, I don't know.

He went round the garden 90 times, in the door, back out the door. I said "Have a chair, sit out in the sun." Well, he nearly bit my head off.

—Hooley, 1985, p. 134

Relatives who were low in negative EE were likely to make very different comments.

I know it's better for her to be on her own, to get away from me and try to do things on her own.

Whatever she does suits me.

I just tend to let it go because I know that when she wants to speak she will speak.

—Ibid.

As research on EE has continued, several findings have emerged:

1. EE in a family may change over time. It may be a product both of the degree of agitation in the patient and of the family interaction style. Half the families high in negative expressed emotion at the patient's first admission are low one year later. A change from high to low negative expressed emotion in a family is associated with lower relapse rates (Hogarty et al., 1986).

TABLE 12-5
Scales of Expressed Emotion

1. *Critical comments about family members.* Criticisms are rated on the basis of content and/or tone. Remarks are considered to be critical if there is a clear and unambiguous statement that the relative dislikes, disapproves of, or resents a behavior or characteristic. The dissatisfaction is expressed intensely and emphatically; the relative must use phrases such as "It annoys me" or "I don't like it." Vocal aspects of speech such as pitch, speed, inflection, and loudness are used to identify critical tone.
2. *Hostility.* Hostility is rated as present when the patient is attacked for what he or she *is* rather than for what he or she *does.* Negative feeling is generalized in such a way that it is expressed about the person him- or herself rather than about particular behaviors or attributes.
3. *Emotional overinvolvement.* Emotional overinvolvement is rated when there is either an exaggerated emotional response to the patient's illness, marked concern reflected in unusually self-sacrificing and devoted behaviors, or extremely overprotective behaviors.
4. *Warmth.* Ratings of warmth are based on the sympathy, concern, and empathy relatives show when talking about the patient, the enthusiasm for and interest in the patient's activities, the number of spontaneous expressions of affection, and the tone of voice used when talking about the patient.
5. *Positive remarks.* Positive remarks are statements that express praise, approval, or appreciation of the behavior or personality of the patient.

Source: From Leff and Vaughn, 1985. Reprinted with permission from the British Journal of Psychiatry.

2. The culture in which people live or from which they come plays a role in the amount of EE they express. In India relatives show relatively lower levels of negative expressed emotion toward patients than that shown by relatives to Anglo-American patients in the United States. Mexican-Americans who live in the United States but who follow traditional cultural practices also show typically lower levels of expressed emotion toward their relatives than do Anglo-Americans (Leff & Vaughn, 1985; Jenkins et al., 1986).
3. EE research also has implications for patients who do not live with their families. High negative expressed emotion is associated with overstimulating treatment and high expectations in foster homes and day-treatment centers, which in turn may lead to high rates of relapse.

EE research has become a focus of controversy for some practitioners and family members because they believe that it blames families for the development of a member's schizophrenia. The research should not be thought of in this way, however. It is focused not on the cause of schizophrenic disorder but on conditions that increase the chance of rehospitalization. The term "expressed emotion" became associated with a negative interactive style because early work showed how negative aspects of EE predict a high *relapse* rate. Later research has shown that warmth and positive comments may also help protect *against* relapse (Leff & Vaughn, 1985). The most important results of the work on EE have been the development of training programs to help families learn how to interact more effectively with patients when

they return from the hospital after an acute episode of schizophrenic disorder.

The term "expressed emotion" can also be misleading because research on negative EE may suggest that families should not express their emotional reactions to each other. What has been found is quite the reverse; in general, a high level of emotional expression in the sense of communicating feelings among family members has been found to help prevent relapse (Spiegel & Wissler, 1986). This finding indicates that some expression of feelings creates a healthier emotional atmosphere for everyone and prevents the festering of anger and irritation that lead to full-blown emotional flare-ups.

In spite of the evidence supporting the EE construct, the meaning of the findings is still not agreed upon by all researchers. Some well-done studies have failed to find that high EE predicts relapse (Parker et al., 1988) or that only some dimensions of EE predict relapse (Barrelet et al., 1990; Leff et al., 1990).

Family Education Programs for family information and training have been found to prevent relapse and rehospitalization (Clarkin, 1989). These training programs provide family members with information about the nature of schizophrenia (diagnosis, symptoms, future expectations), its treatment (both medication and family management), and how the family can work together to take into account both the needs of the patient and the needs of the rest of the family. In some education programs, the patient participates in some or all of the sessions, while in others only the other family members take part. Some programs focus on one family at a time,

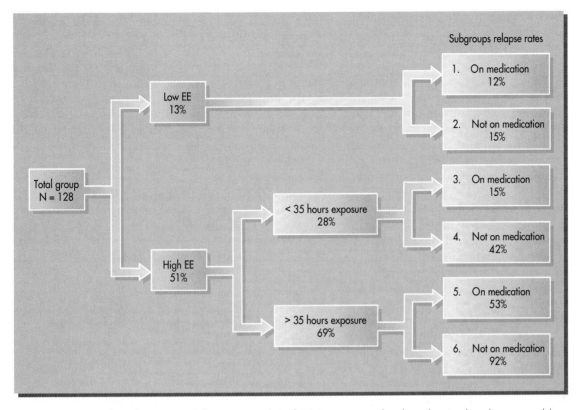

Figure 12-10 The relapse rates (after nine months) of 128 patients with schizophrenic disorder grouped by whether their families were high or low in negative expressed emotion (EE), the amount of time per week they were exposed to EE, and whether or not the patient was taking antipsychotic drugs.

SOURCE: From C. E. Vaughn and J. P. Leff (1976), *British Journal of Psychiatry*, 129, p. 132. Copyright © 1976 by *The British Journal of Psychiatry*. Reprinted by permission.

others combine several family groups. Most programs begin with a discussion of what the diagnosis means, and stress that it is a method of communication rather than a condemnation of the affected person. The therapist may next try to dispel common myths about schizophrenia, such as the idea of split personality. Family members also find it helpful to know about the prevalence of schizophrenia so that they realize they are not alone in their frustration and difficulties.

One aspect of many of these programs that seems especially helpful is a detailed discussion of the common symptoms of schizophrenia such as disordered thought, delusions, hallucinations, and withdrawal, so that family members can understand what the patient is experiencing. The therapist tries to personalize this material, either by having the patient and the family talk about these symptoms and asking the patient to describe those that he or she has experienced, or by using autobiographical accounts similar to the quotations presented in chapter 11 and in this chapter.

Families also receive an explanation of what is known about the psychobiology of schizophrenia to help them understand the underlying mechanisms of the symptoms. Since one of the major goals of these programs is to decrease the feelings of guilt of the family that their behavior in some way caused the illness, most programs stress schizophrenia's genetic aspects (see Box 12-1).

Programs are also likely to stress environmental factors, in the sense that schizophrenic disorder is a condition responsive to stress. The role of the family in managing the stress the patient experiences is emphasized as a way of possibly decreasing symptoms and making relapse less likely. Finally, and perhaps most importantly, family members are given guidelines about how to cope with living with someone with a schizophrenic disorder. Such guidelines might include constructive ways to handle guilt, embarrassment, frustration, and anger. Family members also learn why behavioral tactics that they might be likely to employ may not work, and receive instruction about how to keep the home atmosphere low-keyed, not overstimulating, and adequately structured. Family education can be extremely beneficial. When families know more about the symptoms and typical behaviors associated with schizophrenic disorders, they become more understanding of what the patient is experiencing and often less critical and hostile.

Another way to help families is to focus on the social functioning of the patient through behavioral intervention that may include education, stress management, stress innoculation, and goal planning for all family members, including the patient (Barrowclough & Tarrier, 1990). Before the intervention began in one study using this approach, patients living in families rated high on negative EE were poorer in their social functioning than those with families low in negative EE. At the end of the 9-month intervention, patients from the high negative EE families who were in the experimental group had improved in their social functioning and patients from high negative EE families who were in the control group had declined. The high EE patients in the experimental intervention group also showed a lower rate of relapse than those in the high EE control group. In addition, more high EE family members in the experimental group no longer were so critical and negative, but had changed their status to low EE. These results suggest that the work on EE has resulted in effective interventions for both patients and families.

Relapse Recognition An important skill for both family members and patients to acquire is the ability to detect early warning signs of a potential relapse in schizophrenic disorder. Figure 12-11 illustrates some of the cognitive-perceptual changes that occur or increase when a relapse begins. This often happens in several stages. First, a period of dysphoria or depressed mood occurs, which is followed by increasing psychotic symptoms such as delusions. When these cognitive perceptual changes occur the person affected is likely to react by trying to understand them. As a result he or she may seek help from a doctor or clinic for symptoms that can only be vaguely described. The vague forebodings such patients feel may also intensify the stress they experience and make effective coping even less possible. Both these fears and the increased stress also increase feelings of dysphoria and these together hasten the relapse process.

Although the general process illustrated in Figure 12-11 is likely to be similar for most individuals who experience a relapse in the course of their disorder, different people may show quite different signs and these are not always easy to identify. Because an increase in symptoms is often accompanied by a decrease in insight, some people choose to conceal these changes. Because many patients continue to have residual symptoms even when they improve, it is not always clear to observers that unusual behaviors they see are not just an indication of persisting symptoms, ongoing cognitive

deficits, or drug side-effects. In addition, the characteristics of a beginning relapse may vary greatly from person to person. An effective approach is to identify an oncoming relapse quickly by training both patients and relatives to watch for changes similar to those that led to the initial diagnosis or to past relapses. One way of doing this is through a structured interview to help identify early signs of the disorder for a particular individual. Sample questions that relatives may be asked include:

> *"When did you decide he/she needed help?"*
> *"What was his/her behavior like at the time?"*
> *"Were there changes before that even those that might not seem important?"*
>
> –Adapted from Birchwood, 1992, p. 273

Table 12-6 (see p. 361) provides a sample of the information obtained for one patient from this type of interview. This information can help relatives or the patient seek help more quickly.

Community Support

Because patients may not have a family to return to, other kinds of support programs also need to be provided. These include halfway houses or group homes, day-care facilities, and mental health clinics that provide both treatment and practical help. Some of these supports may be transitional; they help the discharged patient readjust to life in the community. Others are used to help a person who is functioning at a low level stay out of the hospital. Most support programs help people to maintain the same level of adaptive behavior they had at the time of their hospital discharge but not to increase their level of performance. Despite their effectiveness at preventing relapse, good aftercare programs and sheltered living accommodations are in very short supply.

A number of types of therapeutic homelike environments in the community have been shown to be successful in preventing relapse in patients. These residential environments are usually developed around the idea of milieu therapy. **Milieu therapy** refers to providing a therapeutic environment on the part of all those involved with the patient. Milieu therapy has several central functions. The sheltered setting provides support and protection for the person as well as structure and containment. At the same time it provides opportunities for socialization and for validation of the symptoms experienced as part of a schizophrenic disorder. Those working in the milieu setting validate affected persons' feelings by letting them know their delusions or hallucinations are quite real experiences. What they are, how they make the person feel, and what they mean can

Lessening a Family's Guilt over Schizophrenia

Donna Lee and her twin sons, Malcolm and Michael, are participants in a twin study at the National Institute of Mental Health (NIMH). Malcolm is affected with schizophrenia while Michael is healthy. The 25-year-old twins and their mother traveled from their home in Canada to Washington, D.C., for five days of testing that included MRI scans and neuropsychological exams. Before beginning the study in which the Lees took part, researchers at NIMH had identified approximately 150 pairs of identical twins in the United States and Canada in which one twin was healthy and the other had been diagnosed with either schizophrenic disorder or bipolar disorder. As the study progressed 64 twin pairs from this group were brought to Washington, D.C. to take part.

Donna and Michael described some of their feelings when they first learned that Malcolm had been diagnosed with a schizophrenic disorder.

When Malcolm was first hospitalized, Donna said, "I was taken into a room, told he has schizophrenia, and asked if I had any questions. Well, you go into a total state of shock. And nobody sat there and explained exactly what schizophrenia is."

Relatives should receive a thorough explanation of the illness after they've recovered from the initial shock, because at that point, she said, "you're really not hearing anything—all you're hearing is

that one word and you can't think of anything else." . . .

"Don't blame the families," Michael said adamantly, emphasizing the "psychological and emotional damage" such an approach causes. "You're making a bad situation terrible." His mother agreed, adding that many relatives automatically blame themselves anyway. "I didn't know anything about schizophrenia and I blamed myself totally and thoroughly. . . . I sort of let Malcolm walk all over me once I found out what was wrong with him because . . . I thought, I've done this to him."

In Washington the Lees spoke openly about their experiences with mental illness. But at home, Michael said, "I don't really talk about it at all. If I have to say anything, I just say that [Malcolm] has a brain disease."

"I've got relatives that I haven't even gotten in touch with," Donna said, "because I know . . . they have the general view that it's caused by your being a bad parent . . . and also they wouldn't want Malcolm near them."

She added that she's "never even written" to one of her sisters. "She probably knows, but I can't . . . talk to her." Donna's voice trailed off. "We were very close before it happened."

"It's really helped all of us in our family, coming here," Donna commented. Learning that schizophrenia has a biological basis "made me feel better, made my

ex-husband feel better. Even my youngest son is starting to accept it now. And it's made me feel easier with Malcolm to realize that this is just an illness."

Both Donna and Michael Lee had experienced many frustrations in trying to deal with Malcolm after his disorder became apparent, but they were also aware of how much more difficult it had been for him than for them.

"No matter what any of us has gone through, Malcolm has gone through ten times worse," said his mother. He's "tried to commit suicide I don't know how many times since he found out about [his diagnosis]. Because when you think you're different and people avoid you and some are even afraid of you . . . what kind of life have you got to look forward to?"

Still, Michael observed that his twin recently obtained his high school equivalency." . . . [H]e's doing better than some people who aren't plagued with mental disease."

—Adapted from Psychiatric News, March 17, 1989, pp. 2, 34

The experience of the Lees shows the importance of helping family members understand that there are biological causes of schizophrenia in order to avoid needless and crippling guilt. It illustrates how this knowledge can aid families to deal more effectively with the problems that a schizophrenic disorder creates and thus help both the person with the disorder and themselves.

---

all be discussed. In a properly functioning mental health system, such residential treatment facilities—in combination with crisis teams—should be able to prevent much of the need for the traditional psychiatric hospital (Mosher, 1989). Unfortunately, few such systems exist.

Another type of community support is based on supportive intervention that is nonresidential. **Nonresidential support** approach does not try to change behavior, skills, or competence directly. Instead, it accommodates to the individual's level of functioning by finding suitable living or working environments and providing missing functions (Anthony & Liberman, 1986). Such interventions might include support persons who provide companionship or advice so that coping with life

tasks is easier. Many times this approach is combined with a case management approach derived from social work in which the case manager links the person to needed services such as clinics or helps him or her get other services such as housing assistance or vocational or sheltered workshop placement.

Long-Term Outcome Studies

There are two schools of thought regarding the outcome or prognosis for schizophrenia. One is derived from Kraepelin's original concept of dementia praecox (see Box 11-2). This view of schizophrenia as a nonreversible

Figure 12-11 The psychological processes that occur in a relapse of a schizophrenic disorder.

Source: Adapted from Birchwood 1992, p. 268.

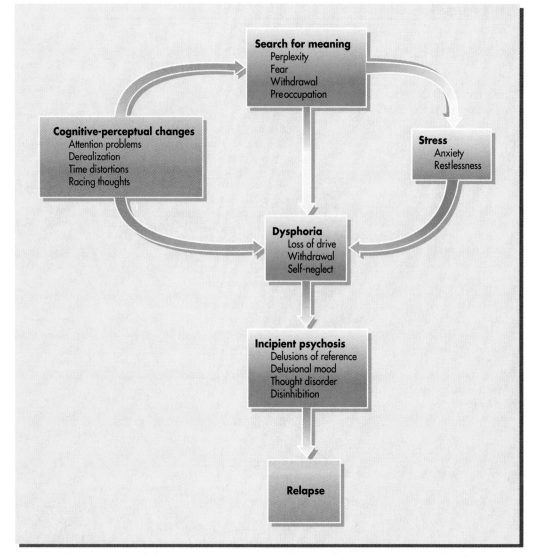

deteriorative disorder assumes that the prognosis is negative. The second viewpoint stems from Bleuler's concept of the schizophrenias, which emphasizes the symptoms rather than the course of the disease. From this viewpoint, a certain number and kind of symptoms are necessary for the diagnosis, but the outcome may range from complete recovery to permanent and severe disability. Currently, a generally accepted view is that some individuals who have been affected by a schizophrenic disorder do fully recover, but that percentage is low (Rund, 1990). However, mental health professionals make a distinction between *recovered* and *cured*. Most of those in the mental-health field do not consider it possible for those who recover from a schizophrenic disorder to be "cured" because they believe that any person who has had a schizophrenic disorder must live with the vulnerability to new psychotic episodes for the rest of his or her life.

Information about whether or not there ever is or can be a complete recovery from schizophrenia is very

important for individuals who have been diagnosed as having a schizophrenic disorder and for their families. The implications are considerable even for those whose behavior seems to have returned to the level they had achieved prior to the initial period of schizophrenic disorder. A letter written by someone who had earlier been diagnosed as having a schizophrenic disorder dramatically illustrates this point.

A few years ago, during my training in medical school, I was hospitalized at a reputable institution and, at some time during my stay, diagnosed as schizophrenic. Fortunately, I am doing very well now, and am pursuing a career in research on schizophrenia. . . . During the years since my hospitalization, however, I have often been fraught with profound guilt over my diagnosis of schizophrenia. . . . I felt that for some people I would be forevermore something of a subhuman creature. I grieved and mourned over my loss for several months. . . . Returning to work as a fellow in a department of psychiatry, I was repeatedly in contact with psychiatrists,

TABLE 12-6
Results of an Interview to Establish a Symptom Pattern Prior to a Relapse or Renewed Period of Psychosis

Informant:	Parents
Date admitted:	25/5/90
Date of relapse:	March 1990 (first episode)
Change first noted:	October 1989

Early Sign	Period prior to relapse
Spending more time alone in bedroom	
Avoiding contact with family; talking less	
Stopped interests/hobbies—listening to music and drawing wildlife	12–20 weeks
Stopped work—"people were picking on him"	
Accused friends of same	
Neglecting personal hygiene—not washing or changing clothes	
Stood in front of mother naked	8–12 weeks
Stealing money from family	
Irritable and argumentative toward family	
Accusing family of reading his mind	
Said he thought the phone was being interfered with	
Laughing for no reason	4–6 weeks
Very preoccupied with TV—sat and stared but did not appear to be watching	

Source: Adapted from Birchwood, 1992, p. 274

Key: Withdrawal/Dysphoria ■

Disinhibition ■

Incipient Psychosis ■

psychologists, and other mental health professionals. Quite frequently amidst such contacts there were derogatory and slanderous remarks of persons labeled as schizophrenic. Dismayed, I soon had repeated dreams in which I had a brain tumor, dreams that were not in the least bit frightening to me. Having an organic disorder seemed far easier to live with then—preferable to experiencing the full psychological impact of this label of schizophrenia. . . . But I continually have a need to ask myself certain questions. Am I now committed to schizophrenia for life? Or is schizophrenia committed to me?

—Anonymous, 1977, p. 4

One frequently asked question is, What happens to people who are diagnosed as schizophrenic? Studies that follow individuals over long periods provide important information about the long-term implications of this diagnosis. However, the definition of schizophrenia has changed over time. Unless we know the particular definition used in the study, the results are hard to interpret. Another drawback of follow-up studies is that, because of their cost, they are often done on the basis of hospital records and the individual is never actually interviewed or personally evaluated. This methodological problem introduces a good deal of uncertainty—for example, did all the record keepers use the same definition of level of adaptation? Despite these problems, long-term follow-up studies provide information of interest to researchers, to clinicians, to those who have received a diagnosis of schizophrenia, and to their families.

A review of long-term follow-up studies done since the early 1970s showed a consistency across their findings (McGlashan, 1988). These studies covered an average period of 10 years since initial diagnosis. The review provided confirmation of the poor long-term outcome for those with a diagnosis of schizophrenia compared to those with other mental illnesses. It also confirmed that the course of schizophrenic illness should not be described as a continuous process of deterioration as some researchers had thought, but rather that the schizophrenic process seemed to bottom out or reach a plateau between five and ten years after the psychosis became apparent. For most of the studies reviewed, the level of recovery achieved five to ten years after the diagnosis was likely to continue unchanged in the future. The studies also showed that the diagnosis of schizophrenia was associated with an increased risk for physical illness, suicide, and mortality not associated with either accidents or suicide.

These follow-up studies showed that none of the treatment approaches used were consistently beneficial in promoting improvement. However, within studies, individual outcomes varied greatly from continuous incapacity to recovery of previous level of function. The important point to recognize is that a substantial number of patients, not just a few unusual cases, do show enough improvement that they no longer currently meet the criteria for a schizophrenic disorder.

Because the diagnostic criteria for schizophrenic disorder have changed in successive editions of the DSM, long-term follow-up studies would be meaningless if only diagnoses were recorded in medical records. Until more is known about the causes of schizophrenia, complete information about all symptoms shown by each patient should be recorded in patient records in addition to the diagnosis. Such records should include not only those symptoms related to the schizophrenic diagnosis, but also others that appear unrelated. Record-keeping like this allows many of those studied, who were diagnosed using older systems, to be rediagnosed on the basis of their original hospital records; thus, meaningful long-term follow-ups are possible.

One good example of the usefulness of this approach is a follow-up study of patients from a hospital in Vermont (Harding et al., 1987a, 1987b). In this study, long-term hospitalized patients who had participated in a comprehensive rehabilitation program and been deinstitutionalized 20 to 30 years earlier were rediagnosed from their records. Those who met the current criteria for schizophrenia were traced and they or their families were interviewed. Between half and two-thirds of these individuals had recovered or were significantly improved. Figure 12-12 shows how many were functioning at least fairly well.

Although many of these people had made a poor adjustment for at least five years after the rehabilitation program, later on many had improved their level of functioning. Some of those who were classified as functioning well apparently did so only because they had learned to live with certain symptoms. These individuals were employed and had good social relationships but still experienced some hallucinations or delusions. Others, who did not work, nevertheless had developed extensive social networks. Because the patients in this study had been hospitalized for up to 25 years and were middle-aged when the rehabilitation program began, these results suggest that for younger, more recently hospitalized patients, the outcome might be even better.

The Vermont study also suggests that schizophrenia, rather than being unremitting, may be affected by prolonged environmental or psychosocial changes. Such changes may have a positive potential if applied in a supportive manner in the course of a stable and continuous care situation in which the patient is not shunted in and out of the hospital setting many times over a long period. The case of John Nash at the beginning of this chapter and the case of Dennis in Box 12-2 offer contrast both in outcome and continuity of care and support.

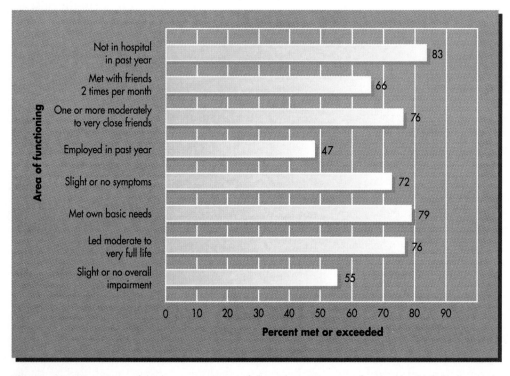

Figure 12-12 Many of the long-term patients followed up 30 years after they had left the hospital had at least a marginally adequate level of functioning. The figure shows the percent of the 168 patients who met or exceeded each criterion.

SOURCE: Data from Harding et al. (1987), *American Journal of Psychiatry*, 144, pp. 718–726.

BOX 12-2

An Unrealized Ideal—Continuity of Care

Although several approaches to treatment of schizophrenia—antipsychotic drugs, behavioral skills training, and changes in the person's living environment and personal relationships—all can have positive effects on decreasing symptoms and helping the person function at a higher level, what is needed for most of those affected by a schizophrenic disorder is a comprehensive program that provides a continuity of care over time. The important elements of such a comprehensive program are listed in Table 12-7.

For many patients, the use of antipsychotic drugs has shortened their first hospital stay by reducing the period during which their psychotic symptoms are most evident. Reducing hospital stays has some very positive effects, since just being hospitalized for a long period, even in the best of institutions, can have negative effects on a person's coping abilities. For that reason, as well as cost factors and concerns about patient rights, increased emphasis has been placed on short hospital stays, mainly to begin and assess drug treatment, followed by discharge to aftercare in the community.

Many patients are repeatedly treated by crisis teams that have the ability to intervene in acute psychosis in the emergency room. While this practice may provide an alternative to hospitalization, many of the follow-up studies have shown that people with a schizophrenic disorder do best when they experience continuity of care over a long period. The case of Dennis, who very likely had been treated in the emergency room on a number of past occasions, illustrates the tragedies that can occur as a function of lack of continuity of care.

Dennis was apprehended by police inside a fast-food restaurant. He had been screaming and throwing tomatoes from the salad bar after he was unable to pay for his order and was asked to leave. The police officers could not calm him, and they felt he was talking in a confusing way about being followed and tortured. After being seen in an emergency room, Dennis was admitted to a public mental hospital. His delusions and auditory hallucinations seemed to respond to medication, and he became cooperative in talking about himself and his treatment history. The hospital staff learned that he had no home or job, but they saw no need to contact his family in California. He was discharged with a prescription, an address for a city shelter, and an appointment slip indicating a time the following week that someone at a nearby clinic could see him. A nurse loaned him money for bus fare, but he never made any of those contacts. There was no further information about him until one day about five weeks later; police in an eastern city called his parents to say Dennis had been killed the night before when he walked in front of a truck on an interstate highway.

—*National Institute of Mental Health, 1991, p. 1*

Patients such as Dennis who experience discontinuous care that lacks ongoing support and offers only piecemeal services are likely to become part of the "revolving door syndrome" (see Figure 12-13). They often have as many as three hospital admissions per year in addition to a large number of emergency room visits (Bellack, 1989). Only a small number of such patients are effectively reintegrated as part of the community. Many continue to be unable to take care of the ordinary tasks of daily living, to manage their own money, or to take their medication as prescribed. They occupy inadequate housing, in general have poor health care, and are easy targets for criminal victimization. The case of Dennis illustrates what may result when poorly functioning people are not provided with continuity of care.

One approach that would serve those individuals better would be to regard and treat schizophrenia as a chronic condition in the same way that other chronic diseases such as diabetes or kidney failure are treated. Patients would benefit from a comprehensive program of long-term care so that they experience some continuity in caregivers and a variety of available coordinated services.

TABLE 12-7
A Comprehensive Care Program Appropriate for Most People with Schizophrenic Disorder

Treatment	Social services
Medication	Income support
Family therapy	Housing
Social skills training	Social support
Medical care	Recreation
Crisis intervention	Continuity of care
Rehabilitation	Active coordination of
Housekeeping	above services
Nutrition and hygiene	
Job training	
Transportation	

Source: Bellack, 1989, p. 7.

Box 12-2 continues on the next page.

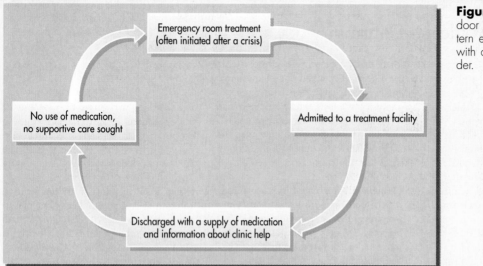

Figure 12-13a The revolving-door treatment and discharge pattern experienced by many persons with a chronic schizophrenic disorder.

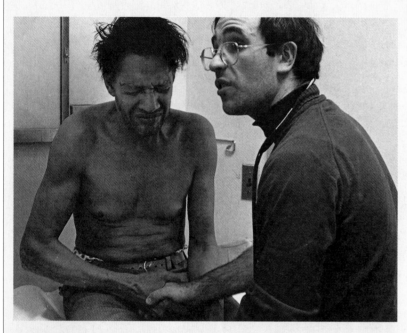

Figure 12-13b The crisis management offered by emergency room care provide for the continuing needs of patients with schizophrenic disorder.

Figure 12-13c Many individuals with schizophrenic disorder are unable to maintain adequate living conditions on their own.

ATTENTION, COGNITION, AND THE SCHIZOPHRENIC PROCESS

Attention Tasks Attention seems to be a central problem for those with schizophrenic disorder. Psychologists study attention problems both to understand more about deficits associated with schizophrenic disorder and also to identify markers for high-risk individuals. Tasks used to study attention include the **Continuous Performance Task, eye-tracking** of slowly moving objects, and the **Stroop task** that measures attention when there are competing sets of stimuli.

Information Processing Tasks Those with a diagnosis of schizophrenic disorder seem to have difficulty in maintaining an internal representation of a prior stimulus when a new one is presented.

Thought Disorder Disordered thought occurs to some extent in most people, but is observed most often in those with schizophrenic disorder. Antipsychotic medication seems to decrease the degree of this disordered thought.

THERAPEUTIC APPROACHES

Antipsychotic Drugs Antipsychotic drugs are the most standard treatment for schizophrenic disorder. For some individuals the drugs appear to suppress ongoing psychotic behavior but may not prevent a relapse or new psychotic episode. A new antipsychotic drug, **clozapine** has fewer unpleasant side effects for patients but must be used with careful monitoring because it may produce bone marrow failure. In general, early treatment with antipsychotic drugs may not only cut short psychotic symptoms but also improve long-term outcome. Noncompliance or stopping of medication is frequent among patients discharged from the hospital after their psychotic symptoms have decreased or because of unpleasant side effects. Whether a person is competent to decide to refuse treatment by medication is a difficult question to answer in schizophrenic disorder because of the disorder's cognitive effects.

Skills Training Social learning theory based on **social skills training** may decrease symptoms, increase social adjustment, and decrease chances of rehospitalization. It does not appear to prevent another psychotic episode. **Self-care skills** related to independent living are also taught by behavioral methods. These have been shown to aid transition to community living. Behavioral techniques have also been used to enhance **cognitive social skills** and to treat disordered cognitions that interfere with problem solving. For example, such training of those with schizophrenic disorder is focused on improving attention and the discrimination of social cues and modifying some of the disordered cognitions that affect the social problem-solving.

Family Interventions Family interventions are effective in preventing relapse and promoting better functioning of those with schizophrenic disorder. **Expressed emotion** (EE) is the term used for the attitudes family members show to others regarding a family member with a schizophrenic disorder. Negative expressed emotion has been associated with an increased rehospitalization rate. Patients whose families are high in negative EE are likely to relapse sooner than those with less critical families. **Family education** programs that educate family members about what to expect in the future, the importance of medication, and ways to reduce stress in family interactions have been found to help prevent relapse and rehospitalization. The programs help the family members gain skills to deal with the patient and also provide them with information about what is known about the psychobiology of schizophrenia. Another important skill for both the patient and the family is **relapse recognition**. This skill allows them to seek help more quickly.

Community Support **Milieu therapy** means that everyone associated with the patient helps to provide a residential therapeutic environment. This provides support and protection for the patient as well as structure and an opportunity for validation of symptoms. Another community support approach is not residential. In that approach the focus is on finding suitable living and working environments for the patient and providing for whatever needs he or she cannot fulfill independently.

LONG-TERM OUTCOME STUDIES

Findings from long-term studies suggest that some people affected by schizophrenia do fully recover, but that the percentage is low. Many others improve greatly but may not reach their former level of adjustment. Even those who do recover are considered to be vulnerable to another episode.

Long-term studies consistently show that a poor long-term outcome is more likely in schizophrenia than in other types of mental illness. The studies also show that five to ten years after the diagnosis of schizophrenic disorder, most people's degree of recovery tends to stabilize and continue unchanged in the future. The studies also show that no one treatment is clearly beneficial for everyone.

CHAPTER THIRTEEN

Jan Sawka, *The Shadow #5*, 1987.
Courtesy of the artist.

COGNITIVE IMPAIRMENT DISORDERS

Bob Oxley, age 39, had been a long distance runner and, until recently, seemed to be in excellent condition. One morning he awoke with the worst headache he had ever had, became too nauseated to eat, and lay in bed caught between dreams and delirium. After a great effort, he dragged himself to his office, but the pain intensified and he could barely call his wife to take him home. When she got him to the hospital, a CT scan detected a white haze of blood in the fluid-filled spaces around his brain. Swollen tissue cast a shadow across both of his frontal lobes. A dye injected into his blood vessels filled a grapelike enlargement that ballooned out from a weakened artery in the front of his brain. Blood had leaked from a tiny tear in this bulge, causing the severe headache, and then clotted—preventing Bob's death. However, Bob was left with a condition called aphasia, in which the individual has a problem finding words and expressing what he might want to say. The aphasia resulted from the fact that the language center in his left frontal lobe had been injured. When Bob wanted to refer to his doctor, he said "blotcher." When asked to name 10 animals he could not utter the names of more than two ("dog" and "cat"). When asked about his work, he said that he worked with "climates" (he was a stockbroker and worked with his clients). In most cases, Bob did not look distressed after his errors.

Ann Martin used to have an enviable memory. Now, at age 58, she forgets recent events and shows poor judgment. (She recently threw out a pair of valuable sterling silver salt and pepper shakers.) Because she can no longer balance her household budget, plan her meals, and take care of herself in other ways, she now lives in a retirement home, even though she is still relatively young. Her condition has been diagnosed as Alzheimer's disease, which is caused by physical degeneration in the brain. This disease results in loss of intellectual ability and changes in personality and behavior.

These two cases show both similarities and differences. They are different because Ann Martin's behavior was the result of a deterioration of brain tissue as the result of a disease process that affected many aspects of her intellectual functioning. Bob Oxley's problem was due to an injury that affected a specific brain function—his ability to translate thoughts into speech. Despite these differences, these two people are similar in that they are each experiencing the effects of changes in the brain.

DSM-IV categorizes mental disorders in terms of clusters of behavioral and psychological features that are associated with distress or disability. The causes of the disorders are usually either unknown or only imperfectly understood. For example, while there is some evidence of central nervous system dysfunction in schizophrenia, affective disorders, and obsessive-compulsive and other disorders, not enough is known to say that they are organically caused. Based on future research, organic factors may come to be regarded as defining features of these disorders or other disorders or be ruled out as specific causes. The disorders we review in this chapter comprise one of the few groupings in DSM-IV that involve both specific behavioral symptoms and known causative factors (Spitzer et al., 1992). In each of them there are characteristic disturbances of consciousness, memory, and/or other cognitive functioning in association with a medical condition or substance (injected, ingested, or inhaled) that is causally related to the disturbance. Establishing the link between the behavioral symptoms and the medical condition or substance is the key element in diagnosing the cognitive impairments we will be describing.

Our knowledge of the conditions that cause these disorders and their specific effects on brain function is increasing, not only because of new tools for study of the living brain, but also because of information about the interaction between organic functioning and personal characteristics and environmental variables. Despite these new techniques and new knowledge, for many people like Bob Oxley and Ann Martin who develop an organic brain disorder, their lives will never be the same again.

The Brain: An Interactional Perspective

The brain is an organ, like the kidney, the heart, or the liver, and organs are known to fail because of hereditary factors as well as environmental ones. Yet, to believe that the brain is merely a series of chemical reactions is to remove humans from any effects of their environment and their own actions. In fact, part of brain functions are "hard-wired" in advance of birth and part are designed to be shaped by experience.

At one time the prevailing view held that the brain grows through childhood, takes its final shape during adolescence, and then slowly ages. New work shows, however, that each area of the brain develops in unique ways throughout life. While some parts of the brain deteriorate, most brain cells continue to form new connections.

Three areas of brain research seem especially pertinent to an understanding of both normal and abnormal behavior:

1. Specifying how the brain grows and maintains itself
2. Identifying the mechanisms by which the brain acquires, stores, and uses information at the cellular and molecular levels, as well as the level of behavior and social interaction
3. Making clear the role played by the brain in monitoring and regulating internal bodily processes

In the past, people looked for physical causes for all forms of maladaptive behavior. If people behaved in odd ways, it was because there was something physically wrong with them. People could be "born criminals" or have "bad blood." Then scientists became aware of the psychological and social causes of behavioral problems. As a result, physical explanations came to be seen as inadequate and even as somewhat simpleminded. Today, however, psychologists are developing a more complete picture of how intertwined the psychological, social, and physical domains of human behavior are.

We learn social skills, interact with others, and acquire personal attitudes within a framework of physical development. Human functioning is influenced by organic events that occur during intrauterine life, the birth process, and the long period of development after birth. The brain may become damaged suddenly—for example, when a person has a stroke or receives a head injury in an accident (see Box 13-1). In other cases certain diseases cause slow deterioration in the brain. These changes in the brain's physical nature, whether they happen quickly or slowly, and whether they involve large or small areas, are often the cause of unusual behavior. Damage to the brain can lead to a wide variety of behavioral problems, depending on what part of the brain is affected and the extent of the damage.

What is known today about brain disorders is consistent with what we have said throughout this text about the interaction among personal and environmental factors, vulnerability, and stress. It would simplify the lives of clinicians and researchers if they could assume that certain types of maladaptation are due to personal variables, others to physical factors, and still others to situational pressures. Unfortunately, such an assumption

Sarah Fell and Her Life Was Changed

One April day 10-year-old Sarah Mon-ahan lost control of her bike and fell. She landed on a spiked piece of farm equipment and a two-inch spike punc-tured her left temple. Today, there is only a small scar, nothing to show the quarter-size hole where the spike shat-tered Sarah's skull and drove bone splinters into her brain. The accident left Sarah permanently brain-damaged, emotionally like a 2-year-old, and acad-emically at the third-grade level (see Figures 13-1 and 13-2). Her moods change in an instant, and she is increas-ingly aggressive toward her family and classmates. Her parents have been advised to lock up scissors and knives. Sarah once pushed her 2-year-old brother into a rock pile, cutting his head and requiring a trip to the emer-gency room. She had no concept she had done anything wrong. Sometimes Sarah hears voices. One evening while the family was watching television, she stood up and yelled, "If you say that again, I'll kill you." No one had said a word.

—Based on *Seattle Times*, March 15, 1991, pp. A1, A3

Figure 13-1 Sarah's external wounds have healed and she appears unaffected by her injury.

Figure 13-2 Sarah and her teacher rejoice in Sarah's success in completing a computer problem.

would be incorrect. Behavior is a joint product of indi-vidual differences and environmental variables. The particular mix of these variables determines how people act and what they think about. There is no standard type of psychological effect for each type and degree of brain defect.

Vulnerability to Brain Disorders

Not only are there many differences in the actual dam-age to the brain that occur in different individuals through injury or disease, but the same amount of brain damage or deterioration can have varying effects. To some degree, these effects depend on the individual's personality and abilities and the social supports avail-able to cushion the organic blow. Thus, there are many cases in which the psychological and behavioral effects of brain injuries and tumors do not conform to what would be expected on the basis of the amount of brain damage suffered.

The following are among the factors that influence vulnerability to brain damage and brain disorders:

1. *Age.* The age at which a brain condition develops can have both long- and short-term effects. Although in some instances an infant brain is better able to compensate for an injury than is an adult brain, the infant brain may also be more sus-ceptible to a variety of pathological conditions. Many behavioral deficits that are caused by damage to the brain in infancy are not noticed until consid-erably later.

2. *Social support.* The presence of caring, accepting peo-ple on whom the individual can rely usually eases adjustment to a brain condition. Social isolation, on the other hand, increases cognitive deficits and, thus, abnormal behavior.

3. *Stress.* The greater the stress, the greater both the cognitive and behavioral deficits will be. Elderly peo-ple with chronic brain conditions often show marked deterioration following a piling up of stressful life events such as retirement or the death of a spouse.

4. *Personality factors.* It is a common clinical observation that some people react with intense anxiety, feelings of depersonalization, paranoid

thinking, defensiveness, and hallucinations to any condition that causes even mild clouding of consciousness and impairment of cognitive and perceptual functioning.

5. *Physical condition.* The site of brain disorder, the rate of onset of the disorder, and the duration of the disorder all influence the clinical picture. In addition, the individual's general level of health plays a role in his or her adjustment.

An individual's psychological state and social relationships at the onset of an organic condition can influence the impact of the condition on his or her behavior. A person with a stable personal life, for example, usually responds differently, and more adaptively, to treatment than does someone in the throes of marital turmoil or financial reversal. When personal problems complicate an organic condition, both medical and psychological treatment may be necessary. In addition to its personal effects, impairment of brain function has a profound influence on interpersonal relationships. For example, people with epilepsy suffer from undesirable social consequences as well as from the seizures themselves.

Because determining the presence and extent of brain damage is complicated by the need to isolate its effects from those caused by personal and social factors, clinicians must avoid overly simple diagnoses. Clearly, a person who is noticeably disoriented, has trouble solving problems, and displays shallow or very changeable moods and emotions is suffering from some sort of behavioral problem. But the primary aspects of the diagnosis—an estimate of the roles played by organic damage, personality, and life stress in causing the disturbance—are not so easily determined.

Assessing Brain Damage

While the list of rare brain disorders is long, many brain disorders that have major impacts on thought and behavior are fairly common. For example, brain injuries, epilepsy, and acute cerebrovascular diseases are more common than schizophrenia and panic disorders (Silver et al., 1990). Consequently, the task of correctly identifying conditions that might be due to brain malfunction is an important one. This task is complicated by the fact that damage to a particular area of the brain can have diverse effects. This point is illustrated in Table 13-1, which lists symptoms often seen in patients who have disorders related to malfunction of the brain's frontal lobes.

A variety of procedures are used in assessing the extent of damage or deterioration of the brain. In addition to a general physical evaluation, clinical tests may

---

TABLE 13–1
Personality and Cognitive Changes in Patients with Disorders Related to Frontal Lobe Malfunctions

Apathy; loss of interest in social interactions
Inattention to personal appearance
Boisterousness; profanity; increased volume of speech
Irritability; violence
Increased risk-taking
Overeating; overdrinking
Reduced capacity to use language, symbols, and logic
Diminished ability to concentrate
Loss of orientation of time or place

Source: Adapted from Silver and others, 1990

---

include a mental-status examination, neuropsychological testing, and both traditional X-rays and newer radiological techniques such as CT and PET scans that provide information on the brain's soft tissues and chemical activity.

Mental-Status and Neuropsychological Testing The **mental-status examination** consists of an interview, which is useful for clinical observation as well as for any statements the individual might make. The mental-status examination is often supplemented by psychological testing and a neurological examination. Clinicians use the mental-status examination to elicit the following information.

1. Level of consciousness—how aware is the individual of what is going on?
2. General appearance (behavior, dress, cooperation)
3. Attention span
4. Orientation with regard to time and place
5. Short-term memory (events of past life or common knowledge)
6. Language (spontaneous speech, comprehension, repetition, reading, writing)
7. Stream of thought—do the individual's ideas fit together logically?
8. Mood
9. Judgment and insight

Use of the mental-status examination is not limited to cases of suspected brain damage. It is employed generally to describe patients' behavior at the time they are seen clinically. It provides an objective record that is important for diagnosis and for assessing the course of a disorder and its subsequent response to treatment. Careful and precise descriptions of behavior, without speculations and inferences, are necessary in recording the mental-status examination. Its results are interpreted in conjunction with information about a patient's history, data from a physical examination, and the results of laboratory tests.

Neuropsychologists use various techniques to assess brain damage and its cause. As discussed in chapter 3, neuropsychology is a relatively new branch of psychology that deals with relationships between behavior and the condition of the brain. Clinical neuropsychologists are particularly interested in the effects of brain lesions on behavior. Neuropsychological tests are used to assess impairment in such areas as awareness of and responsiveness to sensory stimulation, ability to understand verbal communication and to express oneself, and emotional expression. Neuropsychological testing is sensitive to impaired functioning of various regions of the brain.

Brain Imaging Progress in constructing tests to measure disturbances in various regions of the brain has been limited by the lack of direct information about what actually goes on in the brain. As we have seen in previous chapters, new technology using a variety of brain-imaging techniques is rapidly changing this situation. This technology contributes to clarifying the relationship between damage to specific regions of the brain and its effects on psychological functioning. This chapter, which focuses on brain disorders, is a good place to review some of the information about scanning techniques. Figure 13-3 shows the basic principles involved in three of the most widely used scanning techniques—computerized tomography (CT scan), positron emission tomography (PET scan), and magnetic resonance imaging (MRI).

The CT scan provides films that show where injuries, deterioration, or enlargement occurred. The PET scan allows researchers to visualize the activity of different parts of the human brain. A PET scan shows patterns of glucose utilization—an index of brain activity—in different parts of the brain. Much as weather maps show various levels of rainfall, a PET scan shows the levels of glucose metabolism in different brain areas as they vary with the person's mental state and behavior. The PET scan enables scientists to study biochemical changes in the brain that could never be charted before. Whereas the CT scan shows the brain's anatomy, the PET scan reveals the varying strength of biochemical processes that occur in different areas of the brain. The PET scan is the most elegant of the available imaging techniques because of its sensitivity and flexibility. PET scans permit the assessment of metabolic activity and the measurement of neurotransmitter function.

Magnetic resonance imaging (MRI) uses arrays of sensitive detectors placed over the head to locate and

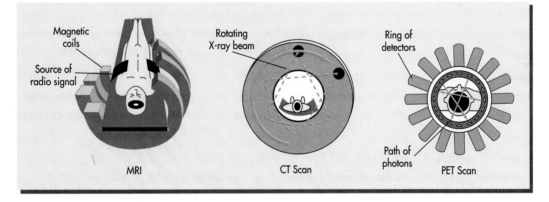

Figure 13-3 Each of the three major scanning techniques used to study the brain produces images in a different way and, as the text explains, each type of scan may have somewhat different uses.

Magnetic resonance imaging (MRI) uses energy in the form of radio waves. After the patient is placed inside the imaging device, a strong magnetic field is created. Under these conditions atoms in each type of tissue resonate differently. A computer uses these resonation patterns to recreate a composite picture or scan.

Computer tomography (CT) operates through a narrowly focused X-ray that is rotated rapidly around the patient's body as the patient lies in the scanner. A computer then builds an image of a thin slice of the body from measures of the radiation passing through the patient as the X-ray source moves from one location to another.

In order to use positron emission tomography (PET) scanning procedures, radioactive chemicals must first be injected into the patient's body. As these chemicals are metabolized and move through the patient's body, they emit positively charged electrons or positrons. Electrons and positrons then collide and emit pairs of photons that create signals by hitting detectors in the apparatus. These signals are then converted by a computer into a map of chemical activity.

measure precise sites of neural activity deep within the brain's furrows and creases. Both the MRI and the CT scan provide visualizations of brain anatomy and possible structural abnormalities. Unlike the CT, which is limited to imaging brain regions in a transverse plane, the MRI can image in all planes.

The Brain and Cognitive Impairment

Many conditions marked by cognitive impairment basically are outgrowths of bodily conditions. From this perspective, the observed psychological syndromes are secondary to physical factors. (Clusters of symptoms that tend to appear together form a **syndrome.**) These symptoms include disturbances in perception, memory, imagination, thought processing, problem-solving skills, and judgment. The most common syndromes involve delirium, dementia, amnesia, intoxication, and withdrawal. This chapter emphasizes disorders marked by delirium, dementia, and amnesia; chapter 14 focuses on intoxication and withdrawal.

Delirium affects the person's state of consciousness or attention, whereas dementia refers to loss of intellectual ability. Delirium is often a short-term condition that is reversible; dementia generally implies a nonreversible and often progressive condition. Amnestic disorders are memory disturbances due either to a medical condition or the effects of a substance (for example, abuse of an illegal drug or a medication).

Delirium

The symptoms of **delirium** include relatively global cognitive impairment, disorientation, and confusion. In delirium, an individual has difficulty mobilizing, focusing, shifting, and sustaining attention. A wide and changeable range of strong emotions that do not seem related to environmental events may be evident.

DSM-IV's diagnostic criteria for delirium are:

1. Disturbances of consciousness (for example, reduced awareness of what is going on in the environment) and reduced ability to focus, sustain, or shift attention.
2. Cognitive deficits and perceptual disturbances (for example, memory loss, disorientation).
3. The symptoms develop over a short period of time (usually, from hours to days, and fluctuate during the course of a day).
4. Evidence that the condition is caused by the direct physiological consequences of a medical condition or intoxication attributable to a psychoactive substance, such as alcohol.

Delirium can occur as a result of either an acute or a chronic brain condition. There are four general organic causes of delirium:

1. Brain disease (for example, an infection or tumor)
2. A disease or infection in another part of the body that affects the brain (for example, a metabolic condition)
3. Intoxication (for example, with alcohol)
4. Withdrawal from a substance to which an individual is addicted (for example, drugs).

Delirium generally accompanies some other serious physical problem; about 10 percent of hospitalized medical and surgical patients (especially those who are elderly) become delirious (Lipowski, 1987). A person who is hospitalized after a heart attack may become delirious because the amount of oxygen the brain receives could depend on whether the patient is sitting up or lying down. Inadequate excretion of body wastes can also cause delirium. For example, if the kidneys fail to function, the toxins that are usually filtered out by the kidneys and excreted in the urine will accumulate in the bloodstream and the blood will have less room for oxygen. As a result of such physical disturbances, the brain begins to starve for oxygen, and symptoms of delirium may occur. The symptoms generally disappear shortly after the precipitating condition has been corrected.

Psychological stress, sleep and sensory deprivation, prolonged immobilization, and severe fatigue are likely to contribute to the onset of delirium and to increase its severity. It is believed that a general derangement of brain metabolism coupled with an imbalance in the neurotransmitters underlie all cases of delirium.

Although everyone has the potential to develop delirium, there appear to be wide variations in susceptibility. Some people become delirious in response to metabolic changes or medications that do not produce delirium in others, whereas others fail to become delirious under metabolic conditions that are likely to produce delirium in most people. The incidence of delirium is highest among old people. It is not known to what extent this increase is a function of age itself rather than the frequency of brain disease and systemic disease in old age.

Patients with brain lesions are especially liable to develop delirium, as are people with long histories of alcohol or drug addiction. Delirium is frequent following surgery—either immediately or after a lucid period of several days—and seems to be due to the physical stress of the surgery itself and to the psychological stress of the surgery and the postoperative period. In a sense, delirium is a threshold phenomenon; that is, each individual may have a specific threshold for this condition. Preexisting brain damage, addiction, and certain chronic medical disorders probably bring people close to this threshold even if they do not exceed it; relatively small metabolic changes may then push the patient over the threshold.

Delirium Tremens

One of the most dramatic examples of delirium can be seen in an acute brain condition called **delirium tremens** (or "the DTs") that may sometimes result from excessive alcohol consumption. People with the DTs may be unable to follow directions like "stick out your tongue" or to attend to events going on around them. In addition to delirium, the DTs are characterized by tremors and visual hallucinations that result in a state of terror. The following excerpt from Mark Twain's *Huckleberry Finn* is a vivid description of the DTs experienced by Pap, a heavy user of alcohol for many years.

I don't know how long I was asleep, but all of a sudden there was an awful scream and I was up. There was Pap looking wild, and skipping around every which way and yelling about snakes. He said they was crawling up his legs; and then he would give a jump and scream, and say one had bit him on the cheek—but I couldn't see no snakes. He started running round and round the cabin, hollering, "Take him off, take him off; he's biting me on the neck." I never see a man look so wild in the eyes. Pretty soon he was all fagged out, and fell down panting; then he rolled over and over wonderful fast, kicking things every which way, striking and grabbing at the air with his hands, and screaming and saying there was devils a-hold of him. He wore out by and by, and laid still awhile, moaning. Then he laid stiller, and didn't make a sound. I could hear the owls and wolves away off in the woods, and it seemed terrible still. He was lying over by the corner. By and by he raised up part way and listened, with his head to one side. He says, very low: "Tramp-tramp-tramp; they're coming after me but I won't go. Oh, they're here, don't touch me—don't! Hands off—they're cold; let go. Oh, let a poor devil alone." Then he went down on all fours and crawled off, begging them to let him alone, and he rolled himself up in his blanket and wallowed in under the old pine table, still a-begging; and then he went to crying. I could hear him through the blanket.

The symptoms of delirium tremens usually are not evident until after the person has stopped drinking. Several aspects of the mechanism that causes its symptoms are not well understood, but the DTs seem to be due to the prolonged interference of alcohol with the metabo-lism of neurons. The condition occurs in about five percent of alcoholics. Regardless of the cause (alcohol, infection, and so on), diffuse slowing of brainwave patterns is a regular finding.

Delirium tremens can last for a week or longer and the affected person usually must be hospitalized. During an episode of the DTs, the patient's physical condition deteriorates and he or she becomes highly susceptible to infections. Tranquilizing drugs and a quiet and orderly environment are essential, since even routine conversations among hospital personnel may frighten the patient and heighten his or her hallucinatory experiences. Renewed ability to sleep and rest usually indicates that an episode of DTs is coming to an end. However, recovery depends on restoration of metabolic equilibrium. In some cases equilibrium cannot be restored and death occurs.

Dementia

I fear I am not in my perfect mind.
Methinks I should know you, and know this man;
Yet I am doubtful; for I am mainly ignorant
What place this is; and all the skill I have
Remembers not these garments; nor I know not
Where I did lodge last night. Do not laugh at me . . .
—Shakespeare, *King Lear*, Act IV, Scene 7

The onset of King Lear's madness shows the symptoms of dementia that people have witnessed for centuries. The essential feature of **brain deterioration,** or **dementia,** is a gradual loss of intellectual abilities that is sufficient to interfere with social or occupational functioning. Memory impairment, decline in ability to exercise good judgment and engage in abstract thinking, loss of self-control, confusion, language and motor problems, and personality changes also occur. Dementia may be progressive, static, or even reversible if an effective treatment is available. Because individuals with dementia are not able to think clearly and often have difficulty making rational judgments, they are particularly vulnerable to physical, psychological, and social stress. Individuals with dementia are more likely than other people to experience delirium.

The onset of dementia is insidious, and the course of the disorder is usually gradual. The term **senile dementia** is often used to refer to the condition when it occurs in people over 65 (see Figure 13-4). Autopsies show that most senile dementias have the characteristics of *Alzheimer's disease,* which will be discussed later in the chapter. If dementia occurs in younger individuals, it is termed **presenile dementia.** In people with this condi-

Figure 13-4 Dementia was not a major public health concern prior to the twentieth century because few people lived beyond the age of 75, and dementia is largely a problem associated with advanced age. Today, more than 50 percent of the entire U.S. population reaches age 75 years and 25 percent live to be 85. The U.S. Census Bureau estimates that by the year 2000 there will be 35 million persons older than 65 years and that by the year 2050 this number will rise to 67 million. A large number of older people in nursing homes have some degree of dementia. The economic impact of dementia is great, running into the billions of dollars each year.

patterns before the onset of senility, including actual and severe psychotic or neurotic reaction patterns, or more likely, tendencies in those directions. These tendencies are made worse by the onset of senility, but they are not caused by it. One common symptom is **confabulation:** when faced with loss of particular memories, the individual fills in memory gaps with detailed, but inaccurate, accounts of his or her activities (Horvath et al., 1989).

Over half of the cases that are diagnosed as senile dementia show various combinations of agitation, paranoid thinking, and schizophreniclike reactions. Depressive features are especially common in cases of dementia and include restlessness at night, irritability, narrowing of interests, and loss of initiative. Table 13-2 lists some of the ways to differentiate dementia from depression. The following case illustrates the combination of symptoms often seen in dementia.

A talented artist was referred by his wife; he had become anxious and mildly depressed when his first symptoms emerged. In many respects he was very fortunate. At the age of 65 he had achieved a national, even international, reputation as an illustrator . . . [he] had devised a special process used to produce color covers and prints. . . . Recognition of his work gained him election to one of the distinguished clubs of artists in the city. There had been some beginning failure in his memory. He complained of some difficulty in the use of his hands and arms, a clumsiness and lack of precision that did not exist before. When first seen, he advised that his father had become senile . . . and had had a slowly progressive course of increasing mental impairment, which the patient feared for himself. . . . He was accompanied on his first visit by his wife. . . . They had been married 30 years and had two daughters, both married. . . .

tion there is a progressive atrophy (degeneration) of brain tissue, and their brainwave patterns are almost invariably abnormal. The individual becomes increasingly subject to lapses of memory, poor judgment, and disorientation. Deterioration in personal habits is common, and behavior may become unpredictable and impulsive. Because the person often remembers past events better than recent ones, he or she seems to live in the past much of the time.

The rate at which behavior is affected and the manner in which it changes are influenced by many factors, not the least of which is the individual's reaction to the physical and psychological deterioration. A sizable percentage of people with dementia seem to undergo profound personality changes. However, these changes may be in degree rather than basic alterations of personality. For these people reconstruction of their earlier personalities may uncover the presence of maladaptive behavior

TABLE 13–2 Signs and Symptoms that Help Distinguish Depression from Dementia	
Dementia	**Depression**
Even progression over months or years	Uneven progression over weeks
Attempts to hide memory loss	Complaints of memory loss
Worse later in day or when fatigued	Often worse in morning, better as day goes on
Unawareness of or minimizing of disability	Awareness of and exaggeration of disability
Abuse of drugs rare	Possible abuse of alcohol or other drugs

Source: Based on Heston and White, 1991

[His wife] declared that at home he had become critical and querulous. He seemed to avoid going out to meet his artist friends. Furthermore, in contrast to his usual self-assurance at his work, he seemed anxious and upset when requested to take on a new contract. His concern over his abilities, his doubts, and even refusal of work were reflected in his relations with his wife. [Over the succeeding months it was learned that she had commenced to drink and did not seem as interested in the care of the house.] Also, he said his daughters were hounding him. Although he was able to talk most interestingly of his past work and life, it was clear that he had difficulty in recalling his earlier visits with his physician, when they occurred, or what had been discussed. The course was slowly progressive. As time went on, the tension and near panic he felt over inability to perform, on the recognition of his slowly progressive impairment of perception and skill, accompanied by much anxiety in meeting his business and social acquaintances, continued to increase. . . . The failure in this mental functioning proceeded slowly. Periods of disorientation were first noticed at night when he arose to go to the bathroom. Some six years after onset he became seriously disturbed, had the delusion that men were attempting to kill him, and hallucinated voices. . . . He would talk to [his wife] of planning a Christmas card, but would forget that his daughters were married. His death, in a local general hospital, occurred quickly from cardiac arrest seven years after he was first seen.

—Kolb and Brodie, 1982, pp. 238–239

Alzheimer's Disease

Dementia is primarily a problem of the aged. For many years most of the problems of older people were lumped together under the heading of "senile disorders." We now know that several different types of psychological and behavioral problems occur among old people. The elderly are vulnerable both to serious consequences of brain changes such as senile dementia and to certain other psychological conditions such as those in which the role of organic factors is much less clear-cut. For example, depressive episodes increase in both frequency and depth in the later years of life (Hamilton, 1989). Depression is likely to be provoked by the beginning of an illness or disability, or the death of a spouse, but given time, most people adjust to these changes. The majority of severe depressions in old age are relapses, although new cases may occur even after the age of 75. Paranoid and hypochondriacal disorders are also common in older people.

Overall, the major clinical challenge facing the elderly is the greater likelihood of disorders in which there is brain degeneration. However, the problems of the elderly also reflect a number of other psychological problems that often accompany increased age. These problems seem to be outgrowths of personal insecurities evoked by such life changes as having to live alone or being supported by others (Hansson & Carpenter, 1994). At the same time, physiological changes may create additional stress as the person seeks to maintain self-esteem and competent, satisfying interactions. It would not be an exaggeration to say that the daily stresses the elderly have to cope with are often so numerous and so severe that they would probably tax the coping resources of young adults.

Dementia often has been regarded as an extreme of the inevitable intellectual decline of people as they get older. This belief has been evaluated and Box 13-2 presents some of the pertinent evidence.

The following account was written by a medical student who had been working with a patient with **Alzheimer's disease** who showed significant cognitive impairment. It conveys some of the reality of this insidious, heartbreaking, malady that is associated with advancing age.

I visited Margo at her home each day. On my way, I'd pick up whatever she needed from the store, or sometimes a treat. Her favorite is peanut butter and jelly sandwiches on white bread. She can devour two in one sitting, especially if milk is at hand. Given her size, this always amazes me.

At the apartment, Margo's Jamaican home attendant, Louise, welcomed me with giggles and smiles, probably because my visit signaled a relief from her duties. It took Louise a few minutes to open the door since it was rigged with an array of locks and chains designed to keep Margo from slipping out in the night. Before the locks were installed, Margo had, on occasion, satisfied her understandable desire to explore the city on her own. We usually found her a couple of days later when we learned of a police report describing a woman in a nightgown seen roaming Central Park. Bad things have happened during these excursions. Does Margo understand that she is locked inside for her own safety? . . .

Margo never called me by name. I never figured out if she just forgot it from one day to the next or whether she ever actually remembered me at all. If I asked her, she would say she knew who I was. But that could have just been adaptive politeness. I probably looked like I wanted to be remembered.

—Firlik, 1991, p. 201

Alzheimer's disease is marked by memory lapses and confusion. Dementia associated with this disease inevitably worsens. One woman said that she did not understand her husband's Alzheimer's condition until the night they gave a dinner party at their home. "It was a very nice evening; we all had a wonderful time. And

Psychological Functioning Over Time

Three points need to be kept in mind about the elderly. One is that there are many examples of successful old people—people who are active, feel that they have something to offer, and make contributions to their families and communities. There is no better example of successful aging than the artist Anna Mary Robertson, better known as Grandma Moses (1860–1961), who first exhibited her paintings at age 78 (see Figure 13-5).

People who age successfully may suffer the physical declines that are frequent among the elderly, but they are resilient and have found ways to work around them. A second point is that there is every reason to believe that most people can adapt successfully to the developmental transitions they encounter throughout life (Schaie, 1989). The third point is that there has been an unfortunate clinical neglect of older people. This is particularly true with regard to their psychological needs. Counseling and psychotherapy for the aged have often been dismissed as a waste of time.

Figure 13-5 Grandma Moses was untrained as an artist and did not start painting in earnest until she was in her seventies. *The Daughter's Homecoming* was painted when she was 87. She did more than just live a long time and paint. She took the commonplaces of daily life, things we rarely look at because they are so homely, and gave them back their sense of wonder. As she looked at her extraordinary life, Grandma Moses said: "I look back on my life like a good day's work, it was done and I felt satisfied with it. I was happy and contented, I know nothing better, and made the best out of what life offered. And life is what we make it, always has been, always will be." Quote from Grandma Moses: *My Life's History* Copyright © 1952 (renewed 1980). Grandma Moses Properties Co., New York.

then as people were getting ready to leave, my husband put on his coat to leave with them. He didn't know he was in his own home." Diagnosis of the disease is based in part on the patient's inability to answer simple questions like "What is the (year) (season) (date) and (month)?" and to perform assigned tasks like, "Count backwards from a given number (like 100) by subtracting 7s" and "Spell the word 'world' backwards." People with Alzheimer's disease forget how to cook, go on wild spending sprees, lose the ability to balance their checkbooks and count change, forget how to drive a car, and lose creative abilities (see Figure 13-7). Nearly total bodily and behavioral deterioration is typical in its final stages.

BOX 13-5

Yet many older people need opportunities to express their reactions to the variety of problems they face and to receive the support and advice of trusted clinicians.

One of the few longitudinal studies of the relationship between age and intellectual functioning is the Seattle Longitudinal Study (Schaie, 1994). The original subjects, who ranged in age from 18 to 67, have now been tested up to six times over a 35-year period. The data from the Seattle Longitudinal Study suggest that there are very great individual differences in intellec-tual change throughout adulthood. Figure 13-6 illustrates some of the results of the study. This figure shows that only for tasks that involve perceptual speed is there a steep decline beginning in young adulthood. Numeric ability shows an early plateau with a steep decline begin-ning in the 60s. The other four abilities reach a plateau by age 53 followed by only modest decline.

There is some evidence concern-ing predictors of good mental function-ing in old age (Schaie, 1989). These include a high level of ability in reading comprehension or verbal fluency, a successful career or some other active involvement through life, and continuing keen mental interests after retirement. Resiliency and having a flexible attitude in middle age is also a predictor of good functioning in later life. There is less mental decline in people who adapt easily to change, who like learning new things, and enjoy going to new places. Simply living with someone with these characteristics can be beneficial. It helps to have a high-functioning spouse.

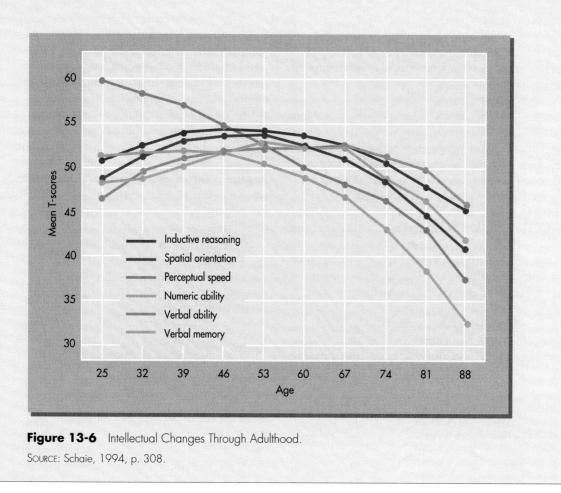

Figure 13-6 Intellectual Changes Through Adulthood.
SOURCE: Schaie, 1994, p. 308.

The challenges confronting those who live with and take care of Alzheimer's patients are considerable. Some of caretakers' most common behavioral concerns for their patients are listed below:

1. *Depression.* Unhappiness and withdrawal are com-mon in Alzheimer's disease patients.

2. *Hostility, belligerence, and aggression.* Alzheimer's patients can be selfish and hostile.

3. *Disorientation.* The Alzheimer's patient will become increasingly confused about people, places, and time.

4. *Wandering.* Wandering and restlessness are common problems.

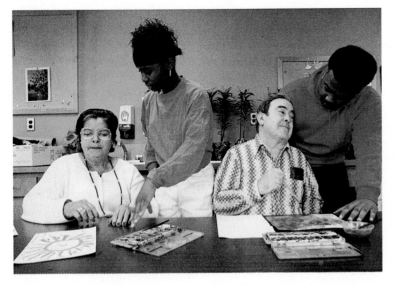

Figure 13-7 College students teach a painting class for Alzheimer's patients at a day care facility. The center plans activities to meet the needs and abilities of each patient.

5. *Anxiety and suspiciousness.* Worries and paranoid thinking occur.

By far the leading cause of mental deterioration among the elderly, Alzheimer's disease probably affects over 10 percent of all people over 65 (Evans et al., 1989). However, estimates concerning the prevalence of the disease vary from study to study depending on the severity of the symptoms used to define dementia. Table 13-3 contains a summary of 22 studies that excluded cases of mild dementia. The table shows how steeply the prevalence rises with age.

The disease tends to run in families and to be more frequent among females than among males. Because most Alzheimer's patients must eventually be placed in institutions, the disease (which has an average duration of about seven years) places tremendous demands on health-care resources. Alzheimer's victims constitute 50 to 60 percent of the 1.3 million people in nursing

homes, accounting for more than half of the many billions of dollars spent annually on nursing home care. The disease will become more common and take an even greater toll as the average age of the U.S. population continues to increase. The part of the population over age 85 is particularly at risk for Alzheimer's disease (Advisory Panel on Alzheimer's Disease, 1991). By the year 2040 the number of people in this age group, the fastest growing segment of the United States population, is expected to be five times greater than it is currently. Based on the proportion of cases currently in that age group, it has been estimated that at that time the number of cases of Alzheimer's disease may exceed 6 million.

Alzheimer's disease is also the most common form of presenile dementia. In these cases also, it usually causes gradual intellectual deterioration with growing lapses of memory (see Table 13-4). The progressive destruction of nervous tissue leads to slurring of speech, involuntary movements of arms and legs, and in some cases, seizures. When the disease manifests itself primarily in the intellectual sphere, the individual may experience great anxiety about the deterioration of his or her abilities.

Research Directions Alzheimer's disease was first identified in 1906 by a German physician, Alois Alzheimer. His patient, a 51-year-old woman, suffered loss of memory, disorientation, and later, severe dementia. After her death, Alzheimer performed an autopsy on her brain and found the two distinctive characteristics of the disease: tangled clumps of nerve cells and patches of disintegrated nerve-cell branches called *plaques*. Because the patients Alzheimer studied were relatively young, he thought the disease to be one of middle age; similar symptoms in elderly people were generally regarded as a natural consequence of aging by Alzheimer and his contemporaries. Today this view has been discarded. Dementias of the Alzheimer's type seem to involve a specific pathological process rather than being a normal consequence of aging. Researchers have looked to many sources for information about possible causes of the disease. There is growing reason to believe that different cases of Alzheimer's disease can spring from different causes. Rather than a single illness, the disease may be a group of closely associated disorders that involve both genetic and nongenetic factors.

Neurochemicals One of the keys to Alzheimer's disease may be a certain type of brain cell, the cholinergic cell, that is involved in memory and learning. These cells release an important chemical messenger called **acetylcholine.** Acetylcholine is a key player

TABLE 13–3 Prevalence of Dementia	
Age	**Prevalence**
60–64	0.7
65–69	1.4
70–74	2.8
75–79	5.6
80–84	10.5
85–89	20.8
90–95	38.6
Source: Keen, 1993	

TABLE 13–4
Phases in the Cognitive Decline Accompanying Alzheimer's Disease

Phase	Examples
1. Complaints of memory deficit	Forgetting names that one formerly knew well
2. Increased cognitive decline and signs of confusion	Losing or misplacing an object of value
3. Moderately severe cognitive decline and intensified confusion (early dementia)	Inability to recall major aspects of one's life, such as the names of close family members
4. Severe cognitive decline and confusion (middle dementia)	Largely unaware of all recent events and experiences
5. Very severe cognitive decline and confusion (late dementia)	Loss of all verbal abilities, need for assistance in eating and toileting

Source: Based on Reisberg, 1985.

in brain activity. When it is released by the cholinergic cell, it stimulates neighboring cells and causes them to release other chemicals and these chemicals in turn influence still other cells. Alzheimer's disease evidently throws a wrench into this process. For reasons that are not yet understood, people with advanced Alzheimer's disease lose up to 80 percent of their cholinergic cells in key brain areas. As a result, there also is a dramatic reduction in the amount of acetylcholine produced in the brain. There is a strong correlation between the amount of loss of acetylcholine or cholinergic cells in an individual's brain and the severity of that person's dementia. One focus of current research is the development of drugs that will increase the formation of acetylcholine, prevent its destruction, or directly stimulate acetylcholine receptors. Current research also suggests that biochemical abnormalities in Alzheimer's disease are not limited to the cholinergic system. There are deficiencies in other systems as well, for example, cell loss in the noradrenergic system which is another chemical messenger system (Advisory Panel on Alzheimer's Disease, 1991; Coyle et al., 1983).

Genes The fact that Alzheimer's disease often occurs in several members of the same family suggests that a genetic factor is at work. Half the immediate family members of patients with Alzheimer's disease may develop the devastating mental disorder if they live into their nineties. Growing evidence indicates that Alzheimer's disease is a hereditary disease, governed by a gene or genes that cause damage to the patient's brain late in life (Corder et al., 1993). Some studies have linked the disease to abnormalities on chromosome 21, which has been identified as the location of the gene for a protein called *beta amyloid* found in the characteristic clumps and plaques of Alzheimer's disease. Laboratory studies have shown that beta amyloid fragments can kill nerve cells. However, it is not completely clear that the

presence of beta amyloid in the brains of those with Alzheimer's disease is the cause, rather than the result of, the process of brain cell degeneration. The degeneration might be due to a protein called *apolipoprotein E* (Apo E). A high percentage of Alzheimer's patients have at least one gene coding for the type of Apo E protein known as *E4*. Apo E4 may be a risk factor for Alzheimer's disease, just as high cholesterol is a risk factor for heart disease (Cotton, 1994).

Screening for hereditary influences in Alzheimer's disease might reveal genetic markers, and it might be possible to identify environmental factors that influence the age of onset and the progress of the disease. However, experts are divided on whether all cases of Alzheimer's disease will turn out to be caused by genes. Research on this topic is complicated by the fact that because the disease occurs so late in life, many people who might be destined to get it die from other causes first.

Alzheimer's Effect on the Family In addition to searching for the causes of Alzheimer's disease, researchers are attempting to find ways of treating not only the patient but caregivers as well. Those who care for people with Alzheimer's disease often experience severe stress. Marian Roach has provided the following description of her reactions and those of her sister, Margaret, to their mother's deterioration as a result of Alzheimer's disease.

I noticed that she had stopped taking phone messages. One friend said she sounded "jealous and hostile." She would abruptly hang up on people. She became obsessed with the plumbing: She would look under the sinks and start to take apart the pipes, convinced there was a drip. She would walk away in the middle of conversation. She became repetitive, depressed.

—Roach, 1983, p. 23

As the deterioration continued, the pressures and emotional strain worsened.

Margaret and I have no relatives but my mother. The decisions we make are made together. Margaret works until 11 at night and on weekends. We have a young woman who lives in the house from Monday through Friday. Another woman comes on Friday and Saturday nights. Yet another takes my mother out—for rides or to the movies—three afternoons a week. But the burden of care is on my patient sister, who manages the schedules and sees my mother daily. I work during the day. I am with my mother on Sundays.

As I have gotten to know this disease, I have felt ashamed at my own embarrassment. I find myself explaining her condition to people, to excuse her behavior. Sometimes I do this in front of her and, for an instant, my mother will look terribly embarrassed. I see it in her face and I feel very unlike a daughter. I feel like a traitor. And then she will forget my explanation of her "memory problem," and her questions and repetitions, along with my embarrassment, will continue. Alzheimer's victims are likely to say or do anything during the stages just before they can do literally nothing for themselves. It is difficult to know what to expect. The anticipation is sometimes the worst part.

I sometimes dread the weekends. I try not to cry in front of Margaret, who tries not to cry in front of me. Margaret and I have discussed the possibility of our contracting the disease. If I get it, I have said that I'd want Margaret to kill me; she has said the same.

—Roach, 1983, p. 31

Research on the particularly stressful aspects of caring for Alzheimer's victims has shown that the sense of lack of control over what will happen next is of great importance. In addition, caregivers feel isolated, unable to deal effectively with the continuing stress, and confused about their own reactions. Support groups and group therapy can be valuable in allowing family members to express their feelings, particularly those that they consider unacceptable (for example, anger and disappointment). The opportunity to compare their experiences with those of other people who are going through the same trial often makes them aware that such feelings are normal and understandable (see Figure 13-8).

The following coping strategies can be useful aids to Alzheimer's caretakers:

1. Try to increase activities that patients formerly enjoyed and can still manage. Try to involve them in such activities, perhaps with another family member or a friend. Talk with them; reminisce about family, friends, and activities.
2. Confronting the situation head-on and trying to reason with Alzheimer's patients will not work.

Figure 13-8 Not only those with Alzheimer's disease, but also other family members, feel the impact of the cognitive and behavioral changes that result from this disorder. Counseling sessions for family members, including the patient, can be helpful to develop strategies for care and also to reduce stress experienced by all family members.

Being reassuring and calm may help to reduce the hostility. Trying to distract the patient with questions about the problem and gradually moving his or her attention to something else may also help.

3. Labeling items, or color coding rooms such as the bathroom or bedroom, can alleviate some problems in the early stages of the disease (see Figure 13-9). Talking in a calm voice and reassuring patients of where they are and whom they are with, may help ease feelings of being lost and alone.
4. Keeping the household free of clutter is a major consideration so that there is not added confusion or harm to the patient as he or she wanders through what was once a familiar environment. Identification bracelets and safety locks are other useful devices for those individuals who are given to wandering. Walking and other physical exercises may help alleviate such problems.
5. Patient fears and anxieties cannot really be dealt with in a rational and normal manner. Identifying what is frightening patients may be helpful, but directly confronting and telling them there is nothing to their concerns will not work. It is often useful to develop calming answers to the situation that is frightening and then to distract the patient to another subject.

Because there is no cure and because of the daily stress experienced by caretakers, Alzheimer's disease is a source of great anxiety for many people. All too often anxiety leads to efforts to deal with a concern or problem by hiding it from other people. It is as if it were

Figure 13-9 Alzheimer's disease has a profound effect, not only on the person who develops it, but also on the lives of all the members of the family. In this home, reminder signs are used to lessen the memory problems Alzheimer's disease creates.

something to be ashamed of. There is a need to bring concerns about Alzheimer's disease into the open so that its reality can be accepted and dealt with in as constructive a way as possible. For this reason, former President Ronald Reagan's announcement in November 1994 that he had the disease was a valuable contribution to public education about the Alzheimer's syndrome (see Figure 13-10). Earlier in their lives, President and Mrs. Reagan's sharing of information about their medical problems proved to be valuable, not only from an educational standpoint, but also as a boost to the morale of other affected people.

Treatment Little progress has been made in the treatment of Alzheimer's disease since Alois Alzheimer's day, and even diagnosis remains difficult. While the patient is alive, the diagnosis must be arrived at by a careful process of elimination. Through brain imaging and other tests, it is possible to determine that the patient has not suffered a series of small strokes and does not have Parkinson's disease, a brain tumor, depression, an adverse drug reaction, or other disorders that can cause dementia. The chances of making an accurate diagnosis of Alzheimer's disease in the living patient have been improved by the finding that 70 to 80 percent of patients with the disease show a characteristic pattern of decrease in metabolic function or cerebral blood flow in

certain areas of the brain (see Figure 13-11). Because no other illness with symptoms of confusion and intellectual deterioration has so far been found that shows this pattern, scanning techniques provide a valuable clue to diagnosis although they do not as yet provide enough information to be certain that the patient has Alzheimer's disease. The only way to be absolutely certain that a patient has the disorder is to examine the brain after death. An autopsy is needed because so far it is the only way to determine whether the plaques and tangles characteristic of the disease are present.

Although much remains to be discovered about this disease, two critical crossroads reached in the approach to treatment for Alzheimer's disease have been (1) the recognition of Alzheimer's disease as a disorder distinct from the normal aging process, and (2) the realization that in developing therapeutic and social interventions for a major illness or disability the concept of *care* can be as important as that of *cure*.

Increasing knowledge about the role of genetic abnormalities in Alzheimer's disease may lead to effective treatment methods. There are several ways in which formation of beta amyloid might be stopped from killing nerve cells in the brain. For example, certain drugs might accomplish this task.

Four scientific and clinical care challenges now face researchers and clinicians who deal with Alzheimer's disease:

Figure 13-10 Former President Ronald Reagan and his wife, Nancy, pose for pictures during his first public appearance after his announcement that he had been diagnosed with Alzheimer's disease.

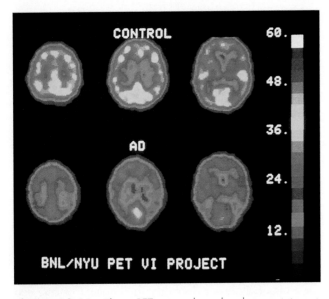

Figure 13-11 These PET scans show the characteristic pattern of decrease in metabolic function seen in the brain of an Alzheimer's patient (*bottom*) compared to that of an age- and sex-matched control (*top*).

1. Determining the fundamental neurobiological causes
2. Developing more effective treatments that would prevent its occurrence and impede or reverse its progression
3. Providing sensitive clinical care for those already diagnosed with Alzheimer's disease
4. Supporting family members throughout the course of the disease with expert advice, treatment, and caring

Pick's Disease

Pick's disease is much less common than Alzheimer's disease. Whereas the risk of Alzheimer's disease increases steadily through adult life, Pick's disease is most likely to develop between the ages of 60 and 70. After that period the risk decreases (Heston & Mastri, 1982). Its symptoms are so similar to those of Alzheimer's disease that it takes an autopsy to tell the two disorders apart. People who have died from Pick's disease show a characteristic form of brain atrophy. Among people over age 40, 24 out of 100,000 can be expected to die of the disease. There appears to be a strong genetic factor, and men are at greater risk of developing the disease than women (Heston et al., 1987).

As is the case with Alzheimer's disease, there are no known cures for Pick's disease or any of the other senile and presenile dementias. The usual treatment consists mainly of emotional support and sedative drugs. Efforts are made to structure the individual's life so that his or her days are uncomplicated and structured so as to avoid pressure and tension. This can also improve the quality of life for those affected by these disorders.

Huntington's Disease

Huntington's disease is a rare hereditary disorder transmitted by a single dominant gene and characterized by progressive degeneration of brain tissue. It can begin at any time from childhood to late in life, but most commonly the onset occurs between the ages of 30 and 50. Four types of symptoms are observed in Huntington's disease: dementia, irritability and apathy, depression, and hallucinations and delusions. In addition, there are *choreiform* movements—involuntary, spasmodic jerking and twisting movements of the neck, trunk, and extremities, and much facial grimacing.

The psychological and behavioral symptoms of Huntington's disease are even more devastating than the physical ones. As the disease develops, the person experiences increasing difficulty in memory storage and retrieval. There is also evidence that intelligence test scores get progressively lower in the period just before the appearance of the characteristic choreiform movements. This suggests that the gene for Huntington's disease does not suddenly "turn on" at the time that the involuntary movements appear.

Impulsiveness in behavior and paranoid and depressive thinking are likely to occur as the disorder progresses and family life becomes disrupted. It is not clear whether these behavioral components of Huntington's disease are organically caused or whether they are psychological reactions to physical deterioration. Recently it has become known that people with Huntington's disease have a deficiency of one neurotransmitter, gamma-amino-butyric-acid (GABA).

The disorder usually begins in middle life, although the onset can occur much earlier. The folksinger and composer Woody Guthrie died in 1967 at the age of 55 after suffering from Huntington's disease for 13 years. As a result of a misdiagnosis, Guthrie had been considered an alcoholic and had been placed in a series of mental hospitals for years before the correct diagnosis was made.

Since the disease is inherited through a single dominant gene, each child of an affected parent has a 50 percent chance of inheriting the disorder. There is no skipping of generations, and until recently there has been no way of distinguishing carriers of the gene from noncarriers until the symptoms appear. The fact that Huntington's disease does not manifest itself until middle life has meant that family members that might be affected by it must spend their childhood, adolescence, and early adult years not knowing whether they will develop the disorder or not.

In the San Luis region of Venezuela, the prevalence

of Huntington's disease is 700 times higher than in the United States. Within a population of about 3,000, about 150 people have been stricken by the disease and 1,500 more have a substantial risk of developing it. This is because San Luis is the home of a handful of families with many affected members. By far the largest of these families is the Soto family, which has the highest known concentration of Huntington's disease of any family in the world. This high incidence of the disease in one family has given scientists an unusual opportunity to study this rare disorder (see Figure 13-12).

By carefully studying the blood of Iris del Valle Soto and other members of her extended family of almost 4,000 people covering eight generations, researchers achieved a startling breakthrough. They identified the location in the chromosome pair (chromosome pair 4) at which the gene for Huntington's disease is located (Wexler et al., 1985). In 1993, the specific gene was identified (Gusella & MacDonald, 1994). This identification was an important first step toward developing a diagnostic test for the disease and perhaps, eventually, a treatment. The diagnostic genetic test is now being used at several clinical centers in Canada and the United States on an experimental basis. As a result of the gene discovery, an even more direct and accurate test for Huntington's disease should be possible and, ultimately, researchers hope, a better understanding of what causes the nerve degeneration that characterizes the disease. A key leader in organizing research on Huntington's disease has been Nancy Wexler, a clinical psychologist and president of the Hereditary Disease Foundation (see Figure 13-13).

Figure 13-13 Ever since learning that her family was affected by Huntington's disease, Nancy Wexler has been a leader in encouraging research into its cause. In 1993 she was given the prestigious Albert Lasker Public Service Award. This citation accompanied the award: "Learning that her family was affected by the disease, she did not bemoan her situation, but rose to the challenge and used her adversity to set her life goal to conquering this late-onset, invariably fatal genetic disorder." In this photograph she is seen with her sister Alice (right), an historian, and her father, Milton, a psychoanalyst.

At present many people who have been offered the currently available test have not chosen to take it. In a study carried out in Canada, those at risk who volunteered to be tested also were assessed for psychological well-being both before the genetic testing and at several intervals afterwards (Hayden, 1991). As might be expected, those who learned that they were likely to develop the disease were very distressed when they first heard this result. However, six months later their psychological state was better than it had been prior to testing although they became distressed whenever they noticed something about their behavior, stumbling over a curb, for instance, that could possibly be an early symptom. People for whom the test indicated freedom from the Huntington's gene were elated at first but then seemed to go into a slump for a variety of reasons. Those who had made irreversible decisions based on concern for their genetic status, for example by being sterilized in order to avoid passing on the Huntington's gene, were particularly negatively affected. Another group negatively affected by the news that they did not carry the gene were

Figure 13-12 Some of the members of a large Venezuelan family whose members are at exceptionally high risk for Huntington's disease enjoy a watermelon party. By donating their DNA for study, family members have helped in the search for the location of the gene that causes this disease.

those who had had unrealistic expectations about how the predictive testing would change their lives. There were similar numbers of negative psychological reactions in the groups that got good and bad news. In general, people who had experienced psychological problems prior to the test had the worst outcome regardless of the test outcome. The results of the study show clearly the importance of including counseling and support services in genetic testing programs.

Parkinson's Disease

Like Huntington's disease, **Parkinson's disease** is progressive and may begin by the age of 50. Its symptoms include tremor, rigidity, an expressionless, masklike facial appearance, and loss of vocal power. A person with Parkinson's disease typically exhibits social withdrawal, reduced intellectual ability, and rigidity in coping with his or her problems. Most Parkinson's patients seem emotionally overcontrolled. As with Huntington's disease, it is difficult to determine how much of the behavioral maladaptation associated with Parkinson's disease is due to organic processes and how much to the patient's psychological reaction to them. The prevalence of the disease is about 250 per 100,000.

There is evidence that the brains of Parkinson's patients are deficient in the neurotransmitter dopamine. Unlike the dementias discussed so far, this disorder can be treated. A drug called *L-dopa* is used to relieve some of the symptoms. One study found that Parkinson's patients treated with L-dopa showed clinical improvement that persisted over a 10-year period (Bauer et al., 1982). A promising advance in understanding Parkinson's disease has been the discovery of a new protein (glial cell line-derived neuro-tropic factor, GDNF) that may promote the secretion of the neurotransmitter, dopamine, and thereby counter the degeneration seen in Parkinson's disease (Weiss, 1993).

Recently, surgeons have carried out tissue implantations into the human brain as a possible way of relieving Parkinson's symptoms. In one case, the right adrenal gland was removed from a 35-year-old man suffering from Parkinson's disease and part of the gland—the medulla—was transplanted to the patient's brain. The hope was that the adrenal tissue would manufacture needed dopamine (Lewin, 1988). While success with tissue implantations has been reported in some cases, there have also been a number of failures. The prospects for use of this procedure for repairing some diseases of the brain are not yet clear.

An illustration of the need to control for variables that might influence the outcome of clinical treatments is a study recently started to determine the effects of using implants of brain cells of aborted fetuses to correct Parkinson's disease in adults. While some researchers have reported success using this surgical approach, some critics have raised the possibility that the power of suggestion (the idea or suggestion that the surgery would relieve or eliminate Parkinson's symptoms) could explain the positive results. The ongoing study will include Parkinson's patients who receive fetal implants and those who do not. The control group will receive sham surgery that will be just like the real surgery but not involve a fetal cell implant. The sham surgery will consist of shaving the patient's head, cutting two oval holes in the skull, and then closing the skull again. Like the real surgery, it is done while the patient is awake, takes about four hours, and requires a hospital stay of a few days. Those who receive the sham operation will be offered the real thing the next year. This study illustrates, not only the need for researchers to control as many variables as possible, but also the ethical issues involved in carrying out sham surgery as a control condition for patients with a serious medical condition.

Brain Trauma: Injuries, Tumors, and Infections

Brain injuries, tumors, and infections can cause serious acute and chronic conditions. Damage to the brain is of central importance in influencing how a person functions.

Injuries and Tumors Traumatic brain injury is a common cause of mental disorders (Silver et al., 1990). Each year in the United States, over 500,000 people suffer severe injuries to the brain. As the case of Sarah Monahan presented in Box 13-1 makes clear, major brain injuries can have profound cognitive and behavioral consequences. Patients with less severe injuries also may suffer from prolonged psychological disability. They may have difficulties in a number of areas of functioning, including work, school, and leisure activities, and may show extreme personality changes.

In addition to head injuries, intracranial growths (brain tumors) can lead to both acute and chronic disorders. In many cases it is difficult to determine how much of the abnormal behavior is a result of damage and how much represents a lifelong behavior pattern or simply a reaction to knowledge of the injury. These factors can interact in many ways. A startling or traumatic event, whether or not it involves physical injury, usually has some specific and symbolic significance for the individual. The term **traumatic neurosis** has been used to describe reactions that follow such an event. A blow to the head that caused little physical damage might be exploited by the injured person, as in some hysterical disorders. The reaction may be reinforced by secondary gains, such as family sympathy or permission to quit one's job. Table 13-5 lists some of the factors that influence the effects of a brain injury.

Brain injuries are usually classified into three groups: **concussions,** or transient states that momentarily change the physical condition of the brain but do not cause structural damage; **contusions,** in which diffuse, fine structural damage—for example, the rupturing of tiny blood vessels—takes place; and **lacerations,** which involve major tears or ruptures in the brain tissue.

Although a concussion might include a temporary loss of consciousness, the person can be expected to recover completely within 24 to 48 hours. Sometimes it is difficult to diagnose precisely the extent of brain injury and its potential effect on brain functioning. A variety of tests and observations are used to analyze each case, including X-ray evidence of skull fracture, a CT scan to determine tissue damage, a test for blood in the spinal fluid, and observation of symptoms such as bleeding from the skull orifices (for example, the ears), throbbing headaches, prolonged loss of consciousness, and sluggish cognitive behavior. Head injuries can lead to highly specific losses in motor or cognitive functioning, with the extent of the loss depending on the kind of injury and where it is located.

Sometimes the brain is injured not by an accident or a blow but by pressure inside the skull, perhaps from a tumor. In such cases the speed with which the intruding body develops also influences the amount of loss. A tumor might grow slowly for a long time before there is evidence of intracranial pressure or behavioral change (see Box 13-3). A good prognosis in cases of brain injury or tumor depends on how early and how accurately the condition is diagnosed and whether an effective treatment for the condition exists.

In some cases in which there is known physical damage, only minor behavioral deficits develop. Apparently some people adapt to minor brain damage better than others do. While brain damage can directly cause maladaptive behavior, it is also possible that the maladaptive behavior can occur simply as a response to the knowledge of having a damaged brain. Furthermore, any type of major injury or traumatic condition might set off a maladaptive psychological reaction.

Tumors produce a variety of physiological and psychological changes because their presence causes a rise in intracranial pressure or interferes with the blood supply to the brain. As with head injuries, the symptoms of tumors depend on their location in the brain. For example, tumors growing in or near the frontal lobes frequently lead to a gradual onset of mental changes, but again, the symptoms depend on the site of the tumor. One group of people with frontal-lobe tumors may become exuberant and euphoric, with their conversation punctuated by laughter and jokes. Another group may show general apathy and slowness in responding. Memory disorders are very common in people with cerebral tumors and are often the first noticeable indication that a problem exists. Researchers are investigating the degree to which training in attentional and cognitive skills can aid in the rehabilitation of brain-damaged individuals.

Early in their development some brain tumors result in changes that neurologists can assess. However, in the absence of other evidence to suggest the presence of a tumor, emphasis on personality and behavioral changes often results in misdiagnosis and the symptoms are attributed to nonorganic factors. The role of organic factors may become evident later. For example, the composer George Gershwin underwent psychoanalysis because he suffered severe headaches. It was not until shortly before his death that the diagnosis of a brain tumor was made.

AIDS Dementia Complex AIDS dementia complex (ADC) is receiving increased attention from neurologists and psychologists because many AIDS patients display cognitive impairment (Dickson & Ranseen, 1990). In addition, some people who are positive for the human immunodeficiency virus (HIV) but have not developed any overt symptoms of AIDS show impairment in neuropsychological testing. The symptoms associated with ADC include: forgetfulness, concentration difficulties, mental slowness, mild motor difficulties, and apathetic, withdrawn behavior. The early symptoms of ADC are similar to the dementias of the elderly and may closely resemble a major depression. (See Table 13-2 for noticeable differences between the dementias and depression.) As ADC progresses, the majority of patients develop a severe dementia with global loss of cognitive functions, severe psychomotor retardation, mutism, and motor weakness. Psychotic symptoms develop in some patients. CT scans of ADC patients reveal cortical atrophy.

ADC is a newly recognized type of dementia. Its early recognition is complicated by its similarities to largely psychological disorders such as depression.

TABLE 13-5
Factors That Influence the Effects of a Brain Injury

1. Age
2. Site of injury
3. Extent of damage
4. Emotional reactions to resulting physical and mental deficits
5. Personality and social competence
6. Social support available after injury

A Malignant Brain Tumor

I don't really understand myself these days. I am supposed to be an average, reasonable, and intelligent young man. However, lately (I can't recall when it started) I have been the victim of many unusual and irrational thoughts. These thoughts constantly recur, and it requires a tremendous mental effort to concentrate on useful and progressive tasks. In March when my parents made a physical break I noticed a great deal of stress. I consulted Dr. Cochran at the University Health Center and asked him to recommend someone that I could consult with about some psychiatric disorders I felt I had. I talked with a doctor once for about two hours and tried to convey to him my fears that I felt overcome by overwhelming violent impulses. After one session I never saw the doctor again, and since then I have been fighting my mental turmoil alone, and seemingly to no avail. After my death I wish that an autopsy would be performed on me to see if there is any visible physical disorder. I have had some tremendous headaches in the past and have consumed two large bottles of Excedrin in the past three months.

This letter was written by Charles Whitman, a student at the University of Texas, on the evening of July 31, 1966. Later that night Whitman killed his wife and his mother. The next morning he went to the tower on the university campus with a high-powered hunting rifle and opened fire. Ninety minutes later he was shot to death, but by that time he had shot 38 people, killing 14, (see Figure 13-14).

Because of the shocking nature of this incident, it attracted widespread attention. There were many attempts to explain Whitman's murderous acts. The letter that Whitman had written provided a number of clues. It referred to intense headaches, and a postmortem examination revealed a highly malignant tumor in a region of the brain that is known to be involved in aggressive behavior. Some experts suggested that Whitman's actions had been caused by brain damage. Most brain tumor victims don't become violent, but the behavioral effects of brain injuries and tumors can sometimes be puzzling and dramatic.

Other experts viewed Whitman's actions as products of the "unusual and irrational thoughts" to which he referred in his letter. A study of Whitman's life revealed that he had had many positive experiences with guns, and some authorities on violent behavior pointed to these experiences as a possible causal factor. Still others cited Whitman's reference to

Figure 13-14 Charles Whitman, shown here in a college photo, killed his wife, mother, and 14 strangers who were hit by bullets he sprayed from a perch high in the tower of the administration building at the University of Texas.

"overwhelming violent impulses" and suggested that those impulses had been bottled up for many years and had finally exploded into action because of the recent life stresses described in his letter.

We cannot be certain which of these potential causes was most important. Perhaps all of them contributed to his actions to varying degrees. The Whitman case dramatically illustrates the many perspectives from which a single act can be viewed and explained.

Because the disorder usually appears in younger people who are not normally expected to develop dementing illnesses, the problem may be misdiagnosed. The typical psychological reactions to a diagnosis of AIDS may further hinder a correct diagnosis of ADC. Because many young individuals have a variety of self-defeating behaviors, such as drug abuse and promiscuous sexual activity at the time they develop ADC, the illness is particularly difficult to treat and to research carefully.

General Paresis Infectious disorders often have an acute onset, although the possibility of slow-acting viral infections should not be ruled out. The central nervous system often is more susceptible to bodily infections than other tissues of the body. Some of these infections do not last long, and successful treatments have been worked out for many of them. If left untreated, however, some infections can lead to irreversible brain disorders.

Untreated **syphilitic infections** are an example of this type of condition. If syphilis is diagnosed before its terminal stages, it can be treated with drugs, usually penicillin. The aim of the drugs is to return the cerebrospinal fluid to normal, which may require many months. These drugs may cure the patient, but the degree of improvement depends on how many neurons were destroyed before the treatment began. When the destruction is great, losses in intellectual functioning cannot be restored.

One of the results of untreated syphilis in its late stage is **general paresis,** or **dementia paralytica,** a progressive deterioration in psychological and motor functioning that results in paralysis, psychosis, and ultimately, death. Among the symptoms of general paresis are loss of cognitive functions, slurring of speech, tremors of the tongue and lips, and poor motor coordination. These symptoms are progressive and eventually lead to a helpless condition. Before the cause and treatment of syphilis were discovered, patients with general paresis represented between one-tenth and one-third of all admissions to mental hospitals.

Because of the negative relationship between the degree of possible improvement and the extent of irreversible brain damage, prompt diagnosis and medical treatment of syphilitic infections is clearly the best approach to reducing the incidence of general paresis.

Amnestic Disorders

Amnestic disorders are disturbances of memory due either to the direct physiological effects of a medical condition or the persisting effects of a substance (drugs, medications, exposure to toxic chemicals). Individuals with an amnestic disorder are impaired in their ability to learn new information or are unable to recall previously learned information or past events. The impairment is particularly evident in the areas of social and occupational functioning and most apparent for verbal and visual tasks that require spontaneous recall. While amnestic disorders have a common core of symptoms, the causes vary depending on the area of the brain affected. An amnestic disorder is often preceded by a period of confusion and disorientation. Most patients with severe amnestic conditions do not have insight into their memory deficit and may actually deny the presence of impairment, even though its presence is obvious to others. The impairment could be transient and of short duration or chronic. In the case of head injuries that cause brain trauma, the patient may be amnestic for the time period before, during, and after injury (see Figure 13-15). Even after relatively minor injuries, many patients complain of headaches, dizziness, fatigue, lack of concentration, and anxiety. In most cases these complaints are of short duration.

The Diversity of Cognitive Impairment Disorders

Delirium, dementia, and amnesia are the three categories of cognitive impairment emphasized in DSM-IV. However, there is a wide diversity of impairments that result from the varied nature of the events causing brain dysfunction (for example, an injury to the brain), their location, and the age of the individual. For this reason, many patients with cognitive impairment do not fit neatly into standard diagnostic categories. Cerebrovascular accidents and epilepsy illustrate the diversity of dysfunctional brain-behavior relationships.

Cerebral Vascular Disorders

Cerebrovascular accidents (CVAs), or **strokes,** are blockages or ruptures of the blood vessels in the cerebrum. When these blood vessels break or are blocked by

Figure 13-15 On Christmas Day, 1985, James McDonnell came home to his wife in Larchmont, New York, after 14 years of amnesia. He had lost his memory after suffering head injuries in two automobile accidents, had gone to Philadelphia, and had found a job in a restaurant. McDonnell said that his memory had returned on Christmas Eve when he bumped his head.

a clot, a portion of the brain is deprived of its supply of oxygen and blood. Extensive damage to the brain and obvious changes in behavior may result. When the affected blood vessels are small and the interference with blood flow is temporary, the symptoms are milder—perhaps only confusion, unsteadiness, and excessive emotionality. Some of the behavioral effects of a stroke may be similar to the dementia that occurs in cases of brain deterioration. However, the symptoms of stroke characteristically have an abrupt onset.

Eric Hodgins, an editor and author, suffered a severe stroke that resulted in aphasia and paralysis of the left side of his body. He later recovered from the aphasia, and wrote about the experience. His account of his stroke vividly portrays the psychological as well as the physical aspects of a severe stroke.

The first thing to be said about it, is that it is like nothing else on earth. . . . The victim-patient is confused, or stunned, or shocked, or unconscious. Whatever his state he is not in good condition to give any fellow layman a clear and coherent account of what happened. Perhaps he can talk—perhaps not. Even with speech, he can't say "It hurts"—because it probably doesn't. So, stroke exists in no focal plane the uninitiated layman can understand or recognize, or on which he can practice his own brand of differen-

tial diagnosis. Thus, as with the traffic accident, a variable period of total confusion elapses after the stroke has struck before the cry goes up, "Somebody get a doctor!" . . .

Unlike other patient types I can think of, the stroke patient goes to the hospital with profound relief, and gladly. Although he is probably not in pain, he is in considerable fear—more than he can express. Something has gone very, very wrong, but "Somebody will fix it": this child-like phrase describes the depth of the patient's need for support and reassurance . . .

In my own case I found it both depressing and infuriating that I encountered no physician with the willingness or capacity to say, as my acute symptoms subsided, "I freely concede you are in a jam—in fact, in several jams. I have no ready-made solutions—but I will help you think your way out of your jams, because I conceive it part of my job, my medical job." Perhaps it is a contentious suggestion that medicine should reach this far out from its examination rooms and its prescription pads to help the stroke patient. But in that case, whose job is it?

—Quoted in Eisenson, 1973, pp. 204–207

Although Hodgins made a stunning recovery, strokes are in fact the third-ranking cause of death after heart attacks and cancer. There are approximately 500,000 new strokes and 200,000 deaths due to strokes in the United States each year. Over 80 percent of these involve people over the age of 65. In addition to age, high blood pressure plays a major role in strokes. The single most important way in which strokes can be prevented is through the treatment and control of high blood pressure. Many clinicians have observed that strokes occur especially often in people who live pressured lives. These people tend to have their strokes while they are relaxing or vacationing. Why strokes occur when stress apparently decreases is unclear.

Vascular Dementia Vascular dementia, or multi-infarct dementia, is caused by a series of minor strokes that occur at different times. The onset is abrupt and the course of the disorder is fluctuating rather than uniformly progressive. The pattern of deficits is "patchy," depending on which areas of the brain have been destroyed. As the condition worsens, the relatively intact areas of intellectual functioning decrease and there is increased disturbance in several functions, including memory, abstract thinking, judgment, and impulse control. Hypertension may be a major factor in multi-infarct dementia. Controlling high blood pressure helps prevent this type of dementia and reduces the likelihood of additional minor strokes when multi-infarct dementia is already present. Vascular dementia is more likely to occur after age 65 than before.

Pellagra and Korsakoff's Syndrome

Vitamin and other nutritional deficiencies can affect the nervous system. For example, **pellagra** is a reversible disease caused by a deficiency of the vitamin niacin (nicotinic acid) or its derivatives. The deficiency affects cells in the area of the cerebral cortex that controls body movement and in other parts of the brain. Symptoms of pellagra are varied, including a skin disorder (the skin looks as if it has been severely sunburned), diarrhea, and psychological deterioration. The signs of psychological impairment are similar to those of anxiety disorders and depression: anxiety, irritability, loss of recent memory, and difficulty in concentration. Untreated cases may result in delirium, hallucinations, and a variety of psychotic behaviors.

The incidence of pellagra has declined sharply in the United States as a result of improved diet, but it is still common in many underdeveloped countries. Chronic alcoholics who have poorly balanced diets may show symptoms of pellagra. On the basis of behavior alone, it is difficult to distinguish between pellagra and conditions such as anxiety or schizophrenia, but when a niacin deficiency is suspected (usually on the basis of skin and digestive symptoms), diagnosis is relatively simple. Except in very severe cases, nutritional therapy is highly effective. The individual is placed on a protein-rich diet that is also high in B vitamins (niacin, thiamine, and vitamin B complex). Mild cases improve noticeably within 48 hours.

While the results of pellagra are reversible with nutritional therapy, sometimes nutritional deficiencies combine with toxic substances to produce substantial and irreversible damage to brain tissue. **Korsakoff's syndrome,** which occurs in some chronic alcoholics, results from a combination of alcoholism and vitamin B_1 (thiamine) deficiency. Recent and past memories are lost, and the person seems unable to form new memories. In addition, there are perceptual deficits, loss of initiative, and confabulation. Delirium tremens frequently is part of the patient's medical history. The longer the vitamin deficiency has persisted, the less responsive the individual will be to vitamin therapy.

Epilepsy

Epilepsy is a transitory disturbance of brain function that develops suddenly, ceases spontaneously, and is likely to reoccur. The form that this disturbance takes depends on the site in the brain at which it originates, the extent of the brain area involved, and other factors. Epilepsy is not a disease but instead is a symptom consisting of recurrent episodes of changes in state of consciousness with or without an accompanying motor or sensory involvement.

Throughout history epilepsy has inspired awe, fear, a sense of mystery, and puzzlement. The Greek physician Hippocrates argued that epilepsy was a naturally caused disease, but for much of modern history it was seen as a sign of demonic possession. Many famous people, including Julius Caesar, the elder William Pitt, and Fyodor Dostoyevsky, had epilepsy. Dostoyevsky, one of the world's great novelists, suffered his first epileptic seizure while he was in prison in Siberia. He believed that the agony of living in chains, the stench, and hard labor had precipitated his attacks, which persisted for years even after he was permitted to leave the prison.

It was the English neurologist Hughlings Jackson (1834–1911) who first accounted for epileptic seizures in terms of brain lesions. He believed that the seizures resulted from excessive discharging by nerve cells in the gray matter of the brain and that irritation of specific areas of the brain caused the particular symptoms manifested by epileptics. Today, we know that many mechanisms, not a single one, may make cells behave abnormally, as they do in epilepsy. The cells involved in epileptic seizures share several abnormal characteristics. During seizures they fire electrical discharges at high rates and in short bursts, with quiet periods in between. In contrast, most normal cells fire fewer discharges spaced more evenly over time. Groups of epileptic cells also tend to fire at the same time, whereas normal cells fire relatively independently of each other. This synchrony of cell discharge is an important factor in a seizure, although how seizures start is poorly understood. It is clear, however, that once a seizure begins, neurons in large portions of the brain fire excessively and simultaneously. Surprisingly, most of the brain's activity recorded between seizures is normal.

Most forms of epilepsy are not believed to be hereditary, but there seems to be a predisposition toward epilepsy in some families. Although it is difficult to give a precise estimate, perhaps half of all cases of epilepsy result from such nongenetic factors as head injuries at birth, infectious diseases of childhood, or brain infections and injuries later in life. The clinical problem of epilepsy is particularly challenging because its solution usually requires establishing the particular combination of causes at work in a given case.

Epilepsy is relatively common and has many forms. Approximately 1 percent of the U.S. population has the condition, and 2 to 3 percent of the population has had a seizure at some time in life. Young children are prone to have seizures, often associated with high fevers. Many children "outgrow" their seizures, but the long-term consequences are not known. Victims of head trauma or brain tumors also are prone to develop epilepsy. The dis-

ease is more common in less affluent countries where health care is poor, because minor or moderate central nervous system infection and trauma are more likely to be neglected.

Researchers put the many forms of epilepsy, which may involve different brain structures, into two categories. Some people with epilepsy have generalized seizures, with electrical activity of unknown origin occurring simultaneously throughout the brain. The second category includes epilepsies in which seizures can be traced to a particular area of the brain—for example, the hippocampus.

Grand Mal and Petit Mal Seizures An epileptic seizure is a result of transient electrical instability of some cells in the brain, which sometimes triggers an "electrical storm" that spreads through part or all of the brain. This electrical activity culminates in a seizure, which can take one of many forms. Many people with epilepsy have only one type of seizure, but a sizable minority experience two or more types. The major types include *grand mal* and *petit mal* seizures and *psychomotor epilepsy*.

The most severe form of epileptic disorder is the **grand mal** (French for "great illness") **seizure** that typically lasts from two to five minutes. This type of attack leaves a painful impression on anyone who witnesses it. The victim of a grand mal seizure displays a set of very striking symptoms. The seizure often begins with a cry, followed by loss of consciousness, falling to the floor, and extreme spasms. These uncontrollable spasms can cause serious harm to the victim. Among the greatest dangers are head injuries and severe biting of the tongue or mouth. The muscular movements of a grand mal seizure are usually preceded by an *aura*, in which the individual experiences a clouded state of consciousness, including feelings of unreality and depersonalization (feelings of strangeness about oneself). The aura may last only a few seconds, but it is often remembered very vividly.

Following the aura, the *tonic phase* of the seizure begins. The body is in an extended position, the eyes remain open, the pupils are dilated, and the corneal and light reflexes are absent. The tonic phase lasts for 15 to 30 seconds and is followed by the *clonic phase*, during which the body alternates between marked muscular rigidity and relaxation. Bladder and bowel control may be lost. Following the convulsive part of a grand mal seizure, there may be a deep sleep that lasts for an hour or two. As the victim regains consciousness, he or she may be bewildered and amnesic. While some grand mal victims have daily attacks, cases have been reported in which there were only a few seizures in an entire lifetime.

In the **petit mal** ("small illness" in French) **seizure,** which is particularly common in children, there is no convulsion. Rather, there is a lapse of consciousness characterized by blank staring and lack of responsiveness lasting up to about half a minute. The individual usually does not lose consciousness. These seizures may occur many times a day.

Petit mal attacks may be difficult to identify unless the person is known to be epileptic or an attack is actually observed. They commonly start in early childhood. Some children have so many attacks daily that they have difficulty attending to what is going on around them. Most petit mal attacks result from disturbances in subcortical brain structures, although the cause of these disturbances is usually unknown.

Psychomotor Epilepsy In psychomotor epilepsy, a type that includes 15 percent of epilepsy cases and is rarely seen in children, the patient retains control of his or her motor functioning but loses the ability to exercise good judgment in carrying out activities. During a psychomotor attack, the individual is in a kind of trance; his or her movements may be repetitive and highly organized but are in fact semiautomatic. Psychomotor seizures may resemble those of petit mal epilepsy, but they last longer (up to two minutes), involve muscle movements related to chewing and speech, and show more clouding of consciousness. The occasional visual hallucinations and the confused state that characterize psychomotor epilepsy are similar to some symptoms of psychosis.

In some cases fear, terror, rage, and depression are among the emotional side effects of psychomotor seizures. These outbursts of emotion come on suddenly. They are apparently automatic and unpremeditated, and they cannot be recalled later. Another feature of this syndrome is inability to shift attention to new objects and situations. There is some evidence suggesting that this syndrome may be associated with temporal lobe lesions; hence, this symptom pattern is referred to as **temporal lobe epilepsy.**

Psychological Factors Over the years there has been much conjecture about the role of psychological factors in epilepsy. Are epileptics helpless victims of their condition, or is it possible that the disease is part of their psychological adjustment to some other aspect of their lives? Clinicians have observed that epileptics' seizures tend to become more frequent when they are confronted with challenges and problems they do not feel competent to handle. In support of this clinical conclusion, research findings have shown that an increased number of stressful life events is associated with an increase in frequency of seizures (Hermann et al., 1990).

From a psychological point of view, the disease often creates overwhelming stress for both epileptics and their families. Much of this stress is related to lack of knowledge about epilepsy, its causes, and its treatment. Other important factors are the role of general life stresses in bringing on seizures and the effect of the stress caused by the ever-present possibility of a seizure, the need to lead a somewhat restricted life, and the stigma that attaches itself to people who are known to be epileptic.

There is increasing recognition of the developmental problems posed by epilepsy. For example, approximately 60 percent of people with epilepsy experience their first seizure before they are 10 years old. This condition represents a major handicap during a formative period of physical and psychological growth. Writer Kurt Eichenwald, who has epilepsy, has described some of his college experiences.

My staring spells—periods of a few seconds of mental absence—had been going on for as long as I could remember. Although I mentioned them to my doctor and my parents occasionally, the events did not seem significant.

Then, in my first semester at college, I was horsing around in the dorm with my roommates, and I fell, hitting my head against a chair. I had a concussion. No one to this day knows if the concussion affected my seizures, but the staring spells soon increased in frequency and severity. I learned they were different from other people's passing moments of distraction.

I remember once, in the dining hall, suddenly realizing everyone was looking at me. My lap was wet. I thought someone had thrown something at me. In fact, I had begun to stare while holding a glass of Coca-Cola in my hand. It had fallen in between my legs and shattered.

—Eichenwald, 1987, p. 30

Later, he began having more major seizures.

I experience what is called an "aura" as random brain cells start to fire. I feel a sense of separation. My head throbs, and I see a flash of lights. Even today, I am not sure of the order of these feelings or the amount of time separating them.

As the electrical firestorm sweeps across my brain, I lose consciousness and fall to the ground. The muscles in my body tighten up and my jaw clenches, the teeth possibly biting and bloodying my lips, tongue, or cheek. My body jerks for a period, usually for less than a minute. During that time, I often get excessive amounts of saliva in my mouth, creating a froth. My breathing becomes irregular, sometimes even stopping. I also can become incontinent.

The convulsion ends, and I fall into a deep, though brief, sleep. As I wake up, another seizure can be triggered, starting the process again.

While unconscious, I do not respond to pain, such as the injection of needles. I have awakened half-frozen in a snowdrift but unaware, until my waking, of the cold.

When fully awake, I am very confused and panicked. Often, it takes time for me to realize a seizure has occurred. I am unsure where I am, who is with me or even what day it is. My speech is broken, and I stutter horribly, so that I am unable to ask questions except of the most patient observers.

—Eichenwald, 1987, p. 31

Treatment There are three major ways to treat epilepsy: drugs, surgery, and psychological management. Certain drugs, such as Dilantin and phenobarbitol, can reduce the frequency and severity of seizures. Unfortunately, there is considerable variation in the way people react to these drugs. The only way to establish the optimal dosage is through trial and error. In some cases the person with epilepsy may use substances (alcohol, for example) that interfere with the effectiveness of anticonvulsive drugs. Several promising experimental drugs now being tested may be more effective and have fewer side effects than drugs currently in use.

If the seizures are a result of some identifiable structural defect and drugs either are not effective or have strong side effects, surgical intervention may be considered. The seizures of temporal lobe epilepsy are especially difficult to control by means of medication, but some studies have reported successful results following removal of parts of the temporal lobe. Because brain surgery entails obvious risks, it is used only when it is clear that some abnormality of brain tissue is causing the seizures. The brain is such a complex structure that it is not always possible to be absolutely certain where the abnormality is, although scanning techniques have helped to localize areas involved. In some cases diagnosed as temporal lobe epilepsy, the temporal lobe has been removed and has been found to have no lesions. For this reason, surgery is seen as a treatment of last resort, to be attempted only after drugs and psychological approaches have failed.

A variety of psychological methods have been used in treating epilepsy. Operant conditioning procedures have been tried successfully with some individuals who cannot be helped by medication. For example, children with epilepsy have been rewarded with attention and care following seizure-free periods. After a seizure occurs, these reinforcers are withdrawn or reduced in strength. Avoiding or changing certain cognitive cues can also be helpful because it is known that the aura preceding a grand mal seizure can be induced by thinking certain thoughts. People with epilepsy who have this form of the disorder can be trained to direct their attention to pleasant thoughts when they feel an aura coming on. Desensitization and relaxation training have been found to be helpful in reducing the frequency of epileptic attacks. Biofeedback, in which patients receive visual or auditory information about their brainwave patterns, can also be an effective treatment.

Many people with epilepsy need help to cope with their condition. Because the disorder frequently begins before adulthood, the emotional responses of the affected person's family must also be dealt with. Often the patient and the family see epilepsy as a kind of disgrace and react to it with shame and guilt. Because an atmosphere of emotional tension and frustration can increase the severity of epileptic seizures, psychotherapy and counseling are frequently recommended both for victims and for their families. Many people still view epilepsy as frightening and mysterious. As a result of such attitudes, a person with epilepsy often feels socially stigmatized. Organizations like the Epilepsy Foundation work to provide information about epilepsy and to decrease occupational, social, and legal discrimination against epileptics. They publicize such facts as the following:

1. People with epilepsy have the same intellectual capabilities as the general population.
2. Between seizures an epileptic person suffers no disturbance in psychological function.
3. Most cases of epilepsy (about 80 percent) can be controlled with anticonvulsive drugs.
4. The genetic factor in epilepsy is probably no greater than in many other common diseases. A person with epilepsy who marries a nonepileptic may expect a 2 percent risk of having a child who also has the disorder. In many cases the risk is even less, especially if the epilepsy is associated with a birth injury or later accident or infection.

An Integrative Approach to Brain Disorders

Because the conditions discussed in this chapter involve actual organic defects, it is tempting to see them as purely medical problems. Why do we consider brain disorders to be different from other organic problems, such as broken arms or gallstones? A physical defect lies at the root of all of these conditions, but the brain has a complex effect on our behavior as well as on our body. This effect is not as clear and predictable as the effects of damage to other parts of the body. Once a broken arm has been set and healed, for example, the person can return to the condition he or she was in before the accident. This is not the case with brain injuries, and it is for this reason that they are of interest to psychologists.

To comprehend the effects of a brain injury on behavior, we require information about the person's life history, personality, and environmental and biophysical factors. We need to identify vulnerability factors in the person's life and indications of his or her ability to be resilient. Purely physical conditions such as broken arms, however, can be treated successfully without such data. Although brain disorders can be treated medically, psychodynamic, behavioral, cognitive, and community concepts are also important in understanding and treating these conditions. Thus, the most fruitful approach to brain disorders is one that integrates knowledge from these diverse fields.

From a psychodynamic perspective, although certain forms of maladaptive behavior may be organically caused, the way people respond to their condition involves psychological factors such as personality, earlier experience, and ways of coping. For example, the more outgoing a person is, the greater the likelihood of improvement in his or her condition. Many cases of brain disorder indicate that an individual's personality at the time of the organic damage has an effect on the degree and form of his or her behavioral deterioration. For example, the content of hallucinations and the ease with which they are expressed depend on personality characteristics.

Behavioral psychologists are less interested in the effects of personality and experience than psychologists who emphasize other perspectives. Behaviorists focus instead on people's ability to adapt to even the most drastic situations. Teaching new responses to compensate for those that have been lost is seen as more important for adjustment than simply helping people accept their new lot in life. Moreover, the way people respond to such training can provide more relevant information about their present psychological state than an examination of their personality before the illness occurred. Because of their emphasis on revising people's maladaptive responses as quickly as possible, behavioral psychologists have a major contribution to make in the treatment of organic brain disorders.

Cognitively oriented psychologists have contributed a variety of techniques to help people in the early stages of dementia deal with the deterioration in their abilities. Memory-aiding techniques such as list making can help Alzheimer's disease victims, for example. Cognitive techniques are also useful in counteracting the depression that often accompanies the development of physical problems and declining intellectual competence.

Damage to the brain and central nervous system would not seem to be a condition that is influenced by community variables. Yet, from all indications, central nervous system dysfunction is not randomly distributed. Cases of brain damage are highly concentrated in the segments of the population lowest in socioeconomic status. Within this group such problems seem to be most prevalent among African-American children. This is true for sociological, not biological, reasons. Poor black infants may become biologically vulnerable shortly after the moment of conception. Inadequate nutrition and prenatal care result in complications of pregnancy, which take their toll in high rates of premature births and congenital defects. These abnormalities include neurological damage that results in impaired intellectual functioning and in behavioral difficulties such as hyperactivity and short attention span. No single complication of pregnancy is more clearly associated with a wide range of neurological dysfunctions than premature birth. For these reasons, those who focus on the community perspective emphasize the prevention of brain disorders through preventive medical care, especially good prenatal care.

The stigma attached to many of the behavioral maladaptations stemming from brain damage often makes the situation worse. People tend to avoid and isolate individuals who are markedly deviant. The behavior of old people provides one of the clearest illustrations of the effects of this social rejection. Mild brain deterioration in a socially rejected older person may lead to greater behavioral maladaptation than moderate deterioration in a person who lives in a friendlier, more accepting environment. From the community perspective, changing people's attitudes toward those who behave differently because of brain disorders can sometimes lessen the behavioral effects of these biological changes.

Cognitive impairment, as seen in delirium, dementia, and amnesia, is a product of events occurring in the brain, but several other factors also play important roles. Psychological and social variables interact with physical condition in determining the individual's level of functioning. A variety of vulnerability and resiliency factors (such as the individual's general condition of health, availability of social support, personality characteristics, coping skills, and interests) influence the impact of brain dysfunction.

THE BRAIN: AN INTERACTIONAL PERSPECTIVE

Areas of brain research that are especially important in understanding normal and abnormal behavior are those dealing with how the brain grows and maintains itself, the mechanisms by which it acquires, stores, and uses information, and the role it plays in monitoring and regulating internal bodily processes.

Vulnerability to Brain Disorders Factors that influence vulnerability to brain damage are age, social support, stress, personality factors, physical conditions of the disorder, and overall health.

Assessing Brain Damage Brain disorders that have important effects on thought and behavior are fairly common, and occur more frequently than such disorders as schizophrenia or panic disorder. The presence of brain damage is assessed by clinical tests, neuropsychological testing, and a variety of scanning techniques. The **mental-status examination** is an interview that assesses a person's general awareness, appearance, mood, and a number of aspects of cognitive functioning. **Neuropsychology** is a branch of psychology that deals with relationships between behavior and the condition of the brain.

The Brain and Cognitive Impairment Conditions marked by cognitive impairment might be due to changes in brain function. Noninvasive imaging techniques are useful in specifying abnormalities in brain anatomy and biochemical processes in different areas of the brain that are linked to disturbances in perception, memory, imagination, thought processes, problem-solving skills, and adjustment.

DELIRIUM

Delirium is a state of relatively global cognitive impairment, disorientation, and confusion, in which a person has difficulty with all aspects of attention. It can occur as a result of many factors, including an acute brain disease or infection, a disease or infection in other parts of the body that affects the brain, intoxication, or withdrawal from an addicting substance. People differ widely in their vulnerability to delirium. **Delirium tremens,** which includes not only the symptoms common to delirium but also tremors and visual hallucinations, may sometimes result from excessive alcohol consumption.

DEMENTIA

Dementia, or **brain deterioration,** involves a gradual loss of intellectual abilities that interferes with normal functioning. Depending on its cause, dementia may be stable, progressive, or reversible. **Senile dementia** refers to this condition if it first occurs after age 65. In younger people, it is called **presenile dementia.** A common symptom of dementia is **confabulation,** in which a person compensates for loss of particular memories by filling in the gaps with inaccurate details.

PSYCHOLOGICAL FUNCTIONING OVER TIME

Elderly persons are at greater risk than the general population for developing disorders involving brain degeneration. They are also at greater risk for depression as a result of increased life stress that may be age-related. It is important to remember, however, that there are many examples of successful aging.

Alzheimer's Disease **Alzheimer's disease** is the most common form of both senile and presenile dementia. This disease's characteristic loss of neurons from the frontal and temporal lobes of the cerebral cortex leads to memory lapses, confusion, and eventual physical and mental deterioration. Research on Alzheimer's disease has focused on neurochemical changes in the brain and on genetic factors. Researchers also have explored ways to help families adapt to the stress of caring for a person with this disease.

Pick's Disease **Pick's disease** is much less common than Alzheimer's disease. This disorder can be diagnosed only at autopsy by a characteristic form of brain atrophy.

Huntington's Disease **Huntington's disease** is a rare hereditary disorder transmitted by a single dominant gene. It results in a progressive degeneration of brain tissue. Its symptoms have been found to be related to a deficiency of one neurotransmitter, GABA, and are thought to be related to a gene pair on chromosome 4.

Parkinson's Disease Symptoms of **Parkinson's disease** are progressive deterioration in intellectual ability, increased rigidity in coping, tremor, and mask-like facial appearance. This disease is believed to be related to a dopamine deficiency and can be treated with the drug L-dopa.

Brain Trauma: Injuries, Tumors, and Infections Brain injuries, tumors, and infections can result in profound cognitive and behavioral consequences. Some of the changed behavior may be the result of psychological factors related to the injury. Such changes are referred to as **traumatic neurosis.** Brain injuries are classified into three groups: **concussions,** which result in transient problems; **contusions,** where there is diffuse damage; and **lacerations,** which involve major tears or ruptures in the brain tissue. Brain tumors can result in a variety of behavioral changes depending on the location of the tumor. AIDS dementia complex (ADC) and general paresis are examples of dementia caused by infections.

AMNESTIC DISORDERS

Amnestic disorders are disturbances of memory due either to a medical condition or the effects of drugs, medications, or exposure to toxic chemicals. People with amnestic disorders have difficulty learning new material and/or recalling previously acquired information. Amnestic impairments can be transient or chronic.

THE DIVERSITY OF COGNITIVE IMPAIRMENT DISORDERS

Many cognitive impairment disorders do not fit neatly into established diagnostic categories. There is wide diversity of cognitive impairments.

Cerebrovascular Accidents Cerebrovascular accidents (CVAs), or **strokes,** are blockages or ruptures of the blood vessels in the cerebrum. Some of the effects may be similar to those of dementia, but the onset is sudden rather than gradual. **Vascular dementia** is caused by a series of minor strokes that occur over a period of time.

Pellagra and Korsakoff's Syndrome Pellagra is a reversible disease caused by a deficiency of the vitamin niacin. Kor-

sakoff's syndrome is the result of a combination of alcoholism and vitamin B_1 deficiency.

Epilepsy Epilepsy is due to an abnormality in brain cell behavior that may have many causes. Some epilepsies are related to generalized seizures and others can be traced to a source in a specific area of the brain. **Grand mal seizures** last several minutes and include loss of consciousness and convulsions. **Petit mal seizures** are lapses of consciousness that last less than a minute and do not include convulsions. **Psychomotor epilepsy** involves a trance-like state lasting up to two minutes and may include outbursts of emotion. Epilepsy may be treated with drugs, surgery, or psychological management depending on the symptoms.

AN INTEGRATIVE APPROACH TO BRAIN DISORDERS

Although brain disorders involve organic problems, knowledge of psychological factors is very important in predicting exactly how a person's behavior will be affected. Each of the psychological perspectives is useful in understanding the impact of these disorders.

CHAPTER FOURTEEN

Raul Guerrero, *Coco Club*, 1989.
Daniel Saxon Gallery, Los Angeles.

SUBSTANCE-RELATED DISORDERS

The gentleman in the corner had been regarded as a true American success, lanky and deep-voiced, brilliant and beloved, the master of all he surveyed. Now, he gazed out defiantly, as if still on the summit, too high to see the cat feces at his feet or the unopened mail or the mirror that would have told him he was master of nothing but his own delusions.

Those who were to thrust the mirror in front of the 62-year-old man, whom I will call James B., were his daughter Isabel, myself, and three of the friends who loved him best.

If James B. had denied his problem, so had we. He had been depressed over the death of his wife and the loss of his architectural business. He had been presenting different excuses to each of us for his growing isolation. He had kept us at bay by clever use of the telephone, until it was cut off for nonpayment of a bill he had never opened.

Yet at last we had gathered into a crisis intervention team and surprised him, hung over, before he could perfect his alibis. . . .

"Daddy, we are here because we love you." Isabel's voice wavered, but the 9-month-old baby on her knee stared at her grandfather unblinkingly. James B., very gingerly, poured out coffee. "I can understand your concern," he said. He had thrown on a shirt—even a tie—but below his bathrobe, his thin, red legs had the look of arms flung down in defeat. "I've had this local flu. I've been going to my doctor for shots every day."

"I checked with your doctor, Daddy, and he hasn't seen you for two years. We think your disease is alcoholism."

All of James B.'s roles now seemed to collide and fall away, revealing the obsession which shone in his eyes like unrequited love. "That's preposterous! My problems have nothing to do with alcohol."

Mel, his former business partner, said he had watched the most brilliant man he had ever known become addled into dull predictability. George, his former chess opponent, blushed and said that James B. had begun to cheat at the game. Lisa, his former lover, tremulously said she was going to marry a man she didn't love because the one she did had not preferred her to the bottle. I reminded him of all the people, including my baby and Isabel's, who could still learn from him.

Coached about the new science of alcohol and the liver, we tried to convince James B. that there was no shame in being an alcoholic.

"Look, can't you understand?" James B. said. "I'm sick, yes; depressed, yes; getting old, yes. But that's all."

"Jim," Mel said, in a voice that resonated with the tension we all felt, "it sounds like you would rather be anything at all than an alcoholic."

After 14 hours of this scenario, some of us began to question whether he really was an alcoholic. Maybe it was some other illness. Then he let spill a few words. "Geez, if I couldn't go down to the pub for a few, I think I'd go nuts!"

"Aaah," Isabel said. "You just admitted it." She put the baby on her father's knee. "Look at your granddaughter. This is your immortality, Daddy, and she needs you. Please don't die. Please choose life, for us."

James B. put his face, the color of gravel, in his hands. No one spoke. When he looked up, he said he would go to a local hospital.

Alcohol is one of a group of substances that have ruined the lives of countless numbers of people. Although there are many differences among them, all of these substances are **psychoactive drugs;** that is, they affect thought, emotions, and behavior. A generalized reduction in goal-directed behavior (for example, going to school or work), together with cognitive deficits (such as inability to concentrate), is a common consequence of prolonged heavy use of a psychoactive substance. As the case of James B. shows, they are capable of causing not only changes in motivation and ability to concentrate and think clearly but also serious physical symptoms. This case also illustrates the tendency of abusers to deny that the substance they are using excessively is a major factor in their problems.

The scope of the problem of substance abuse is suggested by the fact that in 1993 a government survey showed that 11.7 million Americans were drug abusers (*Substance Abuse and Mental Health Services Administration News*, Summer, 1994). The survey found that illicit drug use, heavy drinking, and smoking go hand-in-hand. Twenty-six percent of heavy drinkers and 12 percent of smokers were also illicit drug users. Sixty percent of those who reported current illicit drug use used only marijuana and an additional 16 percent used marijuana plus one or more other illicit drugs. (About 5.1 million people reported using marijuana weekly.) As Figure 14-1 shows, while the numbers of users of illicit drugs had decreased significantly from 1979, the 1993 figures remain large. Ominously, the survey found that only half of youths 12–17 years of age felt there was great risk in using marijuana occasionally, or in trying cocaine, PCP (phencyclidine), or heroin. Teenagers' use of marijuana and alcohol seems to be on the increase (*The New York Times*, December 13, 1994). Thus, the use of addictive substances continues to be a serious problem.

Addiction is a term that has been used to describe the harmful effects of excessive reliance on drugs for pleasure and relief of tension. This term is not used in DSM-IV, which instead focuses attention on substance dependence. DSM-IV contains two broad categories of disorders related to the use of psychoactive substances, the Substance-Use Disorders and the Substance-Induced Disorders.

Substance-Use Disorders

Substance-use disorders include problems associated with using and abusing such drugs as alcohol, cocaine, and heroin that alter the way people think, feel, and behave. There are two subgroups of Substance-Use Disorders, those related to substance dependence and those related to substance abuse.

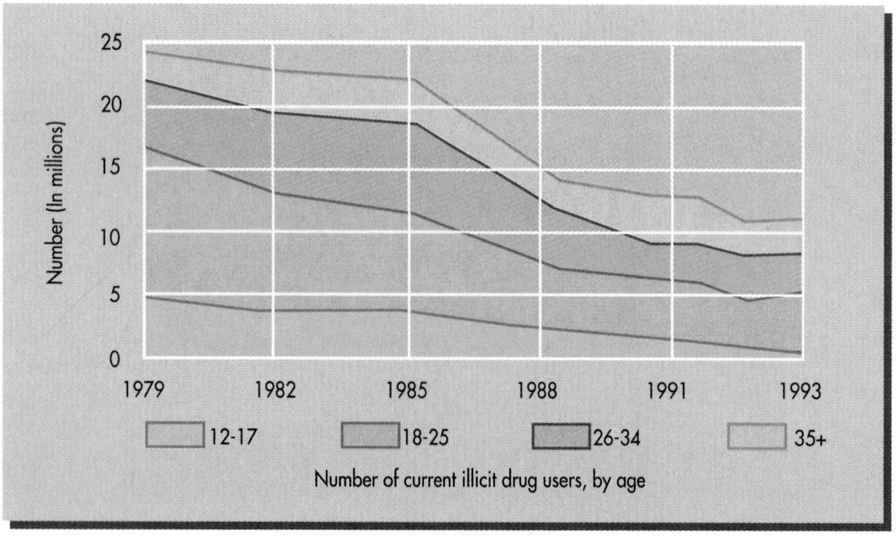

Substance Dependence

DSM-IV defines substance dependence as a maladaptive pattern of substance use that leads to clinically significant impairment or distress. Table 14-1 presents the criteria for this disorder. Cognitive, behavioral, and physiological symptoms define the condition of **substance dependence.** Most individuals with substance dependence have an intense craving for a particular substance. They continue to use it even though doing so exacerbates their substance-related problems. There are alterations in their bodily systems (particularly the nervous system) when

Figure 14-1 Results of *Substance Abuse and Mental Health Services Administration* 1993 Survey.

TABLE 14–1
Criteria for Substance Dependence

The presence of three or more of the following criteria in the same 12-month period establishes the existence of substance dependence.

1. Tolerance, as defined by the need for markedly increased amounts of the substance to achieve the desired effect and a markedly diminished effect with continued use of the same amount of the substance.
2. Withdrawal, as defined by the characteristic withdrawal syndrome for the substance and use of the substance to relieve or avoid withdrawal symptoms.
3. Ingestion of larger amounts or over a longer period than was intended.
4. Persistent desire or unsuccessful effort to cut down or control substance use.
5. A great deal of time spent in activities necessary to obtain the substance, use the substance, or recover from its effects.
6. Elimination or reduction of important social, occupational, or recreational activities that are given up or reduced because of substance use.
7. Continued substance use despite knowledge of having a persistent or recurrent physical or psychological problem that is caused or exacerbated by the substance.

drug use is discontinued, and a need for increased frequency and amount of the substance to get the same effects as previously. Withdrawal symptoms occur if use of the drug is discontinued. Substance-dependent individuals show a distinctive pattern of repeated use that usually results in tolerance, withdrawal symptoms, and compulsive drug taking.

Tolerance means that the person has to use more and more of a substance to get the same effect, or that the same size dose has progressively less effect as time goes by. Reactions to morphine and alcohol are examples of tolerance build-up. The pain-reducing power of morphine decreases if the drug is given over a long period. As alcoholics consume increasing amounts of alcohol, their cell membranes are altered so that less and less of the alcohol permeates the membranes. If less alcohol is actually penetrating cell membranes, an alcoholic may have less alcohol in his or her brain than a normal person with the same blood level of alcohol would. This is interesting in view of the fact that some alcoholics can perform well after consuming an amount of alcohol that would put a nonalcoholic into a coma. Whereas tolerance for alcohol is considerable, it is usually much less extreme than tolerance for some other substances, such as, amphetamines. The degree to which tolerance develops varies greatly across substances.

Withdrawal refers to a particular set of physical symptoms that occur when a person stops or cuts down on the use of a psychoactive substance. The severe physical reaction that occurs when heroin use is curtailed is probably the best-known form of withdrawal. Withdrawal symptoms vary greatly across the classes of substances. Marked and generally easily measured physiological signs of withdrawal are common with alcohol and anxiety-reducing drugs. Withdrawal symptoms are often present, but less apparent, with stimulants such as amphetamines and cocaine.

Compulsive substance use involves behavior related to obtaining the substance, frequently called drug-seeking behavior, and behavior associated with the actual ingestion or use of the substance. Someone who is dependent on a drug gives its use a much higher priority than other behaviors that once had higher value. Substance-dependent individuals may expend inordinate effort and time trying to obtain the substance to which they are dependent, and frequently when it is available they are unable to control the amount they use or the length of time they use it. This lack of control may be manifested by unsuccessful efforts to reduce or stop using the substance despite a persistent wish to do so. They may continue to use the substance, often in situations in which it is physically hazardous to do so, despite the awareness of the serious problems it causes.

Substance Abuse

In **substance abuse** there are recurrent and significant adverse consequences related to the use of substances. These consequences include repeated failure to fulfill major obligations (for example, as a parent), repeated use in situations in which it is physically hazardous to do so, legal problems, and recurrent social and interpersonal problems. The criteria for substance abuse do not include tolerance, withdrawal, or a pattern of compulsive use. Instead, its outstanding features are only the harmful consequences of repeated use. A diagnosis of substance abuse is most likely in individuals who have only recently started taking the substance. Table 14-2 presents DSM-IV criteria for this disorder.

The concepts of substance dependence and substance abuse have been controversial and this controversy has been reflected in DSM changes over the years. In DSM-II the term *dependence* included both psychological and physiological dependence. Psychological dependence had to do with psychologically based substance-seeking behavior that results in a fairly regular schedule of daily or continuous usage, while physiological dependence referred to substance-seeking behavior in which physiologically-based tolerance and withdrawal play key roles. In DSM-III, *dependence* was used only in the physiological sense and required evidence of either tolerance or withdrawal. As we have seen, DSM-IV distinguishes

TABLE 14–2
Criteria for Substance Abuse

The presence of three or more of the following criteria within a 12-month period establishes the existence of substance abuse.

1. Recurrent substance use resulting in a failure to fulfill important obligations (for example, at work, school, or home).
2. Recurrent substance use in situations in which it is physically hazardous to do so (for example, driving an automobile when under the substance's influence).
3. Recurrent substance-related legal problems (e.g., arrests).
4. Continued substance use despite having persistent or recurrent social or interpersonal problems caused or exacerbated by the effects of the substance (for example, physical fights).

between substance dependence and substance abuse. As we have pointed out, the criteria for substance dependence include tolerance, withdrawal, and compulsive use and those for substance abuse are essentially psychological problems and maladaptive behavior (for example, failing to fulfill social or work responsibilities). However, some writers have argued that there is no meaningful distinction between substance abuse and substance dependence and that substance abuse is simply a less severe (and overlapping) variant of substance dependence (Widiger & Smith, 1994). While there is agreement that drug usage becomes a substance use disorder when persons are significantly impaired in their control of this usage, increased knowledge concerning the physiological and psychological aspects of the process will no doubt influence future efforts at classifying these disorders.

Substance-Induced Disorders

Recent ingestion of certain substances can lead to serious behavioral, psychological, and physiological signs and symptoms. Different substances have quite distinctive effects. **Substance intoxication** is usually associated with substance abuse or dependence. However, one or more episodes of intoxication alone are not sufficient for a diagnosis of either substance dependence or abuse. Evidence for recent ingestion of the substance is obtained from physical examination (for example, smell of alcohol on the breath), case history, and analysis of bodily fluids (for example, urine or blood). DSM-IV's criteria for substance intoxication include the development of reversible substance-specific symptoms due to recent ingestion of or exposure to a substance and clinically significant maladaptive behavioral or psychological changes due to the effect of the substance on the central nervous system. The most common indications of intox-

ication are disturbances of perception, wakefulness, attention, thinking, judgment, motor behavior, and interpersonal behavior. The substance, the dose, the history of using the substance, the person's tolerance for the substance, the period of time since the last dose, the person's expectations regarding the substance's effects, and the environment or setting all can influence level of intoxication. **Substance-induced disorders** cause a variety of symptoms that are characteristic of other mental disorders. These symptoms include delirium and psychotic behavior.

Psychologists are interested in substance-use disorders and substance-induced disorders because a person's response to drugs seems to be due to a combination of physiological and psychological factors. Some people can control their use of many psychoactive substances; others seem unable to do so. Some individuals have severe withdrawal symptoms; others do not. The effects that drugs produce also differ from one user to another.

People differ in their vulnerability to the negative effects of particular substances and their resilience when confronted with experiences of substance use. Probably both the personality and physiological characteristics of the user and the environment or setting in which the substance is used influence the reaction observed. This is another case in which the interaction between the person and the situation, which has been referred to so often throughout this book, is important in understanding individual behavior. However, although these individual characteristics have a major influence on a person's response to a mood- or behavior-modifying substance, such substances do have certain general effects that are experienced by most people who use them. Table 14-3 describes some of the effects of six types of psychoactive substances, along with their prominent symptoms and effects of overdose.

To gain an appreciation of the diversity of substance-related disorders, we turn now to a review of the major ones, beginning with problems related to the use of alcohol. In most cultures, alcohol is the most frequently used brain depressant and a cause of serious and widespread interpersonal and health problems.

Alcohol-Related Disorders

Alcohol has been used for recreational, medicinal, and ceremonial purposes for at least ten thousand years. The oldest of all archaeological records contain reference to its use. The **alcohol** that is contained in beer, wine, and hard liquor is a chemical compound known as ethyl alcohol or ethanol. Only ethanol is safe for human consumption—other kinds of alcohol are isopropyl alcohol (rubbing alcohol) and methyl alcohol (wood alcohol). Ethanol is manufactured by two methods, distillation (hard liquors) or fermentation (beer and wine).

TABLE 14–3
Several Types of Substances, Their Effects and Symptoms, and the Consequences of Overdose

Substance	Typical Effects and Symptoms	Consequences of Overdose
Alcohol	Tension reduction followed by depressed physical and psychological functioning.	Disorientation, loss of consciousness, and death at extremely high blood-alcohol levels.
Tranquilizing Drugs	Depressed reflexes and impaired motor functioning, tension reduction.	Shallow respiration, dilated pupils, clammy skin, weak and rapid pulse, coma, possible death.
Amphetamines	Increased alertness, excitation, euphoria, increased pulse rate and blood pressure, sleeplessness.	Agitation, hallucinations, paranoid delusions, convulsions, death.
Heroin	Initial euphoria followed by apathy, drowsiness, "rush" of pleasure, impaired judgment.	Slow, shallow breathing, nausea, clammy skin, vomiting, convulsions, coma, possible death.
LSD	Illusions, hallucinations, distortions in time perception, loss of contact with reality, palpitations.	Psychotic reactions.
Marijuana	Euphoria, relaxed inhibitions, increased appetite, possible disorientation, dry mouth.	Fatigue, possible psychosis.

Despite the different production methods used, the ethanol contained in all these beverages is the same drug. The only difference is in the amount of alcohol as a percentage of total volume. In beer and wine, the percentage usually varies from 3 to 14 percent. In hard liquor, sometimes called distilled spirits, the percentage varies from 40 percent (80 proof) to 75 percent (150 proof). The amount of pure ethanol is generally about the same in a one-ounce shot of whiskey (or other hard liquor), a four-ounce glass of wine, or a twelve-ounce bottle of beer.

In the short term, alcohol acts on the central nervous system as a "blocker" of messages transmitted from one nerve cell to the next. It first affects the frontal lobes of the brain, the seat of inhibitions, reasoning powers, memory, and judgment. After continued consumption, it next affects the cerebellum, the seat of motor muscle control, balance, and the five senses. Finally, it affects the spinal cord and medulla, the seat of involuntary functions such as breathing, heart rate, and body temperature control. If enough alcohol is consumed, to the point of a blood-alcohol level of 0.50 percent or more, the involuntary function system can shut down and the person may die from acute alcohol poisoning.

Excessive Alcohol Use

Negative effects of overuse of alcohol have been considered a serious problem for many years. About 70 percent of adults in America drink alcohol on occasion; 12 percent of these Americans are heavy drinkers, people who drink almost every day and become intoxicated several times a month. More men than women are heavy drinkers. For both men and women, the prevalence of drinking is highest and abstention is lowest in the 21- to 34-year age range. Table 14-4 provides estimates of the percent of alcohol in the blood as a function of amount of alcohol consumed and body weight.

Over the years, the terminology used to describe the excessive use of alcohol has ranged widely. It has been characterized in terms of alcohol dependence, alcohol abuse, as a disease that is essentially an involuntary disability, and alcoholism. Characterizing it as alcoholism usually recognizes that it involves multiple causes, signs, and symptoms that usually include dependence and abuse. DSM-IV defines **physiological dependence on alcohol** in terms of tolerance and symptoms of withdrawal. **Alcohol abuse** is defined in terms of behavioral indicators such as lowered job performance

TABLE 14-4
Are You Drunk?

This table shows the estimated percent of alcohol in the blood according to body weight and the number of drinks consumed. One drink is calculated as equal to one ounce of 100-proof alcohol, a 4-ounce glass of wine, or a 12-ounce bottle of beer. Alcohol in the blood decreases over time. To calculate how much time decreases blood-alcohol level, subtract .015 for each hour that has passed since the first drink.

| Body Weight | \ \ \ \ \ \ Drinks | | | | | | Interpreting the Results | |
	1	2	3	4	5	6	BLOOD ALCOHOL PERCENT	INTOXICATED?
100 lbs.	.038	.075	.113	.150	.188	.225	0.000 to 0.050%	No
120	.031	.063	.094	.125	.156	.188	0.050 to 0.100	Maybe[a]
140	.027	.054	.080	.107	.134	.161	0.100 to 0.150	Probably
160	.023	.047	.070	.094	.117	.141	0.150 and above	Yes
180	.021	.042	.063	.083	.104	.125		
200	.019	.038	.056	.075	.094	.113		
220	.017	.034	.051	.068	.085	.102		
240	.016	.031	.047	.063	.078	.094		

[a]In most states, 0.100 is proof of illegal intoxication.

Source: Government of the District of Columbia.

and poor interpersonal relationships. In **alcohol intoxication** there are clinically significant behavioral and psychological changes (for example, inappropriate sexual or aggressive behavior, slurred speech, incoordination, impaired attention or memory, and coma).

Alcohol and Risk Regardless of the terms employed, there is agreement about the harmful effects for individuals and the community of excessive intake of alcohol. Forty percent of all traffic fatalities (the leading cause of accidental death) are alcohol-related (see Table 14-5). Highway accidents in which alcohol is involved are the primary cause of death for young people. After 18-year-olds received the right to vote in 1971, the legal drinking age was lowered in many states. Studies of auto accident statistics from these states produced convincing evidence that the age reduction had resulted in an increased proportion of auto crashes and fatalities involving youthful drivers. Since 1976, therefore, many states have raised the drinking age. In the 12 months after Michigan raised the drinking age, accidents resulting in death or injury among 18- to 20-year-olds dropped by 28 percent.

Research data show that alcohol is also involved in a high percentage of nontraffic accidents: Almost 50 percent of people who die from falls had been drinking; 52 percent of the fires that lead to adult deaths involved alcohol; and 38 percent of drowning victims had been drinking (*Alcohol and Health*, 1990).

Alcohol and Health Perhaps 20 percent of the total national expenditure for health is alcohol-related. A recent survey found that over 10,000,000 Americans have major problems of alcoholism, most of which

TABLE 14-5
Is It Safe to Drive?

The amount of alcohol that seriously interferes with driving skills varies from person to person, and even an individual's tolerance can vary over time. In general, however, impairment increases with each drink and the subsequent rise in blood-alcohol level. As little as one drink, especially if you do not drink regularly or if you drink on an empty stomach, can make you an unsafe driver.

0.05 Blood-alcohol concentrations of 0.05 percent and above can mean lax thought, judgment, and restraint. There may be a significant increase in mistakes in tasks requiring divided attention. Steering errors increase and vision is affected.

0.10 Around 0.10 percent, virtually all drivers are significantly impaired. Reaction time to novel situations requiring choices is slowed, as are reactions to sounds or visual stimulation. Voluntary motor action is affected, with arm movements, walking, and speech usually becoming noticeably clumsy. At this blood-alcohol level, the likelihood of being involved in a crash is six times that of a sober driver.

0.20 At 0.20 percent, the entire motor area of the brain is significantly depressed, and the person is very drunk. Staggering is likely. Reaction time is even slower, especially in divided-attention tasks. The person may become loud, incoherent, and emotionally unstable. At this level, the risk of a crash is 100 times that of a sober person.

involve physiological dependence (tolerance, withdrawal, and drinking to relieve or avoid withdrawal symptoms) (Grant, 1992). Alcoholism shows several typical patterns: regular daily intake of a large amount, regular heavy drinking confined to weekends, and unpredictable binge drinking (long periods without alcohol interrupted by episodes of heavy drinking lasting for weeks or months). Much excessive use of alcohol that has not reached clinical proportions might be called **problem drinking.** While problem drinking should not be viewed as an inevitable step on the way to alcoholism, one study found that over a four-year period 30 percent of people initially categorized as problem drinkers and alcohol abusers had become alcohol dependent (Hasin et al., 1990). Figure 14-2 shows the change from drinking as part of a social activity to the solitary drinking behavior typical of alcoholism. Box 14-1 presents a first-person account of the downward spiral of an alcoholic.

Alcohol abuse and dependence are linked to physical, as well as behavioral, impairment. Table 14-6 describes the negative effects of alcohol on various bodily organs and systems. When alcohol is abused extensively, brain damage can result. For example, CT scans of young chronic alcoholics show reductions in the density of their left brain hemispheres compared to those of nonalcoholic individuals (Golden et al., 1981). Brain dysfunction is present in from 50 to 70 percent of detoxified alcoholics at the beginning of treatment. Certain cognitive abilities of people who use alcohol only moderately in social situations have been found to be impaired even 24 hours after they last used alcohol (Eckhardt et al., 1981).

The damaging effects of alcohol use by pregnant women on their unborn children has also been clearly documented. Because alcohol freely crosses the placenta, the developing fetus's blood alcohol level will be equal to that of the mother. As a result the child may develop **fetal alcohol syndrome** which produces physical malformations and mental retardation. It was at first thought that fetal alcohol syndrome was related to the mother's heavy alcohol use and to binge drinking in particular. More recent research has shown that even light to moderate alcohol use may have negative effects on the unborn child. (Fetal alcohol syndrome is discussed in detail in chapter 16.)

In addition to what alcohol does to the body, its role in behavioral maladaptation is also powerful (Cox, 1990). This fact is reflected in recent comorbidity data showing that among people with alcohol disorders, another mental disorder appears in 37 percent of cases (Robins & Regier, 1991). Alcohol disorders in men are associated with an eightfold risk for psychotic episodes; in women, there is a threefold risk (Tien & Anthony, 1990). The highest comorbidity rates are for affective, anxiety, and antisocial personality disorders. Comorbidity rates are generally higher in women than men. The causes of high comorbidity rates related to alcohol abuse and dependence have not yet been discovered. When two disorders are associated, the one that occurs first might be a risk for the other. Overall, alcoholism precedes depression in the majority of cases. However, among women, depression comes first (Meyer, 1989).

Surprisingly, alcohol may also have some beneficial effects. Moderate use of alcohol (two ounces per day) may lessen the chances of a heart attack (Ahlawat & Siwach, 1994). It is not clear why this should be the case, but researchers have suggested a number of possibilities. Alcohol may reduce psychological stress, or it

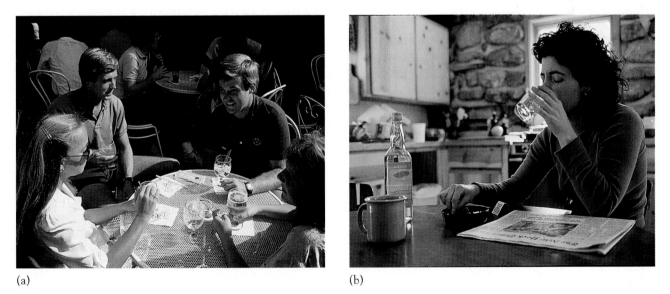

(a)　　　　　　　　　　　　　　　　　　　　　　(b)

Figure 14-2 Drinking takes place in many different settings. *(a)* These couples have incorporated a drink with friends as one aspect of a pleasant social interaction. *(b)* This solitary drinker is likely to be using alcohol as a way of dealing with worries or depressed feelings.

The Downward Spiral of an Alcoholic

My alcoholism took years to develop into a chronic affliction, and during much of that time I went to bars after work, one of the guys. The delusion was gradually reinforced by gravitation. I mingled more and more with other persistent drinkers who took longer and longer to call for their bar tabs. Most of us were actually alcoholics in varying stages of development. The nonalcoholics had long ago selected themselves out. Those of us who remained agreed that we were "normal." Unhappy, but normal.

Alcoholic perceptions are like that, in a hundred insidious and distorting ways. All of them are aimed at protecting a drunkard's notion that he is possessed of free will. My drinking buddies and I agreed that we did not have a drinking problem. Everything in our increasingly narrow world, though, was a problem that required drinking: the wife, the kids, the boss, the government. In dingy watering holes from which everyone with a healthy life to lead had gone home, we conspired to overlook the obvious, that our bodily cells were addicted, and our minds were along for the ride.

Inexorably, the need for alcohol grew, while the lies wore thin. As my alcoholism accelerated, I abandoned most drinking partners and joined the ranks of solitary topers bellied up to countless bars. I lost any sense at all of what would happen after I started drinking; I became completely unpredictable. Some-times I would go home after a couple of drinks (there was usually more booze there). More often, I would join the lineup of other alcoholics at the bar telephone stalls, fumbling with worn-out excuses about unexpected visitors and urgent business meetings.

Sometimes I would simply hole up in my office with a bottle after everyone else had gone home. There simply wasn't anything else in my life. Most frightening of all, I began to suffer alcoholic blackouts during drinking episodes. I would swim back into consciousness with no recollection of where I had been or what I had done. Once, I came to late at night on a downtown city street with my suit trousers slashed down one side by a razor.

---

may promote the formation of substances that help prevent or remove the plaque that can clog coronary arteries. Some researchers and public health officials are concerned that announcing positive effects of alcohol use will be interpreted as a suggestion that drinking is desirable for everyone. They point out that it is premature to recommend alcohol as a heart-attack preventative. A moderate amount for one person may be too much for another because of individual differences in tolerance for alcohol.

Perspectives On Alcohol-Related Disorders

Alcohol-related disorders do not have just one cause. There are many and they often combine to produce bodily, psychological, and behavioral effects. Therefore, it is not surprising that several theoretical perspectives have contributed to research on these disorders.

The Biological View After the first drink, the average person experiences a lessening of anxiety. As more alcohol is consumed, the depressant action of alcohol affects brain functions. The individual staggers, and his or her mood becomes markedly unstable.

Influenced by evidence that heavy drinking leads to a variety of bodily changes, writers have often characterized alcoholism itself as a disease. E. M. Jellinek (1960), often referred to as the father of the modern study of alcoholism, believed that alcoholism is a permanent and irreversible condition and that alcoholics are essentially different from nonalcoholics. Alcoholics, he contended, experience an irresistible physical craving for alcohol. Satisfaction of this craving leads to loss of control as a result of increasing physical dependence on alcohol. Alcoholic individuals feel compelled to continue drinking even after ingesting only a small amount of alcohol. Jellinek believed that the only way alcoholics can return to a normal life is through complete abstinence.

TABLE 14–6
The Effects of Alcohol on the Body

Bodily Organ or System	Effect
Brain	Brain cells are altered, and many die.
	Memory formation is blocked.
	Senses are dulled.
	Physical coordination is impaired.
Stomach and Intestines	Alcohol can trigger bleeding and can cause cancer.
Heart	Deterioration of the heart muscle can occur.
Immune System	Infection-fighting cells are prevented from functioning properly.
	Risk of bacterial disease is increased.
Reproduction	In men: hormone levels change, causing lower sex drive and enlarged breasts.
	In women: menstrual cycles become irregular and ovaries malfunction.

Some of Jellinek's ideas have been questioned on the basis of research findings that seem inconsistent with them. However, Jellinek's concept of alcoholism as a disease did succeed in changing people's attitude toward alcoholics from one of condemnation and blame to one of concern. In addition, it focused researchers' attention on the biological aspects of alcohol abuse.

Genetic Factors in Susceptibility to Alcohol Studies using animals have shown that it is possible to breed strains of mice or rats that differ in the way they metabolize alcohol (Goodwin, 1986). Although the results are clearer for sons than daughters, it has been demonstrated many times that alcoholism runs in human families as well. Sons of alcoholics are about four times more likely to be alcoholic than are sons of nonalcoholics. Adoption studies show this is true even when children have no exposure to their biological parents after the first few weeks of life (Schuckit, 1987). Evidence for genetic predisposition to alcoholism is growing, and it is now widely accepted by researchers that alcoholism can result from the interaction of heredity and environment.

Studies of individuals who had a biological parent with alcoholism but were removed from the alcoholic environment through adoption at an early age have allowed assessment of the relative contributions of genetic and environmental factors in the genesis of alcoholism. Some studies have identified two types of genetic predisposition to alcoholism—*male-limited* and *milieu-limited* (Cloninger et al., 1981). In the male-limited type, susceptibility occurs only in males and early in their lives. In the milieu-limited form, a combination of genetic susceptibility and environmental provocation is needed to produce alcoholism that is usually less severe than the male-limited type.

Researchers are attempting to identify the specific gene or genes that might be linked to alcoholism. Although some researchers believe there are genes specific to alcoholism, others think alcoholism results from a set of biological factors that are heavily influenced by environmental events.

Knowledge that alcoholism has both genetic and environmental components can have important practical applications. If reliable biological indicators of a predisposition toward alcoholism can be found, individuals who have those indicators can know the risks they face and can make informed choices about drinking (see Figure 14-3). Another practical application is improved treatment. It is already clear that alcoholism is not a single disease. By clarifying the nature of various subcategories of alcoholism, genetic studies can point the way to more specific and effective therapies based on the genetic uniqueness of individuals.

Genetic molecular variations in alcohol-metabolizing enzymes are a major area of research on the heredity of alcoholism because a mutation that produces a slight alteration in the molecular structure of these enzymes could be expected to have a pronounced effect on their ability to remove alcohol from the body. Many investigators believe that such studies have the potential of explaining fundamental mechanisms of alcoholism and of identifying genetic markers of susceptibility (Korenman & Barchas, 1993).

Alcohol and the Nervous System Alcohol affects every system of the body, but its greatest, most immediate, and most visible effects are on the central nervous system. All the complex features of an individual—thoughts, emotions, actions—are based on chemical and electrical processes which occur in billions of nerve cells at any instant. Several features of this system could be involved in inherited predisposition to alcoholism.

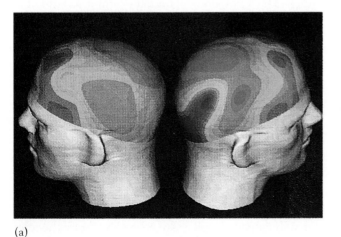

(a)

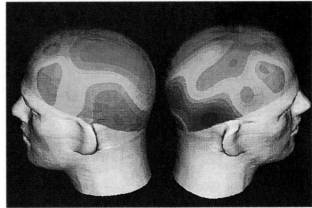

(b)

Figure 14-3 Use of computerized scanning techniques has made it possible to work toward determining patterns of electrical activity in the brain that may identify those at high risk for alcoholism. These maps of differential electrical brain activity in controls (a) and individuals at high risk for alcoholism (b) were constructed by recording event-related brain potentials from 32 scalp electrodes and then using a mathematical computer program to construct the visual images. In the two photos, the electrical activity, represented as color shading, forms a somewhat different pattern for the controls and the at-risk groups. Further research will be needed to determine the role genetic factors play in heightened risk patterns.

Alcohol could interfere with numerous processes involved in nerve cell function, and if there is inherited variation in these processes it could result in either neurochemical vulnerability or resistance to alcoholism. Among the leading neurochemical hypotheses are the following.

- Individuals who are predisposed toward alcoholism might have nerve cell membranes that are less sensitive to the permeability-altering effects of alcohol, which would affect the movement of sodium and potassium ions and the propagation of nerve impulses.
- Predisposition toward alcoholism might be based on inherited variations in the sensitivity of certain enzymes to inhibition by alcohol. This also would affect the transmission of nerve impulses, which depend on the enzyme's regulation of the flow of ions through the nerve cell membrane.
- Predisposition toward alcoholism may be based on inherited variations in the neurotransmitter release and uptake systems involved in the chemical propagation of nerve impulses between nerve cells.
- People who are predisposed to alcoholism may produce abnormal amounts of certain morphinelike compounds that may be involved in alcohol addiction.
- Predisposition toward alcoholism may be based on inherited variations in the brain's neurochemical mechanisms for reinforcing certain behaviors.

Central to several biological theories of the effects of alcohol is the idea that a reward center exists in the brain that mediates all types of reinforcement, including reinforcers such as food and various types of drugs (including alcohol). Consequently, the inherent abuse potential of a given substance is likely to reflect its ability to activate this reward pathway. Controversy exists concerning the precise site of this reward center (Korenman & Barchas, 1993).

Sensitivity to Alcohol Individual sensitivity to the effects of alcohol varies greatly. As noted earlier, some people can remain conscious after drinking a quantity of alcohol that would cause others to pass out, become comatose, or even die. Others are so sensitive to alcohol that just one or two drinks can produce acute discomfort accompanied by obvious physiological changes. These individual variations are probably due to differences in the ability to metabolize alcohol or to innate differences in the central nervous system's sensitivity to alcohol.

When compared with men, women have much less of a specific stomach enzyme (alcohol hydrogenase) that neutralizes and breaks down alcohol. As a result, when a woman and a man drink the same amount, proportionately, for their size and weight, about 30 percent more alcohol enters the woman's bloodstream. When women drink too much alcohol, the small amount of the

enzyme that they do have loses its ability to break down alcohol in the stomach. For alcoholic women, drinking alcohol is essentially the equivalent of injecting it intravenously, bypassing stomach digestion entirely. In male alcoholics, however, the enzyme still can neutralize alcohol, but not so well as in men who do not drink to excess. This enzyme may be one reason that women's livers get diseased more quickly than men's.

A comparison of people of different racial stock may shed light on the genetic component of these differences in alcohol metabolism. There is evidence of a high prevalence of sensitivity to alcohol among people of Asian derivation (Chinese, Japanese, Koreans, Native Americans, and Eskimos). Signs of sensitivity—rapid facial flushing, elevated skin temperature, and increased pulse rate—after consuming moderate amounts of alcohol appear to be common among these groups but are seen in only 5 percent of Caucasians. Studies suggest that these differences are based on genetic variations in the enzymes involved in alcohol metabolism (*Alcoholism: An inherited disease*, 1985).

The Psychodynamic View Psychodynamic theorists often describe the typical person who develops an alcohol problem as an **oral-dependent personality.** They believe that such a person's basic need for oral gratification was not satisfied early in life. This lack of satisfaction resulted in the development of an individual who is driven to secure oral satisfaction through such devices as drinking, smoking, and eating, and whose personality is characterized by self-doubt, passivity, and dependence.

Although there is no conclusive evidence that personality factors are involved in the development of alcoholism, a study reported by Jones (1981) demonstrated a consistent set of personality attributes among some alcoholics. The study drew upon data from a longitudinal research project that had begun when the subjects were ten-and-a-half years old. In middle age the subjects were interviewed about their drinking patterns. Jones found that as adults, male problem drinkers were likely to be described as relatively hostile, submissive, socially unsuccessful, and anxious. In general, these men had been rated as rather extroverted in adolescence. However, at that time they also described themselves as having less satisfactory social relationships and greater feelings of inferiority than did other males in the study. Jones believed that these men were rather impulsive and unsure of themselves in adolescence and that they had difficulty forming deeper, more lasting friendships. Additional longitudinal studies are needed to clarify the roles of personality and psychodynamic factors in alcohol use.

Psychoanalysts see overuse of alcohol and other psychoactive substances as products of neurotic conflict, doubt and anxiety about one's self-worth, and attempts to make up for an impaired self-concept. While they judge certain characteristics (a condemning view of oneself, for example) as a vulnerability to substance overuse, psychoanalysts tend to neglect physiological and social variables that may be vulnerability factors.

Learning Factors According to learning theorists, one reason people drink is that alcohol is reinforcing. People experience effects from drinking alcohol that can cause them to drink again to repeat the experience. Through its effects, alcohol can be a positive reinforcer, producing positive sensations in the brain, or a negative reinforcer, alleviating negative associations, such as anxiety. Studies have shown that some of alcohol's actions in the brain and blood stream can cause an animal to seek alcohol and even to work for it (for example, press a lever) to repeat the experience it elicits. Demonstrating that alcohol is negatively reinforcing, studies have shown that alcohol reduces anxiety in mice placed in an open maze. If mice are given alcohol before being placed in sections of the maze that they would otherwise avoid, they then spend more time in those sections (Grant, 1992). With animal models, researchers are learning which networks of nerve cells are responsible for reinforcement and how it might be modified.

If alcohol alleviates anxiety, then does higher anxiety lead to increased drinking? A study that compared drinking in adolescent rhesus monkeys raised by their mothers with drinking in monkeys raised only with their peers noted that peer-reared monkeys displayed more anxiety-related behaviors and drank more alcohol than mother-reared animals (Higley et al., 1991). However, when the mother-reared monkeys were isolated from one another, an event that caused stress, their levels of drinking increased until they almost matched those of peer-reared animals. Some people drink as a way of coping with problems of living. They learn this behavior through reinforcement (being accepted by friends who value drinking), modeling (seeing others "solve" their problems with alcohol), and other learning mechanisms (see Figure 14-4). Short-term use of alcohol may be reinforcing for many people because of the pleasurable feeling of relaxation it produces. But since drinking is not an effective coping mechanism, their life situation does not improve. Feeling even less able to cope constructively, they increase their maladaptive coping behavior.

It is also possible that alcohol is sought for its short-term excitatory actions and is reinforcing because it makes people "feel good." Like all psychological phenomena, reinforcement has underlying neurochemical mechanisms. Several studies have implicated certain neurochemicals in the reinforcing properties of alcohol. Alcohol may make many people "feel good" because it alters the levels of dopamine and norepinephrine, as well as opioid peptides, in a specific brain region. Sub-

jectively, these neurochemical changes are experienced as excitation, and because that experience can be pleasurable, people will seek alcohol again.

Cognitive Factors Behavior is influenced by expectations about the consequences of behaving in a particular way as well as by what actually does happen. Behavior thus can be shaped and maintained by cognitive appraisals of what has happened and what is likely to happen. A problem drinker learns to expect positive effects from drinking and interprets the experience in that way, despite the fact that the predominant quality of the actual experience is negative.

The importance of expectancy is illustrated by an experiment reported by Marlatt and others (1973). These investigators used a taste-rating task to determine whether drinking rates are affected by the actual presence of alcohol or merely by the expectancy of alcohol. The taste-rating task was an unobtrusive measure of drinking because the person's attention was focused on the taste of the drinks. The drinks used were vodka and tonic, and tonic alone. The subjects were permitted to

Your best friends are the ones who tell you not to drink.

"I was eleven when I started drinking, and I was hooked on it for four years. If I saw a friend drinking today, I'd tell her what I went through. And I'd tell her not to drink."
Alcohol is a drug. And you can get hooked on it. It's a fact. The younger you start, the more

addictive it is and the more damage it can do.
It's not easy to say no. But if you want to be somebody, you have to learn.
To find out more, contact the National Council on Alcoholism in your area. Or write NCA, 12 West 21st Street, New York, NY 10010.

Say no. And say yes to your life.

Figure 14-4 This poster illustrates a modeling approach to discouraging alcohol use with its "Say No" message. Its focus is to help young people resist peer pressure to use alcohol.

drink as much of the beverages as they wished in the time allotted. The researchers found that the only significant determinant of the amount of alcohol consumed was the subjects' expectations regarding what they were drinking; those who expected alcohol drank more. This finding supports a cognitive interpretation of drinking. (Later in the chapter we discuss the applications of this cognitive perspective to therapy for problem drinkers.) Figure 14-5 shows a naturalistic setting for experiments on drinking behavior.

There is evidence that a person's belief about the alcohol content of a drink, regardless of its actual content, can be a significant determiner not only of alcohol consumption but also of various behaviors that may accompany or result from drinking, such as depression, delay of gratification, social anxiety, and sexual responsiveness in men. This evidence comes from studies, like the one described above, using the *balanced placebo design*, in which half of the subjects are given a drink containing alcohol and half are given a nonalcoholic beverage. By varying both drink content and expectancy set, this design permits joint and separate evaluation of the behavioral consequences of a subject's belief that he or she has consumed alcohol and the consequences of actual alcohol consumption.

Social and Community Factors The problem of excessive use of alcohol has sociocultural as well as psychological dimensions. The values and customs of the community influence attitudes toward drinking. In the past, problems of alcohol use were extremely frequent among certain ethnic groups, such as the Irish and Swedish, relatively infrequent for Italians, and particularly infrequent for Jews. Today, however, alcoholism is

decreasing among Irish- and Swedish-Americans but rising among second- and third-generation Italian-Americans and Jews. Changing social customs within the cultural group seem to be a significant factor in these patterns of alcohol consumption.

Rates of alcoholism are low in groups in which the drinking customs, values, and sanctions are well known, agreed to by all, and consistent with the rest of the culture (see Figure 14-6). Among the sociocultural conditions that minimize alcohol problems are the following:

1. Exposure of children to alcohol at an early age in a strong family or religious setting. The alcoholic beverage is served in diluted form (wine as opposed to distilled spirits, for example) and in small quantities.
2. The beverage is considered a food and is served mainly at meals.
3. Drinking is not considered either a virtue—for example, a proof of manhood or virility—or a sin.
4. Abstinence is socially acceptable but excessive drinking or drunkenness is not.

A variety of social and interpersonal factors also influence alcohol consumption. These include the level of stress in the community and in the individual's personal life (Sayette, 1993). Among the personal factors are friendships, family situation, and employment and financial status (Linsky and others, 1985).

An Interactional View During recent years, a more complex biopsychosocial view of alcoholism has developed. At the core of this newer concept of alcoholism is a cycle that results in a perpetuation of harmful drinking. This cycle involves the following elements:

1. Certain vulnerable individuals are more likely to develop alcohol dependence because of biological, psychological, or social predisposing factors (for example, genetics, depression, or peer influence).
2. Heavy drinking is intensified by precipitating factors such as stressful life events or psychological instigators (for example, anxiety or insomnia).
3. The vulnerable individual finds alcohol rewarding, either because of the euphoria produced or the dysphoria assuaged.
4. Alcohol abuse develops as a consequence of these rewarding experiences resulting in tolerance and increased drinking.
5. Physical dependence follows, along with the need to drink to prevent withdrawal symptoms.

Figure 14-5 Student volunteers pose as research participants in an Alcohol Skills Training Program session held at the Behavioral Alcohol Research Laboratory (BARLAB) at the University of Washington.

Figure 14-6 The context in which alcoholic beverages are consumed is an important factor in alcoholism. Drinking wine at family gatherings, like this Jewish Passover ceremony, is much less likely to lead to problem drinking than imbibing in situations in which there is pressure for the individual to "excel at drinking."

6. The addictive cycle is further intensified by persistent physiological craving.
7. Physical dependence mechanisms tend to become reactivated by alcohol ingestion after a period of abstinence, with accompanying reinstatement of the self-defeating cycle.

Perhaps the greatest need in research on substance-related disorders is for consideration of the simultaneous effects of a number of personal, social, and cultural factors on alcohol consumption. It is important to examine the interactive effects of these factors in order to explain current levels of alcohol consumption. For example, two individuals with similar biological vulnerabilities (for example, sensitivity to alcohol) might consume quite different amounts of alcohol depending on social (peer) pressure to participate in drinking parties.

Treatment

The first step in treating alcohol dependence is usually **detoxification,** or "drying out." Detoxification, which usually is carried out in a protected, well-supervised setting such as a hospital, is aimed at removing the effects of a toxic substance (e.g., alcohol) from the body. Physiological withdrawal symptoms often begin 6 to 24 hours after heavy drinking has stopped, although they can occur as soon as alcoholics simply reduce their intake of alcohol. Withdrawal signs can include tremors, delirium, sweating, confusion, increased blood pressure, and agitation. There is no established sobering agent—nothing that counteracts the effects of alcohol or speeds its breakdown and passage out of the body. Many alcoholics can withdraw on their own, but some are so severely dependent that they have to be detoxified—supervised as they go through a gradual withdrawal. Once detoxification is complete, insomnia, depression, and anxiety may persist for weeks or months. However, these conditions usually receive no treatment after the detoxification period has ended.

Most recovery from alcoholism is not the result of treatment. Probably no more than 10 percent of alcohol abusers are ever treated at all, but as many as 40 percent recover on their own. Alcoholics with a stable job and family life have the best chance of recovery; age, sex and the duration of alcohol abuse matter less. An important step in overcoming alcoholism is the alcoholic's acknowledgment of the disorder. As the case of James B. at the beginning of this chapter pointed out, alcohol abusers, feeling ashamed and guilty, often refuse to admit the problem to themselves and try to conceal it from their families and friends, who in turn may avoid acknowledging it for fear of being intrusive or having to take responsibility. It is valuable in clinical inter-views to determine the patient's willingness to admit the seriousness of his or her drinking problem (see Table 14-7).

Denial and obliviousness are not the only sources of misunderstanding. In a society that has so many heavy drinkers, it is not always easy to decide when a drinking problem has become so serious that special help is needed. Alcoholism can be hard to observe day by day, even if it's easily recognizable over a period of years. Patterns of abuse through a lifetime are variable, the symptoms come and go. Alcoholics are not always drinking uncontrollably; some drink only on weekends, and many succeed in remaining abstinent or nearly abstinent for months at a time. In the following sections we describe several treatment programs for problem drinkers and detoxified alcoholics.

The Biological Approach Earlier in the chapter we mentioned that biological theories regarding susceptibility to alcohol might someday lead to effective physical

TABLE 14–7
Determining Extent of Drinking Problem and Alcoholic's Willingness to Admit the Problem—The Initial Steps in Treatment Planning

It is not necessarily useful simply to ask how much a person drinks, because the response is likely to be vague and may be influenced by denial. One of the best ways of determining the extent of denial of the symptoms is a series of questions that can be addressed to alcoholics. Some helpful questions about drinking patterns or habits are the following:

Do you sometimes drink heavily after a disappointment or quarrel?

Do you always drink more heavily when you feel under pressure?

Are you drinking more often without eating?

Do you try to sneak in extra drinks on social occasions?

Have you attempted various ways to control your drinking?

Have you failed to keep promises to yourself to cut down?

Do you avoid your family and close friends while drinking?

Useful questions about feelings include:

Do you feel guilty about your drinking?

Do you want to go on drinking when your friends have had enough?

Do you often regret what you have said or done while drinking?

Do you feel uncomfortable if alcohol is not available in certain situations?

Are you annoyed by the way others talk about your drinking?

If friends or family members can be interviewed these questions might be addressed to them:

Does this person's drinking ever worry or embarrass you?

Does it spoil family holidays?

Does it create a tense atmosphere?

Do you lie to conceal it?

Does he or she try to justify the drinking or avoid discussion of it?

Do you or your children fear physical or verbal assault from this person when he or she is drinking?

Does this person become remorseful and apologize after a drinking episode?

Do others talk about this person's drinking?

---

therapies for alcoholism. While such therapies have not yet been developed, in the past decade research into the pharmacological treatment of alcoholism has become increasingly active. Several drugs have been developed for the treatment for alcohol dependence and are used in the management of withdrawal symptoms, the treatment of certain psychological problems (for example, anxiety) in heavy drinkers, and in other aspects of rehabilitation. Research is also being conducted with the aim of developing a pharmacological agent that might reduce alcohol cravings. Achieving this goal will require more knowledge concerning the behavioral and biological factors that regulate alcohol intake. Several neurotransmitters and neurohormones may play roles in the acquisition, maintenance, and cessation of alcohol consumption. Continued research on the mechanisms underlying these behaviors may yield more clinically useful drug treatments.

Another biological approach to alcohol problems is to alter the body's response to alcohol. The drug disulfiram provides one way to do this because it causes extreme and sometimes violent discomfort (nausea, vomiting, cold sweats) when a person drinks alcohol within 12 hours of taking it. Since disulfiram is self-administered, the success of this technique depends on the individual's motivation to reduce or eliminate drinking. If the person wants to drink, disulfiram therapy will fail. It may be useful, however, as part of a therapeutic approach that also deals with motivations or situational cues that lead to alcohol use.

The Community Approach One outgrowth of the view that alcoholism is a disease, caused perhaps by physiological sensitivity to alcohol, is the belief that the alcoholic needs to avoid alcoholic beverages completely. According to the disease model, losing control of drinking is an involuntary manifestation of an internal addictive disorder. If one drink is enough to set off a drinking binge in alcoholics who want to rehabilitate themselves, that drink must not be taken. Alcoholics Anonymous (AA), the most widely used group treatment for alcoholism, attempts to help the alcoholic resist taking that one drink. Consequently, the AA program is widely recommended by adherents of the disease model.

Alcoholics Anonymous is a community-based approach to alcoholism. There are more than 89,000 groups throughout the world with more than 2,000,000 members in 141 countries. Most members are referred to AA by other AA members and by rehabilitation and counseling programs. AA expects recovering alcoholics to admit their personal powerlessness over alcohol and seek help from a higher power, which can be understood in any way an individual member chooses. Members are urged to pray or meditate to get in touch with that power. They are asked to make a "moral inventory," confess the wrongs they have done, beg forgiveness, make amends, and carry the message to other alcoholics. AA takes the position that anyone who has once been an alcoholic is always an alcoholic; the disease can be arrested by vulnerability is permanent.

The most famous AA slogans are "It's the first drink that gets you drunk," which states the goal of abstinence, and "One day at a time," which places present action before long-term planning. AA members are told that although alcohol is the source of their problems they must assume responsibility for their own recovery. They must also resolve to devote themselves to helping others in need as part of their own rehabilitation.

The effectiveness of AA has not been scientifically documented and methodological problems make such an evaluation difficult. Because many alcoholics drop out of the program, presumably as failures, they are not counted when the percentage of members who successfully abstain is calculated. In addition, not all people with alcohol problems are willing to join AA. Because the organization is committed to the idea of total abstinence from alcohol, individuals who believe they have a problem with alcohol but want to reduce rather than cease their drinking probably would not join the group. Because its members represent a selected population of those with alcohol-related problems their percentage of success in remaining abstinent does not necessarily represent the success rate for all alcohol-dependent people if they belonged to AA.

One of AA's most important rehabilitative ingredients is the social support it provides for members. Members know they can call upon fellow members at any time for aid in resisting the temptations of alcohol. Although AA may not be the right approach for every alcoholic, for those who find it congenial it can be a valuable source of support, belongingness, and security. While not formally affiliated with any professional organization or institution, AA now represents a major referral resource for alcoholic patients.

The Psychodynamic Approach Clinicians who take a psychodynamic perspective advocate psychotherapy for alcoholics. Although there have been some encouraging clinical reports on the usefulness of psychotherapy, research on the topic has not yet produced definitive conclusions. Most studies of psychotherapy with alcoholics are not comparable with respect to such important variables as the setting in which the treatment was applied, the duration of the therapy, and the criteria by which the therapy was evaluated.

The use of psychotherapy to help people with alcohol problems may be limited by the fact that they often need help at odd hours in their efforts to stay sober. The low self-esteem of some overusers of alcohol may be even further lowered by having to depend on people who do not have an alcohol problem.

In the past, psychotherapists believed that alcoholism was merely a symptom of underlying psychological difficulties. The logical conclusion was that such patients would improve in regard to their drinking, if such difficulties were successfully addressed. Today, it is widely recognized that psychotherapeutic exploration for someone who is still drinking not only provides very little benefit but may be barely remembered from one session to the next.

An increasing number of psychodynamically oriented clinicians recognize the value of looking at alcohol problems from the standpoint of the family system rather than the individual. These therapists acknowledge that alcohol abuse not only affects families but is also influenced by how the family interacts and functions as a system. For this reason, it is necessary to find out whether family behavior patterns have been organized and altered to accommodate the unique demands of the alcoholic member. Family therapists view the whole family, not the alcoholic member alone, as the primary patient. While treatment goals vary from case to case, family therapists often focus their attention on restabilizing family behavior after cessation (or reduction) of drinking has taken place. In some cases, a major effort is needed to restructure relationships within the family.

The Learning Approach Learning theorists may make use of **aversive conditioning** in their treatment of alcoholics. Aversive conditioning is based on the principles of classical conditioning (see chapter 3). If a glass of alcohol (conditioned stimulus) regularly precedes an aversive stimulus such as a nausea-producing drug (unconditioned stimulus), the alcohol will eventually elicit some part of the unconditioned response—in this case, vomiting. Once the unpleasant response has been conditioned to alcohol, the habit of avoiding alcohol will be established through operant conditioning. The response of abstinence is strengthened because it reduces the unpleasant feeling (nausea) that the conditioning situation has associated with alcohol. Electric shock is sometimes used in place of nausea-producing drugs in this procedure, but it seems to be less effective. Aversive conditioning approaches often require "booster sessions" because the threat of an unpleasant reaction tends to weaken over time. Long-term follow-up studies are needed to establish the success rate of this therapeutic method.

Another learning approach, **covert sensitization**, uses aversive images and fantasies rather than actual shocks and chemicals. Alcoholic patients are told that they can eliminate their "faulty habit" by associating it with unpleasant stimuli. They are instructed to close their eyes and imagine that they are about to drink an alcoholic beverage. They are then taught to imagine the sensations of nausea and vomiting. If it is repeated often enough, the association between nausea and the sight, smell, and taste of alcohol is presumed to establish a conditioned aversion to alcohol.

The Cognitive Approach Many cognitively based alcohol programs are focused on controlled drinking rather than on abstinence. The **controlled drinking** approach means that the emphasis is on building participants' coping skills so that they can keep their alcohol consumption to the level they have previously determined is acceptable. In this approach, clients are oriented toward monitoring their own behavior by noting the situational and environmental antecedents and consequences of heavy drinking. Their past learning in relation to drinking is reviewed, and their expectations about the effects of alcohol are discussed. Participants in controlled-drinking programs are encouraged to ask themselves questions such as the following:

- At what places am I most likely to overdrink?
- With which people am I most likely to overdrink?
- When am I most likely to overdrink?
- How do I feel emotionally just before I begin to overdrink?

Special emphasis is placed on drinking as a response to stress. This approach makes sense, since a high percentage of people with alcohol problems report that their heavy drinking often begins when they are faced with unpleasant, frustrating, or challenging situations. Improved problem-solving skills, particularly in the area of interpersonal relationships, learning how to anticipate and plan for stressful experiences, and acquiring the ability to say "No, thanks" when offered a drink have been shown to have therapeutic value for alcoholics (Marlatt & Gordon, 1985).

One reason that learning approaches may not be effective is that the short-term effects of alcohol often are positively reinforcing. Only the effects of overconsumption, ending in intoxication, dangerous or socially frowned-upon behavior, or a period of binge drinking have negative-reinforcement properties. The cognitive perspective deals with this problem by focusing the client's thoughts on the consequences of the drinking behavior as well as on the specific situations in which

drinking is most likely to appear tempting. The client and the therapist work together to develop cognitive coping techniques to deal with these situations.

Relapse Prevention While the goal of therapeutic efforts is to help alcoholics stop drinking, or drinking to excess, maintaining sobriety over the long term is also of great importance. Alcoholics who undergo treatment have a high relapse rate. Many go through treatment a number of times or through a number of treatments and still relapse into uncontrolled drinking.

For those who view alcoholism as a disease, a relapse is a failure that the victim is powerless to control. From the cognitive viewpoint, a relapse is a slip or error. The cognitive approach views a relapse as a fork in the road. One fork leads back to the abusing behavior, the other toward the goal of positive change.

Relapse-prevention programs combine a cognitive approach with a variety of treatment procedures designed to change the individual's drinking pattern (Daley & Marlatt, 1992; Marlatt & Gordon, 1985). Such programs can be used whether the goal is abstinence or controlled drinking. The only requirement is that the client make a voluntary decision to change. The relapse-prevention approach assumes that the person experiences a sense of control over his or her behavior as long as the treatment program continues. If the person encounters a high-risk situation, this sense of control is threatened and a relapse is likely. High-risk situations include negative moods such as frustration, anger, or depression; interpersonal conflicts such as an argument with an employer or family member; and social pressure to indulge in drinking. If the person is able to make an effective coping response—for example, denying the offer assertively when friends suggest "just one drink"—the probability of a relapse decreases. Figure 14-7 describes the cognitive-behavioral approach to the relapse process.

An important factor in relapses is the **abstinence-violation effect.** When a relapse occurs, the individual has two kinds of cognitive and emotional responses. One is conflict and guilt; the other is an attribution to temporary situational factors rather than a permanent personal weakness or lack of self-efficacy. An alcoholic who breaks abstinence for the first time may continue to drink after the lapse in order to relieve the conflict and guilt related to the first drink. The individual may also reduce the conflict between the drinking behavior and the goal of avoiding relapses by thinking: "This just proves I'm an alcoholic. I can't control my drinking once I start it." Rather than attributing the lapse to the difficult situation, people who use these cognitions are likely to blame themselves for lack of willpower or inability to resist temptation. Such thoughts increase the probability that a single drink may snowball into a full-strength alcoholic binge and a total relapse.

In addition to viewing any slip into drinking as a

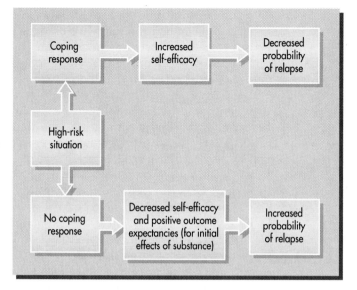

Figure 14-7 A cognitive-behavioral analysis of the relapse process begins with exposure to a high-risk situation. A high-risk situation is any situation that arouses stress, negative emotions, strong urges and temptations, or interpersonal conflict. Having a coping response increases the sense of self-efficacy (feeling that one is in control) and decreases the probability of relapse. Not having a coping response decreases self-efficacy (and heightens the feeling of not being in control) and, together with positive expectations about the favorable effects of the substance, increases the probability of relapse.

temporary lapse and not necessarily a permanent relapse and a sign of personal failure, one of the primary goals of the relapse-prevention program is to train the individual to recognize the early-warning signals that may precede a relapse and to plan and carry out a series of intervention or coping strategies before it is too late. The relapse-prevention technique holds promise not only for alcohol abuse but also for drug use, smoking, and other problems of self-control such as dieting. Its main components—identifying high-risk situations and learning pertinent coping and behavioral skills—are applicable to many types of situations. Table 14-8 lists some ways in which lapses can be handled in a positive manner. Many relapse-prevention programs recommend that individuals carry a card with them listing some coping techniques. Further research is needed that explores short- and long-term effects of relapse-prevention techniques.

Abstinence versus Controlled Drinking A sometimes intense and angry dispute about the necessity for abstinence began in the 1960s when studies reported that some former alcoholics could continue to drink moderately. Most advocates of controlled drinking are behavioral or cognitive-behavioral therapists who see alcohol abuse as a bad habit or a personal or social problem. Defenders of abstinence, including Alcoholics Anonymous and many medical and mental health professionals, believe that loss of control is inevitable for an alcoholic once drinking starts. They tend to regard alcoholism as a disease whose progress can be arrested only by removing the poison that causes it.

Critics of the disease perspective argue that while abstinence can work well for some individuals, it is very hard to live up to; moreover, recovery from alcoholism may not require such a drastic step. One study suggested that alcohol abusers can recover without abstinence (Polich et al., 1980). In this investigation, known as the *Rand study*, over 900 individuals with severe alcohol problems were studied for four years after they had been admitted to one of eight federal alcoholism treatment centers. The researchers found that at the end of this period almost half of the subjects were either abstaining from alcohol or drinking in a controlled manner.

Another longitudinal study also found that some alcohol abusers can return to drinking on a controlled basis without abusing alcohol (Vaillant & Milofsky, 1982). However, subjects who were alcohol-dependent and/or had many alcohol-related problems generally achieved successful results only if they became abstinent (see Figure 14-8).

These findings suggest that there may be two groups of alcohol abusers. Some can successfully resume drinking on a controlled basis. Others must abstain entirely if they are to cope with their alcohol problem. Both studies show that level of abuse before treatment plays an important role in the success of various treatment strategies. However, most researchers in this area would agree that the success rates of treatment procedures are not high enough.

Further research on such issues as the value of abstinence versus controlled drinking needs to be sufficiently complex to take account not only of subjects' drinking

| TABLE 14–8 |
| Learning from a Lapse |

A temporary lapse can be used as an opportunity for learning and need not signal defeat. The first priority is to prevent slips by anticipating high-risk situations and preparing ways to handle them. When a lapse does occur, it helps to carry a card listing coping tactics tailored to personal needs. Such advice might include:

1. Treat the slip as an emergency requiring immediate action.
2. Remember that a slip is not a relapse.
3. Renew your commitment.
4. Review the actions that led to the lapse so you won't repeat them.
5. Make an immediate plan for recovery.
6. Ask someone for help.

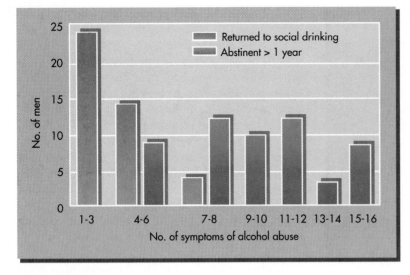

Figure 14-8 A return to controlled social drinking has a greater chance of success if the person has only a few symptoms of alcohol abuse. Only four men who had seven or more problems were able to return to social drinking. Most of these multiproblem people who did not resume alcohol abuse eventually became abstinent.

SOURCE: *Archives of General Psychiatry, 39,* 127–133. Copyright © 1982, American Medical Association.

histories but also of their motivations and expectations about what would constitute success in coping with their drinking problems. For example, how much does abstinence change the life of an alcoholic? Alcoholics in the first few years of abstinence have been compared with returning prisoners of war. Their world is unfamiliar, because they have been living in an environment created by alcohol. Feelings that have been blunted or suppressed come back to trouble them. They have lost a great deal of time and must start where they left off. Being sober, like being free after imprisonment, entails new responsibilities. Alcoholics in the early stages of abstinence thus often suffer from anxiety and depression and may find it difficult to hold a job or preserve a marriage. The resolution of these problems comes when they establish new personal relationships, rebuild old ones, and begin to develop confidence in their power to control their lives (Rosenberg, 1993).

Preventing Alcohol-Related Disorders

Although there has been much research related to the treatment of alcoholism, expert opinions differ concerning which treatments are particularly effective. One difficulty in interpreting the available evidence is that many people (perhaps over 50 percent) who enter alcohol treatment programs drop out of them, and no one knows what happens to these dropouts. Studies compar-

ing inpatient and outpatient programs have produced conflicting results. It is becoming clear that much treatment research has failed to identify differential effectiveness because different types of patients have been lumped together in study populations. Despite conflicting findings concerning treatment programs, a picture of which alcohol abusers are likely to do well, regardless of the treatment, is emerging: people with jobs, stable relationships, minimal psychopathology, no history of past treatment failures, and minimal involvement with other drugs.

Research on treatment for alcoholism is improving and should yield practical results. Preventing alcohol abuse, however, would obviously be better than having to treat it. Unfortunately, less is known about prevention than about treatment. According to some studies, taxes that raise the price of alcohol and therefore reduce a society's total consumption have a more than proportionate effect on serious alcohol abuse. There are usually fewer alcohol problems in countries where the price of alcohol is high relative to the average income. It is less clear whether merely limiting alcohol advertising is effective.

Other community-level strategies that can be useful from the standpoint of prevention are raising the minimum drinking age, regulating the types of outlets and the hours during which alcohol may be sold, establishing tough drinking-and-driving laws, and carrying out various types of educational programs directed at important target groups. Box 14-2 presents information about the scope of the alcohol-abuse problem in one setting, the college campus, and suggests some practical approaches to prevention.

The overuse of alcohol and other drugs during adolescence and early adulthood continues to be a public health problem. The problem is serious because for the developing young adult these substances undermine motivation, interfere with cognitive processes, contribute to debilitating mood disorders, and increase risk of accidental injury or death (Hawkins, Catalano, & Miller, 1992). Researchers have had difficulty developing preventive interventions with long-term staying power and are seeking ways of conceptualizing prevention programs that are likely to be successful. One way of approaching this task is to identify risk factors for overuse and then develop programs aimed at reducing them. Preventing the following risk factors for overuse of alcohol and other psychoactive substances might significantly reduce the problem currently confronting society.

Drinking on Campus

In stark contrast to the purposeful bustle along the hospital corridor that crisp February dawn, a cluster of bewildered students glanced silently at each other as they waited to find out whether Jim Callahan was dead or alive. Full of fear, for him and for themselves, the fraternity brothers replayed the previous night in their minds, again and again. The initiation ritual was supposed to have been funny—a test of the fraternity's power over its new pledges. Wasn't it a good job, to order them to drink "kamikazes" in the frat house basement until they were sick? The freshmen could sleep it off, after all. But when 18-year-old Jim Callahan passed out early on the morning of February 12, 1988, he never woke up.

Later, doctors would explain that Callahan died from acute alcohol poisoning caused by drinking a huge quantity of alcohol in a very short time. He drank about 24 ounces—nearly three-fourths of a liter—in 30 to 45 minutes following a Lambda Chi Alpha pledge-pinning ceremony.

This tragedy took place at Rutgers University, but there have been similar events at other educational institutions (see Figure 14-9). Although drinking among college students as a whole has declined from 89 percent in 1981 to 80 percent in 1991, surveys show that the rate of abusive drinking among college students has held relatively steady. This is in contrast to a decline in the rate of binge drinking among people in the same age group who are not college students (see Figure 14-10). The universities surveyed reported that the number of cases involving alcohol poisoning of students that are treated at medical centers has generally doubled (Celis, 1992).

According to another recent survey, 44 percent of college students are binge drinkers defined as having five drinks in a row for men or four in a row for women on at least one occasion in the two weeks before the survey (Wechsler and others, 1994). At about one-third of the 140 colleges and universities surveyed

more than 50 percent of students were found to be binge drinkers, at another third, fewer than 35 percent were.

One prevention approach taken by two University of Washington researchers, G. Alan Marlatt and John Baer, has been the development of a six-to eight-week college course on sensible approaches to alcohol. Can merely taking a class alter harmful drinking habits? Marlatt and Baer found that course participants significantly reduced their alcohol consumption and maintained that reduction even two years later. Furthermore, two other groups—one that only read the class manual and another that received only brief verbal information—also cut their drinking significantly. These results are even more impressive because all those selected for the class were at high risk for alcohol problems through heavy drinking or factors such as a family history of alcoholism.

This prevention program does not tell students they must abstain from liquor (except for those who are alcoholics), which may be a contributing factor to the program's success. The course provides information from which students can assess whether they have a problem and decide what, if anything, they want to do about it. Emphasis is placed on sensible drinking as a skill. Drinking is compared with driving, both of which can be dangerous if practiced by an unskilled person. The course tells students that, as with driving, one must learn to drink by experience—what, when, where, and how much—one can't learn simply by being told how (Kivlahan and others, 1990). The course also asks students to monitor their own drinking behavior by providing answers to questions such as those in Table 14-9.

In a related approach, Marlatt (1994) used a one-on-one procedure. Called motivational interviewing, it avoids confrontation. Counselors meet individually with freshmen college students who were heavy drinkers in high school (five drinks in at least one setting during the previous month) to give them feedback on their drinking patterns, their beliefs about the effects of alcohol and the risks they face. Sessions are followed by

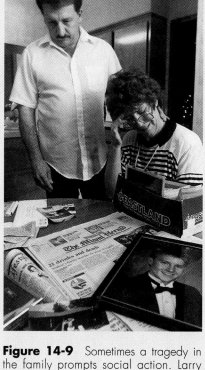

Figure 14-9 Sometimes a tragedy in the family prompts social action. Larry Wooten, a university junior, died as the result of the challenge from an old friend with whom he competed in sports, for grades, and in social activities. The pair challenged each other while watching a football game in a bar as to who could drink more in an hour. Larry drank one more drink than his friend, a total of 23 shots of liquor, but later died as a result. His parents, shown here, have mounted a campaign against alcohol abuse. Their efforts are part of many by parents, fraternities, and universities to try to control the trend toward abusive drinking by college students.

annual check-ups on changes in drinking behavior. Students who participated in this program saw a 68 percent drop in the average quantity of alcohol they consumed two years later. Consumption by a control group of heavy drinkers fell by a moderate 16 percent.

The Social Side of College Drinking

Drinking is a preferred way to socialize; few students drink alone. Those whose

Box continues on the next page.

drinking is getting out of hand are often threatened by those who don't drink. As long as others are consuming alcohol in large amounts, heavy drinkers rationalize that the amount they consume must be all right. Motives for drinking can vary quite a bit, however. For most students, college years are a time of experimenta-tion with a range of adult behaviors; drinking, especially when it is not one's family pattern, is one of these. For some students, college years are also a time for rebellion; under-age drinking is a way to flout the rules that say they are "too young." For some too, on campus as in society in general, drinking is a popular way to relieve stress. Other factors, such as ethnic patterns and heredity, may also play a role in drinking habits.

What Can You Do?

Here are some ways students can help themselves before they drink:

- Before a party, agree as a group on a designated driver—someone who will stay sober.
- Agree on ways to let someone know that he or she is drinking too much.
- Before drinking alcoholic beverages, provide and eat foods high in protein and carbohydrates.
- Pace drinks to one per hour.
- Have nonalcoholic beverages available, and switch to them after you reach your alcohol limit.
- Focus an event on dancing, dinner, or other activities, not on drinking.
- If someone becomes intoxicated, strongly suggest that he or she not drive, and drive the person home yourself or call a taxi. If necessary, let the person sleep overnight on the couch.
- If someone passes out, keep the person on his or her side, not on the back, and call for medical help.

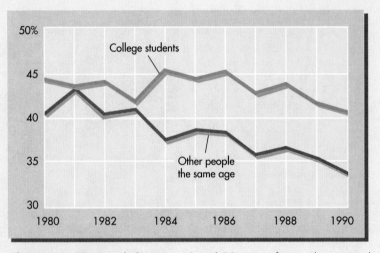

Figure 14-10 People between 19 and 22 years of age who reported that they had drunk at least five alcoholic drinks in a row at some time in the last two weeks.

SOURCE: National Institute of Drug Abuse as published in *The New York Times*, December 21, 1991, p. A8.

TABLE 14–9
Understanding Personal Drinking Patterns is the First Step to Sensible Alcohol Use

In order to help students understand the personal reasons for their alcohol use and the kinds of situations that are likely to lead to more drinking, one assignment to a class on sensible approaches to drinking involves thinking about and answering the following questions. The answers may give each student some important insights into his or her drinking patterns.

Are there any *places* where you are more likely to overdrink?
    (Yes/No) Where?

Are there any *people* with whom you are more likely to overdrink?
    (Yes/No) Who?

Are there any *times* or *days* when you are more likely to overdrink?
    (Yes/No) When?

Are there any *activities* that make it more likely that you will overdrink?
    (Yes/No) Describe them.

Do you think that you overdrink when you are *feeling* certain ways?
    (Yes/No) Describe those feelings.

Could you take a "vacation" from (avoid) any of the places or people involved in your overdrinking?
    (Yes/No) Which ones?

Are there places where you are *less likely* to overdrink?
    (Yes/No) Where?

Are there people with whom you are *less likely* to overdrink?
    (Yes/No) Who?

- Extreme economic deprivation
- Neighborhood disorganization
- Early and persistent behavior problems, including aggressive behavior and hyperactivity
- Poor family management practices
- Family conflict
- Lack of cohesion within the family
- Academic failure
- Social pressure to use drugs
- Alienation and rebelliousness
- Early peer rejection

Other Drugs

Strictly speaking, alcohol is a drug—it is a chemical substance that leads to physiological and psychological changes when ingested. But for most people the word "drugs" means pills, powders, and pot. In addition to alcohol, psychoactive drugs may be classified into several groups: barbiturates and tranquilizers, the opioids, cocaine, amphetamines, psychedelics, phencyclidine (PCP), marijuana, and nicotine.

Barbiturates and Tranquilizers

Barbiturates (such as phenobarbitol) and tranquilizers (such as Valium) are grouped together because they both have a depressing effect on the central nervous system. They probably do this by interfering with synaptic transmission. Either they inhibit the secretion of excitatory neurotransmitters or they cause the release of inhibitory transmitter substances. Both types of drugs reduce anxiety and insomnia and affect a wide range of bodily functions. They are both very popular. Each year Americans consume over 300 tons of barbiturates; tranquilizers are an even bigger business.

Barbiturates, or derivatives of barbituric acid, are prescribed by physicians for relief of anxiety or to prevent convulsions. Mild doses of barbiturates are effective as sleeping pills, although they may actually cause sleep disorders if used over a long period. Higher doses, such as those used by addicted individuals, trigger an initial period of excitement that is followed by slurred speech, loss of coordination, severe depression, and impairment of thinking and memory. Illicit use of barbiturates often occurs in conjunction with the use of other drugs, notably alcohol and heroin. The effects of alcohol and barbiturates are addictive, and this combination is especially dangerous.

The body quickly develops a tolerance to barbiturates and tranquilizers. As tolerance develops, the amount of the substance needed to maintain the same level of intoxication is increased. The margin between an intoxicating dose and a fatal one also becomes smaller (see Figure 14-11). These drugs can cause both physical and psychological dependence. After addiction has developed, sudden abstinence can cause withdrawal symptoms including delirium, convulsions, and death. The following case describes the results of an accidental overdose of one type of barbiturates, secobarbital (Seconal). Because Seconal is packaged in red capsules they are often referred to as *reds*, *red birds*, or *red devils*.

> *Judi A. was a young, attractive girl from a middle-class family who apparently was seeking something that eluded her. She died of an overdose of barbiturates.*
>
> *Judi A. had lived only 17 years, 5 months and 27 days before her nude body was found on a grimy bed which had been made up on the floor of a rundown apartment in Newport Beach [California]. A small pill was found on the bed near the body, another was discovered on the floor.*
>
> *Judi's death was classified as an accident because there was no evidence that she intended to take her own life. Actually it was about as accidental as if she'd killed herself while playing Russian roulette. Judi didn't intentionally take too many reds. She was familiar with them, had taken them before, knew what to expect. She'd even had an earlier scare from a nonfatal overdose. But her mind, clouded by the first few pills, lost count and she ingested a lethal number. She was dying before she swallowed the last pill.*
>
> —Adapted from Hazlett, 1971, p. 1

There are three types of barbiturate abuse.

1. *Chronic intoxication*, in which people obtain prescriptions, often from more than one physician. Initially they seek barbiturates to reduce insomnia and anxi-

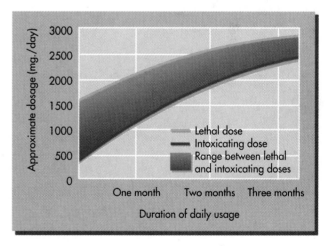

Figure 14-11 The relative relationship between lethal and intoxicating doses of short-acting barbiturates in the blood changes as tolerance develops. Dosages are only approximate because of individual differences in tolerance to the drug and patterns of use.

Source: Adapted from Wesson & Smith, *Barbiturates, Their Uses, Misuse, and Abuses*, (1977), Human Service Press, p. 35.

ety, and may then become addicted to the drugs. Chronic use leads to slurred speech and decreased effectiveness on the job.

2. *Episodic intoxication,* in which individuals take barbiturates orally to produce a "high" or state of well-being.

3. *Intravenous injections,* in which the drug is injected, often in combination with other drugs (such as heroin). Intravenous use produces a "rush" of pleasant, warm, drowsy feelings. Many complications are associated with prolonged use of the drug in this manner.

Relapses are common among barbiturate users because use of the drug is an easy way of escaping tension, anxiety, and feelings of inadequacy.

Some tranquilizers act like barbiturates, while others act quite differently. **Tranquilizers** are derived from several chemical groups. Overuse of tranquilizers is common. They are frequently prescribed to reduce anxiety, and perhaps half a million Americans use them for nonmedical purposes. As with barbiturates, the body develops a tolerance to many tranquilizers. Physical and psychological dependence and serious withdrawal symptoms may occur. Apparently unaware that they are addictive or that they can cause death, many people use tranquilizers freely. Just as they do with barbiturates, the undesirable effects of these substances increase when they are used in combination with alcohol and other drugs.

Valium is a member of the *benzodiazepine* group of tranquilizers. Drugs in this group produce less euphoria than other tranquilizing drugs, so the risk of dependence and abuse is relatively low. Nevertheless, tolerance and withdrawal can develop.

The Opioids

The term **opioid** refers to any natural or synthetic substance that acts on the body in a way that is similar to the action of derivatives of the opium poppy. These substances bind to and act upon opioid receptor sites in the brain. The opioids include a variety of substances, some of which occur naturally while others are synthetic. Heroin is the most well-known synthetic opioid.

Natural Opioids Several forms of opioids that resemble opium and heroin in their effects are manufactured by the brain and the pituitary gland. Three such distinct opioids are the **endorphins, enkephalins,** and **dynorphins.** Some of these substances can also be made artificially for experimental use. Research using natural opioids may provide insights into the mechanisms of pain, pleasure, emotion, and perception. The endorphins have been the most widely studied.

There is already some evidence that when individuals suffering from chronic spinal pain are treated effectively with acupuncture, endorphins are released into the spinal fluid (Jaffe, 1989). The endorphin levels seem to peak at the moments when the pain-relieving effects of the acupuncture are most pronounced.

Study of the endorphins has led to the mapping of the entire opioid-receptor system. The nerves of the brain and spinal cord have been found to contain specific receptor sites to which opioids must bind in order to produce their effects. Morphine and similar drugs block pain signals to the brain because they fit into these receptor sites like a key into a lock.

Work on the possibility that opiod-related disorders may respond to endorphin therapy has begun in several laboratories. Some scientists suspect the existence of a deficiency disease: The addict's craving for and dependence on opioids may be caused by chronic underproduction of natural endorphins. If this is the case, it may be possible to use synthesized endorphins to correct the underlying cause of addiction. Two possibilities might account for endorphin deficiencies. One is that the opioids themselves suppress endorphin production; the other is that some people have a genetically caused deficiency in endorphin production.

While the endorphins have been isolated and examined directly by biochemists, behavioral researchers have been able to study their action either by injecting endorphins into subjects and observing their analgesic (pain-killing) effects or by injecting a drug called *naloxone,* which blocks the effects of the endorphin. If a procedure produces analgesia when naloxone is not used but does not affect pain when naloxone is present, there is indirect evidence that endorphins mediate the pain-reducing effects of the procedure. For example, research done in China has shown that injections of naloxone greatly reduce the analgesic effects of acupuncture.

The Opiates The word **opiate** refers only to drugs of this type that are derived from the juice of the opium poppy, *Papaver somniferum.* Archaeologists think that the opium poppy's seemingly miraculous powers were first discovered by Neolithic farmers on the eastern shores of the Mediterranean Sea. This knowledge spread from Asia Minor across the ancient world, as the drug manufactured from the poppy, *opium,* became a valued commodity. In the seventeenth century opium was praised by a prominent physician as God's greatest gift to humanity for the relief of its sufferings.

In 1804 the most important active ingredient of opium, **morphine,** was identified. Physicians applauded it as a painkiller of known reliability. Opium and its derivatives were also used to treat coughs, diarrhea, fever, epilepsy, melancholy, diabetes, skin ulcers, constipation, and a variety of other ills well into the 1800s.

Many people became addicted to opium and its derivatives after it was given to them for medicinal purposes; nineteenth-century English writers Thomas De Quincy and Samuel Coleridge are examples. Opium derivatives were popular as home remedies, and until the 1860s there were few restrictions on who might sell or purchase them. One of the largest abuses of the drug was to sedate infants. Working mothers and women who tended babies for pay used these home remedies to keep infants sleepy and calm. By the late 1800s many physicians were becoming concerned about the problems of morphine addiction.

Just as morphine was at first considered a safe substitute for opium, **heroin,** which was produced for the first time in 1874 by boiling morphine in acetic acid, was at first hailed as a safe and effective substitute for morphine. This assertion soon proved to be horribly untrue, and today heroin is involved in over 90 percent of narcotic-addiction cases.

Heroin can be injected, smoked, or inhaled. Heroin addicts go through a characteristic sequence of experiences. After the drug is injected, the user feels a "rush" or "flash" as the nervous system reacts to its presence. Addicts describe the rush as an extraordinarily pleasurable sensation, one that is similar in many ways to sexual orgasm, only more intense and involving the whole body. Following the rush, the user experiences the "nods," a lingering state of euphoric bliss. Fatigue, tension, and anxiety fade away. Feelings of inadequacy are replaced by relaxed contentment. One young addict reported that after experiencing his first heroin high he had exclaimed to himself: "Why didn't they tell me such wonderful feelings existed?" A significant number of heroin addicts have stated that unless the world could provide them with a feeling to compensate for the loss of the high, they would never be able to give up heroin. The negative aspects associated with heroin, however, far outweigh the temporary feelings of well-being.

The Effects of Opioids Opioids have both sedative and analgesic effects. The opioids are sometimes called **narcotics,** but because this term is used differently by those who study drugs and by the legal system, it does not always have the same meaning to law enforcement personnel, laypeople, physicians, and scientists.

The opioids cause mood changes, sleepiness, mental clouding, constipation, and slowing of the activity of the brain's respiratory center. An overdose may cause death due to cessation of breathing. The withdrawal reaction can be severe and is manifested by sweating, muscle pains, nausea, vomiting, diarrhea, and other symptoms that may last for two or three days; less severe symptoms may persist for four to six months. Heroin use is likely to be associated with serious deterioration of both the individual's social life and family relations.

Causes of Opioid-Related Disorders A study of Vietnam War soldiers who used heroin heavily during the war found that a high percentage stopped using it when they returned home (Robins, 1993). This showed that, contrary to the widespread assumption that when a person used heroin extensively he or she became "hooked" on it, heroin addicts are not doomed for life. A study conducted in California found that cessation from using opiates is easier for individuals who are in their early thirties or younger (Hser, Anglin, & Powers, 1993). While the precise meaning of these findings is not yet clear, the finding that many veterans who used opiates in Vietnam were able to abstain upon returning home has stimulated interest in the idea that controlled use of at least some substances is possible for some people. Additional support for this view was provided by reports of people who have used opioids in a controlled manner for long periods. Although some users require drugs in increasingly large dosages every day, other daily users seem able to limit their intake. Perhaps the reason that controlled use of opioids has received relatively little attention is that people who are able to achieve such use do not come to the attention of clinicians. In any case, a better understanding of the process of opioid addiction is necessary so that effective social policies—for example, drug use laws and treatment procedures—can be formulated.

At present there are two competing views of opioid addiction: the exposure orientation and the interactional orientation. According to the **exposure orientation,** the cause of addiction is simply exposure to opioids. When a person experiences stress, endorphins are secreted and produce a stress-induced analgesia (increased tolerance for pain). The use of heroin and other opioids may cause a long-term breakdown in the biochemical system that synthesizes the endorphins. An addict may continue to use opioids because drug use has broken down the body's normal pain-relief system. It is also thought that opioid drugs are reinforcing because they postpone painful withdrawal symptoms. This view does not explain why some addicts have severe withdrawal symptoms while others do not. Moreover, some people become seriously addicted to other drugs that do not produce severe withdrawal symptoms, such as nicotine and coffee.

From the **interactional orientation,** both the person and the situation are important factors in the development of addiction: People's characteristics (their expectations, worries, etc.) and the situations they face in life, particularly those that create stress, jointly influence their need for and reactions to drugs. The available evidence is consistent with this interpretation. This view can explain why some military personnel who had served in Vietnam could so easily leave heavy drug use behind when they returned to the United States. In

Vietnam, they were faced with strange people and places, boredom, danger, feelings of helplessness, and other emotions and situations that made their coping mechanisms appear inadequate. Once they had returned home, the situational cues that were related to a craving for opioids were absent.

One recurring finding of research on opioid addicts is that they frequently have severe personality problems (Kosten & Rounsaville, 1986). They suffer particularly from depression and their suicide rate is thought to be five times the average. Depression often continues after withdrawal and even becomes worse. Some authorities believe that the drugs cause depression, and others think that more often depression—or at least a vulnerability to depressive symptoms under stress—leads to opioid abuse when the drugs are available. Depression in addicts may have been overestimated, since there is some evidence that the ones who seek treatment are more depressed than those who do not.

Treatment for Opioid Dependence Clinicians do not agree on how opioid-dependent individuals should be treated. Since the nineteenth century, treatment has consisted primarily of hospitalization for withdrawal from the drug. Aside from being expensive, hospitalization generally seems to be ineffective, although positive findings have been reported in a 20-year follow-up study of hospitalized addicts (Vaillant, 1973). Although 23 percent had died (mostly from unnatural causes) and 25 percent were still known to be using drugs, somewhat more than one-third had achieved stable abstinence, mainly as a result of strict supervision after discharge from the hospital.

There is currently no single accepted standard of treatment for opioid dependence. One difficulty is that opioid dependence is now rarely the sole clinical problem; most patients with opioid dependence also abuse drugs other than opioids and commonly have severe psychological problems as well. Depression, antisocial behavior, and anxiety disorders are among the comorbidity features found in opioid dependence.

Methadone maintenance is the most widely used treatment for opioid addicts. Methadone is a synthetic substance that blocks the effects of heroin. It can be taken orally, prevents withdrawal symptoms for 24 hours, and prevents or decreases the euphoric effects or rushes that occur if heroin is taken while the methadone is active. Its withdrawal effects are also less intense (though somewhat more prolonged) than those of heroin, and their appearance is delayed. While the biochemical and physiological properties of methadone are not fully understood, it apparently blocks all the ordinary effects of morphinelike drugs by competing with them at receptor sites in the central nervous system. Through the use of methadone, the craving for heroin is

relieved. Methadone allows a heroin-dependent person to function in society.

Methadone-maintenance programs seem suitable to a wide range of opioid-dependent individuals, and since they can be carried out on an outpatient basis, they cost less than institutional treatment. However, despite its relative effectiveness methadone maintenance is not universally supported. Critics claim that it does not really cure addicts but merely transfers their dependence from one drug to another.

For all patients not assigned to methadone maintenance, the first step in treatment is a gradual detoxification using decreasing methadone doses. This approach is often attempted with patients who are in treatment for the first time or who have been dependent on opioids for no more than a year or two. Hospitalization may be convenient but is not necessary. It is now standard practice to substitute oral methadone for whatever illegal drug the patient has been taking and then gradually to lower the dose to zero over a period of a week or two as the detoxification proceeds. When the methadone dose becomes very low withdrawal symptoms may intensify and the user may wish to stop the detoxification process. Clonidine, a nonopiate drug originally marketed to lower blood pressure, has proved to be effective at this point in detoxification in easing withdrawal because it acts at some of the same nerve endings as opioids.

Another drug that may be helpful in achieving abstinence is **naltrexone,** which specifically blocks opioid receptors. While the drug is present, it prevents readdiction to heroin and other opioid drugs. It is relatively safe and nontoxic and one dose can last for up to three days. Unfortunately, although it is an excellent treatment for highly motivated patients who prefer to be opioid-free, most street heroin addicts are not interested in naltrexone because it keeps them from getting high. Naltrexone will effectively block the effects of opioids but it does not stop the psychological craving for opioids. The optimum duration of naltrexone therapy has not yet been established, but motivated patients should probably take it for at least three months after detoxification.

Dealing with drug-dependent individuals and with the traffic in illegal drugs is a major problem in many countries. One British program tries to control heroin abuse through a system of outpatient drug-dependence clinics. These clinics give addicts daily maintenance doses not only of methadone but even of heroin and cocaine. By providing a legal daily maintenance dose, the clinics hope to draw these people into contact with the helping system and make it unnecessary for them to support their habit through crime. The ultimate goal is to gradually wean them from the drugs if possible, or at least to stabilize them on a fixed dose of heroin or methadone in a lifetime program. In a ten-year follow-up study of the effectiveness of the system, investigators found that 40 percent of a group of heroin-dependent people who had attended the clinics in 1969 were still attending a clinic and receiving heroin or methadone (Wille, 1981). The majority of these continuing users had been socially stable for at least 10 years. Most of them were employed and were not currently in trouble with the law. Of the group who were no longer attending the clinics, at least half had become abstinent.

There are few follow-up studies from other countries with which these data may be compared. However, the data that exist suggest that the British program is at least as effective as approaches used in other countries (Jaffee, 1985). Moral objections to the government's providing heroin and cocaine for addicts have been a constant threat to the existence of the British program as more than a methadone-maintenance plan.

Is abstinence the solution to the heroin-dependent person's problems? One study suggests that merely abstaining from opioids has disappointingly little effect on the other medical, emotional, and social problems of addicts (Kosten et al., 1987). The subjects of the study were 150 patients who applied for treatment at an addiction clinic. Three-fourths were men, and they had used opioids for an average of 10 years. Two-and-a-half years later the researchers interviewed most of them again. Some were now abstinent, and some were using even more opioids than before; most were in-between.

At the time of the follow-up, the general level of patients' problems had improved and their drug problems had improved the most. However, neither the original severity of the patients' drug problem nor the amount of time they were drug-free during the study predicted the severity of their drug problem at the time of follow-up. The severity of medical, family, and psychological problems of the patients at follow-up also did not predict their levels of drug use at follow-up but instead were related to the original severity of these problems at the beginning of the program.

Based on these results, the authors concluded that addicts need family therapy, psychotherapy for depression, vocational counseling, and other types of treatment at least as much as they need help in achieving abstinence. Psychodynamically and cognitively oriented therapies have been found to be helpful with some opioid-dependent persons, particularly those with long-standing severe psychiatric disorders (Woody et al., 1986).

Cocaine

Cocaine is the main active drug in the leaves of the coca bush that grows on the eastern slopes of the Andes Mountains in South America. The Indians of Peru and Bolivia have used its leaves for centuries to increase endurance and decrease hunger so that they can cope better with the rigors of their economically marginal, high-altitude existence. In 1860 cocaine was isolated and purified.

Like heroin, cocaine initially had a positive, even benign image. Freud, who periodically used cocaine himself, recommended it for use in treating depression and other conditions, including morphine withdrawal. Its use as a local anesthetic led to the discovery of synthetic substitutes with low toxicity, while its use in treating morphine withdrawal indirectly led to self-administration of the drug. From about 1880 to 1900 cocaine was actually an ingredient in some popular brands of soda. Cocaine can be "snorted" or sniffed, smoked (often in a water pipe), or injected intravenously. Cocaine taken by injection is associated with the highest levels of dependence (Gossop et al., 1994).

Cocaine is a naturally-occurring central nervous system stimulant. Whereas the opioids are "downers" that slow the body's responses, cocaine is an "upper" that increases heart rate, raises blood pressure and body temperature, and decreases appetite. It puts the body in an emergency state in much the same way that a rush of adrenaline would in a stressful situation. Although it is not clear how cocaine produces this effect, it is likely that it causes the release of large amounts of dopamine in the brain. Cocaine also affects at least three parts of the brain itself: the cerebral cortex, which governs reasoning and memory; the hypothalamus, which controls appetite, body temperature, sleep, and emotions such as fear and anger; and the cerebellum, which regulates motor activities such as walking and balance.

This case illustrates cocaine psychosis which can result from high dosages of the drug.

After a while, I was convinced that there were people trying to break into my house. I didn't know who they were, but I was sure that people were after me. There was probably some reality to it too, since I really was scared that the police would come in and bust me. The only way that I felt that I could protect myself was by getting a knife. So I started sleeping with a butcher knife next to me. That didn't work for long, though, because I still felt insecure. So I felt that I had to get a gun. Every night, I went to bed with a gun on one side of me and a butcher knife on the other side. I was just waiting for someone to come in the house so that I could blow his brains out. God knows what I was going to do with the knife. I swear, I was a maniac. It wouldn't have mattered who had come to the door. If someone had come to my door at the wrong time to borrow a cup of sugar, I can tell you with 100 percent certainty, he would have been dead.

—Weiss and Mirin, 1987, p. 39

Despite an overall decline in cocaine use, the potency of cocaine products now available is much greater than in the past with the wide availability of **crack** cocaine, a concentrated form of the drug. Crack differs from other forms of cocaine primarily because it is easily vaporized and inhaled and thus its effects have an extremely rapid onset. Crack has greatly increased the use of the drug among adolescents because of its relatively low price. People who use crack experience high-dose, high-intensity effects that greatly increase the probability of extremely negative long term effects such as panic states, toxic psychoses, and paranoid schizophrenia. High-dose effects also include markedly altered perceptions of reality including aggressive or homicidal behavior against imagined persecution by others. Crack represents a serious problem because dependence develops extremely rapidly.

The use of crack has produced one of the great tragedies of the last decade, the birth of thousands of "crack babies." Women who use cocaine in any form during pregnancy are likely to place the fetus at risk because of the greater chance of spontaneous abortion or fetal death late in pregnancy, or the reduction of infant birth weight if the pregnancy is carried to term. These effects are thought to be related to a lack of oxygen and reduced blood flow to the fetus as a result of the intense vasoconstriction or temporary narrowing of the mother's blood vessels induced by the cocaine. Some crack babies are born with visible birth defects, but many more have neurological defects. Nearly all these infants are irritable and difficult to soothe and as a result are less likely to receive adequate mothering. As these crack babies enter the school system, it appears that they have cognitive difficulties in structuring information and also have low tolerance for frustration. Crack babies have been referred to as a "bio-underclass," children for whom a combination of physiological damage and socioeconomic disadvantage may result in a life of inferiority (Rist, 1990). Estimates of the number of babies affected by crack use range from between 50,000 to 200,000 births per year (Julien, 1992).

Cocaine produces feelings of wittiness and hyper-alertness and is often praised by users as being almost risk free: no hangovers like those produced by alcohol, no injection scars like those caused by heroin use, and no lung cancer, which is associated with use of marijuana and tobacco. Unfortunately, its action is more complex and less benign than most users believe. Since its effects are highly reinforcing and psychologically addicting to the user, desire for it is hard to control. A damaging habit usually develops over a period of several months to several years. Compulsive users cannot turn the drug down; they think about it constantly, dream about it, spend all their savings on it, and borrow, steal, or deal to pay for it.

Physical tolerance also develops quickly so an increased dose is needed to produce the same effects, thus increasing the danger of overdose. Users often say that they never quite recapture the euphoria of the first snort. Whether cocaine can be said to produce a withdrawal reaction depends partly on definitions but recent research suggests withdrawal does occur after extensive cocaine use (Grilly, 1989). Researchers are zeroing in on how cocaine produces euphoria and the depression and craving that result from chronic use. The drug interferes with the normal functioning of neurotransmitters, chemicals that activate nerves in an area of the brain associated with pleasurable feelings (Gawin, 1991).

High doses or repeated use of cocaine can produce a state resembling mania, with impaired judgment, incessant rambling talk, hyperactivity, and paranoia that may lead to violence or accidents. There is also an acute anxiety reaction that is sometimes severe enough to be called panic. Serious acute physical reactions are also possible. By constricting blood vessels and increasing the heart rate, cocaine can produce cardiac symptoms, including irregular heartbeat, angina, and myocardial infarction. High doses may also cause nausea, headache, cold sweats, tremors, and fast, irregular, shallow breathing. People who have high blood pressure or damaged arteries may suffer strokes as a result of cocaine use. Table 14-10 summarizes the effects of cocaine use. Death usually results from convulsions followed by paralysis of the brain centers controlling respiration, which in turn leads to cardiac arrest; in serious cases an acute overdose must be treated with oxygen and anticonvulsant drugs. A common cause of death is intravenous injection of a "speedball"—a combination of heroin and cocaine.

Treating Cocaine Dependence The cocaine-dependent person must first become convinced that treatment

---

TABLE 14–10
Effects of Cocaine[a]

1. Euphoria
2. Increased energy
3. Enhanced mental acuity and alertness
4. Increased sensory awareness (sexual, auditory, visual)
5. Decreased appetite
6. Decreased need for sleep
7. Increased self-confidence
8. Impaired judgment
9. Loss of motivation
10. Delusions and paranoid thinking
11. Convulsions
12. A variety of problems in the cardiovascular system including constricted blood vessels, increased heart rate, myocardial infarction, stroke, brain hemorrhages

[a]The effects depend on dosage and degree of habitual use.

is necessary. As in all types of drug and alcohol dependence, more or less subtle forms of denial are common; for example, abusers may want relief for some of the side effects without giving up the habit itself. Sometimes they are induced to come in for treatment only by pressure from family members, employers, or the law. People seek treatment at different stages of dependency, and the severity of the symptoms varies greatly.

Many cocaine users have joined mutual-help groups such as Cocaine Anonymous or Narcotics Anonymous. These programs use more or less the same approach, which was developed from Alcoholics Anonymous: They encourage their members to confide in others who have the same problem, to share their feelings, to make a resolution to overcome dependency, and to support the resolutions of other members. Members admit their powerlessness to control their drug use and seek help from a higher power while taking a "moral inventory" of themselves and pledging abstinence one day at a time.

Many cocaine users have histories of dysfunctional family lives. Cocaine use has been associated with family patterns of alcoholism, domestic violence, separation, or divorce, as well as with physical, sexual, or emotional abuse within the family (Wallace, 1991). In such cases psychotherapy can be an important part of treatment—although psychotherapy alone rarely solves drug problems. **Supportive psychotherapy** is a relationship with a sympathetic professional who provides comfort and encourages the abuser to stay away from sources of cocaine. Interpretive or exploratory psychotherapy can help some abusers understand what functions cocaine has been fulfilling in their lives and find other ways of coping.

A serious problem in treating cocaine dependence is preventing relapse. Abusers usually return to cocaine because it has become a familiar response to certain cues—daily annoyances, family conflict, feelings of boredom, loneliness, anger, depression, sexual stirrings, alcohol intoxication, and the places, people, sights, and sounds that have become associated with the drug. People dependent on cocaine need to learn to avoid places where the drug is available and friends who use it. Sometimes that means finding a new job and a new place to live. Usually they must give up other drugs that arouse a desire for cocaine or reduce the ability to resist it. Behavioral principles can be helpful, for example, by using desensitization to eliminate craving. The cocaine-dependent person might repeatedly be shown hypodermic needles, glass pipe, or films of people using cocaine in the hope that desire for the drug will fade when it is no longer satisfied after exposure to the cues that have come to provide it. In general, recovery is difficult unless a cocaine-dependent person has a stake in something besides the drug.

Amphetamines

Amphetamines, like cocaine, are potent psychomotor stimulants. Various drugs in this group are called speed, crystal, pep pills, bennies, meth, and many other names, depending on the specific active agent. Despite their dissimilar chemical structures, amphetamines and cocaine have many similar properties. They both probably act by influencing the norepinephrine and dopamine receptor systems. This has been demonstrated in research studies using antipsychotic medications that are known to block not only the dopamine receptors but some of the norepinephrine receptors as well. If these antipsychotic medications are given prior to amphetamine or cocaine use, they inhibit most of the behavioral effects of either drug. This suggests that the blocked receptors were those that would otherwise transmit nerve impulses that produce the drug-related responses.

Moderate amphetamine use results in increased wakefulness, alertness, and elevation of mood. Psychomotor performance is improved temporarily, but the improvement may be followed by a compensatory rebound or letdown in which the user feels fatigued, less alert, and somewhat depressed.

The medical uses of amphetamines include suppression of appetite and improvement of mood in mild depressions. Amphetamines are also helpful in treating certain neurological and behavioral disorders. College students who use amphetamines when "cramming" for exams not only notice increased energy and tolerance for sleeplessness but also increased productivity on the next day's exam. Although this may be useful at times, the "improved" performance may not be truly better. Many students have the disillusioning experience of looking at their wondrous performance later and finding it to be of poor quality. The drug impaired their critical thinking at the same time that it increased their output.

High doses of amphetamines have significant effects on the central nervous system and the cardiovascular system; they lead to nervousness, headache, dizziness, agitation, apprehension, confusion, palpitations, and elevated blood pressure. Regular use of large amounts leads to greater tolerance for the drug and increased intolerance for being without it. Users become malnourished, exhausted, careless, and indifferent to normal responsibilities. Their thinking is often characterized by a paranoia that may develop into a full-blown psychosis accompanied by hallucinations. Withdrawal symptoms, if they occur, are mild compared with those that often accompany cessation of opioid use; they also differ qualitatively. Since tolerance for amphetamines develops rapidly, many users inject it into a vein to obtain more intense effects. This high-dose, long-term use of amphetamines is dangerous and self-destructive. Since the initial effects are stimulating and pleasant, unwary individuals often proceed to higher doses and eventually to a state of dependence.

Hallucinogens

Hallucinogens or psychedelics act on the central nervous system to produce alteration of consciousness. They change the user's perceptions of both the internal and the external world. There is usually sensory displacement, which can drastically alter color perception and hearing. Auditory, visual, and tactile hallucinations accompany the experience, along with a changed perception of self. Among the natural hallucinogenic substances are mescaline, psilocybin, and dimethyl tryptamine (DMT). Synthetic psychedelics include diethyltryptamine (STP), and **lysergic acid diethylamide** (LSD). The following case describes some of the effects of LSD.

> A 21-year-old woman was admitted to the hospital after ingesting a large amount of LSD. About half an hour after ingestion she perceived that light affected her strangely and that the bricks in the wall had begun to move in and out. She became frightened when she realized that she was unable to distinguish her body from the chair she was sitting on or from her lover's body. Her fear became more marked as she began to think that she would not get back into herself. At the time of her admission she was hyperactive and laughed inappropriately. Her stream of talk was illogical and her emotions extremely variable. After two days this reaction had ceased, but she was still afraid of the drug and convinced that she would not take it again because of her frightening experience.
>
> —Adapted from Kolb and Brodie, 1982, p. 666

In many cultures hallucinogens have been used for hundreds of years. Mescaline, which is derived from the peyote cactus, and psilocybin, which is obtained from certain mushrooms, are used for religious ceremonies by Indians in Mexico and Central America. West Africans and Congolese have traditionally chewed the ibogaine root, which contains tryptamine, to "release the gods." While epidemiological surveys have found a decline in use of most substances that are abused, major hallucinogenic drugs, predominantly LSD, have maintained a steady, somewhat increasing trend. In 1990, 7.6 percent of the U.S. population reported using a hallucinogenic drug at some time in their lives (Abraham & Aldridge, 1993).

LSD (popularly called "acid") is a colorless, odorless, and tasteless material. Effects are produced by as little as 50 micrograms (a microgram is a millionth of a gram), an amount that in pure form would not be visible to the

naked eye. No legally manufactured LSD is available to the general public, and the output of illegal, often amateur, laboratories is rarely pure LSD. In the course of research on certain groups of therapeutic compounds, LSD was first synthesized in 1938 by Albert Hoffman, a Swiss chemist. His description of the drugs' effects on him in the laboratory gave a more benign view than the case described above.

> I was forced to stop my work in the laboratory . . . and to go home, as I was seized by a particular restlessness associated with the sensation of mild dizziness. On arriving home, I lay down and sank into a kind of drunkenness which was not unpleasant and which was characterized by extreme activity of imagination. As I lay in a dazed condition with my eyes closed (I experienced daylight as disagreeably bright) there surged upon me an uninterrupted stream of fantastic images of extraordinary plasticity and vividness and accompanied by an intense, kaleidoscope-like play of colours. This condition gradually passed off after about two hours.
>
> —Hoffman, 1971, p. 23

The immediate effects of LSD usually last about 8 to 12 hours. The mechanism of its action is not well understood, but it is known to stimulate the sympathetic nervous system and to produce physiological changes like those seen in a person who is aroused, excited, or under stress. The most common subjective effects are euphoria, quick shifts from one mood to another, and altered awareness of the color, size, and shape of stimuli. Time perception is so altered that minutes may seem like hours. Bizarre sensations may be experienced, frequently including feelings of separation or disintegration of some part of the body. The user typically realizes that these effects are due to the drug and are not "out there." Some users experience bewilderment, disorganization, personal and sexual identity confusion, and fears of losing control. They may experience intense emotions that they cannot label. In fact, one of the most unfortunate effects of LSD is the feeling of being overwhelmed by confusing emotions that cannot be sorted out because they are going by so fast.

LSD sometimes produces extreme anxiety or panic reactions. Such "bad trips" are generally short-lived and can often be modified by supportive reassurance. Bad trips may be terminated by appropriate medication and occasionally by hospitalization. The most serious effects of LSD are paranoid symptoms (feelings of being followed, spied on, or persecuted), psychosis resembling that found in schizophrenia, and severe depression that occasionally leads to suicide attempts. Negative effects of a single large dose of LSD may persist for months, require long hospitalization, and resist the usual forms of treatment. The frequency of such reactions is difficult to determine but is probably less than one percent. When such problems arise, it is often difficult to separate the effects of LSD from those of prior drug use, personality characteristics, and a variety of other factors. While users of hallucinogens develop dependence, withdrawal symptoms usually do not occur.

In **post-hallucinogen perceptual disorder** there are "flashbacks": spontaneous recurrences of parts of the LSD experience long after the action of the drug has ceased. Such recurrences can take place in the first few weeks and have been reported as long as two years following the last dose of the drug. It is not clear why these flashbacks occur. One possibility is that LSD causes biochemical changes in the body that last long after drug use. The aftereffects may have serious consequences if they occur in situations that require attentive thinking and decision making.

Treatment for abuse of hallucinogens depends on the severity of the reaction. Severely affected people must have medical attention to prevent cardiovascular or respiratory collapse. If psychotic behavior is present, antipsychotic drugs of the type used to treat schizophrenia may be helpful, although about 10 percent of drug users who become acutely psychotic never recover. Psychologically based therapy, particularly group psychotherapy and supportive drug-free groups, can be helpful because users of hallucinogens often have feelings of low self-worth and use the drugs to improve their relationships with other people. Many of these abusers need psychological help with their social responses so that they can substitute rewarding social experiences for the reinforcement they get from drugs.

Phencyclidine (PCP)

PCP (phencyclidine) has several street names, including "angel dust" and "crystal." It was first developed as an anesthetic in the 1950s. However, it was taken off the market for human use because it sometimes caused disorientation and hallucinations. It is available in a number of forms—a pure, white crystallike powder, a tablet or a capsule. PCP is sometimes sprinkled on marijuana or parsley and smoked. It also can be swallowed, sniffed, or injected. Although PCP is illegal, it is easily manufactured. Users can never be sure what they are buying since it is manufactured illegally. Sometimes it may not even be PCP, but a lethal by-product of the drug.

The effects of PCP depend on how much is taken, the way it is used, and the individual. Effects include increased heart rate and blood pressure, flushing, sweating, dizziness, and numbness. As with hallucinogens, adverse reactions to PCP tend to be more common among individuals with preexisting mental disorders. When large doses are taken, effects include drowsiness, convulsions, and coma. Taking large amounts of PCP can also cause death from repeated convulsions, heart and lung failure, or ruptured blood vessels in the brain.

PCP is classified as a dissociative anesthetic because it makes the individual feel dissociated or detached from the environment. In small doses, it produces insensitivity to pain; in large doses, it produces a comalike state and blank stare. People who take larger doses feel as if they are being bombarded by stimuli. They may lose the ability to distinguish between fantasy and reality and suffer severe intellectual and emotional disorganization. PCP users sometimes develop severe depression or a severe psychotic state that is not easily reversible. Whether these outcomes are a result of the drug alone or of underlying personality characteristics is not clear.

Researchers studying areas of the brain affected by PCP have discovered that PCP can protect the brain from permanent damage after a stroke or heart attack. Scientists do not yet fully understand this process, but they have proven that it works in a series of animal studies. PCP has diverse effects because it works at two different sites on nerve cells, named PCP and sigma receptors, that have quite different characteristics. Pharmaceutical companies are working to develop new synthetic drugs with the same action as PCP but without its undesirable qualities. MK-801, the first compound of this type that is readily available to researchers, has reduced neuronal damage when given before or after trauma to animals (Myers, 1988).

Inhalants

The extensive capillary surface area of the lungs makes inhalation a favored method of administration of many psychoactive substances. In some cases, the effect of inhalation can resemble intravenous injection in its intensity. There is one group of substances for which direct inhalation is virtually the only route of self-administration. The inhalants are volatile substances or organic solvents such as gasoline, lighter fluids, spray paints, and cleaning fluids. Most of these substances are hydrocarbons of some type. Once inhaled, blood levels of most inhalants peak within minutes. There is evidence of tolerance and withdrawal symptoms for inhalants. Users of inhalants report distortion in their perceptions of size, color, and the passage of time. They may briefly develop delusions and hallucinations. As with alcohol, intoxication is accompanied by muscular incoordination and dizziness. Headaches, nausea, coughing, and abdominal pain are often present.

Because of their low cost, easy availability, and ease of concealment, inhalants may for many be the first psychoactive substance used. Inhalant use is generally considered to be more common among younger people (Dinwiddie, 1994). Tolerance to the effects of inhalants and withdrawal symptoms have been reported among heavy users. Recurrent inhalant use may result in the individual giving up or reducing important social, occupational, or recreational activities.

Cannabis

The cannabis plant has been harvested throughout history for its fibers, oils, and psychoactive resin (see Figure 14-12). **Marijuana,** which consists of the dried leaves and flower tops of the plant, is the form in which it is most often used in the United States. The solidified resin, called **hashish** (or, colloquially, "hash"), can also be used to produce psychoactive effects.

Many Americans have used marijuana at least once, in spite of the fact that it is classified as an illegal substance and its cultivation, possession, distribution, and use are prohibited. Despite the prohibitions and the controversy over its safety, the use of marijuana increased sharply during the 1960s and 1970s. This was followed by a decline in the 1990s. Recently, there has been a rise in teenagers' use of marijuana (*The New York Times*, February 6, 1994, p. E. 18). This increase is troubling because new methods of harvesting and processing cannabis plants have made marijuana about 20 times more potent than the marijuana available on the street in the 1960s and 1970s.

Marijuana is not pharmacologically a narcotic,

although in the United States it has been legally classified as one since 1937. The mechanisms of its action are not well understood, but its more common effects have been identified. An important advance in research was the isolation of the major active ingredient in marijuana, THC (delta-9-tetrahydrocannabinol). Only barely detectable concentrations of THC are present in the brain of a rat after one dose. But with repeated administration THC and the products of its metabolism gradually build up so that administration of a single dose is detectable for as long as eight days afterward.

Marijuana can be taken by either eating or smoking parts of the cannabis plant. Smoking is the fastest way to feel the drug's effects. When the smoke is inhaled, it is spread across the surface of the lungs, quickly absorbed into the bloodstream, and carried to the brain in a few seconds. When marijuana is ingested, THC enters the bloodstream from the digestive system and is carried to the liver. There enzymes break it down into other substances, which are carried to the brain by the circulatory system.

Cannabis intoxication usually begins with a "high" feeling followed by such symptoms as inappropriate laughter and grandiosity, lethargy, impairment in short-term memory, impaired judgment, distorted sensory perceptions, impaired motor performance, and distortions in time perception (usually time seems to pass very slowly). These are the reactions of two people who had used marijuana for the first time.

The first time I smoked I had the feeling of being entirely outside of my body, hovering above it and as I was lying on the bed, I was exceptionally conscious of my body for part of the time, realizing how, and feeling how, each individual part was working.

—Berke and Hernton, 1974, p. 97

Doug is a single 25-year-old repairman for a large home appliance company. On weekends he often goes to parties with his girlfriend. Drugs are often available at the parties but he and his girlfriend rarely use them. However, at a recent party one of his friends offered him some marijuana to smoke. His girlfriend, who rarely used drugs, was initially reluctant to participate but finally agreed to join him. The couple lay on a bed and Doug rolled a joint. As they smoked his girlfriend became withdrawn, anxious, and frightened. She stood up but found it difficult to walk and lay back down on the bed feeling even more anxious. Doug stopped smoking and began trying to calm her. Gradually, over the next hour she relaxed and her anxiety changed to a mild sense of euphoria. As the effects of the drug wore off she complained that her mouth was dry and asked Doug to get her

Figure 14-12 Leaves from a cannabis plant.

something to drink. When he returned she said, "I'm starved. Let's get out of here and get something to eat."

Marijuana became popular as a recreational drug partly because it is cheap and readily available but also because many people believe that when used in moderation it is not a risk to physical or mental health. Despite this widespread attitude the federal government has conducted a vigorous and costly campaign to prevent the entry of marijuana into this country. As a result, a great deal of marijuana is grown illegally in the United States and Canada. Several authoritative reports have been issued on the effects of marijuana on health, but scientific controversy and public confusion still exist as to whether marijuana should be legalized or whether the laws against it should be strengthened.

In the early 1980s a committee of the National Academy of Science was asked to make a critical review of current knowledge about the effects of marijuana on health (National Academy of Sciences, 1982). The committee's report concluded that marijuana has a variety of effects, some of which are harmful to human health. Marijuana use causes changes in the heart and circulation that are similar to those caused by stress. These changes might be a threat for individuals with high blood pressure or heart disease. Marijuana smoke causes changes in the lungs that may lead to respiratory problems, but cancer-producing agents in marijuana smoke are even more of a problem. Marijuana smoke contains about 50 percent more carcinogens than does tobacco smoke.

In males, marijuana suppresses the production of male hormones, decreases the size and weight of the prostate gland and testes, and inhibits sperm production, although these effects appear to be reversible. Such specific reproductive effects have not been found for nonpregnant women. In pregnant women, however, THC crosses the placental barrier and may harm the unborn child. It can also be secreted in breast milk, thereby affecting nursing infants. Various studies have shown that marijuana blocks ovulation and can cause birth defects in animals (Jaffe, 1989). The belief that marijuana use is associated with chromosome breaks, which are thought to be indicators of genetic damage, does not appear to be correct. Contradictory evidence exists as to whether the drug causes atrophy or other gross changes in the brain. One particularly important point is that the impairment lasts for four to eight hours after the feeling of intoxication is over. This means that behavior may be affected even when the user is no longer aware of the presence of the drug.

One positive aspect of marijuana and its chemical derivatives is its therapeutic potential. Evidence suggests that marijuana is useful in the treatment of glaucoma, an eye disorder that may cause blindness, and that it helps control the severe nausea and vomiting that accompany chemotherapy for cancer. It may also be useful in treating asthma and certain types of epileptic seizures. However, the stress it puts on the cardiovascular system may make marijuana an inappropriate drug for treating older people.

Government agencies are reluctant to legalize the sale and use of marijuana because of vocal public opposition. Some legalization opponents argue that the most potent deterrent of marijuana use is the possibility of arrest and imprisonment. However, while enforcement of marijuana laws is a major drain on the resources of the criminal justice system, it does not seem to be effective. Some people have proposed licensing the sale of marijuana, as is done with alcohol, and writing laws regulating its potency. Endangering the lives or well-being of others—for example, by operating a motor vehicle while intoxicated—would be penalized, but safe recreational use would not be illegal. Others have suggested eliminating criminal penalties for users but not for sellers of marijuana. Because of the prevalence of its use and the public controversy about whether it should be decriminalized, over 20 percent of the states have dropped criminal penalties for minor marijuana offenses in the last few years. Several other states permit the use of marijuana for certain medical purposes.

There is a great need to base laws and social policies concerning marijuana and other drugs on facts rather than on opinions and fears. Laboratory research and studies of the longer-term effects of drugs and thera-pies are a first step toward providing the facts. Because marijuana is the most frequently used illicit drug in the United States, there is a particular need to develop treatment programs for the disorders it causes. A recent controlled study evaluated the ef-fects of two treatments on the ability of people with marijuana problems to achieve abstinence (Stephens et al., 1994). The treatments were (1) a relapse prevention program similar to those described earlier in the chapter and (2) social support groups. The support groups included opportunities to get and give support and dealt with such topics as coping with mood swings, relating to friends who continue to use marijuana, and maintaining motivation to be abstinent. As Figure 14-13 shows, both treatment approaches were effective. There were significant reductions in marijuana use and nearly two-thirds of the subjects were able initially to achieve abstinence and one-third showed signs of improvement throughout a 12-month posttreatment period.

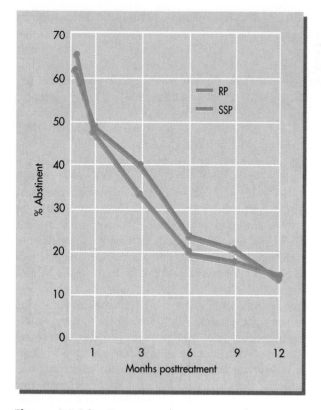

Figure 14-13 Continuous abstinence rates by treatment conditions. RP = relapse prevention; SSP = social support.

SOURCE: Stephens, Roffman, and Simpson, (1994). "Treating Adult Marijuana Dependence." *Journal of Consulting and Clinical Psychology*, 62, p. 97.

Nicotine

I can quit smoking if I wish;
I've done it a thousand times.

—Mark Twain

Nicotine and cancer-causing tars are the only pharmacologically active ingredients in tobacco. Nicotine acts at least in part by directly stimulating certain receptors that are sensitive to the neurotransmitter acetylcholine and as a result exerts powerful effects on the brain and spinal cord, the peripheral nervous system, and the heart. Its initial use causes nausea and vomiting by stimulating the vomiting center in the brain stem as well as receptors in the stomach, but tolerance of this effect develops quickly. Normal doses of nicotine can increase heart rate and blood pressure, and the heart's need for oxygen. If this increased need for oxygen cannot be met, for instance in people who have atherosclerosis or hardening of the arteries, the result may be angina or chest pains or a heart attack. Smoking by pregnant women tends to reduce the birth weight of their babies. In addition to the effects of nicotine,

the tars contained in tobacco are a major cause of lung cancer.

Despite these consequences, smoking is a difficult habit to give up even for those who try (see Figure 14-14). Some smokers experience psychological distress in the form of anxiety and guilt because they cannot stop smoking. The difficulty of giving up tobacco use on a long-term basis may be due to the unpleasant nature of the withdrawal experience, the importance of social or environmental cues, and the highly overlearned nature of the habit (the pack-a-day smoker is reinforced by the rapid effects of nicotine in each of about 75,000 puffs per year). Withdrawal symptoms—irritability, anxiety, headache, excessive appetite, and difficulty in concentrating—do not occur in all smokers, but in some heavy smokers withdrawal symptoms can be detected within two hours after the last cigarette. Since many smokers use cigarettes as a way of coping with stress, it is not clear whether these symptoms are related to the withdrawal of nicotine or whether some of them may be due to psychological characteristics that helped start the addictive behavior.

Primarily due to more public awareness of the negative effects of tobacco, smoking rates have declined in the United States and Canada. Many long-term smokers have given up the habit. Most cigarette smokers who try to quit do so on their own and they are more likely to be successful than those who seek help in quitting through formal programs. Furthermore, persons who seek help tend to be heavier smokers and to have made more cessation attempts than those who quit unaided. While stopping smoking unaided is a simple, direct, and effective path to getting rid of nicotine dependence, special smoking cessation programs have an important role to play. According to one estimate, over 2 million people per year are helped by such programs (Keleman et al., 1990).

Therapeutic efforts to help people stop smoking take several forms. Some of these methods use the biological perspective. From this viewpoint, the problem is not so much that smoking calms the nerves as that nonsmoking sets up the negative reinforcement of withdrawal symptoms, which can be ended by having another cigarette. By resuming the use of cigarettes, the individual is attempting to regulate the nicotine level in his or her body. This may have important physiological effects because nicotine stimulates the release of *central peptides,* hormones that have a powerful effect on key mental and physical functions. This suggests that smokers who are heavily dependent but want to quit smoking may require, on a temporary basis, some pharmacological substitute for the nicotine they are deriving from cigarettes.

Chewing gum containing nicotine was developed to

"Phil suddenly decided to give up everything that was bad for him—no more smoking, drinking, or junk food—and he feels absolutely terrific!"

Figure 14-14 Drawing by Handelsman, © 1985, *The New Yorker Magazine*, Inc.

ease withdrawal from tobacco by providing both an alternate source of nicotine and a substitute oral activity. Nicotine gum probably does not give the same positive pleasure as smoking a cigarette because nicotine is absorbed more slowly through the lining of the mouth than through the lungs. However, the gum may enable a smoker to break the habit in two stages. First the smoker can focus on overcoming the behavioral and psychological components of tobacco dependence without having to cope with nicotine withdrawal at the same time. Linked with each smoker's puffing habits are the many other actions involved in handling cigarettes and responding to cues that call for lighting up. Because smoking is a complex behavior, all components of that behavior need to be addressed in helping a person stop smoking. Once these behavior patterns are controlled, withdrawal from the nicotine gum might be accomplished more easily. Research is needed to evaluate the effects of nicotine gum by itself and in combination with other factors. The available evidence indicates that by itself it makes a positive contribution to smoking cessation and an even more positive one when used in conjunction with coun-

seling programs (Cepeda-Benito, 1993; Orleans & Slade, 1993).

The recently developed nicotine patch also seems promising. A transdermal nicotine patch is a multilayered pad containing the active ingredient nicotine, which is applied to the skin via a pressure-sensitive adhesive (see Figure 14-15). The patch, which must be prescribed by a doctor, administers a controlled dose of nicotine over a 16- or 24-hour period. Doses are maintained for a specified number of weeks and reduced in stages to gradually wean the smoker from nicotine dependence. The total course of nicotine replacement treatment is approximately 90 days but depends on the patch used. A number of pharmaceutical companies manufacture a nicotine patch.

As with nicotine gum, objective evaluation of the nicotine patch is needed. Does it work? Are there side effects? (See Figure 14-16.) The available evidence suggests that it is effective and there are few side effects (Sachs, Sawe, & Leischow, 1993; Tang, Law, & Wald, 1994). The positive effects of both the gum and the patch seem to be maximized when they are combined with counseling that provides support information about the process of quitting, and training in useful skills such as relaxation.

Cognitive research has identified three "stages of change" relevant to smoking cessation (Marlatt & Gordon, 1985). The first stage involves the individual's commitment to making a change and setting goals—for example, stopping smoking. Unfortunately, smokers are often ambivalent about quitting and reluctant to take personal responsibility for quitting. They need help in developing their commitment and motivation to change. Once the individual has made the commitment to stop smoking, a specific plan can be developed and implemented. This second stage is an action phase for actual change. The third stage involves maintenance of change, with relapse prevention playing an important role in maintenance. Change is facilitated when people can identify the situations in which they are most likely to be tempted to smoke, learn cognitive coping techniques as alternatives to smoking, and can use self-reinforcement when they are successful in resisting the temptation to smoke. Table 14-11 summarizes the stages of change concept. Can smokers proceed through these stages themselves or do they require professional assistance? While some people may need professional assistance, available evidence indicates that for many people self-help approaches can be effective (Curry, 1993). Box 14-3 provides some tips that might be useful to smokers

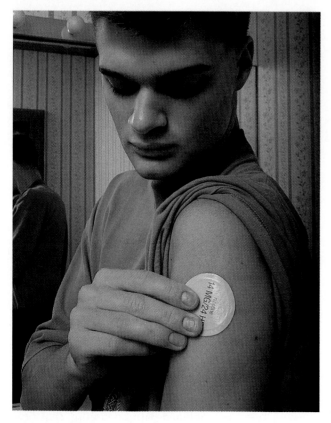

Figure 14-15 A transdermal nicotine patch. This patch administers 14 milligrams during a 24-hour period.

SOURCE: *Alcohol, Drug Abuse, and Mental Health Administration News,* May–June 1992, p. 6.

"Your smoking problem is solved. But now you're addicted to nicotine patches."

Figure 14-16 *The Wall Street Journal,* November 23, 1994, p. A15. Reprinted by permission of Cartoon Features Syndicate, Inc.

who are thinking about quitting. Quitting smoking is not just a matter of will power. It requires awareness of one's vulnerabilities (for example, people are more likely to feel they need to smoke in certain tension-arousing situations) and one's ability to be resilient (for example, to continue efforts to stop smoking even after a relapse).

Caffeine

Is caffeine in the same league as such substances as cocaine and marijuana? Researchers have recently shown that caffeine exhibits the features of a typical psychoactive substance that cause dependence (Strain et al., 1994). Coffee, tea, and cola drinkers are addicted to caffeine in the same way that others are addicted to cigarettes, alcohol, or intravenous drugs. This means that caffeine is the world's most widely used mind-altering drug. Most people consume per day about the amount of caffeine in two cups of coffee. This amount produces a mild, positive effect, including a feeling of well-being and alertness. Higher doses can produce anxiety and nervousness, but these negative effects do not in themselves constitute serious health risks. Using DSM-IV's criteria, a person is caffeine-dependent who develops tolerance, has withdrawal symptoms, uses the substance in spite of aggravation of medical or mental problems, and makes repeated unsuccessful attempts to quit. Many coffee, tea, and cola lovers meet these criteria and are physically dependent on caffeine and will suffer temporary headaches, lethargy, and depression when they stop using it. But of the millions of people who like and use caffeine, only a small, but as yet unknown, percentage are true addicts. Table 14-12 lists the major symptoms of caffeine intoxication.

Substance Dependence and Social Policy

Substance dependence continues to be a major problem throughout the world. Recent developments in the study of pain regulators and pain receptors in the body are providing some valuable clues, particularly in the area of opioid abuse. Information about the health consequences of using some substances—for example, marijuana and tobacco—have decreased their overall use. Some therapeutic procedures, especially those that emphasize cognitive techniques for relapse prevention, show promise as treatments for alcohol and tobacco abuse. Still unanswered, however, is the question of whether social policy should be changed—for example, to decriminalize marijuana or provide maintenance doses for heroin addicts in government clinics. In part

Thinking About Quitting?

Quitting smoking is not just a matter of will power. Planning and effective cognitive strategies can aid in achieving cessation goals.

You Are Not Alone
- Remember that most adult smokers want to quit.

Getting Ready to Quit
- Notice when and why you smoke.
- Change your smoking habits.

- When you want a cigarette, delay having it for one minute.
- Buy one pack of cigarettes at a time and switch to a brand you don't like.
- Set a date for quitting.
- Have a friend quit smoking with you.

Quit Day
- Change your morning routine.
- Get rid of all cigarettes. Put away your ashtrays.

- When the urge to smoke hits, remember the four "Ds": drink water, delay, deep-breathe, and do something else.
- Carry gum, hard candy, or a cinnamon stick with you.
- Reward yourself for getting through the day without smoking.

Staying Smoke-Free
- Take one day at a time.
- If you relapse, don't feel you've failed. Try again. Most smokers try several times before quitting for good.

TABLE 14–11
Stages of Change

1. *Contemplation and commitment.* Usually preceded by a pre-contemplation stage in which people do not see themselves as having a problem ("What's bad about smoking?").
2. *Action.* A specific plan for change is established and implemented (for example, use of nicotine substitutes, activating social support of friends, family, and coworkers).
3. *Maintenance.* Changing smoking patterns takes time, and self-monitoring and relapse prevention strategies are necessary during the action and maintenance phases.

TABLE 14–12
Major Symptoms of Caffeine Intoxication

Presence of five or more of these symptoms, together with ingestion of 150 milligrams of caffeine (more than 2 to 3 cups of coffee) are diagnostic of caffeine intoxication.

Restlessness
Nervousness
Excitement
Insomnia
Flushed face
Excessive need to urinate
Gastrointestinal disturbance
Muscle twitching
Rambling flow of thought and speech
High heart rate
Periods of inexhaustibility and very high energy level
Psychomotor agitation

---

because of lack of knowledge about the consequences of these actions—such as whether they would increase or decrease use of the substance—and in part because of philosophical differences among citizens, lawmakers, and scientists, these policy issues seem likely to remain unresolved.

Substance-related disorders involve psychoactive substances that affect thought, emotions, and behavior. Two categories of disorders are related to these substances: **Substance-use disorders** and **Substance-induced disorders.**

SUBSTANCE-USE DISORDERS

There are two subgroups of Substance-Use Disorders, those related to **substance dependence** and those related to **substance abuse.** In substance dependence there is intense craving for the substance to which the person is addicted and that person shows tolerance, withdrawal symptoms, and compulsive drug-taking. **Tolerance** means that the person has to use more and more of a substance to get the same effect. **Withdrawal** refers to physical symptoms that occur when a person stops or cuts down on the use of a psychoactive substance. **Compulsive substance use** involves drug-seeking behavior—behavior related to obtaining the substance. Substance abuse refers to recurrent and significant adverse consequences related to use of substances.

SUBSTANCE-INDUCED DISORDERS

Ingestion of different substances can lead to serious behavioral, psychological, and physiological symptoms. **Substance intoxication** occurs when recent ingestion of the substance leads to these symptoms. In substance intoxication there are reversible substance-specific symptoms due to recent ingestion. Indications of substance intoxication include disturbances of perception, attention, and thought.

ALCOHOL-RELATED DISORDERS

Ethanol is the only type of **alcohol** intended for human consumption. The ethanol contained in various types of alcoholic drinks—beer, wine, and hard or distilled liquor—is the same drug. However, these types of drinks differ in percentage of their total volume that is made up of alcohol. Alcohol acts on the central nervous system as a blocker of messages from one nerve cell to the next. Initially it acts on frontal lobe functions such as memory and judgment. In greater amounts it affects the cerebellum and motor muscle control. In very large amounts it affects the medulla and spinal cord and the involuntary functions of the body such as breathing and heart rate.

Perspectives on Alcohol-Related Disorders Alcohol-related disorders have multiple causes and there are theories concerning known and possible determinants. Ingestion of alcohol first reduces anxiety and then has a depressant effect on the body. The biological perspective views alcoholism as a permanent and irreversible condition. According to this view a person with alcohol problems must entirely stop drinking in order

to control alcohol use. Researchers believe that there may be a genetic predisposition for alcoholism. People vary greatly in their sensitivity to the effects of alcohol. Women may be more sensitive to alcohol than men because they have less of a specific enzyme that neutralizes alcohol and because of their lower body weight. The psychodynamic perspective suggests that people who abuse alcohol may have an **oral-dependent personality;** that is, they have a larger than normal need for oral gratification because of early life experiences. The learning perspective suggests that, through both social and physiological reinforcement and through modeling, people learn to use alcohol as a way of coping. The cognitive perspective focuses on people's expectations about the effects of alcohol. The community perspective emphasizes the importance of the values and customs of the community in forming attitudes toward alcohol use. The more complex biopsychosocial view considers some individuals to have a predisposition for alcohol dependence and focuses on stress as a precipitating factor in drinking. In this view an addictive cycle develops.

Treatment Treatment for alcohol dependence begins with **detoxification,** "drying out," which is accompanied by physical symptoms of withdrawal. Specific types of drugs have been developed to ease the withdrawal symptoms. A community approach is used by Alcoholics Anonymous, an organization dedicated to helping alcoholics become abstinent and rehabilitate themselves through mutual social support. Individual psychotherapy does not tend to be helpful for alcoholics, but family therapy may be useful to restructure relationships after drinking has stopped. Learning approaches including **aversive conditioning** and covert sensitization have been used to help people stop drinking. In the cognitive approach, drinkers are taught to monitor their behavior and determine the types of situations that are likely to tempt them to drink. **Relapse-prevention programs** help people gain effective coping responses to prevent drinking. These programs also help people cope with the **abstinence-violation effect,** the guilt and self-blame people feel when their coping lapses and they take one or more drinks. Some researchers and therapists believe that some people who have a history of alcohol abuse can learn to practice controlled drinking and use alcohol in moderation. Others believe that abstinence from all alcohol is the only way to deal with problem drinkers.

Prevention Community-level programs regulating access to alcohol and penalizing driving after alcohol use may be helpful. Prevention programs that teach young people about alcohol's effects and that help them to learn effective coping responses in situations where alcohol is served may be even more useful. Development of effective prevention approaches can be facilitated by identification of risk factors for overuse of alcohol (for example, family conflict and neighborhood disorganization).

Barbiturates and Tranquilizers Both barbiturates and tranquilizers have a depressing effect on the central nervous system. Both groups of drugs are especially dangerous in combination with alcohol. **Barbiturates** are often prescribed by physicians to decrease anxiety or prevent convulsions. **Tranquilizers** are derived from several chemical groups. They are overused in the United States. Both barbiturates and tranquilizers are dangerous because tolerance develops and the user often increases the dose to dangerous levels to get the desired effect.

The Opioids Opioids is the term used to describe all drugs with morphinelike effects that bind to the opioid receptors in the brain. Some opioids occur naturally and some are chemically synthesized. Natural opioids include **endorphins, enkephalins,** and **dynorphins,** all of which are manufactured by the brain and the pituitary gland. **Opiates** are members of the opioid group that are derived from the juice of the opium poppy—for example, **morphine** and **heroin.** Opioids cause changes in mood, sleepiness, mental clouding, constipation, and slowing of the activity of the respiratory center in the brain. Opioids are sometimes called **narcotics,** but this term does not have the same meaning to law officers, physicians, scientists, and the public. The withdrawal reaction from opioid use can be severe. According to the **exposure orientation** theory of opioid addiction, the use of opiates shuts down the body's synthesis of natural opioids. The **interactional orientation** holds that the situation in which drugs are used is significant. The most widely used treatment for opioid addicts is **methadone maintenance. Naltrexone,** a drug that blocks opioid receptors, can be used effectively as treatment to prevent readdiction after detoxification.

Cocaine Cocaine, a drug from the leaves of the coca bush, stimulates the central nervous system and increases heart rate, raises blood pressure and temperature, and decreases appetite. It can produce feelings of hyperalertness, but in larger doses can produce a maniclike state, paranoia, and impaired judgment. **Crack** is a more potent form of cocaine that is highly addictive. Cocaine users may benefit from aversive conditioning and contingency contracts. Many cocaine users have dysfunctional families. Mutual help groups similar to Alcoholics Anonymous can be an effective way to provide the social support that is lacking.

Amphetamines Amphetamines are powerful psychomotor stimulants that affect both the central nervous system and the cardiovascular system. In moderate doses they result in wakefulness, alertness, and elevated mood. Tolerance develops rapidly, so many users begin injecting amphetamines to get more intense effects. High doses lead to nervousness, dizziness, confusion, heart palpitations, and elevated blood pressure.

Hallucinogens. Hallucinogens or **psychedelics** produce alterations in consciousness by their action on the central nervous system. Natural hallucinogens include mescaline, psilocybin, and DMT. Synthetic hallucinogens include STP and LSD. Natural hallucinogens have been used in religious ceremonies by many primitive cultures for hundreds of years. Abuse of hallucinogenic drugs can result in respiratory or cardiovascular collapse or in psychotic behavior. Support groups and teaching of social skills seem effective in the prevention of recurrence of hallucinogen use.

Phencyclidine (PCP) PCP is a synthetic chemical that may cause disorientation and hallucinations and make the user feel dissociated from the environment. Users sometimes develop a severe depression or a severe psychotic state that may be difficult to reverse.

Inhalants Inhalants are volatile substances or organic solvents (such as gasoline, spray paints) that can be used to produce changes in perception. Their recurrent use may cause withdrawal from social, occupational, or recreational activities. Inhalants are more commonly used by young people because of their ease of accessibility. Tolerance and withdrawal symptoms occur when inhalants cause dependence.

Cannabis Cannabis use in the form of marijuana has increased recently. **Hashish** is a solidified resin of the cannabis plant. The major active ingredient in cannabis products is THC. Marijuana use impairs motor coordination and perception and affects short-term memory and learning even after the feeling of intoxication from the drug has passed. Treatments involving relapse prevention and social support groups have been found to be effective in helping people with marijuana problems achieve abstinence.

Nicotine Nicotine, a chemical found in tobacco, acts at least in part by directly stimulating certain receptors that are sensitive to the neurotransmitter acetylcholine. Normal doses of nicotine can increase heart rate and blood pressure, and increases the heart's need for oxygen and may cause chest pains or a heart attack in people with atherosclerosis. Despite their knowledge that smoking is hazardous to health, many people find the habit of smoking difficult to give up. Such difficulty may be due to withdrawal symptoms, social and environmental cues, the overlearned nature of the habit, and the frequent reinforcement that is delivered with every puff. Although many smokers are able to quit on their own, smoking cessation programs can be effective for those who would like to quit. Cognitive research has identified three stages of change relevant to smoking cessation. These include commitment to change, implementation of the change, and maintenance of the change with emphasis on relapse prevention. When used along with a counseling program, **nicotine gum** and **nicotine patches** can be helpful in reducing tobacco use.

Caffeine Caffeine can be addictive. It has mind-altering properties and in high doses can cause anxiety and nervousness. Tolerance and withdrawal symptoms also can occur. Symptoms of caffeine intoxication include restlessness, insomnia, high heart rate, and rambling flow of thought and speech.

CHAPTER FIFTEEN

Paul Klee, *Flowers in Stone*, 1939.
Superstock. © 1996 Artists Rights Society, New York/VG BildKunst, Bonn.

DISORDERS OF CHILDHOOD AND ADOLESCENCE

Robbie's difficulties began when he was very young. He is now 13 years old.

His parents want him out of the house. They say he has always been a difficult child and is getting worse. As a toddler, he was very active and stubborn, and attempts to discipline him were usually ineffective. In nursery school he was unusually distractible and impulsive. In early elementary school, teachers reported their concern not only about his distractibility and impulsivity, but also about his aggressive and antagonistic behavior toward other children.

When Robbie was 7, he was seen by a school psychologist and placed in a smaller, more structured classroom . . . [but he] continued to fight with his classmates and was ostracized by them. At times, his parents and teachers sensed . . . his loneliness and low self-esteem, but he was reluctant to discuss these issues.

[As time passed] the situation became worse. Robbie was suspended or expelled from school on numerous occasions. Now in middle school, he attends a class for children with behavioral problems and is working considerably below grade level. He has no friends and engages in no extracurricular activities, having recently been dropped from the soccer team for fighting.

Robbie began smoking at 10, and he now drinks alcohol fairly regularly and uses marijuana and other drugs on occasion. He hangs around with older adolescents and was recently arrested for shoplifting. Robbie says he knows people think he is a "loser" and a troublemaker, but he blames his family and says, "I can't wait to be on my own."

National Advisory Mental Health Council, 1990, p. 8

Anna's behavior was a contrast to Robbie's.

At three years of age, Anna was a quiet child. She spent a great deal of time sucking her thumb and hugging a teddy bear that was almost without fur as a result of constant loving. When her mother went into the bedroom to make the beds, Anna followed. The same things happened when her mother went to the telephone or took the wash out of the washing machine. She cried every day when her mother left her at the day-care center. The teachers there reported much the same behavior that she showed at home. . . . When Anna was 6, she refused to stay in her first-grade classroom unless her mother or grandmother sat in the back of the room.

Deciding to do something about unwanted behavior in a child can be much more agonizing than making a similar decision about an adult. Parents often feel responsible for everything their children do, and may feel especially guilty about admitting that their child has a problem that is serious enough to require professional help. And when parents or others do intervene, they may make things worse by emphasizing a problem that might disappear if it were ignored. On the other hand, many problems are easier to treat in children, since their behavior patterns and interaction styles have not yet become firmly established.

Normal or healthy development comes about through a series of interlocking social, emotional, and cognitive competencies. Competencies at one developmental period not only help the child adapt to the environment, but also help prepare the way for new competencies to come. These developing competencies also integrate the old ones into new patterns of functioning. Pathological development, on the other hand, may be thought of as a lack of growth and integration of these competencies. Because of the important role early competencies play in later ones, an early disturbance may ultimately result in the emergence of a much larger difficulty some years later.

Behavioral problems sometimes interfere with a child's development by delaying the learning of all kinds of academic and social skills. Despite these potential handicaps, however, many children with psychological problems are brought to the attention of mental-health workers only when some crisis occurs. By then the problem may be difficult to treat because it has become so severe that the child had been labeled as a "problem." Withdrawn children like Anna are less likely to be referred for problem behavior than children like Robbie who are extremely active, damage property or belongings, or who in other ways make life difficult for those around them. Yet Anna's behavior may be cause for concern if it continues at the present level.

Because of the interlocking aspects of development over time, attention should be paid to unusual patterns of childhood behavior whether these are hard to live with or not. Antisocial and acting-out behavior and severe reading problems in children are often correlated with adult disorders. Such childhood problems as shyness, fears, tics, nervousness, hypersensitivity, speech defects, and anxiety reactions may leave fewer discernible effects on later development, although adults who had these problems in childhood may be described as at least mildly maladjusted compared to the average person (Rutter & Hersov, 1985).

The Scope of the Problem

According to recent estimates, anywhere from 17 to 22 percent of children under age 18 meet the diagnostic criteria for one or more mental disorders (National Advisory Mental Health Council, 1990). Of these 11 to 14 million children, at least half may be severely handicapped by a disorder, but many of the rest have trouble coping with the demands of school, family, and community.

Some maladaptive behavior in childhood results from normal variations in rates of development. But even these may have long-term effects. Children who develop later than their age-mates often carry feelings of inadequacy and inferiority into adulthood. Personalities of children who are early or late in maturing physically may be permanently affected. Problems can also result from lateness in acquiring cognitive skills. Children who are unable to master academic work when their classmates are ready for it are at a serious disadvantage both in school and in later life, even if they catch up afterward (Figure 15–1). If learning deficits are the product of an untreated learning disability, depression is likely to develop. The depression then may increase the chances of future learning problems. Only about 2 million of the children who need mental health treatment receive it—at best, about 18 percent. In contrast, 74 percent of children suffering from physical handicaps are treated professionally (U.S. Office of Technology Assessment, 1990). In other words, maladaptive behavior in children is a major problem that society is not addressing adequately. Many of the untreated children are likely to develop into seriously mentally ill adults who, if untreated, may have difficulties in their personal lives and in holding jobs. A number of risk factors for childhood disorders have been identified. These factors include parental psychopathology, family discord and divorce, low socioeconomic status, the child's temperamental characteristics, and stressful experiences (Jensen et al., 1990). Child abuse is an especially damaging

Figure 15-1 Learning to write requires a certain degree of coordination and cognitive skill. Children develop these skills at different rates. Those who develop them later than average may be particularly vulnerable to later adjustment problems.

stressor. Abused children have a very high rate of psychological problems (Egeland et al., 1993) (see Box 15–1). For many of these children, problems will extend into adulthood.

Persistence of Childhood Disorders

In the ECA study referred to in previous chapters, those in the community with a diagnosable disorder frequently reported that it had begun during childhood or before the beginning of adulthood (Weissman et al., 1990). Because some critics have suggested that many childhood disorders identified in epidemiological studies may be only transitory problems, it is important to have longitudinal data to determine if these critics may be wrong and that these problems persist over time. A follow-up study of children originally evaluated in a general population survey showed that many childhood disorders tend to persist rather than to disappear naturally over time (Cohen et al., 1993). Children who received a diagnosis at follow-up and who were judged to be severely affected by the diagnosed disorder were also found to have received a diagnosis two and one-half years earlier. For both boys and girls an original diagnosis of attention-deficit/hyperactive disorder, oppositional disorder, conduct disorder, and overanxious disorder tended to persist in all ages. Only major depression did not have a strong pattern of continuation. However, this fact may be related to the characteristics of depression, not to persistence of disorders in childhood. Even in adults depression tends to be a recurring disorder rather than one in which the symptoms persist unbroken over long periods.

Helping troubled youngsters is often problematic because there is lack of understanding of the nature of childhood disorders and their causes. For example, it is

not known whether some disorders of childhood, such as psychoses, depression, and anxiety disorders, are extensions of the adult categories or whether they are separate disorders with different causes. One piece of evidence that suggests that many childhood disorders are distinct from their adult versions is the difference in the sex ratios in these disorders for children and adults. In childhood, boys are affected more often than girls in almost all categories. Beginning in adolescence, however, mood disorders and anxiety disorders are more frequent in women, and there is no sex difference in schizophrenic disorders (Rutter & Garmezy, 1983).

Disruptive Behavior

Disruptive behavior is an obvious indication of a potential problem. Two kinds of children who behave disruptively are of special concern to parents, teachers, and clinicians; children who do not pay attention and seem exceptionally active, and children who behave aggressively, break rules, and cause significant harm to other people and their property. The first type is diagnosed as having *attention-deficit/hyperactivity disorder* while the latter group have a diagnosis of *oppositional defiant disorder* or *conduct disorder*.

Attention-Deficit/Hyperactivity Disorder

Children who are diagnosed with **attention-deficit/hyperactivity disorder** (A-D/HD) have either or both continuing problems of attention and of hyperactivity-impulsivity that are more severe and frequent than those of typical children at the same developmental level. One DSM-IV requirement for this disorder is that at least some hyperactive or inattentive symptoms must have been observed before age 7, even if the diagnosis is made much later. To meet the DSM-IV diagnostic criteria the behaviors must also result in impaired performance in at least two different environments, for instance, both at home and at school. There are several types of A-D/HD. In the *combined type*, both attention deficit and hyperactivity are present. In two subtypes, *predominantly inattentive type* and *predominantly hyperactive-impulsive type*, the person has too few symptoms to meet one of the criteria, so that only the other can be diagnosed (see Table 15-1). To meet the criteria for the inattentive subtype or hyperactivity/impulsivity subtype, at least six of the behavioral features for that subtype must have been present before age 7. To meet the criteria for combined A-D/HD at least six of the behavioral features of each subtype must be identified.

Jimmy illustrates a number of the behaviors seen in a child with an A-D/HD disorder.

Child Abuse and Sexual Abuse Victims and Survivors

Child Abuse

Sometimes parents neglect their children by failing to provide food, clothing, warmth, a clean environment, and the supervision necessary to keep their children safe. Or they may provide these things but express no interest in their children and fail to interact with them more than is absolutely necessary. Neglected children show the effects of lack of parental stimulation. They talk less and make fewer social responses. In addition, they engage in little exploratory or inquisitive behavior. They also are likely to be depressed (Conaway & Hansen, 1989). Child abuse also has negative effects on children but it is quite different from child neglect. Physical **child abuse** includes acts of overt physical violence or excessive punishment and typically occurs in discrete episodes and with a low frequency. Such physical abuse is often accompanied by parental anger as a result of a child's failure to meet parental demands. Another type of child abuse, **sexual abuse**, involves a variety of sexual acts by which an adult, using his or her authority over a child, manipulates and exploits a child.

Physical Child Abuse

Physical child abuse affects at least 350,000 children in the United States every year according to one large epidemiological study (NCCAN, 1988). This is probably a considerable underestimate because it involves only those instances reported to child protective agencies. Three types of strategies have been used to study child abuse. Some studies simply compare rates of history of abuse in two or more samples that differ on a possible abuse outcome, for example, how frequently these people mistreat their own children. A second strategy compares the behavior of subjects with a history of abuse to those without that history on the assumption that any differences observed in their behaviors may be a consequence of abuse. Both these strategies involved retrospective reports of abuse long after it took place. Because such studies are correlational the results cannot establish a casual relationship between abuse and the outcome behav-

ior. Even more of a problem in interpreting the results are the possible biases in the subjects' reports of abuse that arise either through their lack of memory about the abuse events or as a result of their attempts to explain or justify later problem behavior. The third and most desirable strategy calls for prospective research. For example, some researchers have gathered information from subjects both before and after the occurrence of abuse (Egeland et al., 1988). The prospective method does not show as strong a link between physical abuse and problem outcomes as the retrospective method does (Widom, 1989).

It is often possible to detect probable abuse in current families by observing children with their mothers. Even quite young children of abusive mothers behave differently when they are with their mothers compared to children of nonabusing mothers (see Figure 15-2). Physical abuse also impacts children's overall behaviors and skills and produces problems severe enough to handicap them in everyday life. Children who have been physically abused tend to be deficient in motor skills such as those involved in running, skipping, or riding a tricycle. These deficiencies may be caused by their fear of exploring and taking risks, but poor motor development has been noted as early as four months of age, so lack of exploratory behavior is not a complete answer. Abused children also show delayed development of speech and language. Preschool children may be abused for talking, so they simply don't practice speaking. Instead, much of their communication is nonverbal.

The IQs of abused children are lower than might be expected compared to similar nonabused children (Salter et al., 1985). This may be a reflection of the fear of failure and difficulty in paying attention to instructions that seem to handicap abused children's performance in testing situations rather than a reflection of actual intelligence level. On the other hand, the test results may represent an actual delay in their cognitive development resulting from the unpredictable and dangerous environment in which such children live. Instead of being able to concentrate on learning, they are concerned with ways of surviving, and in

addition they may be preoccupied by anxious thoughts and a variety of fantasies. Physically abused children are more likely not only to be more aggressive but also to have a higher rate of both oppositional defiant disorder and conduct disorder (Hansen et al., 1990). Physically abused children are also more likely to be substance abusers in adolescence (Caviola & Schiff, 1988). In addition to problems involving aggression toward others or lack of impulse control, physically abused children are more likely than nonabused children to have emotional problems such as anxiety and depression (Hansen et al., 1990) and to have poorer peer relationships (Dodge et al., 1994).

Physical abuse in childhood may have long-term consequences. Adolescents as well as adults who have been physically abused as children are more likely than those with no history of abuse to show aggression to nonfamily members, including dating partners. Several studies have found that in college student populations both physical abuse in childhood and parental marital violence predicted dating violence in college students (Bernard & Bernard, 1983; Riggs et al., 1990). In one prospective study (McCord, 1983) there was no difference in the rate of adult crime among groups identified as having been abused, neglected, or loved in childhood, but physical abuse by parents was associated with more violent criminal behavior (assault, rape, and murder) when their children reached adulthood.

Although physical abuse can have very negative immediate and long term effects, some individuals show a resiliency that seems to allow them to escape these negative outcomes. A high level of cognitive competency may play a protective role. For example, mothers abused in childhood who did not later abuse their own children had higher IQ scores than a similar group of mothers who did abuse their children (Egeland, 1988). Supportive social relationships, therapy, and fewer stressful life events also seem to provide protection from negative long-term effects (Malinosky-Rummell & Hansen, 1993).

Sexual Abuse and Victimization

Interactions leading to sexual abuse often begin with less intrusive acts such as fondling or sexual kissing. Over time,

BOX 15-1

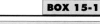

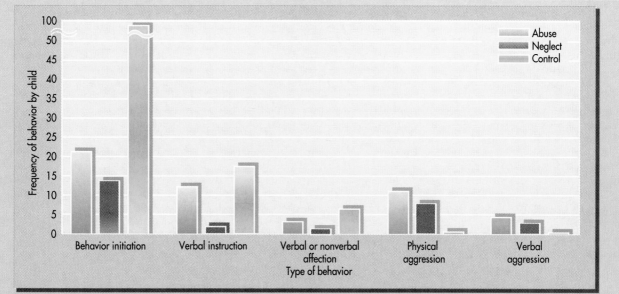

Figure 15-2 Frequency of different types of behaviors by children when they interacted with their mothers who were abusive, neglectful, or from a control group.

SOURCE: Adapted from Bousha & Twentyman, (1984). Mother-child interactional style in abuse, neglect, and control groups. *Journal of Abnormal Psychology*, 93, p. 110.

if access to the child continues to be available, the abusive behaviors progress to oral-genital contact and anal or vaginal penetration.

Although some children are sexually assaulted by strangers, most children are sexually abused by adults they know. As a result, the sexual activity may initially be disguised as a game or normalized through joint viewing of pornographic videotapes or magazines by the child and abusing adult. Abusers usually warn children, sometimes with a threat of force, to keep the activity secret. Disclosure of the abuse often comes accidentally from another victim or through the discovery that the child has developed a sexually transmitted disease.

Four characteristic responses have been suggested to typify the effects of sexual abuse on a child. These include sexual traumatization, stigmatization, betrayal, and powerlessness (Finkelhor, 1988). *Traumatization* refers to the impairment of healthy sexual function, including confusion about sexuality and affection and a tendency to form erotic relationships. *Stigmatization* refers to the victims' tendency to blame themselves for the abusive acts, to feel ashamed and guilty. Feelings of *betrayal* of trust, likely to be experienced especially if the abuser is a family member or other well-known person, can lead to future difficulty in forming relationships and sometimes to

choosing later relationships characterized by exploitation. *Powerlessness* refers to the feelings of helplessness and vulnerability the child feels. Such feelings are associated with regressive behaviors, dissociative disorders, and a variety of anxiety symptoms.

The case of Rosa, age 6, illustrates some of the short-term results of sexual abuse. Rosa had been sexually abused by her father.

Mrs. Torres reported that she separated from Mr. Torres about 6 months ago. . . . Visitation with Rosa by Mr. Torres was irregular until 4 months ago, when he began to pick her up every Saturday and kept her overnight at his mother's home. . . .

Mrs. Torres reported that Rosa began to masturbate excessively about a year ago. It was so noticeable that her kindergarten teacher had discussed it with the mother last spring. Rosa was also labeled "provocative" by the teacher, who reported incidents in which Rosa would pull her pants down in front of boys and try to touch their penises. Mrs. Torres also reported that in the last 4 months, Rosa had been pulling at her underpants. She said that this behavior was especially noticeable on Sundays, after Rosa had been with her father. It was so noticeable that Mrs. Torres tried different detergents

and bought a different type of underpants for Rosa, thinking that these might be causing the irritation.

Mrs. Torres stated that starting about a year ago, Rosa began waking up with nightmares. Rosa had also become extremely oppositional in the last year. . . . Inattentiveness and difficulty concentrating at school had affected [her] performance in school this year.

Mrs. Torres reported that Rosa was increasingly reluctant to go on visitations with her father, coming up with excuses, saying "I'm sick" or "I don't want to go." She would not get dressed sometimes, and then would want to wear lots of clothes, including pants over shorts. Rose was also evidencing some fear of men. She was reluctant to approach her grandfather, with whom she had previously been close, and seemed anxious about being around men.

Strand, 1991, p. 79

Sexual victimization is considered to be a risk factor for mental health problems in childhood (Kendall-Tackett et al., 1993). However, 20 to 50 percent of sexually abused children do not have apparent symptoms when evaluated with measures commonly used to assess child psy-

Box continues on the next page.

chopathology (Spaccarelli, 1994). Some reasons for this variability in outcome have been suggested by research including severity, duration of the abuse, and age when the abuse first occurred (Kendall-Tackett et al., 1993). Despite the importance of these factors, much of the variability in outcome still is unexplained. One way to approach this lack of explanation is to use a model such as that developed by Sameroff and Fiese (1990) (see Figure 15-3). In this view, which illustrates the vulnerability-resilience theme of this book, the victim of sexual abuse will face three categories

of stressful events: the abuse itself, abuse-related events, and disclosure-related events. These stressors include the effects of the abuse itself, problems involved with keeping the secret, heightened family conflict and possible marital separation when the abuse is discovered, and possible further changes based on community reaction to the abuse. The symptoms arising from abuse may be affected by negative cognitive appraisals (self-blame, loss of trust in relationships, beliefs concerning physical damage) and ineffective coping strategies (wishful thinking, cognitive avoidance). The sup-

port resources the child has, as well as his or her relevant personal characteristics, may moderate these strategies and appraisals to make them less damaging or lead to the substitution of more positive self-appraisals to make them less damaging or lead to the substitution of more positive self-appraisals and strategies. By considering all these factors concerning stress, vulnerability, and resiliency, researchers may develop a better understanding of why some children seem to experience fewer negative effects and also of how to develop interventions to help those most affected.

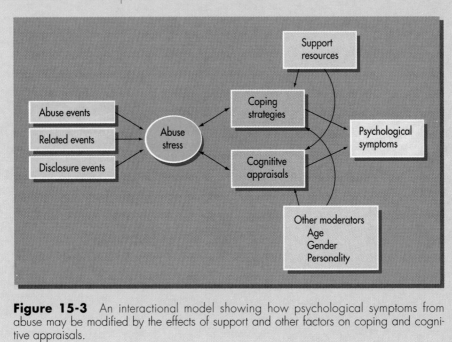

Figure 15-3 An interactional model showing how psychological symptoms from abuse may be modified by the effects of support and other factors on coping and cognitive appraisals.

SOURCE: Adapted from Spaccarelli, 1994, p. 344, originally from Sameroff & Fiese, 1990.

By his second year, he seemed to be ignorant of danger, walking on the edge of counters and hanging from the top shelf of the bookcase. If his mother did not watch him closely in the park, he would wander off. On one occasion, she became involved in discussion with another mother and later found Jimmy on another block, staring in a window and seemingly unaware that he had become lost. Temperamentally, he could be described as a child with a high level of motor activity, fluctuating mood, intensity of reaction, and difficulty adapting to new situations. . . .

In his third-grade class Jimmy sat near the front of the room, where the teacher could quietly direct him and answer his endless stream of questions. As usual, Jimmy made noise (squirming in his seat, humming, and drumming with two pencils) while the teacher was working at the board. His desk was disorganized, with papers falling out and crayons under

the seat that occasionally were ground into the floor. He often did not sit in his seat but positioned himself on his knees and leaned out into the aisle. [His teacher] gave up ordering him to be quiet because threats each day had been greeted with verbal agreement but no change in Jimmy's behavior.

—Garfinkel et al., 1990, pp. 157–158

To meet the DSM-IV criteria these inattentive or hyperactive behaviors must have continued for at least six months before the diagnosis is made and some of them must have been present before age 7. Table 15-1 makes it clear that A-D/HD involves more than the high levels of exuberance and motor activity displayed by many normal children. Estimates of the prevalence of A-D/HD range from 3 to 5 percent of school-age children in the general population and make up from 30 to

TABLE 15-1
Behavioral Features of Attention-Deficit/Hyperactivity Disorder

Inattention

1. Is easily distracted by extraneous stimuli
2. Has difficulty following through on instructions in the absence of close supervision (e.g., fails to finish schoolwork or chores)
3. Has difficulty sustaining attention in tasks or play activities
4. Often does not seem to listen to what is being said to him or her
5. Often loses things necessary for tasks or activities (e.g., toys, pencils)
6. Often fails to give close attention to details and makes careless mistakes in schoolwork or other activities
7. Has difficulty organizing activities and tasks
8. Often avoids or dislikes tasks that require sustained mental effort (such as homework)

Hyperactivity/Impulsivity

Hyperactivity

1. Often leaves seat in classroom or in other situations in which remaining seated is expected
2. Has difficulty playing or engaging in leisure activities quietly
3. Runs about or climbs excessively in inappropriate situations
4. Often fidgets with hands or feet or squirms in seat
5. Often "on the go" or acts as if "driven by a motor"
6. Often talks excessively

Impulsivity

1. Has difficulty awaiting turn
2. Often blurts out answers to questions before they have been completed
3. Often interrupts or intrudes on others

---

40 percent of all referrals to child guidance clinics (Wheeler & Carlson, 1994). Figure 15-4 shows the decrease in the number of cases of A-D/HD per thousand boys after age 10 and illustrates how, until age 18, boys are the predominant group affected by the disorder.

A-D/HD is most often diagnosed during early school years for two probable reasons. First, it is usually hard to establish a positive diagnosis of A-D/HD before a child is 4 or 5 years old because, during this developmental period, some normal behaviors seem similar to the DSM-IV criteria. Second, the school situation makes demands on children that may not have been present in their earlier environments. For instance, children in school are frequently expected to sit quietly, to complete intellectually challenging tasks, and to pay attention while the teacher gives instructions or explains new concepts. These demands may highlight attention difficulties and inability to control activity level.

Consequences of A-D/HD A-D/HD produces two important consequences for children—deficiencies in both academic and social skills. Deficits in attention may have a negative effect on learning because such deficits make it more difficult for children to pick up basic information and concepts. In a school setting this

problem is compounded by distraction and lack of organization in school assignments. In turn, these difficulties may well result in a lack of practice of basic skills, such as those gained by completing sets of arithmetic problems or spelling exercises. As a result of this lack of skill development, school achievement becomes a problem—setting up a spiral of consistently decreasing achievement. Such a decrease can encourage a negative self-view, lowering the child's belief that he or she can succeed at school-related tasks.

Learning by observation in social settings may also be impacted by behaviors characteristic of A-D/HD. One research project that took place at summer camp illustrates the difficulty (Whalen and Henker, 1985). Pairs of boys, one with A-D/HD and one a control, played a game in which they alternated playing the roles of an astronaut and of mission control. The astronaut was to be the follower, to listen carefully to mission control messages, comply with instructions, and give appropriate feedback. Mission control was to be the leader who conveyed the needed information and guided the astronaut. Each boy played the game twice in each role, each time with a different partner. The most interesting finding was that unlike the boys in the control group, the A-D/HD boys did not seem to benefit from the opportu-

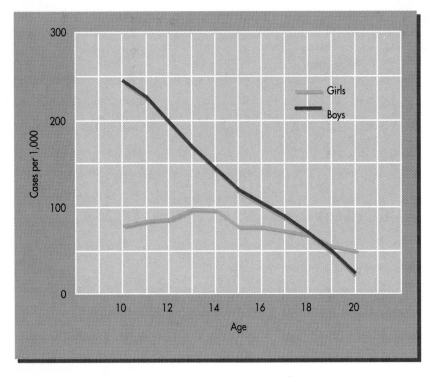

Figure 15-4 Rates of A-D/HD vary by age and sex of child.

SOURCE: Cohen et al. (1993). An epidemiological study of disorders in late childhood and adolescence. *Journal of Child Psychiatry and Psychology*, 34, p. 58.

nity to observe another boy in the more difficult role of mission control before playing the role themselves (see Figure 15-5).

The ability to interact successfully with peers in a social setting is one of the most important aspects of a child's development (Wheeler & Carlson, 1994). Children whose behavior is hyperactive, either with or without attention disorder, also experience roadblocks in social development. Behaviors characteristic of hyperactivity often result in a negative social status for preadolescent children. Hyperactive boys and boys whose major problem is inattention are both likely to be rated as unpopular by their school peers (Carlson et al., 1984). In both attention-deficit and hyperactive groups, the boys are aware of their unpopularity and generally have low self-esteem. In addition to experiencing negative feedback from others and holding negative views of themselves, children with A-D/HD also act as "negative social catalysts" (Whalen & Henker, 1985)—that is, they seem to elicit maladaptive behaviors from others (teachers and peers) around them. In one study, boys with A-D/HD were paired with a boy without a diagnosis. The pair's interactional behavior was then compared with that of control pairs in which neither boy had been diagnosed with A-D/HD (Cunningham & Siegel, 1987). In the pairs that included a boy with A-D/HD *both* boys showed more frequent demands, command statements,

and negative responses than did the boys in the pairs in which neither boy had this diagnosis. This suggested that behaviors characteristic of A-D/HD elicit more demanding and negative behaviors in normal peers that may then serve to reinforce and escalate these behaviors in the child with an A-D/HD diagnosis.

This interaction between a child's behavior and the behavior of another person is frequently seen in family settings as well as in school. Problematic interpersonal interactions are often observed among family members in families that include a child with A-D/HD. Parents of children with this disorder are often noted to be experiencing marital difficulties, high levels of stress, and conflict-laden parent-child interactions (Bernier & Siegel, 1994). While sometimes these characteristics are seen as probable causes of the child's difficulties, they may instead be a result of the catalyzing effect of interacting with a child with an A-D/HD diagnosis (Barkley et al., 1990). In laboratory settings, at least, after children's behaviors change as a result of medication, parents' behaviors also alter (Barkley, 1989). Parents of children with A-D/HD experience more stress and fewer gratifications as parents than most other parents do (Fischer, 1990). Although much of this stress arises from parent-child interactions, another important source of stress comes from people outside the family who may respond negatively to the parents by expressing disapproval either of their parenting skills or of their child's behavior (Bernier & Siegel, 1994).

Teachers also act differently toward A-D/HD children than to their non–A-D/HD peers; the teachers tend to be more intense and controlling. The presence of a child with an A-D/HD disorder in the classroom also seems to alter the teacher's behavior for the whole class so that the rate of the teacher's negative interactions with the other children in the class also increases (Whalen & Henker, 1985). When children with A-D/HD were medicated during school hours, teacher-child interactions were also observed to become more normal.

Possible Causes At present the causes of attention-deficit/hyperactivity disorder are unknown. Although it is a common disorder, it is probably the result of a complex set of factors including genetic inheritance, environmental factors, function in several brain regions, and

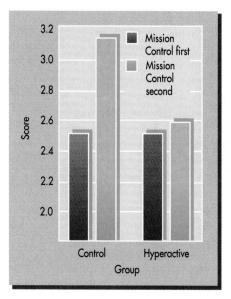

Figure 15-5 Communicative efficiency of boys with A-D/HD and control boys when serving as mission control during the first versus the second game. Both groups of boys performed at about the same level when they played the role of mission control first. In the second game, when they had previously seen another boy in the same role, hyperactive boys showed much less change in their behavior than did the control boys.

SOURCE: Whalen and Hanker, (1985). Cognitive behavioral therapies for hyperactive children: premises, problems, and prospects. *Journal of Abnormal Child Psychology, 13*, p. 469.

level of neurotransmitter activity. Studies of parents also support the idea that A-D/HD is transmitted in families because both mothers and fathers of children with A-D/HD are much more likely to be classified in this category than are parents of children in the control group. Siblings of children with A-D/HD are two to three times as likely to be diagnosed with A-D/HD as controls (Faraone & Biederman, 1994). Second-degree relatives (aunts and uncles of those with A-D/HD diagnosis) have also shown higher rates of hyperactivity diagnosis than were seen in relatives of a control group. Higher rates of school failure and intellectual impairment, compared to controls, have also been found in biological relatives of those with A-D/HD even for those relatives that did not meet criteria for an A-D/HD diagnosis (Faraone et al., 1993). These family studies suggest a genetic basis for A-D/HD and demonstrate a pattern of distribution of the disorder in families that might be consistent with a single major gene as the causal factor.

Although A-D/HD seems to run in families, it is important to distinguish between familial and genetic causes. The closer the genetic relationship, the more the environment also tends to be shared. This results in a confounding of genetic and environmental factors that only twin and adoption studies can clarify. As yet there are few such studies for A-D/HD. Environmental factors cannot be ruled out by the data so far. Genetic models indicate that only about 46 percent of the boys and 32 percent of the girls who would carry such a gene can be expected to develop A-D/HD (Deutsch et al., 1990). This low *penetrance*, as it is called, suggests that both genetic vulnerability and certain environmental stressors are necessary for symptoms to develop.

Since the first descriptions of A-D/HD early in this century, it has been speculated that the disorder has a neurological basis or is at least in part biologically based. This idea has been supported by brain-imaging studies, EEG studies, genetic studies, and studies of response to psychoactive drugs. However, the exact nature of this deficit has not been specified. So far it has not been possible to map certain behavioral descriptors of those with an A-D/HD diagnosis onto particular parts of the nervous system or even onto specific types of cognitive operations (Riccio et al., 1993). Although it has been suggested that the frontal lobes and brain stem as well as the neurotransmitter system (especially dopamine and norepinephrine) may be involved, research findings have not always supported any of these ideas. One area of the brain that has been studied in relation to A-D/HD is the corpus callosum. This area is thought to facilitate communication between the two hemispheres of the brain. It is particularly associated with the allocation of attention and level of arousal of each brain hemisphere. Two studies have demonstrated some differences in size of portions of the corpus collosum for A-D/HD subjects and a comparison group (Giedd et al., 1994; Hynd et al., 1991). In one study these size differences were found to be correlated with children's scores on an impulsivity/hyperactivity scale completed by parents and teachers. Despite such intriguing findings and the possibility of using new and powerful scanning devices, it is doubtful that a single lesion or difference in a brain region can account for the complicated behavioral picture of A-D/HD.

Other suggestions about the causes of A-D/HD include a metabolic dysfunction in the brain (Zametkin et al., 1990), delayed maturation of the central nervous system (Hynd et al., 1991), and complications during pregnancy or birth and illnesses of early infancy (Hartsough & Lambert, 1985).

Treatment By far the most common treatment for hyperactive children is the use of drugs that stimulate the central nervous system such as methylphenidate (Ritalin), dextroamphetamine (Dexedrine), or pemoline (Cylert). Between 80 and 90 percent of all children diagnosed with A-D/HD are thought to have been treated with a central nervous system stimulant drug at some time. A large number of studies reveal that these drugs have positive short-term effects (Pelham, 1993). They take effect quickly (behavioral effects can often be seen within 30 minutes) and wear off quickly (within 4 to 6 hours). Their effectiveness follows a general bell curve or normal curve pattern with the maximum effect at about 2 to 4 hours, depending on the medication used. This effectiveness pattern has important implications for children in classroom settings. The administration of medication should take into account the timing of school activities that cause a child particular difficulties. For example, if a child has problems with social interactions at noon recess, a pill given at breakfast 4 to 5 hours earlier and another administered 30 minutes before recess will not provide much benefit.

Many children treated with these medications show improved classroom behavior with a reduction in class disruption and increased on-task performance. In addition they may complete more of their assigned work and do it with greater accuracy (Pelham, 1993). Figure 15-6 illustrates measures of classroom behavior in a special summer treatment program for children with A-D/HD who received a placebo (nonactive medication) compared to children who received two different levels of methylphenidate medication. The figure shows that several aspects of classroom performance were clearly improved by either level of the medication, although a larger amount of medication did not seem to produce much additional benefit over the smaller dose. Medication may also increase children's prosocial behavior when interacting with a group of peers. It seems to have the clearest effect on children who are the most aggres-

sive (Murphy et al., 1992). The medications were most associated with a decrease in negative behaviors in social group interactions rather than an increase in positive behaviors (see Figure 15-7). Medication does not seem to improve behavioral interactions in a one-to-one situation with another child.

Most research on the effects of medications for A-D/HD has been carried out with young school children. A few studies with older adolescents show that although the medication improved cognitive performance in laboratory tasks, teachers rated classroom improvement as minimal. Moreover, a smaller percentage of these older children showed any improvement, compared to the results of studies with younger children (Klorman et al., 1990). Medication in childhood does not seem to improve outcome in adulthood. When adolescents or adults who received stimulant medication for hyperactivity in childhood are compared with hyperactive children who did not receive such medication, their current adjustment and behaviors do not differ (McMahon, 1994). Although a number of causes for this discouraging finding have been suggested, the reason that temporary improvement does not lead to permanent change remains unclear.

The use of medication, especially medication continued over a long time period, must be considered especially carefully when young children are involved. Medication, even if temporarily helpful, may have possible long-term developmental or growth effects. Thus far it does not appear that the medications for A-D/HD have negative long-term physical effects although, with high dosage, they do seem to inhibit both growth and

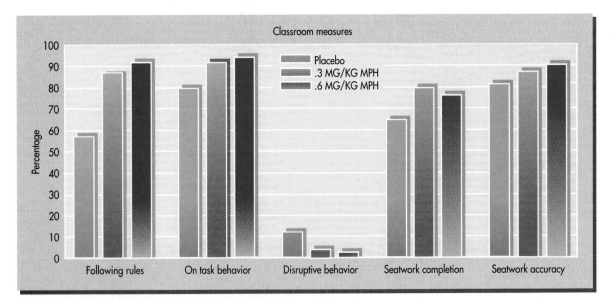

Figure 15-6 Differences in classroom behavior and performance of children with A-D/HD diagnoses who received low or high doses of methylphenidate twice daily compared to a group who received doses of a placebo.

SOURCE: Pelham, 1993, p. 202.

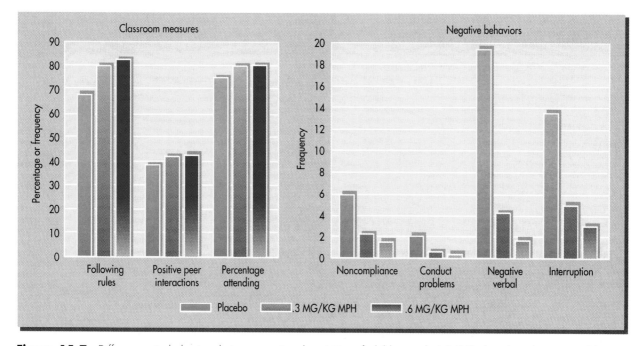

Figure 15-7 Differences in behavior during recreational activities of children with A-D/HD disorder who received low or high doses of methylphenidate twice daily compared to a group who received doses of a placebo.

SOURCE: Pelham, 1993, p. 205.

weight gain (Gittelman-Klein & Mannuzza, 1988). The cause of this effect is not known for certain, but it seems likely to be because the medication reduces appetite and food intake.

Another concern about medication has been that children may be encouraged not to take responsibility for their behavior and attribute any changes to "the pill" rather than their own actions (Henker & Whalen, 1989). Recent research has shown, however, that the type of attributions or causal statements children made about their behavior were related to whether they had been successful or unsuccessful in a particular task—not whether they were using medication at that time. The children tended to take personal credit for good outcomes regardless or whether or not they were receiving medication and to make external attributions (blame their teachers or their medication) for their failures (Hoza et al., 1993).

Because of lack of information about long-term effects of medication, many experts recommend that a behavioral intervention should be established and evaluated before any medication is given. This behavioral approach should include both classroom intervention and parent training (Pfiffner & O'Leary, 1993). Only if the child does not show sufficient improvement after such an approach is established should medication be used. The most effective way to monitor behavioral changes as a result of these interventions is to use rating scales for specific behaviors rather than general overall teacher ratings. Examples of items from one widely used rating scale are shown in Table 15-2.

Behavioral therapy and psychostimulant medication each have areas of effectiveness and areas of weakness. As a result, for many children stimulant medication should be combined with a psychosocial approach. The medications seem most effective in the areas of academic accuracy and productivity while the behavioral modifications including parental training are most effective in changing social behaviors (Pelham, 1993). Both medication and behavioral modification seem to be essential ongoing aspects of treatment in the long term. In all studies carried out so far, the benefits of the combined treatment did not continue when one part of the treatment package was removed. Instead, the effects were reduced to the benefits of the remaining part of the intervention (Pelham, 1993). This means that the medication does not merely enable the behavioral treatment to become effective and that changing the psychosocial environment does not remove the need for medication.

Counseling the parents of children and involving them in the treatment plan and behavioral aspects of the treatment are extremely important. Parents need to be informed about the disorder—including its natural course, possible causes, and likely prognosis with and without treatment. They also should be given practical suggestions for the daily management of their child. For example, parents must learn the importance of avoiding stressful situations known to cause difficulty, overstimulation, and excessive fatigue. Almost all parents can be taught the general principle of structuring the child's environment to include regular routines and proper limits set on the child's behavior. Parental involvement is

TABLE 15-2
Items from the Iowa Conners Teacher's Rating Scale Used to Assess Effects of A-D/HD Medication

Check the column which best describes this child today.

	Not at All	Just a Little	Pretty Much	Very Much
1. Fidgeting				
2. Hums and makes other odd noises				
3. Excitable, impulsive				
4. Inattentive, easily distracted				
5. Fails to finish things he or she starts (short attention span)				

1. To what extent was this child's behavior toward peers like that of a normal child today?
   Very much like a normal child   0   1   2   3   4   5   6   Not at all like a normal child
2. To what extent was this child's behavior toward adults like that of a normal child today?
   Very much like a normal child   0   1   2   3   4   5   6   Not at all like a normal child
3. To what extent did you find interacting with this child today a pleasant experience?
   Very Pleasant   0   1   2   3   4   5   6   Very Unpleasant
4. How well did this child behave in class today?
   Very well   0   1   2   3   4   5   6   Not well at all
5. How well did this child do on his school work today?
   Very well   0   1   2   3   4   5   6   Not well at all

Source: Pelham, 1993, p. 215.

particularly valuable because complete reliance on drugs may reduce the interest of parents and teachers in finding other ways to help. Although some combined medication and behavioral interventions have produced disappointing results, long-term programs that include medication, intensive therapy, classroom behavior management, and education and therapy for parents appear promising as a way to reduce the rate of arrests for serious offenses and institutionalization when the children become adolescents (Satterfield et al., 1987).

Long-Term Outcomes As children and teenagers with an A-D/HD disorder mature, the number and the intensity of their symptoms usually decrease but their level of functioning may remain impaired (Shaffer, 1994). Such childhood signs of motor activity as excessive aimless running, climbing, and jumping up when others remain seated are replaced by general restlessness or what might be described as jittery behavior. Poor work skills and school difficulties that are a product of earlier inattention also may become prominent as children become older. These problems may have long-term implications for success in adulthood—for example, by limiting job possibilities and opportunities for advanced education.

Several studies suggest that most of those who meet the criteria for A-D/HD in childhood still meet the same criteria in midadolescence. However, when these same individuals reach their midtwenties only a few (about 10 percent) meet the full A-D/HD criteria and could be considered clinically impaired by this disorder (Mannuzza et al., 1993). Other research suggests that

A-D/HD effects may continue into adulthood. In one study, 84 adults who had A-D/HD beginning in childhood continued to show the same pattern of psychopathology and disturbances in cognition and function that had been observed when they were children (Biederman et al., 1993). As a result of such findings that suggest continuation of A-D/HD problems in adulthood, DSM-IV criteria for this disorder were modified so that they were also applicable to adults. For example, wording concerning "play" and "school" was changed to include "work" as well. There is strong evidence that A-D/HD is associated with later behaviors that harm others or create problems with the law (Biederman et al., 1991). Drug use disorders are also frequently noted (Mannuzza et al., 1991). A longitudinal study carried out in Sweden showed that a high level of hyperactive behavior (without a formal diagnosis meeting A-D/HD criteria) of boys at age 13 was linked with 10 times the probability of problems and violent offenses when the boys were from 15 to 25 years of age (Klinterberg et al., 1993). However, if A-D/HD is not accompanied at an early age by conduct problems or aggression, then the likelihood of adult antisocial behavior is relatively low (Lilienfeld & Waldman, 1990). An important question requiring further research concerns the link between A-D/HD, conduct disorders, and antisocial personality disorder.

If A-D/HD was not diagnosed in childhood it may be difficult to verify DSM-IV criteria in adulthood. Because the criteria require certain behaviors to be observed before age 7, it may be difficult for adults retrospectively to recall these behaviors accurately. Some individuals who were previously hyperactive may forget or not accurately identify the behaviors. A study of adults who received a hyperactive diagnosis as children showed that one-fifth of them could not remember being hyperactive as children (Mannuzza et al., 1993). Others may magnify their problems with attention or activity in childhood if it helps them justify obtaining a desired treatment (Shaffer, 1994). Another difficulty in identifying A-D/HD in adults is the high rate of comorbidity (coexistence) of A-D/HD and other disorders, such as conduct disorder or learning difficulties. Comorbidity often makes it difficult to decide which of the occurring conditions is the most important cause of the problem, as well as which is the most important focus for treatment.

Oppositional Defiant Disorder and Conduct Disorder

A substantial number (about 24) percent of children with A-D/HD who are referred for treatment may also fit the diagnosis for either oppositional defiant disorder or conduct disorder (McConaughy & Achenbach, 1994).

Oppositional Defiant Disorder In **oppositional defiant disorder** (ODD) the child or adolescent frequently behaves in a negativistic, defiant, disobedient, and hostile way toward authority figures. More specifically, DSM-IV requires at least four of the following behaviors to occur frequently—arguing with adults, defying rules or refusing to comply with adult requests, deliberately annoying others, blaming others for his or her own behaviors or mistakes, being touchy and easily annoyed, being typically angry and resentful, and being spiteful and vindictive toward others. Of course children and adolescents are likely to behave in each of these ways at some times, but to meet the criteria for ODD diagnosis these behaviors must be more frequent than is typical for the child or adolescent's age and must lead to problems in school, work, or social functioning. Table 15-3 summarizes behaviors characteristic of ODD. ODD behaviors are usually seen first at home and then may generalize to other settings. Figure 15-8 shows that in one large epidemiological study the overall rates for boys and girls were not very different (Cohen et al., 1993).

Jeremy's behavior illustrates ODD. At age 9 his mother brought him to a mental health clinic because of his increasing disobedience and problems at school.

Several events that occurred during the previous month had convinced his mother that she must do something about his behavior. Several weeks ago he had sworn at his teacher and was suspended from school for three days. Last week he was reprimanded by the police for riding his three-wheeler in the

---

TABLE 15-3
Behavioral Features of Oppositional Defiant Disorder (ODD)

A pattern, over at least a six-month period, of negativistic, hostile, and defiant behavior that includes at least four of the following:

1. Having frequent loss of temper
2. Having frequent arguments with adults
3. Deliberately defiant or noncompliant with rules and results
4. Deliberately annoying others
5. Blaming others for own behavior
6. Touchy and easily annoyed
7. Angry and resentful
8. Spiteful or vindictive

These behaviors must be serious enough to interfere with functioning in some area—social, school, or work. If the person meets the criteria for conduct disorder or, if over age 18, the criteria for antisocial personality disorder, the ODD diagnosis is not used. It is also not given if the behaviors occur as part of a mood disorder or psychotic disorder.

---

street, something his mother had repeatedly cautioned him about. The next day he failed to use his pedal brakes and rode his bike into a store window, shattering it. He has not been caught in any more serious offenses, though once before he broke a window when he was riding his bike with a friend. Jeremy had been difficult to manage since nursery school. Since that time the problems slowly escalated. Whenever he is without close supervision, he gets into trouble. He has been reprimanded at school for teasing and kicking other children, tripping them, and calling them names. He is described as bad-tempered and irritable, even though at times he seems to enjoy school. Often he appears to be deliberately trying to annoy other children, though he always claims that others have started the arguments. He does not become involved in serious fights, but does occasionally exchange a few blows with another child.

—Spitzer et al., 1989, pp. 307–308

Family factors may play a role in ODD. It seems to be more common in families in which at least one parent has a history of ODD, conduct disorder, A-D/HD, antisocial personality disorder, substance-related disorder, or mood disorder. Serious marital conflict in a family is also associated with ODD. Parent-child relationship factors that may be related to ODD include harsh parental discipline or inconsistent discipline as well as lack of parent involvement with their children and their education. Other factors that may be important are the way parents help their children to become socialized or to modulate their behavior according to the demands of the situation (Frick, 1993).

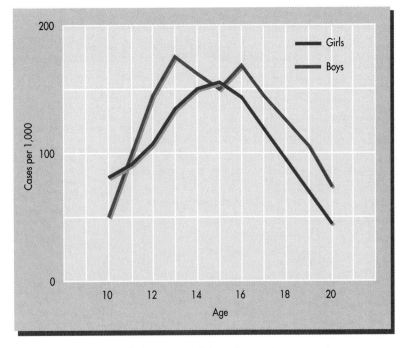

Figure 15-8 Rates of oppositional defiant disorder by age and sex.

SOURCE: Cohen et al. (1993). An epidemiological study of disorders in late childhood and adolescence. *Journal of Child Psychiatry and Psychology, 34,* p. 859.

Conduct Disorder Another category of aggressive behavior that often is more serious in its consequences is conduct disorder. In **conduct disorder** major societal norms are violated and the basic rights of others are often severely violated as well. The case of Robbie at the beginning of this chapter illustrates the serious nature of some behaviors seen in children with conduct disorder. The persistent behaviors typical of conduct disorder include aggressive conduct that causes or threatens harm to people or animals, nonaggressive conduct that causes property damage, theft or major deceitfulness, and serious rule violations. Several of these characteristic behaviors must have occurred in the past year and at least one in the past six months. Table 15-4 lists behavioral characteristics of conduct disorder. Figure 15-9 shows that rates of conduct disorder have a different pattern from rates for ODD as shown in Figure 15-8. For one thing, there are gender differences just as there are in A-D/HD (Figure 15-4). Not only are boys more likely than girls to receive this diagnosis but the age pattern is different. For boys ages 10 to 20 the rating is highest at age 10 and decreases thereafter. For girls, the midteens represent a peak in this behavior although the overall rate is still lower than that for boys (Cohen et al., 1993).

Conduct disorder can begin before age 10 or sometime in adolescence. Those children who develop these behaviors early are predominantly male. They are more likely to go on to develop antisocial personality disorder in adulthood than are the children who develop

conduct disorder in adolescence. Adolescents who develop conduct disorder are likely to have more positive peer relationships than those who develop it in childhood. These adolescents show their conduct-disordered behavior only in the presence of others. Conduct disorder seems to be increasing; current estimates of the prevalence of the disorder range from 6 to 19 percent of the male population under 18 years of age and 2 to 9 percent of the females under that age.

Children who show symptoms of conduct disorder are also likely to have such other problems as learning disorders, mood disorder, and substance abuse disorder. They are also likely to come from families in which harsh discipline, physical or sexual abuse, lack of supervision, and other problems associated with dysfunctional families are common. Some children and adolescents may carry out their aggressive activity on a solitary basis. Others are likely to associate with a delinquent peer group and may be conforming to a group norm. Figure 15-10 shows a humorous view of behavior seen in conduct disorder but does a good job of conveying the seeming enjoyment in harming others. Identifying a conduct disorder can be difficult without knowledge of a variety of aspects of a child's life. In some cases, what appears to be a conduct disorder may

---

TABLE 15-4
Behavioral Features of Conduct Disorder

Three or more of these behavioral criteria must have been present in the last 12 months and at least one in the past 6 months.

1. *Aggression toward people:* including bullying, intimidating, use of weapons, physical cruelty, forced sexual activity, mugging, purse-snatching, and aggression toward animals
2. *Destruction of property:* including fire-setting and other deliberate property destruction
3. *Deceitfulness or theft:* including breaking into a building or car, conning others to obtain goods, stealing items of value
4. *Serious rule violation:* including staying out at night without parents' permission before age 13, running away from home, school truancy before age 13

These behaviors must be severe enough to cause impairment in some area of functioning—social, school, or work. For those over 18 years of age, conduct disorder is diagnosed only if the individual does not meet the criteria for antisocial personality disorder.

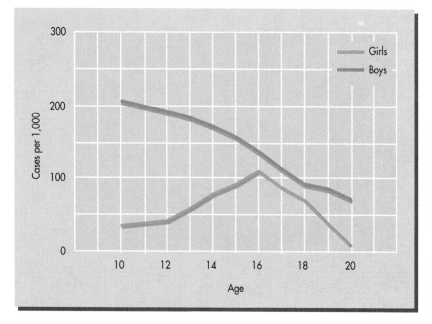

Figure 15-9 Rates of conduct disorder by age and sex.

SOURCE: Cohen et al. (1993). An epidemiological study of disorders in late childhood and adolescence. *Journal of Child Psychiatry and Psychology, 34*, p. 859.

simply be an attempt to adjust to acute or chronic stress. In the situation described below, the boy's misconduct can be interpreted as a jealous battle with his mother and her lover over her affections rather than as a conduct disorder.

Jeffrey, a 14-year-old boy, appeared in family court on a third felony charge. For several months he had stolen and lied, and been physically and verbally abusive and short-tempered. He has also been spending a lot of time lifting weights in an effort to develop strong muscles. Some four months ago his divorced mother began to live with a new man who has been trying to discipline Jeffrey. His mother seems to get some pleasure from his behavior and alternately indulges and punishes him.

Both A-D/HD and ODD are often associated with later development of conduct disorder in adolescence. Conduct disorder, itself, is strongly predictive not only of antisocial personality disorder but also of drug and alcohol abuse disorders in adulthood (Robins & Price, 1991). Figure 15-11 shows that the number of conduct problems in childhood or adolescence is related to the likelihood of developing one of these disorders later.

Treatment Probably the most effective treatment for conduct disorder is prevention. Preventive measures involve helping children to develop skills that will give them successful experiences both as youngsters and as they grow older. A project designed to enhance preschool children's cognitive development provides an example of the importance of learning skills in preventing later delinquent behavior. In a follow-up to this study the children, then adolescents, were compared to a group of similar background who had not attended the special preschool (Schweinhart & Weikart, 1980). Although the intelligence test scores of children who had been in the preschool group did not differ from those of children in the control group, their motivation and achievement in school and their classroom behavior were superior to those of the controls. Even more important in terms of the treatment of conduct disorders, their self-reports of delinquent behavior were much lower than those reported by the controls. These findings suggest that skill building may be an important tool for modifying the aggressive behavior typical of conduct

"The little dears! They still believe in Santa Claus."

Figure 15-10 Charles Addams illustrates the deliberate cruelty to others often practiced by children and adolescents with conduct disorder. Santa's basic rights are about to be violated by his reception into this household.

SOURCE: Drawing by Charles Addams; ©1952, 1980 *The New Yorker Magazine*, Inc.

disorder. If family members are involved in the skill-building program so that they are more likely to reinforce the child's skills at home, school-based programs that teach cognitive or social skills are especially likely to be effective (Miller & Prinz, 1990).

For skill building to be helpful, the way the child customarily evaluates situations must be taken into account. One interesting difference between aggressive and nonaggressive children is that the former show more bias in interpreting the causes of social interactions (Milich & Dodge, 1984). In situations in which the cause was not obvious—for example, being hit on the back with a ball—aggressive children are more likely to interpret the act as hostile. Sometimes this response may be caused by past experiences. For example, a psychologist reported the following incident:

I was treating an aggressive adolescent boy named Rocky twice per week on a long-term basis. We had built a good, warm relationship. One day I saw Rocky in the hallway and approached him from behind as he talked to a peer. I touched him on the shoulder and began to say hello when he turned around and impulsively punched me in the jaw. As soon as he realized whom he had hit, he apologized profusely saying that he thought I must have been another patient on the ward. It was painfully clear to me that Rocky had been perceptually ready to perceive an attack from another.

—Dodge, 1985, p. 93

One way of dealing with these aggressive responses might be to devise interventions that aim at de-biasing perceptions (Kendall et al., 1990). In this type of cognitive-behavioral intervention, children learn to mentally review the answers to a series of questions before acting. These include not only what led up to the situation and what happened, but also the long as well as the short term outcomes of the response that might be made. The children practice the skill of cognitive review by first listening as the instructor reviews appropriate thoughts for a particular situation aloud, then verbally rehearsing appropriate thoughts themselves. As the children learn to apply this technique in other situations they are taught to begin by saying their thoughts aloud. A child might be taught to use the following "think-aloud" procedure when he or she finds a pencil is missing.

Uh oh, my pencil is missing. There, I see that Ronald has it. Now before I go and get it back, let me think about what happened. I'll do it out loud, like my skills leader has told me. Let's see, first I'll say to myself "What happened?"

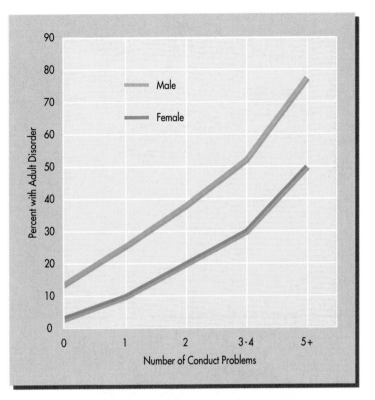

Figure 15-11 The number of conduct problems in childhood is a predictor of the probability of being diagnosed with an externalizing disorder (antisocial personality disorder, drug, or alcohol-use disorder) in adulthood.

SOURCE: Adapted from Robins and Price, 1991, p. 126.

Well, I lost my pencil and Ronald has it. Ronald could have stolen it. Or maybe he just found it and was using it. Or maybe he doesn't know that it is mine. I wonder what Ronald is thinking. I guess I could ask him. I'm not sure which of these is right, but I don't want to get into a fight. I'd rather stay friends with Ronald, because we play basketball together. So I'll give him the benefit of the doubt. Maybe he just found it. I'll go ask him to return it.

—Dodge, 1985, p. 101

For this kind of approach to be effective, the child must have a warm working relationship with a clinician or some other person with whom he or she can have a series of positive social encounters. The positive encounter must happen over and over again to demonstrate to the child that his or her initial negative expectations were not accurate. Even then it may be difficult for the child to generalize the experience to other people, especially peers.

Parents can be effective forces for behavior change but they may need help. Parent training has been effective in preventing progression of the problems of oppositional defiant disorder into the more serious ones of conduct disorder or adult disorders related to aggressive and antisocial behavior. One of the first and best-known parent training programs, developed by Patterson (1975, 1982), uses the social-learning approach. This approach is designed to help prevent coercive interactions between parents and children and works most effectively with preschool and elementary school children. Such family-based interventions do not seem to be as successful with adolescents (McMahon, 1994). One great advantage of parental-training programs is that they enable parents to act as therapists in the child's natural environment. However, a problem with this type of program is that, in many cases, the multiple problems existing in families with a child at risk for conduct disorder make it difficult to secure parent interest and—even if that is present—for parents to carry out the program.

In all the interventions described a common factor seems to be positive, prosocially inclined social support from one or more close relationships. Such social support appears to be one of the principal ways to prevent conduct disorder initially and to keep it from developing into a more serious disorder in adulthood. Although conduct disorder appears to be part of a chain of disorders leading to association with a deviant peer group in the midteens followed by more serious antisocial behavior as an adult, conduct-disordered individuals from harmonious families are less likely to move into deviant peer groups. Choice of a nondeviant romantic partner is also associated with a more supportive relationship and less deviance in adulthood (Quinton et al., 1993). Despite the protection such relationships can afford, those with conduct disorder are less likely to achieve such a supportive relationship because of their negative behaviors toward others, their lack of interpersonal skills, and their frequent association with deviant peers.

Internalizing Disorders

While it is hard not to notice the disruptive behavior of children with hyperactivity and conduct disorder, it may be easy to overlook the problems of children who are quiet and struggle with inner concerns. We might think of hyperactivity and conduct disorders as *externalizing* disorders, and conditions in which anxiety and depression predominate as **internalizing disorders.** While *overt* activity (undesirable behavior) is the outstanding feature of externalizing disorders, *covert* activity (worries, disturbing thoughts) is the clinical problem in internalizing disorders. Internalizing disorders are often difficult to detect and their seriousness may tend to be underestimated by parents and teachers.

The internalizing disorders that are most common in children include several kinds of anxiety disorders—separation anxiety, generalized anxiety, phobias, obsessive-compulsive disorders—and depression. As children grow older, anxiety symptoms may decrease. However, chil-

dren who are very high in anxiety, although they may no longer have an anxiety disorder, seldom move to the low end of the anxiety scale. Depression becomes more frequent in adolescence. Many of these disorders occur in both children and adults, therefore DSM-IV does not generally consider them separately as children's disorders. However, because these disorders may have long-range developmental implications as they occur in childhood it is important that we recognize that they occur in childhood.

Separation Anxiety Disorder

The only anxiety disorder classified by DSM-IV as unique to childhood is **separation anxiety disorder.** Children with this disorder show excessive anxiety or even panic when they are not with major attachment figures, usually parents, or in familiar surroundings. Such children may be unable to stay in rooms by themselves and may refuse to go to school or visit friends' homes. The case of Anna at the beginning of the chapter illustrates some aspects of this disorder. When these children are asked why they are afraid, they may express fear of getting lost and never finding their parents again. Or they may have greatly exaggerated fears of animals, monsters, kidnappers, muggers, and of accidents or illness that may strike them or their parents. Very often such children complain of nausea, headaches, abdominal pains, or rapid heart rate. Sometimes, especially in older children, anxiety or panic is anticipated and seen when the time for the separation approaches.

Children with separation anxiety disorder often have trouble going to sleep and insist that someone stay with them until they do fall asleep. Another way children express this anxiety is by waking during the night and getting into bed with a parent or sibling. Although these children may have no interpersonal difficulties when separation is not an issue, if they are away from home they may be extremely homesick and miserable or even panic. Under such circumstances they withdraw from social activity and are unable to concentrate on work or play.

Possible Causes In early childhood all children experience some separation anxiety (see Figure 15-12). This normal developmental stage is different from the excessive reaction to separation that may occur if older children develop a separation anxiety disorder. Even older children may react strongly at the time of a separation from a parent or other person with whom they have a close relationship without being diagnosed with separation anxiety disorder. This diagnosis is given only if the disturbed behavior lasts an unusually long time—at least four weeks—and results in clinically significant distress or impairment in important aspects of functioning such

Figure 15-12 For the period beginning before an infant's first birthday and extending for about 18 months, most children experience distress when they are about to be separated from a parent. This desire to stay in contact with the attachment figure may have biological roots. Through natural selection, infants of all species who stayed close to their mothers were more likely to survive.

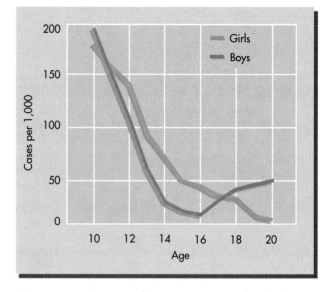

Figure 15-13 Rates of separation anxiety disorder by age and sex.

SOURCE: Cohen et al. (1993). An epidemiological study of disorders in late childhood and adolescence. *Journal of Child Psychiatry and Psychology, 34,* p. 856.

as school or social relationships. It is this lasting quality, rather than the occurrence of distress and concern about separation when it occurs, that distinguishes this disorder. Figure 15-13 shows the steep decline in the rate of separation anxiety after age 10. Although separation anxiety disorder is uncommon in adolescence, if it does begin then it may result in substantial and chronic psychopathology (Clark et al., 1994).

Many times, separation anxiety disorder develops after the child experiences some life stress. This could be a loss through death of a relative or pet or a threatened loss such as a serious illness in the family. Parental separation or divorce or moving to a new neighborhood also may help precipitate this disorder. Why some children have this reaction to stress and others do not is unclear. Neglected children are not likely to develop separation anxiety disorder; instead, children with this disorder are likely to come from families that are caring and close-knit. Some tendency to experience separation

anxiety may run in families: It seems to be more common in close biological relatives of children with the disorder than in the general population.

It may be that children who develop a separation disorder have experienced some difficulties during the attachment process that many theorists believe takes place in the first two years of the child's life. The establishment of a secure attachment is considered important in preventing later psychological disorders, especially depression (Bowlby, 1980). Research on children who were securely attached in infancy shows that as they grow older they become more independent and better able to form good social relationships than children who were anxious or ambivalent in their early attachment.

Treatment The treatment of separation anxiety can be approached in a variety of ways depending on the features of particular cases. Sometimes puppet play and role play with the therapist assuming the role of the child and displaying adaptive reactions to fantasied separations are helpful. The same puppet play technique might be used from a psychodynamic perspective in attempts to deal with the causes of the separation anxiety. In some instances, the key to treatment is a behavioral approach in which an attempt is made to extinguish anxiety by increasing separation time. This approach requires the cooperation of both parents and the child and the help of the therapist in preparing the child for the separation attempts. A common cause of treatment failure with separation anxiety disorder lies in the inability of the parents to cooperate with the therapeutic program by increasing time of separation. This is particularly true when the child lives with a single parent who is socially isolated and highly dependent on the child. It is also a problem if parents have unresolved separation anxiety of their own that makes it difficult for them to stand aside. In such cases, a family therapy approach might be helpful for the child's problem.

Overanxious Disorder of Childhood

Although none of the other anxiety disorders are unique to childhood or adolescence it is important in the understanding of disorders in childhood to know that they may occur during that period. **Overanxious disorder of childhood** is a form of the generalized anxiety disorder found in adults. In this disorder the child or adult experiences excessive apprehension about a number of future events or activities. This worry or anxiety is present most of the time and is accompanied by at least one of the following: restlessness, excessive fatigue, problems in concentration, irritability, muscle tension, and disturbed sleep. Children with this disorder may worry about catastrophic events such as an earthquake or flood. They tend to be perfectionistic, overly compliant, and unsure of themselves. They are often concerned about their competence and how well they are doing even in situations where others are not evaluating them.

Fears and Phobias

Most children's fears disappear as they grow older, even without treatment (see Figure 15-14). On the other hand, some children's fears are intense and disturbing and are appropriate objects of professional concern even if they may disappear spontaneously later. Not only may they cause the child great distress, but they may also interfere with social development. To appreciate the impact of a childhood phobia on the child and her family, imagine Cindy, age 8, who has an unreasonable fear of dogs. She will not go out to play even in her own fenced yard because a dog might come near. She is unable to walk to school or go on errands, so she must be chauffeured everywhere.

Animal phobias, social phobias, and other fears that continue beyond the age at which they normally would disappear can often be treated effectively using a behavioral approach such as systematic desensitization or modeling (see Figure 15-15). At the beginning of therapy the fearful child observes another child or adult interacting in the feared situation. Then, after a number of sessions, the child is encouraged to approach the feared object gradually until finally he or she interacts with it as the model does. This adaptation of social-learning theory, stimulated by the work

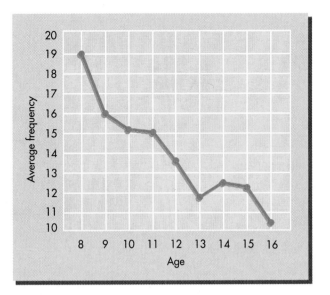

Figure 15-14 Frequency of fears across age.
SOURCE: Based on King et al., 1989.

of Albert Bandura and others (Bandura & Menlove, 1968), is often successful in treating frequently occurring fears.

Modeling of a somewhat different sort, called **symbolic modeling,** can be used to prepare children for frightening and unfamiliar situations such as hospitalization and dental work. This procedure typically uses a realistic film that shows the child what to expect. Studies have shown that symbolic modeling may be an effective aid in reducing anxiety (Melamed & Bush, 1986).

Obsessive-Compulsive Disorder

Obsessions involve the persistent intrusion of intense, unwanted senseless thoughts, while compulsions are marked by repetitive, ritualistic behaviors. Many children engage in mild rituals and obsessions as part of their normal development. Bedtime and dressing rituals are common in toddlers, preschool children, and younger grade school children. Compulsions, such as trivial motor acts, are also common. A young child may stroke a blanket continuously before falling asleep or may suck his or her thumb only at bedtime. Even children's games reflect these rituals. Children often chant rhymes or songs in a repetitive fashion or feel compelled to avoid certain objects, such as sidewalk cracks. Such behaviors rarely are maladaptive in childhood. Sometimes, however, certain acts develop into more disruptive **obsessive-compulsive** and **ritualistic** behaviors that require treatment. Two adolescent patients who were hospitalized because of the severity of their problems are described in the following excerpt.

Figure 15-15 When a child witnesses a trusted person calmly modeling a nonfearful response, he or she may ultimately be able to take the next step and try the behavior, find it does not produce a negative result, and extinguish the former phobic response.

Patient A was a 14-year-old boy who began washing eight to ten times a day after his family moved to a new neighborhood when he was 4. After that, he had only occasional episodes until about two years ago, when he began washing excessively because of fear of sperm on his body.

He also had obsessive thoughts of death and compulsively checked light switches. He had been treated both by psychotherapy and with antipsychotic drugs. At school, he was quiet and unaggressive, participated in many activities, and was a good student. His parents had a mutually supportive relationship and were of middle-class socioeconomic status. All his siblings were well; however, his father was mildly depressed.

Patient B was also 14 years old. For the last two years, she had washed herself excessively, and was preoccupied by number rituals, such as the compulsion to perform all her daily acts in multiples of six. Until her symptoms developed, she had no obsessive traits, was a good student, and had many friends. She had been treated by psychotherapy for one year. Her symptoms began suddenly at a time when her father's business failed. Both parents, of middle-class socioeconomic status, were alcoholic.

—Adapted from Rapoport et al., 1981, p. 1548

These adolescents were part of a long-term National Institute of Mental Health study of children with severe obsessive-compulsive disorder (Flament et al., 1990; Rapaport, 1986). Although when first admitted to the hospital none of the children could function effectively because of the severity of his or her obsessive-compulsive problems, none showed any signs of disordered thinking and all were able to discuss their problems sensibly. Before their symptoms began, their development had not been particularly unusual. In general, they were good, but not outstanding, students and seemed somewhat timid although not excessively withdrawn. In general, the outlook for children who engage in severe obsessive-compulsive behavior is not promising. When followed up several years later, almost 70 percent of those in this long-term study still met the criteria for obsessive-compulsive disorder (Flament et al., 1990). More than half the group were diagnosed at follow-up with a major mood disorder (often with recurrent episodes) and almost half had some form of anxiety disorder. Children affected by obsessive-compulsive disorder are likely to spend much of their day in rituals and obsessive thoughts, which severely restricts their functioning. Although such a severe degree of obsessive-compulsive behavior in childhood is rare, the majority of adults diagnosed with this disorder report retrospectively that their compulsive or obsessive behaviors had begun at least by adolescence and had continued relatively unchanged into adulthood (Zeitlin, 1986).

Treatment For children and adolescents with obsessive-compulsive disorder, treatment may include medication and a variety of behavioral or cognitive therapies. Tricyclic antidepressants and antianxiety medication are frequently used. Recently the antidepressant fluoxetine (Prozac) has been used with some positive results (Tollefson et al., 1994). Behavioral therapy, with or without medication, has also been helpful (March et al., 1994). Some children who were followed up in the NIMH study reported that they had also utilized a "do-it-yourself" behavior therapy in which they exposed themselves to the feared situation while preventing themselves from carrying out their ritualizing behaviors. They believed that this approach was helpful when used over a long period (Flament et al., 1990). They also tried to "keep very busy" with almost any activity and thought that this also helped keep the rituals away. These children believed the psychotherapy they had received was helpful for family problems or personal problems, such as shyness, but was not effective in helping them to decrease their obsessive-compulsive behaviors.

Depression

Helen knew something was wrong with her 12-year-old daughter, but she couldn't quite put her finger on it. Some days Nancy moped in her room, other days she was just quiet. There were times when she had angry outbursts for no reason at all, and she was terribly irritable. In addition, she seemed to have lost interest in eating. At first, Helen wrote it off as typical "preteen stuff." When her husband disagreed, they took Nancy to her pediatrician who referred her to a child psychiatrist. The diagnosis was depression.

Childhood is often pictured as a happy time of little responsibility, endless play, and infinite enjoyment. In fact, though, many children often think such thoughts as: "I'm dumb, ugly, and stupid," "I wish I were dead," and "You don't love me." Studies confirm that many youngsters often feel sad. In one study, about 10 to 12 percent of the 10-year-olds in a school district population were described by parents and teachers as often appearing miserable, unhappy, tearful, or distressed. When the children were interviewed, their responses created the same impression. The prevalence of depressive symptoms identified in such interviews with children has been consistently higher than prevalence estimates obtained by asking parents about their children's symptoms (Barrett et al., 1991). Not only do children report more depression than their parents perceive but generally the children's self-reported symptoms are stable over at least several months (Charmon, 1994). This suggests that children are not reporting temporary moods but rather long-lasting conditions. Table 15-5 lists common signs of depression in children and adolescents.

DSM-IV does not contain a special diagnostic category or description for depression in childhood; instead, it uses the adult criteria with minor modifications. Depressed mood occurs less frequently in young children and becomes more common in adolescence. Prevalence of depression in children of elementary school age is 2 to 5 percent but the pattern varies for boys and girls (Van Hasselt & Hersen, 1994) (see Figure 15-16). Children seen in diagnostic centers for learning problems and children with chronic illnesses also have high rates of depression. Elementary school age children who experience a major depressive episode are likely also to meet the diagnostic criteria for A-D/HD or anxiety disorder, or to show behaviors that meet some but not all the criteria for ODD or conduct disorder. Although depression may occur much earlier, the peak risk period for depression is mid- and late adolescence (Van Hasselt & Hersen, 1994). In adolescence additional types of associated

| TABLE 15-5 |
| Common Signs of Depression in Children and Adolescents |

Although these symptoms may be present in either boys or girls, each symptom tends to be more common in one sex than in the other.

More Common in Girls

1. Body image distortion. Feeling "ugly" or otherwise unattractive
2. Loss of appetite and weight; eating less and eating erratically
3. Lack of satisfaction. Being upset about herself, about life at school and at home, and about social life

More Common in Boys

1. Irritability. Being easily angered and hostile; snapping at family, friends, and teachers
2. Social withdrawal. Ceasing to spend time with friends; spending most of the time alone
3. Drop in school performance. Loss of interest in and enthusiasm about school and other activities

problems include substance-related disorders and eating disorders.

Childhood depression is difficult to define and study because its characteristics are variable depending upon the age of the child and his or her cognitive and social abilities. The specific consequences of childhood-onset

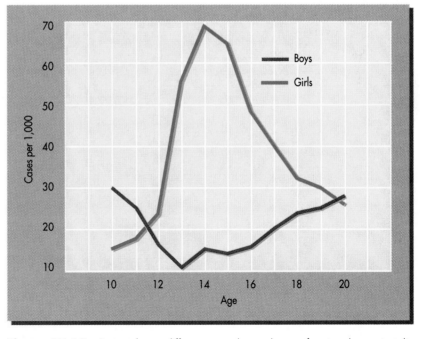

Figure 15-16 Sex and age differences and prevalence of major depressive disorder in childhood and adolescence.

SOURCE: Cohen, et al. (1993). An epidemiological study of disorders in late childhood and adolescence. *Journal of Child Psychiatry and Psychology, 34,* p. 857.

depression on future cognitive and social development are not yet clear, although it is known that depression in children and adolescents may be relatively long-lasting (Kovacs & Goldston, 1991). Figure 15-17 shows that in one study of major depressive disorder in children 9 to 13 years of age, it took one-and-a-half years before 92 percent of children had recovered (Kovacs, 1985). (Major depressive disorder is described in chapter 10.) The chances of another occurrence of depression were also high for this group. Seventy-two percent of these children had a second episode within five years. Some of these children may be expected to continue to experience depression through a large part of their lives. In general, the earlier the onset of the syndrome of depression, the more severe the mood disturbances are likely to be in adulthood (Harrington et al., 1990). In one longitudinal study, several children showed differing but long-continuing patterns of depression (Chess et al., 1983).

At 8 years of age, Harold had been having behavioral problems for a year. He disliked school, was shy, and had few friends. He was moody, quiet, and afraid of new situations. Because there had been several problems in his life—his parents had separated when he was 6 and his mother had been briefly hospitalized for severe depression—it was unclear whether his depression was due to these events or to other causes. Things improved, but at 12 Harold became depressed again and disliked school intensely. At 17 he reported that he could "step into an unhappy mood for no apparent reason" and then would feel tired and irritable and would avoid people. Shortly after this he became severely

depressed for about two weeks and was treated with antidepressant drugs. At 22 he had moved to his own apartment. He made some money mopping floors but was basically supported by his mother. He spent most of his time practicing music—he had taught himself to play the piano, banjo, and guitar. He summarized his existence as going from "slow deadness to acute crisis" and described recurrent depressions at ages 9, 15, 18, and 19, each of which lasted months even when treated with antidepressant drugs.

—Adapted from Chess et al., 1983, pp. 413–414

Sylvia's depression was not noted until she was 21, after months of an intense obsessive preoccupation that her skin and hair were terribly ugly, which was not true. She threatened to drop out of college, and although she had top grades and was attending a top-level school she had changed colleges twice. She was hospitalized briefly and for the next year made many suicidal threats and a few suicidal attempts and then gradually improved.

During her therapy sessions she reported that she had been depressed even as far back as age 8 and had always covered it over with a veneer of cheerfulness and friendliness. This was substantiated by some poems she had written from ages 12 to 15 which were filled with melancholy and hopelessness. She did not report any life events that could explain the cause of her depression, although she did have several family members who had been depressed.

—Adapted from Chess et al., 1983, p. 415

Below, we will look at a few possible causes of long-standing patterns of depression in young people such as Harold and Sylvia.

Possible Causes Depression "runs in families" (Hammen, 1992). This means that many depressed children have depressed parents. Environmental factors are also important; undesirable family environments and poor relationships with parents, siblings, and peers are common in children with mood disorders. Sometimes family tensions and parental divorce bring on symptoms of depression. These symptoms may reflect the child's feelings of hopelessness and helplessness about the situation. Although the conflict of divorcing parents is not a problem a child can solve, the child's attributional style is an important vulnerability factor just as it is in adult depression. That children tend to become depressed when they encounter stressful situations if they use an attributional style in which they blame themselves, or see general or unchanging factors as a cause of their problems, was demonstrated by a study of children in grades three to five whose perceived rejection by peers, actual rejection by peers, and levels of depression were assessed at three time points over the year (Panak & Garber, 1992). Even when the children's initial levels of depression and actual and perceived

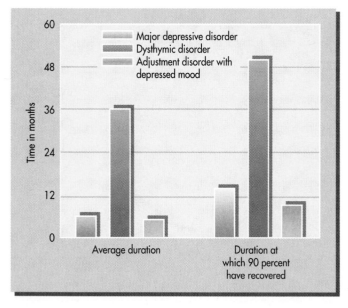

Figure 15-17 Duration of depressive disorders in children.

SOURCE: M. Kovacs (1985). The natural history and course of depressive disorders in childhood. *Psychiatric Annals*, 15, p. 387–389. Reprinted by permission.

peer rejection were taken into account, along with any increase in actual peer rejection over time, the child's tendency to use the attributional style significantly predicted depression a year later. This fact shows the role of attributional style as a vulnerability factor in producing depression.

Treatment Very young children have difficulty describing their emotional states. While fear can be inferred from behavior, facial expressions, and psychological responses, depression is difficult to pinpoint because of the importance of its cognitive components. When interviewing a child about possible depression, it is essential to ask questions in simple, concrete language. For example, few preschoolers spontaneously volunteer they feel sad but will express sad feelings when carefully questioned.

One way to get this information is through use of a structured interview. The "Kiddie SADS," a child's version of an adult interview used in diagnosis of depression, the Schedule for Affective Disorders and Schizophrenia, has been shown to measure depression in children reliably (Chambers et al., 1985). However, because an individual interview with the child by a mental health professional is costly, other less expensive methods of getting information—such as questionnaires—are often used instead. One questionnaire frequently used for screening children is the Children's Depression Inventory (Kovacs & Beck, 1977).

The risk of suicide is a concern in working with depressed children or adolescents. In one study of adult outcome for children and adolescents who had been diagnosed as having a major depressive disorder 10 years earlier, the overall suicide rate for those in the depressed sample was 4.4 percent (Rao et al., 1993). In comparison, no one from either the normal control group or a group diagnosed with some type of anxiety disorder had committed suicide. Of particular significance was the finding that none of the suicides occurred until late adolescence or adulthood, although most of those in the depressed group had first experienced depression about the time of puberty. This suggests that, although suicide may not be an immediate risk for children and early adolescents who are depressed, there is a significant risk as they grow older. Depression in childhood or adolescence also indicates an increased risk for depressive disorder in adulthood, for treatment for that disorder, and for psychiatric hospitalization (Harrington et al., 1990). Despite this heightened risk, adults followed up 18 years after childhood treatment for depression were no more likely than those in a control group to have nondepressive adult psychiatric disorders. This suggests that the causative factors for childhood depression are specific to that disorder rather than indicating a general vulnerability.

Although antidepressant drugs are used to treat depression in children and adolescents as well as in adults, tricyclic antidepressants have not been found to be effective for either children or adolescents in double-blind studies (Ambrosini et al., 1993). It may be that treatment with antidepressants is slower to take effect in adolescents than in adults with the result that treatment periods in these studies were not long enough to show an effect. Another possibility is that depression that begins in childhood or adolescence is a more severe illness and less responsive to treatment than a depressive disorder that begins in adulthood.

Two psychological approaches, interpersonal therapy and cognitive therapy, have produced promising results when used with depressed adolescents (Mufson, 1993; Mufson et al., 1994). Interpersonal therapeutic efforts are focused on problems in the child's or teenager's relationships. In this approach the client is coached on how to express feelings more clearly in troubled relationships, as well as assisted in other interpersonal problem-solving skills. Another promising approach designed to prevent the development of depression in vulnerable children is a cognitive group approach that may be carried out in after-school classes (Clark et al., 1993). In these classes the children learn that they have some control over their moods and that they can change the way they feel by changing the way they think. For example, they might learn to think, "I didn't study hard enough," when receiving a poor test score instead of thinking, "I'm stupid." Other work using social skills training rather than a purely cognitive approach suggests that such training not only provides improvement immediately after treatment but that compared to a group that received supportive therapy the social skills group members continued to progress after the treatment had ended (Fine et al., 1991).

Eating Disorders

Some eating disorders occur in infancy and early childhood. These disorders include **pica,** in which the child persistently eats nonfood substances such as paint, string, leaves, or pebbles, and **rumination disorder of infancy,** in which the infant regurgitates or spits up partially digested food. However, DSM-IV considers these eating disorders of infancy or early childhood to have little in common with the two major eating disorders of most interest to psychologists, anorexia nervosa and bulimia nervosa. Both anorexia and bulimia are especially prevalent throughout adolescence as well as young adulthood, and are more likely to be found in females than in males. Approximately 95 percent of individuals with anorexia and 90 percent of those with bulimia are female (Killian, 1994).

Anorexia Nervosa

Anorexia nervosa's main characteristic is a person's refusal to maintain even a minimally normal body weight. Both the experience and the significance of body weight and body shape are distorted in those with anorexia. Some simply feel grossly overweight even if others view them as thin. Others realize they are thin but still view certain parts of their bodies, often thighs, buttocks, and abdomen, as "too fat." For both groups self-esteem appears to be highly dependent on the appearance of their bodies. They are likely to compulsively weigh themselves, measure their body parts, and persistently use a mirror to check their bodies. They tend to view weight loss as a sign of unusual self-discipline and weight gain as a sign of failure of self-control.

Wendy was 16 years old when her parents insisted that she be seen by the family pediatrician because of severe weight loss. Wendy was 5 feet, 3 inches tall and weighed 78 pounds. She had been dieting for the past 2 years because she had decided, at a weight of 110 pounds, that she was too fat. Wendy had begun menstruating at age 13, but she had not had a menstrual period for the past 1½ years. She indicated that she was not concerned that her periods had stopped, but she was extremely concerned that she was still too fat.

Over the course of her past 2 years' dieting efforts, Wendy had become increasingly strict about how much she would eat, and each mealtime ended in a battle with her parents over her food intake. . . . Typically, her daily food consumption consisted of an egg, a small portion of bread, a carrot stick, and some water or diet soda . . .

As Wendy grew thinner, she became increasingly preoccupied with planning how much she was going to eat each day, and with how to avoid situations in which she would be pressured to eat more than she had planned to. Wendy had begun an exercise program at the time she started dieting, and her daily exercises, carried out in a strictly ordered routine, became lengthier and more strenuous each day. Wendy always swam a given number of laps four times a day. During the summer, she swam these laps outdoors even in lightning or thunder. Over time, even though feeling exhausted, she added an extra swimming session at night without her parents' knowledge, jumping out of her second-story bedroom window to go outside to swim. Wendy felt extremely hungry, tired, and irritable almost all of the time. She was also preoccupied with thoughts of food and how she looked. Her weight continued to drop, and her schoolwork suffered. She stopped interacting with the few girls she had talked to at school and became quite isolated from others.

Despite the efforts of her parents and her pediatrician, Wendy refused to stop dieting. She indicated that she felt extremely good about herself, knowing that she could control her bodily urges to the extent that she would not eat when hungry, and that she could exercise strenuously even though she felt exhausted. Eventually, Wendy was hospitalized for treatment, despite her strong objections that there was nothing wrong with her. Her weight at the time of hospitalization was 68 pounds.

Leon & Dinklage, 1989, p. 206

Although Wendy's behavior of combining low calorie intake and a great deal of exercise is typical for girls and women with anorexia, the relatively small number of men with this diagnosis seem to rely mainly on excessive exercise as a weight-loss or control strategy (Touyz et al., 1993).

The mean age for onset of anorexia nervosa is 17 years of age, but there seem to be two particularly high risk periods, one at age 14 and the other at age 18. Table 15-6 lists the criteria for anorexia used in DSM-IV. In their attempts to understand this disorder, researchers have divided anorexics into subgroups: those who are thin primarily because of restricted food intake (the restricting type) and those who, in addition to restricting food intake, use vomiting and purging with laxatives to maintain low body weight (the binge-eating/purging

---

TABLE 15-6
Anorexia Nervosa

Overall Criteria

1. Refusal to keep body weight at or above 85 percent of the generally recognized normal level for age and height
2. Intense fear of gaining weight or becoming fat even when underweight
3. Disturbance in experience of body weight or shape, undue influence of these factors on self-esteem, or denial of seriousness of health risks of current low body weight
4. If menstruation has begun, the absence of three consecutive menstrual cycles

Associated Behaviors

- Substantial weight loss in a relatively short period
- Continued dieting although individual becomes bone-thin
- Continual setting of new weight goals after one is reached
- Dissatisfaction with appearance, claims of feeling fat, even after weight loss goal is reached
- Isolated dieting rather than participation in a diet group
- Development of unusual interest in food combined with restricted food intake
- Development of strange eating rituals, e.g., cuts food into tiny pieces or measures everything before eating extremely small amounts
- Secret eating
- Obsessiveness about exercising
- Appearance of depression much of the time
- Binging and purging (for one subgroup)

type). Behavior of this binge-eating/purging type is different from behavior of those who have a diagnosis of bulimia (discussed in the next section) because bulimics tend to be of average weight and use purging only to compensate for the extremely high calorie intake during binges.

The primary feature of anorexia nervosa is the obsessive preoccupation with body image and with losing weight. Unlike the true reduction of appetite in depressive disorders, in anorexia there is a conscious and deliberate refusal of food. Those with anorexic disorder are not only preoccupied with weight regulation but also take pride in the ability to control the urge to eat (Mizes, 1990). Individuals with anorexia often either do not see their weight loss, cessation of menstruation, and other symptoms as important or they are defensive about the subject. Despite this apparent lack of concern by those with anorexia about the consequences of their behavior, anorexia disturbs the body's functioning in many ways. It may result in such conditions as retarded bone growth, anemia, dry skin, low body temperature and basal metabolism rate, slow heart rate, and lack of tolerance for cold (Rock & Yager, 1987). If there is vomiting, a number of additional physiological changes are likely to accompany anorexia. One of these, a low level of serum potassium, may cause cardiac arrhythmia, a tendency toward changes in heart rate that can result in death. Vomiting can also damage the esophagus and tooth enamel and increase tooth decay.

Possible Causes While the causes of anorexia are unknown, most clinicians and researchers believe that several risk factors play important roles. Prejudice against being fat is strong and emphasis on thinness is high in many cultural groups. However, since most adolescents are exposed to similar sociocultural pressures, and the prevalence of anorexia is relatively low, other factors may also play a role in the development of the disorder. For instance, some career choices link thinness and achievement. These special populations (notably ballet dancers and fashion models) are especially at risk for the development of anorexia (Goldbloom & Garfinkel, 1990). Another group that seems at risk are elite female athletes, particularly those in sports emphasizing leanness. In a study of more than 600 elite female athletes in Norway, 15 percent met the criteria for an eating disorder (Sundgot, 1994). One group of athletes, women gymnasts, may be particularly at risk (see Figure 15-18). In a study of female collegiate gymnasts only 22 percent of the group reported eating behaviors that could be classified as normal or not disordered. Higher levels of disordered behavior were associated with desire to weigh less, lower self-esteem, and greater endorsement of sociocultural values of thinness (Petrie, 1993).

The binge-eating/purging and restricting subgroups of anorexia may have different causes. Those in the binge-eating/purging group are more likely than those in the restrictor group to abuse alcohol or drugs and to have other problems of impulse control, such as stealing (Leon & Phelan, 1984). Families of those who binge and purge are less stable, have more parental discord and physical health problems, and have experienced more negative events in the recent past. Such families have much higher rates of mood disorders and substance abuse disorders than the families of restrictors (Kog & Vandereycken, 1985, 1989). This relationship suggests that genetic factors may play a role at least in the binge-eating/purging subtype of anorexic disorders. Some researchers have concluded that overall anorexia is intergenerationally transmitted because anorexia nervosa is eight times as common in close relatives of those with this disorder as in relatives of those in a control group of patients with other types of problems (Strober et al., 1990).

Some researchers look to dynamics within the family as a possible cause of anorexia (Minuchin et al., 1978). Minuchin found several common characteristics among families who have a child with anorexic disorder: enmeshment, overprotectiveness, rigidity, and lack of conflict resolution. The enmeshed family is one in which no one can be an individual or have a separate identity and the insistence on togetherness results in the lack of privacy. Tolerance for conflict is also extremely low in these families. Some deny that any differences exist among their members, others deal with differences by shifting conversation to other topics. When such tactics are used, conflicts within the family are not resolved. Instead, natural differences accumulate and stress builds up. Although this characterization of families who have an anorexic child is interesting, some studies have not supported Minuchin's ideas (Palmer et al., 1988).

Other researchers have investigated personality factors that might contribute to anorexia nervosa. Obsessive and inhibited behaviors mixed with impulsivity seem to characterize individuals affected by the disorder (Vitousek & Manke, 1994). One suggestion is that the disorder may appear in biologically vulnerable individuals who have a defensive self-concept and who feel capable of coping with the challenges of adolescence only through repetitive, reward-seeking behaviors that focus on feelings of self-control and emphasize thinness as a criterion for self-worth and success (Sohlberg & Strober, 1994).

Treatment Psychologists have only recently begun to develop treatment plans for anorexia. Treatments range from individual approaches (including psychotherapy and antidepressant medications) to family therapy,

Figure 15-18 Christy Henrich in 1988, five years before her death. By mid-1993 she weighed only 60 pounds. A near-Olympic caliber gymnast, she died at 22 as a result of multiple organ system failure. Her mother commented before her death. "I would say 99 percent of what happened to Christy is because of the sport. All the focus is on the body."

SOURCE: *New York Times*, July 28, 1994, p. C19. Article by Eric Pace.

assertiveness training, and nutritional education. Because most children and adolescents with anorexia and their families do not seek treatment for several years after symptoms have developed, results with children and early adolescents must be inferred from treatment studies dealing with young adults. Overall, antidepressant medication does not seem very helpful in anorexia (Ambrosini et al., 1993). However, preliminary research indicates that fluoxetine (Prozac) may be more successful than either tricyclic or MAO antidepressants in helping to reduce obsessional symptoms and in maintaining weight gain (Kaye et al., 1990).

Two major psychologically based therapeutic approaches used in treating anorexia are behavioral methods and family therapy; these techniques are often used together and combined with nutrition management. In behavioral programs hospital privileges are made dependent on weight gain. While this technique often leads to increases in body weight, it has some negative features. If the weight gain required is too great (some programs have required a half-pound gain per day), patients may develop bulimia and use laxatives and vomiting as a method of weight control (Leon & Phelan, 1984). They are also likely to show poor social adjustment. In addition to such purely behavioral treatments, cognitive-behavioral approaches have also been used. These cognitive methods that focus on the faulty thinking seemingly contributing to the unrealistic body image typical found in those with anorexia are usually combined with other approaches such as nutritional counseling. In such an approach, emphasis is placed on establishing normal eating patterns.

Some researchers have focused on family therapy, especially for younger anorexic individuals. One follow-up reported a recovery rate of 86 percent two-and-a-half years or more after family therapy began (Minuchin et al., 1978). However, this study focused on young girls who had only recently begun to show anorexic symptoms. It is possible that this high recovery rate might not occur among older individuals with anorexia who had developed more established eating (or noneating) habits.

Another study compared the effects of family therapy and ego-oriented individual therapy, each in combination with dietary and medical treatment, in treating female adolescents over a 16-month period (Robin et al., 1994). The family therapy emphasized parental control over eating and weight gain, cognitive restructuring

group therapy, and intensive inpatient or outpatient programs involving all of these approaches. Those with anorexic disorder may also receive coping skills training, and problem solving, and communication training for family members. The individual therapy emphasized building ego strength and autonomy as well as achieving insight into personal emotional blocks related to eating. The individual and family therapy treatments were comparable in reducing body shape dissatisfaction and improved eating attitudes and decreasing eating-related family conflict. However, the family therapy approach produced a greater weight gain.

Longer-term outcome effects achievable through treatment for anorexia were shown by a follow-up study of German adolescents about five years after they had been treated for eating disorders. The study found that 68 percent had recovered, 14 percent still met diagnostic criteria for an eating disorder, and 18 percent had a significant level of symptoms but no longer met all the criteria (Steinhausen & Seidel, 1993). No initial symptom pattern could be found in this study that predicted which individuals would improve.

Bulimia Nervosa

In **bulimia nervosa** binge-eating episodes occur in which large quantities of food are consumed, followed by purging through the use of laxatives, diuretics, medications, fasting, or excessive exercise.

Possible Causes Someone with bulimia nervosa is not extremely thin, instead is usually average or above-average weight. Some anorexic patients may also binge and purge but, in addition, they restrict food intake and are significantly underweight. A person with bulimia is aware of his or her abnormal eating patterns, afraid of being unable to stop eating, and likely to be depressed and self-critical about this behavior. Binge eating must occur at least twice a week for at least three months to meet the diagnostic criteria for this disorder. Some researchers have suggested that bulimia is a type of depression and should be classified as a mood disorder, but as of now there is insufficient evidence to uphold this view (Hinz & Williamson, 1987). We can only say with surety that bulimia, like many other chronic disorders, is often accompanied by depression. The following case gives an example of typical bulimic behavior.

Lisa became bulimic at 18. Her strange eating behavior began when she started to diet. Although she dieted and exercised to lose weight, periodically she ate huge amounts of food and attempted to counter the effects of the extra calories and to maintain her normal weight by forcing herself to vomit.

Lisa often felt like an emotional powder keg, by turns, angry, frightened, and depressed. Sometimes she stole things on impulse; sometimes she drank too much. Sometimes she couldn't stop eating for hours. Unable to understand her own behavior, she thought no one else would either. She felt iso-lated and lonely. Typically, when things were not going well, she would be overcome with an uncontrollable desire for sweets. She literally ate pounds of candy and cake at a time, and often didn't stop until she was exhausted or in severe pain. Then, overwhelmed with guilt and disgust, she would force herself to vomit.

Her eating habits so embarrassed her that she kept them secret until, depressed by her mounting problems, she attempted suicide. Luckily, she didn't succeed. While recuperating in the hospital, she was referred to an eating disorders clinic where she became involved in group therapy. There she received the understanding and help she so desperately needed from others who had bulimia.

The **binge-purge** cycle of overeating and then compensating by use of vomiting or use of laxatives is a central feature of bulimia. Individuals with bulimia may consume prodigious amounts of food during one of these binges. Between 2,000 and 5,000 calories are usually consumed per binge, up to twice as many calories as most people consume in a day. During a binge, easily prepared, high-calorie foods such as potato chips, fast food, bread, and sweets, are the foods of choice, although many binge eaters focus on particular foods. Binges often occur while the person is at home alone watching TV or browsing through a magazine, or in a car or fast-food restaurant. If food runs out during a binge, a person with bulimia may rush out to buy more. Those affected by bulimia tend to eat in an unsystematic manner; they binge, do not eat for a day, and then binge again. Table 15-7 lists some common characteristics of bulimia.

Binge eating is quite common among college women, but clinically significant bulimic behavior is not. And even when the criteria for bulimic behavior are met, the condition may not be long-lasting. Even though bulimia is sometimes described as an epidemic on college campuses, that is not true unless one is referring to self-reported overeating with or without occasional purging. Although two-thirds of college women report eating binges, these are not as severe or frequent as those of bulimics and are not usually accompanied by self-induced vomiting or the use of laxatives. Only 1.3 percent of college women can be classified as bulimic (Schotte & Stunkard, 1987).

Attempts to explain bulimia have focused on the role of negative cognitive-emotional states in bringing on binge episodes. Pressure at work or school and problems with personal relationships often precede binges. Those with bulimia often report their binges to be prompted by stress resulting from contact with certain people, most frequently mothers but sometimes boyfriends, fathers, and sisters (Carrol & Leon, 1981). Two anxiety-related theories of binge eating have been suggested: escape from self-awareness (Heatherton & Baumeister, 1991) and purging theory (Leitenberg et al., 1988). In each

TABLE 15-7
Bulimia Nervosa

Overall Criteria

1. Recurring episodes of binge eating with the following characteristics:
   a. Eating within a discrete period of time a much larger amount of food than most people would eat in similar circumstances and in a similar time period
   b. A sense of lack of control or inability to stop eating during a binge episode
2. Inappropriate compensatory behavior to prevent weight gain including self-induced vomiting, misuse of laxatives, diuretics, enemas or other medications, excessive exercise, fasting periods
3. Binges and compensatory behaviors occurring at least twice a week for at least 3 months
4. Body shape and weight unduly influencing self-view
5. These behaviors occurring not only during episodes of anorexia nervosa

Associated Behaviors

- Consumption of large amounts of food without weight gain
- Drug and alcohol abuse
- Appearance of depression much of the time
- Excessive exercise that interferes with important activities
- Attempts to conceal symptoms

case the behavior is thought to decrease anxiety. Escape theory suggests that binge eaters have such high standards and expectations that, when they fall short of the standards, they become highly self-aware and tend to be preoccupied with unflattering self-views and concern about how others perceive them. Binge eating serves to narrow their attention to the immediate situation and drive out other thoughts. Purging theory suggests that it is the vomiting that reduces the anxiety, not the binges on food. There is some support for each view.

Bulimia may be related to a genetic component of mood disorders, as is suggested by the higher incidence of both mood disorders and alcoholism in relatives of bulimic individuals. It has also been thought to be related to neurotransmitter dysfunction involving the neurotransmitter, serotonin (Wallin & Rissanen, 1994). However, psychological factors may also contribute to bulimic behavior. It seems likely that certain personality factors make some people more vulnerable to family and social experiences that have a negative effect on self-esteem and feelings of self-efficacy. Some theorists have suggested that children who have been seriously abused may be more likely to develop eating disorders (Waller, 1994). Although a number of studies have been carried out to determine if a link between bulimia and abuse

exists, at present the evidence does not suggest such a link (Pope et al., 1994).

Treatment Antidepressant drugs together with a variety of cognitive and behavioral techniques have been used to treat bulimia. The cognitive and behaviorally based treatments focus on breaking the binge-purge cycle either by preventing binges or by preventing purges. The treatments often involve self-monitoring (keeping records of antecedents and consequences related to binge-eating and purging), relaxation training, identifying and modifying cognitive distortions and developing enhanced feelings of self-efficacy, and altering the environment as necessary. One study compared results of three types of therapy (antidepressant medication, cognitive-behavior therapy, and a combination of the two) in a one-year post-treatment follow-up (Agras et al., 1994). In addition, two medication time-periods, a 16-week and a 24-week period, were studied for both the medication and for combination therapies. Seventy-eight percent of those in the combination 24-week treatment group were free of binging and purging behaviors at the one-year follow-up. Only 18 percent of the 16-week antidepressant medication group were free of binging and purging symptoms. (The results for the rest of the groups were intermediate.) Figure 15-19 shows the differences among the groups. The results suggest that—to be effective—antidepressants should be continued for at least 24 weeks. They also showed that the 24-week combination treatment was most effective.

Another behavioral approach that is sometimes advocated is exposure therapy with response prevention of binge behavior (Carter & Bulik, 1994). In this method patients are first instructed to eat a small amount of a food they ordinarily binge on in order to trigger the impulse to binge and then to try to resist that urge (response prevention). The use of exposure techniques have been shown to reduce binging and purging although the treatment remains controversial.

Relapse and the return of symptoms is a serious problem for those who have been successfully treated for bulimia nervosa. In one study, 30 to 40 percent of those who had abstained from binge eating and purging for a minimum of two months were likely to relapse within a period of six to eight months after recovery (Olmsted et al., 1994). Those who had no behaviors associated with bulimia for at least six months after treatment were unlikely to experience another bulimic episode.

How do those who have recovered from bulimia view their recovery? Forty women who had been recovered for a year or more participated in semistructured interviews about factors related to the recovery process (Rorty et al., 1993). Table 15-8 shows the aspects of their eating disorder that the women found most difficult to change and those things they would still like to

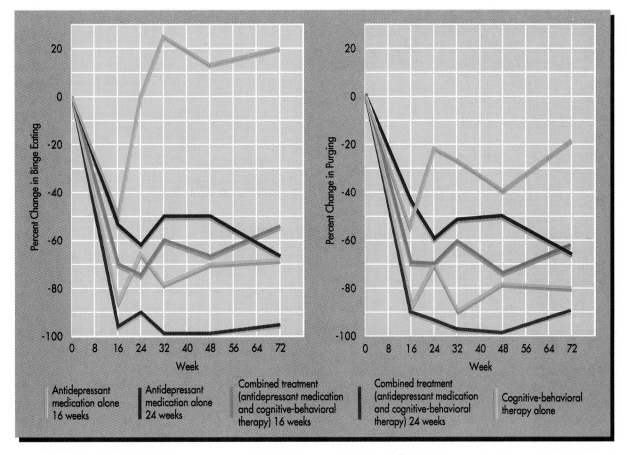

Figure 15-19 Comparative results for antidepressant medication (desipramine), cognitive-behavior therapy, and combined treatment on binging and purging.

SOURCE: Agras, et al. (1994). One year follow-up of psychosocial and pharmacological treatments for bulimia nervosa. *Journal of Clinical Psychiatry, 55,* p. 179–183.

change. In this group, women treated by mental health professionals were more likely to be satisfied with the treatment process than were women treated by general medical practitioners or nutritionists. The former patients were also asked how the important people in their lives had helped or hindered the recovery process. The results are shown in Table 15-9. In general, partners and friends were most likely to be helpful and provided the most emotional support. Mothers were most likely to be viewed as having been actively harmful, and both parents were viewed as providing insufficient emotional support.

Therapy for Children and Adolescents

Although many of the therapeutic approaches developed for adults can be used directly or in slightly modified form with older children and adolescents, frequently the most effective approach to therapy for young children is to work with the parent instead of the child. This type of therapy may have several purposes:

1. To help the parent understand the way children develop and the kinds of behavior typical of different ages.
2. To show the parent adaptive ways to deal with the child—for instance, how to play with a young child or how to use constructive methods of motivation rather than harsh discipline.
3. To suggest ways to improve family interactions that may be causing stress for the parents or the child or both.

When therapy focused on the child seems more appropriate, several differences between therapy for children and for adults must be considered:

1. Children rarely initiate treatment for themselves and typically do not understand the purpose of mental health services. Therefore, some children actively resist being taken for treatment.
2. The child's parents must have ongoing participation

TABLE 15-8
**Behaviors Most Difficult to Change or Behaviors
Still Unchanged at Recovery from Bulimia**

Category	Percent
Most difficult to change:	
Body image problems/desire to be thinner	80
Fear of getting fat	58
Obsessive or negative thoughts in relation to food	55
Urge to binge, purge or diet	48
Lack of awareness of hunger and satiety	23
Nothing is difficult to change	10
Other (e.g., lack of self-acceptance)	15
Still like to change:	
Body image problems/desire to be thinner	68
Fear of getting fat	33
Obsessive or negative thoughts in relation to food	38
Urge to binge, purge, or diet	20
Lack of awareness of hunger and satiety	10
Subject would not like to change anything	13
Other (e.g., self-criticism)	15

Note. Percent of women who spontaneously cited features most difficult/would still like to change.
Source: Adapted from Rorty, Yager, & Rossotto, 1993, p. 257.

in the therapy process. Not only must the parents initiate, continue, and finance treatment, but they usually must modify their own behavior in certain respects.

3. Often children are referred for therapy because they are deviating from the normal pattern of development. This means therapy must be at least partly directed toward helping them to attain those norms

if at all possible.

While many therapeutic approaches for adults have been adapted for use with children, researchers have also developed some methods uniquely suited to young children. Play therapy, storytelling techniques, and parent-administered behavior-modification programs are some therapies specially tailored for children. As in therapeutic interventions with adults, cultural expectations and practices of the family members need to be taken into account. Box 15-2 illustrates the importance of such cultural sensitivity.

Play Therapy

Because young children's limited verbal skills make traditional "talking" therapy inappropriate, many therapists employ **play therapy.** They meet with the child in a playroom and use the child's play activities or play interactions between the child and the therapist as a therapeutic vehicle (see Figure 15-21). Therapists use play to help children act out their feelings, face them, and learn to control them.

Play therapy is especially useful in helping children deal with a recent trauma, for example the experience of sexual abuse, being witness to violence or disaster, parental divorce, or the death of a parent. For example, the father of Cathy, four-and-a-half years old, had recently killed himself. During one session Cathy first played briefly with a doll and then made some "cookie faces" out of modeling clay. One face was misshapen and when the therapist asked her if the faces were like people in her family she put the faces in the bottom of a bowl and later rerolled the clay, destroying them. Then

TABLE 15-9
How Bulimic Patients' Relationships Affected Recovery

Relationship	Percent Agreement in Each Category		
Helped	**Emotional Support**	**Practical Support**	**Not Helpful**
Mother	10	33	90
Father	10	26	90
Sibling(s)	33	3	64
Partner	55	8	39
Friend(s)	45	0	45
Hindered or Harmed	**Insufficient Emotional Support**	**Actively Harmful**	**Not Harmful**
Mother	23	55	20
Father	26	33	44
Sibling(s)	11	37	60
Partner	13	16	68
Friend(s)	0	3	87

Percentages may add up to more than 100 because all categories endorsed by subjects were scored.
Source: Adapted from Rorty, Yager, & Rossotto, 1993, p. 257.

Factors Underlying Successful Assessment, Diagnosis, and Treatment of Children and Adolescents from Diverse Cultural Backgrounds

When children are referred for clinical evaluation or treatment, it is important to understand the cultural beliefs of the family and take these into account. In addition, it is important that the clinician not "jump to conclusions" by assuming a stereotyped view based on limited cultural knowledge rather than by investigating the actual facts concerning the family.

Grace, a withdrawn and overly shy Asian-American 10-year-old, was accompanied to the clinic by her parents for an evaluation session. The clinician, who spoke to the parents to obtain a clinical history, had made the following initial assumptions:

- The family is Chinese because their address is near Chinatown.
- Their dress and demeanor indicate that this is a first-generation, traditional family.
- The family's belief system is based on Confucianism.
- Although the child is withdrawn, she is probably doing well academically.

Canino & Spurlock, 1994, pp 43–44

Acting on these assumptions without further investigation could have denied Grace the help she needed. Fortunately, the clinician did a thorough history taking. This information made it clear that the family were not immigrants but third-generation, nontraditional, Korean-American members of the Roman Catholic religion, who believed that their daughter had a learning disability. Testing did show some

specific learning difficulties and treatment was begun promptly. The experience of this therapist shows that it is important to remember that minority group membership does not automatically imply certain beliefs and attitudes.

Although clinicians should not make unwarranted cultural generalizations, at the same time they need to be aware that cultural beliefs can play an important role in both evaluation of the problem and the acceptability and outcome of treatment. For example, Maria was referred to a clinic because of her disrespectful behavior at home. She was 13 years old and from a Latino family.

[Her parents described her] as confrontational, assertive, and too autonomous. Maria demanded more freedom and openly talked about boys and sex. Her parents' traditional beliefs and childbearing attitudes were in direct opposition to their child's behavior.

(Canino and Spurlock, 1994, p. 46)

Although Maria's parents viewed her behavior as deviant, in contrast

. . . her teachers perceived her as an assertive and independent young woman who felt comfortable exploring difficult issues. They regarded her behavior as an indication of strength. At school Maria had been told to speak up, know her own mind, question what she heard, and be independent.

(Ibid, p. 47)

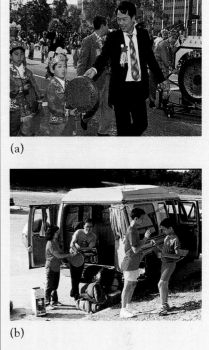

Figure 15-20 Although Asian-American families may participate in activities related to Asian culture (a), they also engage in typically American activities (b). Clinicians need to be aware of both of these dimensions of the lives of Asian-Americans.

After the clinician learned of her parents' and teachers' discrepant views concerning Maria's behavior, a series of meetings for both family and teachers was arranged with a biculturally-sensitive clinician. As a result of the interactions her family was able to understand Maria's behavior in a new way, her teachers became more aware of the family's beliefs and values, and Maria was able to begin to understand the conflicting messages from home and school and develop her own view.

she walked to the sand table. The therapist described what happened next. When Cathy absentmindedly ran her fingers through the sand, she found a figure of a man buried in the sandbox.

C: Look, I found a man in here.

T: You're surprised to find a man buried in the sand.

C: (*Her attention focuses completely on the sand table*

now, her eyes focused, and body turned. She proceeds with intent and with a sense of anxious excitement to check the sand very thoroughly with her fingers for more buried men but does not find another. She leans down and picks up a box of army-type men and tanks and dumps them into the sand. She is silent as she works to clear all the sand aside, and, as she works, it becomes apparent to the therapist she is making room for

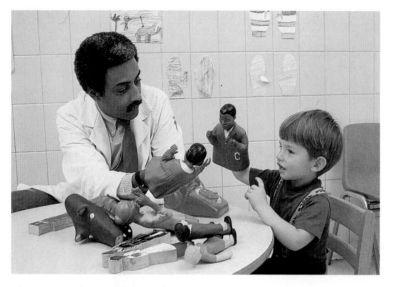

Figure 15-21 Children often communicate better through play than through speech. Play therapy is designed to take advantage of this fact and to give children a symbolic way to express their fears, aggressions, and insecurities.

the box to fit.) I'm making a place for the box to stay.

T: You want it to have a spot there. (*Cathy then takes the tanks out of the sand and places them carefully in the box. With much effort, she piles up the sand and smoothes it up against the box, wedging and blending it into the sandbox.*) It seems you're really working to smooth the sand up to hold the box in place. It's almost like a mountain.

C: (*with pride*) You can see that right! (*She then picks up some of the figures and carefully covers them up with sand with a look of satisfaction.*)

T: Some of the people are buried.

C: Yeah . . . so they can't come out.

T: You want to be sure that they stay buried and no one will dig them up . . . like people in a cemetery are buried and they don't get dug up.

C: Like my dad. He's inside the coffin.

T: In the ground, and no one can dig it up. It stays there in the ground. Is your dad buried in a cemetery too?

C: I think so . . .

T: Where is your dad now?

C: His spirit goes from his body.

T: Where?

C: To heaven.

T: And what about his body?

C: It's in the ground. It's in the ground inside the coffin. The coffin stays in the ground buried. I'd like to see it again.

T: You'd like to see it again, but you can't.

That makes us sad sometimes.

Hurley, 1991, pp. 247–248

Charlie, a 10-year-old boy and his sister were living with their aunt and their mother who had recently been divorced after a marriage characterized by chronic violence. Charlie's mother expressed her anger at the breakup of her marriage by refusing to grant many of Charlie's requests and by threatening not to let him visit his father again. Charlie, on his first visit to the therapist, drew his dysfunctional family as occupants of a spaceship with a crisis in the making and his own foot next to the escape hatch (see Figure 15-22). He described the drawing this way.

It's a spaceship. My sister's at the controls. Mom is up here, reading. Dad is sleeping, and Auntie is below, working . . . she likes to be away from everybody. This is me. The spaceship is going to California [where Charlie's father lived] . . . but we are all going to crash . . . run into a star.

Robinson, 1991, pp. 223–224

Charlie felt helpless and defeated and was frightened by his mother's hostility and anger. He acted out some of these feelings by playing war games with the therapist. He used toy soldiers to fight against the therapist's "troops," built forts from furniture, and made the whole therapy room into a battleground.

Charlie: I've blown away your bunkers. . . . Here come my men to attack.

Therapist: I have nothing to protect me; anything can happen to me now.

C: You take all of these men (*gives me the full complement of soldiers*). Captain [one Rambo-like soldier who grew in power with every battle] will fight them all!

T: The Captain is all by himself; how can he handle all these attackers alone?

Robinson, 1991, pp. 232–233.

The therapist played along by letting Charlie know that he recognized the lopsided odds over which Captain (Charlie) is going to triumph. In these play episodes Charlie always won, but that was not good enough, he had to "wipe out" the therapist in every play encounter. The interactions were used by the therapist to help Charlie express his aggression safely and begin to learn to master it in the presence of a nonreactive and trusted adult.

Figure 15-22 Charlie's family portrait.

SOURCE: Robinson, 1991, p. 224.

Behavioral and Cognitive-Behavioral Therapy

Probably the most often used treatments for children involve behavioral methods of various kinds. Gerald Patterson (1980, 1986) has developed a widely used behavioral therapy for families with a child who behaves overaggressively. The family members are taught the social skills needed to interact in positive reinforcing ways rather than aversively. They are also shown how to teach the child that such overaggressive behaviors will not be tolerated. This no-tolerance policy is demonstrated by their refusal to comply or give in to the coercive demands and by subjecting the child to a time-out procedure in which he or she is removed to another room and required to stay there for a set period of time. This policy, coupled with positive reinforcement for desirable behaviors, has been effective for many families.

Cognitive-behavioral approaches have also been useful, especially in school settings. Children have been taught to identify problems, plan how to deal with them, and then self-monitor their behaviors, sometimes using "think-aloud" techniques in which they self-instruct by giving themselves audible verbal instructions. This training not only improves school performance but also seems to improve behavior at home, according to parent reports (Meyers & Cohen, 1990).

Family Therapy

The family-systems approach to therapy holds that it is the system of family interaction, not one individual, that is disturbed. Even though one person is usually identified as the member with the problem, that person's symptoms are a reflection of a disturbance in a larger family unit. For example, a boy whose behavior was hyperactive was referred for treatment. Although he was labeled as the problem, a look at the family showed a more pervasive difficulty.

In this family the husband and wife did not get along. The husband spent all his time caring for his own dependent parents. He felt burdened by his wife and three children and felt no one looked after his needs. The wife felt neglected and uncared for and got satisfaction from the antics of her youngest child, the boy [referred for treatment]. The other two older children who were well behaved seemed excessively mature in their actions. The problems in this interconnected system could be seen by looking at any of the members, not just at the young boy labeled as hyperactive.

—Andolphi et al., 1983

Family therapy has much in common with the psychodynamic approach because it often focuses on the meanings behind the behavior of each of the family members. The family therapist seeks to get a picture of the actual experience of the problem by the family. What is going on in the family now? What was going on in the family when the problem developed? How have family members responded? The first task of the therapist often is to reframe the child's problem in terms of family dysfunction and help develop alternative, healthier ways of dealing with these issues.

Results of Therapy

Through the use of a technique called **meta-analysis,** a method of quantitatively combining the findings of independent studies, several researchers have summarized research-based therapy studies of children and adolescents in which treatment groups were compared to controls (Weisz et al., 1992). The studies represent a variety of therapeutic approaches including behavior modification, cognitive-behavioral methods, group therapy, client-centered therapy, play therapy, and family therapy. Overall, the results show that therapy in these research studies had consistent beneficial effects for the children involved compared to the outcome for the control groups. In general, the studies were in agreement that the average treated child functioned better than 75 to 80 percent of the control group. In another study of research only with family therapy, the average treated child scored better on behavioral ratings than 69 percent of the control group (Hazelrigg et al., 1987).

Even though therapeutic research projects are difficult, time-consuming, and expensive to carry out, clinic-based studies are even more difficult. One major problem is that random assignment of children to treatment or control groups is usually not possible in clinic-based studies. To compensate for this difficulty, some researchers make comparisons between children treated in clinics and untreated children from the general population who were matched in certain demographic and clinical characteristics. Other comparisons have been made between children who completed therapy and those who dropped out. An analysis of the published results from clinic-based studies did not show statistically significant effects for therapy (Weisz et al., 1992).

Why might this difference between clinic and research study outcomes exist? The difference in methodological control may be one reason. It is also possible that the children in the research treatment studies were less seriously disturbed or that they and their families, because they were voluntary recruits, participated more willingly. Most of the research studies involved children, treatment conditions, and interventions that are not really representative of what is found in conventional clinical practice (Weisz & Weisz, 1989). Most of the children in the studies had not been individually referred for clinical help because of a severe behavioral problem. The therapists who participated in these research studies were specially trained in specific techniques just prior to the study. They also had small client caseloads compared to those found in clinical practice. As a result, the research therapists may have been able to work more effectively. Another, and more encouraging, reason may be that most clinically based studies were carried out some years ago. More recently developed methods—such as those used in the research studies in the meta-analyses—may be more effective. One current task for researchers is to identify the key components of success in child and adolescent therapy studies and test the most effective ways of adopting these components to clinical settings.

CHAPTER SUMMARY

THE SCOPE OF THE PROBLEM

Maladaptive behavior in children is a major problem that society does not adequately address. Risk factors for childhood disorders include parental psychopathology, family discord and divorce, low socioeconomic status, the child's temperament, and stressful experiences. Child abuse is a particularly damaging stressor.

Persistence of Childhood Disorders Many childhood disorders including attention-deficit/hyperactivity disorder, conduct disorder, oppositional defiant disorder, and overanxious disorder tend to persist as the child grows older. Major depression, in children as in adults, tends to recur rather than continuing without a break.

DISRUPTIVE BEHAVIOR

The disruptive behavior category includes children who are exceptionally active and may have problems with attention, as well as children who behave aggressively toward others and cause harm to people and property.

Attention-Deficit/Hyperactivity Disorder Children with attention-deficit/hyperactivity disorder (A-D/HD) display severe or frequent problems in paying attention and impulsive or overactive behaviors that result in impaired performance in at least two environments—for example, school and home. Thirty to forty percent of referrals in child guidance clinics involve A-D/HD. Most of the time the diagnosis occurs during early school years because of the increased demand for attention and sitting quietly that is made in the school setting. Consequences of A-D/HD are deficiencies in both academic and social skills. Behaviors of a child with an A-D/HD disorder seem to produce negative behaviors in others—peers, parents, and teachers—with whom they interact. The course of A-D/HD is unknown at present although genetic inheritance, environmental factors, brain and neurotransmitter functioning all may contribute. By far the most common treatment is the use of stimulant drugs. These seem to have positive, short-term effects on academic productivity but not a long-term outcome. Behavioral therapy including both classroom intervention and parent training is usually recommended as a first step before stimulant drugs are used. Such treatment is especially useful in changing social behaviors. A-D/HD may continue into adulthood, although the behaviors may differ and may no longer meet all the A-D/HD criteria. Adults diagnosed with A-D/HD in childhood or adolescence are more likely to continue to show problems of attention, have limited vocational success, and to be involved in problems with the law to a greater extent than average.

Oppositional Defiant Disorder and Conduct Disorder A child with **oppositional defiant disorder** (ODD) behaves in a negativistic, defiant, disobedient, and hostile way toward authority figures. ODD behaviors usually begin at home and generalize to other situations. The aggressive behavior in **conduct disorder** is more serious than behavior in ODD. In conduct disorder, major societal norms and the basic rights of others are violated. Conduct disorder, especially if developed in childhood, may lead to a diagnosis of antisocial personality disorder in adulthood. Conduct disorder is also associated with other problems—including learning disorders, mood disorder, and substance-abuse disorder—and with growing up in a dysfunctional family where family life may include harsh discipline and physical or sexual abuse. The best way of dealing with oppositional defiant disorder and conduct disorder is prevention. Effective prevention efforts often emphasize skill building as a way of modifying aggressive behavior. An effective cognitive approach focuses on identifying and helping the child modify hostile attributions that may lead to aggressive behavior.

Parent training, especially that based on the social-learning approach, helps to prevent coercive interactions between parents and children. Social support from a nondeviant peer group or romantic partner, if it can be developed, also helps to prevent problems from continuing in adulthood.

INTERNALIZING DISORDERS

In **internalizing disorders** the problems may be covert, that is, related to worries and disturbing thoughts rather than the overt activities of the disruptive behavior disorders. Internalizing disorders include separation anxiety and overanxious disorder of childhood, fears and phobias, obsessive-compulsive disorders, and depression. DSM-IV does not make a distinction between child and adult forms of many of these disorders, but it is important to recognize that they may occur in childhood.

Separation Anxiety Disorder Children who are diagnosed with **separation anxiety disorder** show excessive anxiety or panic when separated from a major attachment figure. This disorder is the only anxiety disorder classified by DSM-IV as unique to childhood.

Overanxious Disorder of Childhood A form of the generalized anxiety disorder found in adults is called **overanxious disorder of childhood.** When this disorder is seen in children the child experiences excessive worry about future events.

Fears and Phobias Many **fears** and **phobias** disappear as children grow older. However, if untreated, they may interfere with social development.

Obsessive-Compulsive Disorders Children often show mild obsessive or compulsive behaviors in the normal course of development. However, **obsessive-compulsive disorder** that involves persistent intrusion of unwanted thoughts and ritualistic behaviors can affect children so severely that they require hospitalization. As these children grow older they often develop symptoms of depression.

Depression Depressive disorder in children tends to be relatively longlasting. Although the symptoms usually improve over time, chances of a recurrence are high. Depression in childhood has been found to increase the likelihood of suicide in late adolescence or early adulthood.

EATING DISORDERS

Anorexia Nervosa Anorexia nervosa is self-induced starvation that occurs even though the person has both physiological and cognitive feelings of hunger. Such people "feel fat" and seem to have distorted body images that lead them to have an obsessive preoccupation with weight loss. Anorexia is most common in middle- and upper-class adolescent females.

Some individuals with an anorexic disorder lose weight by limiting food intake; others (the binge-eating/purging type) use vomiting and laxatives as well as calorie restriction to maintain a significantly lower-than-average body weight. Depression is often a long-term problem for people with anorexia. Treatment approaches most commonly used include behavioral methods and family therapy. Treatment can lead to long-term improvement.

Bulimia Nervosa People who have **bulimia nervosa** practice binge eating although they are likely to be depressed and self-critical about such behavior. The binge eating occurs at least twice a week and is usually accompanied by laxative use or self-induced vomiting for weight control as part of a binge-purge cycle. Binge eaters are also likely to be on weight reducing diets from which their binges represent relapses. Individuals with bulimia may be average, or above average, in weight. Bulimia is thought by some researchers to be a form of depression in which the binges are used to get relief from anxiety and depression. It does not simply represent an eating problem but is associated with poor overall adjustment. Binge behavior often appears to be triggered by stressful interpersonal interactions with close family members. Bulimia is treated with a variety of cognitive and behavioral techniques, group therapy, and antidepressant drugs.

THERAPY FOR CHILDREN AND ADOLESCENTS

With young children the most effective therapeutic approach is often to work with the parents to show them adaptive ways to deal with their child and improve stressful family interactions. Because children often do not initiate therapy themselves, they may be unwilling participants. Parents, who typically initiate and finance the treatment of the child's problems, must usually also be willing to modify their own behavior. In therapy with children and their parents it is important to take the family's cultural beliefs into account.

Play Therapy Interaction with the therapist in a play setting is often the most appropriate direct treatment for young children because of their limited verbal skills.

Cognitive and Behavior Therapies As with adults, cognitive aspects of therapy for children are focused on their distortions of reality, their expectations, and their theories concerning their family and school. Behavioral methods are the most frequently used therapeutic techniques with children. In some cases the parent is trained in behavior modification techniques and becomes a quasi therapist.

Family Therapy The family systems approach focuses on patterns of family interaction rather than the individual as the source of the difficulty. The therapist tries to assess family dynamics and then to develop more adaptive ways for the family to interact.

Results of Therapy Meta-analysis of research-based studies of child therapy shows that such therapy has a beneficial effect for many children.

CHAPTER SIXTEEN

Jaune Quick-to-See Smith, *I See Red: Ten Little Indians II,* 1992
Mixed Media, Collage on paper. 41½" X 29½".
Steinbaum Krauss Gallery.

DEVELOPMENTAL DISORDERS

Peter nursed eagerly, sat and walked at the expected ages. Yet some of his behavior made us vaguely uneasy. He never put anything in his mouth. Not his fingers nor his toys—nothing. More troubling was the fact that Peter didn't look at us, or smile, and wouldn't play the games that seemed as much a part of babyhood as diapers. While he didn't cry, he rarely laughed, and when he did, it was at things that didn't seem funny to us. He didn't cuddle, but sat upright in my lap, even when I rocked him. But children differ and we were content to let Peter be himself. We thought it hilarious when my brother, visiting us when Peter was eight months old, observed that "that kid has no social instincts, whatsoever." Although Peter was a first child, he was not isolated. I frequently put him in his playpen in front of the house, where the school children stopped to play with him as they passed. He ignored them too. . . .

Peter's babbling had not turned into speech by the time he was three. His play was solitary and repetitious. He tore paper into long thin strips, bushel baskets of it every day. He spun the lids from canning jars and became upset if we tried to divert him. Only rarely could I catch his eye, and then saw his focus change from me to the reflection in my glasses. It was like trying to pick up mercury with chopsticks.

—Quoted in Eberhardy, 1967, pp. 257–258

Peter's case is an example of one of the serious developmental disorders known as **autistic disorder.** Autistic disorder (autism) and mental retardation are two developmental disorders that greatly affect children's overall development. Other developmental disorders are more specific: They affect speech (stuttering or difficulties in pronunciation), academic skills (reading disorder, expressive-writing disorder, or arithmetic disorder), or motor skills (coordination disorder). None of these specific disorders has as great an impact on children and their families as do autism and mental retardation.

This chapter is devoted to these two major and pervasive disorders. Both are characterized by significant impairment in several areas of development, including social interaction, communication, the presence of repetitive stereotyped behaviors, interests, and activities. Autistic disorder is diagnosed on DSM-IV's Axis I, whereas mental retardation is diagnosed in Axis II.

Autistic Disorder

Autistic disorder is marked by serious abnormal development in social interaction and communication. Autistic individuals have a very restricted repertory of interests and activities. The case of John in Box 16-1 illustrates several features seen in autistic disorders. These disorders occur at a rate of 2 to 5 cases per 10,000 individuals. Approximately 75 percent of the cases involve some degree of mental retardation and require lifelong care. Rates of autistic disorder are four to five times higher in males than in females, but females are more likely to exhibit more severe mental retardation.

Characteristics of Autistic Behavior

Children with autistic disorder show several kinds of impairment—in social relationships, communication, and activities. Their social interactions are highly unusual. In general, such children have a noticeable lack of awareness of the existence or feelings of others. They may treat people as though they are objects. Autistic children do not seek out an adult for comfort if they are hurt or upset. They don't like to be held and they avoid eye contact. Children with autism prefer solitary play and have a poor understanding of social conventions. Even as young children, autistic children do not enjoy the usual parent-child kiss-and-cuddle routines. For example, they do not wave goodbye or play peek-a-boo, and as toddlers, they do not follow their parents around the house or run to meet them when they come home.

Communication impairment is even more dramatic than impaired social behavior in autism. About half of all autistic children do not develop speech at all. Rather than a response to someone's action or an attempt to get an interaction going, the babble seems to an observer to occur randomly. If they do learn to talk, autistic children's speech is likely to be unusual. For instance, they may simply repeat what is said to them or repeat commercials they have heard on television. They also tend to reverse "you" and "I"; thus, when asking for a drink they might say "You want a drink" instead of "I want a

---

CASE STUDY   **BOX 16-1**

Autistic Disorder

John is five years old. He was referred to a child psychiatrist because of delayed speech development and poor peer relationships. His mother describes him as "living in a shell" and feels he never developed a close, loving relationship with her. He did not begin to speak until the age of three, and even now has a limited vocabulary of only about 200 words. Most of his speech consists of repetitive phrases heard on television, or simple requests or demands. He is unable to initiate or sustain a conversation with peers or adults.

John demonstrates a number of unusual behaviors and interests. For example, he is fascinated with water and often will spend long periods of time intently watching water dripping into a basin. He shows no interest in playing with toys in a usual way but would rather arrange objects in a straight line or else talk jargon to himself while rocking back and forth. He shows little interest in usual children's shows on television; he would rather watch adult game shows. He becomes very upset if furniture is moved around in the house and was inconsolable when his parents bought a new car.

His nursery school teacher says he has an amazing facility for numbers and letters, but she is concerned because he would rather stay by himself than play with other children. John communicates little with his teacher and seems odd and aloof, "in his own world."

When John was three, his mother was told by the family doctor that John probably would grow out of these problems. John's mother senses now that John is suffering from a severe and chronic condition.

Institute of Medicine, 1990, pp. 26–27

---

drink." In addition, their tone of voice may be unusual—singsong or monotonous.

Autistic children have a very narrow range of interests and activities; they may spend a great deal of time spinning objects, flicking their fingers, or twisting or rocking their bodies. Sameness and routine are very important. Moving a piece of furniture or changing the daily routine in any way can be terribly distressing to an autistic child. Table 16-1 lists the major characteristics seen in autistic disorder.

As they grow older, autistic children may spend their time repetitively feeling or smelling objects or lining up items in a row. Bus timetables and the like may be fascinating to them and they sometimes spend hours studying such items. Because autistic children have a tremendous drive to carry out these fixations, the channeling of this behavior into somewhat similar productive activities has been suggested as a therapeutic approach by one woman who has successfully overcome most of her autistic symptoms (Grandin, 1987). Ted Hart illustrates the unusual combination of deficits and abilities frequently observed in cases of autistic disorder. Figure 16-1 contains a photograph of Ted and his father who has devoted his life to helping Ted develop as optimally as possible.

Nineteen-year-old Ted appeared to be developing normally until he was almost three. Then his parents became concerned because he still showed no interest in playing with other children and had begun to use unusual speech patterns and show other unusual behaviors. At nine he could read and remember the spelling of five-syllable Greek names for dinosaurs but he couldn't tie his shoes or differentiate the fantasy on television or in books from reality. He knows the number of toes on exotic animals and names the day of the week a person's birthday will fall on far into the future. Ted has strange and irrational phobias of shower curtains, kites, and chicken soup. Ted's paternal uncle is also autistic.

Ted has been placed in a special center, comes home for holidays, and has made progress. An important goal for the center is to help Ted achieve a measure of independence during his adult life.

Adapted from *Seattle Times*, January 9, 1990, p. H1.

The lives of autistic individuals are limited by their failure to develop peer relationships (they may have little or no interest in establishing friendships), their delay in, or total lack of, the development of spoken language, and an adherence to specific inflexible routines or rituals that serve no discernable function. Their develop-

TABLE 16–1
Clinical Features of Autistic Disorder

Social Interaction

1. Marked lack of awareness of others.
2. Lack of social or emotional reciprocity.
3. Rarely seeks comfort or affection in times of distress.
4. Failure to develop peer relationships.
5. Absent or impaired imitation (lack of responsiveness to modeling).

Communication

1. Delay in or total absence of spoken language with markedly abnormal nonverbal communication (e.g., in eye-to-eye gaze).
2. Failure to use social or emotional cues to regulate communication.
3. Speech abnormalities (pitch, intonation, rate, rhythm, stress).
4. Stereotyped and repetitive use of language or idiosyncratic language (e.g., repeats words or phrases whether or not they have communicative value).

Behavior

1. Insistence on sameness (e.g., distress over small changes).
2. Persistent preoccupation with parts of objects.
3. Stereotyped body movements.
4. Markedly restricted range of interests.
5. Absent or markedly impaired imaginative play.

Figure 16-1 Ted with his father, Charles. Because his older brother was autistic, Charles has been sensitive to the needs of autistic persons for a long time and is a leader in the state of Washington and throughout the country in creating facilities and conditions within communities that will improve the lives of autistic persons. He has written a book that describes his experiences with his brother and son.

SOURCE: Hart, 1989.

mental delays and behavioral abnormalities are usually noticeable prior to age 3.

Autism Versus Childhood Schizophrenia Although autism was originally thought of as a psychosis, it is now considered to be a developmental disorder. However, psychosis can occur in children, and some childhood psychoses may be the same disorder as schizophrenia in adults. Childhood schizophrenia occurs much less frequently than schizophrenia in adulthood and it rarely occurs before age 7 or 8. It is not clear whether schizophrenia that occurs before age 15 has the same consequences and outcome as schizophrenia in adulthood; however, the symptoms are similar and include hallucinations, bizarre fantasies, ideas of being controlled by others, and paranoid ideas. Most researchers and clinicians agree that complete recovery from childhood schizophrenia is unlikely.

Research on Autistic Disorder

Autism was first described by Leo Kanner, a child psychiatrist, in 1943. Kanner presented cases of children who, from the beginning of life, exhibited a unique pattern of behavior in which they were unable to relate in an ordinary way to people and situations. In addition to this "extreme autistic aloneness," he stressed the children's "obsessive desire for the maintenance of sameness." Kanner thought of autism as a child psychosis and believed that most autistic children were basically very intelligent.

We now know that in the majority of cases autism is connected with global mental retardation. Although research on autism usually groups all autistic children together, such children seem to fall into at least two groups: those who are normal or near normal in intelligence and those who function at a retarded level. (Prior, 1992). One important area for future research is the separate study of these two groups who may be very different despite the similarities in their social functioning.

The Psychological Perspective Autistic persons are profoundly impaired in several ways, with cognitive deficits and social and affective deficits being paramount.

Cognitive Deficits While most autistic children can see and hear normally, they respond to sensory input in a distorted way. From a very early age they are either under- or overresponsive to all kinds of stimuli. Often both ways of responding can be seen in the same person. Some of the perceptual disturbances of autistic children seem to decrease with age, especially if the child responds well to treatment for the overall disorder, but there seems to be no doubt that early cognitive development in autistic children is abnormal (Leslie & Frith, 1990).

The most universal symptom of autistic disorder is language disturbance. More than half of all autistic children remain mute, and for those who do speak, specific aspects of language disorder remain. The "I" and "you" reversal is characteristic of autistic speech. Another characteristic is **echolalia** in which the child simply echoes or repeats all or part of what has been said to him or her. Both the language and manner of speaking of autistic children seem mechanical and monotonous.

Autistic children have problems with the social aspects of language, too. Even those who function well have difficulty initiating conversations or maintaining them. The usual kinds of expressions people use for these things, such as, "Speaking of," or "By the way," don't seem to be easy for autistic people to use. They also have trouble in social situations because they seem generally oblivious of their impact on others.

Another indication of the cognitive difficulties of autistic children is their lack of development of symbolic play. Using a stick for a horse or a big box for a playhouse are examples of symbolic play, which usually develops in normal children by about 21 months of age and becomes elaborated as they grow older. At least half of autistic children show a complete absence of symbolic play.

The cognitive problems of autistic children don't seem to be a function of poor memory. Autistic children's short-term recall is not deficient. For instance, when asked to repeat strings of words, verbal autistic children can repeat random meaningless strings as well as they can meaningful sentences (Dawson, 1989). In general, research on cognition suggests that, while their basic input and simple memory may not be impaired, autistic individuals have a problem with higher-level cognitive processing in which stimuli are organized by meaning. Autistic children have more problems with symbolic thought than with real-life examples. For example, one group did better at puzzles that required thinking about alternatives if the material they used was three-dimensional (colored wooden shapes) instead of two-dimensional (line drawings) (Prior & McGillivray, 1980). These cognitive deficiencies are probably related to the absence of symbolic or representational play in autistic children (Wulff, 1985).

Social and Affective Deficits Autistic individuals have abnormal interpersonal relationships that seem to be related to their affective and emotional abnormalities (see Box 16-2). Research studies have shown that the emotional facial expressions, gestures, and vocalizations of autistic children are often idiosyncratic. (Dawson, 1989). Autistic children seem to lack the normal child's ability to coordinate affective expression and behavior. They seem neither to recognize the sig-

Videos of Child's First Birthday Are Tools to Diagnose Autism

Researchers have found home videos shot at children's first birthday parties to be useful in diagnosing autistic disorder (Figure 16-2). They have found that the absence of four behaviors—eye contact, showing an object to another person, pointing to objects, and responding to their own name—identify autistic children with 91 percent accuracy (Osterling & Dawson, 1994). The most predictive behavior of autism is how little the children look at other people. Autistic children just don't make eye contact with the same frequency as do normally developing children.

The research compared the first birthday party videotapes for 11 infants who were later diagnosed as having autistic disorder and 11 normally developing infants. Video footage of first birthdays was chosen for the study over tapes of other activities because parents often can't recall when they shot film or how old their child was at the time. The party setting also reduced, somewhat, the variability in the environment where the children were observed.

The researchers developed a coding system to note the presence or absence of a number of developmentally appropriate behaviors and autisticlike behaviors. Raters, who were unaware of a child's diagnosis, viewed the party videos and coded the number of times a child exhibited each behavior. Using these data, the researchers correctly identified 10 of the 11 autistic children and the same number of the normally developing children. Using just one behavior, looking at another person's face, the researchers were able to correctly classify 77 percent of the children.

Earlier research has shown that about half the parents of autistic children suspected a problem before their infant was a year old and that most parents began expressing concern to their pediatrician by the time their child was 18 months old. Even so, a diagnosis usually isn't made until a child is between 3 and 4.

Diagnosis has been difficult because autistic children, even though many of them have some form of mental retardation, can look very normal physically. Their motor development also occurs at the proper time. At a very young age, a child with autistic disorder may seem like a normal child with a few abnormal behaviors. Staring off into space and rocking back and forth are stereotypical autistic behaviors, but normal kids also do them. Normal children even do head banging. It's common at an early age. But normal kids also make eye contact and point at things, behaviors that are rare in autistic children.

Early identification of autism might provide clues to intervention and relief for worried parents because many of them go from doctor to doctor and clinic to clinic trying to find answers. Most parents feel better when they know what is wrong with their child and how they might do something that is helpful.

(a)

(b)

Figure 16-2 Videotapes made of the first birthday party of an autistic child (a) and a normal (b) child. The child with autism maintains a focus on objects rather than people and is not enjoying the experience with the people around him. In contrast, the normally developing child is looking at the people gathered for the party and sharing affect with them.

nals sent out by other people nor to display normally coherent patterns of feelings. Researchers suggest that they thus fail to participate in the coordinated patterns of feelings and action that usually occur between people. Related to this may be the fact that autistic children have difficulty in imitating a diversity of actions (Hobson, 1989). The abnormal interpersonal relationships that stem from autistic children's social comprehension deficit may lead to impaired verbal ability (Koegel et al., 1994).

The Biological Perspective Many research efforts have focused on identifying a biological cause for autism. Researchers have made significant discoveries, but to date, no biological factor can be said with absolute certainty to be the determining factor. Because of autism's pattern of cognitive disabilities, researchers have focused on the left hemisphere of the brain, where language and symbolic material are assumed to be processed (Dawson, 1989). They have found that the cognitive problems of autistic children, especially those of language, seem different from those that occur from either left-hemisphere or bilateral damage to the brain. These difficulties might be caused by early damage to the limbic system, which then affects other parts of the nervous system. Another possibility is that autism's symptoms can be explained in terms of a dysfunction of behavioral systems in the brain stem that is further distorted by dysfunctioning of the midbrain and the cortex.

Some kind of brain pathology seems likely in autistic individuals, since at least one-fifth of autistic children develop epileptic seizures in adolescence (Deykin & MacMahon, 1979). The risk of seizures is much greater for those autistic children who are severely retarded than for those who are not. Researchers have also noted a correlation between autism and brain injury at or after birth. In a study of 17 sets of identical twins in which only one of each set was autistic, 12 of the affected twins probably had experienced brain damage (for example, from convulsions shortly after birth) (Folstein & Rutter, 1977).

Through modern scanning technology, researchers are seeking to identify specific features of brain anatomy or brain biochemistry that differentiate autistic individuals from other groups. In one study, 18 autistic children and adults underwent nuclear magnetic resonance imaging (MRI), a procedure in which a magnetic field is used to create three-dimensional images of the brain (see chapter 10). When they were compared with people who had either no neurological problems or neurological damage unrelated to autism, 14 of the 18 showed stunted development in a part of the cerebellum known as the superior posterior cerebellar vermis (Piven et al., 1990). The main function of the cerebellum is to coordinate complex movements. It is essential for balance, fine motor control, and muscle coordination. The cerebellar vermis is connected to brain regions that govern attention, arousal level, and the assimilation of sensory information (Courchesne et al., 1988).

Researchers speculate that the stunted development may occur in the first few months after conception or during the first or second years of life. Its causes are also unclear. Possibly the same process that damages the cerebellar vermis also harms other regions of the brain associated with symptoms of autism. Another possibility is that damage to the cerebellum alters the development of related brain regions. The unusual behavior of autistic children might be either a cause or an effect of underdevelopment in the cerebellum and other regions of the brain. According to one theory, autistic behavior is an attempt to relieve persistent overstimulation by uncontrolled brain activity (Dawson, 1989). There is some evidence that autistic persons have a shortage of a type of nerve cell that transmits inhibiting messages from the cerebellum to the cerebral cortex, the seat of thinking and judgment.

Research suggests there may also be a hereditary factor in autism. A survey conducted in Utah found that, while the rate of the disorder is low in the general population, there is a high prevalence among members of an autistic child's family (Ritvo et al., 1989). Among children born after the first autistic child, the rate is close to 9 percent, or 215 times higher than that of the general population. In the rare case of two autistic children born in the same family, the chance of a third child with autism is 35 percent.

There is also evidence that a family history of delayed speech is much more common in families of a child who is autistic (25 percent of all of the families) than in the average family (Bartak et al., 1975). Another clue comes from a study of twins in which one member was autistic. The probability that the other twin would also be autistic or would have other cognitive abnormalities was greatly increased when the twins were monozygotic rather than dizygotic (see Figure 16-3). Knowledge about the genetics of autism suggests that what is inherited is probably not autism but some general tendency to have language or cognitive abnormalities (Rutter & Garmezy, 1983).

It has also been suggested that the parents of autistic children share human leukocyte antigens (HLA). Antigens are substances that stimulate the production of antibodies in the blood. The antibodies are blood proteins generated by the immune system that protect a person against specific microorganisms or toxins in the blood. When antigens of the parents are the same, this may increase the likelihood that the unborn child will be attacked by its mother's immune system (Stubbs et al., 1985). A finding supporting this idea is that mothers of autistic children report a greater frequency of both spontaneous abortions and bleeding during pregnancy;

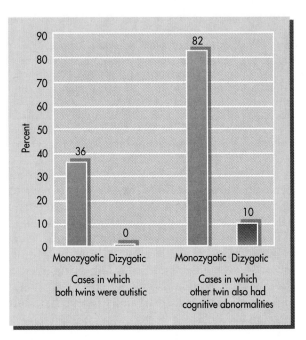

Figure 16-3 Differences between monozygotic and dizygotic twin pairs in which at least one twin is autistic.

SOURCE: Adapted from Folstein & Rutter (1978), p. 226.

these may be due in part to immune system attacks. Although this theory is still somewhat speculative, comparison of HLA antigen samples from parents of autistic children with samples from parents who did not have an autistic child showed the predicted differences. Seventy-five percent of the parents of autistic children shared antigens, but only 25 percent of the control parents did so.

Another area of research focuses on whether prenatal illness of the mother or other prenatal, birth-injury, or postnatal factors are related to autism. So far a variety of findings have been made about these relationships, but no single variable accounts for a large proportion of cases of autism or distinguishes between autistic children and controls (Tsai, 1987).

Therapy

Behavior modification programs have often been used with children who are severely autistic. These programs have shown promise in improving such children's language and self-help skills, which, in turn, improve their chances for social adjustment.

At the beginning of a behavior modification program, it may take 15 to 30 minutes to get a correct response from the child, even for simple tasks such as looking at the instructor on command. Once the child can consistently follow simple commands, he or she may be asked to perform imitative behavior, first by following visual instructions (such as raising an arm when the instructor does) and then by following verbal instructions (such as raising an arm when the instructor asks for that movement). An entire program such as this one takes several hours a day for months at a time. For this reason, at least one parent is trained to work with the child between visits to a professional. As the child progresses, the parent takes over a great deal of the training. Although behavioral approaches help autistic children develop special skills, the children are often unable to generalize the learned responses to other situations.

One follow-up study of children who had participated in intensive behavioral training suggests that this type of treatment may be effective for some autistic children (Lovaas, 1987). As preschoolers, the children were treated by trained therapists for 40 hours a week for at least two years. Their parents were also trained in the treatment procedures so that they could continue the treatment during all the child's waking hours. During the treatment each child's behavioral deficiencies were specifically targeted and special programs to encourage desired behaviors were developed. Some of these are shown in Figure 16-4.

The treatment procedure dealt with high rates of aggressive and self-stimulation behaviors in a graded

series of methods. First these behaviors were ignored. If that did not reduce them, a "time-out" procedure was used in which the activity was interrupted until the child's objectionable behaviors ceased. More acceptable forms of behavior were shaped as replacements. Finally, if these methods were ineffective, the therapist said "no" very loudly or gave the child a slap on the thigh while the undesirable behavior was going on. Despite the therapists' general reluctance to use physically aversive behavior, work on the project showed that this was an essential element in producing behavior change. Children who improved in the program were placed in regular pre-school and primary school programs. The rate of improvement in the intensive therapy group was compared to that for a similar group of children who were given the same type of therapy only 10 hours a week and to that of a group treated in other programs. A comparison of the groups is shown in Figure 16-5.

Children who received the intensive training were more likely to be placed in regular classrooms than children in either of the other two groups. Results for those other two groups—the group that received a limited 10 hour per week intervention and the group that received other types of treatment—were quite similar to each other. Neither of these treatment approaches was found to be nearly as effective as the intensive training in helping autistic children to develop needed skills. The three programs did not differ in improving language skills. Nearly half of the children in each group were placed in classes for those with delayed language. The results of this project suggest that intensive behavioral training may allow some autistic children to reach an average level of functioning, and that this approach is superior to less intensive training and to the usual therapies that autistic children may receive.

Intensive training programs provide opportunities, not only for the recipients to learn new skills, but also for the trainers to acquire insights concerning how the training might be improved. O. Ivar Lovaas, who developed and carried out the project just described, has given a personal example of the accidents and incidental observations from which researchers and clinicians find clues to the improvement of treatment programs. Lovaas describes his work with Beth, who was autistic and possessed only the most minimal language skills.

When one sees a client (or "subject") once or twice a week, one develops a relationship with that person that is very different from seeing a person 6 hours a day, 5 days a week over most of a year. Also, by the time I saw Beth, I had helped raise four children and learned a great deal about how to raise them. By now I was spending much more time with Beth than I had with

(a)

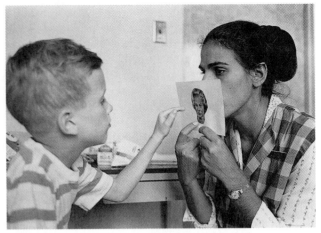

(c)

(b)

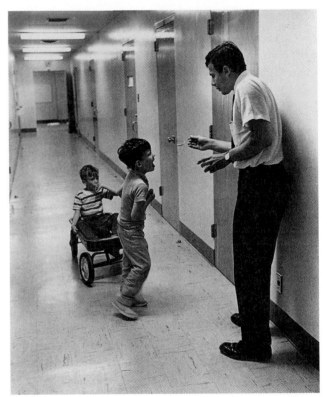

(d)

Figure 16-4 Autistic children receive special learning programs. (*a*) The therapist is hand-prompting a mute child to make the "wh" sound. (*b*) The therapist is using food as a reinforcer for the child to attend to him and make eye contact. (*c*) The therapist is teaching a child to identify parts of the face from a picture after he has learned to name the parts from his face and hers. She uses verbal reinforcement. (*d*) Autistic children have difficulty playing with other children. The therapist is using food to reinforce joint play activity.

my own children, and I had come to consider her as one of my own. One day, while I briefly interrupted Beth and her teacher's play to make a short comment, Beth walked away from us to a steel cabinet, bent over, and violently banged her head against the sharp corner. I would not let any of my own children act like that. Quite impulsively and without any contemplation, I reached over and gave her a whack on her behind with my hand. She stopped suddenly and looked at me, as if to ask, "Is this a psychiatric clinic or isn't it?" I experienced intense fear and guilt as to what I had done. However, Beth paused for about 1 minute, then as if to test me, hit her head once more. I mustered up enough courage to give her one more slap on the behind. At that point, Beth came back over to the teacher and me, and acted very affectionate and sociable. There were no other acts of self-injury that day, or in my presence thereafter. This incident was never planned, and in fact, I would not have planned to do what I did.

Lovaas, 1993, p. 621

Efforts are being made at treating autistic disorder with medications. One study showed that clomipramine, a medication effective in treating obsessive-compulsive disorder, reduced or stopped some

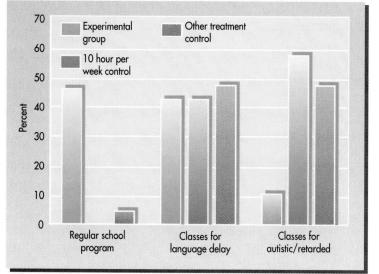

Figure 16-5 School placement at second grade for autistic children who were treated with an intensive behavioral therapy intervention during their preschool years compared to school placement of control groups. Note that none of the children in the 10-hour-per-week control group was able to be placed in a regular classroom.

SOURCE: Data from Lovaas (1987). Copyright © 1987 by the American Psychological Association. Reprinted by permission of the author.

symptoms in autistic children (Gordon et al., 1992). The improvements were seen most strongly in symptoms that resemble compulsions, but in some children the medication also improved their ability to make eye contact and reduced hyperactivity and temper tantrums.

Prospects for Change

As with other children, the intelligence test scores of autistic children predict their school achievement, later occupations, and social status. One key indicator of later outcome is whether the child has developed fairly good language skills by the age of 5.

A follow-up study at a Canadian regional research center of children who had earlier been diagnosed as autistic showed that more than half the children were being cared for in institutions, that most had experienced a persistence of symptoms, and that few were living independently or were capable of holding a job (Wolf & Goldberg, 1986). About 90 percent of the group was mentally retarded.

A few autistic children who have made a good adjustment later in life have written about their experiences and provided some insight into what it must feel like to be autistic. Box 16-3 contains two accounts written by individuals who showed considerable resilience in meeting the challenge of autism. Unfortunately, successful adjustment is achieved by only a small proportion of autistic children. More typical is the case of Bruce:

During his preschool years he was involved in extensive therapy but he remained mute, bizarre, and socially isolated. During Bruce's school years no special program was available, so his mother took special courses to prepare herself to teach him. Through her efforts he learned about 100 words. He never used them voluntarily and relied on simple signs for communication.

At 20 Bruce is physically healthy. He remains mute, but does use signs to express his wishes. As a child, he had unusual skill at assembling puzzle pieces. He still has this ability which helps him in his prevocational training. If left alone he still rocks his body for hours and twirls objects in front of his face, much as he did when he was a preschooler.

—Adapted from Cohen et al., 1978, pp. 68–69

Mental Retardation

Mental retardation, which receives an Axis II diagnosis in DSM-IV, is defined as a significantly below-average level of intelligence measured by an individually administered intelligence test. In mental retardation, a person's social as well as intellectual functioning must be impaired (see Figure 16-6). A DSM-IV diagnosis of mental retardation is indicated when there are deficits in at least two of the following skill areas: communication, self-care, home living, social and interpersonal skills, use of community resources, self-direction, functional academic skills, work, leisure, health, and safety.

Mental retardation is regarded as a chronic, irreversible condition that begins before the age of 18. If intellectual functioning drops to retarded levels after age 18, the problem is classified as a dementia rather than mental retardation.

Although many children with autistic disorder are also retarded, there are several differences between autism and retardation.

1. Retarded children may have a cognitive development that is equal to their social development. In autism the child's social development is always lower than the cognitive development.
2. Retarded children show delays in language but autistic children show severe language deficits and more language deviance.
3. Self-stimulation, preoccupation with visual and auditory stimuli, and bizarre behaviors such as spinning objects and flapping and twirling the body are common in autism but not in retardation.
4. Retarded children are motivated to please adults, but autistic children are not concerned about their impact on others.

BOX 16-3

Coping with Autism

Tony

Tony was referred to a children's clinic when he was 26 months old. He did not speak at all and he did not seem to respond to his parents or the clinic staff in the way a young child might be expected to do; instead he ignored their approaches. His parents said he had always seemed stiff and hard to hold, he never smiled back at them, and he spent most of his time spinning objects or watching his hands as he moved his fingers.

Tony spent several years in a therapeutic nursery school and by age three had learned to communicate although he was severely echolalic. By the time he was six his intelligence test score was just slightly below average. During high school he was very aware of his feelings of being different. He quit high school in tenth grade and joined the army but was quickly discharged for fighting. Then he worked as an assembler in a manufacturing plant. He tried to get a girlfriend, but had been unsuccessful. He said he has difficulties with anxiety, periodic overuse of alcohol, and unusual sensory experiences. This is a portion of what Tony wrote about himself [Tony's original spellings are retained here]: "In school I learned some things very quickly but others were beyond learning comprehension. I used to disrupt the whole class and love to drive the teachers nuts. When I first started talking—five years old—I started talking about an incident that happened a year before. I was obsessed with certain things and played in my own way. I make things with Garbage or Junk and Play with them. I like mechanical Battery Power toys or electronic toys. . . . IN tenth grade I quit school and worked washing cars and work(ed) many other Jobs too. I was verry derpressed and Hyper at wok. I got along with my boss at all my Jobs. I tend to get lazy and had trouble getting along with other people. So in effort to keep my Jobs I avoided many people. I found It a lot easeyer to get along with older people and FEARED People my age because of school. I went into the army and got in lots of Fights with peo-

ple. So I got dicarged. I allso have great Trouble getting thing organized and missunderstand allmost everything. "And had and still have some mental blocks and great difficulty paying attention and listining to people and was verry easly distracted. I damanded to be amused by people and got board verry eas(i)ly and cant deal with stress. And had great difficulty fullfilling oblagations. I woudl hear electronic Noises and have quick siezious in bed and many other physical problems. Often I have to be Force to get things done and verry uncoordinated. And was verry Nervous about everything. And Feared People and Social Activity Greatly . . . I never got Fired from a job. My problems havn't changed at ALL from early childhood. I was Just able to Function. And it still the same today."

—Volkmar and Cohen, 1985, pp. 49, 51

Temple Grandin

Temple Grandin was autistic in childhood but was above average in intelligence, had fewer difficulties than Tony, but still has some characteristics of autism.

I am now 36 years old and work as a consultant, designing livestock facilities for feedlots, ranches, and meat plants throughout the U.S. and abroad. I have also authored articles in both national and international livestock publications. At the present time I am doing research on animal behavior and neurophysiology and working on my doctorate in animal science at the University of Illinois. . . .

At the age of 1½ to 3 I had many of the standard autistic behaviors such as fixation on spinning objects, refusing to be touched or held, preferring to be alone, destructive behavior, temper tantrums, inability to speak, sensitivity to sudden noises, appearance of deafness, and an intense interest in odors. . . .

At the age of 3 to 3½ my behavior greatly improved, but I did not learn to speak until 3½. At the age of 3 to 4 my

behavior was more normal until I became tired. When I became tired, bouts of impulsive behavior would return. . . .

In college I was on the Dean's honor list, but getting through the foreign language requirement was difficult. I scraped by with Ds and Cs. Learning sequential things such as math was also very hard. My mind is completely visual and spatial work such as drawing is easy. I taught myself drafting in six months. I have designed big steel and concrete cattle facilities, but remembering a phone number or adding up numbers in my head is still difficult. I have to write them down. Every piece of information I have memorized is visual. If I have to remember an abstract concept I "see" the page of the book or my notes in my mind and "read" information from it. Melodies are the only things I can memorize without a visual image. I remember very little that I hear unless it is emotionally arousing or I can form a visual image. In class I take careful notes, because I would forget the auditory material. When I think about abstract concepts such as human relationships I use visual similes. For example, relationships between people are like a glass sliding door. The door must be opened gently, if it is kicked it may shatter. If I had to learn a foreign language, I would have to do it by reading, and make it visual.

—Grandin, 1984, pp. 144–145

In 1991, Temple Grandin, who now teaches animal science at Colorado State University and works as an agricultural consultant designing livestock equipment, observed that:

. . . For me and for other autistic people, a challenging career or hobby makes life satisfying. Almost all my friends are people interested in either autism or livestock management. I cannot emphasize enough the importance to a high-functioning autistic person of developing an area of interest and building social contacts through it.

—Grandin, 1991, p. 6

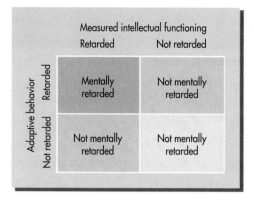

Figure 16-6 Only people who are significantly below average in both intellectual functioning and adaptive behavior are classified as mentally retarded.

Mental retardation can arise as a result of several factors. Genetic and prenatal factors may affect fetal development and result in retardation. Factors related to birth and early postnatal development (for example, traumatic deliveries that cause brain injury and head injuries occurring during infancy or early childhood) may also play roles. Psychosocial factors may be involved either by themselves or in addition to biological factors. Poverty, teenage parenthood, and substance abuse often produce a self-perpetuating familial pattern of retardation. In this chapter, we will review a number of the factors involved in mental retardation. Regardless of the cause or causes, mental retardation usually has a profound effect on the family of the affected child.

Degrees of Mental Retardation

Clinicians use four categories of mental retardation, which are based on intelligence-test scores: *mild, moderate, severe,* and *profound* (see Table 16-2). The following cases illustrate these categories and Table 16-3 presents highest levels of adaptive behavior for each group.

TABLE 16–2 Levels of Mental Retardation		
	IQ	**Percent of All Retardation**
Mild mental retardation	50–70	85
Moderate mental retardation	35–49	10
Severe mental retardation	20–34	4
Profound mental retardation	Below 20	Less than 1

Mild Retardation: Alice is 16 and has been in special classes since preschool. She can feed and dress herself well, but she needs help in deciding on appropriate clothes to wear. She can write simple letters and use the telephone. She can carry on an ordinary conversation, but she does not seem aware of important current events and is unable to talk or write about abstractions. She rides a bicycle and seems well coordinated. She can find her way around her neighborhood but can't go farther without aid. She can cook simple meals and go shopping for specific items by herself.

Moderate Retardation: Bob, age 17, has been in a special educational program since he was six. He can dress himself but needs to be checked over to be sure he is completely dressed before going out. He can go to a nearby store by himself but cannot tell if he has been given the correct change. He cannot take buses alone. In his group home he makes his bed, helps set the table, and sweeps the floor. He works in a sheltered workshop stuffing envelopes. His speech is barely understandable, but he responds to directions and requests.

Severe Retardation: Jason, age 21, has been in educational programs since he was six. He can feed himself with a spoon and can dress himself if the clothing is not too difficult to get on. He gets lost if he goes more than a block from home. He can talk, but his speech is repetitive and his vocabulary small. He enjoys going to the store with others but has no concept of making purchases. He cannot select three objects from a group. Jason has been enrolled in two different shelter workshop programs but has been unable to learn the job routine.

Profound Retardation: Peggy is 30. She has been slow in development since birth and has been in a special educational program since preschool. She cannot dress herself completely. She can use a spoon but not a knife and fork. She does not interact much with other people except by smiling or laughing; she does not talk. She can respond to simple commands like "Come here" and to her name. She spends a great deal of time rocking her body back and forth. Although she likes TV, she pays attention for only brief periods and seems to be watching only the movement.

Biological Causes of Mental Retardation

Mental retardation has many causes, but these may be grouped into two general categories: nonenvironmental factors (including both genetic factors and biological causes such as prenatal exposure to alcohol or birth injuries) and psychosocial reasons. Retarded children who are also **psychosocially disadvantaged** may show no specific disabilities but may resemble their parents in low intellectual achievement. They are likely to experience little intellectual stimulation in their environment, receive poor medical care, and have unhealthful diets and living conditions. Thus, their heredity and/or envi-

TABLE 16–3
Behavior of Retarded Individuals at Various Stages of Development

Level of Retardation	Highest Level of Adaptive Behavior		
	Age 3	Age 9	Age 15 and over
Profound	Drinks from a cup with help; sits unsupported or pulls self up; imitates sounds, repeats Ma-Ma. Indicates knowledge of familiar people and interacts with them nonverbally.	Tries to feed self but spills; can pull off pants and socks; walks alone; uses 4–10 words; may play with others briefly.	Feeds self; can dress except for small buttons and zippers; toilet trained but may have accidents; can climb steps and throw a ball; vocabulary of up to 300–400 words and uses grammatically correct sentences; if nonverbal, may use gestures for communication; understands simple questions and directions; participates in simple group games.
Severe	Feeds self with finger foods; can remove clothes, but often does so inappropriately; stands alone or walks unsteadily; says 1 or 2 words; plays "patty cake" or with toys.	Feeds self with spoon, may be messy; drinks unassisted; may indicate need for toilet; runs and jumps; speaks 2–3 word sentences; interacts with others in simple play.	Feeds self adequately with spoon and fork; can dress with zippers and buttons; is toilet trained. Can run, go up and down stairs alternating feet; may communicate in complex sentences; participates in group activities; does simple tasks and errands.
Moderate	Tries to feed self but spills; can pull off pants and socks; walks alone; uses 4–10 words; may play with others briefly.	Feeds self; can dress except for small buttons and zippers; toilet trained but may have accidents; can climb steps and throw a ball; vocabulary of up to 300–400 words and uses grammatically correct sentences; if nonverbal, may use gestures for communication; understands simple questions and directions; participates in simple group games.	Feeds, bathes, and dresses self; selects daily clothing; can wash and iron own clothes; has good body control; can carry on simple conversation and can interact cooperatively with others; can go on errand without a list; can assume responsibility for simple household tasks.
Mild	Feeds self with spoon, may be messy; drinks unassisted; may indicate need for toilet; runs and jumps; speaks 2–3 word sentences; interacts with others in simple play.	Feeds self adequately with spoon and fork; can dress with zippers and buttons; is toilet trained; can run, go up and down stairs alternating feet; may communicate in complex sentences; participates in group activities; does simple tasks and errands.	Cares for own personal grooming, sometimes with reminders; can go around own neighborhood easily; carries on everyday conversation; writes simple letters and uses telephone; can go shopping, prepare simple meals, and initiate most of own activities.

ronmental experiences may combine to cause their intelligence test scores to fall in the lower end of the distribution.

For a long time it has been thought that most mild mental retardation was usually explained by this combination of heredity and environmental conditions. In contrast, lower intelligence scores—those at moderate, severe, and profound retardation levels—were thought to be the result of some kind of pathology, such as disease, injury, chromosomal abnormality, or specific genetic disorder. Modern epidemiological research has cast doubt on this theory. A Swedish study has shown that at least half and often a much greater proportion of mildly retarded people in the population have some chromosomal defect, specific genetic disease, or some other specific pre- or postnatal disease or injury (Akesson, 1986). This suggests that such factors play a role at all levels of retardation. However, it is also true that compared to people in other retarded groups those in the mildly retarded group are more likely to have family members who also fall in the mildly retarded category. For instance, the IQ scores of the brothers and sisters of one group of retarded children were measured (Nichols, 1984). None of the siblings of the severely retarded children were retarded, but 20 percent of the siblings of mildly retarded children were also retarded (see Figure 16-7). These findings indicate that although there is some overlap, mild and severe cases of mental retardation probably have different causes.

Biological Causes Whenever nonenvironmental causes of retardation are discussed, a number of overlapping terms are used. The predictable gene-based qualities that are transmitted from parents to children are hereditary. However, some of the genes available at the moment of conception are not quite like those of either parent and are called **mutants.** In addition, in certain polygenic disorders, each nonaffected parent may contribute enough pathologically related genes so that together these genes move the child over the threshold from nondisordered to disordered.

Disorders caused by mutations, superthreshold doses of affected genes, and disorders caused by predictable parental contribution are all referred to as **innate.** In addition, certain disorders can be acquired prenatally, for example, as a result of chemical substances passed to the child through the mother's placenta. These factors, together with the innate factors mentioned above, make up what are called **congenital** factors. **Constitutional** factors include all these congenital factors and also factors that are due to illness or injury after birth. Figure 16-8 explains the differences among these terms used to discuss biological causes of retardation.

Hereditary Disorders Some disorders are caused by specific genes that have been identified. If the disorder is caused by a dominant gene, only one gene of that particular gene pair needs to be affected to produce the dis-

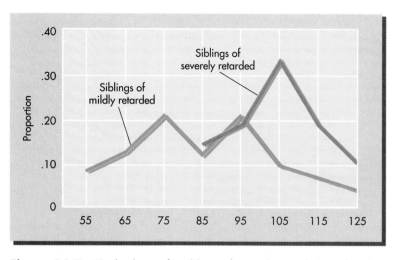

Figure 16-7 IQ distribution for siblings of severely retarded (IQ less than 50) and mildly retarded (IQ 50–69) white children.

SOURCE: Nichols (1984). Familial mental retardation. *Behavior Genetics*, 14, p. 163.

order. In contrast, in recessive disorders, both members of the gene pair must be affected.

The number of known dominant genes that cause severe retardation is small because people who are afflicted by these disorders do not usually have children. Often a mutation, or spontaneous variation in a gene, seems to be responsible for the first case of a dominant gene disorder recognized in a family. In many of these disorders the symptoms do not become apparent immediately after birth. An example of such a disorder is **tuberous sclerosis.** In addition to severe retardation and seizures, this condition produces small fibrous tumors, often beside the nose, as well as internal tumors and skin abnormalities. The seizures may not begin until the child is 3, and the tumors may not appear until several

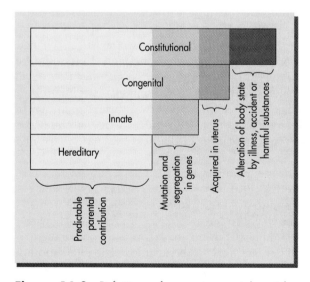

Figure 16-8 Definitions of nonenvironmental contributors to mental retardation.

years later. In some mild cases the tumors appear but retardation may be minimal or absent.

A parent might carry only one recessive gene in a particular gene pair without showing symptoms of the problem transmitted by the gene. If both parents carry the same recessive gene, each of their children has a one in four chance of being affected by the problem and a two in four chance of becoming a carrier like the parents. Many of these inherited problems involve disorders of metabolism.

Phenylketonuria (PKU) is an inherited metabolic disorder in which the body is unable to oxidize the chemical phenylalanine, which therefore accumulates in the body. If this accumulation is allowed to continue, severe mental retardation may result. Very few untreated PKU victims have IQs above 50. If treatment, which involves a restrictive diet, is started early, most of these changes can be prevented, although earlier damage cannot be reversed. Children who received treatment at an early age are usually in the normal range on intelligence tests and neurological examinations, although they score lower on intelligence tests than their siblings did at comparable ages.

Newborn infants can be tested for PKU although, because only 1 in 17,000 children has PKU, the costs of such testing are high per case actually identified. But the costs of caring for the retarded are also high. In one program the saving from detecting and treating each infant with PKU and thus preventing retardation was over $200,000 (Barden et al., 1984). Testing of newborns for PKU is now required in many states.

A lifelong adherence to a restrictive low protein diet is advisable for those with PKU. It had been thought that these children could go off their special diet when they became adults, but it is now known that change to a normal diet has negative long-term effects (Matthews et al., 1986). Adults who go off the diet may develop problems with short-term memory, coordination, and ability to concentrate. Based on this research, teaching dietary management beginning in early childhood can prevent retardation in the next generation (see Figure 16-9).

Before treatment for PKU was developed most people who had PKU did not have children. Now that treatment has saved them from retardation, PKU women are more likely to have children. If pregnant women with PKU do not continue to follow a restrictive diet, their children are likely to be retarded. The retardation does not arise from a particular pair of recessive genes but instead comes from the environmental characteristics within the mother's uterus. A high phenylalanine level

Figure 16-9 Jackie Gnecchi (left) was a member of the first generation of young people with PKU who have reached adulthood without the cognitive damage that results when PKU is untreated. She was born in 1970, soon after newborn screening for PKU became standard practice in hospitals around the country. Beginning when she was two weeks old she received a special diet. She is seen here talking with a social worker at the University of Washington Child Development and Mental Retardation Center who was part of the treatment team that worked with Jackie and her parents.

in the uterus is almost certain to result in severe fetal brain damage. This problem may be avoided or the risk decreased if the PKU mother follows the special low protein diet designed to control blood phenylalanine level.

Tay-Sachs disease, another inherited metabolic disorder, is inevitably fatal. This condition, which is caused by a recessive gene, occurs most often in Ashkenazi Jews whose ancestors came from a small area in Eastern Europe. It causes progressive degeneration of the nervous system, degeneration of the brain, and death, usually before the age of four.

Fragile X syndrome involves a genetically transmitted weakening or break on the X sex chromosome. The syndrome is named *Fragile X* because a small portion at the tip of the X chromosome seems susceptible to breakage under certain conditions. The Fragile X syndrome is the second-most common identifiable cause of mental retardation in males. The most common is Down syndrome, which we will discuss in the next section. Males with the Fragile X syndrome have long faces, big ears, and, as adults, large testes. Men who have this syndrome are more likely than women to be severely retarded. The syndrome usually results in severe to profound retardation, although some of those affected are only mildly retarded. Autistic behaviors and speech problems are often seen in people who have Fragile X syndrome.

Because the Fragile X syndrome is transmitted through the X chromosome, men must inherit the disease from their mothers (Warren & Nelson, 1994). If only one of a woman's X chromosomes is affected by the

Fragile X syndrome the woman may or may not be retarded herself, but she may be a carrier who can transmit the problem to her children. One study examined four generations of one family in which the great-grandmother was a carrier of the disorder (Saul et al., 1982). In the 40 people who were in the next three generations of her family, there were 7 men with Fragile X syndrome, 6 women who were carriers and passed the disorder on to their children, and 9 other women who were potential carriers but who had not yet given birth to a child with the syndrome. Several of these female carriers were at least mildly retarded.

Scientists have recently made the important discovery of the gene that causes the Fragile X syndrome. With this advance, it should now be possible to diagnose the disease unequivocally and to do prenatal genetic screening for the disease. It will also be possible to identify syndrome patients whose retardation or behavioral difficulties had been attributed to factors such as autism or a lack of oxygen during birth. Although no treatments currently exist for the syndrome, identification of the gene will enable researchers to study how the gene operates to influence intelligence and why flaws in it cause retardation.

Down Syndrome: A Chromosomal Disorder More than half of the children who are severely or profoundly retarded have genetic disorders that are not transmitted directly through specific dominant or recessive genes. In these cases, defects of the nonsex chromosomes, or **autosomes,** lead to conditions that cause mental retardation. About one-third have single-gene mutations and most of the remainder have chromosomal mutations or abnormalities. **Chromosomal abnormality** actually occurs in about 10 percent of all conceptions. However, since most of these abnormal fetuses are naturally aborted through miscarriage, only about 1.5 percent of all newborns have such a problem.

The most frequent chromosomal abnormality is **Down syndrome** (named for the physician who first described its symptoms), which occurs about once in every 800 births. Down syndrome is also called **trisomy 21.** The term *trisomy* refers to the presence of three chromosomes of a particular type rather than the usual two. In the case of Down syndrome there are three number 21 chromosomes (shown in Figure 16-10). In addition to Down syndrome, there are other chromosomal abnormalities that are related to retardation: **trisomy 13** and **trisomy 18.** These conditions, which are much rarer than Down syndrome, cause more severe retardation and a shorter life expectancy. The parents of an infant with any of these trisomies face an increased risk of trisomy in future pregnancies.

Children who are affected by Down syndrome have many characteristic physical features that make this disorder easy to recognize. These include a flat face and a

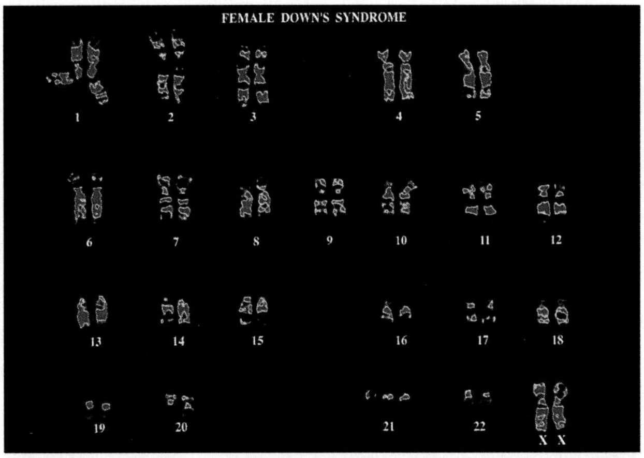

Figure 16-10 Chromosomal abnormalities are detected with relatively high frequency and are the cause of many spontaneous abortions. The most common abnormality in children who are born alive is trisomy 21, which causes Down syndrome. In more than 95 percent of Down syndrome cases there are 47 chromosomes, with 3, rather than 2, twenty-first chromosomes. In a few other cases there are only 46 chromosomes but one member of the number 21 chromosome pair is defective. This figure shows the chromosomal analysis of a girl with Down syndrome. Note the extra chromosome 21 indicated by the arrow.

SOURCE: Adapted from *Facts about Down Syndrome,* U.S. Dept. of Health & Human Services, 1984.

small nose, eyes that appear to slant upward because of small folds of skin at the inside corners, slightly protruding lips and tongue, small ears, and small square hands with short fingers and a curved fifth finger. Children with Down syndrome tend to be shorter than average, with especially short arms and legs in proportion to their bodies. They also are likely to be somewhat obese in childhood and adolescence. Further, such a child is apt to have a congenital heart abnormality.

Children with Down syndrome have about a 99 percent chance of being retarded. There is considerable variability in the level of retardation, however, which may range from mild to severe. In general, Down children seem especially weak in tactile perception, higher-level abstraction and reasoning, and auditory perception.

Programs to provide increased stimulation to very young Down syndrome children have attempted to modify the typical downward trend of development (Cicchetti & Beeghly, 1990). Intervention often begins a few days after birth with physical therapy programs. Programs for young children provide a variety of activities to help develop both physical and cognitive skills (see Figure 16-11). Parents are also trained to take part in activities to stimulate their children.

As infants, Down syndrome children explore their environment in the same ways that other children do. During the preschool period, their development, although slower than that of nonhandicapped children,

short-term memory often mean that information overload occurs, which can result in poor performance. Auditory memory is especially poor, making the child less able to learn from verbal information (Varnhagen et al., 1987). Other problems of Down children that can be major hindrances in pursuing a normal life are inability to comprehend instructions, to pay attention to several things at once, and to express clearly what they are thinking or what they need. Often even older Down syndrome children use a kind of telegraphic speech in which connecting words like "and" or "but" and other words such as prepositions and adverbs are missing. Such a teenager might say "Cat. Jump. Roof. Tree," instead of "The cat jumped off the roof and into the tree."

Because Down syndrome children often learn better by seeing material rather than hearing it, some researchers have tried using computers to improve this telegraphic speech (see Figure 16-12). Teenagers were able to improve their language structure by using special computers that read back what they wrote. One boy, who before the project could only describe his father who had recently died by saying "Dad. Talk. Down. Boom," was able to write: "My father and I went to his office. We would eat lunch and drink Diet 7-Up. I love you, Dad" (Kolata, 1987). Such efforts cannot cure retardation, but can help people function more effectively.

The average adolescent or adult with Down syndrome has the intellectual abilities of a young child. Mental development for people with Down syndrome can continue into their thirties and forties if they are in a stimulating environment (Berry et al., 1984). An increasing number of mentally retarded persons, including some with Down syndrome, are being placed in carefully selected and supervised jobs (see Figure 16-13). However, for many older people with Down syndrome,

Figure 16-11 Enrichment activities for young Down syndrome children may help them achieve far more as they grow older than previously would have been expected. Jason Kingsley (left) and Mitchell Levitz (right) are well-functioning young men who in 1994 wrote a book, *Count Us In,* describing their experiences as persons with Down syndrome. Although there are some skills that have so far eluded them, such as driving a car, they are employed and seem well-adjusted. They and their parents attribute their triumphs over Down syndrome to early stimulation. For example, within 10 days of his birth, Mr. Kingsley's parents began vigorously exercising his arms and legs each time they changed his diaper and they decorated his bedroom with startlingly bright colors and many hanging mobiles.

SOURCE: *The New York Times,* March 20, 1994, p. 13.

seems to follow a similar pattern. One difference is that these children show less exploration behavior and so are not as active in investigating their surroundings. Through their childhood and adolescence, Down syndrome children have poorer muscle tone and coordination than other children. As a result, they are less active, carry out tasks more slowly, and have poorer balance than other children. As Down syndrome children reach school age their delays in physical and cognitive development begin to cause more problems. Deficits in

Figure 16-12 Teaching children with Down syndrome to use computers may be a way to help them overcome some of the problems they have in expressing their thoughts.

aging appears to occur early and brings with it a decrease in cognitive abilities. This may occur because their brains contain fewer neurons than the average, with the result that the normal loss of neurons with aging affects them with unusual severity. Researchers have discovered that the brains of young adults with Down syndrome tend to show plaques and tangles that appear similar although not identical to those found in Alzheimer's disease (see Figure 16-14). As in Alzheimer's disease, these changes seem to be concentrated in the hippocampus, the area of the brain that

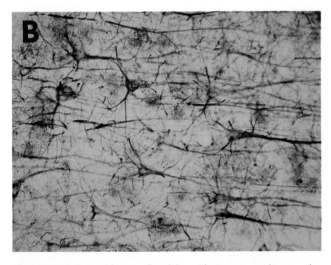

Figure 16-13 A growing number of people with Down syndrome are joining the workforce. This young woman, employed by a large company, is taking inventory in a department store in Atlanta.

SOURCE: *The New York Times*, January 2, 1990. p. 1

Figure 16-14 Almost all adults with Down syndrome who live to be over 30 years of age develop brain lesions (senile plaques and tangles) similar to those seen in patients with Alzheimer's disease. This micrograph of a tissue sample from the brain of a young Down Syndrome patient shows a considerable number of these plaques (brown), although normal neurons (blue) are still present. Courtesy of Drs. Brian Cummings and Patrick Kesslak, Institute for Brain Aging and Dementia, University of California at Irvine.

plays a selective role in learning and memory. About 25 to 40 percent of Down syndrome adults actually become demented, that is, lose their memories and the ability to care for themselves.

The risk of having a child with Down syndrome increases dramatically with the age at which a woman becomes pregnant (see Figure 16-15). It is not clear why age of the mother has this effect. It might be that since women are born with all the eggs they will ever have, the eggs of an older mother may have passed their prime because of aging. Another possibility is that the eggs have been damaged over the years by such influences as medication, radiation, or other harmful substances in the environment. Since older fathers also seem to increase the child's risk for other genetic disorders, researchers are now looking at what factors related to the father's age might produce Down syndrome. Because men's supply of sperm is renewed continually, unlike women's egg supply, the answer does not seem to be in the aging of the genetic material itself.

Techniques are now available for the prenatal diagnosis of Down syndrome. Through **amniocentesis** amniotic fluid is extracted from the sac protecting the fetus and tested for genetic and chromosomal defects. Amniocentesis cannot be used until about the fourth month of pregnancy and the cells must be cultured for two weeks after the test, so the pregnancy is well advanced before the result is known. This means that if the tests show a defect in the fetus the parents may face a very difficult decision over continuing the pregnancy.

Amniocentesis may be suggested if the risk of a

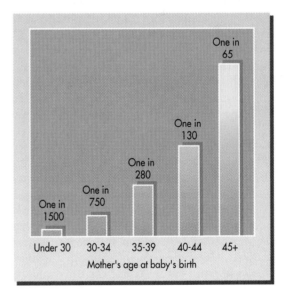

Figure 16-15 The chances of giving birth to a child with Down syndrome increase with the mother's age.

SOURCE: Smith & Wilson (1973), p. 17.

retarded or otherwise genetically damaged child is high—for example, if the mother is over 35 or if there is another child with genetic problems in the family. The results, together with information about the parents' genetic history, are used to counsel parents regarding the probable outcome of the pregnancy. Given this knowledge, the prospective parents can decide to terminate the pregnancy, or they can prepare themselves for the birth of a child with a specific problem. In the majority of cases the procedure reveals that the fetus does not have the defect, and the parents are spared months of needless anxiety.

The Fetal Environment The environment in which the fetus lives before birth is a frequent cause of below-average intellectual functioning. In fact, mental retardation of prenatal origin is the most common of all birth defects. Prenatal factors that have been linked to mental retardation include maternal infections, blood incompatibilities and chronic maternal conditions, chemicals in the fetal environment, radiation, malnutrition, the age of the parents, and maternal stress.

The placental sac surrounding the unborn infant acts as a barrier that prevents many infections from being transferred from the mother to the fetus, but a number of viruses may cross this barrier. About half of all fetuses whose mothers contract the **rubella virus** (German measles) in the first three months of pregnancy are also infected. The virus destroys cells and may interfere with the fetal blood supply. In one group of children of mothers who had rubella while pregnant, about one-third were retarded (Chess, 1978). Rubella can be controlled by a general vaccination program. Retardation can also result if the mother has a bacterial infection such as syphilis or a chronic viral illness such as herpes.

Sometimes biochemical substances in the fetus cause the mother to develop an antibody response to the baby. These antibodies may damage fetal tissues in much the same way that people sometimes reject organ transplants. Some chronic medical conditions in the mother may also cause retardation in the fetus. Hypertension (high blood pressure) and diabetes are examples of chronic disorders that may interfere with fetal nutrition and lead to brain damage. Both of these conditions can be treated in the pregnant woman if they are diagnosed early. Drugs taken by the mother can pass through the placenta to the fetus. Even mild tranquilizers such as Librium are associated with an increase in the rate of serious fetal malformations. In addition, chemicals in the air, food, and water may affect the child before birth.

In recent years alcohol use during pregnancy has become recognized as an important cause of retardation. Even women who drink moderately during pregnancy may have children who are affected to some degree. So far, no safe limits of alcohol use during pregnancy have been established.

Children born to mothers who drink heavily often exhibit **fetal alcohol syndrome** (FAS), a specific set of characteristics that includes retarded growth, physical defects and deformities, mental retardation, and other abnormalities of brain functioning and behavior. In severe cases, facial deformities are apparent at birth or in early childhood: small eyes, drooping eyelids, a short, upturned nose with a low bridge, flat cheeks, a thin upper lip, low-set ears, a receding chin, a bulging forehead, and an unusually large space between the nose and the mouth. Children with FAS are short and thin, with small heads. They grow slowly and their appetite is poor (see Figure 16-16).

Consistent with other evidence, a recent study found an average IQ of 68 in a group of adolescent and adult FAS individuals (Streissguth et al., 1991). Their academic functioning was typically at the second- to fourth-grade level, with arithmetic deficits most common. Poor judgment, distractibility, and difficulty perceiving social cues were frequently noted. The individuals studied

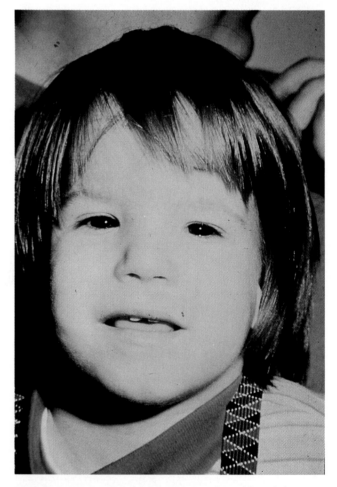

Figure 16-16 This child shows a number of facial characteristics typical of fetal alcohol syndrome.

seemed to have little conception of the future or capacity to learn from experience. They ignored warnings and needed to have the simplest instructions repeated many, many times.

Not all children affected by alcohol in the womb develop the full FAS. If the mother's drinking is only moderately heavy, both physical and mental abnormalities may be subtler. For chronically alcoholic women who have one child with FAS, the chance that another child will also have it is 100 to 400 times higher than in the general population. (Streissguth et al., 1991).

It is hard to say how common fetal alcohol effects are because symptoms range from minor to incapacitating on a continuum without obvious breaks. One estimate of the prevalence rate of the full syndrome is one in 700 live births (Streissguth et al., 1991).

Children affected with FAS face many difficulties because of their cognitive disabilities (Niccols, 1994). Michael Dorris, a professor at Dartmouth College who adopted a boy with FAS, described his son's life in this way:

My son will forever travel through a moonless night with only the roar of wind for company. Don't talk to him of mountains, of tropical beaches. Don't ask him to swoon at sunrises or marvel at the filter of light through leaves. He's never had time for such things, and he does not believe in them. He may pass by them close enough to touch on either side, but his hands are stretched forward, grasping for balance instead of pleasure. He doesn't wonder where he came from, where he's going. He doesn't ask who he is, or why. Questions are a luxury, the province of those at a distance from the periodic shock of rain. Gravity presses Adam so hard against reality that he doesn't feel the points at which he touches it. A drowning man is not separated from the lust for air by a bridge of thought—he is one with it—and my son, conceived and grown in an ethanol bath, lives each day in the act of drowning. For him there is no shore.

—Dorris, 1989, p. 264

Problems at and After Birth Certain conditions occurring at birth are known to increase the probability of mental retardation, although these are not nearly as frequent causes of retardation as some of the prenatal causes. Two of the most common birth complications are **asphyxia,** lack of oxygen, and **prematurity,** birth three weeks or more before term. Some infants do not get enough oxygen during or before the birth process. If death does not result from this asphyxia, seizures, retardation, and other problems are likely to occur. Premature infants usually are low in birth weight. When a child weighs three pounds or less at birth, the risk of retardation as well as health problems becomes much greater. Because adolescents often give birth to small infants and—especially in the case of unmarried mothers—often do not have adequate medical care, their infants are at high risk for retardation and other problems (Andreasen & Black, 1991). For this reason alone, the increase in pregnancies among adolescent girls should be viewed with concern.

Damage to the central nervous system after birth can also cause retardation. Among the causes of such damage are infections, blows to the head, tumors, asphyxiation, and poisons. Some poisonous substances damage the brain cells by depriving them of oxygen. Carbon monoxide, barbiturates, and cyanide work in this way. Other poisons damage specific sites in the brain. Of these, lead, arsenic, and mercury are the most common.

Psychosocial Disadvantage

About three-quarters of all retarded people are in the mildly retarded category. In many of these cases there are no obvious causal factors like the ones just discussed. However, careful epidemiological study often points to some contributing biological factors (Akesson, 1986). In many instances, these mildly retarded individuals cannot be singled out on the basis of their appearance, and often they are not identified as retarded until the early years of school. A very large number of children in this group come from families of low socioeconomic status. Because in many cases their parents' IQs also fall in the mildly retarded range, the question is often asked whether heredity is the predominant factor in their retardation.

Environment has been referred to by some as a threshold variable, meaning that once a certain minimal quality of environment has been reached, further environmental stimulation is unimportant when compared to inherited capability. To put it another way, heredity provides a range of possibilities for the developing child, but the child's level of achievement within that rather wide range might be attributable to the environment in which he or she grows up. The results of many studies show that between 50 and 80 percent of the variation in intelligence factors is due to inheritance and the remainder to environmental influences (Zigler et al., 1984).

Psychosocial Enrichment

Some investigators have tried to manipulate the environment to determine the effect of an enriched environment on children who are thought to have low intellectual potential. In a program carried out in North Carolina, pregnant women with IQs averaging 80 were recruited for study (Ramey & Haskins, 1981). After their babies' births, half of the infants were cared for during the day at an educational day-care center and half were reared at home by their mothers. Both groups of children received medical care and dietary supplements, and their families were given social services if they requested them. At the age of 3, the children in the intervention group had significantly higher IQs than the control group. This difference seemed to be due to a decline in IQs of the control infants during the 12- to 18-month age period. By the time the children were 5 years old, 39 percent of the control group had IQs below 85, whereas only 11 percent of the intervention group had IQs in this range. This study suggests that educational day care beginning before three months of age results in normal intellectual development, at least until the age of 5, for children of high-risk families.

Whether interventions that enrich the environment of economically deprived children who are at risk for retardation have a long-term effect on their intellectual performance is still an open question. Some investigators believe that interventions that begin in the very early years of life, such as the program described above, are most likely to succeed. Others believe that the early period of life is not uniquely critical and that later interventions also have a good chance of success. Most investigators would agree that work with the parents of young children, as well as with the children themselves, enhances the success potential for any program (Garber, 1988).

Typically, intervention programs produce improved scores during and immediately after the program. The same effect can be seen in the increased intelligence-test scores of culturally deprived children after their first year in school. However, in both cases these at-risk children seem to lose their early gains, and in later grades their performance worsens compared to that of other children. This change might be a function of the changing demands of school programs as children grow older. In the higher grades greater emphasis is placed on abstract thinking. This is also true of the content of intelligence test questions aimed at older children. Perhaps many of these at-risk children are deficient in the ability to think abstractly. On the other hand, perhaps the special help in cognitive skills that the children obtained in the program was not complete enough to enable them to use those skills independently or to apply them to more complex levels of problem solving. This area of research is filled with many unanswered questions.

While in the past, retarded people were usually institutionalized for life, the current emphasis is on helping retarded people live more independent lives. The largest group of retarded individuals are classified as mildly retarded and this group has the greatest chance for living in the community on their own or with minimal support. Children who are mildly retarded, because they appear physically similar to other children and may have social or manual skills that partially mask their inability to handle intellectual tasks, may not be identified as retarded until they have been in school for several years. They may even remain unidentified throughout their entire school careers. However, people who are profoundly, severely, or moderately retarded are often identified soon after birth and may ultimately be placed in an institutional setting.

Public Educational Programs School programs for the retarded have changed greatly over the last 35 years. Special classes have been established for severely and moderately retarded students who previously were totally excluded from school programs, and many slow-learner classes for mildly retarded children have been abolished. The children from such classes have been **mainstreamed,** or integrated into regular classes. Both these changes have come about as a result of court decisions in cases dealing with the civil rights of the retarded.

The Education for All Handicapped Children Act of 1975 required public schools to provide free appropriate education to all handicapped children. Because of this law and recent court decisions, school districts are obligated to provide training for severely and profoundly retarded children. Such programs concentrate on basic communication and social skills. Although it is too early to assess whether they improve the child's performance, these programs do seem to prevent many severely and profoundly retarded children from being institutionalized in early childhood. Instead, a large number are now cared for at home, sometimes through adolescence or longer.

School classes for slow learners have been affected by a series of legal decisions, beginning with the *Brown v. Board of Education* case of 1954. In that decision, which marked the end of legally segregated schools and "separate but equal" education, special-education classes were criticized as offering poor education. Students were usually placed in classes for slow learners on the basis of intelligence tests, and critics argued that intelligence tests were unfair to lower-class or minority children because they were heavily loaded with socially and culturally biased items. These items would be familiar to middle-class children but might not be part of the experience of a child from a lower-class or minority family. Pressure to place mildly retarded children in regular classrooms has also come from laws requiring the "least restrictive" placement possible for any given child. There is a growing movement to avoid identifying and labeling the children as retarded because of concern that such labels may stigmatize them. For minority children in particular, it is feared that such labels may be a result of test bias rather than valid estimates of their abilities. Despite the potential benefits of "least restrictive" placement, however, some researchers believe that in certain states children who need special services may be denied them (Zigler & Hodapp, 1991).

Education in a mainstreamed or regular class is believed to be desirable for retarded children because exposure to normal role models and the absence of labeling might help them improve their achievement level and social adjustment. So far, however, this belief has not been supported by research findings. There seems to be little difference in performance between children who have been mainstreamed and those who have been placed in special classes. In one large study, both groups scored in the lowest one percent on standardized tests of reading and arithmetic (Kaufman et al., 1982). Nor does mainstreaming by itself improve the social status of a retarded child. In a study of more than 300 mainstreamed classrooms, the students were asked to rate each other's behavior. The mean rating for the retarded children was one standard deviation below that for their nonretarded classmates (Gottlieb et al., 1978) despite the fact that the basis of the ratings was not the label "retarded" but the *behavior* of the retarded children. Many retarded children lack social skills and an idea of what behaviors are socially appropriate. In addition, because retardation puts children at risk for lower academic performance than others of their age, those who feel they are achieving poorly may express frustration by aggressive behavior or by attention-getting actions that are annoying to their classmates.

Community-Living Programs Emphasis on normalizing the lives of the retarded has increased in recent years. The same changes in the law requiring that even severely retarded individuals receive the least restrictive educational placement possible have been applied to the concept of overall care, too. As a result, many people who have been in institutions for many years have been discharged and have returned to the community. Young children who formerly would have been sent to institutions often live at home and attend special school programs that include job training. At present, more retarded persons in residential care live in small, private facilities than in public institutions. New admissions to large state institutions, especially for children, are becoming increasingly rare.

Deinstitutionalization can have a major impact, not only on retarded individuals, but on their families as well. In one study, residents of a large institution were moved into small community-based living groups because of a court order (Latib et al., 1984). Initially most of their families opposed deinstitutionalization. Many of them had made the decision to institutionalize their relatives many years earlier, often under great stress. In general, they believed that their relatives had reached their highest level of development and had little chance of learning new skills. They thought they were adequately cared for and worried that they would not be protected in small residential settings. They also wondered how long funding would be available for community-based homes. Six months after the move, however, the families felt positive about it. Not only did they feel that deinstitutionalization was good for the member of their family who was now living in the community, but they felt happier themselves.

For retarded individuals who are discharged from large institutions, group homes function both as a permanent home for those who are unable to live independently and as a transition point for those who are learning living skills that will help them live on their own (see Figure 16-17). One problem in opening new group homes is the opposition of potential neighbors. Once the home is established, the opposition generally decreases and the neighbors' unrealistic fears about crime, property values, and quality of life dissipate (Okolo & Guskin, 1984). An important part of community-living programs is the job training offered to residents through subsidized sheltered workshops or special training programs where employees are not expected to work at the pace necessary to be economically feasible (see Figure 16-18).

Vocational and Social Skills Training Knowledge and use of appropriate vocational and social skills are key factors in success both in competitive job environments and in sheltered workshops. Skills training through modeling has been found to be a very effective technique. One study compared the effects of modeling with those of coaching the same skills (LaGreca et al., 1983).

Figure 16-17 In addition to providing shelter, group homes are a place where retarded adolescents and adults learn valuable homemaking and self-management skills.

Figure 16-18 A sheltered workshop offers both a place to learn job skills and a working environment for people who cannot compete for jobs on an equal basis.

Several problem situations were modeled so that prospective workers could learn to identify both problem behaviors and appropriate ways of dealing with such situations.

> You come to work in the morning and can't find one of the materials you need to do your job (for example, the napkins). Inappropriate solution: walk around, talking to coworkers; sit at table and do nothing. Appropriate solution: request help from supervisor politely.
>
> You are working in the morning and the person working next to you is being very loud, talking and laughing. You are finding it hard to concentrate on your work because of the noise. Inappropriate solution: yell at co-worker to "shut up"; throw something at co-worker; insult co-worker; threaten co-worker. Appropriate solution: politely request quiet behavior; ignore co-worker.
>
> —LaGreca et al., 1983, p. 272

The effectiveness of modeling is shown by a comparison with both a coaching group and a control group. After seven weeks on the job only one of the 11 people in the modeling group had been fired. Half of the coaching group had been fired; in the control group, 10 had been fired and only 2 were still on the job.

Another important aspect of retarded people's lives is a supportive network of people. One way to increase the amount of support available is to help the individual learn social skills. Another is to make sure that decisions about living and working conditions take friendships into account. If friendship networks are kept in mind when residents of facilities for the retarded have to be relocated, the outcome is likely to be much better. In one study, residents who had moved to a new home with chosen friends were more sociable several years later than residents who had been separated from friends (Romer & Heller, 1983). They were also better able to care for themselves.

While mentally retarded individuals are being integrated into the community, they are vulnerable to personal, sexual, and financial exploitation. One source of this problem is the tendency of the retarded to answer "yes" to all questions, regardless of content. Such readiness to agree clearly can have negative consequences. For one thing, it means that retarded people are likely to agree to inappropriate or unfair requests.

One way to prevent exploitation of retarded individuals is to pay special attention to teaching them what is expected of a person and how to say "no" (Schilling & Schinke, 1984). For example, participants in a training program for food service workers were taught how to handle their earnings and how to say "no" to people who asked to borrow money. Another problem area is sexual behavior. Training programs have taught retarded people how to recognize and escape from sexually exploitive situations. Mentally retarded individuals also need to be trained to understand what society views as appropriate sexual behavior and to avoid such acts as public masturbation and inappropriate sexual approaches to others.

Psychological and Social Problems

Retarded individuals are likely to experience psychological problems as well as intellectual retardation. In one study, up to 40 percent of retarded children were rated by their parents or teachers as psychologically disturbed (Rutter et al., 1970). Severely retarded children exhibit an even higher rate of disturbance: Nearly half may be diagnosed as having a behavior disorder. The same types of disorders are seen in retarded children as in nonretarded children, although the frequencies of different types of disorders differ in the two groups. Those who are severely retarded are more likely to have a psychosis or to be hyperactive and less likely to have a conduct disorder (Rutter et al., 1975). This difference is probably explained by the likelihood that severely retarded children also have central nervous system damage.

Until the 1800s, little distinction was made between mental retardation and mental illness. However, during the nineteenth century, intellectual deficits came to be viewed as the primary characteristic of mental retardation and emotional impairment as the primary characteristic of psychiatric disorders. Recent research has shown this distinction to be invalid, because the prevalence rate for psychopathology is as great or greater for individuals with mental retardation as for nonretarded persons (Borthwick-Duffy, 1994). At present, theories of psychopathology among mentally retarded individuals lag behind theories developed for the general population. There is a need for appropriate methods to assess the psychological problems of retarded individuals (Matson & Sevin, 1994; Reiss & Valenti-Hein, 1994).

Problems of social adjustment among retarded children living with their parents may be particularly difficult during adolescence. Mildly retarded adolescents in particular tend to be socially isolated and may experience a "friendship void." Most of their contacts with others generally are at school, not in social activities. If they do have social interactions, these tend to be with younger children, not those of the same age (Brier, 1986). In one study, 84 percent of retarded children developed emotional or behavioral problems during adolescence (Zetlin & Turner, 1985). The problems included temper tantrums, violent or destructive behavior, use of drugs and alcohol, and an increase in withdrawal behavior. Many of these problems seemed to be related to the young people's growing awareness of the gap between themselves and other teenagers in terms of expectations for the future and ability to be independent. The retarded adolescents' desire for dating relationships was another source of problems. When these young people became adults, only one-third were still in conflict with their parents. The rest either had adjusted to dependence on their parents or had been able to establish fairly independent life styles that gave them satisfaction.

Retarded individuals often have a low opinion of themselves. When they live in the community this problem becomes more severe because there are more opportunities for comparisons with nonretarded people. In one study, retarded individuals living in an institution were more likely to rate themselves as smart and attractive than retarded people living in a community setting (Gibbons, 1985). Since the intellectual level of those in the institution was lower and the rated attractiveness no different, the community group's exposure to and self-comparisons with nonretarded individuals probably accounted for the difference.

The kinds of problems these adolescents and adults face can be helped by psychotherapy. Family therapy is often used, especially for adolescents. Individual psychotherapy can be useful in the same way that it may be helpful for nonretarded adolescents. Social skills training and job preparation also contribute to adjustment. Such techniques have helped many retarded people to adjust well, marry, and live semiindependent lives (see Figure 16-19).

The Families of Retarded Children

From the parents' point of view, the birth of a mentally retarded child is a stressful and often devastating event. For nine months they have looked forward to the arrival of a healthy, normal child. When those expectations are shattered, they often go through a grieving process similar to that following the death of a family member. In the past, many professionals emphasized the parents' need for help until they could accept the situation. The professionals viewed the process as time-limited. One parent of a retarded child comments on this view.

Parents of retarded people, the theorists tell us, learn to live with their children's handicaps. They go through stages of reaction, moving through shock, guilt, and rejection to the promised land of acceptance and adjustment.

My own experience as the father of a retarded child did not fit this pattern. Instead, it convinced me that most people seriously misunderstand a parent's response to this situation. The standard view does not reflect the reality of parents' experience or lead to helpful conclusions.

Professionals could help parents more—and they would be more realistic—if they discarded their ideas about stages and progress. They could then begin to understand something about the deep, lasting changes that life with a retarded son or daughter brings to parents. And they could begin to see that the negative feelings—the shock, the guilt, and the

Figure 16-19 This photo shows Victor, 30, and Kathy, 29, after they had announced their marriage plans. A few years ago such an announcement would have been almost unthinkable because both Kathy and Victor are retarded.

bitterness—never disappear but stay on as a part of the parent's emotional life.

Most parents, I believe, never fully resolve the complexity of feelings about their child's retardation. They don't "adjust to" or "accept" that fact, at least not in the way psychology books describe it.

—Searl, 1978, p. 27

Many parents of retarded children retain some optimism about their child's future progress while the child is still young. For example, they may overestimate the child's academic potential and underestimate problems in learning. This is illustrated by the observation that parents of young children are more supportive of the concept of mainstreaming (combining children of all abilities into one school program) than parents of older children, who see a greater need for special education programs (Suelzle & Keenan, 1981). In general, just as the grieving process goes on over a lifetime, the parents' acceptance of the severity of their child's disability is not steady and gradual. Instead, problems of acceptance flare up acutely at particular stages in the child's development.

Families of retarded children go through a series of crises as the child reaches various developmental stages. In one survey, three-quarters of the parents described life with their retarded child as a series of ups and progressively greater downs. Only one-quarter described their grief as being healed by time (Wikler et al., 1981). The parents were asked to evaluate the extent to which they were upset at a number of points, including early events such as the time of diagnosis, the time for walking and talking, and decisions on school placement, and later events such as the onset of puberty, the 21st birthday, and discussion and decisions about the care of the child after the parents' death.

When the parents' responses were compared with the predictions of social workers, the results showed that the social workers tended to overestimate the extent to which the parents were upset over the earlier experiences and to underestimate the extent to which they were upset over the later experiences. For example, the social workers overestimated the degree of the parents' upset at the times when the child would normally have been expected to walk, when the child entered a special-education class rather than the regular school program, and when younger siblings surpassed the retarded child in functioning. They markedly underestimated how upsetting the child's 21st birthday was to the parents.

The unmet needs of parents seem to form a U-shaped curve. These needs are high among parents of preschoolers, drop off when the children enter some kind of school program, and rise again, even beyond the original levels, when the children become young adults.

Periods of transition in the children's lives are also associated with increased family stress. Both entry into adolescence and to young adulthood seem particularly stressful to the family. Figure 16-20 shows the stress levels of families with retarded children of different ages. Two samplings two years apart showed similar findings.

In the past, parents of severely retarded children were urged to institutionalize such children shortly after birth, before they had had a chance to become attached to them. More recently, they have been urged to care for their children at home. However, the presence of a retarded child puts great stress on a family. Parents report a sense of loss and hopelessness, a decrease in self-esteem, and increases in shame, guilt, and marital disharmony (Lobato, 1983).

The brothers and sisters of retarded children may also be affected by the child's presence. There has not been much research on these effects. What we do know suggests that the parents of a retarded child often place increased demands on their other children. They are expected to care for the retarded child and to subordinate their needs to those of their sibling. Their parents expect more of them and at the same time often have less time and attention to give them. These children sometimes feel pressure to excel in order to "make up" for their retarded sibling.

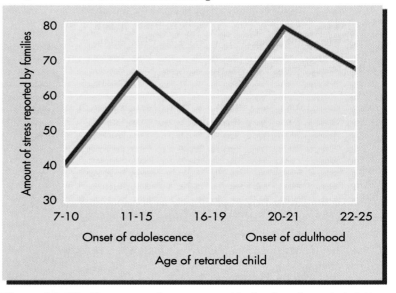

Figure 16-20 The amount of stress reported by families of retarded children varies with the age of the children. Developmental transitions seem to produce especially high levels of stress.

SOURCE: Wikler (1986), p. 705.

Much of the research on the effects of a retarded child on other family members was done some years ago, when many children were institutionalized, and in many cases there were no control groups. This is an area where more facts are needed. What is known at present is that, not surprisingly, the parents' attitudes toward the retarded child and their ways of dealing with the situation have an important effect on their other children's adjustment.

AUTISTIC DISORDER

Autism is a relatively rare disorder, but one with profound effects. Three quarters of those with autistic disorder are retarded.

Characteristics of Autistic Behavior Children with **autistic disorder** are impaired in social relationships, communication, and activities. Many autistic children never develop speech. Those who do may have unusual speech patterns such as **echolalia,** the tendency to reply by repeating back what was said to them. They are likely to spend a great deal of time in repetitive motions or activities. Autism, although originally considered to be a psychosis, is now considered to be a developmental disorder. Psychosis, although rare, does occur in childhood. Childhood schizophrenia, much less common than adult schizophrenia, does not usually occur before age 7 or 8. Although the symptoms are similar, it is not known whether childhood schizophrenia is the same disorder as adult schizophrenia.

Research on Autistic Disorder Language disturbance is the most universal symptom of autism. The autistic person's cognitive problems don't seem to be the result of poor memory, but instead stem from difficulties with higher-level cognitive processing and symbolic thought. Autistic individuals also have social deficits because they seem unable to coordinate affective expression and behavior. This results in an inability to understand the signals sent out by others. Some type of brain pathology seems likely in autism. One fifth of autistic children develop epileptic seizures in adolescence. The likelihood of developing these seizures is much higher in those who are severely retarded. Brain imaging techniques have shown that autistic children may be more likely to have stunted brain development in the cerebellum. If one child in a family is autistic, the chances of autism in subsequent children is much higher than that in the general population. Research on the genetics of autism suggests that what is inherited is some general tendency toward cognitive or language abnormalities rather than autism itself.

Therapy Severely autistic children are often treated by using a behavior modification program. Such programs' success is limited, although it may be successful with a subgroup of autistic children.

Prospects for Change A key predictor of outcome for an autistic child is development of language by age 5. Intelligence test scores predict school and occupational outcome for these children just as they do for nonautistic children.

MENTAL RETARDATION

Mental retardation is defined as a significantly below-average level of intellectual functioning that is accompanied by impaired social functioning. Mental retardation is a chronic, irreversible condition that begins before age 18. Autistic children may also be retarded, but they form a special group that differs from other retarded children in several ways. Retarded children may have comparable levels of social and intellectual development, but autistic children have lower social than cognitive development. Autistic children also show severe language deficits and unusual behaviors that are not common in retardation.

Degrees of Mental Retardation Mental retardation is divided into four levels based on intelligence test scores. These levels are: mild, moderate, severe, and profound retardation. There are two general categories of retardation: One is based on **psychosocial disadvantage** and one on biological factors not related to the child's social environment.

Biological Causes of Mental Retardation Retardation can be a result of a variety of genetic factors: inheritance of certain genes; **mutation** or changes in certain genes or chromosomes caused by a variety of factors; gene contributions from each parent that together move the child over the threshold for retardation; or by chemical substances passed on to the fetus through the mother's placenta. Illness or injury after birth can also cause retardation. Both genetic factors and problems after birth are grouped together and termed **constitutional factors.** Those disorders caused by **dominant** genes require only one gene in the gene pair to produce the effect. Sometimes mutation of a parent's gene causes the first case of a dominant gene disorder found in a family. One example is **tuberous sclerosis.** Disorders caused by specific recessive genes require that the individual inherit that gene from both parents before symptoms appear. Examples of this type of disorder are **phenylketonuria** (PKU) and **Tay-Sachs disease.** Genetic defects carried on the **autosomes,** or nonsex cells, may produce more severe defects than those carried on the chromosome pair that determines sex. One abnormality carried by a sex-cell located gene pair is **Fragile X syndrome,** which is often associated with autistic behaviors and speech problems as well as retardation. **Chromosomal abnormality** occurs in 10 percent of all conceptions, but most of these abnormal fetuses are spontaneously aborted. Of those that are not, the most frequent chromosomal abnormality is **Down syndrome.** Most children with Down syndrome are retarded, but the level of retardation varies. Children with Down syndrome have characteristic physical features and also seem to have specific cognitive deficits. Most cases of Down syndrome are the result of the presence of an extra number-21 chromosome, hence the name trisomy-21. The risk of having a child with Down syndrome increases dramatically with a mother's age. One way to determine if a fetus is affected by a trisomy or a disorder caused by dominant or recessive genes is through **amniocentesis,** an analysis of the amniotic fluid surrounding the fetus.

The most common cause of all birth defects is related to the **prenatal environment.** Retardation can be caused by maternal infections such as **rubella virus** (German measles). If the mother has chronic high blood pressure or diabetes this may also interfere with fetal nutrition and produce retardation. An important cause of retardation is drugs that pass through the mother's placenta. **Fetal alcohol syndrome** (FAS) is an example of an important cause of both physical and mental abnormalities in children. Prematurity, asphyxiation, and accidents may also result in brain damage and retardation.

Psychosocial Disadvantage A large number of children, especially those with mild retardation, come from families of low socioeconomic status. Because many of their parents are also mildly retarded, it is not clear whether the children's retardation is related to heredity, environment, or a combination of both.

Psychosocial Enrichment If children from psychosocially disadvantaged homes are given educational day care from an early age, they are less likely to be classified as retarded on intelligence tests. Little is known about the long-term effects of such programs, however. Another aspect of psychosocial enrichment is the current emphasis on helping retarded people live as independent lives as possible. One way this is done is through public education programs for the retarded. These have changed greatly, largely through the impetus of the Education for All Handicapped Children Act of 1975 that required public schools to provide appropriate education for all handicapped children. Programs include those for severely and profoundly retarded children where the emphasis is on basic communication and social skills. Such programs seem to delay institutionalization for these children because more of them are cared for at home through adolescence or longer. Another legal decision, the *Brown v. Board of Education* case of 1954 not only ended legal racial segregation of schools, but it also placed pressure on schools to integrate or **mainstream** retarded children into their regular classes. Although it was anticipated that mainstreaming retarded children would improve the quality of their educational experience, research findings have not demonstrated that this has happened. Deinstitutionalization efforts have meant that several kinds of living arrangements are possible for many retarded individuals. These arrangements include a return to their families, as well as foster homes, group homes, or nursing homes. For those who can profit from them, sheltered workshops that teach job skills and also may provide subsidized employment have been valuable. Both vocational and social skills training are important for the success of retarded people in all these living and working situations.

Psychological and Social Problems Retarded persons are likely to experience psychological problems. Although these problems are often the same types found in the general population, the frequencies differ. Adolescence is a particularly difficult time for retarded children living at home and for their parents, at least in part because the teenagers experience a growing gap between their social expectations and ability to function independently and the expectations and abilities of nonretarded adolescents. Psychotherapy can be useful in dealing with these problems.

The Families of Retarded Children The birth of a mentally retarded child is usually a major source of stress for parents. Families of retarded children go through a series of crises as the child reaches various developmental stages. Development of the brothers and sisters of a retarded child may be affected significantly by the retarded child's presence in the family.

CHAPTER SEVENTEEN

Rene Magritte, *The Future of Statues*, 1935.
Tate Gallery, London/Art Resource, New York. © 1996
C. Herscovici/Artist Rights Society, New York.

THERAPIES AND THEIR OUTCOMES

Betty Rouse, housewife and mother of three adolescent children, had been in psychotherapy for two years. She had sought therapy because she felt herself to be an unhappy, inadequate person, who, as she put it, "was not good for much besides cooking dinner and chauffeuring the kids around to Scout meetings." During the first several months of therapy, she talked mainly about herself. As time passed, however, her husband Fred was mentioned with increasing frequency and strong emotion. By the end of therapy, Betty concluded that, while many of her problems were of her own making, Fred had consistently made them worse by showing that he saw her as "just a housewife and mother," not as someone who was admirable for her own sake. After trying fruitlessly to talk with Fred about how he always belittled her, Betty concluded that her self-esteem was more important to her than she had ever realized and that Fred would only hinder its growth. With great pain and guilt, mainly because of the effect it might have on the children, Betty decided to get a job, live apart from Fred, and eventually get a divorce. She hoped one day to meet a man who would both love her and value her as a person.

Did Betty Rouse's psychotherapy have good or bad effects? The answer depends on a number of things, including her past life and one's own values. Therapy situations involve a special relationship between a professional clinician and a person with a problem. A therapist's job is difficult and hard to evaluate because each person's problem is unique and because the various therapeutic approaches differ greatly. Would the outcome of Betty Rouse's therapy have been different if she had been seeing a behavior therapist, a biologically oriented psychiatrist, or a family therapist? So many factors are involved that we cannot answer this question but it is possible to make comparisons among the therapeutic approaches used for different types of cases.

It is important to keep in mind the similarities as well as the differences among the various therapeutic approaches. All therapeutic relationships aim to provide clients with certain ingredients that are missing from their lives. Regardless of their therapeutic orientation, all clinicians must deal with the patient's psychological state and with his or her expectation of receiving help. All therapists attempt to form some sort of supportive therapeutic relationship. All clinicians must create a problem-solving setting, communicate their views of the problems presented, and help the client devise possible solutions to those problems.

In preceding chapters we have described major therapeutic approaches to specific types of maladaptive behavior. We have discussed the "talking therapies," such as psychoanalysis and client-centered counseling, in which conversations between the client and the therapist are the vehicle for achieving change; cognitive-behavioral therapies, such as systematic desensitization and building of social skills and confidence in using them, which involve applications of learning and cognitive principles in specially structured clinical situations; and biological therapies, such as antipsychotic, antidepressive, or tranquilizing drugs and electroconvulsive treatments, which are aimed at achieving behavior change through physical means.

Until now, we have focused attention primarily on the particular therapies that seem most pertinent to helping people with certain types of disorders overcome their difficulties. However, there are some general questions about the nature of therapeutic interventions and their effects that require special consideration. The questions include:

- Do most or all of the different therapeutic approaches have common elements? If so, what are they?
- Why is a particular therapy effective for certain types of problems but not for others?
- Would combining different therapeutic approaches yield better results than using each approach by itself?

- What is the process by which therapeutic change comes about?
- On what basis should judgments about the success of therapeutic efforts be made?
- How researchable are issues related to these efforts?

In the following pages, where possible, we will attempt to answer these and other questions about therapies for maladaptive behavior and try to separate what is known from what is not yet known.

The case of a 54-year-old man who participated in a clinical trial of the type described in chapter 1 illustrates the importance of these questions about the nature of therapeutic change and of research on this topic. The aim of the trial was to evaluate a new medication for depression. The trial, which lasted for 12 weeks, was placebo-controlled. Neither patients nor the therapists knew whether the pills the patients were taking had active ingredients or were simply placebos.

> His response during the first week was modestly positive. At week 3 he was remarkably happy, saying he had not felt this way for 5 years. He was rated "markedly improved" with no symptoms of depression from week 4 until completion of the study.
>
> He was a lonely man who knew that he needed but one strong heterosexual relationship to sustain himself. Five years before entering the study he had found the only woman whom he had ever loved. Because she was in the midst of a painful divorce and because he was so ardent in his declarations of affection, she ended their 2-month romance.
>
> During his first week in the study he felt somewhat better and decided to call her. To his amazement, she said, "Maybe we should work on our relationship." He had dinner with her and was delighted that she wanted to continue to see him. He relaxed, stopped worrying, and became less affected by the little things that had been tormenting him. He attributed his dramatic increase in positive mood to "fate"; namely, that she was ready to see him again. He reluctantly admitted that he had initiated the spiral of events associated with the improvement in his mood.

This man was receiving placebos. What caused his improvement? It certainly was not the contents of the inert pills he was taking. A relevant fact is that the trial in which he was participating was conducted in a clinic. Each time he came to the clinic for a new supply of pills he had contact with a clinician who inquired as to how he was getting along. We will never know exactly why improvement took place in this case. It might have been a spontaneous remission—that is, the patient might simply have gotten better in the absence of active treatment. This seems unlikely since the man's depression was long-standing. The improvement might have come about because participation in the clinical trial created hope that he would be helped by doing so. The clinician's questions about how the patient was getting along might have been quite supportive, given how lonely he was. The hope created by coming to the clinic and getting to know the clinician may have given the man enough courage to make an attempt at rekindling the romantic relationship he so desired. This attempt was his alone—and yet the clinical contacts probably played a facilitative role. This man's improvement shows the need for (1) well-controlled evaluations of therapies and (2) large enough numbers of participants so that occasional unexpected improvements of people in placebo conditions do not wash out whatever therapeutic effects the experimental condition might have.

Although we have talked about therapeutic techniques in relation to specific disorders, it is useful to discuss what we know about the various therapeutic methods in general. Doing so will be valuable in two ways. First, reviewing these clinical methods toward the end of the book will highlight how much we have learned along the way and, second, it will lay the groundwork for a discussion of how different therapies are conducted, evaluated, compared, and in some instances, combined. We will start with the psychologically based therapies. These include psychodynamic therapy and psychoanalysis, cognitive therapies, and cognitive-behavioral therapies used either with individuals or with groups. Next, we will survey the uses of biologically based therapies and, finally, cover the effects of hospitalization both in its therapeutic and protective aspects.

Psychotherapy

All forms of psychotherapy involve interchanges between a client and a therapist. These interchanges, which are nonverbal as well as verbal, are aimed at understanding what is on the client's mind. This understanding is then used as a basis for efforts to change the client's maladaptive ways of thinking, reacting to situations, and relating to others.

In the course of their work, and regardless of their theoretical orientations, therapists must perform three tasks: (1) listen, (2) understand, and (3) respond. The therapist listens to the patient in order to learn about his or her preoccupations, worries, and concerns. Listening serves two functions: It lets the therapist hear about topics that the client brings up spontaneously, and it provides information pertinent to the therapist's hypotheses about the client's problems. Listening provides a basis for the therapist's understanding of the client's self-concept and view of the world.

Through listening and understanding, the therapist becomes able to respond. The response might be a question aimed at eliciting more information or it might be a comment. The comment might be an interpretation of what has been going on in the session or in the client's interpersonal relationships. As our review will demonstrate, there are many types of psychotherapy that differ in their theoretical bases, aims, and techniques. Yet, there are also important similarities.

Psychodynamic Therapy and Psychoanalysis

Although psychoanalysis greatly influenced the development of psychodynamic therapy, there are now a great variety of psychodynamic therapeutic approaches. Because psychoanalysis takes a long time and is expensive, only a small fraction of the people who desire it can experience that form of therapy. However, psychoanalytic concepts and techniques are widely used in ways that make them more suitable for the treatment of larger numbers of clients by many psychodynamically-oriented therapists.

Psychodynamic therapy is typically conducted with the client and the therapist sitting facing or almost facing each other. The client is encouraged to review early relationships with parents and significant others, but the therapist also directs attention to the situations facing the client at present. The client is expected to do most of the talking, while the psychodynamic therapist occasionally interjects clarifications to assist the client in understanding the dynamics of the problem that led him or her to seek professional help.

Psychoanalysis is a specific subtype of psychotherapy. Before a psychoanalysis formally begins, the psychoanalyst has a series of sessions with the client to determine the suitability of this therapeutic approach (see Table 17-1). A psychoanalysis requires on the average between two and five years, usually with four to five sessions per week. Over the years, the total number of sessions has increased. In contrast to psychodynamic therapy, the client lies on a couch and the therapist sits out of the client's line of sight in order to avoid distracting the client from the process of free association. In **free association,** the client expresses thoughts and feelings in as free and uninhibited a manner as possible. This expression results in a natural flow of ideas unencumbered by interruptions or explanations. The examination of dreams and fantasies is also important in psychoanalysis to a greater degree than in other psychodynamic therapies. The goal of this examination is **insight** into one's inner life and a more realistic view of the motivations and needs of other people.

After months of talking about her husband as a demanding, overbearing man who was always gloomy, Rose Francis, aged 50, remarked to her therapist: "You know, I guess I

Figure 17-1 Therapists may have negative reactions to patients because of countertransference.

SOURCE: Drawing by D. Reilly; © 1991 *The New Yorker* Magazine, Inc.

The case of Bill Jenkins, a 40-year-old construction supervisor who sought psychotherapy because of the increasing number of arguments he was having with his wife, provides an example of transference.

During the first 20 sessions he described in detail to the therapist frustrations connected with his marital and work situations. In these sessions, he never referred to any thoughts he might have had about the therapist. In the 21st session, Jenkins noticed a small crack in one of the walls of the therapist's office. He said to the therapist: "It looks like the construction company that put up that wall didn't do a very good job." After several uncomfortable pauses, he went on, "You know, Doc, I feel embarrassed saying this but somehow I keep feeling sorry for you, feeling like, in a way, you've been a loser. Like that lousy construction job over there (pointing to the crack in the wall). Some of those construction guys are pretty smart fellows who don't mind taking advantage of innocent people."

The characteristic Jenkins was attributing to the therapist (being a loser) could not have been based on facts available to him because Jenkins knew little about the therapist's background. What he said was the first outward expression of his developing relationship with and fantasies concerning the therapist. In subsequent sessions, Jenkins himself observed the similarity between his pictures of the therapist and his father, who was an alcoholic and a "loser." At one point he said, "It doesn't make sense, does it, for me to see you as being like my father?"

really don't like him." There was a tone of wonder and surprise in her voice when she said this. After recognizing her strong negative feelings toward her husband, Mrs. Francis found it possible to identify and sympathize with some of her husband's worries and concerns. She became better able to see the world through his eyes. The opportunity to tell her therapist, "You know, I guess I really don't like him," enabled Rose to be more accepting of her husband than she had been for years. Gaining insight into negative feelings often enables an individual to be more objective about the situation that gave rise to the feelings in the first place. In this case, Rose was able to ask herself the question, "Why does he behave as he does toward me?" and this thought then allowed her to think about the specific behaviors in the situation rather than about her angry feelings.

An important feature of many forms of psychotherapy is **transference,** the displacement by the client of affect and feelings from one important person (mother, father, spouse) to another—specifically, the therapist. In **positive transference,** the patient feels predominantly friendly and affectionate toward the therapist. In **negative transference** hostility predominates. **Countertransference** refers to the therapist's emotional reactions to a patient. It is important for the success of treatment that the therapist be aware of the countertransference reactions. They may also provide important clues to the client's relationships with others. Psychoanalysts must be analyzed themselves because of the belief that their self-insight will increase their awareness of their countertransference reactions (see Figure 17-1).

In asking that question, Jenkins showed insight and came close to making an interpretation of his behavior toward the therapist (seeing him as a loser like his father). Interpretations of behavior that arise during psychotherapy sessions may be made by either the therapist or the client.

Many people go into psychotherapy expecting to be told what is wrong with them and what to do about it, but psychodynamically-oriented psychotherapists usually limit their intervention to making interpretations when they seem especially appropriate and the client seems unable to make or express them. Through these interpretations, therapists seek to expose areas of conflict, portions of which have been unconscious, and to help the client understand past psychological events. During therapy, individuals may be confronted with an interpretation that they have an interest in not acknowledging. They may become irritated with the therapist for confronting them, and in an effort to protect themselves they may try to think of more acceptable, but incorrect, explanations for their behavior. Most therapists prefer that clients evolve their own interpretations and then use them to achieve self-understanding with the help of the therapist. Psychodynamic treatment is aimed at helping clients place their motivations in perspective and redirect the influence of the motivations on everyday life.

In psychoanalysis, transference and countertransference reactions are ultimately addressed. In other forms of psychotherapy, interpretations of these processes might be less important than dealing with the pressing problems in the client's day-to-day life. This does not mean that transference and countertransference do not occur or that the therapist doesn't think they are important. It means that the therapist has decided to give the highest priority to the problems that the client feels are most crucial. In some cases psychotherapists wish that they could explore certain aspects of the client's thinking but conclude that the client isn't ready to engage in such exploration.

In the initial stages of psychotherapy, tentative answers must be sought to a number of questions:

- Why did the client come to me?
- What are the pressing problems from the client's point of view?
- What underlying or unconscious problems is the client not aware of?
- Will it be possible to help the client explore these underlying problems?

The answers to these questions help the therapist set objectives and decide on tactics for later stages of therapy. The psychodynamic therapist hopes that, as a result of therapy, unconscious conflicts will be exposed and dealt with and that patients will be able to see themselves, their past lives, and people important to them in a more realistic light.

Gaining Access to the Unconscious Psychotherapists who are psychoanalytically oriented usually seek to uncover their patients' forgotten thoughts and emo-

tions. These therapists believe that repressed memories of traumatic experiences contribute to the problems for which clients seek treatment, that the veil of repression lifts as therapy proceeds and previously unaccessible material is dealt with.

One of the questions that arises in connection with efforts to lift this veil is: Are the recovered memories correct? Because the trauma-linked material recovered often pertains to early childhood, it may not be possible to obtain objective confirmation that the recovered memories are true. Did the traumatic events the patient remembers really take place or might the recovered memories be the patient's response to the therapist's suggestions that the traumatic experiences had occurred or might have occurred? Because of the possibility that the allegedly repressed memories are false, several writers have questioned the validity of the idea of the lifting of repression (Loftus, 1993; Loftus & Ketcham, 1994; Ofshe & Watters, 1994). The fallibility and malleability of memory is familiar to anyone who has had his or her vivid recall of a third-birthday party shattered by a grainy home movie. One's present bad life situation (for example, being in an acrimonious marriage) and the need to explain it might well distort a person's memories. In addition, a therapist's beliefs about the causes of a person's psychological problems might also distort memories by directing a patient's thought in a particular direction.

Recovered memories about childhood sexual abuse and other traumatic experiences may well be correct, but what is often lacking is objective evidence of their validity. Without this type of verification it becomes conjectural whether recovered memories are correct, or due to inadequacies of the therapeutic method, to the workings of the patient's or therapist's mind, or to some other factor. Such possibilities make it clear that a significant challenge confronts psychodynamic therapists and researchers: When can memories be trusted? The remembrance of things past can be a mysterious process, with realities and myths blending into a vivid—but, perhaps, incorrect—picture (see Box 17-1). However, one recent study has provided evidence that many people do forget traumatic experiences in childhood (Williams, 1994). The subjects were women with previously documented histories of sexual abuse in childhood. Close to 40 percent of these women did not recall the abuse that had been reported 17 years earlier. Women who were younger at the time of the abuse and those who were molested by someone they knew were more likely to have no recall of the abuse. Long periods with no memory of abuse cannot be taken as evidence that the abuse did not occur. Why people create false memories and why they forget actual events are important topics that require intensive research.

False Memories

Harold I. Lief, a respected and experienced psychiatrist, poses questions that he and many other clinicians are now raising concerning the recovery of unconscious material.

Imagine that you are consulted by parents whose adult daughter has just accused her father of incestuous relations a decade or more after the alleged sexual abuse occurred. Who to believe—the parents or the adult child?

On the one hand, sex abuse is a frequent and frightful experience with potentially disastrous consequences for adult adaptation. On the other hand, a false allegation of incest will rip apart a family, inflicting a blow from which few families can fully recover. What a dilemma for the psychiatrist!

What if you believe that the therapist treating the adult "victim" has unduly influenced the patient by a style of interviewing in which suggestion, perhaps even hypnosis, has been used to elicit

memories of abuse? How reliable are such memories?

The issue of real versus false allegations of child sexual abuse, which haunted Freud, still haunts us today but for different reasons. We need to research the frequency of false accusations, the motives for making them, the role of the therapists in generating them, and the relationship between repressed memories and the process by which they are recalled.

(Lief, 1992, p. 8)

In 1994, a special committee of the American Psychological Association issued a report on memories of abuse. The report acknowledges both the possibility of remembering long-forgotten memories of abuse and of constructing convincing pseudo-memories for events that never occurred. These were the committee's conclusions.

- Controversies about adult recollections should not obscure the fact that

child sexual abuse is a complex, pervasive problem in America that has historically been unacknowledged.
- Most people who were sexually abused as children remember all or part of what happened to them.
- It is possible for memories of abuse that have been forgotten for a long time to be remembered, although the mechanisms by which this might happen are not well understood.
- It is possible to construct convincing pseudo-memories for events that never occurred, although the mechanisms by which this occurs are not well understood.
- There are gaps in knowledge about the processes that lead to accurate or inaccurate recollection of childhood sexual abuse.

The committee also noted the importance of (1) therapists approaching questions of childhood abuse from a neutral position and (2) individuals looking for a psychotherapist to seek a licensed practitioner who has training and experience in the issues for which treatment is sought.

Hypnosis Hypnosis is an approach taken by some psychotherapists as a means of recovering repressed memories and helping patients deal with them. Hypnosis involves a process of inducing a trancelike state in which the person being hypnotized is receptive to suggestions made by the hypnotist. In addition to receptivity to suggestion, the hypnotic state is characterized by an altered state of consciousness in which focused attention and concentration appear to be maximized. The hypnotized person seems exceptionally attentive to inner experience during the hypnotic session. Some psychotherapists use hypnosis for a variety of purposes: to suggest specific changes in thinking or behavior, as an aid in psychotherapy (for example, to help a client overcome anxiety or deal with upsetting ideas), and to enhance relaxation. Although the technique has been used clinically for years, research on hypnosis is in its infancy. There is considerable controversy over what hypnosis actually is and whether it really involves a special trancelike state. Because of its success in inducing states that appear to involve relaxation, it has aroused the interest of behavior therapists as well as psychotherapists (Weitzenhoffer, 1989).

It is now known that hypnosis is an altered state of consciousness—an intense alertness in which the mind

can screen out extraneous matters and focus on particular details. The hypnotic trance is characterized by extreme relaxation and heightened susceptibility to suggestion. It allows people to suspend logical reasoning and draw upon psychological strengths that they do not normally command voluntarily. The focused concentration and heightened suggestibility of the trance state help the individual accept the therapist's directions and come to grips with problems more rapidly.

Hypnotists typically begin their sessions by asking subjects to stare at an object, suggesting in a soothing voice that they are relaxing and becoming hypnotized, and that they will find it easy to comply with the hypnotist's suggestions (see Figure 17-2). In experimental settings this "hypnotic induction" typically lasts for about 15 minutes. If the subjects are willing to be hypnotized, they appear relaxed and drowsy and become responsive to test suggestions from the hypnotist. Afterward they report changes in bodily sensations and claim that they have been hypnotized. People who are susceptible to hypnosis have beliefs and expectations that motivate them to adopt the hypnotic state. They usually have better than average ability to focus attention, as well as a vivid imagination.

While the potential for emotional exploitation or

Figure 17-2 A competent hypnotist can induce a trance in a variety of ways in about 10 minutes. A traditional method is to relax the subject and to direct attention—in a confident, rhythmic, monotonous, repetitive voice—to sensations that are usually ignored: "Your hand is getting heavier and heavier; it feels so heavy it is hard to keep it raised; it is becoming even heavier."

deception is inherent in all forms of psychotherapy and all forms of human influence, this potential is a particular danger of hypnosis. For this reason, therapists disapprove of stage magicians who use hypnosis casually as entertainment. Inappropriate suggestions may create turmoil and conflict even though the patient does not act on them. That kind of harm is most likely when hypnosis is performed for its own sake or for the therapist's gratification. Hypnosis is not a treatment for severe mental disorders such as schizophrenia and major depression, but it has been used for almost everything else—from phobias to sexual problems and psychosomatic illnesses, to bedwetting and nail-biting in children.

Under hypnosis, a person experiences a suspension of critical judgment and a state of heightened suggestibility and responsiveness to social cues. Because of the memories that can be created during this state, it is important that the therapist refrain from unduly influencing the patient. This means asking questions like, "What happens next?" rather than, "How did he sexually abuse you?" Hypnosis allows the patient to turn on memories of traumatic experiences during the psychotherapeutic session, and then shut them off at its conclusion. Although the scientific study of hypnosis is a relatively recent development, much has been learned about how it works and its effects. We now know that there are wide differences among people in their susceptibility to hypnosis. Instances of post-hypnotic amnesia are commonly reported. That is, if told to forget what occurred under hypnosis, some suggestible subjects show an absence of recall until they are later told by the hypnotist that they can remember. Because hypnosis does not seem to be a distinct physiological state and because

hypnotized and nonhypnotized subjects often behave in identical ways, psychologists have sought to understand hypnosis in terms of such psychological processes as dissociation, imagination, and role-playing.

Humanistic and Existential Therapies

Several forms of psychotherapy either disagree with the assumptions of psychoanalytic theory or modify them in certain ways. The neo-Freudians accept most psychodynamic principles but reject the emphasis placed by psychoanalytic theory on instinctual unconscious impulses. **Humanistic therapies** emphasize people's desire to achieve self-respect. **Existential therapies** emphasize the need to confront basic questions of existence, such as: What is the meaning of my life? Am I hiding from myself?

Common to humanistic and existential approaches is a focus on the client's experience in the therapy situation and the view that each individual is the expert concerning his or her unique experience in life. These approaches seek to foster a person's potential for growth, self-determination, and choice. They hold that new awarenesses and the creation of new meanings are the basis of behavioral change. These therapeutic approaches share the view that an effective relationship with the therapist is crucial in bringing about this change.

Humanistic Therapy **Client-centered therapy** is a leading example of the humanistic approach applied to psychotherapy. Carl Rogers, its founder, saw the individual as seeking personal growth but needing the support of an appreciative, accepting therapist. The therapist is a nondirective facilitator who encourages the client's self-exploration and efforts to achieve greater maturity and self-confidence. Whereas in traditional psychodynamic therapy the therapeutic relationship—including transference and countertransference—and the therapist's interpretations help clients solve personal problems, in client-centered therapy a nonjudgmental therapist facilitates the process of self-understanding by serving as a mirror for the client.

As a group, client-centered therapists have been among the leaders in research about what actually goes on in psychotherapy. Rogers saw psychotherapy as a growth process and encouraged objective study of the events that occur as therapy progresses. He recognized that people's ideas and ways of looking at the world influence their emotional lives.

The client-centered therapist believes that perceptions and cognitions determine whether an individual has warm, positive interpersonal relationships or strained relationships that stir up unpleasant emotions. As the client restructures his or her view of the world, troubling emotions such as anxiety and anger become less potent. For example:

> When I started coming here, I saw my problem as anger— toward other people as well as myself. There were times I felt like a seething inferno. You sat there as I ranted and raved and I really appreciated the fact that you listened so attentively to everything I said. Sometimes you would reflect back to me what I had just said, sometimes you would just ask a question about a comment I had made. I don't really know how it happened but I began thinking about why I get so angry at home. Then a lot of things fell into place. I was angry because I was doing things I didn't want to do. I was doing those things out of guilt and obligation. Why should I think I had to be nice to people I can't stand? When I finally realized that I didn't have to do certain things, I became more spontaneous and less angry.

Client-centered therapists believe that people are not innately destructive, but they do have negative feelings. From the client-centered perspective, these feelings are considered to be an outgrowth of externally imposed distortions that force people to alter their behaviors and feelings much as a seed, trapped under a brick, is forced to contort its growth to reach air and sun. Rogers thought of therapy as present-oriented and existential. Labels and diagnoses were not useful. What was needed was **unconditional positive regard,** reflected in the therapist's nonjudgmental, empathetic listening. Whereas a behavior therapist would concentrate on getting clients to change their behavior, a Rogerian therapist would focus on supplying an environment in which the client feels free to express thoughts and feelings. The client-centered therapists assume that unconditional positive regard will increase the client's self-acceptance and self-knowledge, which, in turn, will lead the client to change his or her behavior.

Existential Therapy Existential therapies also emphasize the present and the need to recognize the uniqueness of each client. Existential therapists work as partners with their clients. Many combine humanistic and psychodynamic approaches in dealing with anxiety, its causes, and the defenses that the client erects to cope with it. In this sense, the existential approach is a therapeutic hybrid.

The emphasis of existential therapy is on helping clients come to terms with basic issues concerning the meaning and direction of their lives and the choices by which they shape their own destinies. Like the majority of clinicians who see nonhospitalized clients, most existential therapists work with people who are troubled by anxiety and depression. Existential therapists see their primary role as helping lonely people make constructive choices and become confident enough to fulfill their

unique selves rather than repressing or distorting their experiences.

Existential therapists believe that the task of creating and revising one's life design is lifelong. It is not something that, once accomplished, need never be reexamined or revised. One's own growth and maturing; the contingencies of living with others, each having a somewhat different life design; and the unpredictability of life generally combine to demand repeated attention to one's personal life view. For existential therapists, life always requires that people create, and revise as needed, a framework within which to discover the meanings of living (Bugental & McBeath, 1995).

Gestalt Therapy Gestalt therapy focuses on clients' perceptions of themselves and the world. It is based on the recognition that people unconsciously organize their perceptions as a *Gestalt:* a meaningful, integrated whole. A Gestalt therapist uses a variety of techniques, including role playing, in an effort to stimulate the client to express strong emotions.

Fritz Perls, the founder of Gestalt therapy, stressed the relationships among distorted perceptions, motivations, and emotions. Unlike most humanistic therapists, who stress the importance of unconditional positive regard for the client, Perls (1969) believed that the therapist's main task was to frustrate the client, to make him or her angry enough to fight out conflicts with authority and thereby develop enhanced feelings of self-worth. Perls believed that instead of trying to reconstruct the history of the client's relationships with others as is done in traditional psychodynamic therapy and psychoanalysis, the therapist should stress the client's moment-to-moment experiences as each session progresses.

Gestalt therapists believe that anxiety and personality disorders arise when people dissociate parts of themselves, particularly their need for personal gratification, from awareness. Because dreams often contain clues to dissociated parts of the self, Gestalt therapists encourage discussion and acting out of dreams.

Cognitive Psychotherapy

The **cognitive psychotherapies** use conversation as the vehicle for achieving change, but psychodynamics (such as repression and transference) are not their focus. Rather, they seek to correct misconceptions that contribute to maladjustment, defeat, and unhappiness. Imagine someone who, as a result of the vicissitudes of life, develops a faulty belief to the effect that "no one could possibly like me if I reveal my true self." Such a person is likely to avoid others, refrain from spontaneous behavior, and pine away in loneliness. Another set of circumstances may convince someone that a series of incidents of "bad luck" means that whatever happens next is likely to be disastrous. Thereupon the individual becomes fearful of the immediate future. Or, after many frustrations and conflicts, a person becomes so anxious that he or she is convinced that a "nervous breakdown" is imminent. The person then tries to avoid all stress even though the best approach would probably be coping with normal stresses—since success in handling them would provide the only convincing evidence of mental well-being. As Figure 17-3 indicates, even misconceptions that might seem positive may cause people problems and can also be a focus in cognitive therapy.

Since opinions, beliefs, or conceptions are ordinarily formed on the basis of evidence, adequate or inadequate, we can also assume that beliefs may be modified by evidence. Psychotherapy may, in fact, provide one of the few situations in which individuals are encouraged to think somewhat systematically about their beliefs, particularly their beliefs about themselves. A number of psychotherapeutic approaches share the assumption that maladaptive behavior is a product of unrealistic perceptions and conditions. The various cognitive therapies use different tactics in redirecting the way people see and interpret their experiences, but they all generally reject the Freudian emphasis on the powerful role of unconscious drives.

An early cognitive approach to therapy was developed by George Kelly. Kelly's (1955) **psychology of personal constructs** led him to ask clients to examine the roles they played in interacting with others and the assumptions underlying those roles. In his **fixed-role**

Figure 17-3 Is this the real world? If this man believes that he deserves this sort of hero's welcome all the time, he may need help in coping with the letdowns that will occur when he is not welcomed as a conquering hero.

SOURCE: Drawing by Frascino; © 1987 *The New Yorker* Magazine, Inc.

therapy Kelly encouraged his clients to practice new roles and relationships. Kelly saw people as problem-solvers whose faulty beliefs and assumptions often lead to undesirable solutions to the problems of living. According to Kelly, by encouraging the client to discuss personal constructs and social roles, the therapist helps the client question and reevaluate aspects of his or her life that arouse anxiety.

Another clinical approach based on cognitive theory is Albert Ellis's **rational-emotive therapy.** Ellis (1970) believes that self-defeating thinking is at the root of maladaptive behavior. Such thinking is based on arbitrary, inaccurate assumptions about oneself and others. It is often marked by a preoccupation with "musts": "I *must* always be friendly to people," "I *must* not disappoint my parents," "I *must* be a big success." In rational-emotive therapy these "musts" are seen as causes of emotional arousal, which, if maintained at too high a level for too long a time, result in psychological and physical wearing down. Therapists who adhere to this approach believe that most of these and other self-defeating "musts" are pounded into our heads as children, and we tend to accept them without question. Thus, rational-emotive therapy has two goals: to get people to question these fundamental, but mistaken, beliefs, and then to exchange them for more constructive ones (Rorer, 1989a, 1989b).

During the course of therapy the cognitive therapist actually demonstrates the ways in which unrealistic self-verbalizations can create or worsen emotional problems. The therapist also actively questions and contradicts faulty, unreasonable assumptions by the client and suggests alternative ways of thinking. Role playing is often used, with the therapist demonstrating the behavioral consequences of different types of beliefs.

Aaron Beck's (1976) cognitive therapy is also directed toward the thoughts that underlie intense, persistent emotional reactions. Beck's technique involves frequent, gentle questioning of the client about the basis for what he or she is saying. Beck speaks of "automatic thoughts" that seem to arise by themselves, without reasoning. These thoughts are accepted as valid even though they are not the products of rational consideration of alternatives. Children who simply accept their parents' values without questioning them are engaging in automatic thought. According to Beck, therapy should be aimed at terminating automatic thinking and replacing it with thoughts that result from rational consideration of alternatives.

Beck's cognitive therapy has been used with various forms of maladaptive behavior, but he has specialized in work with depressed people. In this work, emphasis is placed on the irrational ideas that contribute to feelings of depression and thoughts of suicide. The approach basically consists of a collaborative inquiry into the validity of clients' false beliefs about themselves, the world at large, or the future. For example, a client who believes he or she is a worthless individual may be encouraged to offer evidence in support of that view and then be asked to consider possible alternative interpretations of such evidence. In addition, the client might be assigned the task of empirically testing the validity of a depressive belief. Eventually, the weight of evidence should serve to undermine the depressive attitude (Beck & Weishaar, 1989).

The working hypothesis of cognitive therapy is that the best way to solve emotional problems is to alter the patient's thinking through cognitive restructuring. This form of psychotherapy concentrates mainly on the way people perceive the world and how they reason about it in everyday situations. Various techniques are used to expose and correct biased attention and recall, misinterpretation of events and statements, false assumptions, rigid beliefs, unjustified generalizations, inferences based on insufficient evidence, and other errors.

Brief Psychotherapies

Although psychotherapy is often thought of as a lengthy, even leisurely exploration of the inner life, in fact most psychotherapy is relatively brief (fewer than 12 sessions). During recent years there has been an increased trend toward limiting how long psychotherapy lasts (Olfson & Pincus, 1994). Contributing to this trend has been the growth of health insurance programs that pay for patients' psychotherapy but place a limit on the number of therapy sessions for which payments will be made. Brief therapies usually have specific goals or targets, such as helping an individual cope with a pressing problem or distressing life event (for example, the death of a loved one). Today, many therapists who perform brief therapy make use of a variety of techniques and theoretical approaches. Interpersonal therapy illustrates the time-limited approaches that are increasingly being used.

Interpersonal Therapy Interpersonal therapy was originally designed for people suffering from depression. Because of its success with this group, its use is now being extended to other types of problems. It is usually conducted in weekly 50-minute sessions for 12 to 16 weeks. The first step is a structured interview dealing with symptoms, family history, and current and recent events in the patient's life. After this, the therapist makes a tentative diagnosis and discusses it with the patient so that they can agree on a therapy plan.

Interpersonal therapists are especially interested in the interpersonal relationships that play a role in a person's thoughts or mood. For example, some depressed people feel abandoned and hopeless because they are undergoing a delayed or distorted form of mourning. Their lives may have changed radically after a marital separation or death in the family. Interpersonal therapists are attentive to role disputes that may involve incompatible expectations of people who are constantly in one another's company—husbands and wives, parents and children, friends, co-workers, and so on. The word "dispute" may be misleading, since conflicting expectations are usually not made explicit, and the resulting hostility is perpetuated by faulty communication as well as by unreconciled differences. Interpersonal therapists introduce these issues only if the patient hints at them, but they have to listen carefully, because many people are so preoccupied with themselves that they hardly notice other people's expectations and concerns. Where appropriate, the interpersonal therapist helps the patient to reinterpret complaints and examine suppressed feelings and thoughts. Other issues with which interpersonal therapists deal are role transitions (for example, moving, graduating, the birth of a child) and interpersonal deficits (which are often reflected in social isolation).

Unlike many kinds of psychotherapy, interpersonal therapy has been defined and outlined with some precision. For example, there is a published manual for therapists (Klerman et al., 1984). Its goal usually is relief of symptoms within a certain time period.

How Effective Is Psychotherapy?

Many groups have a stake in the evaluation of therapeutic effectiveness. Patients, their families, therapists, researchers, insurance companies, legislators, and planners of mental-health services all want to know about effectiveness. However, evaluating a type of therapy in a given instance is not just a matter of checking its effectiveness generally. A generally effective therapy in the hands of an ineffective therapist could be harmful to patients. Beyond that, there are misdiagnoses that can lead to poor matches between therapies and therapists, on the one hand, and patients, on the other. In some cases, therapy helps a person, but only after one or more frustrating experiences with a therapist who is not helpful. Clearly, evaluating therapies, therapists, and the therapy process are important tasks for clinicians and the public (see Box 17-2).

Given that there are many types of psychotherapy, it is obvious that researchers have their work cut out for them. Obtaining information about therapeutic effectiveness is not easy for a number of reasons. For example, individual therapists differ in their ability to carry out particular therapies. Furthermore, some therapies may be more effective with certain types of patients than others. Psychotherapy is not a single process applied to a single problem. Research on therapy is improving as studies become more complex and incorporate more relevant factors into their research designs. For many reasons, researchers cannot conduct studies on the effectiveness of different therapies in the same way that laboratory studies are usually carried out. Table 17-2 summarizes some of the practical differences between these types of studies.

Before a clinical research project is carried out, there must be agreement on how to measure the results. For example, suppose a researcher intends to assess the effectiveness of a type of psychotherapy designed to reduce the tendency to hallucinate. One way to measure the dependent variable would be to count the number of times people report having hallucinatory experiences. But people might have hallucinations that they did not report, or might make up such experiences just to have something to report. Thus, whereas some clinicians might contend that frequency of reported hallucinations is a reasonable index of the general tendency to hallucinate, others might not be satisfied with this conclusion.

In any research, all groups of subjects must be as similar or equal as possible before the experiment begins. The therapists in the various groups should also be comparable. Most studies of therapy techniques compare a group of people who receive treatment with one or two groups of people who do not. But such comparisons do not show how individuals within the groups are affected by specific aspects of the treatment. Clinicians also need to know how changes in the client's behavior are related to what the clinician does or says.

Because of these complexities and despite hundreds of research studies, there are disagreements about the relative effectiveness of the different psychological therapies. Researchers with different criteria and expectations have obtained different results from such comparisons. For example, after reviewing the literature, Eysenck (1952, 1961) concluded that psychotherapy was an ineffective clinical method. He argued that many apparent successes could be explained by **spontaneous remissions,** in which the client's symptoms would have disappeared in time with or without treatment. Bergin and Lambert (1978) found that psychotherapy had an effect but that the effect was not necessarily positive. Some patients actually seemed to deteriorate because of psychotherapy.

Components of Effective Psychotherapy Overall, the research evidence suggests that psychotherapy is effective—but not enormously so—and that no one psychotherapeutic approach is clearly superior to any other (Lambert & Bergin, 1994). The evidence that in many instances psychotherapy, rather than a particular brand of a psychotherapy, has positive effects has contributed to interest in identifying factors common to different therapies that might be the active ingredients. Particular

emphasis is being placed on therapist variables and the therapist-patient match. The therapist's ability to instill hope in people who are upset may be especially important.

Research on the nature of psychological therapies has explored the characteristics, attitudes, and behavior of the client and therapist in addition to the therapeutic technique used. What goes on in therapy sessions can be characterized in terms of the operation of two sets of factors. **Technique factors** are the procedures employed by the therapist, which may or may not match the descriptions of those procedures found in books and manuals. **Interpersonal factors** refer to the social chemistry or dynamics of the relationship between the therapist and the client. While it would be convenient if technique factors were the only ingredients in therapy, interpersonal factors not only are important but can be decisive in influencing the outcome. For example, a study of treatment for substance-use disorders found that therapists showed widely different rates of effectiveness and that high effectiveness was associated with the therapist's possession of strong interpersonal skills (Najavits & Weiss, 1994).

An example of the importance of interpersonal factors is provided by a study that included groups of trained and untrained therapists (Strupp & Hadley, 1979). One group consisted of experienced professional psychotherapists; the other group, of Vanderbilt University professors who were selected on the basis of their widely recognized interest in their students, their accessibility, and their willingness to listen to and help students solve personal problems. None of the professors had worked in the field of psychology or in any other "helping" profession. The subjects were college students, most of whom complained of anxiety. Each student was assigned to either a professional or a nonprofessional therapist. A third group of subjects constituted a control group. Each control subject went through an assessment procedure, but the start of therapy was delayed.

The study found no significant differences that could be attributed to the type of therapist to which a given client had been assigned. Clients who were treated by either psychotherapists or professors showed more improvement than the control subjects. The measures of change included the students' own ratings, judgments by independent experts, MMPI scores, and clinicians' evaluations of their clients' progress. Favorable outcomes were most prevalent among clients whose therapists actively provided them with information, encouragement, and opinions. The therapists whose clients improved were those who made special efforts to facilitate the discussion of problems, focused on the here and now rather than on early-childhood experiences, and encouraged the client to seek new social activities. Thus, the personal qualities of the therapist clearly are a very important factor in therapeutic process.

Examining the Process of Psychotherapy

Studies of therapeutic effectiveness contain valuable information but by no means tell the whole story of psychotherapy. Also needed are analyses of the ingredients of effective therapy. After all, if something works, we want to know why it works. **Process research** is concerned with the elements of psychotherapy; that is, what actually happens in therapy. This research explores such topics as the following:

1. The therapist-patient relationship;
2. The patient's goals, and whether they change over time (see Figure 17-4);
3. The therapist's goals, and whether they change over time;
4. The content of therapeutic sessions and changes in content over time;
5. Types of emotional expression at different phases of the therapeutic process;
6. How the patient and therapist perceive the sessions;
7. Whether the sessions focus on achieving insight or direct behavior modification.

Researchers who study the therapeutic process seek to identify the events, beliefs, and attitudes in psychotherapy that contribute to patient improvement.

Such improvement is displayed in patients' behavior and feelings. For example, researchers need to determine if therapists' and patients' goals in therapy are the same. There is evidence that psychodynamically-oriented therapists place greater value on the achievement of insight than do their patients. On the other hand, patients rate reassurance and support from the therapist more highly than do their therapists (Llewelyn, 1988). Further inquiry is needed into how patients' and therapists' perceptions

Figure 17-4 "But what if you get me back to reality and I don't *like* it?"

SOURCE: © 1989; reprinted courtesy of Bunny Hoest and *Parade* Magazine.

If psychological therapies are effective in treating specific clinical problems, an important question is, which events in therapy sessions are the active ingredients, the ones that actually bring about change? Evidence from studies like the one just described suggests that the active ingredients might be interpersonal factors and not the therapeutic process as usually described in textbooks. The following characteristics of therapists may influence the process of change and, thus, the outcome of therapy: warmth, friendliness, genuineness, interpersonal style, beliefs, values, and prejudices. In addition to the therapist's personality, his or her age, sex, and socioeconomic background may also play a role in the therapeutic process (see Figure 17-5). The means by which therapists' charac-

teristics are communicated to the client include the therapist's appearance and his or her verbal and nonverbal behavior.

TABLE 17-2
Differences Between Experimental Laboratory Studies and Evaluation of Therapy

Factor	Laboratory Study	Psychotherapy
Independent variables	Usually quite clearly defined	Complex, often difficult to define clearly
Dependent variables	Usually quite clearly defined	Often involve complex set of responses that change over time
Experimental situation	Well-controlled	Not possible to eliminate unexpected events
Other situations	Researchers usually not concerned about what happens to subject outside experimental situation	Therapist is interested in outcome for client outside therapy situation

BOX 17-2

of their relationship and of events in psychotherapy relate to clinical outcomes (Garfield, 1990; Strupp, 1989).

Video and audio recordings of therapy sessions provide objective evidence of the events that take place in them and the tactics employed by therapists. In the following case, the taped session provided this verbatim account as the therapist skillfully enabled the patient to express her fears of being rejected by the therapist.

Therapist: We've gotten to know each other a lot better since our first session. Is there anything you've been afraid to tell me?

Patient: I'm not sure.

Therapist: Sometimes patients are afraid to tell their therapist something, especially if they think it'll put them in a bad light. Could that be true for you?

Patient: Yes. There is something. But I don't want to tell you.

Therapist: How are you predicting I'll react?

Patient: You'll think I'm terrible.

—Beck and Freeman, 1990, p. 268

After a discussion of the patient's fear of rejection and with support from the therapist, the patient revealed a traumatic pattern of childhood sexual abuse of which she felt very ashamed. The discussion that ensued permitted valuable progress to be made in establishing a nondefensive working relationship between the patient and therapist. Had the therapist not taken the initiative in bringing out the patient's fears, the patient might never have been able to experience the therapist's acceptance of her as a person.

In addition to providing support and acceptance, good therapists give their patients the opportunities to learn that the world may not be as punishing a place as they think it is. The therapist may serve as a model who disconfirms the patient's irrational or unnecessarily pessimistic beliefs about the nature of interpersonal relationships—as shown in the following case.

A patient complained that she could not feel close to men. She was burdened by the unconscious belief that unless she was totally compliant with a man's wishes, he would feel insulted and reject her. She soon began to respond to the male therapist in the same way, withdrawing from him out of fear that she might feel forced to accept damaging interpretations or follow bad advice. So

she unconsciously decided that before confronting any other problems she would have to change her belief in the need for compliance. Encouraged by her therapist, she decided to test the belief through trial actions.

Once she questioned some of the therapist's comments and felt relieved when the therapist was not upset; he had passed her test. He pointed out her exaggerated fear of hurting him. As a result, she felt less constrained by her unrealistic belief, less anxious and defensive. She relaxed some of the repression she had maintained in obedience to the belief and recalled that her father used to sulk whenever she challenged him. She then began to challenge the therapist more directly, and at the same time felt more able to cooperate with him. Once she knew that she did not have to agree with his ideas, she could like him and take his ideas seriously. She also began to feel more comfortable with her boyfriend and was able to work on problems she would have been afraid to confront before.

Research on the process of psychotherapy requires evaluation of therapists' ability to form working alliances with patients. Study of therapists, as well as types of therapies, are needed in the scientific study of the therapeutic process.

Meta-Analysis A technique known as **meta-analysis** can be used to summarize the results of many studies. Meta-analysis involves (1) grouping studies in which treatment conditions have been compared with an untreated control condition on one or more measures of outcome; (2) statistically determining the therapeutic effects on different groups using the available measures; and (3) averaging the sizes of the effects across the studies that the researcher wants to compare. In this way groups receiving psychotherapy can be compared with untreated control groups and groups receiving other therapeutic approaches, such as systematic desensitization and behavior modification. Figure 17-6 provides an example of a meta-analysis of 475 studies of the effects of psychotherapy. This meta-analysis showed that the average client receiving therapy was generally better off in a measurable way than 75 percent of people who received no treatment, and was also better off with respect to the alleviation of fear and anxiety than were 83 percent of the untreated controls (Smith, et al., 1980). Subsequent studies have also yielded results showing that patients given psychotherapy

have better outcomes than people in untreated control groups.

Meta-analysis is a way of quantifying outcome measures so that they can be combined over many studies. Whether meta-analysis is the best way to answer questions about therapeutic effectiveness is still being debated.

The number of meta-analytic studies is increasing, and so is their complexity (Rosenthal, 1991). Greater complexity is needed, in part because researchers do not want to be criticized for mixing studies that are not similar. The results of meta-analysis are harder to interpret if the effect sizes from fundamentally different types of studies are lumped together. Perhaps the sharpest criticism of meta-analysis is that comparisons of studies that are methodologically weak can add little to an ultimate evaluation of therapeutic effects. On the other hand, meta-analysis of tighter, more homogeneous studies could prove very enlightening. Unfortunately, so many factors are relevant to therapy outcomes that there are insufficient studies incorporating all these factors to permit the most meaningful meta-analyses. For example, it

(a)

(b)

(c)

Figure 17-5 There is evidence that what goes on early in the patient-therapist relationship may be an important predictor of outcome. Although a patient who has an early negative reaction to his or her therapist may eventually be able to work productively with the therapist, a successful therapeutic outcome is more likely if the reaction is warm and positive. One factor in positive or negative reactions to the therapy situation is the patient's first impression of the therapist. Which of these therapists would you prefer to go to? Rank your preferences and think about the basis for the ranking.

is quite conceivable that certain types of therapy used with certain types of patients are highly effective when certain outcome measures, but not others, are used. The results might be different using other therapies, patients, clinical problems, and outcome measures.

An example of this specificity is research on cognitive therapy as a treatment for panic reactions as well as for depression. In one experiment, 17 patients averaged four panic attacks a week at the start; they had only one a week after six weeks of cognitive therapy and none at all when they completed treatment (Sokol et al., 1989). All were still free of symptoms after a year, and their depression and general anxiety were also greatly reduced. Figure 17-7 illustrates some results of this study. In contrast to the long-term success of cognitive therapy, people given drug treatment for panic attacks tend to relapse within a few months when they are taken off the drug (Sokol et al., 1989). Cognitive therapy has been more successful than most other psychological therapies in the treatment of panic attacks.

Another example of the importance of specificity is a meta-analysis showing that in psychotherapies of fewer than 12 sessions, the nonpsychoanalytic treatments were clearly better than their alternatives, but that when there were more than 12 sessions, the psychoanalytic therapies fared better (Grauwe, 1987). Finally, a meta-analysis of the effectiveness of psychotherapy with children showed that children whose therapy took place as part of a clinical research project had greater and more lasting improvement than children seen in community clinics that were not part of a research project (Weisz et al., 1992).

Cognitive-Behavioral Therapies

So far, we have discussed only those therapies in which conversational interchanges are the primary vehicle used to treat people with problems. We turn now to some psychologically based approaches that are more action-oriented, directed toward changing specific types of maladaptive behavior, and usually follow a carefully laid out plan for strengthening or weakening target responses.

These approaches originally grew out of learning theories dealing with the acquisition and extinction of behavioral responses. They tended to be behavioristic, eschew discussion of mental events, and focus on identifiable stimuli and responses. Cognition, affect, and motivation, since they were not amenable to direct

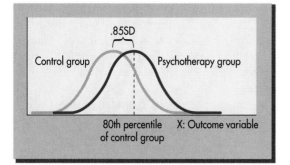

Figure 17-6 Meta-analysis involves the statistical combination of many separate and often very different studies. The figure illustrates the general findings of an analysis that combined 475 controlled studies of therapeutic effectiveness. The average person in the treated group was 0.85 standard deviations above the mean for the control group on the measures used to evaluate therapeutic outcome. This difference is a large one when compared to the effects of many experimental interventions used in psychology or education. For example, cutting the size of a school class in half causes an increase in achievement of 0.15 standard deviation units. The effect of nine months of instruction in reading is an improvement in reading skills of 0.67 standard deviation units.

SOURCE: Mary Lee Smith, Gene V. Glass, and Thomas I. Miller, *The Benefits of Psychotherapy.* The Johns Hopkins University Press, Baltimore/London, 1980. p. 88.

observation, were held to be beyond the purview of psychological inquiry. Terms such as **behavior therapy** and **behavior modification** were used to describe these approaches.

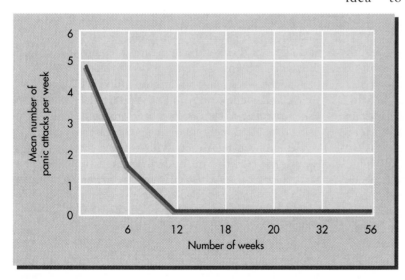

Figure 17-7 Mean number of panic attacks as a function of weeks in treatment.

SOURCE: L. Sokol, A. T. Beck, R. L. Greenberg, F. D. Wright, and R. J. Berchick, Cognitive therapy of panic disorder: A nonpharmacological alternative, *The Journal of Nervous and Mental Disease, 177,* 711–716. Copyright © 1989 by Williams & Wilkins.

Behavior Therapy and Cognitive-Behavior Therapy

Behavior therapy uses operant and classical conditioning-based techniques in efforts to change maladaptive behavior. Table 17-3 lists the basic assumptions of behavior therapy. The operant techniques used in behavior therapy led to an approach referred to as *behavior modification.* The classical conditioning approach resulted in a variety of desensitization techniques used to reduce people's fear of specific situations or particular objects. **Behavior modification** refers to the application of operant learning principles to bring about a specific change in behavior. Although behavior modification originated as a technique based on operant conditioning, combinations of behavioral and cognitive approaches are now the most used approach to programs for behavior change. Operant conditioning methods use schedules of reinforcement and shaping to gradually achieve a desired response. Special prompts might be employed to highlight a situation that calls for a particular response. **Fading** refers to gradual elimination of these special cues when they are no longer needed. Positive reinforcers (such as praise or money) are used to strengthen desired responses. The **token economy** is one of the most common applications of operant principles to modify maladaptive behavior. In a token economy, patients are given reward tokens, such as poker chips, for socially constructive behaviors. The tokens can later be exchanged for desirable items or activities. Extinction procedures and punishment might be used to eliminate undesirable responses. When punishment is employed to eliminate a response, it is a good idea to positively reinforce an alternative, more desirable, response at the same time.

Another major development of recent years is the use of **biofeedback** procedures in which the individual is reinforced whenever a designated change in bodily functioning takes place. Through biofeedback the individual becomes better able to control internal processes, such as body temperature and heart rate, that are related to maladaptation.

Behavior therapy has made important contributions by emphasizing the importance of fine-grained analysis of how individuals react to specific life situations. It has also shown the value of a skills-training orientation to therapy and of specifying therapy outcomes especially relevant for individual patients (Goldfried & Castonguay, 1993).

In the 1970s, as psychology moved in a cognitive direction, it became clear that

TABLE 17-3
Basic Assumptions of Behavior Therapy

1. Most abnormal behavior is acquired and maintained according to the same principles as normal behavior.
2. Most abnormal behavior can be modified through the application of social-learning principles.
3. The current determinants of behavior must be assessed.
4. People are best described by what they think, feel, and do in specific life situations.
5. Treatment methods are precisely specified and objectively evaluated.
6. Treatment outcome is evaluated in terms of generalization to the real-life setting and its maintenance over time.
7. Treatment strategies are individually tailored to different problems in different individuals.
8. Extensive use is made of psychological assistance; from parents and teachers and others, to modify problem behavior in the settings in which it occurs.

Source: Based on O'Leary & Wilson, 1987.

thought processes were frequently as important as environmental influences. As a consequence, interventions were developed to modify cognitions that contribute to maladaptive behavior. The term **cognitive-behavior therapy** refers to these interventions that integrate cognitive and behavioral therapies. Bandura's social-learning theory (see chapter 3), representing an integration of learning and conditioning concepts and a recognition of the importance of symbolic cognitive processes, contributed to the ascendancy of the cognitive-behavioral approach to maladaptive behavior and its treatment.

Cognitive therapies, such as those devised by Kelly and Beck, were developed within traditional psychotherapeutic settings. Cognitive-behavior therapy reflects the increasing interest of therapists in cognitive modification as a means of influencing emotions and behaviors. This approach to therapy makes use of a variety of behavioral techniques, such as a graded program of activities, homework, and role playing, along with an effort to identify and modify unrealistic cognitions. In recent years, cognitive therapists and behavior therapists have freely borrowed techniques from one another. For example, Beck now employs homework assignments in his therapeutic work. Cognitive-behavior therapy builds on behavior therapy.

Psychodynamically oriented therapists often assume that symptoms will disappear after in-depth, lengthy analysis and insight gained about hidden complexes, fantasies, and anxieties. As this joke that pokes fun at these traditional psychodynamic approaches suggests, behavior therapists take a more direct approach to their clients' problems:

A man named John had a maddening compulsion to tear paper. After years of psychoanalysis, John was still tearing paper, and his family was losing all hope. They finally brought John to a new therapist, who walked John around the room, talking quietly to him. When he left the office, John was cured. A year later, John's compulsion was still gone, and the grateful family asked the therapist what he had said to John on that fateful day. The therapist said: "I told him. 'Don't tear paper.'"

Even though they might laugh at this joke, both behaviorally and psychodynamically oriented therapists would perceive it as a great oversimplification of the therapeutic process.

Components of Cognitive-Behavior Therapy

In one sense, cognitive-behavior therapy is not as easily defined as certain other therapies. Psychoanalysts always focus on certain general aspects of their work with patients—for example, transference. On the other hand, cognitive-behavior therapists will use one or several therapeutic interventions that seem appropriate to the needs of particular patients. Let's review some of these therapeutic components.

Relaxation Training Relaxation training often helps people who are tense and generally anxious. In one approach, emphasis is placed on learning to contrast muscular tension with muscular relaxation. In another, meditation procedures are employed. Relaxation therapies appear to be helpful for a variety of psychosomatic disorders, particularly tension headaches and migraine headaches (see chapter 6). However, they usually are not sufficient by themselves. Life styles, social environments, and views of the world can create or compound people's problems in living. Such factors as the quality and nature of available social support and the individual's goals, attitudes, and values often must be addressed. Table 17-4 lists a number of factors that bear on the advisability of using relaxation techniques in a given case.

Research on relaxation skills requires answers to two questions: Has the individual learned the relaxation skill? Does use of the skill lead to beneficial clinical results? Obviously, if the skills were never learned, there would be little reason to expect positive results from relaxation training. Appropriate control groups are needed to provide an adequate basis for judging the effectiveness of the training. There is also a need for studies that explore the effectiveness of relaxation training both alone and in combination with other types of therapy.

Muscular Relaxation Muscular relaxation involves tensing and then relaxing various muscle groups. The individual is encouraged to note the differences between feeling tense and feeling relaxed. Relaxation training is used in many methods of natural childbirth and in yoga. People who have difficulty falling asleep often find that relaxation exercises help them get to sleep more quickly. At first, individuals use relaxation exercises mainly in the therapy situation. But as their ability to relax themselves improves, they are encouraged to perform relaxation exercises in stressful situations that they encounter in everyday life.

Meditation In relaxation training involving meditation, the individual learns to concentrate on a thought, a sensation, a word, an object, or some mental state. Some techniques are very active and require that the person make a strenuous effort to focus on a specific thing. Certain yoga techniques, for example, require that the practitioner maintain specific postures and deliberately control his or her breathing or other bodily functions. Other meditation techniques, such as transcendental meditation (TM), are passive approaches. Practitioners simply remain in a quiet atmosphere and make a relaxed attempt to achieve a state of inner peace. The individual concentrates on a *mantra* (a specially selected word) and tries, but does not strain, to exclude all other thoughts. Most passive techniques are practiced for 20-minute periods each day, typically once in the morning and again before dinner.

Exposure Therapy **Exposure therapies** are based on the principle that continued exposure to anxiety-provoking stimuli will decrease anxiety to manageable levels and reduce phobic responses. **Exposure** consists of a gradual approach to an anxiety-provoking situation. Under such conditions the distress experienced in the situation is kept at a relatively low level.

Exposure to fear-arousing situations is one of the most effective ways of overcoming fear. However, there are positive results only if clients are willing to expose themselves to the situations they are afraid of. Although

in vivo exposure (actually being in the situation) usually works best, **fantasized exposure** (thinking about being in the situation) is also effective. Exposure treatment is appropriate for many unpleasant or disadvantageous emotional responses. If the treatment is effective, improvement can usually be observed within five or six sessions. Figure 17-8 shows the applicability of cognitive-behavioral techniques to the fear of flying.

Flooding is a form of exposure therapy in which the client is exposed to a flood of fear-arousing stimuli that is not terminated simply because the client experiences a high level of tension. In flooding, the clinical session is saturated with frightening thoughts and images in the hope that emotional responses to them will be extinguished through "burnout." If this happens, **extinction** is said to have occurred.

In **implosive therapy** the client experiences higher and higher levels of anxiety through imaginal presentation of scenes depicting behavior and situations that he or she has strenuously avoided in the past. The imagery used in treatment is intended to represent conflict areas that are thought to be the source of the avoidance behavior. The imaginal material used in implosion therapy tends to be much more intense than that used in flooding.

Systematic desensitization combines behavioral training (muscular relaxation) with cognitive activity. It begins with the induction of a relaxed state. While the client is relaxed, he or she imagines scenes related to his or her specific fear. Desensitization begins with scenes or images that are only mildly fear-arousing. The client is encouraged to concentrate on perpetuating the relaxed state while imagining those situations. Once the client

Figure 17-8 Cognitive-behavioral techniques can often take the fear out of flying. An estimated 15 million Americans refuse to board a plane and another 30 million are anxious flyers. Cognitive-behavior therapy programs for fear of flying include in vivo exposure, relaxation exercises, desensitization, and useful cognitive strategies. Here, an airline captain talks with a woman participating in a fear of flying therapy program.

is able to remain relaxed, progressively more upsetting scenes are imagined.

The theory behind systematic desensitization is that the relaxation response competes with previously learned anxiety responses, such as fears and phobias. Research has shown that practicing relaxation when the fear-arousing stimulus is actually present (*in vivo* desensitization) yields superior results to simply imagining the stimulus. Desensitization works best with people who habitually show noticeable increases in physiological arousal (e.g., accelerated heart rate, moist palms) when exposed to the fear-arousing stimulus.

Paradoxical intention is a technique in which the therapist instructs the client to perform behaviors that appear to be in opposition to the client's therapeutic goal. For example, an individual who complains of inability to fall asleep within a satisfactory interval might be asked to remain awake as long as possible. An agoraphobic who cannot go into crowded places for fear of suffering severe heart palpitations might be instructed to go into crowded places and try to become anxious. Paradoxical intention is a relatively new technique that requires more research. It is not yet clear when it is appropriate or why it seems to be effective in particular cases. Perhaps it is effective because it requires the client to maintain the very behavior that he or she seeks to change under conditions that cannot support continuation of that behavior. Exposure to anxiety-provoking situations is an element of paradoxical intention and may contribute to its effectiveness (Shoham-Salomon et al., 1989).

Modeling Often people are unaware that habit controls much of their behavior. Through **modeling,** they can be shown that there are other ways of doing things. Although modeling can take place when an individual observes someone demonstrating specific social skills, it also occurs informally—for example, when children imitate the heroes of television shows. In clinical applications of modeling, demonstrations by models are often combined with **guided rehearsals,** in which the individual is encouraged to imitate the behavior of the model with the model helping whenever necessary. When people imitate the adaptive behavior of models, their new responses are strengthened by positive reinforcement. The success of a modeling program depends on several factors.

1. How carefully the observer attends to the modeled behavior.
2. How well what was observed is retained.
3. The observer's ability to reproduce the modeled behavior.
4. How motivated the observer is to use the modeled behavior.

Live modeling involves direct observation of a model. **Participant modeling,** or **behavioral rehearsal,** goes one step further by requiring the client to practice the behavior, often in interaction with the model. **Symbolic modeling** refers to observation of a model who is presented indirectly through film, video or audio tape, or printed word. **Covert modeling** is a logical extension of symbolic modeling in which the individual is asked to imagine observing a model and a particular consequence. For example, a male cross-dresser was asked to engage in covert modeling by imagining the following scene:

You are standing behind a one-way mirror. You see a bare room except for two single beds with clothes on them. One bed has male clothes on it and the other has female clothes on it. Straight ahead at the other end of the room, you see a door open and a naked man about your age walks into the room. He walks toward the beds which are next to each other about four feet apart. He starts to go toward the bed with the female clothes on it. He looks at the clothes; suddenly you can see a painful expression on his face. He sits down on the bed. Now he starts to sweat and looks sick. He reaches for a bra and he starts to gag. As he puts the bra on he starts to vomit all over the clothes and on himself. He groans in agony as he doubles over and falls down to the ground. He is lying with the bra on and wallowing in vomit.

—Cautela, 1985, p. 93

A covert modeling scene was then presented in which the model puts on the male clothes and looks happy. In general, covert modeling involves constructing scenes or situations in which the client can picture the behavior that is to be changed.

Like other cognitive-behavioral therapies, modeling is often combined with other approaches. For example, while reinforcing adaptive overt behavior, the therapist might help the client acquire more realistic ideas about problem areas. In treating a complex problem such as intense anger in a child, the therapist might: (1) teach the parents to be more effective in reacting to temper tantrums (modeling might be used to accomplish this); (2) help the child identify the situations and thoughts that evoke the tantrums; (3) model cognitive and behavioral responses to stress and frustration that are more effective than anger; and (4) use guided rehearsal and praise to strengthen the child's adaptive behavior.

Assertiveness Training Lack of assertive behavior is often related to deficits in social skills or to interfering emotional reactions and thoughts. If appropriate behaviors are available but are not performed because of anxiety, a useful focus may be on enhancing the client's anxiety management skills. **Assertiveness training** is specifically designed to enhance the interpersonal skills one needs to stand up for one's rights, such as refusing unwanted requests, expressing opinions, and making requests. Assertiveness training is preceded by a careful assessment of the client's responses in certain types of situations. The assessment is designed to answer these questions: What situations are of concern to the client? What does the client typically do in these situations? What are the personal and environmental blocks to more assertiveness in these situations?

Modeling and behavioral rehearsal play important roles in assertiveness training programs (see Figure 17-9). Positive feedback is offered after each rehearsal, and prompting is provided when needed. Homework assignments are used if, as is desirable, the client agrees to carry out tasks that require assertiveness outside the training sessions. If the assertiveness deficits extend over a broad range of social behaviors, a number of training sessions may be needed. However, if the problem is fairly specific, a few sessions may be sufficient.

A particular component of cognitive-behavior therapy, such as assertiveness training, might be completely sufficient by itself in helping someone overcome a specific problem. However, multiple components are frequently required to achieve therapeutic success. Box 17-3 presents a case study that involved several therapeutic components.

How Effective Is Cognitive-Behavior Therapy? Cognitive-behavioral interventions aim to correct people's misconceptions, strengthen their coping skills and feelings of control over their own lives, and facilitate constructive self-talk, or the things people typically say to themselves as they confront different types of situations. For instance, rather than saying "I'll never be able to do all that," they might tell themselves, "I'll just take it one step at a time."

There is growing evidence that cognitive-behavioral training can be quite effective in helping people overcome fears and inhibitions and increase their coping skills (Barlow, 1994). While the mechanism by which this training leads to improvements in behavior has not been completely described, an important factor seems to be the client's sense of self-efficacy, that is, the client's belief that he or she is effective at carrying out tasks. Feelings of self-efficacy increase when individuals acquire new skills, which in turn encourages them to strengthen their skills even further.

Cognitive-behavioral interventions seem to be particularly effective in treating disorders in which anxiety plays a prominent role (Hollon & Beck, 1994). While these results are encouraging, more information is needed concerning the contributions to therapeutic effectiveness of the several components of this approach to clinical intervention (Ilardi & Craighead, 1994). More evidence is also needed concerning cognitive-behavioral interventions as compared to other types of therapy.

Group Therapy

Group approaches to psychotherapy are used not only because they are less costly but because many clinicians believe that therapy can be at least as effective with groups as it is with individuals. One appealing feature of group psychotherapy is that clients can learn both by observing other group members' adaptive and maladaptive attempts to solve personal problems and by comparing their own relationship with the therapist with those of the other members (see Figure 17-10).

Group therapy is usually seen as a means of broadening the application of psychotherapeutic concepts. Some advocates of group psychotherapy believe it may actually produce better results than individual therapy. Groups are particularly effective when they give participants opportunities to acquire new social skills through modeling. Opportunities to rehearse or practice these skills in the group increase the chances that the participants will actually use their newly acquired skills in everyday life. The following are among the most frequently observed features of group therapy:

1. *Self-disclosure*—the opportunity to tell the group about one's personal problems and concerns.
2. *Acceptance and support*—feeling a sense of belongingness and being valued by the group members.
3. *Norm clarification*—learning that one's problems are neither unique nor more serious than is true for other group members.
4. *Social learning*—being able to relate constructively and adaptively within the group.

Figure 17-9 Modeling and behavioral rehearsal can be effective techniques in assertiveness training.

Use of Multiple Cognitive-Behavioral Components

Lisa, a 29-year-old mechanical engineer, sought treatment for chronic anxiety and panic attacks. She had had only two panic attacks, but feared having another one. The first panic attack occurred when she was in the hospital waiting to go home with her new baby. About two weeks later, she had another attack. At the time of the second attack, she and her 7-year-old daughter were at home on a Saturday afternoon with the new baby. Her husband was playing basketball with his friends.

Lisa's therapy extended over 15 sessions. Six months after the end of therapy, Lisa had had no recurrence of panic attacks. Several issues had emerged as the therapist discussed her problem with Lisa. Her husband had a job that required him to be away for two or three nights a week. Because of her husband's absences, Lisa had difficulty doing the overtime work required to meet her job's deadline. Lisa frequently felt overwhelmed by her life's circumstances.

The first thing Lisa's therapist had done was to give her a relaxation tape with the suggestion that she listen to it several times a week. The therapist thought that Lisa might be able to use some of the relaxation strategies presented on the tape to counteract anxiety when it occurred. At about the fourth week of therapy, Lisa reported much less anxiety. At that point, the therapist asked Lisa to keep a log of any negative feelings (such as anger) that she might experience. After three weeks of log-keeping, Lisa came to her therapy session saying that she had noticed for the first time that she felt distressed on the nights when her husband was away from home. Lisa then commented that, in addition to his absences, her husband, although loving and well-meaning, tended not to be very helpful when he was present; he seemed to expect Lisa to do most of the work of holding the family and household together.

Lisa's log-keeping led her to begin keeping a journal, which led to two positive

changes. First, she realized that she needed more help around the house and hired a college student to come help her with the dinnertime bustle several nights a week. Second, when Lisa described some of the events included in her journal, the therapist concluded that Lisa needed to be more assertive in certain situations. The therapist helped Lisa cognitively restructure some of her beliefs. Instead of believing "There's no point in asking for help—I can't get it," Lisa was encouraged to think more positively. After Lisa realized that she might get help if she asked for it, during therapy sessions she and the therapist engaged in role-playing in which Lisa learned and practiced making assertive responses. She came to realize that she tended to ask for too little and to let people off the hook if her request was not immediately met.

This case illustrates the problem-solving approach taken by cognitive-behavior therapists. After completing her cognitive-behavior therapy, Lisa and her husband came together for 10 couples therapy sessions. This contributed to the positive development of their relationship and reduction of her distress level.

Based on Persons (1992)

5. *Vicarious learning*—learning about oneself through the observation of other group members, including the therapist.
6. *Self-understanding*—finding out about one's behavior in the group setting and the motivations contributing to the behavior.

Although group therapy initially was carried out from a psychodynamic perspective, humanistic, cognitive, and behavioral therapists have developed their own group techniques.

The experience of group therapy differs not only because of the theoretical perspective and methods of the group leader, but also because of a number of other factors. These include the types of problems or disorders confronting the group members, the therapeutic goals that have been established, the role the leader takes, the setting in

which the group meets, and the individual characteristics of the group members. Clients are usually screened before being admitted to a therapy group to ensure that

Figure 17-10 Members of a therapy group have opportunities to learn and gather support from other members and from the therapist.

they will be able to participate at an effective level and that they will not be disruptive to the group as a whole. An important factor in many long-term groups in which members enter and leave the group at different times is the presence of a few "senior" members who are doing well and serve as models for identification, stimulate hope, and offer practical advice and suggestions that have helped them improve their situation. These persons often have a special relationship with the group leader, who in turn must take care that the relationship is not seen as excluding others in the group.

Group therapy provides an opportunity for members to observe how their behavior affects other people and to receive personally relevant feedback. To maximize the likelihood that this will happen, group therapists often emphasize not only what members reveal about themselves, but also how the others react to what is said in the group setting. The following account gives an example of this process.

> John, usually a silent member, opened a group meeting with a carefully planned statement about an episode of sexual abuse he had experienced as a child. He told the story in a deliberate manner with a flat expression. When he finished, there were a couple of minutes of silence, whereupon John said, half-jokingly, that he didn't give a damn if the group responded to him or not. Soon the disclosure evoked many reactions in the rest of the group. Another member, Steven, began to weep, recalling a past experience of sexual molestation and its subsequent influence on his sexual identity. Two other members offered him some words of support, which fell on deaf ears: this permitted the leader to point out how hard it is for Steven to accept comfort from others. One member commented that she felt confused by the discrepancy between how much John revealed and his flat, rehearsed manner of revelation. Another member, Mary, had an entirely different set of responses to John: She felt that his overwhelming self-disclosure put pressure on other group members to respond in kind. She resented this pressure and felt manipulated by John. A lively and engaging session ensued, with many complex variations on the theme of self-disclosure.
> —Vinogradov & Yalom, 1990, p. 191

How did John's revelation affect the other members? How did John feel about his self-disclosure? The group leader encouraged John to examine his feelings and to comment on the support offered to him by other group members (both the explicit support of other members and the implicit support of Steven, who revealed similar painful material). The leader also encouraged a discussion of Mary's observations about John's style of delivery and her feelings of having been coerced and manipulated. A productive discussion took place, not so much about the content of John's early sexual abuse, but about how the group functioned in dealing with it. Later sessions suggested that John benefited both

from having made his self-disclosures and from learning about how the other members of the group reacted to them.

Cognitive-Behavioral Group Therapy

The focus of cognitive-behavioral group therapy is on increasing the skills and comfort of people in social situations. Group members role-play specific social situations that they find difficult. The themes of particular sessions are often selected by the therapist from prior knowledge of the members' problems. The therapist may model alternative ways of handling these situations. The role playing is accompanied by social reinforcement and feedback, and homework tasks are assigned. Other techniques are used as well, including graded task assignments, examination of specific types of distortions that may arise in social interactions (such as overgeneralization and imagining catastrophes), and discussion of types of cognitions that have negative and positive influences in group situations.

Cognitive-behavioral group therapy is more highly structured than group therapy conducted along psychodynamic lines. From a psychodynamic point of view, group psychotherapy represents an opportunity to deal with transference in a social situation and to compare one's attitude toward participation in a group with those of other group members. The group is often seen as an extension of the family. For example, a frequent topic that arises in group therapy is the competition of group members for the therapist's attention. A psychoanalyst might see echoes of the members' relationships to parents and siblings in their performances in the group. A cognitively oriented clinician, on the other hand, would be interested primarily in the often irrational ideas of group members concerning what goes on, or should go on, in social situations. Client-centered therapists see the therapist's role in groups as basically the same as in individual counseling; in both situations the therapist is a facilitator of personal growth. Cognitive-behavioral therapists are increasingly using techniques such as modeling and behavior rehearsal in groups.

Family and Marital Therapy

Sometimes therapy focuses on individuals who already constitute a group. Two examples are family therapy and marital therapy.

Family Therapy Family therapy is based on the idea that many problems not only arise from family behavior patterns but also are affected by them. The following are some of the core problems that family therapy addresses:

1. Inability to resolve conflicts, make decisions, or solve problems

2. Chaotic organization and lack of agreed-upon responsibilities
3. Too rigid an organization, resulting in an inability to respond to changing circumstances and stress
4. Overcloseness to the point that individual family members may lose any sense of individuality
5. Lack of emotional ties and communication among family members
6. Failure of the parents to agree on child-rearing practices.

Instead of treating family members individually, the therapist encourages the family to work as a group, dealing together with their attitudes and feelings toward one another and their resistance to cooperation and sharing (see Figure 17-11). Family therapy often provides a valuable forum for airing hostilities, reviewing emotional ties, and dealing with crises. It is important for the therapist to be fair and impartial in discussing disagreements between family members and to bear in mind that families usually are characterized by a hierarchy in which parents are expected to assume some authority and responsibility for the behavior of their children. The degree of hierarchy will vary, depending on the parents' philosophy of child-rearing and the ages of the children. For adolescents and young adults, one important problem may be that their growing independence requires modification of the hierarchical structure.

Most family therapists begin by focusing on here-and-now problems. For example, a 12-year-old boy may be intermittently truant from school, tell lies, and seek out parties on weekends where he had been known to drink beer. The child may complain of parental pressure and repeated criticism, whereas the parents express their fears about the child's unreliability and poor school performance. The therapist seeks to help the family develop plans which the parents and child then can implement together for dealing with these problems. The therapist's approach is designed to minimize guilt, scapegoating, and blame among family members and to maximize open-mindedness and cooperation among them.

Roles in the drama of family life, assumed perhaps out of loyalty or a need for belonging, may become destructive over time yet hard to abandon because they help to maintain the family. For example, a child who takes on the role of a parent because of a mother's or father's incapacity is likely to play this adult role poorly, using authority too harshly or making it a vehicle of rivalry with younger brothers and sisters. Another child may be assigned the role of bad boy so that one of the parents can play disciplinarian. Such roles must be openly recognized and the assignments altered if the family is to become more healthy. The family members often develop an unspoken family mythology that has important effects on all family members. The mythology may be something like, "John is the stupid one," "Father can't work." These myths are especially likely to create conflict when they are incompatible with family ideals or are not accepted by all members of the family. Therapists often find that bringing the myths out in the open in family discussion is helpful in focusing on the problems these distorted role assignments create.

The Family As a System If any single idea could be said to guide family therapy, it is probably the notion of a family system. Human life can be organized hierarchically into systems of varying size and complexity: the individual, the family, the society, the culture. The family is seen as a self-maintaining system which, like the human body, has feedback mechanisms that preserve its identity and integrity by restoring homeostasis—the internal status quo—after a disturbance. A change in one part of the family system thus is often compensated elsewhere. Families have mechanisms for adapting to changed circumstances, and, like individuals, they have biologically and socially determined states of development.

A family that functions poorly cannot adjust to change because its mechanisms are either inflexible or

Figure 17-11 During family therapy sessions, the therapist observes how the members of the family interact. Here, the therapist is using what has just been said by a family member to help the others see how one person's behavior affects other family members.

ineffectual. The family's daily habits and internal communication—its *transactional patterns*, as they are called—harm its individual members. The pathology is in the system as a whole. Individual disorders not only serve as a source of protection and power for the disturbed person but may also preserve the family system and act as a distorted means of communication within that system. They fulfill the same function that neurotic symptoms are said to fulfill for individuals in psychodynamic theory.

Some families are highly interdependent; everyone in them is overresponsive to everyone else. They develop habits of intimate quarreling and complaining that become difficult to change. In other families, the family members have little mutual contact or concern; their boundaries are rigid. Family systems that are too closely knit, or enmeshed, respond too intensely to change; every disturbance may turn into a crisis. Systems in which the family members are distant, or disengaged, do not respond strongly enough; serious problems are ignored and issues are avoided.

Systems theory defines influences as mutual and causality as circular, so family therapists tend to avoid blaming and attributing causes—although there are exceptions to this as to every other generalization about the field. The symptoms of a defective family system are said to take different forms in different members of the system. A husband and wife, for example, may seem to have very different personalities, but this may be due not to their intrinsic characteristics as individuals but rather to their functions within that system. For this reason, family therapists often make limited use of ordinary psychiatric diagnoses, which describe individual pathology, and diagnose family situations instead.

Marital Therapy Marital difficulties contribute, not only to personal unhappiness and family instability, but also to a wide range of mental-health and physical problems. **Marital therapy** is directed toward helping couples overcome their difficulties.

Couples frequently seek marital therapy because one or both of the partners believe that the relationship is troubled or are contemplating ending it through divorce or separation. By seeing the therapist together, the partners can more easily identify problems and alter the ways in which they relate to each other. The main advantage of couple's therapy is that the therapist, as an impartial observer, can actually witness the couple's interactions rather than hearing about them in a secondhand and perhaps one-sided report. Both family therapy and marital therapy can be carried out from one of several perspectives. Family therapy is likely to include behavioral or psychodynamic approaches. Couples therapy often utilizes a cognitive focus as well. Regardless of the type of marital therapy practiced, a current trend is to focus attention on specific relevant issues such as helping the couple increase communication, express feelings, help each other, and enjoy shared experiences.

Marital therapists report distinct patterns of symptoms among couples. In some cases, each partner in a marriage demands too much of the same thing from the other: service, protection, care, and so forth. In other cases, spouses compound each other's problems by complementing each other. One partner takes charge and the other becomes incompetent: an overbearing and emotionally distant husband has a "hysterical" wife whose erratic behavior makes him still more overbearing; a strong, angry wife has a passive, alcoholic husband who is a suitable object of her anger, and that anger makes him even more passive; the husband of a depressed and hypochondriacal woman needs to be a healer and savior. Often marital therapy aims to reveal what is hidden: the passive partner's suppressed anger, the savior's feelings of helplessness.

Psychodrama

Although most group therapy is essentially an expanded, more complicated, and more realistic version of individual therapy, a number of approaches have been designed especially for groups. One of these is **psychodrama,** which was created by Jacob Moreno in the 1920s. Moreno led impromptu activity groups of children in the public gardens of Vienna. He noticed that when the children were encouraged to act out stories instead of merely reading or listening to them, they often displayed unexpected depths of feeling and understanding. He later experimented with a form of theater, the "theater of spontaneity," in which players were encouraged to draw upon their inner resources in creating the dramatic action rather than following a script.

Moreno saw psychodrama as a vehicle for expressing strong emotions, acquiring insight into one's own behavior, and realistically evaluating the behavior of others. Psychodrama is a directive treatment in that the therapist controls the mechanics of the therapy situation. However, it is nondirective in that the emotional content of sessions arises spontaneously from the activities of the participants.

In psychodrama a group of individuals assembles under the leadership of a therapist (often called the director). The group enacts events of emotional significance in order to resolve conflicts and release members from inhibitions that limit their capacity for spontaneous and creative activity, particularly social activity. Behavior therapists use role playing to give clients practice in new social skills, but in psychodrama role-playing tends to be more spontaneous and oriented toward expressing strongly felt emotions (see Figure 17-12).

Figure 17-12 Both role play and psychodrama are effective psychotherapeutic tools. These boys, confined to an institution for juveniles, are shown acting out a situation as the therapist watches.

How Effective Are Group Approaches?

In discussing individual psychotherapy and cognitive-behavioral therapies, we noted that each approach seemed to be effective, but information was lacking on the treatment components that were the active ingredients and the clinical groups for which particular therapies might be most appropriate. For example, while cognitive-behavioral approaches are often quite helpful with people for whom anxiety is a major problem, their effectiveness with many other clinical groups has not yet been demonstrated. Group therapy is even more complex than individual therapy because of the number of people involved. Not surprisingly, less is known about its processes and effectiveness. Lack of agreement about the basic concepts that underlie the processes involved in group therapy has hampered research on its effectiveness (Bednar & Kaul, 1994). The questions: Which treatments work? and When do they work and why? have not yet been answered.

The lack of answers to these questions is more an indication of the complexity of the processes involved and lack of accepted conceptualizations than of demonstrated lack of effectiveness. An increasing number of clinicians and researchers believe that group approaches are promising and likely to be effective and efficient (Scheidlinger, 1994).

A recent review of marital therapy illustrates the current state of knowledge concerning group approaches generally (Jacobson & Addis, 1993). It appears that most kinds of treatments are helping some couples, are leaving substantial numbers of couples unchanged, and appear to have about the same success rates. This conclusion applies to the immediate effects of couples' therapy; much less is known about long-term effects.

Research on the Psychological Therapies

According to recent estimates, over 400 psychological therapies are in use for adults, over 200 for children and adolescents (Kazdin, 1995). These therapies are being used with approximately 300 different forms of abnormal behavior. It is not surprising that we do not yet have answers to all the questions raised about the therapies. Nevertheless, it is a step forward to be aware of the questions for which answers are needed. Table 17-5 lists the major questions for which researchers are seeking answers. Because the future of psychological therapies relies on these answers, we will mention four of the most important issues in research in this area. The first concerns features unique to particular treatments or common to all treatments. The second concerns the criteria by which therapeutic effectiveness is judged. The third relates to comparisons among different therapeutic approaches. The fourth issue concerns cultural and ethnic diversity, a neglected topic that is beginning to receive the attention it deserves.

TABLE 17-5
Questions Toward Which Research on Psychological Treatments Is Directed

- Does the treatment produce therapeutic change?
- What components constitute necessary, sufficient, and facilitative therapeutic change?
- What components or other treatments can be added to enhance therapeutic change?
- What changes can be made in the treatment to increase its effectiveness?
- Which treatment is more or most effective for a particular condition and population?
- On what patient, family, or therapist characteristics does treatment depend for its effectiveness?
- What processes occur in treatment that affect within-session performance and that may contribute to the treatment outcome?

Source: Based on Kazdin, 1995

Common and Unique Features of Therapies

Earlier in the chapter we mentioned the importance of the therapist's ability to instill hope in patients. This ability, regardless of the formal therapeutic techniques used by the therapist, is an important common feature of all therapies. Given the evidence that therapies frequently are effective with patient groups as compared to nontreated groups and that differences among various types of therapy are often not large, it is reasonable to consider the possibility that the therapist, rather than the treatment per se, is the active ingredient. To the extent possible, research on treatment techniques needs to separate the effects of therapist characteristics and the therapist-patient relationship from those attributable to the technique employed. This can be accomplished by careful research planning, use of appropriate statistical methods, and large enough samples.

Therapeutic Outcomes

One of the most important questions in outcome studies is what the criteria for improvement should be. Which are more important, changes in how the client feels and behaves or changes in what he or she thinks about? Would the opinions of the client's family or co-workers be helpful in evaluating improvement? How important is the therapist's evaluation of the outcome? Sometimes the therapist and the client don't agree. Anthony Storr, a British psychoanalyst, gives this example of what he had considered an "unsuccessful" case:

> Some time ago I had a letter from a man whom I had treated some 25 years previously asking whether I would see, or at any rate advise treatment for, his daughter. He assumed, wrongly, that I would not remember him, and, in the course of his letter, wrote as follows: "I can quite truthfully say that six months of your patient listening to my woes made a most important contribution to my life style. Although my transvestism was not cured, my approach to life and to other people was re-oriented and for that I am most grateful. It is part of my life that I have never forgotten."
>
> Looked at from one point of view, my treatment of this man was a failure. His major symptom, the complaint which drove him to seek my help, was not abolished. And yet I think it is clear that he did get something from his short period of psychotherapy which was of considerable value to him. A man does not write to a psychotherapist asking him to see his daughter, 25 years after his own treatment was over, using the terms employed in this letter, unless he believes that what happened during his period of treatment was important.
>
> —Storr, 1980, p. 146

If all the measures of improvement do not agree which is most important? How can we compare studies that use different outcome measures to evalute the effectiveness of various therapies? Clearly, although outcome research is progressing in sophistication, many of the important questions will be difficult to answer. Personal accounts of experiences in psychotherapy provide researchers with hypotheses for future research. Identifying the elements of personal growth and the factors that foster it will contribute to the development of better formal and informal therapies.

It is not unusual for clients to see themselves as cured while their therapists see them as unimproved or even as being worse. Studies of improvement therefore should include three independent measures: the client's evaluation of the progress made; the therapist's evaluation; and the judgments of people who know the client well, such as family members and friends.

Another approach to evaluating the effectiveness of therapy is to assess the resultant behavior change. Although one of the goals of psychotherapy is enhancement of the client's self-awareness and insight, most people would consider therapy a failure if the person's behavior remained the same. It is not enough to be a source of insight.

Changes in overt behavior are easier to describe and assess objectively than changes in attitudes, feelings, and beliefs. But questions remain. To what degree should behavioral change be used as a criterion? Who should determine the kinds and amounts of change desired? How lasting should the change be? How longstanding and disabling has the patient's condition been? It seems reasonable that criteria for success should be related to the difficulty of the hurdle to be overcome. Implicit in this conclusion is the recognition that criteria that are appropriate in one case may be inappropriate in others.

Comparing Therapies

Most of the treatment outcome studies we have mentioned so far involved comparisons between treatment and nontreatment (control) groups. We noted that there is growing support for the conclusion that psychological therapies are worthwhile for many people. What have been the results of head-to-head comparative studies of two or more therapies? Meta-analyses of these studies have revealed a mixed picture. There is a strong tendency for measurements to show no difference among techniques in amount of change produced. However, this is countered by indications that, under some circumstances, cognitive and behavioral methods have superior results although they do not generally differ in efficacy among themselves (Lambert & Bergin, 1994). Research carried out with the intent of contrasting two or more treatments has often shown small differences between outcomes for the groups compared.

In one widely cited comparative study (Sloane et al., 1975), the subjects were college students who had applied for treatment—mostly for anxiety and personality disorders—at a psychiatric outpatient clinic. The goal of the study was to compare the relative effectiveness of behavioral therapy (desensitization, assertiveness training, and so on) and more traditional, short-term, psychodynamically oriented therapy. In addition to these two groups, there was a control group whose members were told that they would have to wait about four months to receive treatment.

The clients were followed up 4 and 12 months after completing therapy. The measures used in the treatment comparisons were derived from interviews with the clients at these times, from the clients' ratings of their own improvement, and from improvement ratings made by an independent assessor. At four months, the psychotherapy and behavioral-therapy groups had improved equally, and significantly more than the waiting-list group. At the one-year follow-up, the behavioral-therapy clients, but not the psychotherapy group, showed some significant improvement with regard to the problems that had led them to seek therapy. However, there were no significant differences between the two groups with regard to social adjustment. The one-year follow-up results were complicated by the fact that some of the clients continued to receive treatment even though the therapy sessions were supposed to end after four months. The researchers concluded that their study provided no clear evidence that behavioral therapy was superior to psychotherapy.

The same researchers reported an interesting additional set of comparisons for some of the subjects in their treatment study (Sloane et al., 1977). One year after beginning treatment, the subjects were mailed questionnaires in which they were asked to rate the importance of 32 factors in the success of their treatment. What was most striking about their responses was the similarity between the psychotherapy and behavioral-therapy groups. Both groups emphasized the importance of gaining insight into one's problems, the client-therapist relationship, the opportunity to give vent to emotions, a sense of trust in the therapist, and the development of confidence. Thus, even though the two treatment approaches are based on different assumptions and use different methods, they were described similarly by the clients. This similarity held both for the sample as a whole and for subgroups of clients who were judged to have responded most positively to the treatments offered them.

In another project, researchers analyzed four studies on the outcome of psychotherapy and concluded that who performs the therapy matters much more than what kind of therapy it is (Luborsky et al., 1986). The studies were conducted at Johns Hopkins University, the University of Pennsylvania, the University of Pittsburgh, and McGill University. Altogether, 25 therapists and 240 patients were involved. In three studies, the patients were average psychiatric outpatients; in the Pennsylvania study, they were heroin addicts taking methadone. The techniques included individual psychodynamic therapy, cognitive-behavioral therapy, and group therapy, all in various combinations and for varying lengths of time. Among the many measures of outcome were judgments of improvement by both patients and therapists and ratings of interpersonal behavior, social adjustment, depression, severity of addiction, and other symptoms.

In all four studies some therapists had a significantly higher success rate than others. Differences among therapists were much greater than differences among therapies in producing a favorable outcome. There was little evidence to show that any individual therapist did better with a particular kind of patient. The researchers suggested that more might be learned about how psychological therapies work by studying the most effective therapists than by comparing different forms of treatment.

Conclusions about the relative effectiveness of therapeutic techniques cannot be drawn from research that is too limited in scope or methodologically weak (see Table 17-6). We noted earlier that there is no best index of clinical outcome. That being the case, research studies should include several measures of outcome, such as clients' self-reports and behavioral measures gathered before and after therapy, as well as expert judgments of clinical progress. There might be significant differences between therapeutic approaches to specific problems with respect to some outcome measures but not others. Furthermore, a therapeutic procedure may be valuable even if it doesn't bring about a complete cure. A person who is less anxious after therapy will be grateful for that benefit despite the failure to achieve a total release from anxiety.

Arguments over the effectiveness of therapeutic programs can be expected to continue for several reasons: people's problems, expectations, and the extent to which their lives can be changed vary; therapists use different methods and have different expectations; and there are no uniform criteria for judging therapeutic effectiveness. Many people are helped by therapy, but some get worse. Even though psychological therapies are not for everyone, they seem to help a sizable number of people sort out their problems and develop new ways of handling stress and the challenges of life.

TABLE 17-6
Key Features of Research on Therapies

1. *Control and comparison groups.* These groups are needed in therapy studies because many influences beyond those that are of special interest to the researcher may be at work during the period covered by therapeutic intervention. Without adequate control or comparison groups, researchers cannot rule out the possibility of alternative explanations such as spontaneous remission.
2. *Sample size.* Because of the need to incorporate a large number of factors in the design of therapy research, sufficiently large sample sizes are needed to allow for appropriate statistical analyses and justifiable inferences from results.
3. *Patient specificity.* Firm conclusions are more likely if subjects are relatively homogeneous in terms of factors that are not the target of the treatment intervention. So many factors may influence outcome that it is important to control as many extraneous variables as possible.
4. *Treatment specificity.* The more clearly defined the treatment or treatments, the more likely it is that reasonable inferences can be drawn from the research. This requires careful specification of the therapeutic techniques used in the research.
5. *Outcome measures.* The more relevant the outcome measures are to the type of case being treated, the more useful the study will be. For example, since obsessive-compulsives rarely hallucinate, there would be little value in using the frequency of hallucinations as an outcome variable. A more useful variable would be the frequency of obsessive thoughts and compulsive behaviors.

Cultural and Ethnic Diversity

Asian-American immigrant parents were concerned that the grades of their only son, a 15-year-old, were falling. The therapist decided that the parents were overcontrolling, overanxious, and overdemanding with a timid adolescent boy who was reluctant to stand up to his parents about his social isolation. The therapist encouraged the boy to argue to convince his parents to allow him to join the school band, participate in after-school sports, choose his own school schedule, and listen to rock music. His mother did not speak English and his father was deferential and seemed to accept the therapist's suggestions. But the parents then terminated the appointments. They said it was because of transportation problems, but the boy indicated that his parents felt the therapist was "too American" and was encouraging disrespect toward them. The therapist had ignored the cultural issues by working with the boy with little attention to the parents' feelings and customs. The approach was not successful.

(Ayres, 1994, p. vi)

We have seen how important it is to compare therapeutic approaches and identify the similarities and differences among them. It is also important to determine the degree to which factors usually not dealt with by psychological theories might be important to the process and outcome of therapy. While most psychological theories have tended to ignore the issue of cultural and ethnic diversity, there is growing reason to believe that the various types of diversity in the population are highly relevant to carrying out treatment and doing research. This issue is important in itself, as well as because of the growing diversity of the population. The United States population includes close to 2 million Native Americans (American Indians), over 30 million African Americans, over 22 million Hispanics (Latinos), and over 7 million Asian Americans. Different cultural groups frequently differ with regard to specific beliefs, attitudes, behaviors, and the types of psychological problems they experience. Cultural differences also are likely to be reflected in how people perceive emotional and physical states. For example, there is evidence that African Americans often blame themselves for their problems, whereas Puerto Ricans often blame others (Casas, 1995).

Cultural and ethnic diversity is particularly relevant to therapeutic practice because different groups within the population frequently have different values and may see themselves and others in disparate ways. For example, insight is not highly valued by all cultural groups; in fact, many Asian American elders believe that thinking too much about something can cause problems. People from lower socioeconomic classes frequently do not perceive insight as appropriate to their life situations and circumstances. Traditional psychodynamic psychotherapy might be less effective for these segments of the population than for middle- and upper-class white people. The usefulness of particular therapies needs to be demonstrated for various cultural and ethnic groups. Research is needed to substantiate the applicability or limitations of traditional and new therapies with respect to minority groups.

Three steps that would improve mental health services for members of minority groups are to (1) increase accessibility to therapy by locating mental health clinics in minority group neighborhoods close to public transportation, (2) employ mental health workers who share the linguistic and cultural backgrounds of the patients, and (3) provide clinicians with training that increases their awareness of the needs of particular groups. An example of this last point is the need for therapists working with Asian Americans to be sensitive to issues of shame and guilt when probing for personal information. To avoid leaving patients with the impression that they have "caused" their problems, therapists must help them understand that people often encounter difficult situations as the result of inevitable and unavoidable circumstances. Because African American families often have extended kinship networks, some therapists have found it appropriate and useful to include members other than just the immediate family in group therapy (Canino & Spurlock, 1994). To provide useful mental health services to children and adults requires that the therapist know enough about their culture for them to feel accepted and understood and also to feel they are active participants in their treatment.

Integration of Psychologically Based Therapeutic Approaches

When therapists who base their techniques on different perspectives discuss their work, there are inevitable differences of opinion. The issues that separate the various schools of thought seem substantial. Should therapists actively direct clients toward behavioral change, or should they focus on the clients' development of insight? Should therapy delve into the past or examine the present? Should its duration be long or short? Despite the different ways in which these questions are answered, there is evidence of a movement toward the integration of therapeutic approaches. "Talking therapies," such as psychodynamic therapy, are placing more emphasis on clients' need to take responsibility for themselves and develop self-mastery. Behavioral therapies are giving increased attention to the cognitive underpinnings of behavioral change. Often this means helping clients acquire insight into their misconceptions about themselves and their social relationships. Many cognitive-behavioral therapists rely heavily on imagery as a means of achieving therapeutic goals. The use of imagery for treatment purposes clearly acknowledges the potentially crucial role of private events.

There is growing evidence that performance-based therapies, in which individuals concretely deal with problematic situations, can be very effective. However, cognitive processes, such as insight, may play an important role in helping people develop more adaptive approaches to their problems of living. As more therapists attend to the relative roles of cognition, emotion, and behavior, steps toward greater integration of therapeutic approaches are becoming noticeable.

Biological Therapies

In chapter 3 we discussed the biological orientation to maladaptive behavior and the therapies that have been generated by this point of view. The most widely used biological therapies today are **electroconvulsive therapy** (ECT) and a growing variety of drugs that influence psychological functioning.

Electroconvulsive Therapy

Until recently, use of ECT had been declining for about 20 years. The basis for the decline was the public's perception (shared by many clinicians) that ECT is dangerous, inhumane, and overused. Some municipalities have urged that its use be restricted. Nevertheless, ECT is now in the midst of a quiet revival. In improved forms, it has emerged as the treatment of choice for the most severe depression when drugs and other therapy fail to help (see chapter 10). Patients for whom ECT is recommended are so severely depressed that they do not eat, sleep very little, and are suicidal. Many suffer from delusions. In about 80 percent of cases, ECT can lift depression within a few weeks (Andreasen & Black, 1991). The response to ECT of Norman Endler described in chapter 10 is an example of the method's effectiveness.

Available evidence suggests that ECT is a relatively safe procedure, particularly when used with anesthetics and muscle relaxants that substantially lessen the traumatic effects of the treatment. Risks are further reduced by applying the electric current to only one side of the head. Several such improvements in reducing ECT's side effects have contributed to its comeback (see Table 17-7). However, there is concern about the cognitive consequences of passing an electric current through a person's head. The major risk is memory loss, although this can be reduced by using ECT on the nondominant side of the brain and in the lowest possible dose (Khan et al., 1993).

Even though it has been used for many years, the mechanism by which ECT works is not yet clear. However, recent evidence suggests that the active ingredients in ECT are the electrical-biochemical events that follow the seizures triggered by the electrical impulses (Hay & Hay, 1990). Progress is now being made in understanding these events.

A clinician who is considering the use of ECT must perform a risk-benefit analysis. On the benefit side is the probability of rapid improvement and, for those who are depressed, the reduced likelihood of death due to suicide. On the risk side, however, are the possibility of death in the course of receiving ECT (this risk is low, with an incidence of about one in 10,000 treatments), the chance of memory impairment (which is short-term and becomes less noticeable with time), and the risk of spontaneous seizures (which are infrequent). In weighing the advantages against the risks, clinicians might reasonably consider ECT when there is severe depression or a possibility of suicide, or when drugs and other therapies are ineffective or seem inappropriate (Coffey & Weiner, 1990).

1. *Length of electrical charge.* Reduced from one second to one twenty-fifth of a second.
2. *Intensity of electrical charge.* Reduced by up to one-half.
3. *Timing of sessions.* Reduced from as often as every day or even two or three a day to no more than three times a week.
4. *Length of treatment.* Formerly, up to 20 sessions or more; now, typically 10 or fewer.
5. *Use of anesthetics and muscle relaxants.* Formerly, no anesthetics or muscle relaxants were used; now both are employed.
6. *Monitoring.* Both brain waves and the electrical functioning of the heart are now monitored, through EEG and EKG.
7. *Placement of electrodes.* Formerly, on both sides of the head; now, on the nondominant side only.

Drug Therapies

Many drugs have been used clinically and in research. Drug treatment has been notably effective with four types of disorders, those in which schizophrenia, mania, depression, and anxiety play important roles:

1. **Antipsychotic drugs** (e.g., phenothiazines) are used primarily to treat people who have a schizophrenic disorder. These drugs are described in chapter 11.
2. **Antimanic drugs** (e.g., lithium) are used to treat those who have a bipolar disorder. Chapter 10 includes a description of these drugs.
3. **Antidepressant drugs** (e.g., tricyclics, MAO inhibitors) are used to treat patients who have been diagnosed as having a mood disorder of the unipolar type, that is, characterized by relatively long-lasting depression but without any history of manic or hypomanic episodes. More information about these drugs is found in chapter 10.
4. **Antianxiety drugs** (e.g., benzodiazepines) are used with people who have a high level or prolonged state of anxiety that is strong enough to incapacitate them or at least cause them difficulty in carrying out many activities of daily life (See chapter 7 for more information about these drugs.)

These types of medication differ in their effectiveness, mechanisms of action, and side effects. The antipsychotic drugs usually produce improvement in 4 to 6 weeks. Antimanic drugs are often effective by themselves, but at times they need to be combined with an antipsychotic drug in highly agitated patients. The effects of antimanic drugs are usually noticeable within

a week. Among the antidepressants, tricyclic drugs are often tried initially, with other types of antidepressants reserved for those patients who do not respond to the tricyclics. The therapeutic effects of the antidepressants usually require between 2 and 4 weeks to be apparent. Antianxiety drugs, whose therapeutic effects may be noticed within a week, are usually employed for limited time periods (up to a few months) to avoid the problem of drug dependence.

Although psychoactive drugs have helped many people live normal or almost normal lives and the safety of their use has improved, there are many unanswered questions about them. A number of risks must still be considered including a variety of side effects. Depending on the drug employed, side effects may include drowsiness, confusion, nightmares, poor appetite, insomnia, blurred vision, lethargy, and changes in blood pressure. Some of the drugs may be fatal if the patient's condition is not monitored regularly and some of the drugs expose the patient to the risk of having a fatal overdose available.

Like those of psychological therapies, the effects of drug therapy are not always predictable. Factors such as age, sex, and genetic background can influence a person's response to a drug. The effectiveness of a particular drug may also depend on how it is metabolized, whether the patient takes it as prescribed, and whether other drugs are being taken at the same time.

Drug Research Clinicians who prescribe drugs want to maximize their therapeutic effects and minimize their undesirable consequences. These goals require the use of carefully designed research procedures. First, extensive preliminary research is done to study the effects of varying doses of a drug on laboratory animals. If these tests suggest that the drug is effective and does not have harmful side effects, if properly used, the drug is administered to human beings under carefully controlled conditions. If these results are also positive, the drug may be approved for large-scale clinical trials in which its effectiveness is scientifically compared with other treatment methods.

Clinical trials involving drugs and other therapeutic procedures can be complex and costly, and may extend over many years (see chapter 1). They often include samples of subjects located throughout the country and even the world. They require careful planning, decisions about dependent measures, recruitment of subjects and their random assignment to the various treatment conditions, use of placebo conditions if possible, and assuring that all clinical personnel are "blind" to the assigned treatment whenever possible (see Figure 17-13).

Controlled clinical trials of most drugs used in the treatment of maladaptive behavior indicate an average effectiveness rate of about 70 percent (Erickson &

Figure 17-13 Placebos may just be "sugar-pills," but they often do have noticeable effects.

SOURCE: *The Wall Street Journal*, October 14, 1994, p. 11. Reprinted by permission of Cartoon Features Syndicate, Inc.

Goodwin, 1994). Although several drugs in a category (for example, antidepressants) may be about equal in effectiveness, there still are significant variations in individual responses to a particular drug.

How Effective Are Biological Therapies?

Many disorders can be treated effectively with ECT or medications. ECT is often helpful for severe depression. Antipsychotic drugs are used extensively in treating schizophrenia. It is widely accepted that these drugs are highly effective, particularly in the short term. However, a substantial percentage of patients with schizophrenic disorder relapse and a moderate percentage become chronic and socially disabled. Perhaps the most important problem associated with drug treatment of schizophrenia is the adverse effects of these medications. The risk of tardive dyskinesia increases with cumulative dose and duration of treatment. Lithium is useful in treating manic episodes and several types of drugs, such as the tricyclics, are helpful in many cases of depression. The tricyclics are also effective in treating panic disorders.

Many advances have been made in the development of biological therapies. Despite these advances, much work remains to clarify the causes and mechanisms of mental disorders and to determine their optimal forms of treatment. Combinations of interventions may provide the best means of treating these disorders.

Combining Therapeutic Approaches Although evidence suggests that the various psychological approaches to treating cases that do not involve extreme psychopathology are all often effective, one should not conclude that it makes no difference which techniques are employed in clinical work. Psychological therapies have been less successful with serious conditions such as schizophrenia, some types of affective disorders, alcoholism, and drug abuse. However, psychological therapies can play an important role in treating some of these conditions when used in combination with biologically based treatments like drug therapy and ECT. The value of the psychological component of these combinations frequently lies in helping the patient deal realistically with problems of day-to-day living. For example, social-skills training has been used effectively to help psychotic individuals taking antipsychotic drugs to adjust better to hospital or community settings. Perhaps as more is learned about the distinctive features of particular therapies, it will be possible to combine them in ways that are optimal for clients (see Figure 17-14).

Researchers are devoting increasingly greater efforts to studying the effectiveness of therapeutic programs that include both medications and psychological interventions. Depression and panic disorders have received the most attention. Medications and psychological interventions often seem to be equally effective, but combined treatment may have advantages for some patients (Beitman, 1993). One study found that providing cognitive therapy while patients were taking antidepressant medications resulted in half the relapse rate of patients who received only medications (Evans et al., 1992). Another study found that a family therapy intervention combined with drug therapy for hospitalized bipolar disorder patients yielded better results than for drug therapy alone (Clarkin et al., 1990). A similar facilitative effect for unipolar patients was not obtained. **Multi-modal treatment** that combines different approaches to clinical intervention has recently been

"I UTILIZE THE BEST FROM FREUD, THE BEST FROM JUNG AND THE BEST FROM MY UNCLE MARTY, A VERY SMART FELLOW."

Figure 17-14

SOURCE: © 1983 by Sidney Harris—*The Wall Street Journal.*

recommended for several conditions, including substance-use disorders, borderline disorders, anxiety disorders, and schizophrenia (Koenigsberg, 1993; Liberman & Green, 1992; Mavissakalian, 1993; Najavits & Weiss, 1993).

Combined therapies need not be limited to integrating biologically and psychologically based treatments. There might be considerable merit in combining features of different psychological interventions (see Box 17-3). Some members of a family might not only participate in family therapy, but also receive some form of individual therapy. This seems a reasonable approach when we note that individual psychopathology and family dysfunction are almost always interdependent. In the following case, drug therapy for a wife led to the couple's therapy and, ultimately, to family therapy.

A 43-year-old, depressed, married woman with two children responded positively to imipramine after 3 weeks of treatment. She denied that her relationship to her husband played any role in her symptoms and, in fact, claimed, "We have excellent communication." Her psychiatrist asked about her husband's response to the imipramine. She replied, "He hasn't said anything." This response was at odds with her claim that they had excellent communication. The psychiatrist asked her husband to come to the next session. In that session, the husband reported that he had told her how pleased he was with the change in her mood but, "Perhaps I didn't state it very clearly." In couples therapy they explored the husband's dysphoria about work, and his fear of burdening his depressed wife with more difficulties. They had difficulty communicating at home because their children repeatedly interrupted their conversations. Their children also dominated much of the decision making. Their psychiatrist worked with them in regaining a parental hierarchy over the children by suggesting that they exclude the children from major decisions and by fostering parental discussion and agreement about managing the children's behavior.

(Beitman, 1993, p. 651)

Utilizing techniques derived from many different perspectives, clinicians might make it possible to improve significantly the quality of the treatments they provide.

Hospitalization

Serious psychological illness may require hospitalization not only because the hospital provides round-the-clock care but also because it can offer all the complex therapies that a patient might need. But while some comprehensive mental hospitals provide an enriched program of therapies, offering such benefits as psychotherapy, drug therapy, and active social, educational, and recreational programs, the budgets of most state hospitals do not permit such varied fare. As a result, many patients in state hospitals receive drugs but few psychological therapies, and live in a relatively impoverished, unstimulating social environment. This is unfortunate because a hospital can be a place that helps a person cope with a crisis and experience personal growth.

No matter what kind of hospital is available, the major reasons for psychiatric hospitalization are as follows.

1. Behavior that poses a threat to self or others.
2. Behavior that is intolerable to members of the patient's community.
3. Failure of outpatient treatment and the hope that inpatient treatment will reverse the process.
4. A treatment procedure that requires a degree of control that is possible only in a hospital.
5. Withdrawal from alcohol or drugs.
6. Physical illness that is complicated by a mental disorder that requires continuous care.

Researchers have studied the kinds of hospital activities that are helpful to patients when they are not in an acute phase of their disorder. One experiment compared a fairly traditional mental hospital routine with a routine based on social-learning principles (Paul & Lentz, 1977). Under the traditional routine, patients spent six percent of their time taking drugs, five percent in classes and meetings, and 63 percent in unstructured activities. This last percentage represents a great deal of boredom and a waste of therapeutic opportunities. Under the social-learning routine, however, 59 percent of the patients' time was devoted to classes, meetings, and structured activities. Only 12 percent of their time was unstructured. The ward employed a token economy to motivate the patients to engage in productive behavior. A comparison of the effects of the two approaches showed that the social-learning group had a significantly higher percentage of discharges to the community than the traditional group. However, regardless of the treatment used, only a small percentage of the patients were able to function in a self-supporting way.

Research on the process of resocialization may contribute answers to such questions as, what steps could help chronic patients adjust successfully to the community? Gordon Paul has suggested ten steps that mental hospitals might take to provide greater happiness and effectiveness among patients, higher morale among staff members, and a more positive social-rehabilitation role for the institution.

> 1. *Emphasize a "resident" rather than "patient" status through informal dress of staff, open channels of communication in all directions, and broad (but clear) authority structure.*

2. *Make clear, through a set of rules and attitudes, that the residents are responsible human beings; are expected to follow certain minimal rules of group living; and are expected to do their share in participating in self-care, work, recreational, and social activities.*

3. *Utilize step systems which gradually increase the expectations placed on the residents in terms of their degree of independence and level of responsibility, with community return emphasized from the outset.*

4. *Encourage social interactions and skills and provide a range of activities as well as regular large and small group meetings.*

5. *Emphasize clarity of communication, with concrete instruction in appropriate behavior and focus on utilitarian "action" rather than "explanation."*

6. *Provide opportunity to practice vocational and housekeeping skills, with feedback, and specific training in marketable skills when needed.*

7. *Reacquaint residents with the "outside world" by exposing them to the community and bringing in community volunteers for discussions.*

8. *Identify the specific unique areas for change and support in concrete terms for each individual.*

9. *Prepare residents and significant others to live in mutually supportive ways in the community through prerelease training and scheduled aftercare.*

10. *When no significant other exists, train and release residents in groups of two to three as a "family" to provide significant others for one another.*

—Paul, 1969, p. 91

The effectiveness of a hospital depends on the needs of its residents, the quality and scope of its programs, and the community and family resources available to the patient. Because of variations in all of these areas, it is not surprising that there are strong differences of opinion about the effectiveness of hospitalization. When all factors are considered, it seems reasonable to conclude that some severely disturbed people can benefit from life in a socially active, therapeutic hospital. The precise percentage of currently institutionalized individuals who might benefit from this experience is very difficult to estimate.

If a ward is run mainly to satisfy the staff, or if a latent goal of the hospital is to maintain order and stability in the institution, the patients get the message. No therapy takes place because patients' behavior is aimed at minimizing conflict with the system and disruption of routine.

An unfortunate hospitalization is a special kind of experience whose mark may be visible long after its completion. It can increase patients' sense that they bear a stigma and make it easy for them to acquire "sick roles"—that is, to come to see themselves as sick people who will always have to be taken care of. It can also lead to a weakening of social and work skills. When these things happen, patients become less able to function in the community.

When complete hospitalization is not required, **partial hospitalization** may be employed (Rosie, 1987). This may include either day or night hospitalization and perhaps evening and weekend care in the hospital.

Day hospitals are used to provide treatment for patients who can live at home but need the structure and social interaction available in the treatment center. Day hospitals also allow members of the patients' families to function more normally because they can carry on their usual activities during the day. Day hospitals often concentrate on teaching social and interpersonal behaviors as well as helping patients learn practical skills such as how to use the bus system or a pay telephone. They may also include training in basic work skills so that patients can get jobs in sheltered workshops that will provide the satisfaction of doing useful work and some payment as well.

Evening, night, and weekend programs are designed primarily to help hospitalized patients make the transition from the hospital to the community. Such programs are especially useful for people who are able to return to their jobs, schools, or training programs but do not have adequate family or social supports to go from inpatient to outpatient status without a partially protected transition period. The concept of night hospitals has gained some acceptance, but relatively few such hospitals have been established on a formal basis.

Over the past few decades hospitalizations for mental illness have become less frequent. While this fact in itself is not necessarily undesirable, public hospital beds available to people with low incomes have declined in number, while there has been an increase in private hospitals (Dorwart et al., 1991). As a consequence, access to hospital care is unevenly distributed in the population. Patients in public hospitals are being discharged after shorter periods of hospitalization, largely because of the effectiveness of psychoactive drugs and an increase in efforts to return patients to the community as quickly as possible. This **deinstitutionalization** process can be a boon to personal development if the individual has a good place to live, sufficient social support, and supervision when needed. Unfortunately, many people who have been discharged from mental hospitals live in furnished rooms in undesirable neighborhoods, are socially isolated, and receive little professional help beyond brief contacts with physicians who prescribe antipsychotic drugs.

The lack of adequate care in the community for chronic mental patients has contributed to the large numbers of homeless people in American cities. Thousands of deinstitutionalized people have nowhere to live. They wander about city centers, sleep where they can, and carry their belongings with them. While the problem of homelessness is complex, the "dumping" of deinstitutionalized people on a community only contributes to human misery. We will look further at this problem in the next chapter.

CHAPTER SUMMARY

PSYCHOTHERAPY

No matter what their theoretical orientations psychotherapists perform three tasks: listening, understanding, and responding to the client.

Psychodynamic Therapy and Psychoanalysis Psychoanalysis is a special type of psychodynamic therapy carried on by specially trained therapists who use the technique of free association and place special emphasis on the examination of both dreams and fantasies. All psychodynamically oriented therapists emphasize insight, the understanding of one's inner life, as the goal of psychotherapy. They use the interpretation of transference, the client's displacement of affect and feeling about others onto the therapist, as an important part of therapy. They also take into account countertransference, the therapist's emotional response to the client. Some psychotherapists use the trancelike state of hypnosis to uncover and deal with material their patients have repressed.

Humanistic and Existential Therapies Humanistic therapies place emphasis on people's desire to achieve self-respect. An example of a humanistic therapy is Rogers's client-centered therapy, which stresses a nondirective, nonjudgmental approach in which the therapist provides an atmosphere of unconditional positive regard. The therapy is focused on increasing clients' self-acceptance and self-knowledge as a way to facilitate changes in their behavior. Existential therapies emphasize clients' needs to confront basic questions regarding the meaning and direction of their lives. Existential therapies are likely to combine humanistic and psychodynamic techniques. Perls's Gestalt therapy stresses that problems arise when people dissociate parts of themselves, especially their needs for personal gratification, from awareness.

Cognitive Psychotherapy The theory of cognitive psychotherapy is that the best way to alter emotional problems is to alter the client's thinking through cognitive restructuring. An early cognitive approach was Kelly's psychology of personal constructs, which focused on the roles people played in interacting with others and the assumptions underlying those roles. Kelly developed fixed-role therapy, in which clients were encouraged to practice new roles and relationships. Ellis originated rational-emotive therapy, which emphasizes the need for clients to question and change their self-defeating thinking and mistaken beliefs. Beck's cognitive therapy focuses on automatic thoughts that may govern behavior although they are not produced by rational considerations. The client and therapist jointly explore the validity of the clients' false beliefs about themselves, the world at large, and the future.

Brief Psychotherapies Most psychotherapy involves fewer than 12 sessions. Health insurance programs that pay for patients' psychotherapy are providing pressure to keep psychotherapy as brief as possible. Brief psychotherapy usually has specific goals or targets, such as helping patients deal with currently important problems in their lives. Interpersonal therapy is a brief type of psychotherapy that originally was used for depression but is now being extended to other problems. It emphasizes the key social relationships in a person's life.

How Effective Is Psychotherapy? Research on its effectiveness indicates that overall it is somewhat helpful to patients. For a wide range of clinical problems, no one psychotherapeutic approach is clearly superior to any other. The therapist's characteristics and approach are important factors in the success of psychotherapeutic interventions. Meta-analysis is a statistical procedure used to summarize the results of therapy outcome studies.

COGNITIVE-BEHAVIORAL THERAPIES

Behavior Therapy and Cognitive-Behavior Therapy Behavior therapy, the forerunner of cognitive-behavioral therapies, began as a way of using operant and classical conditioning techniques to change behavior. Behavior modification developed from the operant techniques. Many operant conditioning methods use reinforcement and shaping to gradually achieve a desired response. Fading is the process of eliminating special cues used in the shaping process. A token economy uses operant methods to reinforce desired behaviors. Biofeedback is a method used to develop control of internal processes. Desensitization used in the treatment of phobias and other fears was developed from the classical conditioning techniques.

Components of Cognitive-Behavior Therapy Cognitive-behavior therapies are interventions that integrate cognitive and behavioral therapies. The interventions include relaxation training, meditation, exposure therapy, modeling and assertiveness training. Depending on the case, these interventions are used by themselves or in combination.

In **relaxation training** the relaxation effect is achieved either by focusing on muscle groups or through meditation techniques.

Exposure therapy is based on the idea that continuous exposure to anxiety-provoking stimuli will decrease anxiety. **Flooding** is a form of exposure therapy in which the client is exposed to a high level of fear arousing stimuli that is not terminated just as a function of client anxiety. Flooding is based on the idea that **extinction** of the fears will occur if the client remains in the anxiety-provoking situation long enough. In **implosive therapy** the client imagines scenes of behaviors or situations that he or she has avoided in the past and then experiences the intense anxiety these create until that anxiety is extinguished. **Systematic desensitization** combines muscular relaxation with cognitive activity in which the client imagines a series of increasingly anxiety arousing scenes related to specific fears. **In vivo desensitization** involves the same techniques when the fear-arousing stimulus is actually present. **Paradoxical intention** is a treatment in which the clinician asks the client to perform exactly the behavior the client is trying to stop.

Modeling is a "how to" approach that involves the demonstration of the behaviors involved in specific social skills for the client. The procedure may be carried out through **live modeling** or the direct observation of the model, **symbolic modeling** or observation of a recorded performance of the model, or **covert modeling** in which the client is asked to imagine observing a model and the consequences of the model's behavior. **Guided rehearsals** allow the client to practice the modeled behavior. **Assertiveness training** is the use of modeling and rehearsal to teach a person the interpersonal skills needed to keep them from being imposed on by others.

Cognitive-behavioral interventions seem to be particularly effective in treating disorders in which anxiety plays a prominent role. More information is needed concerning which therapeutic components contribute the most to therapeutic effectiveness.

GROUP THERAPY

Group therapy sessions include a group of several usually with similar problems who meet together with a therapist in regular sessions. In addition to being lower in cost than individual therapy, group therapy may be more effective for some problems. Group membership provides acceptance and support, normative information about behaviors and feelings, and an opportunity to learn through modeling and behavioral rehearsal. Group therapy is likely to be carried out from either a psychodynamic or a cognitive-behavioral perspective.

Cognitive-Behavioral Group Therapy The focus of **cognitive-behavioral group therapy** is on development of social skills and comfort in social situations.

Family and Marital Therapy Both family therapy and marital therapy focus on individuals who already constitute a group. Family therapists view the family as a system. In family therapy the family members work together with the therapist to deal with their attitudes and feelings toward each other and to understand how the behavior of each affects the others. Marital therapy can be viewed as a subtype of family therapy. Family therapy is likely to include psychodynamic or cognitive-behavioral approaches.

Psychodrama Psychodrama is a special kind of group therapy in which the group acts out events of emotional significance in order to express strongly-felt emotions.

How Effective Are Group Approaches? Perhaps because of its complexity (more than one patient), less is known about the effectiveness of group therapy than individual therapeutic approaches. More information is needed concerning the basic concepts applicable to the group process and the active ingredients of group therapy. Most group approaches seem to be helpful for at least some people and large differences in effectiveness have not been found for the various group therapy approaches.

RESEARCH ON THE PSYCHOLOGICAL THERAPIES

Common and Unique Features of Therapies An important task for researchers is to distinguish common features of various therapeutic approaches from the unique features of particular therapies. There is growing reason to believe that it is necessary to separate the effects of the therapist's characteristics and the therapist-patient relationship from those attributable to the particular therapeutic procedures used. **Process research** in psychotherapy is concerned with understanding how each of the elements of the therapeutic effort affect the outcome for the patient.

Therapeutic Outcomes One of the most important questions in studies of therapy is what the outcome measures should be. Possible choices are the therapist's opinion, the client's behavior or feelings, or the view of others such as family members or co-workers. There is often disagreement about outcome among these different sources.

Comparing Therapies There is a strong trend toward no difference between therapeutic approaches in amount of change produced. However, in some cases cognitive-behavioral approaches appear to be superior. There is considerable difference in the success of individual therapists, even those that use the same therapeutic approach. In general, psychological approaches have been found to be useful in cases without extreme psychopathology. Psychological therapies are often not successful alone in the treatment of schizophrenia, bipolar disorder, alcoholism, and drug abuse, but frequently produce a better result when used in combination with drug therapies than the drug therapies produce when used alone. Studies that compare several therapies are needed, but are complex and costly.

Recognizing Cultural and Ethnic Diversity Because of growing cultural and ethnic diversity within the population it is important for therapists to become more aware of the values, beliefs, and needs of particular groups, such as African Americans, Hispanics, Native Americans, and Asian Americans. Research is needed to determine the degree to which cultural and ethnic factors play important roles in processes and outcomes of therapeutic interventions.

INTEGRATION OF PSYCHOLOGICALLY BASED THERAPEUTIC APPROACHES

Aspects of many of the different therapeutic approaches have been found to be useful. Most therapists believe that therapeutic techniques addressing emotion, cognition, and behavior are all important in helping clients. As a result there is a trend toward a greater integration of therapeutic techniques based on the different perspectives.

BIOLOGICAL THERAPIES

Electroconvulsive Therapy Electroconvulsive therapy (ECT) is most likely to be used for severe depression, especially as treatment for those who are at high risk for suicide, when drugs and other types of therapy have failed to help.

Drug Therapies Four general types of drugs have been found to be effective in treating mental disorders: **antipsychotic drugs, antimanic drugs, antidepressant drugs,** and **antianxiety drugs.** Before drugs can be used to treat patients the medications must be thoroughly tested for effectiveness and for negative side effects. Drugs and other therapeutic procedures are evaluated through **clinical trials** that compare outcomes for patients who receive different treatments.

How Effective Are Biological Therapies? ECT and medications are often effective in treating particular disorders. Some medications are effective short-term but not long-term. Some drugs can have serious side effects—for example, the development of tardive dyskinesia in schizophrenic individuals treated with certain antipsychotic drugs. More information is needed concerning the mechanisms by which biological therapies affect behavior. Researchers are exploring the possibility that combinations of biological and psychological intervention are more effective than either intervention by itself. There is evidence that this might be the case. There is also evidence suggesting that combinations of psychological interventions can be more effective than the interventions by themselves.

HOSPITALIZATION

Some of the reasons that psychiatric hospitalization is recommended include behavior that poses a threat to self or others, failure of outpatient treatment, or a treatment procedure that requires a high degree of control. As a result of the **deinstitutionalization** movement of the past several decades, hospital treatment in the United States has become less frequent and those who are hospitalized tend to remain there for shorter periods of time.

CHAPTER EIGHTEEN

Sherri Silverman, *Ladders of Light #7: Yellow Hands,* 1992.
Superstock.

SOCIETY'S RESPONSE TO MALADAPTIVE BEHAVIOR

Ann Jackson had taught at Buchanan High School for eight years. She was 33 years old, still had some ideals, and had a reputation among both students and faculty of being a nice person. She was also a discouraged person who too often felt she wasn't able to reach several of her students. One who fell into this group was 16-year-old Bill Hadley. Bill paid little attention in class, did not complete assignments, and frequently did not show up at all. But what worried Ann Jackson the most was what she knew about Bill's activities outside class. Other students were afraid of him because of his imposing size, his bullying attitude, and his history of antisocial behavior. He had had numerous contacts with the police for a variety of reasons. He had been accused of puncturing the tires of a dozen cars parked along a street, extorting money from other students, and shoplifting at neighborhood stores. The most serious offense was a severe beating Bill had given to another student. According to those present at the fight, Bill was in such an uncontrollable rage that he couldn't stop hitting and kicking the other student even though it was evident that the student was helpless and in pain, and he started fighting with the spectators when they intervened. Ann Jackson couldn't get Bill out of her mind. She continually worried about what was going to happen to him.

Relatively small problems have a way of becoming big problems if nothing is done about them. Ann Jackson wished that something could be done to redirect Bill Hadley's life while he was still young, but she didn't know what she, the school, or the community could do now or what could have been done earlier to prevent Bill's current unhappiness, anger, and counterproductive behavior.

Many well-meaning and intelligent people feel helpless when confronted with obvious mental distress in another individual. At the same time, everyday life is full of examples of people who are able to either help people in distress or help prevent distress from occurring. In the following example an exceptionally accomplished young college graduate was found to have had a chaotic, stress-inducing family life. Yet an informal relationship with a neighboring family had given him valuable opportunities for personal growth.

He came from an extremely disturbed home setting in which every member of his family except himself had been hospitalized for severe mental illness; and yet he had graduated from a renowned university with honors, had starred on the football team, and was unusually popular. During his government training he was held in the highest esteem by staff members and was rated as best liked and most likely to succeed by his peers.

In examining this young man's history we discovered that during his elementary school years he had essentially adopted a neighborhood family as his own and spent endless hours with them. Certain characteristics of this family appear most significant. They were a helping family in the sense that love emanated from them and was freely available to all. Of special significance for the fellow under consideration was his relationship with a boy in the family, a year older than he, who formed for him a positive role model with whom he closely identified. . . .

An even more crucial factor was his relationship with the mother in this family, who became his guide, counselor, and chief source of emotional nurturance. His reports indicate that while this relationship was intense, it was not symbiotic, and seemed to foster his independence and self-development. Although there are probably few like her, she represents a dimension of socially indigenous therapy that may be more significant than is usually recognized. Her home became a neighborhood gathering place. It might be characterized as an informal therapy agency, a kitchen clinic.

—Bergin & Lambert, 1978, pp. 149–150

In this chapter we discuss the role played by society in dealing with deviance and preventing problems of living. People have vulnerabilities that keep them from being able to handle challenges along life's path and from developing optimal skills. What can society do to prevent personal vulnerabilities from ruining people's lives? What can society do to minimize the negative effects on the individual and the community of vulnerabilities created either by biological or environmental factors? Not much can be done about factors such as a person's heredity and brain structure, but some of the unfortunate aspects (poverty, parental abuse) of people's lives stem from their environment and, to some extent, might be subject to modification.

Vulnerability and resilience have been a theme throughout this book. Society has a role to play, not only in reducing personal vulnerabilities, but also in fostering resilience (Coie et al., 1993). Resilience is not a static trait but rather the ability to use internal or external resources. New vulnerabilities and/or strengths may emerge during developmental transitions throughout the life course. The community can play a role in prevention, as well as in fostering resilience in both children and adults. While the negative effects of poverty seem to be cumulative and increase as children get older, there is good reason to believe that the promotion of a person's sense of competence and self-esteem is one of the key ingredients in any prevention process and that supportive relationships are especially valuable in promoting resilience (Werner, 1993).

Types of Prevention

Throughout this book we have considered methods of assessing, treating, and caring for individuals with behavior problems, but we have only briefly mentioned the possibility that the actual occurrence of maladaptive behavior in the population can be reduced. This is the focus of *prevention*.

Levels of Prevention

"An ounce of prevention is worth a pound of cure" is a well-known truism. Why, then, aren't preventive measures more common? In some cases it is not clear what steps are needed to achieve the goal of prevention, and in others society does not seem willing or able to take the needed steps. Prevention of mental or physical disorder can take place on three levels.

These three types of prevention span the entire range of mental health interventions from the universality of primary prevention; to the selective interventions of secondary prevention; to tertiary prevention, which essentially amounts to treatment.

Primary prevention is concerned with the general reduction of new cases of disorders and is administered to everyone in a particular population, for instance all students at a school or all pregnant women whether or not they might be at particular risk. Scientific information about cause and effect is very important in primary prevention. For example, knowledge of the possibility of harm to the unborn child has persuaded many women not to smoke or drink during pregnancy. Physicians are much more careful about prescribing medication for pregnant women because of information linking even seemingly harmless drugs with birth defects. And knowledge of the harmful effects of nicotine addiction has led psychologists to conduct research on ways to discourage children from beginning to smoke cigarettes. Another example of primary prevention is premarital counseling. Marital problems and divorce are highly correlated with maladaptive behavior. Premarital counseling is aimed at encouraging couples to anticipate any problems and to develop ways of coping with them before marriage.

Secondary prevention is more selective than primary prevention because it is limited to a subgroup of the population that is at a higher than average risk for developing a mental disorder, with psychological, social, or biological factors as the basis for determining risk. The aim of secondary prevention is to reduce the potential disability of an existing abnormal condition. For example, if a child with phenylketonuria (PKU) is identified early, a special diet can prevent serious retardation. Children who are behind in intellectual and social development as a result of living in homes where little stimulation and individual attention are available can be helped to gain more normal development through special enrichment programs. These programs can help the child catch up in the developmental process and gain skills that will make later school achievement more likely. Another example of secondary prevention is providing support groups for people who have recently experienced a traumatic event.

Whereas secondary prevention efforts are directed to "at-risk" people, the focus of **tertiary prevention** is people already diagnosed as having an illness (Institute of Medicine, 1994). Tertiary prevention is aimed at reducing the impairment that has resulted from a given disorder or event. This is achieved through rehabilitation and resocialization. For example, behavioral therapy for a hyperactive child may help him or her become more attentive in school and more accepted by other children despite the continuing problems associated with the condition. Counseling or group therapy after a traumatic event such as injury and permanent paralysis from an automobile accident may provide the social supports that reduce a person's vulnerability to the added stress of coping with the new disability. Rehabilitation of those who have committed crimes is another important area of tertiary prevention. Often offenders serve a prison sentence and are discharged back into the community without either adequate skills of impulse-control or the practical skills to get a job. The same difficult transitional situation is often faced by people who have been hospitalized for a schizophrenic disorder and later discharged directly into the community without any further attention or support.

Preventive measures have been developed in many cases in which biophysical factors are known to cause maladaptive behavior. However, the effects of detrimental social factors have frequently been ignored or neglected. It is much easier to detect and control the effects of an enzyme deficiency in newborn infants than it is to detect and control the pervasive influence of poverty and racism. But ignoring these causes and correlates of maladaptive behavior will not decrease their influence.

When prevention methods are successful, risk factors that lead to abnormal behavior are reduced or eliminated. In general, priority in efforts to achieve prevention is given to serious conditions that have high rates of incidence, and for which effective methods are available. For example, prevention efforts have been directed at one of the most serious and prevalent maladaptive behaviors of childhood, juvenile delinquency.

Juvenile delinquency is a legal term used to designate lawbreaking by minors. Each year between four and five percent of American teenagers, or approximately 1,300,000, are referred to the courts for suspected offenses other than traffic violations (Dryfoos, 1990) (see Figure 18–1). The following case gives an example of the troubled youngsters to whom the police, the legal system, and the community must respond.

Carl is a 16-year-old high school dropout who was placed in a locked correctional institution for seven months. He had been charged with breaking and entering, robbery, and parole violation offenses in which he admitted involvement. He first started getting into trouble at age 12 when he assaulted two women during a purse-snatching incident. By the time he entered high school, he had been in juvenile court for offenses involving theft, destruction of property, and unauthorized use of an automobile. When he was fifteen, he and his friends broke into an appliance store, and stole several color TVs, tape recorders, and portable radios. Carl's father is an accountant and his mother is a high school teacher. Carl describes himself as a "bad ass." He thinks his parents believe that hanging around with the wrong people is the source of his many difficulties with established authority and the law.

Delinquent behavior seems to have many causes, ranging from poor living conditions to a psychopathic or antisocial personality disorder to psychosis. Some of the following conditions have also been identified with delinquency.

1. Poor physical and economic conditions in the home and neighborhood.

(a)   (b)

(c)

Figure 18-1 Helping juvenile offenders to become productive members of society is a challenge to the court system, to those who work to rehabilitate these young people, and to society as a whole. (a) The judge often tries to assess the adolescent's attitudes about the offense. (b) Some juveniles can be treated most effectively in a residential institution where they are removed from their everyday environments and can receive intensive treatment. (c) Another effective way of helping some young offenders is to require that they spend time in community service rather than institutionalizing them.

2. Rejection or lack of security at home.
3. Exposure to antisocial role models within or outside the home, and antisocial pressures from peer-group relationships.
4. Lack of support for achievement in school.
5. The expectation of hostility on the part of others.

Juvenile delinquency can be approached at different levels of prevention. Primary prevention often takes the form of programs aimed at improving living conditions and school achievement. For example, provision of low-cost subsidized housing that would enable families to move into low crime areas might provide less exposure to other delinquents. Special school programs that make individualized instruction available to help children with deficiencies in academic skills might not only help them become successful in school but might also have a long-term positive effect on their lives by giving them hope for the future as well as later opportunities for success. Although such programs are important and can be helpful to potential delinquents, perhaps the most effective primary prevention comes about through personal relationships. There is some evidence that if children growing up in high-crime areas have a positive role model, their behavior may be more influenced by that person than by their antisocial peers. When this happens, it is often because of the opportunity to observe and practice the cognitive and behavioral coping skills demonstrated by the role model.

Secondary prevention programs concentrate on young people who have shown early signs of delinquency. For example, there might be a special intervention focused on helping youngsters who have committed minor nonviolent offenses (such as theft or truancy) behave less impulsively.

Sometimes changing delinquent behavior might be classified as tertiary prevention. The youth might be involved in seriously maladaptive behavior. The following case presents an example of the type of preventive measures that may be taken in such a situation.

A 14-year-old boy was referred to a therapist by the court because he had set several large grass fires that had endangered houses. He could not explain his behavior, and neither could his parents since he had always behaved responsibly at home.

The boy's family was seen for six family-therapy sessions. These sessions revealed that the family could not discuss problems openly but tended to communicate nonverbally. Several recent family crises had caused tension. The father seemed to handle his unhappiness by withdrawing from the family into club activities. The son seemed to express his anger at family problems by setting fires. Once they began to meet in therapy sessions and these problems became evident, all of the family members were able to change their behavior. One year later there had been no more fire-setting.

—Based on Eisler, 1972, pp. 77–78

At all levels of prevention, the problems of delinquency and the therapeutic treatment of delinquents are far from solved. The number of delinquents who go on to commit more antisocial acts is high. Different approaches work best with different types of cases, but as yet all methods produce more failures than successes. Understanding delinquency requires a better grasp of the variables involved in the interaction between the person and the situation.

Situation-focused and Competency-focused Prevention Prevention can be approached from two perspectives. **Situation-focused prevention** is aimed at reducing or eliminating the environmental causes of disordered behavior, while **competency-focused prevention** is concerned with enhancing people's ability to cope with conditions that might lead to maladaptive behaviors. Situation-focused approaches seek to change the environment, for example, by making it less stressful. Competency-focused approaches seek to strengthen people's coping skills so as to make them more resistant should various types of stress-arousing situations arise.

Divorce is a common example of a stress-arousing situation. Its occurrence has increased dramatically over the last several decades and has resulted in changes in life styles and in the environments in which children are brought up. Nearly half of all children living in the United States can expect to spend some time—an average of about six years—living in a single-parent family. Divorce and parental discord are related to impaired functioning and social behavior in children. Divorced people are likely to be overrepresented among people who make suicide attempts, become alcoholics, go through periods of depression, and seek help from mental-health professionals.

Programs are needed that can reduce the likelihood of maladjustment in divorced couples and their children. An example of such a program is one developed for newly separated individuals. The program provided the participants with psychological support and special training over a six-month period after the separation (Bloom & Hodges, 1988). Staff members made themselves available to participants when advice and counseling were needed. Training was provided in such practical areas as employment and child-rearing. Compared with newly separated people who did not participate in the program, the participants experienced less anxiety, fatigue, and physical illness, along with improved coping ability. There was some evidence that the intervention program was more effective for women than for men. Participants' comments after the program ended suggested that their knowledge that interested people and special services were available if needed may have been the most powerful ingredient in the program. Future research will be needed to determine the long-term effects on both parents and children of programs that are designed to reduce the traumatic effects of an inevitably distressing situation.

Although the program just described can be seen as a competency-focused approach, it was activated only after the participants had already taken steps toward divorce. Another type of competency-focused prevention effort might aim to strengthen skills that are important in interpersonal relationships, particularly with one's spouse, long before thoughts of divorce might arise. The idea behind such an effort would be to increase coping skills and thereby enable couples to handle the stresses of marriage in more effective ways.

Early-education programs also illustrate competency-focused prevention. Their aim is to prevent or reduce problems in subsequent years. One project began with the frequent observation that maladapted children (and adults) tend to have weak interpersonal cognitive problem-solving skills (Shure & Spivack, 1982, 1987). These skills include the ability to identify problems and feelings (in oneself and others), to think of alternative solutions to a problem, to see relationships between alternative approaches and the achievement of goals, and to appreciate the consequences of one's actions (Shure, 1992). Interpersonal problem-solving skills can be thought of as mediating effective behavioral adjustment as well as fostering academic competence (see Figure 18–2).

Figure 18-2 Children often act directly. When they want something they take it, or they express displeasure by hitting another child. Cognitive games created by a team of researchers attempt to create greater empathy with others and in this way change the self-centered aggressive behavior often seen in childhood.

The following is an excerpt from one of the lessons used by Spivack and his co-workers in teaching young children to be more sensitive to their feelings and those of others.

Now this is just a game. *Have each child hold a toy previously used from trinket box.* Peter, you snatch Kevin's toy from him.

Kevin, how do you feel about that? *Kevin responds.*

Peter, now let him have it back.

Now, how do you feel, Kevin? *After child answers, repeat with other pairs.*

Use a picture of a firetruck. Larry, how would going for a ride on this firetruck make you feel? *Let child respond.*

Let's pretend that a man came and drove the truck away and you could NOT have a ride. How would you feel now? *Same child responds.*

Now let's pretend he came back and said, "Okay, now you can go for a ride." How would that make you feel? *Same child responds.*

Use a picture of a ball. How do you think Steven might feel if we let him play with this ball? *Group answers.*

Maybe he would feel happy and maybe he would not feel happy. Let's find out. How can we find out? *Encourage children to ask.*

Let's pretend someone came along and threw the ball out the window so Steven could not play with it anymore. Now how do you think Steven might feel?

He might feel sad or he might feel mad. How can we find out?

Encourage children to ask.

—Spivack et al., 1976, pp. 183–184

These researchers found that behavioral adjustment was positively influenced by training in cognitive and social skills. This positive effect was greatest for children who originally seemed most maladjusted, and positive results were still evident a year later. In a related project inner-city mothers who were given training in interpersonal cognitive problem-solving skills were able to pass their training on to their children. Research with older children and adults supports the idea that the skills involved in academic and social effectiveness are learnable. Furthermore, it has been shown that improved teacher training—for example, teaching them to reinforce students' adaptive behavior—contributes to a more productive learning environment in the classroom. Sometimes situation-focused and competency-focused prevention efforts can occur as part of the same project. An approach that involves parenting classes and a chance to earn a high school diploma for teen age mothers combined with in-school day care for their children provides a competency focus for the mothers and situation-focused prevention for their preschool

children (see Figure 18–3). Because the mothers have few financial resources, few job-related skills, and usually lack maturity and knowledge about how to care for their children, the children are at high risk. For instance, in addition to earning a high school diploma and acquiring job-related skills, the young mothers in the Teenage Pregnancy and Parenting Program (TAPP) at an alternative high school in Seattle take courses in nutrition, anger management, household finances, and child rearing. Participants say the TAPP program also provides a support group and a gathering place for young mothers.

Sites of Prevention

This chapter especially emphasizes research that is relevant to the prevention of maladaptive behavior. Where data are lacking, we speculate about the use of social experimentation. We do not attempt a comprehensive analysis of all the components of a complex social structure; instead, we direct our attention toward three areas that definitely affect the growth and development of children and adults: the family, the school, and the community.

We are in a period of major changes within the family. Of the 12 million children under the age of 3 in the United States today, a staggering number are affected by one or more risk factors that make healthy development more difficult (*Starting Points*, 1994). The changes include:

- In 1960, only 5 percent of all births in the United States were to unmarried mothers. The figure today is over 26 percent.
- Every year about 1 million adolescents become pregnant.

Figure 18-3 High-school day care facilities provide young mothers with a chance to earn a diploma and learn both work-related and parenting skills.

- Divorce rates are rising. Almost half of all children can expect to experience a divorce during childhood and to live an average of five years in a single-parent family.
- Children are increasingly likely to live with only one parent, usually the mother. In 1960, fewer than 10 percent of all children under the age of eighteen lived with one parent; the figure today is 25 percent. Fathers are increasingly absent from the home.
- The number of children in foster homes is close to 500,000.
- One in four children under the age of three (nearly 3 million children) live in families with incomes below the federal poverty line.
- Pressures on both parents to work mean that they have less time with their young children; more than half of mothers of infants now work outside the home.

The Family

Parents play a significant role in their children's development because of the genes they contribute and the environment they provide. This environment begins in the uterus during the nine months before birth. Whatever can improve prenatal care and thus reduce the incidence of premature birth and other foreseeable difficulties might help reduce several types of problems, such as low intelligence. Improved prenatal and neonatal care can be expected to reduce brain damage, which, among other conditions, is related to certain types of epilepsy.

From the standpoint of prevention, the family is important because much of the child's earliest learning and development takes place within the family setting. Self-help groups can be useful for parents of young children. These groups provide parents with a way of understanding the typical ways that children behave as well as a way of learning about how others have coped successfully with child-rearing problems. Meeting with others with similar interests also provides an important opportunity for social relationships with other adults, something that is often lacking for parents with young children. Parents' ideas about child-rearing and the development process make important contributions to the day-to-day environment of children (see Figure 18–4). The relationship between certain parental practices and aggression in children demonstrates the effect of parental attitudes on their children. Many aggressive children come from homes in which the parents make the child feel insecure and rejected, bombard the child with commands, taunts,

and threats, and teach the child that force is the only way to get what is wanted. The following parenting practices have been linked reliably to children's aggression (Perry et al., 1990):

1. *Monitoring failures.* Parents of aggressive and delinquent children are less aware of their children's whereabouts, activities, and social contacts.
2. *Parental aggression.* Many aggressive children come from homes in which at least one parent is exceptionally violent.
3. *Permissiveness.* Parents of aggressive children frequently decline to set limits on their children's behavior and are ineffective at stopping their children's deviant behavior.
4. *Inconsistency.* Inconsistency both between parents and within one parent in disciplinary practices have been implicated in aggressive development.
5. *Rejection.* Highly aggressive individuals often have a history of parental rejection.

Because parents' behavior may play a role in their children's problems, many clinicians who specialize in treating childhood disorders stress the importance of parenting training, family therapy, or in some cases, therapeutic work with the parents as the most effective way of helping children. However, some parents experience tremendous, and often unwarranted, personal guilt if their children develop problems (see Figure 18–5).

The following are some additional examples of the influence parents with certain disorders may have on their children (Rutter, 1988). Children of psychotic parents are slow in developing speech and bladder control, have more eating and sleeping problems, and are more likely to be delinquent than other children. Alcoholic

Figure 18-4 A self-help or mutual support group for parents of young children can provide both learning opportunities and social support.

WHAT WENT WRONG?

Never owned dog?

Had strange middle name?

Johnny Xerxes Miller

Did not learn to play a musical instrument?

Too much fruit salad in early life?

R. Chast

Figure 18-5 Some well-intentioned, overly conscientious parents worry too much about what children need early in life to lay the groundwork for a good life later. On the other hand, there are parents who do not devote enough attention to their children's needs.
SOURCE: Drawing by R. Chast; © 1987 *The New Yorker* Magazine, Inc.

parents have a disproportionately large number of hyperactive children, and alcoholic mothers are over-represented among mothers of babies with low birth-weight and low IQs. There is also a relationship between criminality in parents and delinquency in their children.

Child Abuse In chapter 15, we discussed the scope of the child abuse problem. Children who have been phys-ically abused, malnourished, and neglected by their par-ents are more prone to various forms of maladaption than other children. Under certain circumstances even "normal" parents—that is, parents who are not obvi-ously disturbed—can have negative effects on their chil-dren's development. One of the most tragic examples of this is child abuse.

Child abuse varies in degree and is often hidden from

view by embarrassed and ashamed parents. But thou-sands of children, many under three years of age, are seriously—often fatally—mistreated each year. When emotional abuse is included as well as physical abuse, the figure becomes much larger. A sizable percentage of abuse cases involve sexual assault.

Abusive parents tend to be less intelligent and more aggressive, impulsive, immature, self-centered, tense, and self-critical than nonabusive parents. They are more likely to have been abused themselves as children; thus, child abuse is a vicious cycle (Cicchetti & Carlson, 1989). Table 18–1 lists family characteristics often asso-ciated with child abuse. The physical and psychological damage done to children by abusive parents can some-times be observed immediately.

An abusive parent is usually a very troubled person who seems to be a victim of uncontrollable impulses and frustrations. The following is an excerpt from a group therapy session in which the participants were mothers who had abused their children.

Mother 1:   *I was just at my breaking point and I knew if I didn't get help somewhere, it would just go on and on and end up a vicious circle. I think that everyone who has had this problem at one time has thought "my goodness, I must be the only person in the world that feels this way." And when I found out that I wasn't, that was a load off my mind.*

Therapist: *Feels what way?*

TABLE 18–1
Characteristics of Abusing Families

Parents' Histories

Experience of abuse or neglect
Lack of affection from parents
Large families
Married as teenagers

Current Family Situation

Socially isolated, parents lack social support
Marital discord
Parental impulsivity
Parental retardation or illiteracy
Stressful living conditions (e.g., inadequate housing)

Parents' Approach to Child-rearing

Infrequent praise of children
Strict demands on child
Low level of child supervision
Early toilet training
Maternal dislike of caretaking
Parental disagreements over child-rearing practices

Source: Based on Nietzel and Himelein, 1986.

Mother 1:	Desperation with their children. Not knowing how to cope. Afraid that you would just lose control completely and knock their head off, you know. I think we were all brought up to believe that women are supposed to have children and they're supposed to have the mother-instinct and if you don't have it, there is something definitely wrong. And I think it took this group to make me realize that women just aren't born with the mother-ing instinct . . . that has helped me.
Another mother:	If you're going to pound your child, the best thing to do is separate yourself from your child.
Mother 1:	That's fine to say, but what if you're like me and you can go on beautifully for a month, two months, three months and all of a sudden like last week I was feel-ing just fine and I cleaned house like I do every Monday . . . I got all them damn floors waxed and _____ wakes up from her nap and she couldn't get her body shirt undone so she got all upset and she wet all over my new waxed floor. And I just went berserk and I threw her around like she had killed somebody, because right at that moment I just snapped, I didn't feel it coming. I was fine, everything was hunky-dory, nothing was wrong, I wasn't in a bad mood, there was no warning . . .

This type of behavior is typical of abusive parents. Behavioral training in impulse control and coping skills can be helpful for parents who want to stop harming their children. Numerous kinds of prevent-ive programs have been attempted. These include parental education and the use of parents as thera-pists. A promising mutual-aid approach is Parents Anonymous (PA), an organization modeled after the social support approach of Alcoholics Anonymous (see chapter 14).

An example of preventive research on abuse is a study in which abusing parents received training in par-enting skills (Wolfe et al., 1981). The parents' training consisted of reading about effective parenting tech-niques, observing modeled demonstrations of how to handle common child-rearing problems, and learning relaxation and other coping skills. In addition, project staff members made weekly home visits to help the par-ents implement what they had learned. When parents who participated in this program were compared with a control group of abusers, the parents in the special pro-gram showed significant improvement in parenting skills. A follow-up showed that none of the specially treated abusers harmed their children during the year after their participation in the program. This study sug-gests that effective child management skills can be taught to abusive parents with a relatively small invest-ment of time and labor.

Similarly, encouraging results were obtained in a study in which the subjects were 400 pregnant women who had at least one of a cluster of risk factors for child abuse (teenaged, poor, unmarried, first pregnancy) (Olds & Henderson, 1989). The pregnant women were ran-domly assigned to four treatment groups. The first group was a "no intervention" control, which included a screening of the child at one and two years of age. The second group included these screenings and provided free transportation to prenatal and well-baby medical appointments. The third group built upon that plan by adding to it nine visits to the home by a nurse during the pregnancy. The fourth group extended regular nurse's visits to the child's second birthday. The nurse's visits were designed to promote linkage with formal service agencies when appropriate and to enhance the social support of the mother (and father, when present). Furthermore, the nurse provided parenting and health education and consultation. Finally, clarification of values around social and family issues was included. Clearly, the fourth group received relatively broad and intensive family services.

The clearest benefits were reaped by the subjects who received the most extensive treatment. Nineteen per-cent of those in the control group abused or neglected their children within the first two years of life. In con-trast, only four percent of those in the group who received long-term nurses' visits maltreated their chil-dren. The other two groups had better results than did the control group, but these were not nearly as impres-sive as the results for the group that received the extended intervention. Other evidence of the extended intervention's effectiveness were also found for scolding rates, provision of appropriate play materials, and avoid-ance of restriction. Moreover, their children showed a trend toward better developmental progress and fewer emergency room visits than their peers in the control group. These findings suggest that a comprehensive intervention program can prevent child maltreatment and promote good parenting in groups at high risk for parenting dysfunction.

There have been many programs directed toward pre-venting child abuse (MacMillan et al., 1994a; MacMil-lan et al., 1994b). The most effective programs seem to be those that involve (1) home visits in which parents can receive training in how to interact with their chil-dren and (2) monitoring of the situation in the home.

Spouse Abuse "To have and to hold . . . to love and to cherish. . . . " This sentiment reflects the feelings of most people toward marriage—but these feelings are not shared by everyone. Beginning in the 1970s, largely as a result of the women's movement, attention has been drawn to the problem of **spouse abuse,** particularly the plight of abused women—those who are browbeaten psychologically as well as those who are physically assaulted—who cower in bedrooms and kitchens, are patched up in emergency rooms, and, not infrequently, are beaten, shot, or stabbed to death in their own living rooms. Spouse abuse occurs in several million homes in the United States each year and more than 8 percent of homicides involve the killing of one spouse by another. An estimated 25 to 30 percent of all women with a spouse or cohabiting partner have been beaten at least once while in such a relationship (Sadock, 1989).

Twenty-nine percent of the women murdered in the United States in 1992 were killed by a husband, exhusband, or suitor (Reiss & Roth, 1994). The type of person who is a batterer tends to become a stalker after the breakup of the relationship, a situation in which the woman frequently concludes (correctly) that her situation can become more perilous if she tries to leave. Cultural acceptance is a contributing factor. Many cultures have an unwritten code that the husband can command and deserves to control the wife. The wife's personal fear is only one of the factors that lead many to tolerate the abuse. Economic dependence, desire to preserve the home, and concern about separation from the children add to the reasons for a woman's unwillingness to leave or to press charges even when the police intervene after an urgent call for help. There is also a generational influence; 80 percent of batterers were the sons of batterers who observed their fathers abusing their mothers. Women threaten and, in fact, kill their husbands or exhusbands, but in smaller numbers and sometimes to protect themselves.

There are data that indicate batterers in upper income and educational groups respond to an appropriate punishment after the first call to the police (Reiss & Roth, 1944). Judicial leniency at this stage is no help to the batterer or to society. There are also data indicating that counseling is valuable to many at this early stage. Why these two approaches are helpful to some and unhelpful to others is worthy of further research. The generational transmission brings up the question of nature or nurture: Does a son who sees his mother battered conclude that it is an acceptable norm, or is he repelled but has an uncontrollable temper that overcomes logical processes? Again, good scientific data could help greatly in these areas.

A woman who has been abused over a long period is afraid. Fear might be a woman's first and most immediate feeling during or after a beating, but other negative feelings may surface when she is not in physical danger. The abused woman is likely to develop doubts about herself. She might wonder whether she is justified in fearing for her life and calling herself "abused." Most likely, however, a woman who thinks or feels that she is being abused is probably correct.

An abused woman may also feel guilty, even though she has done nothing wrong. An abused wife may feel responsible for her husband's violence because she believes she may have provoked him in some way. She then places the blame on herself instead of on her abuser. Along with the feelings of being a failure, both as a woman and in her marriage, may come a real fear of being trapped and powerless.

A wife abuser tends to be filled with anger, resentment, suspicion, and tension. He also, underneath all his aggressive behavior, can be insecure and feel like a loser. He may use violence to give vent to the bad feelings he has about himself or his lot in life. Home is one place where he can express those feelings without punishment to himself. If he were angry with his boss and struck him, he would pay the price; but all too often he gets away without any penalty when he beats his wife. One study found that compared with nonabusive husbands, abusive husbands were less assertive in social relationships than their wives, more likely to have been abused as children and more likely to have witnessed spouse abuse between their own parents (Rosenbaum & O'Leary, 1981).

Efforts to help abused spouses include not only emergency care, safety, and shelter but also long-range planning. Because abused spouses need to develop better feelings about themselves—that is, change their self-image—they need to strengthen their self-related positive cognitions. Counseling often emphasizes the following types of self-statements.

- I am not to blame for being beaten and abused.
- I am not the cause of another person's violent behavior.
- I do not have to take it.
- I deserve to be treated with respect.
- I do have power over my own life.
- I can use my power to take good care of myself.
- I can make changes in my life if I want to.
- I am not alone. I can ask others to help me.
- I deserve to make my own life safe and happy.

The three levels of prevention can all be applied to spouse abuse. Premarital counseling is an example of primary prevention; marital counseling to reduce discord illustrates secondary prevention; and providing abused spouses with safety, shelter, and counseling exemplifies tertiary prevention.

Parental Conflict and Divorce

John's parents divorced when he was 3. Shortly thereafter, his father all but dropped out of his life, visiting only occasionally and never for more than a few hours. When John was 7, his mother remarried, and the family moved halfway across the country. He was 11 before he saw his father again.

As visitations became more regular, John's mother began criticizing her ex at every possible opportunity. The more she criticized, the more John became his father's apologist. When he was 15, convinced the grass was greener on the other side of the fence, John went to live with his dad. That arrangement, however, lasted little more than a year. Realizing he had a better relationship with his father when he wasn't living with him, John again packed his bags and spent his last year of high school with his mother and stepfather.

John's story is, unfortunately, not that unusual. There is growing evidence that parental conflict and divorce have adverse effects on children's development (Cummings & Davies, 1994). However, these effects can be reduced by taking certain preventive steps (Wallerstein, 1991).

Research on this topic is complicated, because it is not possible to separate the effects of divorce from the effects of family conflict and parental inadequacy. Divorce might be regarded as a special case of family conflict in which legal dissolution of the family results. While divorce is public and measurable, parental conflict occurs mainly in private and cannot be reduced to a statistic. Researchers have tried to pinpoint the kinds of negative outcomes that family conflict tends to promote. Boys in most cases have been found to be more obviously vulnerable than girls are and they often respond in more easily noticed ways. Common reactions in boys are increased aggression, troubled peer relations, and lack of impulse control (Cherlin et al., 1991).

The degree to which divorce is upsetting to children has been recognized for a long time. Children of divorced parents show up much more frequently in psychiatric outpatient clinic populations than their proportion in the population would predict. Even children in nonclinical samples are likely to exhibit dramatic divorce-related changes in play behavior and relationships with others (Hetherington, 1991). Not only do children have to deal with their own stress, but they must cope with parents who are also experiencing high levels of stress and whose own emotional health and financial well-being may have significantly deteriorated. Children and their parents must adjust to new living and custody arrangements (see Figure 18-6). Research and the clinical experience of many therapists and counselors has provided some ideas that may help parents soften the blow of divorce for their children.

(a)

(b)

Figure 18-6 Divorce has many effects on the lives of both parents and children. The majority of children live with their mothers, often in reduced economic circumstances. Children may have infrequent contact with their noncustodial parent and that relationship may be based on what are often rather superficial interactions but little ongoing attention. (a) A single mother prepares a meal for her children. (b) A child and noncustodial father spend an afternoon together on an outing.

1. *Tell the children ahead of time.* This lets them prepare for one parent's moving out.
2. *Tell the children the reasons that the decision was made.*

This helps prevent children's frequent belief that they were the cause of the breakup. Make the explanation brief but honest and suitable for the age of the child.

3. *Emphasize that the divorce is a permanent decision*. Many children harbor the belief that their parents will eventually get back together.

4. *Explain what changes there will be in the child's life*. These may include moving, a new school, and much less money to spend. Emphasize the positive challenge of adapting to the new situation.

5. *Let the children be free to express their anger*. This is an effective way to prevent long-term problems. At the same time, the parents should avoid using their children as a dumping ground for their own sense of anger or despair. Instead, they should share their negative feelings with an adult friend or with a therapist or counselor.

6. *Avoid forcing the child to choose between the parents or to take sides*. Custody and visitation rights that are fair to both parents should be agreed upon. Both parents should make continued contact with the children a high priority.

Parental Training While parents sometimes fail to help their children develop optimally, there are numerous instances in which they can play very positive roles. For example, there is growing evidence that parents can be trained to respond therapeutically to their children's behavioral problems. Training parents to be effective behavior-change agents has positive consequences for children's development (Kramer, 1990). Not only can the parent help the child learn needed cognitive or social skills, but because the parent learns to help in a positive way, the relationship between the parent and child can be improved. Training parents in helping skills can change the child's view of the parent from that of someone who is not satisfied with the child's behavior to someone supportive who cares about the child and is helping the child to change the situation to achieve a positive outcome. The main techniques for bringing this about are modeling, behavioral rehearsal, and reinforcement (see Figure 18-7).

Programs for parents in fostering desirable behavior in children who exhibit the more common types of problem behavior can be effective. For example, one child continually tried to command and control the behavior of his parents ("You go over there and I'll stay here"). When his parents learned to identify and differentially respond to this autocratic behavior, its frequency declined. The child became more socially cooperative when his parents ignored his commands; they also gave him special attention when he cooperated. Parents and teachers of highly aggressive boys have been taught to note the occurrence of particular types of

Figure 18-7 This mother is teaching her child, who is a slow learner, how to write her name. Notice how the mother uses modeling, and the mother's reinforcement of the child's progress.

undesirable behavior and to reduce its frequency through the use of reinforcement and other appropriate behavioral techniques (Patterson, 1982).

The School

School districts, schools, and classrooms are larger and more complex social systems than families. Often they seem unwieldy and unmanageable. However, in some cases it is more feasible to attack problems of behavior in the school situation than in the home.

Early Detection Programs Teachers, school psychologists, and social workers can cite many instances in which longstanding family problems are not identified until the child reaches school age. But even when a problem is recognized at school, it may not be possible to deal with it effectively. The parent may refuse to cooperate with the school, or the realities of the child's life may make any significant change in his or her condition impossible—for example, if the child's home is unstable because of continual fighting between the parents or because the parents are immature and irresponsible.

Despite such barriers, early-detection projects in schools have attempted to identify children on the basis of their current behavior and school performance who are likely to have more severe adjustment problems later in life. The results of these projects show that early observation of the child, together with data available to school mental-health workers (for example, nurses' notes, teachers' reports, and test scores), can predict later psychological difficulties. In addition, classmates' ratings of each other seem to have predictive value. On the basis of such information, secondary prevention studies have been carried out to help vulnerable children before their problems become serious enough to require clinical help. For example, in one project nonprofessional aides worked under close professional supervision for an entire school year with children who were judged to be at risk for school maladjustment. The children who received this one-to-one contact showed significant changes in a number of areas, including social and academic skills and overall adjustment (Chandler et al., 1984). Special training for teachers, workshops to help parents develop their child-rearing skills, and carefully planned in-school and after-school activity programs can help prevent a significant number of behavior disorders in children (Bond & Compas, 1989; Cowen & Hightower, 1990).

Dropping Out Some children are never comfortable in school, and by the time they reach high school they are ready to leave. The dropout problem is a social as well as an educational one. In prosperous times, when jobs are not difficult to obtain, the economic cost to the dropout may not seem great. However, when competition in the job market intensifies, poorly educated, unskilled people tend to fall by the wayside.

An example of primary prevention is a study aimed at teaching cognitive and social skills to high school students (Sarason & Sarason, 1981). The school in which the research was conducted had a history of high dropout and delinquency rates and a low percentage of graduates who went on to college. The research was carried out in class sessions as part of a regular course. The basic procedure involved using modeling to demonstrate social and cognitive skills, followed by rehearsal of the modeled behavior. The subjects saw demonstrations of the cognitive antecedents of effective behavior (for example, deciding between alternative courses of action) and effective overt responses (such as how to ask a teacher a question). Repeated emphasis was placed on the links between thought and action. The following is an excerpt from a modeling videotape that was shown in the experimental program ("Jim's cognitions" refers to voiceovers in which Jim's thoughts were spoken aloud).

Tom:	Hey Jim, you want to go down to Green Lake fourth period?
Jim:	What are you gonna do down at Green Lake?
Tom:	A bunch of us are gonna take the afternoon off and party it up.
Jim:	I don't think I can go. Sixth period Mr. Smith is reviewing for the algebra exam.

Tom:	What about coming over and staying until sixth?
Jim:	Well, I kind of like Mr. Jones's class. Besides, it's too hard to get to Green Lake and back in an hour and forty minutes. I could come after school.
Tom:	You know Lydia is going to be there.
Jim:	(with noticeable interest): She is?
Tom:	Yeah. And by the time school is over, who knows if the party will still be there. We might go over to someone's house.
Jim's cognitions:	Gee, I really want to go to that party. Maybe I can get up the nerve to ask Lydia out. But I should stay for that algebra review, at least. The test will be hard enough without missing the review.
Tom:	You know, it is Friday afternoon and a beautiful day.
Jim's cognitions:	I wish Tom would let me make my own decision. This isn't easy. Maybe I could study hard this weekend. Then I won't need to go to the review. But will I really study Saturday?
Tom:	Well, are you going to come?
Jim:	I don't know, Tom. I'll have to think about it some more. Maybe I'll see you there fourth. If not, I'll probably come later.
Tom:	Okay, I hope you come.

One year after the completion of the study, the experimental subjects had better school-attendance records, less tardiness, and fewer referrals to school counselors and psychologists because of behavioral problems than similar students who did not participate in the program.

Table 18-2 lists certain measures schools can take to prevent dropping out.

The Community

There is growing evidence that early intervention in the lives of children can build the resilience needed to withstand stress and the difficulties of living under unfavorable conditions. Since 1965, Head Start has combined developmentally oriented child care with community involvement, support of parents, and provision of nutrition, health care, and social services. It has served 3- to 5-year-old children from low-income families who need an extra boost to be ready for school and appears to have been effective (*Starting Points*, 1994). There is also evidence of effectiveness for multifaceted community interventions with older children. For example, juvenile

1. Early identification of high-risk students is essential, with particular attention to transition difficulties, such as from junior
   high to senior high school.
2. Small-size classes appear to be especially beneficial to high-
   risk students.
3. Individualized attention and instruction are necessities for
   children with problems in school.
4. Teachers should have reasonable but high expectations for
   behavior and achievement and be sensitive to gender, race,
   and cultural issues.
5. Counseling services are needed by potential dropouts who
   often have personal and family problems.

Source: Based on Dreyfoos, 1990.

delinquency has been reduced through combinations of
early family support, special educational programs, and
community opportunities to participate in pro-social
activities (Yoshikawa, 1994).

After people leave school they are pretty much on
their own. Most of their activities are not supervised by
authority figures, and a certain degree of independence
is expected of them. At the same time, they are
expected to fit into the community by working and by
adhering to societal laws, values, norms, and priorities.

The World of Work Work is the major postschool
activity for most people. Finding employment that is
satisfying and sufficient to earn a livelihood is obviously
a major ingredient in an individual's satisfaction with
life. This seems particularly important in view of evidence that economic conditions such as poverty, unemployment, and underemployment can affect the
incidence of stressful life events, which in turn can
cause health and behavioral problems. A number of
studies have shown that low socioeconomic status is
associated with a high frequency of stressful events and
the lack of adequate methods for coping with them
(Eron & Peterson, 1982). Thus, it is not necessarily
socioeconomic status by itself that causes problems, but
rather the life events and poor coping skills that are correlated with this status.

Regardless of socioeconomic status, unemployment
can cause psychological as well as economic problems.
Brenner (1973, 1984) has reported that when employment levels decline, admissions to state mental hospitals
rise. He also found that economic reverses are correlated
with increases in death rates from a variety of conditions, including suicide, homicide, and cirrhosis of the
liver, a disorder that is often associated with heavy alcohol use. The physical and physiological effects of unem-

ployment are not necessarily immediate. The entire
impact of a rise in unemployment might not be felt for
several years after it occurred. People who have multiple
stressors in their lives at the time that they lose their
jobs run the greatest risk of some sort of breakdown.

How can maladaptive work behavior be prevented?
A study by Ross and Glaser (1973) compared several
variables related to childhood experiences and the
home environments of two groups of male residents of a
ghetto in a large city. Both groups grew up under decidedly disadvantaged circumstances, but while half continued to live in poverty, the other half managed to
change their lives for the better in significant ways.
There were two successful "A" groups consisting of
African-American and Mexican-American men and
two unsuccessful "B" groups of the same ethnic makeup.
The A groups had worked more or less steadily during
the two years preceding the study; the B groups had
been unemployed or underemployed. The investigators
hypothesized that parental attitudes and aspirations
made the difference between people who did and did
not overcome the developmental barriers posed by
poverty and discrimination.

Interviews with respondents in the two groups
uncovered a number of differences that supported the
hypothesis and were consistent for both ethnic groups.
Members of the A groups received greater support,
encouragement, and discipline at home. They also had
developed a sense of self-esteem through involvement in
productive activities. The results indicate the need to
help relatively unsuccessful people overcome low self-
esteem and self-confidence. Another personality characteristic of members of the B groups that might be
modified through imaginative programs is their dependence on approval from peers. We might expect that
many unproductive people would benefit from a close
relationship with a nonpeer—teachers, athletic coaches,
or employment counselors, for example—who would
make demands, motivate achievement, provide information about productive skills, and act as both models and
reinforcers of good performance.

Community Agencies Every person is influenced by
the way in which society and its institutions are organized. Although some institutions are concerned with
specific segments of the population (for example, day-
care centers, schools, social centers for senior citizens),
several are capable of reaching a majority of the society's
members. Because of our tendency to take these institutions for granted, we may lose sight of their potential for
contributing to personal growth and reducing the likelihood of maladaptation. For example, a public library
can be a powerful force in a person's life by providing
access to books that can offer young people positive
models and a broader view of the world. If the library

can also provide positive personal experiences, these may make important contributions to the prevention of maladaptive behavior (see Box 18-1).

Sometimes community support comes about informally. Most people deal with everyday crises in the best way they can using available resources. Just as we don't go to a doctor every time we have a sniffle, we don't run to a clinical psychologist every time we are upset. The availability of nonprofessional "therapists" may be one reason for this. For example, people like hairdressers and bartenders do a lot of therapeutic listening to the troubles of their customers (Cowen, 1982). However, some social institutions have been specifically assigned the task of handling crises.

Although they are not usually included in lists of mental-health workers, police officers frequently modify behavior—whether for good or ill and whether they are aware of it or not. Police officers are not in a position to remove the causes of crime, but as their skills in human relations develop, their contributions to the prevention of crime could increase. A crime prevention experiment in New York City provided some information about the effects of increasing police officers' psychological sophistication and expertise (Bard, 1970). The focus of training and preventive work was on handling family disputes, since a high percentage of violent crimes are committed by close relatives. Another reason for developing more skill in handling family disturbances is that 22 percent of fatalities and 40 percent of injuries to police officers occur while they are intervening in these situations (see Figure 18-9). Psychological training does help police officers handle violence more effectively. In addition, it can help them deal with many other problems, such as the usually harmless but often bizarre behavior of former mental hospital patients, with more tact and discretion.

Suicide Prevention Aside from the police, many communities offer specialized programs directed toward people who are going through a personal crisis or who share particular types of problems. For example, suicide and crisis prevention centers have been established in many communities (see Figure 18-10). The purpose of these centers is to encourage troubled people to seek help, either through telephone contact or in person. Such efforts may provide a means of reducing social isolation and bringing destructive and self-destructive thoughts out into the open. However, because it usually is not possible to conduct well-controlled studies of sudden crisis events such as potential suicides, there is continuing debate about the nature and effectiveness of crisis prevention centers. One study presented evidence suggesting that suicide-prevention centers do lower suicide rates, particularly among young white females (Miller et al., 1984). There is also evidence that crisis hotlines reach segments of the population (for example, many adolescents) often not served by traditional mental-health interventions (Garland & Zigler, 1993).

Many suicides can be prevented if friends and relatives recognize the danger signs and take appropriate actions. Some of these signs are listed in Table 18-3. There is no specific treatment for those who make suicide attempts, because the reasons for those attempts are extremely varied. Therapists who treat clients at risk for suicide must show that they are not surprised or discouraged by the client's suicidal urges. Several strategies are often employed by therapists to deal with the possibility of suicide. One approach is to be very active and tell the client to get rid of pills, guns, ropes, or other potential means of suicide. Therapists must also be available at all times and may ask the client to call if he or she is uncertain about controlling suicidal impulses. Sometimes it is helpful to insist that the client make an explicit promise not to commit suicide. Because people contemplating suicide often are not thinking clearly and see no other options open to them, the therapist can be helpful in suggesting other possibilities to solve the problem. When a therapist or other person is in contact with someone threatening suicide, bargaining may be useful. For instance, someone threatening to jump from a high place can be urged to delay and keep all options open by discussing the problem. Sometimes—despite these efforts—it is necessary, if physically possible, to intervene to save the life of a potential suicide (see Figure 18-11).

The prevention of suicide requires knowledge of the profile of people at risk for suicide. Studies have shown that people who commit suicide are nearly all psychologically disturbed (Murphy, 1988). There is a sharp rise in the incidence of suicide in the first few weeks following discharge from mental hospitals. Studies reveal that 40 to 50 percent of those who commit suicide are clinically depressed and another 25 percent are alcoholics. These figures suggest that the major group at risk is a particular, highly recognizable, specific segment of the population. Bearing this profile in mind, Table 18-4 lists some important contributions to suicide prevention that can be made by clinicians, family, and friends.

To prevent suicide, if family members or friends see any warning signs they should not hesitate to take action by asking questions such as "Are you very unhappy?" "Do you have a plan about taking your life?" "Do you think you really don't want to live anymore?" Asking direct questions about suicide doesn't put ideas into someone's head. Instead it may be a lifesaving measure if the answers are taken seriously. Both family and friends often don't believe that such statements might be acted upon or they may be too frightened to take action. If the suicidal threat seems immediate, the nearest suicide prevention center (usually listed under "suicide" or "crisis" in the phone book) should be contacted.

Kenneth Clark and Arthur Schomburg

Kenneth Clark, an influential educator and psychologist, made a significant contribution to American history by influencing the course of school desegregation. In making its historic 1954 decision declaring segregated schools unconstitutional, the Supreme Court relied on the results of Clark's research demonstrating that African Americans had negative attitudes toward other African Americans and that these negative attitudes, in part, were products of segregated schools and segregated communities. The development of Clark's distinguished career was aided at an early age by his contact with a librarian at the New York Public Library who became an important model and source of support for him and who helped him appreciate his African American heritage (see Figure 18-8).

I met Schomburg when I was about twelve years old, a crucial period in my life. It was at this time I clearly recognized that I was not ever going to be able to compete with my classmates in athletic skills.

I went to the library not only to escape the athletic competition, but also to escape the streets.

On one of my trips to the library, I decided that I was going to go upstairs to the third floor to the forbidden and mysterious area reserved for adults. I fully expected to be turned away unceremoniously. As I climbed the last flight of stairs, I felt the excitement of an interloper. I was prepared for the risk of either a polite or a more direct rejection. When I entered the room, a large man, whom I later came to know as Arthur Schomburg, got up from his desk and came over to me and smiled. He didn't ask me what I wanted. He merely put one arm around my shoulder and assumed that I was interested in the books. We went over to a table and sat down and began to talk. . . . We talked about books. We talked about wonderful things: about the history of human beings, about the contributions of Negroes which were to be found in books. He showed me portraits of Negroes who had contributed something important.

Figure 18-8 Kenneth Clark during an interview on an NBC telecast.

On that first day of meeting Schomburg, I knew I had met a friend. He accepted me as a human being and through his acceptance helped me to share his love of, and his excitement in, the world of books.

—Clark, 1965

Suicide Postvention Suicide **postvention** refers to efforts to help those who knew the person who died. Suicides among young people are often particularly shocking and difficult for those who knew them to understand. If the person who killed him or herself was part of a larger group, for instance a student in school, the whole group may feel the impact of the death. Those who knew the person may have many conflicting feelings of anger, guilt, and shock. The suicide act may also take on a certain glamour among some other students who see it as an exciting and glamorous way to deal with problems. In order to help the survivors and to prevent future suicides, programs involving professionals, school faculty, and students can be very effective. One such program used in schools after a student suicide is the Suicide Prevention Project of the New Jersey Community Mental Health Center at Piscataway. The **postvention** program has three basic principles.

1. Nothing should be done to glamorize or dramatize a suicide.
2. Doing nothing can be as dangerous as doing too much.

3. The students cannot be helped until the faculty is helped.

The postvention team usually meets first with school administrators, then with the faculty, and finally with all the members of the student group. During these meetings all participants have a chance to challenge their own feelings of guilt or self-blame by learning something about the dynamics of adolescent suicide. They also have opportunity to express the varying emotions that are typical after a suicide—shock, guilt, anger, and anxiety. Table 18-5 summarizes the postvention process and goals.

The Challenge of Prevention

At the beginning of this chapter we said that prevention can take more than one form. It can involve taking the steps needed to keep a disorder from arising in the first place as well as efforts to limit its impact on the life of the individual. In this sense prevention and treatment are closely related. Common to both is the concept of vulnerability. Vulnerability arises when an individual's

Figure 18-9 Police officers frequently must intervene in family disputes. This officer is trying to calm a domestic disturbance.

Figure 18-10 Crisis hotlines and suicide-prevention centers provide help for people who feel unable to cope with events in their lives. Sometimes just talking to an understanding listener is all that is needed. If more help is required, hotline staffers can provide callers with additional resources for assistance.

TABLE 18–3
Warning Signs of Suicide

Verbal comments. Statements such as "I wish I'd never been born," and "You'll be sorry when I'm gone," should be taken just as seriously as the direct threat, "I'm going to kill myself."

Behavior changes. These cover a wide range and include giving away treasured possessions, taking life-threatening risks, and having frequent accidents. Other signs may be complaints of intense loneliness or boredom, a marked increase in agitation or irritability, or getting into trouble with the police. There may also be the more customary signs of depression: changes in appetite and sleep habits, complaints of inability to concentrate, and withdrawal from friends and from favorite activities.

Situational factors. Inability to communicate with family and friends, recent problems at work or school, end of a love relationship, and recent involvement with drugs or alcohol all increase the situational risk for suicide.

personal characteristics are insufficient to deal with the situation. The challenge of prevention is the identification of opportunities for growth and stability and the provision of such opportunities to people who need them. These opportunities differ depending on the nature of the people to be served. For example, as they grow older, children need situations that give them increasing opportunities for independence. On the other hand, the aged usually need increasing care and attention.

Society inevitably must be involved in meeting the challenge of prevention because it controls or influences so many of the situations of modern life. We have seen many examples of the impact of community and social forces on our lives. Certain types of maladaptive behavior (for example, phobias and delusions) can be attacked on an individual basis with the clinical methods we have described (psychotherapy, behavioral therapy, drugs). But lasting solutions to many problems of living require social change. Children living in crowded slum apartments or with abusive or neglectful parents have only limited opportunities to generalize from what they learn in a stimulating school or preschool program. Medication may help deinstitutionalized patients hallucinate less frequently, but they still need a supportive environment and a chance to acquire new social and occupational skills.

Preventing maladaptive behavior and responding therapeutically to it when it does occur require an examination of society, its

Figure 18-11 Sometimes emergency physical intervention is necessary to prevent suicide. This woman had threatened to jump from a ledge outside her third floor apartment. Police and paramedics had to pull her to safety after their attempts to persuade her to reenter the building failed.

components, and how they are interrelated. This examination should include elements that a community lacks as well as positive steps that it may take. Examples of such steps are houses for runaway children, drop-in centers for teenagers, and crisis centers. Virtually all such programs have been started by citizens without government support, and, at least initially, on a nonprofessional basis. As a result of such efforts, professionals in many areas have broadened the scope of their clinical

---

TABLE 18–4
Steps to Preventing Suicide

1. Heightened awareness (for example, by family physicians) of the roles that depression, alcoholism, and other factors play in suicidal risk.
2. Early treatment of the psychological problems that underlie suicide attempts.
3. Careful questioning about suicidal intention ("Do you ever wish you were dead?", "Do you ever think about harming yourself or taking your life?", "Have you ever made a suicide attempt?")
4. Hospitalization of individuals who are known to have formulated a plan to kill themselves.
5. Removal of all access to firearms whenever the slightest hint of suicide is detected.
6. Restricted access of high-risk individuals to drugs that can be lethal in high doses.
7. Follow-up of high-risk individuals after treatment.

Source: G. E. Murphy, Prevention of suicide in *American Psychiatric Press Review of Psychiatry*, 7, edited by A. J. Frances and R. E. Hales, Washington, D.C., American Psychiatric Press. Copyright © 1988 American Press, Inc. pp. 403–421.

---

services and have increased their involvement in community programs.

Paraprofessionals

Programs have also been created to train and use nonprofessionals and paraprofessionals for significant roles in a variety of community settings. A wide culture-related gap often exists between middle-class professional workers (clinical psychologists, psychiatrists, and social workers) and people from lower socioeconomic groups who need help. Much of the success of **paraprofessionals** seems to be due to similarities between their backgrounds and those of their clients. For this reason, some community psychologists devote a major portion of their activities to training paraprofessionals.

Paraprofessionals vary widely in age, education, and cultural background. They often make up a large part of the staff in neighborhood service centers, residential youth centers, and mental-health programs in both urban and rural areas. There they may serve as bridges between an established agency and a target group in the community that the agency has failed to serve effectively. Although relatively little research has been done on how to select, train, and evaluate the effectiveness of these workers, it has been shown that in some situations paraprofessionals may be as effective as the experts (Hattie et al., 1984). The responsibilities of paraprofessionals and their role in professional and community power structures need to be defined.

Self-Help Groups

Self-help groups can also contribute to prevention. For many human problems there are no easy answers or easy cures, but there is an alternative to coping with them alone. Millions of people whose problems and needs are not met through formal health care, social services, and counseling programs can find the hope and personal support they need in self-help groups. Within these groups, whose members share common concerns, they are offered the understanding and help of others who have gone through similar experiences. People like those in the following examples might find the help they need by contacting the appropriate group.

Margaret and Bill are parents of a young child diagnosed with terminal cancer. For two years they have shared suffering, dashed hopes, and heartbreak. In spite of caring friends and professional support, they feel alone in their grief.

Jean is a divorced mother who has custody of her three

TABLE 18–5
The Postvention Process

Student Reaction	Postvention Staff Response
1. Shock. Students may initially appear remarkably unreactive. In fact, they are in a state of shock and not yet able to accept the reality of the suicide.	1. Staff needs to assume a stance of anticipatory waiting, acknowledging the shock and showing a willingness to talk about the suicide when students are ready. Hill (1984) suggests waiting 24 to 48 hours before initiating more direct action.
2. Anger and projection. Students will look for someone to blame. Initially, this may be directed at important adults in the victim's life, including school staff. "Why did they let it happen?"	2. Some expressions of anger must be allowed. Staff members may share the similar feeling they have had. However, at the same time, reality must be introduced. There are limits on how much one person can be responsible for actions of another.
3. Guilt. Typically, students who knew the victim may move from blaming others to blaming themselves. "If only I had talked to him more."	3. Here, particularly, staff can be helpful by sharing their own similar reactions. And again, the reality principle is also introduced. One person cannot assume total responsibility for the act of another.
4. Anger at victim. This is a common reaction by students, even those not closely connected to the victim. "How could he do this to us?"	4. Staff needs to give permission for such expressions by normalizing them, perhaps tempered by questioning if the victim fully realized the impact of his act.
5. Anxiety. Students will begin worrying about themselves. "If he could kill himself because he was upset, maybe I (or my friends) could too."	5. Discussion should be guided towards helping students differentiate between themselves and the victim and towards other options for problem-solving.
6. Relief. Once the normal distortions of feelings are resolved, students can allow themselves to feel the sadness of the loss and begin the healing process.	6. Staff must guard against encouraging a pseudo-mourning process before students have worked at resolving their conflicts over the suicide.

Source: Lamb & Dunne-Maxim, 1987, p. 257

children. She now finds herself overwhelmed by the problems of single parenthood. Her teenage son has become difficult to handle and she is increasingly discouraged in trying to provide for her children's needs and the demands of her job.

Roger has a serious drinking problem. He has been fired from two jobs in the last year and is deeply in debt. He has lost the respect of his family and friends. He entered treatment at an alcoholism clinic but began to drink again two months after the treatment ended. He realizes that his addiction is ruining his life but feels helpless to control it.

As social beings, all of us need to be accepted, cared for, and emotionally supported; we also find it satisfying to care for and support those around us. Within the most natural "self-help networks"—families and

friends—we establish the one-to-one contact so important to our happiness and well-being. This informal support is such a basic part of our social character that we tend to take it for granted, but it clearly influences our ability to handle distressing events in our lives. Many of our daily conversations are actually mutual counseling sessions in which we exchange the reassurance and advice that help us deal with routine stresses. In fact, research scientists have found that there is a strong link between the strength of our social support systems, our health, and our response to illness (see Figure 18-12). Further research is needed to determine when, under what conditions, and for which types of problems self-help groups are most effective (Videka-Sherman & Lieberman, 1985). Table 18-6 lists some of the charac-

Figure 18-12 Self-help groups are based on the belief that some problems can be helped the most through mutual support from those who have experienced the same difficulties. In this photo, a support group for women who have had breast cancer meets to hear a presentation and to talk about ways of dealing with the experience of being a cancer patient.

teristics of self-help groups and ways in which they benefit their members. Some self-help groups are well known and have been in existence for many years. An example of such a group is Alcoholics Anonymous. Based on the success of this group, similar groups such as Gamblers Anonymous have been formed to help people with other types of problems. A group that is focused on the rehabilitation of mentally troubled persons is Compeer. This organization, with headquarters in Rochester, New York, began with ten mental patients and ten vol-

TABLE 18–6
Self-Help Groups

The Major Characteristics of Self-Help Groups

1. Avoidance of professional leadership and direction
2. A homogeneous membership that has a common problem, affliction, or deviant status
3. Meeting places outside such traditional therapy settings as hospitals and clinics
4. Open-ended membership in which the group's composition is rarely constant

Ways in Which Self-Help Groups Benefit Their Members

1. Emotional support and understanding
2. An accepting reference group that reduces social isolation
3. Information and advice
4. Models of how to cope effectively with stress
5. Enhancement of members' awareness of alternatives available in dealing with problems

unteers. It is now active in most states and in Canada as well. Compeer has helped more than 10,000 mentally and emotionally handicapped people. Mentally ill persons are put in contact with a "compeer"—a volunteer—who spends at least one hour per week with the client for a year. The volunteers, who invariably become the clients' friends, undergo brief training, meet with the clients' therapists if needed, and submit written monthly reports. Compeer seems to significantly cut the rate of clients' reentry to a mental institution. Its success may be attributed to the social support provided in frequent informal and meaningful contacts with a caring friend.

Community Psychology

Community psychology is concerned with the role of social systems in preventing human distress and maladaptive behavior. Community psychologists attempt to work in settings that have an impact on prevention. For example, they might serve as human-relations consultants to a police department, work to increase the skills of individuals who staff welfare offices, or develop prevention programs in homes or schools. Outreach programs are aimed at either preventing breakdowns or dealing with problems in the community before more drastic treatment programs, such as hospitalization, become necessary. Making communities livable requires good ideas about social planning as well as awareness that various segments of the population, including the aged, minorities, and the unemployed, have special needs. Community psychologists are interested in the environmental facts of life in particular communities as well as the impact of those facts on individual lives.

Treatment in the Community

Whether people receive mental-health services in the community or in institutions, society has a definite interest in how those services are provided, their effectiveness, and their cost. The mix of available services can influence not only the recipients' sense of well-being but also their economic productivity. Many people who would otherwise have to be hospitalized could remain in the community if facilities that provide additional social support and supervision were available. A study released in 1994 by the New York State Commission on the Quality of Care for the Mentally Disabled found that nearly 40 percent of all patients discharged from mental hospitals are rehospitalized within six months. Part of the problem is that many former patients deteriorate in the community because of inadequate services. The inadequacy of community services is one reason more than 30,000 seriously mentally ill individuals—with schizophrenia, manic-depressive psychoses, and other severe disorders—are confined to jails on any given day.

A basic component of the needed services is affordable, supportive housing. Although the supply of either is very small, there are two types of housing for the mentally ill: (1) **custodial housing** and (2) **alternative housing.** Custodial housing (boarding houses, nursing homes, and special-care homes) tend to be large facilities financed and often run by cities, counties, and states with little or no rehabilitation programs. They often have an institutional atmosphere similar to that of hospitals. Alternative housing (halfway houses, group homes, co-ops) tends to be small and focused on rehabilitation and community integration. Most alternative housing programs encourage residents to become involved in making decisions about the selection of new residents and upkeep of the home. Staff members with training in social work or psychiatric rehabilitation often work in the home. The main aim of alternative housing facilities is to prevent hospitalization and improve the quality of life. Some supported housing facilities have private apartments in which the resident is a legal tenant with support coming in from outside.

The Oxford House concept illustrates a type of innovative living arrangement that seems to be effective. The original Oxford House in Washington, D.C. was developed for the rehabilitation of drug addicts and alcoholics, and there are now more than 500 similar facilities throughout the country. Each Oxford House is self-run, with no professional staff such as counselors or house managers. Every resident has one vote, and all participate in running the house, with officers rotating every six months. That eliminates "us against them" sentiments and the addict's traditional resentment of authority, fosters responsibility and, as residents' leadership and self-management skills grow, self-confidence. Every resident must pay his or her own way; established houses help new houses get started. Unlike traditional halfway houses, that often have short time limits, residents can stay as long as they like, if they pay their rent and follow the number one rule: sobriety. Relapse means automatic expulsion. (They can reapply, but only after 30 days of sobriety.)

Oxford House residents have many vulnerabilities and often lack resilience (75 percent have served jail time; 60 percent have been homeless during their addiction). Its success might not be generalizable to groups who are not drug addicts and alcoholics. For that reason experiments in housing and rehabilitation with diverse groups is needed. The halfway house or community lodge has been tried with patients discharged from mental hospitals. In one study, a group of institutionalized patients volunteered to move from the mental hospital to a lodge in the community (Fairweather and others, 1969). The members decided who their leaders would be and the work that each would perform. Initially, extensive supervision was needed, and the group frequently found it necessary to seek help. However, as time passed, the lodge patients significantly increased their employment level and the length of time they were able to be out of the hospital. The median percentage of time in full employment for the lodge group was as high as 70 percent, while virtually all of the control subjects were totally unemployed. Unfortunately, funding for this type of facility is rarely available from public sources, private organizations, or health or insurance coverage of patients.

Problems with Community Programs

A look at one mentally ill woman's journey through the mental health system illustrates many problems endemic to community programs. Writer Susan Sheehan (1982) followed the story of Sylvia Frumkin over nearly 20 years of treatment. Frumkin (the name is fictitious, but the story is true) had a long and disheartening journey through what is commonly called "the system." In fact, she encountered the disjointed, fragmented, and ineffective system at every turn. Following her first psychotic break in 1964 at the age of 15, she was repeatedly hospitalized or placed in various types of institutions. At different times she was diagnosed as manic-depressive or with a schizophrenic disorder, either undifferentiated or paranoid type. At one time or another she was given individual psychotherapy, antipsychotic medications, lithium, insulin coma therapy, electroconvulsive therapy, "Christian psychotherapy," and megavitamin therapy. Over the years she saw a constantly changing array of therapists, each often for a very short period. These therapists treated her with nearly every available medication, sometimes without reference to her history, and they sometimes changed, suddenly decreased, or altogether stopped her medication in a seemingly arbitrary manner.

Sylvia Frumkin was not the kind of patient most therapists enjoy; she was described as slovenly, unappreciative, and uncooperative. She drained the energies of clinical personnel by being loud, abusive, and even violent during the acute phases of her illness. Even when she was not acutely ill, Frumkin was characterized by a staff member as "arrogant, nasty, and demanding." As Figure 18-13 shows, Sylvia Frumkin experienced 45 changes in treatment settings in 17 years. She was repeatedly bounced back and forth between her family home, various hospital settings, and community residential facilities. She was admitted 27 separate times to

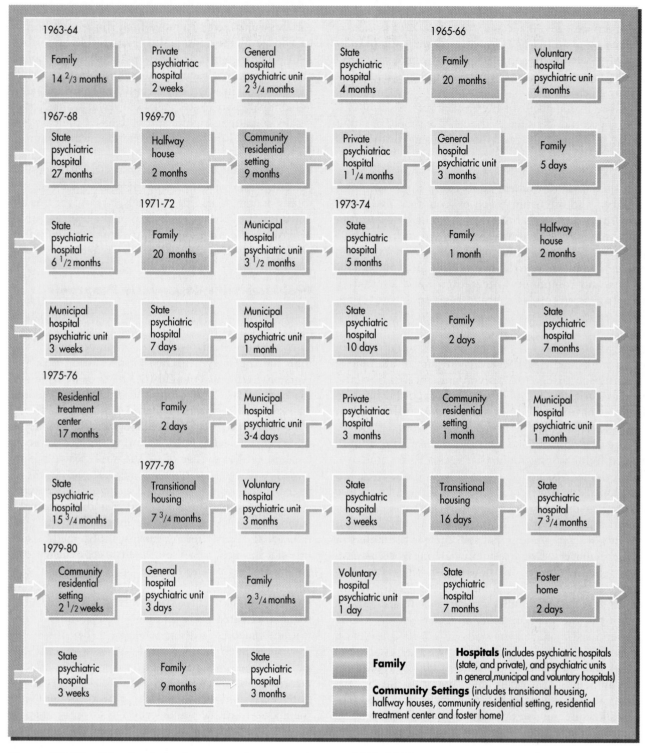

Figure 18-13 Sylvia Frumkin's odyssey as a chronic mental patient, 1963–1980.

SOURCE: Moran, A. E., Freedman, R. I., and Sharfstein, S. S., The journey of Sylvia Frumkin: A case study for policymakers, *Hospital and Community Psychiatry, 35,* 887–893, 1984. Copyright © 1984, the American Psychiatric Association. Reprinted by permission.

eight different hospitals (state, municipal, general, voluntary, and private), where she spent a total of nine years. She spent almost seven years in a state hospital. For slightly less than six years she lived with her family, cycling in and out of their home nine different times. She spent a total of three years in several different types of community settings, such as halfway houses, a foster home, a YWCA residence and a religious community.

The cost of her care was estimated to be $636,000 in 1982 and would be considerably greater today if the costs of inflation were taken into account.

Unfortunately, Sylvia Frumkin's story is not unique. There are an estimated 1.7 to 2.4 million chronically mentally ill people in the United States. Policy makers and the public can learn a great deal from the experiences of people like Sylvia Frumkin. Her story clearly illustrates the profound impact of chronic mental illness on patients, families, and communities, as well as on the staggering costs of providing care. It may well be that Frumkin would have continued to deteriorate even if the conditions of her treatment had been more favorable, but the behavior of the system certainly seems to have been a contributing factor. In her various hospitalizations, Frumkin never experienced a prolonged relationship with a caring person. She perceived no one as having her interests continuously at heart during a period of 17 years. Cases like Frumkin's have led mental-health workers, judges, and other government officials to think about ways to reform both the system and the laws that place disturbed individuals in public institutions.

Improving Treatment in the Community

Experiments designed to improve the mix of available mental-health services are sorely needed but are rare. The Massachusetts Mental Health Center provides an alternative for patients who traditionally would have been admitted and retained on inpatient services. In the system all patients who are thought to need inpatient hospitalization are first admitted to a day hospital. Those who do not require residential facilities return to their homes or community living situations at night and on weekends. Those who are admitted for day hospitalization but are found to require 24-hour inpatient care because they are dangerous or unable to care for themselves are transferred to an acute intensive-care unit within the hospital. As soon as is warranted by the clinical situation, these patients are returned to the day hospital or to a day hospital and dormitory inn.

The dormitory-inn is a special facility that provides care for patients for whom the intensive-care unit is no longer appropriate, who need treatment in the day hospital, and who have no other place to sleep. It is a time-limited residence with an anticipated three-week length of stay (Gudeman et al., 1985). The development of this type of facility clearly reflects growing awareness of the need for an expanded array of treatment facilities in the community. The opportunity for resocialization is an important element of these programs. Also of importance is the ability of the program to adapt to the special needs of its residents and workers. Halfway houses can, at a lower cost to society, increase the personal freedom

and self-confidence of many former mental-hospital patients and decrease the stigma attached to mental illness.

Although the concept of community care for the chronically mentally ill is a good one, as chapter 17 pointed out, most deinstitutionalized people have simply been dumped into communities that fear them because of their eccentric behaviors and do not look after them in any systematic way.

Once the mentally ill are out on their own, they will more than likely stop taking their medications. The lack of professional care on the streets and the effects of alcohol and other drug abuse are further serious complications. They may now be too disorganized to extricate themselves from living on the streets—except by exhibiting blatantly bizarre or disruptive behavior that leads to their being taken to a hospital or jail (see Figure 18-14).

Few deinstitutionalized people are given the vocational training, guidance in self-care, recreation, or opportunities for socializing that are required for any sort of meaningful existence. The need for follow-up care, the hard realities of insufficient funding, the impact of patients on communities, and the uncertainties as to what constitutes effective community programs have all been largely ignored. As a result, a growing number of people who would otherwise be enthusiastic about deinstitutionalization have become at least somewhat disillusioned.

One consequence of the large number of failures of deinstitutionalization has been an increase in readmissions to state hospitals. Patients now stay in the hospital for shorter periods but, because of their inability to function in the community, return more often. About half of the patients who are released from state hospitals are readmitted within a year of discharge.

What lessons can be learned from the way deinstitutionalization has been practiced up to now? Perhaps the most important lesson of the bad experiences of the past two decades is that deinstitutionalization as it is now being carried out is not helpful to many individuals. As happens so often, society neglects many of the basics needed to reach a worthy objective. More money and more trained personnel are needed.

More education is also essential. Public-information programs about mental illness and retardation and more citizen involvement in planning for the reentry of former patients into the community can help make deinstitutionalization a positive experience for both the patients and the community. The entry of formerly hospitalized patients into the neighborhood has frequently been perceived as a threat, even though the overwhelming majority of ex-mental patients and retarded individuals are harmless (Rabkin, 1979). Nothing can arouse negative feelings in a neighborhood

Legal Aspects of Treatment and Prevention

In this and the previous chapter we have discussed ways to help people avoid having problems and, if that isn't possible, to overcome them to the extent possible. Because people live in groups, the community has an interest in preventing behavior that is maladaptive. Although historically it has not always been the case, governmental bodies now have laws that deal with both helping people who behave deviantly and protecting the public from the dangers posed by certain types of deviant individuals (for example, criminals). In reality, such laws may be problematic if our judgment of what constitutes help happens to be wrong or if the person doesn't want to be helped.

Institutionalization

The process of placing a person in an institution is called **commitment.** Prisoners are committed to prisons for punishment, and mental patients are committed to mental hospitals for treatment. **Criminal commitment** of an individual to a mental hospital may occur when a criminal act is legally declared to be a result of insanity and it is determined that the interests of society and the individual would be best served by commitment to a mental hospital rather than to a prison. Some mental patients voluntarily commit themselves, but others are involuntarily hospitalized through a legal procedure called **civil commitment.** Civil commitment can only be carried out if a person is judged to be a risk to him- or herself or to others. The forced institutionalization of a person poses serious problems. On the one hand, civil commitment aims at providing help, but to do that, it may deprive the person of basic human rights.

One example of the logistical difficulties posed by commitment laws is the case of Anna May Peoples, a Seattle woman who was diagnosed as having paranoid schizoprenia. Because of her paranoia, she said, she took refuge in the city's Public Safety Building. Peoples made the building her home for two years, but authorities had to dismiss trespassing charges against her. She was judged not competent to stand trial, but not dangerous enough to institutionalize (see Figure 18-15). A newspaper article described her situation as follows.

. . . But the 64-year-old transient was arrested again last night, charged again with criminal trespass for being in the Public Safety Building after hours. Officers escorted her out

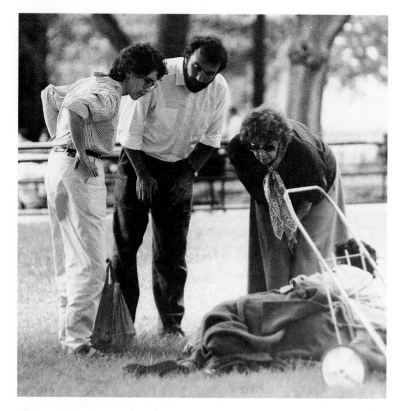

Figure 18-14 Workers from Project Help, a New York program for the homeless, talk with a homeless person to determine whether he is severely mentally ill and needs hospitalization. Project Help uses an active outreach program to identify those who are in need of help, provides immediate treatment, and places them in community residences, group homes, or their own apartments. Unfortunately, because of their serious and chronic mental illnesses, about 30 percent of homeless people aided by Project Help have ended up back on the streets.

more effectively than the proposed establishment of a halfway house or aftercare center in the vicinity. Yet there is no evidence that simply being a discharged mental patient makes a person more likely to commit crimes or endanger the community. However, there is an increasing tendency to place people with criminal records in mental hospitals, and people with previous arrest records are likely to be arrested again after they are discharged from mental hospitals.

The problems of the chronically mentally ill living in the community require a comprehensive system of care that includes:

1. An adequate number of supervised community-housing settings
2. Community clinical services ranging from professional mental-health workers who can provide crisis intervention to hospitalization for acute conditions
3. Recognition of the importance of families in treatment, along with adequate support for family members as well as for the patient.

Figure 18-15 Anna May Peoples, caught between the technicalities of legal incompetence and lack of dangerousness, waits to hear her fate during a court appearance.

of the building at 10:45 P.M., then arrested her five minutes later when she came back in.

To the consternation of the Police Department, Peoples insists on making her home in the building at Third Avenue and James Street. She bathes in the restroom sinks, dresses in the elevators, and sleeps on the rock-hard floors.

One night, police found her naked in an elevator. Another time, she fell asleep and plunged through a plate-glass door.

Social workers tried to find the woman a home, but Peoples refused help. She preferred the Public Safety Building, despite being dragged out by police on various occasions.

—Adapted from Guillen, 1982, p. B1

Criminal Commitment To convict a person of a crime, the state must establish beyond a reasonable doubt not only that the person committed the prohibited act but also that the act was committed with criminal intent. If criminal intent cannot be proven, the insanity defense becomes possible. The concept of insanity is often confused with that of competence to stand trial. **Insanity** refers to a person's state of mind at the time that an act was carried out, while **competency** refers to a person's state of mind at the time of a judicial proceeding. In a legal sense, an **incompetent person** is one who lacks the capacity to consult with a lawyer and to understand the nature of legal proceedings. Both insanity and competency are legal terms whose applicability in a given case is determined by a judge after considering all evidence, including the opinons of expert witnesses.

Insanity is a legal term, not a psychiatric diagnosis. Early English law did not recognize insanity as an excuse for criminal behavior. However, by the thirteenth century proof of criminal intentions was necessary to convict a person of a felony. If accused individuals could prove that they were completely "mad," they could successfully defend themselves against a criminal charge. In

1843 Daniel M'Naghten, a Scottish wood-turner, assassinated Edward Drummond, secretary to the prime minister of England. He was found not guilty because the judges stated that he was "labouring under such a defect of reason, from disease of the mind, as not to know the nature and quality of the act he was doing; or, if he did know, that he did not know he was doing what was wrong."

This ruling, known as the **M'Naghten rule,** became the "right and wrong" test of insanity and was widely adopted. As belief in this interpretation grew, statutes were introduced that permitted the court to defer sentencing decisions until the offender could be studied and recommendations made to the judge. Psychiatrists, psychologists, social workers, and probation officers became advisers to the court. Sentencing became more flexible, and parole was used increasingly.

An example of an attempt to invoke the M'Naghten rule occurred in the case of Jack Ruby, who was convicted of the murder of President Kennedy's assassin, Lee Harvey Oswald, in 1964. In appealing his death sentence, Ruby claimed that he suffered from psychomotor epilepsy and that this prevented him from determining right and wrong. However, this claim was rejected by the judge and Ruby was found legally sane. He eventually died in prison.

The M'Naghten rule and subsequent court decisions have been controversial largely because of the difficulty defining precisely what knowing right from wrong really means. Contrasting with the M'Naghten rule's emphasis on the "right and wrong" test is the idea of the **irresistible impulse,** according to which the person could not control his or her behavior. The **Durham rule** states that a person is not criminally responsible if the criminal act was the product of mental disease or mental defect. None of these rules about the nature of insanity is without ambiguities and difficulties.

In 1962 the American Law Institute (ALI) proposed a set of guidelines that have since been incorporated into the laws of several states. The ALI's guidelines focus on impairment that grows out of a defendant's mental illness and include the following ideas:

1. *A person is not responsible for criminal conduct if at the time of such conduct as a result of mental disease or defect he lacks substantial capacity either to appreciate the criminality (wrongfulness) of his conduct or to conform his conduct to the requirements of law.*
2. *. . . The terms "mental disease or defect" do not include an abnormality manifested only by repeated criminal or otherwise antisocial conduct.*

—American Law Institute, 1962, p. 66

The Insanity Defense With each passing year, the ALI guidelines have gained increased acceptance throughout the country. In 1983, in the case of *Jones v. United States*, the Supreme Court ruled that people who are found not guilty by reason of insanity can be held indefinitely in a mental hospital under a less rigorous standard of proof of dangerousness than is required for civilly committed individuals. The Court ruled that acquitted insanity defendants "constitute a special class that should be treated differently."

The number of insanity defenses that are successful is very small. In the entire state of New York, for example, there are on the average fewer than 50 successful insanity defenses each year. Thus, the insanity defense contributes only a tiny fraction to the problem of crime in the United States. In part, this is because juries have difficulty applying the fine legal points involved in the insanity defense. The following excerpt from a news article illustrates this point.

> Roderick Stoudamire, whose previous trial ended in a hung jury three months ago, was found guilty in Superior Court today of first-degree murder in the stabbing death last summer of a woman jogger at Seward Park.
>
> The jury of six women and six men announced its verdict for the second trial at 10:40 A.M. in a courtroom packed with spectators. They deliberated about five hours.
>
> The jury also found Stoudamire guilty of assaulting two other women joggers.
>
> Stoudamire, 16, had pleaded not guilty by reason of insanity. It was his insanity defense that caused the deadlock in the first trial. After deliberating more than two days, jurors in that case said they were confused by the definition of criminal insanity, and could not decide whether it applied to Stoudamire.
>
> The tall, slender youth sat quietly, usually with a vacant look on his face, as witnesses testified during both of the long and often dramatic trials. He wore the same look this morning when the decision against him was read.
>
> A mistrial was declared in the youth's first trial after jurors announced they were deadlocked. In that trial, ten said they did not believe Stoudamire was legally insane, while the two others said they were convinced the youth was schizophrenic and voted to acquit him.
>
> —Horne, 1979, p. C11

Understandably, the public remembers highly publicized cases in which the insanity defense is invoked and someone who has clearly committed a crime is found not guilty by reason of insanity (see Figure 18-16). Sometimes such people are released after a short hospitalization, and later commit another crime.

In 1981, John Hinckley, Jr.'s acquittal by reason of insanity from charges of attempting to assassinate then President Ronald Reagan caused many people to question the fairness of the insanity defense. The American Psychiatric Association argued that people should be acquitted for insanity only if they have a serious mental disorder such as psychosis. Those who have personality disorders—for example, antisocial personality disorder—or abuse drugs or alcohol should be held responsible for their actions. The Association further stated that expert witnesses should not be allowed to testify about whether the defendant was able to control his or her behavior (*Psychiatric News*, February 4, 1983). The use of expert opinion poses profound interpretive problems. So far none of the guidelines that have been proposed for dealing with the problem of insanity have provided a completely satisfactory solution.

During the trial of Hinckley, the barrage of contradictory expert testimony damaged the image of psychiatry in the public mind. Those who would abolish the insanity defense believe that one way to end this type of spectacle would be to restrict psychiatric testimony to evidence of mental abnormality that bears on the defendant's conscious awareness and perception—his or her "intent" to commit the crime. Other testimony concerning more subtle impairments of understanding, judgment, or behavior control would no longer be relevant at the guilt stage of the trial, but could be introduced at the time of sentencing. Another proposal calls for a pool of expert witnesses to be selected by the court. These experts would no longer testify for the prosecution or the defense. Instead, the impartial panel would attempt to arrive at a conclusion regarding the defendant's mental state when the crime was committed.

Three states (Montana, Idaho, and Utah) have abolished the insanity defense. In 1994 the United States Supreme Court held that there is no constitutional violation when defendants are denied the defense. Although most other states are unlikely to abolish the insanity defense, controversy continues to surround it. Modifications can be expected in laws concerning its applicability.

Civil Commitment All 50 states have civil commitment laws. These laws are based on the doctrine of **parens patriae** (Latin for "parenthood to the state"), according to which the state can act in what it takes to be the best interest of a minor or of an adult who is incapacitated. The principal features of the process are a petition, a hearing, and a decision about the place to which the individual is to be committed. In some states, the judgments of psychiatrists are decisive in reaching commitment decisions. In others, physicians who are not psychiatrists play dominant roles. Until fairly recently, standards for commitment were loosely worded and protections for the patient either did not exist or were ignored. Then, in a 1979 decision (*Addington v. Texas*),

(a)

(b)

(c)

(d)

Figure 18-16 Edmund E. Kemper, III, (a) was acquitted by reason of insanity from the charge of murdering his grandparents in 1964, and was released from a mental hospital in 1969 as "cured"; he later murdered six college students, his mother, and one of her friends—for which he was found sane and guilty. Dennis Sweeney (b) was sent to the Mid-Hudson Psychiatric Center when a judge accepted his plea of "not guilty by reason of mental disease" for killing Congressman Allard Lowenstein in 1980. After the slaying of his parents, Gregory Shaddy (c) was acquitted by reason of insanity; he spent two years in a hospital and was then pronounced cured and released. The case of John W. Hinckley, Jr., (d) revived debate over the insanity defense after he was acquitted from the charge of attempting to assassinate President Ronald Reagan in 1981 and was committed to a mental hospital.

the U.S. Supreme Court ruled that people may not be committed to mental institutions unless the state has presented "clear and convincing" evidence that they require hospitalization.

Growing awareness of abuses like the one described in the following newspaper article led to reforms of commitment codes in many states. The patient in this article had been sent to a medical hospital during a severe attack of asthma in 1956. Twenty days later she was committed to a county mental hospital. She was not discharged until 1960, even though the staff of the mental hospital had considered her sane since 1957. *The New York Times* gave the following report of the proceedings at her release trial.

At today's hearing in Judge Pindar's court, Dr. John J. Scott, assistant medical director of the county medical hospital, testified that as far back as 1957, at a hospital staff conference, Miss Dean had been adjudged sane.

Asked why she had not been released in view of her many requests for her freedom since that time, Dr. Scott said that the woman was without relatives and it had been feared that she would become a public charge.

When a patient at the hospital, Miss Dean performed the duties of a registered nurse, without pay.

Miss Dean's release was effected through the effort of a friend, who remembered that Raymond H. Chasan, a lawyer, had won the release of another mental patient in 1947, under somewhat similar circumstances.

—Copyright© 1960 by The New York Times Company. Reprinted by permission

All civil commitment laws involve two judgments: whether the individual is suffering from a disabling mental illness and whether he or she is dangerous. The first criterion is relatively easy to establish. The second is more of a problem. "Dangerousness" refers to the potential to inflict harm on other people as well as on oneself. Judging how dangerous a person might be is often a difficult matter.

In the beginning, Jane's older neighbor seemed friendly enough.

Stuart, who lived alone, would often stop to chat. Sometimes he'd borrow a gardening tool, or Jane would borrow one from him. But two years ago, the relationship changed dramatically.

Stuart, who is in his 60s, became infatuated with Jane, 36. He recited Bible verses to her, then broke into her home while she was gone. He wrote Jane long love letters, tried to

accost her and kiss her in church, and attempted to lure her three children into his house with candy and baseball cards.

He bought an expensive van identical to Jane's, and said he was planning to kidnap Jane and her children and drive them across the country.

—Based on *Seattle Times*, August 27, 1990, pp. A1, A5

Is Stuart harmless, or a serious danger to his neighbors? Although a judge declared Stuart harmless, he subsequently was jailed for several misdemeanors and also harassed Jane over a long period of time.

Because dangerousness involves a prediction of future behavior, its application to individual cases creates enormous problems. Can a clinical expert tell the court whether a person is dangerous and when he or she has stopped being dangerous?

In 1985 a 22-year-old accountant was pushed in front of a speeding subway train at rush hour. A large team of doctors, nurses, and technicians operated on her for 22 hours, trying to save her life and repair her severe head injuries and numerous broken bones. Her assailant, who had been held by another subway rider until police arrived, turned out to be a 19-year-old unemployed woman with a history of mental problems. She had been released from a psychiatric ward less than a month before her crime, despite violent behavior while incarcerated and a psychiatrist's warning that she was dangerous. On two occasions she had attacked fellow patients and had to be subdued by means of a straitjacket.

Although the psychiatrist in this case was correct in thinking that the 19-year-old woman was dangerous, available evidence suggests that clinicians' predictions of whether a given individual will do something dangerous in the future are often inaccurate. Mental health specialists can do the best job of predicting dangerous behavior that might occur in the near future, but even then studies show they are only from 40 to 60 percent accurate (Appelbaum, 1991). For longer term predictions the record is much worse. In several studies that followed patients over several years, only 14 to 35 percent of those considered to be potentially dangerous to others were actually arrested for violent crimes. At present, the best indication of future dangerousness is dangerousness in the past unless the particular circumstances that led to the past behavior no longer exist.

Studies of dangerousness have consistently found that few patients are dangerous only to others. In a study of one thousand patients seen in psychiatric emergency rooms, only 4 percent were dangerous to others, three times that many were suicidal or dangerous to themselves, and only 0.6 percent were dangerous only to others and not to themselves (Appelbaum, 1991).

The goal of protecting the rights of people who might be committed to an institution against their will is accepted by all. However, it is by no means clear how to protect those rights while simultaneously assuring the welfare of the individual and of society. At present, civil commitments seem to be increasing in frequency. This trend is being reinforced by recent court decisions that have emphasized the *parens patriae* role of the state in treating a patient for his or her own good. Also contributing to the trend is the failure of many states to develop community treatment networks to supplement hospital systems, as well as health insurance programs that provide only marginal subsidies for outpatient care.

The Historical Context of Civil Commitment. How a community responds at any given time to mentally ill people who need help varies depending on current social values, legal decisions, and judgments about the potential danger of people harming themselves or others. During the late nineteenth and early twentieth centuries, most states enacted involuntary commitment laws to provide care for those mentally ill individuals who needed it but, because of their mental illness, could not recognize their need. Hospitalization and treatment of the mentally ill, even without the patient's informed consent, were considered necessary to help a person in need. Beginning about 30 years ago, changing values led to new laws that emphasized the civil liberties of individuals. Involuntary commitment came to be seen as state action that resulted in the loss of an individual's constitutionally protected right to liberty. Not only did grounds for commitment become more restrictive but many legal authorities argued that only a compelling governmental interest could justify the loss of liberty occasioned by commitment. Many states changed their involuntary commitment laws to require a finding of mental illness and dangerousness to self or to others as the only grounds for commitment. Most mental health agencies adopted policies of short-term hospitalization whenever possible in response to court rulings that patients have the right to the least restrictive alternative to hospitalization.

Recently, because of the public's concerns about community safety, most states have enacted laws authorizing outpatient commitment of mentally ill individuals who are not dangerous but are likely to deteriorate and become dangerous if they do not receive treatment. Patients subjected to outpatient commitment can be ordered to take medications and to keep appointments at mental health centers. Laws dealing with outpatient commitment reflect the state's increased willingness to use its commitment authority to seek treatment compliance of noninstitutionalized patients. Recent laws have also given mental health practitioners more power and responsibility to care for the mentally ill through the involuntary civil commitment system. Changes in laws concerning both inpatient and outpatient commitment reflect tensions within society concerning the need to help individuals requiring help and also to protect the community.

The Rights of Patients

In the not-so-distant past, people were treated as if admission to a mental hospital justified taking away all their rights. However, according to court decisions over the past 20 years, patients' rights must be upheld and adequate treatment must be provided. In a 1971 case that attracted national attention (*Wyatt v. Stickney*), a court ruled that a state must provide adequate treatment for mental hospital patients who are confined involuntarily. Beyond recognizing the patient's right to treatment, the court specified basic hospital staffing ratios and qualifications and also required individualized treatment plans.

In a 1975 Supreme Court decision (*O'Connor v. Donaldson*), Kenneth Donaldson was awarded compensatory and punitive damages of $38,500 against two staff psychiatrists at the Florida State Hospital because they had not provided adequate treatment for him during the 14 years of his involuntary commitment. The significance of the *O'Connor v. Donaldson* ruling was its recognition that hospitalized people who are not dangerous have a constitutional right to treatment. Whether or not a dangerous patient has a similar right has not yet been decided. The *O'Connor v. Donaldson* decision strengthened the rights of involuntarily hospitalized patients, but it did not make the task of determining whether or not a patient is dangerous any easier.

The courts have opened the door to long-overdue improvement in the treatment of the mentally ill. A federal judge in New Jersey ruled that an involuntarily committed mental patient who objected to the drug therapy administered to him may not be forced to take the medicine (*Rennie v. Klein*, 1978). Since drugs now constitute the primary mode of behavior control in institutions, and virtually all involuntarily committed patients are routinely given antipsychotic medications, this and similar rulings may have widespread effects on the way in which treatment is defined in state institutions. In addition to strengthening patients' right to get treatment (and their right to refuse it), the courts have also supported patients' right to receive the least restrictive treatment available. The "least restrictive treatment" is only as restrictive and confining as is necessary to achieve the purposes of the commitments.

Increasingly, both patients and judges are questioning the safety and effectiveness of present-day treatment methods. Physical treatments such as drugs and electroconvulsive therapy do have the potential to cause permanent injury. Certain patients appear to deteriorate as a result of receiving psychotherapy. Some experts also believe that behavior-modification procedures such as token economies are too coercive. Some critics believe that merely being institutionalized is therapeutically counterproductive, regardless of the quality of the institution. Until recently a hospital's power to deny patients the right to examine their own files was taken for granted. Now patients can see their charts, but some hospitals do not voluntarily tell patients that they are entitled to do so.

As the rights of patients have been extended, the requirement of informed consent has been strengthened. **Informed consent** requires that patients receive adequate information about the nature of a planned treatment before they agree to submit to it. The clinician must communicate this information in language that is meaningful to the patient, rather than in medical jargon, and must clearly explain the potential risks and benefits, including any discomfort that might arise from the treatment. Frequently, if the patient is incompetent to evaluate the information provided (for example, because of a psychotic condition), a lawyer assigned to look out for the patient's interests plays a role in the decision-making process. The requirement of informed consent applies to people who serve as subjects in experiments as well as to patients who are undergoing treatment. Patients and experimental subjects both have the right to terminate their participation in treatment or research even if they had previously consented to participate.

Should patients have the right to discontinue treatment that most people would agree was helping them? The difficulty of answering this question can be seen in this daughter's account of her mother's changed behavior after discontinuing the use of antipsychotic medication. Her mother came to New York to join her children after being discharged from a mental institution in Kansas. She was taking Haldol, an antipsychotic drug.

On Haldol Mother's behavior improved tremendously, and we even harbored false hopes of her return to normal living. We never suspected that she might cease taking medication and regress. . . .

Not only did Mother rediscover art and music in New York, but she soon became familiar with the liberal New York laws regarding "patients' rights." She refused to continue to take Haldol and slowly began the reverse trip to "No Man's Land," where she now dwells. The first sign of her decompensation was a refusal to come to my apartment, and then she rejected me completely. Next the manager of her middle class apartment hotel asked us to remove her. She was annoying the guests with her outbursts. She had become known to all the shopkeepers on the block as "The Crazy Lady of West 72nd Street." Looking like a zombie, she paraded down West 72nd Street, accusing aunts, uncles, and brother of stealing her father's fortune, screaming at people who frightened her. . . .

Whether or not it's preferable for her to be forcefed Haldol and incarcerated in Kansas or allowed to do as she pleases in liberal New York, as destructive as her life is now, is paradoxical. She was not able to enjoy life and pursue her artistic interests in the former situation, but she is even less able to do so in the latter. Without medication, she can only exist. I believe that basically she is less free in her present life, a prisoner of her delusions and paranoia. My brother, however, disagrees. He thinks that Mother is better off having the choice to live as she wishes, wandering aimlessly in the streets, constructing the world to fit her delusions.

—Adapted from Lanquetot, 1984, p. 471

The institutionalization of children brings with it special problems that the courts are only beginning to address. Among the questions that must be considered are: How much freedom may parents exercise in seeking to institutionalize a son or daughter? When, and under what conditions, can the state institutionalize children against the parents' will? What procedures are needed to protect the child's rights? What are those rights? The United States Supreme Court has ruled that parents may commit their children to state institutions as long as "neutral fact-finders" approve. The quality of the treatment provided is an important factor in approving institutionalization for children as well as for adults. For example, questions have been raised concerning the constitutionality of institutions for the mentally retarded that provide little or no special training.

The issue of informed consent in therapy has been recognized most clearly in the case of biological treatments such as electroconvulsive therapy, but it is also relevant to the psychological therapies. Whenever possible, the goals of therapy should be determined jointly by the therapist and the client, without undue influence exerted by the therapist. Should a therapist encourage a young man to go to college because the client's parents, who are paying the therapy bills, want him to? The client should be the main concern of the therapist, but external influences like the parents' desires might become coercive factors in treatment. Clinicians also must not unduly impose their personal values on the therapy they offer to clients. A respectful attitude toward the client, an undogmatic approach, and healthy questioning of therapeutic tactics are important ingredients in all types of treatment.

A Final Word

In chapter 2 we traced the history of abnormal psychology and noted the enormous conceptual changes that have taken place over the centuries. This concluding chapter, perhaps more than any other in the book, illustrates the optimistic outlook of many researchers and therapists today. It is easy to point out the gaps in our knowledge: Why does schizophrenia primarily occur in the late teens and early twenties? What causes panic attacks? What can be done about senility? But perhaps more significant than the lack of knowledge implied by these questions is the current consensus that (1) the scientific method can fruitfully be applied to them, and (2) the resulting knowledge can be used to reduce the occurrence of maladaptive behavior. Another positive development is the increased willingness of court judges, mental health professionals, and the public to examine and reevaluate principles by which care is provided to the mentally ill.

There are many leads to effective prevention, but systematic research is needed to develop effective interventions. While the preventive approaches reviewed in this chapter seem promising, only scientific studies can validate them.

The formula for achieving prevention might be written $P = K \times W$. Prevention (P) is achieved when the needed knowledge (K) is available and society has the will (W) to use that knowledge to prevent unwanted outcomes. One of the great achievements of the present era is the widespread awareness that little good and much harm is done by blaming or stigmatizing people for their abnormalities, whether physical or behavioral. One of the great challenges is finding a way to motivate both individuals and society to do things to increase happiness, personal effectiveness, and the common good of the human family.

At many points through the book we have observed the ability of some people to cope with adversity and even become stronger as a result. As the challenge of resilience—the ability to bounce back—is joined with the challenge of vulnerability and the personal, social, and biological characteristics that put us at risk, the field of abnormal psychology will be able to contribute even more than it has thus far to an understanding of the human condition.

TYPES OF PREVENTION

Prevention efforts can be focused at several different points on the problem development time line.

Levels of Prevention **Primary prevention** focuses on reducing new cases that would otherwise occur in a population. The role of **secondary prevention** is to reduce the potential impact of an existing abnormal condition by decreasing its duration, intensity, or the disability it creates. **Tertiary prevention** is aimed at reducing the disability that has already resulted from a disorder or event. **Situation-focused prevention** is aimed at reducing or eliminating the environmental causes of maladaptive behavior. The emphasis of **competency-focused prevention** is enhancing people's abilities to cope with the conditions that can lead to maladaptive behavior. Either of these approaches might be applied to divorce, an example of a stressful situation that often leads to maladaptive behavior. Early education programs illustrate a competency-focused prevention. The training they provide in cognitive and social skills facilitates the child's early school adjustment and may also have positive long-term effects.

SITES OF PREVENTION

The Family The family is an important focus for prevention efforts. Parents affect their children's development from the moment of conception, through the genes they contribute, the prenatal environment, and the physical and psychological environment in which the children grow up. Parenting practices that have been linked to aggressive behavior in children include failure of supervision or monitoring, aggressive or abusive behavior, overpermissiveness, inconsistency, and rejection. Parental conflict and divorce are also areas where interventions at any of the three prevention levels can be helpful to the entire family. **Child abuse** and **spouse abuse** are other examples of harmful behaviors that can be treated by intervention at all levels of prevention. For some other types of problems parents can be trained to act as therapists toward their children.

The School Many family problems, behavior problems, and problems associated with learning are not identified until a child begins school. Special interventions by the classroom teacher and by school mental-health workers can prevent many behavior disorders in children. Interventions that strengthen children's social and cognitive skills can also help prevent their later dropping out of school.

The Community Community agencies or organizations can provide satisfying experiences for children that may help them develop positive interests and skills. They can bring children into contact with caring adults as well as provide access to new ideas. Police officers may play an important role in prevention. They may serve as positive role models and if trained in prevention techniques may help deter family violence by defusing confrontations. Crisis and suicide prevention centers can lower suicide rates and reduce social isolation. Suicide **postvention** programs are designed to help those who knew the person who died. They are usually presented in organizational settings to help those who knew and worked with the suicide victim deal with feelings of guilt and anger and to decrease the chances of additional suicides.

THE CHALLENGE OF PREVENTION

Prevention of maladaptive behavior and providing appropriate therapeutic responses when it does occur have implications for our basic social institutions as well as for specific programs for groups or treatment with individuals.

Paraprofessionals **Paraprofessionals,** who do not themselves have specialized mental health training but who are similar in cultural background to those to be served, often make important contributions to prevention and treatment.

Self-Help Groups **Self-help groups** made up of people with a common problem can be helpful to many people who experience extreme stress or loss.

Community Psychology **Community psychology** is concerned with the role of social systems and community environment in prevention.

TREATMENT IN THE COMMUNITY

An integrated network of community services can help prevent hospital readmission for the chronically mentally ill. Communities also may prevent institutionalization by making adequate treatment facilities and housing such as group homes available.

Problems with Community Programs Community programs need to provide integrated treatment and support services as well as more continuity in service delivery for those who have chronic problems with maladaptive behavior.

Improving Treatment in the Community A variety of treatment programs can offer alternatives to full time residential hospitalization. These include partial hospitalization through day hospitals or dormitory inns. Once patients are discharged from the hospital half-way houses an adequate case management system can be important in keeping them out of the hospital. Although deinstitutionalization has helped to empty hospitals of long term patients, the lack of funding of alternative programs has resulted in an increased frequency of read-missions of patients to hospitals for short term stays. Treatment programs of all types should offer support for family members as well as the patient and recognize the importance of families in treatment.

LEGAL ASPECTS OF TREATMENT AND PREVENTION

Institutionalization Commitment, or placement in an institution, may be either voluntary when patients agree to enter the hospital or involuntary when they are hospitalized through a legal procedure called **civil commitment. Criminal commitment** of a person to a mental hospital may occur when that person's criminal act is legally declared to be the result of insanity and it is in the interests of society to protect itself. **Insanity** is a legal term that refers to a person's state of mind when a criminal act was carried out; **competency** refers to a person's state of mind at the time of a judicial proceeding. A legally **incompetent person** lacks the capacity to consult a lawyer and to understand what the legal proceeding is about. The insanity defense arose from the recognition that a crime was not necessarily a deliberate violation of social norms but might be a result of a psychological disturbance. Although the number of successful insanity defenses is very small, the defense has been the source of controversy of many years. The **M'Naghten rule,** or the knowledge of right and wrong test of insanity, was widely used for many years. More recently, the American Law Institute proposed a set of guidelines that have been incorporated into the laws of many states. The American

Psychiatric Association has argued that people should be acquitted for insanity only if they have a severe disorder such as a psychosis. Civil commitment laws are based on the doctrine of **parens patriae,** the idea that the state can act in the best interest of a minor or incapacitated adult. The process includes a petition, a hearing, and a decision about the place of commitment. Current law requires that the state present "clear and convincing" reasons why hospitalization is required. Patient rights while hospitalized have also been the focus of court decisions. The state must provide adequate treatment for those who are confined involuntarily. In addition court decisions have upheld patients' rights to refuse specific types of treatment.

The Rights of Patients Patients' rights include the right of **informed consent** which means that they must have explained to them the nature of the treatment and its possible benefits and negative consequences before they agree to the treatment. They also have the right to terminate the treatment even if they had previously consented to it.

A FINAL WORD

The social need for prevention is one of the most powerful motivators for research in the field of abnormal psychology. The formula for prevention can be expressed: Prevention equals necessary knowledge multiplied by the will of society to use that knowledge.

Abnormal psychology Study of deviant and maladaptive behaviors.

Abstinence-violation effect The reaction of conflict and guilt when an individual fails to resist the temptation to indulge in a behavior that he or she is trying to stop—for example, using alcohol. This response often triggers a binge or total relapse.

Acetylcholine Chemical involved in the transmission of nerve impulses.

Acid Slang term for LSD.

ACTH See *adrenocorticotrophic hormone*.

Acute Stress Disorder A reaction to stress in which the symptoms appear during the month following the stressor. If the symptoms continue past one month, the diagnosis is changed to post traumatic stress disorder (PTSD).

Adaptation Dynamic process by which an individual responds to his or her environment and the changes that occur within it; ability to modify one's behavior to meet changing environmental requirements. Adaptation to a given situation is influenced by one's personal characteristics and the type of situation. Term often used in a biological, Darwinian sense.

Addictive behavior The presence of a repetitive habit pattern that is associated with problems in the personal and social spheres as well as the risk of disease. This behavior must be perceived by the person and by others to be out of control.

Adjustment An individual's ability to harmonize with the environment.

Adjustment disorder Maladaptive reaction to a particular stressful condition that results in impaired functioning and symptoms in excess of what might be a normal response to the stressor. The reaction must occur soon after the beginning of the stress and the reaction can be expected to decrease when the stressor ceases.

Adjustment disorder with depressed mood Depression that occurs as a result of an identifi-

able life event and that is expected to disappear when the event's impact ceases. (Not classified as mood disorder.)

Adoption studies An attempt to understand the genetics of a disorder and separate them from the effects of environment by comparing children adopted in infancy whose biological parents are affected by a disorder with adopted children without such heredity.

Adrenal cortex The outer layer of the adrenal gland; a source of hormone secretion in the body.

Adrenal corticosteroids Hormones released by the adrenal cortex which affect the body's response to stress.

Adrenaline A secretion of the adrenal glands; also called *epinephrine*.

Adrenal medulla One of the two principal parts of the adrenal glands, the part of the endocrine system located just above the kidneys. A principal function is the secretion of hormones in emergency-type situations.

Adrenocorticotrophic Hormone (ACTH) Hormone secreted by the pituitary gland that goes to the adrenal cortex to release adrenal corticosteroids, chemicals that stimulate the body's response to stress.

Affect Emotion, feeling, or mood: pleasant or unpleasant, intense or mild; also, a tone of feeling accompanying a thought.

Affective disorder See *mood disorder*.

Agoraphobia Pathological fear of open spaces.

AIDS dementia complex (ADC) A type of dementia that is secondary to the development of the autoimmune disease syndrome (AIDS) or positive status of the human immunodeficiency virus (HIV).

Alcohol abuse The overuse of alcohol that results in lowered job performance and lowered quality of interpersonal relationships.

Alcohol amnestic disorder Another term for Korsakoff's disease or syndrome.

Alcohol intoxication The appearance of clinically significant behavioral and psychological changes such as inappropriate sexual or aggressive behavior, slurred speech, decreased coordination, impaired attention or memory, or coma.

Alcoholism Alcohol dependence or addiction.

Allergen The substance that causes an allergic reaction by causing antibodies to attack the immune system.

Allergy An abnormal immune system reaction to an ordinarily harmless substance.

Alpha wave A particular kind of electrical brain activity often seen when a person is tense and the frequency of which decreases with drowsiness or relaxation.

Alprazolam A tranquilizing drug derived from the benzodiazepine group. Used to treat panic disorder.

Alzheimer's disease Chronic brain disorder, occurring as early as the fourth decade of life and involving progressive destruction of nervous tissue, which results in slurring of speech, involuntary muscular movements, and gradual intellectual deterioration with growing lapses of memory.

Amnesia Total or partial memory loss—often acute—following emotional or physical trauma.

Amnesia, continuous A type of dissociative disorder in which the person is unable to recall any events that occurred after a specific point in time. The disorder includes lack of memory for the present.

Amnesia, dissociative Extensive, but selective memory losses without any evidence of organic changes or injuries.

Amnesia, generalized A rarely occurring type of dissociative disorder in which there is total failure to recall the person's past life.

Amnesia, selective A type of dissociative disorder in which a person can recall some but not all of the events that occurred during a particular time period.

Amnesia, systematized A dissociative disorder in which the loss of memory is restricted to certain categories of information rather than to particular time periods.

Amnestic disorders Memory disturbances due to either a medical condition or the persistent effects of some chemical substance.

Amniocentesis Technique of removing a sample of amniotic fluid from a pregnant woman and analyzing it to determine whether there are chromosomal defects in the fetus.

Amphetamines Nervous system (particularly cerebral cortex) stimulants, such as dexedrine, which bring a sense of well-being and exhilaration. The stimulation effect is succeeded by fatigue and depression. Psychologically but probably not physiologically addicting.

Anal stage Stage of psychosexual development in which the child derives intense pleasure from activities associated with elimination.

Anencephaly A condition in which a child is born without a developed brain.

Angina pectoris Periodic chest pains resulting from an insufficient supply of oxygen to the heart. A type of coronary heart disease.

Anomaly A deviation from the norm; an abnormality.

Anorexia nervosa An intense and irrational feeling of being fat that leads to excessive restriction of food intake and weight loss that may be life threatening. Usually occurs in adolescence or early adulthood and is much more common in females than males.

Anorgasmia In women, the inability to achieve an orgasm after a normal level of sexual excitement.

Antianxiety drugs Commonly called *tranquilizers*. Used to calm anxious people.

Antidepressant drugs General term for a number of drugs used to relieve depression and to elevate mood.

Antigens Foreign substances that, when introduced into the body, induce the formation of antibodies and then react with these antibodies in a specifiable manner.

Antimanic drugs A family of drugs based on a compound of lithium carbonate that is used to treat mania, bipolar disorder, and some depressions.

Antipsychotic drugs Group of chemical compounds used to treat individuals who show severely disturbed behavior and thought processes, especially in cases of schizophrenia.

Antisocial personality disorder Characterized by continuous, chronic, antisocial behavior beginning before the age of 15 and continuing into adult life. Diagnosis not made until person reaches age 18. Behavior tends to impair the rights of others and to be characterized by an impaired capacity for close relationships.

Anxiety An affect with both psychological and physiological aspects. Generally, an unpleasant emotional state accompanied by physiological arousal and the cognitive elements of apprehension, guilt, and a sense of impending disaster. Distinguished from fear, which is an emotional reaction to a specific or identifiable object.

Anxiety disorder Formerly called *neurosis* or *neurotic disorder*. Characterized by some form of anxiety as the most prominent symptom. Includes panic disorders, phobic disorders, obsessive-compulsive disorder, generalized anxiety disorders, and reactions to stressors.

Aphasia Partial or total loss of the ability to convey thoughts through speech.

Appetitive Referring to a physical craving or desire.

Asexual Characterized by lack of response to sexual stimulation and lack of interest in sexual activity.

Asphyxia Unconsciousness or death caused by a lack of oxygen. May result in retardation or seizures as a result of brain damage.

Assertiveness training Combined cognitive and behavioral approach designed to increase the frequency of aggressive behavior that is socially desirable.

Assessment Information gathering aimed at describing and predicting behavior. Assessment specialists devise tests that measure various aspects of behavior.

Assessment interview Same as diagnostic interview.

Assessment study A study aimed at gathering information to describe a particular group in which variables are not manipulated. Such data can be used for prediction and are usually expressed in the form of correlations between variables.

Assortative mating The tendency for people to marry those who have similar characteristics to their own. For instance, persons with chronic schizophrenia tend to marry individuals who have a schizophrenic spectrum disorder or other psychotic disorder. This genetic loading must be taken into account when estimating genetic risk for a variety of disorders.

Asthma Disorder of a chronic nature, often psychophysiological in nature, characterized by coughing, wheezing, breathing difficulty, and a feeling of suffocating.

Atherosclerosis A disorder caused by a build up of plaque (deposits on the blood vessel walls) that narrow the vessels and result in insufficient blood supply to the heart.

Attention-deficit/hyperactivity disorder (A-D/HD) Severe and frequent problems of either or both attention to tasks or hyperactive and impulsive behavior. Some symptoms must have been observed before age 7. May be of combined type with both types of symptoms or of either the predominantly inattentive type or the predominantly hyperactive-impulsive type.

Attribution A term used by social psychologists to describe the way a person assigns responsibility for cause and effect.

Aura Clouded state of consciousness, accompanied by feelings of unreality, which precedes an epileptic attack. Also, the sensory, motor, or mood disturbance preceding migraine headache.

Authentic behavior Term used by

some existential theorists to describe behavior dictated by a person's own goals rather than by the goals of society.

Autistic Term used to describe a certain type of schizophrenic thought pattern characterized by self-centered thinking understandable only to the individual.

Autistic disorder A developmental disorder usually occurring early in childhood characterized by severe impairment in social relationships, communication, and activity. Frequently includes mental retardation.

Autistic savant One of a small number of persons who have the symptoms of autism, but who have special aptitudes that are remarkable, not only compared to people with the same diagnosis, but compared to the aptitudes of the ordinary person.

Autoerotic asphyxia The self-limiting of oxygen into the body in order to increase sexual sensations. May result in death because of impaired judgment about when to release the oxygen restriction as a result of lessened cognitive function due to the oxygen deprivation.

Autoerotic practices Sexual stimulation practiced by an individual on him or herself.

Autonomic reactivity Excessive action of the sympathetic and parasympathetic portions of the autonomic nervous system.

Autonomic system Functional division of the nervous system concerned with visceral activities, smooth muscles, and endocrine glands. Name comes from the fact that it was formerly thought to function independently of the central nervous system.

Autosome Chromosome that does not determine the sex of the individual.

Aversion therapies Group of behavior therapies which attempt to condition avoidance responses in patients by pairing the behavior to be extinguished with punishing stimuli—for example, electric shock, social criticism, drugs that cause vomiting. Also known as *aversive conditioning*.

Aversive conditioning See *aversion therapies*.

Avoidance response Attempt to leave a situation in which an aversive stimulus is expected to occur.

Avoidant personality disorder Characterized by social withdrawal based on fear of social rejection.

Axon Part of the cell that transmits impulses away from the cell body and across the synapse to the dendrites of another cell.

Balanced placebo design An experimental design in which some subjects receive an inactive substance and others a psychoactive substance. Part of each group is led to expect that they have received the other category of substance and part of each group is accurately informed about what substance they are given.

Baquet A water-filled tub used by Mesmer as a focus for treatment of hysterical complaints.

Barbiturates Family of drugs that depress central nervous system action and may be addictive.

Baseline observation Operant conditioning procedure in which an initial rate of some response is established. Can be used for descriptive purposes or as a control condition before introducing behavior modification procedures and subsequent response-rate comparisons.

BEAM See *brain electrical activity mapping*.

Bedlam Noisy uproar or confusion. A word derived from conditions at Bethlehem Hospital, an institution for the insane.

Behavioral assessment The objective recording of particular categories of observable behavior prior to beginning behavior therapy. The assessment may take place in specially contrived situations or under real life conditions.

Behavioral coping What a person actually does when confronted by a stressor.

Behavioral medicine An area focused on ways to improve health, treatment, and rehabilitation by using behavioral techniques to help people adopt generally healthier ways of living and to follow treatment plans for specific problems. Also focuses on helping health care

providers improve their service delivery.

Behavioral rating scale for Children A type of rating scale designed to be used by untrained observers to quantify different aspects of children's behavior.

Behavior change experiment The test of a therapeutic manipulation to determine whether the individual's maladaptive behavior is lessened.

Behavior genetics Study of the transmission of certain kinds of behavior through selective mating.

Behaviorism School of psychology whose adherents contend that the study of overt and observable behaviors provides the only legitimate data of science. Covert events, such as consciousness, are disregarded or considered only as mediation processes between stimulus and response contingencies.

Behavior modification Type of therapy based on the principles of operant conditioning.

Behavior therapy Includes several techniques of behavior modification based on laboratory-derived principles of learning and conditioning. Behavior therapies focus on modifying overt behaviors with minimal reference to internal or covert events.

Benzodiazepines Group of drugs, such as Librium and Valium, used primarily to treat anxiety.

Bereavement The state of having lost someone through death.

Beta amyloid A protein found in the clumps and plaques of cells typically found in the brains of Alzheimer's disease patients. Although the protein has been shown to kill nerve cells it is not clear whether its presence may reflect the cause or effect of Alzheimer's disease.

Binet tests The intelligence test concept originated by Binet in which the person tested is asked to complete a variety of tasks that assess reasoning, ability to follow directions, and judgment. The results originally were based on the concept of the intelligence quotient or IQ as the ratio of test score or mental level to chronological age but are now computed in terms of how much the person's score deviates from the mean of scores for that particular chronological age.

Binge-purge cycle The sequence of extreme overeating followed by self-induced vomiting or the use of laxatives. The central feature of bulimia nervosa. Sometimes also seen in anorexia nervosa but then carried out in association with a generally limited food intake that keeps weight significantly below the established normal range.

Biofeedback Method for inducing behavioral change in which the client learns to alter autonomic nervous system responses by monitoring them on recording instruments.

Biological perspective Theoretical perspective that suggests that all disorders, physical or behavioral, have biological causes. Causes may lie in heredity, genetic accident, or bodily infection or trauma.

Biopsychosocial model Interactional view that emphasizes the interaction among biological, psychological, and social factors in determining behavior and body functioning.

Bipolar I disorder Includes at least one episode of mania, and in most patients, one or more major depressive episodes.

Bipolar II disorder A type of bipolar disorder in which the person has experienced at least one major depressive episode and one hypomanic episode but has never had a manic episode or cyclothymia.

Bipolar disorder Mood disorder in which the individual experiences both periods of mania and periods of depression. Formerly called *manic-depressive order*.

Bisexual Someone who is sexually attracted to members of both sexes.

Bisexual behavior The preference, at different times, for male and for female sex partners.

Bodily assessment Measures of some aspects of an individual's physiological state, for example heart rate, blood pressure, or amount of sweating. Many of these can be assessed automatically on a continuous basis over time.

Body dysmorphic disorder An extreme preoccupation with a minor or imagined physical flaw that the individual views as a defect or deformity.

Booster session An additional treatment carried out after a period of time has elapsed since the original treatment series. Intended to counteract any weakening of the treatment effect.

Borderline personality disorder Characterized by impulsive and unpredictable behavior and marked shifts in mood. Instability may affect personal relationships, behavior, mood, and image of self.

Bottom-up studies In the study of hereditary factors in disorder, this approach focuses first on identifying children with a disorder and then investigates the clinical status of their parents and other relatives. Contrast with *top-down studies*.

Brain deterioration See *dementia*.

Brain electrical activity mapping (BEAM) A technique for study of electrical brain activity in which the electrical impulses are summarized in color maps.

Brain imaging techniques A variety of non-intrusive computer-based techniques that provide views of the structural or metabolic activity in the living brain.

Brainstem Portion of the central nervous system that includes the hindbrain, midbrain, and forebrain up to the thalamus.

Briquet's syndrome Another name for somatization disorder.

Bulimia nervosa Frequent episodes of binge eating by individuals of average or above average weight. Purging or self-induced vomiting is often employed by the individual at the end of the eating session.

Burnout Condition found most often among people in the helping professions whose work involves intense interpersonal contact. Symptoms include loss of effectiveness and self-confidence and the general feeling of inability to deal with particular situations.

Caffeine Crystalline compound that is found in coffee, tea, and kola nuts

and which acts as a stimulant of the central nervous system and also as a diuretic.

Cannabis Plant whose resin produces a psychoactive substance. In solid form the resin is called *hashish*.

Cardiovascular disorder Disorder affecting the blood vessel system and the heart.

Case manager Person assigned by a social service agency to help a person link up with essential services and to provide some general supervision.

Case study Detailed observations of a client's behavior, symptoms, and reported thoughts over a period of time with inferences about cause and effect supplied by the clinician. Often called clinical method.

Catatonic schizophrenia Type of schizophrenic disorder characterized by psychomotor disturbance. Often takes the form of body rigidity or posturing. Other behavior may include waxy flexibility or mutism.

Catecholamines Group of hormones, including epinephrine, norepinephrine, and dopamine, that are important in the response to stress. Some catecholamines are produced in the brain, where they are important in nerve transmission.

Categorical model An approach to classification used in the *Diagnostic and Statistical Manual*. In this method the diagnosis may be made if a certain number of criteria are satisfied, rather than requiring all criteria to be met.

Cell body The part of the cell that contains the nucleus.

Central nervous system (CNS) Brain and spinal cord; does not include the nerve trunks and their peripheral connections.

Cerebellum Portion of the brain consisting of two hemispheres located behind and above the medulla; coordinates motor activities and maintains bodily equilibrium.

Cerebral cortex Convoluted layer of gray matter of the brain; outer layer of the cerebrum.

Cerebral hemispheres One of the two lateral halves of the cerebrum or upper part of the brain.

Cerebral ventricles Cavities in the brain that are connected to the central canal of the spinal cord and contain cerebrospinal fluid.

Cerebrovascular accident (CVA) Rupture or blockage of blood vessels in the cerebrum that disrupts or prevents blood flow. Commonly referred to as a *stroke*.

CHD See *coronary heart disease*.

Child abuse Harm, usually physical, deliberately inflicted on children by their parent(s), often by repeated beatings.

Child neglect Failure by the caretaker to provide a child with healthful environment, adequate food, clothing, or supervision.

Choline acetylcholine transferase Enzyme that forms acetylcholine.

Chorionic villus sampling A method of determining genetic damage in the fetus.

Chromosomal anomaly Abnormality in chromosome structure or number of chromosomes.

Chromosomes Gene-bearing structures within cells.

Chronic care model A type of full time or day hospitalization in which an attempt is made to improve the patient's level of social skills and to reduce symptoms. Expectations for patient change are limited to improvement rather than recovery.

Civil commitment Commitment of a person to an institution based on a judgment that the person is a potential danger to him or herself and/or to others.

Classical conditioning Pavlov's experimental method by which a conditioned stimulus is paired with an unconditioned stimulus. Procedure involves presenting the two stimuli in close temporal proximity. The first, or unconditioned, stimulus elicits a reflex. After a number of trials the second, or conditioned, stimulus acquires the potentiality of evoking a similar reflex.

Classification The establishment of a hierarchical system of categories based on the relationship or presumed relationship among the things

to be classified, for instance, disorders of behavior and cognition.

Client-centered therapy Carl Rogers' therapeutic approach, which views the subject matter of psychotherapy as the client's world of immediate experience that should be approached from the client's frame of reference. In the Rogerian system, the therapist's main task is to create the opportunity for the individual to achieve a reorganization of his or her subjective world and to reach self-actualization.

Clinical method Case study of the individual through observation. May rely heavily upon intuitive judgments of the clinician rather than upon experimentation and systematic measurement.

Clinical psychologist Psychologist, usually a Ph.D. or Psy.D., who has special training and skills in assessing and treating maladaptive behavior.

Clinical trial The use of a research design including one or more experimental groups and a control group in testing the usefulness of a particular approach in treatment of patients.

Clinician Professional who deals directly with the examination or treatment of patients or clients.

Clitoris In females, a small organ at the front of the vulva that is highly sensitive to sexual stimulation. The analogue of the penis in the male.

Clonic phase An aspect of seizure activity in which there is rapid alternation of muscle contractions and muscle relaxation.

Clozapine One of the so called "new generation" of antipsychotic drugs that may be effective with some patients not helped by early types of antipsychotic drugs. Has potentially risky side effects unless carefully monitored.

Cluster headache Very painful headaches that peak quickly and often last no more than an hour. Long pain free periods tend to alternate with series of headaches over a day or week.

Cocaine Stimulant with a number of characteristics in common with the amphetamines.

Codeine Derivative of opium that is less potent than morphine.

Cognitive assessment Specification and enumeration of the typical thoughts that precede, accompany, and follow maladaptive behavior. Used in research and by cognitive behavior therapists especially in working with depressed individuals.

Cognitive-behavioral interventions A therapeutic approach that includes structured training sessions and prescribed exercises to help clients change maladaptive behavior by changing specific types of thoughts about themselves and others that typically occur in certain situations.

Cognitive coping skills Particular ways of thinking that aid in behaving effectively in stressful situations.

Cognitive distortion model *of depression* Proposed by Aaron Beck and suggests that depression is a disorder of thought.

Cognitive modification Technique whereby individuals learn to modify maladaptive thought patterns or to substitute new internal dialogues for old maladaptive ones.

Cognitive perspective Point of view that considers behavior to be the result of information processing and problem solving. Emphasis is on mental processes of which the individual is aware or can easily become aware.

Cognitive process variables The mechanisms by which people formulate the expectations and evaluations that are present within awareness. The processes themselves are usually not available to the individual.

Cognitive product variables Self-critical automatic thoughts and attributions and pessimistic future expectations that often characterize cognitions of depressed persons. They are generally within the person's awareness and can be reported on directly.

Cognitive psychology Study of human beings as information processors and problem solvers. Focus has recently been extended from the traditional studies of memory, attention, and problem solving to include the effects of personality factors and emotions on learning and performance.

Cognitive psychotherapy A talking therapy that is focused on clarifying the client's belief system and how it relates to maladjustment and unhappiness. The focus is on challenging inaccurate and maladaptive beliefs.

Cognitive rehearsal Procedure in which a client learns to rehearse ways to handle problem situations mentally. Such rehearsal makes it easier for the client to behave effectively in the actual situations.

Cognitive restructuring A technique used by Albert Ellis and other cognitive therapists in which the client is made aware of a connection between unrealistic thoughts and the maladaptive behavior these evoke. Clients are helped to develop more rational ways of looking at their behavior.

Cognitive schema. See *schemata*.

Cognitive set A person's habitual way of viewing the world and distorting it in terms of his or her personality characteristics and expectations.

Cognitive triad Description of depression in terms of negative thinking about oneself, the current situation, and the future. Part of Beck's cognitive distortion model.

Coming out Term used by homosexuals to indicate the occasion of openly declaring their sexual orientation.

Commitment Placement in an institution, usually without the consent of the person committed, through a legal procedure. See also *civil commitment, criminal commitment*.

Communication deviance Term referring to the inability of a person to maintain a shared focus of attention with another. Studied in parent-child communications in families with a schizophrenic child.

Community perspective Viewpoint that much maladaptive behavior results from poor living conditions, discrimination, and so on. Emphasis is on preventive activities.

Community psychology Branch of applied psychology concerned with modifying both the individual and the structure of the social system to produce optimal benefits for both society and the individual. Community psychologists are often primarily interested in preventing maladaptive behavior.

Co-morbidity The significant overlap or co-occurrence of symptoms and conditions in different disorders. The common finding of co-morbidity in depression and anxiety, for instance, makes it important to understand the relationship between these two disorders.

Competency May refer to adequacy of coping skills. In a legal sense refers to whether a person who is the object of a legal proceeding has the capacity to profit from consultation with a lawyer and to understand the purpose of the legal proceedings.

Competency-focused prevention Actions to prevent maladaptive behavior through helping those at risk develop coping skills.

Compulsive behavior Characterized by an individual's need to repeat a series of acts again and again even though he or she perceives them as senseless and interfering with desirable activities.

Compulsive substance abuse Behavior that is focused on drug seeking to the detriment of other parts of the individual's life.

Computerized axial tomography (CT scan) Technique that uses a narrow beam of x-rays to photograph an area of the body from many angles. A computer then analyzes this information to provide a clear picture of soft tissues as well as the tissue seen in conventional x-rays.

Concordance Term describing the degree of relationship among twins and other family members with respect to a given characteristic or trait. They are referred to as *concordant* if they both show a particular trait; if they do not, the pair is described as *discordant* for that trait.

Concussion Head injury that does not cause lasting structural damage. Rate of recovery is proportional to the severity of the injury.

Conditioned response (CR) In classical conditioning, the response that occurs after training has taken place and after the conditioned stimulus has been presented.

Conditioned stimulus (CS) In classical conditioning, the neutral stimu-

lus that does not elicit a response prior to training.

Conditioning See *classical conditioning; operant conditioning*.

Conduct disorder Diagnostic classification for those under 18 who commit antisocial acts. Adults may also be classified this way if they do not meet the criteria for the antisocial personality disorder.

Confabulation The process of filling in missing memories with fabricated information; to replace forgotten facts with fantasy.

Congenital Characteristics that are either innate or acquired, usually through chemical action, while the child is in the uterus.

Conscious Aspects of one's mental life of which a person is aware at any particular time.

Constitutional Any characteristics acquired by heredity, uterine environment, or illness or injury at or after birth.

Continuous Performance Test Test of sustained visual attention in which the subject is required to indicate whenever a certain stimulus is presented and to ignore all other stimuli.

Controlled drinking approach A therapeutic approach to decreasing overuse of alcohol by teaching clients coping skills, self-monitoring of behavioral antecedents of heavy drinking, and altered expectations concerning the effects of alcohol.

Contusion Brain condition in which diffuse structural damage has occurred (e.g., rupture of blood vessels). Typically, cerebrospinal fluid pressure is raised, causing such symptoms as coma and stupor.

Conversion disorder Type of somatoform disorder in which there is a loss or change in physical functioning that suggests a physical disorder but seems to be a direct expression of a psychological conflict.

Coping Contending with difficulties and overcoming them.

Coping skills The characteristic way a person deals with difficulties or stress. Commonly used skills include task-directed activity, working on a problem step by step, appropriate control of emotion.

Coping style Characteristic way a person deals with the stimuli in his or her environment.

Coronary heart disease (CHD) Disorder in which one or more of the coronary arteries is partially or totally obstructed by deposits. This results in a temporary or permanent cut off of blood to portions of the heart muscle.

Correlation Degree of correspondence between two variables; a statistical index of covariation that varies from $+1.00$ to -1.00.

Correlational study Type of research in which the relationship of two or more characteristics is measured. No statement about cause and effect can be made from correlational research.

Cortex Outer layer of an organ such as the cerebrum, cerebellum, or adrenal gland.

Corticotrophin-releasing factor (CRF) Substance secreted by the hypothalamus that releases the chemical ACTH when it reaches the pituitary gland.

Countertransference Psychoanalytic term that refers to the therapist's emotional reactions to the patient. See also *transference*.

Covert Behavior that is internal and not directly observable. Includes unexpressed thoughts and feelings and other conscious and unconscious mental phenomena.

Covert modeling Learning through imagining how someone else would perform a task or by anticipating what response might be given to certain types of behavior.

Covert sensitization Behavioral therapy in which anxiety is created toward a particular stimulus situation that is likely to produce undesirable behavior. Usually the stimulus is paired with cognitions relating to the possible negative consequences if the person continues a given behavior. A treatment often used in changing the focus of sexual excitement.

CPT See *Continuous Performance Test*.

Crack A street name for a smokable form of very potent, concentrated cocaine.

Criminal commitment Commitment of a person to an institution based on a judgment that the person is guilty of a criminal act and is also legally insane.

Crisis A decisive turning point in a series of events.

Criteria The standards against which behaviors are measured.

Cross-cultural approach Method of studying the causes of various psychological and physical problems by studying their occurrence in a variety of cultures and then attempting to identify factors that are correlated with high and low frequency of the problems.

Cross-fostering study Method of evaluating hereditary factors in behavioral disorders by comparing frequency of a disorder in groups with genetic vulnerability reared by healthy adoptive parent(s) and groups without known genetic vulnerability reared by adoptive parent(s) who have a particular behavior disorder.

Cross-sectional study Research design in which different groups are sampled at the same time and the results compared. Technique often used to study human development.

CT scan See *computerized axial tomography*.

Culture General values, attitudes, achievements, and behavior patterns shared by members of the same society.

Cyclothymic disorder A long lasting disorder that includes both mania and depressive episodes, neither of which meet the criteria for major episodes. Lasts for at least 2 years.

Cytomegalovirus One of a number of viral diseases which, if present in a pregnant woman, may result in retardation and other congenital problems in the child.

Date rape Rape committed by a person who is a social acquaintance of the person who is raped.

Day hospitalization Treatment approach used for either chronic or acutely ill patients or for patients in need of rehabilitation. Patients attend a hospital program during the day and return home in the evening. Activities during the day are focused on social skills and practical problem solving.

Defense mechanism (ego defense) Psychoanalytic term for various psychic operations used by the ego to avoid awareness of unpleasant and anxiety-provoking stimuli. The ego selectively uses defense mechanisms to ward off anxiety originating in the id, the superego, or dangers in external reality.

Deficiency needs According to Maslow, the most basic needs of life, which must be met before higher needs, such as social and intellectual needs, can be considered.

Deinstitutionalization Movement whose purpose is to remove patients from large mental hospitals and to obtain treatment and sheltered living conditions for them in the community.

Deinstitutionalize Efforts to remove from care-giving institutions all those individuals who do not present a clear danger to others or to themselves.

Delirium Condition characterized by a confused mental state, usually resulting from shock or fever, accompanied by alterations in attention and by hallucinations, delusions, and incoherence.

Delirium tremens Acute delirium caused by overdoses of alcohol and consisting of severe alterations in consciousness and attention. Also referred to as the DTs.

Delusion Incorrect belief maintained despite clear evidence to the contrary.

Delusional disorder The presence of a persistent but not bizarre delusion that is not due to any other mental disorder such as schizophrenia. Apart from the delusion, the person's behavior is not obviously unusual.

Dementia Progressive atrophy of brain tissue that results in lapses of memory, poor judgment, and disorientation. Called *presenile dementia* if it occurs before age 65, and *senile dementia* if it begins after age 65.

Dementia paralytica Another term for general paresis.

Dementia praecox Older term for schizophrenia; used by Kraepelin to emphasize the early onset and irreversibility of the disorder as he defined it.

Demographic The description of human populations in terms of growth, density, distribution, and vital statistics.

Dendrite Branched part of a cell that serves as a receptor for nerve impulses from the axons of other cells and transmits them toward the cell body.

Denial Defense mechanism that allows rejection of elements of reality that would be consciously intolerable; negation of experiences or reality through unacceptance.

Deoxyribonucleic acid See *DNA*.

Dependent personality disorder Characterized by an inability to make major decisions and a belittling of a person's own abilities and assets. Intense discomfort is experienced if the person remains alone for more than a brief period.

Dependent variable Aspect of behavior which changes according to manipulation of the independent variable in an experiment.

Depersonalization Feelings of unreality or a loss of personal identity; often experienced as one's being someone else or as watching oneself in a movie.

Depression Pervasive feeling of sadness that may begin after some loss or stressful event, but that continues long afterwards. Inappropriate thought patterns that generalize every event as a calamity are characteristic.

Depressive disorder Depressive symptoms that meet diagnostic criteria for either a single episode of major depression, or recurrent episodes. If manic or hypomanic behavior has been observed in the past, depressed symptoms should not be classified as a major depression even if they meet the other criteria.

Descriptive statistics Procedures used to summarize groups of individual observations. The most common descriptive statistics are measures of central tendency (e.g., mean) and measures of variability (e.g., standard deviation).

Desensitization hypothesis The idea that antidepressant drugs are effective because they reduce abnormal sensitivity in the catecholamine receptors of people who are depressed.

Determinism The philosophical idea that all acts are the inevitable result of what has happened before and that human choice or free will plays no role in what happens.

Detoxification Ridding the body of the particular toxic substance that is causing the problem. In drug or alcohol detoxification, withdrawal signs are usually experienced as the amount of toxic substance declines.

Developmental disorder One of a group of disorders that involve distortions in the development of basic psychological functions that are involved in social skills, language, perception, and motor behavior. The disorder can be pervasive and involve many functions (e.g., autism) or specific and involve only a single aspect of development (e.g., developmental arithmetic disorder).

Dexamethasone Suppression Test Chemical test used in an attempt to differentiate depressed individuals who may be helped by different treatments.

Dexedrine See *dextroamphetamine*.

Dextroamphetamine Stimulant drug (e.g., Dexedrine) sometimes used in the treatment of hyperactivity.

Diagnosis Classification of behavior disorders in terms of relatively homogeneous groups based on similar behaviors or correlates. Shorthand description of the behavioral and personality correlates associated with a particular classification. In medicine, the act or process of deciding the nature of a diseased condition.

Diagnostic and Statistical Manual (DSM) Classification system for abnormal behavior published by the American Psychiatric Association. The system, currently called DSM-IV, is generally used in the United States for official diagnostic and record keeping purposes.

Diagnostic interview Interview designed to gather information and assess behavior, usually for the purpose of determining seriousness and outcome or deciding what treatment approach would be appropriate.

Diagnostic Interview Schedule (DIS) A structured interview used in the diagnosis of mental disorders.

Diastolic Term used to describe the blood pressure reading at the time the heart dilates to allow more blood to enter.

Diathesis-stress theory The idea that only people with an underlying vulnerability to a disorder will develop that disorder when they are exposed to overwhelming stress. This approach is used particularly in understanding why some people develop symptoms of one of the schizophrenic spectrum disorders when exposed to stress.

Diazepam One of the benzodiazepines, a group of antianxiety tranquilizers. Known by trade name, Valium.

Dimensional model An approach to classification that focuses on patterns of characteristics to determine profiles of characteristics that differentiate the different categories. The Minnesota Multiphasic Personality Inventory is used in this way.

Discordant Term often used in twin studies to describe particular characteristics on which the twins differ. Characteristics that are the same for both are referred to as *concordant*.

Disorders of infancy, childhood, or adolescence Conditions that begin at one of these developmental periods in a person's life.

Disorganized schizophrenia (hebephrenic type) Type of schizophrenia distinguished by incoherent speech and flat, incongruous, or silly affect. Often associated with extreme oddities of behavior such as gesturing or grimacing.

Displacement Defense mechanism in which an emotional attitude is transferred from one object to a substitute object.

Dissociative disorder Sudden, temporary alteration in the functions of consciousness, identity, or motor behavior in which some part of one or more of these functions is lost. If consciousness is affected, the person cannot remember important personal events. If identity is affected, a new identity that dominates behavior is temporarily assumed. If motor behavior is affected, then consciousness and/or identity are also affected. Wandering behavior is the most common resulting motor behavior.

Dissociative identity disorder A disorder in which a person assumes alternate personalities. Also called multiple personality disorder.

Divalproex A drug used in research studies to treat bipolar disorder. May be helpful to some patients for whom lithium was not an effective treatment.

Dizygotic twins Fraternal twins developed from two fertilized eggs. The two individuals have the same genetic relationship as any pair of siblings.

DNA Abbreviation for deoxyribonucleic acid, a complex chemical found in chromosomes within living cell nuclei. The sequence of its units determines genetic inheritance.

Dominant gene Member of the gene pair that determines whether the individual will show the trait controlled by that gene. Other member of the pair may be the same (also dominant) or different (recessive).

Dopamine One of the neurotransmitters included under the category of catecholamines and also under the larger category of monoamine neurotransmitters.

Dopamine hypothesis Idea that schizophrenia involves an excess of the neurotransmitter dopamine at certain sites in the brain.

Double-blind method Experimental design used in drug research. Neither the subjects nor the experimenters know whether the medications given to different comparison groups are active or inert (placebos).

Down syndrome Condition related to some inequality in the chromosome pair designated as number 21. Usually associated with a trisomy, or presence of an extra chromosome in addition to the usual pair. Also called trisomy 21.

Drug therapy Use of a variety of psychoactive drugs to treat different types of maladaptive behavior. Drugs are most often used to treat schizophrenia, bipolar disorder, some depressions, and anxiety. Drug treatment is often combined with other types of therapy.

DSM See *Diagnostic and Statistical Manual.*

DST See *dexamethasone suppression test.*

DTs See *delirium tremens.*

Dymorphin One of the naturally occurring opioids in the body that are part of a signaling system related to pain, mood regulation, and learning.

Dyspareunia (functional) Type of sexual dysfunction in which persistent and recurrent genital pain is associated with coitus without any apparent physical cause.

Dysphoria Feelings of anxiety, depression, and restlessness.

Dysphoric mood Characterized by symptoms of depression, sadness, feeling blue and hopeless.

Dysthymia A longstanding depressed mood accompanied by loss of interest and lack of pleasure in situations which most people would find enjoyable.

Dysthymic disorder Long-lasting chronic depressed mood or loss of pleasure in most usual activities. Does not meet the criteria for a major depressive episode.

Echolalia Meaningless repetition of words.

ECT See *electroconvulsive therapy.*

EEG See *electroencephalogram.*

Efficacy expectation The belief that one can successfully carry out a particular behavior.

Ego In psychoanalytic theory, the part of the psyche which makes up the self or the "I." Part of the psyche that is conscious and most closely in touch with reality and that functions as the "executive officer" of the personality.

Ego boundaries, loss of A state of being unable to distinguish between oneself and another person as separate individuals each of whom has his/her own unique thoughts and feelings. Often associated with feelings of being controlled by others. May be found in schizophrenic disorder or borderline personality disorder.

Electroconvulsive therapy (ECT) Treatment for depression in which electrical current is passed through a patient's head. Used if a quick treatment is needed because of a high suicide risk or if antidepressant drugs have not been effective.

Electroencephalogram (EEG) Graphic record of minute electrical impulses arising from brain cells. Measured by an electronic device called an *electroencephalograph.*

Encephalitis Inflammation of the white matter of the brain. Symptoms include visual failure, mental deterioration, and spastic paralysis.

Encopresis Repeated voluntary or involuntary bowel movements of normal consistency that occur in inappropriate surroundings and are not a result of any organic disorder.

Endocrine Referring to any of the ductless glands of the body. These pass their secretions directly from the gland cells to the bloodstream.

Endorphin Pain-killing substance that occurs naturally in the brain.

Enkephalin A protein that naturally occurs in the body and that produces a morphine-like activity.

Epidemiological research Studies designed to link the occurrence of a disorder with a specified population. One focus of this research is the study of the association between mental disorders and various population variables. Results are often expressed in terms of *incidence*, or the number of new cases that appear during a specific time period, and *prevalence*, the number of cases that currently exist within the population.

Epidemiology The scientific study of the associations between diseases or behavioral deviations and social class variables, geographical variables, or environmental variables. These associations, derived from the study of large population groups, help to suggest possible causes for the health problems observed.

Epilepsy Transitory disturbance of brain function which is characterized by a sudden onset and loss of consciousness and which may involve tonic and clonic muscle spasms. Epileptic seizures may be minor (petit mal) or major (grand mal) and tend to recur.

Epinephrine One of the hormones secreted by the adrenal medulla, active in emotional excitement and in response to stress.

Erectile disorder Type of sexual dysfunction in which the male is occasionally or chronically unable to achieve or maintain a penile erection. The condition may have physical or psychological causes. Also known as *impotence*.

Erectile dysfunction See *erectile disorder*.

Erogenous zone Parts of the body sensitive to sexual stimulation.

Escape response The attempt to get out of an unpleasant or aversive situation.

Etiology Assignment of a cause; scientific study of causes and origins of maladaptive behavior.

Excitement (sexual) The initial response to sexual stimulation marked by vaginal lubrication or penile erection.

Exhibitionism Exposure of the genitals in public for purposes of obtaining sexual pleasure and gratification.

Exhibitionist One who practices exhibitionism.

Existential therapy Type of psychotherapy which uses both humanistic and psychodynamic approaches. Emphasis is placed on each person's ability to affect his or her life course by the particular choices made.

Exit event A psychological loss of social support through death, divorce, or the breakup of a relationship.

Exorcism Expelling of evil spirits.

Experiment A study using the experimental method.

Experimental method Study of the factors influencing a result by the manipulation of one or more experimental variables rather than simply observing what occurs naturally.

Exposure Requiring the client to participate in anxiety-provoking situations under supportive supervision until the anxiety response is extinguished. Based on the classical conditioning approach.

Exposure orientation In drug addiction, the idea that addiction is brought about by an environment that provides availability of drugs.

Exposure therapy Behavioral therapy that has as its basic element maintaining contact with or imagining contact with the feared stimulus.

Expressed emotion (EE) A measure of emotional involvement and attitudes of family members when talking about a behaviorally disturbed family member.

Expressed trait A trait that dominates in the individual and is determined either by at least one dominant gene or by a pair of recessive genes. If only one recessive gene is present the individual has the potential to pass on a genetic characteristic, but that characteristic is not observable in the person him or herself.

Extinction Weakening of a response following removal of reinforcement.

Eye-tracking movements Study of smooth pursuit and saccadic eye movements as an individual attempts to visually follow a rhythmically moving stimulus. One goal of such study is to uncover genetic markers of vulnerability.

Factitious disorder Symptoms, either fabricated or self-induced, that are designed to produce attention and care from medical personnel.

Fading Technique for gradually eliminating cues used in behavior modification after an individual begins to achieve a desired response.

Family study Study of characteristics of a group of related individuals to uncover genetic patterns.

Family systems approach A therapeutic approach in which the disturbance experienced by the client is viewed as the result of the way the family interacts rather than a problem caused by the client alone.

Family therapy Specialized type of group therapy in which the members of the family of the client all participate in group-treatment sessions. The basic idea is that the family, not just the individual client, has to alter behavior to solve the problem.

Fantasized exposure Exposure therapy in which the upsetting stimuli are imagined rather than presented in actuality.

Fetal alcohol syndrome Condition that may occur in the children of alcoholic mothers or mothers who used excessive alcohol during pregnancy. Characterized by retardation and unusual physical characteristics.

Fetishism Sexual deviation in which sexual interest is centered upon some body part or inanimate object which becomes capable of stimulating sexual excitement.

First rank symptoms Group of symptoms described by Kurt Schneider in an attempt to establish clear behavioral criteria for schizophrenia. A basis of the DSM-III-R definition of schizophrenic disorders. Also reflected in DSM-IV.

Fixation Inappropriately strong attachment for someone or something. Also refers to an abnormal arrest of development during infancy or childhood which persists in adult life as an inappropriate constellation of attitudes, habits, or interests.

Fixed-role therapy Cognitive approach developed by George Kelly in which the client is asked to practice or try out new roles in relationships.

Flashback The reexperiencing of hallucinations or other perceptual symptoms which had originally occurred while the person was intoxicated by a psychoactive substance.

Flooding Behavioral therapeutic technique used particularly in the treatment of phobias. Treatment consists of exposing the client to the feared stimulus until the fear response has been extinguished.

Follow-up study A method in which individuals listed at one point in time are contacted again at a later time to reassess behavior so that any changes can be noted.

Four humours The four body fluids (blood, black bile, yellow bile, and phlegm) that were thought by the ancients to play a role in character and temperament.

Fragile X syndrome An abnormality of the X chromosome that is the most frequent cause of mental retardation except for Down syndrome.

Free association Basic technique of the psychoanalytic method by which a patient expresses his or her thoughts as freely and in as uninhibited a manner as possible. Free associations provide a natural flow of thought processes unencumbered by interruptions or explanations.

Frontal lobe Portion of each cerebral hemisphere involved in abstract thinking processes.

Fugue state Flight from reality in which the individual may leave his or her present environment and life situation and establish a new lifestyle in another geographical location. Such a person is usually totally amnesic concerning his or her past life, although other abilities remain unimpaired; he or she may appear essentially normal to others.

Full Scale IQ One of three intelligence test scores obtained from any of the Wechsler tests. This IQ score takes into account both verbal ability and performance and spatial skills.

Fully functioning person Term used by Carl Rogers to describe the optimal level of adjustment at which an individual can function with minimal anxiety.

GABA Term for gamma-amino-butyric-acid, a neurotransmitter. A deficiency of GABA, associated with hereditary causes, is thought to be involved in Huntington's disease.

Galvanic skin response (GSR) Change in the electrical resistance of the skin. This response serves as a dependent variable in conditioning and is used in lie detector tests.

Gastrointestinal disorders Disorders of the digestive system, the stomach, and intestines.

Gay Term used to describe a homosexual lifestyle by those who feel the term homosexual has too many negative connotations.

Gender identity Basic feature of personality encompassing an individual's conviction of being male or female.

Gender-identity disorder (transsexualism) Disorder in which the individual has a strong desire to become a member of the opposite sex by changing his or her anatomical structure.

Gender-identity disorder of childhood A disorder occurring before puberty in which the child shows intense distress over its assigned sex. Such children may deny their assigned sex or assert that they will develop the genital characteristics of the opposite sex.

Gender nonconformity in childhood Situation in which the child is primarily interested in the activities culturally associated with the opposite sex. Not necessarily associated with later sexual deviance.

Gene Microscopic structure in the chromosome; physical unit of hereditary transmission.

General adaptation syndrome Concept proposed by Selye. Three-stage reaction of an organism to excessive and prolonged stress, including (1) an alarm or mobilization reaction; (2) a resistance stage; and (3) a final stage of exhaustion.

Generalized anxiety disorder Persistent anxiety that lasts at least 1 month and includes several of the following: motor tension, autonomic hyperactivity, apprehensive expectation, vigilance, and scanning. The symptoms do not include phobias, panic attacks, obsessions, or compulsions.

General paresis See *paresis*.

Genetic counseling The giving of information about risk for inheritance of certain disorders based on general information about heredity, knowledge of family history, and genetic characteristics of the person or couple seeking information.

Genetic heterogeneity In genetics, the idea that more than one gene is necessary for the inheritance of a characteristic. However, the genes each have a separate effect, not an additive one.

Genetic specificity A gene pattern that is unique to a particular disorder or group of disorders.

Global assessment of functioning (GAF) The measure, on Axis V of DSM-IV, of an individual's overall psychological, social, and occupational functioning.

Glove anesthesia Condition in which a person cannot move or feel the part of the arm and hand that a glove would normally cover.

Grand mal Severe form of epilepsy involving major convulsive attacks and loss of consciousness.

Grief Sorrow, usually over a loss.

Group home A sheltered living environment that may be either transitional or permanent. Often used for retarded persons and those with chronic schizophrenia. Emphasis is on self-care and self-regulation to the extent the individual's ability and condition permit.

Group hysteria Hysterical symptoms, often of a conversion disorderlike nature, that seem to spread contagiously through a group of individuals.

Group therapy Psychotherapy of several persons at the same time in small groups.

Guided mastery A therapeutic approach in which the therapist enhances the client's feelings of self-efficacy through modeling, information, or suggestions.

Guided rehearsal Aspect of modeling in which the client practices the previously modeled behavior and is coached by the therapist in order to improve the performance.

Gyri Raised portions of the brain's surface between the sulci. (Plural of gyrus.)

Habituation Decrease of the orienting response after the repeated presentation of a stimuli.

Halfway house Transitional living facility that accommodates, for a short period of time, newly discharged psychiatric patients or those who have functioned maladaptively.

Hallucination Sensory perception in the absence of an external stimulus. Hallucinations are usually visual ("seeing things") but may occur in other sensory modalities as well.

Hallucinogen General name for a group of drugs or chemicals capable of producing hallucinations.

Halo effect Tendency to rate an individual improperly high or low on a particular factor because of prior information or a general impression of the individual.

Hashish Hallucinogenic substance that is the solidified resin of *cannabis sativa* (marijuana).

Headache, cluster Headaches that occur in groups over a relatively short time period. Each headache is very painful for several minutes and fades away completely within an hour.

Headache, migraine Severe headache caused by a constriction followed by a dilation of the cranial artery. Usually preceded by some sensory or emotional cues called an *aura*. The disorder is thought to have some stress-related components.

Health psychology Area of psychology concerned both with calling attention to ways that disease can be prevented by changing living habits and with helping people modify behavior that increases health risk.

Hebephrenic schizophrenia See *disorganized schizophrenia*.

Helplessness See *learned helplessness*.

Hereditary Qualities transmitted from parent to child through genetic transmission.

Heredity The process by which characteristics of an organism are basically determined by genes received from the parents.

Heroin Extremely addictive opiate derived from morphine.

Herpes virus hominus (herpes simplex) Chronic viral illness which, if present in a pregnant woman, may cause retardation and other congenital malformations in her child.

Heterocyclics Recent terminology used to describe the overall group comprising the tricyclics and second generation antidepressants and to distinguish them from the monoamine oxidase inhibitor group of antidepressant medications.

Heterosexual Characterized by attraction to the opposite sex.

Hierarchy of needs View, especially as described by Abraham Maslow, that certain basic needs of the individual must be met before the person becomes interested in such topics as personal growth and self-actualization.

High-risk study Research strategy entailing the longitudinal study of persons who might be vulnerable to breakdown.

Histrionic personality disorder Characterized by overly reactive behavior of a histrionic, exhibitionistic type. Individuals with this disorder are egocentric and self-absorbed and usually have poor sexual adjustment.

Homeostasis Maintenance of equilibrium and constancy among the bodily processes.

Homosexual A person who prefers to engage in sexual activity with persons of his or her own sex and who continues this behavior over a long period of time.

Homosexual behavior Sexual activity between persons of the same sex.

Hopelessness Negative expectations that may be characteristic of a person who is at risk for suicide. The Beck Hopelessness Scale has been used as a predictor of suicide risk.

Hopelessness depression A suggested subtype of depression in which attributional style is important in producing the depressed state.

Hormones Glandular secretions that function as coordinators of bodily reactions to external events and body growth and development.

Humanistic-existentialist perspective Idea that all individuals are unique and should be free to make their own choices about life directions. Emphasizes the creative freedom and potential of the individual.

Humanistic therapies Psychotherapies with special emphasis on human beings' fundamental desires to obtain self-respect and their needs for it. Carl Rogers' approach is an example.

Huntington's disease Uncommon degenerative disease occurring in families. Symptoms include jerking and twisting movement, facial grimaces, and psychotic symptoms. Also called Huntington's chorea.

Hyperactivity See *attention-deficit/ hyperactivity disorder*.

Hypertension High blood pressure, usually considered a psychophysiological disorder.

Hypervigilance Tendency to constantly survey the environment for negative stimuli. A coping mecha-

nism often used by avoidant personalities and by anxious individuals.

Hypnosis Altered state of consciousness induced by suggestion. Ranges from mild hypersuggestibility to deep, trancelike states.

Hypochondriasis (Hypochondria) Disorder in which a person is preoccupied by fear of disease and worries a great deal about his or her health without any realistic cause.

Hypomania A disorder characterized by unusual elevation in mood that is not as extreme as that found in mania.

Hypomanic episode A distinct period of elevated expansive or irritable mood and other manic behaviors that is not severe enough to greatly impair social or occupational functioning and does not require hospitalization.

Hypothalamus Part of the brain that lies below the thalamus. Controls various activities of the autonomic nervous system, including regulation of body temperature.

Hypothesis A statement of relationship or cause and effect stated in terms that allow a scientific test.

Hypothesis-testing experiment Evaluation of the correctness of an idea by experimental test.

Hypothetical construct Inferred intermediate mechanism; a concept conceived of as having properties of its own (e.g., a memory trace).

Hysteria Presence of a physical problem without any physical causes. A person with hysteria is called an *hysteric*.

Hysteric Term used by Charcot to describe an individual who complains of organic symptoms such as pain, blindness, or paralysis for which no organic cause can be found.

Id In psychoanalysis, that division of the psyche which is a repository of all instinctual impulses and repressed mental contents. Represents the true unconscious or the "deepest" part of the psyche.

Identification Feeling of association with another person or group such that an individual takes on the viewpoint and viewpoint of the other(s).

Idiot Term formerly used for a retarded

individual whose intelligence fell in the lowest measurable range.

Imipramine One of the tricyclic drugs used in the treatment of some depressed individuals.

Immune system Body system that fights disease through inactivation of foreign substances by means of lymphocyte cells.

Implicit learning Learning that derives from observations of behavior that are analyzed and interpreted some time after they actually occurred.

Implosive therapy Behavior therapy technique based on the principle of extinction. Client is repeatedly presented with strong anxiety-provoking stimuli until he or she no longer reacts in an anxious manner.

Impotence Failure of a male to attain or maintain a penile erection even when sexually excited.

Impulse control disorder A disorder in which the person seems unable to resist impulses (gambling, stealing, fire setting) that do not occur as part of any other disorder.

Impulse control disorder not classified elsewhere A disorder that clearly has the characteristics of impulse control but does not meet the criteria for any of the types specified.

Impulsive Characterized by a lack of forethought or planning.

Inauthentic behavior According to existential theorists, the determination of behavioral goals by others, not one's self.

Incest Sexual relations between close family members, such as brother and sister or parent and child.

Incidence A count of the number of new cases that begin during a certain period of time; used in epidemiology. Contrast with *prevalence*.

Incompetent person Legal term used to describe individuals who are not able to understand the meaning of legal proceedings in which they are involved and who are unable to consult with an attorney in a way that might assist their defense.

Increased-stress theory Idea that the negative impact of the condition of poverty and crime make mental ill-ness, especially schizophrenia, more likely because of the increased pressures of living. Contrast with *social selection theory*.

Independent variable Experimental factor (e.g., time of food deprivation) that is manipulated or altered in some manner while others are held constant.

Index case Term used in the study of genetics to indicate the individual with a disorder whose heredity is under study.

Indoleamine Type of neurotransmitter of the monoamine group—e.g., serotonin—that appears especially closely related to mood.

Infantile sexuality View held by Sigmund Freud that children as well as adults have sexual feelings and experience erotic stimulation.

Inferential statistics Methods based on the laws of probability that are used to draw conclusions about relationships among variables studied.

Inflexibility Inability to change; in personality, those coping styles habitually used even if they are unsuitable to a given situation.

Information processing A view of cognitive behavior that compares the human senses and brain function and behavior to a computer.

Informed consent Requirement that patients must be given adequate information about the benefits and risks of planned treatments before they agree to the procedures.

Inhibited sexual excitement A sexual disorder characterized by either low sexual desire or aversion to sexual activity. In men, this disorder means failure to achieve or maintain an erection sufficient to complete sexual intercourse.

Innate Characteristics acquired through general inheritance or the mutation of a gene or genes passed on from the parent.

Insanity Legal term connoting mental incompetence, inability to distinguish "right from wrong," and inability to care for oneself.

Insight Self-knowledge; understanding the significance and purpose of one's motives or behavior, including the ability to recognize inappropriateness and irrationality.

Intellectualization A defense mechanism in which a person separates the description or meaning of an event from its emotional impact.

Intelligence test Standardized test used to establish an intelligence-level rating by measuring an individual's ability in a variety of tasks including information, word meaning, concept formation, and various performance skills.

Interactional orientation (*in addiction*) The idea that both aspects of the person and of the situation are important in determining whether addiction will occur. People who may use drugs while they are in a long term stressful situation may not show signs of addiction such as withdrawal when they transfer to a less stressful environment in which the cues that accompanied drug use are absent.

Interactional view of behavior Viewpoint that directs attention to the joint effects or interactions of many of the variables emphasized by different theoretical viewpoints in producing abnormal behavior.

Internalizing disorders A group of childhood disorders that are characterized less by overt activity than by cognitive activity consisting of worries or disturbing thoughts.

Interpersonal factors In therapy refers to the relationship between the therapist and the client as a consequence of the personalities of the two rather than as a result of the techniques the therapist uses.

Interpersonal psychotherapy A form of psychotherapy that focuses on increasing clients' social effectiveness and the extent that they feel cared about by others.

Intervening variable An inferred variable functionally connected with antecedents and consequences; such variables are abstractions and have no properties other than those defined by the empirical data.

Interview See *diagnostic interview; therapeutic interview*.

Intravenous injection The injection of a drug or chemical directly into the bloodstream by inserting a hollow needle into a vein.

Intoxication Mental disorder and the presence of maladaptive behavior due to the use and present effect on the body of some substance. The most common behavior changes are inattention and impaired thinking, judgment, emotional control, and motor activity.

Intrapsychic conflict Lack of acceptance of certain areas of thought or emotion that make it necessary for an individual to attempt to keep some material out of awareness.

In vivo exposure A technique used in cognitive therapy or desensitization in which the individual practices adaptive cognitions or relaxation behavior in the actual presence of the anxiety-producing object or situation.

Irrational thought Ideas and beliefs that are derived from emotional response rather than reasoning.

Isolation Defense mechanism by which inconsistent or contradictory attitudes and feelings are walled off from each other in consciousness. Similar to repression, except that in isolation the impulse or wish is consciously recognized, but is separated from present behavior; in repression, neither the wish nor its relation to action is recognized. Intellectualization is a special form of isolation.

Juvenile delinquency Violations of the law committed by children and adolescents (usually defined as persons 18 years of age or younger).

Kappa statistic A type of reliability index that corrects for chance agreement to provide a true estimate of reliability.

Karyotype A microphotograph of an individual's chromosomes in a standard array.

Kaufman Assessment Battery for Children (K-ABC) An intelligence test for children that is based on ideas from cognitive psychology and neuropsychology to measure simultaneous and sequential processing abilities. Designed to be less culturally biased than conventional intelligence tests.

Kinsey Report First detailed statistical report that attempted to present the variations in human sexual behavior from a descriptive, scientific view.

Korsakoff's syndrome Chronic brain disorder precipitated by a vitamin deficiency stemming from alcoholism. Characterized by marked disorientation, amnesia, and falsification of memory.

Labeling Cognitive device by which a person classifies his or her own emotional responses as a way of controlling behavior, especially in stress-producing situations. Also, a way people are categorized by others, a way of stereotyping.

La belle indifference Marked lack of concern about one's disability, occasionally seen in patients with conversion disorder.

Laceration Gross tear or rupture in tissue. Cerebral lacerations may occur through head injuries.

Latency period According to Freud, the period from age 5 until adolescence during which the child's sexual impulses are not a primary focus of his or her pleasure-seeking activities.

Learned helplessness Acquired belief in one's helplessness to deal with a situation or control one's environment. Concept has been applied to explain depression in humans.

Learning perspective Idea that what one experiences is the most important aspect of behavior, which is considered as a product of stimulus—response relationships. One group of learning theorists was called behaviorists.

Lesbianism The practice of homosexual behavior by women.

Librium (chlordiazepoxide) Tranquilizer often prescribed for anxiety problems.

Limbic system Part of the brain that controls visceral and bodily changes associated with emotion; also regulates drive-motivated behavior. Lower parts of the cerebrum.

Lithium (lithium carbonate) Chemical salt used in the treatment of bipolar disorder.

Live modeling Learning through direct observation of another person who performs the act or acts which are to be learned.

Locus, gene The characteristic position within a chromosome in which a particular gene pair are located.

Locus of control Personality characteristic described by Julian Rotter in which an individual believes either that he or she has the power to affect the outcome of situations (internal locus of control) or that he or she has little control over what happens (external locus of control).

Longitudinal study Research strategy based on observing and recording the behavior of people over periods of time. Involves obtaining measures on the same people either continuously or at specific or regular intervals.

LSD (Lysergic acid dimethylamide) Chemically produced synthetic hallucinogen with psychotomimetic properties.

Lunatic Term used in the past to describe the insane. The word *luna* (moon) refers to the old belief that those who were insane were moonstruck.

Lycanthropy Term for the magical change believed to overcome individuals and cause them to behave like wolves.

Lymphocyte A general term that includes several types of cells in the immune system that fight disease.

Magnetic resonance imaging (MRI) A method by which electromagnetic radiation is used to visualize and measure anatomy in the living person.

Magnetic resonance spectroscopy (MRS) Measurement of tissue chemistry and metabolic function in living organisms through the use of electromagnetic radiation emitted from these chemical changes.

Mainstreaming An educational policy in which children with physical and mental disabilities participate at least to some degree in regular school classes. Some special classes during the school day may be provided that are focused on their special learning difficulties.

Major depressive disorder or episode A severe depression characterized by dysphoric mood as well as poor appetite, sleep problems, feelings of restlessness or being slowed down, loss of pleasure, loss of energy, feelings of inability to concentrate or indecisiveness, recurrent thoughts of death or suicide attempts. These occur without mood-incongruent delusions or hallucinations and are not due to schizophrenia, paranoid disorder, organic mental disorder, or recent death of a loved one.

Maladaptive behavior Behavior that deals inadequately with a situation, especially one that is stressful.

Male limited Hereditary pattern that seems to be transmitted only from fathers and only to male offspring.

Malingering Behavior designed to get financial or other rewards by pretending to have some disorder. Contrast with *factitious disorder.*

Mania Euphoric, hyperactive state in which an individual's judgment is impaired.

Manic depressive psychosis See *bipolar disorder.*

Mantra See *meditation.*

MAO inhibitor See *Monoamine oxidase inhibitor.*

Marijuana Substance derived from the leaves or flowering tops of the cannabis plant. Smoking it leads to a dreamy state of altered consciousness in which ideas are disconnected, uncontrollable, and plentiful. Under the influence of marijuana, behavior is impulsive and mood is elevated.

Marital therapy A subtype of group therapy in which a couple meets together with a therapist in an attempt to improve the couple's interaction.

Markers Biological or behavioral characteristics that may make it possible to identify people who are vulnerable to certain disorders.

Masochism Deviation in which sexual pleasure is attained from pain inflicted on oneself, from being dominated, or from being mistreated.

Masochist One who practices masochism.

Masturbation Self-stimulation of the genitals for the purposes of deriving sexual pleasure.

Mediator A link (for example, between a stimulus and the resulting behavior).

Meditation The technique of relaxing through concentrating on a thought, sensation, or special word or mantra.

Medroxyprogesterone acetate (MPA) A chemical used to reduce the level of male sex hormone in the blood which is used experimentally for treating some of the paraphilias. Trade name Depo-provera.

Meninges Any of the membranes enclosing the brain or spinal cord in vertebrates.

Meningitis Inflammation of any or all of the meninges of the brain and spinal cord. Usually caused by a bacterial infection.

Mental age The age equivalent at which a person's intelligence behavior places him or her. Contrasted to chronological age, the person's actual age as determined by birth date. The ratio between the two [(MA ÷ CA) × 100] was the original formulation of the intelligence quotient.

Mental retardation Intellectual functioning significantly below average. Generally defined as an intelligence test score of 70 or below together with a poor level of social functioning. The degree of retardation is further defined by intelligence test score range.

Mental-status examination An interview, sometimes supplemented with psychological and neurological tests, used to assess an individual's intellectual function and ability to interact appropriately with the environment.

Meta-analysis Technique used to combine the data from many studies in a meaningful way. Has been used to investigate the effects of psychotherapy on clients.

Metacognition A person's knowledge of his or her own cognitive processes and the products of these processes.

Methadone Synthetic chemical whose action is similar to that of morphine. Because its use allegedly does not lead to escalation of dosage, it is prescribed by some authorities as a treatment for heroin addiction.

Methadone maintenance Use of methadone as a substitute for heroin. Methadone prevents withdrawal and

suppresses the desire for heroin, although methadone also has undesirable side effects.

Method factors Variations in results that are caused by the way a study was conducted, the type of questionnaire used, or other factors not associated with a real difference in what has been measured.

Methylphenidate Stimulant drug (e.g., Ritalin) sometimes used in the treatment of hyperactivity.

Migraine headache A severe headache, often on one side only, accompanied by nausea and dilation of the cranial artery. These headaches are usually preceded by a sensory, motor, or mood disturbance called an aura.

Milieu-limited Term for a hereditary pattern in which a disorder seems to appear only under certain environmental conditions.

Milieu therapy Effort to provide a totally therapeutic environment within an institution by enlisting the efforts of all staff members as providers of some form of therapeutic contact.

Mind Human consciousness as shown in thought, perception, and memory. Reflects the artificial dichotomy often made between mind and body.

Minnesota Multiphasic Personality Inventory (MMPI) Self-report personality questionnaire designed to facilitate psychiatric diagnosis.

M'Naghten rule Legal precedent in English law, originating in 1843, which provides for acquittal if an accused person is found to be not responsible for the crime—that is, if he or she could not distinguish between "right and wrong." The rule did not take into account that a person might be held to be insane even though he or she knew the difference between right and wrong.

Modeling Behavior learned or modified as a result of observing the behavior of others. Learner does not have to make the observed response him- or herself, or be reinforced for making it, to learn the new behavior. Term used interchangeably with observational learning. See also *covert, live,* and *symbolic modeling.*

Monoamine neurotransmitter
Type of neurotransmitter with a distinctive single amino acid (NH_2) in its molecular structure. There are two types of monoamines: catecholamines and indoleamines.

Monoamine oxidase (MAO)
Enzyme in the neuron receptors that inactivates the various amines, including the catecholamines.

Monoamine oxidase (MAO) inhibitor One of a group of drugs used to treat depression. Works by preventing the degrading of monoamines and thus allowing more norepinephrine and serotonin to collect at the receptor sites.

Monogenic (single-gene) theory
Refers to theory of inheritance in which a gene at one particular locus (e.g., one site on a chromosome) is sufficient to produce an inherited characteristic.

Monozygotic twins Identical twins developed from one fertilized egg.

Mood disorder One of a group of disorders primarily affecting emotional tone. Can be depression, manic excitement, or both. May be episodic or chronic.

Moral treatment Technique of treating mental-hospital patients which prevailed in the nineteenth century. Emphasized removal of restraints, allowing religious conviction, and ensuring humanitarian treatment.

Morphine Principal derivative of opium which has been used extensively to relieve pain.

Mosaicism The condition in which all a person's cells do not have the same chromosome count as a result of an error in cell division in the fertilized egg.

MRI see *magnetic resonance imaging*

MRS see *magnetic resonance spectroscopy*

Multiaxial classification system
System that rates an individual separately on a number of different criteria or axes. The DSM system is an example.

Multiaxial diagnostic system A multiaxial classification system developed to diagnose disordered behavior.

Multifactorial polygenic model
Theory that a number of genes from a variety of loci may combine to produce a particular characteristic or disorder.

Multi-infarct dementia See *vascular dementia*.

Multiple personality disorder
See *dissociative identity disorder*.

Munchausen syndrome A factitious disorder in which the person pretends to have a particular disorder in order to get medical treatment. Involves faking of symptoms, and often self-injury.

Muscle contraction headache
See *tension headache*.

Mutant A cell in which the hereditary material has been altered. This mutation may be spontaneous (occurring naturally) or induced by internal factors such as radiation and certain chemicals.

Mutation Sudden change in the composition of a gene, which usually causes abnormal characteristics in the progeny.

Myocardial infarction Tissue damage to the heart muscle from a drastic decrease in the amount of blood that reaches the heart; commonly called a heart attack.

Naloxone A drug that blocks the pain relieving effects of endorphins.

Naltrexone A drug that prevents readdiction to heroin and other opioids by blocking opioid receptors.

Narcissism Term for self-love or self-absorption derived from the Greek myth about Narcissus who fell in love with what he thought was a water nymph but was in reality his own reflection in a pond.

Narcissistic personality disorder Characterized by a sense of self-importance and a preoccupation with fantasies of unlimited success. Individuals are preoccupied with how well they are doing and how well others think of them. Disorder is often accompanied by depressed mood.

Narcotics Legal term for addicting drugs, the most common of which are the opiates, derived from the Oriental poppy.

Narrow criteria In schizophrenia, research criteria that exclude those who clearly have experienced a schizophrenic process but who have not had the symptoms for an extended period of time and who are presumed to have a possible positive outcome. These criteria may make outcome prediction better but may not add to a complete understanding of the schizophrenic process.

Natural disaster Overwhelming event caused by the forces of nature rather than human intervention—for example, a tornado, earthquake, or flood.

Natural fool Old term for a retarded person. It means one who is born deficient in judgment.

Negative symptoms, in schizophrenia Symptoms characterized by behavior deficits such as flattened affect, poverty of speech and apathy. Sometimes called Type II schizophrenia.

Negative transference Feelings of hostility a client carries over from earlier relationships into his or her relationship with a therapist.

Neoanalyst Theorist who agrees with a revised version of Freud's concepts.

Neo-Freudian Pertaining to former followers of Freud who departed in several major doctrinal ways from orthodox psychoanalysis. Whereas ego psychologists view themselves as psychoanalysts, neo-Freudians may not. Prominent among the neo-Freudians are Adler, Jung, and Sullivan. Their writings emphasize the social and cultural determinants of behavior.

Neuroleptic drugs Name for a group of psychoactive drugs that are used to treat schizophrenic disorders. These reduce psychotic symptoms but may have side effects resembling neurological disorders.

Neurologist Specialist in the diagnosis and treatment of disorders of the nervous system.

Neuron Individual nerve cell.

Neuropsychology Branch of psychology dealing with brain-behavior relationships.

Neuroscience An interdisciplinary field of science that is focused on understanding the relationship between brain structure and function and behavior, affect, and cognitions.

Neurosis Older term for what is now called *anxiety disorder*.

Neurotic depression Older term for *dysthymic disorder*.

Neurotransmitter Chemical product of the nervous system that makes possible the movement of the nerve impulse across the synapse.

Nicotine Volatile psychoactive substance that is the chief active chemical in tobacco.

Nocturnal penile tumescence (NPT) Enlargement and erection of the penis that occurs during rapid-eye-movement sleep.

Non compos mentis Latin term meaning not of sound mind and therefore not legally responsible.

Nonresidential support A treatment format in which support is provided through assistance with finding living quarters, job placements, and other necessities rather than supplying support in a residential milieu.

Non-shared environment Term used in the study of twins or siblings to contrast the environmental effects that both experience in the family with those that differ because of unique events, personal characteristics, or experiences or relationships outside the family.

Nontranssexual gender identity disorder Persistent discomfort about one's assigned sex; frequently involves cross dressing or fantasies about cross dressing. Differs from transsexualism in that there is no persistent preoccupation to acquire the primary and secondary sexual characteristics of the other sex.

Norepinephrine Hormone also called *noradrenalin*, produced by the adrenal medulla. One of the catecholamine group.

NPT See *nocturnal penile tumescence*.

Object relations The psychoanalytic approach that focuses attention on the emotional bonds between persons rather than on a person's view of him or herself.

Observational research A method in which no variables are manipulated and relationships are studied as they naturally occur. Contrast with *experimental method*.

Obsessive behavior Characterized by preoccupation with a particular type of thought that keeps occurring repetitively.

Obsessive-compulsive behavior Behavior that combines ritualistic behavior and compulsive thinking.

Obsessive-compulsive disorder Characterized by recurrent obsessions and/or compulsions, often accompanied by depression or anxiety.

Obsessive-compulsive personality disorder Distinguished by lack of ability to express warmth, a stiff and formal way of relating to others, and extreme perfectionism that leads an individual to focus on details rather than on the whole picture.

Occipital lobe Major division of either cerebral hemisphere located in the dorsal area.

Occupational activities Diagnosed on Axis V of DSM. This information provides an assessment of how well a person is currently functioning.

Operant conditioning Form of conditioning in which a desired response occurs and is subsequently reinforced to increase its probability of more frequent occurrence; also called *instrumental conditioning*.

Operant response Response originally occurring rarely that has been increased in frequency through reinforcement.

Opiate Natural or synthetic substance that is similar in action to morphine or other derivatives of the opium poppy.

Opioid Drug with a morphine-like action. Can be either a natural or synthetic substance.

Oppositional defiant disorder Although less serious than conduct disorder, this disorder is characterized by negative behaviors and unwillingness to accept the authority of others. Often develops into conduct or mood disorder.

Oral dependent Psychodynamic term to describe individuals who secure a major part of their psychological gratification from such activities as eating, drinking, and smoking, and who may show dependent personality characteristics.

Oral stage First developmental stage of infancy, during which pleasure is derived from lip and mouth contact with need-fulfilling objects (e.g., breast).

Organic affective syndrome Abnormal changes in mood thought to be the result of changes in brain metabolism or toxic conditions.

Organic anxiety syndrome Panic attacks or generalized anxiety thought to be causally related to some specific organic factor.

Organic brain syndrome Group of symptoms characteristic of acute and chronic brain disorders.

Organic defect theory Idea that a particular bodily organ that is working improperly is the cause of maladaptive behavior.

Organic delusional syndrome Delusional thinking that occurs as the result of some organic condition, often associated with abuse of a variety of substances including amphetamines, cannabis, and hallucinogens.

Organic hallucinosis Hallucinations caused by some organic factor. Often the result of use of hallucinogenic drugs or large quantities of alcohol.

Organic mental disorder Brain dysfunction based on either aging or the ingestion of substances that affect brain activity. May be temporary or permanent.

Organic personality syndrome Diagnosis used when major personality changes occur that are believed to be the result of some change in or injury to brain tissue.

Organismic point of view Pertaining to the organism as a whole rather than to particular parts. Behavior is considered an interrelated and interactive function of the integrated organism.

Organ-susceptibility hypothesis Idea that emotional stress might cause a psychophysiological problem in a bodily organ in a particular individual because that organ had some inherent weakness.

Orgasm Third stage of sexual response, which involves rhythmic muscular contractions and high physical arousal. In the male, ejaculation of semen takes place during this stage.

Orienting response Measurable psychophysiological changes that come about when a person notices an environmental stimulus and prepares to receive some information from it.

Overanxious disorder of childhood A childhood disorder in which excessive or unrealistic worry is observed concerning performance or competence. Form of generalized anxiety disorder.

Overgeneralization According to Aaron Beck, characteristic way of thinking found in some depressed individuals. Tendency to exaggerate the meaning of an event into a general principle.

Panic disorder Type of anxiety disorder characterized by recurring panic or anxiety attacks and extreme nervousness not necessarily related to exposure to threatening situations.

Paradigm A model or example.

Paradoxical intention Therapeutic technique in which the client is instructed to perform behaviors that seem to be counter to the therapeutic goal. For instance, someone who is afraid of crowds may be instructed to go into a crowd and concentrate on feeling as fearful as possible.

Paranoid disorder Disorder characterized by the persistence of delusions that are usually well organized; does not include prominent hallucinations, incoherent speech, thought derailment, or many of the delusions associated with schizophrenia.

Paranoid personality disorder Personality disorder similar in some ways to schizoid personality disorder, but notable for extreme sensitivity in interpersonal relationships; suspicious, jealous, and stubborn behavior; and a tendency to use the defense mechanism of projection.

Paranoid schizophrenia Type of schizophrenia characterized by persistent delusions, often either grandiose or accusatory.

Paraphilia Sexual deviation that involves choice of inappropriate sex partners or inappropriate goals for the sex act. Pedophilia, sadism, and voyeurism are examples.

Paraprofessional Term used to describe workers who have received certain basic training that enables them to perform tasks formerly performed by professional workers. Paraprofessionals often come from the same communities and educational backgrounds as the people whom they treat or aid.

Parasuicide Term used to describe any act that does not end in death in which a person deliberately causes self-injury or takes a drug overdose with the apparent intention of suicide.

Parens patriae Legal doctrine that gives the state power to act in what it believes to be the best interest of an incapacitated adult or a minor.

Parental affective style A measure of negative feelings expressed by family members as the family discusses upsetting problems together. Compare with *expressed emotion*.

Paresis Chronic and progressively deteriorating brain condition caused by syphilitic infection and characterized by loss of cognitive and motor functions, speech disorder, and eventual death.

Parietal lobe Middle division of each cerebral hemisphere of the brain, behind the central sulcus, above the fissure of Sylvius, and in front of the parieto-occipital fissure.

Parkinson's disease Chronic and progressive neurological disorder characterized by motor tremor, rigidity, loss of vocal power, and psychotic symptoms. Believed to be caused by an acquired defect in brain metabolism.

Partial hospitalization Use of either day, night, or weekend hospital care for patients who do not need 24-hour care. Designed particularly to aid transition back to the community. Also used to prevent complete hospitalization if the family can provide partial care, for instance, outside of their own working hours.

Participant modeling Therapeutic procedure in which the response is first demonstrated for the client, who then produces the same response with suggestions from the therapist.

Passive-aggressive personality disorder Usually characterized by aggressive behavior exhibited in passive ways (e.g., pouting). Three types are often distinguished: (1) passive-aggressive type: hostility and aggression expressed by passive means such as obstructionism, stubbornness, inefficiency, and procrastination; (2) aggressive type: hostility and aggressiveness expressed directly through temper tantrums, destructive behavior, argumentativeness, and negativism; and (3) passive-dependent type: characterized by overdependency, helplessness, indecisiveness, and the childlike tendency to cling to others. Reactions are grouped together on the basis that they seem to represent different reactions to common-core conflicts over dependency and aggression.

Pathology Disease or abnormal physical condition.

PCP (phencyclidine) Hallucinogenic drug popularly known as "angel dust."

Pedophile Person 16 years of age or older who engages in sexual activity with one or more prepubescent children.

Pedophilia Sexual deviation in which an adult desires or engages in sexual relations with a child. May be either homosexual or heterosexual in nature.

Pellagra Chronic disease caused by niacin deficiency. Symptoms include skin eruptions, digestive disturbances, and disturbances of the nervous system which may cause psychotic-like behavior.

Penetrance Percentage of cases in which a particular trait or characteristic, derived from a specific gene, will manifest itself in subsequent organisms of the species.

Pepsinogen Substance found in the gastric system that is converted to a digestive enzyme by hydrochloric acid in the digestive system. Individuals with high natural pepsinogen levels are prone to develop ulcers under stressful conditions.

Peptide A compound containing two or more amino acids linked together in a specific chemical fashion.

Performance anxiety (sexual) High degree of concern in males about the ability to maintain an erection until orgasm. The anxiety has a negative effect on sexual performance.

Performance IQ One of the two subscores of the Wechsler intelligence test series. Reflects ability to solve puzzles, copy designs, and perform other similar tasks.

Peripheral nervous system System that includes all outlying nerve structures not included in the central nervous system.

Personal constructs A term originated by George Kelly for categories used by someone about his or her personal effectiveness in acting in specific or general types of situations.

Personality Particular constellation of attributes that defines one's individuality.

Personality disorder Deeply ingrained, inflexible, maladaptive patterns of thought and behavior which persist throughout a person's life.

Personality inventories Paper-and-pencil tests in which the person describes him- or herself by answering a series of true-false questions or by rating a series of self-descriptive phases. Most personality inventories yield several scores, each of which is intended to describe an aspect of personality.

Personal maladaptation Perception by an individual of personal dissatisfactions and concerns that interfere with happiness but not significantly with social adjustment or work achievement.

Pervasive developmental disorder A life-long disorder in which the quality of the person's social interactions, communication skills, and ability to engage in imaginative activities and other cognitive tasks is impaired. Autistic disorder is one subtype of this disorder that has been defined so far.

Petit mal Mild form of epilepsy which involves partial alterations of consciousness.

PET scan See *positron emission tomography*.

Phallic stage Stage of psychosexual development during which a child begins to perceive his or her body as a source of gratification. Feelings of narcissism are heightened during this period.

Phenobarbitol Barbiturate sometimes used as a sedative and in the control of epileptic seizure activity.

Phenothiazine One of a family of antipsychotic drugs.

Phenylketonuria (PKU) Form of mental retardation caused by a metabolic deficiency.

Phobia Excessive or inappropriate fear of some particular object or situation which is not in fact dangerous.

Phobic disorder Type of anxiety disorder mainly characterized by irrational and highly specific fears (for example, of dirt, water, high places).

Phototherapy The use of exposure to very bright light for several hours a day as a treatment for seasonal depression.

Phrenology Obsolete theory that different psychological behaviors were related to different parts of the brain and that these could be assessed by touching the surface of the skull.

Physical disorder Term used to refer to a medical as opposed to a psychological problem. Included in the DSM system on Axis IV.

Physiognomy The art of judging human character or personality from facial features.

Physiological dependence Development of tolerance to increased amounts of alcohol or other substance and symptoms of withdrawal if the use of the substance is ended.

Pica Repeated eating of nonnutritive substances such as paint, clay, animal droppings, or laundry starch at a time when there is no evidence of hunger, malnutrition, or aversion.

Pick's disease Type of progressive dementia caused by atrophy of the cerebral cortex.

Placebo Inactive or inert substance that is presented as effective remedy for some problem in order to determine what role suggestibility plays in symptom change.

Placebo effect Changes in behavior as a result of the expectancy that a placebo, or inactive substance, is an active or "real" drug; type of suggestion effect.

Plaque Abnormal structure found in nerve cells of individuals who have Alzheimer's disease.

Plateau stage Second stage of sexual response, which includes increases in heart rate and muscle tension as well as swelling of genital tissue.

Play therapy Treatment approach used with children; based on the assumption that young children can express thoughts and fantasies more directly in play than through verbal means.

Pleasure principle Psychoanalytic term for the regulatory mechanism for mental life that functions to reduce tension and gain gratification. Principle that governs the functioning of the id to obtain gratification without regard to reality considerations.

Polygenic model Theory in genetics that several genes at different loci must interact to produce a particular inherited characteristic.

Polygraph Instrument that measures emotional responses through physiological reactions, such as blood pressure and galvanic skin response. Commonly called a *lie detector*.

Population genetics Study of the ways genes are distributed in a population through the mating of individuals.

Positive reinforcer See *reinforcer*.

Positive symptoms, in schizophrenia Generally, symptoms that show behavioral excesses: hallucinations, delusions, bizarre behavior, and so forth. Sometimes called Type I schizophrenia.

Positive transference Carrying over of positive feelings about other relationships onto the therapist-client relationship.

Positron emission tomography (PET) Technique for studying the dynamic chemical activity of the brain by using a scanning device that produces a series of cross-sectional images of the brain.

Post-hallucinogen perceptual disorder The experience of spontaneous flashbacks related to prior hallucinatory experiences associated with LSD use.

Posttraumatic psychosis Psychotic symptoms that appear suddenly after an injury to the brain or a stressful life event.

Posttraumatic stress disorder (PTSD) Development of symptoms in response to events of such severity that most people would be stressed by them. Symptoms often include a feeling of numbness in response or psychological reexperiencing of the event in thoughts, dreams, or nightmares.

Postvention A therapeutic intervention in which survivors are given supportive treatment.

Poverty of content A characteristic of some schizophrenic speech in which little information is transmitted through speaking because of factors such as vagueness of meaning, repetition of phrases, or inappropriate degree of abstraction of the thoughts expressed.

Preconscious Thoughts that are not held in a person's mind at a particular time but which can easily be brought into awareness.

Premature ejaculation Inability of the male to inhibit ejaculation long enough for his female partner to experience orgasm.

Prematurity Before the expected time. In referring to infants, birth before the completion of the usual gestation period. Prematurity is a risk factor for psychological as well as physical difficulties later in development.

Premorbid adjustment Achievement level and adjustment to interpersonal activities shown by an individual earlier in life before a disorder becomes apparent.

Presenile dementia See *dementia*.

Prevalence Information concerning the number of cases of a particular disorder that are ongoing at any particular time. Contrast term with *incidence*.

Primary appraisal First stage of assessing the meaning of a situation. In this stage the situation is interpreted as threatening or harmless. In the following stage, secondary appraisal, the individual decides how to deal with the situation.

Primary classification In the DSM system, the problem diagnosed on Axis I.

Primary degenerative dementia Dementia which is the specific result of a disease process rather than an additional symptom resulting from some other disorder.

Primary prevention Efforts at preventing the development of maladaptation by removing factors that might cause it to develop.

Primary process thinking Primary cognitive mode, characteristic of infants and children, that is not based on rules of organization or logic. The presence of primary process thinking, free association in its purest form, is characteristic of the id. Primary process thought is illogical, is entirely pleasure oriented, has no sense of time or order, and does not discriminate between reality and fantasy. Compare with *secondary process thinking*.

Primitive emotion node A hypothetical memory unit that organizes memories related to a particular mood.

Problem drinking Term for the pattern of alcohol abuse that does not include alcohol dependence or physiological addiction.

Process research In psychotherapy research, the attempt to understand what happens during the course of psychotherapy in contrast to interest only in the desirability of the outcome.

Prognosis Forecast; probable course and outcome of a disorder.

Projection Defense mechanism that involves attributing to others the undesirable characteristics or impulses which belong to, but are not acceptable to, oneself.

Projective technique Ambiguous stimulus materials that elicit subjective responses of an associative or fantasy nature. So named because an individual is believed to "project" aspects of his or her personality into the task. Tasks may include inkblot interpretation (Rorschach Test), and various associative completion techniques (word association, incomplete sentences).

Prototypal approach The use of a checklist in making a diagnostic decision. If more than a predetermined number of characteristics are found, the diagnosis is made. As a result people with the same diagnosis may have different sets of characteristics.

Prozac A trade name for the drug fluoxetine. Used to treat depression and anxiety. Considered to be useful in some other disorders. Considerable controversy has surrounded its use.

Psilocybin One of the two psychoactive substances isolated from the psilocybin mushroom.

Psychedelic drug A drug that is able to alter sensory perceptions.

Psychiatric nurse A registered nurse who has taken specialized training in the care of those with mental illness.

Psychiatric social work Field of social work in which the professional specializes in helping those with maladaptive behaviors in a clinical, usually medical, setting.

Psychiatric social worker A person with a graduate degree in social work and specialized training in treating and practically assisting both patients with behavioral problems and their families.

Psychiatrist Physician with postgraduate training in the diagnosis and treatment of emotional disorders.

Psychic determinism Principle of causality, one of the basic assumptions of psychoanalysis, which states that all events, overt and covert, are determined by prior and often multiple mental events.

Psychoactive drug Term including several types of drugs that may reduce maladaptive behavior. Includes antipsychotic, antianxiety, and antidepressant drugs.

Psychoactive substance A chemical that affects a person's thoughts, emotions, and behavior.

Psychoactive substance-induced organic mental disorder Organic changes that occur as a result of the use of psychoactive substances.

Psychoactive substance use disorders Behavioral or cognitive problems that are related to the use of some substance that affects the emotions, cognitions, and behavior such as alcohol, marijuana, and cocaine.

Psychoanalysis Term has three meanings: (1) theory of psychology and psychopathology developed by Freud from his clinical experiences with patients; (2) procedure for investigating the mental life, conflicts, and coping processes, which employs the techniques of free association, dream analysis, and interpretation of transference and resistance phenomena; and (3) form of therapy that uses the psychoanalytic procedure and the theories of personality and psychopathology just described.

Psychodrama Method of group therapy in which individuals both act out their emotional responses in situations they find difficult and also practice new, constructive roles.

Psychodynamic perspective Point of view that emphasizes thoughts and emotions as the most important determiners of behavior. Basic ideas come from the work of Sigmund Freud.

Psychodynamic therapy A therapeutic approach based on the psychodynamic perspective originating in the theories of Freud, but not limited to psychoanalysis.

Psychogenic Adjective referring to symptoms for which an organic cause cannot be specified.

Psychogenic amnesia Disturbance in the ability to recall important personal information in the absence of an organic disorder and without the assumption of a new identity such as that found in a psychogenic fugue.

Psychogenic fugue See *fugue state.*

Psychogenic pain disorder Characterized by severe pain that does not have an identifiable physical cause.

Psychoimmunology Study of the relationship between changes in immune system functioning and psychological events.

Psychological dependence Habit or need that requires continued or repeated administration of a drug to produce pleasure or to avoid conflict.

Psychological factors affecting physical condition Another

term used for psychophysiological disorders or psychosomatic disorders.

Psychological functioning Ratings of both current functioning and highest level of functioning achieved in the past are recorded on Axis V of the DSM. This information helps to determine how handicapped the person currently is by the disorder as well as the potential for change.

Psychological numbing Reduced capacity for emotion, and symptoms of apathy, withdrawal, and depression. These are likely to occur after a disaster.

Psychological perspective View that maladaptive behavior is caused by problems of perception, cognition, or emotion rather than by biological causes.

Psychological tests Procedures to measure in a standardized way some aspect of behavior such as intelligence or personality characteristics.

Psychology of personal constructs The approach of George Kelly, who was interested in helping his clients understand the unique way in which they viewed themselves and other people and also to see that their behavior was designed to fill certain roles. Kelly urged his clients to try out new roles rather than be stuck in nonadaptive ways of interacting.

Psychometric Refers to measures of psychological functioning.

Psychomotor Term used to describe muscular action resulting from prior mental activity, especially conscious mental activity.

Psychomotor epilepsy Trancelike state with recurring episodes of confusion during which repetitive and semiautomatic muscle movements occur. Often accompanied by confusion and visual hallucinations.

Psychoneuroimmunology A field of scientific specialization devoted to an understanding of the relationships among behavior, neural activity, and the immune system.

Psychopath Term used by Hervey Cleckley to describe antisocial individuals who have a certain set of characteristics including charm, lack of anxiety or guilt, poor judgment, and failure to learn from experience.

Psychopharmacology Study of the effects of drugs on psychological functioning and behavior.

Psychophysiological assessment Measurement of various body functions such as blood pressure, heart rate, breathing, and galvanic skin response in an attempt to understand feelings and emotions. One commercial use is the polygraph or lie detector.

Psychophysiological (psychosomatic) disorder Physical pathology and actual tissue damage that results from continued emotional mobilization of the body during periods of sustained stress.

Psychophysiology of behavior Study of the relationship between observed behavior and the functions of the central and peripheral nervous systems.

Psychosexual disorder Deviant sexual thoughts and/or behavior that are either personally anxiety-provoking, or are injurious to others.

Psychosexual stage One of several developmental stages of life as defined by Sigmund Freud. These differ in terms of the source of primary gratification and include oral, anal, phallic, and genital stages.

Psychosis (plural: psychoses) Disorder that includes any of the following: delusions, hallucinations, incoherence, repeated derailment of thought, marked poverty of thought content, marked illogicality, and grossly disorganized or catatonic behavior.

Psychosocial disadvantage Growing up in an intellectually, culturally, and financially impoverished environment.

Psychosocial stressor Feeling of stress arising from relationships with other people in the environment.

Psychosomatic disorder See *psychophysiological disorder.*

Psychosomatic hypothesis Idea popular in the 1930s and 1940s that physical symptoms can be caused by an inability to express strong emotions.

Psychotherapy General term referring to psychological, verbal, and expressive techniques used in treating maladaptive behavior. The client works on resolving inner conflicts and modifying his or her behavior by means of verbal interchanges with the therapist. Insight into feelings and behavior is the goal of most psychotherapy.

Psychotic An adjective indicating the presence of psychosis.

Psychotic disorder A disorder in which there is gross impairment in reality testing and the creation of a new reality. Psychotic disorders include schizophrenia, delusional disorders, some organic mental disorder, and some mood disorders.

Psychotic disorder not otherwise specified Disorder in which psychosis is clearly present but which do not fit the criteria for any of the specific types of psychoses.

Punishment Aversive stimulus given as a result of an undesired behavior in an attempt to suppress that behavior in the future.

Rape Sexual intercourse accomplished by force and without the partner's consent.

Rape-relief center Organization, often composed in part of volunteers, designed to provide information about medical and legal services for those who have been raped and also to offer psychological support for the victims.

Rating scale Type of test in which a person can indicate on a scale the degree of his or her agreement with each item.

Rational approach Idea that only the use of reason and not experimental evidence or observation is the prime source of truth.

Rational-emotive therapy Therapy developed by Albert Ellis to modify unrealistic and illogical thought.

Rational thinking Based on reasoning and logic, not on observation or experimental evidence.

Reaction formation Defense mechanism that enables the individual to express an unacceptable impulse by transforming it into its opposite.

Recessive gene Member of a gene pair which determines the characteristic trait or appearance of the individual only if the other member of the pair matches it. Compare to *dominant gene*.

Recognition A measure of information retention in which the subject is asked to select which of several stimulus items have been presented previously.

Refractory period (sexual) In males, the period after orgasm when no additional arousal can occur. Females may or may not have a refractory period.

Regress To go backward or return to an earlier level of functioning. Interpreted in psychoanalytic theory as a defense mechanism. See *regression*.

Regression Defense mechanism characterized by a return to earlier and more primitive modes of responding. Through regression, the ego returns to an earlier developmental phase of functioning which had met with some success.

Rehabilitation model A type of full time or day treatment in which attention is given to improving social and vocational functioning. The treatment is usually of limited length but may last longer than acute care.

Reinforcement Any event (stimulus) which, if contingent upon response by an organism, changes the probability that the response will be made again. Reinforcements may be positive (reward) or negative (aversive) and may be presented according to a prescribed schedule (continuous, intermittent). May also be primary (drive reducing—e.g., food) or secondary (derived from prior association with a primary reinforcer—e.g., money, praise).

Reinforcer A consequence of behavior that makes it more likely the behavior will occur again. A *positive reinforcer* achieves this result by provoking a reward or pleasure. A *negative reinforcer* is a stimulus that ceases when the desired behavior is performed. See also *punishment*.

Relapse prevention In treatment of alcohol problems from a cognitive viewpoint, the emphasis on identifying problem situations and helping the client to identify coping devices that may give him or her a feeling of control over such situations.

Relational assessment Testing instruments to assess a person's key social relationships.

Relaxation training Series of specified exercises that the client learns to perform in order to remove a tension response that may be characteristic in certain situations.

Reliability The tendency of a measure or procedure to produce the same results when administered on two different occasions. Also refers to the internal homogeneity of a multiple-item test.

Remission Cessation of the symptoms of a disorder. Implies that the basic problem may still exist.

REM sleep Stage of sleep characterized by rapid eye movements and a characteristic brain-wave pattern. Reducing the amount of REM sleep can help decrease some types of depressive symptoms.

Repression Psychoanalytic defense mechanism that involves a "stopping-thinking" or not-being-able-to-remember response. Repression actively forces traumatic events, intolerable and dangerous impulses, and other undesirable mental affects out of consciousness into the less-accessible realm of the unconscious.

Resilience The ability to bounce back after stress. Capacity to function effectively in situations where others might develop maladaptive behavior.

Resolution phase The period after sexual orgasm in which the arousal decreases and the body's physiological status returns to normal.

Retardation Level of intellectual functioning that is significantly below average and is accompanied by an inability to behave adaptively in society because of this lack of cognitive ability.

Retarded ejaculation Inhibition of the sexual response of males that results in an inability to eject semen even when sexually excited.

Rheumatoid arthritis Chronic joint disease with inflammation caused by immune-system activity.

Risk factor A personal characteristic that is correlated with some disorder. Indicates an increased probability that the person will develop a particular type of problem or illness. People with high risk factors are said to be especially vulnerable to a particular disorder.

Ritalin See *methylphenidate*.

Ritualistic behavior Behavior that follows a series of prescribed actions that are repeated even though they may be maladaptive. Thought to be a way of reducing anxiety.

Role playing In psychotherapy, a technique that requires an individual to enact a social role other than his or her own, or to try out new roles. In sociology, an individual's assumption of the role expected of him or her in a particular type of situation.

Rorschach inkblots Projective test developed by Hermann Rorschach in which the individual is shown a series of ambiguous inkblots and asked to describe what is seen in them.

Rubella virus Virus which, if present in a pregnant woman, particularly during the first 3 months of pregnancy, can cause retardation and other congenital disorders in her child; commonly called *German measles*.

Rumination disorder of infancy Disorder in which partially digested food is brought up into the infant's mouth without nausea or vomiting. The infant loses weight or fails to gain weight after a period of normal functioning.

Saccadic eye movement Quick jerks of the eye interspersed with steady fixations that are under voluntary control.

SAD See *seasonal affective disorder*.

Sadism Sexual deviation in which sexual gratification is obtained through inflicting physical pain on other people.

Sadist One who practices sadism.

Sadistic personality disorder A longstanding behavioral pattern in which the person seems to enjoy inflicting psychological or physiological suffering on other people or on animals. The disorder differs from sexual sadism because the sadistic behavior is not carried out for sexual arousal.

Schedule A plan of what will happen and the time it is to occur.

Schema (plural, Schemata) An hypothesized cognitive structure that organizes knowledge related to a particular situation or domain.

Schemata The plural of *schema*. Schemata are the expectations people have as to the way others behave and the appropriate behaviors for various types of situations. A person's schemata are important in addition to what actually occurred in determining the way that he or she will respond to particular types of situations.

Schizoaffective disorder Separate category from either schizophrenia or affective disorders for individuals who show depressive or manic symptoms as well as those of thought disorder.

Schizoid personality disorder Classification used for withdrawn individuals who are not disturbed by their lack of social relationships. These people have flat emotional responses and often seem cold and detached.

Schizophrenia See *schizophrenic disorders*.

Schizophrenia, episodic type with residual symptoms A stage of schizophrenic disorder in which psychotic features, especially hallucinations or delusions, are currently not prominent but in which eccentric behavior, illogical thinking, social withdrawal, and other features of schizophrenia may continue to be observed.

Schizophrenia in remission A lessening or disappearance of symptoms that had been apparent when the person was diagnosed as having a schizophrenic disorder. The term reflects the view that schizophrenia is a life-long disease for which there is no cure, only the possibility of at least temporarily reduced symptoms.

Schizophrenic disorders Group of disorders that always involves at least one of the following at some time: delusions, hallucinations, or certain characteristics of thought disorder.

Schizophrenic spectrum disorder One of a group of disorders including schizotypal and paranoid personality disorders, and sometimes schizoaffective disorder, atypical psychosis, and paranoid disorder, which

are thought by some researchers to be produced by the same genetic factors as schizophrenia. Used as an explanation for the fact that the incidence of narrowly defined schizophrenia alone is less than would be expected by monogenetic theory.

Schizotypal personality disorder Shows some of the symptoms of schizophrenia, but not in as extreme a form. People with this disorder include those formerly diagnosed as having simple schizophrenia. Differs from schizoid personality disorder in that it includes eccentricities of communication and behavior not seen in that group.

Seasonal affective disorder (SAD) A form of affective disorder in which depression is more likely to occur in winter when the hours of natural light are limited and mania is more likely to occur in spring and summer when the number of hours of daylight are at a maximum. Depression of this type is often treated with phototherapy (the use of bright lighting).

Secondary appraisal Second stage of appraisal of a situation in which an individual considers the kind of action necessary and whether he or she has the skills to deal with the situation.

Secondary prevention Efforts directed toward detecting early signs or symptoms to prevent a more serious condition.

Secondary process thinking Psychoanalytic concept referring to organized, logical, and reality-oriented adult thinking. Whereas primary process thinking is characteristic of the id and is based on the pleasure principle, secondary process thought is an ego function based on the reality principle.

Second-generation antidepressants A group of more recently developed antidepressants that do not have the three-ring chemical structure of the tricyclic antidepressants.

Second rank symptoms Those symptoms classified by Schneider as typical of schizophrenia but which are also found in other psychotic disorders.

Selective serotonin receptive inhibitors A category of antidepressant drugs that have somewhat fewer side effects than the tricyclic group.

Self-actualization Synonymous with self-fulfillment. Process by which the development of one's potentials and abilities is achieved.

Self-determination Viewpoint of existential theorists that individuals have control of their own lives through the choices they make.

Self-help group A group of people with the same problem who meet together to share experiences and ways to handle situations in an attempt to help themselves improve their own ability to cope with these problems.

Self-monitoring Keeping detailed records of one's behavior.

Self-observations Records kept by the client or patient that detail the frequency of certain specified types of behavior and usually include any specific environmental factors or personal thoughts that occurred just before, during, or after the behavior.

Self-psychology A theory developed by Kohut that considers the individual's self-concept as the central organizing factor in psychological development.

Self-regulation Technique of controlling one's own behavior through internal reinforcement often in the form of cognitions.

Senile dementia See *dementia*.

Sensate focus Approach to sex therapy advocated by Masters and Johnson in which an individual learns to focus on erotic sensation to the exclusion of other stimuli.

Sensorimotor Pertaining to the functions of the sensing and motor activities of the individual—for example, the sensorimotor nerves.

Sentence completion test Projective test in which the client is presented with a series of incomplete sentences and is asked to complete each one.

Separation anxiety disorder Some children's irrational fear of being apart from the parent(s) because of worries of what will happen to themselves or to their parent(s) in their absence.

Serotonin (5HT) One of a group of chemical neurotransmitters that implement neural transmission across the synapse. Thought to be involved in some types of depression.

Sex offender Term used for individuals who come into contact with the legal system because of their practice of sexual deviations that are prohibited by law.

Sex-reassignment surgery Surgery in which male or female genital organs are removed and facsimiles of genital organs of the opposite sex are created. Surgery is usually combined with hormone treatment to modify secondary sexual characteristics.

Sexual disorders Includes two types—paraphilias and sexual dysfunction. The first relates to obtaining sexual satisfaction through inappropriate partners or activities. The second is the inability to carry out normal sexual activities because of physiological difficulties thought to have psychological causes.

Sexual dysfunction Problems in one or more phases of sexual intercourse that decrease the pleasure derived by the participants or make successful culmination impossible.

Shaman Inspired priest or medium who can summon up and communicate with good and evil spirits.

Shaping Basic process of operant conditioning involving the reinforcement of successively closer approximations to a desired behavior.

Sheltered workshops Organizations, often run by charitable groups, that provide job training and experience and sometimes long term jobs for those unable to compete in the marketplace because of physical or mental disability.

Simple phobia Relatively rare type of phobia that involves irrational fear not related to either unfamiliar situations or social interactions; for example, fear of shut-in places (claustrophobia) or fear of specific animals.

Simple schizophrenia See *schizotypal personality disorder*.

Single photon emission computed tomography (SPECT) An imaging technique that measures cerebral blood flow and neurochemical changes that occur with different types of brain activity.

Situation-focused prevention Actions to prevent maladaptive behavior through changing aspects of the environment. For example, providing after-school activities to keep children off the street or changing to non-leaded paint as a way to prevent children from ingesting lead and possibly developing retardation.

Sleep disorders Disorders characterized either by problems with the amount, quality, and timing of sleep, or by abnormal events occurring during sleep such as night terrors or sleepwalking.

Smooth pursuit eye movements Type of essentially involuntary movement that occurs when an individual visually follows the movements of a rhythmically moving object such as a pendulum.

Social causation theory Theory that maladaptive behavior is a result of poor economic circumstances, poor housing, and inadequate social services.

Social facilitation Acquisition of social competence skills through observing the behavior of others.

Social intervention Treatment approach that involves not only interacting with the client but also attempting to modify the client's environment at home or at work.

Social learning theories Refers to several similar theoretical viewpoints which hold that social behavior and inner thoughts and feelings are learned through social interactions.

Social phobia Type of irrational fear of situations in which a person will be exposed to the scrutiny of others. Most common types are fear of blushing, public speaking, eating in public, writing in public, and using public toilet facilities.

Social relationships Those interpersonal relationships that play a role in a person's life. Assessed on Axis V of DSM.

Social role The function a particular person plays in society, which is determined by the particular role he or she fills. Most people have a variety of overlapping social roles, such as an occupational role, several family roles, and perhaps some recreational roles as well.

Social selection theory Idea that the lower socioeconomic class contains many people who drifted there from higher classes because of their poor functioning. Higher incidence of maladaptive behavior in the lower class is explained in this way.

Social skills training Behavioral or cognitive-behavioral therapeutic approach that emphasizes learning more effective ways of interacting with other people in a variety of situations.

Social support The positive aspects of interpersonal ties that assist in coping and promote both physical and mental health.

Somatic system Part of the peripheral nervous system that sends nerve impulses from the sense organs to the muscles that determine voluntary movement.

Somatic therapy Treatment, such as drugs, surgery, or electroconvulsive therapy, that directly affects a person's physical state.

Somatization disorder (Briquet's syndrome) Disorder characterized by a variety of dramatic but vague complaints that are often chronic and which have no discernible physical cause.

Somatoform disorders Characterized by physical symptoms that suggest a physical disorder but for which there are (1) no organic findings to explain the symptom and (2) strong evidence or suggestion that the symptoms are linked to psychological factors or conflicts; formerly called *hysterical neurosis* or *conversion reaction*.

Sonogram See *ultrasound scanning technique*.

Specific developmental disorder Problems in specific area of development not due to another more general disorder such as retardation or autism. Examples are reading disorder, arithmetic disorder, inability to articulate certain sounds clearly.

Specificity The now discredited idea that specific types of emotional conflicts and types of stress are associated with the development of certain physical conditions in vulnerable persons.

SPECT See *Single photon emission computed tomography*

Spectrum concept The idea that several differently classified disorders may be caused by the same general genetic pattern. These disorders are then considered genetically related.

Spina bifida A condition in which the spinal cord does not close over the nerve column during the prenatal period. The amount of the spinal column that remains open determines how many nerves will be affected. This condition is often associated with an abnormal buildup of pressure of spinal fluid in the brain which can produce retardation unless it is surgically treated.

Splitting Term used to describe the inability of the borderline individual to integrate the positive and negative experiences he or she has with another individual into a coherent relationship. A term used by object relations theorists.

Spontaneous remission Disappearance of symptoms or maladaptive behavior in the absence of therapeutic intervention.

Spouse abuse Physical harm done to wives or husbands by their marital partners. Physical assaults by husbands on wives are most common. Abuse may also be psychological.

Squeeze technique Technique used in sex therapy to assist the male in retarding ejaculation by gently squeezing the end of the penis when ejaculation is imminent.

Standardized interview See *structured interview*.

Stanford-Binet Modification of the Binet test developed at Stanford University by Louis Terman, which has been the Binet format most often used in North America.

Statutory rape Crime defined as having sexual intercourse with someone below the age of legal consent. Force is not necessarily involved.

Stereotypy Development of a ritualized or highly repetitive behavior.

Sometimes seen as a result of stress or of the use of certain drugs such as amphetamines.

STP (2, 5 dimethoxy-4-methyl amphetamine) Hallucinogenic agent similar to LSD.

Straight jacket Confining garment used to bind the arms tightly against the body. Often used for violent patients.

Stress Feeling or reaction individuals have when faced with a situation that demands action from them, especially action that may be beyond their capabilities.

Stressor Source of stress, pressure, or strain. Something that upsets the equilibrium of an organism.

Stroke See *cerebrovascular accident*.

Stroop effect The greater difficulty in ignoring words and attending to color on the Stroop task than the reverse.

Stroop Task A measure of selective attention in which color names are presented written either in black or the color named or written in a color of ink unlike the color named. The Stroop effect measures the relative difficulty or reaction time when the subject is asked to ignore the word versus ignore the color. Those with schizophrenic disorder show a greater Stroop effect than do nonpatient controls.

Structured Clinical Interview (SCID) A diagnostic interview that is less structured than the widely used Diagnostic Interview Schedule (DIS). The SCID allows the interviewer to ask follow-up questions based on clinical judgment.

Structured interview Also called a standardized interview. An interview procedure in which the interviewer is given a set of instructions that includes definitions of symptoms, numerical ratings for different symptom severities, a series of questions related to each type of symptoms, a set of topics to be covered, and information about how extensively the interviewer is to probe for information about each type of question. The interviewer is allowed flexibility in ordering of the questions.

Sublimation Defense mechanism and developmental concept which involves the refinement or redirection of undesirable impulses into new and more socially acceptable channels. Whereas displacement involves an alteration in choice of object, sublimation alters both the aim (unacceptable drive) and the object to a socially acceptable ones.

Substance abuse Use of a psychoactive substance to the degree that a severe and long-lasting impairment in function results.

Substance abuse disorder A severe and long-lasting impairment resulting from use of a psychoactive substance.

Substance dependence A pattern of substance use that leads to clinically significant impairment or distress that includes cognitive, behavioral, and physiological symptoms.

Substance-induced organic mental disorder Result of direct effects on the central nervous system of mood- or behavior-modifying substances. Examples are intoxication or drug-withdrawal symptoms.

Substance intoxication The distinctive but reversible effects of the ingestion or exposure to certain substances as a result of their effect on the central nervous system. Common effects include disturbances in perception, wakefulness, attention, thinking, judgment, motor behavior, and interpersonal behavior.

Substance-use disorders This category consists of two subgroups, substance dependence and substance abuse. Both include problems associated with using and abusing alcohol and illegal drugs.

Sulci (singular: sulcus) Shallow valleys on the surface of the brain separating the convolutions.

Superego Structure of the psyche in psychoanalytic theory which is developed by internalization of parental standards and by identification with parents. Contains two parts: the ego-ideal and the conscience. The ego-ideal represents the total of positive identifications with accepting and loving parents and desired standards of excellence and good conduct. The conscience includes those attitudes and values which are moralistic (good-bad) in nature.

Support group Group of individuals with the same or similar problems who meet to discuss their problems and how to deal with them.

Supportive therapy Brief form of psychotherapy in which the therapist provides acceptance for the patient and affords him or her some opportunity to be dependent.

Surrogate parent model An example of milieu intervention in which a patient lives for a few weeks during a critical phase of a disorder such as schizophrenia with a carefully screened couple who have been successful parents and who are trained to work with patients in crisis.

Survival guilt Feeling that it is unfair to be alive when others in the same situation have died. Overwhelming feelings of guilt, unworthiness, and helplessness.

Symbolic modeling Learning through watching film or videotaped sequences of someone performing the act or acts to be learned or alternately learning appropriate responses through listening to audiotapes or reading text.

Symptom disorder Disorders diagnosed on Axis I of the Diagnostic and Statistical Manual. These disorders have symptoms that may come and go unlike the disorders diagnosed on Axis II which generally continue throughout life.

Synapse Point at which a nerve impulse passes from an axon of one neuron to the dendrite of another neuron.

Synaptic vesicle Container on the axon terminal button that serves as a storage point for a chemical neurotransmitter.

Syndrome A group of symptoms that often appear together.

Syphilitic infection Chronic infectious venereal disease, transmitted through direct contact, caused by a spirochete, *Trepenema pallidum*.

Systematic desensitization Learning-theory-based therapeutic technique in which a client is first trained in muscle relaxation and then imagines a series of increasingly anxiety-provoking situations until he or she no longer experiences anxiety while thinking about the stimuli. Learning principle involved is reciprocal inhibition, according to which two incompatible responses (e.g., anxiety and relaxation) cannot be made simultaneously by one person.

Systolic Term used to describe the blood pressure reading at the time the heart contracts to drive the blood through. Compare to *diastolic*.

Tactile Referring to the sense of touch.

Tangles Abnormal structures found in nerve cells of individuals who have Alzheimer's disease.

Tarantism Uncontrollable urge to dance, believed to be the result of the bite of a tarantula. This was frequent in Southern Italy from the fifteenth to seventeenth centuries.

Tardive dyskinesia Disorder involving uncontrolled body movements, often of the lips and tongue, that may result from treatment with antipsychotic drugs.

TAT See *Thematic Apperception Test*.

Tay-Sachs disease Inherited metabolic disorder, inevitably fatal, that causes progressive deterioration of the nervous system.

Technique factors The particular procedures used by a therapist in treating a client. Distinguished from the effects of the therapist's personality on the treatment.

Temperament The general nature of a person consistent across time and situations that is thought to arise from constitutional factors present at birth.

Temporal lobe Part of the cerebral hemisphere lying behind the temples and below the lateral fissure in front of the occipital lobe.

Tension headache Probably the most common form of headache; characterized by bandlike pains and tender scalp. Gradual in onset and often long lasting. Thought to be a result of stress.

Tertiary prevention Efforts aimed at reducing the impairment that may result from a given disorder.

Test anxiety Unusually apprehensive response to evaluative situations. Often a factor in poor performance because of worry and interfering thoughts.

THC (tetrahydrocannabinol) Major active ingredient in marijuana.

Thematic Apperception Test (TAT) Projective test consisting of somewhat ambiguous pictures. Subject is asked to tell a story about each picture. From these stories personality dynamics are inferred.

Theoretical perspective The particular set of beliefs or ideas that determine what people notice in behavior, how they interpret what they observe, and how they believe problems should be approached.

Therapeutic interview Interaction between a client and therapist although perhaps including other family members as well. Designed to help promote change in behavior and attitudes.

Thorazine Trade name for chlorpromazine, one of a group of tranquilizing drugs used in the treatment of schizophrenia.

Thought stopping A cognitive technique that uses a specific command as a distraction to end a period of obsessive thinking.

Tic Involuntary, repetitive, rapid muscle contractions often occurring in the face. Thought to be related to tension and anxiety.

Tolerance (drug) Condition in which an individual must use increasing doses of a substance to produce the same physiological effect.

Tonic phase Phase of seizure in which the body is extended and stiff and during which reflexes to light and to pressure on the cornea are absent. See also *clonic phase*.

Top-down studies In the study of heredity factors in disorder, this approach focuses first on identifying parents with a particular diagnosis and then ascertaining the clinical status of their children.

Tranquilizing drugs Drugs (for example, of the chlorpromazine and phenothiazine families) which are used to reduce agitation and anxiety. Drug action inhibits the activities of the hypothalamus.

Transference Psychoanalytic term that refers to the displacement of affect from one person to another. Patterns of feelings and behavior originally experienced with significant figures in childhood are displaced or attached to individuals in one's current relationships (e.g., a psychotherapist). Current person is reacted to as if he or she were some significant other from the respondent's past. Transference reactions may be positive or negative.

Translocation The breaking off of a piece of one chromosome and the attachment of that piece to another chromosome. May result in the transmission of too much genetic material to the child of a person with a translocation.

Transdermal patch A multilayered pad applied to the skin with adhesive that allows gradual absorption by the body of medication or chemicals over a prolonged period. Often used to administer decreasing amounts of nicotine to individuals who are attempting to stop cigarette smoking.

Transsexualism Intense desire or need to change one's sexual status, including anatomical structure.

Transvestism Sexual deviation in which an individual derives gratification from wearing the clothing of the opposite sex.

Traumatic neurosis Psychological symptoms that occur after a traumatic event but which are not a direct result of physical injury.

Trephination Process of making a circular hole in the skull. In early times this was done to allow evil spirits to escape.

Tricyclics Group of drugs used to treat depression. An example is imipramine. Common trade names of tricyclic drugs are Tofranil and Elavil.

Trisomy Occurrence in an individual of three chromosomes of one kind rather than the usual pair. Usually associated with an abnormality of some type.

Trisomy 13 Presence of three number 13 chromosomes rather than the usual pair. Occurs in one of every 5000 births and causes severe mental retardation and a number of specific physical defects. Only about 18 percent of affected infants survive the first year.

Trisomy 18 Presence of three number 18 chromosomes rather than the usual pair. The next most common trisomy after trisomy 21. Occurs in one of every 3000 births. Most such infants die before birth; only 10 percent of those born alive survive to age 1. Results in severe retardation and many physical abnormalities.

Trisomy 21 See *Down syndrome*.

Tuberous sclerosis Disorder caused by a dominant gene and characterized by severe retardation, seizures, and the appearance of small, fibrous tumors.

Type A Personality A behavior pattern characterized by extremes of competitiveness, striving for achievement, restlessness, hyper-alertness, explosiveness of speech, tenseness of facial muscles, and feelings of being under pressure of time and of bearing excess responsibility that is associated with a high risk of coronary heart disease.

Type B Personality A behavior pattern characterized by the opposite extremes of the behavior of a Type A personality, thought to be at low risk for coronary heart disease.

Ulcer Sore on the skin or internal mucous tissue that results in the death of the tissue involved.

Ultrasound scanning technique The use of sound waves to produce a visual image of a fetus or of the form and action of body organs. Also called *sonogram*.

Unauthentic behavior According to existentialist theory, that behavior governed not by an individual's desire but by the desires of other people.

Unconditional positive regard Term used by Carl Rogers to emphasize the importance of a therapist's unqualified acceptance of a client as a person of worth.

Unconditioned response (UCR or UR) In classical conditioning, the response that occurs automatically, before training, when the unconditioned stimulus is presented.

Unconditioned stimulus (UCS or US) In classical conditioning, the stimulus that automatically elicits the desired response before training has taken place.

Unconscious Out of awareness; mental contents that can be brought to awareness only with great difficulty (or not at all).

Undifferentiated type schizophrenia Clearly psychotic symptoms that either do not fit any of the other categories of schizophrenia or that meet the requirements for more than one category.

Undoing Defense mechanism aimed at negating or atoning for some disapproved impulse or act.

Unipolar disorder Term for an affective disorder in which only depression occurs and there is no history of episodes of mania.

Vaginal Pertaining to the vagina, the passage leading from the external genital opening to the uterus in female mammals.

Vaginismus (functional) Type of sexual dysfunction in women in which an involuntary spasm of the muscles of the outer third of the vagina interferes with sexual activity.

Validity In statistics, the extent to which a test measures what it is intended to or purports to measure.

Validity, external An experimental situation that is perceived to relate closely to a real world situation.

Valium One of the minor tranquilizing drugs often prescribed to reduce anxiety.

Vascular dementia The deficits in intellectual function that may result from a series of minor strokes occurring over a period of time. Also called multi-infarct dementia.

Venereal disease Contagious disease (for example, syphilis and gonorrhea) contracted through sexual intercourse.

Ventricles System of communicating cavities in the brain that are linked with the central canal of the spinal cord.

Verbal IQ One of the two subscores of the Wechsler intelligence test series. Tests reflect general information or knowledge and the ability to make abstractions.

Vesicle Storage area in the nerve endings that holds neurotransmitter chemicals.

Vicarious learning Learning that occurs merely by watching the behavior of others.

Visual analogue scales (VAS) A type of rating scale used to assess a variety of subjective phenomena by using portions of a line to represent a personal perception of the phenomena.

Voyeurism (scopophilia) Attaining sexual gratification from observing the sexual behavior of others. Synonymous with *peeping tomism*.

Vulnerability Conditions, either internal or external, that make a person more likely to be affected adversely by stress. Factors include heredity, personality, lack of coping skills, previous negative life events, and some negative environmental factors.

WAIS See *Wechsler Adult Intelligence Scale*.

Wechsler Adult Intelligence Scale (WAIS-R) A widely used individually administered intelligence test for those over 16 years of age. A series of subtests of different types yield a Verbal IQ, Performance IQ, and Full Scale IQ.

Wechsler Intelligence Scale for Children (WISC-III) Intended for children between ages 6 and 16. Uses the same general format as the Wechsler Adult Intelligence Scale and provides Verbal, Performance, and Full Scale IQs.

Wechsler Preschool and Primary Scale of Intelligence (WPPSI) Intended for children between ages 3 and 7. Uses the same general format as the Wechsler Adult Intelligence Scale and provides Verbal, Performance, and Full Scale IQs.

WISC See *Wechsler Intelligence Scale for Children*.

Withdrawal Physiological changes, varying from mild to extremely unpleasant, that take place after an individual's discontinuation of a habit-forming substance. The symptoms of heroin withdrawal are perhaps best known.

Word association test Projective technique in which a list of words is presented one by one. Client is asked to respond to each item with the first word that comes to mind.

WPPSI See *Wechsler Preschool and Primary Scale of Intelligence*.

X-linked dominance Genes carried on the X sex chromosome that determine a characteristic by their presence. Females have two X chromosomes. Males have one X and one Y chromosome. This means that characteristics that are a result of X-linked dominance can occur in males only through inheritance from the mother. In females it can be inherited from either parent.

Abbey, A. (1991). Acquaintance rape and alcohol consumption on college campuses: How are they linked? *Journal of American College Health, 39,* 165–169.

Abel, G., Becher, J., & Cunningham-Rathner, J. (1988). Multiple paraphiliac diagnoses among sex offenders. *Bulletin of the American Academy of Psychiatry and the Law, 16,* 153–168.

Abraham, H. D., & Aldridge, A. M. (1993). Adverse consequences of lysergic acid diethylamide. *Addiction, 88,* 1327–1334.

Abraham, K. (1968). Notes on the psychoanalytic investigation and treatment of manic-depressive insanity and allied conditions (1911). In K. Abraham, *Selected papers of Karl Abraham.* New York: Basic Books.

Abrams, D. B., & Wilson, G. T. (1979). Effects of alcohol on social anxiety in women: Cognitive versus physiological processes. *Journal of Abnormal Psychology, 88,* 161–173.

Abrams, S. (1973). The polygraph in a psychiatric setting. *American Journal of Psychiatry, 130,* 94–98.

Abramson, L. Y., Metalsky, G. I., & Alloy, L. B. (1989). Hopelessness depression: A theory-based subtype of depression. *Psychological Review, 96,* 358–372.

Acierno, R. E., Hersen, M., & Van Hasselt, V. B. (1993). Interventions for panic disorder: A critical review of the literature. *Clinical Psychology Review, 13,* 561–578.

Adamson, J. (1989). An appraisal of the DSM-III system. *Canadian Journal of Psychiatry, 34,* 303–310.

Adler, G., & Buie, D. (1979). Aloneness and borderline psychopathology: The possible relevance of child development issues. *International Journal of Psychoanalysis, 60,* 83–96.

Advisory Panel on Alzheimer's Disease. DHHS Pub. No. (ADM)91-1791. Washington, DC: Superintendent of Documents, U.S. Government Printing Office.

Agras, W. S., Rossiter, E. M., Arnow, B., Telch, C. F., Raeburn, S. D., Bruce, B., & Koran, L. M. (1994). One-year follow-up of psychosocial and pharmacologic treatments for bulimia nervosa. *Journal of Clinical Psychiatry, 55,* 179–183.

Agras, W. S., Taylor, O. B., Kraemer, H. C., Allen, R. A., & Schneider, M. S. (1980). Relaxation training: Twenty-four hour blood pressure reductions. *Archives of General Psychiatry, 37,* 859–863.

Ahlawat, S. K. & Siwach, S. B. (1994). Alcohol and coronary artery disease. *International Journal of Cardiology, 44,* 157–162.

Akesson, H. O. (1986). The biological origin of mild mental retardation. *Acta Psychiatrica Scandinavica, 74,* 3–7.

Akhtar, S. (1987). Schizoid personality disorder: A synthesis of developmental, dynamic, and descriptive features. *American Journal of Psychotherapy, 41,* 499–518.

Akhtar, S. (1990). Paranoid personality disorder: A synthesis of developmental, dynamic, and descriptive features. *American Journal of Psychotherapy, 44,* 5–25.

Akiskal, H. S. (1985). Interaction of biologic and psychologic factors in the origin of depressive disorders. *Acta Psychiatrica Scandinavica, 74* (Suppl. 319), 131–139.

Akiskal, H. S. (1994). Dysthymia: Clinical and external validity. *Acta Scandinavica Psychiatrica, 83* (Suppl. 383), 19–23.

Alcohol and Health (1990). Rockville, MD: National Institute of Alcohol Abuse and Alcoholism.

Alcoholism: An inherited disease. (1985). Rockville, MD: National Institute of Alcohol Abuse and Alcoholism.

Alford, B. A., & Beck, A. T. (1994). Cognitive therapy of delusional beliefs. *Behavior Research and Therapy, 32,* 369–380.

Alford, B. A., Beck, A. T., Freeman, A., & Wright, F. D. (1990). Brief focused cognitive therapy of panic disorder. *Psychotherapy, 27,* 230–234.

Alnaes, R., & Torgersen, S. (1993). Mood disorders: Developmental and precipitating events. *Canadian Journal of Psychiatry, 38,* 217–224.

Ambelas, A. (1987). Life events and mania: A special relationship. *British Journal of Psychiatry, 150,* 235–240.

Ambrosini, P. J., Bianchi, M. D., Rabinovich, H., & Elia, J. (1993). Antidepressant treatments in children and adolescents I. Affective disorders. *Journal of the American Academy of Child and Adolescent Psychiatry, 32,* 1–6.

American Law Institute. (1962). *Model penal code: Proposed official draft.* Philadelphia: American Law Institute.

American Psychiatric Association (1994). *Diagnostic and Statistical Manual of Mental Disorders* (4th ed.) (*DSM-IV.*). Washington, DC: American Psychiatric Association.

Anderson, D. J., Noyes, R., Jr., & Crowe, R. R. (1984). A comparison of panic disorder and generalized anxiety disorder. *American Journal of Psychiatry, 141,* 572–575.

Anderson, E. A. (1987). Preoperative preparation for cardiac surgery facilitates recovery, reduces psychological distress, and reduces the incidence of acute postoperative hypertension. *Journal of Consulting and Clinical Psychology, 55,* 513–520.

Andreasen, N. C., & Black, D. W. (1991). *Introductory text of psychiatry.* Washington, DC: American Psychiatric Press.

Andreasen, N. C., & Grove, W. (1979). The relationship between schizophrenic language, manic language, and aphasia. In J. Gruzelier & P. Flor-Henry (Eds.), *Hemisphere symmetries of function in psychopathology.* Amsterdam: Elsevier/North Holland.

Anonymous. (1977). Psychosocial implications of schizophrenic diagnoses (personal account). *Schizophrenia Bulletin, 3,* 4(b).

Anthony, W. A., & Liberman, R. P. (1986). The practice of psychiatric rehabilitation: Historical, conceptual, and research base. *Schizophrenia Bulletin, 4,* 622–635.

Appelbaum, P. S. (1991). What are the current standards for involuntary commitment to a mental hospital? *Harvard Mental Health Letter, 7* (11), 8.

Arieti, S., & Bemporad, J. (1978). *Severe and mild depression.* New York: Basic Books.

Aronow, E., & Resnikoff, M. (1976). *Rorschach content interpretation.* Orlando, FL: Grune & Stratton.

Aronson, T. A., & Shukla, S. (1987). Life events and relapse in bipolar disorder. The impact of a catastrophic event. *Acta Psychiatrica Scandinavica, 57,* 571–576.

Asaad, G., & Shapiro, B. (1986). Hallucinations: Theoretical and clinical overview. *American Journal of Psychiatry, 143,* 1088–1097.

Askildsen, E. C., Watten, R. G., & Faleide, A. O. (1993). Are parents of asthmatic children different from other parents? *Psychotherapy and Psychosomatics, 60,* 91–99.

Awad, A. G. (1989). Drug therapy in schizophrenia—Variability of outcome and prediction of response. *Canadian Journal of Psychiatry, 34,* 711–720.

Ayres, W. H. (1994). Foreword. In I. A. Canino & J. Spurlock, *Culturally diverse children and adolescents: Assessment, diagnosis, and treatment* (pp. vi–vii). New York: Guilford.

Bancroft, J. (1994). Homosexual orientation: The search for a biological basis. *British Journal of Psychiatry, 164,* 437–440.

Bandura, A. (1978). The self-system in reciprocal determinism. *American Psychologist, 33,* 344–358.

Bandura, A. (1981). Cultivating competence, self-efficacy, and intrinsic interest through proximal self-motivation. *Journal of Personality and Social Psychology, 41,* 586–598.

Bandura, A. (1986). *Social foundations of thought and action: A social cognitive theory.* Englewood Cliffs, NJ: Prentice Hall.

Bandura, A., & Menlove, F. L. (1968). Factors determining vicarious extinction of avoidance behavior through symbolic modeling. *Journal of Personality and Social Psychology, 8,* 99–108.

Bandura, A., & Schunk, D. H. (1981). Cultivating competence, self-efficacy, and intrinsic interest through proximal self-motivation. *Journal of Personality & Social Psychology, 41,* 586–598.

Bard, M. (1970). Alternatives to traditional law enforcement. In F. Korten, S. W. Cook, & J. I. Lacey, *Psychology and the problems of society.* (Eds.) Washington, DC: American Psychological Association (pp. 128–132).

Barden, H. S., Kessel, R., & Schuett, V. E. (1984). The costs and benefits of screening for PKU in Wisconsin. *Social Biology, 31,* 1–17.

Barefoot, J. C., Peterson, B. L., Dahlstrom, W. G., Siegler, I. C., Anderson, N. B., & Williams, R. B., Jr. (1991). Hostility patterns and health implications: Correlates of Cook-Medley Hostility Scale scores in a national survey. *Health Psychology, 10,* 18–24.

Barefoot, J. C., Siegler, I. C., Nowling, J. B., Peterson, B. L., Haney, T. L., & Williams, R. B., Jr. (1987). Suspiciousness, health, and mortality: A follow-up study of 500 older adults. *Psychosomatic Medicine, 49,* 450–457.

Barkley, R. A. (1989). Hyperactive girls and boys: Stimulant drug effects on mother-child interactions. *Journal of Child Psychology and Psychiatry, 39,* 379–390.

Barkley, R. A., Fischer, M., Edelbrock, C., & Smallish, L. (1990). The adolescent outcome of hyperactive children diagnosed by research criteria, I: An eight-year prospective follow-up study. *Journal of the American Academy of Child and Adolescent Psychiatry, 29,* 546–557.

Barlow, D. H. (1994). Psychological interventions in the era of managed competition. *Clinical Psychology, 1,* 109–122.

Barlow, D. H., Brown, T. A., & Craske, M. G. (1994). Definitions of panic attacks and panic disorder in the DSM-IV: Implications for research. *Journal of Abnormal Psychology, 103,* 553–564.

Barlow, D. H., Craske, M. G., Cerny, J. A., & Klosko, J. S. (1989). Behavioral treatment of panic disorder. *Behavior Therapy, 20,* 261–282.

Barlow, D. H., DiNardo, P. A., Vermilyea, B. B., Vermilyea, J., & Blanchard, E. B. (1986). Co-morbidity and depression among the anxiety disorders: Issues in diagnosis and classification. *Journal of Nervous and Mental Disease, 174,* 63–72.

Baron, M., Gruen, R. S., & Romo-Gruen, J. M. (1992). Positive and negative symptoms: Relation to familial transmission of schizophrenia. *British Journal of Psychiatry, 161,* 610–614.

Baron, M., & Risch, N. (1987). The spectrum concept of schizophrenia: Evidence for a genetic-environmental continuum. *Journal of Psychiatric Research, 21,* 257–267.

Barrelet, L., Ferrero, F., Szigethy, L., Giddey, C., & Pellizzer, G. (1990). Expressed emotion and first-admission schizophrenia. Nine-month follow-up in a French cultural environment. *British Journal of Psychiatry, 156,* 357–362.

Barrett, M. L., Berney, T. P., Bhate, S. R., Famuyiwa, O. O., Fundudis, T., Kolvin, I., & Tyner, S. (1991). Diagnosing childhood depression. Who should be interviewed—parent or child? *British Journal of Psychiatry, 159,* (Suppl. 11), 22–27.

Barrowclough, C., & Tarrier, N. (1990). Social functioning in schizophrenic patients. I. The effects of expressed emotion and family intervention. *Social Psychiatry and Psychiatric Epidemiology, 25,* 125–129.

Bartak, L., Rutter, M., & Cox, M. (1975). A comparative study of infantile autism and specific developmental receptive language disorder. I. The children. *British Journal of Psychiatry, 126,* 127–145.

Bartrop, R. W., Luckhurst, E., Lazarus, L., Kiloh, L. G., & Penny, R. (1977). Depressed lymphocyte function after bereavement. *Lancet, 1,* 834–836.

Bauer, R. B., Stevens, C., Reveno, W. S., & Rosenbaum, H. (1982). L-Dopa treatment of Parkinson's disease: A ten year follow-up study. *Journal of the American Geriatric Society, 30,* 322–325.

Beck, A. T. (1967). *Depression: Clinical, experimental and theoretical aspects.* New York: Hoeber.

Beck, A. T. (1970). Role of fantasies in psychotherapy and psychopathology. *Journal of Nervous and Mental Disease, 150,* 3–17.

Beck, A. T. (1976). *Cognitive therapy and the emotional disorders.* New York: International Universities Press.

Beck, A. T., Brown, G., Berchick, R. J., Stewart, B. L., & Steer, R. A. (1990). Relationship between hopelessness and ultimate suicide: A replication with psychiatric outpatients. *American Journal of Psychiatry, 147,* 190–195.

Beck, A. T., Brown, G., Steer, R. A., Eidelson, J. L., & Riskind, J. H. (1987). Differentiating anxiety and depression: A test of the cognitive content-specificity hypothesis. *Journal of Abnormal Psychology, 96,* 179–183.

Beck, A. T., & Emery, G. (1985). *Anxiety disorders and phobias: A cognitive perspective.* New York: Basic Books.

Beck, A. T., Freeman, A., & Associates (1990). *Cognitive therapy of personality disorders.* New York: Guilford.

Beck, A. T., Rush, A. J., Shaw, B., & Emery, G. (1979). *Cognitive therapy of depression.* New York: Guilford.

Beck, A. T., Steer, R. A., Kovacs, M., & Garrison, B. (1985). Hopelessness and eventual suicide: A ten year prospective study of patients hospitalized with suicidal ideation. *American Journal of Psychiatry, 142,* 559–563.

Beck, A. T., & Weishaar, M. (1989). Cognitive therapy of anxiety, in A. Freeman, K. M. Simon, L. E. Beutler, & H. Arkowitz, eds., *Comprehensive handbook of cognitive therapy.* New York: Plenum.

Beck, J. C. (1994). Epidemiology of mental disorder and violence: Beliefs and research findings. *Harvard Review of Psychiatry, 2,* 1–6.

Beck, J. G., & Barlow, D. H. (1984). Current conceptualizations of sexual dysfunction: A review and an alternative perspective.

Clinical Psychology Review, 4, 363–378.

Becker, R. E. (1990). Social skills training. In A. S. Bellack & M. Hersen (Eds.), *Comparative treatments for adult disorders.* New York: Wiley.

Bednar, R. L. & Kaul, T. J. (1994). Experiential group research: Can the cannon fire? In A. E. Bergin and S. L. Garfield (Eds.), *Handbook of psychotherapy and behavior change* (4th ed.). New York: Wiley.

Beers, C. (1908). *A mind that found itself.* Garden City, NY: Doubleday.

Beitman, B. D. (1993). Afterword to Section IV. In J. M. Oldham, M. B. Riba, & A. Tasman (Eds.), *Review of Psychiatry* (Vol. 12, pp. 651–654). Washington, DC: American Psychiatric Press.

Beitman, B. D. (1993). Pharmacotherapy and the stages of psychotherapeutic change. In J. M. Oldham, M. B. Riba, & A. Tasman (Eds.). *Review of Psychiatry* (Vol. 12, pp. 521–539). Washington, DC: American Psychiatric Press.

Bell, Q. (1972). *Virginia Woolf: A biography.* New York: Harcourt Brace.

Bellack, A. S. (1989). A comprehensive model for treatment of schizophrenia. In A. S. Bellack, ed., *A clinical guide for the treatment of schizophrenia.* New York: Plenum.

Bellack, A. S., & Muesler, K. T. (1993). Psychosocial treatment for schizophrenia. *Schizophrenia Bulletin, 19,* 317–336.

Bemporad, J. R., & Vasile, R. G. (1990). Psychotherapy. In A. S. Bellack and M. Hersen, eds., *Comparative treatments for adult disorders.* New York: Wiley.

Bender, L. (1938). A visual motor Gestalt test and its clinical use. *American Orthopsychiatric Association Research Monographs,* No. 3.

Benson, D. F., Miller, B. L., & Signer, S. F. (1986). Dual personality associated with epilepsy. *Archives of Neurology, 43,* 471–474.

Benson, H. (1977). Systemic hypertension and the relaxation response. *New England Journal of Medicine, 296,* 1152–1156.

Bentall, R. P., Haddock, G., & Slade, P. D. (1994). Cognitive behavior therapy for persistent auditory hallucinations: From theory to therapy. *Behavior Therapy, 25,* 51–66.

Bentler, P. M., & Prince, C. (1969). Personality characteristics of male transvestites. *Journal of Abnormal Psychology, 74,* 140–143.

Bentler, P. M., & Prince, C. (1970). Psychiatric symptomatology in transvestites. *Journal of Clinical Psychology, 26,* 434–435.

Benton, M. K., & Schroeder, H. E. (1990). Social skills training with schizophrenics: A meta-analytic evaluation. *Journal of Consulting and Clinical Psychology, 58,* 741–747.

Bergin, A. E., & Garfield, S. L. (Eds.) (1994). *Handbook of psychotherapy and behavior change* (4th ed.). New York: John Wiley.

Bergin, A. E., & Lambert, M. J. (1978). The evaluation of therapeutic outcomes. In S. L. Garfield, & A. E. Bergin (Eds.), *Handbook of psychotherapy and behavior change: An empirical analysis* (2nd ed.). New York: John Wiley.

Berke, J., & Hernton, C. (1974). *The cannabis experience.* London: Peter Owen.

Bernard, M. L., & Bernard, J. L. (1983). Violent intimacy: The family as a model for love relationships. *Family Relations, 32,* 283–286.

Bernier, J. C., & Siegel, D. H. (1994). Attention-deficit hyperactivity disorder: A family and ecological systems perspective. *Families in Society, 75,* 142–151.

Berry, P., Groeneweg, G., Gibson, D., & Brown, R. I. (1984). Mental development of adults with Down syndrome. *American Journal of Mental Deficiency, 89,* 252–256.

Bertelsen, A., & Gottesman, I.I. (1986). Offspring of twin pairs discordant for psychiatric illness. *Acta Geneticae Medicae et Gemellogiae, 35,* 310.

Beumont, P. J. (1993). Anorexia nervosa in males: A report of 12 cases. *Australian and New Zealand Journal of Psychiatry, 27,* 512–517.

Bibring, E. (1953). The mechanism of depression. In P. Greenacre (Ed.), *Affective disorders.* New York: International.

Biederman, J., Faraone, S. V., Spencer, T., Wilens, T., Norman, D., Lapey, K. A., Mick, E., Lehman, B. K., & Doyle, A. (1993). Patterns of psychiatric comorbidity, cognition, and psychosocial functioning in adults with attention deficit hyperactivity disorder. *American Journal of Psychiatry, 150,* 1792–1798.

Birchwood, M. Early intervention in schizophrenia: Theoretical background and clinical strategies. *British Journal of Clinical Psychology, 31,* 257–278.

Black, J. L. (1993). ECT: Lessons learned about an old treatment with new technologies. *Psychiatric Annals, 23, (1),* 7–14.

Blazer, D., Hughes, D., & George, L. D. (1987). Stressful life events and the onset of a generalized anxiety syndrome. *American Journal of Psychiatry, 144,* 1178–1183.

Bleuler, E. (1915/1950). *Dementia praecox or the group of schizophrenias* (J. Zinkin, trans.). New York: International Universities Press.

Bloom, B. L., & Hodges, W. F. (1988). The Colorado Separation and Divorce Program: A preventive intervention program for newly separated persons. In R. H. Price, E. L. Cowen, R. P. Lorian, & J. Ramos-McKay (Eds.), *Fourteen ounces of prevention: A casebook for practitioners.* Washington, DC: American Psychological Association.

Blumenthal, R. (1993). Omission of author's residence proves embarrassing. *New York Times,* Dec. 5, p. Y20.

Bohman, M., Cloninger, C. R., Sigvardsson, S., & von Knorring, A. L. (1982). Predisposition to petty criminality of Swedish adoptees I. Genetic and Rh environmental heterogeneity. *Archives of General Psychiatry, 39,* 1233–1241.

Bohmfalk, G. C. (1991). No laughing matter. *Journal of the American Medical Association, 265,* 1245.

Bond, L. A., & Compas, B. E. (1991). *Primary prevention and promotion in the schools.* Newbury Park, CA: Sage Publications.

Boor, M. (1982). The multiple personality epidemic. *Journal of Nervous and Mental Disease, 170,* 302–304.

Booth-Butterfield, M. (Ed.), (1991). *Communication, cognition, and anxiety.* Newbury Park, CA: Sage Publications.

Bornstein, R. F. (1992). The dependent personality: Developmental, social, and clinical perspectives. *Psychological Bulletin, 112,* 3–23.

Borthwick-Duffy, S. A. (1994). Epidemiology and prevalence of psychopathology in people with mental retardation. *Journal of Consulting and Clinical Psychology, 62,* 17–27.

Bousha, D. M., & Twentyman, C. T. (1984). Mother-child interactional style in abuse, neglect, and control groups: Naturalistic observations in the home. *Journal of Abnormal Psychology, 93,* 106–114.

Bowden, C. L. (1993). The clinical approach to the differential diagnosis of bipolar disorder. *Psychiatric Annals, 23,* 57–63.

Bowden, C. L., Brugger, A. M., Swann, A. C., Calabrese, J. R., Janicak, P. G., Petty, F., Dissaver, S. C., Davis, J. M., and others

(1994). Efficacy of divalproex vs. lithium and placebo in the treatment of mania. *Journal of the American Medical Association, 271*, 918–924.

Bowlby, J. (1980). *Loss, sadness, and depression*. New York: Basic Books.

Boyd, J. H., Rae, D. S., Thompson, J. W., Burns, B. J., Bourdon, K., Locke, B. Z., & Regier, D. A. (1990). Phobia: Prevalence and risk factors. *Social Psychiatry and Psychiatric Epidemiology, 25*, 314–323.

Braff, D. L. (1989). Sensory input deficits and negative symptoms in schizophrenic patients. *American Journal of Psychiatry, 146*, 1006–1011.

Braff, D. L. (1993). Information processing and attention dysfunctions in schizophrenia. *Schizophrenia Bulletin, 19*, 233–259.

Breier, A., Buchanon, R. W., Irish, D., & Carpenter, W. T. Jr. (1993). Clozapine treatment of outpatients with schizophrenia: Outcome and long-term response patterns. *Hospital and Community Psychiatry, 44*, 1145–1149.

Brenner, H. D. (1989). The treatment of basic psychological dysfunctions from a systemic point of view. *British Journal of Psychiatry, 155* (Suppl. 5), 74–83.

Brenner, H. D., Boker, W., Hodel, B., & Wyss, H. (1989). Cognitive treatment of basic pervasive dysfunctions in schizophrenia. In S. C. Schulz and C. A. Tamminga (Eds.) *Schizophrenia: Scientific progress* (pp. 358–367). New York: Oxford University Press.

Brenner, H. D., Hodel, B., Genner, R., Roder, V., & Corrigan, P. (1992). Biological and cognitive vulnerability factors in schizophrenia: Implications for treatment. *British Journal of Psychiatry, 161*, 154–163.

Brenner, M. H. (1973). *Mental illness and the economy*. Cambridge, MA: Harvard University Press.

Brenner, M. H. (1984). *Estimating the effects of economic change on national health and social well-being*. (Joint Economic Committee of the U.S. Congress). Washington, DC: U.S. Government Printing Office.

Breslau, N., & Davis, G. C. (1993). Migraine, physical health and psychiatric disorder: A prospective epidemiologic study in young adults. *Journal of Psychiatric Research, 27*, 211–221.

Breslow, N., Evans, L., & Langley, J. (1985). On the prevalence and roles of females in the sadomasochistic subculture: Report of an empirical study. *Archives of Sexual Behavior, 14*, 303–317.

Breslow, N., Evans, L., & Langley, J. (1986). Comparisons among heterosexual, bisexual, and homosexual male sadomasochists. *Journal of Homosexuality, 13*, 83–107.

Brewerton, T. D., Krahn, D. D., Hardin, T. A., Wehr, T. A., & Rosenthal, N. E. (1994). Findings from the Seasonal Pattern Assessment Questionnaire in patients with eating disorders and control subjects: Effects of diagnosis and location. *Psychiatry Research, 52*, 71–84.

Breznitz, S. (1988). The seven kinds of denial. In C. D. Spielberger, I. G. Sarason, & P. B. Defares (Eds.), *Stress and Anxiety* (Vol. 11. pp. 73–90), Washington, D.C.: Hemisphere.

Brier, N. (1986). The mildly retarded adolescent: A psychosocial perspective. *Developmental and Behavioral Pediatrics, 7*, 320–323.

Brown, G. W., Bifulco, A. & Harris, T. O. (1987). Life events, vulnerability and onset of depression: Some refinements. *British Journal of Psychiatry, 150*, 30–42.

Brown, T. A., Barlow, D. H., & Liebowitz, M. R. (1994). The empirical basis of generalized anxiety disorder. *American Journal of Psychiatry, 151*, 1272–1280.

Browne, A., & Finkelhor, D. (1986). Impact of child sexual abuse: A review of research. *Psychological Bulletin, 99*, 66–77.

Brownell, K. D., Hayes, S. C., & Barlow, D. H. (1977). Patterns of appropriate and deviant sexual arousal: The behavioral treatment of multiple sexual deviations. *Journal of Consulting and Clinical Psychology, 45*, 1144–1155.

Buchsbaum, M. S. (1993). Positron-emission tomography and brain activity in psychiatry. In J. M. Oldham, M. B. Riba, & A. Tasman (Eds.), *Review of Psychiatry* (Vol. 12, pp. 461–485). Washington, DC: American Psychiatric Press.

Bugental, J. F. T., & McBeath, B. (1995). Depth existential therapy: Evolution since World War II. In B. Bongar and L. E. Beutler (Eds.), *Comprehensive textbook of psychotherapy: Theory and practice* (pp. 111–122). New York: Oxford University Press.

Burnside, J. W. (1987). The diary. *Journal of the American Medical Association, 257*, 1802.

Butcher, J. N. (1990). *The MMPI-2 in psychological treatment*. New York: Oxford University Press.

Butler, G. (1989). Issues in the application of cognitive and behavioral strategies to the treatment of social phobia. *Clinical Psychology Review, 9*, 91–106.

Cahill, C., Llewelyn, S. P., & Pearson, C. (1991). Treatment of sexual abuse which occurred in childhood: A review. *British Journal of Clinical Psychology, 30*, 1–12.

Caldwell, C. B., & Gottesman, I. I. (1990). Schizophrenics kill themselves too: A review of risk factors for suicide. *Schizophrenia Bulletin, 16*, 571–589.

Calhoun, L. G., & Allen, B. G. (1991). Social reactions to the survivor of a suicide in the family: A review of the literature. *Omega, 23*, 95–107.

Cameron, N. (1963). *Personality development and psychopathology*. Boston: Houghton Mifflin.

Campbell, S. S., & Gillin, J. C. (1987). Sleep measures in depression: How sensitive? How specific? *Psychiatric Annals, 17*, 647–653.

Canino, I. A., & Spurlock, J. (1994). *Culturally diverse children and adolescents: Assessment, diagnosis, and treatment*. New York: Guilford.

Cannon, T. D., & Mednick, S. A. (1993). The schizophrenia high-risk project in Copenhagen: Three decades of progress. *Acta Psychiatrica Scandinavica, 370*, 33–47.

Carlson, C. L., Lahey, B. B., & Neeper, R. (1984). Peer assessment of the social behavior of accepted, rejected, and neglected children. *Journal of Abnormal Child Psychology, 12*, 187–198.

Carlson, C. L., Pelham, W. E., Milich, R., & Dixon, M. J. (1992). Single and combined effects of methylphenidate and behavior therapy on classroom behavior, academic performance and self-evaluations of children with attention deficit-hyperactivity disorder. *Journal of Abnormal Child Psychology, 9*, 43–54.

Carlson, C. L., Pelham, W. E., Milich, R., & Hoza, B. (1993). ADHD boys' performance and attributions following success and failure: Drug effects and individual differences. *Cognitive Therapy and Research, 17*, 269–287.

Carrol, K., & Leon, G. R. (1981). The bulimia-vomiting disorder within a generalized substance abuse pattern. Paper presented at the 15th Annual Convention of the Association for the Advancement of Behavior Therapy, Toronto.

Carroll, B. J. (1985). Dexamethasone Suppression Test: A review of contemporary confusion. *Journal of Clinical Psychiatry, 46*, 13–24.

Carter, F. A., & Bulik, C. M. (1994). Exposure treatments for bulimia nervosa: Procedure, efficacy, and mechanisms. *Advances in Behavioral Research and Therapy, 16,* 77–129.

Casas, J. M. (1995). Counseling and psychotherapy with racial/ethnic minority groups in theory and practice. In B. Bongar and L. E. Beutler (Eds.), *Comprehensive textbook of psychotherapy: Theory and practice* (pp. 311–335). New York: Oxford University Press.

Casey, R. J., & Berman, J. S. (1985). The outcome of psychotherapy with children. *Psychological Bulletin, 98(2),* 388–400.

Caspi, A. & Elder, A. H., Jr., (1988). Early personality and life disorganization. In E. M. Hetherington, R. M. Lerner, & M. Perlmutter (Eds.), *Child development in life-span perspective.* Hillsdale, NJ: Lawrence Erlbaum Associates.

Catalan, J., Hawton, K., & Day, A. (1990). Couples referred to a sexual dysfunction clinic: Psychological and physical morbidity. *British Journal of Psychiatry, 156,* 61–67.

Cautela, J. R. (1985). Covert modeling. In A. S. Bellack & M. Hersen (Eds.), *Dictionary of behavior therapy techniques.* New York: Pergamon.

Caviola, A. A. & Schiff, M. (1988). Behavioral sequelae of physical and/or sexual abuse in adolescents. *Child Abuse and Neglect, 12,* 181–188.

Celis, W. (1991). As fewer students drink, abuse of alcohol persists. *The New York Times,* December 31, 1991, 1, A8.

Cepeda-Benito, A. (1993). Meta-analytical review of the efficacy of nicotine chewing gum in smoking treatment programs. *Journal of Consulting and Clinical Psychology, 61,* 822–830.

Chalkley, A. J., & Powell, G. E. (1983). The clinical description of forty-eight cases of sexual fetishisms. *British Journal of Psychiatry, 142,* 292–295.

Chambers, W. J., Puig-Antich, J., Hirsch, M., Paez, P., Ambrosini, P. J., Tabrizi, M. A., & Davies, M. (1985). The assessment of affective disorders in children and adolescents by semi-structured interview. *Archives of General Psychiatry, 42,* 696–702.

Chandler, C. L., Weissberg, R. P., Cowen, E. L., & Guare, J. (1984). Long term effects of a school-based secondary prevention program for young maladapting children. *Journal of Consulting and Clinical Psychology, 52,* 165–170.

Charman, T. (1994). The stability of depressed mood in young adolescents: A school based survey. *Journal of Affective Disorders, 30,* 109–116.

Cherlin, A. J., Furstenberg, F. F., Chase-Lansdale, P. L., Kiernan, K. E., Robins, P. K., Morrison, D. R., & Tietler, J. O. (1991). Longitudinal studies of effects of divorce on children in Great Britain and the United States. *Science, 252,* 1386–1389.

Chesney, M. A., & Rosenman, R. H. (Eds.) (1985). *Anger and hostility in cardiovascular and behavioral disorders.* Washington, D.C.: Hemisphere.

Chess, S. (1978). The plasticity of human development. *American Academy of Child Psychiatry, 17,* 80–91.

Chess, S. (1990). Pathogenesis of the adjustment disorders: Vulnerabilities due to temperamental factors. In J. D. Noshpitz & R. D. Coddington (Eds.), *Stressors and the adjustment disorders.* New York: John Wiley.

Chess, S., Thomas, A., & Hassibi, M. (1983). Depression in childhood and adolescence: A prospective study of six cases. *Journal of Nervous and Mental Disease, 171,* 411–420.

Christopher, I.C. (1993). Psychosocial factors and immunity in nonhuman primates: A review. *Psychosomatic Medicine, 55,* 298–308.

Chuang, H. T., Devins, G. M., Hunsley, J., & Gill, M. J. (1989). Psychosocial distress and well-being among gay and bisexual men with human immunodeficiency virus infection. *American Journal of Psychiatry, 146,* 876–880.

Cicchetti, D., & Beeghly, M. (1990). *Children with Down Syndrome: A developmental perspective.* Cambridge, England: Cambridge University Press.

Cicchetti, D., & Carlson, V. (1989). *Child maltreatment: Theory and research on the causes and consequences of child abuse and neglect.* New York: Cambridge University Press.

Clark, D. B., Smith, M. G., Neighbors, B. D., Skerlec, L. M., & Randall, J. (1994). Anxiety disorders in adolescence: Characteristics, prevalence, and comorbidities. *Clinical Psychology Review, 14,* 113–137.

Clark, D. M., Salkovskis, P. M., Hackmann, A., Middleton, H., Anastasiades, P., & Gelder, M. (1994). A comparison of cognitive therapy, applied relaxation and imipramine in the treatment of panic disorder. *British Journal of Psychiatry, 164,* 749–769.

Clark, K. A. (1965). A role for librarians in the relevant war against poverty. *Wilson Library Bulletin,* Sept. 1965 (Quoted in A. MacLeod, *Growing up in America.*) Rockville, MD: National Institute of Mental Health.

Clarkin, J. F. (1989). Family education. In A. S. Bellack (Ed.), *A clinical guide for the treatment of schizophrenia.* New York: Plenum.

Clarkin, J. F., Glick, I. D., Haas, G. L., Spencer, J. H., Lewis, A. B., Peyser, J., Demane, N., Good-Ellis, M., Harris, E., & Lestelle, V. (1990). A randomized clinical trial of inpatient family intervention: V. Results for affective disorders. *Journal of Affective Disorders, 18,* 17–28.

Clayton, P. J. (1990). Bereavement and depression. *Journal of Clinical Psychiatry, 51,* 34–38.

Clementz, B. A., Sweeney, J. A., Hirt, M., & Haas, G. (1991). Phenotypic correlations between oculomotor functioning and schizophrenia-related characteristics in relatives of schizophrenic probands. *Psychophysiology, 28,* 570–578.

Clinton, J. J. (1993). From the Agency for Health Care Policy and Research. *Journal of the American Medical Association, 270,* 172.

Cloninger, C. R., Bohman, M., & Sigvardsson, S. (1981). Inheritance of alcohol abuse. *Archives of General Psychiatry, 38,* 861–868.

Coe, C. L. (1993). Psychosocial factors and immunity in nonhuman primates: A review. *Psychosomatic Medicine, 55,* 298–308.

Coffey, C. E., & Weiner, R. D. (1990). Electroconvulsive therapy: An update. *Hospital and Community Psychology, 41,* 515–521.

Coffey, C. E., Weiner, R. D., Djang, W. T., Figiel, G. S. (1991). Brain anatomic effects of electroconvulsive therapy: A prospective magnetic imaging study. *Archives of General Psychiatry, 48,* 1013–1021.

Cohen, D. J., Caparulo, B. K., & Shaywitz, B. A. (1978). Neurochemical and developmental models of childhood autism. In G. Serban (Ed.), *Cognitive defects in the development of mental illness.* New York: Brunner/Mazel.

Cohen, J. D., & Servan-Schreiber, D. (1992). Context, cortex, and dopamine: A connectionist approach to behavior and biology in schizophrenia. *Psychological Review, 99,* 45–77.

Cohen, L. H. (1988). *Life events and psychological functioning: Theoretical and methodological issues*. Newbury Park, CA: Sage Publications.

Cohen, M. E., Robins, E., Purtell, J. J., Altmann, M. W., & Reed, D. E. (1953). Excessive surgery in hysteria. *Journal of the American Medical Association, 151*, 977–986.

Cohen, P., Cohen, J., & Brook, J. (1993) An epidemiological study of disorders in late childhood and adolescence—II. Persistence of disorders. *Journal of Child Psychiatry and Psychology, 34*, 869–877.

Cohen, P., Cohen, J., Kasen, S., Velez, C. N., Hartmark, C., Johnson, J., Rojas, M., Brook, J. & Streuning, E. L. (1993). An epidemiological study of disorders in late childhood and adolescence—I. Age- and gender specific prevalence. *Journal of Child Psychiatry and Psychology, 34*, 851–867.

Cohen, R. A. (1975). Manic-depressive illness. In A. M. Freedman, J. I. Kaplan, & B. J. Sadock (Eds.), *Comprehensive textbook of psychiatry*, 2nd ed. Baltimore, MD: Williams & Wilkins.

Cohen, S., & Williamson, G.M. (1991). Stress and infectious disease in humans. *Psychological Bulletin, 109*, 5–24.

Cohen, S., Tyrrell, D. A. J., & Smith, A. P. (1991). Psychological stress and susceptibility to the common cold. *New England Journal of Medicine, 325*, 606–612.

Coie, J. D., Watt, N. F., West, S. G., Hawkins, D., Asarnow, J. R., Markman, H. J., Ramey, S. L., Shure, M. B., & Long, B. (1993). The science of prevention: A conceptual framework and some directions for a national research program. *American Psychologist, 48*, 1013–1022.

Cole, N. (1985). Sex therapy—A critical appraisal. *British Journal of Psychiatry, 147*, 337–351.

Conaway, L. P., & Hansen, D. J. (1989). Social behavior of physically abused and neglected children: A critical review. *Clinical Psychology Review, 9*, 627–652.

Condray, R., & Steinhauer, S. R. (1992). Schizotypal personality disorder in individuals with and without schizophrenic relatives: Similarities and contrasts in neurocognitive and clinical functioning. *Schizophrenia Research, 7*, 33–41.

Conte, J. R., Sorenson, E., Fogarty, L., & Rosa, J. D. (1991). Evaluating children's reports of sexual abuse: Results from a survey of professionals. *American Journal of Orthopsychiatry, 61*, 428–437.

Corder, E. H., Saunders, A. M., Strittmatter, W. J., Schmechel, D. E., Gaskell, P. C., Small, F. W., Roses, A. D., Haines, J. L., & Pericak-Vance, M. A., (1993). Gene dose of apolipoprotein E Type 4 in late onset families. *Science, 261*, 921–924.

Cornblatt, B. A., & Keilp, J. G. (1994). Impaired attention, genetics, and the pathophysiology of schizophrenia. *Schizophrenia Bulletin, 20*, 31–46.

Cornblatt, B. A., Lenzenweger, M. F., & Erlenmeyer-Kimling, L. L. (1989). The Continuous Performance Task, identical pairs version: II. Contrasting attentional profiles in schizophrenic and depressed patients. *Psychiatry Research, 29*, 65–85.

Coryell, W., Endicott, J., Reich, T., Andreasen, N., & Keller, M. (1984). A family study of bipolar II disorder. *British Journal of Psychiatry, 145*, 49–54.

Cotton, P. (1994). Constellation of risks and processes seen in search for Alzheimer's clues. *Journal of the American Medical Association, 271*, 88–91.

Council on Scientific Affairs, American Medical Association. (1986). Polygraph. *Journal of the American Medical Association, 256*, 1172–1175.

Courchesne, E., Young-Courchesne, N., Press, G. A., Hesselink, J. R., & Jernigan, T. L. (1988). Hypoplasia of cerebellar vermal lobules VI and VII in autism. *New England Journal of Medicine, 318*, 1349–1354.

Cowen, E. L. (1982). Help is where you find it: Four informal helping groups. *American Psychologist, 37*, 385–395.

Cowen, E. L., & Hightower, A. D. (1990). The Primary Mental Health Project: Alternative approaches in school-based preventive intervention. In T. B. Gutkin & C. R. Reynolds (Eds.), *Handbook of school psychology*. New York: John Wiley.

Cox, B. J. (1990). Substance abuse and panic-related anxiety: A critical review. *Behavior Research and Therapy, 28*(5), 385–393.

Coyle, J. T., Price, D. L. C., & DeLong, M. R. (1983). Alzheimer's disease: A disorder of cortical cholinergic innervation. *Science, 219*, 1184–1190.

Coyne, J. C., Kessler, R. C., Tal, M., Turnbull, J., Wortman, C. B., & Greden, J. F. (1987). Living with a depressed person. *Journal of Consulting and Clinical Psychology, 55*, 347–352.

Cromwell, R. L. (1993). Searching for the origins of schizophrenia. *Psychological Science, 4*, 276–279.

Crosby, D. (1989). First person account: Growing up with a schizophrenic mother. *Schizophrenia Bulletin, 15*, 507–509.

Crow, T. J. (1994). Prenatal exposure to influenza as a cause of schizophrenia. *British Journal of Psychiatry, 164*, 588–592.

Crowe, M. J., Gillan, P., & Golombok, S. (1981). Form and content in the conjoint treatment of sexual dysfunction: A controlled study. *Behaviour Research and Therapy, 19*, 47–54.

Crowe, M. J., & Jones, M. (1992). Sex therapy: The successes, the failures, the future. *British Journal of Hospital Medicine, 48*, 474–479.

Cummings, E. M., & Davies, P. (1994). *Children and marital conflict: The impact of family dispute and resolution*. New York: Guilford.

Cummings, J. L. (1993). The neuroanatomy of depression. *Journal of Clinical Psychiatry, 54*: 11 (Suppl.), 14–20.

Cunningham, C. E., & Siegel, L. S. (1987). Peer interactions of normal and attention-deficit-disordered boys during free-play, cooperative task, and simulated classroom situations. *Journal of Abnormal Child Psychology, 15*, 247–268.

Curry, S. J. (1993). Self-help interventions for smoking cessation. *Journal of Consulting and Clinical Psychology, 61*, 790–803.

Daley, D. C., & Marlatt, G. A. (1992). Relapse prevention: Cognitive and behavioral interventions. In J. H. Lowinson, P. Ruiz, & R. B. Millman (Eds.), *Substance abuse: A comprehensive textbook* (2d ed.) (pp. 533–542). Baltimore, MD: Williams & Wilkins.

Dam, H., Molin, J., Bolwig, T. G., Wildschiodtz, G., & Mellerup, E. T. (1994). Development of winter depression and the effect of light therapy. *Nordic Journal of Psychiatry, 48*, 75–79.

Davey, G. C. L. (1992). Classical conditioning and the acquisition of human fears and phobias: A review and synthesis of the literature. *Advanced Behavioral Research Theory, 14*, 29–66.

Davis, G. E., & Leitenberg, H. (1987). Adolescent sex offenders. *Psychological Bulletin, 101*, 417–427.

Dawson, G. (Ed.) (1989). *Autism: Nature, diagnosis, and treatment*. New York: Guilford.

DeFries, Z., Jenkins, S., & Williams, E. C. (1964). Treatment of disturbed children in foster care. *American Journal of Orthopsychiatry, 34*, 615–624.

Deluty, R. H. (1988–89). Physical illness, psychiatric illness and the acceptability of suicide. *Omega: The Journal of Death and Dying, 1,* 79–91.

deMontigny, C., Chaput, Y., & Blier, R. (1990). Modification of serotonergic neuron properties by long-term treatment with serotonin reuptake blockers. *Journal of Clinical Psychiatry, 51,* Suppl. B., 4–8.

Demos, J. P. (1982). *Entertaining Satan: Witchcraft and the culture of early New England.* New York: Oxford University Press.

De Nike, L. D., & Tiber, N. (1968). Neurotic behavior. In P. London & D. Rosenhan (Eds.), *Foundations of abnormal psychology.* New York: Holt, Rinehart & Winston.

de Ruiter, C., Rijken, H., Garssen, B., van Schaik, A., & Kraaimaat, F. (1989). Comorbidity among the anxiety disorders. *Journal of Anxiety Disorders, 3,* 57–68.

Deutsch, A. (1948). *The shame of the states.* New York: Arno.

Deutsch, C. K., Matthysse, S., Swanson, J. M., & Farkas, L. G. (1990). Genetic latent structure analysis of dysmorphology in attention deficit disorder. *Journal of the American Academy of Child and Adolescent Psychiatry, 29,* 189–194.

Deutsch, S. I., & Davis, K. L. (1983). Schizophrenia: A review of diagnostic and biological issues. II. Biological issues. *Hospital and Community Psychiatry, 34,* 423–437.

Deykin, E. Y., & MacMahon, B. (1979). The incidence of seizures among children with autistic symptoms. *American Journal of Psychiatry, 136,* 1310–1312.

Dickson, L. R., & Ranseen, J. D. (1990). An update on selected organic mental syndromes. *Hospital and Community Psychiatry, 41,* 290–300.

Didion, J. (1979). *The white album.* New York: Simon & Schuster.

Digdon, N., & Gotlib, I. H. (1985). Developmental considerations in the study of childhood depression. *Developmental Review, 5,* 162–199.

Dimsdale, J. E. (1988). A perspective on Type A behavior and coronary disease. *New England Journal of Medicine, 318,* 110–112.

Dinwiddie, S. H. (1994). Abuse of inhalants: A review. *Addiction, 89,* 925–939.

Docter, R. F. (1988). *Transvestites and transsexuals.* New York: Plenum.

Dodge, K. A. (1985). Attributional bias in aggressive children. *Advances in Cognitive Behavioral Research and Therapy, 4,* 73–110.

Dodge, K. A., Pettit, G. S., & Bates, J. E. (1994). Effects of physical maltreatment on the development of peer relations. *Development and Psychopathology, 6,* 43–55.

Dohrenwend, B. P., Levav, I., Shrout, P. E., Schwartz, S., Naveh, G., Link, B. G., Skodol, A. E., & Stueve, A. (1992). Socioeconomic status and psychiatric disorders: The causation-selection issue. *Science, 255,* 946–952.

Dollard, J., & Miller, N. (1950). *Personality and psychotherapy.* New York: McGraw-Hill.

Dorian, B., & Garfinkel, P. E. (1987). Stress, immunity and illness—a review. *Psychological Medicine, 17,* 393–407.

Dorris, M. (1989). *The broken cord.* New York: Harper & Row.

Dorwart, R. A., Schlesinger, M., Davison, H., Epstein, S., & Hoover, C. (1991). A national study of psychiatric hospital care. *American Journal of Psychiatry, 148,* 204–210.

Dryfoos, J. G. (1990). *Adolescents at risk.* New York: Oxford University Press.

Dunner, D. L. (1987). Stability of Bipolar II affective disorder as a diagnostic entity. *Psychiatric Annals, 17,* 18–20.

Dykman, B. M., Horowitz, L. M., Abramson, L. Y., & Usher, M. (1991). Schematic and situational determinants of depressed and nondepressed students' interpretation of feedback. *Journal of Abnormal Psychology, 100,* 45–55.

Easton, K. (1959). An unusual case of fugue and orality. *Psychoanalytic Quarterly, 28,* 505–513.

Eaton, W. W., Kessler, R. C., Wittchen, H. U., & Magee, W. J. (1994). Panic and panic disorder in the United States. *American Journal of Psychiatry, 151,* 413–420.

Eberhardy, F. (1967). The view from "the couch." *Journal of Child Psychology and Psychiatry, 8,* 257–263.

Eckardt, M. J., Harford, T. C., Kaelber, C. T., Parker, E. S., Rosenthal, L. S., Ryback, R. S., Salmoiraghi, G. C., Vanderveen, E., & Warren, K. R. (1981). Health hazards associated with alcohol consumption. *Journal of the American Medical Association, 246,* 648–666.

Egeland, B. (1988). Breaking the cycle of abuse: Implications for prediction and intervention. In K. D. Browne, C. Davies, & P. Stratton (Eds.), *Early prediction and prevention of child abuse.* New York: John Wiley.

Egeland, B., Carlson, E., & Sroufe, L. A. (1993). Resilience as process. *Development and Psychopathology, 5,* 517–528.

Egeland, B., Jacobvitz, D., & Sroufe, L. A. (1988). Breaking the cycle of abuse. *Child Development, 59,* 1080–1088.

Egolf, B., Lasker, J., Wolf, S., & Potvin, L. (1992). The Roseto effect: A 50-year comparison of mortality rates. *American Journal of Public Health, 82,* 1089–1092.

Eichenwald, K. (1987). Braving epilepsy's storm. *New York Times Magazine,* January 11, 30–36.

Eisenson, J. (1973). *Adult aphasia: Assessment and treatment.* Englewood Cliffs, NJ: Prentice-Hall.

Eisler, R. M. (1972). Crisis intervention in the family of a firesetter. *Psychotherapy: Theory, research and practice, 9,* 76–79.

Eldred, S. H., Bell, N. W., Longabaugh, R., & Sherman, L. J. (1964). Interactional correlates of chronicity in schizophrenia. *Psychiatric Research Report 19,* December, 1–12. Washington, DC: American Psychiatric Association.

Eliot, R. S., & Buell, J. C. (1983). The role of the CNS in cardiovascular disorders. *Hospital Practice,* May, 189–199.

Elkin, I. (1994). The NIMH treatment of depression collaborative research program: Where we began and where we are. In A. E. Bergin and S. L. Garfield (Eds.), *Handbook of psychotherapy and behavior change* (pp. 114–139). New York: John Wiley.

Elkin, I., Shea, T., Watkins, J. Imber, S. D., Sotsky, S. M., Collins, J. F., Glass, D. R., Pilkonis, P. A., Leber, W. R., Docherty, J. P., Fiester, S. J., & Parloff, M. B. (1989). NIMH Treatment of Depression Collaborative Research Program, I: General effectiveness of treatments. *Archives of General Psychiatry, 46,* 971–982.

Ellenberger, H. F. (1970). *The discovery of the unconscious.* New York: Basic Books.

Ellicott, A., Hammen, C., & Gitlin, M. (1990). Life events and the course of bipolar disorder. *American Journal of Psychiatry, 47,* 1194–1198.

Ellis, A. (1962). *Reason and emotion in psychotherapy.* New York: Lyle Stuart.

Ellis, A. (1970). Rational-emotive therapy. In L. Hersher (Eds.), *Four psychotherapies.* New York: Appleton-Century-Crofts.

Ellis, B., & Heiman, J. R. M. (1992). Marital and psychological adjustment in the context of a sexual dysfunction. *University of Washington Medical Center Update,* October 1992, 1–2.

Endler, N. S. (1990). *Holiday of darkness*. New York: Wiley-Interscience.

Engel, G. L. (1977). The need for a new medical model: A challenge for biomedicine. *Science, 196,* 129–136.

Emmelkamp, P. M. G., Van Der Helm, M., Van Zanten, B. L., & Plochg, I. (1980). Treatment of obsessive-compulsive patients: The contribution of self-instructional training to the effectiveness of exposure. *Behavior Research and Therapy, 18,* 61–66.

Epstein, A. W. (1965). Fetishism. In R. Slovenko (Ed.), *Sexual behavior and the law*. Springfield, IL: Thomas.

Erickson, H. M., & Goodwin, D. W. (1994). Pharmacologic interventions. In B. Van Hasselt and M. Hersen (Eds.), *Advanced Abnormal Psychology*. New York: Plenum Press.

Erikson, E. H. (1975). *Life history and the historical moment*. New York: W. W. Norton.

Erlenmeyer-Kimling, L. (1987). Biological markers for the liability to schizophrenia. In H. Helmchen & F. A. Henn (Eds.), *Biological perspectives of schizophrenia*. New York: John Wiley.

Erlenmeyer-Kimling, L., & Cornblatt, B. A. (1993). A summary of attentional findings in the New York High-Risk Project. *Journal of Psychiatric Research, 26,* 405–426.

Erlenmeyer-Kimling, L., Cornblatt, B. A., Rock, D., Roberts, S., Bell, M., & West, A. (1994). The New York High-Risk Project: Anhedonia, attentional deviance, and psychopathology. *Schizophrenia Bulletin, 19,* 141–153.

Eron, L. D. (1987). The development of aggressive behavior from the perspective of a developing behaviorism. *American Psychologist, 42,* 435–442.

Eron, L. D., & Peterson, R. A. (1982). Abnormal behavior: Social approaches. In M. R. Rosenzweig & L. W. Porter (Eds.), *Annual Review of Psychology, 33*. Palo Alto, CA: Annual Reviews.

Evans, D. E., Funkenstein, H. H., Albert, M. S., Scherr, P. A., Cook, N. R., Chown, M. J., Hebert, L. E., Hennekens, C. H., & Taylor, J. O. (1989). Prevalence of Alzheimer's disease in a community population of older persons: Higher than previously reported. *Journal of the American Medical Association, 262,* 2551–2556.

Evans, J., Williams, J. M., O'Loughlin, S., & Howells, K. (1992). Autobiographical memory and problem-solving strategies of parasuicide patients. *Psychological Medicine, 22,* 399–405.

Evans, M. D., Hollon, S. D., DeReubis, R. J., Piasicki, J. M., Grove, W. M., Garvey, M. J., & Tuason, V. B. (1992). Differential relapse following cognitive therapy and pharmacotherapy for depression. *Archives of General Psychiatry, 49,* 802–808.

Everson, M. D., & Boat, B. W. (1994). Putting the anatomical doll controversy in perspective: An examination of the major uses and criticisms of the dolls in child sexual abuse evaluations. *Child Abuse and Neglect, 18,* 113–129.

Exner, J. E. (1994). *The Rorschach: A comprehensive system* (3rd ed.). New York: Wiley.

Eysenck, H. J. (1952). The effects of psychotherapy: An evaluation. *Journal of Consulting Psychology, 16,* 319–324.

Eysenck, H. J. (1961). The effects of psychotherapy. In H. J. Eysenck (Ed.), *Handbook of abnormal psychology*. New York: Basic Books.

Faedda, G. L., Tondo, L., Teicher, M. H., Baldessarini, R. J., Gelbard, H. A., & Floris, G. F. (1993). Seasonal mood disorders. Patterns of seasonal recurrence in mania and depression. *Archives of General Psychiatry, 50,* 17–23.

Fairweather, G. W., Sanders, D. H., Maynard, H. C., Kessler, D. L., & Bleck, D. S. (1969). *Community life for the mentally ill: An alternative to institutional care*. Chicago: Aldine.

Faraone, S. V., & Biederman, J. (1994). Is attention deficit hyperactivity disorder familial? *Harvard Review of Psychiatry, 1,* 271–287.

Faraone, S. V., Biederman, J., Krifcher-Lehman, B., Spencer, T., Norman, D., & Seidman, L. (1993). Intellectual performance and school failure in children with attention deficit hyperactivity disorder and in their siblings. *Journal of Abnormal Psychology, 102,* 616–623.

Faraone, S. V., Kremen, W. S., & Tsuang, M. T. (1990). Genetic transmission of major affective disorders: Quantitative models and linkage analyses. *Psychological Bulletin, 108,* 109–127.

Faraone, S. V., & Tsuang, M. T. (1985). Quantitative models of the genetic transmission of schizophrenia. *Psychological Bulletin, 98,* 41–66.

Fauman, M. A. (1994). *Study guide to DSM-IV*. Washington, DC: American Psychiatric Press.

Feehan, M., McGee, R., & Williams S. (1993). Mental health disorders from age 15 to age 18 years. *Journal of the American Academy of Child and Adolescent Psychiatry, 32,* 1118–1126.

Feldman, M. D., & Ford, C. V. (1993). *Patient or pretender: Inside the strange world of factitious disorders*. New York: John Wiley.

Figiel, G. S., Krishnan, R. R., & Doraiswamy, M. (1990). Subcortical structural changes in ECT-induced delirium. *Journal of Geriatric Psychiatry and Neurology, 3,* 172–176.

Fine, S., Forth, A., Gilbert, M., & Haley, G. (1991). Group therapy for adolescent depressive disorder: A comparison of social skills and therapeutic support. *Journal of the American Academy of Child and Adolescent Psychiatry, 30,* 79–85.

Finkelhor, D. (1988). The trauma of sexual abuse: Two models. In G. E. Wyatt & G. J. Powell (Eds.) *Lasting effects of child sexual abuse* (pp. 61–82). Newbury Park, CA: Sage.

Fischer, M. (1990). Parenting stress and the child with attention deficit hyperactivity disorder. *Journal of Clinical Child Psychology, 19,* 337–346.

Firlik, A. D. (1991). Margo's logo. *Journal of the American Medical Association, 265,* 201.

Fischer, G. J. (1986). College student attitudes toward forcible date-rape: I. Cognitive predictors. *Archives of Sexual Behavior, 15,* 457–466.

Flament, M. F., Koby, E., Rapoport, J. L., Berg, C. J., Zahn, T., Cox, C., Denckla, M., & Lenane, M. (1990). Childhood obsessive-compulsive disorder: A prospective follow-up study. *Journal of Child Psychology and Psychiatry, 31,* 363–380.

Folstein, S., & Rutter, M. (1977). Infantile autism: A genetic study of 21 twin pairs. *Journal of Child Psychology and Psychiatry, 18,* 297–321.

Folstein, S., & Rutter, M. (1978). A twin study of individuals with infantile autism. In M. Rutter & E. Schopler (Eds.), *Autism: A reappraisal of concepts and treatment*. New York: Plenum.

Fossey, E., & Shapiro, C. M. (1992). Seasonality in psychiatry: A review. *Canadian Journal of Psychiatry, 37,* 299–308.

Frances, A. J., & Klein, D. F. (1982). Anxious, precise, demanding man seeks help soon after marriage. *Hospital and Community Psychiatry, 33,* 89–90.

Frances, R. J., & Widiger, T. (1986). The classification of personality disorders: An overview of problems and solutions. *Annual Review of Psychiatry, 5,* 240–257.

Frank, E., Anderson, C., & Rubinstein, D. (1978). Frequency of sexual dysfunction in "normal" couples. *New England Journal of Medicine, 299,* 111–115.

Franks, L. (1985). The story of "James B." *New York Times Magazine,* Oct. 20, p. 48.

Freeman, A., Simon, K. M., Beutler, L. E., & Arkowitz, H. (Eds.), (1989). *Comprehensive handbook of cognitive therapy.* New York: Plenum.

Freud, S. (1930). Civilization and its discontents. In J. Strachey (Ed.), *The standard edition of the complete psychological works of Sigmund Freud,* Vol. 21. London: Hogarth.

Freud, S. (1951). A letter from Freud (April 9, 1935). *American Journal of Psychiatry, 107,* 786–787.

Freud, S. (1957). (originally published 1917) Mourning and melancholia. In J. Strachey (Ed.), *The standard edition of the complete psychological works of Sigmund Freud,* vol. 14. London: Hogarth.

Freud, S. (1969). *Collected works,* Vol. 5. New York: Basic Books.

Frick, P. J. (1993). Childhood conduct problems in a family context. *School Psychology Review, 22,* 376–385.

Friedberg, J. (1977). Shock treatment, brain damage, and memory loss: A neurological perspective. *American Journal of Psychiatry, 134,* 1010–1014.

Friedman, H. S., & Booth-Kewley, S. (1987). The "disease-prone personality." *American Psychologist, 42,* 539–555.

Friedman, M., & Rosenman, R. (1974). *Type A behavior and your heart.* New York: Knopf.

Fromuth, M. E. (1986). The relationship of childhood sexual abuse with later psychological and sexual adjustment in a sample of college women. *Child Abuse and Neglect, 10,* 5–15.

Fuller, A. K. (1989). Child molestation and pedophilia: An overview for the physician. *Journal of the American Medical Association, 261,* 602–606.

Gabbard, G. O. (1985). The role of compulsiveness in the normal physician. *Journal of the American Medical Association, 254,* 2926–2929.

Garber, H. L. (1988). *The Milwaukee Project: Preventing mental retardation in children at risk.* Washington, DC: American Association on Mental Retardation.

Gardos, G., Casey, D. E., Cole, J. O., Perenyi, A., Kocsis, E., Arato, M., Samson, J. A., & Conley, C. (1994). Ten-year outcome of tardive dyskinesia. *American Journal of Psychiatry, 151,* 836–841.

Garfield, S. L. (1990). Issues and methods in psychotherapy process research. *Journal of Consulting and Clinical Psychology, 58,* 273–280.

Garfinkel, B. D., Carlson, G. A., & Weller, E. B. (1990). *Psychiatric disorders in children and adolescents.* Philadelphia: Saunders.

Garland, A. F., & Zigler, E. (1993). Adolescent suicide prevention: Current research and social policy implications. *American Psychologist, 48,* 169–182.

Garmezy, N. (1993). Children in poverty: Resilience despite risk. *Psychiatry: Interpersonal & Biological Processes, 56,* 127–136.

Gawin, F. H. (1991). Cocaine addiction: Psychology and neurophysiology. *Science, 251,* 1580–1586.

Gelder, M., Gath, D., & Mayou, R, (1989). *Oxford textbook of psychiatry,* 2nd ed. Oxford, England: Oxford University Press.

George, M. S., Ketter, T. A., & Post, R. M. (1993). SPECT and PET imaging in mood disorders. *Journal of Clinical Psychiatry, 54:* 11 (Suppl.), 6–13.

George, M. S., Ring, H. A., & Costa, D. C. (1991). *Neuroactivation and neuroimaging with SPECT.* London, England: Springer-Verlag.

Gershon, E. S., Berrettini, W. H., & Goldin, L. R. (1989). Mood disorders: Genetic aspects. In H. I. Kaplan & B. J. Sadock (Eds.), *Comprehensive textbook of psychiatry,* 5th ed. Baltimore: Williams & Wilkins.

Gershon, E. S., Hamovit, J., Guroff, J. J., Dibble, E., Leckman, J. F., Sceery, W., Targum, S. D., Nurnberger, J. I., Goldin, L. R., & Bunney, W. E., Jr. (1982). A family study of schizoaffective, bipolar I, bipolar II, unipolar and normal control probands. *Archives of General Psychiatry, 39,* 1157–1167.

Ghaemi, S. N., & Pope, H. G. (1994). Lack of insight in psychotic and affective disorders: A review of empirical studies. *Harvard Review of Psychiatry, 2,* 22–33.

Gibbons, F. X. (1985). Stigma perception: Social comparison among mentally retarded persons. *American Journal of Mental Deficiency, 90,* 98–106.

Giedd, J. N., Castellanos, F. X., Casey, B. J., Kozuch, P., King, A. C., Hamburger, S. D., & Rapoport, J. L. (1994). Quantitative morphology of the corpus callosum in attention deficit hyperactivity disorder. *American Journal of Psychiatry, 151,* 665–669.

Gill, J. J., Price, V. A., Friedman, M., Ihoresen, C. E., Powell, L. H., Ulmer, D., Brown, B., & Drews, F. R. (1985). Reduction in Type-A behavior in healthy middle-aged American military officers. *American Heart Journal, 110,* 503–514.

Gill, M., McGuffin, P., Parfitt, E., Mant, R., Asherson, P., Collier, D., Vallada, H., Powell, J., Shaika, S., Taylor, C., Sargeant, M., Clements, A., Nanko, S., Takazawa, N., Llewellyn, D., Williams, J., Whatley, S., Murray, R., & Owen, M. (1993). A linkage study of schizophrenia with DNA markers from the long arm of chromosome 11. *Psychological Medicine, 23,* 27–44.

Gittelman, R., & Klein, D. F. (1984). Relationships between separation anxiety and panic and agoraphobic disorders. *Psychopathology, 17* (Suppl.), 56–65.

Gittelman-Klein, R., & Mannuzza, S. (1988). Hyperactive boys almost grown up III. Methylphenidate effects on ultimate height. *Archives of General Psychiatry, 45,* 1131–1134.

Glaser, R., & Kiecolt-Glaser, J. (Eds.) (1994). *Handbook of human stress and immunity.* San Diego, CA: Academic Press.

Goffman, E. (1959). *The presentation of self in everyday life.* New York: Doubleday.

Gold, G. (1974). *The White House transcripts.* New York: Bantam Books.

Goldberg, T. E., Greenberg, R. D., Griffin, S. J., Gold, J. M., Kleinman, J. E., Pickar, D., Schulz, S. C., & Weinberger, D. R. (1993). The effect of clozapine on cognition and psychiatric symptoms in patients with schizophrenia. *British Journal of Psychiatry, 162,* 43–48.

Goldbloom, D. S., & Garfinkel, P. E. (1990). Eating disorders: Anorexia nervosa and bulimia nervosa. In B. D. Garfinkel, G. A. Carson, & E. B. Weller (Eds.), *Psychiatric disorders in children and adolescents.* Philadelphia: Saunders.

Golden, J. C., Graver, B., Blose, I., Berg, R., Coffman, J., & Bloch, S. (1981). Differences in brain densities between chronic alcoholic and normal control patients. *Science, 211,* 508–510.

Golden, K. M. (1977). Voodoo in Africa and the United States. *American Journal of Psychiatry, 134,* 1425–1427.

Goldfried, M. R., & Castonguay, L. G. (1993). Behavior therapy: Redefining strengths and limitations. *Behavior Therapy, 24,* 505–526.

Goldstein, M. J. (1985). Family factors that antedate the onset of schizophrenia and related disorders: The results of a fifteen-year prospective longitudinal study. *Acta Psychiatrica Scandinavica Supplementum,* No. 319, *71,* 7–18.

Goodwin, D. W. (1986). Genetic factors in the development of alcoholism. *Psychiatric Clinics of North America, 9,* 427–433.

Goodwin, F. K., & Jamison, K. R. (1987). Bipolar disorders. In R. E. Hales & A. J. Frances (Eds.), *American Psychiatric Association Annual Review,* vol. 6. Washington, DC: American Psychiatric Press.

Goodwin, F. K., & Jamison, K. R. (1990). *Manic-depressive illness.* New York: Oxford University Press.

Goodyer, I., Kolvin, I., & Gatzanis, S. (1985). Recent undesirable life events and psychiatric disorder in childhood and adolescence. *British Journal of Psychiatry, 147,* 517–523.

Gordon, C. T., Rapoport, J. L., Hamburger, S. D., & State, R. C. (1992). Differential response of seven subjects with autistic disorder to clomipramine and desipramine. *American Journal of Psychiatry, 149,* 363–366.

Gosselin, C., & Wilson, G. (1980). *Sexual variations.* New York: Simon & Schuster.

Gossop, M. Griffiths, P., Powis, B., & Strang, J. (1994). Cocaine: Patterns of use, route of administration, and severity of dependence. *British Journal of Psychiatry, 164,* 660–664.

Gostin, L. O., Lazzarini, Z., Alexander, D., Brandt, A. M., Mayer, K. H., & Silverman, D. C. (1994). HIV testing, counseling, and prophylaxis after sexual assault. *Journal of the American Medical Association, 271,* 1436–1444.

Gotlib, I. H. & Colby, C. A. (1987). *Treatment of depression.* New York: Pergamon Press.

Gotlib, I. H., & McCann, C. D. (1984). Construct accessibility and depression: An examination of cognitive and affective factors. *Journal of Personality and Social Psychology, 47,* 427–439.

Gottesman, I. I. (1991). *Schizophrenia genesis: The origins of madness.* New York: Freeman.

Gottesman, I. I., & Goldsmith, H. H. (1994). Developmental psychopathology of antisocial behavior: Inserting genes into its ontogenesis and epigenesis. In C. A. Nelson (Ed.), *Threats to optimal development: Integrating biological, psychological, and social risk factors.* Hillsdale, NJ: Lawrence Erlbaum.

Gottlieb, J., Semmel, M. I., & Veldman, D. J. (1978). Correlates of social status among mainstreamed mentally retarded children. *Journal of Educational Psychology, 70,* 396–405.

Graham, J. R. (1993). *MMPI-2: Assessing personality and psychopathology* (2nd ed.). New York: Oxford University Press.

Grandin, T. (1984). My experiences as an autistic child and review of selected literature. *Journal of Orthomolecular Psychiatry, 13,* 144–174.

Grandin, T. (1987). Motivating autistic children. *Academic Therapy, 22(3),* 297–302.

Grandin, T. (1991). Overcoming autism: A first person account. *Harvard Mental Health Letter,* March 4–7.

Grant, B. F. (1992). Prevalence of the proposed DSM-IV alcohol use disorders: United States, 1988. *British Journal of Addiction, 87,* 309–316.

Grauwe, K. (1987). *The Bern meta-analysis of outcome studies: Dynamic vs. non-dynamic therapies.* Paper presented at the meeting of the Society for Psychotherapy Research, Ulm, Germany.

Green, E. (1972). Biofeedback for mind/body self-regulation: Feeling and creativity. *Biofeedback and self-control.* Chicago: Aldine.

Green, M. F. (1993). Cognitive remediation in schizophrenia: Is it time yet? *American Journal of Psychiatry, 150,* 178–187.

Green, R. (1974). *Sexual identity conflicts in children and adults.* New York: Basic Books.

Green, R. (1987). *The "sissy boy syndrome" and the development of homosexuality.* New Haven: Yale University Press.

Greenberg, R. P., Bornstein, R. F., Greenberg, M. D., & Fisher, S. (1992). A meta-analysis of antidepressant outcome under "blinder" conditions. *Journal of Consulting and Clinical Psychology, 60,* 664–669.

Greenfeld, J. A. (1970). A child called Noah. *Life,* October 26, 60–72.

Grillon, C., Courchesne, E., Ameli, R., Geyer, M. A., & Braff, D. L. (1990). Increased distractibility in schizophrenic patients. *Archives of General Psychiatry, 47,* 171–179.

Grilly, D. (1989). *Drugs and human behavior.* Boston: Allyn and Bacon.

Grinker, R. (1979). *Historical perspectives on depression.* Roche Laboratories Professional Services Department.

Grove, W. M., Clementz, B. A., Iacono, W. G., & Katsanis, J. (1992). Smooth pursuit ocular motor dysfunction in schizophrenia: Evidence for a major gene. *American Journal of Psychiatry, 149,* 1362–1368.

Gudeman, J. E., Dickey, B., Hellman, S., & Buffett, W. (1985). From inpatient to inn status: A new residential model. *Psychiatric Clinics of North America, 8,* 461–469.

Guillen, T. (1982). Competency ruling frees Safety Building squatter. *Seattle Times,* Jan. 27, B1.

Gunderson, J. G. (1984). *Borderline Personality Disorder.* Washington, DC: American Psychiatric Press.

Gunderson, J. G., Ronningstam, E., & Bodkin, A. (1990). The diagnostic interview for narcissistic patients. *Archives of General Psychiatry, 47,* 676–680.

Gunderson, J. G., & Zanarini, M. C. (1987). Current overview of the borderline diagnosis. *Journal of Clinical Psychiatry, 48(8)* (Supplement), 5–11.

Gusella, J. F., & MacDonald, M. E. (1994). Huntington's disease and repeating trinucleotides. *New England Journal of Medicine, 330,* 1450–1451.

Guze, B. H., Baxter, L. R., Schwartz, J. M., Szuba, M. P., & Liston, E. H. (1991). Electroconvulsive therapy and brain glucose metabolism. *Convulsive Therapy, 7,* 15–19.

Haaga, D. A. (1987). Treatment of the Type A behavior pattern. *Clinical Psychology Review, 7,* 557–574.

Haaga, D. F., Dyck, M. J., & Ernst, D. (1991). Empirical status of cognitive theory of depression. *Psychological Bulletin, 110,* 215–236.

Hackett, T. P., & Cassem, N. H. (1975). The psychologic reactions of patients in the pre- and post-hospital phases of myocardial infarction. *Postgraduate Medicine, 57,* 43–46.

Hagnell, O., & Rorsman, B. (1980). Suicide in the Lunby study: A controlled prospective investigation of stressful life events. *Neuropsychobiology, 6,* 319–322.

Hall, G. C. (1990). Prediction of sexual aggression. *Clinical Psychology Review, 10(2),* 229–245.

Hamer, D. H., Hu, S., Magnuson, V. L., Hu, N., & Pattatucci, A. (1993). A linkage between DNA markers on the X chromosome and male sexual orientation. *Science, 261*, 321–327.

Hamilton, E., & Abramson, L. 1983. Cognitive patterns and major-depressive disorders: A longitudinal study in a hospital setting. *Journal of Abnormal Psychology, 92*, 173–184.

Hamilton, M. (1982). Symptoms and assessment of depression. In E. S. Paykel (Ed.), *Handbook of affective disorders*. Edinburgh: Churchill-Livingston.

Hamilton, M. (1989). Mood disorders: Clinical features. In H. I. Kaplan & B. J. Sadock (Eds.), *Comprehensive textbook of psychiatry*, 5th ed. Baltimore: Williams and Wilkins.

Hammen, C. (1992). Cognitive, life stress, and interpersonal approaches to a developmental psychopathology model of depression. *Development and Psychopathology, 4*, 189–206.

Hammond, L. K., & Deluty, R. H. (June, 1991). *Attitudes of clinical psychologists, psychiatrists, and oncologists toward suicide*. Paper presented at the annual meeting of the American Association of Applied and Preventive Psychology, Washington, DC.

Hansen, D. J., Conaway, L. P., & Christopher, J. S. (1990). Victims of child physical abuse. In R. T. Ammerman & M. Hersen (Eds.), *Treatment of family violence: A sourcebook* (pp. 17–49). New York: John Wiley.

Hansson, R. O., & Carpenter, B. N. (1994). *Relationships in old age*. New York: Guilford.

Harding, C. M., Brooks, G. W., Ashikaga, T., Strauss, J. S., & Breier, A. (1987a). The Vermont longitudinal study of persons with severe mental illness, I: Methodology, study sample and overall status 32 years later. *American Journal of Psychiatry, 144*, 718–726.

Harding, C. M., Zubin, J., & Strauss, J. S. (1987b). Chronicity in schizophrenia: Fact, partial fact or artifact. *Hospital and Community Psychiatry, 38*, 477–486.

Hare, R. D., & Forth, A. E. (1985). Psychopathy and lateral preferences. *Journal of Abnormal Psychology, 94*, 541–546.

Harrington, R., Fudge, H., Rutter, M., Pickles, A., & Hill, J. (1990). Adult outcomes of childhood and adolescent depression. *Archives of General Psychiatry, 47*, 465–473.

Harris, T. O. (1992). Social support and unsupportive behaviors. In H. O. F. Veiel & U. Baumann (Eds.), *The meaning and measurement of social support* (pp. 171–192). New York: Hemisphere.

Harrow, M., Goldberg, J. F., Grossman, L. S., & Meltzer, H. Y. (1990). Outcome in manic disorders: A naturalistic follow-up study. *Archives of General Psychiatry, 47*, 666–671.

Hart, C. (1989). *Without reason*. New York: Harper and Row.

Hartsough, C. S., & Lambert, N. M. (1985). Medical factors in hyperactive and normal children: Prenatal, developmental and health history findings. *American Journal of Orthopsychiatry, 55*, 190–201.

Harvard Mental Health Letter. (1990). Panic disorder: Part I. Boston. 7(3), 1.

Hasin, D. S., Grant, B., & Endicott, J. (1990). The natural history of alcohol abuse: Implications for definitions of alcohol use disorders. *American Journal of Psychiatry, 147*, 1537–1541.

Hattie, J. A., Sharpley, C. F., & Rogers, H. J. (1984). Comparative effectiveness of professional and paraprofessional helpers. *Psychological Bulletin, 95*, 534–541.

Hawkins, J. D., Catalano, R. E., & Miller, J. Y. (1992). Risk and protective factors for alcohol and other drug problems in adolescence and early adulthood: Implications for substance abuse prevention. *Psychological Bulletin, 112*, 64–105.

Hay, D. P., & Hay, L. K. (1990). The role of ECT in the treatment of depression. In C. D. McCann & N. S. Endler (Eds.), *Depression: New directions in theory, research, and practice*. 255–272. Toronto: Wall & Emerson.

Hayden, M. R. (1991). *Predictive testing for Huntington's disease*. Paper presented at the International Congress of Human Genetics in Washington, DC.

Haynes, S. G., Feinleib, M., & Kannel, W. B. (1980). The relationship of psychological factors to coronary heart disease in the Framingham study: III. Eight-year incidence of coronary heart disease. *American Journal of Epidemiology, 111*, 37–58.

Hazelrigg, M. D., Cooper, H. M., & Borduin, C. M. (1987). Evaluating the effectiveness of family therapies: An integrative review and analysis. *Psychological Bulletin, 101*, 428–442.

Hazlett, B. (1971). Two who played with death—and lost the game. *Los Angeles Times*, November 1, 5.

Heatherton, T. F., & Baumeister, R. F. (1991). Binge eating as escape from self-awareness. *Psychological Bulletin, 110*, 86–108.

Hecht, H., von Zerssen, D., Krieg, C., Possi, J., & Witchen, H. (1989). Anxiety and depression: Comorbidity, psychopathology, and social functioning. *Comprehensive Psychiatry, 30*, 420–433.

Heikkinen, M., Aro, H., & Lonnqvist, J. (1993). Life events and social support in suicide. *Suicide and Life-Threatening Behavior, 23*, 343–358.

Helzer, J. E., Robins, L. N., & McEvoy, L. (1987). Posttraumatic stress-disorder in the general population. *New England Journal of Medicine, 317*, 1630–1634.

Helzer, J. E., Robins, L. N., McEvoy, L. T., Spitznagel, E. L., Stolzman, R. K., & Farmer, A. (1985). A comparison of clinical and diagnostic interview schedule diagnoses. *Archives of General Psychiatry, 42*, 657–666.

Helzer, J. E., Spitznagel, E. L., & McEvoy, L. (1987). The predictive validity of lay diagnostic interview schedule diagnoses in the general population. *Archives of General Psychiatry, 44*, 1069–1077.

Henderson, A. S. (1992). Social support and depression. In H. O. F. Veiel & U. Baumann (Eds.), *The meaning and measurement of social support* (pp. 85–92). New York: Hemisphere.

Henker, B., & Whalen, C. K. (1989). Hyperactivity and attention deficits. *American Psychologist, 44*, 216–223.

Herbert, T. B., & Cohen, S. (1993). Depression and immunity: A meta-analytic review. *Psychological Bulletin, 113*, 472–486.

Herbert, T. B., & Cohen, S. (1993). Stress and immunity in humans: A meta-analytic review. *Psychosomatic Medicine, 55*, 364–379.

Hermann, B. P., Whitman, S., Wyler, A. R., Anton, M. T., & Vanderzwagg, R. (1990). Psychosocial predictors of psychopathology in epilepsy. *British Journal of Psychiatry, 156*, 98–105.

Herold, E. S., & Way, L. (1983). Oral-genital sexual behavior in a sample of university females. *Journal of Sex Research, 19*, 327–338.

Hersen, M., Gullick, E. L., Matherne, P. M., & Harbert, T. L. (1972). Instructions and reinforcement in the modification of a conversion reaction. *Psychological Reports, 31*, 719–722.

Heston, L. L., & Mastri, A. R. (1982). Age of onset of Pick's and Alzheimer's dementia: Implications for diagnosis and research. *Journal of Gerontology, 37*, 422–424.

Heston, L. L., & White, J. (1991). *The vanishing mind: A practical guide to Alzheimer's disease and other dementias.* New York: W. H. Freeman.

Heston, L. L., White, J. A., & Mastri, A. R. (1987). Pick's disease. *Archives of General Psychiatry, 44,* 409–411.

Hetherington, E. M. (1991). The role of individual differences and family relationships in children's coping with divorce and remarriage. In P. A. Cowan & E. M. Hetherington (Eds.), *Family transitions.* Hillsdale, NJ: Lawrence Erlbaum Associates.

Higley, J. D., Hasert, M. F., Suomi, S. J., & Linnoila, M. (1991). *Nonhuman primate model of alcohol abuse: Effects of early experience, personality, and stress on alcohol consumption.* Proceedings of the National Academy of Sciences of the United States of America.

Hilgard, E. R. (1986). *Divided consciousness.* New York: John Wiley.

Hinshaw, S. P., Lahey, B. B., & Hart, E. L. (1993). Issues of taxonomy and comorbidity in the development of conduct disorder. *Development and Psychopathology, 5,* 31–49.

Hinz, L. D., & Williamson, D. A. (1987). Bulimia and depression: A review of the affective variant hypothesis. *Psychological Bulletin, 102,* 150–158.

Hirschfeld, R. M. A., Shea, M. T., & Weise, R. (1991). Dependent personality disorder: Perspectives for DSM-IV. *Journal of Personality Disorders, 5,* 135–149.

Hobson, R. P. (1989). Beyond cognition: A theory of autism. In G. Dawson (Ed.), *Autism: Nature, diagnosis, and treatment.* New York: Guilford.

Hodgkinson, P. E., & Stewart, M. (1991). *Coping with catastrophe.* London, England: Routledge.

Hoenig, J. (1984). Schneider's first rank symptoms and the tabulators. *Comprehensive Psychiatry, 25,* 77–87.

Hofer, M. A. (1984). Relationships as regulators: A psychobiologic perspective on bereavement. *Psychosomatic Medicine, 46,* 183–197.

Hoffman, A. (1971). LSD discoverer disputes "chance factor" in finding. *Psychiatric News, 16,* 23–26.

Hogarty, G. E., Anderson, C. M., Reiss, D. J., Kornblith, S. J., Greenwald, D. P., Javna, C. D., Madonia, M. J., & the EPICS Schizophrenia Research Group. (1986). Family psychoeducation, social skills training, and maintenance chemotherapy in the aftercare treatment of schizophrenia I. *Archives of General Psychiatry, 43,* 633–642.

Holland, A., & Gosden, C. (1990). A balanced chromosomal translocation partially co-segregating with psychotic illness in a family. *Psychiatry Research, 32,* 1–8.

Hollon, S. D., & Beck, A. T. (1994). Cognitive and cognitive-behavioral therapies. In A. E. Bergin and S. L. Garfield (Eds.), *Handbook of psychotherapy and behavior change* (4th ed.) (pp. 428–466). New York: John Wiley.

Hollon, S. D., & Kendall, P. C. (1980). Cognitive self-statements in depression: Development of an automatic thoughts questionnaire. *Cognitive Therapy and Research, 4,* 383–396.

Hollon, S. D., DeRubeis, R. J., Evans, M. D., Wiemer, M. J., Garvey, M. J., Grove, W. M., & Tuason, V. B. (1992). Cognitive therapy and pharmacotherapy for depression. *Archives of General Psychiatry, 49,* 774–781.

Holzman, P. S. (1978). Cognitive impairment and cognitive stability: Toward a theory of thought disorder. In G. Serban (Ed.), *Cognitive defects in the development of mental illness.* New York: Brunner/Mazel.

Holzman, P. S., Kringlen, E., Matthysse, S., Flanagan, S. D., Lipton, R. B., Cramer, S., Levin, S., Lange, K., & Levy, D. L. (1988). A single dominant gene can account for eye tracking dysfunctions and schizophrenia in offspring of discordant twins. *Archives of General Psychiatry, 45,* 641–647.

Hooley, J. M. (1985). Expressed emotion: A critical review of the literature. *Clinical Psychology Review, 5,* 119–139.

Horne, J. (1979). Defendant found guilty of murdering jogger. *Seattle Times,* May 31, C11.

Horowitz, M. J. (1974). Stress response syndromes. *Archives of General Psychiatry, 31,* 768–781.

Horowitz, M. J. (1986). Stress-response syndromes: A review of posttraumatic and adjustment disorders. *Hospital and Community Psychiatry, 37,* 241–249.

Horvath, T. B., Siever, L. J., Mohs, R. C., & Davis, K. (1989). Organic mental syndromes and disorders. In H. I. Kaplan & B. J. Sadock (Eds.), *Comprehensive textbook of psychiatry,* 5th ed. Baltimore: Williams and Wilkins.

Horwitz, A. V. (1984). The economy and social pathology. *Annual Review of Sociology, 10,* 95–119.

Houghton, J. F. (1980). One personal experience: Before and after mental illness. In J. G. Rabkin, L. Gelb, & J. B. Lazar (Eds.), *Attitudes toward the mentally ill: Research perspectives.* Rockville, MD: National Institute of Mental Health.

Houghton, J. F. (1982). First person account: Maintaining mental health in a turbulent world. *Schizophrenia Bulletin, 8,* 548–552.

Howland, R. H., & Thase, M. E. (1993). A comprehensive review of cyclothymic disorder. *The Journal of Nervous and Mental Disease, 181,* 485–493.

Howland, R. H., & Thase, M. E. (1991). Biological studies of dysthymia. *Biological Psychiatry, 30,* 283–304.

Hoza, B., Pelham, W. E., Milich, R., Pillow, D., & McBride, K. (1993). The self-perceptions and attributions of attention deficit hyperactivity disordered and nonreferred boys. *Journal of Abnormal Child Psychology, 21,* 271–286.

Hser, Y. I., Anglin, M. D., & Powers, K. (1993). A 24-year follow-up of California narcotics addicts. *Archives of General Psychiatry, 50,* 577–584.

Hurley, D. J. (1991). The crisis of paternal suicide: Case of Cathy, age 4-1/2. In N. B. Webb (Ed.), *Play therapy with children in crisis* (pp. 237–253). New York: Guilford.

Hurt, S. W., & Clarkin, J. F. (1990). Borderline personality disorder: Prototypic typology and the development of treatment manuals. *Psychiatric Annals, 20,* 13–18.

Hyde, J. S. (1994). *Understanding human sexuality.* New York: McGraw-Hill.

Hynd, G. W., Hern, K. L., Voeller, K. K., & Marshall, R. M. (1991). Neurobiological basis of attention-deficit hyperactivity disorder (ADHD). *School Psychology Review, 20,* 174–186.

Hynd, G. W., Semrud-Clikeman, M., Lorys, A. R., Novery, E. S., & Eliopulos, D. (1991). Corpus callosum morphology in attention deficit-hyperactivity disorder (ADHD): Morphometric analysis of MRI. *Journal of Learning Disabilities, 24,* 141–146.

Iacono, W. G., & Clementz, B. A. (1993). A strategy for elucidating genetic influences on complex psychopathological syndromes (with special reference to ocular motor functioning and schizophrenia). In L. J. Chapman, J. P. Chapman, & D. C. Fowles (Eds.) *Progress in experimental psychopathology research* Vol. 16, (pp. 11–65). New York: Springer.

Iacono, W. G., & Koenig, W. G. R. (1983). Features that distinguish the smooth-pursuit eye-tracking performance of schizophrenic, affective disorder, and normal individuals. *Journal of Abnormal Psychology, 92,* 29–41.

Ilardi, S. S., & Craighead, W. E. (1994). The role of nonspecific factors in cognitive-behavior therapy for depression. *Clinical Psychology, 1,* 138–156.

Institute of Medicine (1990). *Research on children and adolescents with mental, behavioral, and developmental disorders.* Rockville, MD: National Institute of Mental Health.

Institute of Medicine (1994). *Reducing risks for mental disorders: Frontiers for preventive intervention research.* Washington, DC: National Academy Press.

Jackson, J. S. (Ed.) (1991). *Life in Black America.* Newbury Park, CA: Sage.

Jacob, R. G., Wing, R., & Shapiro, A. P. (1987). The behavioral treatment of hypertension: Long-term effects. *Behavior Therapy, 18,* 325–352.

Jacobs, B. L. (1994). Serotonin, motor activity and depression-related disorders. *American Scientist, 82,* 456–463.

Jacobson, N. S., & Addis, M. E. (1993). Research on couples and couple therapy: What do we know? Where are we going? *Journal of Consulting and Clinical Psychology, 61,* 85–93.

Jaffee, J. H. (1985). Opioid dependence. In H. I. Kaplan & B. J. Sadock (Eds.), *Comprehensive textbook of psychiatry,* 4th ed., vol. 1. Baltimore: Williams and Wilkins.

Jaffee, J. H. (1989). Drug dependence: Opioids, nonnarcotics, nicotine (tobacco), and caffeine. In H. I. Kaplan & B. J. Sadock (Eds.), *Comprehensive textbook of psychiatry, 5th ed.* Baltimore: Williams and Wilkins.

Jamison, K. R. (1989). Mood disorders and seasonal patterns in British writers and artists. *Psychiatry, 52,* 125–134.

Jeffries, J. J. (1993). Ethical issues in drug selection for schizophrenia. *Canadian Journal of Psychiatry, 38,* Supplement 3, S70–S74.

Jellinek, E. M. (1960). *The disease concept of alcoholism.* New Haven: Hillhouse Press.

Jemmott, J. B., III, & Locke, S. E. (1984). Psychosocial factors, immunologic mediation, and human susceptibility to infectious diseases: How much do we know? *Psychological Bulletin, 95,* 78–108.

Jenkins, J. H., Karno, M. N., de la Selva, A., Santana, F., Tellis, C., Lopez, S., & Mintz, J. (1986). Expressed emotion, maintenance psychotherapy and schizophrenic relapse among Mexican-Americans. *Psychopharmacology Bulletin, 22,* 621–627.

Jenkins, J. H., Kleinman, A., & Good, B. J. (1991). Cross-cultural studies of depression. In J. Becker and A. Kleinman (Eds.), *Psychosocial aspects of depression.* Hillsdale, NJ: Lawrence Erlbaum.

Jensen, P. S., Bloedau, L., Degroot, J., Ussery, T., & Davis, H. (1990). Children at risk: I. Risk factors and child symptomatology. *Journal of American Academy of Child Adolescent Psychiatry, 29,* 51–59.

Johnson, J., Weissman, M. M., & Klerman, G. L. (1990). Panic-disorder, comorbidity, and suicide attempts. *Archives of General Psychiatry, 47,* 805–808.

Johnstone, E. C., & Geddes, J. (1994). How high is the relapse rate in schizophrenia? *Acta Psychiatrica Scandinavica Supplementum, 382,* 6–10.

Jones, M. C. (1981). Midlife drinking patterns. Correlates and antecedents. In D. H. Eichorn (Ed.), *Present and past in middle life.* New York: Academic Press, 223–242.

Joseph, J. G., Caumartin, S. M., Margalittal, M. P. H., Kirscht, J. P., Kessler, R. C., Ostrow, D. G., & Wortman, C. B. (1990). Psychological functioning in a cohort of gay men at risk for AIDS: A three-year descriptive study. *The Journal of Nervous and Mental Disease, 178,* 607–615.

Judd, L. L. (1990). Putting mental health on the nation's agenda. *Hospital and Community Psychiatry, 41,* 131–134.

Julien, R. M. (1992). *A primer of drug action,* 6th ed. New York: Freeman.

Kane, J. M. (1993). Understanding and treating psychoses: Advances in research and therapy. *Journal of Clinical Psychiatry, 54,* 445–452.

Kane, J. M. (1994). Efficacy, mechanisms, and side effects of typical and atypical neuroleptics. In N. C. Andreason (Ed.), *Schizophrenia: From mind to molecule* (pp. 173–188). Washington, DC: American Psychiatric Press.

Kaplan, H. S. (1974). *The new sex therapy: Active treatment of sexual dysfunctions.* New York: Quadrangle Books.

Kaplan, H. S. (1979). *Disorders of sexual desire.* New York: Simon & Schuster.

Kapur, S., Mieczkowski, T., & Mann, J. J. (1992). Antidepressant medications and the relative risk of suicide attempt and suicide. *Journal of the American Medical Association, 268,* 3441–3445.

Kaslow, N. J., Doepke, K. J., & Racusin, G. R. (1994). Depression. In V. B. VanHasselt & M. Hersen (Eds.), *Advanced abnormal psychology.* New York: Plenum Press.

Kaufman, A. S. (1990). *Assessing adolescent and adult intelligence.* Boston: Allyn & Bacon.

Kaufman, A. S., & Kaufman, N. L. (1983). *Kaufman Assessment Battery for Children: Interpretive manual.* Circle Pines, NM: American Guidance Service.

Kaufman, M. J., Agard, J. A., & Semmel, M. I. (1982). *Mainstreaming: Learners and their environments.* Baltimore: University Park Press.

Kawachi, I., Colditz, G. A., Ascherio, A., Rimm, E. B., Giovannucci, E., Stampfer, M. J., & Willett, W. C. (1994). Prospective study of phobic anxiety and risk of coronary heart disease in men. *Circulation, 89,* 1992–1997.

Kaye, W. H., Weltzin, T. E., Hsu, L. K., & Bulik, C. M. (1991). An open trial of fluoxetine in patients with anorexia nervosa. *Journal of Clinical Psychiatry, 52,* 464–471.

Kazdin, A. E. (1995). Methods of psychotherapy research. In B. Bongar and L. E. Beutler (Eds.), *Comprehensive textbook of psychotherapy: Theory and practice* (pp. 405–433). New York: Oxford University Press.

Keen, J. (1993). Dementia: Questions of cost and value. *International Journal of Geriatric Psychiatry, 8,* 369–378.

Kegan, R. G. (1986). The child behind the mask: Sociopathy as developmental delay. In W. H. Reid, D. Dorr, J. I. Walker, & J. W. Bonner (Eds.), *Unmasking the Psychopath.* New York: W. W. Norton.

Keith, S. J., Regier, D. A., & Rae, D. S. (1991). Schizophrenic disorders. In L. N. Robins & D. A. Regier (Eds.), *Psychiatric disorders in America: The epidemiological catchment area study.* New York: The Free Press.

Keller, M. B. (1990). Diagnostic and course of illness variables pertinent to refractory depression. In A. Tasman, S. M.

Goldfinger, & C. A. Kaufmann, *Review of Psychiatry* (vol. 9). Washington, DC: American Psychiatric Press.

Kelly, G. A. (1955). *The psychology of personal constructs* (vols. 1 & 2). New York: W. W. Norton.

Kendall-Tackett, K. A., Williams, L. M., & Finkelhor, D. (1993). Impact of sexual abuse on children: A review and synthesis of recent empirical studies. *Psychological Bulletin, 113*, 164–180.

Kendall, P. C., Reber, M., McLeer, S., Epps, J., & Ronan, K. R. (1990). Cognitive-behavioral treatment of conduct-disordered children. *Cognitive Therapy and Research, 14*, 279–289.

Kendall, P. C., & Wilcox, L. E. (1978). Self-control in children: Development of a rating scale. *Journal of Consulting and Clinical Psychology, 47*, 1020–1029.

Kendell, R. E. (1983). Schizophrenia. In R. E. Kendall & A. K. Zealley (Eds.), *Companion to psychiatric studies*. Edinburgh: Churchill Livingstone.

Kendler, K. S., & Diehl, S. R. (1993). The genetics of schizophrenia: A current genetic-epidemiological perspective. *Schizophrenia Bulletin, 19*, 261–285.

Kendler, K. S., Gruenberg, M., & Tsuang, M. T. (1985). Psychiatric illness in first-degree relatives of schizophrenic and surgical control patients. *Archives of General Psychiatry, 42*, 770–779.

Kendler, K. S., Heath, A., Martin, N. G., & Eaves, L. J. (1986). Symptoms of anxiety and depression in a volunteer twin population: The etiologic role of genetic and environmental factors. *Archives of General Psychiatry, 43*, 213–221.

Kendler, K. S., Neale, M. C., Kessler, R. C., Heath, A. C., & Eaves, L. J. (1992). Familial influences on the clinical characteristics of major depression: A twin study. *Acta Psychiatrica Scandinavica, 86*, 371–378.

Kendler, K. S., Neale, M. C., Kessler, R. C., Heath, A. C., & Eaves, L. J. (1993). A twin study of recent life events and difficulties. *Archives of General Psychiatry, 50*, 789–796.

Kennedy, S., Kiecolt-Glaser, J. K., & Glaser, R. (1990). Social support, stress, and the immune system. In B. R. Sarason, I. G. Sarason, & G. R. Pierce (Eds.), *Social support: An interactional view*. New York: John Wiley.

Kenyon, K. (1979). A survivor's notes. *Newsweek*, April 30, 17–B10.

Kernberg, O. F. (1975). *Borderline conditions and pathological narcissism*. New York: Jason Aronson.

Kessler, R. C., McGonagle, K. A., Zhao, S., Nelson, C. B., Hugh, M., Eshleman, S., Wittchen, H. U., & Kendler, K. S. (1994). Lifetime and 12-month prevalence of DSM-III-R psychiatric disorders in the United States. *Archives of General Psychiatry, 51*, 8–19.

Kety, S. S., Rosenthal, D., Wender, P. H., Schulsinger, F., & Jacobson, B. (1978). The biological and adoptive families of adopted individuals who become schizophrenic: Prevalence of mental illness and other characteristics. In L. C. Wynne, R. L. Cromwell, & S. Matthysse (Eds.), *The nature of schizophrenia: New approaches to research and treatment*. New York: Wiley.

Kety, S. S., Wender, P. H., Jacobsen, B., Ingraham, L. J., Rosenthal, D., Jannson, L., Faber, B., & Kinney, D. (1994). Mental illness in the biological and adoptive relatives of the schizophrenic adoptees. Replication of the Copenhagen Study in the rest of Denmark. *Archives of General Psychiatry, 51*, 442–455.

Khan, A., Mirolo, M. H., Hughes, D., & Bierut, L. (1993). Electroconvulsive therapy. *Psychopharmacology, 16*, 497–513.

Kiecolt-Glaser, J. K., & Glaser, R. (1992). Stress and the immune system: Human studies. In A. Tasman and M. B. Riba (Eds.), *Review of Psychiatry* (Vol. 11, pp. 169–179). Washington, DC: American Psychiatric Press.

Killian, K. D. (1994). Fearing fat: A literature review of family systems understandings and treatments of anorexia and bulimia. *Family Relations, 43*, 311–318.

Kilmann, P. R., Sabalis, R. F., Gearing, M. I., Bukstel, L. H., & Scovern, A. W. (1982). The treatment of sexual paraphilias: A review of outcome research. *Journal of Sex Research, 18*, 193–252.

King, N. J., Ollier, K., Iacuone, R., Schuster, S., Bays, K., Gullione, E., & Ollendick, T. H. (1989). Fears of children and adolescents: A cross-sectional Australian study using the Revised Fear Survey Schedule for children. *Journal of Child Psychology and Psychiatry, 30*, 775–784.

Kirmayer, L. J., Robbins, J. M., & Paris, J. (1994). Somatoform disorders: Personality and the social matrix of somatic distress. *Journal of Abnormal Psychology, 103*, 125–136.

Kivlahan, D. R., Marlatt, G. A., Fromme, K., Coppel, D. B., & Williams, E. (1990). Secondary prevention with college drinkers: Evaluations of an alcohol skills training program. *Journal of Consulting and Clinical Psychology, 58*, 805–810.

Klein, M. H., Benjamin, L. S., Rosenfeld, R., Treece, C., Husted, J., & Greist, J. H. (1993). The Wisconsin Personality Disorders Inventory: Development, reliability, and validity. *Journal of Personality Disorders, 7*, 285–303.

Klerman, G. L., Weissman, M. M., Ouellette, R., Johnson, J., & Greenwald, S. (1991). Panic attacks in the community: Social morbidity and health care utilization. *Journal of the American Medical Association, 265*, 742–746.

Klerman, G. L., Weissman, M. M., Rounsaville, B. J., & Chevron, E. S. (1984). *Interpersonal therapy of depression*. New York: Academic Press.

Klinterberg, B. A., Andersson, T., Magnusson, D., & Stattin, H. (1993). Hyperactive behavior in childhood as related to subsequent alcohol problems and violent offending: A longitudinal study of male subjects. *Personality and Individual Differences, 15*, 381–388.

Klorman, R., Burmaghin, J. T., Fitzpatrick, M. A., & Borgstedt, A. D. (1990). Clinical effects of a controlled trial of methylphenidate on adolescents with attention deficit disorder. *Journal of the American Academy of Child and Adolescent Psychiatry, 26*, 702–709.

Kluft, R. P. (1988). The dissociative disorders. In J. A. Talbott, R. E. Hales, & S. C. Yudofsky (Eds.), *The American Psychiatric Association textbook of psychiatry*. Washington, DC: American Psychiatric Press.

Kluft, R. P. (1991). Multiple personality disorder. In A. Tasman & S. M. Goldfinger (Eds.), *Review of psychiatry* (vol. 10). Washington, DC: American Psychiatric Press.

Kneip, R. C., Delamater, A. M., Ismond, T., Milford, C., Salvia, L., & Schwartz, D. (1993). Self- and spouse ratings of anger and hostility as predictors of coronary heart disease. *Health Psychology, 12*, 301–307.

Knowles, P. A. L., & Prutsman, T. D. (1968). *The case of Benjie*. Unpublished manuscript, Florida Atlantic University.

Koegel, L. K., Valdez-Menchaca, M. C., & Koegel, R. L. (1994). Autism: Social communication difficulties and related behaviors. In V. B. Van Hasselt and M. Hersen (Eds.), *Advanced Abnormal Psychology*. New York: Plenum Press.

Koenigsberg, H. W. (1993). Combining psychotherapy and pharmacotherapy in the treatment of borderline disorders. In J. M. Oldham, M. B. Riba, and A. Tasman (Eds.), *Review of Psychiatry* (vol. 12). Washington, DC: American Psychiatric Press.

Kog, E., & Vandereycken, W. (1985). Family characteristics of anorexia nervosa and bulimia: A review of the research literature. *Clinical Psychology Review, 5,* 159–180.

Kog, E., & Vandereycken, W. (1989). Family interaction in eating disorder patients and normal controls. *International Journal of Eating Disorders, 8,* 11–23.

Kolata, G. (1987). The poignant thoughts of Down's children are given voice. *New York Times,* December 22, 15.

Kolb, L. D., & Brodie, H. K. H. (1982). *Modern clinical psychiatry,* 10th ed. Philadelphia: W. B. Saunders.

Konner, M. (1989). Homosexuality: Who and why? *New York Times Magazine,* April 2, 60–61.

Koopman, C., Classen, C., & Spiegel, D. (1994). Predictors of posttraumatic stress symptoms among survivors of the Oakland/Berkeley, California, firestorm. *American Journal of Psychiatry, 15,* 888–894.

Korenman, L. G., & Barchas, J. D. (Eds.) (1993). *Biological basis of substance abuse.* New York: Oxford University Press.

Koss, M. P. (1993). Detecting the scope of rape: A review of prevalence research methods. *Journal of Interpersonal Violence, 8,* 198–222.

Koss, M. P., & Oros, C. J. (1982). Sexual experiences survey: A research instrument investigating sexual aggression and victimization. *Journal of Consulting and Clinical Psychology, 50,* 455–457.

Kosten, T. R., & Rounsaville, B. J. (1986). Psychopathology in opioid addicts. *Psychiatric Clinics of North America, 9,* 515–532.

Kosten, T. R., Rounsaville, B. J., & Kleber, H. D. (1987). Multidimensionality and prediction of treatment outcome in opioid addicts: 2.5-year follow-up. *Comprehensive Psychiatry, 28,* 3–13.

Kovacs, M. (1985). The natural history and course of depressive disorders in childhood. *Psychiatric Annals, 15,* 387–389.

Kovacs, M., & Beck, A. T. (1977). An empirical-clinical approach toward a definition of childhood depression. In J. G. Schulterbrandt & A. Raskin (Eds.), *Depression in childhood: Diagnosing treatment and conceptual models.* New York: Raven Press.

Kovacs, M., & Goldston, D. (1991). Cognitive and social cognitive development in depressed children and adolescents. *Journal of the American Academy of Childhood and Adolescent Psychiatry, 30,* 388–392.

Kraepelin, E. 1909–1913. *Psychiatrie,* 8th ed. Leipzig: J. A. Barth.

Kraepelin, E. (1921). *Clinical psychiatry: A textbook for students and physicians.* Trans. A. R. Desfendorf. New York: Macmillan.

Krakowski, A. J. (1982). Stress and the practice of medicine: II. Stressors, stresses, and strains. *Psychotherapy and Psychosomatics, 38,* 11–23.

Kramer, J. J. (1990). Training parents as behavior change agents: Successes, failures, and suggestions for school psychologists. In T. B. Gutkin & C. R. Reynolds (Eds.), *Handbook of school psychology.* New York: John Wiley.

Kringlen, E. (1981). Stress and coronary heart disease. *Twin Research 3: Epidemiological and clinical studies.* New York: Alan R. Liss.

Kupfer, D. J., Ulrich, R. F., Coble, P. A., Jarrett, D. B., Grochocinski, V. J., Doman, J., Matthews, G., & Borbely, A. A. (1985). Electroencephalographic sleep of younger depressives. *Archives of General Psychiatry, 42,* 806–810.

Lacks, P. (1984). *Bender-Gestalt screening for brain dysfunction.* New York: John Wiley.

Laffal, J. (1965). *Pathological and normal language.* New York: Atherton.

Lagreca, A. M., Stone, W. L., & Bell, C. R., III. (1983). Facilitating the vocational-interpersonal skills of mentally retarded individuals. *American Journal of Mental Deficiency, 88,* 270–278.

Lahey, B. B., Applegate, B., McBurnett, K., Biederman, J., Greenhill, L., Hynd, G. W., Barkley, R. A., Newcorn, J., Jensen, P., Richters, J., et al. (1994). DSM-IV field trials for attention deficit hyperactivity disorder in children and adolescents. *American Journal of Psychiatry, 151,* 1673–1685.

Lahey, B. B., Carlson, C. L., & Frick, P. J. (1994). Attention deficit disorder without hyperactivity: A review of research relevant to DSM-IV. In T. A. Widiger, A. J. Frances, W. Davis, & M. First (Eds.), *DSM-IV Sourcebook* (Vol. 1). Washington, DC: American Psychiatric Press.

Lahey, B. B., Schaughency, E. A., Strauss, C. C., & Frame, C. L. (1984). Are attention deficit disorders with and without hyperactivity similar or dissimilar disorders? *Journal of the American Academy of Child Psychiatry, 23,* 302–309.

Lamb, F., & Dunne-Maxim, K. (1987). Postvention in schools: Policy and progress. In E. J. Dunne, J. L. McIntosh, & K. Dunne-Maxim (Eds.), *Suicide and its aftermath: Understanding and counseling the survivors.* 245–262. New York: Norton.

Lambert, M. J., & Bergin, A. E. (1994). The effectiveness of psychotherapy. In A. E. Bergin and S. C. Garfield (Eds.), *Handbook of psychotherapy and behavior change* (4th ed.). New York: John Wiley.

Lanquetot, R. (1984). First person account: Confessions of the daughter of a schizophrenic. *Schizophrenia Bulletin, 10,* 467–471.

Lansky, M. R. (1988). Common clinical predicaments. In J. F. Clarkin, G. L. Haas, & I. D. Glick (Eds.), *Affective disorders and the family: Assessment and treatment* (pp. 213–238). New York: Guilford.

LaRoche, C., Cheifetz, P., Lester, E. P., Shibur, L. D., Tommaso, E., & Engelsmann, F. (1985). Psychopathology in the offspring of parents with bipolar affective disorders. *Canadian Journal of Psychiatry, 30,* 337–343.

Latib, A., Conroy, J., & Hess, C. M. (1984). Family attitudes toward deinstitutionalization. *International Review of Research on Mental Retardation, 12,* 67–93.

La Trobe, U., & Bandoora, V. (1991). Multidimensionality of the content of female sexual fantasy. *Behavior Research and Therapy, 29,* 179–189.

Laumann, E. O., Gagnon, J. H., Michael, R. T., & Michaels, S. (1994). *The social organization of sexuality.* Chicago: University of Chicago Press.

Lazarus, A. A. (1971). *Behavior therapy and beyond.* New York: McGraw-Hill.

Lazarus, R. S. (1991). *Emotion and adaptation.* New York: Oxford University Press.

Leaf, P. J., Weissman, M. M., Myers, J. K., Tischler, G. L., & Holzer, C. E., III. (1984). Social factors related to psychiatric disorder: The Yale Epidemiological Catchment Area Study. *Social Psychiatry, 19,* 53–61.

Lear, M. W. (1988). Mad malady. *New York Times Magazine*, July 3, 21.

Leff, J., & Vaughn, C. (1981). The role of maintenance therapy and relatives' expressed emotion in relapse schizophrenia: A two-year follow-up. *British Journal of Psychiatry, 139,* 102–104.

Leff, J., & Vaughn, C. (1985). *Expressed emotion in families.* New York: Guilford Press.

Leff, J. P., Wig, N. N., Bedi, H., Menon, D. K., Kuipers, L., Korten, A., Ernberg, G., Day, R., Sartorious, N., & Jablensky, A. Relatives' expressed emotion and the course of schizophrenia in Chandigarh: A two year follow-up of a first contact sample. *British Journal of Psychiatry, 156,* 351–356.

Lehrer, P. M., & Murphy, A. I. (1991). Stress reactivity and perception of pain among tension headache sufferers. *Behavioral Research and Therapy, 29,* 61–69.

Leitenberg, H., Rosen, J. C., Gross, J., Nudelman, S., et al. (1988). Exposure plus response-prevention treatment of bulimia nervosa. *Journal of Consulting & Clinical Psychology, 56,* 535–541.

Leon, G. R., & Dinklage, D. (1989). Obesity and anorexia nervosa. In T. H. Ollendick and M. Hersen (Eds.), *Handbook of child psychopathology* (pp. 247–264). New York: Plenum.

Leon, G. R., & Phelan, P. W. (1984). Anorexia nervosa. In B. Lahey & A. Kazdin (Eds.), *Advances in Clinical Child Psychology, 8,* 81–111.

Leslie, A. M., & Frith, U. (1990). Prospects for a cognitive neuropsychology of autism: Hobson's choice. *Psychological Review, 97,* 122–131.

LeVay, S. (1991). A difference in hypothalamic structure between heterosexual and homosexual men. *Science, 253,* 1034–1037.

Levine, R. V., Lynch, K., Myake, K., & Lucia, M. (1989). The Type A city: Coronary heart disease and the pace of life. *Journal of Behavioral Medicine, 12,* 509–524.

Levine, S. B. (1980). Psychiatric diagnosis of patients requesting sex reassignment surgery. *Journal of Sex and Marital Therapy, 6,* 164–173.

Lewin, R. (1988). Cloud over Parkinson's therapy. *Science, 240,* 390–392.

Lewinsohn, P. M., Mischel, W., Chaplain, W., & Barton, R. (1980). Social competence and depression. The role of illusory self-perceptions. *Journal of Abnormal Psychology, 89,* 203–212.

Lewis, G., David, A., Andreasson, S., & Allebeck, P. (1992). Schizophrenia and city life. *The Lancet, 340,* 137–140.

Liberman, R. P., & Corrigan, P. W. (1993). Designing new psychosocial treatments for schizophrenia. *Psychiatry, 56,* 238–249.

Liberman, R. P., & Green, M. F. (1992). Whither cognitive therapy for schizophrenia? *Schizophrenia Bulletin, 18,* 27–35.

Lief, H. I. (1992). Psychiatry's challenge: Defining an appropriate therapeutic role when child abuse is suspected. *Psychiatric News,* August 21, p. 1092.

Lilienfeld, S. O., & Waldman, I. D. (1990). The relation between childhood attention-deficit hyperactivity disorder and adult antisocial behavior reexamined: The problem of heterogeneity. *Clinical Psychology Review, 10,* 699–725.

Lilienfeld, S. O., Waldman, I. D. & Israel, A. C. (1994). A critical examination of the use of the term and concept of *comorbidity* in psychopathology research. *Clinical Psychology, 1,* 71–83.

Liljefors, I., & Rahe, R. H. (1970). An identical twin study of psychosocial factors in coronary heart disease in Sweden. *Psychosomatic Medicine, 32,* 523–542.

Lindemalm, G., Korlin, D., & Uddenberg, N. (1986). Long-term follow-up of "sex change" in 13 male to female transsexuals. *Archives of Sexual Behavior, 15,* 187–210.

Linehan, M. M. (1987). Dialectical behavior therapy for borderline personality disorder. *Bulletin of the Menninger Clinic, 51,* 261–276.

Linehan, M. M. (1989). Cognitive and behavior therapy for borderline personality disorder. In A. Tasman, R. E. Hales, & A. J. Frances (Eds.), *Annual Review of Psychiatry,* vol. 8. Washington, DC: American Psychiatric Press.

Linehan, M. M. (1993). *Cognitive-behavioral treatment of borderline personality disorder.* New York: Guilford.

Linehan, M. M., Armstrong, H. E., Suarez, A., Allmon, D., & Heard, H. L. (1991). Cognitive behavioral treatment of chronically parasuicidal borderline patients. *Archives of General Psychiatry, 48,* 1060–1064.

Linehan, M. M., Heard, H. L., & Armstrong, H. E. (1993). Naturalistic follow-up of a behavioral treatment for chronically parasuicidal borderline patients. *Archives of General Psychiatry, 50,* 971–974.

Linehan, M. M., Tutek, D. A., Heard, H. L., & Armstrong, H. E. (1994). Cognitive-behavioral treatment for chronically parasuicidal borderline patients: Interpersonal outcomes. *American Journal of Psychiatry, 151,* 1771–1776.

Lingjaerde, O. (1983). The biochemistry of depression. A survey of monoaminergic, neuroendocrinological, and bio-rhythmic disturbances in endogenous depression. *Acta Psychiatrica Scandinavica Supplementum, 302,* 36–51.

Linsky, A. S., Straus, M. A., & Colby, J. P., Jr. (1985). Stressful events, stressful condition and alcohol problems in the United States: A partial test of Coles' theory. *Journal of Studies on Alcohol, 46,* 72–80.

Lipowski, Z. J. (1987). Delirium (acute confusional states). *Journal of the American Medical Association, 258,* 1789–1792.

Lipschitz, A. (1990). *College suicide: A review monograph.* New York: American Suicide Foundation.

Lipsius, S. H. (1987). Prescribing sensate focus without proscribing intercourse. *Journal of Sex and Marital Therapy, 13,* 106–116.

Llewelyn, S. P. (1988). Psychological therapy as viewed by clients and therapists. *British Journal of Clinical Psychology, 27,* 223–237.

Livesley, W. J., Schroeder, M. L., Jackson, D. N., & Jang, K. L. (1994). Categorical distinctions in the study of personality disorder: Implications for classification. *Journal of Abnormal Psychology, 103,* 6–17.

Lobato, D. (1983). Siblings of handicapped children: A review. *Journal of Autism, 13,* 347–364.

Loftus, E. G. (1993). The reality of repressed memories. *American Psychologist, 48,* 518–537.

Loftus, E. G., & Ketcham, K. (1994). *The myth of repressed memory: False memories and accusations of sexual abuse.* New York: St. Martin's.

LoPiccolo, J. (1994). The evolution of sex therapy. *Sexual and Marital Therapy, 9,* 5–7.

Loranger, A. W., Sartorius, N., Andreoli, A., Berger, P., Buichheim, P., Channabasavanna, S. M., Coid, B., Dahl, A., Diekstra, R. F. W., Ferguson, B., Jacobsberg, L. B., Mombour, W., Pull, C., Ono, Y., & Regier, D. A. (1994). The international personality disorder examination. *Archives of General Psychiatry, 51,* 215–224.

Lovaas, O. I. (1987). Behavioral treatment and normal educational and intellectual functioning in young autistic children. *Journal of Consulting and Clinical Psychology, 55*, 3–9.

Lovaas, O. I. (1993). The development of a treatment-research project for developmentally disabled and autistic children. *Journal of Applied Behavior Analysis, 26*, 617–630.

Lovejoy, M. (1982). Expectations and the recovery process. *Schizophrenia Bulletin, 8*, 605–609.

Luborsky, L., Crits-Christoph, P., McLellan, T., Woody, G., Piper, W., Liberman, B., Imber, S., & Pilkonis, P. (1986). Do therapists vary much in their success? Findings from four outcome studies. *American Journal of Orthopsychiatry, 56*, 501–512.

Lukoff, D., Lu, F., & Turner, R. (1992). Toward a more culturally sensitive DSM-IV: Psychoreligious and psychospiritual problems. *The Journal of Nervous and Mental Disease, 180*, 673–682.

Luntz, B. K., & Widom, C. S. (1994). Antisocial personality disorder in abused and neglected children grown up. *American Journal of Psychiatry, 151*, 670–674.

Maccoby, E., & Maccoby, N. (1954). The interview: A tool of social science. In G. Lindzey (Ed.), *Handbook of social psychology*. Cambridge, MA: Addison-Wesley, 449–487.

MacDougall, J. M., Dembroski, T. M., & Krantz, D. S. (1981). Effects of types of challenge on pressor and heart rate responses in Type A and B women. *Psychophysiology, 18*, 1–9.

MacMillan, H. L., MacMillan, J. H., Offord, D. R., Griffith, L., & MacMillan, A. (1994). Primary prevention of child physical abuse and neglect: A critical review. Part I. *Journal of Child Psychology and Psychiatry, 35*, 835–856.

MacMillan, H. L., MacMillan, J. H., Offord, D. R., Griffith, L., & MacMillan, A. (1994). Primary prevention of child sexual abuse: A critical review. Part II. *Journal of Child Psychology and Psychiatry, 35*, 857–876.

Mahl, G. L. (1968). Gestures and body movements in interviews. In J. M. Shlien (Ed.), *Research in psychotherapy: Proceedings of the third conference*. Washington, DC: American Psychological Association.

Mahoney, E. R. (1983). *Human sexuality*. New York: McGraw-Hill.

Maj, M., Pirozzi, R., & Kemali, D. (1989). Long-term outcome of lithium prophylaxis in patients initially classified as complete responders. *Psychopharmacology, 98*, 535–538.

Malarkey, W. B., Kiecolt-Glaser, J. K., Pearl, D., & Glaser, R. (1994). Hostile behavior during marital conflict alters pituitary and adrenal hormones. *Psychosomatic Medicine, 56*, 41–51.

Malgady, R. G., Rogler, L. H., & Tryon, W. W. (1992). Issues of validity in the Diagnostic Interview Schedule. *Journal of Psychiatric Research, 26*, 59–67.

Malinosky-Rummell, R., & Hansen, D. J. (1993). Long-term consequences of childhood physical abuse. *Psychological Bulletin, 114*, 68–79.

Mannuzza, S., Klein, R. G., Bonagura, N., Malloy, P., Giampino, T. L., & Addalli, K. A. (1991). Hyperactive boys almost grown up. *Archives of General Psychiatry, 48*, 77–83.

Mannuzza, S., Klein, R. G., Bessler, A., Malloy, P., & LaPadula, M., Biederman, J., Faraone, S. V., Spencer, T., Wilens, T., & LaPadula, M. (1993). Adult outcome of hyperactive boys: Educational achievement, occupational rank, and psychiatric status. *Archives of General Psychiatry, 50*, 565–576.

Manuck, S. B., Morrison, R. L., Bellack, A. S., & Polefrone, J. M. (1985). Behavioral factors in hypertension, cardiovascular responsivity, anger, and social competence. In M. A. Chesney & R. H. Rosenman (Eds.), *Anger and hostility in cardiovascular and behavioral disorders*. Washington, DC: Hemisphere.

March, J. S., Mulle, K., & Herbel, B. (1994). Behavioral psychotherapy for children and adolescents with obsessive-compulsive disorder: An open trial of a new protocol-driven treatment package. *Journal of the American Academy of Child and Adolescent Psychiatry, 33*, 333–341.

Marengo, J. T., Harrow, M., Lanin-Kettering, I., & Wilson, A. (1986). Evaluating bizarre-idiosyncratic thinking: A comprehensive index of positive thought disorder. *Schizophrenia Bulletin, 12*, 497–510.

Markowitz, J., Brown, R., Sweeney, J., & Mann, J. J. (1987). Reduced length and cost of hospital stay for major depression in patients treated with ECT. *American Journal of Psychiatry, 144*, 1025–1029.

Marks, I. M. (1978). *Living with fear*. New York: McGraw-Hill.

Marks, I. M. (1987a). Behavioral aspects of panic disorder. *American Journal of Psychiatry, 144*, 1160–1165.

Marks, I. M. (1987b). *Fears, phobias, and rituals: Panic, anxiety, and their disorders*. New York: Oxford University Press.

Marlatt, G. A. (1994). *Binge drinking in adolescents and young adults—a harm-reduction approach*. Invited address, American Psychological Association annual convention, Los Angeles, CA.

Marlatt, G. A., Demming, B., & Reid, J. B. (1973). Loss of control drinking in alcoholics: An experimental analogue. *Journal of Abnormal Psychology, 81*, 233–241.

Marlatt, G. A., & Gordon, J. R. (1985). *Relapse prevention: Maintenance strategies in the treatment of addictive behaviors*. New York: Guilford.

Marten, P. A., Brown, T. A., Barlow, D. H., Borkovec, T. D., Shear, M. K., & Lydiard, R. B. (1993). Evaluation of the ratings comprising the associated symptom criterion of DSM-III-R generalized anxiety disorder. *Journal of Nervous and Mental Disorder, 181*, 676–682.

Maser, J. D., & Cloninger, C. R. (Eds.), (1990). *Comorbidity of mood and anxiety disorders*. Washington, DC: American Psychiatric Press.

Masters, W. H., & Johnson, V. E. (1966). *Human sexual response*. Boston: Little, Brown.

Masters, W. H., & Johnson, V. E. (1970). *Human sexual inadequacy*. Boston: Little, Brown.

Masters, W. H., & Johnson, V. E. (1979). *Homosexuality in perspective*. Boston: Little, Brown.

Masters, W. H., Johnson, V. E., & Kolodny, R. C. (1985). *Human sexuality*, 2nd ed. Boston: Little, Brown.

Matson, J. L., & Sevin, J. A. (1994). Theories of dual diagnosis in mental retardation. *Journal of Consulting and Clinical Psychology, 62*, 6–16.

Mattes, J. A., & Gittlesman, R. (1983). Growth of hyperactive children on maintenance regimen of methylphenidate. *Archives of General Psychiatry, 40*, 317–321.

Matthews, W. S., Barabas, G., Cusak, E., & Ferrari, M. (1986). Social quotients of children with phenylketonuria before and after discontinuation of dietary therapy. *American Journal of Mental Deficiency, 91*, 92–94.

Mavissakalian, M. R. (1993). Combined behavioral and pharmacological treatment of anxiety disorders. In J. M. Oldham, M. B. Riba, and A. Tasman (Eds.), *Review of Psychiatry* (Vol. 12, pp. 565–584). Washington, DC: American Psychiatric Press.

McClelland, D. C., Ross, G., & Patel, V. (1985). Exam stress and immunoglobulin levels. *Journal of Human Stress, 11*, 52–59.

McConaughy, S. H., & Achenbach, T. M. (1994). Comorbidity of empirically based syndromes in matched general population and clinical samples. *Journal of Child Psychology and Psychiatry, 35*, 1141–1157.

McCord, J. (1983). A forty-year perspective on effects of child abuse and neglect. *Child Abuse and Neglect, 7*, 265–270.

McGhie, A. & Chapman, J. (1961). Disorders of attention and perception in early schizophrenia. *British Journal of Medical Psychology, 34*, 103–116.

McGlashan, T. H. (1986). Schizotypal personality disorder. *Archives of General Psychiatry, 43*, 329–334.

McGlashan, T. H. (1988). A selective review of recent North American long-term follow-up studies of schizophrenia. *Schizophrenia Bulletin, 14*, 515–542.

McGlashan, T. H. (1994). Psychosocial treatments of schizophrenia. In N. C. Andreason (Ed.), *Schizophrenia: From mind to molecule* (pp. 189–218). Washington, DC: American Psychiatric Press.

McGlashan, T. H., & Fenton, W. S. (1992). The positive-negative distinction in schizophrenia: Review of natural history validators. *Archives of General Psychiatry, 49*, 63–72.

McGue, M., & Gottesman, I. I. (1989). Genetic linkage in schizophrenia: Perspectives from genetic epidemiology. *Schizophrenia Bulletin, 15*, 453–464.

McGue, M., Gottesman, I. I., & Rao, D. C. (1985). Resolving genetic models for the transmission of schizophrenia. *Genetic Epidemiology, 21*, 99–110.

McGuffin, P., Reveley, A., & Holland, A. (1982). Identical triplets: Nonidentical psychosis? *British Journal of Psychiatry, 140*, 1–6.

McMahon, R. J. (1994). Diagnosis, assessment, and treatment of externalizing problems in children: The role of longitudinal data. *Journal of Consulting and Clinical Psychology, 62*, 901–917.

McNally, R. J. (1987). Preparedness and phobias: A review. *Psychological Bulletin, 101*, 283–303.

McNally, R. J. (1990). Psychological approaches to panic disorder: A review. *Psychological Bulletin, 108*, 403–419.

Meana, M., & Binik, Y. M. (1994). Painful coitus: A review of female dyspareunia. *The Journal of Nervous and Mental Disease, 182*, 264–272.

Meisler, A. W., & Carey, M. P. (1990). A critical reevaluation of nocturnal penile tumescence monitoring in the diagnosis of erectile dysfunction. *The Journal of Nervous and Mental Disease, 178*, 78–89.

Melamed, B. G., & Bush, J. P. (1986). Parent-child influences during medical procedures. In S. M. Auerbach and A. L. Stolberg (Eds.), *Crisis intervention within children and families*. Washington, DC: Hemisphere.

Mellor, C. S. (1970). First rank symptoms of schizophrenia. *British Journal of Psychiatry, 177*, 15–23.

Meloy, J. R. (1992). Revisiting the Rorschach of Sirhan Sirhan. *Journal of Personality Assessment, 58*, 548–570.

Meltzer, H. Y. (1993). New drugs for the treatment of schizophrenia. *Psychiatric Clinics of North America, 16*, 365–385.

Merikangas, K. R. (1990). Comorbidity for anxiety and depression: Review of family and genetic studies. In J. D. Maser and C. R. Cloninger (Eds.), *Comorbidity of mood and anxiety disorders*. Washington, DC: American Psychiatric Press.

Messer, I. (1994). *Tactical police officers stress study*. College Station, TX: Unpublished doctoral dissertation.

Meuwissen, I., & Over, R. (1991). Multidimensionality of the content of female sexual fantasy. *Behaviour Research and Therapy, 29*, 179–189.

Meyer, J. (1990). Guess who's coming to dinner this time? A study of gay intimate relationships and the support for those relationships. *Journal of Homosexuality, 18*, 59–82.

Meyer, R. (1989). Typologies. In *Treatments of psychiatric disorders* (Vol. 2). Washington, DC: American Psychiatric Association.

Meyers, A. W., & Cohen, R. (1990). Cognitive-behavioral approaches to child psychopathology: Present status and future directions. In M. Lewis & S. M. Miller (Eds.), *Handbook of developmental psychology* (pp. 475–485). New York: Plenum.

Mezzich, J. E., Ahn, C. W., Fabrega, H., Jr., & Pilkonis, P. A. (1990). Patterns of psychiatric comorbidity in a large population presenting for care. In J. D. Maser & C. R. Cloninger (Eds.), *Comorbidity in anxiety and mood disorders*. Washington, DC: American Psychiatric Press.

Mikail, S. F., Henderson, P. R., & Tasca, G. A. (1994). An interpersonally based model of chronic pain: An application of attachment theory. *Clinical Psychology Review, 14*, 1–16.

Miklowitz, D. J., & Stackmman, D. (1992). Communication deviance in families of schizophrenic and other psychiatric patients: Current state of the construct. *Progress in Experimental Personality and Psychopathology Research, 15*, 1–46.

Milich, R., & Dodge, K. A. (1984). Social information processing in child psychiatric populations. *Journal of Abnormal Child Psychology, 12*, 471–490.

Miller, G. E., & Prinz, R. J. (1990). Enhancement of social learning family interventions for childhood conduct disorders. *Psychological Bulletin, 108*, 291–307.

Miller, H. L., Coombs, D. W., Leeper, J. D., & Barton, S. N. (1984). An analysis of the effects of suicide prevention facilities on suicide rates in the United States. *American Journal of Public Health, 74*, 340–343.

Miller, M. W. (1994). Listening to Eli Lilly: Prozac hysteria has gone too far. *Wall Street Journal*, March 30, pp. B1, B7.

Miller, N. E. (1992). Some examples of psychophysiology and the unconscious. *Biofeedback and Self-Regulation, 17*, 3–16.

Millon, T. (1986). The avoidant personality. In R. Michels and J. O. Cavenar, Jr. (Eds.), *Psychiatry*, vol. 1. New York: Basic Books.

Minuchin, S., Rosman, B., & Baker, L. (1978). *Psychosomatic families: Anorexia nervosa in context*. Cambridge, MA: Harvard University Press.

Mirsky, A. F., & Bakay Pragnay, E. (1984). Brainstem mechanisms in the processing of sensory information: Clinical symptoms, animal models and unit analysis. In D. E. Sheer (Ed.), *Attention: Theory, brain functions and clinical applications*. Hillsdale, NJ: Erlbaum.

Mitchell, P., Mackinnon, A., & Waters, B. (1993). The genetics of bipolar disorder. *Australia and New Zealand Journal of Psychiatry, 27*, 560–580.

Mizes, J. S. (1990). Criterion-related validity of the Anorectic Cognitions Questionnaire. *Addictive Behaviors, 15*, 153–163.

Mohr, D. C., & Beutler, C. E. (1990). Erectile dysfunction: A review of diagnostic and treatment procedures. *Clinical Psychology Review, 10*, 123–150.

Moldin, S. O., Scheftner, W. A., Rice, J. P., Nelson, E., Knesevich, M. A., & Akiskal, H. (1993). Association between major depressive disorder and physical illness. *Psychological Medicine, 23,* 755–761.

Moltz, D. A. (1993). Bipolar disorder and the family: An integrative model. *Family Process, 32,* 409–423.

Money, J. (1987). Sin, sickness, or status? Homosexual gender identity and psychoneuroendocrinology. *American Psychologist, 42,* 384–399.

Moore, C. (1989). Evaluation of sexual disorders. *Treatment of psychiatric disorders* (vol. 3). Washington, DC: American Psychiatric Association.

Moos, R. H. (1974). *Family Environment Scale.* Palo Alto, CA: Consulting Psychologists Press.

Moran, A. E., Freedman, R. I., & Sharfstein, S. S. (1984). The journey of Sylvia Frumkin: A case study for policymakers. *Hospital and Community Psychiatry, 35,* 887–893.

Moran, Lord C. M. W. (1966). *Winston Churchill: The struggle for survival, 1940–1965.* Boston: Houghton Mifflin.

Morris, J. (1974). *Conundrum.* New York: Harcourt, Brace, & Jovanovich.

Morrison, R. L., & Wixted, J. T. (1989). Social skills training. In A. S. Bellack (Ed.), *A clinical guide for the treatment of schizophrenia.* New York: Plenum.

Morrissey, J. P., & Goldman, H. H. (1986). Care and treatment of the mentally ill in the United States: Historical developments and reforms. *American Association of Political and Social Sciences, 484,* 12–28.

Mosher, L. R. (1989). Community residential treatment: Alternatives to hospitalization. In A. S. Bellack (Ed.), *A clinical guide for the treatment of schizophrenia.* New York: Plenum.

Mueser, K. T., Bellack, A. S., Douglas, M. S., & Morrison, R. L. (1991). Prevalence and stability of social skill deficits in schizophrenia. *Schizophrenia Research, 5,* 167–176.

Mueser, K. T., & Berenbaum, H. (1990). Psychodynamic treatment of schizophrenia: Is there a future? *Psychological Medicine, 20,* 253–262.

Mufson, L. (1993). *Interpersonal psychotherapy for depressed adolescents.* New York: Guilford.

Mufson, L., Moreau, D., Weissman, M. M., Wickramaratne, P., Martin, J., & Samoilov, A. (1994). Modification of interpersonal psychotherapy with depressed adolescents (IPT-A): Phase I and II studies. *Journal of the American Academy of Child and Adolescent Psychiatry, 33,* 695–705.

Murphy, D. A., Pelham, W. E., & Lang, A. R. (1992). Aggression in boys with attention deficit disorder: Methylphenidate effects on naturalistic observations of aggression, response to provocation in the laboratory, and social information processing. *Journal of Abnormal Child Psychology, 20,* 451–466.

Murphy, G. E. (1988). Prevention of suicide. In A. J. Frances & R. E. Hales (Eds.), *Review of psychiatry,* vol. 7. Washington, DC: American Psychiatric Press.

Murray, H. A. (1943). *Thematic apperception test: Pictures and manual.* Cambridge, MA: Harvard University Press.

Myers, J. (1988). Drug controls heart/stroke damage. *Alcohol, Drug Abuse, and Mental Health Administration, 14*(9), 1–2.

Nagata, D. (1989). Long-term effects of the Japanese American internment camps: Impact upon the children of the internees. *Journal of the Asian American Psychological Association, 13,* 48–55.

Najavits, L. M., & Weiss, R. D. (1994). Variations in therapist effectiveness in the treatment of patients with substance use disorders: An empirical review. *Addiction, 89,* 679–688.

Name withheld (1993). Walking with my specter. *Journal of the American Medical Association, 268* (25), 149, 151.

Nasar, S. (1994). The lost years of a Nobel laureate. *New York Times,* Sunday, November 13, Section 3, pp. 1, 8.

National Academy of Sciences. (1982). *Marijuana and health.* Washington, DC: National Academy Press.

National Advisory Mental Health Council (1990). *National plan for research on child and adolescent mental disorders.* Rockville, MD: National Institute of Mental Health.

National Center on Child Abuse and Neglect (1988). *Study of national incidence and prevalence of child abuse and neglect: 1988.* Washington, DC: U.S. Department of Health and Human Services.

National Institute of Mental Health. (1990). *Mental health, United States, 1990.* (DHHS Publication No. ADM 90–1708). Washington, DC: US Government Printing Office.

National Institute of Mental Health. (1991). Caring for people with severe mental disorders: A national plan of research to improve services. (DHHS Publication No. ADM 91–1762). Washington, DC: US Government Printing Office.

Needles, D. J., & Abramson, L. Y. (1990). Positive life events, attributional style, and hopefulness: Testing a model of recovery from depression. *Journal of Abnormal Psychology, 99,* 156–165.

Neimeyer, G. J., & Neimeyer, R. A. (1985). Relational trajectories: A personal construct contribution. *Journal of Social and Personal Relationships, 2,* 325–349.

Nemiah, J. C. (1988). Psychoneurotic disorders. In A. M. Nicholi (Ed.), *The new Harvard guide to modern psychiatry,* 2nd ed. Cambridge, MA: Harvard University Press.

Nemiah, J. C., & Uhde, T. W. (1989). Phobic disorders. In H. I. Kaplan & B. J. Sadock, eds., *Comprehensive textbook of psychiatry,* 5th ed. Baltimore: Williams & Wilkins.

Neugebauer, R. (1979). Medieval and early modern theories of mental illness. *Archives of General Psychiatry, 36,* 477–483.

Niccols, G. A. (1994). Fetal alcohol syndrome: Implications for psychologists. *Clinical Psychology Review, 14,* 91–111.

Nichols, P. L. (1984). Familial mental retardation. *Behavior Genetics, 14,* 161–170.

Nicholson, I. R., & Neufeld, R. W. J. (1992). A dynamic vulnerability perspective on stress and schizophrenia. *American Journal of Orthopsychiatry, 62,* 117–130.

Nietzel, M. T., & Himelien, M. J. (1986). Prevention of crime and delinquency. In B. A. Edelstein and L. Michelson (Eds.), *Handbook of prevention.* New York: Plenum.

North, C. S., Smith, E. M., & Spitznagel, E. L. (1994). Posttraumatic stress disorder in survivors of a mass shooting. *American Journal of Psychiatry, 151,* 82–88.

Noshpitz, J. D., & Coddington, R. D. (Eds.), (1990). *Stressors and the adjustment disorders.* New York: John Wiley.

Nuechterlein, K. H. (1983). Signal detection in vigilance tasks and behavioral attributes among offspring of schizophrenic mothers and among hyperactive children. *Journal of Abnormal Psychology, 92,* 4–28.

O'Callaghan, E., Gibson, T., Colohan, H. A., Buckley, P., Walshe, D. G., Larkin, C., & Waddington, J.L. (1992). Risk of schizophrenia in adults born after obstetric complications and their association with early onset of illness: A controlled study. *British Medical Journal, 305,* 1265–1269.

O'Callaghan, E., Gibson, T., Colohan, H. A., Walshe, D. G., Buckley, P., Larkin, C., & Waddington, J. L. (1991). Season of birth in schizophrenia. Evidence for confinement of an excess of winter births to patients without a family history of mental disorder. *British Journal of Psychiatry, 158,* 764–769.

O'Donoghue, E. G. (1914). *The story of Bethlehem Hospital from its foundation in 1247.* London: T. Fisher.

Ofshe, R., & Watters, E. (1994). *Making monsters: False memories, psychotherapy, and sexual hysteria.* New York: Scribners.

Ogden, J. A. H. (1947). *The Kingdom of the Lost.* London: Bodley Head.

Okolo, C., & Guskin, S. (1984). Community attitudes toward community placement of mentally retarded persons. *International Review of Research in Mental Retardation, 12,* 25–66.

Olds, D. C., & Henderson, C. (1989). The prevention of mal-treatment. In D. Cicchetti & V. Carlson (Eds.), *Child maltreatment: Theory and research on the causes and consequences of child abuse and neglect.* New York: Cambridge University Press.

O'Leary, A. (1990). Stress, emotion, and human immune function. *Psychological Bulletin, 108,* 363–382.

O'Leary, K. D., & Wilson, G. T. (1987). *Behavior therapy: Application and outcome.* Englewood Cliffs, NJ: Prentice-Hall.

Olfson, M., & Pincus, H. A. (1994). Outpatient psychotherapy in the United States, II: Patterns of utilization. *American Journal of Psychiatry, 151,* 1289–1294.

Olmsted, M. P., Kaplan, A. S., & Rockert, W. (1994). Rate and prediction of relapse in bulimia nervosa. *American Journal of Psychiatry, 151,* 738–743.

O'Neal, J. M. (1984). First person account: Finding myself and loving it. *Schizophrenia Bulletin, 10,* 109–110.

Orleans, C. T., & Slade, J. (Eds.) (1993). *Nicotine addiction: Principles and management.* New York: Oxford University Press.

Osterling, J., & Dawson, G. (1994). Early recognition of children with autism: A study of first birthday home videotapes. *Journal of Autism and Developmental Disorders, 24,* 247–257.

Othmer, E., & Othmer, S. C. (1994). *The Clinical Interview Using DSM-IV* (Vol. 1). Washington, DC: American Psychiatric Press.

Ottaviani, R., & Beck, A. T., (1987). Cognitive aspects of panic disorders. *Journal of Anxiety Disorders, 1,* 15–28.

Otten, A. L. (1994). People patterns. *The Wall Street Journal,* November 9, 1994, p. B1.

Palmer, R. L., Oppenheimer, R., & Marshall, P. D. (1988). Eating disordered patients remember their parents: A study using the Parental Bonding Instrument. *International Journal of Eating Disorders, 7,* 101–106.

Panek, W. F., & Garber, J. (1992). Role of aggression, rejection, and attributions in the prediction of depression in children. *Development and Psychopathology, 4,* 145–165.

Parker, G., & Hadzi-Pavlovic, D. (1990). Expressed emotion as a predictor of schizophrenic relapse: An analysis of aggregated data. *Psychological Medicine, 20,* 961–964.

Patten, S. B. (1991) Are the Brown and Harris "Vulnerability Factors" risk factors for depression. *Journal of Psychiatric Neuroscience, 16,* 267–271.

Patterson, C. J. (1992). Children of lesbian and gay parents. *Child Development, 63,* 1025–1042.

Patterson, G. R. (1982). *Coercive family processes.* Eugene, OR: Castalia Press.

Patterson, G. R. (1986). Performance models for antisocial boys.

Meeting of the American Psychological Association. *American Psychologist, 41,* 432–444.

Patterson, G. R. (1975). *Families with aggressive children.* Eugene, OR: Castalia Press.

Paul, G. L. (1969). Chronic mental patient: Current status-future directions. *Psychological Bulletin, 71,* 81–93.

Paul, G. L., & Lentz, R. J. (1977). *Psychosocial treatment of chronic mental patients: Milieu versus social-learning programs.* Cambridge, MA: Harvard University Press.

Paykel, E. S. (1991) Depression in women. *British Journal of Psychiatry, 158,* 22–29.

Pelham, W. E., Jr. (1993). Pharmacotherapy for children with attention-deficit hyperactivity disorder. *School Psychology Review, 22,* 199–227.

Perls, F. S. (1969). *Gestalt therapy verbatim.* Lafayette, CA; Real People Press.

Perry, D. G., Perry, L. C., & Boldizar, J. P. (1990). Learning of aggression. In M. Lewis & S. M. Miller (Eds.), *Handbook of developmental psychopathology.* New York: Plenum Press.

Persad, E. (1990). Electroconvulsive therapy in depression. *Canadian Journal of Psychiatry, 35,* 175–182.

Persky, V. W., Kempthorne-Rawson, J., & Shekelle, R. B. (1987) Personality and risk of cancer: 20-year follow-up of the Western Electric Study. *Psychosomatic Medicine, 49,* 435–449.

Persons, J. B. (1992). A case formulation approach to cognitive-behavior therapy: Application to panic disorder. *Psychiatric Annals, 22,* 470–473.

Petrie, T. A. (1993). Disordered eating in female collegiate gymnasts: Prevalence and personality/attitudinal correlates. *Journal of Sport and Exercise Psychology, 15,* 424–436.

Pfiffner, L. J., & O'Leary, S. G. (1993) Psychological treatments: School-based. In J. L. Matson (Ed.), *Handbook of hyperactivity in children.* Boston: Allyn & Bacon.

Pfohl, B. (1991). Histrionic personality disorder: A review of available data and recommendations for DSM-IV. *Journal of Personality Disorders, 5,* 150–166.

Pierce, G. R., Sarason, I. G., & Sarason, B. R. (1991). General and relationship-based perceptions of social support: Are two constructs better than one? *Journal of Personality and Social Psychology, 61,* 1028–1039.

Piercey, B. P. (1985). First person account: Making the best of it. *Schizophrenia Bulletin, 11,* 155–157.

Pinel, P. (1969). *Traite' medico-philosophique sur Palienation mentale,* 2nd ed. Paris: Brossen, 1809; as quoted in W. Riese, 1968, *The legacy of Philippe Pinel.* New York: Springer.

Piven, J., Berthier, M. L., Starkstein, S. E., Nehme, E., Pearlson, G., & Folstein, S. (1990). Magnetic resonance imaging evidence for a defect of cerebral cortical development in autism. *American Journal of Psychiatry, 147,* 734–739.

Plakun, E. M., Burkhardt, P. E., & Muller, A. P. (1985). Fourteen-year follow-up of borderline and schizotypal personality disorders. *Comprehensive Psychiatry, 26,* 448–455.

Plomin, R., Owen, M. J., & McGuffin, P. (1994). The genetic bases of complex human behaviors. *Science, 264,* 1733–1739.

Polich, J. M., & Armor, D. J. (1980). *The course of alcoholism: Four years after treatment.* Santa Monica, CA: Rand.

Pope, H. G., Jr., Jonas, J. M., Hudson, J., Cohen, B. M., & Gunderson, J. G. (1983). The validity of DSM-III borderline personality disorder. *Archives of General Psychiatry, 40,* 1319–1323.

Pope, H. G., Mangweth, B., Negrao, A. B., Hudson, J. I., & Cord, T. A., (1994). Childhood sexual abuse and bulimia nervosa: A comparison of American, Austrian, and Brazilian women. *American Journal of Psychiatry, 151,* 732–737.

Powell, C. (1991). Robert Lowell: The search for the father in madness and poetry. *Australian and New Zealand Journal of Psychiatry, 25,* 375–382.

Prentky, R. A., & Knight, R. A. (1991). Identifying critical dimensions for discriminating among rapists. *Journal of Consulting and Clinical Psychology, 59,* 643–661.

Presley, A. S., Grubb, A. B., & Semple, D. (1982). Predictors of successful rehabilitation in long-term patients. *Acta Psychiatrica Scandinavica, 66,* 83–88.

Prince, V. C. (1967). *The transvestite and his wife.* Los Angeles: Argyle Books.

Prior, M. R. (1992). Childhood autism: What do we know and where should we go? *Behaviour Change, 9,* 96–103.

Purcell, K., Brady, K., Schal, H., Muser, J., Molk, L., Gordon, N., & Means, J. (1969). The effect on asthma in children of experimental separation from the family. *Psychosomatic Medicine, 31,* 144–164.

Putnam, F. W. (1991). Dissociative phenomena. In A. Tasman & S. M. Goldfinger (Eds.), *Review of Psychiatry* (vol. 10). Washington, DC: American Psychiatric Press.

Quinton, D., Pickles A., Maughn, B., & Rutter, M. (1993). Partners, peers, and pathways: Assortative pairing and continuities in conduct disorder. *Development and Psychopathology, 5,* 763–783.

Rabkin, J. G. (1979). Criminal behavior of discharged mental patients: A critical appraisal of the research. *Psychological Bulletin, 86,* 1–27.

Ragland, D. R., & Brand, R. J. (1988). Type A behavior and mortality from coronary heart disease. *New England Journal of Medicine, 318,* 65–69.

Raine, N. V. (1994). Returns of the day. *New York Times Magazine,* October 2, p. 34.

Ramey, C. T., & Haskins, R. (1981). The modification of intelligence through early experience. *Intelligence, 5,* 43–57.

Rao, U., Weissman, M. M., Martin, J. A., & Hammond, R. W. (1993). Childhood depression and risk of suicide: A preliminary report of a longitudinal study. *Journal of the American Academy of Child and Adolescent Psychiatry, 32,* 21–27.

Rapaport, K., & Burkart, B. R. (1984). Personality and attitudinal characteristics of sexually coercive college males. *Journal of Abnormal Psychology, 13,* 216–221.

Rapoport, J., Elkins, R., Langer, D. H., Sceery, W., Buchsbaum, M. S., Gillin, J. C., Murphy, D. L., Zahn, T. P., Lake, R., Ludlow, C., & Mendelson, W. (1981). Childhood obsessive-compulsive disorder. *American Journal of Psychiatry, 138,* 1545–1554.

Rapoport, J. L. (1989). *The boy who couldn't stop washing.* New York: Dutton.

Raz, S., & Raz, N. (1990). Structural brain abnormalities in the major psychoses: A quantitative review of the evidence from computer imaging. *Psychological Bulletin, 108,* 93–108.

Reich, W. (1949). (originally published 1933) *Character analysis.* New York: Orgone Institute Press.

Reisberg, B. (1985). Alzheimer's disease updated. *Psychiatric Annals, 15,* 319–322.

Reid, W. H. (1986). Antisocial personality. In R. Michels & J. O. Cavenar, Jr. (Eds.), *Psychiatry* (vol. 1). New York: Basic Books.

Reid, W. H., & Balis, G. U. (1987). Evaluation of the violent patient. In R. E. Hales & A. J. Frances (Eds.), *American Psychiatric Association Annual Review* (vol. 6). Washington, DC: American Psychiatric Press.

Reiss, A. J., & Roth, S. A. (Eds.) (1994). *Understanding and preventing violence.* Washington, DC: National Academy Press.

Reiss, S., & Valenti-Hein, D. (1994). Development of a psychopathology rating scale for children with mental retardation. *Journal of Consulting and Clinical Psychology, 62,* 28–33.

Rekers, G. A. (1977). Assessment and treatment of childhood gender problems. In B. B. Lahey & A. E. Kazdin (Eds.), *Advances in clinical child psychology* (vol. 1). New York: Plenum.

Repucci, N. D., & Haugaard, J. J. (1989). Prevention of child sexual abuse. *American Psychologist, 44,* 1266–1275.

Research on mental illness and addictive disorders. (1985). *American Journal of Psychiatry, 142* (supplement), 9–41.

Riccio, C. A., Hynd, G. W., Cohen, M. J., & Gonzalez, J. J. (1993). Neurological basis of attention deficit hyperactivity disorder. *Exceptional Children, 60,* 118–124.

Rice, D. P., & Miller, L. S. (1992). *The economic burden of schizophrenia.* Paper presented at the Sixth Biennial Research conference on the Economics of Mental Health, Bethesda, MD, 1–17.

Riggs, D. S., O'Leary, K. D., & Breslin, F. C. (1990). Multiple correlates of physical aggression in dating couples. *Journal of Interpersonal Violence, 5,* 61–73.

Rist, M. C. (1990). The shadow children. *American Schoolboard Journal,* January 19–24.

Ritvo, E. R., Jorde, L. B., Mason-Brothers, A., Freeman, B. J., Pingree, C., Jones, M. B., McMahon, W. M., Petersen, P. B., Jenson, W. R., & Mo, A. (1989). The UCLA-University of Utah epidemiologic survey of autism: Recurrence risk estimates and genetic counseling. *American Journal of Psychiatry, 146,* 1032–1036.

Roach, M. (1983). Another name for madness. *New York Times Magazine,* Jan. 16, 22–31.

Robin, A. L., Siegel, P. T., Koepke, T. Moye, A. W., & Tice, S. (1994). Family therapy versus individual therapy for adolescent females with anorexia nervosa. *Journal of Developmental and Behavioral Pediatrics, 15,* 111–116.

Robins, L. N. (1993). Vietnam veterans' rapid recovery from heroin addiction: A fluke or normal expectation? *Addiction, 88,* 1041–1054.

Robins, L. N., Helzer, J. E., Croghan, J., & Ratcliff, K. S. (1981). National Institute of Mental Health Diagnostic Interview Schedule. *Archives of General Psychiatry, 38,* 381–389.

Robins, L. N., & Price, R. K. (1991). Adult disorders predicted by childhood conduct problems: Results from the NIMH Epidemiological Catchment Area Project. *Psychiatry, 54,* 116–132.

Robins, L. N., & Regier, D. A. (1991). *Psychiatric disorders in America: The epidemiological catchment area.* New York: The Free Press.

Robinson, H. (1991). Visitation with divorced father provokes reemergence of unresolved family conflicts: Case of Charlie, age 10. In N. B. Webb (Ed.), *Play therapy with children in crisis* (pp. 219–236). New York: Guilford.

Rock, C. L., & Yager, J. (1987). Nutrition and eating disorders: A primer for clinicians. *International Journal of Eating Disorders, 6,* 267–280.

Roder, V., Eckman, T. A., Brenner, H. D., Kienzie, N., & Liberman, R. P. (1990). Behavior therapy. In M. I. Herz, S. J. Keith, & J. P. Docherty (Eds.), *Handbook of schizophrenia: Psychosocial treatment of schizophrenia* (Vol 4, pp. 107–134). Amsterdam: Elsevier.

Rogers, C. R. (1951). *Client-centered therapy.* Boston: Houghton-Mifflin.

Rogers, C. R. (1959). A theory of therapy, personality, and interpersonal relationships as developed in the client-centered framework. In S. Koch (Ed.), *Psychology: A study of a science* (vol. 3). New York: McGraw-Hill.

Rogers, C. R. (1980). *A way of being.* Boston: Houghton-Mifflin.

Rogers, J. G., Voullaire, L., & Gold, H. (1982). Monozygotic twins discordant for trisomy 21. *American Journal of Medical Genetics, 11,* 143–146.

Rogler, L. H., & Hollingshead, A. B. (1965). *Trapped: Families and schizophrenia.* New York: John Wiley.

Romer, D., & Heller, T. (1983). Social adaptation of mentally retarded adults in community settings: A social-ecological approach. *Applied Research in Mental Retardation, 4,* 303–314.

Rorer, L. G. (1989a). Rational-emotive theory: I. An integrated psychological and philosophical basis. *Cognitive Therapy and Research, 13,* 475–492.

Rorer, L. G. (1989b). Rational-emotive theory: II. Explication and evaluation. *Cognitive Therapy and Research, 13,* 531–548.

Rorschach, H. (1942). *Psychodiagnostic: Methodik and ergebnisse eines wahrnehmungs-dianostichen experiments,* 2nd ed. (P. Lemkau & B. Kronenberg, trans.) Berne and Berlin: Huber, 1932; republished: New York: Grune & Stratton.

Rorsman, B., Grasbeck, A., Hagnell, O., Lanke, J., Ohman, R., Ojesjo, L., & Otterbeck, L. (1990). A prospective study of first-incidence depression: The Lundby study, 1957–1972. *British Journal of Psychiatry, 156,* 336–342.

Rorty, M., Yager, J., & Rossotto, E. (1993). Why and how do women recover from bulimia nervosa? The subjective appraisals of forty women recovered for a year or more. *International Journal of Eating Disorders, 14,* 249–260.

Rosenbaum, A., & O'Leary, K. D. (1981). Marital violence: Characteristics of abusive couples. *Journal of Consulting and Clinical Psychology, 49,* 63–71.

Rosenberg, H. (1993). Prediction of controlled drinking by alcoholics and problem drinkers. *Psychological Bulletin, 113,* 129–139.

Rosenblum, L. A., & Paully, G. S. (1987). Primate models of separation-induced depression. *Psychiatric Clinics of North America, 10,* 437–447.

Rosenman, R. H., Brand, R. J., Jenkins, C. D., Friedman, M., Straus, R., & Wurm, M. (1975). Coronary heart disease in the Western Collaborative Group Study. *Journal of the American Medical Association, 233,* 872–877.

Rosenthal, D. (Ed.). (1963). *The Genain quadruplets: A case study and theoretical analysis of heredity and environment in schizophrenia.* New York: Basic Books.

Rosenthal, D., Wender, P. H., Kety, S. S., Schulsinger, F., Welner, J., & Ostergaard, L. (1968). Schizophrenics' offspring reared in adoptive homes. In D. Rosenthal & S. S. Kety (Eds.), *The transmission of schizophrenia.* Oxford: Pergamon Press.

Rosenthal, D., Wender, P. H., Kety, S. S., Schulsinger, F., Welner, J., & Reider, R. (1975). Parent-child relationships and psychopathological disorder in the child. *Archives of General Psychiatry, 32,* 466–476.

Rosenthal, N. E., Sack, D. A., Gillin, J. C., Lewy, A. J., Goodwin, F. K., Davenport, Y., et al. (1984). Seasonal affective disorder: A description of the syndrome and preliminary findings with light therapy. *Archives of General Psychiatry, 41,* 72–80.

Rosenthal, R. (1991). *Meta-analytical procedures for social research* (2nd ed.). Beverly Hills, CA: Sage.

Rosie, J. S. (1987). Partial hospitalization: A review of recent literature. *Hospital and Community Psychiatry, 38,* 1291–1299.

Ross, H. L., & Glaser, E. M. (1973). Making it out of the ghetto. *Professional Psychology, 4,* 347–356.

Rosvold, H. E., Mirsky, A. F., Sarason, I. G., Bransome, E. D., & Beck, L. H. (1956). A continuous performance test of brain damage. *Journal of Consulting Psychology, 20,* 343–350.

Rothblum, E. D. (1994). "I only read about myself on bathroom walls": The need for research on the mental health of lesbians and gay men. *Journal of Consulting and Clinical Psychology, 62,* 213–220.

Rothschild, A. J. (1993). The Dexamethasone Suppression Test in psychiatric disorders. *Psychiatric Annals, 23,* 662–670.

Roy, A. (1986). Depression, attempted suicide, and suicide in patients with chronic schizophrenia. *Psychiatric Clinics of North America, 9,* 193–206.

Ruberman, J. W., Weinblatt, E., Goldberg, J. D., & Chaudhary, B. S. (1984). Psychological influences on mortality after myocardial infarction. *New England Journal of Medicine, 311,* 552–559.

Ruch, L. O., Gartrell, J. W., Amedeo, S. R., & Coyne, B. J. (1991). The Sexual Assault Symptom Scale: Measuring self-reported sexual assault trauma in the emergency room. *Psychological Assessment, 3,* 3–8.

Rund, B. R. (1990). Fully recovered schizophrenics: A retrospective study of some premorbid and treatment factors. *Psychiatry, 53,* 127–139.

Rupp, A., & Keith, S. J. (1993) The costs of schizophrenia. *Psychiatric Clinics of North America, 16,* 413–423.

Rush, A. J., & Weissenburger, J. E. (1994). Melancholic symptom features and DSM-IV. *American Journal of Psychiatry, 151,* 489–498.

Rush, A. J., Beck, A. T., Kovacs, M., et al. (1982) Comparison of the effects of cognitive therapy and pharmacotherapy on hopelessness and self-concept. *American Journal of Psychiatry, 139,* 862–866.

Russell, D. E. H. (1984). The prevalence and seriousness of incestuous abuse: Step fathers vs. biological fathers. *Child Abuse and Neglect, 8,* 15–22.

Rutter, D. R. (1985). Language in schizophrenia: The structure of monologues and conversations. *British Journal of Psychiatry, 146,* 399–404.

Rutter, J. (1991). Nature, nurture, and psychopathology: A new look at an old topic. *Development and Psychopathology, 3,* 125–136.

Rutter, M., Cox, A., Tupling, C., Berger, M., & Yule, W. (1975). Attainment and adjustment in two geographical areas: I. The prevalence of psychiatric disorder. *British Journal of Psychiatry, 126,* 493–509.

Rutter, M., & Garmezy, N. (1983). Developmental psychopathology. In P. Mussen (Ed.), *Handbook of child psychology* (vol. 4). New York: John Wiley.

Rutter, M., Graham, P., & Yule, W. (1970). A neuropsychiatric study in childhood. *Clinics in Developmental Medicine*, Nos. 35/36. London: Heinemann.

Rutter, M., & Hersov, L. (1985). *Child and adolescent psychiatry: Modern approaches*. Oxford, England: Blackwell Scientific Publications.

Rutter, M., & Shaffer, D. (1980). DSM-III: A step forward or back in terms of the classification of child psychiatric disorders. *Journal of the American Academy of Child Psychiatry, 19*, 371–394.

Sabat'e, O., Campion, D., d'Amato, T., Martres, M. P., Sokoloff, P., Giros, B., Leboyer, M., Jay, M., Guedj, F., & Thibaut, F. (1994). Failure to find evidence for linkage or association between the dopamine D3 receptor gene and schizophrenia. *American Journal of Psychiatry, 151*, 107–111.

Sachs, D. P., Sawe, U., & Leischow, S. J. (1993). Effectiveness of a 16-hour transdermal nicotine patch in a medical practice setting, without intensive group counseling. *Archives of Internal Medicine, 153*, 1881–1890.

Sackeim, H. A., Devanand, D. P., & Prudic, J. (1992). Medication resistance as a predictor of ECT outcome and relabs. *American College of Neuropsychopharmacology Abstracts of Panels and Posters, 51*.

Sackeim, H. A., Prudic, J., & Devanand, D. P. (1990). Treatment of medication-resistant depression with electroconvulsive therapy. In A. Tasman, S. M. Goldfinger, & C. A. Kaufmann (Eds.), *Review of psychiatry* (vol. 9). Washington, DC: American Psychiatric Press.

Sackeim, H. A., & Wegner, A. Z. (1986). Attributional patterns in depression and euthymia. *Archives of General Psychiatry, 43*, 553–560.

Sadock, V. A. (1989). Normal human sexuality and sexual disorders. In H. I. Kaplan & B. J. Sadock (Eds.), *Comprehensive textbook of psychiatry*, 5th ed. Baltimore: Williams & Wilkins.

Sadock, V. A. (1989). Rape, spouse abuse, and incest. In H. I. Kaplan & B. J. Sadock, eds., *Comprehensive textbook of psychiatry*, 5th ed. Baltimore: Williams & Wilkins.

Salter, A. C., Richardson, C. M., & Kairys, S. W. (1985). Caring for abused preschoolers. *Child Welfare, 64*, 343–356.

Sameroff, A. J., & Fiese, B. H. (1990). Transactional regulations and early intervention. In S. J. Meisels & J. P. Shonkoff (Eds.), *Handbook of early childhood intervention* (pp. 119–149). Cambridge, England: Cambridge University Press.

Sanders, C. M. (1993). Risk factors in bereavement outcome. In M. S. Stroebe, W. Stroebe, & R. O. Hansson (Eds.), *Handbook of bereavement*. Cambridge, England: Cambridge University Press.

Sanderson, W. C., & Barlow, D. H. (1990). A description of patients diagnosed with DSM-III-R generalized anxiety disorder. *The Journal of Nervous and Mental Disease, 178*, 588–591.

Santayana, G. (1905–1906). *The life of reason*. New York: Scribner.

Sarason, I. G. (1979). Three lacunae of cognitive therapy. *Cognitive Therapy and Research, 3*, 223–235.

Sarason, I. G., Johnson, J. M., & Siegel, J. M. (1978). Assessing the impact of life stress: Development of the Life Experiences Survey. *Journal of Consulting and Clinical Psychology, 46*, 932–946.

Sarason, I. G., Levine, H. M., Basham, R. B., & Sarason, B. R. (1983). Assessing social support: The Social Support Questionnaire. *Journal of Personality and Social Psychology, 44*, 127–139.

Sarason, I. G., & Sarason, B. R. (1981). Teaching cognitive and social skills to high school students. *Journal of Consulting and Clinical Psychology, 49*, 908–919.

Sarason, I. G., & Sarason, B. R. (Eds.) (1985). *Social support: Theory, research and applications*. Dordrecht, The Netherlands: Martinus Nijhof.

Sarason, I. G., Sarason, B. R., & Pierce, G. R. (1990). Social support: The search for theory. *Journal of Social and Clinical Psychology, 9*, 133–147.

Sartorius, N., & de Girolamo, G. (1991). Preface to a special issue. *Schizophrenia Bulletin, 17*, 401–405.

Sartorius, N., Ustun, T. B., Costa-e-Silva, J. A., Goldberg, L, Lecrubier, Y., Ormel, J., Von Korff, M., & Wittchen, H. U. (1993). An international study of psychological problems in primary care. Preliminary report from the World Health Organization Collaborative project on "Psychological Problems in General Health Care." *Archives of General Psychiatry, 50*, 819–824.

Sass, L. A. (1987). Introspection, schizophrenia, and the fragmentation of self. *Representations 19*, 1–34.

Satterfield, J. H., Satterfield, B. T., & Schell, A. M. (1987). Therapeutic interventions to prevent delinquency in hyperactive boys. *Journal of the American Academy of Child and Adolescent Psychiatry, 26*, 56–64.

Saul, R. A., Stevenson, R. I., Simensen, R. J., Wilkes, G., Alexander, W., & Taylor, H. (1982). Fragile X syndrome in South Carolina. *Journal of the South Carolina Medical Association, 78*, 475–477.

Sayette, M. A. (1993). An appraisal-disruption model of alcohol's effects on stress responses in social drinkers. *Psychological Bulletin, 114*, 459–476.

Schafer, R. (1948). *Clinical application of psychological tests*. New York: International Universities Press.

Schaie, K. W. (1989). The hazards of cognitive aging. *The Gerontological Society of America, 29*, 484–493.

Schaie, K. W. (1994). The course of adult intellectual development. *American Psychologist, 49*, 304–313.

Schalling, D. (1978). Psychopathy-related personality variables and the psychophysiology of socialization. In R. D. Hare & D. Schalling (Eds.), *Psychopathic behavior: Approaches to research*. Chichester, England: John Wiley.

Schatzberg, A. F. (1991). Psychotic (delusional) major depression: Should it be included as a distinct syndrome in DSM-IV? *American Journal of Psychiatry, 149*, 733–745.

Scheidlinger, S. (1994). An overview of nine decades of group psychotherapy. *Hospital and Community Psychiatry, 45*, 217–225.

Schilling, R. F., & Schinke, S. P. (1984). Maltreatment and mental retardation. In J. M. Berg (Ed.). *Perspectives and progress in mental retardation* (vol. 1). Baltimore, MD: University Park Press.

Schnall, P. L., Pieper, C., Schwartz, J. E., Karasek, R. A., Schlussel, Y., Devereux, R. B., Ganau, A., Alderman, M., Warren, K., & Pickering, T. G. (1990). The relationship between "job strain," workplace diastolic blood pressure, and left ventricular mass index. *Journal of the American Medical Association, 263*, 1929–1972.

Schoenman, T. J. (1984). The mentally ill witch in textbooks of abnormal psychology: Current status and implications of a fallacy. *Professional Psychiatry, 15*, 299–314.

Schotte, D. E., & Stunkard, A. J. (1987). Bulimia vs. bulimic behaviors on a college campus. *Journal of the American Medical Association, 258,* 1213–1215.

Schuckit, M. A. (1987). Biological vulnerability to alcoholism. *Journal of Consulting and Clinical Psychology, 55,* 307–309.

Schuldberg, D. (1993). Personal resourcefulness: Positive aspects of functioning in high-risk research. *Psychiatry, 56,* 137–152.

Schwartz, A. J., & Whitaker, L. C. (1990). Suicide among college students: Assessment, treatment, and intervention. In S. J. Blumenthal & D. J. Kupfer (Eds.), *Suicide over the life cycle: Risk factors, assessment, and treatment of suicidal patients.* Washington, DC: American Psychiatric Press.

Schweinhart, L. J., & Weikart, D. P. (1980). *Young children grow up.* Ypsilanti, MI: High/Scope.

Scull, A. (1993). *The most solitary of afflications: Madness and society in Britain 1700–1900.* New Haven, CT: Yale University Press.

Searl, S., Jr. (1978). Stages of parent reaction to the birth of a handicapped child. *Exceptional Parent,* (April), 23–27.

Segal, Z. V. (1988). Appraisal of the self-schema construct in cognitive models of depression. *Psychological Bulletin, 103,* 147–162.

Segal, Z. V., & Swallow, S. R. (1994). Cognitive assessment of unipolar depression: Measuring products, processes and structures. *Behavior Research and Therapy, 32,* 147–158.

Seidman, S., & Rieder, R. O. (1994). A review of sexual behavior in the United States. *The American Journal of Psychiatry, 151,* 330–341.

Seligman, M. E. P. (1971). Phobias and preparedness. *Behavior Therapy, 2,* 307–320.

Seligman, M. E. P. (1974). Depression and learned helplessness. In R. J. Friedman & M. M. Katz (Eds.), *The psychology of depression: Contemporary theory and research.* Washington, DC: V. H. Winston.

Seligman, M. E. P. (1975). *Helplessness: On depression, development, and death.* San Francisco: W. H. Freeman.

Selye, H. (1976). *The stress of life,* rev. ed. New York: McGraw-Hill.

Shaffer, D. (1994). Attention deficit hyperactivity disorder in adults. *American Journal of Psychiatry, 151,* 633–638.

Shaffer, J. W., Graves, P. L., Swank, R. T., & Pearson, T. A. (1987). Clustering of personality traits in youth and the subsequent development of cancer among physicians. *Journal of Behavioral Medicine, 10,* 441–447.

Shapiro, D. (1965). *Neurotic styles.* New York: Basic Books.

Shapiro, D. A., Barkham, M., Rees, A., Hardy, G. E., Reynolds, S., & Startup, M. (1994). Effects of treatment duration and severity of depression on the effectiveness of cognitive-behavioral and psychodynamic-interpersonal psychotherapy. *Journal of Consulting and Clinical Psychology, 62,* 522–534.

Shea, M. T., Elkin, I., Imber, S. D., Sotsky, S. M., Watkins, J. T., Collins, J. F., Pilkonis, P. A., Beckham, E., Glass, D. R., Dolan, R. T., & Parloff, M. B. (1992). Course of depressive symptoms over follow-up: Findings from the National Institute of Mental Health Treatment of Depression Collaborative Research Program. *Archives of General Psychiatry, 49,* 782–787.

Shea, S. C. (1988). *Psychiatric interviewing: The art of understanding.* Philadelphia: Saunders.

Sheehan, S. (1982). *Is there no place on earth for me?* Boston: Houghton Mifflin.

Shekelle, R. B., Raynor, W. J., Ostfeld, A. M., Garron, D. C.,

Bieliauskas, L. A., Liv, S. C., Maliza, C., & Oglesby, P. (1981). Psychological depression and 17-year risk of death from cancer. *Psychosomatic Medicine, 43,* 117–125.

Shengxian L., & Phillips, M. R. (1990). Witch doctors and mental illness in Mainland China: A preliminary study. *American Journal of Psychiatry, 147,* 221–224.

Sherman, B. (1985). The new realities of "date rape." *New York Times,* Oct. 23, 17.

Shoham-Salomon, V., Avner, R., & Neeman, R. (1989). You're changed if you do and changed if you don't: Mechanisms underlying paradoxical interventions. *Journal of Consulting and Clinical Psychology, 57,* 590–598.

Shore, E. R. (1989). What I learned about community psychology from my bout with cancer. *The Community Psychologist, 23,* 25.

Shumaker, S. A., & Czajkowski, S. M. (Eds.) (1994). *Social support and cardiovascular disease.* New York: Plenum.

Shumaker, S. A., & Hill, D. R. (1991). Gender differences in social support and physical health. *Health Psychology, 10,* 102–111.

Shure, M. B., & Spivack, G. (1982). Interpersonal problem-solving in young children: A cognitive approach to prevention. *American Journal of Community Psychology, 10,* 341–356.

Shure, M. B., & Spivack, G. (1987). Competence-building as an approach to prevention of dysfunction: The ICPS model. In J. A. Steinberg & M. M. Silverman (Eds.), *Preventing mental disorders: A research perspective.* Rockville, MD: National Institute of Mental Health.

Siever, L. J., Bernstein, D. P., & Silverman, J. M. (1991). Schizotypal personality disorder: A review of its current status. *Journal of Personality Disorders, 5,* 178–193.

Siever, L. J., & Coursey, R. D. (1985). Biological markers for schizophrenia and the biological high risk approach. *Journal of Nervous and Mental Disease, 173,* 4–16.

Siever, L. J., & Kendler, K. S. (1986). Schizoid/schizotypal/paranoid personality disorders. In R. Michels and J. O. Cavenar, Jr. (Eds.), *Psychiatry* (vol. 1). New York: Basic Books.

Silver, J. M., Hales, R. E., & Yudofsky, S. C. (1990). Psychiatric consultation to neurology. In A. Tasman, S. M. Goldfinger, & C. A. Kauffmann, eds., *Review of psychiatry,* vol. 9. Washington, DC: American Psychiatric Press.

Silverman, M. M. (1993). Campus student suicide rates: Fact or artifact?—A review. *Suicide and Life-Threatening Behavior, 23,* 329–342.

Silverstein, M. L., & Harrow, M. (1981). Schneiderian first-rank symptoms in schizophrenia. *Archives of General Psychiatry, 38,* 288–293.

Skinner, B. F. (1959). A case history in scientific method. In S. Koch (Ed.), *Psychology: A study of a science,* vol. 2. New York: McGraw-Hill.

Sklar, L. S., & Anisman, H. (1981). Stress and cancer. *Psychological Bulletin, 89,* 369–406.

Skodol, A. E. (1989). *Problems in differential diagnosis.* Washington, DC: American Psychiatric Press.

Skultans, V. (1979). *English madness.* London: Routledge & Kegan Paul.

Sloane, R. B., Staples, F. R., Whipple, K., & Cristol, A. H. (1977). Patients' attitudes toward behavior therapy and psychotherapy. *American Journal of Psychiatry, 134*(2), 134–137.

Sloane, R. B., Staples, F. R., Yorkston, N. J., Whipple, K., & Cristol, A. H. (1975). *Short-term analytically oriented psychother-*

apy versus behavior therapy. Cambridge, MA: Harvard University Press.

Smith, D. W., & Wilson, A. A. (1973). *A child with Down's syndrome (mongolism)*. Philadelphia: Saunders.

Smith, E. M., North, C. S., McCool, R. E., & Shea, J. M. (1990). Acute postdisaster psychiatric disorders: Identification of persons at risk. *American Journal of Psychiatry, 147,* 202–206.

Smith, M., Wasmuth, J., McPherson, J. D., Wagner, C., Grandy, D., Civelli, O. and others. (1989). Cosegregation of an 11q11-9p22 translocation with affective disorder: Proximity of the dopamine D2 receptor gene relative to the translocation breakpoint. *American Journal of Human Genetics, 45,* A220.

Smith, M. L., Glass, G. V., & Miller, T. I. (1980). *The benefits of psychotherapy*. Baltimore: Johns Hopkins University Press.

Smith, R. N. (1982). *Dewey and his times*. New York: Simon & Schuster.

Smith, T. W. (1982). Irrational beliefs on the cause and treatment of emotional distress: A critical review of the rational-emotive model. *Clinical Psychology Review, 2,* 505–522.

Sohlberg, S., & Strober, M. (1994). Personality in anorexia nervosa: An update and a theoretical integration. *Acta Psychiatrica Scandinavica, 89* (Suppl. 378), 1–16.

Sokol, L., Beck, A. I., Greenberg, R. L., Wright, F. D., & Berchick, R. J. (1989). Cognitive therapy of panic disorder: A nonpharmacological alternative. *The Journal of Nervous and Mental Disease, 177,* 711–716.

Sokoloff, P., Giros, B., Martres, M. P., Bouthenet, M. L., & Schwartz, J. C. (1990). Molecular cloning and characterization of a novel dopamine receptor as a target for neuroleptics. *Nature, 347,* 146–151.

Solomon, S. D., Gerrity, E. T., & Muff, A. M. (1992). Efficacy of treatments for posttraumatic stress disorder: An empirical review. *Journal of the American Medical Association, 268,* 633–638.

Solovay, M. R., Shenton, M. E., & Holzman, P. S. (1987). Comparative studies of thought disorders. *Archives of General Psychiatry, 44,* 13–20.

Spaccarelli, S. (1994). Stress, appraisal, and coping in child sexual abuse: A theoretical and empirical review. *Psychological Bulletin, 116,* 340–362.

Spanos, N. P. (1978). Witchcraft in histories of psychiatry: A critical analysis and an alternative conceptualization. *Psychological Bulletin, 85,* 417–439.

Spanos, N. P. (1994). Multiple identity enactments and multiple personality disorder: A sociocognitive perspective. *Psychological Bulletin, 116,* 143–165.

Spiegel, D., Bloom, J. R., Kraemer, H. C., & Gottheil, E. (1989). Effect of psychosocial treatment on survival of patients with metastatic breast cancer. *Lancet,* October 14, 888–891.

Spiegel, D., & Wissler, T. (1986). Family environment as a predictor of psychiatric rehospitalization. *American Journal of Psychiatry, 143,* 56–60.

Spiegel, D. A. (Ed.) (1994). *Dissociation.* Washington, DC: American Psychiatric Press.

Spiegel, D. A. (1994). Does cognitive behavior therapy assist slow-taper alprazolam discontinuation in panic disorder? *American Journal of Psychiatry, 151,* 876–881.

Spiegel, D. A., Roth, M., Weissman, M., Lavori, P., Gorman, J., Rush, J., & Ballenger, J. (1993). Alprazolam and exposure alone and combined in panic disorder with agoraphobia: A controlled study in London and Toronto. *British Journal of Psychiatry, 162,* 788–789.

Spitzer, R. L., Gibbon, M., Skodol, A. E., Williams, J. B. W., & First, M. G. (1989). *DSM-III-R casebook.* Washington, DC: American Psychiatric Press.

Spitzer, R. L., Skodol, A. E., Gibbon, M., & Williams, J. B. W. (1981). *DSM-III casebook.* Washington, DC: American Psychiatric Association.

Spitzer, R. L., Skodol, A. E., Gibbon, M., & Williams, J. B. W. (1983). *Psychopathology: A casebook.* New York: McGraw-Hill.

Spitzer, R. L., First, M. B., Williams, J. B. W., Kendler, R., Pincus, H. A., & Tucker, G. (1992). Now is the time to retire the term "organic mental disorders." *American Journal of Psychiatry, 149,* 240–244.

Spitzer, R. L., Williams, J. B. W., Gibbon, M., & First, M. B. (1992). The structured clinical interview for DSM-III-R (SCID): I. History, rationale, and description. *Archives of General Psychiatry, 49,* 624–629.

Spivack, G., Platt, J. J., & Shure, M. B. (1976). *The problem-solving approach to adjustment.* San Francisco: Jossey-Bass.

Spring, B., Lemon, M., Weinstein, L., & Haskell, A. (1989). Distractibility in schizophrenia: State and trait aspects. *British Journal of Psychiatry, 155,* 63–68.

St. Clair, D., Blackwood, D., Muir, W., Carothers, A., Walker, M., Spowart, G., Cosden, C., & Evans, H. J. (1990). Association within a family of balanced autosomal translocation with major mental illness. *Lancet, 336,* 13–16.

Stark, K. D., Humphrey, L. L., Crook, K., & Lewis, K. (1990). Perceived family environments of depressed and anxious children: Child's and maternal figure's perspectives. *Journal of Abnormal Child Psychology, 18,* 527–547.

Starting Points: Meeting the needs of our youngest children. (1994). New York: Carnegie Corporation of New York.

Stein, M., Schleifer, S. J., & Keller, S. E. (1987). Psychoimmunology in clinical psychiatry. In R. E. Hales & A. J. Frances (Eds.), *American Psychiatric Association annual review* (vol. 6). Washington, DC: American Psychiatric Press.

Stein, M. B., Walker, J. R., & Forde, D. R. (1994). Setting diagnostic thresholds for social phobia: Considerations from a community survey of social anxiety. *American Journal of Psychiatry, 15,* 408–412.

Steinhauer, S. R., Zubin, J., Condray, R., Shaw, D. B., Peters, J. L., & van Kammen, D. P. (1991). Electrophysiological and behavior signs of attentional disturbance in schizophrenics and their siblings. In C. A. Tammings and S. C. Schulz, *Advances in Neuropsychiatry and Psychopharmacology* (vol. 1) *Schizophrenia Research* (pp. 169–178). New York: Raven Press.

Steinhausen, H. C., & Seidel, R. (1993). Outcome in adolescent eating disorders. *International Journal of Eating Disorders, 14,* 487–496.

Stephens, R. S., Roffman, R. A., & Simpson, E. E. (1994). Treating adult marijuana dependence: A test of the relapse prevention model. *Journal of Consulting and Clinical Psychology, 62,* 92–99.

Stone, M. H. (1980). *The borderline syndromes.* New York: McGraw-Hill.

Stone, M. H. (1986). Borderline personality disorder. In R. Michels and J. O. Cavenar, Jr. (Eds.), *Psychiatry* (vol. 1). New York: Basic Books.

Stone, M. H., Stone, D. K., & Hurt, S. W. (1987). The natural history of borderline patients treated by intensive hospitalization. *Psychiatric Clinics of North America, 10,* 185–206.

Storr, A. (1980). *The art of psychotherapy.* New York: Methuen.

Storr, A. (1988). Churchill: The man. In A. Storr (Ed.), *Churchill's black dog, Kafka's mice, and other phenomena of the human mind.* New York: Grove Press.

Strain, E. C., Mumford, G. K., Silverman, K., & Griffiths, R. R. (1994). Caffeine dependence syndrome: Evidence from case histories and experimental evaluations. *Journal of the Medical Association, 272,* 1043–1048.

Strand, V. C. (1991). Victim of sexual abuse: Case of Rosa, age 6. In N. B. Webb (Ed.), *Play therapy with children in crisis* (pp. 69–91). New York: Guilford.

Streissguth, A. P., Aase, J. M., Clarren, S. K., Randels, S. P., LaDue, R. A., & Smith, D. F. (1991). Fetal alcohol syndrome in adolescents and adults. *Journal of the American Medical Association, 265,* 1961–1967.

Strober, M., Lampert, C., Morrell, W., Burroughs, J., & Jacobs, C. (1990). A controlled family study of anorexia nervosa: Evidence of familial aggregation and lack of shared transmission with affective disorders. *International Journal of Eating Disorders, 9,* 239–253.

Stroebe, M. S., Stroebe, W., & Hansson, R. O. (Eds.) (1993). *Handbook of bereavement.* Cambridge, England: Cambridge University Press.

Stroop, J. R. (1935). Studies of interference in serial verbal reaction. *Journal of Experimental Psychology, 18,* 643–662.

Strupp, H. H. (1989). Psychotherapy: Can the practitioner learn from the researcher? *American Psychologist, 44,* 717–724.

Stubbs, E. G., Ritvo, E. R., & Mason-Brothers, A. (1985). Autism and shared parental HLA antigens. *Journal of Child Psychiatry, 24,* 182–185.

Suddath, R. L., Christison, G. W., Torrey, E. F., Casanova, M. F., & Weinberger, D. R. (1990). Anatomical abnormalities in the brains of monozygotic twins discordant for schizophrenia. *New England Journal of Medicine, 322,* 789–794.

Suelze, M., & Keenan, V. (1981). Changes in family support networks over the life cycle of mentally retarded persons. *American Journal of Mental Deficiency, 86,* 267–274.

Sunahara, R. K., Seeman, P., Van Tol, H. H., & Niznik, H. B. (1993). Dopamine receptors and antipsychotic drug response. *British Journal of Psychiatry* (Suppl.) *22,* 31–38.

Sundgot, B. J. (1994). Risk and trigger factors for the development of eating disorders in female elite athletes. *Medicine and Science in Sports and Exercise, 26,* 414–419.

Suomi, S. J., & Harlow, H. F. (1972). Social rehabilitation of isolation-reared monkeys. *Developmental Psychology, 6,* 487–496.

Suomi, S. J., & Harlow, H. F. (1978). Early experience and social development in Rhesus monkeys. In M. E. Lamb (Ed.), *Social and personality development.* New York: Holt, Rinehart and Winston.

Swanson, J. W., Holzer, C. E., III, Ganju, V. K., & Jono, R. T. (1990). Violence and psychiatric disorder in the community: Evidence from the epidemiologic catchment area surveys. *Hospital and Community Psychiatry, 41,* 761–770.

Swedo, S. E., Leonard, H. L., Rapoport, J. L. (1992). Childhood-onset obsessive compulsive disorder. *Psychiatric Clinics of North America, 15,* 767–775.

Swett, C., Jr., Surrey, J., & Cohen, C. (1990). Sexual and physical abuse histories and psychiatric symptoms among male psychiatric outpatients. *American Journal of Psychiatry, 147,* 632–636.

Takei, N. T., Sham, P., O'Callaghan, E., Murray, G. K., Glover, G., & Murray, R. M. (1994) Prenatal exposure to influenza and the development of schizophrenia: Is the effect confined to females? *American Journal of Psychiatry, 151,* 117–119.

Tang., J. L., Law, M., & Wald, N. (1994). How effective is nicotine replacement therapy in helping people to stop smoking? *British Medical Journal, 308,* 21–26.

Teicher, M. H., Glod, C. A., & Cole, J. O. (1993). Antidepressant drugs and the emergence of suicidal tendencies. *Drug Safety, 8,* 186–212.

Teicher, M. H., Glod, C., & Cole, J. O. (1990). Emergence of intense suicidal preoccupation during fluoxetine treatment. *American Journal of Psychiatry, 147,* 207–210.

Teplin, L. A., Abram, K. M., & McClelland, G. M. (1994). Does psychiatric disorder predict violent crime among released jail detainees?: A six-year longitudinal study. *American Psychologist, 49,* 335–342.

Terkelsen, M. D., & Grosser, R. C. (1990). Estimating clozapine's cost to the nation. *Hospital and Community Psychiatry, 41,* 863–869.

Thoresen, C. E., Friedman, M., Gill, J. J., & Ulmer, D. K. (1982). The recurrent coronary prevention project: Some preliminary findings. *Acta Medica Scandinavica, 68,* 172–192.

Thorndike, R. L., Hagen, E. P., & Sattler, J. M. (1986). *The Stanford-Binet intelligence scale: Guide for administration and scoring.* Chicago, IL: Riverside.

Tien, A. Y., & Anthony, J. C. (1990). Epidemiological analysis of alcohol and drug use as risk factors for psychotic experiences. *The Journal of Nervous and Mental Disease, 178,* 473–480.

Tienari, P., Lahti, I., Sorri, A., Naarala, M., Moring, J., Kaleva, M., Wahlberg, K. E., & Wynne, L. C. (1990). Adopted-away offspring of schizophrenics and controls: The Finnish adoptive family study of schizophrenia. In L. Robins & M. Rutter (Eds.), *Straight and devious pathways from childhood to adulthood.* New York: Cambridge University Press.

Tienari, P., Wynne, L. C., Moring, J., Lahti, I., Naarala, M., Sorri, A., Wahlberg, K. E., Saarento, O., Seitamaa, M., & Kalveva, M. (1994). The Finnish adoptive family study of schizophrenia: Implications for family research. *British Journal of Psychiatry Supplement, 23,* 20–26.

Tollefson, G. D., Rampey, A. H., Potvin, J. H., Jenike, M. A., Rush, A. J., Kominguez, R. A., Koran, L. M., Shear, M. K., Goodman, N. & Gerduso, L. A. (1994). A multicenter investigation of fixed-dose fluoxetine in the treatment of obsessive-compulsive disorder. *Archives of General Psychiatry, 51,* 559–567.

Tomb, D. A., & Christensen, D. D. (1987). *Case studies in psychiatry for the house officer.* Baltimore: Williams & Wilkins.

Torgersen, S. (1979). The nature and origin of common phobic fears. *British Journal of Psychiatry, 134,* 343–351.

Torgersen, S., Onstad, S., Skre, I., Edvardsen, J., & Kringlen, E. (1993). "True" schizotypal personality disorder: A study of co-twins and relatives of schizophrenic probands. *American Journal of Psychiatry, 150,* 1661–1667.

Torrey, E. F., & Bowler, A. (1990). Geographical distribution of insanity in America: Evidence for an urban factor. *Schizophrenia Bulletin, 16,* 591–604.

Torrey, E. F., Bowler, A. E., Taylor, E. H., Gottesman, I. I. (1994).

Schizophrenia and manic-depressive disorder. New York: Basic Books.

Torrey, E. F. (1994). Violent behavior by individuals with serious mental illness. *Hospital and Community Psychiatry, 45,* 653–662.

Touyz, S. W., Kopec-Schrader, E. M., & Beumont, P. J. (1993). Anorexia nervosa in males: A report of 12 cases. *Australian and New Zealand Journal of Psychiatry, 27,* 512–517.

Touyz, S. W., Kopec-Schrader, E. M., Vitousek, K., & Manke, R. (1994). Personality variables and disorders in anorexia nervosa and bulimia nervosa. *Journal of Abnormal Psychology, 103,* 137–147.

Tsai, L. Y. (1987). Pre- peri-, and neonatal factors in autism. In E. Shopler & G. B. Mesibov (Eds.), *Neurobiological issues in autism.* New York: Plenum.

Turner, S. M., Beidel, D. C., & Costello, A. (1987). Psychopathology in the offspring of anxiety disorders patients. *Journal of Consulting and Clinical Psychology, 55,* 229–235.

Turner, S. M., Beidel, D. C., Darcu, C. V., & Keys, D. J. (1986). Psychopathology of social phobia and comparison to avoidant personality disorder. *Journal of Abnormal Psychology, 95,* 389–394.

Uba, L. (1994). *Asian Americans: Personality patterns, identity, and mental health.* New York: Guilford.

Vachon, L. (1989). Respiratory disorders. In H. I. Kaplan & B. J. Sadock, (Eds.), *Comprehensive textbook of psychiatry,* 5th ed. Baltimore: Williams & Wilkins.

Vaillant, G. E. (1973). A 20-year follow-up of New York narcotic addicts. *Archives of General Psychiatry, 29,* 237–241.

Vaillant, G. E. (1984). The disadvantages of DSM-III outweigh its advantages. *American Journal of Psychiatry, 14,* 542–545.

Vaillant, G. E., & Milofsky, E. S. (1982). Natural history of male alcoholism: IV. Paths to recovery. *Archives of General Psychiatry, 39,* 127–133.

Vaillant, G. E. (1994). Ego mechanisms of defense and personality psychopathology. *Journal of Abnormal Psychology, 103,* 44–50.

Vargas, J. S. (1990). B. F. Skinner—The last few days. *Journal of Applied Behavior Analysis, 23,* 409–410.

Varma, S. L., & Sharma, I. (1993). Psychiatric morbidity in the first-degree relatives of schizophrenic patients. *British Journal of Psychiatry, 162,* 672–678.

Varnhagen, C. K., Das, J. P., & Varnhagen, S. (1987). Auditory and visual memory span: Cognitive processing by TMR individuals with Down's syndrome or other etiologies. *American Journal of Mental Deficiency, 91,* 398–405.

Vaughn, C. E., & Leff, J. P. (1976). The influence of family and social factors on the course of psychiatric illness. *British Journal of Psychiatry, 129,* 125–137.

Vaughn, C. E., Snyder, K. S., Jones, S., Freeman, W. B., & Falloon, I. R. H. (1984). Family factors in schizophrenic relapse. *Archives of General Psychiatry, 41,* 1169–1177.

Veiel, H. O. F., Brill, G., Hafner, H., & Welz, R. (1988). The social supports of suicide attempters: The different roles of family and friends. *American Journal of Community Psychology, 16,* 839–861.

Videka-Sherman, L., & Lieberman, M. (1985). The effects of self-help and psychotherapy intervention on child loss: The limits of recovery. *American Journal of Orthopsychiatry, 55,* 70–82.

Vinogradov, S., Dishotsky, N. I., Doty, A. K., & Tinklenberg, J. R. (1988). Patterns of behavior in adolescent rape. *American Journal of Orthopsychiatry, 58,* 179–187.

Vinogradov, S., & Yalom, I. D. (1990). Self-disclosure in group psychotherapy. In G. Stricker & M. Fisher (Eds.), *Self-disclosure in the therapeutic relationship.* New York: Plenum.

Virkkunen, M. (1983). Insulin secretion during the glucose tolerance-test in antisocial personality. *British Journal of Psychiatry, 142,* 598–604.

Vitousek, K., & Manke, F. (1994). Personality variables and disorders in anorexia nervosa and bulimia nervosa. *Journal of Abnormal Psychology, 103,* 137–147.

Volavka, J., Crowner, M., Brizer, D., Convit, A., Van Praag, H., & Suckow, R. F. (1990). Tryptophan treatment of aggressive psychiatric inpatients. *Biological Psychiatry, 28,* 728–732.

Volkmar, F. R., & Cohen, D. J. (1985). The experience of infantile autism: A first-person account by Tony W. *Journal of Autism and Developmental Disorders, 15,* 47–54.

Vollhardt, L. T. (1991). Psychoneuroimmunology: A literature review. *American Journal of Orthopsychiatry, 61,* 35–47.

Volvaka, J. (1990). Aggression, electroencephalography, and evoked-potentials: A critical review. *Neuropsychiatry, Neuropsychology, and Behavioral Neurology, 3,* 249–259.

Walker, L. E. (1984). *The battered woman syndrome.* New York: Springer.

Wallace, B. C. (1991). *Crack cocaine.* New York: Brunner/Mazel.

Wallace, M. (1994). Schizophrenia—a national emergency: Preliminary observations on SANELINE. *Acta Psychiatrica Scandinavia, 89* (Suppl.), 33–35.

Waller, G. (1994). Childhood sexual abuse and borderline personality disorder in the eating disorders. *Child Abuse and Neglect, 18,* 97–101.

Wallerstein, J. S., & Kelly, J. B. (1990). Surviving the breakup: How children and parents cope with divorce. NY: Basic Books.

Wallin, M. S., & Rissanen, A. M. (1994). Food and mood: Relationship between food, serotonin and affective disorders. *Acta Psychiatrica Scandinavica, 89,* 377 (Suppl.), 36–40.

Ward, S. R., Chapman, R., Cohn, E., White, S., & Williams, K. (1991). Acquaintance rape and the college social scene. *Family Relations, 40,* 65–71.

Warren, S. T., & Nelson, D. L. (1994). Advances in molecular analysis of fragile X syndrome. *Journal of the American Medical Association, 271,* 536–554.

Watson, J. B. (1925). *Behaviorism.* New York: Norton.

Weary, G., & Edwards, J. A. (1994). Social cognition and clinical psychology: Anxiety, depression, and the processing of social information. In R. S. Wyer, Jr., and T. K. Srull (Eds.), *Handbook of Social Cognition* (Vol 2). Hillsdale, NJ: Laurence Erlbaum Associates.

Weaver, T. L., & Clum, G. A. (1993). Early family environments and traumatic experiences associated with borderline personality disorder. *Journal of Consulting and Clinical Psychology, 61,* 1068–1075.

Wechsler, D. (1955). *Manual for the Wechsler Adult Intelligence Scale.* New York: Psychological Corporation.

Wechsler, D. (1958). *The measurement and appraisal of adult intelligence,* 4th ed. Baltimore: Williams & Wilkins.

Wechsler, H., Davenport, A., Dowdall, G., Moeykens, B., & Castillo, S. (1994). Health and behavioral consequences of binge drinking in college. *Journal of the American Medical Association, 272,* 1672–1677.

Weinberg, T. S. (1978). Sadism and masochism: Sociological perspectives. *Bulletin of the American Academy of Psychiatry and Law, 6,* 284–295.

Weinberg, T. S., & Falk, G. (1980). The social organization of sadism and masochism. *Deviant Behavior, 1,* 370–393.

Weinberg, T. S., Williams, C. J., & Moser, C. (1984). The social constituents of sadomasochism. *Social Problems, 31,* 379–389.

Weiner, D. B. (1979). The apprenticeship of Philippe Pinel: A new document, "Observations of Citizen Pussin on the Insane." *American Journal of Psychiatry, 136,* 1128–1134.

Weiner, D. B. (1992). Philippe Pinel's "Memoir on Madness" of December 11, 1794: A fundamental text of modern psychiatry. *American Journal of Psychiatry, 149,* 725–732.

Weiner, H. (1991). From simplicity to complexity (1950–1990): The case of peptic ulceration—I. Human Studies. *Psychosomatic Medicine, 53,* 467–490.

Weiner, H., Cancro, R., Lehmann, H. E., & Frazier, S. H. (1989). Psychopharmacologic treatments. In *Treatments of psychiatric disorders: A task force report of the American Psychiatric Association.* Washington, DC: American Psychiatric Association.

Weiss, R. (1993). Promising protein for Parkinson's. *Science, 260,* 1072–1073.

Weiss, R. D., & Mirin, S. M. (1987). *Cocaine.* Washington, DC: American Psychiatric Press.

Weissman, M. M. (1990). Panic and generalized anxiety: Are they separate disorders? *Journal of Psychiatric Research, 24,* 157–162.

Weissman, M. M. (Spring 1993). The epidemiology of personality disorders: A 1990 update. *Journal of Personality Disorders* (Spring Suppl.), *1,* 44–62.

Weissman, M. M., Bland, R. C., Canino, G. J., Greenwald, S., Hwu, H. G., Lee, C. K., Newman, S. C., Oakley-Browne, M. A., Stipic, M. R., Wickramaratne, P. J., Wittchen, H. U., & Yeh, E. K. (1994). The cross national epidemiology of obsessive compulsive disorder: The Cross National Collaborative Group. *Journal of Clinical Psychiatry, 55,* 5–10.

Weissman, M. M., Bruce, M. L., Leaf, P. J., Florio, L. P., & Holzer, (1990). Affective disorders. In L. N. Robins and D. A. Regier (Eds.), *Psychiatric disorders in America.* New York: Free Press.

Weissman, M. M., Gershon, E. S., Kidd, K. K., Prussof, B. A., Leckman, J. F., Dibble, E., Hamovit, J., Thompson, W. D., Pauls, D. L., & Guroff, J. J. (1984). Psychiatric disorder in the relatives of probands with affective disorders. *Archives of General Psychiatry, 41,* 13–21.

Weisz, J. R., & Weiss, B. (1989). On "dropouts" and "refusers" in child psychotherapy: Reply to Garfield. *Journal of Consulting and Clinical Psychology, 57,* 170–171.

Weisz, J. R., & Weiss, B. (1993). *Effects of psychotherapy with children and adolescents.* New York: Sage.

Weisz, J. R., Weiss, B., & Donenberg, G. R. (1992). The lab versus clinic: Effects of child and adolescent psychotherapy. *American Psychologist, 47,* 1578–1585.

Weitzenhoffer, A. M. (1989). *The practice of hypnotism.* New York: Wiley.

Weltzin, T. E., Hsu, L. K. G., & Kaye, W. H. (1990). *An open trial of fluoxetine in anorexia nervosa: Maintenance of body weight and reduction of obsessional features.* Abstract presented at the fourth International Conference on Eating Disorders, New York, NY, April 28.

Wender, P. H., Rosenthal, D., Kety, S. S., Schulsinger, F., & Welner, J. (1974). Cross-fostering: A research strategy for clarifying the role of genetic and experiential factors in the etiology of schizophrenia. *Archives of General Psychiatry, 30,* 121–128.

Werdegar, D., Sokolow, M., Perloff, D. B., Riess, F., Harris, R. E., Singer, T., & Blackburn, H. W., Jr. (1967). Portable recording of blood pressure: A new approach to assessments of the severity and prognosis of hypertension. *Transactions of the Association of Life Insurance Medical Directors of America, 51,* 93–173.

Werner, E. E. (1993). Risk, resilience, and recovery: Perspectives from the Kauai Longitudinal Study. *Development and Psychopathology, 5,* 503–515.

Werner, E. E., & Smith, R. S. (1992). *Overcoming the odds: High-risk children from birth to adulthood.* Ithaca, NY: Cornell University Press.

Wesson, D. R., & Smith, D. E. (1977). *Barbiturates: Their use, misuse, and abuse.* New York: Human Services Press.

Wewers, M. E., & Lowe, N. K. (1990). A critical review of visual analogue scales in the measurement of clinical phenomena. *Research in Nursing and Health, 13*(4), 227–236.

Wexler, N. S., Gusella, J. F., Conneally, P. M., & Housman, D. (1985). Huntington's disease and the new genetics: A preview of the future for psychiatric disorders. In H. A. Pincus & H. Pardes (Eds.), *The integration of neuroscience and psychiatry.* Washington, DC: American Psychiatric Press.

Whalen, C. K., & Henker, B. (1985). The social worlds of hyperactive (ADDH) children. *Clinical Psychology Review, 5,* 447–478.

Wheeler, J., & Carlson, C. L. (1994). The social functioning of children with ADD with hyperactivity and ADD without hyperactivity: A comparison of their peer relations and social deficits. *Journal of Emotional and Behavioral Disorders, 2,* 2–12.

Wheeler, L., & Miyake, K. (1992). Social comparison in everyday life. *Journal of Personality and Social Psychology, 62,* 760–773.

Whitehead, W. E., Blackwell, B., & Robinson, A. (1978). Effects of diazepam on phobic avoidance behavior and phobic anxiety. *Biological Psychiatry, 13,* 59–64.

Widiger, T. A. (1991). DSM-IV reviews of the personality disorders: Introduction to special series. *Journal of Personality Disorders, 5,* 122–134.

Widiger, T. A., & Smith, G. T. (1994). Substance use disorder: Abuse, dependence and dyscontrol. *Addiction, 89,* 267–282.

Widiger, T. A., Frances, A., & Trull, T. J. (1987). A psychometric analysis of the social-interpersonal and cognitive perceptual items for the schizotypal personality disorder. *Archives of General Psychiatry, 44,* 741–745.

Widom, C. S. (1978). A methodology for studying noninstitutionalized psychopaths. In R. D. Hare & D. A. Schalling (Eds.), *Psychopathic behavior: Approaches to research.* Chichester, England: John Wiley.

Widom, C. S. (1989). Does violence beget violence: A critical examination of the literature. *Psychological Bulletin, 106,* 3–28.

Wikler, L. M. (1986). Periodic stresses of families of older mentally retarded children: An exploratory study. *American Journal of Mental Deficiency, 90,* 703–706.

Wikler, L. M., Wasow, M., & Hatfield, E. (1981). Chronic sorrow revisited. *American Journal of Orthopsychiatry, 51,* 63–70.

Wille, R. (1981). Ten year follow-up of a representative sample of London heroin addicts: Clinic attendance, abstinence, and mortality. *British Journal of Addiction, 76,* 259–266.

Williams, J. B. W., Gibbon, M., First, M. B., Spitzer, R. L., Davies,

M., Borus, J., Howes, M. J., Kanes, J., Pope, H. G., Jr., Rounsaville, B., & Wittchen, H. U. (1992). The structured clinical interview for DSM-III-R (SCID): II. Multisite test-retest reliability. *Archives of General Psychiatry, 49,* 630–636.

Williams, L. M. (1994). Recall of childhood trauma: A prospective study of women's memories of child sexual abuse. *Journal of Consulting and Clinical Psychology, 62,* 1167–1176.

Willick, M. S. (1994) Schizophrenia: A parent's perspective—Mourning without end. In N. C. Andreasen (Ed.), *Schizophrenia from mind to molecule.* (pp. 5–20). Washington, DC: American Psychiatric Press.

Winokur, G., Coryell, W., Akiskal, H. S., Endicott, J., Keller, M, & Mueller, T. (1994) Manic-depressive (bipolar) disorder: The course in light of a prospective ten-year follow-up of 131 patients. *Acta Psychiatrica Scandinavica, 89,* 102–110.

Winston, A., Laikin, M., Pollack, J., Samstag, L. W., McCullough, M. A. L., & Muran, J. C. (1994). *American Journal of Psychiatry, 151,* 190–194.

Wise, T. N. (1985). Fetishism—etiology and treatment: A review from multiple perspectives. *Comprehensive Psychiatry, 26,* 249–257.

Wittchen, H. U., Zhao, S., Kessler, R. C., & Eaton, W. W. (1994). DSM-III-R generalized anxiety disorder in the National Comorbidity Survey. *Archives of General Psychiatry, 51,* 355–364.

Wolf, L., & Goldberg, B. (1986). Autistic children grow up: An eight to twenty-four year follow-up study. *Canadian Journal of Psychiatry, 31,* 550–556.

Wolf, S., & Bruhn, J. G. (1993). *The power of clan: The influence of human relationships on heart disease.* New Brunswick, NJ: Transaction Publishers.

Wolfe, D. A., Sandler, J., & Kaufman, K. (1981). Competency-based parent training program for child abusers. *Journal of Consulting and Clinical Psychology, 49,* 633–640.

Woody, G. E., McLellan, A. T., Luborsky, L., & O'Brien, C. P. (1986). Psychotherapy for substance abuse. *Psychiatric Clinics of North America, 9,* 547–562.

Woolf, L. (1964). *Beginning again: An autobiography of the years 1911 to 1918.* New York: Harcourt.

Woolf, V. (1978). *The letters of Virginia Woolf* (N. Nicholson and J. Trautman (Eds.), New York: Harcourt.

Wu, J. C., Gillin, J. C., Buchsbaum, M. S., & Hershen, T. (1992). Effect of sleep deprivation on brain metabolism of depressed patients. *American Journal of Psychiatry, 149,* 538–543.

Wulff, S. B. (1985). The symbolic and object play of children with autism: A review. *Journal of Autism and Developmental Disorders, 15,* 139–147.

Wyatt, R. C., & Livson, N. (1994). The not so great divide? Psychologists and psychiatrists take stands on the medical and psychosocial models of mental illness. *Professional Psychology: Research and Practice, 25,* 120–131.

Wyatt, R. J. (1991). Neuroleptics and the natural course of schizophrenia. *Schizophrenia Bulletin, 7,* 325–351.

Wysocki, J. J., & Sweet, J. J. (1985). Identification of brain-damaged, schizophrenic, and normal medical patients using a brief neuropyschological screening battery. *International Journal of Clinical Neuropsychology, 7,* 40–49.

Yoshikawa, H. (1994). Prevention as cumulative protection: Effects of early family support and education on chronic delinquency and its risks. *Psychological Bulletin, 115,* 28–54.

Young, J. E., Beck, A. T., & Weinberger, A. (1993) Depression. In D. H. Barlow, (Ed.), *Clinical handbook of psychological disorders* (2d ed.) (pp. 240–277). New York: Guilford.

Young, M. A., Fogg, L. F., Scheftner, W. A., & Fawcett, J. A. (1994). Interactions of risk factors in predicting suicide. *American Journal of Psychiatry, 151,* 434–435.

Zahn, T. P., & Carpenter, W. T., Jr. (1978). Effects of short-term outcome and clinical improvement on reaction time in acute schizophrenia. *Journal of Psychiatric Research, 14,* 59–68.

Zalewski, C., & Archer, R. P. (1991). Assessment of borderline personality disorder: A review of MMPI and Rorschach findings. *Journal of Nervous and Mental Disease, 179,* 338–345.

Zametkin, A. J., Nordahl, T. E., Gross, M., King, A. C., Semple, W. E., Rumsey, J., Hamburger, S., & Cohen, R. M. (1990). Cerebral glucose metabolism in adults with hyperactivity of childhood onset. *The New England Journal of Medicine, 323,* 1361–1366.

Zanarini, M. C., Gunderson, J. G., Marino, M. F., Schwartz, E. O., & Frankenburg, F. (1988). DSM-III disorders in the families of borderline patients. *Journal of Personality Disorders, 2,* 292–302.

Zeitlin, H. (1986). *The natural history of psychiatric disorder in children.* Oxford England: Oxford University Press.

Zetlin, A. G., & Turner, J. L. (1985). Transition from adolescence to adulthood: Perspectives of mentally retarded individuals and their families. *American Journal of Mental Deficiency, 89,* 570–579.

Zigler, E., Bulla, D., & Hodapp, R. (1984). On the definition and classification of mental retardation. *American Journal of Mental Deficiency, 89,* 215–230.

Zigler, E., & Hodapp, R. M. (1991). Behavioral functioning in individuals with mental retardation. *Annual Review of Psychology, 42,* 29–50.

Zigler, E., & Levine, J. (1983). Hallucinations vs. delusions: A developmental approach. *Journal of Nervous and Mental Disorder, 171,* 141–146.

Zimmerman, M. (1994). Diagnosing personality disorders: A review of issues and research methods. *Archives of General Psychiatry, 51,* 225–245.

Zimrin, H. (1986). A profile of survival. *Child Abuse and Neglect, 10,* 339–349.

Zubin, J., Magaziner, J., & Steinhauer, S. R. (1983). The metamorphosis of schizophrenia: From chronicity to vulnerability. *Psychological Medicine, 13,* 551–571.

Zubin, J., & Spring, B. (1977). Vulnerability—a new view of schizophrenia. *Journal of Abnormal Psychology, 86,* 103–126.

Zubin, J., Steinhauer, S. R., Day, R., & van Kammen, D. P. (1985). Schizophrenia at the crossroads: A blueprint for the 80s. *Comprehensive Psychiatry, 26,* 217–240.

Chapter 1: 7 Suzanne DeChicco/New York Times Pictures. 13 (top) Nubar Alexanian/Woodfin Camp & Associates; (middle) Bernard Gotfryd/Woodfin Camp & Associates; (bottom) Spencer Grant/Monkmeyer Press. 25 (top) University of Wisconsin, Harlow Primate Laboratory; (bottom) University of Wisconsin, Harlow Primate Laboratory.

Chapter 2: 34 Kal Muller/Woodfin Camp & Associates. 35 American Museum of Natural History. 36 Smithsonian Institution. 37 Bettmann. 38 Bettmann. 39 (top) James H. Karales/Peter Arnold, Inc.; (bottom) Bettmann. 40 "St. Catherine exorcising a possessed woman." © Denver Art Museum, Samuel H. Kress Foundation Collection. 41 (bottom) Historical Pictures Service, Inc., Chicago. (top) Scala/Art Resource. 42 National Library of Medicine. 43 (top, right) Courtesy of the Victoria and Albert Museum, London. With permission of the Bethlem Royal Hospital, Kent; (bottom, right) *Melancholy Madness* © Victoria and Albert Museum, London. With permission of Bethlem Royal Hospital, Kent; (left) Hulton Deutsch Collection Limited. 44 Wellcome Institute. 45 (top) National Library of Medicine; (bottom) Bettmann. 46 Culver Pictures, Inc. 47 (top) PH Archives; (middle) PH Archives; (bottom) PH Archives; (bottom, right) National Library of Medicine. 48 (top) George M. Cushing Photography. (bottom) PH Archives. 49 "1880s art therapy workshop." Printed with permission of The Institute of Pennsylvania Hospital, PA. 50 National Mental Health Institution. 51 National Library of Medicine.

Chapter 3: 60 David Parker/Science Photo Library/Photo Researchers, Inc. 61 Bob Sacha. 67 Professor Marcus E. Raichle. 69 (top) Oscar Burriel/Latin Stock/Science Photo Library/Photo Researchers, Inc.; (bottom) Philippe Plailly/Science Photo Library/Photo Researchers, Inc. 72 Bettmann. 82 B. F. Skinner Foundation. 83 Spencer Grant/Picture Cube, Inc. 86 Chuck Painter/Stanford University News Service. 87 Courtesy of Aaron T. Beck. 88 Carl Rogers Memorial Library.

Chapter 4: 105 (left) Jeff Kaufman/FPG International; (right) Michael Newman/Photoedit. 112 Lew Merrim/Monkmeyer Press. 113 Kaufman Assessment Battery for Children by Alan S. Kaufman and Nadeen

L. Kaufman. © 1983 American Guidance Service, Inc., 4201 Woodland Road, Circle Pines, Minnesota 55014. Reproduced with permission of the Publisher. All rights reserved. 116 (left) Ken Karp/PH Archives; (right) Bob Daemmrich/Stock Boston. 117 Harvard University Press. 119 (left) Cary Wolinsky/Stock Boston; (right) C. Glassman/The Image Works. 120 David E. Dempster/David E. Dempster. 122 Spacelabs Medical, Inc.

Chapter 5: 128 Richard Sheinwald/AP/Wide World Photos. 131 Reuters/Bettmann. 136 Bob Mahoney/The Image Works. 137 Rhoda Sidney. 138 AP/Wide World Photos. 144 Dr. Arshad Husain. 146 AP/Wide World Photos.

Chapter 6: 155 Robert Brenner/Photoedit. 157 (left) Sarah Putnam/Picture Cube, Inc.; (right) Bob Daemmrich/The Image Works. 158 Jamie Francis/AP/Wide World Photos. 160 UPI/Bettmann. 161 (top) Pierre Boulat/COS/Woodfin Camp & Associates; (bottom) Robert Goldstein/Photo Researchers, Inc. 170 Joan C. Fahrenthold/AP/Wide World Photos.

Chapter 7: 182 Phil Huber/New York Times Pictures. 185 AP/Wide World Photos. 190 (left) Columbus Museum of Art, Ohio; George Tooker. American b. 1920. *Cornice*. ca. 1949. Tempera on panel. 24 x 15 1/2. Museum purchase: Howard Fund; (right) Monkmeyer/Mahon/Monkmeyer Press. 191 Monkmeyer/Siteman/Monkmeyer Press. 196 Michael P. Gadomski/Photo Researchers, Inc. 197 Bob Daemmrich/The Image Works.

Chapter 8: 213 James Lemass/Picture Cube, Inc. 216 Leinwand/Monkmeyer Press. 220 Trustees of the British Museum. 224 (top, left) UPI/Bettmann; (top, right) Henry Grossman/Life Magazine, Time Warner, Inc.; (bottom) PH Archives. 225 (top) Mariette Pathy Allen; (bottom) AP/World Wide Photos. 228 Alon Reininger/Woodfin Camp & Associates. 231 Erin N. Calmes. 232 Jacques Chenet/Woodfin Camp & Associates.

Chapter 9: 242 Fay Torresyap/Stock Boston. 245 Dagmar Fabricius/Uniphoto. 247 Chuck Pulin/Star File. 254 Vinnie Fish/Black Star. 260 Liamute Druskis/PH Archives.

Chapter 10: 269 (top) Phil Huber/Black Star; (bottom) Alan Tannenbaum/Sygma. 275 Jacob Lawrence, *Depression*, 1950. Tempera on paper, 22 x 30 1/2 in. (55.9 x 77.5 cm). Gift of David M. Solinger. Collection of Whitney Museum of American Art, New York. Photo by Geoffrey Clements. 278 Dr. Michael E. Phelps. 279 Dr. Mark S. George, M. D./Dr. Mark S. George, M. D. 280 Northern Light Technologies. 283 U. S. Dept. of Health & Human Services. 288 Bettmann. 290 Roz Levin Photography. 291 Will & Deni McIntyre/Photo Researchers, Inc. 299 (left) Bettmann; (middle) UPI/Bettmann; (right) AP/World Wide Photos. 306 Reuters/Bettmann.

Chapter 11: 316 (top) UPI/Bettmann; (bottom) Mario Cabrera/AP Wide World Photos. 319 Shepard Sherbell/SABA Press Photos, Inc. 322 (left) The Granger Collection; (middle) Bettmann; (right) Archiv der Universität Heidelberg/German Information Center. 323 Al Vercoutere. 325 Psychology Today Magazine. 326 (top) Dr. Monte S. Buchsbaum, M. D.; (middle, left) Dr. Monte S. Buchsbaum, M. D.; (middle, middle) Dr. Monte S. Buchsbaum, M. D.; (middle, right) Psychology Today Magazine; (bottom, middle) Dr. Monte S. Buchsbaum, M. D.; (bottom, right) Psychology Today Magazine. 327 (top, left) Dr. Monte S. Buchsbaum, M. D.; (top, middle) Dr. Monte S. Buchsbaum, M. D.; (top, right) Dr. Monte S. Buchsbaum, M. D.; (bottom, left) Dr. Monte S. Buchsbaum, M. D.; (bottom, middle) Dr. Monte S. Buchsbaum, M. D. 331 Daniel R. Weinberger, M. D. 332 (top) Hank Morgan/Rainbow; (bottom, left) Hank Morgan/Rainbow; (bottom, right) Hank Morgan/Rainbow.

Chapter 12: 344 Denise Applewhite/Sygma. 364 (middle) Barbara Pfeffer/Peter Arnold, Inc.; (bottom) Owen Franken/Stock Boston.

Chapter 13: 369 (left) Jim Berry/Seattle Times; (right) Jim Berry/Seattle Times. 374 Abigail Heyman. 376 Anna Mary Robertson (Grandma) Moses, *The Daughter's Homecoming*. Copyright © 1989, Grandma Moses Properties Co., New York, and the Lauren Rogers Museum of Art, Laurel, Mississippi. 378 Richard Falco/Black Star. 380 SIU/Peter Arnold, Inc. 381 (top) Lynn Johnson/Black Star; (bottom) Mark J. Terrill/AP/Wide World Photos. 382 Mony DeLeon/Peter Arnold, Inc. 383 (bottom) Steve Uzzell, III; (top) Mark Peterson/SABA Press Photos, Inc. 386 AP/Wide World Photos. 387 N. Y. Daily News.

Chapter 14: 403 (left) Paul Mozell/Stock Boston; (right) Michael Weisbrot/Stock Boston. 405 (left) PH Archives; (right) PH Archives. 407 National Council on Alcoholism Inc. 408 Mary Levin/University Photography. 409 Shackman/Monkmeyer Press. 415 John Moran/New York Times Pictures. 426 PH Archives. 430 Billy E. Barnes/Stock Boston.

Chapter 15: 437 Mary Kate Denny/Photoedit. 452 George Goodwin/Monkmeyer Press. 454 Peter Vandermark/Stock Boston. 460 Don Ipock/AP/Wide World Photos. 465 (top) Laima Druskis/Stock Boston; (bottom) Bob Daemmrich/Stock Boston. 466 Michal Heron/Woodfin Camp & Associates. 467 Drawing from Robinson, Howard (1991), "Visitation with Divorced Father Provokes Reemergence of Unresolved Family Conflicts: Case of Charlie, Age 10," p. 224 in N. B. Webb (ed.), *Play Therapy with Children in Crisis*, New York: Guildford. Reprinted by permission.

Chapter 16: 473 Tom Reese/Seattle Times. 475 (top) Julie Osterling and Geraldine Dawson/Irwin G. Sarason; (bottom) Julie Osterling and Geraldine Dawson/Irwin G. Sarason. 478 (top, left) Allan Grant Productions; (bottom, left) Allan Grant Productions; (top, right) Allan Grant Productions; (bottom, right) Allan Grant Productions. 484 CDMRC Outlook. 485 Biophoto Associates/Science Source/Photo Researchers, Inc. 486 (top) Chris Maynard/New York Times Pictures; (bottom) Mike Greenlar/The Image Works. 487 (top) National Down Syndrome Congress; (bottom) Patrick Kesslak. 488 Psychology Today Magazine. 491 Alan Carey/The Image Works. 492 Bill Aron/Photoedit. 493 AP/Wide World Photos.

Chapter 17: 505 David E. Dempster. 512 (top, left) Goldberg/Monkmeyer Press; (bottom, left) Zigy Kaluzny/Tony Stone Images; (top, right) James Prince/Photo Researchers, Inc. 515 N. Rowan/The Image Works. 517 David E. Dempster. 518 Sygma. 520 Bob Daemmrich/The Image Works. 522 Bob Daemmrich/Stock Boston.

Chapter 18: 538 (top, left) Comstock; (top, right) F. Paolini/Sygma; (bottom) Jacques Chenet/Woodfin Camp & Associates. 539 Goodwin/Monkmeyer Press. 540 Alon Reininger/Woodfin Camp & Associates. 541 Carey/The Image Works. 545 (top) Michael Newman/Photoedit; (bottom) Tony Freeman/Photoedit. 546 Robert Brenner/Photoedit. 550 AP/Wide World Photos. 551 (top) Bob Daemmrich/Stock Boston; (bottom) David E. Dempster. 552 George Rizer/AP/Wide World Photos. 554 James Wilson/Woodfin Camp & Associates. 558 Jim Estrin/New York Times Pictures. 559 Cole Porter/Seattle Times. 561 (top, left) UPI/Bettmann; (top, right) UPI/Bettmann; (bottom, left) UPI/Bettmann; (bottom, right) UPI/Bettmann.

Name Index

A

Aase, J.M., 488, 489
Abbey, A., 136
Abel, G., 232
Abraham, H.D., 424
Abraham, K., 279
Abrams, D.B., 24
Abrams, S., 123
Abramson, L.Y., 286, 287
Achenbach, T.M., 447
Acierno, R.E., 204
Adamson, J., 101
Addalli, K.A., 454
Addis, M.E., 522
Adler, G., 255
Agard, J.A., 491
Agras, W.S., 168, 463, 464
Ahlawat, S.K., 403
Ahn, C.W., 205
Akesson, H.O., 483, 489
Akhtar, S., 245, 247
Akiskal, H.S., 273, 275, 300
Albert, M.S., 378
Alderman, M., 168
Aldridge, A.M., 424
Alexander, D., 231
Alexander, W., 485
Alford, B.A., 201, 354
Alleback, P., 338
Allen, B.G., 305
Allen, R.A., 168
Allmon, D., 256
Alloy, L.B., 286
Alnaes, R., 282
Altmann, M.W., 172
Ambelas, A., 301
Ambrosini, P.J., 457, 460
Amedeo, S.R., 135
Ameli, R., 345
Anastasiades, P., 204, 457
Anderson, C.M., 216, 356
Anderson, D.J., 185
Anderson, E.A., 130
Anderson, N.B., 164
Andersson, T., 446
Andolphi, M., 467
Andreasen, N.C., 202, 300,
    318, 489, 526
Andreasson, S., 342
Andreoli, A., 245
Angelo, C., 467
Anglin, M.D., 427
Anisman, H., 169
Anrow, B., 463
Anthony, J.C., 403
Anthony, W.A., 360

Anton, M.T., 390
Antoni, M.H., 133
Appelbaum, P.S., 562
Arato, M., 352
Archer, R.P., 254
Arieti, S., 292
Arkowitz, H.S., 131
Armor, D.J., 413
Armstrong, H.E., 256
Arnow, B., 463
Aro, H., 303
Aronson, T.A., 304
Asaad, G., 317
Asarnow, J.R., 436
Ascherio, A., 162
Asherson, P., 329
Ashikaga, T., 362, 363
Askildsen, E.C., 170
Avner, R., 516
Awad, A.G., 351
Ayers, W.H., 525

B

Bakay Pragay, E., 346
Baker, L., 459, 460
Baldessarini, R.J., 281
Balis, G.U., 10, 261
Bancroft, J., 214
Bandura, A, 86, 453
Barabas, G., 484
Barchas, J.D., 405, 406
Bard, M., 549
Barden, H.S., 484
Barefoot, J.C., 164
Barkham, M., 296
Barkley, R.A., 442
Barlow, D.H., 183, 184, 186,
    199, 204, 205, 221, 226, 517
Baron, M., 320, 329
Barrelet, L., 356
Barrett, M.L., 455
Barrowclough, C., 358
Bartak, L., 476
Barton, R., 287
Barton, S.N., 549
Bartrop, R.W., 70
Basham, R.B., 132
Bates, J.A., 438
Bauer, R.B., 384
Baumeister, R.F., 461
Baxter, L.R., 291
Becher, J., 232
Beck, A.T., 10, 86, 87, 190,
    201, 221, 260, 265, 283,
    284, 285, 294, 304, 353,
    457, 507, 508, 511, 512,
    513, 517

Becker, R.E., 293
Bednar, R.L., 522
Beeghly, M., 485
Beers, C., 50
Beidel, D.C., 202, 262
Beiderman, J., 446
Beitman, B.D., 527, 529
Bell, C.R., 491, 492
Bell, M., 339
Bell, N.W., 16
Bell, Q., 303
Bellack, A.S., 164, 168, 352,
    363
Bemporad, J.R., 282, 292
Bender, L., 111
Benjamin, L.S., 114
Benson, D.F., 148
Benson, H., 168
Bentall, R.P., 354
Bentler, P.M., 225
Benton, M.K., 354
Berchick, R.J., 512, 513
Berenbaum, H., 351
Berg, C.L., 454
Berg, R., 403
Berger, M., 492
Berger, P., 245
Bergin, A.E., 509, 523, 534
Berke, J., 426
Bernard, J.L., 438
Bernard, M.L., 438
Berney, T.P., 455
Bernier, J.C., 442
Bernstein, D.P., 249
Berrettini, W.H., 268
Berry, P., 486
Bertelson, A., 300
Berthier, M.L., 486
Bessler, A., 447
Beumont, P.J., 458
Beutler, C.E., 217
Beutler, L.E., 131
Bhate, S.R., 455
Bianchi, M.D., 457, 460
Bibring, E., 282
Biederman, J., 443, 447
Bieliauskas, L.A., 169
Bierut, L., 526
Bifulco, A., 288
Binik, Y.M., 217
Birchwood, M., 358, 360, 361
Black, D.W., 203, 489
Black, J.L., 295
Blackburn, H.W., 122
Blackwell, B., 204
Blackwood, D., 330
Blanchard, E.B., 204

Bland, R.C., 194
Blazer, D., 184
Bleck, D.S., 555
Blesser, A., 446
Bleuler, E., 319, 346
Bloch, S., 403
Bloedau, L., 436
Bloom, B.L., 539
Bloom, J.R., 169
Blose, I., 403
Blumenthal, R., 315
Boat, B.W., 230
Bodkin, A., 251
Bohman, M., 258, 405
Bohmfalk, G.C., 140
Boker, W., 354
Boldizar, J.P., 541
Bolwig, T.J., 284, 285
Bonagura, N., 446
Bond, L.A., 547
Booth-Butterfield, M., 120
Borbely, A.A., 282
Borduin, C.M., 467
Borgstedt, A.D., 444
Borkovec, T.D., 184
Bornstein, R.F., 262
Borthwick-Duffy, S.A., 493
Borus, J., 110
Bourdon, K., 189
Bousha, D.M., 439
Bouthenet, M.L., 332
Bowden C.L., 300, 306
Bowlby, J., 286, 452
Bowler, A.E., 8, 330, 333, 337
Boyd, J.H., 189
Brady, K., 170, 171
Braff, D.L., 344, 345
Brand, R.J., 163
Brandt, A.M., 231
Breier, A., 352, 362, 363
Brenner, H.D., 351, 353, 354
Brenner, M.H., 548
Breslau, N., 160
Breslin, F.C., 438
Breslow, N., 227, 228
Brewerton, T.D., 284
Breznitz, S., 129
Brier, N., 493
Brill, G., 307
Brodie, H.K.H., 375, 424
Brook, J., 436, 442, 447, 448,
    449, 452, 455
Brooks, G.W., 363, 368
Brown, B., 167
Brown, G., 288, 304
Brown, R.I., 486
Brown, T.A., 184, 186, 205

Birth order, 62
Bisexuality, 210, 211, 214, 222
  and sadomasochism, 227
Bizarre behavior, in schizotypal
  personality disorder, 243
Blood pressure, 122, 167, see
  also hypertension
  and marital conflict, 155
  nicotine and, 428
Blushing, fear of, 191
Bodily assessment, 121–123,
  125
Body dysmorphic disorders,
  173, 178
Body image, 459
Body language, in assessment,
  106–107
Borderline personality disorder,
  238, 247–252, 263, 267
  causes of, 249–250
Brain, 63–65
  in abnormal behavior, 36
  adaptation in, 65
  deterioration, 368
  left hemisphere, 475
  Pick's disease, 382
  reward center, 406, 407
  scans of, 330
  systems of, 66
Brain anatomy, and
  homosexuality, 214
Brain atrophy, 393
Brain damage, 369, 541
  from alcohol use, 403
  assessment of, 370
  in autistic disorder, 475, 477
  eye tracking in, 347
  in schizophrenic disorder,
  320
  in syphilis, 387
Brain deterioration, see
  dementia
Brain disorders, vulnerability,
  393
Brain dysfunction, and
  depression, 277
Brain electrical activity, in
  schizophrenic disorder, 345
Brain imaging, 67, 69, 371, 393
  in Alzheimer's disease, 381
  techniques of, 123
Brain infections, 384
Brain injuries, 384
Brain lesions:
  and delirium, 372
  eye tracking in, 347
Brain potentials, 63
Brain reward system, 64–65
Brain structure, in
  schizophrenic disorder,
  330
Brain trauma, 384–387, 393
  amnestic disorder in, 387
Brain tumor, 384
  and aggression, 376
  and epilepsy, 389

Brain wave, and antisocial
  personality disorder,
  254–259
Breathalyzer test, 25
Breuer, Joseph, 72
Brief psychotherapy, 508
Briquet's syndrome, 171, 177
Broad Street pump, 9
Brown v. Board of Education,
  490, 497
Bulimia nervosa, 457, 460,
  461–463, 469
Burton, Robert, 42

C

Caffeine, 429–430, 433
Caffeine-dependence, 430
Cancer, 164–165
  and stress, 177
Cannabis, 426–428, 433
Cardiovascular disorder,
  162–167, 177
Cardiovascular system:
  and amphetamine use, 423
  hallucinogens and, 425
  and marijuana, 427
Care, continuity of, 363
Case management, as
  treatment, 359
Case study method, 19, 30
Castrophizing, 86
Catatonic behavior, 320
Catatonic excitement, 341
Catatonic rigidity, 318, 341
Catatonic type, of
  schizophrenic disorder, 323,
  341
Catecholamines, 177, 276
  in coronary heart disease,
  162
Categorical model, of
  classification, 262
Causal attributions, 308
Causation, multiple, 71
Central nervous system, 62, 92
  and amphetamine use, 423
  and attention-deficit/
  hyperactivity disorder,
  443
  cocaine and, 421
  and mental retardation, 489,
  492
  and morphine, 419
Central nervous system
  damage, and community
  factors, 392
Central tendency, measures of,
  26, 30
Cerebellar vermis, 476
Cerebellum:
  cocaine and, 421
  in autistic disorder, 476
Cerebral cortex:
  cocaine and, 421
  cortex, 63

Cerebral ventricle, 341
Cerebrospinal fluid, 330
Cerebrovascular accident, 387,
  394
Charcot, Jean Martin, 51, 154
Chemical system, of brain, 66
Child abuse, 6, 9, 20, 437,
  438–439, 542–543, 565
  and eating disorder, 462
Child rearing skills, 540
Child sexual abuse, 230–232,
  see also pedophilia
Childhood disorders, 99, 435,
  468
Children:
  gender identity disorder in,
  221–222
  institutionalization of, 564
  treatment of, 46
Children's Depression
  Inventory, 457
Chlorpromazine, 297
Cholinergic system, 379
Choreiform movement, in
  Huntington's disease, 382
Chromosomal abnormality,
  485, 496
Chromosomal defect, in
  mental retardation, 483
Chromosome pair 11, 300
Chromosome pair 21, 60, 92
Chromosome pair 4, 383, 393
Chromosome pair 6, 300
Chromosome X, 300, 485
Chromosomes, 324, 328
  anomalies of, 60
Chronic illness, and
  depression, 455
Chronic mental illness, 557
Circadian rhythm, 278
Civil commitment, 559, 566
Civil rights, and mental illness,
  13
Classical conditioning, 80–81,
  82, 92
  as alcohol abuse treatment,
  411
Classification, 96–103, 124
  of personality disorders,
  261–262
  process of, 103–124
  research on, 102, 124
Classification system,
  characteristics of, 97
Classroom intervention, 565
Client factors, in diagnosis,
  103
Client-centered therapy, 505,
  531
Clinical contacts, 29
  reasons for, 11–12
Clinical judgment, 97
  study of, 102–103
Clinical psychologist, 14, 29
Clinical scales, of MMPI-2,
  113

Clinical trials, 23, 500,
  527–528, 533
Clinician factors, in diagnosis,
  103
Clomipramine, 204, 478, see
  also tricylic drugs
Clonidine, 412
Close relationships, and
  depression, 271
Clozapine, 352, 365
Cluster headaches, 159, 160
Cocaine, 398, 421–423, 433
  withdrawal symptoms, 399
Cocaine Anonymous, 423
Cognitions, 507
  abstract, 490
  in anxiety, 285
  in depression, 283, 284, 285
  disordered, 348
  histories of, 85
  and maladaptive behavior,
  507
  in obsessive-compulsive
  disorder, 195
  and psychoactive drugs, 398
  in schizophrenic disorder,
  354
  in substance intoxication,
  400
Cognitive abilities:
  and aging, 376
  and alcohol use, 403
Cognitive accuracy, in
  depression, 287
Cognitive appraisals, and
  abuse, 440
Cognitive approach, to alcohol
  abuse, 412
Cognitive assessment, 120, 125
Cognitive behavior therapy,
  200, 204, 207, 293, 308,
  512–518, 526, 532, see also,
  cognitive therapy
  effectiveness of, 517
  skill training in, 354
Cognitive behavioral
  intervention, and conduct
  disorder, 450
Cognitive behavioral therapy:
  for anorexia, 460
  for children, 467
  of sexual dysfunction, 220
Cognitive coping techniques,
  for smoking cessation, 429
Cognitive deficits, 372
  in autistic disorder, 474
  in schizophrenic disorder,
  353–354
Cognitive development:
  and child abuse, 438
  in Down syndrome, 485
  in fetal damage syndrome,
  488–489
Cognitive disorders, 9
Cognitive distortions, 87, 295
  and bulimia, 462

in depression, 283–285, 308
Cognitive dysfunction, in schizophrenic disorder, 349
Cognitive factors, in alcohol use, 407–408
Cognitive functioning, in head injury, 385
Cognitive group therapy, 457
Cognitive impairment, 372, 387–392
disorders of, 394
factors in, 392
Cognitive impairment disorders, 367–394
Cognitive Interference Questionnaire, 120
Cognitive modification, 150, 151
Cognitive perspective, 58, 84–88, 93, 200–203, 518
on antisocial personality disorder, 259
on anxiety disorder, 207
and brain disorder, 392
on depression, 283–287
in family therapy, 521
on sexual dysfunction, 220
Cognitive processing, in autistic disorder, 496
Cognitive processes, 514
role of, 59
Cognitive psychotherapy, 506–508, 531
Cognitive rehearsal, 200, 201, 202, 207
Cognitive restructuring, 87, 201, 204, 207
and anorexia, 460
Cognitive skills, 540
training, 547
Cognitive social learning theory, 84
Cognitive social skills, 365
Cognitive strategies, to smoking cessation, 430
Cognitive theories, 59, 87–88, 202
Cognitive therapy, 469, 528
in borderline personality disorder, 251
for bulimia, 462
for cocaine use, 423
for depression, 287, 293–297, 308, 457
and hopelessness, 304
for opioid addiction, 420
for schizophrenia, 354
Cognitive triad, 283, 308
Cohort effect, in depression, 269–270
Collaborative study, of depression, 295
College students, alcohol use of, 423–4245
Coma, and drug use, 425
Combined therapies, 533

and depression, 295, 308
for personality disorder, 261
Commitment, 558, 566
civil, 560
involuntary, 562, 563
outpatient, 562
Communication:
in autistic disorder, 472–473
in family therapy, 520
in schizophrenic disorder, 318, 340
Communication deviance, 340, 341
Communication training:
and anorexia, 461
in sexual dysfunction, 219
Community, 565
treatment facilities in, 562
treatment in, 13, 554–558, 565
Community agencies, as prevention, 548
Community approach:
to alcohol treatment, 409
to prevention, 414
Community care, 37
Community factors:
and alcohol use, 408
and coronary heart disease, 166
in schizophrenic disorder, 341
Community interventions, with children, 548
Community perspective:
on alcohol abuse, 432
on brain damage, 392
on brain disorder, 392
Community psychology, 89, 93, 554, 565
Community services, 555, 558
Community support, 365, 565
for schizophrenic disorder, 358–359
Community-cultural perspective, 58, 89–90, 93
Community-living programs, 491
Comorbidity, 204, 205, 207
with alcohol, 403
in attention-deficit/hyperactivity disorder, 447
Compeer, 554
Competence, 536
Competency, 566
legal, 352, 365, 559
Competency-focused prevention, 565
Compulsion, 193, 194, 206
in childhood, 453
Compulsive behavior, 2, see also obsessive-compulsive personality disorder, obsessive-compulsive anxiety disorder

in exhibitionism, 228
Compulsive rituals, 195, 196
exposure therapy for, 199
Compulsive substance, 432
Computed tomography (CT), 59, 67, 277, 291, 370, 371, 372, 393
Computer electroencephalagraphic tomography scans (CET), 327
Concordance, in twin studies, 61
Concussion, of brain, 385, 393
Conditioned response, 80, 81
Conditioned stimulus, 80, 81
Conditioning, aversive, 411
Conditioning procedures, in anxiety disorder, 199
Conduct disorder, 437, 438, 447–451, 468
and depression, 455
and oppositional defiant disorder, 447
Conduct problems, in adjustment disorder, 139
Confabulation, 374, 393
in Korsakoff's syndrome, 388
Conflict:
and anxiety, 196
and bodily response, 155
intrapsychic, 73
and mental illness, 41
parental, 545
unconscious, 503
Confounding, 27, 30
Confusion, in Alzheimer's disease, 375
Congenital factors, in mental retardation, 483
Conscious-unconscious dimension, 73, 92
Consciousness, 372
hypnosis and, 504
level of, 370
Consent, informed, 352, 563
Constitutional factors, in mental retardation, 483
Continuous Performance Task, 344, 345, 346, 365
Control:
environmental and stress, 168
loss of, 195
Control group, 23
Control scales, of MMPI-2, 113–114
Controlled drinking, 412, 413
Contusion, of brain, 385
Conversion disorder, 172, 177
Convulsions, and drug use, 425
Coping, 5–8, 124, 128, 131
alcohol use as, 407, 413
in avoidant personality disorder, 258

in dependent personality disorder, 258
in depression, 283
with pain, 174–175
in personality disorder, 261
process of, 130, 139
with stress, 98
training, 539
Coping skills, 6, 29, 129–132, 151, 155–156, 263
and cognitive-behavioral intervention, 517
and stress, 149
training in, 543
and vulnerability, 392
Coping skills training, and anorexia, 459
Coping strategies, for caretakers, 380
Coronary bypass, coping with, 130
Coronary heart disease, 162–167
Corpus callosum, and attention-deficit/hyperactivity disorder, 443
Correlation coefficient, 26–27
Correlational study method, 19, 20, 30
Cortical atrophy, in AIDS, 386
Corticotrophin-releasing factor (CRF), 66
Cortisol, 276
Counseling psychologist, 14
Counseling:
for attention-deficit/hyperactivity disorder, 445–446
marital, 544
premarital, 544
Countertransference, 502, 503, 531
Couples therapy, see marital therapy
Covert events, 71
Covert sensitization, 226–227, 411
and paraphilia, 229
Crack babies, 422
Crack cocaine, 421, 433
Creativity, and bipolar disorder, 298–303, 306
Crime, and abuse, 438
Crime prevention, 549
Criminal commitment, 558, 559, 566
Crisis hotlines, 549
Crisis prevention centers, 549
Crisis teams, as hospital alternatives, 359
Criteria factors, in diagnosis, 103
Critical periods, in brain development, 65
Cross-cultural comparisons, 104–105

Sexual disorders, 100, see also sexual dysfunction
Sexual dysfunction, 214, 216, 218, 233
  Kaplan approach, 220–221
  Masters and Johnson approach
  and rape, 135
  treatment of, 218–221, 233
  treatment effectiveness, 221
Sexual excitement, inhibited, 233
Sexual exploitation, in mental retardation, 492
Sexual gratification, 73
Sexual orientation, 214
Sexual preference, 211, 212–214
Sexual-reassignment surgery, 222–223
Sexual victimization, 438–440
Sexuality, Freud's view of, 73
Shakespeare, William, 42
Shaman, 34, 54
Shaping, 82, 513
Sheltered workshops, 359, 491
Ship of Fools, 45
Short-term therapy, 524
Shyness, 5, 436
Side effects:
  of antidepressants, 289
  drug, 527
  of lithium, 302
  of medication, 320
Significance, level of, 30
Single photon emission computed tomography (SPECT), 67, 277
Sirhan, Sirhan, 116
Situation-focused prevention, 565
Skill training, 551
  for alcohol use, 423
  and brain disorder, 392
  for schizophrenic disorder, 351
Skills, self-care, 353
Skinner, B.F., 82, 198
Sleep, 67
  problems with, 272, 274, 278
  rapid eye movement, 215
  in substance intoxication, 400
Sleep deprivation, and delirium, 372
Sleep disorder, 68–69, 100
  due to a general medical condition, 68
  related to another mental disorder, 68
Sleep problems, in adjustment disorder, 139
Sleep terror disorder, 69
Smoking cessation, 429, 430, 433

Smoking cessation programs, 429
Social change, and coronary heart disease, 167
Social competence, and hypertension, 167–168
Social cues, 354
  discrimination of, 365
Social disorganization, and maladaptive behavior, 89
Social environment, and maladaptive behavior, 89
Social facilitation, 84
Social factors, and alcohol use, 408
Social intervention, 150, 151
Social isolation
  and health, 165
  in schizoid personality disorder, 242
  in schizophrenia, 313
Social learning, 518, 530
  in parent training, 451
Social learning theory, 83–84, 92, 353
  of childhood phobia, 453
Social networks, and recovery, 361
Social phobia, 191–192, 206
Social policy, and substance dependence, 430
Social relationships:
  in autistic disorder, 472, 474
  in avoidant personality disorder, 257
  in mental retardation, 493, 497
Social roles, 90, 93
  in cognitive therapy, 507
Social selection theory, 89, 338, 341
Social skills, 133, 540
  and alcohol use, 406
  and attention-deficit/ hyperactivity disorder, 441
  in avoidant personality disorder, 258
  cognitive, 354
  and conduct disorder, 449–450
  and depression, 283
  in mental retardation, 491
  in schizoid personality disorder, 242
Social skills training, 365, 547
  for depression, 292, 457
  in mental retardation, 491–492, 493
  in schizophrenic disorder, 352–354
Social support, 8, 89, 91, 121, 132–133, 151, 154, 177, 341, 438, 469, 517, 543, 548
  and alcohol treatment, 411
  and brain disorder, 369

  and bulimia, 463
  and cancer, 169
  for caretakers, 382
  and conduct disorder, 451
  and coronary heart disease, 166
  and cultural differences, 89
  and depression, 270, 271
  and gender, 270, 271
  and mental retardation, 492
  in stress, 149
  and suicide, 303
  in treatment process, 501
  and vulnerability, 392
Social-causation theories, 89
Social withdrawal, 20–21
  in adjustment disorder, 139
  in Parkinson's disease, 384
Socioeconomic status, and schizophrenic disorder, 338
Socrates, 37
Sodium lactate, 186
Somatic system, 62
Somatic therapies, 14
Somatization disorders, 171–172, 177
Somatoform disorders, 100, 154, 171–175, 177
Soto family, 383
Special education, 491, 548
Specific phobia, 189–190, 206
SPECT, 291
Spectrum concept, 333, 341
Speech:
  delay of, 476
  disordered, 317–318
  disorganized, 319
  oddity in, 244
  in schizophrenia, 313
  in schizophrenic disorder, 318
  slurring of, 378
Speech content, poverty of, 318
Spinoza, Baruch, 42
Splitting, 79, 251
Spontaneous remission, 509
Spouse abuse, 232, 544, 565
Squeeze technique, 219
Stages, of psychosexual development, 73–75
Stalking, 544
Standard deviation, 26, 30
Stanford-Binet scales, 110
Startle response, 142
State hospitals, 13
Stereotypes, 465
  cultural, 52
Steroids, and mania, 297
Stigma:
  of brain disorder, 392
  in epilepsy, 390, 391
  of mental illness, 3–4, 29
Stigmatization, 439
Stimulant drugs:
  amphetamines, 423

  cocaine, 421
Stimulants, for attention-deficit/ hyperactivity disorder, 444
Stimulus-response view, of behavior, 80
Storytelling techniques, 464
STP, 433
Stress, 5–6, 9, 28, 89, 91, 128–150, 151, 177, 196, 197, 207, 267, 287, 324, 333, 341, 368, 440, 539, 548
  AIDS risk and, 214
  and alcohol use, 407, 408
  and anxiety, 182
  and borderline personality disorder, 250
  and brain disease, 375
  and brain disorder, 369, 370
  and cancer, 169
  of caretakers, 379–380
  and colds, 157–158
  and community factors, 338
  coping with, 130
  and delirium, 372
  in dementia, 373
  and depression, 270, 282
  in dissociative disorder, 144
  in epilepsy, 390
  full life events and CHD, 161
  glandular response to, 66
  and heart attack, 162
  and illness, 155–158, 177
  and immune system, 70
  job-related, 168
  and maladaptive behavior, 89, 90
  and manic episode, 300–301
  ongoing, 271
  from parental divorce, 545
  of parents, 442
  in patient families, 354
  physical effects of, 134
  and schizophrenic disorder, 336–338, 361
  in schizophrenic disorder, 336–338, 341, 349, 357
  and separation anxiety disorder, 452
  situational aspects of, 135
  and smoking for, 428
  and voyeurism, 228
Stress disorder, acute, 143
Stress innoculation, 357
Stress management, 357
Stressful environment, in schizophrenic disorder, 333
Stressful events, and depression, 309
Stressors, on DSM Axis IV, 99
Stroke, 368, see also cerebrovascular accidents
  and cocaine use, 422
  depression in, 278
  and PCP, 429

Information Needed for DSM-IV Diagnosis

Diagnosis involves determining whether a clinical problem meets the criteria for a particular disorder. In making a diagnosis, a clinician compares available information about a case with the DSM-IV criteria. The presence of symptoms, problems, and characteristics of a person's life specified in the criteria are diagnostic.

However, diagnosis using DSM-IV can be a complex process because its coverage (the number and types of disordered behaviors it includes) has increased greatly compared with earlier diagnostic systems. Many symptoms are applicable to several types of disorders, and clinicians need to keep in mind the types of information pertinent to the various types of disorders. In a given case, the presence of a significant inconsistency with the criteria for a particular diagnosis might preclude its use.

FOUR EXAMPLES OF INFORMATION NEEDED TO MAKE DIAGNOSTIC DECISIONS

Anxiety Disorders

Individuals suffering from anxiety disorders experience intense anxiety, worry, and apprehension, and often develop avoidance behavior, ritual acts, and repetitive thoughts.

A 30-year-old office worker complains of dizziness, sweating palms, and heart palpitations. He says he constantly feels tense and worried, and often has difficulty concentrating. Although his wife sees him as a nervous person, he tries to hide his symptoms from her.

The clinician should determine:

- Current and past history of anxiety, worry, and apprehension
- Current stress and past traumatic events
- The frequent development of avoidance behavior, ritual acts, or repetitive thoughts
- Sleep disturbance, bad dreams
- Physical complaints
- Previous and current mental and emotional disorders
- Compulsive behaviors or rituals

Substance-Related Disorders

Individuals with substance-related disorders experience adverse behavioral, social psychological, and physiological effects caused by seeking or using one or more substances such as alcohol and cocaine.

A 27-year-old dental assistant says she drinks heavily in order to sleep nights. She often feels lonely and is tense when she is not drinking. A friend describes her as being "unstable." Her mother had a severe drinking problem.

The clinician should determine:

- Identity of substance(s) used
- History of substance(s) used
- History of substance-use emergencies and treatment
- Cognitive impairment (for example, confusion, disorientation)
- Physiological signs (for example, rapid heart rate, dilation of eye pupils)
- Psychomotor agitation or retardation
- Changes in mood, perception, and thought
- Changes in personality, mood, anxiety
- Results of urine drug screening, blood-alcohol level
- Changes in social or family life
- Current and past legal problems